ICDM 2001

Proceedings

2001 IEEE International Conference on Data Mining

29 November – 2 December 2001

San Jose, California

Sponsored by

IEEE Computer Society Technical Committee on
Pattern Analysis and Machine Intelligence (TCPAMI)

IEEE Computer Society Task Force on Virtual Intelligence (TFVI)

Corporate Sponsors

Insightful Corporation, Seattle, Washington

Microsoft Research, San Francisco, California

NARAX Inc., Golden, Colorado

Springer-Verlag, New York, New York

StatSoft Inc., Tulsa, Oklahoma

Edited by

Nick Cercone, University of Waterloo

T.Y. Lin, San Jose State University

Xindong Wu, University of Vermont

IEEE
COMPUTER
SOCIETY

Los Alamitos, California

Washington   Brussels   Tokyo

IEEE Computer Society Order Number PR01119
ISBN 0-7695-1119-8
ISBN 0-7695-1120-1 (case)
ISBN 0-7695-1121-X (microfiche)
Library of Congress Number 2001087761

Additional copies may be ordered from:

IEEE Computer Society	IEEE Service Center	IEEE Computer Society
Customer Service Center	445 Hoes Lane	Asia/Pacific Office
10662 Los Vaqueros Circle	P.O. Box 1331	Watanabe Bldg., 1-4-2
P.O. Box 3014	Piscataway, NJ 08855-1331	Minami-Aoyama
Los Alamitos, CA 90720-1314	Tel: + 1 732 981 0060	Minato-ku, Tokyo 107-0062
Tel: + 1 714 821 8380	Fax: + 1 732 981 9667	JAPAN
Fax: + 1 714 821 4641	http://shop.ieee.org/store/	Tel: + 81 3 3408 3118
http://computer.org/	customer-service@ieee.org	Fax: + 81 3 3408 3553
csbooks@computer.org		tokyo.ofc@computer.org

Editorial production by Danielle C. Young

Cover art production by Joe Daigle/Studio Productions

Printed in the United States of America by The Printing House

IEEE
COMPUTER
SOCIETY

Table of Contents

2001 IEEE International Conference on Data Mining (ICDM 2001)

Regular Papers

vi

Posters

Welcome from the Steering Committee Chair

Welcome to IEEE Data Mining 2001, the first IEEE International Conference on Data Mining (ICDM'01)! On behalf of the ICDM Steering Committee and the ICDM'01 Conference Committee, I would like to thank you for coming to ICDM'01, and I wish you have a great time in San Jose, the heart of the Silicon Valley.

With the support of both world-renowned experts and new researchers from the international data mining community, ICDM'01 has received an overwhelming response compared to any other data mining related conference this year: 365 paper submissions, 8 workshop proposals, and 29 tutorial proposals. The ICDM Steering Committee anticipates that ICDM will soon be recognized as one of the very best conferences in the field. In addition to business oriented data mining, ICDM has an equal emphasis on engineering, scientific, and medical data for which domain knowledge plays a significant role in knowledge discovery and refinement. ICDM will be held annually, in different regions of the world. It seeks to promote close collaboration with regional data mining conferences, and promote the entire data mining field.

As a new conference, ICDM provides us with the unique advantage of being able to learn from the experiences of other conferences and from the onset to set our standards high. For example, the ICDM Steering Committee has established a database of "Established Researchers in Data Mining." Each person in our database has a solid publication record. This database is used by ICDM organizers of each year to identify and invite first-rate researchers to become members of the program committee. The availability of this database would save time in identifying appropriate candidates and ensure that our program committee is comprised of the highest quality of researchers, including both established researchers and rising stars.

Compared to other data mining related conferences, ICDM is truly international, and the presentation of research is the primary focus of the ICDM conference. Papers exploring new directions receive a careful and supportive review at each ICDM conference. Also, we will make special efforts to encourage local participants each year, so that each ICDM conference will have a flavor of its locality.

Data mining is an emerging and interdisciplinary field. ICDM covers broad and diverse topics related to the design, analysis and implementation of data mining theory, systems and applications. These include, but are not limited to, the following areas:

- Foundations and principles of data mining
- Data mining algorithms and methods in traditional areas (such as classification, clustering, probabilistic modeling, and association analysis), and in new areas
- Data and knowledge representation for data mining
- Modeling of structured, textual, temporal, spatial, multimedia and Web data to support data mining
- Complexity, efficiency, and scalability issues in data mining
- Data pre-processing, data reduction, feature selection and feature transformation
- Statistics and probability in large-scale data mining
- Soft computing (including neural networks, fuzzy logic, evolutionary computation, and rough sets) and uncertainty management for data mining
- Integration of data warehousing, OLAP and data mining
- Man-machine interaction in data mining and visual data mining
- Artificial intelligence contributions to data mining
- High performance and distributed data mining
- Machine learning, pattern recognition and automated scientific discovery
- Quality assessment and interestingness metrics of data mining results
- Process centric data mining and models of data mining process
- Security and social impact of data mining
- Emerging data mining applications, such as electronic commerce, Web mining and intelligent learning database systems

Organizing the conference needs teamwork. First, I would like to thank the Program Chairs, Workshops Chair, Tutorials Chair, Panels Chair, Publicity Chair and Local Arrangements Chair for their countless hours devoted to various conference activities. My sincere gratitude goes to Jerome H. Friedman (Stanford University), Jim Gray (Microsoft Research, The 1999 Turing Award Winner), Pat Langley (Institute for the Study of Learning and Expertise, USA) and Benjamin W. Wah (University of Illinois, Urbana-Champaign, President of the IEEE Computer Society) for agreeing to present invited talks that will cover different perspectives of data mining. Last but not the least, I would like to thank all Steering Committee members, Program Committee members, additional reviewers, authors, and attendees for your contribution and participation. Without you, we cannot have the conference.

Xindong Wu

ICDM Steering Committee Chair
ICDM'01 Conference Chair

Message from the Program Chairs

One of the prime reasons why businesses, government, universities and society are undergoing rapid and fundamental change as the new millennium begins can be summed up succinctly - the Internet.

The amount of information available over the Internet is huge. Navigating through the Internet, gaining access to relevant information in a timely, efficient manner is, at best, problematic. Adding value, for example, the online use of decision support, is becoming increasingly important. How we reach an accord with the increasing amount of information available over the Internet provides at least the following problems for solution:

- intelligent agents, particularly those equipped with data mining capabilities;
- multi-modality interfaces and Internet retrieval systems;
- data mining for marketing; and
- effective data mining and online analytic mining for efficient use of the Internet.

In addition to the usual economic and technological reasons, new ideas from agent technology, data mining, collaborative work, etc. will form important characteristics of modern Internet access.

Performance characteristics will determine a Web site's success. If access is slow or queued, "customers" are unlikely to wait. The resource implications of a network such as the Internet are extraordinary and growing and the dependence on security, performance, reliability and service places additional burdens on service providers; these resource implications also place a premium on intelligent solutions to these problems. Primary among these solutions is data mining.

That is not to ignore ethical, legal, social and policy issues; these are important. The Pandora's Box of potential problems, the ethical, legal, social and policy issues related to the Internet also provide for a wide variety of practitioners from many disciplines to participate in new research.

Our conference is about Data Mining, a frequently controversial intelligent systems technology. And although there have been many reported "success" stories surrounding data mining (most direct marketing companies and many biotech companies use some form of data mining, and there are thousands of such applications worldwide), many data mining projects remain in the realm of research: high potential reward, accompanied by high risk. Continued success in data mining depends on continued research.

Welcome to ICDM'01, the 2001 IEEE International Conference on Data Mining, held at the Doubletree Hotel, San Jose, California, USA from November 29 - December 2, 2001. For a first time conference, the response has been overwhelming. ICDM'01 received 365 submissions from 36 countries. Less than a third of the papers came from the United States (120 papers). Other countries contributing include: China (25), Australia (24), Japan (22), Taiwan (21), Canada (20), United Kingdom (18), France (13), Germany (12), Hong Kong (10), Spain (10), Singapore (9), Finland (7), Brazil (7), Italy (6), Korea (6), Chile (3), Israel (3), Netherlands (3), Vietnam (3), Czech Republic (2), Egypt (2), Greece (2), Poland (2), Portugal (2), Russia (2), Slovenia (2), Argentina (1), Belgium (1), Cuba (1), India (1), Malaysia (1), Mexico (1), Romania (1), Turkey (1), and Zaire (1). Just fewer than 20% of the submissions were accepted as regular papers, 72 papers in all and another 11% were accepted as poster papers, or 40 additional papers. Subsequently 3 poster papers were withdrawn. ICDM'01 is further supplemented by two workshops, Text Mining (TextDM 2001) and Integrating Data Mining and Knowledge Management, two tutorials, Text and Data Mining for Bioinformatics and Mining Time Series Data. Four invited speakers have graciously accepted invitations to make special presentations at ICDM'01, Jerome H. Friedman, Jim Gray, Pat Langley and Benjamin W. Wah.

Any conference of this size and magnitude cannot be successful without the hard work of many individuals. We would like to acknowledge the great effort put forward by our Program Committee and Steering Committee (listed separately) for their reviewing efforts and for their advice. We join our Conference Chair in thanking our Tutorials Chair Chris Clifton, our Workshops Chair Johannes Gehrke, our Panels Chair Ramamohanarao Kotagiri, our Publicity Chair Ning Zhong, and our Local Arrangements Chair Xiaohua (Tony) Hu. We reserve special thanks for the fine overall organization, guidance and timing of our General Chair Xindong Wu. We thank PhD student Richard Relue of the Colorado School of Mines who developed Web files for handling electronic paper submissions and on-line registrations. Finally, but not least, we thank Wen Gao of Waterloo for helping facilitate the reviewing efforts of the program chairs.

We are grateful to our sponsors for their generous support of ICDM'01; we thank ICDM'01 corporate sponsors: Microsoft Research, Insightful Corporation, NARAX Inc., Springer-Verlag, StatSoft Inc. Finally, we extend a special appreciation to the Institute for Electrical and Electronics Engineers (IEEE) for sponsoring ICDM'01. It would appear from the response generated that their sponsorship and the help that they provided are amply justified. We truly hope that you will take the time and enjoy the conference.

Nick Cercone and T.Y. Lin

Program Co-Chairs, 2001

Conference Organization

Conference Chair:

Xindong Wu, University of Vermont, USA

Program Committee Chairs:

Nick Cercone, University of Waterloo, Canada
T.Y. Lin, San Jose State University, USA

ICDM'01 Workshops Chair:

Johannes Gehrke, Cornell University, USA

ICDM'01 Tutorials Chair:

Chris Clifton, MITRE, USA

ICDM'01 Panels Chair:

Ramamohanarao Kotagiri, University of Melbourne, Australia

ICDM'01 Publicity Chair:

Ning Zhong, Maebashi Institute of Technology, Japan

ICDM'01 Local Arrangements Chair:

Xiaohua (Tony) Hu, Vigilance Inc., USA

Steering Committee

Xindong Wu, Chair, University of Vermont, USA

Max Bramer, University of Portsmouth, UK

Nick Cercone, University of Waterloo, Canada

Ramamohanarao Kotagiri, University of Melbourne, Australia

Katharina Morik, University of Dortmund, Germany

Gregory Piatetsky-Shapiro, KDnuggets, USA

Philip S. Yu, IBM T.J. Watson Research Center, USA

Ning Zhong, Maebashi Institute of Technology, Japan

Program Committee

Nick Cercone, Co-Chair, University of Waterloo, Canada

T.Y. Lin, Co-Chair, San Jose State University, USA

Daniel Barbara, George Mason University, USA

Roberto Bayardo, IBM Almaden Research, USA

Philip Chan, Florida Institute of Technology, USA

Surajit Chaudhuri, Microsoft Research, USA

Arbee L.P. Chen, National Tsing Hua University, Taiwan

Ming-Syan Chen, National Taiwan University, Taiwan

Christopher W. Clifton, The MITRE Corporation, USA

Andrea Danyluk, Williams College, USA

Guozhu Dong, Wright State University, USA

Saso Dzeroski, Jozef Stefan Institute, Slovenia

Tom Fawcett, Hewlett-Packard Labs, USA

Jerome Friedman, Stanford University, USA

Matjaz Gams, Jozef Stefan Institute, Slovenia

Johannes Gehrke, Cornell University, USA

Clark Glymour, Carnegie-Mellon University, USA

Jim Gray, Microsoft Research, USA

Petr Hajek, Academy of Sciences, Czech Republic

Howard J. Hamilton, University of Regina, Canada

David Hand, Imperial College, UK

David Heckerman, Microsoft Research, USA

Se June Hong, IBM Research, USA

Xiaohua (Tony) Hu, Vigilance Inc., USA

Kien Hua, University of Central Florida, USA

Eamonn Keogh, University of California, Irvine, USA

Joerg-Uwe Kietz, Swiss Life, Switzerland

Willi Klosgen, GMD, Germany

Yves Kodratoff, University Paris-Sud, France

Raghu Krishnapuram, IBM India Research Labs

Vipin Kumar, University of Minnesota - Minneapolis, USA

Laks V.S. Lakshmanan, IIT - Bombay, India

Non-PC Reviewers

Ada Wai-chee Fu
Aijun An
Ajay Dhawale
Akiko Aizawa
Alex Tuzhilin
Amit A. Nanavati
Andreas Prodromidis
Aran Lunzer
Arkadiusz Wojna
Arnaud Giacometti
Asanobu Kitamoto
Ayman Ammoura
Aysel Ozgur
Baptiste Jeudy
Bernard Zenko
Bilgehan Uygar Oztekin
C.J. Butz
Carsten Lanquillon
Catherine Wen
Chi-Hoon Lee
Chris Drummond
Chung-Wen Cho
Dale Schuurmans
Damien Brain
David Cheung
David Coufal
Dimitrios Gunopulos
Dominik Slezak
Dominique Laurent
G. Ozsoyoglu
Gautam Das
George Chang
George Forman
Graham Williams
Grant Weddell
Grzegorz Góra
Haixun Wang
Hasan M. Jamil
Honghua Dai
Hongjun Lu
Hui Xiong
Huiyuan Shan

Hung Son Nguyen
Hung-Chen Chen
I. Kramosil
James Bailey
Jaroslaw Stepaniuk
Jean-Francois Boulicaut
Jia-Lien Hsu
Jia-Ling Koh
Jian Pei
Jianchao Han
Jimmy Hunag
Jinyan Li
Jiong Yang
John Holt
Jun He
K. Krishna
Katherine G. Herbert
Kenro Aihara
Krishna P Chitrapura
Lei Yu
Levent Ertoz
Limsoon Wong
Ljupco Todorovski
Lorenza Saitta
Lotfi Lakhal
Luiza Antonie
Mahesh V. Joshi
Manoranjan Dash
Marcin Szczuka
Masaru Kitsuregawa
Michael Steinbach
Michael Wong
Michihiro Kuramochi
Mohammad El-Hajj
Mounir Tantaoui
Nina Mishra
Ning-Han Liou
Oliver Ritthoff
Pang-Ning Tan
Patrick Marcel
Paul Munteanu
Pauray S.M. Tsai

Periklis Andritsos
Peter Andreae
Peter Brockhausen
Ramdev Kanapady
Rohan Baxter
Rosine Cicchetti
Sachindra Joshi
Saharon Rosset
Saurabh Singhal
Sen Zhang
Shichao Zhang
Shin'ichi Satoh
Show-Jane Yen
Songmao Zhang
Soumya Ray
Sridhar Rajagopalan
Srinivasan Parthasarathy
Stefan Haustein
Stefan Rüping
Svetlana Kiritchenko
Takashi Matsuda
Takuya Wada
Tatiana Semenova
Tetsuya Yoshida
Tim Hansell
Tony Abou-Assaleh
Viet Phan-Luong
Vinayaka Pandit
W. Fan
Wei Wang
Weinan Wang
Weiqiang Lin
Xiaowei Yan
Xiong Wang
Yang Xiang
Yi-Hung Wu
Ying Sai
Yingwei Wang
Yitong Wang
Zhenmei Gu
Zili Zhang

REGULAR

On Effective Conceptual Indexing and Similarity Search in Text Data

Charu C. Aggarwal
IBM T. J. Watson Research Center
Yorktown Heights, NY 10598
charu@us.ibm.com

Philip S. Yu
IBM T. J. Watson Research Center
Yorktown Heights, NY 10598
psyu@us.ibm.com

Abstract

Similarity search in text has proven to be an interesting problem from the qualitative perspective because of inherent redundancies and ambiguities in textual descriptions. The methods used in search engines in order to retrieve documents most similar to user-defined sets of keywords are not applicable to targets which are medium to large size documents, because of even greater noise effects stemming from the presence of a large number of words unrelated to the overall topic in the document. The inverted representation is the dominant method for indexing text, but it is not as suitable for document-to-document similarity search, as for short user-queries. One way of improving the quality of similarity search is Latent Semantic Indexing (LSI), which maps the documents from the original set of words to a concept space. Unfortunately, LSI maps the data into a domain in which it is not possible to provide effective indexing techniques. In this paper, we investigate new ways of providing conceptual search among documents by creating a representation in terms of conceptual word-chains. This technique also allows effective indexing techniques so that similarity queries can be performed on large collections of documents by accessing a small amount of data. We demonstrate that our scheme outperforms standard textual similarity search on the inverted representation both in terms of quality and search efficiency.

1. Introduction

In recent years, the large amounts of data available on the web has made effective similarity search and retrieval an important problem. Similarity indexing has uses in many web applications such as search engines or in providing close matches for user queries. A related problem is that of document-to-document similarity queries, in which the target is an entire document, as opposed to a small number of words for a specific user query. Such a system has considerable use in *recommender systems* in library or web ap-

plications, in which it is desirable to find the closest matches to a document which is currently being browsed. Other examples include personalized systems which can perform *information filtering*: a process which studies the long term access pattern by the user, and fetches the pages which are most consistent with his profile.

Similarity search is often used for short user queries in search engines such as *Yahoo!*, *Lycos*, *Google* and *AltaVista* [13] in which closest sets of matches are found to sets of keywords specified by the user. For such applications, the documents are represented in the form of an *inverted index* [11]. Other access methods [7] such as signature files exist, though the inverted representation seems to have become the method of choice in the information retrieval domain. The inverted representation consists of lists of Document Identifiers, one for each word in the lexicon. For each word w, its list contains all the document identifiers, such that the corresponding documents contain it. In addition, meta-information on word-frequency, position, or document length may be stored along with each identifier. For each user query, it suffices to examine the Document IDs in the inverted lists corresponding to the words in the query (or *target*). Details on how the similarity function is actually calculated for the relevant documents may be found in [11].

Similarity search has proven to be an interesting problem in the text domain because of the unusually large dimensionality of the problem as compared to the size of the documents. For example, a typical document collection on the world-wide web may have hundreds of thousands of words. This is significantly more than the average size of a document on the world-wide web. Considerable correlations between words exist because of synonymity and different descriptions of the same underlying latent concepts. Thus, two documents containing very different vocabulary could be similar in subject material. Similarly, two documents sharing considerable vocabulary could be topically very different. While applying the method to search engines (which is a special application of similarity search, in which the target document contains very few words), this problem is

3

observed in the form of retrieval incompleteness and inaccuracy. For example, while querying on *cats* one may miss documents containing a description on the *feline* species, which do not explicitly contain the word *cat*. In many cases, the target may contain a multitude of concepts and subjects, which can be inferred only from the aggregate distribution of words in the document. Another well known problem is that of *polysemy*, in which the same word could refer to multiple concepts in the description (The word *virus* could refer to a computer virus, or to a biological virus.) Clearly, the ambiguity of the term can be resolved only by viewing it in the context of other terms in the document. In general, it is a challenging problem to design similarity functions for high dimensional applications [8] because of the fact that the aggregate behavior of high dimensional feature vectors contains a lot of information which cannot be inferred from individual attributes.

A well known method for improving the quality of similarity search in text is called *Latent Semantic Indexing* [6], in which the data is transformed into a new *concept space*. This concept space depends upon the document collection in question, since different collections would have different sets of concepts. Latent semantic indexing is a technique which tries to capture this hidden structure using techniques from linear algebra. The idea in LSI is to project the data into a small subspace of the original data such that the noise effects of synonymy and polysemy are removed. The advantageous effects of the conceptual representation extend to problems well beyond the text domain [2, 3]. A detailed description of the effects of conceptual representation may be found in [2, 6, 9].

LSI transforms the data from the sparse indexable representation (with the inverted index) in a very high overall dimensionality to a representation in the real space which is no longer sparse. Even though the new representation is of much lower overall dimensionality (typically about 200 or so dimensions are needed to represent the concept space), it is beyond the capacity of spatial indexing structures to handle effectively. Thus, we are presented with a difficult choice: if the data is represented in original format using the inverted index, it is less effective for performing document-to-document similarity search; on the other hand, when the data is transformed using latent semantic indexing, we have a data set which cannot be indexed effectively. Therefore, if we have a very large collection of documents, we would either be reduced to using a sequential scan in order to perform conceptual similarity search, or have to do with lower quality search results using the original representation and ignore the problems of synonymy and polysemy.

Another difficulty in performing document-to-document queries effectively is that a large fraction of the words in the target document are unrelated to the general subjects in it. Such words increase the noise effects, and reduce the likelihood of good search results. This is a problem that even latent semantic indexing cannot resolve very effectively. In addition to these issues, it is clear that the performance of the inverted representation of documents worsens with increasing number of words in the target document. In the search engine application it may be typical for a well-formulated query to contain words which are specialized enough, so that each of the relevant inverted lists contain only a small number of Document Identifiers. This is certainly not the case in a typical target document, where it is inevitable that some words may have substantially large inverted lists; yet cannot be ignored. Accessing these lists may significantly worsen the performance of an inverted representation when applied to a document-to-document query.

In this paper, we will discuss a technique which represents documents in terms of *conceptual word-chains*, a method which admits both high quality similarity search and indexing techniques. We will compare our technique to standard similarity search on the inverted index in terms of quality, storage, and search efficiency. We will show that the scheme achieves good qualitative performance at a low indexing cost. We note that our system is similar in spirit to the independently developed concept indexing technique [10]; which focusses on the dimensionality reduction problem; here we focus mainly on the efficiency and efffectiveness of the similarity indexing process.

This paper is organized as follows. The remainder of this section is devoted to related work, a formal description of the contributions of this paper, and some preliminary definitions and notations. In section 2, we show how to represent the documents in the concept space. In section 3, we discuss the indexing search technique used for the purpose of this paper. Section 4 discusses how the word-chains defining the concept space are created. The empirical results are illustrated in section 5, while section 6 contains the conclusions and summary.

1.1. Contributions of this paper

In this paper, we discuss a new method for conceptual similarity search for text using word-chaining which admits more efficient document-to-document similarity search than the standard inverted index, while preserving better quality of results. The technique also results in much lower storage requirements because it uses a compressed representation of each document. This low storage requirement in turn translates to higher search efficiency. Thus, we demonstrate that our scheme outperforms the standard similarity methods on text on all three measures: quality, storage, and search efficiency. This is also the first piece of work which treats the performance and quality issues of textual similarity search in one unified framework.

1.2. Preliminaries

In order to represent documents, we used the vector space representation in which each document is represented as a vector of words together with normalized term frequencies. Specifically, each document can be represented as a term vector of the form $\bar{a} = (a_1, a_2, \ldots a_n)$. Each of the terms a_i has a weight w_i associated with it, where w_i denotes the normalized frequency of the word. We used the standard $tf\text{-}idf$ normalization, in which less frequently occuring words in the aggregate collection are given higher weight. Details of the normalization process may be found in [11]. The *concatenation* of two documents is defined by appending one document with the other. Thus, if $\bar{a} = (a_1, \ldots a_n)$ be the weights in the vector space representation of document A, and $\bar{b} = (b_1, \ldots b_n)$ be the weights in the vector space representation of document B, then the concatenation of documents A and B is given by $(a_1 + b_1, \ldots a_n + b_n)$.

The similarity between two documents may be measured by using the *cosine* measure. The cosine similarity between two documents with weight vectors $U = (u_1, \ldots u_n)$, and $V = (v_1, \ldots v_n)$ is given by:

$$cosine(U, V) = \frac{\sum_{i=1}^{n} f(u_i) \cdot f(v_i)}{\sqrt{\sum_{i=1}^{n} f(u_i)^2} \cdot \sqrt{\sum_{i=1}^{n} f(v_i)^2}} \quad (1)$$

Here $f(\cdot)$ is a damping function such as the square-root or logarithm.

A *word-chain* is a set of closely related words along with a weight for each of the words. For example, a word-chain (along with corresponding weights) for military-related vocabulary could be:
army (75), troops (35), regiment (13), barracks (5),....
Typically, we expect the word-chain to contain a small number [1] of words which are semantically related to a given topic. This is somewhat similar to an automatically-generated thesaraus. For the purpose of our paper, we will treat a word-chain as a meta-document, and therefore all of the above notations and definitions for document representation and similarity are also applicable to a word-chain.

2. Defining the Conceptual Representation

There are a large number of objective functions such as the dice coefficient, jaccard coefficient, and cosine coefficient which are used to measure similarity between text documents [11]. There is not much consensus on the relative quality of the different ways of calculating similarity. The cosine function used in this paper is one of the more well known ones. However, what is common to all these techniques is that they are all susceptible to the redundancies, ambiguities and noise effects in textual descriptions.

In our paper, we change the representation of the document *at the attribute level* by defining new sets of attributes corresponding to concepts which have semantic significance. Each of these concepts is defined by a word-chain, which in turn is generated using the aggregate behavior of the document collection being indexed. For the time-being we will skim over the issue of how these word-chains are actually generated, and assume that each of them is a meta-document containing closely related words with weights representing relative frequency of occurance. More about word-chain generation will be discussed in a later section. Thus, a one-to-one correspondence exists between the new set of attributes defined and the word-chains. Let us assume that the number of such attributes is k^*. The larger the document collection available, the easier it is to generate sets of word-chains which reflect the different semantic concepts in the document collection. This is a useful property, since indexing is more critical for larger applications. Let us assume that the vector space representation of the set of of k^* word-chains are denoted by $\overline{v_1} \ldots \overline{v_{k^*}}$. Note that some of the word-chains may have overlapping vocabulary, corresponding to the fact that there may often be some relationship between the concepts in the collection. Let us also assume that $\bar{u}$ is the vector space representation of a given document. Then, in the conceptual coordinate system, the coordinate along the axis v_i is given by $max\{0, cosine(\bar{u}, \overline{v_i}) - t\}$. Here $t \in (0, 1)$ is a suitably defined constant which we shall define as the *activation threshold*. We will have more to say about this value later. The coordinate value thus calculated is the *conceptual strength*.

In order to intuitively understand the concept space, let us try to get a feel for what the coordinates corresponding to a given document refer to. Since each word-chain contains a set of semantically related words (or topical vocabulary), the conceptual strength of document with respect to a word-chain defines how closely the document matches this vocabulary. Thus, if a document contains a multitude of subjects which have sufficient presence, then this is reflected by non-zero conceptual strengths for each of the corresponding attributes. For example, a document X on a military hospital may share vocabulary from two of the word-chains out of the many attributes. These two attributes may correspond to the fact that it is a military related document, and that it is a document related to the medical profession. This description is more amenable to topical similarity search than a text description, since another document on military hospitals may not share a significant amount of text with X, and a document sharing a considerable amount of text with X unrelated to military hospitals may be a very poor

---

[1] As we will see in the empirical section, the typical size of a word-chain is about 50 words.

Algorithm *Search(Target Concepts* $C = \{c_1, \ldots c_r\}$,
    Strength: $\{t_1, \ldots t_r\}$*)*
begin
Initialize hash table as empty;
for each $i \in \{c_1, \ldots c_r\}$ **do**
  begin
  for each document j indexed by concept i
      in the inverted representation **do begin**
    if entry for document j does not exist in the hash table
        then create entry for j in hash table and initialize entry value to 0;
    add $\frac{t_i \cdot q_{ij}}{\sqrt{L_j} \cdot \sqrt{L^t}}$ to the entry for document j in the hash table;
    end;
  end;
Return the document with largest hash table entry;
end

Figure 1. Searching for the Closest Conceptual Neighbor

match. In the conceptual vector-space representation, the length of each vector is k^*, and the corresponding weights represent the conceptual strength. Let $A = (a_1, \ldots a_{k^*})$ and $B = (b_1, \ldots b_{k^*})$ be the coordinates of two points in the concept space. Then the conceptual cosine C-cosine between the two documents is defined in a similar way as the cosine function without the application of damping. Therefore, we have:

$$\text{C-cosine}(A, B) = \sum_{i=1}^{k^*} a_i \cdot b_i / \left(\sqrt{\sum_{i=1}^{k^*} a_i^2} \cdot \sqrt{\sum_{i=1}^{k^*} b_i^2} \right).$$
$$(2)$$

3. Indexing and Searching the Conceptual Representation

In the conceptual representation, when the word-chains are reasonably well-separated, a given document is likely to share substantial vocabulary with only a few of the word-chains. In terms of the coordinate representation, this means that only a few of the components are likely to be strongly positive, while most components are zero.

The definition of the conceptual strength introduced in the previous section ensures that when the similarity of a document to a word chain is less than a certain amount called the *activation threshold* (denoted by t), the corresponding conceptual strength for that coordinate is zero. The aim is to create a conceptual representation which summarizes the information in the document in terms of a small number of concepts which are specific to the particular collection in question. The use of an activation threshold ensures that even though a document may share a tiny amount of vocabulary from many word-chains, these correspond to the noise-effects stemming from words which are not generally related to the dominant topics in it. Furthermore,

even though the document may share only a small amount of noisy vocabulary from each such word-chain, the sum of the noise effects over all the different word chains could be considerable. In effect, only a nicely filtered fraction of the vocabulary (corresponding to the dominant subjects) may be used in order to create the non-zero components in the conceptual representation. Such words are the *topical words* of that document.

One way of viewing conceptual representation is as a compressed representation of the documents which reduces the inherent noise effects of ambiguity, redundancy and unrelated vocabulary in a document. Latent semantic indexing achieves the noise reduction by picking a small subspace of the original data which shows the maximum variation in the distribution of the features. However, it does not achieve the compression effects since the documents are mapped to arbitrary numbers in the real domain. This also makes the data impossible to index because of the nature of the high dimensional representation.

Once the conceptual coordinates of each document have been determined, an inverted index of the new representation may be created. In this case, we have an inverted list for each of the k^* concepts corresponding to the word-chains. The document identifiers on a list are those documents which have a non-zero conceptual strength for the corresponding concept. The small number of positive components in the conceptual representation makes the data indexable, since the inverted representation is dependant upon the sparsity of the data. Along with each document ID j pointed to by each concept i, we also store the following information: (1) The *conceptual strength* q_{ij} for concept i in document j. (2) The *conceptual length* of document j, which is denoted by $L_j = \sum_{(i:\text{ concept } i \in \text{ document } j)} q_{ij}^2$, and is one of the terms in the denominator of the conceptual cosine function.

Let $\{c_1, \ldots c_r\}$ be the set of concepts in the target document, and $\{t_1, \ldots t_r\}$ be the strength of the corresponding concepts. Our similarity search algorithm uses the meta-information in the inverted index [11]. Let L^t be the length of the target document. We say that a document is *touched* by the target, if it has at least one concept, which is in the target (In other words, its ID occurs on at least one of the inverted lists corresponding to that concept.). Then the algorithm builds a hash table of all documents which are touched by the target by examining the inverted lists one by one, and inserting document IDs in the hash table. When the document j from the inverted list for concept c_p ($1 \leq p \leq r$) is being examined, it keeps updating a similarity count entry for each document in the hash table by adding $\frac{t_p \cdot q_{c_p j}}{\sqrt{L_j} \cdot \sqrt{L^t}}$ to the corresponding hash table entry. At the end of the scan, for each document j which has been touched by the target, the value of the corresponding entry in the hash table will

6

Algorithm *ConceptualWordChains(Documents: D, NumberOfChains: k^*,*
Integer: ActivationThreshold)
{ $\mathcal{W}$ = set of word chains; $\mathcal{C}_i$ = set of documents
   related to words chain $W_i \in \mathcal{W}$ }
{ $\mathcal{D}$ = set of all documents }
begin
 $\mathcal{W}$ = A randomly chosen set of n_0 documents;
 $ChainLength = StartChainLength$;
 while ($n_0 > k^*$)
 do begin
  $(\mathcal{D}, \mathcal{C}_1, \ldots \mathcal{C}_{n_0})$ =*MatchDocuments*($\mathcal{W}, \mathcal{D}, ActivationThreshold$);
  $\mathcal{W}$ =*FindWordChains*($\mathcal{C}_1, \ldots \mathcal{C}_{n_0}, ChainLength$);
  $\mathcal{W}$ =*RemoveChains*($\mathcal{W}, \mathcal{C}_{n_0}$);
  $\mathcal{W}$ =*ConsolidateChains*($\mathcal{W}, \max\{n_0 \cdot \gamma, k^*\}$);
  $n_0 = \max\{n_0 \cdot \gamma, k^*\}$;
  $ChainLength = \max\{FinalChainLength, ChainLength * \theta\}$;
  { $\theta < 1$ indicates the rate at which the number of words
     in each chain reduces in an iteration }
 end;
end

Figure 2. Word-chain Creation

be given by $\sum_{(p: \text{concept } c_p \in \text{document } j)} \frac{t_p \cdot q_{cpj}}{\sqrt{L_j} \cdot \sqrt{L^i}}$. This is
the conceptual cosine (C-cosine) between the target and the
document j. The search method is illustrated in the Figure 1. This method for calculating similarity directly from
the meta-information in the inverted index can be adapted
to textual similarity search on the original document for
certain objective functions; though many IR systems use
the inverted representation to identify the documents which
should be accessed from the database, and then separately
access the vector space representation in order to calculate
similarity.

4. Generating the Conceptual Space

It is important to understand that the success of this
method depends upon the finding of well separated word-
chains which contain sets of closely correlated words. The
concept of using word clustering for specific problem of text
classification has been discussed by Baker and McCallum
[5]. However, the applicability of that technique is restricted
to the classification problems where the documents are already labelled. In our technique we concentrate on finding
word-chains in an unsupervised way by iteratively creating
word clusters and collections of documents associated with
these clusters.

A good number of algorithms are known in the literature for performing text clustering [4, 1], though the focus
of our technique is slightly different in terms of being able
to find clusters on the *words* as opposed to the documents.
Furthermore, there may be overlaps on the words in the different concepts. The method takes as input the activation
threshold which is the user-defined limit on when a con-

cept can be considered to be present in a document. This is
the same value which is used during the process of building the inverted index and performing the similarity search.
This activation threshold is useful in finding semantic relationships between the documents in the collection and the
intermediate word-chains generated by the algorithm.

Our overall algorithm is an iterative one in which word-
chains are used as representatives for grouping semantically
related documents. In each iteration, the vocabulary in the
word-chains is refined so that the resulting meta-document
contains more and more tightly related sets of words. In
the first iteration, each word-chain W_i is simply the set of
words in an arbitrary document from the collection. The
number of such chains is n_0. The exact value of n_0 is determined by the running time considerations, which will be
discussed in a later section. At this point, closely related
documents to each word-chain are found and collected in a
set. Specifically, for word-chain W_i the set of semantically
related documents to it is denoted by $\mathcal{C}_i$. A document may
belong to multiple sets in $\{\mathcal{C}_1 \ldots \mathcal{C}_{n_0}\}$. These in turn are
used in order to re-create each word-chain W_i by retaining
the dominant vocabulary of $\mathcal{C}_i$. The number of words retained in each iteration is denoted by $ChainLength$. The
algorithm starts with a larger value of $ChainLength$, and
gradually reduces it in each iteration as the word-chains get
more refined, and a smaller number of words are required
in order to isolate the subject in a word-chain. This technique of finding closely related documents by iteratively refining both word-chains and document assignments to such
chains is an effective technique for the creation of closely
related groups of words. In each iteration, we keep consolidating chains which are close enough to belong to the same
topic, so that we do not have concepts which are too similar in their vocabulary. At the same time we keep removing
the chains which do not have enough matching documents,
which corresponds to the fact that such concepts are not
well represented in the aggregate behavior of the collection.

The overall algorithm for generation of word-chains is illustrated in Figure 2. We assume that the set of word-chains
available to the algorithm at any stage is denoted by $\mathcal{W}$ and
the documents which are being used in order to create the
word-chains are denoted by $\mathcal{D}$. In each iteration, we assign
a random sample $\mathcal{R}$ of the documents to their most semantically related word-chains in $\mathcal{W}$. The reason for picking
a random sample $\mathcal{R}$ is that the assignment procedure re-
quires $n_0 \cdot |\mathcal{R}|$ similarity functions calculations, where n_0 is
the number of word-chains. This may dominate the running
times. Therefore, picking a random sample size which is inversely proportional to the current number of word-chains
n_0 balances the running time in each iteration. Furthermore,
larger sample sizes are chosen in later iterations, when it is
more critical to calculate word-chains in a more accurate
and refined way. The particular value of the random sam-

ple used for our algorithm was $k^* \cdot |\mathcal{D}|/n_0$. This value of the random sample size chosen ensures that in the last iteration, when $n_0 = k^*$, the entire document collection is used. A document is assigned to all the word-chains in $\mathcal{W}$, to which the similarity of the document is larger than the activation threshold. Thus, a document could get assigned to multiple chains, corresponding to the different subjects in it. At the end of this procedure, the sets of documents $(\mathcal{C}_1, \ldots \mathcal{C}_{n_0})$ are returned, which corresponds to the different word-chains.

After the assignment procedure, we create a word-chain W_i out of each group $\mathcal{C}_i$. To do so, we concatenate the documents in each semantically related group which was created in the assignment process, and we project out the words with the least weight from the corresponding meta-document. This ensures that only the terms which are frequently occuring within that group of semantically related documents are used in the word-chain. The number of terms in the word-chains reduces by a geometric factor θ in each iteration. We shall refer to this value θ as the *projection factor*. This is because in the first few iterations, when the word-chains are not too refined, a larger number of dimensions need to be retained in the projection in order to avoid premature loss of information. In later iterations, the word-chains become more refined and it is possible to project down to a fewer number of words.

In each iteration, we reduce the number of word-chains by the *chain-consolidation factor* γ by consolidating very closely related chains. This reduces the likelihood of redundancy in the semantic representation of the documents, when expressed in terms of the final word chains (similar to the problem of synonymy). The merging process is implemented using a simple single linkage clustering method. Each word-chain is represented by a node in an undirected graph, and the similarity between each pair of word-chains is calculated. Edges are added to the graph in decreasing order of similarity, until there are $n_0 \cdot \gamma$ connected components. The new reduced set of word-chains are then re-created by concatenating the chains corresponding to each such component. Although the simple linkage process is somewhat naive, it is very fast and effective for values of the consolidation factor $\gamma \geq 0.1$. This is because single-linkage methods are very effective for cases when a small number of merges are performed before recalculation of nearest neighbors. The projection factor θ was picked in a way, so that the reduction of the initial chain length to the final chain length occured in the same number of iterations as the reduction of the number of word-chains from n_0 to k^*. In order for this to happen, the following relationship must be satisfied: $\log_\gamma(n_0/k^*) = \log_\theta(FinalChainLength/StartChainLength)$.

Some of the word-chains may turn out to be meaningless and consist of unrelated words. Such word-chains attract very few documents from the original set during the matching process. In order to find which word-chains should be removed, we calculated the mean μ and standard deviation σ of the distribution of documents in the groups $\mathcal{C}_i$ for $i \in \{1, \ldots n_0\}$. We discard all those word-chains W_i from $\mathcal{W}$ such that the number of documents in $\mathcal{C}_i$ is less than the threshold value of $\mu - r \cdot \sigma$. Here r is a parameter, which defines the statistical level of significance at which one would like to remove the poorly-defined chains.

5. Empirical Results

We used a scan of the *Yahoo!* taxonomy from November 1996. This taxonomy contained a total of 167193 documents, over a lexicon of approximately 700,000 words. Each document in this taxonomy contained an average of about 80 to 100 distinct words from the lexicon. The very commonly occuring terms (or stop words) had already been removed from this lexicon. In addition, we removed words which rarely occured in the collection. Specifically, any words which occured in the entire collection less than 6 times was removed. Most of these words turned out to be misspellings or creative variations of ordinary words, which had no significance in the similarity indexing process. The resulting lexicon contained approximately 80,000 words.

Since the inverted representation is the primary data structure which provides indexing capabilities for text, we compared our scheme to it. Most of the results in this paper compare the widely used cosine textual function and its conceptual analogue (see Equations 1 and 2). For the textual cosine, the square-root damping function[2] was used and the inverse-document-frequency (idf) normalization [11] was used in order to weight the importance of the different words. We evaluated the textual similarity function against the conceptual method for both quality and efficiency.

5.1. Quality

This is difficult to measure because of its inherently non-quantitative nature. Therefore, we will provide evidence of the effectiveness of the conceptual technique in an indirect way. We will use the class labels on the *Yahoo!* data set in order to check how well the retrieved results matched the target. If it is assumed that the manually defined *Yahoo!* class labels reflect topical behavior well, then the relationship between the class labels of the target and search results can provide very good evidence of search quality. We found that the conceptual technique was able to match the documents well in terms of overall subject matching, whereas the textual representation was often mislead by the noise effects of individual words. Since

---

[2]The square-root damping function was slightly better than the logarithmic damping function in our empirical tests.

Target Document	Textual Neighbor	Conceptual Neighbor
@Arts@Architecture@Architects	@Arts@Architecture@Architects (16%) @Arts@Architecture (24%) @Arts (36%)	@Arts@Architecture@Architects (34%) @Arts@Architecture (47%) @Arts (58%)
@Arts@Art_History@Artists	@Arts@Art_History@Artists (16%) @Arts@Art_History (29%) @Arts (38%)	@Arts@Art_History@Artists (29%) @Arts@Art_History (44%) @@Arts (49%)
@Arts@Dance	@Arts@Dance (19%) @Arts (28%)	@Arts@Dance (44%) @Arts (55%)
@Government@Military@Air_Force	@Government@Military@Air_Force (18%) @Government@Military (29%) @Government (36%)	@Government@Military@Air_Force (33%) @Government@Military (48%) @Government (51%)
@Health@Nursing	@Health@Nursing (19%) @Health (29%)	@Health@Nursing (31%) @Health (48%)
@Recreation@Sports@Tennis	@Recreation@Sports@Tennis (17%) @Recreation@Sports (29%) @Recreation (30%)	@Recreation@@Sports@Tennis (32%) @Recreation@Sports (45%) @Recreation (48%)
@Science@Biology@Botany	@Science@Biology@Botany (18%) @Science@Biology (25%) @Science (31%)	@Science@Biology@Botany (32%) @Science@Biology (42%) @Science (51%)
Overall Average 20 categories	Lowest level class (16%) One level higher (28%)	Lowest level class (28%) One level higher (47%)

Table 1. Matching of the subjects in target and nearest neighbors

the focus of this paper is in measuring the quality and coherence of the nearest neighbor obtained from conceptual indexing, we need some hard criterion for quantification of such qualitative measurements. To do so, we used the $Yahoo!$ class labels associated with the documents. We compared the class labels in the retrieved results to the class labels of all levels of the $Yahoo!$ hierarchy in the target. Specifically, we computed the $p = 20$ closest neighbors to the target, and calculated the percentage of neighbors from the same or a hierarchically related class. The results are presented in Table 1. The first column indicates the class label of the target document; whereas the second and third columns indicate some statistics of the class distributions of the search results for the textual and conceptual neighbors respectively for all levels of the $Yahoo!$ hierarchy which are related to the target. For example, for a target document in the @Arts@Architecture@Architects category, we would try to find the percentage of neighbors belonging to each of the subtrees of $Yahoo!$ corresponding to @Arts@Architecture@Architects, @Arts@Architecture, and @Arts respectively. Clearly the percentage of matching neighbors would always be higher while trying to make a partial match with a hierarchically related node. The values reported in each entry of Table 1 are determined by averaging over all targets in the corresponding $Yahoo!$ class. It is also apparent that it is goodness for these accuracy numbers to be as high as possible, if we assume that $Yahoo!$ class labels reflect topical behavior well.

As illustrated in Table 1, an exact match between the class labels of the target document and the nearest neighbors was found a very small percentage of the time for the textual nearest neighbor. We note that we are only using the matching percentage of class labels of an unsupervised similarity search procedure in order to demonstrate the qualitative advantages of conceptual similarity. (Therefore the results from supervised classifiers are a bound on the kind of accuracy one could hope to qualitatively achieve with a simple unsupervised nearest neighbor technique.) The accuracy of the textual neighbor ranged in the vicinity of 14-19% over the different categories. On the other hand, the accuracy for the conceptual nearest neighbor ranged between 30-40%. The accuracy numbers varied considerably over the different categories. In each case, the conceptual neighbor always dominates the effectiveness of the textual neighbor. The test results for the hierarchical relationship of the retrieved documents to the target were similar. In these cases the percentage accuracies for the textual nearest neighbor varied between 25-29%, whereas the numbers for the conceptual nearest neighbor were in the range of 45-50%. Furthermore, the conceptual neighbor performed much better in each of the individual cases.

5.2. Storage Requirements and Search Efficiency

On generating the conceptual space, we found that each document contained about 5-10 concepts. On the other hand, the average document contained about 100 words. This is a dramatic reduction in the space required to store and index documents. This results in savings both in terms of storage efficiency and computational efficiency of disk

Method	Result
Textual	426 676 (IDs Accessed)= 5.1 MB
Conceptual	9032 (IDs Accessed)= 108 KB

Table 2. Search Efficiency for the two methods

accesses. The original set of 167,000 documents required a total of about 87.7 MB in the inverted representation, whereas the conceptual representation required only 8.3 MB. This translates to more than an order of magnitude improvement in the space required for storage. These improved storage requirements also translate to greater efficiency during query time in two ways: (**1**) In the textual representation, some of the inverted lists are very long because of relatively commonly occuring words (which are not stop words). These inverted lists contribute to a substantial portion of the access time. This is never the case in the conceptual representation. (**2**) Each of the target documents contains a fewer number of concepts; so fewer number of the inverted lists need to be accessed.

Since the inverted representation is used by both the schemes, it follows that the search efficiency may be determined easily by calculating the number of document IDs (including repetitions) which were accessed by each of the methods. The number of ID accesses and corresponding disk access requirements are illustrated in Table 2. The numbers are averaged over 1000 queries for each case. As we see from Table 2, each similarity search query in the textual representation required an access of 426,676 documents IDs from the inverted index, which sums to a total of about 5.1 MB. This is an exceptionally high access requirement for a *single query*. Note that the number of document IDs accessed is more than the number of documents in the collection, corresponding to the fact that the same ID occured on multiple lists. The number of distinct IDs accessed for each query averaged at about 10% of the total documents. The reason for this exceptionally large number of documents being accessed is that some words are more frequent in the document collection than others (but are important enough to be not considered stop-words). The lists for these words add significantly to the access cost. The use of the inverted representation ensures that the search efficiency requirements scale linearly with the size of the document collection. Thus, an access requirement of 5.1 MB per query for a moderately sized collection of 167,000 documents does not bode well for the performance on much larger collections. In contrast, the conceptual indexing technique requires the access of an average of 9032 document IDs per query. This is about 108 KB per query and more than an order of magnitude improvement over the textual

indexing technique.

6. Conclusions and Summary

In this paper, we discussed a new method for conceptual indexing and similarity search of text. The techniques discussed in this paper can be used for dramatically improving the search quality as well as search efficiency. Although our technique is designed with a focus on document-to-document similarity queries, the techniques are also applicable to the short queries of search engines. This work provides an integrated view of qualitatively effective similarity search and performance efficient indexing in text; an issue which has not been addressed before in this domain.

References

[1] C. C. Aggarwal, S. C. Gates, P. S. Yu. On the Merits of Using Supervised Clustering for building Categorization Systems. *ACM SIGKDD Conference*, 1999.

[2] C. C. Aggarwal. On the Effects of Dimensionality Reduction on High Dimensional Similarity Search. *ACM PODS Conference*, 2001.

[3] C. C. Aggarwal, S. Parthasarathy. Mining Massively Incomplete Data Sets by Conceptual Reconstruction. *ACM KDD Conference*, 2001.

[4] P. Anick, and S. Vaithyanathan. Exploiting Clustering and Phrases for Context-based Information Retrieval. *ACM SIGIR Conference*, 1997.

[5] L. Douglas Baker, A. K. McCallum. Distributional Clustering of words for Text Classification. *ACM SIGIR Conference*, 1998.

[6] Dumais S., Furnas G., Landauer T. Deerwester S., Using Latent Semantic Indexing to improve information retrieval. *ACM SIGCHI Conference, 1988.*

[7] C. Faloutsos Access Methods for Text. *ACM Computing Surveys* 17, 1, March 1995.

[8] A. Hinneburg, C. C. Aggarwal, D. A. Keim. What is the Nearest Neighbor in High Dimensional Spaces? *Proceedings of the VLDB Conference*, 2001.

[9] J. Kleinberg, A. Tomkins. Applications of Linear Algebra in Information Retrieval and Hypertext Analysis. *ACM PODS Conference*, 1999.

[10] G. Karypis, E.-I. Han. Concept Indexing: A Fast Dimensionality Reduction Technique with Applications to Document Retrieval and Categorization. *CIKM Conference*, 2000.

[11] G. Salton, M. J. McGill. Introduction to Modern Information Retrieval. *Mc Graw Hill*, New York, 1983.

[12] H. Schutze, C. Silverstein. Projections for efficient document clustering. *ACM SIGIR Conference*, 1997.

[13] http://www.altavista.com, http://www.lycos.com, http://www.yahoo.com http://www.google.com

Comparisons of Classification Methods for Screening Potential Compounds

Aijun An
Department of Computer Science
York University
Toronto, Ontario M3J 1P3 Canada
aan@cs.yorku.ca

Yuanyuan Wang
Department of Statistics and Actuarial Science
University of Waterloo
Waterloo, Ontario N2L 3G1 Canada
y32wang@uwaterloo.ca

Abstract

We compare a number of data mining and statistical methods on the drug design problem of modeling molecular structure-activity relationships. The relationships can be used to identify active compounds based on their chemical structures from a large inventory of chemical compounds. The data set of this application has a highly skewed class distribution, in which only 2% of the compounds are considered active. We apply a number of classification methods to this extremely imbalanced data set and propose to use different performance measures to evaluate these methods. We report our findings on the characteristics of the performance measures, the effect of using pruning techniques in this application and a comparison of local learning methods with global techniques. We also investigate whether reducing the imbalance in the training data by up-sampling or down-sampling would improve the predictive performance.

1 Introduction

High throughput screening (HTS) is a technique in which predicting extreme values is more important than predicting low or mid-ranged values [15]. HTS has been used in drug discovery to screen large numbers of potential compounds against a biological target. Biotechnology advances, such as newly developed synthetic methods and better assay techniques, make it possible to screen tens of thousands to hundreds of thousands of compounds at the early stage of drug design. For example, in the application this paper presents, nearly 30,000 compounds have been assayed to discover their biological activities for protecting human cells from HIV infection. However, it is impractical to test every available compound against every biological target. Pharmaceutical companies now have of order one million compounds in their databases, and combinatorial chemistry can generate similar numbers of new compounds. Therefore, there is a great need to optimize this high throughput screening process by developing methods that can identify promising compounds from a large chemical inventory on the basis of a relatively smaller set of tested compounds. One approach is to use the data from tested compounds to relate biological activity to molecular descriptors of chemical structures. Discovering this structure-activity relationship helps biologists and chemists make decisions on which compounds are most likely to be highly active, so that they can speed up the searching process [17].

Many techniques can be used to discover the structure-activity relationship based on a set of tested compounds. For example, Jones-Hertzog *et al* [8] applied the recursive partitioning technique for building decision trees to model the structure-activity relationship. King *et al* [9] applied an inductive logic programming program to discover the structure-activity relationship. Neural networks have also been applied [3]. A major challenge in modeling this structure-activity relationship is that, although the data set may contain a large number of tested compounds, active compounds are often rare. For example, in the data set that we are working on for discovering a compound's activity in protecting human cells from HIV infection, only 2% of the compounds are active. Therefore, we are facing with a problem of learning from an extremely imbalanced data set. Learning with this kind of imbalanced data set presents problems to learning systems, problems which are not revealed when the systems work on relatively balanced data sets. Since most inductive learning algorithms assume that maximizing accuracy on a full range of cases is the goal [13], these systems exhibit accurate prediction for the majority class cases, but very poor performance for cases associated with the low frequency class. A solution to this problem is to reduce the imbalance in the data set by using different sampling techniques, such as data reduction or "down-sampling" techniques that remove only majority class examples [10] and "up-sampling" techniques that duplicate the training examples of the minority class or create new examples by corrupting existing ones with artificial noise [6]. An alternative to balancing the classes is to develop a learning algorithm that is intrinsically insensitive to

11

class distribution in the training set [12]. An example of this kind of algorithm is the SHRINK algorithm [11] that finds only rules that best summarizes the positive examples (of the small class), but makes use of the information from the negative examples.

In this paper, we investigate several existing data mining and statistical methods for modeling the structure-activity relationship based on an extremely imbalanced data set. The methods include a decision tree learning method, a rule induction method, a neural network method, a k-nearest neighbor method and a few regression methods. Our objective is as follows. First, we would like to determine how each of these methods reacts to the extremely imbalanced class distribution and which of these methods is most appropriate for this kind of learning problem. Second, we would like to evaluate these methods using different performance measures and determine whether there is correlation between the performance measures. Third, we would like to investigate whether pruning techniques that are often used in the decision tree and decision rule learning to avoid overfitting would help improve the predictive performance on imbalanced data sets. Finally, we would like to investigate whether reducing the imbalance in the training data by upsampling or down-sampling would improve performance.

2 The Data Set

The study was performed with a data set of nearly 30,000 compounds obtained from GlaxoSmithKline (GSK). The data were collected by the National Cancer Institute (NCI) in an effort to discover new compounds capable of inhibiting the HIV virus. The response variable indicates the activity status of the compounds as confirmed by the Developmental Therapeutics Program (DTP) AIDS anti-viral screen which measures how a compound protects human CEM cells from HIV-1 infection. The activity measure for each compound has three levels: 0 (inactive), 1 (moderately active), and 2 (active). The six descriptor variables were generated by GlaxoSmithKline chemists and are continuous variables called BCUT numbers which describe the structure of the compounds such as their surface area, bounding patterns, charges, and hydrogen bond donor and acceptor ability. They were calculated based on the work by Burden [4], who discovered that the compounds with similar structures have similar BCUT values.

The data set is very unbalanced. There are 215 active compounds, 393 moderately active compounds and the rest (29,204) are inactive. Our initial analysis of the data indicated that the inactives have a very complex distribution in the space of each pair of the descriptors and the active compounds are located in regions where there are many inactive ones. Because some of the methods we evaluated were designed to handle a binary response and there are relatively few compounds in the two active categories, we combined the active and moderately active compounds into one group. As a result, the data set contains 608 active compounds, which are about 2% of the compounds in the data set, and the rest are inactive compounds. To evaluate the modeling methods, the data set is further randomly split into a training and a test set. The training and test sets are of equal size and are both comprised of 304 active compounds and 14602 inactive compounds.

3 Performance Measures

Our objective is to evaluate some data mining and statistical classification methods on the data set. For each method, we build a classification model based on the training set and then test the model on the test set. A simple way to test the model is to classify the compounds in the test set and collect the classification accuracy as the performance measure. However, since it is the active compounds that are of interest and the active compounds occupy a very small percentage of the data, accuracy on the entire test set is not an appropriate performance measure for this application. Furthermore, simply classifying compounds is not sufficient. The domain experts would like the compounds in the test set to be presented to them in decreasing order of a prediction score with the highest prediction indicating the most probably active compound so that the compounds that are most likely to be active can be assayed in their labs first. Due to this reason, for each method being evaluated, we have to find a way to assign a prediction score to a test case and rank the cases according their scores. To be cost effective, it is preferred that a high proportion of the compounds ranked highest are actually active.

To evaluate the predictive performance of this kind, a popular measure is the *hit rate*, which is the proportion of active compounds or "hit" amongst those selected [15]. In this paper, we use three performance measures to evaluate the methods. First, we propose to use *average hit rate*, which is defined as the average of the hit rates at the points where active compounds are correctly recognized in a ranked list. The average hit rate has the similar definition to the performance measure of *average precision* used in information retrieval[1]. The second measure we use is called *hit curves*, which depicts the number of active compounds versus the number of compounds selected from a ranked list. With a hit curve we would like to show the performance on the highest region of a ranked list. Therefore, we restrict the number of selected compounds to be no more than 500. The third performance measure we use is *ROC*

---

[1] Finding active compounds from a large collection of compounds is similar to finding relevant documents from a large collection of documents in information retrieval. Both tasks have a highly skewed class distribution and output a ranked list of objects.

curves [14], which depict how the percentage of correctly recognized active compounds depends on the percentage of the incorrectly classified inactive compounds. ROC curves illustrate tradeoffs between true positive rates and false positive rates with respect to the active compounds. Given a ranked list, a ROC curve shows the predictive performance on the whole region of the list.

4 Description of Classification Models

We evaluate the following data mining and statistical methods for discovering classification models from data. Since it is necessary to output a ranked list of test examples in the prediction phase, we also describe the ranking criterion that we used for each method.

4.1 ELEM2

ELEM2 [1] is a rule induction algorithm that generates a set of classification rules by selecting attribute-value pairs from data. The learning strategy used in ELEM2 is a sequential covering method, which sequentially learns a single conjunctive rule, removes the examples covered by the rule, then iterates the process until all positive examples of a class are covered or until no rule can be generated. The result of the learning process for one class is a disjunctive set of conjunctive rules. ELEM2 also has an option to use a post-pruning technique that removes some attribute-value pairs from the condition part of a rule to avoid over-fitting. To post-prune a rule, ELEM2 computes a rule quality value for the rule according to one of the rule quality formulas described in [2]. In post-pruning, ELEM2 checks each attribute-value pair in the rule in the reverse order in which they were selected to determine if removal of the attribute-value pair will decrease the rule quality value. If not, the attribute-value pair is removed and the procedure checks all the other pairs in the same order again using the new rule quality value resulting from the removal of that attribute-value pair to discover whether another attribute-value pair can be removed. This procedure continues until no pair can be removed.

The rules generated by ELEM2 can be used to classify new examples in a test set. To apply ELEM2 to identify active compounds in our particular application, we design a ranking procedure that calculates a numerical score for each test example and ranks the test examples according to both their predicted classes and their scores. The score is called *ranking score* and measures an example's likelihood of belonging to a class, e.g., the category of active compounds in our particular application. To define the ranking score of an example e with respect to a class C, we first compute a matching score between e and a rule r of C using $MS_C(e, r) = \frac{m}{n} \times Q(r)$, where n is the number of attribute-value pairs that r contains, m is the number of attribute-value pairs in r that are matched with e, and $Q(r)$ is the rule quality value of r. The ranking score of e with respect to C is defined as

$$RS(e, C) = \sum_{i=1}^{k_1} MS_C(e, r_i) - \sum_{j=1}^{k_2} MS_{\neg C}(e, r_j),$$

where r_i is a rule of C, k_1 is the number of rules of C, r_j is a rule of classes other than C, and k_2 is the number of this kind of rules.

The ranking algorithm of ELEM2 ranks the test examples according to both the predicted class label (produced by ELEM2's classification program) for the example and the ranking score of that example with respect to a specified class C, e.g., the active compounds. It places test examples that are classified into the specified class C in front of other test examples and ranks the examples in each group in decreasing order of their ranking scores with respect to C.

4.2 Classification Trees

We use a Classification and Regression Tree (CART) program implemented in S [5] to test the performance of decision trees on our data set. Using binary recursive partition, a decision tree method successively splits the data along coordinate axes of predictors. At each division, the resulting two subsets of data are as homogeneous as possible with respect to the response of interest. In S, the splitting criterion is *deviance*, which measures the homogeneity of the two subsets. Let p_{ij} denote the probability of one observation in subset i to be in class j and n_{ij} denote the number of observations that are in subset i and belong to class j. The deviance of subset i is defined as $D_i = -2 \sum_j n_{ij} \log p_{ij}$. The deviance of the subtree generated by the split is defined as $D = \sum_i D_i$. The split that minimizes D is chosen. The default setting in S uses the following two constraints to stop further splitting the data:

(1) there must be at least 10 observations in a node; and

(2) the node deviance must be at least 1% of the root node deviance.

We call the trees generated with this default setting *default trees*. A *pure tree* can be constructed by removing these two constraints to allow the tree to perfectly adapt to the training data. In our experiments, we evaluate both kinds of trees on our data set.

To rank the examples in the test set, we calculate a score for each terminal node of a tree. A test example is assigned the score of the terminal node it falls in. Examples in the test set are ranked according to their assigned scores. To calculate the score for a terminal node in a default tree, we first calculate the estimated hit rate for the node as $\hat{p} = \frac{n_{active}}{n}$, where n_{active} is the number of active compounds in the training set that fall in the node and n is the number of compounds falling in the node. To account for uncertainty in $\hat{p}$, we assume a Binomial model for responses in each terminal node and calculate a 95% one-sided confidence interval or lower bound, $\hat{p_{lb}}$, for the true hit rate p. The $\hat{p_{lb}}$ score is large if $\hat{p}$ is large and there are many compounds in a node. We use the $\hat{p_{lb}}$ score to rank terminal nodes and test examples for a default tree. For a pure tree, we rank terminal nodes and test examples according to the node size, which is the number of active compounds in the training set that fall in the node.

4.3 k-Nearest Neighbor

K-nearest neighbor (kNN) classification is a very simple but powerful algorithm. For each case in the test set, a kNN method finds k nearest points in the training set according to a distance measure and assigns a predicted class to the test case by using a (weighted) vote among the k selected neighbors. In our experiment, k is determined by using leave-one cross-validation on the training data and Euclidean distance is used as the distance measure to find k nearest neighbors. Votes for the active compounds from the k nearest neighbors relative to all the votes can be regarded as the probability of the test case to be in the class of active compounds. This probability is used to rank test cases.

4.4 Logistic Regression Model

Logistic Regression Model (LRM) is a special case of generalized linear models and it is a popular model to handle data with binary response. LRM assumes

$$\log\left(\frac{p}{1-p}\right) = b_0 + b_1 x_1 + b_2 x_2 + ... + b_n x_n, \quad (1)$$

where p denotes the probability that the observed case (represented by $x_1, x_2, ..., x_n$) is in the category of interest and b's are the parameters to be estimated from the training data. In the prediction phase, the probability, p, that a test case is in the category of interest can be calculated with the estimated b's. Test cases are then ranked according to their probabilities of being in this category, which is the category of active compounds in our application.

4.5 Generalized Additive Model

The Generalized Additive Model (GAM) used in our study is an extension to the logistic regression model. In GAM, each predictor x_i in (1) is replaced by a smooth func-

tion, $f_i(x_i)$, where $i = 1, ..., n$, as follows:

$$\log\left(\frac{p}{1-p}\right) = b_0 + f_1(x_1) + f_2(x_2) + ... + f_n(x_n), \quad (2)$$

where $f_1, f_2, ...$ and f_n are smoothing splines which can be estimated from the training set.

4.6 Neural Networks

A feed-forward neural network [16] with one hidden layer of 9 nodes is used in our study. It is the simplest but the most common form of neural networks. The neural network can output an estimated probability that a test case is in a category of interest. We use this probability to rank test cases.

4.7 MARS

In Multivariate Adaptive Regression Splines (MARS), a multiple regression function is approximated using linear splines and their tensor products. Detailed description of MARS can be found in [7].

5 Empirical Comparison of Modeling Methods

To evaluate the above data modeling methods, we randomly split our data set four times, resulting in four training-test data splits. The training and test sets in each split are of equal size and both consist of 304 active and 14602 inactive compounds.

5.1 Results

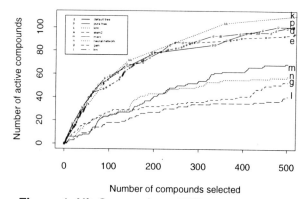

Figure 1. Hit Curves from Different Methods

Figure 1 compares the methods using hit curves for one random training-test data split[2]. From these hit curves, we

---

[2] The curves for three other splits are similar

14

can observe that *default tree, pure tree*, ELEM2[3] and the *k*-nearest neighbor method have the lead, followed by MARS and the neural network method. The worst performance is given by GAM and LRM.

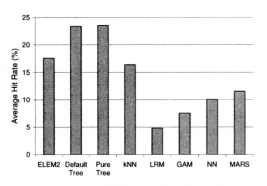

Figure 2. Average Hit Rates for the 8 Methods

Figure 2 compares the methods in terms of average hit rates. The average hit rate for each method is obtained by averaging the average hit rates on 4 random training-test data splits. It can be easily observed from the figure that the two tree methods take the lead, followed by ELEM2 and kNN, which in turn followed by MARS and the neural network method. LRM has the worst performance.

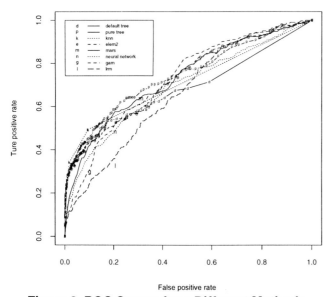

Figure 3. ROC Curves from Different Methods

Figure 3 presents the ROC curves produced by the 8 methods on one random training-test data split[4]. ROC curves illustrate the performance on the entire region of a

---

[3] ELEM2 has an option for choosing a rule quality formula. The result presented here is from using the $C2$ rule quality formula [2].

[4] The results on three other random splits are similar.

---

ranked list. The 8 curves cross each other and there is no single method dominating all the time. However, we can generally say that at the very beginning, pure tree, default tree, ELEM2 and kNN are among the best and their curves overlap, then the kNN method outperforms others and later the pure tree and GAM pick up the lead. MARS is also a good method in this comparison even if its top ranking performance displayed in hit curves is not as good. The LRM method remains the lowest in ROC curves, which is consistent with its ranking in terms of top ranking performance. Another observation we obtain from these ROC curves is that default trees are not as good as pure trees, which conflicts with observations from many other applications that smaller trees usually give better performance.

5.2 Discussion

It is obvious that hit curves depict the top ranking performance, while ROC curve illustrate the performance on the entire region of a ranked list. However, it was not obvious at what region of a ranked list the average hit rate is good at measuring the performance. By comparing our results on average hit rates with the results on hit curves, we observe that the average hit rate actually measures the top ranking performance. For our data set, we can roughly say that it measures the performance for the top 200 compounds in a ranked list even if the definition of average hit rate is based on the entire region. This observation can be explained by analyzing the definition of average hit rate. An active compound that ranks higher makes larger contribution to the value of the average hit rate. A low ranking active compound has a very small weight in the computation of the average hit rate.

In terms of the modeling methods we compare, we observe that local methods, including the classification tree methods, ELEM2 and kNN, which are good at capturing the local behavior and interactions in the data, are more successful techniques, outperforming all the other methods. These local methods are more general, flexible and make minimal assumptions about the underlying relationships. They are able to focus on very local regions with concentrations of active compounds. In kNN, strong local behavior in this data set is also indicated by the fact that an optimal k is chosen by using cross-validation on the training data.

Among the other methods we evaluate, LRM is a popular model for problems with binary response variables. However, it assumes that the log odd of the probability of active response, instead of inactive response, can be well approximated by a linear combination of the BCUT numbers. This assumption is unrealistic for the data that have only six predictors and may have a lot of large noises. GAM incorporates adaptive smoothing (smoothing splines) on each predictor into the data model, which results in a better performance than LRM. MARS allows not only non-linear effects within predictors but also some interactions among them. Feed-forward neural networks can also be seen as a method to parameterize a fairly general non-linear function [16]. We have observed from our experiments that both MARS and feed-forward neural networks give better performance than LRM and GAM on our data set.

6 Pruning vs No-pruning

We noticed from the above results that the pure tree method is comparable to the default tree method in terms of average hit rates and hit curves. In terms of ROC curves, it is obvious that the pure tree outperforms the default tree. Therefore, we can say that the pure tree performs as well as or better than the default tree in terms of top ranking performance and it is better than the default tree in terms of the performance in the entire region of the ranked list. This finding was a surprise to us because a pure tree perfectly adapts to the training data and it is usually considered to be overfitting the data. In many other applications, smaller trees, rather than overfitting trees, are preferable. A possible reason for our finding is that conventional criteria used in learning algorithms, such as misclassification rates, accuracy measurements or deviance, often assume that target classes have a balanced distribution.

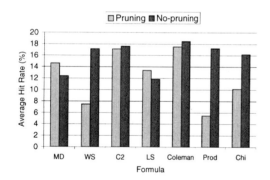

Figure 4. Comparison of Pruning with No-pruning

To further test the results, we conducted experiments with ELEM2 using different rule quality formulas. A rule quality formula is used in the post-pruning process of ELEM2 to determine whether an attribute-value pair in a rule should be removed to avoid overfitting. Description of the rule quality formulas used in ELEM2 can be found in [2]. Figure 4 shows the average hit rates of ELEM2 using different rule quality formulas with or without the pruning

technique[5]. The results indicate that for most of the rule quality formulas, such as *WS, Prod, Chi, C2* and *Coleman*, no-pruning produces better average hit rates than pruning. Only for formulas *MD* and *LS*, pruning is beneficial. However, these two formulas, even with the pruning option, are not as competitive as some other formulas on this imbalanced data set. The best performances are given by formulas *Coleman* and *C2*, indicating that *Coleman* and *C2* better handle the imbalance in the data set and that the pruning technique is not beneficial when the data is extremely imbalanced.

7 Balancing the Data

Another objective of this research is to discover whether reducing the imbalance in the training data would improve the predictive performance for the 8 modeling methods we have evaluated. To reduce the imbalance in the training data, we conducted both up-sampling and down-sampling. For up-sampling, we created 6 additional training sets by duplicating the examples of active compounds to increase the prevalence of active compounds in the training data. Percentages of active compounds in these 6 training sets are 4%, 8%, 14%, 25%, 40% and 50%, respectively. The original distribution of active compounds is 2%. Figure 5 illustrates the average hit rates versus the percentage of active compounds in the training data for the 8 modeling methods. From the curves we can observe that only for the pure tree method, balancing the data by up-sampling increases the performance. However, the increases are small and are not considered as significant. For other methods, balancing the data is not beneficial. The curves for the LRM and GAM methods are flat, indicating that they are not sensitive to the changes in the distribution of the data. MARS and the feed-forward neural network method are sensitive to the changes. The performance for these two methods can be increased by up-sampling. But their performance can also be decreased if the "right" distribution is not chosen. For the kNN method, the performance is decreasing at the beginning and is later flattened as the percentage of the active compounds increases. This is because in kNN k is chosen by using cross-validation and as the active compounds are being duplicated many times, k is consistently determined to be 1 because too many duplicated active compounds are in the training data.

We also conducted experiments with down-sampling for reducing the imbalance in the data. For down-sampling, we keep all the active compounds in the training data and randomly select a subset of inactive compounds. We created 13 down-sampled training sets. Each of the training sets contains $n \times 304$ inactive compounds, where n changes

---

[5] The results in the figure are the average over 4 random training-test data splits.

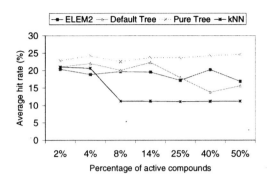

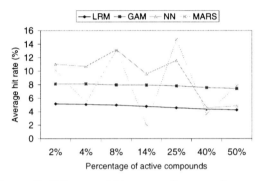

Figure 5. Effects of Up-sampling on Average Hit Rates

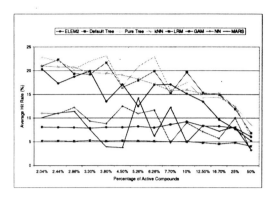

Figure 6. Effects of Down-sampling on Average Hit Rates

from $1, 3, 5, 7, ...,$ until 40. Consequently, the percentage of active compounds in the training set changes from $50\%, 25\%, 16.7\%, 12.5\%, ...,$ until 2.4%. In the original training data, the percentage of active compounds is 2.04%. Our experimental results for down-sampling is shown in Figure 6. The horizontal axis represents the percentage of active compounds in the down-sampled training data. The left-most point represents the true distribution of the data. As the percentage of active compounds increases, the size of training data decreases because of more inactive compounds are removed due to down-sampling. The curves describe the changes of average hit rates with respect to the changes in the percentage of the active compounds for the 8 modeling methods. We can observe that all the methods reach their lowest average hit rates when the data become perfectly balanced (50%). This is because too much information is lost by reducing the number of inactive compounds to be the same as active compounds. It can also be observed that LRM and GAM are not sensitive to the changes in training data since their curves are pretty much flat. The performance for the kNN method consistently decreases as the more and more inactive compounds are removed from the training data. For ELEM2, none of the down-sampled training sets improves the performance. For each of the tree methods, small improvement can be seen

at two points. But, generally, their performance decreases. For MARS and the neural network method, down-sampling can help, but it can also decrease the performance compared to using the original training set.

8 Conclusions

We have compared a number of classification methods on an extremely imbalanced data set for modeling the structure-activity relationship to identify active compounds for drug discovery. Among the methods we evaluated, local methods, such as the tree methods, the ELEM2 rule induction method and the kNN method, which are able to identify local behaviors and interactions, outperform other methods in terms of measures for the top ranking performance. Among the local methods, the pure tree method is robust in that it performs well on all the four data splits and that it does not only outperform others in the top region, but is also among the best methods evaluated on the entire region of the ranked list.

The pure tree's outstanding performance over the default tree indicates that the pre-pruning technique used in the default tree learning to avoid overfitting the data is not beneficial. This result is consistent with the results obtained from ELEM2 that uses post-pruning techniques to prevent the rules from overfitting the data. We found that for most of the rule quality formulas tested, especially those that give the best performance in the imbalanced data set, post-pruning does not improve the predictive performance. This conclusion needs to be further tested on other imbalanced data sets to determine whether the result is unique for our application.

We also found in this research that reducing the imbalance in the training data by either up-sampling or down-sampling does not increase the predictive performance for most of the evaluated methods. Only for MARS and the neural network method, the performance can be improved at certain points of up-sampling or down-sampling. At other points, the performance can be decreased. Therefore, careful selection of up-sampling or down-sampling points in terms of percentage of active compounds in the training data is necessary for using the up-sampling or down-sampling technique with MARS and neural networks. Cross-validation may be used in this selection.

In terms of performance measures used in our evaluation, ROC curves are good at depicting the performance in the entire region of a ranked list. Both hit curves and average hit rates are good at measuring the top ranking performance, which is considered to be important for our application. A benefit of using average hit rates is that it is easy to rank the methods being compared, while hit curves may cross each other multiple times, which makes it hard to determine which method is actually better overall. The measure of average hit rate can also be easily incorporated into a learning algorithm as a criterion for doing some sort of selection. For example, we may use the average hit rate as a criterion in cross-validation for determining an optimal tree size in the tree post-pruning process. This is one of the items we will work on in the future. We expect that a "right" criterion in pruning can lead to better performance.

Acknowledgment
This research is supported by the Natural Sciences and Engineering Research Council of Canada (NSERC). We would also like to thank Nick Cercone, Hugh Chipman and William Welch for their suggestions on this work.

References

[1] An, A. and Cercone, N. 1998. "ELEM2: A Learning System for More Accurate Classifications." *Proceeding of the 12th Canadian Conference on Artificial Intelligence*, Vancouver, Canada.

[2] An, A. and Cercone, N. 2000. "Rule Quality Measures Improve the Accuracy of Rule Induction: An Experimental Approach", *Proceedings of the 12th International Symposium on Methodologies for Intelligent Systems*, Charlotte, NC. 119-129.

[3] Andrea, T.A. and Kalayeh, H. 1991. Application of Neural Networks in Quantitative Structure-Activity Relationships of Dihydrofolate Reductase Inhibitors. *J. Med. Chem.*, Vol.34, 2824-2836.

[4] Burden, F.R. 1989. "Molecular Identification Number for Substructure Searches". *Journal of Chemical Information and Computer Sciences*, Vol.29, 225-227.

[5] Clark, L.A., Pregibon, D. 1991 "Tree-Based Models" in *Statistical Models in S*, edited by J. M. Chambers and T. J. Hastie. Wadsworth & Brooks/cole Advanced Books & Software Pacific Grove, California.

[6] DeRouin, E., Brown, J., Beck, H., Fausett, L. and Schneider, M. 1991. "Neural Network Training on Unequally Represented Classes", In Dagli, C.H., Kumara, S.R.T. and Shin, Y.C. (eds.), *Intelligent Engineering Systems Through Artificial Neural Networks*, ASME Press. 135-145.

[7] Friedman, J.H. 1991. "Multivariate Adaptive Regression Splines", *The Annals of Statistics*, 19, 1-141.

[8] Jones-Hertzog, D.K., Mukhopadyay, P., Keefer, C.E., Young, S.S. 2000. "Use of Recursive Partitioning in the Sequential Screening of G-protein-coupled Receptors". *Journal of Pharmacological and Toxicological Methods*, Vol.42. No.1999, 207-215.

[9] King, R.D., Muggleton, S., Lewis, R.A. and Sternberg, M.J.E. 1992. "Drug Design by machine learning: The use of inductive logic programming to model the structure-activity relationships of trimethoprim analogus binding to dihydrofolate reductase". *Proc. Natl. Acad. Sci.*, Vol.89, No.23.

[10] Kubat, M. and Matwin, S. 1997. "Addressing the Curse of Imbalanced Training Sets: One-Sided Sampling". *Proceedings of the Fourteenth International Conference on Machine Learning*, Morgan Kaufmann. 179-186.

[11] Kubat, M., Holte, R. and Matwin, S. 1997. "Learning when Negative Examples Abound," *Proceedings of ECML-97*, Springer. 146-153.

[12] Kubat, M., Holte, R. and Matwin, S. 1998. "Machine Learning for the Detection of Oil Spills in Satellite Radar Images", *Machine Learning*, 30, pp.195-215.

[13] Provost, F. 2000 "Machine Learning from Imbalanced Data Sets", *Invited paper for the AAAI'2000 Workshop on Imbalanced Data Sets*,

[14] Provost, F. and Fawcett, T. 2001. "Robust Classification for Imprecise Environments", *Machine Learning*, 42, 203-231.

[15] Tatsuoka, K., Gu, C., Sacks, J. and Young, S.S. 1998. Predicting Extreme Values in Large Datasets. *Journal of Computational and Graphical Statistics*.

[16] Venables, W.N., and Ripley, B.D. (1999).*Modern Applied Statistics with S-plus*, 3rd edition. New York : Springer, c1999.

[17] Wang, Y., Chipman, H.A., Welch W.J. (2001) "Mining Nuggets from High Throughput Screening Data" a paper presented at the annual meeting of the Statistical Society of Canada (SSC) in 2001.

Knowledge Discovery from Diagrammatically Represented Data

Michael Anderson
Department of Computer and Information Sciences
Fordham University
Bronx, NY 10458
anderson@trill.cis.fordham.edu

Abstract

Knowledge discovery from diagrammatic data can be facilitated by a language that permits queries on such data. Such a language (Diagrammatic SQL) is being developed to expedite the development of an autonomous artificially intelligent agent with a capacity to deal with diagrammatic information. This language is described and examples of how it can be used to facilitate diagrammatic data mining are detailed.

1. Introduction

In our ongoing investigation into the development of an agent with full diagrammatic reasoning capabilities comparable to those of human beings, we are currently focusing our attention on systems that allow users to pose queries against diagrams, seeking responses that require information to be inferred from diagrams — *diagrammatic information systems (DIS)* [3,4]. We are developing a core diagrammatic information system that remains diagram and domain independent, capable of accepting domain dependent diagrammatic and non-diagrammatic knowledge. In this way, each body of knowledge produces a new instantiation of the diagrammatic information system knowledgeable in the particular domain and diagram types represented by this knowledge. Our first instantiation of a diagrammatic information system, for example, is informed about *cartograms* (maps representing information as grayscale or color shaded areas) of the United States (Figure 1). Other domains might include suites of diagrams representing systems such as automobiles, the human body, integrated circuits, buildings, ships, etc.

An important facet of this research has been the development of a language in which to express queries against diagrammatic information. *Diagrammatic SQL (DSQL)* [3] is our extension to Structured Query Language (SQL) that supports querying of diagrammatic

information. Just as SQL permits users to query information in relations of a relational database, DSQL permits a user to query information in diagrams. We have chosen to extend SQL for use as our query language for a number of reasons. The grammar of SQL has a remarkable fit to the uses we wish to make of it. It is a reasonably intuitive language that allows specification of *what* data you want without having to specify exactly *how* to get it. It is a well-developed prepackaged technology whose use permits us to focus on more pressing research issues. SQL's large installed base of users provides a ready and able audience for a fully developed version of DSQL. As DSQL extends SQL, the SQL substrate can be used to query non-diagrammatic information, permitting heterogeneous data retrieval. The availability of immediate and imbedded modes provide means to use the system responses for both direct human consumption and further machine processing. Lastly, the availability of natural language interfaces to SQL will allow a diagrammatic information system to provide an even more intuitive interface for its users.

An interesting outgrowth of the development of DSQL is the capability of using this language to facilitate knowledge discovery from diagrammatic information. Given a database of diagrams, DSQL can be used to perform a number of data mining tasks including data cleaning, integration of heterogeneous data, retrieval of data relevant to the data mining task at hand, diagrammatic concept hierarchies development, generalization of diagrams through these hierarchies, computation of interestingness measures of discovered knowledge, and visualization of the discovered patterns.

2. A diagrammatic information system

As an example of a diagrammatic information system and its use of DSQL, consider the diagram in Figure 1. This is a cartogram (from The Weather Channel web site

Figure 1. Optimal planting in late May

http://www.weather.com) that depicts, in five colors, regions in the United States where it was optimal to plant various crops in late May, 2000. As detailed in the accompanying key, dark red denotes tomatoes and annuals, yellow denotes corn and beans, dark green denotes broccoli, light green denotes potatoes and lettuce, and light red denotes strawberries. Given this diagram as input to the system, as well as the semantics of the colors in this particular diagram, posing the query "Which states had regions optimal for planting strawberries in late May?" elicits the diagram in Figure 2 as a response from the system. In this diagrammatic response, each state that had regions optimal to plant strawberries in late May is represented by its shape in black positioned where the state lies within the United States.

Figure 1 is input to the system as a *pixmap* (pixel map) and stored as such. The system is supplied with the semantic mapping of the colors of the diagram to the crop types present and diagrams of these colors are stored. Using this information, the input diagram can then be parsed into five diagrams, each comprised of a single color. Each of these diagrams represents, then, the location of the optimal planting of a particular crop within the United States in late May. Figure 3, for example, shows the diagram resulting from this parsing that represents the locations of optimal planting regions for strawberries in the United States in late May.

A priori diagrammatic knowledge required to respond to this example query is comprised of a set of diagrams that represent the shape and locations of each state within the United States. Figure 4 is an example of such a diagram that shows the location of the state of New York within the United States by marking its area on the map in black. There are forty eight such state diagrams (along with a diagram for the capital region) as this domain pertains to the continental United States only. The one-time effort of developing this set of diagrams is small when weighed against the fact that it can be used to query *all* past, present, and future US diagrams on the Weather Channel web site.

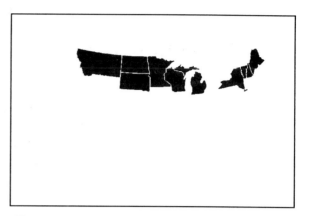

Figure 2. Response to query: "Which states had regions optimal for planting strawberries in late May?"

The query "Which states had regions optimal for planting strawberries in late May?" is presented to the system as the DSQL query :

DSELECT state FROM us
WHERE crop = strawberries AND season = late_may

Intuitively, this query requests that the system display all states in the US that satisfy the condition that they contain a region in which strawberries are planted in late May.

The response to this query is generated by comparing each of the state diagrams with the diagram representing strawberries in late May using primitives derived from the theory of inter-diagrammatic reasoning (detailed in the next section). When a state diagram intersects the late May strawberry diagram, the semantics of the domain dictate that that state contains a region that was optimal for planting strawberries in late May. All such states are then accumulated onto a single diagram and presented to the user as the response to the query.

In this manner, diagrammatic responses can be generated for a wide variety of queries concerning crops in the United States including "Which states did not have regions optimal for planting broccoli in late May?", "How many states had regions optimal for planting corn and beans in late May?", "Did Rhode Island have a region optimal for planting strawberries in late May?", "Which crop had regions optimally planted in late May in the most states?", "Did any states have regions optimal for planting strawberries and potatoes in late May?", "Which states had regions that were optimal for planting either corn or tomatoes in late May?", "Did more states have regions optimal for planting strawberries than tomatoes in late May?", "Which states had regions optimal for planting corn but not potatoes in late May?" , etc.

After a concise description of the theory that provides the foundation for DSQL, we use this example system to show how DSQL can help facilitate knowledge discovery from diagrammatic information.

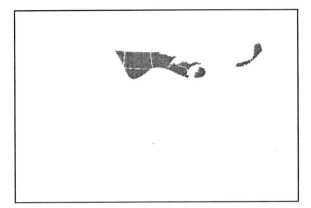

Figure 3. Location of optimal planting regions for strawberries in late May

3. Inter-diagrammatic reasoning

Our currently chosen approach gleans knowledge from diagrams by directly manipulating spatial representations of them. This approach is motivated by noting that, given diagrams directly input as pixmaps — an ability required of an autonomous diagrammatically capable agent — any translation into other representations will require some form of direct manipulation of these pixmaps. In many cases, this translation is superfluous. Given this approach, we store input pixmaps directly with no further abstraction. This strategy not only allows us to manipulate these spatial representations directly but, should the need arise, it will allow us to translate to any other representations as required. We use, as a basis for this direct manipulation of diagrams, an *inter-diagrammatic reasoning* approach.

Inter-diagrammatic reasoning (IDR) [3,5,6,7] defines diagrams as *tessellations* (tilings of finite subsets of two-dimensional space). Individual *tesserae* (tiles) take their values from an I, J, K valued subtractive CMY color scale. Intuitively, these CMY (Cyan, Magenta, Yellow) color scale values (denoted $v_{i,j,k}$) correspond to a discrete set of transparent color filters where i is the cyan contribution to a filter's color, j is the magenta contribution, and k is the yellow contribution. When overlaid, these filters combine to create other color filters from a minimum of WHITE ($v_{0,0,0}$) to a maximum of BLACK ($v_{I-1, J-1, K-1}$).

IDR leverages the spatial and temporal coherence often exhibited by groups of related diagrams for computational purposes. Like diagrams are combined in ways that produce new like diagrams that infer information implicit in the original diagrams. The following unary operators, binary operators, and functions provide a set of basic tools for the process of IDR.

IDR binary operators take two diagrams, d_1 and d_2, of equal dimension and tessellation and return a new diagram where each tessera has a value v that is some

Figure 4. Location of New York in the US

function of the values of the two corresponding tesserae, $v_{i1, j1, k1}$ and $v_{i2, j2, k2}$, in the operands.

- *OR*, denoted $d_1 \vee d_2$, returns the *maximum* of each pair of tesserae where the maximum of two corresponding tesserae is defined as $v_{max(i1,i2), max(j1, j2), max(k1,k2)}$.

- *AND*, denoted $d_1 \wedge d_2$, returns the *minimum* of each pair of tesserae where the minimum of two corresponding tesserae is defined as $v_{min(i1,i2), min(j1,j2), min(k1,k2)}$.

- *OVERLAY*, denoted $d_1 + d_2$, returns the *sum* of each pair of tesserae where the sum of values of corresponding tesserae is defined as $v_{min(i1+i2, I-1), min(j1+j2, J-1), min(k1+k2, K-1)}$.

- *PEEL*, denoted $d_1 - d_2$, returns the *difference* of each pair of tesserae the difference of values of corresponding tesserae is defined as $v_{max(i1-i2, 0), max(j1-j2, 0), max(k1-k2, 0)}$.

- *NOT*, denoted $\neg d$, is a one place operator that returns the value of $\infty - d$, where ∞ (the *maximum diagram*) denotes a diagram equal in tessellation to d containing all BLACK-valued tesserae.

- *NULL*, denoted $\eta(d)$, is a one place Boolean function taking a single diagram that returns TRUE if $d = \emptyset$, where $\emptyset$ (the *null diagram*) denotes a diagram equal in tessellation to d containing all WHITE-valued tesserae, else it returns FALSE.

- *ACCUMULATE*, denoted $a(d, ds, o)$, is a three place function taking an initial diagram, d, a set of diagrams of equal dimension and tessellation, *ds*, and the name of a binary diagrammatic operator, *o*, that returns a new diagram which is the accumulation of the results of successively applying o to d and each diagram in *ds*.

- *MAP*, denoted $\mu(f, ds_1,...,ds_n)$, is an $n+1$ place function taking an n-place function f and n sets (of equal cardinality) of diagrams of equal dimension and tessellation, ds_i, that returns the set of values resulting from application of f to each corresponding n diagrams in $ds_1,...,ds_n$.

- *FILTER*, denoted $\phi(f, ds)$, is a two place function

taking a Boolean function, f and a set of diagrams of equal dimension and tessellation, *ds*, that returns a new set of diagrams comprised of all diagrams in *ds* for which f returns TRUE.

- *ISOLATE*, denoted $\iota(d,d_{i,j,k})$, is a binary operator taking two diagrams d and $d_{i,j,k}$ (a diagram covered in $v_{i,j,k}$-valued tesserae) that returns a diagram where tesserae corresponding to those in d with value $v_{i,j,k}$ ($v_{i,j,k} \neq$ WHITE) have a non-WHITE value and all other tesserae are WHITE. This is compound operator whose functionality is achieved by creating a diagram $d_{BLACK-1}$ covered in BLACK - 1 valued tesserae, and returning the value of $\neg$ $((d - d_{i,j,k}) \lor (d_{i,j,k} - d))$ - $d_{BLACK-1}$.

DSQL queries are compiled into equivalent IDR operations and these are executed to produce appropriate responses. For example, the query "Which states had regions optimal for planting strawberries in late May?" can be represented in IDR operators as:

$\alpha(\emptyset, \phi(\lambda(x)$
$\quad \sim\eta(\alpha(\emptyset,\mu(\iota,\phi(\lambda(y) (y = \text{late\_may}), \text{season}),$
$\quad\quad\quad \phi(\lambda(z) (z = \text{strawberries}), \text{crop})), +)$
$\quad \land x, \text{states}), +).$

4. Knowledge discovery with DSQL

Discovery of knowledge in data, diagrammatic or otherwise, can be decomposed into a sequence of steps: *data cleaning* (removal of noise and inconsistent data), *data integration* (combining of multiple data sources), *data selection* (retrieval of relevant data), *data transformation* (conversion of data into appropriate forms for mining), *data mining* (extraction of patterns in data), *pattern evaluation* (computation of the interestingness of patterns), and *knowledge presentation* (visualization of patterns) [11]. DSQL facilitates each of these steps for knowledge discovery in diagrammatic data.

4.1. Data cleaning

Diagrammatic data is subject to both pixel-level noise (when dealing with pixmaps) and knowledge-level noise. Pixel-level noise relates to inconsistencies in the data that arise from file reading errors, scanning errors, etc. As this noise is difficult both to detect and remove, the system must accommodate it through the specification of thresholds instead of absolutes. Knowledge-level noise relates to irrelevant aspects of diagrammatic data. Figure 1, for example, contains much information that is irrelevant to the system's current goals including The Weather Channel logo, title and key, non-US geography, and bodies of water. DSQL removes this noise from consideration by the nature of its a priori knowledge — only regions of the diagram that are of interest are represented in this knowledge. Figure 5 shows these queriable regions in the current domain with

knowledge-based noise removed.

4.2. Data integration

Sources for data to be mined may differ in various ways including their physical locations, logical configurations, storage and access paradigms, and representation schemes.

DSQL's SQL substrate permits querying of all SQL-accessible data and enables DSQL to query both diagrammatic and non-diagrammatic data simultaneously. Thus DSQL can be viewed as an inter-lingua abstraction that can be use to achieve integration of diagrammatic and non-diagrammatic data by furnishing a homogeneous interface to this data. Given appropriate data sources, DSQL permits queries on heterogeneous data such as "What was the *average temperature* of states that had regions optimal for strawberries in late May?" or "Of those states that had regions optimal for planting tomatoes in late May, which had the *highest per captia income*?" For example, this latter query can be expressed by imbedding it into a SQL query that uses the list of states returned by DSQL to query the per capita income of the relation as follows:

```
SELECT MAX(pci) FROM us WHERE state IN
(DSELECT state FROM us
WHERE crop = tomatoes AND  season = late_may)
```

4.3. Data selection

As data mining an entire data set indiscriminately can be time consuming and return many patterns irrelevant to the data mining task at hand, DSQL, by its very nature, provides a means to select relevant data subsets. The query detailed previously is an example of the retrieval of such a subset. Further, given its data integration capabilities, DSQL can draw this subset from both diagrammatic and non-diagrammatic data.

4.4. Data transformation

It is often useful to the discovery process to provide background knowledge concerning the domain of the data to be mined and this knowledge is often provided as concept hierarchies or mappings from sets of low-level data to higher-level more general concepts [10].

The a priori knowledge providing the location, shape, and size of states within the United States is an example of one layer of a diagrammatic concept hierarchy. It maps sets of pixels (low-level data) into states (higher level concepts). DSQL can facilitate creation of further levels of concept hierarchies through its CREATE VIEW feature as a DSQL diagrammatic view can serve as a generalization of the diagrams from which it is created. For example, the following DSQL statement creates the view shown in Figure 6:

```
CREATE VIEW newengland AS
```

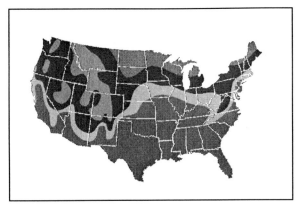

Figure 5. Planting diagram with noise removed

Figure 6. DSQL newengland view

```
DSELECT state FROM us
WHERE state = connecticut OR state = maine
OR state = massachusetts OR state = newhampshire
OR state = vermont OR state = rhodeisland
```

Using this view, any state in the set {Connecticut, Maine, Massachusetts, New Hampshire, Vermont, Rhode Island} can be represented more generally by the diagrammatic concept of *newengland*. Generalizations from the tessarae level (pixels, in the current example) to diagrams (sets of tesserae) to sets of diagrams can permit pattern discovery and presentation at more meaningful and understandable levels.

4.5. Data mining

Methods for finding patterns in cleaned, integrated, selected , and transformed data can be classified into two categories: *descriptive data mining*, where the object is to construct a concise description of the general properties of a set of data, and *predictive data mining*, where the object is to construct a model that can be used to help predict the behavior of new data sets [13].

Continuing our investigation into the application of machine learning techniques to diagrammatic data [8], we are currently exploring predictive data mining from temporal diagrammatic data [2]. Given a sequence of related diagrams representing change in some characteristics over time, how can earlier values for these characteristics be used to predict later values? Our current approach induces rules based upon the values for various characteristics for the relevant data set over the sequence of given diagrams. DSQL permits retrieval of diagrammatic data across the search space of these characteristics and comparison of this data to the data relevant to the data mining tasks. An example is presented in the next section.

4.6. Pattern evaluation

Not all patterns discovered through data mining are equally interesting. Less interesting patterns can be

pruned by interestingness measures that estimate the simplicity, certainty, utility, and novelty of discovered patterns. Two such measures are confidence and support [1]. *Confidence* is a measure of certainty that assesses the validity of the pattern. Given a rule *if A then B*, the confidence of that rule can be expressed as the number of data items containing both A and B divided by the number of data items containing A. *Support* is a measure of utility that assesses the potential usefulness of a pattern. Given a rule *if A then B*, the support of that rule can be expressed as the number of data items containing both A and B divided by the number of total data items.

DSQL facilitates the computation of both confidence and support by providing a means to count the number of items that satisfy a given condition. Both measures are computed using DSQL queries in the example data mining task that follows.

4.7. Knowledge presentation

Finally, interesting patterns found via data mining must be visualized in ways that make the discovered knowledge clear. The visual nature of DSQL responses can be exploited to help provide such visualizations. In the following example, DSQL provides a straightforward means to visualize the confidence and support of the discovered knowledge.

5. An example

Figures 7 and 8 are cartograms from The Weather Channel web site that depict, in various colors, regions in the United States where it was optimal to plant various crops in late April, 2000 and early May, 2000. As detailed in the accompanying key, in Figure 7 orange denotes citrus, dark red denotes tomatoes and annuals, yellow denotes corn and beans, dark green denotes broccoli, light green denotes peas and onions, pink denotes strawberries, and blue denotes regions too cold to plant anything. In Figure 8, red denotes tomatoes and annuals, yellow denotes corn and beans, dark green

Figure 7. Optimal planting in late April

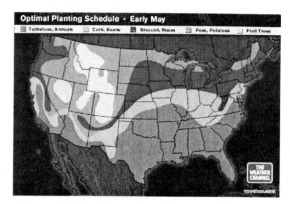

Figure 8. Optimal planting in early May

denotes broccoli and roses, light green denotes peas and potatoes, and pink denotes fruit trees.

Together with Figure 1, these three cartograms can be viewed as a portion of a database of time-sequence data concerned with optimal planting of crops in the US. The order of this data is based upon the time of year to which each cartogram pertains — late April (Figure 7), early May (Figure8), and late May (Figure 1).

Given this database, we set for ourselves the predictive knowledge discovery task of finding indicators earlier in the sequence that can help predict which states will have regions optimal for planting strawberries at the end of the sequence in late May. The example more concretely illustrates DSQL's use in each knowledge discovery step previously discussed.

5.1. Data cleaning and integration

As stated previously, DSQL removes noise from diagrammatic data by specification of a priori knowledge that focuses only on the relevant portions of that diagrammatic data. In this case, this a priori knowledge consists of diagrams representing the shape, size, and location of each state in the continental Unites States.

As we are currently investigating DSQL's purely diagrammatic aspects, the current example does not make use of its data integration capabilities.

5.2. Data selection and transformation

Data relevant to the current knowledge discovery task is retrieved by posing the query "Which states are optimal for planting strawberries in late May?" In DSQL:

DSELECT state FROM us

WHERE crop = strawberries AND season = late_may
The result of this query is shown in Figure 2 comprised of the following set of states: {Maine, Michigan, Minnesota, Montana, New Hampshire, New York, North Dakota, South Dakota, Vermont, Wisconsin}

In this example, data is transformed by a priori knowledge providing the location, shape, and size of

states within the United States mapping sets of pixels (low-level data) into states (higher level concepts).

5.3. Data mining

The strategy used to find the desired predictors is to query previous seasonal diagrams for the states that contain regions for each of the crops represented in each diagram. These responses, then, are compared with task relevant data retrieved during data selection and those responses that do not contain a significant subset of the task relevant data are removed from further consideration. The remaining set of queries is then combined to induce a rule and that rule is evaluated for interestingness.

To begin, the late April diagram is queried, via DSQL, for states that contain regions optimal to plant each of the crops it represents (including "no crop"). These queries include "Which states have regions optimal for planting citrus?", "Which states have regions optimal for planting tomatoes and annuals?", etc.

Given a tolerance level of 100% (i.e. responses are removed that do not return a data set of which the entire set of task relevant data retrieved during data selection is a subset), only one such query for late April is retained: "Which states have regions that are optimal for planting fruit trees in late April?" In DSQL:

DSELECT state FROM us

WHERE crop = fruit_trees AND season = late_april
This query returns the diagram shown in Figure 9.

Next, the early May diagram is queried, via DSQL, for states that contain regions optimal to plant each of the crops it represents. Again, given a tolerance level of 100%, only one such query for early May is retained: "Which states have regions that are optimal for planting peas and potatoes in early May?" In DSQL:

DSELECT state FROM us

WHERE crop=peaspotatoes AND season= early_may
This query returns the diagram shown in Figure 10.

As each of these queries elicits a response that matches the task relevant data exactly, the conditions represented

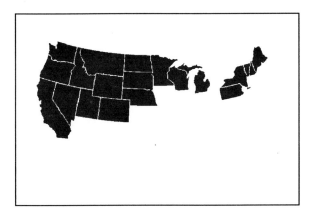

Figure 9. Response to query: "Which states had regions optimal for planting fruit trees in late April?"

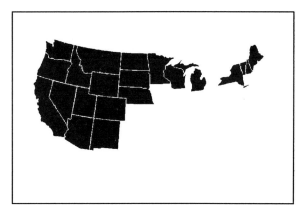

Figure 10. Response to query: "Which states had regions optimal for planting peas and potatoes in early May?"

by the queries represent likely predictors for a state containing a region optimal for planting strawberries in late May. That is, states that contained regions optimal for planting strawberries in late May contained regions optimal for planting fruit trees in late April and peas and potatoes in early May. As we are interested in predicting optimal strawberry planting regions from past observations, we are interested in validating the induced rule: "If a state has regions optimal for planting fruit trees in late April and peas & potatoes in early May, then it has regions optimal for planting strawberries in late May."

5.4. Pattern evaluation

Evaluating the interestingness of this rule requires establishing its simplicity, certainty, utility, and novelty. Its simplicity can be established through a count of conjuncts used in the rules antecedent — we deem two to be within our simplicity threshold. Further, we deem the rule novel in that it is at least so to us. We establish certainty via computation of the rule's measure of confidence and its utility via computation of the rule's measure of support.

To compute the confidence measure of this rule, DSQL is used to query the database for 1) the number of states that satisfy the antecedent of the induced rule ("state has regions optimal for planting fruit trees in late April and peas & potatoes in early May") and 2) the number of states that satisfy both the antecedent and consequent of the induced rule ("If state has regions optimal for planting fruit trees in late April and peas & potatoes in early May, then it has regions optimal for planting strawberries in late May"). The confidence measure equals the first count divided by the second count. The following DSQL query returns the first count:

```
DSELECT COUNT (state) FROM us
WHERE   (crop = fruit_trees AND season =late_april)
```

AND (crop = peaspotatoes AND season = early_may)
The result of this query is 19, the number of states that satisfy it. The following DSQL query returns the second count:

```
DSELECT COUNT (state) FROM us
WHERE   (crop = fruit_trees AND season =late_april)
AND (crop = peaspotatoes AND season = early_may)
AND (crop = strawberries AND season = late_may)
```

The result of this query is 10, the number of states that satisfy it. The confidence measure is then 10/19 or 52.6%, deeming the rule correct about half the time.

The measure of support is computed by dividing the second count from above (number of states satisfying both the antecedent and consequent of the rule) by the total number of states in the database. The following DSQL query returns the count of all states (including Washington, D.C.):

```
DSELECT COUNT (state) FROM us
```

The result of this query is 49. The measure of support is then 10/49 or 20.4% deeming the rule useful for about a fifth of the database.

5.5. Knowledge presentation

To help clarify the rule, DSQL queries can be used to help visualize the confidence and support of the discovered knowledge. These queries are identical to those used to determine the interestingness measures except that diagrams are returned instead of counts. States that satisfy the antecedent of the induced rule, as displayed in Figure 11, are returned by the first query. States that satisfy both the antecedent and consequent of the rule, as displayed in Figure 2, are returned by the second query.

6. Conclusion

We have shown how a language that can be used to query diagrammatic data can be useful in knowledge discovery

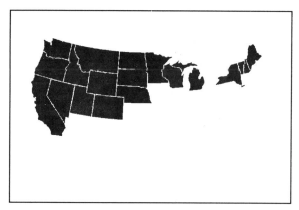

Figure 11. States satisfying the antecedent of the rule

tasks on this data. Other related data mining approaches include data mining on spatial databases [9], multimedia databases [12], and mining the World Wide Web [14]. Our approach differs from typical spatial databases in that high level semantics are provided for raster level data instead of simply descriptions of points, lines, polygons, etc. Further, multimedia databases, while permitting queries upon raster data, do so at relatively primitive levels of abstraction such as color, basic shape, texture, etc. Again, the higher level of abstraction provided by our approach (arising from its domain specificity) differentiates it.

To conclude, this is but a step in our attempt to provide agents with diagrammatic reasoning capabilities. Such a capability will be required of autonomous agents that interact with an environment rife with such representations and unsophisticated users whose expectations for human-like interaction are unbounded. Those agents able to interact with diagrammatic information in their environment and engage in two-way diagrammatic communication with users will clearly exhibit a higher degree of autonomy and naturalness of human-machine interfacing than those not so able.

7. Acknowledgments

This material is based upon work supported by the National Science Foundation under grant number IIS-9820368.

8. References

[1] Agrawal, R., Imielinski, T. and Swami, A., 1993. Database Mining: A Performance Perspective. *IEEE Transactions on Knowledge and Data Engineering*, 5:914-925.

[2] Agrawal, R. and Srikant, R., 1995. Mining Sequential Patterns. In Proceedings of 1995 International Conference on Data Engineering (ICDE '95), pp. 3-14, Taipei, Taiwan, March.

[3] Anderson, M. 1999. Toward Diagram Processing: A Diagrammatic Information System. In Proceedings of the 16th National Conference on Artificial Intelligence, Orlando, Fl. July.

[4] Anderson, M. 2000. Diagrammatic Reasoning and Mathematical Morphology. In Proceedings of the AAAI Spring Symposium on Smart Graphics, Stanford, CA. March.

[5] Anderson, M. and Armen, C. 1998. Diagrammatic Reasoning and Color. In Proceedings of the AAAI Fall Symposium on Formalization of Reasoning with Visual and Diagrammatic Representations, Orlando, FL. October.

[6] Anderson, M. and McCartney, R. 1995. Inter-diagrammatic Reasoning. In Proceedings of the 14th International Joint Conference on Artificial Intelligence, Montreal, Canada. August.

[7] Anderson, M. and McCartney, R. 1996. Diagrammatic Reasoning and Cases. In Proceedings of the 13th National Conference on Artificial Intelligence, Portland, OR. August.

[8] Anderson, M. and McCartney, R. 1997. Learning from Diagrams. *Journal of Machine Vision and Graphics*, Vol. 6, No. 1.

[9] Ester, M., Kriegel, H.-P. and Sander, J., 1997. Spatial Data Mining: A Database Approach. In Proceedings of the International Symposium on Large Spatial Databases, pp. 47-66, Berlin, Germany, July.

[10] Han, J. and Fu, Y., 1994. Dynamic Generation and Refinement of Concept Hierarchies for Knowledge Discovery in Databases. In Proceedings of the 1994 AAAI Workshop Knowledge Discovery in Databases (KDD '94), pp. 157-168, Seattle, WA. July.

[11] Han, J. and Kamber, M., 2001. *Data Mining: Concepts and Techniques*. Morgan Kaufmann Publishers, San Francisco, CA.

[12] Subrahmanian, V.S., 1998. *Principles of Multimedia Database Systems*. San Francisco: Morgan Kaufmann.

[13] Weiss, S.M. and Kulikowski, C.A., 1991. *Computer Systems that Learn: Classification and Prediction Methods from Statistics, Neural Nets, Machine Learning, and Expert Systems*. San Mateo, CA: Morgan Kaufmann.

[14] Zaïane, O.R. and Han, J., 1998. Querying the World-Wide Web for Resources and Knowledge. In the Proceedings of the International Workshop on Web Information and Data Management (WIDM '98), pp. 9-12, Bethesda, MD, November.

Integrating E-Commerce and Data Mining: Architecture and Challenges

Suhail Ansari, Ron Kohavi, Llew Mason, and Zijian Zheng

Blue Martini Software
2600 Campus Drive
San Mateo, CA, 94403, USA

{suhail,ronnyk,lmason,zijian}@bluemartini.com

Abstract

We show that the e-commerce domain can provide all the right ingredients for successful data mining. We describe an integrated architecture for supporting this integration. The architecture can dramatically reduce the pre-processing, cleaning, and data understanding effort often documented to take 80% of the time in knowledge discovery projects. We emphasize the need for data collection at the application server layer (not the web server) in order to support logging of data and metadata that is essential to the discovery process. We describe the data transformation bridges required from the transaction processing systems and customer event streams (e.g., clickstreams) to the data warehouse. We detail the mining workbench, which needs to provide multiple views of the data through reporting, data mining algorithms, visualization, and OLAP. We conclude with a set of challenges.

Note: A long version of this paper is also available [1].

1. Introduction

In *Measuring Web Success* [2], the authors claim that "Leaders will use metrics to fuel personalization" and that "firms need web intelligence, not log analysis."

Data mining tools aid the discovery of patterns in data[1] and E-commerce is the killer-domain for data mining. It is ideal because many of the ingredients required for successful data mining are easily satisfied: data records are plentiful, electronic collection provides reliable data, insight can easily be turned into action, and return on investment can be measured. To really take advantage of this domain, however, data mining must be integrated into the e-commerce systems with the appropriate data transformation bridges from the transaction processing system to the data warehouse and vice-versa. Such integration can dramatically reduce the data preparation time, known to take about 80% of the time to complete an analysis [3]. An integrated solution can also provide users with a uniform user interface and seamless access to metadata.

2. Integrated Architecture

In this section we give a high level overview of a proposed architecture for an e-commerce system with integrated data mining. Details of the most important parts of the architecture and their advantages appear in following sections. The described system is an ideal architecture based on our experiences at Blue Martini Software. In our proposed architecture there are three main components, *Business Data Definition*, *Customer Interaction*, and *Analysis*. Connecting these components are three data transfer bridges, *Stage Data*, *Build Data Warehouse*, and *Deploy Results*. The relationship between the components and the data transfer bridges is illustrated in Figure 1. Next we describe each component in the architecture and then the bridges that connect these components.

In the *Business Data Definition* component, the e-commerce business user defines the data and metadata associated with their business. This data includes merchandising information (e.g., products, assortments, and price lists), content information (e.g., web page templates, email templates for campaigns, articles, images, and multimedia) and business rules (e.g., personalized content rules, promotion rules, and rules for cross-sells and up-sells). From a data mining perspective the key to the *Business Data Definition* component is the ability to define a rich set of attributes (metadata) for any type of data. For example, products can have attributes like size, color, and targeted age group, and can be arranged in a hierarchy representing categories like men's and women's, and sub-categories like shoes and shirts. As another example, web page templates can have attributes indicating whether they show products, search results, or are used as part of the checkout process. Having a diverse set of available attributes is not only essential for data mining, but also for personalizing the customer experience.

The *Customer Interaction* component provides the interface between customers and the e-commerce business. Although we use the example of a web site throughout this paper, the term customer interaction applies more generally to any sort of interaction with customers. This interaction could take place through a web site (e.g., a marketing site or a web store), email marketing campaigns, cus-

---

[1] In this paper, we use the term *data mining* to denote the wider process, sometimes called *knowledge discovery*, which includes multiple disciplines, such as preprocessing, reporting, exploratory analysis, visualization, and modeling.

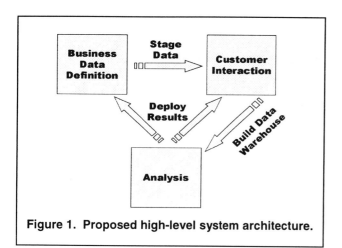

Figure 1. Proposed high-level system architecture.

tomer service (via telephony or email), wireless application, or a bricks-and-mortar point of sale system. For effective analysis of all of these data sources, a data collector needs to be an integrated part of the *Customer Interaction* component. To provide maximum utility, the data collector should not only log sale transactions, but it should also log other types of customer interactions, such as web page views for a web site, opening of emails sent out as part of a campaign, etc. Further details of the data collection architecture for the specific case of a web site are described in Section 3. To illustrate the utility of this integrated data collection let us consider the example of an e-commerce company measuring the effectiveness of its web banner advertisements on other sites geared at attracting customers to its own site. A similar analysis can be applied when measuring the effectiveness of advertising or different personalization on its own site.

The cost of a web banner advertisement is typically based on the number of "clickthroughs." That is, there is a fee paid for each visitor who clicks on the banner advertisement. Many e-commerce companies measure the *effectiveness* of their web banner advertisements using the same metric, the number of clickthroughs, and thus fail to take into account the *sales generated* by each referred visitor. If the goal is to sell more products then the site needs to attract buyers rather than browsers. A Forrester Research report [2] stated *"Using hits and page views to judge site success is like evaluating a musical performance by its volume."* We have seen the ratio of generated sales to clickthroughs vary by as much as a factor of 20 across a company's web banner advertisements. One advertisement generated five times as much in sales as another advertisement, even though clickthroughs from the former advertisement were one quarter of the clickstreams from the latter. The ability to measure this sort of relationship requires conflation of multiple data sources.

The *Analysis* component provides an integrated environment for decision support utilizing data transformations, reporting, data mining algorithms, visualization, and OLAP tools. The richness of the available metadata gives the *Analysis* component significant advantages over horizontal decision support tools, in both power and ease-of-use. For instance, the system automatically knows the type of each attribute, including whether a discrete attribute's values are ordered, whether the range of a continuous attribute is bounded, and textual descriptions. For a web site, the system knows that each customer has web sessions and that each web session includes page views and orders. This makes it a simple matter to compute aggregate statistics for combinations of customers, sessions, page views, and orders automatically. We examine the integrated analysis component in more detail in Section 4.

The *Stage Data* bridge connects the *Business Data Definition* component to the *Customer Interaction* component. This bridge transfers (or *stages*) the data and metadata into the *Customer Interaction* component. Having a staging process has several advantages, including the ability to test changes before having them implemented in production, allowing for changes in the data formats and replication between the two components for efficiency, and enabling e-commerce businesses to have zero downtime.

The *Build Data Warehouse* bridge links the *Customer Interaction* component with the *Analysis* component. This bridge transfers the data collected within the *Customer Interaction* component to the *Analysis* component and builds a data warehouse for analysis purposes. The *Build Data Warehouse* bridge also transfers all of the business data defined within the *Business Data Definition* component (which was transferred to the *Customer Interaction* component using the *Stage Data* bridge). The data collector in the *Customer Interaction* component is usually implemented within an On-Line Transaction Processing (OLTP) system, typically designed using entity relation modeling techniques. OLTP systems are geared towards efficient handling of a large number of small updates and short queries. This is critical for running an e-commerce business, but is not appropriate for analysis [4, 5], which usually requires full scans of several very large tables and a star schema design which business users can understand. For data mining, we need to build a data warehouse using dimensional modeling techniques. Both the data warehouse design and the data transfer from the OLTP system to the data warehouse system are very complex and time-consuming tasks. Making the construction of the data warehouse an integral part of the architecture significantly reduces the complexity of these tasks. In addition to typical ETL (Extract, Transform and Load) functionality, the bridge supports import and integration of data from both external systems and syndicated data providers (e.g., Acxiom). Since the schema in the OLTP system is controlled by the architecture, we can automatically convert the OLTP schema to a multi-dimensional star schema that is optimized for analysis.

The last bridge, *Deploy Results*, is the key to closing the loop and making analytical results actionable. It provides the ability to transfer models (e.g., association rules or collaborative filtering), scores or predicted values (e.g., classification or regression results), and new attributes constructed using data transformations (e.g., lifetime value) back into the *Business Data Definition* and *Customer Interaction* components for use in business rules for personalization.

3. Data Collection

This section describes the data collection component of the proposed architecture. This component logs customers' transactions (e.g., purchases and returns) and event streams (e.g., clickstreams). While the data collection component is a part of every customer touch point (e.g., web site, customer service applications, and wireless applications), in this section we will describe in detail the data collection at the web site. Most of the concepts and techniques mentioned in this section could be easily extended to other customer touch points.

3.1. Clickstream Logging

Most e-commerce architectures rely on web server logs or packet sniffers as a source for clickstream data. While both these systems have the advantage of being non-intrusive, allowing them to "bolt on" to any e-commerce application, they fall short in logging high-level events and lack the capability to exploit metadata available in the application [6]. For each page that is requested from the web server, there are a huge number of requests for images and other content on the page. Since all of these are recorded in the web server logs, most of the data in the logs relates to requests for image files that are mostly useless for analysis and are commonly filtered out. Because of the stateless nature of HTTP, each request in a web log appears independent of other requests, so it becomes extremely difficult to identify users and user sessions from this data [7, 8, 9, 10]. Since the web logs only contain the name of the page that was requested, these page names have to be mapped to the content, products, etc., on the page. This problem is further compounded by the introduction of dynamic content where the same page can be used to display different content for each user. In this case, details of the content displayed on a web page may not even be captured in the web log. The mechanism used to send request data to the server also affects the information in the web logs. If the browser sends a request using the "POST" method, then the input parameters for this request are not recorded in the web log.

Packet sniffers try to collect similar data by looking at data "on the wire." These techniques still have problems identifying users (e.g., same visitor logging in from two different machines) and sessions. Also, given the myriad ways in which web sites are designed it is extremely difficult to extract logical business information by looking at data streaming across a wire. To further complicate things, packet sniffers can't see the data in areas of the site that are encoded for secure transmission and thus have difficulty working with sites (or areas of a site) that use SSL (Secure Socket Layer). Such areas of a site are the most crucial for analysis including checkout and forms containing personal data. In many financial sites including banks, the entire site is secure thus making packet sniffers that monitor the encrypted data blind and essentially useless, so the sniffers must be given access to data prior to encryption, which complicates their integration.

Collecting data at the application server layer can effectively solve all these problems. Since the application server serves the content (e.g., images, products and articles), it has detailed knowledge of the content being served. This is true even when the content is dynamically generated or encoded for transmission using SSL. Application servers use cookies (or URL encoding in the absence of cookies) to keep track of a user's session, so "sessionizing" the clickstream is trivial. Since the application server also keeps track of the user, using login mechanisms or cookies, associating the clickstream with a particular visitor is simple. The application server can also be designed to keep track of information absent in web server logs including pages that were aborted (user pressed the "stop" button while the page was being downloaded), local time of the user, speed of the user's connection and if the user had turned their cookies off. This method of collecting clickstream data has significant advantages over both web logs and packet sniffers.

3.2. Business Event Logging

The clickstream data collected from the application server is rich and interesting; however, significant insight can be gained by looking at subsets of requests as one logical event or episode [7, 11]. We call these aggregations of requests *business events*. Business events can also be used to describe significant user actions like sending an email or searching [2]. Since the application server has to maintain the context of a user's session and related data, the application server is the logical choice for logging these business events. Business events can be used to track things like the contents of abandoned shopping carts, which are extremely difficult to track using only clickstream data. Business events also enable marketers to look beyond page hit-rates to *micro-conversion rates* [12]. A micro-conversion rate is defined for each step of the purchasing process as the fraction of products that are successfully carried through to the next step of the purchasing process. Two examples of these are the fraction of product views that resulted in the product being added to the shopping cart and the fraction of products in the shopping cart that successfully passed through each phase of the checkout process. Thus the integrated approach proposed in this architecture gives marketers the ability to look directly at product views, content views, and product sales, a capability far more powerful than just page views and clickthroughs.

Some interesting business events that help with the analyses given above include: adding items to, or removing items from the shopping cart, initiating checkout, finishing checkout, search, and registration. The search keywords and the number of results for each of these searches that can be logged with the search events give marketers significant insight into the interests of their visitors and the effectiveness of the search mechanism.

Another touch point that can make significant use of business events is campaign management. Campaign Management can use business events to track the sending of an email to a specific user for a specific campaign. Business Events can also be used to track the opening of these emails, submission of survey forms sent out in the email, and user click-through on the emails resulting in visits to the web site. These business events coupled with the users' clickstream data give a comprehensive picture of the user's behavior across multiple touch points. Similarly, a business event can be collected each time that a rule or model is used in personalization and these events, coupled with the shopping-cart/checkout events, can give an excellent estimate of the effectiveness of each type of personalization.

3.3. Effective Sampling Techniques

One of the challenges in collecting clickstream and business events is the volume of data generated. It is not uncommon for a site to have tens of millions of page requests a day. Add to this the data collected for specific events to track behavior and the effectiveness of personalization and the size of this data can easily grow into hundreds of millions of records. Collecting all this data may be infeasible both from a storage perspective and the impact this may have on the performance of the web site. One solution to this problem is to sample the data at the point of collection, and only collect a subset of the data. Straightforward percentage based sampling of requests however, has disastrous implications, as this results in the recording of incomplete sessions. Even sampling at the session level is not recommended since this may result in only a percentage of a user's sessions being recorded. This prevents the tracking and analysis of repeat visitors and their behavior among other things. Our architecture supports the sampling of this data at the cookie level.

4. Analysis

This section describes the analysis component of our architecture. We start with a discussion of data transfor-

mations, followed by analysis techniques including reporting, data mining algorithms, visualization, and OLAP. The data warehouse is the source data of analyses in our architecture. Although dimensional modeling is usually a prerequisite for analysis, our experience shows that many analyses require additional data transformations that convert the data into forms more amenable to data mining.

4.1. Data Transformations

As we mentioned earlier, the business user can define product, promotion, and assortment hierarchies in the *Business Data Definition* component. Figure 2 gives a simple example of a product hierarchy. This hierarchical information is very valuable for analysis, but few existing data mining algorithms can utilize it directly. Therefore, we need data transformations to convert this information to a format that can be used by data mining algorithms. One possible solution is to add a column indicating whether the item falls under a given node of the hierarchy. Let us use the product hierarchy shown in Figure 2 as an example. For each order line or page request containing a product SKU (Stock Keeping Unit), this transformation creates a Boolean column corresponding to each selected node in the hierarchy. It indicates whether this product SKU belongs to the product category represented by the node. Figure 3 shows the enriched row from this operation.

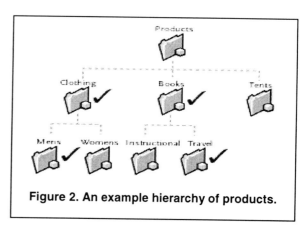

Figure 2. An example hierarchy of products.

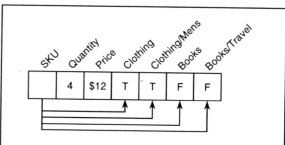

Figure 3. Data record created by the add product hierarchy transformation.

Since customers are the main concern of any e-commerce business, most data mining analyses are at the customer level. That is, each record of a data set at the final stage of an analysis is a customer signature containing all the information about the customer. However, the majority of the data in the data warehouse is at other levels such as the order header level, the order line level, and the page request level. Each customer may have multiple rows at these levels. To make this detailed information useful for analyses at the customer level, aggregation transformations are necessary [13]. Here are some examples of aggregated attributes that we have found useful:

- How much is each customer's average order amount above the mean value of the average order amount for female customers?
- What is the total amount of each customer's five most recent purchases over $30?
- What is the frequency of each customer's purchases?
- What is the recency of each customer's purchases (the number of days since the last purchase)?

Some of these attributes are very difficult to construct using standard SQL statements, and need powerful aggregation transformations. We have found RFM (Recency, Frequency, and Monetary) attributes particularly useful for the e-commerce domain.

E-commerce data contains many date and time columns. We have found that these date and time columns convey useful information that can reveal important patterns. However, the common date and time format containing the year, month, day, hour, minute, and second is not often supported by data mining algorithms. Most patterns involving date and time cannot be directly discovered from this format. To make the discovery of patterns involving dates and times easier, we need transformations which can compute the time difference between dates (e.g., order date and ship date), and create new attributes representing day-of-week, day-of-month, week, month, quarter, year, etc. from date and time attributes.

Based on the considerations mentioned above, the architecture must support a rich set of transformations.

4.2. Reporting, Algorithms, and Visualization

In this section we discuss the importance of reporting, analytical algorithms and data visualization. Basic reporting is a bare necessity for e-commerce. Through generated reports, business users can understand how a web site is working at different levels and from different points of view. Example questions that can be answered using reporting are:

- What are the best selling products?
- What are the most frequent failed searches?
- What are the conversion rates by brand?
- What are the top referrers by sales amount?
- What are the top abandoned products?

Our experience shows that some reporting questions such as the last two mentioned above are very hard to answer without an integrated architecture that records both event streams and sales data.

Beyond basic reporting, we have found simple attribute statistics based on distributions, averages, minima and maxima for continuous attributes and top distinct values (with counts and percentages) for discrete attributes to be extremely useful. Given that typical e-commerce data contains many hundreds of attributes it is important to be able to quickly identify interesting attributes based on their distribution (e.g., attributes with a single populated value or with a uniform distribution are typically uninteresting). It is also useful to be able to examine the distributions of attributes against a given target attribute. Again, it is important to be able to reduce the number of attributes that need to be examined by identifying those attributes that are correlated with the target attribute.

Model generation using data mining algorithms is a key component of the architecture. Classification, regression, clustering, sequence analysis, association rules, and collaborative filtering all reveal patterns about customers, their purchases, page views, etc. By generating models, we can answer questions like:

- What characterizes customers that prefer certain promotions to others?
- What characterizes customers that accept cross-sells and up-sells?
- What characterizes visitors that do not buy?
- What articles generate sales for particular products?
- How do the navigation paths differ for browsers and buyers?

Models can be used for business insight, generating scores and predictions (to be later used in personalization) or can be directly deployed to the *Customer Interaction* component to form the basis of a real-time personalization or recommendation engine.

Based on our experience, in addition to automated data mining techniques, it is necessary to provide interactive model modification tools to support business insight. Models either automatically generated or created by interactive modifications can then be examined or evaluated on test data. The purpose is to let business users understand their models before deploying them. For example, we have found that for rule models, measures such as confidence, lift, and support at the individual rule level and the individual conjunct level are very useful in addition to the overall accuracy of the model.

Given that humans are very good at identifying patterns from visualized data, visualization and OLAP tools can greatly help business users to gain insight into business problems by complementing reporting tools and data mining algorithms. Our experience suggests that visualization tools are very helpful in understanding generated models and web site operational data. For example, on real client data, we have seen that plotting a bar-chart of the number of sessions by day of the week has shown that traffic is higher on Tuesday and Wednesday.

To understand why this was so, it was interesting to look at a heat-map as shown in Figure 4. The x-axis is date (one value for every day) while the y-axis is the hour of the day. Each intersection therefore represents an hour on a given day and its color (shade of gray) is assigned

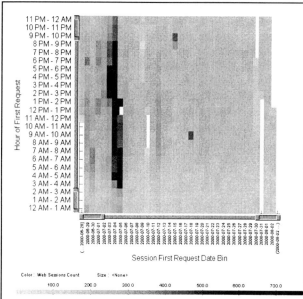

Figure 4. A heat-map showing the date, hour of day, and session count in gray.

based on the number of sessions that started at that hour. The heat-map quickly reveals that the reason for the spike on Tuesday is the July 4th holiday, when traffic increased dramatically. It is also instructive to look at the white spaces in the figure, on July 10th and July 30th-July 31st. These indicate site downtime and prior to that downtime there is relatively little traffic at the site (lighter grays).

4.3. Closed Loop Interaction Management

One of the primary advantages of this integrated architecture is closing the loop on customer interactions, analysis and personalization. This is arguably the most difficult part of the knowledge discovery process to implement in a non-integrated system. However, the shared metadata across all three components means that results can be directly reflected in the data that defines the e-commerce company's business.

The architecture supports several personalization engines that run within the *Customer Interaction* component. Rules defined by marketing users can be deployed for offering promotions to visitors, or displaying specific products or content to a certain type of visitor. These rules

can be based on several different types of data, including customer attributes, customer shopping and browsing history, and the current shopping basket. Data mining models (such as those based on association rules or collaborative filtering) can be deployed from the *Analysis* component to provide real-time dynamic recommendations for products, assortments or even content. The architecture can also use control groups so that personalization is only activated for a fraction of the target visitors. This enables analysts to directly look at sales or results for visitors when the rules were and were not activated. As an example of closing the loop, customers can be scored on their propensity to accept a cross-sell and the site can be personalized based on these scores. Clickstream data, business events and other transactional data can then be analyzed to measure the effectiveness of these cross sells. These results can then be used to further improve the model and new scores can then be used in personalizing the site. Managing email campaigns is another good example of closing the loop. A recent Forrester report says that email personalization and list quality are key factors in determining the effectiveness of email campaigns [14]. As an example, consider two email campaigns sent out with two different promotional offers in them. The *Customer Interaction* component enables business users to track the success of these campaigns at multiple levels like the number of users that opened each email, clicked through on each email, and actually used the promotion to make a purchase. Using the analysis component, users can delve into the details of customers that responded to each kind of promotional offer and further tune the segmentation model (lists) for different types of promotions and campaigns. Similarly, the content used in the emails can also be targeted to a specific, more granular, customer segment. In this way the integrated architecture allows business users to personalize interactions, track user responses, measure success, get insight into the effect of the personalization, calculate ROI and further personalize the interactions, effectively closing the loop.

5. Challenges

In this section we describe several challenging problems based on our experiences in mining e-commerce data. The complexity and granularity of these problems differ, but each represents a real-life area where we believe improvements can be made. Except for the first two challenges, the problems deal with data mining algorithmic challenges.

Make Data Mining Results Comprehensible

Business users, from merchandisers who make decisions about the assortments of products to creative designers who design web sites to marketers who decide where to spend advertising dollars, need to understand the results of data mining. Few data mining models, however, are easy to understand. Classification rules are the easiest, followed by classification trees. A visualization for the Naïve-Bayes classifier [15] was also easy for business users to understand in the second author's past experience.

The challenge is to define new types of models and ways of presenting them to business users.

Make Data Mining Process Accessible

The ability to answer a question given by a business user usually requires some data transformations and technical understanding of the tools. Our experience is that even commercial report designers and OLAP tools are too hard for most business users. Two common solutions are (i) provide templates (e.g., reporting templates, OLAP cubes, and recommended transformations for mining) for common questions, something that works well in well-defined vertical markets, and (ii) provide the expertise through consulting or a services organization. The challenge is to find ways to empower business users so that they will be able to serve themselves.

Support Multiple Granularity Levels

Data collected in a typical web site contains records at different levels of granularity. Page views are the lowest level with attributes such as product viewed and duration. Sessions include attributes such as browser used, initiation time, referring site, and cookie information. Each session includes multiple page views. Finally, customer attributes include name, address, and demographic attributes. Each customer may be involved in multiple sessions.

Mining at the page view level by joining all the session and customer attributes violates the basic assumption that records are independently and identically distributed. If we are trying to build a model to predict who visits page X, and Joe happens to visit it very often, then we might get a rule that if the visitor's first name is Joe, they will likely visit page X. The rule will have multiple records (visits) to support it, but it clearly will not generalize beyond the specific Joe. This problem is shared by mining problems in the telecommunication domain [16]. The challenge is to design algorithms that can support multiple granularity levels correctly.

Utilize Hierarchies

Products are commonly organized in hierarchies. A product hierarchy is usually three to eight levels deep. A customer purchases individual products, but generalizations are likely to be found at higher levels (e.g., families or categories). Some algorithms have been designed to support tree-structured attributes [17], but they do not scale to large product hierarchies. The challenge is to support such hierarchies within the data mining algorithms.

Scale Better: Handle Large Amounts of Data

Yahoo! has over 1.2 billion page views per day [18]. The challenge is to find useful techniques (other than sampling) that will scale to this volume of data. Are there aggregations that should be performed on the fly as data is collected?

Support and Model External Events

External events, such as marketing campaigns (e.g., promotions and media ads), and site redesign change patterns in the data. The challenge is to be able to model such events, which create new patterns that spike and decay over time.

Detect Robots and Crawlers

Robots and crawlers can dramatically change clickstream patterns at a web site. For example, Keynote (www.keynote.com) provides site performance measurements. The Keynote robot can generate a request multiple times a minute, 24 hours a day, 7 days a week, skewing the statistics about the number of sessions, page hits, and exit pages (last page at each session). Search engines conduct breadth first scans of the site, generating many requests in short duration. Identifying such robots to filter their clickstreams is a non-trivial task, especially for robots that pretend to be real users.

Support Slowly Changing Dimensions

Visitors' demographics change: people get married, their children grow, their salaries change, etc. With these changes, their needs, which are being modeled, change. Product attributes change: new choices (e.g., colors) may be available, packaging material or design change, and even quality may improve or degrade. These attributes that change over time are often referred to as "slowly changing dimensions" [4]. The challenge is to keep track of these changes and provide support for such changes in the analyses.

Handle date/time and cyclical attributes

Significant numbers of date and time attributes are collected from clickstreams and order data. Few algorithms handle these properly. Some algorithms consider them to be unique streams, rendering them useless. Others look at the date as a continuous attribute, which is useful but makes it hard to capture specific intervals since splits typically occur on a single threshold. A combination of a date and time attribute is more useful than date alone, but rarely supported. One transformation commonly done to dates is to convert them to other attributes, such as day of week. However, cyclical attributes, such as day of week and hour of the day, need to be recognized as a special type because it does not make much sense to look at day-of-week greater than Tuesday. It would be much better to capture a consecutive range of days, such as Saturday to Sunday.

Today, the alternative is typically to specifically construct such attributes as Weekend or Morning (from hour).

6. Summary

We proposed an architecture that successfully integrates data mining with an e-commerce system. The proposed architecture consists of three main components: *Business Data Definition*, *Customer Interaction*, and *Analysis*, which are connected using data transfer bridges. This integration effectively solves several major problems associated with horizontal data mining tools including the enormous effort required in pre-processing of the data before it can be used for mining, and making the results of mining actionable. The tight integration between the three components of the architecture allows for automated construction of a data warehouse within the *Analysis* component. The shared metadata across the three components further simplifies this construction, and, coupled with the rich set of mining algorithms and analysis tools (like visualization, reporting and OLAP) also increases the efficiency of the knowledge discovery process. The tight integration and shared metadata also make it easy to deploy results, effectively closing the loop. Finally we presented several challenging problems that need to be addressed for further enhancement of this architecture.

Acknowledgments

We would like to thank other members of the data mining and visualization teams at Blue Martini Software, and Cindy Hall. We wish to thank our clients for sharing their data with us and helping us refine our architecture and improve Blue Martini's products.

References

[1] Suhail Ansari, Ron Kohavi, Llew Mason, and Zijian Zheng, Integrating E-Commerce and Data Mining, *Blue Martini Software Technical Report*, 2001. Available from the articles section of http://developer.bluemartini.com.

[2] Eric Schmitt, Harley Manning, Yolanda Paul, and Joyce Tong, Measuring Web Success, *Forrester Report*, November 1999.

[3] Gregory Piatetsky-Shapiro, Ron Brachman, Tom Khabaza, Willi Kloesgen, and Evangelos Simoudis, An Overview of Issues in Developing Industrial Data Mining and Knowledge Discovery Applications, *Proceeding of the second international conference on Knowledge Discovery and Data Mining*, 1996.

[4] Ralph Kimball, *The Data Warehouse Toolkit: Practical Techniques for Building Dimensional Data Warehouses*, John Wiley & Sons, 1996.

[5] Ralph Kimball, Laura Reeves, Margy Ross, Warren Thornthwaite, *The Data Warehouse Lifecycle Toolkit : Expert Methods for Designing, Developing, and Deploying Data Warehouses*, John Wiley & Sons, 1998.

[6] Ron Kohavi, Mining e-commerce data: The good, the bad, and the ugly (invited industrial track talk). In Foster Provost and Ramakrishnan Srikant, editors, *Proceedings of the Seventh ACM SIGKDD International Conference on Knowledge Discovery and Data Mining*, August 2001. http://robotics.Stanford.EDU/users/ronnyk/goodBadUglyKDDItrack.pdf

[7] Robert Cooley, Bamshad Mobashar, and Jaideep Shrivastava, Data Preparation for Mining World Wide Web Browsing Patterns, *Knowledge and Information Systems*, 1, 1999.

[8] Bettina Berendt, Bamshad Mobasher, Myra Spiliopoulou, and Jim Wiltshire, Measuring the Accuracy of Sessionizers for Web Usage Analysis, *Workshop on Web Mining at the First SIAM International Conference on Data Mining*, 2001.

[9] J. Pitkow, In search of reliable usage data on the WWW, *Sixth International World Wide Web Conference*, 1997.

[10] Shahana Sen, Balaji Padmanabhan, Alexander Tuzhilin, Norman H. White, and Roger Stein, The identification and satisfaction of consumer analysis-driven information needs of marketers on the WWW, *European Journal of Marketing*, Vol. 32 No. 7/8 1998.

[11] Osmar R. Zaiane, Man Xin, and Jiawei Han, Discovering Web Access Patterns and Trends by Applying OLAP and Data Mining Technology on Web Logs, *Proceedings of Advances in Digital Libraries Conference (ADL'98)*, Santa Barbara, CA, 1998.

[12] Stephen Gomory, Robert Hoch, Juhnyoung Lee, Mark Podlaseck, Edith Schonberg, Analysis and Visualization of Metrics for Online Merchandizing, *Proceedings of WEBKDD'99*, Springer 1999.

[13] B. Mobasher, H. Dai, T. Luo, M. Nakagawa, Y. Sun, and J. Wiltshire, Discovery of Aggregate Usage Profiles for Web Personalization, *Proceedings of KDD'2000 Workshop on Web Mining for E-Commerce - Challenges and Opportunities (WEBKDD'2000)*, p. 1-11, 2000.

[14] Jim Nail, Chris Charron, Tim Grimsditch, and Susan Shindler, The Email Marketing Dialogue, *Forrester Report*, January 2000.

[15] Barry Becker, Ron Kohavi, and Dan Sommerfield. Visualizing the Simple Bayesian Classifier, Chapter 18, pages 237-249, *Information Visualization in Data Mining and Knowledge Discovery*, Morgan Kaufmann, Publishers, San Francisco, 2001.

[16] Saharon Rosset, Uzi Murad, Einat Neumann, Yizhak Idan, and Gadi Pinkas, Discovery of Fraud Rules for Telecommunications: Challenges and Solutions, *Proceedings of the Fifth ACM SIGKDD International Conference on Knowledge Discovery and Data Mining*, 1999.

[17] Hussein Almuallim, Yasuhiro Akiba, and Shigeo Kaneda, On Handling Tree-Structured Attributes, *Proceedings of the Twelfth International Conference on Machine Learning*, p.12-20, 1995.

[18] *Yahoo! Inc. Second Quarter 2001 Financial Results*, July 11, 2001.

Classification with Degree of Membership: A Fuzzy Approach

Wai-Ho Au   Keith C.C. Chan

Department of Computing
The Hong Kong Polytechnic University
Hung Hom, Kowloon, Hong Kong
E-mail: {cswhau, cskcchan}@comp.polyu.edu.hk

Abstract

Classification is an important topic in data mining research. It is concerned with the prediction of the values of some attribute in a database based on other attributes. To tackle this problem, most of the existing data mining algorithms adopt either a decision tree based approach or an approach that requires users to provide some user-specified thresholds to guide the search for interesting rules. In this paper, we propose a new approach based on the use of an objective interestingness measure to distinguish interesting rules from uninteresting ones. Using linguistic terms to represent the revealed regularities and exceptions, this approach is especially useful when the discovered rules are presented to human experts for examination because of the affinity with the human knowledge representation. The use of fuzzy technique allows the prediction of attribute values to be associated with degree of membership. Our approach is, therefore, able to deal with the cases that an object can belong to more than one class. For example, a person can suffer from cold and fever to certain extent at the same time. Furthermore, our approach is more resilient to noise and missing data values because of the use of fuzzy technique. To evaluate the performance of our approach, we tested it using several real-life databases. The experimental results show that it can be very effective at data mining tasks. In fact, when compared to popular data mining algorithms, our approach can be better able to uncover useful rules hidden in databases.

1. Introduction

Classification is an important topic in data mining research [2, 9-12, 24, 26]. The problem is concerned with the mining of a set of production rules that can allow the values of an attribute in a database to be accurately predicted based on those of other attributes [1-2, 16, 19, 22, 24]. For example, we are given a customer database with each record characterized by such attributes as income, car-owned, and plan-subscribed, a rule that could be discovered can be "90% of high-income customers who own a Jeep are subscribes of Plan B; 3% of all customers have both characteristics." The discovery of such a rule could be important to a marketing manager who may, as a result, concentrate on promoting Plan B among high-income Jeep owners.

For data mining to be effective, an algorithm should be able to handle linguistic or fuzzy variables. This is because the ability to do so would allow some interesting patterns to be more easily discovered and expressed. For example, if crisp boundaries are defined for "high-income" in the above rule, there is a possibility that it may not be interesting at all as the support and confidence measure is dependent to a large extent on the definitions of boundaries. Despite its importance, many data mining algorithms (e.g., [1-4, 16, 18-19, 22, 24-25]) were not developed to handle fuzzy data or fuzzy rules. They were used mainly to deal with categorical and quantitative attributes. In particular, when dealing with quantitative attributes, their domains are usually divided into equal-width or equal-frequency intervals. In most cases, the resulting intervals are not too meaningful and are hard to understand.

To deal with fuzzy data and fuzzy rules, we present a new approach, which employs *linguistic terms* to represent regularities and exceptions discovered, in this paper. These linguistic terms can be defined as fuzzy sets so that, based on their membership functions, either categorical or quantitative data, can be transformed by fuzzification. To deal with these fuzzified data so as to discover fuzzy rules, this approach utilizes the idea of *residual analysis* [5-8]. With it, our approach is able to reveal interesting associations hidden in the database without the need for users' to supply some subjective thresholds. In other words, unlike many data mining algorithms (e.g., [1-4, 16, 18-19, 22, 24-25]) that only discover rules with consequent consisting only of categorical or discretized crisp-boundary quantitative attributes, our approach is able to discover rules with consequent composing of linguistic terms. This allows the prediction of attribute values to be associated with degree of membership. Consequently, our approach is able to deal with the cases that an object can belong to more than one class. For example, a person can suffer from cold and fever to certain extent at the same time. Furthermore, the use of linguistic terms to represent the discovered rules also allows quantitative values to be inferred.

The rest of this paper is organized as follows. In Section 2, we provide a brief description of how existing algorithms can be used for classification and how fuzzy techniques can be applied to the data mining process. The details of our approach are given in Section 3. To evaluate the performance of this approach, we applied it to several real-life databases. The results of the experiments are discussed in Section 4. Finally, in Section 5, we provide a summary of the paper.

2. Related work

Among the different approaches to solving the classification problem, decision tree based algorithms (e.g., [1-2, 19, 21-22]) are the most popular. Other than the use of decision tree based algorithms, techniques that have been developed to mine association rules can also be used for classification (e.g., [16]).

It is important to note that the intervals involved in quantitative association rules may not be concise and meaningful enough for human experts to obtain nontrivial knowledge. *Linguistic summaries* introduced in [27] express knowledge in linguistic representation, which is natural for people to comprehend. In addition to linguistic summaries, the applicability of fuzzy modeling techniques to data mining has been discussed in [13]. Furthermore, an information-theoretic fuzzy approach has been proposed in [17] to discover unreliable data in databases. Nevertheless, these fuzzy techniques have not been developed for classification.

An approach, which combines symbolic decision trees with approximate reasoning offered by fuzzy representation, has been proposed in [14] for building *fuzzy decision trees*. Based on a set of predefined fuzzy linguistic variables, a method for constructing fuzzy decision trees and a number of inference procedures based on conflict resolution in rule-based systems and efficient approximate reasoning methods have been presented in [14]. Given a database, this approach can be used to build a fuzzy decision tree and the resulting tree can be used for inference.

An empirical comparison of our approach with C4.5 [21] (a decision tree based approach), CBA [16] (an association rule mining approach), and FID [14] (a fuzzy decision tree approach) on several real-life databases will be given in Section 4 below.

3. A fuzzy approach for data mining

Our approach is capable of mining fuzzy rules in large databases without any need for user-specified thresholds or mapping of quantitative into binary attributes. A fuzzy rule describes an interesting relationship between two or more linguistic terms. The definition of linguistic terms is presented in Section 3.1. The details of this approach are then given in Section 3.2. In Section 3.3, we describe how interesting fuzzy rules can be identified. A confidence measure, called *weight of evidence* [5-8] measure, is then defined in Section 3.4 to provide a means for representing the uncertainty associated with the fuzzy rules. In Section 3.5, we describe how to predict unknown values using the discovered fuzzy rules.

3.1. Linguistic terms

Given a set of records, $\mathcal{D}$, each of which consists of a set of attributes $\mathcal{I} = \{I_1, ..., I_n\}$, where I_v, $v = 1, ..., n$, can be quantitative or categorical. For any record, $d \in \mathcal{D}$, $d[I_v]$ denotes the value i_v in d for attribute I_v. For any quantitative attribute, $I_v \in \mathcal{I}$, let $dom(I_v) = [l_v, u_v] \subseteq \mathfrak{R}$ denote the domain of the attribute. Based on the fuzzy set theory, a set of linguistic terms can be defined over the domain of each quantitative attribute. Let us therefore denote the linguistic terms associated with some quantitative attribute, $I_v \in \mathcal{I}$ as $\mathcal{L}_{vr}$, $r = 1, ..., s_v$, so that a corresponding fuzzy set, L_{vr}, can be defined for each $\mathcal{L}_{vr}$. The membership function of the fuzzy set is denoted as $\mu_{L_{vr}}$ and is defined as:

$$\mu_{L_{vr}} : dom(I_v) \rightarrow [0, 1]$$

The fuzzy sets L_{vr}, $r = 1, ..., s_v$, are then defined as:

$$L_{vr} = \begin{cases} \displaystyle\sum_{dom(I_v)} \frac{\mu_{L_{vr}}(i_v)}{i_v} & \text{if } I_v \text{ is discrete} \\[2ex] \displaystyle\int_{dom(I_v)} \frac{\mu_{L_{vr}}(i_v)}{i_v} & \text{if } I_v \text{ is continuous} \end{cases}$$

for all $i_v \in dom(I_v)$. The degree of membership of some value $i_v \in dom(I_v)$ with some linguistic term $\mathcal{L}_{vr}$ is given by $\mu_{L_{vr}}$.

Note that $I_v \in \mathcal{I}$ can also be categorical and crisp. In such case, let $dom(I_v) = \{i_{v1}, ..., i_{vm_v}\}$ denote the domain of I_v. In order to handle categorical and quantitative attributes in a uniform manner, we can also define a set of linguistic terms, $\mathcal{L}_{vr}$, $r = 1, ..., m_v$, for each categorical attribute, $I_v \in \mathcal{J}$, where $\mathcal{L}_{vr}$ is represented by a fuzzy set, L_{vr}, such that

$$L_{vr} = \frac{1}{i_{vr}}$$

Using the above technique, we can represent the original attribute, $\mathcal{J}$, using a set of linguistic terms, $\mathcal{L} = \{\mathcal{L}_{vr} \mid v = 1, ..., n, r = 1, ..., s_v\}$ where $s_v = m_v$ for categorical attributes. Since each linguistic term is represented by a fuzzy set, we have a set of fuzzy sets, $L = \{L_{vr} \mid v = 1, ..., n, r = 1, ..., s_v\}$. Given a record, $d \in \mathcal{D}$, and a linguistic terms, $\mathcal{L}_{vr} \in \mathcal{L}$, which is, in turn, represented by a fuzzy set, $L_{vr} \in L$, the degree of membership of the values in d with respect to $\mathcal{L}_{vr}$ is given by $\mu_{L_{vr}}(d[I_v])$. In other words, d is characterized by the term $\mathcal{L}_{vr}$ to the degree $\mu_{L_{vr}}(d[I_v])$. If $\mu_{L_{vr}}(d[I_v]) = 1$, d is completely characterized by the term $\mathcal{L}_{vr}$. If $\mu_{L_{vr}}(d[I_v]) = 0$, d is not characterized by the term $\mathcal{L}_{vr}$ at all. If $0 < \mu_{L_{vr}}(d[I_v]) < 1$, d is partially characterized by the term $\mathcal{L}_{vr}$.

Realistically, d can also be characterized by more than one linguistic term. Let φ be a subset of integers such that $\varphi = \{v_1, ..., v_m\}$ where $v_1, ..., v_m \in \{1, ..., n\}$, $v_1 \neq ... \neq v_m$ and $|\varphi| = h \geq 1$. We further suppose that $\mathcal{J}_\varphi = \{I_v \mid v \in \varphi\}$. Given any $\mathcal{J}_\varphi$, it is associated with a set of linguistic terms, $\mathcal{L}_{\varphi r}$, $r = 1, ..., s_\varphi$ where $s_\varphi = \prod_{v \in \varphi} s_v$.

Each $\mathcal{L}_{\varphi r}$ is defined by a set of linguistic terms, $\mathcal{L}_{v_1 r_1}, ..., \mathcal{L}_{v_m r_m} \in \mathcal{L}$. The degree, $\lambda_{\mathcal{L}_{\varphi r}}(d)$, to which d is characterized by the term $\mathcal{L}_{\varphi r}$ is defined as:

$$\lambda_{\mathcal{L}_{\varphi r}}(d) = \min(\mu_{L_{v_1 r_1}}(d[I_{v_1}]), ..., \mu_{L_{v_m r_m}}(d[I_{v_m}]))$$

$\mathcal{D}$ can then be represented by a set of fuzzy data, $\mathcal{F}$, which is characterized by a set of linguistic attributes, $\mathcal{L} = \{\mathcal{L}_1, ..., \mathcal{L}_n\}$. For any linguistic attribute, $\mathcal{L}_v \in \mathcal{L}$, the value of $\mathcal{L}_v$ in a record, $t \in \mathcal{F}$, is a set of ordered pairs such that

$$t[\mathcal{L}_v] = \{(\mathcal{L}_{v1}, \mu_{v1}), ..., (\mathcal{L}_{vs_v}, \mu_{vs_v})\}$$

where $\mathcal{L}_{vk}$ and μ_{vk}, $k \in \{1, ..., s_v\}$, are a linguistic term and its degree of membership, respectively.

For any record, $t \in \mathcal{F}$, let $o_{\mathcal{L}_{pq}\mathcal{L}_{\varphi k}}$ be the degree to which t is characterized by the linguistic terms $\mathcal{L}_{pq}$ and $\mathcal{L}_{\varphi k}$, $p \notin \varphi$. $o_{\mathcal{L}_{pq}\mathcal{L}_{\varphi k}}$ is defined as:

$$o_{\mathcal{L}_{pq}\mathcal{L}_{\varphi k}} = \min(\mu_{L_{pq}}, \mu_{L_{\varphi k}}) \qquad (1)$$

We further suppose that $deg_{\mathcal{L}_{pq}\mathcal{L}_{\varphi k}}$ is the sum of degrees to which records in $\mathcal{F}$ characterized by the linguistic terms $\mathcal{L}_{pq}$ and $\mathcal{L}_{\varphi k}$. $deg_{\mathcal{L}_{pq}\mathcal{L}_{\varphi k}}$ is given by:

$$deg_{\mathcal{L}_{pq}\mathcal{L}_{\varphi k}} = \sum_{t \in \mathcal{F}} o_{\mathcal{L}_{pq}\mathcal{L}_{\varphi k}} \qquad (2)$$

Based on the linguistic terms, we can apply our approach to mine fuzzy rules in fuzzy data and present them to human users in a way that is much easier understood. Due to the use of fuzzy technique blurring the boundaries of adjacent intervals of numeric qualities, our approach is resilient to noise such as inaccuracies in physical measurements of real-life entities.

3.1.1. An illustrative example. In this section, we illustrate how a relation in a relational database can be transformed to a fuzzy relation based on the linguistic terms. Let us consider a sample relation shown in Figure 1.

Age	MaritalStatus	Salary
23	U	40,000
29	M	43,000
33	M	55,000
35	U	64,000
55	M	62,000

Figure 1. A sample relation.

Let us further suppose that the Married attribute, which is a categorical attribute, is represented by two linguistic terms defined as:

$$Unmarried = \frac{1}{U} \quad \text{and} \quad Married = \frac{1}{M}$$

For the remaining two quantitative attributes, Age and Salary, they are represented by the linguistic terms given in Figure 2.

Based on these linguistic terms, the sample relation is transformed to a fuzzy relation shown in Figure 3. Instead of mining interesting rules from the original relation, we perform data mining in the resulting fuzzy relation.

37

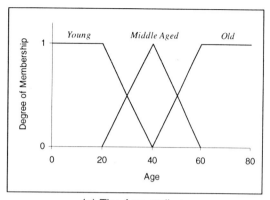

(a) The Age attribute

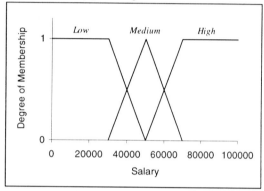

(b) The Salary attribute

Figure 2. The definitions of linguistic terms.

Age	MaritalStatus	Salary
{(Young, 0.85), (Middle Aged, 0.15)}	{(Unmarried, 1)}	{(Low, 0.5), (Medium, 0.5)}
{(Young, 0.55), (Middle Aged, 0.45)}	{(Married, 1)}	{(Low, 0.35), (Medium, 0.65)}
{(Young, 0.35), (Middle Aged, 0.65)	{(Married, 1)}	{(Medium, 0.75), (High, 0.25)}
{(Young, 0.25), (Middle Aged, 0.75)}	{(Unmarried, 1)}	{(Medium, 0.3), (High, 0.7)}
{(Middle Aged, 0.25), (Old, 0.75)}	{(Married, 1)}	{(Medium, 0.4), (High, 0.6)}

Figure 3. The resulting fuzzy relation.

3.2. The fuzzy data mining algorithm

It is important to note that a fuzzy rule can be of different orders. A first-order fuzzy rule can be defined to be a rule involving one linguistic term in its antecedent; a second-order rule can be defined to have two; and a third-order rule can be defined to have three linguistic terms, etc. Our approach is given in Figure 4 below.

To mine interesting first-order rules, our approach makes use of an objective interestingness measure introduced in Section 3.3 below. After these rules are discovered, they are stored in R_1 (Figure 4). Rules in R_1 are then used to generate second-order rules that are then stored in R_2. R_2 is then used to generate third-order rules

that are stored in R_3 and so on for 4th and higher order. Our approach iterates until no higher order rule can be found.

The function, $interesting(\mathcal{L}_{pq}, \mathcal{L}_{\varphi k})$, computes an objective measure to determine whether the relationship between $\mathcal{L}_{pq}$ and $\mathcal{L}_{\varphi k}$ is interesting. If $interesting(\mathcal{L}_{pq}, \mathcal{L}_{\varphi k})$ returns true, a fuzzy rule is then generated by the *rulegen* function. For each rule generated, this function also returns an uncertainty measure associated with the rule (see Section 3.4). All fuzzy rules generated by *rulegen* are stored in $\mathcal{R}$ that will then be used later for prediction or for the users to examine.

1) $R_1 = \{\text{first-order fuzzy rules}\};$
2) **for**$(m = 2; |R_{m-1}| \neq \phi, m + +)$ **do**
3) **begin**
4) $C = \{\text{each condition in the antecedent of } r \mid r \in R_{m-1}\};$
5) **forall** φ composed of m elements in C **do**
6) **begin**
7) **forall** $t \in \mathcal{T}$ **do**
8) **forall** $(\mathcal{L}_{pq}, \mu_{pq}) \in t[\mathcal{L}_p], (\mathcal{L}_{\varphi k}, \mu_{\varphi k}) \in t[\mathcal{L}_\varphi], p \notin \varphi$ **do**
9) $deg_{\mathcal{L}_{pq}\mathcal{L}_{\varphi k}} + = \min(\mu_{pq}, \mu_{\varphi k});$
10) **forall** $(\mathcal{L}_{pq}, \mu_{pq}) \in t[\mathcal{L}_p], (\mathcal{L}_{\varphi k}, \mu_{\varphi k}) \in t[\mathcal{L}_\varphi], p \notin \varphi$ **do**
11) **if** $interesting(\mathcal{L}_{pq}, \mathcal{L}_{\varphi k})$ **then**
12) $R_m = R_m \cup rulegen(\mathcal{L}_{pq}, \mathcal{L}_{\varphi k});$
13) **end**
14) **end**
15) $\mathcal{R} = \bigcup_m R_m;$

Figure 4. The fuzzy data mining algorithm.

3.3. Discovering interesting rules in fuzzy data

In order to decide whether a relationship between a linguistic term, $\mathcal{L}_{\varphi k}$, and another linguistic term, $\mathcal{L}_{pq}$, is interesting, we determine whether

$$\Pr(\mathcal{L}_{pq} \mid \mathcal{L}_{\varphi k}) = \frac{\text{sum of degrees to which records characterized by } \mathcal{L}_{\varphi k} \text{ and } \mathcal{L}_{pq}}{\text{sum of degrees to which records characterized by } \mathcal{L}_{\varphi k}} \quad (3)$$

is *significantly different* from

$$\Pr(\mathcal{L}_{pq}) = \frac{\text{sum of degrees to which records characterized by } \mathcal{L}_{pq}}{M} \quad (4)$$

where $M = \sum_{u=1}^{s_p} \sum_{i=1}^{s_\varphi} deg_{\mathcal{L}_{pu}\mathcal{L}_{\varphi i}}$. If this is the case, we consider the relationship between $\mathcal{L}_{\varphi k}$ and $\mathcal{L}_{pq}$ interesting.

The significance of the difference can be objectively evaluated based on the idea of an *adjusted residual* [5-8] defined as:

$$d_{\mathcal{L}_{pq}\mathcal{L}_{\varphi k}} = \frac{z_{\mathcal{L}_{pq}\mathcal{L}_{\varphi k}}}{\sqrt{\gamma_{\mathcal{L}_{pq}\mathcal{L}_{\varphi k}}}} \tag{5}$$

where $z_{\mathcal{L}_{pq}\mathcal{L}_{\varphi k}}$ is the *standardized residual* [5-8] and is given by:

$$z_{\mathcal{L}_{pq}\mathcal{L}_{\varphi k}} = \frac{deg_{\mathcal{L}_{pq}\mathcal{L}_{\varphi k}} - e_{\mathcal{L}_{pq}\mathcal{L}_{\varphi k}}}{\sqrt{e_{\mathcal{L}_{pq}\mathcal{L}_{\varphi k}}}} \tag{6}$$

where $e_{\mathcal{L}_{pq}\mathcal{L}_{\varphi k}}$ is the sum of degrees to which records are expected to be characterized by $\mathcal{L}_{\varphi k}$ and $\mathcal{L}_{pq}$. It is defined as:

$$e_{\mathcal{L}_{pq}\mathcal{L}_{\varphi k}} = \frac{\sum_{i=1}^{s_\varphi} deg_{\mathcal{L}_{pq}\mathcal{L}_{\varphi i}} \sum_{u=1}^{s_p} deg_{\mathcal{L}_{pu}\mathcal{L}_{\varphi k}}}{M} \tag{7}$$

and $\gamma_{\mathcal{L}_{pq}\mathcal{L}_{\varphi k}}$ is the *maximum likelihood estimate* [5-8] of the variance of $z_{\mathcal{L}_{pq}\mathcal{L}_{\varphi k}}$ and is given by:

$$\gamma_{\mathcal{L}_{pq}\mathcal{L}_{\varphi k}} = \left(1 - \frac{\sum_{i=1}^{s_\varphi} deg_{\mathcal{L}_{pq}\mathcal{L}_{\varphi i}}}{M}\right)\left(1 - \frac{\sum_{u=1}^{s_p} deg_{\mathcal{L}_{pu}\mathcal{L}_{\varphi k}}}{M}\right) \tag{8}$$

If $d_{\mathcal{L}_{pq}\mathcal{L}_{\varphi k}} > 1.96$ (the 95 percentiles of the normal distribution), we can conclude that the discrepancy between $\Pr(\mathcal{L}_{pq} \mid \mathcal{L}_{\varphi k})$ and $\Pr(\mathcal{L}_{pq})$ is significantly different and hence the relationship between $\mathcal{L}_{\varphi k}$ and $\mathcal{L}_{pq}$ is interesting. Specifically, the presence of $\mathcal{L}_{\varphi k}$ implies the presence of $\mathcal{L}_{pq}$. In other words, it is more likely for a record having both $\mathcal{L}_{\varphi k}$ and $\mathcal{L}_{pq}$.

3.4. Uncertainty representation

Given that a linguistic term $\mathcal{L}_{\varphi k}$ is associated with another linguistic term $\mathcal{L}_{pq}$, we can form the following fuzzy rule.

$$\mathcal{L}_{\varphi k} \Rightarrow \mathcal{L}_{pq} [w_{\mathcal{L}_{pq}\mathcal{L}_{\varphi k}}]$$

where $w_{\mathcal{L}_{pq}\mathcal{L}_{\varphi k}}$ is the *weight of evidence* measure that is defined as follows.

Since the relationship between $\mathcal{L}_{\varphi k}$ and $\mathcal{L}_{pq}$ is interesting, there is some evidence for a record to be characterized by $\mathcal{L}_{pq}$ given it has $\mathcal{L}_{\varphi k}$. The weight of evidence measure is defined in terms of an information theoretic measure known as *mutual information*. Mutual information measures the change of uncertainty about the presence of $\mathcal{L}_{pq}$ in a record given that it has $\mathcal{L}_{\varphi k}$ is and, in turn, defined as:

$$I(\mathcal{L}_{pq} : \mathcal{L}_{\varphi k}) = \log \frac{\Pr(\mathcal{L}_{pq} \mid \mathcal{L}_{\varphi k})}{\Pr(\mathcal{L}_{pq})} \tag{9}$$

Based on mutual information, the weight of evidence measure is defined in [5-8] as:

$$\begin{aligned} w_{\mathcal{L}_{pq}\mathcal{L}_{\varphi k}} &= I(\mathcal{L}_{pq} : \mathcal{L}_{\varphi k}) - I(\bigcup_{i\neq q}(\mathcal{L}_{pi} : \mathcal{L}_{\varphi k})) \\ &= \log \frac{\Pr(\mathcal{L}_{\varphi k} \mid \mathcal{L}_{pq})}{\Pr(\mathcal{L}_{\varphi k} \mid \bigcup_{i\neq q}\mathcal{L}_{pi})} \end{aligned} \tag{10}$$

$w_{\mathcal{L}_{pq}\mathcal{L}_{\varphi k}}$ can be interpreted intuitively as a measure of the difference in the gain in information when a record with $\mathcal{L}_{\varphi k}$ characterized by $\mathcal{L}_{pq}$ and when characterized by $\mathcal{L}_{pi}$, $i \neq q$. The weight of evidence measure can be used to weigh the significance or importance of fuzzy rules.

Given that $\mathcal{L}_{\varphi k}$ is defined by a set of linguistic terms, $\mathcal{L}_{v_1 k_1}, \ldots, \mathcal{L}_{v_m k_m} \in \mathcal{L}$, we have a high-order fuzzy rule as follows:

$$\mathcal{L}_{v_1 k_1}, \ldots, \mathcal{L}_{v_m k_m} \Rightarrow \mathcal{L}_{pq} [w_{\mathcal{L}_{pq}\mathcal{L}_{\varphi k}}]$$

where $v_1, \ldots, v_m \in \varphi$.

3.5. Predicting unknown values using fuzzy rules

Given a record, $d \in dom(I_1) \times \ldots \times dom(I_p) \times \ldots \times dom(I_n)$, let d be characterized by n attribute values, $\alpha_1, \ldots, \alpha_p, \ldots, \alpha_n$, where α_p is the value to be predicted. Let $\mathcal{L}_p$, $p = 1, \ldots, s_p$, be the linguistic terms corresponding to the class attribute, I_p. We further let l_p be a linguistic term with domain $dom(l_p) = \{\mathcal{L}_{p1}, \ldots, \mathcal{L}_{ps_p}\}$. The value of α_p is given by the value of l_p. To predict the correct value of l_p, our approach searches the fuzzy rules with $\mathcal{L}_{pq} \in dom(l_p)$ as consequents. For any combination of attribute values, α_φ, $p \notin \varphi$, of d, it is characterized by a linguistic term, $\mathcal{L}_{\varphi k}$, to a degree of compatibility, $\lambda_{\mathcal{L}_{\varphi k}}(d)$, for each $k \in \{1, \ldots, s_\varphi\}$. Given those rules implying the assignment of $\mathcal{L}_{pq}$, $\mathcal{L}_{\varphi k} \Rightarrow \mathcal{L}_{pq}[w_{\mathcal{L}_{pq}\mathcal{L}_{\varphi k}}]$, for all $k \in \zeta \subseteq \{1, ..., s_\varphi\}$, the evidence for such assignment is given by:

$$w_{\mathcal{L}_{pq}\alpha_\varphi} = \sum_{k \in \zeta} w_{\mathcal{L}_{pq}\mathcal{L}_{\varphi k}} \cdot \lambda_{\mathcal{L}_{\varphi k}}(d) \qquad (11)$$

Suppose that, of the $n - 1$ attribute values excluding α_p, only some combinations of them, $\alpha_{[1]}, ..., \alpha_{[j]}, ..., \alpha_{[\beta]}$ with $\alpha_{[j]} = \{ \alpha_i \mid i \in \{1, ..., n\} - \{p\} \}$, are found to match one or more rules, then the overall weight of evidence for the value of I_p to be assigned to $\mathcal{L}_{pq}$ is given by:

$$w_q = \sum_{j=1}^{\beta} w_{\mathcal{L}_{pq}\alpha_{[j]}} \qquad (12)$$

As a result, the value of α_p is given by $\{(\mathcal{L}_{p1}, w_1), ..., (\mathcal{L}_{pq}, w_q), ..., (\mathcal{L}_{ps_p}, w_{s_p})\}$. When a crisp value is to be assigned to α_p, the following methods are used depending on I_p is categorical or quantitative.

In case that I_p is categorical, l_p is assigned to $\mathcal{L}_{pc}$ if

$$w_c > w_g, g = 1, ..., s_p' \text{ and } g \neq c \qquad (13)$$

where s_p' ($\leq s_p$) is the number of linguistic terms implied by the rules. α_p is therefore assigned to $i_{pc} \in dom(I_p)$.

If I_p is quantitative, a new method is used to assign an appropriate value to α_p. Given the linguistic terms, $\mathcal{L}_{p1}, ..., \mathcal{L}_{ps_p}$, and their overall weight of evidence, $w_1, ..., w_{s_p}$, let $\mu'_{L_{pu}}(i_p)$ be the weighted degree of membership of $i_p \in dom(I_p)$ to the fuzzy set L_{pu}, $u \in \{1, ..., s_p\}$. $\mu'_{L_{pu}}(i_p)$ is given by:

$$\mu'_{L_{pu}}(i_p) = w_u \cdot \mu_{L_{pu}}(i_p) \qquad (14)$$

where $i_p \in dom(I_p)$ and $u = 1, ..., s_p$. The defuzzified value, $F^{-1}(\bigcup_{u=1}^{s_p} L_{pu})$, which provide an appropriate value for α_p is then defined as:

$$F^{-1}(\bigcup_{u=1}^{s_p} L_{pu}) = \frac{\int_{dom(I_p)} \mu'_{L_{p1}\cup...\cup L_{ps_p}}(i_p) \cdot i_p di_p}{\int_{dom(I_p)} \mu'_{L_{p1}\cup...\cup L_{ps_p}}(i_p) di_p} \qquad (15)$$

where $\mu'_{X \cup Y}(i) = \max(\mu'_X(i), \mu'_Y(i))$ for any fuzzy sets X and Y. For quantitative predictions, we use *root-mean-squared error* as a performance measure. Given a set of test records, D, let n be the number of records in D. For any record, $r \in D$, let $[l, u] \subset \Re$ denote the domain of the class attribute. We further let t_r be the target value of the class attribute in r and o_r be the value predicted by our approach. The root-mean-squared error, rms, is defined as

$$rms = \sqrt{\frac{1}{n} \sum_{r \in D} \left(\frac{t_r - l}{u - l} - \frac{o_r - l}{u - l} \right)^2} \qquad (16)$$

4. Performance Analysis

To evaluate the effectiveness of our approach, we tested it using several real-life databases: a *credit card* database, a *diabetes* database, and a *social* database. For each experiment, each of these databases was divided into two datasets with records in each dataset randomly selected. The mining of rules was performed on one of them. The other dataset was reserved for testing. For each such testing dataset, the values of the attributes to be predicted were deleted. The rules discovered by mining the other dataset was then used to predict the deleted attribute values. The predicted values are then compared against the original values to see if they are the same. If it is the case, an accuracy count is incremented. Based on this accuracy count, the percentage accuracy for our approach, C4.5 [21] (a decision tree based approach), CBA [16] (an association rule mining approach), and FID [14] (a fuzzy decision tree approach) are computed. The experiments performed for each of the databases were repeated ten times and the percentage accuracy, averaged over the ten trials, were recorded and are presented in the following sections.

4.1. The *credit card* database

The *credit card* database [20] contains data about credit card applications. It consists of 15 attributes of which one of them, the Success attribute, is concerned with whether or not an application is successful. The meaning of these attributes are not known as the names of the attributes and their values were changed by the donor of the database to meaningless symbols to protect confidentiality of the data. Out of the 15 attributes, 6 are quantitative and 9 are categorical. Each of the 6 quantitative attributes was represented by 4 linguistic terms for our approach and FID.

There are altogether 690 records in the database. For experiments, we randomly selected 30% (i.e., 207 in total) of them for testing by deleting from them the values of the Success attribute. Each of our approach, C4.5, CBA, and FID, was then used to mine rules from the rest of the database (70% or 483 records). The discovered rules were then used to predict the missing Success values in the test records. This procedure of randomly selecting different sets of records for data mining and testing was repeated ten times. The percentage accuracy was computed for each trial and the percentage accuracy averaged over these ten trials is given in Table 1. Of the four different approaches, our approach performed better then C4.5, CBA, and FID by 6.3%, 3.9%, and 30.9%, respectively.

4.2. The *diabetes* database

The *diabetes* database [23] contains 768 patient records. These records are characterized by 9 attributes including one denoted Test-results. Test-results contains either a "1" (tested positive for diabetes) or a "2" (tested negatively for diabetes). The other attributes are all quantitative. Each of these quantitative attributes was represented by 4 linguistic terms for our approach and FID. A total of 30% of the records were randomly selected from the database and the values of Test-results in these records deleted. Using each of our approach, C4.5, CBA, and FID, rules were mined from the remaining 70% of the data. These rules were then used to determine the values of Test-results in the test dataset. This testing procedure was repeated ten times for each of our approach, C4.5, CBA, and FID and the percentage accuracy, averaged over the ten trials, were determined. Of these different approaches, our approach performed better than C4.5, CBA, and FID by 3.8%, 3.2%, and 15.6%, respectively (Table 1).

4.3. The *social* database

The *social* database [15] contains data collected by the US Census Bureau. The data in the database were divided into two sets by the donor of the data. The first dataset, which consists of 32,561 records, where used for data mining whereas the second dataset, which consists of 16,281 records, were used for testing. The records in the database are characterized by 15 attributes. Of these attributes, 6 are quantitative. Each of these quantitative attributes was represented by 4 linguistic terms for our approach and FID. The remaining 9 attributes are all categorical.

Using each of our approach, C4.5, CBA, and FID, predictive modeling rules were mined from the dataset for data mining. These rules were then used to predict the values of the Salary attribute in the test data. The percentage accuracies for the four approaches are given in Table 1. Of these different approaches, our approach

performed better than C4.5, CBA, and FID by 0.5%, 1.7%, and 62.3%, respectively.

Unlike the case with the *credit card* and the *diabetes* databases, it should be noted that testing was not repeated for this particular database. This is because the records for data mining and for testing were fixed by the donor rather than randomly selected.

4.4. Discussion

In summary, our approach performed better than C4.5, CBA, and FID in the above cases. It achieved an average accuracy of 84.1% and is better than C4.5 by 3.5%, CBA by 2.9%, and FID by 36.2%. If we define a baseline accuracy to mean the accuracy obtained by simply assigning the most frequently occurring values to the attributes being predicted, the baseline accuracy for the *credit card* database is 55.5%, the *diabetes* database is 65.1%, and the *social* database is 76.1%. For all the databases, the accuracies of the rules discovered by our approach, C4.5, and CBA are significantly higher than the baseline accuracy. For the *credit card* database, the accuracy of FID is only marginally higher than the respective baseline accuracy. For the *diabetes* database, the accuracy of FID is marginally lower than the baseline accuracy. For the *social* database, the accuracy of FID is significantly lower than the baseline accuracy.

Table 1. Average percentage accuracy.

| Databases | Percentage Accuracy | | | |
	Our Approach	C4.5	CBA	FID
credit card	88.9%	82.6%	85.0%	58.0%
diabetes	77.6%	73.8%	74.4%	62.0%
social	85.9%	85.4%	84.2%	23.6%
Average	84.1%	80.6%	81.2%	47.9%

5. Conclusions

In summary, we have presented a fuzzy approach that can be used for mining interesting rules for classification with degree of membership. This approach represents the revealed regularities and exceptions using linguistic terms. The use of linguistic terms allows human users to better understand the discovered rules because of the affinity with the human knowledge representation. Furthermore, our approach is capable of finding interesting relationships among attributes without any subjective input required of the users. The effectiveness of it has been evaluated using several real-life databases. The experimental results show that our approach can be very effective at data mining tasks. In fact, in the experiments we performed, our approach was found to be able to predict more accurately than C4.5, CBA, and FID.

References

[1] R. Agrawal, S. Ghost, T. Imielinski, B. Iyer, and A. Swami, "An Interval Classifier for Database Mining Applications," in *Proc. of the 18th Int'l Conf. on Very Large Data Bases*, Vancouver, British Columbia, Canada, 1992, pp. 560-573.

[2] R. Agrawal, T. Imielinski, and A. Swami, "Database Mining: A Performance Perspective," *IEEE Trans. on Knowledge and Data Engineering*, vol. 5, no. 6, pp. 914-925, 1993.

[3] R. Agrawal, T. Imielinski, and A. Swami, "Mining Association Rules between Sets of Items in Large Databases," in *Proc. of the ACM SIGMOD Int'l Conf. on Management of Data*, Washington D.C., 1993, pp. 207-216.

[4] R. Agrawal and R. Srikant, "Fast Algorithms for Mining Association Rules," in *Proc. of the 20th Int'l Conf. on Very Large Data Bases*, Santiago, Chile, 1994, pp. 487-499.

[5] W.-H. Au and K.C.C. Chan, "An Effective Algorithm for Discovering Fuzzy Rules in Relational Databases," in *Proc. of the 7th IEEE Int'l Conf. on Fuzzy Systems*, Anchorage, Alaska, 1998, pp. 1314-1319.

[6] W.-H. Au and K.C.C. Chan, "FARM: A Data Mining System for Discovering Fuzzy Association Rules," in *Proc. of the 8th IEEE Int'l Conf. on Fuzzy Systems*, Seoul, Korea, 1999, pp. 1217-1222.

[7] K.C.C. Chan and W.-H. Au, "Mining Fuzzy Association Rules," in *Proc. of the 6th Int'l Conf. on Information and Knowledge Management*, Las Vegas, Nevada, 1997, pp. 209-215.

[8] K.C.C. Chan and W.-H. Au, "Mining Fuzzy Association Rules in a Database Containing Relational and Transactional Data," in A. Kandel, M. Last, and H. Bunke (Eds.), *Data Mining and Computational Intelligence*, Heidelberg, Germany; New York, NY: Physica-Verlag, 2001, pp. 95-114.

[9] M.-S. Chen, J. Han, and P.S. Yu, "Data Mining: An Overview from a Database Perspective," *IEEE Trans. on Knowledge and Data Engineering*, vol. 8, no. 6, pp. 866-883, 1996.

[10] U.M. Fayyad, "Mining Databases: Towards Algorithms for Knowledge Discovery," *Bulletin of the Technical Committee on Data Mining*, vol. 21, no. 1, 1998, pp. 335-341.

[11] U.M. Fayyad, G. Piatetsky-Shapiro, and P. Smyth, "From Data Mining to Knowledge Discovery: An Overview," in U.M. Fayyad, G. Piatetsky-Shapiro, P. Smyth, and R. Uthurusamy (Eds.), *Advances in Knowledge Discovery and Data Mining*, Menlo Park, CA: AAAI/MIT Press, 1996, pp. 1-34.

[12] J. Han and M. Kamber, *Data Mining: Concepts and Techniques*, Morgan Kaufmann, 2001.

[13] K. Hirota and W. Pedrycz, "Fuzzy Computing for Data Mining," *Proc. of the IEEE*, vol. 87, no. 9, pp. 1575-1600, 1999.

[14] C.Z. Janikow, "Fuzzy Decision Trees: Issues and Methods," *IEEE Trans. on Systems, Man, and Cybernetics – Part B: Cybernetics*, vol. 28, no. 1, pp 1-14, 1998.

[15] R. Kohavi, "Scaling Up the Accuracy of Naive-Bayes Classifiers: A Decision Tree Hybrid," in *Proc. of the 2nd Int'l Conf. on Knowledge Discovery and Data Mining*, Portland, Oregon, 1996.

[16] B. Liu, W. Hsu, and Y. Man, "Integrating Classification and Association Rule Mining," in *Proc. of the 4th Int'l Conf. on Knowledge Discovery and Data Mining*, New York, NY, 1998.

[17] O. Maimon, A. Kandel, and M. Last, "Information-Theoretic Fuzzy Approach to Data Reliability and Data Mining," *Fuzzy Sets and Systems*, vol. 117, pp. 183-194, 2001.

[18] H. Mannila, H. Toivonen, and A.I. Verkamo, "Efficient Algorithms for Discovering Association Rules," in *Proc. of the AAAI Workshop on Knowledge Discovery in Databases*, Seattle, Washington, 1994, pp. 181-192.

[19] M. Mehta, J. Rissanen, and R. Agrawal, "SLIQ: A Fast Scalable Classifier for Data Mining," in *Proc. of the 5th Int'l Conf. on Extending Database Technology*, Avignon, France, 1996.

[20] J.R. Quinlan, "Simplifying Decision Trees," *Int'l J. of Man-Machine Studies*, vol. 27, pp. 221-234, 1987.

[21] J.R. Quinlan, *C4.5: Programs for Machine Learning*, San Mateo, CA: Morgan Kaufmann, 1993.

[22] J. Shafer, R. Agrawal, and M. Mehta, "SPRINT: A Scalable Parallel Classifier for Data Mining," in *Proc. of the 22nd Int'l Conf. on Very Large Data Bases*, Mumbai (Bombay), India, 1996.

[23] J.W. Smith, J.E. Everhart, W.C. Dickson, W.C. Knowler, and R.S. Johannes, "Using the ADAP Learning Algorithm to Forecast the Onset of Diabetes Mellitus," in *Proc. of the Symp. on Computer Applications and Medial Cares*, 1983, pp. 422-425.

[24] P. Smyth and R.M. Goodman, "An Information Theoretic Approach to Rule Induction from Databases," *IEEE Trans. on Knowledge and Data Engineering*, vol. 4, no. 4, 1992, pp. 301-316.

[25] R. Srikant and R. Agrawal, "Mining Quantitative Association Rules in Large Relational Tables," in *Proc. of the ACM SIGMOD Int'l Conf. on Management of Data*, Montreal, Canada, 1996, pp. 1-12.

[26] S.M. Weiss, *Predictive Data Mining: A Practical Guide*, San Francisco, CA: Morgan Kaufmann, 1998.

[27] R.R. Yager, "On Linguistic Summaries of Data," in G. Piatetsky-Shapiro and W.J. Frawley (Eds.), *Knowledge Discovery in Databases*, Menlo Park, CA: AAAI/MIT Press, 1991, pp. 347-363.

[28] L. Zadeh, "Fuzzy Sets," *Inform. Control*, vol. 8, pp. 338-353, 1965.

Provably Fast Training Algorithms for Support Vector Machines[*]

José L. Balcázar
Departament de Llenguatges i Sistemes Informàtics,
Univ. Politècnica de Catalunya
Campus Nord, Jordi Girona Salgado 1-3, 08034 Barcelona, Spain

Yang Dai
Dept. of Bioengineering (MC063)
University of Illinois at Chicago
851 S. Morgan Street, Chicago, IL 60607–7052, USA

Osamu Watanabe
Dept. of Mathematical and Computing Sciences,
Tokyo Institute of Technology
Meguro-ku Ookayama, Tokyo 152-8552, Japan

Abstract

Support Vector Machines are a family of data analysis algorithms, based on convex Quadratic Programming. We focus on their use for classification: in that case the SVM algorithms work by maximizing the margin of a classifying hyperplane in a feature space. The feature space is handled by means of kernels if the problems are formulated in dual form. Random Sampling techniques successfully used for similar problems are studied here. The main contribution is a randomized algorithm for training SVMs for which we can formally prove an upper bound on the expected running time that is quasilinear on the number of data points. To our knowledge, this is the first algorithm for training SVMs in dual formulation and with kernels for which such a quasilinear time bound has been formally proved.

---
[*]The first author started this research while visiting the Centre de Recerca Matemàtica of the Institute of Catalan Studies in Barcelona, and is supported by the IST Programme of the EU under contract number IST-1999-14186 (ALCOM-FT), EU EP27150 (Neurocolt II), Spanish Government PB98-0937-C04 (FRESCO), and CIRIT 1997SGR-00366. The second author conducted this research while at the Dept. of Mathematical and Computing Sciences, Tokyo Institute of Technology, and is supported by a Grant-in-Aid (C-13650444) from the Ministry of Education, Science, Sports and Culture of Japan, and a start-up fund from Dept. of Bioengineering, University of Illinois at Chicago. The third author started this research while visiting the Centre de Recerca Matemàtica of the Institute of Catalan Studies in Barcelona, and is supported by a Grant-in-Aid for Scientific Research on Priority Areas "Discovery Science" from the Ministry of Education, Science, Sports and Culture of Japan. We want to thank for their help Emo Welzl, Nello Cristianini, and John Shawe-Taylor.

1. Introduction

The *Support Vector Machine* (SVM in short) is a modern mechanism for two-class classification, regression, and clustering problems. Since the present form of SVM was proposed [CV95], SVMs have been used in various application areas, and their classification power has been investigated in depth from both experimental and theoretical points of view [CST00]. An important feature is that their way of working, by identifying the so-called support vectors among the data, offers important contributions to a number of problems related to Data Mining.

Indeed, the outcome of the training phase of a SVM is a set of weights associated to the input data; the weight is null on all data except the support vectors. In most situations only a small fraction of the data become support vectors, and it can be rigorously proven that the same outcome of the training is obtained if one only uses support vectors instead of all the data points. Therefore SVMs can be used for data summarization. It has been experimentally shown [SBV95] that, for some relevant tasks, the set of support vectors is stable in the sense that several different SVM-based classifiers ended up all choosing large ratios of common support vectors; thus, indeed this suggests that the support vectors are capturing the essentials of the data set. Finally, in a phase of data cleaning, outliers are easily detected by monitoring the growth of the weights. A more detailed, accessible survey of the method and references to applications to data mining and many other tasks is [BC00].

The three main characteristics of SVMs are: first, that

they minimize a formally proven upper bound on the generalization error; second, that they work on high-dimensional feature spaces by means of a dual formulation in terms of kernels; and, third, that the prediction is based on hyperplanes in these feature spaces, which may correspond to quite involved classification criteria on the input data, and which may handle misclassifications in the training set by means of soft margins.

The bound on the generalization error, to be minimized through the training process, is related to a data-dependent quantity (the margin, which must be maximized) but is independent of the dimensionality of the space: thus, the so-called "curse of dimensionality", with its associated risk of overfitting the data, is under control, even for infinite-dimensional feature spaces.

The handling of objects in high-dimensional feature space is made possible (and reasonably efficient) through the use of the important notion of "kernel" [BGV92]. If the maximization of the margin is expressed in dual form, it turns out that the only operations needed on data, both to train the SVM and to classify further data, are scalar products. A kernel is a function that operates on the input data but has the effect of computing the scalar product of their images in the feature space: this allows one to work implicitly with hyperplanes in highly complex spaces. We will come back to duality in section 5, and we defer the detailed explanation of the last feature, the soft margins approach, to the next section.

Algorithmically, the problem amounts to solving a convex quadratic programming (QP in short) problem; actually, it was proved in [SBV95] that a similar technique is able to help choosing a kernel. However, to scale up to really large data sets, the standard QP algorithms alone are inappropriate since their running times grow too fast [BC00].

Thus, many algorithms and implementation techniques have been developed for training SVMs efficiently. Among the proposed speed-up techniques, those called "subset selection" have been used as effective heuristics already from the earliest papers eventually leading to SVM, including [BGV92]. Roughly speaking, a *subset selection* is a technique to speed-up SVM training by dividing the original QP problem into small pieces, thereby reducing the size of each QP problem. Well-known subset selection techniques [CST00] are chunking, decomposition, and sequential minimal optimization [Pla99] (SMO in short), which may be combined with a reduction on the data on the basis of so-called guard vectors [YA00]. In particular, SMO has become popular because it outperforms the others in several experiments. Though the performance of these subset selection techniques has been extensively examined, no theoretical guarantee has been given on the efficiency of algorithms based on these techniques. As far as the authors know, the only positive theoretical results are the convergence (i.e.,

termination) of some of such algorithms [Lin01, KG01].

Yet another recent alternative, the Reduced Support Vector Machine [LM01], proposes to use only a single random subsample of data points, and to combine it to all the data points through kernel-computed scalar products in feature space. Our approach has some resemblance with this one in that a random selection of a small number of data points is made; however, in our algorithms, this is done repeatedly by filtering the selection through a probability distribution that evolves according to the results of the previous phases.

In a previous paper [BDW01], we have proposed to use random sampling techniques that have been developed and used for combinatorial optimization problems. An important drawback of our previous algorithm in [BDW01], or, rather, of its analysis, based on the beautiful Simple Sampling Lemma of [GW00], is that the algorithm is analyzed in primal form, and that the analysis of its running time is not valid, in principle, for its natural dual counterpart. The reason is that the linearly many new variables that appear as Lagrange multipliers in the dual formulation increase the dimensionality too much. Additionally, the analysis depended on certain unproven combinatorial hypothesis.

The contribution of this paper is a randomized subset selection scheme that improves on our previous algorithm in that it can be applied in dual form, and in that the theorem that bounds the expected number of rounds does not depend on any combinatorial hypotheses. The running time is polynomial (of low degree) in the dimension n of the input space and quasilinear, $O(m \log m)$, on the number m of data points, for m larger enough than n. This complexity-theoretic analysis suggests that its scalability properties to truly large data sets may raise a hope to bring the SVM methodology closer to the requirements of data mining tasks.

It must be said, though, that the algorithm proposed here suffers an important loss in performance in case of having many outliers (compared with the dimensionality of the data). This was to be expected since, of course, highly non-separable input data causes a lot of algorithmic difficulty.

2. Support Vector Machines, Optimization, and Random Sampling

Here we explain some basic notions on SVM and random sampling techniques necessary for our discussion. For additional explanations on SVM, see, e.g., the textbook [CST00] or the survey [BC00]; and for random sampling techniques, see the survey [GW00].

The training problem for two-class classification SVM can be phrased as follows. Given is a set of labeled examples; we have to come up with a hyperplane separating the positive examples from the negative examples with the largest possible margin, i.e., maximal separation from all

Max Margin (P1)

$$\min. \ \frac{1}{2}\|\boldsymbol{w}\|^2 - (\theta_+ - \theta_-)$$

w.r.t. $\boldsymbol{w} = (w_1, ..., w_n), \theta_+, \text{and } \theta_-,$

s.t. $\boldsymbol{w} \cdot \boldsymbol{x}_i \geq \theta_+ \ \text{if } y_i = 1, \ \text{and}$

$\boldsymbol{w} \cdot \boldsymbol{x}_i \leq \theta_- \ \text{if } y_i = -1.$

Max Soft Margin (P2)

$$\min. \ \frac{1}{2}\|\boldsymbol{w}\|^2 - (\theta_+ - \theta_-) + D \cdot \sum_i \xi_i,$$

w.r.t. $\boldsymbol{w} = (w_1, ..., w_n), \theta_+, \theta_-, \text{and } \xi_1, ..., \xi_m$

s.t. $\boldsymbol{w} \cdot \boldsymbol{x}_i \geq \theta_+ - \xi_i \ \text{if } y_i = 1,$

$\boldsymbol{w} \cdot \boldsymbol{x}_i \leq \theta_- + \xi_i \ \text{if } y_i = -1, \ \text{and } \xi_i \geq 0.$

Figure 1. Two Optimization Problems

the data points. Intuitively, the maximal margin separator does not unnecesarily lie towards either class, and this is the intuitive reason why it could generalize better; more formal reasons were mathematically proved by Vapnik and others, and can be found in [CST00].

A possible formalization for the problem is as follows. Suppose that we are given a set of m examples $\boldsymbol{x}_i, 1 \leq i \leq m$, in some n dimensional space, say $\mathbb{R}^n$. Each example $\boldsymbol{x}_i$ is labeled by $y_i \in \{1, -1\}$, the classification of the example. The *SVM training problem* we will discuss in this paper essentially consists in solving the optimization problem (P1) in Figure 1. Here we follow [BB00] and use their formulation. The problem can be restated with a single threshold parameter as given in [CV95]. We are assuming here that we are in the separable case, i.e. indeed a hyperplane separating the two classes of examples exists; the nonseparable case, which is our main topic, will be discussed shortly.

Remarks on Notations. Throughout this paper, we use X to denote the set of examples, and let n and m denote the dimension of the example space and the number of examples respectively. Also we use i for indexing examples (and their labels), and $\boldsymbol{x}_i$ and y_i to denote the ith example and its label respectively. The range of i is always $\{1, ..., m\}$.

By the *solution* of (P1), we mean the hyperplane that achieves the minimum cost. Given a solution, its support vectors are the data points $\boldsymbol{x}_i$ for which, at the solution, the corresponding inequality is tight: $\boldsymbol{w} \cdot \boldsymbol{x}_i = \theta_+$ if $y_i = 1$, and $\boldsymbol{w} \cdot \boldsymbol{x}_i = \theta_-$ if $y_i = -1$. We also consider partial problems of (P1) that minimize the target cost under some subset of constraints. A solution to such a partial problem of (P1) is called a *local solution* of (P1) for the subset of constraints.

An important feature of SVM is that they are also applicable to the nonseparable case. More precisely speaking, for nonseparable data we can take two positions: (i) the case

where we consider that a hyperplane is too weak a classifier for our given examples, and that we should be able to fit them better nonlinearly; and (ii) the case where we consider that there are some erroneous examples, or outliers, which we should somehow identify and allow to be misclassified. Of course, a nonlinear classifier may be better at classifying them correctly, but, in case we suspect they are erroneous, the more adaptive the classifier is, the better it can adapt to the errors; we might not want it to. The usability of SVM is due to the fact that we can balance both positions.

The first subcase is solved by the SVM approach by mapping examples into a high-dimensional space; we come back to this point later on. The second subcase is solved by relaxing constraints by introducing slack variables or "soft margin error" [CV95]. Thus, we also consider the generalization of the problem (P1), corresponding to the soft margin hyperplane separation problem: it is (P2) in Figure 1.

For a given set X of examples, suppose we solve the problem (P2) and obtain the optimal hyperplane. Then an example $\boldsymbol{x}_i \in X$ is called an *outlier* if it is misclassified with respect to this hyperplane and the optimal margins: equivalently, $\xi_i > 0$. Throughout this paper, we use ℓ to denote the number of outliers. The soft margin parameter D determines the degree of influence of the outliers. Note that D should be fixed in advance; that is, D is a constant throughout the training process.

Again, the concept of support vector for (P2) is defined in terms of tight inequalities: $\boldsymbol{w} \cdot \boldsymbol{x}_i = \theta_+ - \xi_i$ if $y_i = 1$, and $\boldsymbol{w} \cdot \boldsymbol{x}_i = \theta_- + \xi_i$ if $y_i = -1$. It is not difficult to see that outliers are a fortiori support vectors.

2.1. LP-type Optimization Problems and the Sampling Lemma

We explain now, briefly, the essentials of the abstract framework for discussing randomized sampling techniques that was given by Gärtner and Welzl [GW00]. Randomized sampling techniques, particularly, the Sampling Lemma below, are applicable for many "LP-type" problems. LP stands for Linear Programming. Here we use $(\mathcal{D}, \phi)$ to denote an abstract LP-type problem, where $\mathcal{D}$ is a set of elements and ϕ is a function mapping any $\mathcal{R} \subseteq \mathcal{D}$ to some value space. In the case of our problem (P1), for example, we can regard $\mathcal{D}$ as X and define ϕ as a mapping from a given subset R of X to the local solution of (P1) for the subset of constraints corresponding to R. As an LP-type problem, we require $(\mathcal{D}, \phi)$ to satisfy certain conditions. Here we omit the explanation and simply mention that our example case clearly satisfies these conditions.

For any $\mathcal{R} \subseteq \mathcal{D}$, a *basis* of $\mathcal{R}$ is an inclusion-minimal subset $\mathcal{B}$ of $\mathcal{R}$ such that $\phi(\mathcal{B}) = \phi(\mathcal{R})$. The *combinatorial dimension* of $(\mathcal{D}, \phi)$ is the size of the largest basis of $\mathcal{D}$. We will use δ to denote the combinatorial dimension. For the problem (P1), each basis is a minimal set of support vectors. The combinatorial dimension of (P1) is $n + 1$ since the two bias parameters θ_+ and θ_- are not independent.

Consider any LP-type problem, and any subset $\mathcal{R}$ of $\mathcal{D}$. A *violator* of $\mathcal{R}$ is an element e of $\mathcal{D}$ such that $\phi(\mathcal{R} \cup \{e\}) \neq \phi(\mathcal{R})$. An element e of $\mathcal{R}$ is *extreme in* $\mathcal{R}$ if $\phi(\mathcal{R} - \{e\}) \neq \phi(\mathcal{R})$. In our case, for any subset R of X, let $(\boldsymbol{w}, \theta_+, \theta_-)$ be a local solution of (P1) obtained for R. Then $\boldsymbol{x}_i \in X$ is a *violator* of R, or (more directly) a *violator* of $(\boldsymbol{w}, \theta_+, \theta_-)$, if the constraint corresponding to $\boldsymbol{x}_i$ is not satisfied by $(\boldsymbol{w}, \theta_+, \theta_-)$.

Consider again any LP-type problem $(\mathcal{D}, \phi)$. Let $\mathcal{U}$ be a set consisting u elements of $\mathcal{D}$. $\mathcal{U}$ may be a *multiple set*, a set containing some element more than once. In order to discuss the case where elements of $\mathcal{D}$ are chosen into $\mathcal{R}$ according to some possibly nonuniform probability, we will use $\mathcal{U}$ as domain instead of $\mathcal{D}$, and will consider simply that $\mathcal{R}$ is a subset of $\mathcal{U}$. Though obvious, the following relation is important: e violates $\mathcal{R}$ iff e is extreme in $\mathcal{R} \cup \{e\}$.

Define $v_{\mathcal{R}}$ and $x_{\mathcal{R}}$ to be the number of violators and extremes of $\mathcal{R}$ in $\mathcal{U}$ respectively. The following bound, which is also easy from the definition, is important: $x_{\mathcal{R}} \leq \delta$.

We are ready to state the Sampling Lemma. The idea, and its algorithmic application as in our theorem 2 below, is already in the literature (see the references in [BDW01]).

Lemma 1 *Let $(\mathcal{D}, \phi)$ be any LP-type problem. Assume some weight scheme u on $\mathcal{D}$ that gives an integer weight to each element of $\mathcal{D}$. Let $u(\mathcal{D})$ denote the total weight. For a given r, $0 \leq r < u(\mathcal{D})$, we consider the situation where a set of r elements of $\mathcal{D}$ has been chosen randomly, according to their weights. Let $\mathcal{R}$ denote the set of chosen elements, and let $v_{\mathcal{R}}$ be the weight of violators of $\mathcal{R}$. Then we have the following bound on the expected value of $v_{\mathcal{R}}$:*

$$\mathrm{Exp}(v_{\mathcal{R}}) \leq \frac{u(\mathcal{D}) - r}{r + 1} \cdot \delta. \tag{1}$$

See [GW00] for the proof, additional explanations, variations for other sampling schemas, important related results such as tail bounds, and applications of this Lemma.

2.2. Preliminary Algorithmics

Consider first the separable case (P1). We can solve this optimization problem by using a standard general quadratic programming algorithm. In most applications, however, the number m of examples is much larger than the dimension n (in other words, many more constraints than variables). This is the situation where randomized sampling techniques are effective. We first describe how to adapt the general-purpose randomized algorithm from [GW00], which works for arbitrary LP-type problems.

procedure OptMargin
  set weight $u(\boldsymbol{x}_i)$ to be 1 for all examples in X;
  $r \leftarrow 6\delta^2$;
  repeat
    $R \leftarrow$ choose r examples from X
      randomly according to u;
    let $(\boldsymbol{w}, \theta_+, \theta_-)$ be a solution of (P1) for R;
    $V \leftarrow$ the set of violators in X of the solution;
    if $u(V) \leq u(X)/(3\delta)$ **then**
      double the weight $u(\boldsymbol{x}_i)$ for all $\boldsymbol{x}_i \in V$;
  until $V = \emptyset$;
  return the last solution;
end-procedure.

Figure 2. A First Randomized Algorithm

The idea is simple. Pick a certain number of examples from X and solve (P1) under the set of constraints corresponding to these examples. We choose examples randomly according to their "weights", where initially all examples are given the same weight. Clearly, the obtained local solution is, in general, not the global solution, and it does not satisfy some constraints; in other words, some examples are misclassified by the local solution. Then double the "weight" of such misclassified examples, and then pick some examples again randomly according to their weights. If we iterate this process several rounds, the weight of "important examples", which are support vectors in our case, grows exponentially fast, and hence, they are likely to be chosen. Note that, once all support vectors are chosen at some round, then the local solution of this round is the true one, and the algorithm terminates at this point. By using the Simple Sampling Lemma, we can prove that the algorithm terminates in $O(n \log m)$ rounds on average.

We describe more precisely the algorithm in Figure 2. We use u there to denote a weight scheme that assigns some integer weight $u(\boldsymbol{x}_i)$ to each $\boldsymbol{x}_i \in X$. For this weight scheme u, consider a multiple set U containing each example $\boldsymbol{x}_i$ exactly $u(\boldsymbol{x}_i)$ times. Note that U has $u(X)$ ($= \sum_i u(\boldsymbol{x}_i)$) elements. Then by "choose r examples randomly from X according to u", we mean to select a set of examples uniformly at random from all $\binom{u(X)}{r}$ subsets of U.

For analyzing the efficiency of this algorithm, we use the Simple Sampling Lemma 1. From it, we can prove the following bound (see [BDW01]).

Theorem 2 *The average number of iterations executed in the OptMargin algorithm is bounded by $6\delta \ln m = O(n \ln m)$. (Recall that $|X| = m$ and $\delta = n + 1$.)*

We want to apply a similar technique for the nonseparable case. Furthermore, we want to do it in such a way that the only operations acting on the data points are scalar products, and we want the output hyperplane to be defined as a linear combination of the data points, so that classifying a new point amounts again only to scalar products as operations on data points. The reasons why the formulations in terms of scalar products allow one to use kernels (and thus obtain highly nonlinear actual classifiers) are carefully described in, e.g., [BC00] and [CST00].

3. Alternative Formulations

To go on we need an alternative formulation of (P2) given in [BDW01], and based on an intuitive geometric interpretation of (P2) that has been given by Bennett and Bredensteiner [BB00] after the Wolfe dual of (P2). Let Z be the set of *composed examples* $\boldsymbol{z}_I$ that are defined as $\boldsymbol{z}_I = (\boldsymbol{x}_{i_1} + \boldsymbol{x}_{i_2} + \cdots + \boldsymbol{x}_{i_k})/k$, with some k distinct elements $\boldsymbol{x}_{i_1}$, $\boldsymbol{x}_{i_2}$, ..., $\boldsymbol{x}_{i_k}$ of X with the same label (i.e., $y_{i_1} = y_{i_2} = \cdots = y_{i_k}$). The label y_I of the composed example $\boldsymbol{z}_I$ inherits its members'. Throughout this note, we use I for indexing elements of Z and their labels. The range of I is $\{1, ..., M\}$, where $M \stackrel{\text{def}}{=} |Z|$; each such I can be identified with a set $I = \{i_1, \ldots, i_k\} \subseteq \{1, \ldots, n\}$. Note that $M \leq \binom{m}{k}$. For each $\boldsymbol{z}_I$, we use z_I to denote the set of original examples from which $\boldsymbol{z}_I$ is composed. Note also that these composed examples are sort of mass centers of all groups of k homogeneously labeled initial data points.

Then the resulting composed examples, for large enough k, may be linearly separable, even if the initial data are not; for instance, in the extreme case where $k = m_+$ (where m_+ is the number of positive examples), the set of positive composed examples consists of only one point. (In some unlikely cases a positive composed example might coincide with a negative one; a slight perturbation of the data avoids this case.) We can formulate now:

Max Margin for Composed Examples (P5)

min. $\frac{1}{2}\|\boldsymbol{w}\|^2 - (\eta_+ - \eta_-)$
w.r.t. $\boldsymbol{w} = (w_1, ..., w_n)$, η_+, and η_-,
s.t. $\boldsymbol{w} \cdot \boldsymbol{z}_I \geq \eta_+$ if $y_I = 1$, and
$\boldsymbol{w} \cdot \boldsymbol{z}_I \leq \eta_-$ if $y_I = -1$.

We keep the name (P5) for consistency with [BDW01], to ease the comparison of our new algorithm with our previous paper. Note that the combinatorial dimension of (P5) is $n + 1$, the same as that of (P1). The difference is that we have now $M = O(m^k)$ constraints, which is quite large. On the other hand, except for the margin parameters η_+ and η_-, it follows from [BB00] (see also [BDW01]) that the remaining values of the optimal solution (i.e. $\boldsymbol{w}^\star$) coincide for (P2) and (P5).

This situation is suitable for the sampling technique, and the same algorithm can be applied. Suppose now that we use OptMargin of Figure 2 for solving (P5). Since the combinatorial dimension is the same, we can use $r = 6(n+1)^2$

as before. From our analysis, the expected number of iterations is $O(n \ln M) = O(kn \ln m)$. That is, we need to solve QP problems with $n + 2$ variables and $O(n^2)$ constraints for $O(kn \ln m)$ times. Although this is not bad at all, there are unfortunately some serious problems. The algorithm needs, at least as it is, a large amount of time and space for "book keeping" computation. First of all, we have to keep weights of all M composed examples in Z. Secondly, for finding violators and for modifying weights, we have to go through Z, which takes at least $O(M)$ steps. Also it is not so easy to choose composed examples randomly according to their weights. Solutions to these problems were obtained in [BDW01], but the proof of the running time of the resulting algorithm depended on an unproven hypothesis.

Thus we head towards the main contribution of this paper, a new algorithm, based on a nontrivial geometric lemma, that handles only m weights and avoids searching for violators on all of Z, and at the same time uses only scalar products on data points, so that it combines with any desired kernel. However, before describing it we need to analyze some properties of the solutions of (P5).

4. Properties of the Solutions

For a given example set X, let Z be the set of composed examples. Let $(\boldsymbol{w}^\star, \theta_+^\star, \theta_-^\star)$ and $(\boldsymbol{w}^\star, \eta_+^\star, \eta_-^\star)$ be the solutions of (P2) for X and (P5) for Z respectively, sharing $\boldsymbol{w}^\star$ as indicated above. Let $X_{\text{err},+}$ and $X_{\text{err},-}$ denote respectively the sets of positive and negative outliers. That is, $\boldsymbol{x}_i$ belongs to $X_{\text{err},+}$ (resp., $X_{\text{err},-}$) if and only if $y_i = 1$ and $\boldsymbol{w}^\star \cdot \boldsymbol{x}_i < \theta_+^\star$ (resp., $y_i = -1$ and $\boldsymbol{w}^\star \cdot \boldsymbol{x}_i > \theta_-^\star$). We use ℓ_+ and ℓ_- to denote respectively the number of positive and negative outliers. From now on, we assume that our constant k is larger than both ℓ_+ and ℓ_-, and that in fact problem (P5) is linearly separable. Let $X_{\text{err}} = X_{\text{err},+} \cup X_{\text{err},-}$.

The problem (P5) is regarded as the LP-type problem $(\mathcal{D}, \phi)$, where the correspondence is as in (P1) except that Z is used as $\mathcal{D}$ here. Let Z_0 be a basis of Z. In order to facilitate understanding, we assume nondegeneracy throughout the following discussion. Note that every element of the basis is extreme in Z. Hence, we call elements of Z_0 *final extremers*. By definition, the solution of (P5) for Z is defined by the constraints corresponding to these final extremers.

By analyzing the Karush-Kuhn-Tucker (in short, KKT) condition for (P2), in [BDW01] we showed:

Lemma 3 *Let $\boldsymbol{z}_I$ be any positive final extremer, i.e., an element of Z_0 such that $y_I = 1$. Then the following properties hold: (a) $\boldsymbol{w}^\star \cdot \boldsymbol{z}_I = \eta_+^\star$. (b) $X_{\text{err},+} \subseteq z_I$. (c) For every $\boldsymbol{x}_i \in z_I$, if $\boldsymbol{x}_i \notin X_{\text{err},+}$, then we have $\boldsymbol{w}^\star \cdot \boldsymbol{x}_i = \theta_+^\star$.*

The corresponding facts hold, *mutatis mutandis*, for negative final extremers.

procedure ComposedMargin
$u_i \leftarrow 1$, for each i, $1 \le i \le m$;
$r \leftarrow 6\delta^2$;
loop
    $R' \leftarrow$ choose r elements from X randomly
        according to their weights;
    $R \leftarrow$ the set of composed examples from Z
        consisting only of points from R';
    $(\boldsymbol{w}, \eta_+, \eta_-) \leftarrow$ the solution of (P5) for R;
    compute θ_+ and θ_- from the local solution;
    $Y \leftarrow$ the set of points from $X - R'$
        misclassified by $(\boldsymbol{w}, \theta_+, \theta_-)$;
    check the stopping condition
        and exit loop if it holds;
    if $u(Y) \le u(X)/(3\delta)$ **then**
        $u_i \leftarrow 2u_i$ for each $\boldsymbol{x}_i \in Y$;
    end loop;
    return the last solution $(\boldsymbol{w}, \theta_+, \theta_-)$;
end procedure.

Figure 3. A Second Randomized Algorithm

5. New Algorithms

Throughout this section, we assume that k is large enough so that the composed examples make up a linearly separable data set; the combinatorial dimension will be now $\delta = k(n + 1)$ (actually we only need that δ upper-bounds the combinatorial dimension; we have also a preliminary argument, that will be described in future work, according to which $\delta = k + n + 1$). Again X is the set of input data and Z is the set of composed examples. Our algorithms must find a maximal margin separator of these composed examples. Fix a set Z_0 of combined examples that is a minimal set of support vectors for the true solution. We will denote by X_0 the set of input points that belong to some composed example in Z_0, so that again $|X_0| \le \delta$. Also note that, again, the solution of the separable maximal margin problem on Z_0 is the global solution. Therefore, any local solution that differs from the global solution must misclassify at least one element of Z_0. This is essentially because, by convexity, any locally optimal solution that is globally feasible is globally optimal. Here again misclassification means that the corresponding inequality does not hold.

The algorithm in Figure 3 essentially implements the intuition just described. The computation of θ_+ and θ_- is made according to lemma 3 (c), by finding the largest distance from $\boldsymbol{w}$ to a point $\boldsymbol{x}_i$ that belongs to a final extremer of the local solution. We use the same template for two algorithms according to two different stopping conditions. Consider first stopping condition A:

    classify all composed examples
        according to $(\boldsymbol{w}, \eta_+, \eta_-)$;
    exit the loop if all of them are correctly classified;

Thus the algorithm first finds a local solution from the sample, and then tests it on all the composed examples. By the previous paragraph, it is partially correct: if it ever stops, the solution it returns is the global solution.

It is a very slow algorithm, since at each iteration it runs over all $M = m^k$ composed examples. Thus we will not analyze its running time; but its partial correctness as argued will make it easier to argue the correctness of the next algorithm using the second stopping condition. Indeed, the separable problem is on the composed examples but we do not want to scan them all in search for violators, but instead do it on the original data points X.

Thus we consider a faster algorithm that runs over the input data points instead, in search of misclassified points: this is the algorithm of Figure 3 with the stopping condition B (we will connect both stopping conditions below):

    exit the loop if all the points in $X - R'$
        are correctly classified ($Y = \emptyset$);

From Lemma 1, we can bound the expected number of violators as $k(n + 1)/r + 1 \cdot u(U) \le u(U)/(6\delta)$. Again by Markov's inequality, on average one out of each two iterations will be successful. So it remains to bound the number of successful iterations. By the same argumentation that supports theorem 1 [BDW01], it follows that, as soon as we prove that each successful stage doubles the weight of some point from X_0, we guarantee the upper bound $t < 3\delta \log m$ on the expected number of rounds. The fact we need to complete the analysis will be a corollary of the proof of the lemma in the next section.

5.1. Equivalence of the Stopping Conditions

We prove now that indeed each successful iteration doubles the weight of at least one element of X_0, and that whenever the algorithm of Figure 3 stops (using the stopping condition B), it has found the true optimal solution. We know this holds for stopping condition A, but for B it is not immediate at all, since it is quite different (and cheaper to compute). We prove this fact as a separate geometric lemma.

Lemma 4 *The stopping conditions are equivalent; i.e., the following two facts are equivalent:*

1. *There exists $\boldsymbol{x} \in X - R'$ misclassified by $(\boldsymbol{w}, \theta_+, \theta_-)$;*

2. *There exists a composed example $\boldsymbol{z}$ misclassified by $(\boldsymbol{w}, \eta_+, \eta_-)$.*

Proof. Suppose that there is a positive misclassified point $\boldsymbol{x}_p$ in $X - R'$, the negative case being analogous. This means that $\boldsymbol{w} \cdot \boldsymbol{x}_p < \theta_+$. Pick a final extremer $\boldsymbol{z}_0$ of the local solution on composed examples. Its corresponding inequality is tight: $\boldsymbol{w} \cdot \boldsymbol{z}_0 = \eta_+$. Note that lemma 3 applies since all composed examples made up from R' are in R. Thus, it contains all misclassified points in R', and there are remaining points $\boldsymbol{x} \in z_0$ fulfilling $\boldsymbol{w} \cdot \boldsymbol{x} = \theta_+$. (The assumption that k is larger than the number of misclassified points is used here.) Construct $\boldsymbol{z}_1$ by replacing one such $\boldsymbol{x} \in z_0$ by $\boldsymbol{x}_p$. By linearity, $\boldsymbol{w} \cdot \boldsymbol{z}_1 < \boldsymbol{w} \cdot \boldsymbol{z}_0 = \eta_+$, so $\boldsymbol{z}_1$ is misclassified by $(\boldsymbol{w}, \eta_+, \eta_-)$.

Conversely, let $\boldsymbol{z}_p$ be a positive composed example misclassified by $(\boldsymbol{w}, \eta_+, \eta_-)$: $\boldsymbol{w} \cdot \boldsymbol{z}_p < \eta_+$. Pick again a final extremer $\boldsymbol{z}_0$ of the local solution. Then we argue first that some misclassified point $\boldsymbol{x}_p$, with $\boldsymbol{w} \cdot \boldsymbol{x}_p < \theta_+$, is in z_p but not in z_0. Indeed, z_0 consists only of points $\boldsymbol{x}$ with $\boldsymbol{w} \cdot \boldsymbol{x} \leq \theta_+$. The correctly classified elements of $\boldsymbol{z}_p$ (if any) have $\boldsymbol{w} \cdot \boldsymbol{x} \geq \theta_+$. Thus, if all misclassified points in z_p are accounted for in z_0, we obtain $\boldsymbol{w} \cdot \boldsymbol{z}_p \geq \boldsymbol{w} \cdot \boldsymbol{z}_0 = \eta_+$, which is not the case.

Thus, some $\boldsymbol{x}_p \in z_p$ is misclassified and not in z_0. But, by lemma 3 (b), all misclassified points of R' are in z_0, and thus $\boldsymbol{x}_p \notin R'$, as was to be shown. $\square$

Finally, we need to argue that at least one point in X_0 gets doubled at each nonterminal successful iteration, except the last one. Note first that, if all the composed examples from points in X_0 are correctly classified by the local solution, as we have already said, there can be no misclassified composed examples of Z at all and, by the previous lemma, the algorithm will end. Thus, the composed example z_p used to start the proof of the lemma (backwards direction) can be actually selected to be composed of points in X_0. Thus, the point $\boldsymbol{x}_p$ that we find in the proof of the lemma is in X_0, is misclassified, and is not in R' as the lemma proves. Thus it doubles weight, and this, combined with a more-or-less standard application of Lemma 1, completes the proof. In this way we can obtain:

Theorem 5 *The algorithm in Figure 3, with stopping condition B, obtains the maximal margin hyperplane in less than $6\delta \log m$ rounds on average.*

The tail bounds given in [GW00] prove additionally that the probability of deviation from the average is exponentially small.

6. Dual Coordinates and our Final Algorithm

The dual formulation is obtained by introducing one more variable, the Lagrangian multiplier, for each inequality, i.e. for each data point, differentiating with respect to the primal variables, and equating to zero the derivatives. Thus, the dual variables are coefficients affecting the data points. It can be seen that the dual formulation only needs scalar products among data points, so that a kernel can be used instead; and the outcome defines the hyperplane as a linear combination of data points, so that classifying

procedure OptMargin
set weight $u(\boldsymbol{x}_i)$ to be 1 for all examples in X;
$r \leftarrow 6\delta^2$;
repeat
    $R \leftarrow$ choose r examples from X
        randomly according to u;
    let $(\boldsymbol{w}, \theta_+, \theta_-, \xi)$ be a solution of (P2) for R;
    $V \leftarrow$ the set of violators in $X - R$ of the solution;
    if $u(V) \leq u(X)/(3\delta)$ **then**
        double the weight $u(\boldsymbol{x}_i)$ for all $\boldsymbol{x}_i \in V$;
until $V = \emptyset$;
return the last solution;
end-procedure.

Figure 4. A Last Randomized Algorithm

new points only needs computing scalar products with data points. Moreover, the optimal value of the Lagrangian multiplier is only nonzero for the support vectors. See [CST00].

We export now the ideas of the previous sections to the dual framework: we first sample, then move into dual form, and then consider composed examples only on the sample (or on their images in feature space). This allows us to introduce a quantity of additional variables (Lagrange multipliers) that is independent of m. Once a local solution is available, the points left unsampled are checked against it, to double the weight of those that led to wrong classifications. Indeed, although it is not fully trivial, it can be seen that all the steps of the algorithm in Figure 3 with stopping condition B can be run only implicitly on the feature space if the kernel is used judiciously.

But there is still a somewhat surprising alternative: instead of translating our last algorithm into dual form, we can actually come back to Figure 2! Indeed, by the analysis of [BB00], we know that the optimal $\boldsymbol{w}^\star$ is the same for (P5) and for (P2). Thus, we can simply sample R input data points, solve (P2) on R (in dual form to use kernels), and, according to stopping condition B, check for violators *only* in $X - R$. Thus, we obtain a simple algorithm, Figure 4, which is similar to the one in Figure 2, but without the assumption of separability. Lacking this assumption means we solve (P2) instead of (P1) to find the local solution, since (P1) may well be unfeasible, and then test the local solution only on the unsampled points, since some sampled points actually do violate it. Another subtle difference is the initial value of the constant δ, where the dependence of k is hidden. The algorithm in Figure 4 has the same performance guarantees as indicated in the previous theorem, even when the local solution is found in dual form with kernels.

7. Conclusions and Further Remarks

We have developed here more algorithms for training support vector machines in such a way that we can formally prove rigorous fast convergence results, in the common case of having much larger data sets than the dimension. This continues the research initiated in our previous paper [BDW01]. The advantage of our last algorithm here is the possibility of using it in dual formulation, which is a key to the use of a major feature of support vector machines, namely kernels into feature spaces. The algorithm has been formally proved to have a very mild dependence of the number of data points, although its dependence on the number of outliers for the nonseparable case may become a cause of slow computation. It needs the prior knowledge of a parameter k corresponding to the influence of outliers: all soft margin implementations of SVM need one similar parameter. However, in general there is no clue as to how to choose it, whereas in our case it has a clear intuitive meaning: k must be such that the sets of homogeneously labeled k-wise mass-centers are linearly separable, or at least an upper bound on such a value.

We have not mentioned experimental validations. Experiments conducted by Norbert Martínez with several variants of our previous algorithms based on the Sampling Lemma indicated that these were competitive with other chunking and decomposition schemas but did not show an spectacular behavior improvement yet. Thus, we have focused on deepening the theoretical understanding of the combinatorial process. Still, we do not think a naive implementation of the algorithm in Figure 4 will be competitive immediately: there is some more work to be done in finding the best possible value of δ, where the current bottleneck resides; a lot of care has to be invested in the interaction with the local problem solver, and dedicated data structures allowing fast sampling under the filtered probability distribution could be designed.

We can enumerate easily several more issues worth further work. First, there may be other possible ways of analyzing the algorithm in [BDW01]; similarly, there could be other possible ways to analyze our final algorithm here. Second, [GW00] contains other applications of sampling to LP-type problems, some of which look promising for advances in SVMs in case we can map them into dual convex quadratic programming. Third, there is an interesting possibility of not using a true QP subroutine for the local problems, but accepting instead suboptimal solutions: would the sampling rounds make up for this? Overall, we believe that further work may lead to new algorithms with better scale-up properties, applicable to very large datasets with reasonable running times.

References

[BDW01] J. L. Balcázar, Y. Dai, and O. Watanabe, A random sampling technique for training support vec-

tor machines, in *Proc. Algorithmic Learning Theory* (ALT'01), 2001.

[BB00] K. P. Bennett and E. J. Bredensteiner, Duality and geometry in SVM classifiers, in *Proc. the 17th Int'l Conf. on Machine Learning* (ICML'2000), 57–64.

[BC00] K. P. Bennett and C. Campbell, Support Vector Machines: Hype or Hallelujah?, SIGKDD *Explorations* Newsletter 2, 2 (2000).

[BGV92] B. E. Boser, I. M. Guyon, and V. N. Vapnik, A training algorithm for optimal margin classifiers, in *Proc. Int. Conf. on Computational Learning Theory* (COLT'92), 144–152, 1992.

[Lin01] C. J. Lin, On the convergence of the decomposition method for support vector machines, *IEEE Trans. on Neural Networks*, 2001, to appear. (Also available from http://www.csie.ntu.edu.tw/~cjlin/papers/.)

[CV95] C. Cortes and V. Vapnik, Support-vector networks, *Machine Learning* 20, 273–297, 1995.

[CST00] N. Cristianini and J. Shawe-Taylor, *An Introduction to Support Vector Machines*, Cambridge University Press 2000.

[GW00] B. Gärtner and E. Welzl, A simple sampling lemma: Analysis and applications in geometric optimization, *Discr. Comput. Geometry*, 2000, to appear. (Also available from http://www.inf.ethz.ch/personal/gaertner/publications.html.)

[KG01] S. S. Keerthi and E. G. Gilbert, Convergence of a generalized SMO algorithm for SVM classifier design, Technical Report CD-00-01, Dept. of Mechanical and Production Eng., National University of Singapore, 2000. (Available from http://guppy.mpe.nus.edu.sg/~mpessk/svm/conv_ml.)

[LM01] Y.-J. Lee and O. L. Mangasarian, RSVM: Reduced Support Vector Machines, in *Proc. First SIAM International Conference on Data Mining*, 2001.

[Pla99] J. Platt, Fast training of support vector machines using sequential minimal optimization, in *Advances in Kernel Methods – Support Vector Learning* (B. Scholkopf, C. Burges, and A. J. Smola, eds.), MIT Press, 185–208, 1999.

[SBV95] B. Schölkopf, C. Burges, and V. Vapnik, Extracting support data for a given task, in *Proc. First Int. Conf. on Knowledge Discovery and Data Mining* (KDD'95), 252–257, 1995.

[YA00] M.-H. Yang and N. Ahuja, A geometric approach to train support vector machines, in *Proc. IEEE Conf. Computer Vision and Pattern Rec.*, 2000, 430–437.

Who Links to Whom: Mining Linkage between Web Sites

Krishna Bharat, Bay-Wei Chang, Monika Henzinger
Google Inc.
Mountain View, CA 94043, USA
{krishna,bay,monika}@google.com

Matthias Ruhl
MIT Laboratory for Computer Science
Cambridge, MA 02139, USA
ruhl@theory.lcs.mit.edu

Abstract

Previous studies of the web graph structure have focused on the graph structure at the level of individual pages. In actuality the web is a hierarchically nested graph, with domains, hosts and web sites introducing intermediate levels of affiliation and administrative control. To better understand the growth of the web we need to understand its macro-structure, in terms of the linkage between web sites. In this paper we approximate this by studying the graph of the linkage between hosts on the web. This was done based on snapshots of the web taken by Google in Oct 1999, Aug 2000 and Jun 2001. The connectivity between hosts is represented by a directed graph, with hosts as nodes and weighted edges representing the count of hyperlinks between pages on the corresponding hosts. We demonstrate how such a "hostgraph" can be used to study connectivity properties of hosts and domains over time, and discuss a modified "copy model" to explain observed link weight distributions as a function of subgraph size. We discuss changes in the web over time in the size and connectivity of web sites and country domains. We also describe a data mining application of the hostgraph: a related host finding algorithm which achieves a precision of 0.65 at rank 3.

1. Introduction

The web is a hierarchically nested graph, with domains, web sites, and individual pages introducing different levels of affiliation and administrative control. A web page is the elementary unit. Pages usually tend to be under the editorial control of a single *entity* (person or organization). A *web site* is a collection of web pages affiliated to a single entity. A *domain* (short for top-level domain) consists of a collection of web hosts, all of which share the same last token in the host name (e.g., .com or .uk). Most domains are associated with individual countries, though there are large domains such as .com and .net that are not geographical.

Previous studies [4, 3, 8] of the web graph structure have focused on the graph structure at the level of individual pages. However, web sites might introduce a more appropriate level of abstraction:

- Documents are frequently represented by multiple web pages. For example, documents authored with Microsoft Powerpoint are often published as a chain of inter-linked web pages. Consequently, the full *hyperdocument* rather than the individual pages may be the right level of granularity for analysis. Bibliometric studies analyze the citation or cocitation between authors, usually considering linkage to or from an author's work in aggregate. To study web authors analogously, web sites may be the right level.

- Since the entity that owns a web site has control over all parts, the content within a site may be reorganized or revised periodically without significantly changing the semantics or linkage relative to the rest of the web. This argues for separating the analysis of inter- and intra-site linkage.

- Concerns have been raised about accessibility of content on the web. E.g., in [8] it was shown that the "distance" between pages on the web is quite large with often no directed path being available.[1] This fails to account for the fact that within a given web site there are implicit paths from all pages to the "root page" (users often truncate the path of the URL to navigate to the root page), from which there should be author-designed paths to all local content. Thus navigation within a web site is often less challenging than would appear from a naive analysis of the linkage. If we assume that sites are internally fully navigable, then the inter-linkage between sites becomes the main factor in determining the accessibility of web-wide content.

- Since generating pages is cheap, some sites may generate a large number of pages (potentially an infinite number which are dynamically generated), skewing statistical properties that people may want to study.

In this paper we attempt to study the web on the web site level. However, determining which pages belong to the

---

[1] Note that search engines provide random access to web content which these studies do not currently account for.

same web site is an open problem, although some heuristic approaches have been proposed, see e.g. [15]. We approximate each web site by all the pages with the same host name[2] and study the following weighted *hostgraph*: Each node represents a web host, and each directed edge represents the hyperlinks from pages on the source host to pages on the target host. The weight of the edge corresponds to the number of such hyperlinks.

Which properties between web hosts are interesting to study? (a) Obviously one wants to determine its size in terms of nodes and edges and observe how it changes over time. (b) Since the "average degree of separation" on the web has received considerable attention on the page level [4, 8] it is interesting to study it in this coarser grain abstraction. (c) It is also interesting to see how the host level abstraction relates to the domain level abstraction, specifically to study the linkage of hosts in different domains. (d) Previous work [12, 8] has shown the Zipfian nature of the indegree and outdegree distribution of the page graph. It is therefore an interesting question whether the hostgraph distributions are Zipfian as well. This evidence of self-similarity would support the conjecture by previous researchers [8] that the web graph has a fractal nature.

Our main contribution in this paper is the abstraction of a hostgraph, intended as a tool to study the web's properties and extract useful structures from it. To the best of our knowledge such an abstraction has not been previously defined in the literature, and nor has it been explictly computed and used for analyzing the web. We present data from three experiments (Section 2) to confirm that the web graph studied at this level exhibits many of the properties observed at the page graph level (Section 4). We use the data to suggest a host-level "copy model" (Section 7) to explain the connectivity seen in the hostgraph, as an extension of a previous page-level copy model. We look at accessibility of content on the web at the host level (Section 3) factoring out intra-site navigability. To understand the effects of language and geography on the web structure we look at the connectivity between top level domains (Section 5). In addition to its use as a analytical tool, we intended the hostgraph to be a suitable resource for data mining. We illustrate this with examples of extracting related hosts based on linkage and co-citation (Section 6). Section 8 discusses related work.

2. Datasets

For a given snapshot of the web, a hostgraph can be computed as follows. In a linear scan through all pages, for every cross-host link we write the corresponding ordered pair

---

[2]Note that this is just a heuristic since a web site can be comprised of many host names (e.g., www.intel.com and support.intel.com can both be considered part of the Intel web site) and inversely a host can host many web sites, (e.g., members.aol.com is a collection of web sites of individuals and small organizations).

	Oct 1999	Aug 2000	Jun 2001
Web pages (millions)	128.99	604.37	1,292
Hyperlinks (billions)	1.27	5.54	19.46

Table 1. Web graphs underlying the hostgraphs.

of hosts to a log. At the end of the pass, the log is sorted and in a linear scan contiguous occurrences of each distinct ordered host pair are counted. Each ordered host pair corresponds to an edge in the hostgraph, and the occurrence count in the log corresponds to its weight.

We ran our experiments with three snapshots of the web, which were subsets of crawls by Google in October 1999, August 2000, and June 2001. In each case the dataset was restricted to the set of hosts reachable from a well known reference host with high in and out degree in the hostgraph. We used www.w3.org, which hosts the web site of the World Wide Web Consortium, as our reference host. The exact choice of reference host is unimportant as long as we are certain that it is part of the central strongly connected component in the hostgraph, which includes all the major international hubs. E.g., using www.cern.ch, www.yahoo.com, or www.dmoz.org as the reference host would have produced exactly the same hostgraph since they can both reach and are reachable from www.w3.org by a directed path of inter-host hyperlinks.

For the June 2001 data set this restricted the number of nodes in the hostgraph to 12.8 million and the number of edges to 395 million. The sum of all the edge weights (i.e., the number of links between the hosts in the web graph) was 4.7 billion. This hostgraph was computed from a web graph consisting of 1.3 billion web pages, which were connected by 19.5 billion hyperlinks. It follows that 14.8 billion edges, or 76% of the edges, link to pages on the same host. In fact, this figure has stayed constant at 76% across the three hostgraphs.

Below we give the data for the data sets. Table 1 shows the number of web pages and their links that are contained in the hostgraphs.

Table 2 gives aggregate statistics for the three hostgraphs. Row 3 counts the set of hyperlinks between pages on distinct hosts, which corresponds to the sum of edge weights in the hostgraph, whereas row 2 counts the set of distinct edges in the hostgraph, ignoring weights.

Row 5 counts the number of hosts which are in the strongly connected component of www.w3.org, i.e., hosts which can reach www.w3.org as well as be reached by www.w3.org through a directed path of hostgraph edges. Note that the existence of a path in the hostgraph does not imply that there is a path in the page-based web graph, although the reverse is true. Hence, this only provides an upper bound on the number of hosts in the largest strongly

		Oct 99	Aug 00	Jun 01
1	Nodes (hosts) in the graph (millions)	3.9	10.4	12.8
2	Edges in the hostgraph (millions)	75.2	262.6	395.2
3	Cross-host hyperlinks ($\Sigma Edgewts$) (billions)	0.31	1.35	4.75
4	Percentage of intra-host hyperlinks	76%	76%	76%
5	Strongly connected component size (mill.)	1.5	7.6	8.5

Table 2. Hostgraphs used in the measurements.

	Oct 99	Aug 00
Estimated unweighted average distance between hosts	4.11	5.27
Estimated weighted average distance between hosts	3.31	3.71

Table 3. Average distances between hosts.

connected component in the web graph.

In the following we will use *indegree* to represent the number of distinct edges incident on a node in the host-graph (i.e., the number of distinct hosts which link to the corresponding host), and *weighted indegree* the sum of their edge weights incident on a node (i.e., the number of hyper-links to pages on corresponding host from other hosts) and likewise for *outdegree* and *weighted outdegree*.

3. Average Distance Between Hosts

The *distance* between two hosts is the length of the short-est path between them measured in number of edges. We es-timated the average distance between any two hosts for two of the graphs. To estimate the average distance we picked 5000 random hosts from the strongly connected component containing `www.w3.org` and computed for each host the distance from it to every other host in the host graph. The average distance was computed by averaging the individual distances observed.

As Table 3 shows, the average distance increased from roughly 4 in the Oct 1999 dataset to roughly 5 in the Aug 2000 dataset. A possible explanation is that new hosts are not linked to as much as older hosts and thus the path to them is longer.

Let DW be the average number of cross-host links tra-versed by the shortest path between two pages in the web graph.

Note that the average distance DH in the host graph is in general neither an upper nor a lower bound for DW in the web graph: DH is not an upper bound on DW since the

shortest path in the web graph might not be the one that min-imizes the cross-host links. DH is not a lower bound on DW since it is averaged over all pairs of hosts while DW is aver-aged over all pairs of pages. Consider for example a graph where the hosts form a chain, while almost all pages are contained in two adjacent hosts forming one large clique. Then DW will be close to 1 while DH will be linear in the number of hosts.

Because of this, we also estimated the weighted aver-age distance where each host is weighted by the number of pages on it. The weighted average distance is a true lower bound on DW. It is not an upper bound by the same ar-gument as for the unweighted average distance. Table 3 shows that the weighted average distance has increased as well. Note that the weighted average is smaller than 4, i.e. smaller the unweighted average. It follows that the pages are not equally spread out over the hosts, but that instead there is a "core" of hosts whose average distance is smaller than 4 that contains most of the pages.

4. Inverse Power Law Distributions

Previous papers have observed that various properties of the web graph follow a Zipfian distribution (a function of the form $1/n^k$): Kumar et al. [14] show that the fraction of web pages with indegree i is roughly proportional to $1/i^2$. Barbarasi and Albert [4] report a Zipfian exponent of 2.1 for the indegree distribution and they also show that the fraction of web pages with outdegree i is roughly propor-tional to $1/i^{2.45}$. In a recent paper Broder et al. [8] reported an indegree exponent of 2.1 and an outdegree exponent of 2.72. They also showed that the fraction of connected com-ponents in the undirected graph has a Zipfian distribution.

We show that the link structure at a coarser granularity, namely at the level of hosts and domains, also follows a Zipfian distribution. More specifically, the fraction of hosts of the host graph with weighted indegree i is (roughly) pro-portional to $1/i^{1.62}$ and the fraction of hosts of the host-graph with weighted outdegree i is (roughly) proportional to $1/i^{1.67}$. We plot these functions in Figure 1[3]. In Sec-tion 6 we give a possible explanation why the values for low weighted degree nodes are smaller than predicted by the Zipfian distribution.

We also investigated the distribution of weighted in- and out- degrees for subsets of the hosts in the hostgraph, namely for top level domains such as .com and .uk. For each such subset the weighted indegree and outdegree dis-tributions are again Zipfian. However, the size of the Zipfian exponent increases with the number of hosts in the domain. Figure 2 plots the Zipfian exponent for weighted indegrees and outdegrees versus the log of the number of hosts in the

---

[3]The "hump" in the second graph is due to a "spam" cluster of 200,000 highly interconnected hosts

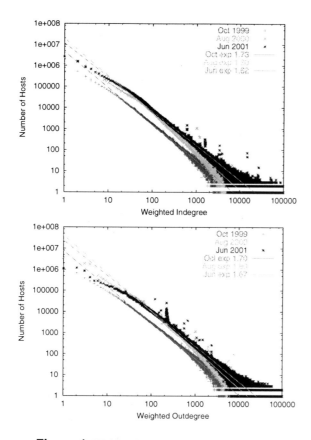

Figure 1. Weighted degrees are Zipf distributed.

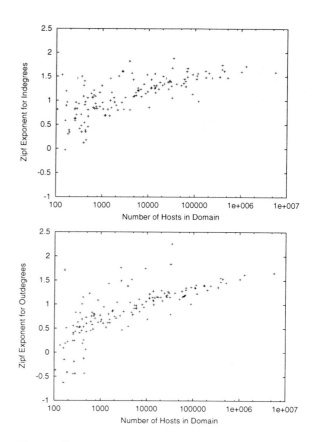

Figure 2. Plots of Zipf exponent for weighted indegree and outdegree distributions as a function of domain size for the 144 largest top level domains.

domain. Both Zipfian exponents seem to slowly increase with the logarithm of the size of the domain, suggesting an exponent of the form $a + b\log n$ where n is the number of hosts in the domain. In Section 7 we provide a possible explanation for this behavior.

Lastly, the distribution of edge weights in the hostgraph, i.e., the number of distinct hyperlinks between ordered pairs of hosts, is Zipf distributed (see Figure 3).

5. Country Domain Linkage

Table 4 shows some of the affinity between top level country domains in the June 2001 hostgraph. The 20 source domains with the highest weighted outdegree are included in the table; the .com domain is also included for comparison. For each source domain, we list the percentage of weighted outdegree into the same domain, into the .com domain, and into the four most highly linked country domains from that source domain.

In every case, there is a much higher number of links within the domain than to any other country domain; in fact, the next highest country domain typically receives around 1% of all links, in comparison to the 50-90% of intradomain links. There is also a much higher number of links to the

.com domain, and even .net, and .org domains (not shown) usually have higher linkage than other countries, (on the order of 3-7%).

The table also shows that, of the country domains, .de and .uk dominate. This is due to the size of those domains – there are more hosts in each of these two domains than any other country domain except for .jp. With so many web pages in .de and .uk, it's simply more likely that a host will point into those domains. .jp may not be as highly linked to due to language differences.

If we ignore the presence of .de and .uk in each country domain's top link destinations, we see that two other trends emerge. The first is that there is often strong geographical connections between a source domain and its most highly linked to domains. For example, Germany's most highly linked to domains are Switzerland, Austria, the Netherlands, and France. Norway's are Sweden, Denmark, Estonia, Soviet Union, and Finland. New Zealand's is Australia.

The linkages are not always reciprocal, however. For example, while China's top linkages are to Taiwan, Japan,

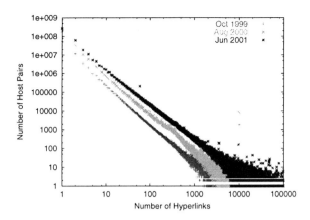

Figure 3. Edge weights are Zipf distributed.

	% of Weighted Outdegree					
	com	**self**	**1**	**2**	**3**	**4**
com	82.9		net 6.5	org 2.6	jp 0.8	uk 0.7
au	27.0	58.8	**uk** 1.0	ch 0.5	**ca** 0.4	de 0.3
br	17.8	69.1	uk 0.4	**pt** 0.4	de 0.4	**ar 0.2**
ca	19.4	65.2	uk 0.6	**fr** 0.4	se 0.3	de 0.3
cn	15.8	74.1	tw 0.4	**jp** 0.2	de 0.2	**hk** 0.1
cz	8.1	82.4	**sk** 1.0	**de** 0.7	uk 0.4	ch 0.1
de	16.0	71.2	uk 0.8	ch 0.6	**at** 0.5	**nl** 0.2
dk	13.8	73.0	uk 1.1	**de** 1.0	int 0.7	no 0.7
es	38.9	42.3	de 1.3	uk 1.0	**fr** 0.5	int 0.3
fr	20.9	61.9	**ch** 0.9	de 0.8	**uk** 0.7	**ca 0.5**
it	19.3	64.6	**de** 1.0	uk 0.7	**fr** 0.4	ch 0.3
jp	17.4	74.5	to 0.8	**cn** 0.6	uk 0.2	de 0.1
kr	26.5	57.1	**jp 0.6**	uk 0.5	de 0.3	to 0.3
nl	21.2	61.7	**de** 1.3	uk 1.1	**be** 0.6	to 0.5
no	16.1	65.6	de 1.2	**se** 0.9	uk 0.7	**dk** 0.6
pl	4.2	92.2	**de** 0.2	uk 0.1	ch 0.1	nl 0.1
ru	10.0	84.9	**ua** 0.4	**su** 0.2	uk 0.2	de 0.2
se	22.6	60.0	nu 1.6	uk 0.9	de 0.7	to 0.6
tw	22.0	66.0	to 1.3	au 0.6	**jp 0.6**	ch 0.4
uk	34.2	45.9	de 0.7	**ca 0.5**	jp 0.3	se 0.3
us	34.4	33.1	**ca 0.6**	**uk 0.5**	au 0.2	de 0.2

Table 4. Most frequently linked to domains from country domains.

and Hong Kong, and Hong Kong's are to Taiwan and China, China and Hong Kong do not show up in Taiwan's linkages until positions 5 and 6 (again ignoring .de and .uk). As another example, New Zealand's position on Australia's list is not first, but fourth. Political and economic relationships might explain these asymmetries.

The other trend is that language affiliations can override geographical affiliations. The strongest example of this is Brazil's top linkage to Portugal, and Portugal's to Brazil. Spain doesn't appear in Portugal's linkages until position 5, despite its strong geographical connection to Portugal. There is also a strong English language affinity among US, UK, Australia, and New Zealand. Examples like this support the intuition that linkages on the web are strongly influenced by shared language.

6. Mining Related Web Hosts

A natural extension of previous work in connectivity based web data mining would be to look at ways to extract significant relationships between hosts on the web based on connectivity within the hostgraph. Previously Bharat et al. [5] explored the use of similarity in outdegree distributions between hosts to find mirrored web sites. This technique proved to be too weak to find mirrors. However, we found that it often yielded pairs of related or affiliated hosts, rather than true mirrors. This led us to using the hyperlink structure of the hostgraph to discover related web hosts.

We examined two other forms of relatedness in the hostgraph.

6.1. Relatedness by Link Frequency

A simple technique to find related hosts is based on the pruning of edges in the hostgraph based on edge weight. Only strong edges remain, revealing connections between hosts that are stronger than mere citation.

We pruned all edges in the graph with weight less than 500. Quantitatively this reduced the set of edges to 139,900 pairs in August 2000 (i.e., the number of ordered host pairs with at least 500 individual hyperlinks between their pages), and to 34,600 in Oct 1999.

We identified several explanations for strongly connected host pairs that didn't seem to be otherwise related:

Large Hosts: Large hosts like `www.geocities.com` and `members.aol.com` have high mutual edge weights by virtue of their immense size.

Boilerplate: Some hosts use a page template on all pages. If this template has cross-host links it leads to a high edge weight. (E.g., mirrors of Open Directory tend to point to `www.dmoz.org` on every directory page.)

Multi-Host Sites: A site that spans multiple hosts may have many references between the hosts; e.g., `archive.soccerage.com` had 17 million links in the August dataset to `www.soccerage.com`.

Spam: A large factor is the activities of "search engine optimizers" who try to manufacture highly connected graphs to promote specific web sites (especially for pornography).

Affiliate Programs: Web sites like Amazon encourage third party web sites to host pages that link back to

Rank	Score	URL
1	70.25	www.lufthansa.com
2	52.21	www.klm.com
3	29.47	www.british-airways.com
4	18.21	www.swissair.com
5	14.18	www.iberia.com
6	12.25	www.britishairways.com
7	10.00	www.aircanada.com
8	9.95	www.aa.com
9	7.96	www.singaporeair.com
10	6.37	www.ual.com

Table 5. Related hosts for www.airfrance.com.

content on their site (e.g., specific books), rewarding them for the traffic sent through.

In addition to citation we could also use co-citation to identify affiliated or related parts of the web.

6.2. Relatedness by Co-citation

Dean and Henzinger [10] showed that cocitation analysis on the web graph works well for finding related web pages. Their best algorithm achieved a precision @ 10 of 0.4. We extended the idea to the hostgraph. Our approach is as follows:

Let B be a set of up to 100 hosts that point to a given host S with outlink count < 50. We impose this limitation on outlink count since hosts which link to lots of other hosts tend to introduce noise due to spurious co-citation. We consider a host, C, a *candidate* if it is pointed to by at least 4 hosts in B. Let $BS(C)$ be the hosts in B that point to C.

We compute for each candidate, C, a score which is use to rank potential hosts, as follows:

$$SCORE(C) = K(C) \cdot \Sigma_{X \in BS(C)} \frac{WT(X,S) \cdot WT(X,C)}{\text{outdeg}(X)^2}$$

where

$$K(C) = \frac{|BS(C)|^2}{\max\{1, \text{indeg}(C)/\text{indeg}(S)\}}.$$

Note that $K(C)$ boosts candidates that are frequently co-cited with the start host, and simultaneously reduces the bias towards candidates that are highly popular link targets (i.e, candidates with high inlink counts). Both proved invaluable in improving precision.

For example on the query www.airfrance.com the algorithm gives the following results. We list them together with their score in table 5.

We collected the output of the algorithm for 100 randomly chosen hosts for which at least 1 related host was

generated. The top 3 results in each case were hand evaluated to compute the fraction of the returned results that were useful. Of these 21 would not load or were in a foriegn language, 14 were pornographic or spam hosts, and of the remaining (159 pairs) 65% were found to be relevant. In other words our algorithm has a *precision at 3 of 0.65*.

7. Web Graph Modeling

7.1. Previous Graph Evolution Models

In recent years, a number of evolutionary models have been proposed to explain the structure of the web [12, 8]. Each model consists of a random process that creates a graph having properties similar to properties of the web, namely, Zipfian degree distributions and a large number of small bipartite cliques. Such modeling is useful for a variety of reasons. First, the process can explain how the web actually evolves, which might be helpful for companies exploiting the web structure, such as search engines. Secondly, this can prompt further research, such as analyzing or modeling sociological and economic issues surrounding the internet.

Traditionally, these models were page-based, i.e. nodes corresponded to single pages, and edges corresponded to links between them. We first describe a model introduced for the page graph called the "copy model". We then adapt it directly to the hostgraph setting. However, we show that this model does not agree with two key observations that we made on the hostgraph. We then propose a modified model for the hostgraph to accommodate both observations.

A first version of the "copy model" was introduced in [12]. Kumar et al [13] slightly modified it and analyzed it in detail. They showed that the model predicts a Zipfian indegree distribution. We present the second model:

- The web graph is created by adding one node u (i.e., a page) at a time, with a fixed outdegree d.

- Link destinations of u are randomly chosen:

  – First, one picks a random existing node v.

  – Then for $i = 1, 2, \ldots, d$, the i-th link of u points to a random existing node with probability α, and to the destination of v's i-th link with $1 - \alpha$.

This corresponds to an author creating a new webpage on a topic by copying links from an already existing webpage. It has the natural effect that a page with many links pointing to it already is more likely to receive additional links pointing to it than a page that nobody links to.

This model can be used on the hostgraph (since the intuition holds) except for two unexplained observations:

1. The observed indegree distribution is almost, but not entirely Zipfian (see Figure 1). While the observed

frequencies agree almost perfectly with the prediction for high indegree hosts, the number of small indegree hosts is considerably smaller than predicted by the model. E.g., see Figure 1 where the data points fall below the line representing the Zipfian distribution.

2. The exponent in the Zipfian distribution in the copy model depends only on α, and so stays constant independent of the size of the web. As we observed in Figure 2, when restricted to individual countries these Zipfian exponents actually depend on the number of hosts in the particular country.

We now discuss how the copy model can be modified to account for these observations.

7.2. Our Hostgraph Model

We next suggest a modification to the copy model that would explain why we observe fewer hosts of low indegree than predicted by the model and also provide a possible explanation for the different Zipfian exponents. We call the model the "re-link model".

- As before, the web graph is created in discrete time steps. At each time step, with probability β, we select a random already existing node, u, and add new additional out links to it. These out links are computed as follows:

  - First, one picks a node v at random among all already existing nodes. Second, one picks d random outgoing edges from v.
  - Then for $i = 1, 2, \ldots, d$, the i-th new link of u points to a random existing node with probability α, and to the destination of the i-th link picked from v with probability $1 - \alpha$.

- With probability $1 - \beta$, we add a new node and then add out-links to it, just as in the copy model.

This model captures the fact that the web not only changes by adding hosts, but also by hosts changing what other hosts they link to ("re-linking"). It is different from the copy model because it makes it possible to add new links without adding new hosts. Since new hosts start out with indegree 0, this reduces the number of low indegree hosts in comparison to the copy model. The parameter β controls how many new hosts are created. If β = 0 the re-link model reduces to the copy model.

To verify our intuition we generated a graph of 1,000,000 nodes with $d = 7$ and α = 0.05 using the re-link model. Figure 4 shows the indegree distribution for various values of β. The larger β becomes, the smaller the probability that a new host is created and the more edges a graph with 1,000,000

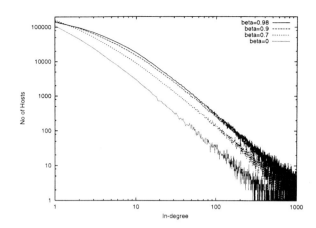

Figure 4. indegree distribution as predicted by the "re-link model" with varying β values.

nodes has. Thus, the curve flattens for low indegree hosts. Additionally, the curve becomes steeper, i.e., the Zipfian exponent increases. One reason might be that hosts quickly grow from small indegree to medium indegree while it takes them longer to become large indegree hosts.

Thus, the model also provides a possible explanation for different Zipfian exponents for different domains. Different domains can have different β values which leads to different Zipfian exponents. The Zipfian exponent grows inversely as β. One way to interpret the parameter β is to say that it reflects the *cost* of establishing a new host versus creating new links from an already existing host. This cost can vary in different domain - the lesser developed the domain, the higher the cost of adding a new host is likely to be and hence the higher the β value. The higher the β value, the lower the Zipfian exponent, which explains the distributions seen in Figures 2.

8. Related Work

There is related work in the area of evolution of the web as well as in web graph analysis.

In the area of web evolution, Pitkow et al [17] presented a model that explains some factors in the survival and change dynamics of documents. Cho et al [9] computed the lifespan of pages in five different domains, namely .gov, .net, .org, .edu, and .com, and showed that it varies widely. Smaller studies on how often web pages change were performed by Wills et al [19] and Douglis et al [11]. Huberman et al [1] presented a theory for the growth dynamic of the Web that takes into account the growth rates in the number of pages per site, as well as the fact that new sites are created at different times. Brewington [7] developed a different model of web page changes.

In the area of web graph analysis, Barbarasi et al [4] estimated the diameter of the Web and presented the Zipfian indegree and outdegree distributions of web pages (see also comments by Adamic et al [2] on this work.) Kumar et al [14] presented various properties of the web graph, one of them being the Zipfian distribution of indegrees as well. They also showed that the web contains a large number of small bipartite cliques. Kleinberg et al [12] presented a copy model, which was analyzed in detail in [13]. Broder et al. [8] analyzed the structure of the graph of web pages and predicted the shape of the web. They also gave a new estimate of the web's diameter disagreeing with Barbarasi et al.

9. Conclusions and Future Work

Our main contribution is the notion of the hostgraph, both as an abstraction to study the web, and as an explictly computed data-structure for use in profiling the growth of the web and for web data mining applications. We show that the hostgraph exhibits many of the properties of the web graph, providing another example of the fractal nature of web connectivity. A key contribution is the observation that the distributions of indegrees and outdegrees within top level domains of the web seem correlated with the size of the domain. We provide a modified "copy model" to explain this. We show, using three examples (data from Oct 1999, Aug 2000 and Jun 2001) that preserving host connectivity information can be useful in web monitoring and growth tracking. We present comparisons of changes in web site size and connectivity, inter-domain connectivity and web diameter estimate, to illustrate this. The host graph was also intended as a resource of data mining. We demonstrate how co-citation at the level of hosts can be mined and describe an algorithm which outputs related hosts with a precision of 0.65 at rank 3.

The hostgraph is only an approximation of what we would really like to compute - a graph of web sites. To achieve this one would need to combine multiple hosts under the some domain into the same node, which is not hard to do. One would also need to identify hosts that contain individual web sites, e.g., educational institutions which host web sites belonging to students, and decompose them. This is an open problem. Several link based page clustering approaches have been taken in the past to extract aggregates from hypertext, including strong connectivity [6], clustering based on routes likely to be taken by users [18], and spreading activation computations [16]. A combination of these techniques could be used in the future to decompose large host such as `geocities.com` into actual web sites. This, and the collapsing of multiple hosts that share the same domain, will allow for the creation of "site graph" that more accurately reflects the linkage between web sites.

Acknowledgements: We would like to thank Daniel Dulitz for computing the June hostgraph data.

References

[1] L. Adamic and B. Huberman. Evolutionary dynamics of the world wide web. *Nature*, September 1999.

[2] L. Adamic and B. Huberman. Scaling behavior on the world wide web. *Science*, 286, October 1999.

[3] R. Albert, H. Jeong, and A.-L. Barabasi. Diameter of the world wide web. *Nature*, 401:130–131, September 1999.

[4] A. Barabasi and R. Albert. Emergence of scaling in random networks. *Science*, 286:509, October 1999.

[5] K. Bharat, A. Broder, J. Dean, and M. Henzinger. A comparison of techniques to find mirrored hosts on the www. *Journal of the American Society for Information Science*, 2000.

[6] R. Botafogo and B. Shneiderman. Identifying aggregates in hypertext structures. In *Proc. Hypertext '91*, Dec. 1991.

[7] B. Brewington and G. Cybenko. How dynamic is the web? In *Proc. 9th WWW Conference*, 2000.

[8] A. Broder, R. Kumar, F. Maghoul, P. Raghavan, S. Rajagopalan, R. Stata, A. Tomkins, and J. Wiener. Graph structure in the web. In *Proc. 9th WWW Conference*, 2000.

[9] J. Cho and H. Garcia-Molina. The evolution of the web and implications for an incremental crawler. In *VLDB 2000*.

[10] J. Dean and M. Henzinger. Finding related pages in the world wide web. In *Proc. 8th WWW Conference*, 1999.

[11] F. Douglis, A. Feldmann, B. Krishnamurthy, and J. Mogul. Rate of change and other metrics: a live study of the world wide web. In *Proc. USENIX Symposium on Internet Technologies and Systems*, 1997.

[12] J. Kleinberg, S. R. Kumar, P. Raghavan, S. Rajagopalan, and A. Tomkins. The web as a graph: Measurements, models, and methods. In *Proc. ICCC*, 1999.

[13] R. Kumar, P. Raghavan, S. Rajagopalan, D. Sivakumar, A. Tomkins, and E. Upfal. Stochastic models for the web graph. In *Proc. Conference on Foundations of Computer Science (FOCS)*, 2000.

[14] R. Kumar, P. Raghavan, S. Rajagopalan, and A. Tomkins. Trawling the web for cyber communities. In *Proc. 8th WWW Conference*, 1999.

[15] W. Li, N.F. Ayan, O. Kolak, and Q. Vu. Constructing multi-granular and topic-focused web site maps. In *Proc. 10th WWW Conference*, 2001.

[16] P. Pirolli, J. Pitkow, and R. Rao. Silk from a sow's ear: Extracting usable structure from the web. In *Proc. ACM SIGCHI*, 1996.

[17] J. Pitkow and P. Pirolli. Life, death, and lawfulness on the electronic frontier. In *Proc. ACM SIGCHI*, 1997.

[18] K. Tajima, K. Hatano, T. Matsukura, R. Sano, and K. Tanaka. Discovery and retrieval of logical information units in web (invited paper). In *Proc. ACM Digital Library Workshop on Organizing Web Space (WOWS)*, 1999.

[19] C. Wills and M. Mikhailov. Towards a better understanding of web resources and server responses for improved caching. In *Proc. 8th WWW Conf*, 1999.

Better Rules, Fewer Features:
A Semantic Approach to Selecting Features from Text.

Catherine Blake and Wanda Pratt
Information & Computer Science
University of California, Irvine
{cblake, pratt}@ics.uci.edu

Abstract

The choice of features used to represent a domain has a profound effect on the quality of the model produced; yet, few researchers have investigated the relationship between the features used to represent text and the quality of the final model. We explored this relationship for medical texts by comparing association rules based on features with three different semantic levels: (1) words (2) manually assigned keywords and (3) automatically selected medical concepts. Our preliminary findings indicate that bi-directional association rules based on concepts or keywords are more plausible and more useful than those based on word features. The concept and keyword representations also required 90% fewer features than the word representation. This drastic dimensionality reduction suggests that this approach is well suited to large textual corpus of medical text, such as parts of the Web.

1. Introduction

Selecting features that are necessary and sufficient is critical if you are to construct a model that can accurately predict future events or describe a problem space. In addition, each individual feature should be **informative**; that is, it clearly captures some aspect of the problem space. Intuitively, models based on informative features will be easier to interpret than models based on uninformative features. For text, the feature representation is tightly coupled to model quality because they are embedded in natural language. Unlike traditional numeric, categorical, and Boolean data types, a textual resource must first be transformed to an alternative representation before a data-mining technique can be applied.

We designed an experiment to understand the relationship between the quality of features used to represent text and the quality of a descriptive model (as measured by plausibility and usefulness). We describe the quality of features in terms of **semantic richness**. For example, *breast cancer* is a disease occurring in a particular part of the body. If a text-mining system represented this phrase using the two individual features *breast* and *cancer*, it would not capture the meaning of the phrase *breast cancer*. Our approach uses a concept feature identified with the entire phrase *breast cancer*, which also captures the semantically equivalent expression *neoplasm of the breast*. We call this approach a semantic approach because it uses a semantic model to determine the features, rather than simply identifying commonly occurring phrases in text. Thus, we say that the concept feature *breast cancer* is semantically richer than the individual features *breast* and *cancer*.

For a model based on text to be valid, our first requirement is that it be **plausible**, that is 'seemingly reasonable or probable' [1]. Clearly, no one will use a system that produces implausible models. For example, neurologists were unwilling to follow decision rules that violated monotonicity constraints, where the neurologist expected an increase (decrease) in an attribute to correspond to an increase (decrease) in a predictive variable[2]. We argue that a model based on text must be plausible before it can be either meaningful or interesting.

Our second requirement is that the generated model be **useful**. By useful, we refer to task-specific usefulness, such as 'would this rule be useful if you were treating a patient with breast cancer?' Although usefulness is a stated goal of data mining [3], it is rarely included as a metric in evaluation, perhaps because it is inherently subjective. Our work explicitly measures the usefulness of a model based on text.

Our hypothesis is that increasing the information content (semantic richness) of features used to represent text will correspond to an increase in the plausibility and usefulness of the descriptive model produced. We used features at three different semantic levels: (1) words (2) manually assigned keywords and (3) automatically selected medical concepts. The model we used was a set of bi-directional association rules. In addition to model quality, our goal was to study the effect of dimensionality when features have varying levels of semantic richness.

2. A Text Mining Scenario

As the amount of text available in electronic form continues to increase at an alarming rate, the tools to manage these textual resources effectively will become critical. Consider **MEDLINE**, a bibliographical database of medical abstracts from conferences and journals that contains more than 11 million entries[4]. The National Library of Medicine (**NLM**), who maintains this resource, estimates that more than 400,000 additional references will be added during 2001 (8,000 new entries each week). Although access to abstracts or the full-text of articles in more than 4,000 biomedical journals has the potential to be useful for medical researchers, the quantity and unstructured nature of this information often results in information overload. Text mining has the potential to reduce information overload by providing a user with patterns from the underlying text.

Our scenario starts with a medical researcher who wants to learn about breast-cancer treatments. She could search MEDLINE to retrieve bibliographic details of documents related to the topic, however if she spent only 1 minute on each abstract and worked 10 hours a day it would take her a month to read the 19,167 related abstracts. Clearly reading every abstract is infeasible. If her task related to a specific treatment, then she would provide additional constraints to narrow the search space. However, her goal is to learn about treatments; thus, it is unreasonable to assume that she knows the names of the available treatments.

A text-mining system would enable her to understand treatments by providing a model of the important relationships within the published scientific literature. The model, which would be at a finer level of granularity than the entire abstract, might identify a co-occurrence between a treatment and its side effects. For example, *Docetaxel*, a chemotherapy drug that destroys cancerous cells, sometimes destroys cells that grow at a fast rate, such as those responsible for hair growth; thus, a patient may suffer from Alopecia (hair loss). A rule associating *Docetaxel* with *alopecia* would be useful to our medical researcher because it would help her understand the nature of the treatments available for breast cancer. Further, co-occurrences previously unreported in any individual study would be of particular interest. Let us use an example from a different domain. Tengs and Osgood found evidence that impotence correlated with smoking. They discovered this correlation by using clinical trials that did not specifically analyze the relationship between impotence and smoking, but rather studied impotence, and happened to report tobacco usage[5]. Although they used a manual rather than an automated approach, we believe that a text-mining system should also identify a correlation between concepts that are not the primary focus of an individual study.

3. Related Work

Identifying informative features from natural language (text) can be difficult; thus, existing approaches use semantically poor features, such as words[6-14]. This approach has the advantage of being domain independent and easy to implement; it has the disadvantage of producing the same number of attributes as the size of the vocabulary. The Apriori algorithm requires potentially 2^m item sets where m is the number of terms in the vocabulary (see section 5). Although it is unlikely that every term will appear in every textual resource, (the condition that makes 2^m item sets necessary in practice), the number of features can seriously impede the application of this data-mining algorithm.

A representation that does not account for natural language characteristics, such as synonymy or polysymy, could cause a data-mining system to generate a misleading model. Consider the phrase *hair loss*, which is synonymous with the medical term *alopecia*. The actual number of times that this concept occurs is the number of times that either *hair loss* or *alopecia* occurs in the text, but a word-based representation would distribute the count between the three features *hair*, *loss*, and *alopecia*. Thus, the word-based count would be smaller than the actual number of occurrences of the medical concept *alopecia*. The word-based representation could also over estimate the count for a concept. The word-based feature count for *hair* would also include the number of times that the expression *hair loss*, *hair gain* and *hair color* occurred in the collection. In contrast, a concept representation would unify the expression *hair loss* with *alopecia* and thus account for synonymy. Although you could augment a word-based system with list of synonymous word pairs such as *nausea* and *queasiness*, it is unclear if this would be effective in removing the influence of synonymy that is present in text.

Other researchers have explored the use of manually assigned keywords. For example, Feldman and colleagues used keywords as features for the generation of association rules[15-17]. However, they did not evaluate the effect of their feature-selection method on the plausibility or usefulness of the generated rules, but rather they determined the time it took to generate the rules. The drawbacks of approaches that use manually assigned keywords are that (1) it is time consuming to manually assign the keywords (2) the keywords are fixed (i.e., they do not change over time or vary based on a particular user) (3) if the keywords are manually assigned, they are subject to discrepancy (4) the textual resources are constrained to only those that have keywords.

Other researchers have used representations of medical concepts that are similar to ours for automatically determining a diagnosis category based on a textual description of a patient's clinical report[18]. They used a physician's diagnosis, also based on the clinical report, as a gold standard, and found that the automatically determined diagnoses based on concepts were more accurate than those based on words. We use the same extensive medical knowledge base; however, our approach identifies concepts from free-form text in scientific abstracts, rather than from clinical reports. Their work also relates more closely to a text categorization task than the text-mining scenario outlined in section 2.

Other studies have examined the effect of feature selection from text on learned models[19,20]. However, these studies use statistical techniques with no semantic component for feature-selection. In addition, the studies measured the performance of their approach on a document-categorization task, rather than the text-mining task in section 2.

Other related research has focused on constructing techniques to improve the quality of text-mined association rules. Most of these approaches first generate a set of rules, and then apply pruning or ranking techniques, such as 'interestingness' [14,21-25]. We consider metrics as a group, rather than ranking individual rules. We anticipate that the average interestingness for rules based on semantically richer representations would be higher than for a semantically poorer representation. We consider plausibility to be a necessary but not sufficient condition for interestingness. Several systems enable users to provide expectations to a system, and then rank rules with respect to how they differ from the users' expectations[24,25]. Although this approach enables a rule ranking for a particular user, it requires considerable effort from users to specify their expectations, such as *the overall instruction ratings are higher than the overall course ratings*[22]. Users are also required to give the degree of belief, a probability; however, there is strong evidence that people are not good at estimating such probabilities [26].

Although we agree that ordering the rules could be valuable, we advocate ranking in conjunction with using informative features. We would be surprised if a plausible and useful rule would ever use the feature 'is'; yet, according to the results of one study based on the χ^2 ranking, the correlation between the features *government*, *is*, and *number* was ranked the most interesting [27].

4. Feature Extraction

In our experiments, we varied the semantic richness of the features used to represent the title and abstract of each bibliographic reference. We now describe the process that we used to generate each of the feature sets.

4.1. Concept Features

Few researchers would claim that a word representation is optimal, but the difficulty of automated natural-language understanding has limited our ability to use a richer representation scheme. Unlike many natural-language systems, our system does not use a part-of-speech tagger to identify candidate phrases. Instead, it uses a heuristic approach to break each sentence in the document's title and abstract into a set of clauses. It separates a sentence into a set of clauses based on **stopwords**; words, such as *the*, *in* and *it*, that occur frequently in text but are not meaningful. We used a generic list of stopwords that was developed for information retrieval purposes[28], and we added to this list numbers, days of the week, and month names. We also developed and included a second set of 31 medical stopwords that occur frequently but are not meaningful, such as *study* and *test*.

We used an existing knowledge base, the **Unified Medical Language System (UMLS)** to map each clause to a medical concept. The UMLS (which was created and is maintained by the NLM) consists of three components: (i) a semantic network that links each concept to one of 132 high-level concepts called semantic types (e.g. the concept Tamoxifen, a chemotherapy drug, has a semantic type of Organic Chemical), (ii) the **Metathesaurus**, a medical thesaurus that contains synonymy and hierarchical links among about 800,000 concepts and 1.9 million concept names and (iii) the SPECIALIST lexicon, which provides lexical information on 140,000 concepts. For example, the UMLS maps the clause *MR-guidance* to the concept *magnetic resonance imaging guidance*.

The last step was to impose semantic constraints on the concepts provided by the UMLS so that the concepts related to findings and treatments. Based on the semantic type hierarchy, we, selected the following types as suitable: *Therapeutic or Preventive Procedure*; *Sign or Symptom*; *Pharmacologic Substance*; *Neoplastic Process*; *Amino Acid, Peptide, or Protein*; *Antibiotic or Organic Chemical*.

---

1. ConceptList ← θ
2. For each sentence in the title and abstract
3.   For each clause in the sentence
4.   concept List ← + UMLS concept using the clause
5.   End for
6. End for
7. ConceptList ← constrain using semantic types

Figure 1 – Concept Extraction Process

Any knowledge-based approach such as ours is clearly dependent on the comprehensiveness and quality of the knowledge it is based on. To assess the quality of our clause-concept mappings, we manually reviewing the original 367 concepts provided by the UMLS. We identified 18 (5%) blatant mismatches and have since notified the NLM. We also noticed that some clauses were mapped to a concept that was more specific or more general than the original clause (e.g., *tolerated* was mapped to the concept *maximum tolerated dose*, and *hematologic recovery* to the concept *recovery from disease*). Although such errors affect model quality, we did not remove these concepts from our feature set.

4.2. Keyword Features

Employees of the NLM assign 10-12 keywords from a controlled vocabulary to each bibliographic reference in the MEDLINE database. Documents are indexed, organized and retrieved using this medical ontology (the **Medical Subject Headings**, or **MeSH**). In addition to the 19,270 MeSH terms, the employees also use 3-4 of the 800 available subheadings (or qualifiers) to index the medical literature. A qualifier provides specific details about the application of a MeSH term in a document. For example, the qualifier *drug effects*, when added to the MeSH term *Liver*, indicates that the article or book is not about the liver in general, but rather is specifically about the effect of drugs on the liver. We used both the MeSH terms and qualifiers as our keyword features.

4.3. Word Features

Researchers generally use word features to represent text [9,11,12,27]. We used the same stopwords as those used to generate concepts, that is a generic set of stopwords [29] augmented with numbers, months, days of the week and 31 medical stopwords.

The approach most often used is to remove stopwords, and then do word **stemming**, a process that removes a word's prefixes and suffixes. Instead of using a generic stemming algorithm, such as Porter's, we used the Lexicon Variant Generator (lvg), a stemming tool

provided by NLM that was specifically designed for the medical domain. In addition to removing suffixes and prefixes (such as unifying both *analyzed* and *analyzing* to *analyze*), lvg unifies morphological changes (such as transforming *wound* to *wind*). We applied pre-processing operations in the following order: convert to lower-case, remove stopwords, strip genitive or possessive, strip punctuation, uninflect, canonicalize. We then removed duplicates of the same canonical form from each abstract.

5. Generation of Association Rules

Following the scenario in section 2, we started with the 19,167 abstracts from MEDLINE that relate to the query *breast cancer treatment*. We then selected the most recent 100 abstracts from this set. We discarded 9 abstracts because they did not have MeSH terms that corresponded to a treatment, and we did not want irrelevant documents to bias our results. The title and abstract of the remaining 91 articles were used to generate the word and concept features. We used the MeSH terms and qualifiers of those documents as the keyword features. Table 1 shows the rules that we used in our experiment.

	Rules based on Word Features	Rules based on Keyword Features	Rules based on Concept Features
1.	Axillary ↔ Background	Drug therapy ↔ Human	Doxorubicin ↔ Prekallikrein
2.	Metastatic ↔ Toxicity	Disease-free survival ↔ Survival analysis	Alopecia ↔ Methotrexate
3.	Grade ↔ Response	Antineoplastic agents, phytogenic ↔ Paclitaxel	Chemotherapy-Oncologic Procedure ↔ stage IV breast cancer
4.	Chemotherapy ↔ Result	Drug therapy ↔Therapeutic use	Carcinoma of Breast ↔ Vinorelbine
5.	Advance ↔ Phase	Lymph Nodes ↔ Radionuclide Imaging	Anorexia ↔ Progressive disease
6.	Blue ↔ Detection	Cyclophosphamide ↔ Methotrexate	Nausea ↔ Stable disease
7.	Cancer ↔ Trial	Antineoplastic agents, phytogenic ↔ Infusions, intravenous	Docetaxel ↔ Neoplasm Metastasis
8.	Milligram ↔ Toxicity	Antineoplastic agents, combined ↔ Breast Neoplasms	Cyclophosphamide ↔ Lymphocyte antigen CD69
9.	Conclusion ↔ Studied	Support, Non-U.S. Govt ↔ Treatment Outcome	Fatigue ↔ Granulocyte Colony-Stimulating Factor
10.	Conclusion ↔ Trial	Adolescence ↔ Lung Neoplasms	Docetaxel ↔ Pain
11.	Common ↔ Tamoxifen	Aged ↔ Drug therapy	Fatigue ↔ Nausea
12.	Advance ↔ Grade	Etiology ↔ Radiotherapy	Doxorubicin ↔ Paclitaxel
13.	Conclusion ↔ Dose	Adolescence ↔ Nausea	Enterotoxin F, Staphylococcal ↔Stable disease
14.	Median ↔ Respectively	Postmenopause ↔ Tamoxifen	Paclitaxel ↔ Vinorelbine
15.	Nausea ↔ Vomit	Lung neoplasms ↔ Nausea	Nausea ↔ Stage IV Breast Cancer
16.	Cancer ↔ Method	Antineoplastic Agents, Combined ↔ Drug Therapy	Axillary Lymph Node Dissection ↔ Secondary Malignant Neoplasm of Lymph Node
17.	Baseline ↔ Questionnaire	Disease-free survival↔Prospective studies	Gemcitabine ↔Vomiting
18.	Breast ↔ Cancer	Aged, 80 and over ↔ Postmenopause	Lymphocyte antigen CD69 ↔ Myalgia
19.	Dose ↔ Phase	Aged ↔ Therapeutic use	Enterotoxin F, Staphylococcal ↔ Gemcitabine
20.	Progressive ↔ Stable	Female ↔ Pathology	Anthracycline Antibiotics ↔ Epirubicin

Table 1 The bi-directional association rules used in our evaluation.

To identify patterns in the text, we used the popular data-mining technique of generating association rules. An **association rule** is of the form A→B, which means "thepresence of A implies the presence of B", where A is the set of antecedents and B is the consequent set. An individual rule identifies a co-occurrence between the antecedent and consequent sets. Each association rule has an associated level of support and confidence. The **support** is the probability that both A and B occur in a textual resource. For example, if 89% of the abstracts contained both the words *breast* and *cancer*; then the support of the association rule *breast→cancer* is 89%. The **confidence** is the probability that B will occur given that A has already occurred. We constrain the rules to those with a single feature in each of the antecedent and consequent sets. We define a **bi-directional association rule** (indicated by ↔) as one that satisfies the support and confidence levels in both directions (i.e., both A→B and B→A have support and confidence greater than the minimum that was set by the user).

We used Borgelt's implementation of the Apriori algorithm to generate association rules on each feature set separately[30,31]. The computationally intensive component of the Apriori algorithm is to identify the **item sets,** those features that occur with a frequency greater than the specified minimum level of support. The algorithm then generates rules that satisfy the minimum level of confidence based on these item sets. We used only bi-directional rules in our experiments.

6. Experiments

Our goal was to determine whether using features of differing semantic richness has an effect on the plausibility or usefulness of bi-directional association rules based on those features. We used two perspectives on plausibility and usefulness, a physician's and the consumer information available from the American Cancer Society's website on breast cancer treatment [32].

	Support (%)	Confidence (%)	Bi-directional Rules
Word	6	48	213
Keyword	4	32	104
Concept	2	16	156

Table 2 – We lowered the minimum support and confidence because the semantically richer representations had fewer features.

Fewer features are required to represent an abstract as a set of concepts, rather than as a set of words. To produce the same number of rules, you would have to lower the support so that approximately the same number of abstracts would satisfy the minimum support and confidence constraints. Therefore, to select a subset of

rules for our experiment, we imposed different minimum support and confidence levels for each feature set. We did not select the rules with the highest support and confidence because there is growing evidence that these metrics do not capture interestingness [14,21,22]. We did attempt to control for support and confidence by generating a set of approximately 100 to 200 bi-directional association rules for each feature set. We then randomly selected 20 rules from each feature set for inclusion in the evaluation (see Table 1 for the rules used in this evaluation). We considered three ways of controlling for support and confidence: (1) fix support and lower confidence (2) fix confidence and lower support (3) fix the ratio of support and confidence. As we did not have a principled way to determine the relative importance of support and confidence, we chose to fix the ratio between the two parameters. We set the ratio based on the default values in Borgelt's implementation [30] to 1:8 (see Table 2 for specific values).

6.1. Assessment

We asked an experienced physician to evaluate the bi-directional association rules in Table 1. We provided the physician with definitions of the medical terms used in the associations because he was not an expert in breast cancer. We assumed that if there was a plausible relationship between the features, then a physician could write down that relationship. Thus, we asked him to state any relationship that he found. We instructed him to answer question B based on plausibility and question C, based on usefulness using a scale of *not at all*, *not really*, *neutral*, *mostly*, and *definitely*. We used the same scale for question D, which attempted to uncover the novelty of the rule. Figure 2 shows the exact questions asked.

(1) Physician Questions:
    (A) The relationship between these concepts could be …
    (B) Do you agree that the relationship in (A) is plausible?
    (C) How useful would knowing this relationship be if you were treating a patient with Breast Cancer?
    (D) Do you agree that this correlation contributes to scientific knowledge on Breast Cancer treatment?

(2) Consumer Questions:
    (A) The relationship between these concepts could be …
    (B) Do you agree that the relationship in (A) is strongly implied?
    (C) How useful is the relationship in (A) with respect to Breast Cancer Treatment?

Figure 2 – Questions asked for each bi-directional association rule to measure plausibility and usefulness from a physician's perspective (1) and with respect to consumer information on available breast cancer treatment (2).

Our second perspective on the plausibility and usefulness of the rules was with respect to basic health information.

We used the American Cancer Society's (ACS) web page of breast cancer treatments as our gold standard. For each rule, we searched the ACS web page for any information that would relate the antecedent and consequent features. As with the first experiment, responses to (B) and (C) were expressed using a scale of *not at all, not really, neutral, mostly,* and *definitely.* Figure 2 shows the exact questions that we asked. The person doing this evaluation (the first author) was not familiar with breast cancer treatments, so they also referred to the definitions provided to the physician.

7. Results and Discussion

Our preliminary results indicate that bi-directional association rules based on keyword or concept features are more plausible and more useful than association rules generated on words. Although this increase is not statistically significant, our concept and keyword representation had the additional benefit of 90% fewer features than a word representation.

We start with an example of two plausible useful rules generated with concept features: *alopecia↔Methotrexate* and *alopecia↔Tamoxifen.* Both Methotrexate and Tamoxifen are chemotherapy drugs associated with hair loss. Neither the word nor the keyword representations identified this relationship with our minimum support and confidence (see Table 1) even though the word features *hair, loss* and *alopecia* occurred in 2, 7 and 6 abstracts respectively. In contrast, the concept representation detected that *hair loss* is synonymous with *alopecia* and accurately recorded that this concept occurred 8 times in our set of abstracts; thus, the concept approach successfully identified this plausible, useful rule. We recognize that eventually *hair↔Methotrexate* would have emerged from the word-based rules if we lowered the minimum support and confidence. However, it is unlikely that a user would be willing to sift through many low quality rules to locate this relationship.

7.1. Physician Assessment

We grouped the physician's plausibility ratings of *mostly* and *definitely* into the general category of *plausible.* Correspondingly, we considered rules to be implausible if he rated them *not at all, not really* or *neutral.* We used the same approach to group usefulness ratings.

	Plausible (%)	Useful (%)	Plausible and Useful (%)
Word	10 (50)	6 (30)	5 (25)
Keyword	17 (85)	11(55)	10 (50)
Concept	13 (65)	13 (65)	9 (45)

Table 3 – Plausible and useful ratings of bi-directional association rules with respect to a physician.

The results show that rules based on concept features produced more useful rules than those based on either keyword or word features. Conversely, he considered rules based on keyword features to be more plausible than rules based on concept or word features (see Table 3). We use an example to illustrate that it may be reasonable for the physician rate a rule as useful, even though he did not consider the rule plausible. The physician rated the rule between *blue* and *detection,* which was generated from word-based features, as *not really plausible,* but *definitely useful.* His possible relationship was 'Color of test marker and diagnosis of disease' and he annotated 'if it existed' next to the usefulness question. Although plausibility estimates the degree to which the current medical literature supports the association, usefulness reflects the value of a rule if it did exist. In this example, the physician doubted the plausibility of the relationship but recognized its usefulness if it existed.

The physician was unable to specify any relationship for 10 of the 60 associations. Of the ten, seven were from word features, thus suggesting that word-based associations are neither understandable nor plausible. Although we used lexical tools that were specifically developed for the medical domain, only 5 of the 20 associations rules for word features were considered to be both plausible and useful by the physician.

To express the quality of the associations, we used the information retrieval metric **precision**, which in this case is the number of association rules that are plausible and useful divided by the total number of rules evaluated. The precision of rules with respect to both plausibility and usefulness was 25%, 50% and 45% for word, keyword, and concept features respectively. Thus, the concept and keyword features appear to improve the quality of generated associations.

In addition to evaluating the plausibility, we attempted to capture how novel or insightful each association was, by asking the question 'Do you agree that this correlation contributes to scientific knowledge on breast cancer treatment?' If we group *mostly* and *definitely* into the insightful category, the physician rated 5 rules as insightful that were generated on word features and 8 rules each for keyword and concept features. After inspecting these rules, however, we believe that the physician misinterpreted this question. For example, the physician rated the association between *Docetaxel* (a chemotherapy drug) and *Neoplasm Metastasis* (when cancer spreads to other parts of the body) as a contribution to scientific knowledge, but the American Cancer Society's web page lists *Docetaxel* as a known chemotherapy drug for treating breast cancer; thus, we believe this rule is not novel. This discrepancy reflects the difficulty in developing accurate methods to measure subjective attributes such as novelty or insightfulness.

7.2. Consumer Health Assessment

When compared to consumer information, rules generated from concept features were more plausible and more useful than associations generated using either word or keyword features. The plausibility and usefulness of associations with respect to basic information on breast cancer treatment was overall slightly lower than that from a physician's perspective. Precision with respect to usability and plausibility was 15%, 30% and 85% for word, keyword and concept features respectively. When considering only plausibility, precision increases to 40%, 60% and 90%. The precision when considering usefulness only, is close to the precision of both metrics, specifically 15%, 35% and 85% for word, keyword and concept representation respectively.

	Plausible (%)	Useful (%)
Word	8 (40)	3 (15)
Keyword	12 (60)	7 (35)
Concept	18 (90)	17 (85)

Table 4 – Plausible and useful ratings of rules with respect to consumer health information.

No plausible explanation could be found between the antecedent and consequent for twenty-two of the sixty bi-directional association rules. Twelve of these associations were based on word features. Eight associations were based on keywords and only the remaining two were based on concept features. We assume that there are more unexplained rules in this survey than for a physician because of a lack of formal medical training by the person doing the assessment. We used lexical tools specifically developed for the medical domain, but only 3 of the 20 associations rules for word features were considered useful.

7.3. Dimensionality Reduction

Although the increase in the number of plausible and useful rules is encouraging, the results are not statistically significant. The improvement is more impressive when you consider the drastic reduction in the number of features required to represent the problem space. We summarize the dimensionality reduction in Table 5.

We found that a keyword representation reduced the average number of features by 26% from 76 to 20. The concept representation reduced the average number of features required to represent the title and abstract by 90% to only 8. Both the concept and keyword representations required 84% fewer distinct terms. This reduction has important implications to the running time of computationally expensive data-mining techniques. Data-mining algorithms often require data in a matrix format. Storing the 91 titles and abstracts in this experiment, as a matrix would require 194,012 cells if you used word

features and 31,759 cells if you used concepts. This reduction becomes increasing important if all 19,167 articles related to breast cancer treatments were used, or if the full-text of the articles was considered.

	Average unique features	Distinct terms	Abstract-Feature Pairs
Word	76	2132	6932
Keyword	20	351	1856
Concept	8	349	1161

Table 5 – Feature selection has a drastic effect on the dimensionality required to represent the domain.

The concept representation reduced the number of abstract-feature pairs by 83% compared to the keyword approach that had a 73% reduction. Despite smaller space requirements, rules produced using keyword and concept features were more plausible and useful than rules generated over words.

8. Future Work

As we mentioned in the related work section, several researchers have explored approaches to rank rules based on interestingness. We also plan to extend our approach to prune or rank rules based on semantic information, such as the semantic relations from the UMLS. Association rules show only that a correlation has occurred between concepts. We are planning to augment this relationship with semantic information. Consider rule 17 in Table 1, where *Gemcitabine* has a semantic type of *Pharmacologic Substance* and *Vomiting* has the semantic type *Sign or Symptom*. A valid semantic relationship between these two semantic types is *treats*: a *Pharmacologic Substance* **treats** a *Sign or Symptom*. We will continue to explore the subjective qualities of a model by interviewing additional physicians. Finally, we plan to conduct experiments on the full text of a document instead of using only the title and abstract. Such experiments will improve our understanding of the impact of the dimensionality reduction with a concept representation.

9. Conclusion

Our hypothesis was that increasing the semantic richness of features used to represent text would have a positive effect on the plausibility and usefulness of a set of bi-directional association rules. Our initial findings support this hypothesis. Specifically, our physician found only 25% of the rules based on word features to be useful and plausible compared with 50% and 45% for keywords and concepts respectively. It was unclear which of the two semantically richer representations were preferred however, because the physician evaluated rules based on keywords to be the most plausible, and rules based on concepts to be the most useful. The consumer information analysis also supported our hypothesis; the concept-based rules were clearly more plausible and useful than either the keyword or the word representations.

Although the increased model quality was not statistically significant, the 90% reduction in the number of features suggests that the semantically rich keywords or concepts features will enable association rules to be generated more efficiently. The keyword representation constrains the suitable text to those with keywords, but this constraint does not apply to the concept representation. Thus, the concept approach would be suitable to apply to any large corpus of medical text, such as portions of the web.

10. Acknowledgements

We thank Dr. Tony Greenberg, Craig Evans, and Henry Wasserman for their help with the evaluation. This work was supported by the University of California's Life Science Informatics grant #L98-05.

11. References

[1] H. W. Fowler and F. G. Fowler, *The Concise Oxford Dictionary of Current English*, 9th ed. Oxford: Clarendon Press, 1995.

[2] M. Pazzani, S. Mani, and W. R. Shankle, "Comprehensible knowledge-discovery in databases", 19th Annual Conference of the Cognitive Science Society, pp.235-238, 1997.

[3] U. Fayyad, G. Piatetsky-Shapiro, P. Smyth, and R. Uthurusamy, *Advances in Knowledge Discovery and Data Mining*, AAAI Press, 1996.

[4] National Library of Medicine, Available at http://www.nlm.nih.gov, 2001.

[5] T. Tengs and N. D. Osgood, "The link between smoking and Impotence: Two Decades of Evidence", *Preventive Medicine*, vol. 32, pp.447-452, 2001.

[6] R. Feldman, "Practical Text Mining", PKDD-98, p487, 1998.

[7] R. Ghani, R. Jones, D. Mladenic, K. Nigam, and S. Slattery, "Data Mining on Symbolic Knowledge Extracted from the Web", *KDD-2000 Workshop on Text Mining*, 2000.

[8] U. Hahn and K. Schnattinger, "Knowledge Mining from Textual Sources", CIKM'97, Las Vegas, pp.83-90, 1997.

[9] B. Lent, R. Agrawal, and R. Srikant, "Discovering Trends in Text Databases", KDD'97, pp.227-230, 1997.

[10] U. Y. Nahm, "Text Mining with Information Extraction: Mining Prediction Rules from Unstructured Text", Thesis proposal, University of Texas, Austin, 2001.

[11] G. W. Paynter, I. H. Witten, S. J. Cunningham, and G. Buchanan, "Scalable browsing for large collections: a case study", 5th Conf. Digital Libraries, Texas, pp.215-218, 2000.

[12] I. H. Witten, Z. Bray, M. Mahoui, and W. J. Teahan, "Text mining: a new frontier for lossless compression", Data Compression Conference, pp.198-207, 1999.

[13] H. Ahonen, O. Heinonen, M. Klemettinen, and A. I. Verkamo, "Applying Data Mining Techniques for Descriptive Phrase Extraction in Digital Document Collections", IEEE Form of Research and Technology Advances on Digital Libraries, pp.2-11, 1998.

[14] M. Klemettinen, H. Manila, P. Ronkianen, H. Toivonen, and A. I. Verkamo., "Finding Interesting rules from Large Sets of discovered association rules", CIKM'94, Maryland, USA, pp.401-407, 1994.

[15] R. Feldman and I. Dagan, "Knowledge Discovery in Textual Databases (KDT)", ECML-95 Workshop on Knowledge Discovery, Crete, Greece, pp.175-180, 1995.

[16] R. Feldman, I. Dagan, and H. Hirsh, "Mining text using keyword distributions", *Journal of Intelligent Information Systems: Integrating Artificial Intelligence and Database Technologies*, vol. 10, pp.281-300, 1998.

[17] R. Feldman and H. Hirsh, "Mining associations in text in the presence of background knowledge", KDD-96, Portland, USA, pp.343-346, 1996.

[18] A. Wilcox, G. Hripcsak, and C. Friedman, "Using Knowledge Sources to Improve Classification of Medical Text Reports", (poster) *KDD-2000 Workshop on Text Mining*, 2000.

[19] Goldberg, "CDM: an approach to learning in text categorization", *International Journal on Artificial Intelligence Tools (Architectures, Languages, Algorithms)*, vol. 5, pp.229-153, 1996.

[20] Y. Yang and J. P. Pedersen, "A Comparative Study on Feature Selection in Text Categorization", ICML'97, 1997.

[21] Silberschatz and A. Tuzhilin, "On Subjective Measures of Interestingness in Knowledge Discovery", KDD'95, 1995.

[22] A. Silberschatz and A. Tuzhilin, "What Makes Patterns Interesting in Knowledge Discovery Systems", *IEEE Transactions on Knowledge and Data Engineering*, vol. 8, pp.970-974, 1996.

[23] R. J. Bayardo and R. Agrawal, "Mining the Most Interesting Rules", KDD'99, San Diego, pp.145-154, 1999.

[24] B. Padmanabhan and A. Tuzhilin, "Unexpectedness as a Measure of Interestingness in Knowledge Discovery", *Decision Support Systems*, vol. 27, pp.303-318, 1999.

[25] B. Liu, W. Hsu, and Y. Ma, "Pruning and summarizing the discovered associations", KDD'99, CA, pp.125-134, 1999.

[26] A. Tversky and D. Kahneman, "Judgment under uncertainty: Heuristics and biases", *Science*, vol. 185, pp.1124-1131, 1974.

[27] S. Brin, R. Motwani, and C. Silverstein, "Beyond Market Baskets: Generalizing Association Rules to Dependence Rules", KDD'98, pp.39-68, 1998.

[28] M. Sanderson, "Stop word list", Available at http://www.dcs.gla.ac.uk/idom/ir_resources/, 1999.

[29] S. J. Nelson, W. D. Johnston, and B. L. Humphreys, "Chapter 11: Relationships in Medical Subject Headings (MeSH)", Available at http://www.nlm.nih.gov/mesh/meshrels.html, 2001.

[30] C. Borgelt, "Apriori Implementation", Available at http://fuzzy.cs.uni-magdeburg/~borgel, 1999. .

[31] R. Agrawal, H. Mannila, R. Srikant, H. Toivonen, and I. Verkamo, "Fast Discovery of Association Rules," in *Advances in Knowledge Discovery and Data Mining*, U. Fayyad, G. Piatetsky-Shapiro, P. Smyth, and R. Uthurusamy, Eds. AAAI/MIT Press, 1995.

[32] American Cancer Society, "Treatment of Breast Cancer Consumer Information", Available at http://www3.cancer.org/cancerinfo, 2001.

Significance Tests for Patterns in Continuous Data

Richard J. Bolton
Imperial College
Department of Mathematics
180 Queen's Gate, London, UK
r.bolton@ic.ac.uk

David J. Hand
Imperial College
Department of Mathematics
180 Queen's Gate, London, UK
d.j.hand@ic.ac.uk

Abstract

In this paper we consider the question of uncertainty of detected patterns in data mining. In particular, we develop statistical tests for patterns found in continuous data, indicating the significance of these patterns in terms of the probability that they have occurred by chance. We examine the performance of these tests on patterns detected in several large data sets, including a data set describing the locations of earthquakes in California and another describing flow cytometry measurements on phytoplankton.

1. Introduction

Data mining is the process of seeking structures in large data sets [5, 6]. Such structures have been divided usefully into the large and small scale. Large-scale structures, summarising global features of a data set, are often called *models*; model building has been the focus of statistical investigation over many decades. Small-scale structures, typically referring to structures that are local in the space of measured variables, are called *patterns*. Pattern detection as an area of formal investigation is a relatively recent development – unlike model building, which could be developed for hand application on small data sets, the search procedures implicit in pattern detection required the advent of the computer. Tools for pattern detection have been developed in parallel in several areas, including association rule analysis, genomic sequence analysis, clickstream analysis, and fraud detection. Such has been the rate of progress in these areas – driven by urgent commercial and scientific needs – that many pattern detection algorithms have been developed. However, detecting a pattern is but the first step. A vital subsequent question, once a potential local structure has been flagged as of interest, is that of whether the pattern represents some real underlying aspect of the data generating mechanism, or is merely a feature of

chance fluctuation in the data which happen to have been observed. It is this question that is the focus of the present paper. In particular, we describe significance tests for patterns. We do not pretend that our method provides the definitive answer to the question of uncertainty in pattern detection; however, we demonstrate a statistical approach that contributes a practical solution to this problem.

Patterns are variously described in the literature. Broadly speaking, for our purposes a pattern may be defined as a recurring configuration of features describing the objects under investigation. The recurrence may be in different objects (e.g. anomalous sequences of credit card transactions), or may be at different positions in the feature set describing a given object (e.g. a nucleotide sequence in DNA). We adopt a definition that subsumes these and other definitions. We define a pattern as a data vector identifying an anomalously high local density of objects [1, 5]. This definition can be applied to most data types, from temporal sequences to static databases, provided some metric measuring the similarity of objects can be defined.

The algorithm that we use to find local peaks of probability density is that described in [1] (and which we now call the PEAKER algorithm). This algorithm finds estimates of the probability density of the data at each of the objects, and then examines each object in turn, to see if it lies at a local peak of the probability density function (pdf). To illustrate, take an arbitrary object P. A local region is defined about P, in terms of the L closest objects to P. These L closest objects to P are examined to see if any of them has a higher estimated pdf than the estimate at P. If none do – if the pdf estimate at P is larger than that at any of its L nearest neighbors – then object P lies at a local pdf peak or mode. The algorithm requires the specification of the method for estimating the probability density and the choice of L. In fact, of course, any monotonic transformation of the pdf estimate will do – we are not concerned with the absolute values, but only their relative size. Taking advantage of this invariance, we use the reciprocal of the average Euclidean distance from P to its k nearest neighbors as our estimate. Adams *et al.* [1] describe some experiments on choice of k and L. In the examples described below, we set k independently of L, but quite small relative to the size of the data set, as we do not want to miss any structure in low density regions of the data. However, any values other than the ones we use, or indeed, any other choice of method of pdf estimation, could be used without affecting our method of significance testing, which does not depend on this choice.

Once we have detected these modes, we wish to know whether they are true patterns, or simply artefacts of random error in the data. That is, we want to attach a measure of statistical significance to a mode such that we can provide evidence that this mode is a pattern. To do this, we apply statistical tests under the null hypothesis that the data are locally uniform and identify departures from this hypothesis that indicate 'peakedness' in the density. This tells us the probability that we would get such a configuration if the data were uniform, with the alternative that the data are 'peaked' and thus a pattern. We describe three different test statistics, and discuss features of these tests and their implementation

2. Distributional Assumptions

PEAKER identifies local modes of probability density. The question we now want to answer is whether such a mode is likely to have arisen if the background distribution (in the region covered by the L nearest objects to the mode) is uniform. We thus define test statistics measuring departure from uniformity and derive their distributions. In particular, since we are interested in alternative hypotheses that favour leptokurtosis (peakedness), our test statistics are measures of leptokurtosis. The result of such a test will be a significance value indicating the probability of observing such an extreme measure of leptokurtosis if the underlying distributions were truly locally uniform. It will be immediately apparent that issues of multiple testing will complicate the conclusions. We discuss these issues below.

Since our basic mode finding algorithm is based on nearest neighbor methods, we also use such concepts to define our test statistics. Nearest neighbor methods have been used for clutter removal in spatial point processes [3], but not as yet for assessing the significance of the features that they leave behind. In particular, when defining our tests, we summarize the distances of the L nearest objects to the mode using measures such as means and medians. The distributions of these can be evaluated under the null hypothesis of uniformity, and we can compute the probability of observing values as extreme as those we do observe (in fact, in the case of the mean and

median, this translates into the probability of observing values as *small* as those we do observe). We give the details below. First, however, it is useful to establish some distributional machinery.

Suppose we have a continuous multivariate data set with dimensionality d (i.e. d variables). The volume, V_R, of a d-dimensional hypersphere of radius R is given by:

$$V_R = \frac{2\pi^{d/2} R^d}{d\Gamma(d/2)}$$

where $\Gamma(a)$ is the Gamma function.

We are ultimately interested in the distribution of the distances of objects from the center of this hypersphere when these objects are uniformly distributed within a hypersphere of radius R. However, this distribution is easier to derive if we first define a variable based on volumes. Draw an object from a uniform distribution over the hypersphere of radius R, and let V be the random variable defined as the volume of a hypersphere with same center as the original hypersphere and radius the distance from the center to the object. The probability density function for V can be written as:

$$\Pr(V = v) = f(v) = \frac{d\Gamma(d/2)}{2\pi^{d/2} R^d}; \quad 0 \le v \le V_R$$

where $\Gamma(\cdot)$ is the gamma function. We can relate the random variable, V, to the random variable, X, defined as the distance from the center of the hypersphere by the equation:

$$V = \frac{2\pi^{d/2} X^d}{d\Gamma(d/2)}$$

And we can write the probability density function of X as follows:

$$f(x) = f(v)\frac{dv}{dx} = \frac{d\Gamma(d/2)}{2\pi^{d/2} R^d} \cdot \frac{2d\pi^{d/2} x^{d-1}}{d\Gamma(d/2)} = \frac{dx^{d-1}}{R^d}; \quad 0 \le x \le R$$

We can also see that $Y_1 = \frac{x}{R} \sim Beta(d,1)$, and $Y_2 = Y_1^d = \left(\frac{x}{R}\right)^d \sim U(0,1)$, results that will come in useful when formulating significance tests. Remember that in these formulations R is a constant and *not* a random variable.

3. Significance Tests

Suppose that we have a sample of n objects within a d-dimensional hypersphere of radius R; that is, we have

68

n random variables, $X_1, ..., X_n$ representing the distances of the objects from the center of the hypersphere, from which we obtain the corresponding functions of X, $(Y_1)_1, ..., (Y_1)_n$ and $(Y_2)_1, ..., (Y_2)_n$, as described in the previous section. We now seek test statistics for departure from uniformity that highlight high density towards the center of the hypersphere.

3.1. Mean of Y_1

The mean of Y_1, is calculated by the equation $\overline{Y_1} = \frac{1}{n} \sum_{i=1}^{n} (Y_1)_i$; however, the distribution of $\overline{Y_1}$ is not easily obtained. Finding the distribution of the sum of Beta distributions is a hard problem as the probability and moment generating functions cannot be characterized in a closed form and so cannot be used to derive the distribution of $\overline{Y_1}$. We choose instead to use Central Limit Theorem results to characterize the distribution as an approximate normal distribution. Hence

$$\overline{Y_1} \overset{CLT}{\sim} N\left(\frac{d}{d+1}, \frac{d}{(d+2)(d+1)^2 n} \right)$$

and we can test the standardized normal random variable

$$Z = \frac{\overline{Y_1} - \frac{d}{d+1}}{\sqrt{\frac{d}{(d+2)(d+1)^2 n}}}$$

against the *lower* tail probabilities of the standard Normal distribution, as a pattern will have an abundance of shorter distances and thus a small value of $\overline{Y_1}$ associated with it. The probability value (significance level) associated with this test is thus $P(Z \le z) = F(z)$. When we talk of a significance level of $\alpha\%$ we mean that there is less than $\alpha\%$ chance that the observed result is due to chance. Note that the normal approximation appears to hold quite well, even for small values of n and large values of d.

3.2. Mean of Y_2

We can obtain the probability density function of the mean of Y_2, $\overline{Y_2} = \frac{1}{n} \sum_{i=1}^{n} (Y_2)_i$, in exact form [7]:

$$f_{\overline{Y_2}}(y) = \sum_{j=0}^{n-1} \frac{n}{(n-1)!}\left[(ny)^{n-1} - \binom{n}{1}(ny-1)^{n-1} + ... + (-1)^j \binom{n}{j}(ny-j)^{n-1} \right] I_{(j/n,(j+1)/n]}(y)$$

such that

$$F_{\overline{Y_2}}(y) = \sum_{j=0}^{n-1} \frac{1}{n!}\left[(ny)^n - \binom{n}{1}(ny-1)^n + ... + (-1)^j \binom{n}{j}(ny-j)^n \right] I_{(j/n,(j+1)/n]}(y)$$

Using this distributional result we can calculate lower tail probabilities for $\overline{Y_2}$. As with the mean of Y_1, a low value of $\overline{Y_2}$ indicates that the data are concentrated towards the center of the hypersphere and the significance level associated with this test is $F_{\overline{Y_2}}(y)$.

3.3. Median of Y_2

Standard results show us that if we have a random sample of n objects from a probability density function $f(\cdot)$, with cumulative distribution function $F(\cdot)$, and order statistics $X_{(1)} \le X_{(2)} \le ... \le X_{(n)}$ then the distribution of the αth order statistic, X_α is given by

$$f_{X_{(\alpha)}}(x) = \frac{n!}{(\alpha-1)!(n-\alpha)!}\left[F(x) \right]^{\alpha-1}\left[1 - F(x) \right]^{n-\alpha} f(x)$$

The median value is given by $X_{((n+1)/2)}$ if n is odd, or by $\frac{1}{2}\left(X_{(n/2)} + X_{((n/2)+1)} \right)$ if n is even. It follows that, for odd n, the median M of the random variable Y_2 has probability density function

$$f_M(m) = \frac{n!}{(\frac{n-1}{2})!(\frac{n-1}{2})!} m^{\frac{n-1}{2}} (1-m)^{\frac{n-1}{2}} ; \qquad 0 \le m \le 1$$

so that, in fact, $M \sim Beta(\frac{n+1}{2}, \frac{n+1}{2})$. For n even, the distributional result is more complicated, being a linear combination of the sum of two Beta distributions. This distribution can be calculated, but for reasonably large n we suspect that there is very little difference in the forms for n odd and even.

We have an exact distribution for M since $R, d > 0$:

$$M = median\left(\left(\frac{X_1}{R}\right)^d, ..., \left(\frac{X_n}{R}\right)^d \right) = \left(\frac{median(X_1, ..., X_n)}{R} \right)^d \sim Beta\left(\frac{n+1}{2}, \frac{n+1}{2}\right)$$

If there is a region of high density around our object point, then M will be smaller than we would expect than if the data were uniformly distributed on the hypersphere. We can compare values of M with the lower tail probabilities of the Beta distribution for appropriate values of n.

Note: We replace n with $(L-1)$ in all of these tests to obtain significance tests for modes detected by PEAKER with the radius, R, of the local region defined as the distance to the Lth nearest neighbor. The null hypothesis is valid for the $(L-1)$ nearest neighbors, given our choice of R.

4. Edge Effects

Situations in which the ranges of the variables have sharp cut-off values, or which have clusters of objects with sharp edges, can cause difficulties. Our tests are based on the null hypothesis that the modes being tested are at the center of hyperspheres containing objects generated from a uniform distribution. This null hypothesis led us to deduce the form for the distribution of the distance of objects from the central mode. Unfortunately, if the hypersphere is centerd near a sharp edge, the distribution of the distance of objects from its center no longer has the same distribution (the further objects are taken from a distorted distribution). In such situations, if we were to apply the significance tests to every object, there would be artificially inflated values of the k-nearest neighbor distance due to edge effects, something that is commonly seen with nearest neighbor methods in spatial statistics. This means that objects near the boundaries of a cluster or a region will have artificially deflated values of the significance statistics and these boundary objects will appear more significant than they actually are. We can illustrate this with a data set containing 10,000 objects uniformly and independently distributed over $[-1,1]^5$. Figure 1 shows those objects with a significance level of 0.05% after applying the $\overline{Y}_2$ statistic with $L=100$ nearest neighbors.

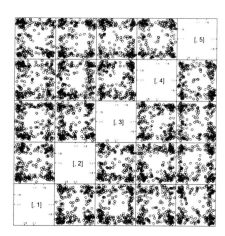

Figure 1. Scatterplot Matrix of significant objects at 0.05% level.

The concentrations of objects at the corners of the plot show that edge effects are particularly evident here. In spatial statistics, there are many approaches to coping with these edge effects. One solution is a toroidal wrap-

around of the data such that no object is, in effect, on an edge. This is a practical solution but not so easy to justify in higher dimensions. We also note that a object on the edge of a cluster will display edge effects that will not be removed by a wrap-around of the whole data set. For example, in Figure 2 we have a data set in two dimensions with 10,000 objects uniformly distributed over four unit squares. Figure 3 shows the objects significant at the 1% level after the toroidal wrap around has removed edge effects.

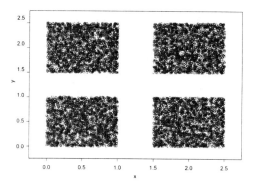

Figure 2. Full data set

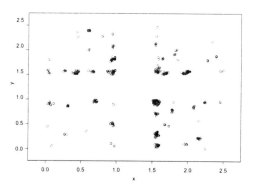

Figure 3. Objects significant at 1% level

The central edges have artificially deflated values of the $\overline{Y}_2$ statistic and thus appear more significant, whereas the outside edge effects have been (mostly) removed. This edge effect increases greatly with increasing dimension and increasing numbers of objects.

We note that objects that are precisely on an edge or a corner are not necessarily affected by edge effects. In this case, the nearest neighbors all lie in a volume arc of the hypersphere centered at the object in question. Within this arc, the assumptions of the distribution of the radius still hold. However, an object a short distance from the edge will have nearest neighbors in a small radius sphere, but next nearest neighbors only on one side (see Figure 4), thus artificially reducing the mean nearest neighbor distance. This is why one approach to edge correction in spatial statistics is to examine only those objects within a 'guard area' such that edge effects are not encountered.

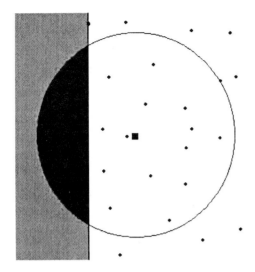

Figure 4. Illustration of edge effect

5. Correction of Significance Values for Multiple Testing

We have already mentioned the fact that significance values will be affected by multiple testing due to the large number of peaks explored. However, the first correction we must make arises because any objects selected by PEAKER are by definition extreme within their local region; these objects have a higher density than their L nearest neighbors. Consequently, we can say that such an object is more likely to be a pattern (or 'peak') than these L nearest neighbors, and thus more likely to have more extreme values of the test statistic than these L neighbors. A high local density is implied by small nearest neighbor distances, especially as these tests are functions of the local density. The statistical tests that we have discussed will only provide us with correct significance values if we apply them to a randomly selected object, so we must correct for the extremeness of each mode.

In our tests we are interested in small values of the statistic and so we want the distribution of the minimum of $L+1$ realizations of the statistic. If $F(\cdot)$ is the CDF of the test statistic in question, then the CDF of the minimum of a sample of $(L+1)$ of these statistics is given by:

$$F_{\min}(\cdot) = 1 - [1 - F(\cdot)]^{L+1}$$

Of course, the underlying assumption in this distributional result is that the objects are independent and identically distributed. Unfortunately, this assumption of

independence will not necessarily be true as our tests are all functions of the other L objects in the sample, which will be more dependent the closer an object is to the 'peak' object. $F_{\min}(\cdot)$ is thus a conservative estimate of the CDF.

For example, we find that an object is a peak amongst its 50 nearest neighbors and we apply test $\overline{Y}_2$, finding that $F(\overline{Y}_2) = 0.0097$. This would suggest statistical significance at the 1% level; however, taking into account the multiple testing aspect, we have $F_{\min}(\overline{Y}_2) = 0.392$, a far less convincing result!

When we run the PEAKER algorithm for a certain value of L we will often identify more than one peak. We need to take into account all of these peaks when performing statistical tests; that is, we must account for the effects of multiple testing once again. This time, however, the correction depends on the number of peaks that PEAKER identifies. Suppose we identify P peaks, then the adjusted value of the CDF for the test statistic is given by

$$F_{adj}(\cdot) = 1 - [1 - F(\cdot)]^{(L+1)P}$$

For this result we assume that peaks are distributed independently of each other.

If we set PEAKER to search through multiple values of L, we encounter more multiple testing problems that are harder to account for, as issues of independence are less clear. The consideration of how this variation of L affects the test statistics is continuing work.

6. Choice of Tests

The significance tests available to us are:

$\overline{Y}_1$, the mean of $\left(\frac{Y}{R}\right)$.

$\overline{Y}_2$, the mean of $\left(\frac{Y}{R}\right)^d$,

$median(Y_2)$, the median of $\left(\frac{Y}{R}\right)^d$,

The last two tests can be compared with exact distributions, whereas the first only has an approximate distribution, albeit a very accurate one even for a relatively small number of nearest neighbors. We prefer the second and third tests and we apply these to the data sets in the examples below.

The combination of the PEAKER algorithm with the statistical tests is referred to from here on as PEAKER+ (PEAKER-Plus).

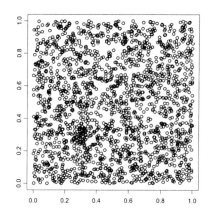

Figure 5. Art2 data.

7. Results

We ran PEAKER+ on two artificial and two real data sets. The first artificial data set, Art1, consists of 2,000 objects generated from a uniform distribution on $U[0,1] \times U[0,1]$. The second artificial data set, Art2 (Figure 5), consists of Art1 appended with 50 objects from a multivariate normal distribution:

$$MVN\left(\begin{pmatrix} 0.3 \\ 0.3 \end{pmatrix}, \begin{pmatrix} 0.025^2 & 0 \\ 0 & 0.025^2 \end{pmatrix}\right)$$

These added objects constitute a peak above the background noise of Art1, although it is not clear from the plot whether the peak is significantly different from the background noise. We set $k = 20$ and $L = 50, 100$ and 200 to represent 'small', 'medium' and 'large' peaks; note that the smaller value of L was set to equal the number of objects in the peak and the medium value was set at twice the number of objects in the peak. We also employed the toroidal wrap-around to remove edge effects.

The number of peaks found and the minimum value of F_{adj} for the mean and median test statistic for data set Art1 are shown in Table 1. No peaks were identified as being significant at anything more extreme than the 99% level, which is reassuring for a data set consisting entirely of random noise. The same experiment was run on Art2 and results shown in Table 2.

L	# of Peaks	Min F_{adj} ($\overline{Y}_2$)	Min F_{adj} ($median(Y_2)$)
50	29	0.999	0.981
100	15	1.000	1.000
200	11	1.000	1.000

Table 1. Results from running PEAKER+ on Art1.

L	# of Peaks	Min F_{adj} ($\overline{Y}_2$)	Min F_{adj} ($median(Y_2)$)
50	28	0.999	0.978
100	14	0.0000376	0.000693
200	9	0.00754	0.285

Table 2. Results from running PEAKER+ on Art2.

Similar results to those for Art1 were obtained for $L = 50$, but the peak is recognized at $L = 100$ with a significance level of approximately 0.004% for the mean test and 0.07% for the median test. The peak is less significant at the $L = 200$ level, and the median test suggests that there is not enough evidence here to suggest that the peak is not a feature of random variation in the data. As we include more objects in the test region, so the peak becomes more likely to have arisen through some random effect in the data. The object identified as a peak with $L = 100$ had co-ordinates (0.300,0.308) to 3 significant figures, showing that the pattern has been correctly identified. No other objects flagged as peaks in Art2 were found to be significant different from a uniform distribution under the tests.

The Quakes data set consists of the longitude and latitude measurements of all 2,049 earthquakes with Richter intensity above 2.5 in California, USA recorded between 1962 and 1981. Patterns found here may indicate an unusually high density of earthquakes in a local region, as opposed to earthquakes that occur randomly in the region. Again, we set $k = 20$ but this time we varied L over smaller values than those we used in the artificial data sets in order to find peaks with smaller support. The number of peaks significant at the 5% level found by PEAKER+ for these parameter values on the Quakes data is shown in Table 3.

L	# of Peaks	#$F_{adj} < 0.05$ ($\overline{Y}_2$)	#$F_{adj} < 0.05$ ($median(Y_2)$)
25	38	7	10
50	19	10	9
100	13	8	6

Table 3. Results from running PEAKER+ on Quakes data.

The following plots show peaks significant at the 5% level for the $\overline{Y}_2$ statistic, together with their local regions for $L = 25$ (Figure 6) and $L = 50$ (Figure 7). The grey triangles with white centers represent peaks significant at the 5% level. These peaks are surrounded by a grey circle representing their local region as defined by the Lth nearest neighbor distance; the different sized local regions reflect the densities of objects in different areas. The grey circles with white centers represent peaks found by

PEAKER+ that are *not* significant at the 5% level; we have little evidence to suggest that these patterns are not simply the result of random fluctuation in the data.

The value of L is an indication of the level of support for a pattern, so our choice of L reflects the pattern size if a peak is flagged as being significant. In Figure 6, many peaks are flagged but only a few are significant. In some cases, peaks that look like they should be patterns are not significant (for example, the upper left peak). They are not significant for this level of L; however, this is not to say that they will not be significant at some other level of L. We see in Figure 7, that the upper left peak is now significant, whereas the three significant peaks on the left-hand side in Figure 6 are not significant for $L = 50$. By eye, we can sometimes find objects that look like they are not features of random variation, but by applying PEAKER+ we can find peaks and assess their significance for particular values of L, also identifying patterns that the naked eye may miss.

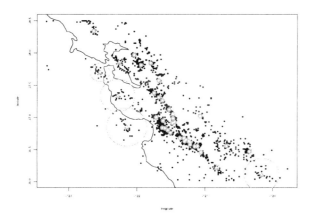

Figure 6. Quakes data set with significant peaks. k = 20, L = 25.

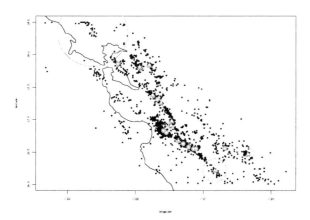

Figure 7. Quakes data set with significant peaks. k = 20, L = 50.

The Crpret1 data set is made up of five (standardized) measurements on each of 10,000 phytoplankton cells through analytical flow cytometry. These measurements are forward light scatter (FSC), 90° light scatter (SSC), depolarized/horizontally polarized light scatter (FL1), orange fluorescence (FL2) and red fluorescence (FL3) (see [4] for more details). Patterns here may indicate small groups of phytoplankton with unusual characteristics.

We set $k = 20$ and recorded results for $L = 25$, 50 and 100, to discover small patterns in the data. Results in Table 4 suggest that there are 2 significant peaks at the 5% level for $L = 50$ and that either one or both of these peaks are also significant for $L = 30$, depending on which test we use. No peaks are significant at the larger $L = 100$ level.

L	# of Peaks	# $F_{adj} < 0.05$ ($\overline{Y}_2$)	# $F_{adj} < 0.05$ ($median(Y_2)$)
25	56	1	2
50	35	2	2
100	21	0	0

Table 4. Results from running PEAKER+ on Crpret1 data.

A scatterplot matrix (Figure 8) appears to confirm the presence of these two patterns in the data. The dense cluster to the top of the FL3 axis (9909 objects) contains no small significant patterns within it, something that we have no way of knowing simply by looking at the plot.

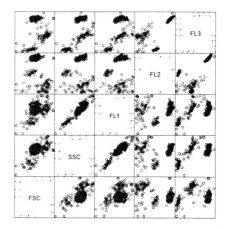

Figure 8. Scatterplot matrix of Crpret1 data.

8. Conclusion

The main parameter of interest in the statistical tests for PEAKER+ is the number of nearest neighbors, L, that define the local region. We have seen that patterns are significant for some values of L but not for others and we realize that it is tempting to vary L until a 'most significant' value is reached. However, we reiterate that this action renders the significance tests meaningless in their current form, as we must once again account for multiple testing to obtain valid significance values. Increasing the number of multiple tests requires accurate tail probability estimates that are increasingly sensitive to error. We are currently investigating an approach that would allow such variation of L.

We observed differences in significance values between results for the mean and median test over all data sets, especially as L increased. This is due to the different distributions of the statistics. The distribution of $median(Y_2)$ has a larger variance and heavier tails than the distribution of $\overline{Y}_2$. Estimates of the significance levels for peaks are thus generally more conservative for $median(Y_2)$ but the estimates themselves have greater variance. However, for large values of L an estimate of the significance value using $median(Y_2)$ would be more robust to edge effects.

In a setting where we are analysing spatial data, such as the Quakes data above, we may also be interested in patterns over certain geographical areas. A possibility here would be to define the local region by area rather than by support. However, since the density of objects often varies considerably over different areas, the significance tests will consider different numbers of objects for each peak. It is not clear whether we can account for multiple testing in the same way when we consider this inconsistency. If this can be overcome then such an approach can be useful for spatial data. However, we feel that varying the local region according to L, and thus the support of a peak, is more easily transferred to multivariate data and thus has wider application.

Of course, others have also developed statistical tests for patterns – though, as we noted in the introduction, the field is a relatively new one. Most other work appears to be based on computing the probability of the occurrence of patterns when the features are categorical. Examples, in a genomic context, are given in [2] and [8]. Our work generalizes this, permitting approximate matches and continuous data.

In summary, PEAKER+ is a data mining algorithm that provides the answer to the most important question we should ask ourselves whenever we discover patterns in data containing any element of uncertainty: are these patterns real?

Acknowledgements

We are grateful to Dr G Tarran of the Plymouth Marine Laboratory, UK, who generated the Crpret1 data used in this paper.

References

[1] N. M. Adams, D. J. Hand, and R. J. Till. Mining for classes and patterns in behavioural data. To appear in *Journal of Operational Research*, 2001.

[2] K. Atteson. Calculating the exact probability of language-like patterns in biomolecular sequences. In *Proceedings of the 6th International Conference on Intelligent Systems for Molecular Biology*, pages 17-24, 1998.

[3] S. Byers and A. E. Raftery. Nearest-neighbor clutter removal for estimating features in spatial point processes. *Journal of the American Statistical Association*,93(442):577-584, 1998.

[4] G. S. Collins and W. J. Krzanowski. Nonparametric discriminant analysis of phytoplankton species using data from analytical flow cytometry, submitted for publication, 2001.

[5] D. J. Hand, G. Blunt, M. G. Kelly, and N. M. Adams. Data Mining for fun and profit (with discussion), *Statistical Science*, 15(2):111-126, 2000.

[6] D. J. Hand, H. Mannila, and P. Smyth. *Principles of data mining*, MIT Press, 2001.

[7] A. M. Mood, F. A. Graybill, and D. C. Boes. *Introduction to the theory of statistics (3rd Edition)*. McGraw-Hill, Singapore, 1974.

[8] M. Tompa. An exact method for finding short motifs in sequences, with application to the ribosome binding site problem. In *Proceedings of the 6th International Conference on Intelligent Systems for Molecular Biology*, pages 262-271, 1999.

Distributed Web Mining using Bayesian Networks from Multiple Data Streams

R. Chen
School of EECS
Washington State University
Pullman, WA 99163, USA
rchen@eecs.wsu.edu

K. Sivakumar
School of EECS
Washington State University
Pullman, WA 99163, USA
siva@eecs.wsu.edu

H. Kargupta
Department of CSEE
Univ. of MD Baltimore County
Baltimore, MD 21250, USA
hillol@csee.umbc.edu

Abstract

We present a collective approach to mine Bayesian networks from distributed heterogenous web-log data streams. In this approach we first learn a local Bayesian network at each site using the local data. Then each site identifies the observations that are most likely to be evidence of coupling between local and non-local variables and transmits a subset of these observations to a central site. Another Bayesian network is learnt at the central site using the data transmitted from the local site. The local and central Bayesian networks are combined to obtain a collective Bayesian network, that models the entire data. We applied this technique to mine multiple data streams where data centralization is difficult because of large response time and scalability issues. Experimental results and theoretical justification that demonstrate the feasibility of our approach are presented.

1. Introduction

The World Wide Web (WWW) is growing at an astounding rate. In order to optimize tasks such as Web site design, Web server design, and to simplify navigation through a Web site, the analysis of how the Web is used is very important. Web server log contains records of user interactions when request for the resources in the servers is received. This contains a wealth of data for the analysis of web usage and identifying different patterns.

In an increasingly mobile world, the log data for an individual user would be distributed among many servers. For example, consider a subscriber of a wireless network who travels frequently and uses her PDA and cell phone to do business and personal transactions; her transactions go through different servers depending upon her location during the transaction. The PDA has very limited memory and communication ability, and her wireless service provider could offer more personalized service by paying careful attention to her needs and tastes. This may be useful for choosing the instant messages appropriate for her interests and physical location. In this scenario, the web log files of the user are distributed in different sites of the service provider. Since these log files are very large, it's not feasible to transmit them to a central site for analysis. Moreover, these transaction data are heterogeneous. There is no guarantee that the user will perform the same type of transactions at every location. The user may choose to perform a wide variety of transactions at different sites. Therefore the features defining the transactions observed at different sites are likely to be different in general although we may have some overlap. Traditional data mining approach to this problem is aggregating all the log files to a central site before analysis. This would involve substantial data communication, large response time, and this approach does not scale well. A collective learning approach, that builds an overall model for the data based on local models, is a more logical approach.

In this paper, we consider a Bayesian network (BN) to model the user log data, which is distributed over different sites. Specifically, we address the problem of learning a BN from heterogenous distributed data. We propose a collective data mining (CDM) approach introduced earlier by Kargupta et. al. [19, 22]. Section 2 provides some background and reviews existing literature in related area. Section 3 presents our approach to distributed web log mining using a BN. An approach to learn a global BN from distributed data, with selective data transmission is presented. Experimental results are presented in Section 4. Finally, we provide some discussions and concluding remarks in Section 5.

2. Background and related work

In this section, we first illustrate the difference between homogenous and heterogenous databases. We then review important literature related to BNs and web mining and provide a brief review of BNs.

Distributed data mining (DDM) must deal with different possibilities of data distribution. Different sites may contain data for a common set of features of the problem domain. In case of relational data this would mean a consistent database schema across all the sites. This is the homogeneous case. In the general case the data sites may be *heterogeneous*. In other words, sites may contain tables with different schemata. Different features are observed at different sites. Let us illustrate this case with relational data. Table 1 shows two data-tables at site X. The upper table contains weather-related data and the lower one contains demographic data. Table 2 shows the content of site Y, which contains holiday toy sales data. The objective of the DDM process may be detecting relations between the toy sales, the demographic and weather related features. In the general heterogeneous case the tables may be related through different sets of key indices. In this paper, we consider the heterogenous data scenario described above. For a web log mining application, the key that can be used to link together observations across sites could be produced using either a "cookie" or the user IP address (in combination with other log data like time of access).

Table 1. Heterogeneous case: Site X with two tables, one for weather and the other for demography.

City	Temp.	Humidity	Wind chill
Spokane	32	48%	12
Portland	51	86%	4
Vancouver	47	52%	6

City	State	Size	Avg. earning	Prop. of small businesses
Spokane	WA	Medium	Medium	0.022
Portland	OR	Large	High	0.017
Vancouver	BC	Medium	Medium	0.031

Table 2. Heterogeneous case: Site Y with one table for holiday toy sales.

State	Best Selling Item	Price	Items Sold
WA	Snarc Action Figure	47.99	23K
OR	Super Squirter	24.99	142K
BC	Light Saber	19.99	5K

2.1. Related Work

We first review important literature on learning using BNs. A BN is a probabilistic graphical model that represents uncertain knowledge [30, 21]. Learning parameters of a BN from complete data is discussed in [5]. Learning parameters from incomplete data using gradient methods is discussed in [4]. Lauritzen [26] has proposed an EM algorithm to learn BN parameters, whereas Bauer et. al. [3]

describe methods for accelerating convergence of the EM algorithm. Learning using Gibbs sampling is proposed in [16]. The Bayesian score to learn the structure of a BN is discussed in [11]. Learning the structure of a BN based on the Minimal Description Length (MDL) principle is presented in [24]. Learning BN structure using greedy hill-climbing and other variants is introduced in [18], whereas Chickering [9] introduced a method based on search over equivalence network classes. Learning the structure of BN from incomplete data, is considered in [10, 6, 13]. See [5, 14, 24] for discussion on how to sequentially update the structure of a network as more data is available. In [25] the authors report a technique to automatically produce a BN from discovered knowledge using a distributed approach.

An important problem is how to learn the BN from data in distributed sites. The centralized solution to this problem is to download all datasets from distributed sites. Kenji [23] worked on the homogeneous distributed learning scenario. In this paper, we address the heterogenous case, where each site has data about only a subset of the features. To our knowledge, there is no significant work that addresses the heterogenous case.

Several work on mining data streams has also been reported [12, 17]. Hulten et. al. [20] and Venkatesh et. al. [31] has considered mining time-varying data streams.

The concept of applying data mining algorithm to web log was proposed in [7, 28]. Chen et. al. [7] introduce the concept of maximal forward reference, whereas Mannila et. al. [28] propose discovering frequent episodes from web log. In [1] the sequential pattern mining technique is used to discover user patterns. In [15] the authors use probabilistic relational models to optimize web site design, whereas Pazzani [29] uses a naive Bayesian classifier to learn user preference. Some work on web personalization for mobile users has been reported by Anderson et. al. [2].

2.2. A brief review of Bayesian networks

A BN is a probabilistic graph model. It can be defined as a pair $(\mathcal{G}, p)$, where $\mathcal{G} = (\mathcal{V}, \mathcal{E})$ is a directed acyclic graph (DAG). Here, $\mathcal{V}$ is the node set which represents variables in the problem domain and $\mathcal{E}$ is the edge set which denotes probabilistic relationships among the variables. For a variable $X \in \mathcal{V}$, a parent of X is a node from which there exists a directed link to X. Figure 1 is a BN called the ASIA model (adapted from [27]). All the variables in this model are binary. Let $pa(X)$ denote the set of parents of X, then the conditional independence property can be represented as follows: $P(X \mid \mathcal{V} \backslash X) = P(X \mid pa(X))$. This property can simplify the computations in a BN model. For example, the joint distribution of the set of all variables in $\mathcal{V}$ can be written as a product of conditional probabilities as follows:

$$P(\mathcal{V}) = \prod_{X \in \mathcal{V}} P(X \mid pa(X)). \qquad (1)$$

The set of conditional distributions $\{P(X \mid pa(X)), X \in \mathcal{V}\}$ are called the parameters of a Bayesian network. If variable X has no parents, then $P(X \mid pa(X)) = P(X)$ is the marginal distribution of X. The ordering of variables constitutes a constraint on the structure of a Bayesian network. If variable X appears before variable Y, then Y can not be a parent of X.

Two important issues in using a Bayesian network are: (a) learning a BN and (b) probabilistic inference. Learning a BN involves learning the structure of the network (the directed graph), and obtaining the conditional probabilities (parameters) associated with the network. Once a BN is constructed, we usually need to determine various probabilities of interest from the model. This process is referred to as probabilistic inference. BN is an important tool to model

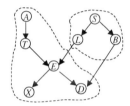

Figure 1. ASIA Model

probabilistic or imperfect relationship among problem variables. It is a promising tool to model customer usage patterns in web data mining applications, where specific user preferences can be modeled as in terms of conditional probabilities associated with the different features.

3. Collective Bayesian learning

In the following, we discuss our collective approach to learning a BN that is specifically designed for a distributed data scenario.

The primary steps in our approach are: (a) Learn local BNs (local model) involving the variables observed at each site based on local data set, (b) At each site, based on the local BN, identify the observations that are most likely to be evidence of coupling between local and non-local variables. Transmit a subset of these observations to a central site, (c) At the central site, a limited number of observations of all the variables are now available. Using this, learn a non-local BN consisting of links between variables across two or more sites, (d) Combine the local models with the links discovered at the central site to obtain a collective BN.

The non-local BN constructed at the central site would be effective in identifying associations between variables

across sites, whereas the local BNs would detect associations among local variables at each site. The conditional probabilities can also be estimated in a similar manner. Those probabilities that involve only variables from a single site can be estimated locally, whereas the ones that involve variables from different sites can be estimated at the central site. Finally, a collective BN can be obtained by taking the union of nodes and edges of the local BNs and the non-local BN and using the conditional probabilities from the appropriate BNs.

It is quite evident that learning probabilistic relationships between variables that belong to a single local site is straightforward and does not pose any additional difficulty as compared to a centralized approach.[1] The important objective is to correctly identify the coupling between variables that belong to two (or more) sites. These correspond to the edges in the graph that connect variables between two sites and the conditional probability(ies) at the associated node(s). In the following, we describe our approach to selecting observations at the local sites that are most likely to be evidence of strong coupling between variables at two different sites.

3.1 Selection of samples for transmission to global site

For simplicity, we will assume that the data is distributed between two sites and will illustrate the approach using the BN in Figure 1. The extension of this approach to more than two sites is straightforward. Let us denote by $\mathcal{A}$ and $\mathcal{B}$, the variables in the left and right groups, respectively, in Figure 1. We assume that the observations for $\mathcal{A}$ are available at site A, whereas the observations for $\mathcal{B}$ are available at a different site B. Furthermore, we assume that there is a common feature ("key" or index) that can be used to associate a given observation in site A to a corresponding observation in site B. Naturally, $\mathcal{V} = \mathcal{A} \cup \mathcal{B}$.

At each local site, a local BN can be learned using only samples in this site. This would give a BN structure involving only the local variables at each site and the associated conditional probabilities. Let $p_A(.)$ and $p_B(.)$ denote the estimated probability function involving the local variables. This is the product of the conditional probabilities as indicated by (1). Since $p_A(x)$, $p_B(x)$ denote the probability or likelihood of obtaining observation x at sites A and B, we would call these probability functions the likelihood functions $l_A(.)$ and $l_B(.)$, for the local model obtained at sites A and B, respectively. The observations at each site are ranked based on how well it fits the local model, using the local likelihood functions. The observations at site A with large likelihood under $l_A(.)$ are evidence of "local re-

---

[1]This may not be true for arbitrary Bayesian network structure. We will discuss this issue further in the last section.

77

lationships" between site A variables, whereas those with low likelihoods under $l_A(.)$ are possible evidence of "cross relationships" between variables across sites. Let $S(A)$ denote the set of keys associated with the latter observations (those with low likelihood under $l_A(.)$). In practice, this step can be implemented in different ways. For example, we can set a threshold ρ_A and if $l_A(x) \le \rho_A$, then $x \in S_A$. The sites A and B transmit the set of keys S_A, S_B, respectively, to a central site, where the intersection $S = S_A \cap S_B$ is computed. The observations corresponding to the set of keys in S are then obtained from each of the local sites by the central site.

The following argument justifies our selection strategy. Using the rules of probability, and the assumed conditional independence in the BN of Figure 1, it is easy to show that:

$$
\begin{aligned}
P(\mathcal{V}) = P(\mathcal{A}, \mathcal{B}) &= P(\mathcal{A} \mid \mathcal{B})P(\mathcal{B}) \\
&= P(\mathcal{A} \mid nb(\mathcal{A}))P(\mathcal{B}),
\end{aligned} \tag{2}
$$

where $nb(\mathcal{A}) = \{B, L\}$ is the set of variables in $\mathcal{B}$, which have a link connecting it to a variable in $\mathcal{A}$. In particular,

$$
\begin{aligned}
P(\mathcal{A} \mid nb(\mathcal{A})) = P(A)P(T \mid A)P(X \mid E)P(E \mid T, L) \\
\times P(D \mid E, B).
\end{aligned} \tag{3}
$$

Note that, the first three terms in the right-hand side of (3) involve variables local to site A, whereas the last two terms are the so-called *cross terms*, involving variables from sites A and B. Similarly, it can be shown that

$$
\begin{aligned}
P(\mathcal{V}) = P(\mathcal{A}, \mathcal{B}) &= P(\mathcal{B} \mid \mathcal{A})P(\mathcal{A}) \\
&= P(\mathcal{B} \mid nb(\mathcal{B}))P(\mathcal{A}),
\end{aligned} \tag{4}
$$

where $nb(\mathcal{B}) = \{E, D\}$ and

$$
\begin{aligned}
P(\mathcal{B} \mid nb(\mathcal{B})) = P(S)P(B \mid S)P(L \mid S)P(E \mid T, L) \\
\times P(D \mid E, B).
\end{aligned} \tag{5}
$$

Therefore, an observation $\{A = a, T = t, E = e, X = x, D = d, S = s, L = l, B = b\}$ with low likelihood at both sites A and B; i.e. for which both $P(\mathcal{A})$ and $P(\mathcal{B})$ are small, is an indication that both $P(\mathcal{A} \mid nb(\mathcal{A}))$ and $P(\mathcal{B} \mid nb(\mathcal{B}))$ are large for that observation (since observations with small $P(\mathcal{V})$ are less likely to occur). Notice from (3) and (5) that the terms common to both $P(\mathcal{A} \mid nb(\mathcal{A}))$ and $P(\mathcal{B} \mid nb(\mathcal{B}))$ are precisely the conditional probabilities that involve variables from both sites A and B. In other words, this is an observation that indicates a coupling of variables between sites A and B and should hence be transmitted to a central site to identify the specific coupling links and the associated conditional probabilities.

In a sense, our approach to learning the cross terms in the BN involves a selective sampling of the given dataset that is most relevant to the identification of coupling between the sites. This is a type of *importance sampling*, where we select the observations that have high conditional probabilities corresponding to the terms involving variables from both sites. Naturally, when the values of the different variables (features) from the different sites, corresponding to these selected observations are pooled together at the central site, we can learn the coupling links as well as estimate the associated conditional distributions. These selected observations will, by design, not be useful to identify the links in the BN that are local to the individual sites. This has been verified in our experiments (see Section 4).

The proposed collective approach to learning a BN is well suited for a scenario with multiple data streams. Suppose we have an existing BN model, which has to be constantly updated based on new data from multiple streams. First, at each local site, the new data is tested for how well its fits with the local BN. If there is an acceptable statistical fit, that observation is used to update the local conditional probability estimates. Otherwise, it is transmitted to the central site, where it is used to update the appropriate conditional probabilities of the cross terms. These updates are then used to update the overall BN model. Note that transmitting the BN updates would involve a significantly lower communication as compared to transmitting the local data streams to a central site.

4 Experimental Results

We tested our approach on three different datasets — ASIA model, real web log data, and simulated web log data. We present our results for the three cases in the following subsections.

4.1 ASIA Model

This experiment illustrates the ability of the proposed collective learning approach to correctly obtain the structure of the BN (including the cross-links) as well as the parameters of the BN. Our experiments were performed on a dataset that was generated from the BN depicted in Figure 1 (ASIA Model). The conditional probability table is a multidimensional array, where the dimensions are arranged in the same order as ordering of the variables, viz. $\{A, S, T, L, B, E, X, D\}$. Table 3 depicts the conditional probabilities of ASIA model. It is laid out such that the first dimension toggles fastest (all variables are binary).

We generated 6000 observations from this model, which were split into two sites as illustrated in Figure 1 (site A with variables A, T, E, X, D and site B with variables S, L, B). Note that there are two edges ($L \to E$ and $B \to D$) that connect variables from site A to site B, the rest of the six edges being local.

Table 3. (The conditional probabilities for the ASIA model

A	0.99	0.01						
S	0.5	0.5						
T	0.1	0.9	0.9	0.1				
L	0.3	0.6	0.7	0.4				
B	0.1	0.8	0.9	0.2				
E	0.9	0.1	0.1	0.01	0.1	0.9	0.9	0.99
X	0.2	0.6	0.8	0.4				
D	0.9	0.1	0.1	0.01	0.1	0.9	0.9	0.99

Table 4. The estimated conditional probabilities of local site A and local site B

Local A				
A	0.99	0.01		
T	0.10	0.84	0.90	0.16
E	0.50	0.05	0.50	0.95
X	0.20	0.60	0.80	0.40
D	0.55	0.05	0.45	0.95
Local B				
S	0.49	0.51		
L	0.30	0.59	0.70	0.41
B	0.10	0.81	0.90	0.19

Local BNs were constructed using a conditional independence test based algorithm [8] for learning the BN structure and a maximum likelihood based method for estimating the conditional probabilities. The local networks were exact as far as the edges involving only the local variables. We then tested the ability of the collective approach to detect the two non-local edges. The estimated parameters of these two local Bayesian network are depicted in Table 4. Clearly, the estimated probabilities at all nodes, except nodes E and D, are close to the true probabilities given in Table 3. In other words, the parameters that involve only local variables have been successfully learnt at the local sites.

A fraction of the samples, whose likelihood are smaller than a selected threshold T, were identified at each site. The samples with likelihood less than some threshold (T_A at site A, T_B at site B) at both sites were sent to a central site. The central site learns a non-local BN based on these samples. Finally, a collective BN is formed by taking the union of edges detected locally and those detected at the central site. The error in structure learning of the collective BN is defined as the sum of the number of correct edges missed and the number of incorrect edges detected. This is done for different thresholds. Figure 2 (left) depicts this error as a function of the fraction of samples communicated. It is

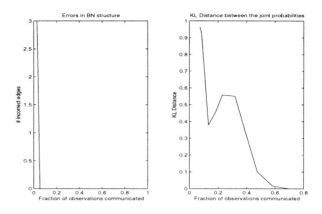

Figure 2. Performance of collective BN: (left) structure learning error (right) parameter learning error.

clear that the exact structure can be obtained by transmitting about 5% of the total samples. Next we assessed the accuracy of the estimated parameters. For the collective BN, we used the parameters from local BN for the local terms and the ones estimated at the central site for the cross terms. This was compared with the performance of a BN learnt using a centralized approach. Figure 2 (right) depicts the KL distance $d(p_{cntr}(\mathcal{V}), p_{coll}(\mathcal{V}))$ between the joint probabilities computed using our collective approach and the one computed using a centralized approach. Clearly, even with a small communication overhead, the estimated conditional probabilities based on our collective approach is quite close that obtained from a centralized approach.

4.2 Webserver Log Data

In the second experiment, we used data from real world domain — a web server log data. This experiment illustrates the ability of the proposed collective learning approach to learn the parameters of a BN from real world web log data. Web server log contains records of user interactions when request for the resources in the servers is received. Web log mining can provide useful information about different user profiles. This in turn can be used to offer personalized services as well as to better design and organize the web resources based on usage history.

In our application, the raw web log file was obtained from the web server of the School of EECS at Washington State University — http://www.eecs.wsu.edu. There are three steps in our processing. First we preprocess the raw web log file to transform it to a session form, which is amenable to our application. This involves identifying a sequence of logs as a single session, based on the IP address (or cookies if available) and time of access. Each session corresponds to the logs from a single user in a single web session. We consider each session as a data sample.

Then we categorize the resource (html, video, audio etc.) requested from the server into different categories. For our example, based on the different resources on the EECS web server, we considered eight categories. They are E–EE Faculty, C-CS Faculty, L-Lab and facilities, T-Contact Information, A-Admission Information, U-Course Information, H-EECS Home, and R-Research. These categories are our features. In general, we would have several tens (or perhaps a couple of hundred) of categories, depending on the webserver. This categorization has to be done carefully, and would have to be automated for a large web server. Finally, each feature value in a session is set to one or zero, depending on whether the user requested resources corresponding to that category. An 8-feature, binary dataset was thus obtained, which was used to learn a BN.

A central BN was first obtained using the whole dataset. Figure 3 depicts the structure of this centralized BN. We then split the features into two sets, corresponding to a scenario where the resources are split into two different web servers. Site A has features E, C, T, and U and site B has features L, A, H, and R. We assumed that the BN structure was known, and estimated the parameters (probability distribution) of the BN using our collective BN learning approach. Figure 4 shows the KL distance between the central BN and the collective BN as a function of the fraction of observations communicated. Clearly the parameters of collective BN is close to that of central BN even with a small fraction of data communication.

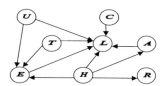

Figure 3. Bayesian Network Structure learnt from Web Log Data

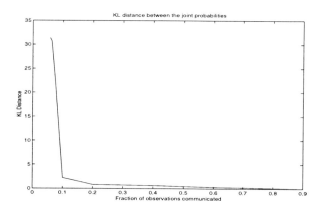

Figure 4. KL distance between joint probabilities for webserver log data

4.3   Simulated log data

This experiment illustrates the scalability of our approach with respect to number of sites, features, and observations. To this end, we generated a large dataset to simulate web log data. We assume that the users in a wireless network can be divided into several groups, each group having a distinct usage pattern. This can be described by means of the (conditional) probability of a user requesting resource i, given that she has requested resource j. A BN can be used to model such usage patterns. In our simulation, we used 43 features (nodes in the BN) and generated 10000 log samples. The structure of the BN is shown in Figure 5. These 43 features were split into four different sites as follows — Site 1: $\{1, 5, 10, 15, 16, 22, 23, 24, 30, 31, 37, 38\}$, Site 2: $\{2, 6, 7, 11, 17, 18, 25, 26, 32, 39, 40\}$, Site 3: $\{3, 8, 12, 19, 20, 27, 33, 34, 41, 42\}$, Site 4: $\{4, 9, 13, 14, 21, 28, 29, 35, 36, 42, 43\}$.

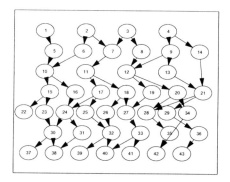

Figure 5. Structure of BN for web mining simulation

We assumed that the structure of the Bayesian network was given, and tested our approach for estimating the conditional probabilities. The KL distance between the conditional probabilities estimated based on our collective BN and a BN obtained using a centralized approach was computed. In particular, we illustrate the results for the conditional probabilities at four different nodes: 24, 27, 38, and 43. Note that the first two conditional probabilities represent cross terms, whereas the last two conditional probabilities represent local terms. Given that these are conditional probabilities, we compute the sum over all the possible values of $\{Node18, Node19\}$, of the KL distance between p_{coll} and p_{cntr}, estimated using our collective approach and the centralized approach, respectively. Figure 6 (top left) depicts the KL distance $\sum_{Node18, Node19} d(p_{\text{cntr}}(Node27 \mid Node18, Node19), p_{\text{coll}}(Node27 \mid Node18, Node19))$, between the two estimates. Figure 6 (top right) depicts a similar KL distance for $Node24$. Clearly, even with a small data communication, the estimates of the conditional probabilities of the cross-terms, based on our collective approach,

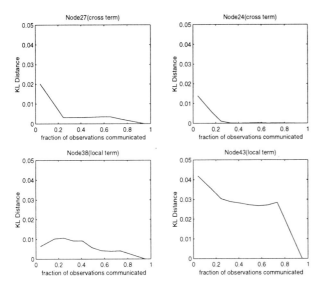

Figure 6. KL distance between conditional probabilities for simulated web log data experiment

is quite close to that obtained by the centralized approach.

To further verify the validity of our approach, the transmitted data at the central site was used to estimate two local conditional probabilities of $Node38$ and $Node43$. The corresponding KL distances are depicted in the bottom row of Figure 6 (left: node 38 and right: node 43). It is clear that the estimates of these probabilities is quite poor, unless a substantial fraction of the data is transmitted. Our experiments clearly demonstrates that our technique can be used to perform a biased sampling for discovering relationships between variables across sites. This simulation also illustrates the fact that the proposed approach scales well with respect to number of nodes, samples, and sites.

5. Discussions and Conclusions

We have presented an approach to learning BNs from distributed heterogenous data. This is based on a collective learning strategy, where a local model is obtained at each site and the global associations are determined by a selective transmission of data to a central site. In our experiments, the performance of the collective BN was quite comparable to that obtained from a centralized approach, even for a small data communication. To our knowledge, this is the first approach to learning BNs from distributed heterogenous data.

Our experiments suggest that the collective learning scales well with respect to number of sites, samples, and features .

We now discuss some limitations of our proposed approach, which suggest possible directions for future work.

Hidden node at local sites: For certain network structures, it may not be possible to obtain the correct (local) links, based on local data at that site. For example, consider the ASIA model shown in Figure 1, where the observations corresponding to variables A, T, E, and X are available at site A and those corresponding to variables S, L, B, and D are available at site B. In this case, when we learn a local BN at site B, we would expect a (false) edge from node L to node D, because of the edges $L \rightarrow E$ and $E \rightarrow D$ in the overall BN and the fact that node E is "hidden" (unobserved) at site B. This was verified experimentally as well. However, the cross-links $L \rightarrow E$ and $E \rightarrow D$ were still detected correctly at the central site, using our "selctively sampled" data. Therefore, it is necessary to re-examine the local links after discovering the cross-links. In other words, some post-processing of the resulting overall BN is required to eliminate such false local edges. Note, however, that we do not encounter this problem in the examples presented in Section 4.

Assumptions about the data: As mentioned earlier, we assume the existence of a key that links observations across sites. Moreover, we consider a simple heterogenous partition of data, where the variable set at different sites are non-overlapping. We also assume that our data is stationary (all data points come from the same distribution) and free of outliers. These are simplifying assumptions to derive a reasonable algorithm for distributed Bayesian learning. Suitable learning strategies that would allow us to relax of some of these assumptions would be an important area of research.

Structure Learning: Even when the data is centralized, learning the structure of BN is considerably more involved than estimating the parameters or probabilities associated with the network. In a distributed data scenario, the problem of obtaining the correct network structure is even more pronounced. The "hidden node" problem discussed earlier is one example of this. As in the centralized case, prior domain knowledge at each local site, in the form of probabilistic independence or direct causation, would be very helpful. Our experiments on the ASIA model demonstrate that the proposed collective BN learning approach to obtain the network structure is reasonable, at least for simple cases. However, this is just a beginning and deserves careful investigation.

Performance Bounds: Our approach to "selective sampling" of data that maybe evidence of cross-terms is reasonable based on the discussion in Section 3 (see eq. (2)-(5)). This was verified experimentally for the three examples in Section 4. Currently, we are working towards obtaining bounds for the performance of our collective BN as compared to that obtained from a centralized approach, as a function of the data communication involved.

Acknowledgements: This work was partially supported by NASA under Cooperative agreement NCC 2-1252.

References

[1] R. Agrawal and R. Srikant. Mining sequential pattern. In *Proceedings of the International Conference on Data Engineering*, pages 3–14, Taipei, 1995.

[2] C. R. Anderson, P. Domingos, and D. S. Weld. Personalizing web sites for mobile users. In *Proceedings of the 10th World Wide Web Conference on World Wide Web*, Hong Kong, 2001.

[3] E. Bauer, D. Koller, and Y. Singer. Update rules for parameter estimation in Bayesian networks. In D. Geiger and P. Shanoy, editors, *Proceedings of the Thirteenth Conference on Uncertainty in Artificial Intelligence*, pages 3–13. Morgan Kaufmann, 1997.

[4] J. Binder, D. Koller, S. Russel, and K. Kanazawa. Adaptive probabilistic networks with hidden variables. *Machine Learning*, 29:213–244, 1997.

[5] W. Buntine. Theory refinement on Bayesian networks. In B. D. D'Ambrosio and P. S. amd P. P. Bonissone, editors, *Proceedings of the Seventh Annual Conference on Uncertainty in Artificial Intelligence*, pages 52–60. Morgan Kaufmann, 1991.

[6] P. Cheeseman and J. Stutz. Bayesian classification (autoclass): Theory and results. In U. Fayyad, G. P. Shapiro, P. Smyth, and R. S. Uthurasamy, editors, *Advances in Knowledge Discovery and Data Mining*. AAAI Press, 1996.

[7] M. Chen, J. Park, and P. Yu. Data mining for path traversal patterns in a web enviroment. In *Proceedings of 16th International Conference on Distributed Computing Systems*, pages 385–392, 1996.

[8] J. Cheng, D. A. Bell, and W. Liu. Learning belief networks from data: An information theory based approach. In *Proceedings of the Sixth ACM International Conference on Information and Knowledge Management*, 1997.

[9] D. M. Chickering. Learning equivalence classes of Bayesian network structure. In E. Horvitz and F. Jensen, editors, *Proceedings of the Twelfth Conference on Uncertainty in Artificial Intelligence*. Morgan Kaufmann, 1996.

[10] D. M. Chickering and D. Heckerman. Efficient approximation for the marginal likelihood of incomplete data given a Bayesian network. *Machine Learning*, 29:181–212, 1997.

[11] G. F. Cooper and E. Herskovits. A Bayesian method for the induction of probabilistic networks from data. *Machine Learning*, 9:309–347, 1992.

[12] P. Domingo and G. Hulten. Mining high-speed data streams. In *Proceedings of the Sixth International Conference on Knowledge Discovery and Data Mining*, pages 71–80, Boston, 2000. ACM Press.

[13] N. Friedman. The Bayesian structural EM algorithm. In G. F. Cooper and S. Moral, editors, *Proceedings of the Fourteenth Conference on Uncertainty in Artificial Intelligence*. Morgan Kaufmann, 1998.

[14] N. Friedman and M. Goldszmidt. Sequential update of Bayesian network structure. In D. Geiger and P. Shanoy, editors, *Proceedings of the Thirteenth Conference on Uncertainty in Artificial Intelligence*. Morgan Kaufmann, 1997.

[15] L. Getoor and M. Sahami. Using probabilistic relational models for collaborative filtering. In *Proceedings of WE-BKDD*, 1999.

[16] W. Gilks, S. Richardson, and D. Spiegelhalter. *Markov chain Monte Carlo in practice*. Chapman and Hall, 1996.

[17] S. Guha, N. Mishra, R. Motwani, and L. O'Callaghan. Clustering data streams. In *Proceedings of the Annual Symposium on Foundations of Computer Science*. IEEE, 2000.

[18] D. Heckerman and D. Gieger. Learning Bayesian networks: A unification for discrete and Gaussian domains. In P. Besnard and S. Hanks, editors, *Proceedings of the Eleventh Conference on Uncertainty in Artificial Intelligence*, pages 274–284. Morgan Kaufmann, 1995.

[19] D. Hershberger and H. Kargupta. Distributed multivariate regression using wavelet-based collective data mining. Technical Report EECS-99-02, School of EECS, Washington State University, 1999. To be published in the Special Issue on Parallel and Distributed Data Mining of the Journal of Parallel Distributed Computing, Guest Eds: Vipin Kumar, Sanjay Ranka, and Vineet Singh.

[20] G. Hulten, L. Spencer, and P. Domingos. Mining time-changing data streams. In *Proceedings of the Seventh International Conference on Knowledge Discovery and Data Mining (to appear)*, San Francisco, 2001. ACM Press.

[21] F. Jensen. *An Introduction to Bayesian Networks*. Springer, 1996.

[22] E. Johnson and H. Kargupta. Collective, hierarchical clustering from distributed, heterogeneous data. In *Lecture Notes in Computer Science*, volume 1759, pages 221–244. Springer-Verlag, 1999.

[23] Y. Kenji. Distributed cooperative Bayesian learning strategies. In *Proceedings of the Tenth Annual Conference on Computational Learning Theory*, pages 250–262, Nashville, Tennessee, 1997. ACM Press.

[24] W. Lam and F. Bacchus. Learning Bayesian belief networks: An approach based on the MDL principle. *Computational Intelligence*, 10:262–293, 1994.

[25] W. Lam and A. M. Segre. Distributed data mining of probabilistic knowledge. In *Proceedings of the 17th International Conference on Distributed Computing Systems*, pages 178–185, Washington, 1997. IEEE Computer Society Press.

[26] S. L. Lauritzen. The EM algorithm for graphical association models with missing data. *Computational Statistics and Data Analysis*, 19:191–201, 1995.

[27] S. L. Lauritzen and D. J. Spiegelhalter. Local computations with probabilities on graphical structures and their application to expert systems (with discussion). *Journal of the Royal Statistical Society, series B*, 50:157–224, 1988.

[28] H. Mannila, H. Toivonen, and A. Verkamo. Discovering frequent episodes in sequences. In *Proceedings of the Second International Conference on Knowledge Discovery and Data Mining*, pages 210–215, Portland, 1996.

[29] M. Pazzani, J. Muramatsu, and D. Billsus. Syskill & Webert: Identifying interesting web sites. In *Proceedings of the National Conference on Artificial Intelligence*. 1996.

[30] J. Pearl. *Probabilistic Reasoning in Intelligent Systems*. Morgan Kaufmann, 1988.

[31] G. Venkatesh, J. Gehrke, and R. Ramakrishnan. DEMON: Mining and monitoring evolving data. *IEEE Transactions on Knowledge and Data Engineering*, 13(1):50–63, 2001.

A Hypergraph Based Clustering Algorithm for Spatial Data Sets

Jong-Sheng Cherng and Mei-Jung Lo
Department of Electrical Engineering
Da Yeh University
Changhwa, Taiwan, R.O.C.
E-mail : jscherng@mail.dyu.edu.tw

Abstract

Clustering is a discovery process in data mining and can be used to group together the objects of a database into meaningful subclasses which serve as the foundation for other data analysis techniques.

In this paper, we focus on dealing with a set of spatial data. For the spatial data, the clustering problem becomes that of finding the densely populated regions of the space and thus grouping these regions into clusters such that the intracluster similarity is maximized and the intercluster similarity is minimized. We develop a novel hierarchical clustering algorithm that uses a hypergraph to represent a set of spatial data. This hypergraph is initially constructed from the Delaunay triangulation graph of the data set and can correctly capture the relationships among sets of data points. Two phases are developed for the proposed clustering algorithm to find the clusters in the data set.

We evaluate our hierarchical clustering algorithm with some spatial data sets in which contain clusters of different sizes, shapes, densities, and noise. Experimental results on these data sets are very encouraging.

Keywords：Data Mining, Clustering, Hypergraph.

1. Introduction

Nowadays, to make a business more competitive, the business management relies progressively on the collection and mining of various data. These data could be derived from a number of different reports collected periodically or different consumer behaviors. In mining valuable information from the data, clustering plays an essential and important role. Clustering is a discovery process in data mining [3, 14] and can be used to group together the objects of a database into meaningful subclasses which serve as the foundation for other data analysis techniques.

In this paper, we focus on dealing with a set of spatial data. The spatial data sets could be the city locations of the global route map of an airline company, the locations of expensive houses in a city, or even the locations of electronic modules in a tiny integrated circuit chip. For these data sets, the clustering problem becomes that of finding the densely populated regions of the space and thus grouping these regions into clusters such that the intracluster similarity is maximized and the intercluster similarity is minimized. Many clustering techniques exist for finding dense clusters in a set of spatial data, such as K-means [9], PAM [11], CLARANS [12], DBSCAN [6], CURE [7], ROCK [8], and CHAMELEON [10]. The method in K-means [9] tries to assign data points to clusters such that the mean square distance of data points to the centroid of the assigned cluster is minimized. This centroid based approaches can, of course, deal with data set in Euclidean space, however, they could fail for data set in an arbitrary similarity space. The medoid based methods of PAM [11] and CLARANS [12] try to search representative points (*i.e.*, medoids) so as to minimize the sum of the distances of data points to their closest medoid, and can work for data sets in an arbitrary similarity space. However, neither PAM and CLARANS nor K-means can find the genuine clusters for data set in which some data points in a given cluster are closer to the center of another cluster than to the center of their own cluster, *e.g.*, the shapes of clusters are not convex. DBSCAN [6] is a well-known spatial clustering technique that has been shown to find clusters of arbitrary shapes by defining a cluster to be a maximum set of density-connected points. DBSCAN can find the genuine clusters of different shapes as long as the evaluation of the density of the clusters can be correctly made in advance and the density of clusters is uniform. On the other hand, agglomerative hierarchical clustering techniques CURE [7] and ROCK [8] use a static model to choose the most similar clusters to merge in the hierarchical clustering. In CURE, instead of using a single centroid for representing a cluster, a certain number of representative points are selected to represent a cluster. The similarity between two clusters is measured by the similarity of the closest pair of the representative points belonging to different clusters. One major drawback of CURE is that it does not consider the homogeneity within the clusters to be merged. In ROCK, the similarity between two clusters is measured by comparing the aggregate inter-connectivity of two clusters against a user specified static inter-connectivity model. Like CURE, ROCK could fail to find the genuine clusters if the choice of parameters in the static model is incorrect with respect to the data set being clustered, or if the characteristics of clusters in the data set are not completely captured by the static model. Recently, a hierarchical clustering technique called CHAMELEON [10] is presented to discover natural clusters of different shapes and sizes. It uses k-nearest neighbor graphs to model the data sets to capture the neighborhoods of data points dynamically. The similarity between two clusters is measured based on a dynamic model. In the clustering process, two clusters are merged only if the inter-connectivity and closeness between two clusters are high relative to the internal inter-connectivity of the clusters and closeness of data points within the clusters. Although CHAMELEON can effectively find more natural clusters than previous works [6-9, 11, 12], there are rooms for looking for more effective techniques for modeling spatial data as well as cluster similarity.

In this paper, we develop a novel hierarchical clustering algorithm that uses a hypergraph to represent a set of spatial data, in which vertices represent data points and weighted hyperedges represent similarities among the data points. This hypergraph is initially constructed from the Delaunay triangulation graph of the data set and can correctly capture the relationships among sets of data points. Two phases are developed for the proposed clustering algorithm to find the clusters in the data set. During the first phase, a large number of relatively small subclusters are found to be used as the seeds for the second phase. During the second phase, a hierarchical clustering technique is first used to merge the seeds to obtain larger subclusters and then to repeatedly merge these subclusters to form the genuine clusters.

The rest of the paper is organized as follows. Section 2 gives an overview of our hierarchical clustering algorithm. Section 3 gives details on how to model the spatial data set by using hypergraph model. Section 4 presents two-phase approach in detail. Experimental results are presented in Section 5. Finally, Section 6 gives a conclusion.

2. Hierarchical Clustering Algorithm

In this section, we propose a novel hierarchical clustering algorithm for finding the densely populated regions of the space and thus grouping these regions into clusters. Figure 1 illustrates an overview of the overall approach used by the proposed clustering algorithm to find the genuine clusters in a spatial data set.

The following shows the proposed hierarchical clustering heuristic consisting of two phases.

Algorithm 1 *Two_Phase_Clustering*
begin

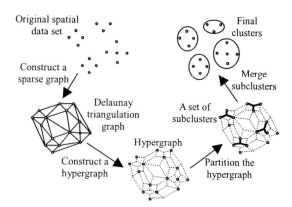

Figure 1: The proposed clustering framework.

call *Delaunay_Triangulation*(V) to obtain a Delaunay triangulation graph $G(V, E)$;
call *Hypergraph*(G) to obtain a hypergraph $G_H(V_H, E_H)$ of G;
call *Seed*(G_H) to obtain a set of seeds { S_1, S_2, ..., S_i };
set the clustering Φ = { S_1, S_2, ..., S_i };
set *highest_level* to be false;
set the initial value of *m_ratio*;
call *Hierarchical_Clustering*(G_H, Φ, *m_ratio*, *highest_level*) to obtain a genuine clusters { C_{g1}, C_{g2}, ..., C_{gk} };
return the genuine clusters { C_{g1}, C_{g2}, ..., C_{gk} };
end

In Algorithm 1, the *Delaunay_Triangulation* procedure first accepts a set of 2D spatial data V of n points as input. Of course, each data point has its corresponding 2D coordinate. The *Delaunay_ Triangulation* procedure constructs the Delaunay triangulation graph $G(V, E)$ based on the construction of Voronoi diagram of V. The graph $G(V, E)$ is a sparse graph representation of V, which allows our clustering algorithm to scale to large data sets. Furthermore, there exists available characteristics in $G(V, E)$ for extracting the similarities between data points. The *Hypergraph* procedure is subsequently applied on G to obtain a hypergraph $G_H(V_H, E_H)$, in which vertices represent data points and weighted hyperedges represent similarities among the data points. This hypergraph is used to represent the set of data and can correctly capture the relationships among sets of data points. In fact, the construction of the Delaunay triangulation graph $G(V, E)$ is crucial for the generation of a hypergraph being capable of modeling data set properly.

After generating the hypergraph G_H, two phases are developed for the proposed clustering algorithm to find the clusters in G_H. At the first phase, the *Seed* procedure is used to find a large number of relatively small subclusters { S_1, S_2, ..., S_i }. These subclusters will be used as the seeds for the second phase. At the second phase, the *hierarchical_clustering* procedure is applied to first merge the seeds to obtain larger subclusters and then to repeatedly merge those similar subclusters to form the genuine clusters { C_{g1}, C_{g2}, ..., C_{gk} } in a hierarchical fashion. In our approach, the connectivity and proximity between clusters are used as a measure of the similarity. Besides, the internal structures of the clusters themselves are also evaluated for mergence. In other words, two clusters are merged only if the connectivity and proximity between both are high relative to the internal connectivity and internal proximity within the two clusters. That is, we try to maintain the homogeneity within the clusters and the heterogeneity between clusters during the second phase.

3. Modeling the Spatial Data

In our hierarchical clustering algorithm, the graph representation of the data set is based on the hypergraph model. A hypergraph $G_H(V_H, E_H)$ is an extension of a graph in the sense that each hyperedge can connect more than two vertices. In our model, each vertex $v_{Hi} \in V_H$ represents a data point, and each hyperedge $e_{Hi} \in E_H$ corresponds to a set of related data points. A hyperedge represents a relationship (affinity) among subsets of data set and the weight of the hyperedge reflects the strength of this relationship. A key problem in modeling of data points as hypergraph is the determination of related data points that can be grouped as hyperedges and determining weights of each such hyperedge. Now a hypergraph clustering algorithm is used to find a clustering of the vertices such that the corresponding data points in each cluster are highly related and the weight of the hyperedges cut by the clustering is minimized.

Hypergraphs provide more benefits over graphs in modeling spatial data set. One of the major advantages is that the hypergraph model allows us to effectively represent important relations among data points in a sparse data structure on which computationally efficient clustering approaches can be used to find clusters of related data points. Another advantage of the hypergraph model is its ability to provide great promise for clustering data in larger dimensional space.

The relationship among the data points can be based on the concept of shared neighbors [8], the *k*-nearest neighbor [10], or a distance metric defined for pairs of data points. In our clustering algorithm, the Delaunay triangulation graph $G(V, E)$ corresponding to the set of data V is constructed to capture the relationship. Figure 2 illustrates the Voronoi Diagram and Delaunay

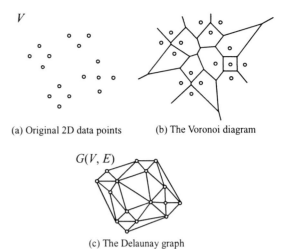

(a) Original 2D data points   (b) The Voronoi diagram

(c) The Delaunay graph

Figure 2: The Voronoi diagram and Delaunay graph from an original 2D data points.

triangulation graph of a simple data set. In fact, Delaunay triangulation graph is the straight-line dual of the Voronoi diagram and is a triangulation of the 2D data points. Each triangle contains three data points. Basically, the shape and the total length of the three edges of a triangle represent the degree of proximity among the corresponding three data points. Therefore, triangles with different configurations correspond to different relationships among their corresponding three data points.

With the Delaunay triangulation graph $G(V, E)$, each weighted hyperedge in the hypergraph $G_H(V_H, E_H)$, representing a relationship among subsets of data set, can be constructed as follows. Each hyperedge $e_{Hi} \in E_H$ connects vertices of a triangle in G and therefore, has three data points connected. However, if the total length of the three edges of a triangle is far larger than other triangles, the hyperedge corresponding to this triangle will be discarded in G_H for the consideration of relatively low relationship among the corresponding three data points. The assignment of a hyperedge weight is based on the configuration of the corresponding triangle. Thus, the weight of a hyperedge e_{Hi} is computed as

$$W(e_{Hi}) = \frac{\sum_{e \in T_{Hi}} length(e)}{\sum_{e \in T_{Hi}} (length(e))^2} \qquad (1)$$

where function $length(e)$ gives the length of edge e that belongs to the corresponding triangle T_{Hi} of e_{Hi}. The high weight value suggests that the total length of the three edges of T_{Hi} should be small and T_{Hi} should approximate equilateral triangle. In other words, if the distances between the three vertices of T_{Hi} are shorter and more uniform than those of most triangles, hyperedge e_{Hi} has larger weight to represent higher similarity between the three vertices of T_{Hi}.

There are two advantages of generating weighted hyperedges using the Delaunay triangulation graph $G(V, E)$. Firstly, data points that are far apart could be completely disconnected in the hypergraph G_H. Secondly, G captures the concept of proximity dynamically. In a dense region, the neighborhoods of data points are defined narrowly and hence the hyperedge weights tend to be large. In a sparse region, the neighborhoods of data points are defined more widely and hence the hyperedge weights tend to be small. In other words, the density of the region is recorded as the weights of the hyperedges.

4. Two-Phase Approach

Our hierarchical clustering algorithm consists of two distinct phases. The purpose of the first phase is to find a set of seeds for the second phase. Each seed contains a number of data points. The purpose of the second phase is to discover the genuine clusters in the data set by merging together subclusters in the clustering hierarchy. In the following, we present the details for these two phases of the proposed clustering algorithm.

4.1. Phase One: Finding the Seeds

In Algorithm 1, the *Seed* procedure generates the seeds (*i.e.*, initial subclusters) by using a hypergraph partitioning algorithm to divide the hypergraph G_H of the data set into a large number of partitions such that the total weight of the hyperedges that straddle partitions is minimized. Since each hyperedge in G_H represents the similarity among data points, a partitioning algorithm that minimizes the edge-cut effectively minimizes the relationship among data points across the resulting partitions.

Iterative improvement based partitioning techniques [4, 5] have been developed for fast and accurate partitioning of hypergraphs. Extensive experiments arising in VLSI application domain have been shown that iterative improvement partitioning algorithms are very effective in capturing the global structure of the hypergraph and hence are capable of finding a partitioning with a small edge-cut. In our current implementation, the cluster-movement single-level two-way partitioning algorithm MMP [4] based on the iterative improvement technique is used to partition the hypergraph into a large number of subclusters. By using MMP, a cluster can be divided into two subclusters with size constraints imposed. In other words, these two subclusters can contain different number of data points.

The *Seed* procedure generates the seeds as follows. Initially, all data points form a single cluster. The procedure then repeatedly selects the largest subcluster among the current set of subclusters and applies MMP for bipartitioning. Note that in each bipartitioning process, the maximum tolerable size ratio of the two obtained subclusters is fixed and is set to 0.2 in current implementation. This process terminates when the number of data points in the largest subcluster is fewer then a specified value *seed_size*, which sets a threshold to bound the size of each seed formed in G_H. In general, the values of *seed_size* should be different for different data sets. Consequently, *seed_size* is set to a fixed ratio of the total number of data points in our clustering algorithm.

4.2. Phase Two: Hierarchical Clustering

Once the fine-grain clustering solution is obtained by the *Seed* procedure, Algorithm 1 goes to an agglomerative hierarchical clustering that merges together these small subclusters by finding the pairs of subclusters that are the most similar.

Algorithm 2 *Hierarchical_Clustering*(G_H, Φ, *m_ratio*, *highest_level*)
Begin
  if (*highest_level* = true) **then** return the clustering Φ ;
  else
    begin
      call *Bottom_Up_Clustering*(G_H, Φ, *m_ratio*, *highest_level*) to obtain a set of subclusters { C_1', C_2', ..., C_j' };
      set $\Phi = \{ C_1', C_2', ..., C_j' \}$;
      scale the value of *m_ratio*;
      call *Hierarchical_Clustering*(G_H, Φ, *m_ratio*, *highest_level*) to obtain a set of clusters $\Phi = \{ C_{g1}, C_{g2}, ..., C_{gk} \}$;
      return the clustering Φ ;
    end
end

Algorithm 3 *Bottom_Up_Clustering*(G_H, Φ, *m_ratio*, *highest_level*)
begin
  $i = 1$;
  while ($i <=$ total number of subclusters) **do**
    begin
      find a subcluster C_j having connections with C_i that maximizes *similarity*(C_i, C_j);
      if ((such a C_j exists) and (*similarity*(C_i, C_j) > specified threshold)) **then**
        record the pair of subclusters C_i and C_j and the

value of *similarity*(C_i, C_j) for C_i;
$i = i + 1$;
end
create a sorted list L to save obtained pairs of subclusters in nonincreasing order of similarity;
total number of merged subclusters *m_total* is set to zero;
$i = 1$;
while ((m_total / total number of subclusters) < m_ratio) and (L is not empty)) **do**
   begin
      select the pair of subclusters with largest similarity from L to form a new cluster C_i' and then remove this pair of subclusters from L;
      $m\_total = m\_total + 2$;
      $i = i + 1$;
   end
if ($m\_total = 0$) **then**
   begin
      set *highest_level* to be true;
      return *highest_level* and the original clustering { C_1, C_2, ..., C_i };
   end
else return *highest_level* and new obtained clustering { C_1', C_2', ..., C_j' };
end

The *Hierarchical_Clustering* procedure described in Algorithm 2 generates the genuine clusters as follows. In fact, bottom-up clustering process described in Algorithm 3 is used to merge most similar subclusters at each level of the clustering hierarchy. To solve the clustering problem efficiently, only subclusters having connections are considered to merge. Therefore, for a given subcluster C_i, the algorithm first identifies all subclusters having connections with C_i and then finds a subcluster C_j from them that maximizes *similarity*(C_i, C_j) (defined below). If such a C_j exists and the computed value of *similarity*(C_i, C_j) is larger than a specified threshold, record the value of *similarity*(C_i, C_j) for C_i. The above process is applied to all subclusters in the same level of the clustering hierarchy. Once every subcluster has been given the opportunity to merge with one of its adjacent subclusters, we then begin to merge pairs of subclusters with larger similarity. The entire process is repeated from the lower level to the higher level until no satisfied subclusters can be found to merge. The similarity between C_i and C_j can be evaluated by the following equation:

$$similarity(C_i, C_j) = connectivity(C_i, C_j)^\alpha \times$$
$$proximity(C_i, C_j)^\beta \qquad (2)$$

where

$$connectivity(C_i, C_j) = \frac{\sum_{\substack{e_{Hi} \in \{e_H| \\ e_H \cap C_i \neq \varnothing, \\ e_H \cap C_j \neq \varnothing\}}} W(e_{Hi})}{MIN\left[\sum_{\substack{e_{Hi} \in \{e_H| \\ e_H \cap C_i \neq \varnothing\}}} W(e_{Hi}), \sum_{\substack{e_{Hi} \in \{e_H| \\ e_H \cap C_j \neq \varnothing\}}} W(e_{Hi})\right]} \times$$

$$\frac{1}{\sum_{\substack{e_{Hi} \in \{e_H| \\ e_H \cap C_{i1} \neq \varnothing, \\ e_H \cap C_{i2} \neq \varnothing\}}} W(e_{Hi}) + \sum_{\substack{e_{Hi} \in \{e_H| \\ e_H \cap C_{j1} \neq \varnothing, \\ e_H \cap C_{j2} \neq \varnothing\}}} W(e_{Hi})} \qquad (3)$$

and

$$proximity(C_i, C_j) = \frac{\sum_{\substack{e_{Hi} \in \{e_H| \\ e_H \cap C_i \neq \varnothing, \\ e_H \cap C_j \neq \varnothing\}}} \frac{W(e_{Hi})}{N_{C_i, C_j}}}{\sum_{\substack{e_{Hi} \in \{e_H| \\ e_H \cap C_{i1} \neq \varnothing, \\ e_H \cap C_{i2} \neq \varnothing\}}} \frac{W(e_{Hi})}{N_{C_{i1}, C_{i2}}} + \sum_{\substack{e_{Hi} \in \{e_H| \\ e_H \cap C_{j1} \neq \varnothing, \\ e_H \cap C_{j2} \neq \varnothing\}}} \frac{W(e_{Hi})}{N_{C_{j1}, C_{j2}}}} \qquad (4)$$

In Equation 2, α and β are user specified parameters and the similarity between C_i and C_j is a function of the connectivity and proximity between them. If $\alpha > \beta$, a higher emphasis is given to the connectivity. And if $\alpha < \beta$, a higher emphasis is given to the proximity. The first term in Equation 3 is a measure of the relative connection strength between C_i and C_j. In the numerator of the first term, the summation represents the total contributed weight of the hyperedges connecting C_i and C_j, and in the denominator, the minimum of the total contributed weight of the hyperedges connecting C_i and the total contributed weight of the hyperedges connecting C_j is considered. The second term in Equation 3 is devised to encourage merging subclusters that have relative lower intra-connectivities. The intra-connectivity of a subcluster C_i can be evaluated by dividing C_i into two roughly equal parts C_{i1} and C_{i2} and computing the weighted sum of hyperedges connecting two parts. Here, the MMP bipartitioner [4] has made it possible to find the intra-connectivity of a subcluster quite efficiently.

In Equation 4, the relative proximity between C_i and C_j is measured as the ratio of the proximity between C_i

and C_j and the sum of the intra-proximities of subclusters C_i and C_j, *i.e.*, the ratio of the average weight of the hyperedges connecting C_i and C_j and the average weights of the hyperedges connecting two parts C_{i1} and C_{i2} of C_i and two parts C_{j1} and C_{j2} of C_j. Again, MMP is applied to partition subclusters C_i and C_j for the evaluation of their intra-proximities. Note that, in Equation 4, $N_{C_i C_j}$ denotes the number of hyperedges connecting C_i and C_j. In the experiments, Equation 2 gives a good measurement of similarity between two subclusters of different shapes, densities, sizes, and noise.

In Algorithms 2 and 3, *m_ratio* denotes a merging ratio parameter specifying the fraction of subclusters to be merged in each level of the bottom-up clustering process. The merging methods in [2] find maximal matchings, which generally force *m_ratio* to be 1. However, maximal matching can result in quick clustering process (*i.e.*, result in too few levels of clustering hierarchy) and hence prevent reaching an optimal clustering result. To effectively control the speed of clustering, in each hierarchy level, the bottom-up merging process stops when a certain fraction of subclusters has been merged. In our current implementation, the values of *m_ratio* are set to be large at the beginning to allow more subclusters to be merged first, and will be gradually decreased in the following levels to prevent result in a local optimal solution.

5. Experimental Results

We first applied the proposed hierarchical clustering algorithm to five 2D data sets as shown in Fig. 3. These five data sets, containing 6000 to 10000 2D data points, have clusters of different shapes, densities, sizes, and noise. In the experiments, same parameter values are used for all five data sets. We set *m_ratio* = 0.95 to specify 95% of subclusters to be merged in the lowest level of the bottom-up clustering process, and subsequently, the value of *m_ratio* is scaled down by a ratio of 0.9 in the following levels. On the other hand, the parameters α and β in Equation 2 are set to be 1.5 and 2.5, respectively, to give higher emphasis on the proximity.

Figure 4 shows the clusters found by our hierarchical clustering algorithm for each one of the five data sets. The data points in different clusters are represented using different colors. Note that the proposed algorithm is capable of identifying the genuine clusters in all data sets. In the case of DS1, five clusters have been found, each of which corresponds to a genuine cluster in DS1. In particular, the data points connecting the two ellipsoids are combined into the left ellipsoid. Of course, these data points could be combined into the right ellipsoid if the

sequences of merging subclusters in the early levels of clustering hierarchy are adjusted. In the case of DS2, two clusters have been found. In the case of DS3, eleven clusters have been found and six of which correspond to the genuine clusters in DS3, and the rest five clusters contain outlier points and noise. Note that in DS3, since each genuine cluster has parts of its data points strongly connected with clusters containing outlier points and noise, it is difficult to completely distinguish data points between genuine clusters and nongenuine clusters without knowing the characteristics of data set in advance. In the case of DS4, eleven clusters have been found and nine of which correspond to the genuine clusters in DS4. The found 'C' shaped cluster contains some outlier data points because these outlier points have strong connections with data points of genuine cluster. This situation occurs in many regions in DS4. In the clustering solutions of DS3 and DS4, there exist many nongenuine clusters. The reason for this is that a relative large number of outlier points and noise are located in the neighborhood and hence the clustering algorithm can not determine whether the cluster is a genuine cluster or not. Finally, in the case of DS5, eight clusters have been found and each of which corresponds to a genuine cluster. From the experimental results, our hierarchical clustering algorithm demonstrates its effectiveness on finding 2D clusters of arbitrary size, shape, and density, and its capability on tolerating outlier data points and noise. Figures 5 and 6 illustrate the results of CURE and CHAMELEON for comparison. Our clustering algorithm outperforms CURE which can fail to find the genuine clusters in the data sets. On the other hand, our clustering algorithm is competitive with CHAMELEON which have generated better results than many recent state-of-the-art spatial data clustering algorithms.

Besides clustering 2D data sets, we have extended our algorithm to deal with 3D data sets. Figure 7 shows a 3D test data set containing 20000 3D data points. In this case, five 3D clusters have been found and each of which corresponds to a genuine cluster in the original data set. In the experiment, the 3D data points are also modeled as a hypergraph where each weighted hyperedge is constructed from the generalized Voronoi diagram and Delaunay graph.

6. Conclusion

In this paper, we have presented a novel hierarchical clustering algorithm which finds the densely populated regions of the space and groups these regions into clusters such that the intracluster similarity is maximized and the intercluster similarity is minimized. The clustering algorithm uses a hypergraph to represent a set of spatial data. This hypergraph is initially constructed from the Delaunay triangulation graph of the data set and can correctly capture the relationships among sets of data points. The measurement of the similarity between two clusters is based on the connectivity and proximity among corresponding data points, and it has been well-defined in our clustering algorithm. Experimental results obtained indicate that our hierarchical clustering algorithm can discover natural spatial clusters of different sizes, shapes, densities, and noise.

References

[1] C. Berge, Graphs and Hypergraphs, American Elsevier, 1976.

[2] T. Bui, C. Heigham, C. Jones, and T. Leighton, "Improving the performance of the Kernighan-Lin and simulated annealing graph bisection algorithms," in *Proc. ACM/IEEE Design Automation Conf.*, pp. 775-778, 1989.

[3] M. S. Chen, J. Han, and P. S. Yu, "Data mining: An overview from database perspective," *IEEE Trans. on Knowledge and Data Eng.*, Vol. 8, No. 6, pp. 866-883, Dec. 1996.

[4] J. S. Cherng, S. J. Chen, and J. M. Ho, "Efficient bipartitioning algorithm for size-constrained circuits," in *Proc. IEE Computers and Digital Techniques*, Vol. 145, No. 1, pp. 37-45, Jan. 1998.

[5] S. Dutt and W. Geng, "VLSI circuit partitioning by cluster-removal using iterative improvement techniques," in *Proc. IEEE Int. Conf. Computer-Aided Design*, pp. 194-200, 1996.

[6] M. Ester, H. P. Kriegel, J. Sander, and X. Xu, "A density-based algorithm for discovering clusters in large spatial databases with noise," in *Proc. of the Second Int'l Conference on Knowledge Discovery and Data Mining*, Portland, OR, 1996.

[7] S. Guha, R. Rastogi, and K. Shim, "CURE: An efficient clustering algorithm for large databases," in *Proc. of 1998 ACM-SIGMOD Int. Conf. on Management of Data*, 1998.

[8] S. Guha, R. Rastogi, and K. Shim, " ROCK: A robust clustering algorithm for categorical attributes," in *Proc. of the 15th Int'l Conf. on Data Eng.*, 1999.

[9] A. K. Jain and R. C. Dubes, Algorithms for clustering data, Prentice Hall, 1988.

[10] G. Karypis, E. H. Han, and V. Kumar, "Chameleon: Hierarchical clustering using dynamic modeling," *IEEE Computer*, Vol. 32, No. 8, pp. 68-75, Aug. 1999.

[11] L. Kaufman and P. J. Rousseeuw, Finding groups in data: An introduction to cluster analysis, John Wiley & Sons, 1990.

[12] R. Ng and J. Han, "Efficient and effective clustering method for spatial data mining," in *Proc. of the 20th VLDB Conference*, pp. 144-155, Snatiago, Chile, 1994.

[13] F. P. Preparata and M. Shamos, Computational geometry an introduction, Texts and Monographs in Computer Science.

[14] M. Stonebraker, R. Agrawal, U. Dayal, E. J. Neuhold, and A. Reuter, "DBMS research at a crossroads: The vienna update, in *Proc. of the 19th VLDB Conference*, pp. 688-692, Dublin, Ireland, 1993.

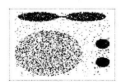

DS1: 8000 data points

DS2: 6000 data points

DS3: 8000 data points

DS4: 10000 data points

DS5: 8000 data points

Figure 3: The five 2D test data sets.

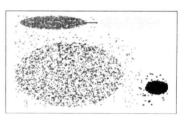
DS1 (5 clusters)

DS2 (2 clusters)

DS3 (11 clusters)

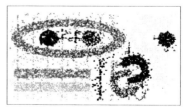
DS4 (11 clusters)

DS5 (8 clusters)

Figure 4: The clustering solutions of proposed algorithm for the five 2D data sets.

DS3 (10 clusters)

DS4 (9 clusters)

DS5 (8 clusters)

Figure 5: The clustering solutions of CURE for data sets DS3, DS4, and DS5.

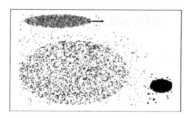

DS1 (6 clusters)

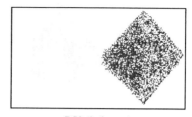

DS2 (2 clusters)

DS3 (11 clusters)

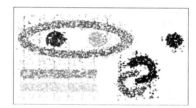

DS4 (11 clusters)

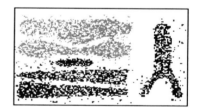

DS5 (8 clusters)

Figure 6: The clustering solutions of CHAMELEON for the five 2D data sets.

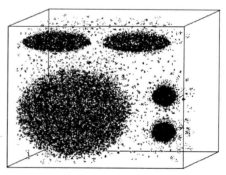

20000 data points

Figure 7: The 3D test data set.

Efficient Determination of Dynamic Split Points in a Decision Tree

David Maxwell Chickering
Microsoft Research
Redmond WA, 98052-6399
dmax@microsoft.com

Christopher Meek
Microsoft Research
Redmond WA, 98052-6399
meek@microsoft.com

Robert Rounthwaite
Microsoft Research
Redmond WA, 98052-6399
robertro@microsoft.com

Abstract

We consider the problem of choosing split points for continuous predictor variables in a decision tree. Previous approaches to this problem typically either (1) discretize the continuous predictor values prior to learning or (2) apply a dynamic method that considers all possible split points for each potential split. In this paper, we describe a number of alternative approaches that generate a small number of candidate split points dynamically with little overhead. We argue that these approaches are preferable to pre-discretization, and provide experimental evidence that they yield probabilistic decision trees with the same prediction accuracy as the traditional dynamic approach. Furthermore, because the time to grow a decision tree is proportional to the number of split points evaluated, our approach is significantly faster than the traditional dynamic approach.

1 Introduction

Decision trees have proven to be useful tools for both solving classification tasks and for modeling conditional probability distributions. The literature is rich with studies of various decision-tree learning systems. Examples of such systems include CLS (Hunt, Marin and Stone [8]), CART (Breiman, Friedman and Olshen [1]), ID3 (Quinlan [11]), C4.5 (Quinlan [10]) and SLIQ (Mehta, Agrawal and Risanen [9]) to name just a few.

When a *predictor* variable (that is, a variable that is included as a decision in the tree) is continuous, the learning algorithm (conceptually) converts the values of that variable into two or more discrete bins. For example, a node in a decision tree may test whether or not the value of a continuous predictor is greater than some threshold; defining the threshold effectively converts the continuous variable into a binary one.

Methods for discretizing continuous predictor variables can generally be classified as either *static* or *dynamic*. Static discretization methods discretize all of the continuous predictors before the decision tree is learned, and the same "buckets" that result are used throughout the tree. Dynamic discretization methods, on the other hand, determine the discretization dynamically as the decision tree is being constructed. Thus, the threshold(s) used in one part of the tree for a particular continuous variable can be different from those used in another part of the tree.

Dougherty, Kohavi, and Sahami [5] examine the relative performance of various discretization techniques when learning both naive-Bayes models and decision trees.[1] Rather surprising, they show that the performance of C4.5 across a number of datasets did not degrade significantly when a particular static discretization algorithm was used instead of the usual dynamic discretization algorithm of C4.5.

Although we have not performed a formal study similar to Dougherty et al. [5], we have found that in the domains we work with, dynamic discretization is, in fact, noticeably superior to static discretization. This discrepancy can perhaps be explained because we usually both learn and use decision trees for the purpose of *prediction*, whereas the algorithms mentioned above learn and use decision trees for the purpose of *classification*. The distinction is that for prediction, the goal of the learning algorithm is to identify the correct conditional probability distribution of the target variable, whereas the goal of classification is to identify the correct label of the target variable. As described by (e.g) Cowell [4] in the context of Bayesian networks, models that result from optimizing these two criteria may be very different.

A second reason to prefer dynamic discretization is that the discretization itself can be interesting to a data analyst. For example, suppose we learn a decision tree for predicting whether or not a customer will buy a certain product, based on known attributes for that customer. It could be interesting that a good discretization of salary for males is different than a good discretization for females, and that by exam-

---

[1]Daugherty et al. [5] use the terms "global" and "local" to refer to static and dynamic, respectively.

ining that difference the analyst might gain insight into the domain.

The traditional dynamic approach to discretization is to allow splits on arbitrary values of predictor variables. In practice, because tree growing is directed by a scoring criterion, algorithms typically only consider predictor values that yield different scores. For example, algorithms often use values that actually occur in the data, or midpoints between pairs of consecutive values that actually occur in the data. To identify these potential split points efficiently, algorithms typically consider predictor values in sorted order. There are two standard methods: (1) for each leaf under consideration for a split, re-sort the data that "drops down" to that leaf by the values for each continuous predictor, or (2) maintain a sorted list of record pointers for each continuous predictor, and propagate the appropriate portions of the list to the children when a split is applied. Method (1) requires numerous expensive sorts that can significantly slow down the algorithm, particularly as the data grows large. Method (2) requires space that scales with the product of the number of records in the data and the number of continuous predictors. Furthermore, the initial sorts of the data may require a prohibitive amount of time.

In this paper, we present a number of simple methods for performing dynamic discretization. As opposed to the traditional approaches, these methods efficiently identify only a small number of potential split points for each continuous predictor variable. Unlike the traditional approach—where the number of split points depends on the number of values in the data, and where sorting contributes super-linear overhead in either time or space—our methods scale linearly in both the number of continuous predictor variables and the size of the data. Two of our methods generate split points using simple summary statistics from the data; these statistics can be gathered in time that is linear in the size of the relevant data. The third method generates split points by dividing the predictor values into k-tiles, which for a constant number of split points can be accomplished in time that grows linearly with both the size of the relevant data and the number of continuous predictors. In Section 2, we introduce notation and provide details on the standard methods for dynamic discretization.

The paper is organized as follows. In Section 3, we describe our methods and discuss their time and space complexity. In Section 4, we provide experimental evidence that some of the proposed methods work as well as the standard methods when trees are evaluated using the prediction accuracy (i.e. the log-likelihood of a holdout set). Finally, in Section 5, we conclude with a discussion of future work.

2   Background and Notation

In this section, we provide background information about decision trees and present our notation.

A probabilistic decision tree T is a structure used to encode a conditional probability distribution of a target variable Y, given a set of predictor variables $\{X_1, ..., X_n\}$. The structure is a tree, where each internal node I stores a mapping from the values of a predictor variable X_j to the children of I in the tree. Each leaf node L in the tree stores a conditional probability distribution for Y given some subset of the values of the predictor values.

For a given set of predictor values $\{x_1, ..., x_n\}$, we obtain the probability $p(Y|X_1 = x_1, ..., X_n = x_n)$ by starting at the root of T and using the internal-node mappings to traverse down the tree to a leaf node. We refer to the mappings in the internal nodes as *splits*. When an internal node I maps values of the predictor variable X_j to its children nodes, we say that X_j is the *predictor* variable of node I, and that I *is a split on* X_j.

For example, Figure 1 shows a decision tree for a probability distribution $p(Y|X_1, X_2, X_3)$. In the Figure, X_1 and X_3 are continuous predictor variables defined on the real line, and Y and X_2 are binary (with values 1 and 2). Assume that we would like to traverse the decision tree to extract the probability $p(Y|X_1 = 12.3, X_2 = 2, X_3 = 2.4)$. We start at the root node, and see that this node is a split on X_2. Because $X_2 = 2$ in the conditioning set of our probabilistic query, the traversal moves next to the right child of the root. This node is a split on X_1, which equals 12.3 in the query, so we move next to the left child. Finally, because $X_3 = 2.4$ (and consequently greater than zero), we finish the traversal by moving to the right child which is a leaf node. The conditional probability is stored in the leaf, and we conclude that $p(Y = 1|X_1 = 12.3, X_2 = 2, X_3 = 2.4) = 0.2$ and $p(Y = 2|X_1 = 12.3, X_2 = 2, X_3 = 2.4) = 0.8$.

Algorithms for learning decision trees from data typically try to maximize a scoring criterion by repeatedly replacing leaf nodes by internal splits. The majority of the classification-tree learning algorithms greedily replace each leaf node with the split that yields the highest entropy in the data. After this initial "growing phase", the tree is then pruned back by greedily eliminating leaves using (e.g.) a holdout score on a test data set.

In the experiments presented in Section 4, we instead apply the greedy growing phase using a Bayesian scoring criterion described in detail by Chickering, Heckerman and Meek [2]. This criterion avoids over-fitting by (both explicitly and implicitly) penalizing model complexity, and consequently no pruning phase is needed.

For almost all scoring criteria, including entropy and the Bayesian criterion we use, the score for replacing a leaf

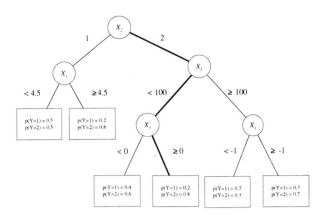

Figure 1. Example decision tree for the distribution $p(Y|X_1, X_2, X_3)$

node L by a split is a function of the subset of the training dataset that is said to be *relevant* to L: For any record in a training dataset, the case is "dropped down" the tree by traversing the tree the same way as was accomplished in the example above, using the values of the variables in the record. For every case that ends up at leaf node L, the case is said to be relevant to L.

For discrete-valued predictors, a typical candidate split considered by the learning algorithm is a binary split, where one child corresponds to exactly one of the discrete states, and the other child corresponds to all other states. Another type of discrete split is a complete split, where there is exactly one child corresponding to every value of the discrete predictor. The most general type of split maps subsets of the predictor's values to different children.

For continuous variables, the children of split nodes correspond to intervals of the predictor variable. In principle, for a given number of children (two in the example above), there are an infinite number of possible intervals that a split could define due to the fact that the interval boundaries are continuous. In the tree shown in Figure 1, for example, the left child node of the split on X_1 could correspond to $< c$ and the right child could correspond to $\geq c$, for any threshold c in the continuous range of predictor variable X_1. The number of interval-defining thresholds that can be distinguished by most scoring criteria, however, is limited by the number of examples in the training data that are relevant to the given leaf. Furthermore, Fayyad and Irani [6] prove that, for the entropy scoring criterion on a discrete target variable, only a restricted set of thresholds can ever achieve the maximum score, and consequently only this set need be considered when using a greedy search. As a result, split points are typically chosen as the midpoint between successive predictor values in the training data or as a specific predictor value in the training data.

For simplicity, we consider only *binary* splits on continuous predictors so we can concentrate our discussion on the problem of identifying a single split point (i.e. threshold). We note, however, that all of the methods for choosing a good split point can be used directly to choose multiple split points (see, e.g. Fayyad and Irani [6], for a discussion of methods for choosing multiple split points).

The standard method for choosing candidate split points for a split on leaf node L is as follows. For each continuous predictor X_i, we visit all of the records relevant to L *in sorted X_i order*, and consider for split points those values that are half-way between the X_i values in each pair of consecutive records. The optimization of Fayyad and Irani [6] allows us to avoid *scoring* all possible split points, but it still requires us to examine the records in sorted order.

There are two methods for handling the ordering requirement: (1) whenever a node N is considered for expansion, we can perform a separate sort of the data records relevant to N on each continuous predictor, or (2) we can pre-sort all of the records on each continuous predictor, retaining the sort information that can then be propagated through the tree.

Let m denote the number of records in the training data, and let m_L denote the number of these records that are relevant to node L in the decision tree. Let γ denote the number of continuous predictor variables. Method (1) requires time $O(\gamma \cdot m_L \log m_L)$ for each node L considered for splitting in the algorithm. For large γ and large datasets, this time overhead can be prohibitive. If the sort is done in-place on the data records, method (1) requires no additional space. Method (2) avoids the per-node sort, but incurs an initial $O(\gamma \cdot m \log m)$ time hit for the initial sort, and requires $O(\gamma \cdot m)$ space to retain the individual sort order for each continuous predictor. For large γ and large m, either the time overhead or space overhead (or both) may be prohibitive.

3 Some Efficient Discretization Methods

In this section, we describe three simple methods for identifying split points that have time and space complexities that grow linearly with the number of relevant records. All three methods use a common approach to discretization which we call the *quantile approach*. Using this approach, we assume a distribution over split point values at each node in the decision tree, and choose the split points such that this distribution is divided into equal-probability regions.

3.1 Gaussian Approximation

The first method, which we call the *Gaussian approximation* method, requires only that the mean and standard deviation of each continuous predictor be known for the data records relevant to each leaf node in the tree being considered for a split. These statistics can be gathered easily whenever the data is being "dropped down" to the children of a newly-formed split. For each record dropped down to leaf node L, a running sum and running sum of squares for each continuous predictor is updated within L, and when all data has reached L the mean and standard deviation are derived from these sums.

We derive the split points for each continuous predictor X_j at leaf node L as follows. First, we choose the number of split points k to consider. This choice may be made dynamically (i.e. via model selection), or as is shown to work reasonably in the following section, we can pre-define k for all predictors in all nodes before running the learning algorithm. Second, we choose the split points that yield $k+1$ equal-density regions of the domain of X_j, under the (usually bad) assumption that X_j is distributed normally in the cases relevant to L. In particular, let $\{c_1, ..., c_k\}$ denote the set of k split points. We choose c_i as

$$c_i = \mu_L + \sigma_L \cdot \Phi^{-1}\left(\frac{i}{k+1}\right)$$

where Φ^{-1} is the inverse of the cumulative distribution function of the standard Gaussian, and μ_L and σ_L are the mean and standard deviation, respectively, of the values of X_j relevant to L.

Given γ continuous predictors and m_L relevant records at leaf L, this calculation requires $O(\gamma)$ space to store the Gaussian sufficient statistics and $O(\gamma \cdot m_L + k)$ time to identify the k split points.

3.2 Uniform Approximation

The second method for computing split points is similar to the first except that we choose equal-density regions of the predictor domain under the (again, usually bad) assumption that the predictor is distributed uniformly between its minimum and maximum value. As in the Gaussian-approximation method, we can easily accumulate the necessary statistics for each predictor—which in this case are simply the minimum and maximum values—as the data is dropped down to children nodes during learning. For a continuous predictor X_j with minimum and maximum values $\min(j)$ and $\max(j)$, respectively, the uniform-approximation approach chooses, for a given k, the split points $\{c_1, ..., c_k\}$ such that:

$$c_i = \min(j) + i \cdot \frac{\max(j) - \min(j)}{k+1}$$

The space and time complexities of this approach are identical to those of the Gaussian-approximation method.

3.3 K-tile method

In our third and final method for computing split points, we choose the continuous split points using k-tiles. This corresponds to the quantile approach using the empirical distribution function. That is, for continuous predictor X_j, we choose split points $\{c_1, ..., c_k\}$ such that there are (approximately) $m_L \cdot \frac{i}{k+1}$ records with $X_j \leq c_i$ and $m_L \cdot \frac{k-i}{k+1}$ records with $X_j > c_i$.[2] For example, if $k = 1$, the method simply chooses the median value of X_j in the records relevant to L. As in the previous methods, we can pre-compute k for all nodes and all predictors.

There are well-known algorithms that identify the jth-smallest value in a list of m elements. In Section 4, we use a well-known implementation that runs in time $O(m)$ on average rather than a more complicated (but also well-known) implementation that runs in time $O(m)$ in the *worst* case. See (e.g.) Cormen, Leiserson and Rivest [3] for a description of both implementations. These algorithms operate in space that is $O(m_L)$, although the average-case $O(m_L)$ implementation can work on the original data records in-place, resulting in no additional space requirement. For small k, we can call such an algorithm k separate times for each continuous predictor, yielding a total time complexity of $O(k \cdot \gamma \cdot m_L)$ to identify all split points for all predictors at leaf L. If k is of the same order as $\log m_L$, it is probably faster to simply sort the records for each X_i. In this case, we have essentially the same algorithm that is commonly used in practice, except that we consider only k split points instead of all possible ones.

4 Experiments

In this section, we present experimental results that suggest that two of our methods of selecting split points result in trees that have better prediction accuracy than trees that are learned when considering all possible split points. In addition, our methods significantly reduce the time needed to learn trees.

We ran experiments using five real-world datasets. Our selection of datasets was influenced by the fact that for small data sets, our optimizations will not provide a significant *absolute* speedup because the standard techniques will already provide adequate performance. We chose the first three datasets because they were the largest data sets from the UC Irvine repository that were included in the study by Mehta et al. [9]. These datasets were *German*, *Hypothyroid*, and *Sick-Euthyroid* and contain 1000, 3163, and 3163 records, respectively. In terms of speed, even these largest datasets are too small to warrant using our approach; as we see below, even when we use the full-blown sorting ap-

---

[2] There may be no such split point that satisfies these conditions exactly.

94

proach, trees in these domains can be learned in less than three seconds. We include the results here simply to provide more evidence that we can achieve good prediction accuracy without considering all possible split points.

The fourth dataset, *Census*, was extracted from the United States Census Bureau. The data consists of the values for a set of 37 demographic variables for approximately 300,000 citizens. Eleven of these demographic variables are continuous. The fifth dataset, *Media Metrix*, contains demographic and internet-use data for about 5,000 people during the month of January 1997. There are 24 demographic variables in this dataset, six of which are continuous. There are 13 categorical variables that indicate the type of the web page (e.g. educational, news).

The first three (small) datasets were originally collected for the purpose of predicting a single output variable. For the German dataset, the goal is to predict whether or not a person has good credit. For Hypothyroid and Sick-Euthyroid, the goal is to predict whether or not a person has a specific medical problem. As a result, we evaluate our approaches by learning a single decision tree for the appropriate target variable in these domains.

In contrast, Census and Media Metrix are datasets collected with no such obvious prediction task; for such datasets, probabilistic decision trees are important for exploratory data analysis and density estimation (e.g. Heckerman, Chickering, Meek, Rounthwaite and Kadie, 2000). In particular, we assume that every variable in the domain is a target variable, and we learn a separate decision tree for each. As a result, these datasets effectively provide an "independent" learning problem for each variable.

To evaluate the performance of our discretization methods on a particular dataset, we first divided the dataset into a training set (consisting of a random sample of roughly 70 percent) and a test set (consisting of the remainder). For the Census dataset, we further sub-sampled the training set so that our trees were learned using roughly 20,000 records. Next, we ran a series of trials to evaluate predictive accuracy, relative to the traditional sorting method, as a function of the number of split points k. In particular, for the ith trial, we (1) set $k = 2^i - 1$, (2) learned a decision tree for each target variable in the domain, and (3) evaluated the average relative increase in predictive accuracy that resulted from using k split points over sorting the data and using all possible split points.

To measure the predictive accuracy of a tree built to predict Y_j, we took the average log probability or log density that the tree assigned to the given value y_j in each test case. The average relative increase in predictive accuracy for a particular dynamic split algorithm was computed as follows. Let s_j denote the predictive accuracy of tree j using the traditional sorting method, and let $a_j(k)$ denote the predictive accuracy of the jth tree using the given method with

k split points. The relative increase in predictive accuracy for tree j, $r_j(k)$ is defined as

$$r_j(k) = \frac{a_j(k) - s_j}{|s_j|}$$

For a discrete target variable Y_j, r_j is simply the relative increase in the average number of bits needed to encode an observation of Y_j.

The average increases reported in the figures for Census and Media Metrix below are the simple average of $r_j(k)$ for those trees that had a continuous split using at least one method. For the Census data, there were 31 such trees, and for the Media Metrix data, there were 16 such trees.

As mentioned in Section 1, we used a greedy learning algorithm in conjunction with a Bayesian scoring criterion. We grew trees using binary splits only. For discrete predictors, we used the method where the first child corresponds to one state and the second child corresponds to all others.

For discrete target variables, we learned multinomial distributions in the leaf nodes, and used a flat Dirichlet parameter prior. For continuous target variables, we chose either a Gaussian distribution or a log-Gaussian distribution ahead of time for all leaves of the tree; the choice was made based on which distribution had a better maximum-likelihood fit on the marginal. If we chose a log-Gaussian distribution, we implemented the learning algorithm by simply taking the log of the target variable in each case. Next, we standardized the (possibly logged) data so that the target had mean zero and standard deviation one. We learned Gaussian distributions in the leaf nodes for the standardized values, using a Normal-Wishart parameter prior that had a prior mean of zero (equivalent sample size one) and a prior precision of one (equivalent sample size two). After learning these Gaussian distributions, we transformed the parameters to correspond to the original data space. We used a structure prior of the form κ^f, where f is the number of free parameters of the tree structure. For the three small datasets and for Census, we used $\kappa = 0.1$, and for Media Metrix, we used $\kappa = 0.01$; these values have proven to work well in previous (unrelated) experiments in these domains. We also used the non-Bayesian rule that a split is never applied if one of the resulting leaves has less than 10 relevant records.

Figure 2 shows the results of our experiments for all of the datasets. For the three small datasets, each point corresponds to a single learning instance. For the Census dataset results in Figure 2(d), each point is an average across the 31 trees for which at least one method resulted in a split on a continuous variable. Similarly, for the Media Metrix dataset results in Figure 2(e), each point is an average across the 16 trees for which at least one method resulted in a split on a continuous variable. In all five plots, the zero axis corresponds to a zero increase in predictive accuracy. In other words, this line corresponds to performance that is equiva-

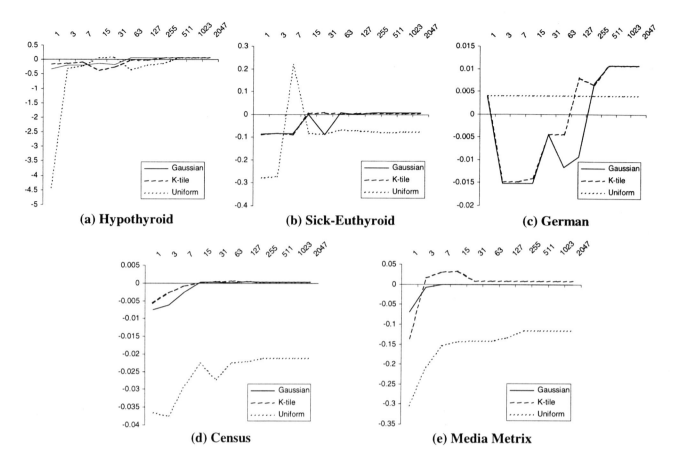

Figure 2. Relative increase in predictive accuracy (y-axis) for all of the data sets as a function of the number of split points k (x-axis) for the three proposed methods.

lent to the method of sorting and scoring all predictor values. As k grows large, all three of the methods should converge to something very close to this line because, at some point, every split point considered by the sorting method will be available for consideration by the other algorithms. It is possible, however, for the asymptotic performance of the Gaussian- and uniform-approximation methods to converge to some non-zero value; because the performance is measured on a test set, arbitrary choices of split points that have identical scoring criterion values for the training set may result in different prediction accuracy on the test set. As the size of the training data grows large, we expect such differences to be minimal. Note that the k-tile method, implemented using midpoints instead of endpoints as described, will be equivalent to the sorting method as soon as k is equal to one less than the number of cases for the given leaf.

For the small datasets Hypothyroid and Sick Euthyroid, the Gaussian-approximation and the k-tile method both worked as well as the full sort method using only a few split points. Although in the German data set the relative predic-

tion accuracy appears not to be very monotonic in k, note that none of the approximations are ever less that a percent and a half worse than the full sort method. We believe the variance in the accuracies in the German domain are a result of the small sample size.

In none of the small datasets did the full sort method take longer than three seconds to construct the tree. Although the approximation techniques are faster, it does not make sense to adopt an approximation technique to speed up an algorithm that is already extremely fast.

We now turn our attention to the results for the Census dataset and the Media Metrix dataset. Both the Gaussian-approximation method and the k-tile method worked as well as the full-blown sorting method using only a few split points. In particular, we see that in both domains, these methods attain or surpass the sorting approach using only 15 split points.

In Figure 3 and Figure 4, we show the running times for all algorithms as a function of the number of split points, for Census and Media Metrix, respectively. Note that both axes are on a logarithmic scale in both figures. The time to learn in these domains grows roughly linearly in k (for $k > 511$), and the three approximation approaches all take about the same time. We expect that in domains with more continuous variables, the k-tile approach, although still linear in k, will prove to take longer in practice.

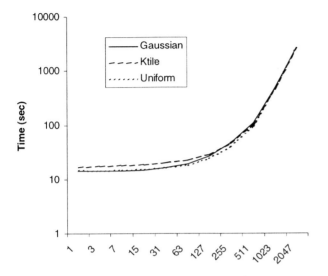

Figure 3. Time in seconds to learn all trees in the Census domain as a function of the number of split points k for the three proposed methods.

Although the k-tile method seems to be the best for Media Metrix and small k, the Gaussian approach works almost as well on the Media Metrix trees and just as well (for $k \geq 15$) on the census trees. The results also show that the uniform-approximation approach does not work well in these domains.

In Figure 5, we show the relative accuracy, using 15 split points, for each of the 31 trees in the Census domain that had at least one split using one of the three methods. Similarly, in Figure 6, we show the relative accuracy, using 15 split points, for each of the 16 trees in the Media Metrix domain that had at least one split using one of the three methods.

5 Conclusions and Future Work

We have presented three methods that dynamically determine split points for continuous predictor variables in a decision tree. We have given experimental evidence that the predictive accuracy of the trees that result from using two of them—namely, the Gaussian-approximation method and the k-tile method—are competitive with the standard approach of scoring all possible split points, while using only 15 split points.

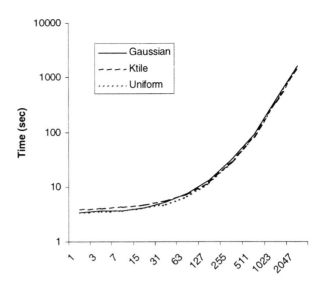

Figure 4. Time in seconds to learn all trees in the Media Metrix domain as a function of the number of split points k for the three proposed methods.

The predictive-accuracy plots that we presented in the previous section show the gain, as a function of the number of split points, that we get if we commit to the number of split points prior to running the learning algorithm. Alternatively, we could incorporate a model-selection step in the learning algorithm that decides (dynamically) how many split points to use at each split in the decision tree. We expect some modest gains in accuracy and potentially some gain in running time were we to implement such an approach.

As mentioned in Section 3, all three of our split-point selection methods can be viewed as identifying quantiles in predictor-variable distributions. It might be interesting to investigate and evaluate alternative, computationally tractable distributions. Additionally, we could try randomly sampling potential split points from predictor-variable distributions.

Finally, we point out that in many data sets, the majority of the time that the learning algorithm spends growing a decision tree is spent scoring candidate splits. If this is the case, then our methods can save time not only by spending less computation *identifying* split points to score, but by spending less time scoring splits by virtue of the fact that so few split points are needed for good accuracy.

Acknowledgments

The Media Metrix dataset for this paper was generously provided by Media Metrix. We thank the anonymous re-

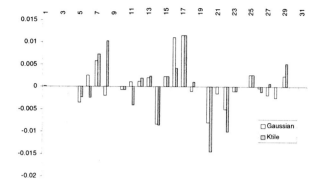

Figure 5. Relative increase in predictive accuracy, corresponding to a fixed $k = 15$, for the 31 trees in the Census data for which at least one methods resulted with a split on a continuous variable.

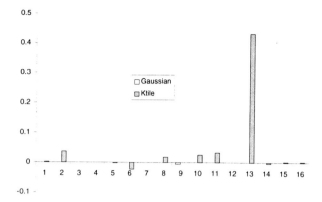

Figure 6. Relative increase in predictive accuracy, corresponding to a fixed $k = 15$, for the 16 trees in the Media Metrix data for which at least one methods resulted with a split on a continuous variable.

viewers for useful comments.

References

[1] L. Breiman, J. Friedman, R. Olshen, and C. Stone. *Classification and Regression Trees.* Wadsworth & Brooks, Monterey, CA, 1984.

[2] D. Chickering, D. Heckerman, and C. Meek. A Bayesian approach to learning Bayesian networks with local structure. In *Proceedings of Thirteenth Conference on Uncertainty in Artificial Intelligence,* Providence, RI, pages 80–89. Morgan Kaufmann, August 1997.

[3] T. H. Cormen, C. E. Leiserson, and R. L. Rivest. *Introduction to Algorithms.* The MIT press, 1990.

[4] R. G. Cowell. On searching for optimal classifiers among Bayesian networks. In *Proceedings of the Eighth International Workshop on Artificial Intelligence and Statistics,* pages 175–180, January 2001.

[5] J. Dougherty, R. Kohavi, and M. Sahami. Supervised and unsupervised discretization of continuous features. In A. Prieditis and S. Russell, editors, *Proceedings of the Twelfth International Conference on Machine Learning,* pages 194–202. Morgan Kaufman, 1995.

[6] U. M. Fayyad and K. B. Irani. Multi-interval discretization of continuous-valued attributes for classification learning. In *Proceedings of the 13th International Joint Conference on Artificial Intelligence,* pages 1022–1029. Morgan Kaufmann, 1993.

[7] D. Heckerman, D. M. Chickering, C. Meek, R. Rounthwaite, and C. Kadie. Dependency networks for inference, collaborative filtering, and data visualization. *Journal of Machine Learning Research,* 1:49–75, October 2000.

[8] E. B. Hunt, J. Marin, and P. T. Stone. *Experiments in Induction.* Academic Press, New York, NY, 1966.

[9] M. Mehta, R. Agrawal, and J. Rissanen. SLIQ: A fast scalable classier for data mining. In *Proceedings of the Fifth International Conference on Extending Database Technology,* pages 18–32, March 1995.

[10] J. Quinlan. Programs for machine learning, 1993.

[11] J. R. Quinlan. Induction of decision trees. *Machine Learning,* 1:81–106, 1986.

Efficient Yet Accurate Clustering

Manoranjan Dash   Kian Lee Tan
School of Computing
National University of Singapore
{manoranj,tankl}@comp.nus.edu.sg

Huan Liu
Dept of Computer Sci. & Engg.
Arizona State University
hliu@asu.edu

Abstract

In this paper we show that most hierarchical agglomerative clustering (HAC) algorithms follow a 90-10 rule where roughly 90% iterations from the beginning merge cluster pairs with dissimilarity less than 10% of the maximum dissimilarity. We propose two algorithms – 2-phase and nested – based on partially overlapping partitioning (POP). To handle high-dimensional data efficiently, we propose a tree structure particularly suitable for POP. Extensive experiments show that the proposed algorithms reduce the time and memory requirement of existing HAC algorithms significantly without compromising in accuracy.

1. Introduction

Clustering is the process of grouping similar objects into clusters or classes. It is an important data exploration task used in diversified areas such as market segmentation in business, gene categorization in biology, spatial discovery, document classification on the WWW for information discovery. In data mining, it can be used as a stand-alone tool to gain insight into the distribution of data, or alternatively it can be used as a preprocessing step for other data mining tasks such as classification. In a recent KDNuggets poll clustering was voted as the most frequent data mining task.

A prominent type of clustering algorithm is hierarchical clustering. It outputs a *dendrogram* that shows a hierarchy of agglomerations or divisions. Hierarchical algorithms can be agglomerative or divisive. Hierarchical agglomerative clustering (HAC) starts with each point in a separate cluster and iteratively merges the closest pair of clusters until there remains only one cluster. The divisive type is the reverse of HAC. Computation needed in an HAC algorithm to go from one level to another is usually simpler than a divisive algorithm [11]. In this paper we will focus on HAC. HAC algorithms are non parametric - assume little about data, natural and simple in grouping objects, and capable of finding clusters of different shapes, such as spherical and

arbitrary, just by changing the similarity measure. However, their time and memory complexities are deterrents in data mining applications. Time complexities are quadratic or higher for many algorithms; memory complexity is either linear or quadratic in the number of objects N depending on whether a dissimilarity matrix is used. Techniques used to overcome these limitations can be broadly categorized as sampling, summarizing, and partitioning. Sampling technique is used in CURE [9], CLARANS [13]. Summarizing technique is used in BIRCH [17], Bradley et al. [4]. Sampling is robust in finding large distinct clusters but are criticized for missing out small yet useful clusters. Summarizing techniques reduce large datasets to a small summary which is then used for clustering. Although a summary of a large dataset reduces the computational cost significantly but they can only produce approximate clusters and does not guarantee correct labeling. Moreover, these techniques still require to run the traditional algorithm over a sample or a summary. Partitioning techniques are proposed in [14] in association with parallel hierarchical clustering. These partitioning methods are straightforward and do not reduce the complexity of sequential processing. CURE [9] uses simple partitioning techniques to speed up the clustering process at the expense of accuracy.

In this paper, we examine techniques for efficient yet accurate clustering. The main idea comes from our observation that most HAC algorithms follow a 90-10 rule where roughly 90% iterations from the beginning merge cluster pairs with dissimilarity less than 10% of the maximum dissimilarity. Moreover, initial iterations are significantly more costly than later iterations. In this paper, we propose two novel algorithms that exploit these characteristics using the concept of partially overlapping partitioning (POP) where each partition overlaps others uniformly. These algorithms output accurate dendrograms while significantly reducing the time and memory complexities by a factor of number of partitions (p). To apply POP efficiently to high-dimensional data, we construct a hierarchy of Voronoi diagrams called hpc – hyperplane clustering – tree. POP with hpc-tree is suitable when memory is limited and its parallel version is far superior than existing parallel algorithms. The proposed approach can be easily modified for efficient density-based and other types of clustering that are based on neighborhood search. Among other benefits, the 90-10 rule is used to boost the performance and accuracy of existing cluster validation methods.

The remainder of the paper is organized as follows. Section 2 describes the 90-10 rule. Section 3 describes POP. Section 4 introduces hpc-tree. Section 5 gives the details of performance study. Section 6 concludes the paper.

2. Motivation

We assume that a dataset contains N objects or data points, where each point x is described by an M-tuple $x = (x_1, ..., x_M)$ of real numbers where M is the number of attributes or dimensions. Dissimilarity between two data points containing real data is typically measured by their distance. We shall restrict our discussion to *Euclidean* distance measure and discuss other types in [6].

2.1. The 90-10 Rule

We run centroid type HAC method over a 2-D dataset with 100 clusters (clusters are distributed randomly) and some noise. In the centroid type, each cluster is represented by its centroid and the cluster pair having closest centroids are merged in each iteration. Based on the HAC results we have plotted Figure 1 showing *distance, size,* and *time* plots. X-axes of these plots stand for percentage of iterations of HAC while Y-axes stand for the closest pair distance in *distance plot*, size of the larger cluster of the closest pair in *size plot*, and time taken until the corresponding iteration in *time plot*. *Distance plot* has a mirror-L shape because the closest pair distance is very small except for the last several iterations. *Size plot* has a similar shape because the size of the merged clusters are very small except for the last several iterations. *Time plot* shows that the initial iterations are much costlier than the iterations towards the end because initially there are more clusters to merge than that towards the end. We call these observations *90-10 rule* which states that:

roughly 90% iterations from the beginning merge clusters that are separated by less than 10% of the maximum closest pair distance.

Extensive experiments with real-world, bench-mark, high-dimensional, multi-resolution, skewed, and noisy datasets show that 90-10 rule holds if the dataset has some clusters and majority of data points are in the clusters. As clustering applications implicitly assume that data is not uniformly distributed but has some clusters in it, the 90-10 rule is true for most clustering applications.

2.2. Different Similarity Metrics

Similarity between two clusters is measured by different metrics which are broadly categorized as *geometric* and *graph*. We examine their adherence to the 90-10 rule.

Geometric Metrics: These metrics represent each cluster by a single representative point. Examples are centroid, median and Ward's minimum variance [15] methods. These methods represent each cluster by its centroid. Centroid and median methods measure similarity of two clusters by the distance between their centroids. Centroid method gives equal weight to each point in the two clusters whereas median method gives equal weight to each cluster. Ward's minimum variance method merges the pair of clusters with the least increase in the sum of square error. All three methods follow the 90-10 rule.

Graph Metrics: In contrast to geometric type, a graph metric considers each point in a cluster to be its representative. Examples are single link, complete link and average link. In single link, dissimilarity between two clusters is the minimum distance between points in the two clusters. In complete link, dissimilarity between two clusters is the maximum distance between points in the two clusters. Average link method measures the dissimilarity between two clusters as the average distance between points in the two clusters. Experiments show that complete and average link methods follow 90-10 rule just like the geometric metrics. Although single link method follows the 90-10 rule for datasets that have well formed clusters, it violates the rule when clusters are connected by a chain of points due to the *chaining effect* [11].

In summary, metrics that follow 90-10 rule merge clusters of small size and of close proximity until last several iterations when they merge a few large and distant clusters. We use centroid method to explain the proposed approach and to conduct experiments.

2.3. Existing HAC Algorithms

The first centroid algorithm proposed uses a dissimilarity matrix that stores dissimilarities between clusters. In each iteration, the dissimilarity matrix is searched to find the closest pair of clusters. Let us call this 'step 1'. For n ($n = N...2$) remaining clusters in an iteration, it requires $O(n^2)$ time to search through the dissimilarity matrix, and for $N - 1$ iterations this step takes $O(N^3)$ time. After merging the closest pair, dissimilarity matrix is updated by deleting the column entries for the closest pair and by creating a new row for the new cluster by determining distance from other clusters. Let us call this 'step 2'. For n clusters in an iteration, this step takes $O(n)$ time to update, and so for $N - 1$ iterations it takes $O(N^2)$ time. Hence the overall time complexity of the algorithm is $O(N^3)$. The memory

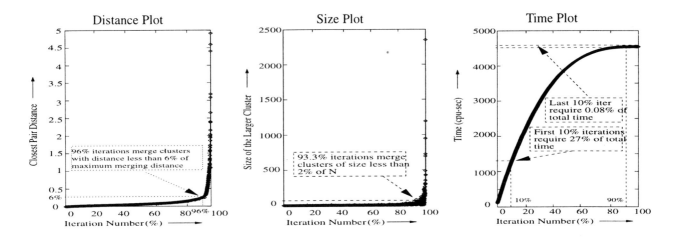

Figure 1. Important Observations about HAC

required is $O(N^2)$ because of the dissimilarity matrix. This simple algorithm can be improved by maintaining a nearest neighbor array that stores nearest neighbor for each cluster. This way, *step 1* requires only to find the minimum of the nearest neighbor distances from the nearest neighbor array in $O(n)$ time for n clusters in any iteration. But, *step 2* requires $O(n^2)$ time in each iteration if a naive nearest neighbor algorithm of $O(n)$ time complexity is used. Day and Edelsbrunner [7] suggested two ways to improve the time complexity of this algorithm by improving *step 2*'s complexity. Type (1) – By obtaining an improved bound on the required number of nearest neighbor updates: If the number of clusters to update after an iteration is α then the overall complexity becomes $O(\alpha N^2)$. Using geometric preliminaries they proposed an upper bound for α as $2(3^M - 2)$ where M is the number of dimensions. Type (2) – By obtaining an improved bound on the time required for each update: They suggested using a heap-based priority queue that requires $O(\log n)$ time for each insert and delete operation on a priority queue. This results in an overall time complexity of $O(N^2 \log N)$.

Anderberg [1] classified hierarchical algorithms into 'stored matrix' and 'stored data' types. Stored matrix algorithms maintain a dissimilarity matrix whereas stored data algorithms calculate the dissimilarities as required. A major distinction is that stored matrix methods are preferred when memory is sufficient to store the dissimilarity matrix of size $O(N^2)$, otherwise stored data is the way out. Type (2) algorithm of Day and Edelsbrunner that uses priority queues is a stored matrix method while type (1) algorithm is more suitable as stored data if M is not large and if memory is not enough to store dissimilarity matrix. In this paper, priority queue algorithm is used to describe the proposed techniques, but complexity analysis and experiments are done for the above different types of algorithms.

3. Hierarchical Clustering Using POP

The 90-10 rule of HAC is due to the mirror-L shape of the distance plot as shown in Figure 1. The distance plot has a sharp turning point at the right end after which only a few iterations remain. As the closest pair distance at this turning point is very small compared to the maximum closest pair distance, *partially overlapping partitioning* (POP) technique can be applied for efficient and accurate HAC.

3.1. 2-Phase Algorithm

We propose a new 2-phase algorithm for HAC based on POP. In *phase 1* data is partitioned into p number of overlapping cells. The region of overlapping is called δ-region where δ is the separating distance. Figure 2 (A) shows an axis-parallel POP that divides the data-space uniformly into p cells. The basic idea is, in each iteration, the closest pair is found for each cell, and from those the overall closest pair is found. If the overall closest pair distance is less than δ then the pair is merged and the priority queues (or the nearest neighbor array depending on the algorithm employed) of only the container cell are updated. If the closest pair or the merged cluster is in a δ-region then the priority queues of the affected cells are also updated. *Phase 1* terminates when the closest pair distance exceeds δ. *Phase 2* merges the remaining clusters of *phase 1* using the traditional algorithm, thus completing the dendrogram. By setting δ to the closest pair distance at the turning point of distance plot, a large number of small clusters are merged in *phase 1* that uses POP while only a small number of larger clusters are merged in *phase 2* that uses the traditional algorithm. This way the overall computational time is reduced significantly. The algorithm is given below.

Algorithm: 2-phase using Priority Queue
Input: Data (N,M), p, δ
Output: Dendrogram
/* Phase 1 */
1. divide the data into p number of overlapping cells
2. Create priority queues P for each cell
3. repeat
4.   for each cell get its closest pair
5.   determine overall closest pair (C_1, C_2)
6.   if $dist(C_1, C_2) > \delta$ go to 10
7.   merge C_1 and C_2, update corresponding P
8.   update P of the affected cells, if any
9. until $dist(C_1, C_2) > \delta$
/* Phase 2: k' – #Remaining Clusters after Phase 1 */
10. merge k' clusters by traditional HAC
11. return dendrogram

Accuracy As POP ensures that *any pair with distance less than δ must reside together in at least one cell*, and as *phase 2* is the traditional method itself, 2-phase algorithm guarantees correct dendrogram. Note that ties between the closest pair distances can produce different dendrograms because there is no unique way of resolving them.

Complexity Analysis To simplify the analysis, we assume equal size of cells and δ-regions. The original priority queue algorithm proposed by Day and Edelsbrunner [7] had an overall time complexity $O(N^2 \log N)$ and memory complexity $O(N^2)$. On the other hand, 2-phase algorithm has an overall time complexity $O((N - k') * (\beta + 1) * (\frac{N}{p} + |\delta|) \log(\frac{N}{p} + |\delta|)) + O(k'^2 \log k')$ assuming $\log(\frac{N}{p} + |\delta|)$ to be greater than p where k' is the number of clusters remaining after *phase 1* and β is the average number of cells affected (other than the container cell) in each iteration. The memory complexity is $O(p * (\frac{N}{p} + |\delta|)^2)$ or $O(k'^2)$ whichever is larger. If δ is set to the closest pair distance at the turning point of distance plot, then both $|\delta|$ and k' are very small. So, if we do not consider $|\delta|$ and k', then the time complexity becomes $O(N * (\beta + 1) * \frac{N}{p} \log \frac{N}{p})$, i.e., $O((\beta + 1) * \frac{N^2}{p} \log \frac{N}{p})$ (gain factor $= \log_{\frac{N}{p}} N \times \frac{p}{\beta+1}$), and the memory complexity is $O(p * \frac{N^2}{p^2})$, i.e., $O(\frac{N^2}{p})$ (gain factor $= p$). The average number of affected cells including the container cell is $\beta + 1$. Its value depends on the data distribution: in the worst case, it is 2^M when each agglomeration affects maximum possible number of cells for M dimensions while in the best case it is just 1 when each agglomeration affects only its container cell. Experiments show $\beta + 1$ is small and, for all test datasets in this paper, it is less than 2.

Detailed complexity analysis of dissimilarity matrix method and 'stored data' method are given in [6]. Table 1 compares the time and memory complexities of existing algorithms and 2-phase algorithm.

3.2. Nested Algorithm

The performance of the 2-phase algorithm depends on the number of partitions p and overlapping width δ. For a fixed p, a small δ will leave behind a large k' number of clusters for the traditional algorithm of *phase 2* whereas a large δ will spend time unnecessarily in partitioning in *phase 1* even when the number of remaining clusters is very small for traditional algorithm of *phase 2* to handle efficiently. The following figure shows that value 'c' is an ideal δ at which the 2-phase algorithm gives optimum performance. Note that c is the distance corresponding to the sharp turning point of the distance plot. [1]

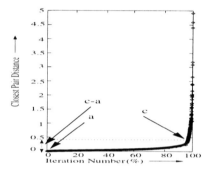

For an efficient 2-phase algorithm it may not be easy to guess an ideal c value properly though. Sampling may be helpful in the following way: take a random sample and obtain its distance plot. The c values of the distance plots for the sample and the whole data almost match because a sample typically increases the small intra-cluster distances while retaining the large inter-cluster distances. This is also the reason why, in general, the sampling approach has been effective for clustering. But the problem with this approach is that a user is required to run the algorithm an additional time over the sample data, and then needs to detect the ideal δ value from the distance plot.

We propose a nested algorithm that dynamically sets the δ and p values. It starts with a very small δ and gradually increases it until there remains very few or just one cluster. As δ increases, p which is set to a high value in the beginning is reduced. Experiments show that the nested algorithm is more efficient than the 2-phase algorithm even when δ is set to the ideal value for the 2-phase scheme. The reason is nested method improves the POP efficiency further by dividing the difference $(c-a)$. Hence we use the nested algorithm in the rest of the paper.

---

[1] In contrast, nearest neighbor search will gain maximum for label 'a' because any pair of points with distance less than a must be found together in at least one of the cells. Hence, we see successful application of POP in clustering is different from that in nearest neighbor search.

Type of Algorithm	Traditional Algorithm	2-Phase Algorithm*	Gain Factor$=\frac{Traditional}{Proposed}$
Time Complexity			
Stored Matrix– Similarity Matrix	$O(N^3)$	$O(\frac{N^3}{p})$	p
– Priority Queues	$O(N^2 \log N)$	$O((\beta+1)*\frac{N^2}{p}\log\frac{N}{p})$	$\log_{\frac{N}{p}} N \times \frac{p}{\beta+1}$
Stored Data	$O(\alpha*N^2)$	$O((\beta+1)*\alpha*\frac{N^2}{p})$	$\frac{p}{\beta+1}$
Memory Complexity			
Stored Matrix – Similarity Matrix	$O(N^2)$	$O(\frac{N^2}{p})$	p
– Priority Queues	$O(N^2)$	$O(\frac{N^2}{p})$	p
Stored Data	$O(N)$	$O(N)$	1

Table 1. Comparison between 2-phase and Traditional Algorithms; *: After Simplification

Complexity Analysis: Time complexity of nested algorithm after simplification, with a nested sequence $<p_j,\delta_j>$ for $j=1...s$ where p_j and δ_j are p and δ values in the jth nested iteration respectively, is $\sum_{j=1}^{s}\left((n_j-n_{j+1})O((\beta+1)*\frac{n_j}{p_j}\log\frac{n_j}{p_j})\right)$. Similarly, memory complexity is $\max_{j=1...s}[p_j*O((\frac{n_j}{p_j}+|\delta_j|)^2)]$, and after simplification it becomes $\max_{j=1...s}[O(\frac{n_j^2}{p_j})]$. See [6] for detailed analysis.

4. High-Dimensional Data and hpc-tree

High-dimensional data poses problems for the simple axis-parallel partitioning technique of the previous section. If a single dimension is used to partition the data, then the δ distance in single dimension will be too small in high-dimensional space which reduces the efficiency drastically. If all (or several) dimensions are used to partition the space and if each is divided into at least two, then for M dimensions there will be 2^M partitions; e.g. for $M=20$ there will be $2^{20}\approx 10^6$, for $M=100$ there will be $2^{100}\approx 10^{30}$ (!) partitions. Most of the partitions will be empty, even when number of data points N is large.

There are two important arguments, both for and against, efficient partitioning of high-dimensional data. They are on nearest neighbor search which is closely linked to the problem of finding clusters in the data. In [16], it is shown that almost all partitioning schemes for efficient nearest neighbor search in high-dimensional data fail if the data is distributed uniformly. A clustering application implicitly assumes that data is not uniformly distributed but has clusters in it, and so the assumption of uniform distribution will be irrelevant for this paper. The other study in [2] argues that some partitioning techniques can still be efficient if there are clusters in high-dimensional data. The authors argue that as dimensionality increases the points within a cluster must be increasingly closer than points in different clusters.

While constructing an efficient partitioning scheme for POP, the following properties should be observed: (1) $|\delta|$ should be small, (2) time spent in distributing points and determining affected partitions should be small, and (3) partitions should not hold too many or too few points. In OptiGrid [10] an optimal hyper-plane partitioning scheme is defined for implementing grid-based clustering. This is not applicable for POP as a main goal of OptiGrid is not to break any cluster. This objective can distribute a large number of points in a single partition violating the criterion 3 and resulting in poorer POP performance. An efficient way to satisfy criterion 2 is a tree structure that needs $O(\log n')$ number of comparisons on average to distribute a point and to determine the affected partitions where n' is the number of nodes in the tree. One way to satisfy criterion 1 is to use Voronoi diagram which partitions the space into cells, directed by a set of *split* points $Q = q_1, q_2, ...$ such that for each cell corresponding to point q_i, the points x in that cell are nearer to q_i than to any other split point in Q. Hence, by constructing a hierarchy of Voronoi diagrams, all the above criteria can be satisfied. We call such a structure as hpc – *hyper plane clustering* – tree where the top or root node gives a brief summary of the whole data and is split to several Voronoi cells which are split as well and so on. A challenging aspect of hpc-tree is the selection of split points in each level. In [5] a hierarchical structure of Voronoi diagram called GNAT is proposed for efficient nearest neighbor search in high-dimensional data. In GNAT, split points are chosen randomly and user is required to specify the number of split points in each level of the hierarchy. Wrong selection of split points results in unbalanced tree leading to disproportionate distribution among the cells and poor POP performance. An ideal split point should be a summary of the points that belong to the corresponding Voronoi cell. In the literature, there are different methods of creating summary of data (e.g. CF-tree (BIRCH [17] and Bradley et al's method [4]). CF-tree is more suitable for hpc-tree because of its hierarchical structure. An artifact of CF-tree is that it does not guarantee that a parent node is the

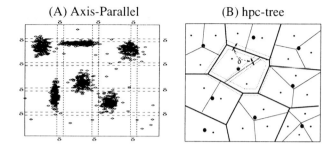

(A) Axis-Parallel   (B) hpc-tree

Figure 2. POP: Axis-Parallel and hpc-tree

closest parent of all of its children which is necessary for hpc-tree.

POP and hpc-tree   The overall construction process of hpc-tree is as follows:
Step 1: Create CF-tree and get the split points (i.e., summary points) of different levels;
Step 2: In each level remove split points with distance less than δ from some other split point;
Step 3: Starting with the root assign each split point to its closest parent.

The leaf nodes (a node consists of a split point among other information) of hpc-tree are the partitions of POP. Starting with the root, for each data point, the path that contains the nearest child is descended until the leaf level is reached. If a point does not belong to δ-boundary of any node of the path, then it is assigned to only one leaf node as a non-boundary point. Otherwise, each affected node is descended and the point is assigned to all the affected leaf nodes as a boundary point, and so on. A simple example of hpc-tree is illustrated in Figure 2 (B). In the 1st level only the root exists which is not shown in the figure. In level 2, there are 9 nodes with heavier split points and thicker boundary lines. The 3rd level has finer split points and thinner boundary lines. The dashed lines show the boundary of width δ for one branch of the hpc-tree. Unlike the axis-parallel partitioning where it is easy to determine the neighboring cells of a data point, in hpc-tree each boundary point stores pointers to the affected partitions. Nested partitioning can use the same hpc-tree for different δ if the minimum separation between the split points is not less than the new δ; otherwise, the tree is reconstructed with the new δ.

The algorithm is similar to the nested algorithm of previous section. It requires an additional *ThresPts* parameter to specify a threshold for average number of points in each cell. If after any nested iteration the average number of points becomes less than *ThresPts* then the tree height is reduced by 1. This will reduce p, the number of leaf nodes in the tree, and hence will increase the average. The default value for *ThresPts* is two.

Complexity Analysis Building hpc-tree: Time complexity of building an hpc-tree is $O(N*B*(1+\log_B n')+\log_2 \frac{N}{N_0} * (\frac{M}{ES})*B*(1+log_B n')+(\log_B n')^2+N*n')$ where size of CF-tree and hpc-tree are assumed to be equal – and it is n' – although hpc-tree is typically smaller than CF-tree, the number of partitions p is equal to the number of leaf nodes and $p \approx \frac{B-1}{B}n'$ where B is the branching factor of CF-tree, M is the memory allocated for CF-tree, ES is the CF entry size, N_0 is the number of data points loaded into memory initially. See [6] for detailed analysis. As for I/O, BIRCH requires a little more than one scan to build the CF-tree. Building hpc-tree requires one scan to distribute the points among the cells. Nested POP with hpc-tree: Complexity analysis of axis-parallel partitioning discussed in Section 3 holds here.

Accuracy: Arguments of accuracy discussed in Section 3 also apply here.

5. Experimental Study

We conducted an extensive performance study to determine the effectiveness of the proposed algorithms over the traditional algorithms. Priority queue algorithm is implemented for stored matrix type and nearest-neighbor array method for stored data type. The proposed approach uses nested POP with hpc-tree. Performance is measured by the time taken (total time including the time required to create CF-tree) and, wherever relevant, by the memory occupied.

Parameter Setting Performance of the proposed approach is largely affected by p and δ. **p**: It is affected by the size of hpc-tree which in turn is affected by the size of the CF-tree. To create CF-tree one needs to run only the first two phases of BIRCH. According to the authors of BIRCH, size of CF-tree is affected by *memory and page sizes*: smaller (larger) page size tends to decrease (increase) the running time, and produces fewer (more) leaf nodes. Similarly, as memory size increases the tree size increases together with the running time. We ran extensive experiments to suggest good values for page and memory sizes. It was found that cpu time does not vary more than ±20% for a wide range of values. To avoid poor performance, the two parameters should not be set too low or too high. Some insight on what is too low and too high for these parameters are: do not set these two so low that the average number of points per partition is more than 20 or so high that it is less than 5; a proper page size for 2-D data is 256 and it should be increased with the number of dimensions; a proper memory size for a 2-D data with $N = 6k$ is 80Kbytes and it should increase with data size. δ: Initially δ is set to a very small value; if the user finds it difficult to set then a possible initial value is 0. For the next nested iteration, set δ

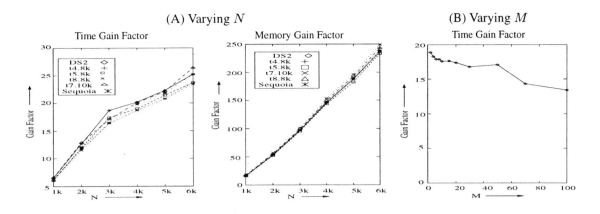

Figure 3. Stored Matrix: Time and Memory Gain Factor (= $\frac{Traditional}{Proposed}$)

to $(1+\delta_{incr})$ times the last closest pair distance which exceeded the previous δ. δ_{incr} can be varied for performance tuning. In the experiments, δ_{incr} is set to 0.1.

5.1. Scalability

Scalability tests are done by varying N and M. Synthetic and benchmark datasets are used for the tests. Synthetic datasets are DS2 (taken from BIRCH [17]), t4.8k, t5.8k, t8.8k, t7.10k (taken from CHAMELEON [12] and CURE [9]). Benchmark dataset is SEQUOIA used in DB-SCAN [8]. These datasets have different shapes of clusters (e.g. arbitrary and Gaussian) and different noise levels (SEQUOIA has very high noise level).

5.1.1 Stored Matrix

Varying N: N varies from 1k to 6k (traditional algorithm required more memory than that is available in our server higher size) while M is 2. Figure 3(A) shows the *time* and *memory* gain factors (i.e., $\frac{traditional}{proposed}$). Expectedly, the time gain factor increases with N as the time complexity of the traditional algorithm $O(N^2 \log N)$ increases faster with N than that of the proposed algorithm $\sum_{j=1}^{s} ((n_j - n_{j+1})O((\beta + 1) * \frac{n_j}{p_j} \log \frac{n_j}{p_j}))$.

Memory gain factor increases with N as well because memory complexity of traditional algorithm $O(N^2)$ increases faster than that of the proposed algorithm $\max_{j=1...s} O(\frac{n_j{}^2}{p_j})$.

Varying M: The number of dimensions M is varied from 2 to 100 for DS2 dataset while N was set to 3k. Figure 3(B) shows the time gain factor (memory comparison is not reported as increase in M does not affect the memory required for priority queues which only stores the dissimilarities). Increasing M does not affect the time performance of the priority queue algorithm much as the dominant time consum-

ing step of updating priority queues is mostly independent of M. Hence, the gain factor does not increase and instead remains unchanged or decreases a little.

5.1.2 Stored Data

Figures 4(A) and (B) show time performance of memory and disk based algorithms for stored data type respectively. Memory comparison is not shown as the memory requirements of the two algorithms are almost equal.

Memory Based

Varying N: Results show that cpu time of the traditional algorithm with complexity of $O(\alpha N^2)$ increases much faster than that of the proposed algorithm with complexity $\sum_{j=1}^{s} ((n_j - n_{j+1})O((\beta + 1) * \alpha * \frac{n_j}{p_j}))$.

Varying M: In contrast to the results for stored matrix where the time gain factor did not increase with M, in stored data memory-based type the gain factor increases rapidly with increasing M. The reason is M has a direct effect on the performance for stored data type algorithms where dissimilarities are calculated on demand.

Disk Based

Varying N and M: The time gain factors are much higher than that for memory based type. The reason is traditional algorithm spends significantly more time in I/O than the proposed methods.

5.2. UCI ML Repository Datasets

The proposed methods are evaluated on several Irvine datasets [3] that has continuous attribute values and no missing value and relatively large N. Due to large memory requirement of traditional stored matrix algorithms, stored data memory-based method is applied. The following table shows significant time gain factor for artificial character, image segmentation and pen digits datasets.

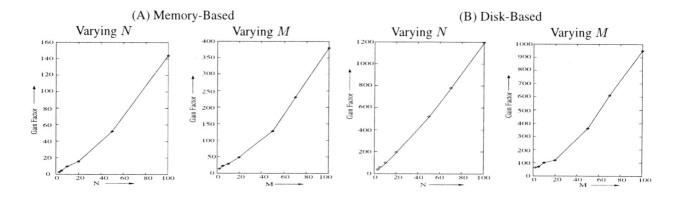

Figure 4. Stored Data: Time Gain Factor

Datasets	N	M	Gain Factor
Character	61,313	7	47.4
Pen Digits	10,992	16	9.4
Image Segmentation	2310	19	4.5

5.3. Scope of POP

The proposed approach is applicable to other clustering methods such as density-based clustering DBSCAN [8] and CURE [9]. In [6] we give details of these algorithms and their comparison with the original algorithms. In general, we argue that the proposed method is applicable to all clustering algorithms that are based on neighborhood search.

6. Conclusion and Future Work

In this paper we studied efficient yet accurate clustering. The key idea comes from a 90-10 rule of HAC algorithms. Partially overlapping partitioning (POP) exploits this characteristic and reduces the time and memory complexities of existing HAC algorithms significantly. For high-dimensional data we propose hpc-tree that is based on the idea that a hierarchy of Voronoi diagrams is a suitable structure for POP. Experimental results showed that the gain factor (both time and memory) increases with the size of dataset. In general, the proposed approach is suitable for clustering algorithms which are based on neighborhood search. In [6] we describe some other aspects of the proposed approach including parallelization, limited memory, cluster validation. Preliminary results show that the proposed methods remains superior over existing methods. We foresee that the proposed approach can be used for extracting natural clusters.

References

[1] M. R. Anderberg. *Cluster Analysis for Applications.* Academic Press, New York, 1973.

[2] K. Beyer, J. Goldstein, R. Ramakrishnan, and U. Shaft. When is "nearest neighbor" meaningful? In *Proceedings of ICDT*, pages 217–235, 1999.

[3] C. Blake and C. Merz. UCI repository of machine learning databases. http://www.ics.uci.edu/~mlearn/MLRepository.html, 1998.

[4] P. S. Bradley, U. Fayyad, and C. Reina. Scaling clustering algorithms to large databases. In *Proceedings of KDD*, 1998.

[5] S. Brin. Near neighbor search in large metric spaces. In *Proceedings of VLDB*, 1995.

[6] M. Dash, K. L. Tan, and H. Liu. Efficient clustering and its validation. http://www.comp.nus.edu.sg/~manoranj/research.html.

[7] W. H. E. Day and H. Edlesbrunner. Efficient algorithms for agglomerative hierarchical clustering methods. *Journal of Classification*, 1(1):7–24, 1984.

[8] M. Ester, H. P. Kriegel, J. Sander, and X. Xu. A density-based algorithm for discovering clusters in large spatial databases with noise. In *Proceedings of KDD*, 1996.

[9] S. Guha, R. Rastogi, and K. Shim. CURE: An efficient clustering algorithm for large databases. In *Proceedings of ACM SIGMOD*, pages 73–84, 1998.

[10] A. Hinneburg and D. A. Keim. Optimal grid-clustering: towards breaking the curse of dimensionality clustering. In *Proceedings of VLDB*, 1999.

[11] A. K. Jain and R. C. Dubes. *Algorithm for Clustering Data*, chapter Clustering Methods and Algorithms. Prentice-Hall Advanced Reference Series, 1988.

[12] G. Karypis, E.-H. Han, and V. Kumar. CHAMELEON: A hierarchical clustering algorithm using dynamic modeling. *IEEE Computer*, 32:68–75, 1999.

[13] R. T. Ng and J. Han. Efficient and effective clustering methods for spatial data mining. In *Proceedings of VLDB*, 1994.

[14] C. F. Olson. Parallel algorithms for hierarchical clustering. *Parallel Computing*, 21:1313–1325, 1995.

[15] J. J. H. Ward. Hierarchical grouping to optimize an objective function. *Journal of the American Statistical Association*, 58:236–244, 1963.

[16] R. Weber, H.-J. Schek, and S. Blott. A quantitative analysis and performance study for similarity-search methods in high-dimensional spaces. In *Proceedings of VLDB*, 1998.

[17] T. Zhang, R. Ramakrishnan, and M. Livny. BIRCH: An efficient data clustering method for very large databases. In *Proceedings of ACM SIGMOD* pages 103–114, 1996.

A Min-max Cut Algorithm for Graph Partitioning and Data Clustering

Chris H.Q. Ding[a], Xiaofeng He[a,b], Hongyuan Zha[b], Ming Gu[c], Horst D. Simon[a]

[a] NERSC Division, Lawrence Berkeley National Laboratory
University of California, Berkeley, CA 94720

[b] Department of Computer Science and Engineering
Pennsylvania State University, University Park, PA 16802

[c] Department of Mathematics
University of California, Berkeley, CA 94720

{chqding,hdsimon}@lbl.gov, {xhe,zha}@cse.psu.edu, mgu@math.berkeley.edu

Abstract

An important application of graph partitioning is data clustering using a graph model — the pairwise similarities between all data objects form a weighted graph adjacency matrix that contains all necessary information for clustering. Here we propose a new algorithm for graph partition with an objective function that follows the min-max clustering principle. The relaxed version of the optimization of the min-max cut objective function leads to the Fiedler vector in spectral graph partition. Theoretical analyses of min-max cut indicate that it leads to balanced partitions, and lower bonds are derived. The min-max cut algorithm is tested on newsgroup datasets and is found to outperform other current popular partitioning/clustering methods. The linkage-based refinements in the algorithm further improve the quality of clustering substantially. We also demonstrate that the linearized search order based on linkage differential is better than that based on the Fiedler vector, providing another effective partition method.

1 Introduction

Graph partitioning has very broad range of applications. At one end are the near-regular graphs, the mesh of a 2D surface of an airfoil or a 3D engine cylinder. Partitioning such a mesh into subdomains for distributed memory processors is a common task. Popular software packages for this partitioning task are developed [17, 16]. At another end are the graphs generated from the World Wide Web. These graphs are highly irregular or random, and node degrees vary dramatically. Partitioning the web graph is useful to automatically identify topics from the retrieved webpages for a user query [15].

Here we emphasize graph partition as data clustering using a graph model. Given the attributes (coordinates) of the data points in a dataset and the similarity or affinity metric between any two points, the symmetric matrix containing similarities between all pairs of points forms a weighted adjacency matrix (weight matrix) of an undirected graph. Thus the data clustering problem becomes a graph partition problem.

The data clustering point of view of graph partitioning helps to define more appropriate criteria for partitioning. In the simplest MINcut algorithm, a connected graph is partitioned into two subgraphs with the cutsize (cut set) minimized. However, MINcut often results in a skewed cut, i.e., a very small subgraph is cut away [4]. Various constraints are introduced, such as the *ratio cut* [4, 14], the *normalized cut* [22], etc. to circumvent the problem. However, skewed cuts still occur when the overlaps between clusters are large.

In this paper, we propose a new graph partition method based on the min-max clustering principle: the similarity or association between two subgraphs (cut set) is minimized, while the similarity or association within each subgraph (summation of similarity between all pairs of nodes within a subgraph) is maximized. These two requirements can be satisfied simultaneously with a simple min-max cut function. We present a number of theoretical analyses of min-max cut, and show that min-max cut always leads to more balanced cuts than the ratio cut and the normalized cut.

Like many other methods, the optimal solution to the graph partition problem is NP-complete because of the combinatoric nature of the problem. An effective approach is to consider continuous relaxation of such problems. An example is to compute a principal direction/component (principal eigenvector of the weight matrix), and find a cut point along this direction so that all points on one side belong to one subgraph, and all points on the other side belong to another subgraph. This establishes a linear search order on which the min-max cut can be efficiently applied to search the optimal cut.

The relaxed version of the min-max cut function optimization leads to a generalized eigenvalue problem. The second lowest eigenvector, also called the Fiedler vector, provides a linear search order (Fiedler order). Thus the min-max cut algorithm (we call it Mcut algorithm) provides both a well-defined objective and a clear procedure to search for the optimal solution. We test the algorithm on a number of newsgroup text datasets and compare it with several current methods. The Mcut algorithm outperforms others.

We introduce a linkage difference metric that effectively identifies nodes near the cut. We find many nodes sitting on the wrong side of the optimal cutpoint, i.e., they have higher linkage to the other cluster than the one they are currently assigned to. Swapping them to the correct side, the objective function is reduced and the clustering accuracy is improved substantially.

It is generally believed that the Fiedler order provides the best known linearized order to search for the optimal cut. Here we find a linkage differential order that provides a *better* ordination than the Fiedler order. Searching based on linkage differential order consistently outperforms those based on the Fiedler order. The linkage differential order start from any existing clustering results and iteratively improves the ordering and therefore the clustering.

2 Min-max cut

Given a weighted graph $G = G(E, V)$ with node set V, edge set E and weight matrix W, we wish to partition it into two subgraphs A, B using the min-max clustering principle — minimize similarity between clusters and maximize similarity within a cluster. This is a sound principle well established in statistics, data mining and machine learning areas. The similarity or association between two nodes is their edge weight W_{uv}. Thus the similarity between subgraphs A, B is the cutsize

$$\text{cut}(A, B) = W(A, B) \qquad (1)$$

where

$$W(A, B) = \sum_{u \in A, v \in B} W_{uv}, \quad W(A) \equiv W(A, A). \qquad (2)$$

Similarity or association within a cluster (subgraph A) is the sum of all edge weights within A: $W(A)$. Note that the weight W_{uu} on node u is included in $W(A)$, which is important for some applications. Thus the min-max clustering principle requires we minimize $\text{cut}(A, B)$ while maximizing $W(A)$ and $W(B)$ at the same time. All these requirements can be simultaneously satisfied by the following objective function,

$$\text{Mcut} = \frac{\text{cut}(A, B)}{W(A)} + \frac{\text{cut}(A, B)}{W(B)}. \qquad (3)$$

We call this new objective function the min-max cut function or Mcut for short. Mcut is inspired by previous works on spectral graph partition [21, 14, 22] (see section 3). It turns out that the continuous relaxation of Eq.(3) must be solved in a way that is different from existing graph partition relaxations [21, 14, 22]. To reveal the solution, we reorder the rows and columns of W conformally with subgraphs A and B such that

$$W = \begin{pmatrix} W_A & W_{A,B} \\ W_{B,A} & W_B \end{pmatrix}. \qquad (4)$$

Let $\mathbf{x}$ and $\mathbf{y}$ be vectors conformally partitioned with A and B, i.e., $\mathbf{x} = (1 \cdots 1, 0 \cdots 0)^T$, $\mathbf{y} = (0 \cdots 0, 1 \cdots 1)^T$.

It follows from Eqs.(1,2) that

$$\begin{aligned} \text{cut}(A, B) &= \mathbf{x}^T (D - W) \mathbf{x} = \mathbf{y}^T (D - W) \mathbf{y}, \quad (5) \\ W(A) &= \mathbf{x}^T W \mathbf{x}, \quad W(B) = \mathbf{y}^T W \mathbf{y}. \end{aligned}$$

Hence the objective function (3) can be rewritten as

$$\text{Mcut} = \frac{\mathbf{x}^T (D - W) \mathbf{x}}{\mathbf{x}^T W \mathbf{x}} + \frac{\mathbf{y}^T (D - W) \mathbf{y}}{\mathbf{y}^T W \mathbf{y}}. \qquad (6)$$

Observe that in Eq.(6), Mcut is invariant under changes of $\|\mathbf{x}\|_2$ and $\|\mathbf{y}\|_2$, and

$$\mathbf{x}^T D \mathbf{y} = 0 \quad \text{and} \quad \mathbf{x}^T W \mathbf{x} > 0, \mathbf{y}^T W \mathbf{y} > 0.$$

Taking these relations into account, we obtain a useful lower bound on (3) in Theorem 1 below. Observe that the problem Eq.(6) can be relaxed into the following optimization problem

$$\min \quad \frac{\widehat{\mathbf{x}}^T (I - \widehat{W}) \widehat{\mathbf{x}}}{\widehat{\mathbf{x}}^T \widehat{W} \widehat{\mathbf{x}}} + \frac{\widehat{\mathbf{y}}^T (I - \widehat{W}) \widehat{\mathbf{y}}}{\widehat{\mathbf{y}}^T \widehat{W} \widehat{\mathbf{y}}} \qquad (7)$$

subject to $\|\widehat{\mathbf{x}}\|_2 = \|\widehat{\mathbf{y}}\|_2 = 1$, $\widehat{\mathbf{x}}^T \widehat{\mathbf{y}} = 0$, $\widehat{\mathbf{x}}^T \widehat{W} \widehat{\mathbf{x}} > 0$, $\widehat{\mathbf{y}}^T \widehat{W} \widehat{\mathbf{y}} > 0$, where $\widehat{W} = D^{-1/2} W D^{-1/2}$ and $\widehat{\mathbf{x}} = D^{1/2} \mathbf{x}/|D|^{1/2}$, $\widehat{\mathbf{y}} = D^{1/2} \mathbf{y}/|D|^{1/2}$. The conditions that $\widehat{\mathbf{x}}^T \widehat{W} \widehat{\mathbf{x}} > 0$ and $\widehat{\mathbf{y}}^T \widehat{W} \widehat{\mathbf{y}} > 0$ are necessary since $\widehat{W}$ in general is an indefinite matrix. Let the largest 2 eigenvalues of $\widehat{W}$ be λ_1, λ_2. $\lambda_1 = 1$ by construction. We have the following (proof omitted).

Theorem 1. Assume that $\lambda_1 + \lambda_2 > 0$. Let vectors $\widehat{\mathbf{x}}$ and $\widehat{\mathbf{y}}$ solve problem Eq.(7). Choose $\widehat{U}$ to be any column orthogonal matrix such that $\widehat{Q} = \left(\widehat{\mathbf{x}}, \widehat{\mathbf{y}}, \widehat{U} \right)$ is an $n \times n$ orthogonal matrix. Then $\widehat{Q}^T \widehat{W} \widehat{Q} = \begin{pmatrix} \begin{pmatrix} \alpha & \gamma \\ \gamma & \alpha \end{pmatrix} & \mathbf{0} \\ \mathbf{0} & \widetilde{W} \end{pmatrix}$, where $\alpha = (\lambda_1 + \lambda_2)/2$, $|\gamma| = |\lambda_1 - \lambda_2|/2$.

It follows from Theorem 1 that both ratios of (7) are equal at the optimal solution:

$$\frac{\widehat{\mathbf{x}}^T (I - \widehat{W}) \widehat{\mathbf{x}}}{\widehat{\mathbf{x}}^T \widehat{W} \widehat{\mathbf{x}}} = \frac{\widehat{\mathbf{y}}^T (I - \widehat{W}) \widehat{\mathbf{y}}}{\widehat{\mathbf{y}}^T \widehat{W} \widehat{\mathbf{y}}} = \frac{2}{\lambda_1 + \lambda_2} - 1, \qquad (8)$$

and the optimal value is Mcut $= 4/(\lambda_1 + \lambda_2) - 2$.

Since Eq.(7) is a continuous relaxation of Eq.(3), the fact that the two terms in (7) are equal at optimal solution suggests that the two terms of Eq.(3) should also be rather "close" to each other, implying $W(A)$ should be "close" to $W(B)$. Hence the resulting clusters tend to have similar weights and are thus balanced. This is one indication that Mcut is a desired objective function for data clustering (see sections 4 and 7 for more discussions).

2.1 Fiedler linear search order

The solution to partition problem can be represented by an indicator vector $\mathbf{q}$, where the nodal value of $\mathbf{q}$ on node u is $q_u = \{a, -b\}$, depending on $u \in A$ or B. Finding the optimal partition is NP-complete. A well-known and effective solution is to first compute a linear search order and then find a cut point along this index order that minimizes the Mcut objective. Theorem 1 implies that the solution vectors $\mathbf{x}, \mathbf{y}$ must lie in the eigenspace of $\widehat{W}$. The first eigenvector $\mathbf{z}_1 = D^{1/2} e$, $e = (1, \cdots, 1)^T$ with the largest eigenvalue $\lambda_1 = 1$ does not match $\mathbf{q}$. The second eigenvector $\mathbf{z}_2$ of $\widehat{W}$ satisfies $\mathbf{z}_2^T \mathbf{z}_1 = 0$ and has positive and negative elements, therefore is a good approximation of $\mathbf{q}$.

More directly, we can show that

$$\min_{\mathbf{q}} \mathrm{Mcut}(A, B) = \min_{\mathbf{q}} \frac{J_N(A, B)}{1 - J_N(A, B)/2} \Rightarrow \min_{\mathbf{q}} J_N(A, B)$$

where

$$J_N(A, B) \equiv J_N(\mathbf{q}) = \frac{\mathbf{q}^T (D - W) \mathbf{q}}{\mathbf{q}^T D \mathbf{q}}. \quad (9)$$

Relaxing q_u to real number in $[-1, 1]$, the solution for minimizing Rayleigh quotient $J_N(\mathbf{q})$ is given by

$$(D - W) \mathbf{q} = \zeta D \mathbf{q}, \quad (10)$$

subject to $\mathbf{q}^T e = 0$. The solution to this generalized eigenvalue problem is the second eigenvector $\mathbf{q}_2$, called the Fiedler vector, and the corresponding eigenvalue ζ_2 is called the Fiedler value. Sorting the Fiedler vector provides the desired linear search order. Furthermore, we obtain a lower bound for the Mcut objective,

$$\min_{\mathbf{q}} \mathrm{Mcut}(A, B) \geq \frac{\zeta_2}{1 - \zeta_2/2}. \quad (11)$$

Note this bound is the same as the optimal Mcut value in Eq.(8), because $\zeta_i = 1 - \lambda_i$, and $4/(\lambda_1 + \lambda_2) - 2 = 4/(2 - \zeta_2) - 2 = \zeta_2/(1 - \zeta_2/2)$.

3 Related work on spectral graph partition

Spectral graph partitioning is based on the properties of eigenvectors of the Laplacian matrix $L = D - W$, first developed by Donath and Hoffman [8] and Fiedler [11, 12], and recently populated by the work of Pothen, Simon and Liu [21]. The objective of the partitioning is to minimize the cut size $J(A, B) = \mathrm{cut}(A, B)$ with the requirement that two subgraphs have the same number of nodes: $|A| = |B|$. Using indicator variable x_u, $x_u = \{1, -1\}$ depending on $u \in A$ or B, the cutsize is

$$\mathrm{cut}(A, B) = \sum_{e_{uv} \in E} \frac{(x_u - x_v)^2}{4} W_{uv} = \frac{\mathbf{x}^T (D - W) \mathbf{x}}{2}. \quad (12)$$

Relax x_u from $\{1, -1\}$ to continuous value in $[-1, 1]$, minimizing $\mathrm{cut}(A, B)$ is equivalent to solve the eigensystem

$$(D - W) \mathbf{x} = \lambda \mathbf{x}. \quad (13)$$

Since the trivial $\mathbf{x}_1 = \mathbf{e}$ is associated with $\lambda_1 = 0$, the second eigenvector $\mathbf{x}_2$, the Fiedler vector, is the solution.

Hagen and Kahng [14] remove the requirement $|A| = |B|$ and show that the Fiedler vector provides a good linear search oerder to the ratio cut (Rcut) partitioning criteria[4]

$$\mathrm{Rcut} = \frac{\mathrm{cut}(A, B)}{|A|} + \frac{\mathrm{cut}(A, B)}{|B|}. \quad (14)$$

The use of generalized eigensystem from Eq.(13) to Eq.(10) has been studied by a number of authors [9, 5, 22]. Chung [5] especially emphasizes the advantage of using normalized Laplacian matrix which leads to Eq.(10). Shi and Malik [22] propose the normalized cut,

$$\mathrm{Ncut} = \frac{\mathrm{cut}(A, B)}{\deg(A)} + \frac{\mathrm{cut}(A, B)}{\deg(B)} \quad (15)$$

where $\deg(A) = \sum_{u \in A} d_u$ is the sum of node degrees, which is also called the *volumn* [5] of subgraph A, in contrast to the size of A. They show that Ncut can be reduced to $\mathrm{Ncut}(A, B) = J_N(\mathbf{q})$ in Eq.(9). Therefore, Ncut uses the same linear search order based on $\mathbf{q}_2$ as Mcut objective. Following the same analysis, we obtain a lower bound for the Ncut objective,

$$\min_{\mathbf{q}} \mathrm{Ncut}(A, B) \geq \zeta_2. \quad (16)$$

Here Rcut, Ncut and Mcut objective functions are first *prescribed* by motivating considerations and then the linear order of the Fiedler vector of (normalized) Laplacian matrix is argued to be the appropriate search order (by relaxing discrete indicator variables). It is important to note that the same objective functions can be automatically obtained as the eigenvalues of the Fiedler vector using a perturbation analysis on the (normalized) Laplacian matrix [6]. This further strengthens the connection between objective function and the Fiedler vector.

Beside spectral partitioning methods, other recent partitioning methods seek to minimize the sum of subgraph diameters, see [7] or k-center problem [1] for examples. There are other clustering methods that use singular value decompositions, for example [10].

4 Random graph model

Perhaps the most important feature of the Mcut method is that it tends to produce balanced cut, i.e., the resulting clusters (subgraphs) have similar sizes. Here we use the random graph model [3, 4] to illustrate this point. Suppose we have a uniformly distributed random graph with n nodes. For this random graph, any two nodes are connected with probability p. We consider the four objective functions, the MINcut, Rcut, Ncut and Mcut. We have the following

Theorem 2. For random graphs, MINcut favors highly

skewed cuts, i.e., very uneven sizes. Mcut favors balanced cut, i.e., both subgraphs have the same sizes. Rcut and Ncut show no size preferences.

Proof. We compute the object functions for the partition of G into A and B. Note that the number of edges between A and B are $p|A||B|$ on average. We have

$$\text{MINcut}(A, B) = p|A||B|$$

For Rcut, we have

$$\text{Rcut}(A, B) = \frac{p|A||B|}{|A|} + \frac{p|A||B|}{|B|} = p(|A| + |B|) = np.$$

For Ncut, since all nodes have the same degree $(n-1)p$,

$$\text{Ncut}(A, B) = \frac{p|A||B|}{p|A|(n-1)} + \frac{p|A||B|}{p|B|(n-1)} = n/(n-1).$$

For Mcut, we have

$$\text{Mcut}(A, B) = \frac{|B|}{|A| - 1} + \frac{|A|}{|B| - 1}$$

We now minimize these objectives. Clearly, MINcut favors $|A| = n - 1$ and $|B| = 1$ or $|B| = n - 1$ and $|A| = 1$, both are skewed cuts. Minimizing $\text{Mcut}(A, B)$, we obtain a balanced cut: $|A| = |B|$. Rcut and Ncut objectives have no size dependency and no size preference, which also implies possible unstable results. This completes the proof.

5 Mcut algorithm

The algorithm for partitioning a graph into two subgraphs becomes the following.

1. Compute the Fiedler vector from Eq.(10). Sort nodal values to obtain the Fiedler order.

2. Search for the optimal cut point corresponding to the lowest Mcut based on the Fiedler order.

3. Do linkage-based refinements (see section 8).

The computation of the Fiedler vector can be quickly done via the Lanczos method [20]. A fast software package for this calculation, LANSO, is available online (http://www.nersc.gov/~kewu/planso.html). The Lanczos iteration has computational complexity of $O(|E| + |V|)$.

6 Experiments

Document clustering has been popular in analyzing text information. Here we perform experiments on newsgroup articles in 20 newsgroups. We focus on three datasets, each has two newsgroups:

```
1/2:    alt.atheism/comp.graphics
10/11:  rec.sport.baseball/rec.sport.hockey
18/19:  talk.politics.mideast/talk.politics.misc
```

(The newsgroup dataset together with the `bow` toolkit for processing is available online[19]).

Word-document matrix X is first constructed. 2000 words are selected according to the mutual information between words and documents

$$I(w) = \sum_d p(w, d) \log_2[p(w, d)/p(w)p(d)]$$

where w represents a word and d represents a document. Words are stemmed using [19]. Standard `tf.idf` scheme for term weighting is used and standard cosine similarity between two documents d_1, d_2 $\text{sim}(d_1, d_2) = d_1 \cdot d_2/|d_1||d_2|$ is used. When each document, column of X, is normalized to 1 using L_2 norm, document-document similarities are calculated as $W = X^T X$. W is interpreted as the weight/affinity matrix of the undirected graph. From this similarity matrix, we perform the clustering as explained above.

For comparison purpose, we also consider three other clustering methods: the ratio cut [4, 14], the normalized cut [22] (see section 3) and the principle direction divisive partitioning (PDDP) [2]. PDDP is based on the idea of principle component analysis (PCA) applied to the vector-space model on X. First X is centered, i.e., the average of each row (a word) is subtracted. Then the first principle component is computed. The loadings of the documents (the projection of each document on the principle axis) form a 1-dim linear search order. This provides a heuristic very similar to the linear search order provided by the Fiedler vector. Instead of searching through to find a minimum based on some objective function, PDDP partitions data into two parts at the center of mass.

To increase statistics, we perform these two-cluster experiments in a way similar to cross-validation. We divide one newsgroup A randomly into K_1 subgroups and the other newsgroup B randomly into K_2 subgroups. Then one of the K_1 subgroups of A is mixed with one of the K_2 subgroups of B to produce a dataset G. The graph partition methods are run on this dataset G to produce two clusters. Since the true label of each newsgroup article is known, we use accuracy, percentage of newsgroup articles correctly clustered, as a measure of success. This is repeated for all $K_1 K_2$ pairs between A and B, and the accuracy is averaged. In this way, every newsgroup articles is used the same number of times. The mean and standard deviation of accuracy are listed.

In Table 1, the clustering results are listed for balanced cases, i.e., both subgroups have about 200 newsgroup articles. Mcut performs about the same as Ncut for newsgroups NG1/NG2, where the cluster overlap is small. Mcut performs substantially better than Ncut for newsgroups NG10/NG11 and newsgroups NG18/NG19, where the cluster overlaps are large. Mcut performs slightly better than PDDP. Rcut always performs the worst among the 4 methods and will not be studied further.

In Table 2, the clustering results are listed for unbalanced cases, i.e., one subgroup has about 300 newsgroup articles and another subgroup has about 200. This is generally a harder problem due to the unbalanced prior distributions. In this case, both Mcut and Ncut perform reasonably well, no clear deterioration is seen, while the performance of PDDP clearly deteriorated. This indicates the strength of Mcut method using graph model. Mcut consistently performs better than Ncut for cases where the cluster overlaps are large.

Dataset	Mcut	Ncut	Rcut	PDDP
NG1/NG2	97.2±1.1	97.2±0.8	63.2±16.2	96.4±1.2
NG10/NG11	79.5±11.0	74.4±20.4	54.9±2.5	89.1±4.7
NG18/NG19	83.6±2.5	57.5±0.9	53.6±3.1	71.9±5.4

Table 1: Accuracy (%) of clustering experiments using Mcut, Rcut, Ncut and PDDP. Each test set G is a mixture of 400 news articles, 200 from each newsgroup.

Dataset	Mcut	Ncut	PDDP
NG1/NG2	97.6 ± 0.8 %	97.2± 0.8 %	90.6 ± 2.1%
NG10/NG11	85.7 ± 8.3 %	73.8± 16.6 %	87.4 ± 2.6%
NG18/NG19	78.8 ± 4.5 %	65.7± 0.5 %	59.6 ± 2.4%

Table 2: Accuracy of clustering experiments using Mcut, Ncut and PDDP. Each test set G is a mixture of 300 news articles from one newsgroup and 200 news articles from the other newsgroup.

7 Skewed cut

We further study the reasons that Mcut consistently outperforms Ncut in large overlap cases. A key observation is that Ncut can be written as

$$\text{Ncut} = \frac{\text{cut}(A,B)}{W(A) + \text{cut}(A,B)} + \frac{\text{cut}(A,B)}{W(B) + \text{cut}(A,B)}, \quad (17)$$

since $\deg(A) \equiv \sum_{u \in A, \, v \in G} W_{uv} = W(A) + \text{cut}(A,B)$. Thus, Ncut sometimes cuts out a set with a very small weight, i.e., a skewed cut, because $\text{cut}(A,B)$ in the denominators help to produce a smaller Ncut value.

We examine several cases and one specific case is shown in Figure 1. The cut points for Mcut and Ncut and relevant quantity are listed in Table 3. Ncut has two pronounced valleys, and produces a skewed cut. while Mcut has a very flat valley and gives balanced cuts. Further examination shows that in both cases, the cutsizes obtained in Ncut are equal or bigger than the weight (self-similarity) of the smaller cluster as listed in Table 3. In the example of Figure 1, Ncut produces a cutsize of 262.7, much larger than the weight $W(B,B) = 169$. In these cases, clearly the Ncut objective [see Eq.(17)] is not appropriate. In the Mcut objective, the cutsize is absent in the denominators; this provides a balanced cut.

These case studies provide some insights to these graph partition methods. Prompted by these studies, here we provide further analysis and derive general conditions under which a skewed cut will occur. Consider

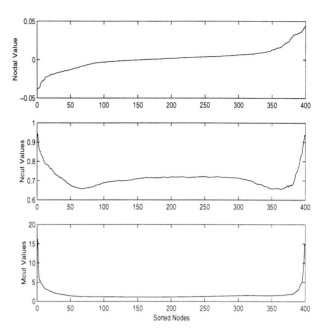

Figure 1: Top: Nodal values of sorted Fiedler vector. Middle: Ncut values as the cut point moves from $i_{cut} = 1, 2, ...n$. Bottom: Mcut values. A dataset from NG18/NG19 in Table 1.

Method	i_{cut}	cut(A,B)	W(A,A)	W(B,B)
Ncut	364	262.7	5312.6	169.0
Mcut	141	1026.6	1488.9	2464.7

Table 3: Cut point, cutsize, within cluster similarities for the case in Figure 1.

the balanced cases where $W(A) \simeq W(B)$. Let

$$\text{cut}(A,B) = f \cdot \langle W \rangle, \quad \langle W \rangle = \frac{1}{2}(W(A) + W(B)),$$

where $f > 0$ is the average fraction of cut relative to within cluster associations.

In the case when the partition is optimal, A and B are exactly the partitioning result. The corresponding Ncut value is

$$\text{Ncut}_0 = \frac{\text{cut}(A,B)}{W(A) + \text{cut}(A,B)} + \frac{\text{cut}(A,B)}{W(B) + \text{cut}(A,B)} \simeq \frac{2f}{1+f} \quad (18)$$

For a skewed partition A_1, B_1, we have $W(A_1) \ll W(B_1)$, and therefore $\text{cut}(A_1,B_1) \ll W(B_1)$. The corresponding Ncut value is

$$\text{Ncut}_1 \simeq \frac{\text{cut}(A_1,B_1)}{W(A_1) + \text{cut}(A_1,B_1)}. \quad (19)$$

Using Ncut, a skewed or incorrect cut will happen if $\text{Ncut}_1 < \text{Ncut}_0$. Using Eqs.(18, 19), this condition is satisfied if

$$\text{Ncut}: \quad W(A_1) \geq (\frac{1}{2f} - \frac{1}{2})\text{cut}(A_1,B_1)$$

We can repeat the same analysis using Mcut and calculating Mcut_0 and Mcut_1. The condition for a skewed cut using Mcut is $\text{Mcut}_1 < \text{Mcut}_0$, which is

$$\text{Mcut}: \quad W(A_1) \geq \frac{1}{2f}\,\text{cut}(A_1, B_1).$$

For large overlap case, say, $f = 1/2$, the conditions for possible skewed cut are:

$$\text{Ncut}: \quad W(A_1) \geq \text{cut}(A_1, B_1)/2$$
$$\text{Mcut}: \quad W(A_1) \geq \text{cut}(A_1, B_1)$$

The relevant quantity is listed in Table 4. For datasets newsgroups 10-11, and newsgroups 18-19, the condition for skewed Ncut is satisfied most of the time, leading to many skewed cuts and therefore lower clustering accuracy in Tables 1,2. For the same datasets, condition for skewed Mcut is not satisfied most of time, leading to more correct cuts and therefore higher clustering accuracy.

Dataset	cut(A,B)	W(A,A)	W(B,B)	f
NG1/NG2	549.4	1766.4	1412.5	0.346
NG10/NG11	772.8	1372.8	1581.0	0.523
NG18/NG19	1049.5	2093.9	1665.5	0.558

Table 4: Average values of cut(A,B), W(A,A), W(B,B) and the fraction in three datasets using Mcut.

8 Linkage-based refinements

The heuristic linear search order provided by the Fiedler vector is generally a good heuristic, as the results shown above. Nevertheless, it may not necessarily be the perfect one. Here we explore this point and find an effective refinement method which substantially improves the quality of graph partitioning.

The linear search order provided by sorting the Fiedler vector $\mathbf{q}$ implies that nodes on one side of the cut point must belong to one cluster: if $q_u \geq q_v \geq q_w$ where u, v, w are nodes, then the linear search will not allow the situation that u, w belong to one cluster and v belongs to the other cluster. Such a strict order is not necessary. In fact, in large overlap cases, we expect some nodes could be moved to the other side of the cut while lowering the overall objective function.

How to identify those nodes near the cut? For this purpose, we define linkage ℓ as a closeness or similarity measure between two subgraphs (clusters):

$$\ell(A, B) = W(A, B)/W(A)W(B) \qquad (20)$$

here $W(A), W(B)$ are for normalization purpose so that $\ell(A, B)$ is insensitive to cluster weights (this is motivated by the *average linkage* $\ell(A, B) = W(A, B)/|A||B|$ in hierarchical agglomerative clustering. Following the spirit of min-max cut, we replaced $|A|, |B|$ by $W(A), W(B)$). For a single node u, its linkage to subgraph A

is $\ell(A, u) = W(A, u)/W(A)$. Now we can identify the nodes near the cut. If a node u is well inside a cluster, u will have a large linkage with the cluster, and a small linkage with the other cluster. If u is near the cut, its linkages with both clusters should be close. Therefore, we define the linkage difference

$$\Delta\ell(u) = \ell(u, A) - \ell(u, B). \qquad (21)$$

A node with small $\Delta\ell$ should be near the cut and is a possible candidate to be moved to the other cluster.

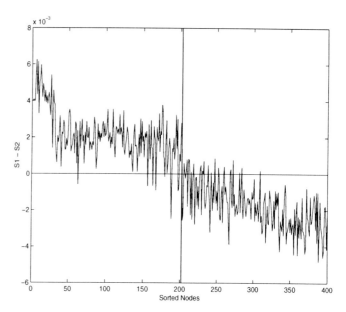

Figure 2: Linkage difference of all nodes. The vertical line indicates the cutpoint using Mcut. Nodes on the left forms cluster A and nodes on the right forms cluster B.

In Figure 2, we show linkage difference $\Delta\ell$ for all nodes. The vertical line is the cut point. It is interesting to observe that not only many nodes have small $\Delta\ell$, but quite a number of nodes whose $\Delta\ell$ have the wrong signs (e.g., $\Delta\ell(u) < 0$ if $u \in A$, or, $\Delta\ell(v) > 0$ if $v \in B$). For example, node #62 has a relatively large negative $\Delta\ell$. This implies node #62 has a larger linkage to cluster B even though it is located in cluster A (left of the cutpoint). Indeed, if we move node #62 to cluster B, the objective function is reduced. Therefore we find a better solution.

After moving node #62 to cluster B, we try to move another node with negative $\Delta\ell$ from cluster A to cluster B depending on whether the objective function is lowered. In fact, we move all nodes in cluster A with negative $\Delta\ell$ to cluster B if the objective function is lowered. Similarly we move all nodes in cluster B with positive $\Delta\ell$ to cluster A. This procedure of swapping nodes is called the "linkage-based swap". It is implemented by sorting the array $s(u)\Delta\ell(u)$ [$s(u) = -1$ if $u \in A$ and $s(u) = 1$ if $u \in B$] in decreasing order to provide a priority list and then moving the nodes, one by one. The greedy move starts from the top of the list to the last node u where $s(u)\Delta\ell(u) \geq 0$. This swap reduces the objective function and increases the partitioning quality. In Table 5, the effects on clustering accuracy due to the swap are listed. In all cases, the accuracy increases. Note that in the large overlap cases, NG9/NG10, NG18/NG19, the accuracy increase about 10% over the Mcut without refinement.

If $s(u)\Delta\ell(u) < 0$ but close to 0, node u is in the correct cluster, although it is close to the cut. Thus we select the smallest 5% of the nodes with $s(u)\Delta\ell(u) < 0$ as the candidates, and move those which reduce Mcut objective to the other cluster. This is done in both cluster A and B. We call this procedure "linkage-based move". Again, these moves reduce Mcut objective and therefore improve the solution. In Table 5, their effects on improving clustering accuracy are shown. Adding together, the linkage bassed refinements improve the accuracy by 20%. Note the final Mcut results are about 30-50% better than Ncut and about 6-25% better than PDDP (see Tables 5 and 1).

Dataset	Mcut	+Swap	+Swap+Move
NG1/NG2	97.2 ± 1.1%	97.5 ± 0.8 %	97.8 ±0.7%
NG10/NG11	79.5 ±11.0%	85.0 ± 8.9 %	94.1 ±2.2%
NG18/NG19	83.6 ± 2.5%	87.8 ± 2.0 %	90.0 ±1.4%

Table 5: Improvements of clustering accuracy due to linkage-based refinements for Mcut alone, Mcut plus swap, and Mcut plus swap and move over 5% smallest $\Delta\ell$ on both sides of the cutpoint.

9 Linkage differential order

It is generally believed that the Fiedler order provides the best known linearized order to search for the optimal cut (although delicate counter examples exist [13, 23]). Is there a linear search order better than the Fiedler order?

Our analysis in previous sections suggests a new linear search order. Given the linkage difference in Figure 2, we see that quite a few nodes far away from the cut point have wrong $\Delta\ell$ signs, that is, they belong to the other subgraph. This strongly suggests that the Fiedler order is not necessarily the best linear search order. In fact, we can sort linkage difference $\Delta\ell$ to obtain a linear order different from the Fiedler order, which will be referred to as *linkage differential* (LD) order. The search to find the best Mcut cut point based on this new LD order represents another improvement over the standard Mcut method.

The results are given in Table 6. We see that the Mcut values obtained on this new order are lower than that based on the Fiedler order. The clustering accuracy also increases substantially. The quality of the clustering based on this new order is slightly better than the results obtained by using Mcut+swap in Table 5. Therefore, we find a new linear order that leads to better graph partitioning than that provided by the Fiedler order.

Note that the LD order does not depend on the Fiedler order. For example, we can obtain the LD order based on the principal direction in PDDP. Furthermore, the LD order can be recursively applied to the clustering results obtained from an earlier LD order for further improvements.

Dataset	Acc(F)	Acc(LD)	Min(F)	Min(LD)
NG1/NG2	97.2 ± 1.1%	97.6±0.8%	0.698	0.694
NG10/NG11	79.5 ±11.0%	87.2±8.0%	1.186	1.087
NG18/NG19	83.6 ± 2.5%	89.2±1.8%	1.126	1.057

Table 6: Improvements on accuracy (2nd and 3rd columns) due to the linkage differential (LD) order over Fiedler order (F). Improvements on min(Mcut) values are also shown. (4th and 5th columns).

10 Hierarchical divisive Mcut

So far in this paper, we focus on bisection a graph into two subgraphs. If more subgraphs or clusters are desired, one can recursively apply Mcut and related refinement to each subgraph, until certain stopping criteria is met, either the desired number of clusters is reached or min(Mcut) value is above certain pre-defined value.

Once the recursive division is stopped, some refinements along the lines discussed in section 8 should be applied. This is because even if during each bisection step, all nodes are optimally partitioned, the final partition is not necessarily optimal, since they are not obtained directly according to the optimal Mcut objective

$$\text{Mcut}_K = \frac{\text{cut}(G_1, \bar{G_1})}{W(G_1)} + \frac{\text{cut}(G_2, \bar{G_2})}{W(G_2)} + \cdots + \frac{\text{cut}(G_K, \bar{G_K})}{W(G_K)}.$$

when G is partitioned into K subgraphs, $G_1, \cdots, G_K$. Note that for $K \geq 3$, each term in Mcut_K will be larger than that in $K = 2$ cases because $\text{cut}(G_p, \bar{G_p}), p = 1, \cdots K$ will increase on average while the weight (self-similarity) $W(G_p)$ will decrease. Thus, Mcut_K would differ from Ncut_K [22] much more than in the $K = 2$ cases [cf. Eq.(17)]. From the analysis regarding balanced cuts in previous sections, Ncut is more likely to produce skewed cuts. Therefore, Mcut is essential in K−way partition.

When applying the refinements on $K \geq 3$ clusters, one may apply the 2-way linkage-based refinement *pairwisely* on all pairs of clusters[18]. However, a direct K-way linkage-based refinement procedure may be adopted: Assume a node u currently belongs to cluster G_i. The linkage difference $\Delta\ell_{ij}(u) = \ell(u, G_j) - \ell(u, G_i)$ for all other K−1 clusters are computed. The smallest $\Delta\ell_{ij}(u)$ and the corresponding cluster id are stored as an entry in a priority list. This is repeated for all nodes so every entry of the list is filled. The list is then sorted according to $\Delta\ell_{ij}(u)$ to obtain the final priority list. Following the list, nodes are then moved one after another to the appropriate clusters if the overall Mcut_K objective is reduced. This completes one pass. For $K \geq 3$, several passes may be necessary.

11 Summary

We introduce the Mcut algorithm for graph partition. It is shown that the min-max objective function follows the clustering principle and produces balanced partitions, compared to many skewed cuts produced by Ratio cut, Nornmalized cut and PDDP algorithms in cases of large cluster overlaps. The linkage difference metric effectively identifies those nodes near the cut, which leads to effective refinement procedures. Finally, the new linkage differential order is shown to provide a better linear search order than the best known Fiedler order. Many datasets such as text information are represented by bipartite graphs. Mcut algorithm can also be applied to the bi-clustering model[24] on these bipartite graph problems.

Acknowledgements. This work is supported in part by Office of Science, Office of Laboratory Policy and Infrastructure, of Department of Energy under contract DE-AC03-76SF00098 through an LDRD grant and NSF Grant CCR-9001986.

References

[1] P.K. Agarwal and C.M. Procopiuc. Exact and approximation algorithms for clustering. *Proc. 9th ACM-SIAM Symposium on Discrete Algorithms*, pages 658–667, 1998.

[2] D. Boley. Principal direction divisive partitioning. *Data mining and knowledge discovery*, 2:325–344, 1998.

[3] B. Bollobas. *Random Graphs*. Academic Press, 1985.

[4] C.-K. Cheng and Y.A. Wei. An improved two-way partitioning algorithm with stable performance. *IEEE. Trans. on Computed Aided Desgin*, 10:1502–1511, 1991.

[5] F.R.K. Chung. *Spectral Graph Theory*. Amer. Math. Society, 1997.

[6] C. Ding, X. He, and H. Zha. A spectral method to separate disconnected and nearly-disconnected web graph components. *Proc. 7th ACM Int'l Conf Knowledge Discovery and Data Mining (KDD 2001)*, pages 275–280, August 2001.

[7] S. Doddi, M.V. Marathe, S. S. Ravi, D. S. Taylor, and P. Widmayer. Approximation algorithms for clustering to minimize the sum of diameters. *Nordic Journal of Computing, 7(3):185, Fall 2000*, Fall 2000.

[8] W.E. Donath and A. J. Hoffman. Lower bounds for partitioning of graphs. *IBM J. Res. Develop.*, 17:420–425, 1973.

[9] R. V. Driessche and D. Roose. An improved spectral bisection algorithm and its application to dynamic load balancing. *Parallel Computing*, 21, 1995.

[10] P. Drineas, A. Frieze, R. Kannan, S. Vempala, and V. Vinay. Clustering in large graphs and matrices. In *Proc. 19th ACM-SIAM Symposium on Discrete Algorithms*, 1999.

[11] M. Fiedler. Algebraic connectivity of graphs. *Czech. Math. J.*, 23:298–305, 1973.

[12] M. Fiedler. A property of eigenvectors of non-negative symmetric matrices and its application to graph theory. *Czech. Math. J.*, 25:619–633, 1975.

[13] S. Guattery and G. L. Miller. On the quality of spectral separators. *SIAM Journal of Matrix Anal. Appl.*, 19(3), 1998.

[14] L. Hagen and A.B. Kahng. New spectral methods for ratio cut partitioning and clustering. *IEEE. Trans. on Computed Aided Desgin*, 11:1074–1085, 1992.

[15] X. He, H. Zha, C. Ding, and H.D. Simon. Web document clustering using hyperlink structures. *Tech Report CSE-01-006*, April 2001.

[16] B. Hendrickson and R. Leland. Chaco mesh partitioning software. *http://www.cs.sandia.gov/CRF/chac.html*.

[17] G. Karypis and V. Kumar. Metis graph partitioning software. *http://www-users.cs.umn.edu/ karypis/metis/*.

[18] B. W. Kernighan and S. Lin. An efficient heuristic procedure for partitioning graphs. *The Bell System Tech. J.*, 1970.

[19] A. McCallum. Bow: A toolkit for statistical language modeling, text retrieval, classification and clustering. *http://www.cs.cmu.edu/mccallum/bow*, 1996.

[20] B. N. Parlett. *The Symmetric Eigenvalue Problem*. SIAM Press, 1998.

[21] A. Pothen, H. D. Simon, and K. P. Liou. Partitioning sparse matrices with egenvectors of graph. *SIAM Journal of Matrix Anal. Appl.*, 11:430–452, 1990.

[22] J. Shi and J. Malik. Normalized cuts and image segmentation. *IEEE. Trans. on Pattern Analysis and Machine Intelligence*, 2000.

[23] D.A. Spielman and S.-H. Teng. Spectral partitioning works: Planar graphs and finite element meshes. *Proc. 37th IEEE Conference on Foundations of Computer Science,*, 1996.

[24] H. Zha, X. He, C. Ding, M. Gu, and H.D. Simon. Bipartite graph partitioning and data clustering. *Proc. 10th Int'l Conf. Information and Knowledge Management (CIKM 2001)*, Nov. 2001.

Preprocessing Opportunities in Optimal Numerical Range Partitioning

Tapio Elomaa
Department of Computer Science, P.O. Box 26
FIN-00014 University of Helsinki, Finland
elomaa@cs.helsinki.fi

Juho Rousu
Department of Computer Science, P.O. Box 26
FIN-00014 University of Helsinki, Finland
rousu@cs.helsinki.fi

Abstract

We show that only the segment borders have to be taken into account as cut point candidates in searching for the optimal multisplit of a numerical value range with respect to convex attribute evaluation functions. Segment borders can be found efficiently in a linear-time preprocessing step. With Training Set Error, which is not strictly convex, the data can be preprocessed into an even smaller number of cut point candidates, called alternations, when striving for the optimal partition. We show that no segment borders (resp. alternations) can be overlooked with strictly convex functions (resp. Training Set Error) without risking to lose optimality. Our experiments show that while in real-world domains significant reduction in the number of cut point candidates can be obtained for Training Set Error, the number of segment borders is usually not much lower than that of boundary points.

1. Introduction

In classifier induction discretization of numerical domains is a potential time-consumption bottleneck, since in the general case the number of possible partitions is exponential in the number of candidate cut points within the domain.

In this paper we consider *class-driven* partitioning in which knowledge of the class labels of the examples is used. Moreover, we are only concerned with *univariate* discretization methods, where only one attribute is partitioned at a time. More specifically, we study *context-free* methods, where — in addition to the class label — only the value of the attribute at hand is considered. In *context-dependent* methods [14, 16] the distance of instances, as measured by all attributes, is taken into account in the quality criteria.

With many commonly used evaluation functions numerical attribute value ranges can be optimally partitioned in quadratic time in the number of candidate cut points using a dynamic programming algorithm [12, 20, 8], but only the

Training Set Error (*TSE*) is known to optimize in linear time [12, 1, 2]. Even quadratic-time evaluation may be too much if the number of potential cut points is high, hence, pruning out as many cut point candidates as possible before embarking on the search is preferable [11, 20, 8, 9, 6]. Preprocessing does not improve the worst-case asymptotic efficiency of the optimal multisplitting task [10]. In this paper we explore further enhancement possibilities and limitations of efficient preprocessing.

It is known that only a subset of the *boundary points* [11] — the so-called *segment borders* [9] — needs to be examined in searching for the optimal partition of a numerical value range with respect to many commonly-used functions. In this paper we show that this linear-time preprocessing applies to all functions that satisfy Jensen's inequality [7]. Moreover, for *TSE* examining only a subset of segment borders is enough.

There are many different relevant definitions of partition optimality. One can look for any partition that optimizes the value of the evaluation function being used, or search for the globally optimal partition with as few intervals as possible. One can, further, explicitly restrict the arity of a partition to some upper bound k and then look for the optimal one among the partitions fulfilling this restriction. An even stricter restriction is to search for the optimal partition of some fixed arity k.

Section 2 discusses partitions of numerical value ranges and their optimality with respect to evaluation functions. In Section 3 we recapitulate the known preprocessing opportunities for common evaluation functions. Section 4 considers the consequences of Jensen's inequality for concave and strictly concave functions. We show that a partition which has all example segments as its intervals is the unique minimal globally optimal partition of any value range with respect to any strictly concave function. We examine *TSE* separately in Section 5. It is proved that for it suffices to examine points in which the class majority changes in between two adjacent segments. In Section 6, we study empirically the reduction of cut point candidates that can be obtained for *TSE*. Finally, Sections 7 and 8 conclude the paper.

115

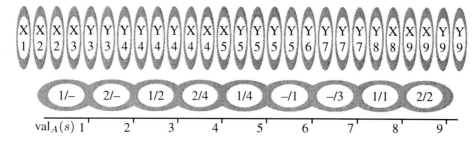

Figure 1. A sequence of examples sorted according to the value of a numerical attribute (above). The class labels (X and Y) of the examples are also shown. The sequence of example bins with the respective class distributions (below). Partition cut points can be set at the bin borders.

2. Optimality of a partition

A *partition* $\biguplus_{i=1}^{k} S_i$ of S consists of k non-empty, disjoint subsets and covers the whole domain. When splitting a set S of examples on the basis of the value of an attribute A, there is a set of thresholds $\{T_1, \ldots, T_{k-1}\} \subseteq R_A$, where R_A is the value range of the attribute A, that defines a partition $\biguplus_{i=1}^{k} S_i$ for the sample in an obvious manner:

$$S_i = \begin{cases} \{s \in S \mid \mathrm{val}_A(s) \leq T_1\} & \text{if } i = 1, \\ \{s \in S \mid T_{i-1} < \mathrm{val}_A(s) \leq T_i\} & \text{if } 1 < i < k, \\ \{s \in S \mid \mathrm{val}_A(s) > T_{k-1}\} & \text{if } i = k, \end{cases}$$

where $\mathrm{val}_A(s)$ is the value of attribute A in example s.

A partition is *optimal* if it optimizes the value of the evaluation function being used. In machine learning algorithms there are many different attribute evaluation functions. Let us consider, for the time being, the very simple function Training Set Error, or *TSE*.

The *majority* class $\mathrm{maj}_C(S)$ of sample S is its most frequently occurring class. The number of *disagreeing* instances, those in the set S not belonging to its majority class, is given by $\delta(S) = |\{s \in S \mid \mathrm{val}_C(s) \neq \mathrm{maj}_C(S)\}|$. Training Set Error is the number of training instances falsely classified in the partition when all intervals are labeled by their majority class. For a partition $\biguplus_i S_i$ of S it is defined as

$$TSE\left(\biguplus_{i=1}^{k} S_i\right) = \sum_{i=1}^{k} \delta(S_i).$$

If one could make its own partition interval out of each example, this partition would have zero misclassification rate. However, one cannot discern between all examples. Only examples that differ in the value of the attribute under consideration can be separated from each other. Consider, for example, the data set shown in Fig. 1. There are 27 examples ordered by an integer-valued attribute A. The examples are instances of two classes; X and Y. Partition cut points can only be set on those points where the value of A changes. Therefore, we can preprocess the data into *bins*. There is one bin for each separate value of attribute A. Within each bin we record the class distribution of the instances belonging to it.

The sequence of bins has the minimal attainable misclassification rate. However, the same rate can usually be obtained with a smaller number of intervals, as we will show in later sections. Moreover, it is usually advisable to restrict the number of intervals, or the *arity* of the partition, at the expense of few misclassifications.

Let Π_{R_A} be the set of all partitions of value range R_A and $P \in \Pi_{R_A}$. Then by $|P|$ we denote the arity of P and by $F(P)$ the value of P with respect to evaluation function F. Let $\mathrm{OPT}^k(R_A, F)$ be the set of optimal partitions of the numerical value range R_A with respect to evaluation function F such that the partitions have at most k intervals. In other words $\mathrm{OPT}^k(R_A, F)$ is

$$\{P \in \Pi_{R_A} \mid k \geq |P| \wedge \forall P' \in \Pi_{R_A} : F(P) \leq F(P')\}.$$

From a member of $\mathrm{OPT}^k_{\min}(R_A, F)$ it is further required that it has as few intervals as any optimal partition;

$$\{P \in \mathrm{OPT}^k(R_A, F) \mid \forall P' \in \mathrm{OPT}^k(R_A, F) : |P| \leq |P'|\}.$$

In practice the maximum number of intervals has the upper bound V, the number of bins in the range.

One can define many different versions of the optimal multisplitting problem. From the practical point of view the interesting ones are the following.

Globally optimal: Find an optimal partition $P \in \mathrm{OPT}^V(R_A, F)$. It is sufficient to return any optimal partition, be it of any arity.

Minimal globally optimal: Find an optimal partition $P \in \mathrm{OPT}^V_{\min}(R_A, F)$ such that its arity is at most that of any other optimal partition of R_A.

Bounded arity optimal: Find an optimal partition $P \in \mathrm{OPT}^k(R_A, F)$ such that $|P| \leq k \leq V$. It is sufficient to return any bounded arity optimal partition as long as its arity is at most k.

Minimal bounded arity optimal: Find a bounded arity optimal partition $P \in \mathrm{OPT}^k_{\min}(R_A, F)$ such that its arity is at most that of any other bounded arity optimal partition of R_A.

Fixed arity optimal: Find an optimal partition $P \in \mathrm{OPT}^k(R_A, F)1$ such that $|P| = k$, where $k \leq V$.

Example Consider the numerical value range shown in Fig. 1. As already observed, the partition with all bins as separate intervals is one of the globally *TSE*-optimal partitions $\mathrm{OPT}^9(R_A, TSE)$ for this numerical value range. It has nine intervals and makes 7 misclassifications. However, it is not a $\mathrm{OPT}^9_{\min}(R_A, TSE)$ partition, because there is one partition with only two intervals that obtains only the same misclassification rate or *TSE*-value: the one in which the two first bins make up the first interval and the remaining bins are gathered into the second interval.

Observe that the 3-optimal partition also has score 7. Since this is the globally optimal score, it must also be bounded arity optimal $\mathrm{OPT}^3(R_A, TSE)$. However, the partition is not minimal bounded arity optimal $\mathrm{OPT}^3_{\min}(R_A, TSE)$ because of the existence of the binary partition with the same *TSE*-score.

3. Pruning of cut points in preprocessing

As discussed above, the partition containing all bins as its intervals is a globally optimal partition for *TSE*. The same actually holds for all convex (and concave) evaluation functions (see the next section). However, it is possible to preprocess the numerical value range into an often radically smaller number of example groups without losing the possibility to recover optimal partitions.

The processing of a numerical value range R_A starts with sorting the examples along the range and by recording the class distributions of the examples that have the same numerical value for the attribute A, thus, belonging to the same bin. The class distribution information suffices to evaluate the goodness of the partition, the actual example set does not need to be maintained.

To construct *blocks* of examples we merge together adjacent class uniform bins with the same class label (see Fig. 2) [8]. The *boundary points* [11] of the value range are the borders of its blocks. Block construction still leaves all bins with a mixed class distribution as their own blocks.

It has been proven that many well-known attribute evaluation functions cannot obtain their optimal value within a block of examples. The evaluation functions that are known

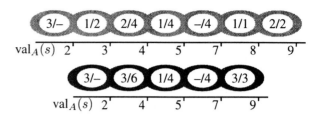

Figure 2. The blocks (above) and segments (below) in the sample of Fig. 1. Block borders are the boundary points of the range R_A and segment borders are a subset of them.

to have optimal partitions defined by boundary points are *Average Class Entropy*, *Information Gain* [17], *Gain Ratio* [17], *Normalized Distance Measure* [15], *Gini Index* [5], *Training Set Error*, and the *MDL-measure* of Wallace and Patrick [19].

From bins we obtain *segments* of examples by combining adjacent bins with an equal relative class distribution (see Fig. 2). Segments group together adjacent mixed-distribution bins that have equal relative class distribution. Also adjacent class uniform bins fulfill this condition; hence, uniform blocks are a special case of segments and segment borders are a subset of boundary points.

Elomaa and Rousu [9] have shown that for the above-mentioned attribute evaluation functions (with the exception of the MDL-measure) only segment borders need to be examined. So the search space of the algorithms can be limited to the combinations of the remaining cut point candidates. When the evaluation function is *cumulative* [12, 8], that is, takes the form of a sum, the combinations can be checked in quadratic time using dynamic programming. Not all common evaluation functions possess this property. For example, the non-convex functions Gain Ratio and Normalized Distance Measure do not belong to this class of functions.

4. Optimal partitions of strictly convex evaluation functions

Many of the most widely used attribute evaluation functions are either *convex* (upwards) or *concave* (i.e., convex downwards) [4, 13, 8]; both are usually referred to as convex functions.

Definition A function $f(x)$ is said to be *convex* over an interval (a, b) if for every $x_1, x_2 \in (a, b)$ and $0 \leq \rho \leq 1$,

$$f(\rho x_1 + (1 - \rho)x_2) \leq \rho f(x_1) + (1 - \rho)f(x_2).$$

A function f is said to be *strictly convex* if equality holds only if $\rho = 0$ or $\rho = 1$.

A function f is *concave* if $-f$ is convex.

Let X be a variable with domain $\mathcal{X}$. Let E denote the expectation. In the discrete case $EX = \sum_{x \in \mathcal{X}} p(x)x$, where $p(x) = \mathbf{Pr}\{X = x\}$.

Theorem 1 (Jensen's inequality [7]) *If f is a convex function and X is a random variable, then*

$$Ef(X) \geq f(EX).$$

If f is strictly convex, then the above inequality implies that $X = EX$ with probability 1, i.e., X is a constant.

For a concave function Jensen's inequality is reversed. Thus, for a concave f, substituting discrete expectation, the inequality becomes

$$\sum_{x \in \mathcal{X}} p(x)f(x) \leq f\left(\sum_{x \in \mathcal{X}} p(x)x\right). \quad (1)$$

Jensen's inequality does not restrict the probability distribution underlying the expectation. It is enough that all probabilities $p(x)$, $x \in \mathcal{X}$, are non-negative and sum up to 1.

Typically, partition ranking functions give each interval a score using an *impurity* function [5], which tries to estimate the class coherence of the interval. The interval scores are usually weighted relative to the sizes of the intervals. Thus, a common form of an evaluation function F is

$$F\left(\biguplus_i S_i\right) = \sum_i \frac{|S_i|}{|S|} I(D_{S_i}), \quad (2)$$

where D_S is the relative class frequency distribution of the set S and I is an impurity function. By relative class frequency distribution of the set S we mean the vector $\langle P(c_1, S), \ldots, P(c_m, S) \rangle$ in which $c_1, \ldots, c_m$ are the possible values of the class attribute C and $P(c, S)$ stands for the proportion of elements of S that have class c: $|\{s \in S \mid \text{val}_C(s) = c\}|/|S|$. Now, $|S_i|/|S| \geq 0$ for all i and $\sum_i(|S_i|/|S|) = 1$ and Eq. 1 can be applied here. Furthermore, because we identify samples with their class distributions, $D_S = \sum_i(|S_i|/|S|)D_{S_i}$ and we get the following result.

Corollary 1 *If the impurity function I is concave, then*

$$F\left(\biguplus_i S_i\right) \leq F(S), \quad (3)$$

in which $F(S)$ is the score of the unpartitioned data. Thus, any splitting of the data can only decrease the value of F and splitting on all cut points will lead to the best score.

Moreover, for strictly concave I, the equality holds only if $D_{S_i} = D_{S_j}$ for all $i \neq j$. Therefore, merging together adjacent segments will always result in a partition with a worse score.

By considering a convex, rather than a concave, evaluation function for which optimization means maximization and reversing the inequalities of equations 1 and 3, it is observed that also then any partitioning leads to a better score.

Examples of commonly used attribute evaluation functions that are strictly convex or concave are Average Class Entropy, Information Gain, and Gini index.

Let the *full segment partition* of a numerical value range be the one in which each segment of the range constitutes a partition interval. By Corollary 1 strictly convex and concave functions must have a globally optimal partition defined by segment borders. Next we show that this partition, in fact, is the *unique* minimal globally optimal partition with respect to such functions.

Theorem 2 *For any strictly concave function F the full segment partition of any value range is the unique minimal globally optimal partition.*

Proof Let P be an arbitrary partition of a value range R_A. Let P' be obtained from P by adding a cut point on each segment border that is not in P. Each new cut point defines two intervals to P'. By the strict concavity of F and Corollary 1, $F(P') \leq F(P)$. Adding a further cut point to P' cannot improve the score of the partition, since it must introduce two new intervals with an equal relative class frequency distribution. Therefore, P' is an optimal partition of R_A.

Next, we remove from P' all cut points that are not on segment borders to obtain partition P''. The intervals on both sides of a cut point that is removed must have the same relative class frequency distribution. Thus, $F(P'') = F(P')$. Obviously P'' is the full segment partition of R_A.

No more cut points can be removed from P'' without changing the F-score, because all adjacent intervals now have different relative class distributions and F is strictly concave. Hence, P'' must be minimal.

The claim follows because P and R_A are arbitrary. $\square$

Bounding the arity of the partition below the number of segments means that the full segment partition cannot be considered as an alternative. However, many concave functions have non-positive second derivatives. This will help us to restrict our attention on segment borders even when the partition arity is bounded. Elomaa and Rousu [9] gave an explicit proof for a couple of such functions; the proof below applies to all such functions.

The following proof (and some subsequent ones) concerns binary partitioning. However, for evaluation functions of the form (2) the theorem applies to the multi-interval case as well, since moving the cut point within an embedded binary partition affects only the corresponding two terms in the impurity score. The other terms in the multisplit are not

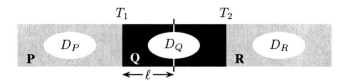

Figure 3. The proof setting considers partitioning of the sample $P \cup Q \cup R$ within segment Q. Dividing Q at any point results in two subsets with equal relative class distributions.

affected by moving the cut point within the example segments under consideration (see [8, 9] for a more thorough treatment of this topic).

Theorem 3 *For an impurity function F with a second derivative that is non-positive everywhere, there is a partition in $\text{OPT}^k(R_A, F)$, where k and R_A are arbitrary, such that its cut points are segment borders.*

Proof Let P, Q, and R be example sets separated by cut points T_1 and T_2. Let the set Q be composed of a single example segment. Let us consider splitting the sets P, Q, and R in two intervals so that the cut point is situated inside Q or on its borders. Let us denote by $\ell \in [0, 1]$ the fraction of Q situated to the left of the cut point (see Fig. 3).

The class distribution of the left-hand side of the cut is $|P| D_P + \ell |Q| D_Q$. Thus, the class distribution of the left-hand side of the partition moves along a line segment $[|P| D_P, |P| D_P + |Q| D_Q]$ in the space of class distributions. Since F has second derivative that is non-positive everywhere, F is concave along the line segment. Hence, the local minima lie at the end points of the line segment; that is, on T_1 and T_2.

By symmetry, also the right-hand side of the split forms a concave curve, and the quality of the split is concave over $[T_1, T_2]$, because the sum of two concave functions is also concave. Hence, no local minimum can lie inside the segment Q. □

Based on the above theorem, it is sufficient to restrict one's attention to segment borders in bounded arity optimization given a strictly convex attribute evaluation function. Whether two segments should be separated or not in a bounded arity partition cannot be decided by looking at the (relative) class distributions of the segments alone. One needs to take into account as well the *context* in which the segments are. A context consists of the example set preceding the pair of segments and that following it.

Theorem 4 *For any strictly concave function F and every pair of example segments P and Q, there is a context O, R such that partition $(O \cup P) \uplus (Q \cup R)$ is optimal.*

Proof Because P and Q are segments, their relative class distributions D_P and D_Q are different. Let us consider the context O, R such that $O = R = P \cup Q$. Then

$$
\begin{aligned}
F(O \uplus (P \cup Q \cup R)) &= F((O \cup P \cup Q) \uplus R) \\
&= F(O \cup P \cup Q \cup R) \\
&\geq F((O \cup P) \uplus (Q \cup R)),
\end{aligned}
$$

because of the strict concavity of F. □

Because of Theorem 4 one cannot prune away segment borders without taking into account the placement of the other cut points. Thus, it seems that developing a general subquadratic preprocessing scheme for operating on a subset of segment borders is difficult.

5. Optimal partitions of Training Set Error

TSE is not a strictly concave function [10]. Therefore, Corollary 1 and Theorem 4 do not tell us anything about the function's *minimal* globally optimal partition, although, Theorem 3 and the earlier explicit proof [9] show that only segment borders need to be considered. We prove that some segment borders can, indeed, be disregarded when trying to find optimal partitions with respect to *TSE*.

Let a segment *majority alternation point* be the border in between two consecutive segments that have different majority classes. For example in the data set of Fig. 2 there is only one majority alternation, in between the first and the second segment. Majority alternations help to find *TSE*-optimal partitions.

Theorem 5 *The partition defined by segment majority alternations is the unique minimal globally optimal partition with respect to TSE.*

Proof Let P be the partition defined by segment majority alternations. It is easy to check that P has the same misclassification rate as the full segment partition. Thus, P is globally optimal with respect to *TSE*.

To see that P is minimal as well, let us first show that all majority alternation points must be cut points in the minimal globally optimal partition of *TSE*. Let R_A be an arbitrary value range (with at least one majority alternation) and $M \in \text{OPT}_{\min}^V(R_A, TSE)$ be such that it does not contain all majority alternation points. Let Q be an interval of M containing the majority alternation points $a_1, \ldots, a_n$, which are not a part of the partition. Because the majority class of segments changes at the majority alternation points, partitioning Q into $n + 1$ subintervals at these majority alternations reduces misclassification of Q and, thus, gives a better partition than M. This contradicts the optimality of M. Therefore, any minimal globally optimal partition has a cut point in each majority alternation point.

Let us now assume that the minimal globally optimal partition M has also other cut points than majority alternations. Let c be one such extra cut point. Now c is in between two consecutive majority alternation points a_i and a_{i+1}. Thus, the majority classes in both sides of c are the same, and the partition intervals $(a_i, c]$ and $(c, a_{i+1}]$ have the same class label. Removing c will not affect the number of misclassifications, but reduces the arity of the partition. Hence, the existence of c contradicts the minimality of partition M. If there are more than one extra cut points in between a_i and a_{i+1}, the intervals induced by all of them have the same majority class, and all of them can be removed without affecting the misclassification of the partition. □

The segments of a value range can be identified in a left-to-right scan through the sorted example sequence. Thus, also majority alternation points can be found in linear time with respect to the number of examples in the sample. As shown in Theorem 5, as a consequence, the unique minimal globally optimal partition can also be found in linear time.

However, when a bounded arity optimal partition is required, examining majority alternation points alone does not suffice, one has to consider the frequency of the minority classes as well. In the following, we show how the concept of a majority alternation point can be generalized so that handling the bounded arity case becomes possible.

Let A and B be two adjacent example segments with relative class frequency distributions $D_A = \{a_1, \ldots, a_k\}$ and $D_B = \{b_1, \ldots, b_k\}$, respectively. There is a segment *alternation point* in between A and B if there is no index set $I = \{i_1, \ldots, i_k\}$ such that $a_{i_1} \geq a_{i_2} \geq \cdots \geq a_{i_k}$ and $b_{i_1} \geq b_{i_2} \geq \cdots \geq b_{i_k}$. In other words, an alternation occurs, if ordering of all the classes in descending order of frequency is different in the two segments. Clearly, a majority alternation is a special case of an alternation. In the two-class setting the two concepts coincide. Thus the number of alternations is always at least as high as that of majority alternations.

Next we show that, analogously to Theorem 3, only alternations need to be considered when searching for the TSE-optimizing partition.

Theorem 6 *For each value range R_A and each k there is an optimal partition in $\mathrm{OPT}^k(R_A, TSE)$ that is defined on segment alternations.*

Proof Let O, P, Q, and R form a sequence of subsets along the value range R_A. Let the relative class distributions of sets O and R, D_O and D_R, be arbitrary and let $D_P = \{p_1, \ldots, p_m\}$ and $D_Q = \{q_1, \ldots, q_m\}$ be such that there is no alternation point in between the sets P and Q.

Let us consider now splitting the set into two intervals and labeling the left-hand side with class h and the right-hand side with class j. Let $\delta_{h,j}(S \uplus \ldots)$ denote the error of a binary partition with S as the left-hand side and all remaining segments as the right-hand side. Respectively, $\delta_{h,j}(\ldots \uplus S)$ has S as the right hand. Furthermore, let $\delta_j(S)$ denote the error of subset S with respect to class j.

The errors of the partitions are

$$\delta_{h,j}(O \uplus \ldots) = \delta_h(O) + \delta_j(P) + \delta_j(Q) + \delta_j(R)$$
$$\delta_{h,j}((O \cup P) \uplus \ldots) = \delta_h(O) + \delta_h(P) + \delta_j(Q) + \delta_j(R)$$
$$\delta_{h,j}((\ldots \uplus R) = \delta_h(O) + \delta_h(P) + \delta_h(Q) + \delta_j(R).$$

By assumption, the point in between P and Q is not a segment alternation. Therefore, from the definition of a segment alternation it follows that for any pair of classes h and j, $1 \leq h, j \leq m$, either 1) $p_h \leq p_j$ and $q_h \leq q_j$ or 2) $p_h \geq p_j$ and $q_h \geq q_j$. In the first case $\delta_h(P) \geq \delta_j(P)$ and, consequently,

$$\delta_{h,j}(O \uplus (P \cup Q \cup R)) \leq \delta_{h,j}((O \cup P) \uplus (Q \cup R)).$$

In the second case $\delta_h(Q) \leq \delta_j(Q)$, and

$$\delta_{h,j}((O \cup P \cup Q) \uplus R) \leq \delta_{h,j}((O \cup P) \uplus (Q \cup R)).$$

Hence, the partition $(O \cup P) \uplus (Q \cup R)$ is at most as good as the two other partitions. Since the classes h and j and the sets O and R are arbitrary, we have shown that in any partition a cut point that is not a segment alternation, can be replaced with another cut point without increasing the error. □

The consequence of the above theorem is that only those cut points that are alternations need to be considered when looking for the bounded arity optimal *TSE* partition. Hence the sample can be processed into intervals separated by alternation points. Note that this can be done in time $O(Gm \log_2 m)$, where G is the number of example segments, if the decreasing frequency order of the classes is determined by sorting the relative class frequency vector. The time requirement, obviously, is linear in the size of the data, but not in the number of the classes m. However, the number of classes is typically small.

Analogously to Theorem 4, we can show that no alternations can be proven suboptimal without considering the context in which the cut point is; that is, which other cut points are present.

Theorem 7 *For each segment alternation there is a context in which it is the TSE-optimal cut point.*

Proof Let us consider the pair of segments P and Q in the context O, R. Let there be a pair of classes h and j for which it holds that $p_h \geq p_j$ and $q_h \leq q_j$. That is, there is a segment alternation in between P and Q. Now, let the class distribution of O be such that j is the majority class of $O \cup P \cup Q$. Note that distributions of this kind are easily generated by choosing O to be large enough and consist of instances of a single class j. Now, $\delta_h(Q) \geq \delta_j(Q)$ and, consequently,

$$\delta_{h,j}((O \cup P \cup Q) \uplus R) \geq \delta_{h,j}((O \cup P) \uplus (Q \cup R)).$$

Similarly, the class distribution of R can be set so that h is the majority class of $P \cup Q \cup R$. Therefore,

$$\delta_{h,j}(O \uplus (P \cup Q \cup R)) \geq \delta_{h,j}((O \cup P) \uplus (Q \cup R)).$$

Thus, the optimal cut point in this case is the alternation in between P and Q. Since h and j are arbitrary, the claim follows. □

The above theorem shows that the usefulness of an alternation point cannot be judged by examining the two neighboring subsets alone. Hence, the existence of a linear-time preprocessing scheme to prune out alternations from the set of possible cut points seems unlikely.

6. Empirical experiments

In this section we examine segment alternations with real-world data. We test for 28 well-known data sets from the UCI data repository [3] what are the relations of average numbers of bin borders, boundary points, segment borders, segment alternations, and majority alternations per numerical attribute.

Fig. 4 depicts the results of the experiment. The number of segment borders is only slightly smaller than that of boundary points. A striking result is that those domains, where there are many classes (e.g., Abalone, Auto insurance, Letter recognition, and Yeast), the number of segment alternations is not much smaller than that of segment borders. The number of majority alternations, though, is somewhat smaller. However, this result is not really surprising, because the more there are classes the less common it is that two adjacent segments have the same frequency order for all of them. The majority class may still be the same in two adjacent segments, even though the number of classes is high.

There is no difference in the number of alternations and majority alternations on two-class domains (e.g., Adult, Australian, Breast Wisconsin, etc.), which is clear from their definition. For some two-class domains (e.g., Breast Wisconsin, Euthyroid, Heart Hungarian, and Hypothyroid) the number of alternations and majority alternations is significantly lower than that of segment borders (ca. 75%). Hence, one can expect important time savings for *TSE* by processing alternations rather than segment borders. On other multiclass domains (e.g., Annealing, Heart Cleveland, Letter Recognition, Satellite, Vehicle, and Yeast) there is a significant difference in the numbers of alternations and majority alternations.

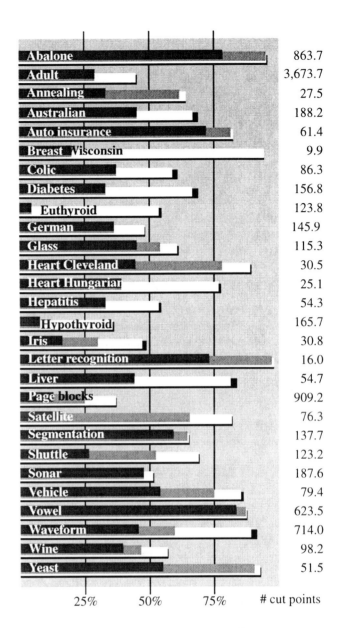

	# cut points
Abalone	863.7
Adult	3,673.7
Annealing	27.5
Australian	188.2
Auto insurance	61.4
Breast Wisconsin	9.9
Colic	86.3
Diabetes	156.8
Euthyroid	123.8
German	145.9
Glass	115.3
Heart Cleveland	30.5
Heart Hungarian	25.1
Hepatitis	54.3
Hypothyroid	165.7
Iris	30.8
Letter recognition	16.0
Liver	54.7
Page blocks	909.2
Satellite	76.3
Segmentation	137.7
Shuttle	123.2
Sonar	187.6
Vehicle	79.4
Vowel	623.5
Waveform	714.0
Wine	98.2
Yeast	51.5

Figure 4. The average number of bin borders (the figures on the right) and the relative numbers of boundary points (black bars below), segment borders (white bars), segment alternation points (gray bars), and majority alternations (dark gray bars on top) per numerical attribute of the domain.

7. Discussion

We saw above that only segment borders need to be examined when searching for any bounded arity optimal partition of a convex or concave evaluation function. Hence, only a well-defined subset of boundary points needs to be examined as cut point candidates. Processing the data into a sequence of example segments can be done in linear time. Preprocessing the data into segments rather than using all the cut points can result in a speed-up of 40–90% [18].

For the Training Set Error function, which is not strictly convex, only alternation points have to be examined in bounded-arity partitioning and a subset of them, majority alternations, are the only cut point candidates in global optimization. On some real-world domains the number of alternation points was discovered to be significantly smaller than that of segment borders. Therefore, practical enhancements can be expected from using alternation points rather than segment borders. However, since *TSE* optimization only requires a linear time [1, 2], careful implementation is needed to harvest the benefit.

Let us still illuminate the significance of the lower bound results for the number of cut point candidates presented in Theorems 3 and 7. The results show that the optimality of an alternation point (or a segment border) cannot be decided by looking at the neighboring example segments alone. Instead, one must consider the context of the cut point, i.e., the neighboring cut points to the left and right. However, since there is a quadratic number of such contexts, one cannot enumerate all of them in a reasonable time. In any case, a linear-time algorithm seems to be out of reach. Using significantly more than a linear time is not fruitful either, because the complexity of the subsequent multisplit search phase is usually quadratic. Moreover, the question of the optimality of a segment border (or an alternation) becomes conditional on the bound on split arity. Since the full segment (and full majority alternation) partition is the minimal globally optimal partition, when the arity bound is very close to the number of segments (or majority alternations), only very few segment borders (and majority alternation points) are suboptimal. Hence, in general, no further savings can be obtained.

8. Conclusion

Examining segment borders — a subset of boundary points — is sufficient in searching for the optimal partition of a value range with respect to a convex evaluation function. The evaluation function Training Set Error, which is not strictly convex, even lets us ignore some of the segment borders; only majority alternations and alternation points need to be considered when searching for the global and bounded arity optimum, respectively.

On the other hand, we were able to show that no segment borders can be ignored with strictly convex functions and in bounded arity partitioning no alternations can be ignored with *TSE* without considering the placement of adjacent cut points. Hence, the limits of fast preprocessing for strictly convex functions and *TSE* seem to have been reached.

References

[1] P. Auer. *Optimal Splits of Single Attributes*. Inst. for Theoretical Computer Science, Graz Univ. of Technology, 1997.

[2] A. Birkendorf. On fast and simple algorithms for finding maximal subarrays and applications in learning theory. In *Computational Learning Theory*, volume 1208 of *LNAI*, pages 198–209. Springer, 1997.

[3] C. L. Blake and C. J. Merz. *UCI Repository of Machine Learning Databases*. Dept. of Information and Computer Science, Univ. of California at Irvine, 1998.

[4] L. Breiman. Some properties of splitting criteria. *Machine Learning*, 24(1):41–47, 1996.

[5] L. Breiman, J. H. Friedman, R. A. Olshen, and C. J. Stone. *Classification and Regression Trees*. Wadsworth, Pacific Grove, CA, 1984.

[6] D. Coppersmith, S. J. Hong, and J. R. M. Hosking. Partitioning nominal attributes in decision trees. *Data Mining and Knowledge Discovery*, 3(2):197–217, 1999.

[7] T. M. Cover and J. A. Thomas. *Elements of Information Theory*. John Wiley & Sons, New York, N.Y., 1991.

[8] T. Elomaa and J. Rousu. General and efficient multisplitting of numerical attributes. *Machine Learning*, 36(3):201–244, 1999.

[9] T. Elomaa and J. Rousu. Generalizing boundary points. In *Proc. 17th Natl. Conf. on Artificial Intelligence*, pages 570–576. AAAI Press, 2000.

[10] T. Elomaa and J. Rousu. On the computational complexity of optimal multisplitting. *Fundamenta Informaticae*, 47:in press, 2001.

[11] U. M. Fayyad and K. B. Irani. On the handling of continuous-valued attributes in decision tree generation. *Machine Learning*, 8(1):87–102, 1992.

[12] T. Fulton, S. Kasif, and S. Salzberg. Efficient algorithms for finding multi-way splits for decision trees. In *Proc. 12th Intl. Conf. on Machine Learning*, pages 244–251. Morgan Kaufmann, 1995.

[13] R. J. Hickey. Noise modelling and evaluating learning from examples. *Artificial Intelligence*, 82(1–2):157–179, 1996.

[14] S. J. Hong. Use of contextual information for feature ranking and discretization. *IEEE Transactions on Knowledge and Data Engineering*, 9(5):718–730, 1997.

[15] R. López de Màntaras. A distance-based attribute selection measure for decision tree induction. *Machine Learning*, 6(1):81–92, 1991.

[16] H. Nguyen and A. Skowron. Boolean reasoning for feature extraction problems. In *Foundations of Intelligent Systems*, volume 1325 of *LNAI*, pages 117–126. Springer-Verlag, 1997.

[17] J. R. Quinlan. Induction of decision trees. *Machine Learning*, 1(1):81–106, 1986.

[18] J. Rousu. *Efficient Range Partitioning in Classification Learning*. PhD thesis, Dept. of Computer Science, Univ. of Helsinki, 2001.

[19] C. S. Wallace and J. D. Patrick. Coding decision trees. *Machine Learning*, 11(1):7–22, 1993.

[20] D. Zighed, R. Rakotomalala, and F. Feschet. Optimal multiple intervals discretization of continuous attributes for supervised learning. In *Proc. 3rd Intl. Conf. on Knowledge Discovery and Data Mining*, pages 295–298. AAAI, 1997.

Using Artificial Anomalies to Detect Unknown and Known Network Intrusions

Wei Fan*
IBM T.J.Watson Research
Hawthorne, NY 10532
weifan@us.ibm.com

Matthew Miller, Salvatore J. Stolfo
Computer Science, Columbia University
New York, NY 10027
{mmiller,sal}@cs.columbia.edu

Wenke Lee
College of Computing, Georgia Tech
Atlanta, GA 30332
wenke@cc.gatech.edu

Philip K. Chan
Computer Science, Florida Tech
Melbourne, FL 32901
pkc@cs.fit.edu

Abstract

Intrusion detection systems (IDSs) must be capable of detecting new and unknown attacks, or anomalies. We study the problem of building detection models for both pure anomaly detection and combined misuse and anomaly detection (i.e., detection of both known and unknown intrusions). We propose an algorithm to generate artificial anomalies to coerce the inductive learner into discovering an accurate boundary between known classes (normal connections and known intrusions) and anomalies. Empirical studies show that our pure anomaly detection model trained using normal and artificial anomalies is capable of detecting more than 77% of all unknown intrusion classes with more than 50% accuracy per intrusion class. The combined misuse and anomaly detection models are as accurate as a pure misuse detection model in detecting known intrusions and are capable of detecting at least 50% of unknown intrusion classes with accuracy measurements between 75% and 100% per class.

1 Introduction

Classification and anomaly detection are two common data analysis tasks. *Anomaly detection* tracks events that are inconsistent with or deviate from events that are known or expected. For example, in intrusion detection anomaly detection systems flag observed activities that deviate significantly from established normal usage profiles. On the other hand, classification systems use patterns of well-known classes to match and identify known labels for unlabeled datasets. In intrusion detection, classification of known attacks is also called *misuse detection*.

Anomaly detection systems are not as well studied, explored, or applied as classification systems. Most of the leading commercial intrusion detection systems (IDSs) employ solely misuse detection techniques, which use patterns of "known" attacks to detect intrusions. However, as anecdotes of serious break-ins to major government, military, and commercial sites have shown, our adversaries, knowing that intrusion prevention and detection systems are installed in our networks, will always be attempting to develop and launch "new" attacks. Last year's Distributed Denial-of-Service (DDOS) attacks have caused major disruptions for services provided over the Internet.

In the generation of classification models, training data containing instances of known classes is often available for training (or human analysis) and the goal is simply to detect instances of these known classes. Anomaly detection, however, relies on data belonging to one single class (such as purely *normal* connection records) or limited instances of some known classes with the goal of detecting all unknown classes. It is difficult to use traditional inductive learning algorithms for such a task, as most are only good at distinguishing the boundaries among all given classes of data. In this paper, we explore the use of traditional inductive learning algorithms for anomaly detection by working from the dataset level. We present methods for generating artificial anomalies based on known classes to coerce an arbitrary machine learning algorithm to learn hypotheses that separate all known classes from unknown classes. We discuss the generation of anomaly detection models from pure normal data, and also discuss the generation of combined misuse and anomaly detection models from data that contains known classes. We apply the proposed approaches to network-based intrusions.

---

*This work was completed when the author was a PhD student at Columbia University

123

The rest of the paper is organized as follows. Section 2 discusses the motivation for artificial anomaly generation and the different methods. In Sections 3-6, we evaluate our methods using RIPPER [2], an inductive rule learner, trained and tested with the 1998 DARPA Intrusion Detection Evaluation dataset. Section 7 reviews related work in anomaly detection. Section 8 offers conclusive remarks and discusses avenues for future work.

A longer version of this paper can be found at http://www.cs.columbia.edu/~wfan

2 Artificial Anomaly Generation

A major difficulty in using machine learning methods for anomaly detection lies in making the learner discover boundaries between known and unknown classes. Since we begin without any examples of anomalies in our training data (by definition of the task of anomaly detection), a machine learning algorithm will only uncover boundaries that separate different known classes in the training data. This behavior is intended to prevent overfitting a model to the training data. Learners only generate hypotheses for the provided class labels in the training data. These hypotheses define decision boundaries that separate the given class labels. To achieve generalization and avoid overfitting, learning algorithms usually do not specify a boundary beyond what is necessary to separate known classes.

Some learners can generate a default classification for instances that are not covered by the learned hypothesis. The label of this default classification is often defined to be the most frequently occurring class of all uncovered instances in the training data. It is possible to modify this default prediction to be *anomaly*, signifying that any uncovered instance should be considered anomalous. It is also possible to tune the parameters of some learners to coerce them into learning more specific hypotheses. However, our experimentation with these methods does not yield a reasonable performance.

The failure of using more specific hypotheses and modifying a model's default prediction has motivated us to propose *artificial anomaly generation* for such a task. Artificial anomalies are injected into the training data to help the learner discover a boundary around the original data. All artificial anomalies are given the class label *anomaly*. Our approach to generating artificial anomalies focuses on "near misses," instances that are close to the known data, but are not in the training data. We assume the training data are representative; hence near misses can be safely assumed to be anomalous. Our artificial anomaly generation methods are independent of the learning algorithm, as the anomalies are merely added to the training data.

Input: D; Output: D'.

1. let F = set of all features of D.
2. let V_f = set of unique values of some feature $f \in F$.
3. let $D' = \emptyset$.
4. for each $f \in F$:
   - let $countV_{max}$ = the number of occurrences of the most frequently occurring value in V_f.
   - for each $v \in V_f$:
     – let $countV$ = the number of occurrences of v in D.
     – loop $i : countV < i \leq countV_{max}$:
       * let d = a randomly chosen datum $d \in D$.
       * let v_f = the value of feature f for d.
       * replace v_f with a randomly chosen value v' s.t. $v' \neq v \wedge v' \neq v_f$ to create d'.
       * $D' \leftarrow D' \cup \{d'\}$.
5. return D'.

Note: The algorithm can be modified to take a factor, n, and produce $n \times |D|$ artificial anomalies.

Figure 1. Distribution-Based Artificial Anomaly (DBA2) Generation Algorithm

2.1 Distribution-based Artificial Anomaly

Since we do not know where the exact decision boundary is between the known and anomalous instances, we assume that the boundary may be very close to the existing data. To generate artificial anomalies close to the known data, a useful heuristic is to randomly change the value of one feature of an example while leaving the other features unaltered.

Some regions of known data in the instance space may be sparsely populated. We compare sparse regions to small islands, and dense regions to large islands, in an ocean. To avoid overfitting, learning algorithms are usually biased towards discovering more general hypotheses. Since we only have known data, we want to prevent hypotheses from being *overly* general when predicting these known classes. That is, sparse regions may be grouped into dense regions to produce singularly large regions covered by overly general hypotheses. Using our analogy, small islands are unnecessarily grouped into large islands to form apparently larger islands. It is possible to produce artificial anomalies around the edges of these sparse regions and coerce the learning algorithm to discover the specific boundaries that distinguish these regions from the rest of the instance space. In other words, we want to generate data that will amplify these sparse regions.

Sparse regions are characterized by infrequent values of individual features. To amplify sparse regions, we proportionally generate more artificial anomalies around sparse regions depending on their sparsity using a proposed algorithm presented in detail in Figure 1. Assuming that the value v of some feature f is infrequently present in the dataset, we calculate the difference between the number of occurrences of v, $countV$, and the number of occurrences of the most frequently occurring value v_{max} of the given feature, $countV_{max}$. We then randomly sample $countV_{max} - countV$ data points from the training set. For each data point d in this sample, we replace the value of feature f, v_f, with any v' such that $v' \neq v \wedge v' \neq v_f$ to generate an artificial anomaly, d'. The learning algorithm used will then specifically cover all instances of the data with value v for feature f. This anomaly generation process is called *distribution-based* artificial anomaly generation or DBA2, as the distribution of a feature's values across the training data is used to selectively generate artificial anomalies.

2.2 Filtered Artificial Anomalies

In the above discussion, we assume that artificial anomalies do not intersect with any known data. We could always check for collision with known instances, but this is a very expensive process. Another approach is to filter artificial anomalies with hypotheses learned on the original data. We use the training set plus an initial generation of artificial anomalies to learn a model. We then evaluate this model over previously generated artificial anomalies and remove any anomalies classified as some known class. This process is repeated until the size of the the set of artificial anomalies remains relatively stable.

3 Experimental Setup

For generation of our models, we have chosen to use RIPPER [2], an inductive decision tree learner. RIPPER can learn both *unordered* and *ordered* rulesets. The use of these types of rulesets in IDSs has been discussed in our previous work [3]. In all reported results, unless clearly stated, we always use an *unordered* RIPPER ruleset and inject an amount of distribution-based artificial anomalies equal to the size of the training set (i.e., we use DBA2 with $n = 1$).

Our experiments use data distributed by the 1998 DARPA Intrusion Detection Evaluation Program, which was conducted by MIT Lincoln Lab (available from the UCI KDD repository as the 1999 KDD Cup Dataset). We use the same taxonomy for categorization of intrusions as was used by the DARPA evaluation. This taxonomy places intrusions into one of four categories: denial of service (DOS), probing (PRB), remotely gaining illegal remote access to a local account or service (R2L), and local user gaining illegal root access (U2R). The DARPA data were gathered from a simulated military network and includes a wide variety of intrusions injected into the network over a period of 7 weeks.

Table 1. Intrusions, Categories and Sampling

U2R	R2L	DOS	PRB
buffer_overflow	ftp_write	back	ipsweep
loadmodule	guess_passwd	land	nmap
multihop	imap	neptune	portsweep
perl	phf	pod	satan
rootkit	spy	smurf	
	warezclient	teardrop	
	warezmaster		

Table 2. Anomaly Detection Rate and False Alarm Rate of Pure Anomaly Detection

%a_{ttl}	94.26
%far	2.02

(a)

	%a		%a
buffer_overflow	100.00√	ftp_write	50√
loadmodule	66.67√	guess_passwd	100.00√
multihop	57.14√	imap	83.33√
perl	-	phf	100.00√
rootkit	10.00	spy	-
		warezclient	64.25√
		warezmaster	80.00√
U2R	47.06√	R2L	66.67√
back	100.00√	ipsweep	-
land	75.00√	nmap	-
neptune	80.52√	portsweep	4.81
pod	9.62	satan	0.32
smurf	99.94√		
teardrop	-		
DOS	94.31√	PRB	1.34

√: significant or %a ≥ 50%

(b)

The data were then processed into connection records using MADAM ID [9]. A 10% sample was taken which maintained the same distribution of intrusions and normal connections as the original data (this sample is available as kddcup.data.10% from the UCI KDD repository). We used 80% of this sample as training data and left the remaining 20% unaltered to be used as test data for evaluation of learned models.

4 Pure Anomaly Detection

For pure anomaly detection, we learned a model using all available *normal* connections augmented by DBA2 anomalies generated from these normal connections. We refer to this collection as dataset$_0$. RIPPER learns a large number of rules for both *normal* and *anomaly* from this dataset.

4.1 Results

Table 2 shows the results of the pure anomaly detection model. We use detection rate and false alarm rate to evaluate performance. Anomaly detection rate, or percentage of occurrences of some unknown intrusion i that are detected as anomalies, is defined as $\%a_i = \frac{|A \cap W_i|}{|W_i|} \times 100\%$, where A is the set of all predicted anomalies and W_i is the set of occurrences of label i in the dataset. We omit the subscript i where the meaning is clear from the context. Similarly, we calculate cumulative anomaly detection rate over all unknown intrusions ($\%a_{ttl}$) and cumulative anomaly detection rate over different categories of unknown intrusions (such as $\%a_{u2r}$). Also, we measure the false alarm rate ($\%far$) of anomalous classifications. This is the percentage of predicted anomalies that are *normal* connections, and is defined as $\%far = \frac{|A \cap W_{normal}|}{|A|} \times 100\%$. If a measurement has a value of 0, we represent it with "−" to enhance readability of the presented tables.

The cumulative anomaly detection rate over all intrusions and false alarm rate are shown in Table 2(a). The anomaly detection model successfully detects 94.26% of all anomalous connections in the test data and has a false alarm rate of 2.02%. To examine the performance for specific intrusion classes and categories, the anomaly detection rate ($\%a$) for each class and category is shown in Table 2(b). The anomaly detection model is capable of detecting most intrusion classes, even though there are no intrusions at all in the training set. A total of 17 out of 22 intrusion classes (all non-null measurements) are detected as anomalies. For 13 out of 22 intrusions (all entries highlighted by $\sqrt{}$), the proposed method catches at least 50% of all occurrences. There are 3 intrusions (*guess_passwd, buffer_overflow* and *phf*) that our approach is capable of detecting perfectly (i.e., $\%a = 100\%$). These 3 intrusions belong to the more harmful U2R and R2L categories. The anomaly detection rates of all 4 categories of intrusions indicate that, in general, each category is successfully detected. In 3 out of 4 categories (U2R, R2L and DOS), the model detects more than 50% of all intrusion occurrences of that category, and it is important to note that these three categories are potentially more damaging than PRB.

5 Combined Misuse and Anomaly Detection

Pure anomaly detection might still have high false alarm rate; the boundaries implied by artificial anomalies can be sharpened by real intrusions. Separate modules for anomaly and misuse detection will not be as efficient as one single module that detects misuse and anomaly in the same time. All these have motivated us to explore the use of artificial anomalies for such as task.

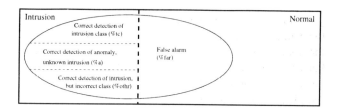

Figure 2. Relationship of Metrics

We learn a single ruleset for combined misuse and anomaly detection. The ruleset has rules to classify a connection to be *normal*, one of the known intrusion classes, or *anomaly*. In order to evaluate this combined approach, we group intrusions together into 13 small *clusters* (details can be found in the longer version of the paper). We create datasets (dataset$_i$, $1 \leq i \leq 12$)[1] by incrementally adding each cluster$_i$ into the *normal* dataset and re-generating artificial anomalies. This is to simulate the process of the invention of new intrusions and their incorporation into the training set. We learn models that contain misuse rules for the intrusions that are "known" in the training data, anomaly detection rules for unknown intrusions in left-out clusters, and rules that characterize normal behavior.

Each cluster contains intrusions that require similar features for effective detection. Clusters should not be confused with the attack categories in our taxonomy. One example of a cluster contains the following intrusions: *buffer_overflow, loadmodule, perl* and *rootkit*. These intrusions all attempt to gain unauthorized root access to a local machine and require features such as *root_shell* (whether a root shell is obtained) and *su_flag* (an indication of whether the su root command been used, in any of its derivations). Some clusters have completely disjoint feature sets, yet some intersect slightly. A model that is trained to detect intrusions from one cluster may have difficulties detecting intrusions from another cluster. For clusters with intersecting feature sets, we hope that a model learned using training instances of intrusions from some cluster may be used to detect intrusions of other clusters as anomalies.

Before explaining our results, we must define some frequently used terms. Any intrusion class that appears in the training data is a *known intrusion*. Similarly, any intrusion class not in the training set is an *unknown intrusion*, or *true anomaly*. *Predicted anomalies* include *true anomalies* and may also include instances of *known intrusions* and *normal*. We use *anomaly* to refer to *predicted anomaly* where our intention is clear from context.

5.1 Results

Our results for combined misuse and anomaly detection methods are shown in Figures 3-5 and Tables 3-4. Based on the outcome of detection, we calculate the following measurements: true class detection rate ($\%tc$), anomaly detection rate ($\%a$), and other class detection rate ($\%othr$). The relationship of these metrics is shown in the Venn diagram in Figure 2. The outside rectangle represents the set of data to be evaluated and the inside ellipse depicts the set of alarms generated by our learned detection models. True class detection rate measures the percentage of connection class i (*normal* or intrusions) being correctly predicted as its true class, and is defined as $\%tc = \frac{|P_i \cap W_i|}{|W_i|} \times 100\%$, where P_i is the set of predictions with label i. $\%a$ is defined as in Section 4.1, but it can be measured for both known and unknown intrusions or intrusion categories that are predicted as anomalies. Other class detection rate, or the rate of detection as another class of intrusion, is the percentage of occurrences of intrusion i that are detected as some class of intrusion other than its true label or anomaly, and is defined as $\%othr = \frac{\sum_{i' \neq i} |P_{i'} \cap W_i|}{|W_i|} \times 100\%$. Additionally, total detection rate is defined as $\%ttl = \%tc + \%a + \%othr$.

We examine our results from several perspectives. First, it is important to see how the proposed method influences the true class detection rate ($\%tc$) of known intrusions. Ideally, using artificial anomalies should allow anomaly detection to classify true anomalies without degrading the performance of detecting known intrusions with misuse rules. Second, we evaluate the effectiveness of detecting true anomalies. Third, we examine whether anomalous classification can compensate for low detection rates of known intrusions by misuse rules. Finally, we show the false alarm rates of anomaly detection in different test settings.

True Class Detection The true class detection rates of models learned with and without DBA2 are shown in Figure 3. The x-axis shows each dataset, ranging from dataset$_1$ to dataset$_{12}$ as explained in Section 5. We see that the curves for R2L, DOS and PRB are indistinguishable. The difference in U2R curves is reasonably small as well[2]. This observation shows that the proposed DBA method does not deteriorate the effectiveness of detecting particular categories of known intrusions. Next, we examine the efficacy of our approach in detecting anomalies.

True Anomaly Detection In analysis, we consider an anomaly detection model to be *significant* for a particular

---

[1]We leave out the 13th cluster for testing.

[2]Note that there are only 34 U2R instances in the test data. Disagreements in just a few examples can make significant difference in $\%tc$.

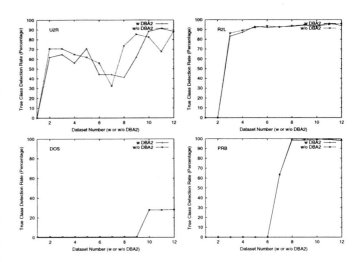

Figure 3. Comparison of True Class Detection Rate (%tc) of Datasets w. and w/o DBA2

Table 3. Percentage of Significant True Anomaly Detections

Dataset	0	1	2	3	4	5	6
Anomaly Types	22	21	17	14	13	12	11
Significant	13	15	14	10	8	9	7
%	59	71	82	71	62	75	64

Dataset	7	8	9	10	11	12
Anomaly Types	10	7	6	5	4	2
Significant	8	6	5	5	3	2
%	80	86	83	100	75	100

detection class if $\%a \geq 50.00\%$. Across 12 experiment settings, there are 122 truly anomalous cases (or 122 intrusions types in 12 experiment settings not included in the training data), and among them, 92 are significant; this is more than 75%. For each experiment setting, the percentage of cases that are significant is shown in Table 3; most are at least 70%.

Next, we study the effectiveness of anomaly detection on different categories of true anomalies. We measure anomaly detection rate ($\%a$) of true anomalies in each intrusion category and all true anomalies (TTL). The results are presented in Table 4. As shown in the upper rightmost curve and the last row of the table under "TTL," the true anomaly detection rate for all true anomalies remains relatively constant as we inject more clusters of intrusions. The curves for U2R, R2L and PRB categories are more bumpy than DOS because the anomaly detection model catches more in one category and fewer in the others.

Table 4. Percentage of True Anomalies Detected as Anomalies ($\%a$)

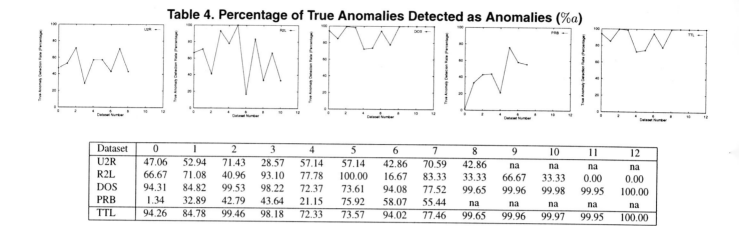

Dataset	0	1	2	3	4	5	6	7	8	9	10	11	12
U2R	47.06	52.94	71.43	28.57	57.14	57.14	42.86	70.59	42.86	na	na	na	na
R2L	66.67	71.08	40.96	93.10	77.78	100.00	16.67	83.33	33.33	66.67	33.33	0.00	0.00
DOS	94.31	84.82	99.53	98.22	72.37	73.61	94.08	77.52	99.65	99.96	99.98	99.95	100.00
PRB	1.34	32.89	42.79	43.64	21.15	75.92	58.07	55.44	na	na	na	na	na
TTL	94.26	84.78	99.46	98.18	72.33	73.57	94.02	77.46	99.65	99.96	99.97	99.95	100.00

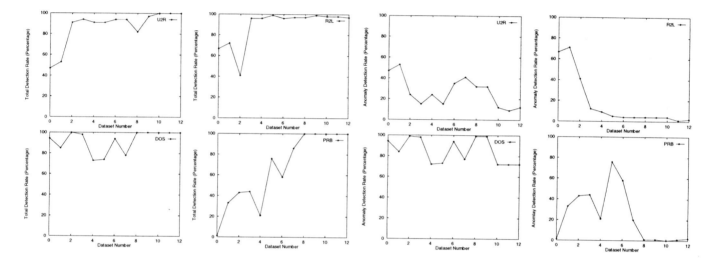

Figure 4. Total Detection Rate ($\%ttl$)

Figure 5. Percentage of Known Intrusions and True Anomalies Detected as Anomalies (%a)

Known Intrusions Detected As Anomalies It is interesting to determine if the proposed approach can prove effective in detecting un-classified known intrusions as anomalies. We consider an anomaly detection method to *significantly compensate* for misuse detection if either the anomaly detection increases the total rate of detection to nearly 100% ($\%tc + \%a \simeq 100\%, \%tc < 100\%$) or $\%a \geq 0.25 \times \%tc$ when $\%tc$ is very low. In 12 experiment settings, there are 88 cases that are candidates for compensation (i.e., $\%tc < 100\%$). Among them, 76 cases (or 86%) are significantly compensated by being detected as anomalies. In 5 of the remaining 12 cases, the intrusions are detected as some other intrusion, leaving no room for anomaly detection to provide any compensation. In Figure 4, we show the total percentage of detection ($\%ttl$) for all 4 categories of intrusions. As expected, there is a general trend of increase. Comparing Figure 4 with Figure 3, we can see a significan higher total detection rate than true class detection rate,

which is mostly attributed to known intrusions being detected as anomalies.

Overall Performance In the above discussion, we have covered the performance of true anomaly detection and misuse detection compensation. We now examine the combined overall performance of detecting both true anomalies *and* known intrusions. The results over all 4 intrusion categories are shown in Figure 5. As expected, there is a general trend of decrease in $\%a$ when the datasets are augmented with more clusters of intrusions. This is caused by the fact that we have learned misuse rules for more intrusions, leaving less room for these intrusions to be detected as anomalies. The shape of the anomaly detection rate curves is somewhat inversely related to their respective true class detection curves in Figure 3. This relationship is explained by the observation that $1 - \%tc$ is an indication of the amount of additional detection that anomaly detection can provide. These decreasing and inverse relationships apply throughout the U2R, R2L and DOS curves, and can be seen in the PRB curves for $dataset_{6-12}$. As we see in Figure 3, as more intrusion clusters are used to augment the *normal* data, the true class detection rates for both U2R and R2L increases and leave less room for anomaly detection to compensate. This explains the generally decreasing tendency of U2R and R2L $\%a$ curves. For DOS attacks, the true class detection rate only rises from 0 to 30% after $dataset_9$, and there is still sufficient room for compensation by anomaly detection — this explains the flatness of the DOS $\%a$ curve in Figure 5. For PRB, the rise in $\%tc$ takes place after $dataset_6$, which is also when we see the complimentary decrease in $\%a$ for $dataset_{6-12}$. The slight bumpiness of the U2R $\%a$ curve is due to the inverse bumpiness of U2R $\%tc$ curve in Figure 3. The slight bumpiness of the DOS and PRB curves are most likely caused by insufficient feature values available when learning a decision boundary for anomalies.

The false alarm rate of anomalous classifications are uniformly below 0.40% (details shown in the longer version of this paper). This confirms that nearly all detected anomalies are either true anomalies or known intrusions. Additionally, the $\%tc$ rates of *normal* connections (or *normal* correctly classified as *normal*) are over or near 99.00%. These observations show the utility of the anomaly detection approach in building highly precise models.

Effects of Cluster Ordering We performed two tests to verify that our results are not influenced by the order in which clusters are added to the training sets. One test is to reverse the cluster ordering as in the previous section, and the other one is a random ordering totally different from the original or second orderings. The results have confirmed that our results are indeed not influenced by cluster order.

6 Additional Issues

We have experimented with different amounts of injected artificial anomalies ($n = 1.5$ or 2). The general trend is that as we increase the injection amount, $\%tc$ of *normal* connections decreases slightly and $\%far$ increases slightly. When the amount of injected artificial anomalies increases, there are more artificial anomalies than normal connections in the training data and the learning algorithm tends to generate more *anomaly* rules. In general, however, the proposed algorithm is not sensitive to the amount of artificial anomalies in the training data.

We experimented with the use of other forms of RIPPER rulesets ($+freq$ and $given$, both of which are *ordered* rulesets). $+freq$ rulesets classify connections in order of increasing frequency followed by *normal*, with a default clas-

sification of *anomaly*. For *given*, we used the following rule order: *normal*, *anomaly* and alphabetically ordered intrusion classes (essentially arbitrary). The results gathered for the use of a $+freq$ ruleset are very close to the detailed results given for our *unordered* rulesets. It is interesting to observe that the *given* rulesets are similar to *unordered* rulesets at later datasets (when more than 3 clusters of intrusions are added to the normal data). However, in the first 2 datasets ($dataset_1$ and $dataset_2$), the anomaly detection is more likely to classify known intrusions as anomalies. This is due to the fact that anomaly rules appear before intrusion rules.

We experimented with the filtering method for DBA2 as proposed in Section 2.2. The generated artificial anomalies were filtered 3 times with a resulting reduction of between 1% and 3% each time. We did not see any significant improvement in performance using this method. We also experimented with filtering anomalies generated using the naive approach and observed that no artificial anomalies were removed at all. The main conclusion to be drawn from these filtering experiments is that most artificial anomalies are truly anomalous, and do not collide with known training data.

7 Related Work

SRI's IDES [6] measures abnormality of current system activity from the probability distributions of past activities. The activities they monitored are host events (e.g., CPU utilization and file accesses); in our work, we monitor network events. Forrest et al. [4] record frequent subsequences of system calls that are used in the execution of a program (e.g., sendmail). Absence of subsequences in the current execution of the same program from the stored sequences constitutes a potential anomaly. Lane and Brodley [8] used a similar approach but they focused on an incremental algorithm that updates the stored sequences and used data from UNIX shell commands. Lee [9], using a rule learning program, generated rules that predict the current system call based on a window of previous system calls. Abnormality is suspected when the predicted system call deviates from the actual system call. Ghosh and Schwartzbard [5] proposed using a neural network to learn a profile of normality. Similar to our approach, random behaviors are generated to represent abnormality for training purposes. Unlike our approach, each of their input features is a distance value from an exemplar sequence of BSM [14] events. This study is one of the first attempts in applying machine learning algorithms to network events for anomaly detection.

Algorithms for anomaly detection and misuse detection have traditionally been studied separately. In SRI's EMERALD [12], anomaly and misuse detection algorithms are encased in separate system components, though their output responses are correlated to generate alarms by the *resolver*. Ghosh and Schwartzbard [5] applied neural networks to both anomaly and misuse detection and compared their relative performance. One of our unique goals in this paper is to study the combination of anomaly and misuse detection in one model to improve overall performance.

We are not aware of closely related work in the generation of training data belonging to an unknown opposite class. Given unlabeled instances, Nigam et al. [13] assigned labels to them using a classifier trained from labeled data and put them in the training set for another round of training. In a skewed distribution scenario, Kubat and Matwin [7] attempted to remove majority instances too close to and too far from the decision boundary. Maxion and Tan [11] used conditional entropy to measure the regularity in the training set and have shown that it is easier to detect anomalies for data with high regularity. Lee and Xiang [10] also applied entropy to determine how hard it is to learn a model of normality and abnormality. Chang and Lippman [1] applied voice transformation techniques to add artificial training talkers to increase variabilities.

8 Conclusion and Future Work

Recent hacker activity has made evident the importance of network-based intrusion detection. Anomaly detection of unknown intrusions is an important and difficult area of IDS. In this paper, we studied the problems of using artificial anomalies to detect unknown and known network intrusions. We proposed a distribution-based anomaly generation algorithm that has proven effective in building anomaly and combined misuse and anomaly detection models that successfully detect known and unknown intrusions.

One assumption of DBA2 is that each dimension (i.e., feature) can be treated individually. In other words, we examine and generate anomalies "dimension by dimension." A possible variation of the algorithm could consider multiple dimensions concurrently or give each dimension a different weight depending on its importance.

References

[1] Eric Chang and Richard Lippmann. Using voice transformations to create additional training talkers for word spotting. In Tesauro et al, editor, *Advances in Neural Processing Systems 7*. MIT Press, 1995.

[2] William Cohen. Fast effective rule induction. In *Proceedings of Twelfth International Conference on Machine Learning (ICML-95)*, pages 115–123. Morgan Kaufman, 1995.

[3] Wei Fan, Wenke Lee, Salvatore Stolfo, and Matthew Miller. A multiple model approach for cost-sensitive intrusion detection. In *Proceedings of Eleventh European Conference on Machine Learning (ECML-00)*, Barcelona, Spain, May 2000.

[4] Stephanie Forrest, Steven A. Hofmeyr, Anil Somayaji, and Thomas A. Longstaff. A sense of self for UNIX processes. In *Proceedings of IEEE Symposium on Security and Privacy 1996*, 1996.

[5] Anup K. Ghosh and Aaron Schwartzbard. A study in using neural networks for anomaly and misuse detection. In *Proceedings of USENIX Security Symposium 1999*, 1999.

[6] Harold Javitz and Alfonso Valdes. The SRI IDES statistical anomaly detector. In *Proceedings of IEEE Symposium on Security and Privacy*, page 1991, 1991.

[7] Miroslav Kubat and Stan Matwin. Addressing the curse of imbalanaced training sets: One sided selection. In *Proceedings of Fourteenth International Conference on Machine Learning (ICML-97)*, pages 179–186. Morgan Kaufmann, 1997.

[8] Terrane Lane and Carla Brodley. Approaches to online learning and concept drift for user identification in computer security. In *Proceedings of Fourth International Conference on Knowledge Discovery and Data Mining (KDD-98)*, pages 259–263, 1998.

[9] Wenke Lee. *A Data Mining Framework for Constructing Features and Models for Intrusion Detection Systems*. PhD thesis, Columbia University, June 1999.

[10] Wenke Lee and Dong Xiang. Information-theoretic measures for anomaly detection. In *The 2001 IEEE Symposium on Security and Privacy*, Oakland, CA, May 2001.

[11] Roy A Maxion and Kymie M.C. Tan. Benchmarking anomaly-based detection systems. In *International Conference on Dependable Systems and Networks*, pages 623–630, June 2000.

[12] Peter G. Neumann and Philip A. Porras. Experiments with EMERALD to date. In *Proceedings of 1999 USENIX Workshop on Intrusion Detection*, 1999.

[13] Kamal Nigam, Andrew McCallum, Sebastian Thrun, and Tom Mitchell. Learning to classify text from labeled and unlabeled documents. In *Proceedings of Fifteenth National Conference on Artificial Intelligence (AAAI-98)*, 1998.

[14] SunSoft. *SunSHIELD Basic Security Module Guide*. SunSoft, Mountain View, CA, 1995.

Using Rule Sets to Maximize ROC Performance

Tom Fawcett

Hewlett-Packard Laboratories

1501 Page Mill Road

Palo Alto, California 94304

tfawcett@acm.org

Abstract

Rules are commonly used for classification because they are modular, intelligible and easy to learn. Existing work in classification rule learning assumes the goal is to produce categorical classifications to maximize classification accuracy. Recent work in machine learning has pointed out the limitations of classification accuracy: when class distributions are skewed, or error costs are unequal, an accuracy maximizing rule set can perform poorly. A more flexible use of a rule set is to produce instance scores indicating the likelihood that an instance belongs to a given class. With such an ability, we can apply rulesets effectively when distributions are skewed or error costs are unequal. This paper empirically investigates different strategies for evaluating rule sets when the goal is to maximize the scoring (ROC) performance.

1. Introduction

Rules are commonly used in data mining because of several desirable properties: they are simple, intuitive, modular, and straightforward to generate from data. Some work concentrates on association rule mining, in which individual rules are valued for the insight they can bring. Another area of work, termed *classification rule learning*, strives to generate rules that collectively have good classification performance [6]. It is the use of rules for classification with which this paper is concerned. Existing methods strive to optimize classification decisions, usually by maximizing accuracy (or equivalently, minimizing error rate) on a training set. They usually try to construct small, compact rule sets while achieving high accuracy.

Recent work in machine learning and data mining has demonstrated problems with using accuracy as a metric [11]. It can be irrelevant or misleading when classes are imbalanced or when misclassification costs are unequal. Ideally, costs should be taken into account and accuracy max-

imization should be replaced with cost minimization. If error costs and class distributions are known exactly, a cost minimizing problem can sometimes be transformed into an accuracy maximizing one. However, in many cases neither costs nor class distributions are known exactly, and both can change over time and over contexts [9, 5]. As conditions change, a high accuracy rule set may produce sub-optimal classifications. Data mining that uses rules for real world classification tasks will eventually face these problems.

One way to allow flexibility under uncertain conditions is to use probabilities. Instead of requiring that a classifier produce a hard (discrete) class decision for each instance, we can use the classification model to generate an estimated probability that an instance belongs to a specific class. Given such probabilities, simple decision theory can be used to generate thresholds under various assumptions of error costs and class distributions. This enables robust classification systems that can operate in uncertain and changing environments [10].

Probabilistic classification has been investigated with other model classes such as neural networks [14] and ensembles of decision trees [8, 21]. These models tend to be much more complex than rule sets and may not have rules' appealing properties of modularity and intelligibility. An open question in data mining is how to use a set of rules to produce reliable instance probabilities. This approach raises issues of how to generate scores from rules, how to combine scores from different rules, and how to select rules for inclusion in a rule set.

This paper explores these issues empirically. We employ the area under an ROC curve (commonly referred to as the AUC) to evaluate and compare strategies [2]. The remainder of this paper is structured as follows. We begin by discussing ROC curves and the AUC as a tool for measuring instance scoring performance. We discuss rules and rulesets, and how they can be used for classification. We then describe a number of experiments investigating the use of classification rules for scoring instances. We conclude by discussing future work and some related issues.

131

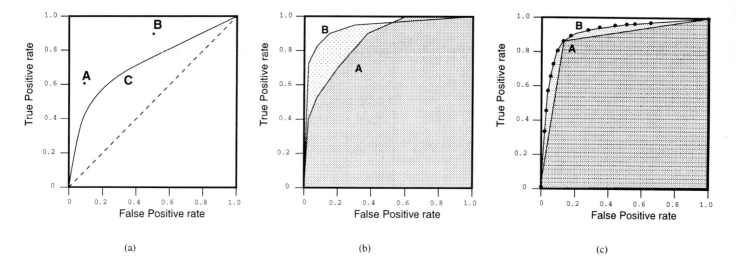

| (a) | (b) | (c) |

Figure 1. ROC graphs and area under ROC curves.

2. ROC graphs and the AUC

To evaluate probabilistic classifiers we adopt Receiver Operating Characteristics (ROC) analysis. ROC graphs have long been used in signal detection theory to depict the tradeoff between hit rates and false alarm rates of classifiers [4, 17]. ROC analysis has been extended for use in visualizing and analyzing the behavior of diagnostic systems [16].

A discrete classifier applied to a test set generates two important statistics. The **True Positive rate** (also called hit rate and recall) of a classifier is:

$$\text{TP rate} \approx \frac{\text{positives correctly classified}}{\text{total positives}}$$

The **False Positive rate** (also called false alarm rate) of the classifier is:

$$\text{FP rate} \approx \frac{\text{negatives incorrectly classified}}{\text{total negatives}}$$

On an ROC graph, TP rate is plotted on the Y axis and FP rate is plotted on the X axis.

A discrete classifier—one that outputs only a class label—produces an *(FP rate,TP rate)* pair, so it corresponds to a single point in ROC space. Classifiers A and B in Figure 1a are discrete classifiers.

Several points in ROC space are useful to note. The lower left point $(0,0)$ represents the strategy of never issuing a positive classification; such a classifier commits no false positive errors but also gains no true positives. The opposite strategy, of unconditionally issuing positive classifications, is represented by the upper right point $(1,1)$. Any

classifier that randomly guesses the class will produce performance on the diagonal line $y = x$. The point $(0, 1)$ represents perfect classification. Informally, one point in ROC space is better than another if it is to the northwest (TP rate is higher, FP rate is lower, or both) of the first.

The diagonal line $y = x$ represents the strategy of randomly guessing a class, and any classifier that appears in the lower right triangle performs worse than random guessing. This triangle is therefore usually empty.

Classifiers can often be coerced into producing a probability estimate or numerical rank for each instance. Such a *ranking* or *scoring* classifier can be used with a threshold to produce a binary classifier: if the classifier output is above the threshold, the classifier produces a **Y**, else a **N**. Each threshold value produces a different point in ROC space, so varying the threshold from $-\infty$ to $+\infty$ produces a curve through ROC space. An ROC curve illustrates the error tradeoffs available with a given classifier. Figure 1a shows the curve of a probabilistic classifier, C, in ROC space. A more thorough discussion of ROC curves may be found in Provost and Fawcett's article [10].

An important point about ROC graphs is that they measure the ability of a classifier to produce good *relative* instance rankings. A classifier need not produce accurate, calibrated probability estimates; it need only produce relative accurate scores that serve to discriminate positive and negative instances. Thus, although this paper refers to rule sets used as probabilistic classifiers, these classifiers only need to produce good relative scores.

2.1. Area under an ROC curve (AUC)

An ROC curve is a two-dimensional depiction of classifier performance. To compare classifiers we often want to reduce ROC performance to a single number representing average expected performance. A common method is to calculate the area under the ROC curve, abbreviated **AUC** [2, 7]. Since the AUC is a portion of the area of the unit square, its value will always be between 0 and 1.0. However, because random guessing produces the diagonal line between $(0, 0)$ and $(1, 1)$, which has an area of 0.5, no realistic classifier should have an AUC less than 0.5.

The AUC has an appealing statistical property: the AUC of a classifier is equivalent to the probability that the classifier will rank a randomly chosen positive instance higher than a randomly chosen negative instance. This is equivalent to the Wilcoxon test of ranks [7]. It is possible for a high-AUC classifier to perform worse in a specific region of ROC space than a low-AUC classifier, but in practice the AUC performs very well and is often used when a general measure of predictiveness is desired.

Figure 1b shows the areas under two ROC curves, A and B. B has greater area and therefore better average performance. Figure 1c shows the area under the curve of a binary classifier A and a scoring classifier B. Classifier A represents the performance of B when B is used with a single, fixed threshold. Though the performance of the two is equal at the fixed point (B's threshold), B's performance becomes inferior to A further from this point.

2.2. AUC with multiple classes

The two ROC axes represent tradeoffs between false positives and true positives with two classes. ROC analysis has been extended to multiple classes [15], but the result in general is non-intuitive and computationally expensive. In practice, n classes are commonly handled by producing n different ROC graphs. Let C be the set of all classes. ROC graph i plots the classification performance using class c_i as the positive class and all other classes $c_{j \neq i} \in C$ as the negative class. Each such graph yields an AUC area.

For a single probabilistic classifier this produces n separate curves with n different AUC values. The AUC values can be combined into a single weighted sum where the weight of each class c_i is proportional to the class's prevalence in the training set:

$$AUC_{total} = \sum_{c_i \in C} AUC(c_i) \cdot p(c_i)$$

3. Rules and classification

A rule is a conjunction of conditions, the satisfaction of which implies membership in a class. For simplicity, consider a two-class problem with classes **p** and **n**. An example of a simple rule and some of its performance statistics is:

$$\mathbf{x_1} \wedge \mathbf{x_2} \wedge \mathbf{x_3} \longrightarrow \mathbf{p}$$
TP=15, P=100, TPrate=.15
FP=2, N=200, FPrate=.01

The second line specifies that within the dataset, 15 **p** examples satisfy $x_1 \wedge x_2 \wedge x_3$ (True Positives). There are 100 **p** examples altogether, yielding a true positive rate (TPrate) of .15. The rule matches two **n** examples (False Positives). There are 200 **n** examples altogether, yielding a false positive rate (FPrate) of .01.

3.1. Rule sets

For the purpose of classification, rules are usually aggregated into a rule set. When the set is ordered this is called a *decision list* [13]. To classify an instance, each rule in the list is tried in sequence, and the first rule whose conditions are satisfied determines the hypothesized class. A decision list is an "**if-then-elseif-...-else-**" formulation of a boolean concept. General cases usually appear toward the end of the list with more specific cases (exceptions) placed at the front. If no rule matches, the final classification is the most prevalent class.

Given a decision list and an instance set, a 2×2 confusion matrix can be generated, representing the classification performance:

		Hypothesized class	
		p	n
Actual	**p**	TP	FN
class	**n**	FP	TN

This adds the TN (True Negatives) and FN (False Negatives) statistics. From this matrix we can estimate the error rate of the classifier:

$$\begin{aligned} \text{Error rate} &= \frac{FP + FN}{TP + TN + FP + FN} \\ \text{Accuracy} &= 1 - \text{Error rate} \end{aligned}$$

Error rate weights FP and FN equally. If we have separate error cost functions $c(FP)$ and $c(FN)$, we instead want to measure expected cost:

$$\text{Cost} = FP \cdot c(FP) + FN \cdot c(FN)$$

Given such cost functions, simple decision analysis provides a way to determine each instance's optimal classification, if we can get an estimate of its class probability. For each instance I we should hypothesize the positive class **p** if:

$$[1 - p(\mathbf{p}|I)] \cdot c(FP) \; < \; p(\mathbf{p}|I) \cdot c(FN)$$

Note that the prior $p(\mathbf{p})$ is incorporated into the posterior estimate $p(\mathbf{p}|I)$. To minimize overall error cost, we thus need a way to estimate instance probabilities $p(\mathbf{p}|I)$. Given the statistics of a matching rule, we can generate a probability estimate simply as

$$p(\mathbf{p}|I) \approx \frac{\text{TP}}{\text{TP} + \text{FP}}$$

This measure is commonly called the *confidence* of the rule. This equation is often used in a Laplace corrected form:

$$p(\mathbf{p}|I) \approx \frac{\text{TP} + 1}{\text{TP} + \text{FP} + |C|}$$

Laplace correction smoothes probability estimates when the number of instances covered by a rule is small.

As mentioned above, we do not need accurate instance probabilities $p(\mathbf{p}|I)$ to make the classification decision. We only need good relative instance scores. Given a test set and knowledge of performance conditions, we can derive a suitable threshold [10].

3.2. Resolving rules

If rules were mutually exclusive, each instance would match at most one rule and a probability estimate could be taken directly from the rule's confidence. However, rules can overlap and multiple rules may "claim" an instance, resulting in potentially conflicting classifications and instance scores. Resolving these into a single class and score is called the *resolution problem*. Given the information available from each rule, a number of strategies can be enumerated:

1. **Random selection (RAND)**. A random matching rule is chosen, and its class and confidence are used as the winning class and score. RAND provides a baseline against which other strategies may be compared.

2. **First matching rule (FIRST)**. Each rule in a list is tested in turn and the first matching rule wins. The rule's class and confidence become the winning class and score. This strategy is appropriate when order is imposed, as in decision lists [13]. When rules are sorted by decreasing confidence, this method selects the highest confidence rule.

3. **Equal voting (VOTE)**. Each rule is tested, and every matching rule contributes a single vote for its class. The majority class wins. The score assigned to the instance is the fraction of votes won by the majority.

4. **Weighted voting (WVOTE)**. This is similar to VOTE, but each matching rule votes with a strength of its confidence. The class with the highest summed confidence wins, and the score is the average confidence.

The rationale for weighted voting is that high confidence rules should have more influence than lower confidence ones.

5. **Lowest false positive rate (LFPR)**. Among matching rules, the rule with the lowest false positive rate is selected. Its class and confidence are used as the class and score. The rationale for LFPR is to choose the matching rule that has the least chance of committing a false positive error.

With each method, if no rule fires on an instance, the majority class is used and the majority class prevalence is used as the instance score.

4. Experiments

Given the discussion above, we investigate the following questions:

1. Is instance scoring really necessary for good AUC performance? Perhaps rule sets already produce good classification performance throughout ROC space. Some prior work has found this not to be true with other model classes [11], but this hypothesis is worth testing this hypothesis with rule set classifiers.

2. What is the effect of various rule set resolution strategies on a rule set's instance scores?

3. How well do rules perform relative to other methods for scoring instances?

4.1. Rule induction methods

Two rule induction methods were used in the experiments below. They are fairly different in operation and in results.

C4.5rules [12] is a companion program to C4.5 which creates rule sets by post-processing decision trees. C4.5rules begins by constructing a rule from each path to a leaf node, with each attribute test in the path becoming a conjunct in the rule. This results in potentially a large number of rules, but the initial set of rules is mutually exclusive. C4.5rules then examines the rules, testing each conjunct to determine whether it is necessary; if rule accuracy is unaffected, the conjunct is deleted. After deleting conjuncts, the resulting rule set is no longer mutually exclusive and exhaustive, so C4.5rules performs several final steps for improving the rule set. Finally it groups the rules by class, based on the number of false positive errors committed by each class subgroup. In the experiments reported here, both C4.5 and C4.5rules were used with their default settings.

Dataset	Resolution strategies					Number of rules	
	RAND	**FIRST**	**LFPR**	**VOTE**	**WVOTE**	**Generated**	**Fired**
Breast-wisc	69.9 ± 6.8	50.1 ± 0.5	97.6 ± 1.3	95.1 ± 2.6	94.7 ± 3.4	306.5	112.3
Car	74.0 ± 2.7	61.7 ± 7.0	92.3 ± 1.7	71.2 ± 4.5	94.3 ± 1.4	107.6	6.6
Cmc	63.2 ± 3.8	63.7 ± 4.1	63.7 ± 4.2	61.9 ± 4.3	63.9 ± 4.0	196.6	3.2
Covtype	69.0 ± 1.9	64.4 ± 3.8	72.9 ± 2.1	66.6 ± 1.8	73.3 ± 1.5	1416.6	32.2
Crx	70.0 ± 7.5	75.0 ± 4.3	83.9 ± 5.1	88.4 ± 5.0	90.2 ± 4.2	758.5	69.8
German	58.2 ± 4.7	67.1 ± 4.9	66.2 ± 5.3	62.3 ± 5.6	71.9 ± 4.9	807.5	36.0
Glass	68.4 ± 10.1	70.1 ± 9.1	71.2 ± 10.0	74.4 ± 10.0	71.7 ± 10.5	183.7	35.0
Image	88.8 ± 2.1	86.0 ± 4.1	93.3 ± 1.4	80.9 ± 2.4	92.3 ± 1.6	811.4	66.2
Kr-vs-kp	66.2 ± 3.0	52.9 ± 3.9	92.6 ± 1.5	84.8 ± 3.3	88.8 ± 2.4	2328.3	340.0
Mushroom	90.1 ± 1.8	53.4 ± 2.5	100.0 ± 0.0	99.4 ± 0.1	99.9 ± 0.1	2362.2	131.7
Nursery	90.2 ± 0.6	93.7 ± 0.4	97.1 ± 0.2	93.6 ± 0.6	96.0 ± 0.3	606.6	12.1
Promoters	51.8 ± 12.6	47.1 ± 20.6	72.6 ± 13.3	76.8 ± 14.4	83.5 ± 16.2	7432.2	334.0
Sonar	48.3 ± 11.2	57.0 ± 11.0	59.4 ± 13.7	63.5 ± 12.4	65.8 ± 12.8	10075.7	1869.2
Splice	57.8 ± 2.3	45.9 ± 2.5	74.6 ± 2.2	70.6 ± 2.8	87.3 ± 1.6	8406.8	214.9

Table 1. Mean and standard deviation of AUCs using RL rules with various resolution strategies. The final two columns give the average number of rules generated and the average number of rules fired on each instance.

RL [3] is a MetaDENDRAL-style rule learner that performs a general-to-specific search of the space of conjunctive rules. This type of rule-space search is described in detail by Webb [18]. RL uses a beam search for rules whose coverage and confidence are above user-defined thresholds. In the experiments reported here, a beamsize of 100 was used along with rule constraints of confidence greater than 0.60, coverage greater than two instances, and no more than four conjuncts per rule. A Laplace corrected version of the confidence equation was used, to compensate for small sample sizes.

With its default settings, RL only finds rules that cover examples not previously covered by other rules. In these experiments, RL was allowed to generate redundant rules in order to experiment with the effects of rule overlap. It is important to note that, unlike C4.5rules, RL does not try to produce a rule set that maximizes classification accuracy.

4.2. Datasets

Fourteen data sets were selected from the UCI Repository [1]. In general, datasets were avoided that had extreme class skews since the purpose of this paper is not to experiment with learning under skewed distributions. Datasets were chosen that could produce reasonable performance with standard rule learners.

Each experiment reported below was performed using 10-fold cross-validation on the datasets. Means and standard deviations of the experimental results are given. For readability, AUCs are reported as percentages of the total possible so they range from 0 to 100 instead of 0 to 1.

4.3. The effect of resolution strategy

Tables 1 and 2 show the effect of different rule resolution strategies using rules from RL and C4.5rules, respectively. Several observations can be made from these results. From the last two columns in each table we can see that RL generated far more rules for each dataset than C4.5rules did, in some cases by one or two orders of magnitude. Also, the number of rules fired on average per instance is far greater for RL than for C4.5rules, indicating that rule contention is considerably higher for the rule sets created by RL. Neither result is surprising. The RL parameters were chosen so that it would generate a large number of overlapping rules, resulting in high contention. On the other hand, C4.5rules begins with a set of mutually exclusive rules; although rules can overlap after conjunct deletion, they will not otherwise conflict.

The results of this contention are seen in the effect of the resolution strategy. There is little difference between resolution strategies with the C4.5rules results because there is little contention to resolve. The RL results in Table 1 show much greater variability.

The differences between resolution strategies are evaluated more carefully in Table 3, in which they are compared in pairs using the mean AUC for each dataset shown in Table 1. Results are given for both the Sign Test (which ignores difference magnitudes) and the Wilcoxon Matched-Pair Signed-Ranks Test (which takes magnitude into account). Each test result is the probability that the first strategy is indistinguishable from the second in performance. RAND and FIRST both perform poorly, and are indeed virtually indistinguishable in performance. Uni-

Dataset	Resolution strategies					Number of rules	
	RAND	**FIRST**	**LFPR**	**VOTE**	**WVOTE**	**Generated**	**Fired**
Breast-wisc	96.6 ± 3.2	97.6 ± 3.0	97.5 ± 2.9	95.8 ± 2.9	97.4 ± 3.6	8.2	2.2
Car	97.6 + 0.7	98.4 ± 0.7	98.4 ± 0.7	96.3 ± 0.8	98.3 ± 0.7	78.6	1.3
Cmc	66.1 ± 5.4	66.8 ± 5.0	66.6 ± 5.2	67.0 ± 2.6	66.5 ± 4.9	39.1	1.2
Covtype	81.5 ± 1.2	83.1 ± 1.5	82.6 ± 1.4	80.3 ± 1.2	82.2 ± 1.4	63.5	1.6
Crx	89.1 ± 3.7	90.9 ± 2.6	89.2 ± 4.2	84.7 ± 3.3	90.1 ± 3.4	12.9	1.9
German	68.2 ± 9.0	68.1 ± 9.7	67.6 ± 10.1	67.7 ± 8.4	67.9 ± 9.6	23.4	1.1
Glass	76.9 ± 5.0	77.1 ± 5.2	77.1 ± 5.2	75.8 ± 8.7	75.7 ± 5.9	12.2	1.0
Image	99.0 ± 0.5	99.1 ± 0.5	99.1 ± 0.5	98.0 ± 0.5	99.0 ± 0.5	28.6	1.5
Kr-vs-kp	99.7 ± 0.2	99.9 ± 0.1	99.9 ± 0.1	99.5 ± 0.4	99.7 ± 0.2	26.3	1.9
Mushroom	100.0 ± 0.0	100.0 ± 0.0	100.0 ± 0.0	99.8 ± 0.0	100.0 ± 0.0	11.5	1.2
Nursery	99.7 ± 0.1	99.8 ± 0.1	99.8 ± 0.0	99.6 ± 0.1	99.8 ± 0.1	336.8	1.6
Promoters	89.2 ± 10.0	89.4 ± 10.6	89.9 ± 11.2	88.9 ± 9.9	88.4 ± 12.8	8.0	1.2
Sonar	77.7 ± 11.6	78.2 ± 12.3	77.7 ± 10.9	76.4 ± 11.2	77.8 ± 13.7	9.1	1.3
Splice	97.1 ± 0.7	97.5 ± 0.6	97.4 ± 0.6	97.2 ± 0.8	97.2 ± 0.7	76.2	2.3

Table 2. Mean and standard deviation of AUCs using C4.5rules with various resolution strategies. The final two columns give the average number of rules generated and the average number of rules fired on each instance.

form unweighted voting (VOTE) performs better. The two measures that take rule statistics into account, LFPR and WVOTE, perform best of all. WVOTE appears to have an advantage over LFPR in these domains but the difference is statistically inconclusive.

Pair	Wins-Ties-Losses	Sign test	WMPSR test
RAND vs FIRST	8-0-6	0.791	0.194
RAND vs LFPR	0-0-14	0.000	0.000
RAND vs VOTE	4-0-10	0.180	0.011
RAND vs WVOTE	0-0-14	0.000	0.000
FIRST vs LFPR	1-0-13	0.002	0.000
FIRST vs VOTE	4-0-10	0.180	0.013
FIRST vs WVOTE	0-0-14	0.000	0.000
LFPR vs VOTE	10-0-4	0.180	0.194
LFPR vs WVOTE	5-0-9	0.424	0.153
VOTE vs WVOTE	2-0-12	0.013	0.003

Table 3. Pairwise comparisons of the results of resolution strategies from Table 1.

4.4. Benefits of instance scoring

Another question is whether instance scoring is useful. Perhaps the classification done by C4.5rules is already sufficient to provide good performance over the entire ROC space. To evaluate this hypothesis, the AUC performance of the C4.5rules was measured as if the rules were evaluated directly for classification; that is, as if they were interpreted by the `consultr` program that comes with C4.5.

This evaluation produces a single "accuracy point" in ROC space. This constitutes an ROC curve whose area can be measured. If probabilistic interpretation of rules has benefits for predictiveness, we might expect a situation as shown in Figure 1c, where classifier B (probabilistic) has a larger area than classifier A (discrete).

Figure 2 shows ROC curves from a C4.5rules rule set on the Covtype domain. Discrete classification yields an FP rate of .13 and a TP rate of .70. Connecting this point to $(0, 0)$ and $(1, 1)$ yields an ROC "curve" with flat sides. If the same rules are used for instance scoring, a curve of greater area can be produced, as shown in the figure. At the accuracy point the two strategies are close in performance, but elsewhere in ROC space the instance scoring strategy exhibits a substantial predictive advantage. This can be seen in the "bowing out" of the scoring curve, which has greater area than the discrete classification curve. This means that as conditions change away from the accuracy point, e.g., the class distribution becomes skewed or one type of error becomes more costly, instance scoring will have a definite advantage.

Table 4 compares these AUCs across the UCI domains. "AUC using consultr" is the AUC from discrete classification and "AUC using WVOTE" is the AUC using instance scoring with WVOTE. On nearly every dataset the WVOTE AUC exceeds the corresponding AUC that would result from direct classification. The results pass both the Sign and Wilcoxon tests at $p < .05$. This demonstrates that using rules to score instances results in a measurable predictive benefit over what would be realized from interpreting them as direct classification rules.

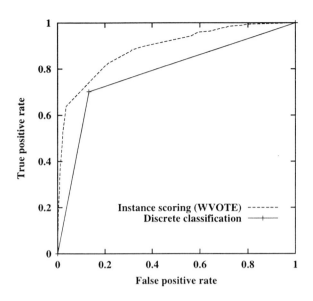

Figure 2. ROC curves of the Covtype domain

Dataset	AUC using `consultr`	AUC using WVOTE
Breast-wisc	95.6 ± 3.4	97.3 ± 3.6
Car	95.3 ± 2.2	98.3 ± 0.7
Cmc	65.1 ± 2.7	66.4 ± 4.9
Covtype	76.0 ± 2.7	82.2 ± 1.4
Crx	85.6 ± 4.8	90.2 ± 3.4
German	64.4 ± 3.4	68.4 ± 9.9
Glass	74.4 ± 7.5	75.5 ± 6.0
Image	97.7 ± 0.7	99.0 ± 0.5
Kr-vs-kp	99.6 ± 0.4	99.7 ± 0.2
Mushroom	100.0 ± 0.0	100.0 ± 0.0
Nursery	98.8 ± 0.3	$99.8 \pm .1$
Promoters	90.1 ± 11.0	88.9 ± 13
Sonar	73.9 ± 6.8	76.9 ± 14
Splice	94.8 ± 1.3	97.2 ± 0.7

Table 4. Comparisons of AUCs under direct classification ("AUC using consultr") and under instance scoring ("AUC using WVOTE").

4.5. Comparison with Naive Bayes

Finally, how well do rules perform against other probability estimation techniques? Rules have various desirable qualities such as modularity and intelligibility, but these qualities are shared by other model classes as well, such as Naive Bayes and linear threshold units. How do rules compare?

Table 5 shows ROC performance of Naive Bayes[1] and rules from C4.5rules using WVOTE resolution. In general, rules appear to perform better than simple Naive Bayes. This observation passes a Sign test ($p < 0.05$), though it does not pass the Wilcoxon test at an acceptable level.

It is possible that more complex model classes such as decision tree ensembles [8, 21] or neural networks [14] would produce better probability estimates than rules do. However, these model classes are more complex and expensive, and lack some of the appealing characteristics of classification rules.

5. Discussion and Future Work

This paper has demonstrated that rules, commonly used for direct classification, can also be used effectively for probability estimation. In fact, when used this way their predictive performance increases. In general, they are competitive with a simple probability estimation method such as Naive Bayes. It is likely that further experimentation with the rule generation methods would result in better absolute performance from rules.

Several important issues have been left unaddressed in this paper.

Even when rule generation is efficient and effective, classification performance can benefit from rule selection, and this is an area of ongoing work. Wilkins and Ma [19] proved that optimal rule selection is NP-hard because overlapping rules can have "sociopathic" interactions; therefore, practical rule selection techniques must be heuristic. The field of machine learning would benefit from a systematic study of heuristic rule selection methods.

The experiments in this paper employed two standard rule learning methods, C4.5rules and RL, but neither was designed to maximize AUC performance. An open question is how rule *generation* should be altered to produce rule with good AUC performance. Various ideas have been proposed, such as starting with a high confidence bias and dynamically adjusting it based on feedback from AUC performance. To our knowledge, no such research has been seriously pursued.

Finally, a related issue is how best to learn rules when one or more classes is rare. Induction under skewed distributions is an important open issue in machine learning that has received attention recently. The datasets used in this study were chosen to be fairly balanced in order to sidestep this issue so that off-the-shelf rule induction methods could be used. Research on other model classes with skewed data sets should provide valuable insights on rule induction as well.

---

[1]Because Naive Bayes is representationally equivalent to a linear threshold unit, no separate test was done.

Dataset	AUC (Naive Bayes)	AUC (C4.5rules)
Breast-wisc	93.1 ± 5.5	97.3 ± 3.6
Car	92.3 ± 2.2	98.3 ± 0.7
Cmc	64.1 ± 5.8	66.4 ± 4.9
Covtype	81.5 ± 2.4	82.2 ± 1.4
Crx	87.6 ± 4.3	90.2 ± 3.4
German	77.1 ± 4.5	68.4 ± 9.9
Glass	74.0 ± 8.7	75.5 ± 6.0
Image	95.6 ± 0.9	99.0 ± 0.5
Kr-vs-kp	95.1 ± 0.8	99.7 ± 0.2
Mushroom	99.8 ± 0.1	100.0 ± 0.0
Nursery	98.0 ± 0.2	$99.8 \pm .1$
Promoters	97.7 ± 4.0	88.9 ± 13
Sonar	76.1 ± 13.0	76.9 ± 14.3
Splice	99.2 ± 0.6	$97.2 \pm .7$

Table 5. Probability estimation: Naive Bayes versus rules from C4.5rules using WVOTE

6. Acknowledgments

Discussions with Foster Provost were helpful in clarifying some rule learning issues. Two anonymous reviewers provided valuable comments. I thank Ross Quinlan for making C4.5 and C4.5rules available for non-commercial use; I thank Foster Provost for making the RL program available; and I thank the Weka project [20] for making their software available.

Much open source software was used in this work. I wish to thank the authors and maintainers of XEmacs, TEX, LATEX, Perl and its many user-contributed packages, and the Free Software Foundation's GNU Project. Scripts for the Sign and Wilcoxon tests were written by Rob van Son.

References

[1] C. Blake and C. Merz. UCI repository of machine learning databases, 1998. http://www.ics.uci.edu/~mlearn/MLRepository.html.

[2] A. P. Bradley. The use of the area under the ROC curve in the evaluation of machine learning algorithms. *Pattern Recognition*, 30(7):1145–1159, 1997.

[3] S. Clearwater and F. Provost. RL4: A tool for knowledge-based induction. In *Proceedings of the Second International IEEE Conference on Tools for Artificial Intelligence*, pages 24–30. IEEE CS Press, 1990.

[4] J. P. Egan. *Signal Detection Theory and ROC Analysis*. Series in Cognitition and Perception. Academic Press, New York, 1975.

[5] T. Fawcett and F. Provost. Activity monitoring: Noticing interesting changes in behavior. In Chaudhuri and Madigan, editors, *Proceedings on the Fifth ACM SIGKDD International Conference on Knowledge Discovery and Data Mining*, pages 53–62, San Diego, CA, Aug. 1999.

[6] A. Freitas. Understanding the crucial differences between classification and discovery of association rules – a position paper. *KDD Explorations*, 2(1):65–69, June 2000.

[7] J. A. Hanley and B. J. McNeil. The meaning and use of the area under a receiver operating characteristic (ROC) curve. *Radiology*, 143:29–36, 1982.

[8] F. Provost and P. Domingos. Well-trained PETs: Improving probability estimation trees. CeDER Working Paper #IS-00-04, Stern School of Business, New York University, NY, NY 10012, 2001.

[9] F. Provost and T. Fawcett. Analysis and visualization of classifier performance: Comparison under imprecise class and cost distributions. In *Proceedings of the Third International Conference on Knowledge Discovery and Data Mining (KDD-97)*, pages 43–48, Menlo Park, CA, 1997. AAAI Press.

[10] F. Provost and T. Fawcett. Robust classification for imprecise environments. *Machine Learning*, 42(3):203–231, Mar. 2001.

[11] F. Provost, T. Fawcett, and R. Kohavi. The case against accuracy estimation for comparing induction algorithms. In J. Shavlik, editor, *Proceedings of the Fifteenth International Conference on Machine Learning*, pages 445–453, San Francisco, CA, 1998. Morgan Kaufmann.

[12] J. R. Quinlan. *C4.5: Programs for machine learning*. Morgan Kaufmann, 1993.

[13] R. L. Rivest. Learning decision lists. *Machine Learning*, 2:229–246, 1987.

[14] S. Santini and D. A. Bimbo. Recurrent neural networks can be trained to be maximum a posteriori probability classifiers. *Neural Networks*, 8(1):25–29, 1995.

[15] A. Srinivasan. Note on the location of optimal classifiers in n-dimensional ROC space. Technical Report PRG-TR-2-99, Oxford University Computing Laboratory, Oxford, England, 1999.

[16] J. Swets. Measuring the accuracy of diagnostic systems. *Science*, 240:1285–1293, 1988.

[17] J. A. Swets, R. M. Dawes, and J. Monahan. Better decisions through science. *Scientific American*, 283:82–87, October 2000.

[18] G. Webb. OPUS: An efficient admissible algorithm for unordered search. *Journal of Artificial Intelligence Research*, 3:383–417, 1995.

[19] D. C. Wilkins and Y. Ma. The refinement of probabilistic rule sets: sociopathic interactions. *Artificial Intelligence*, 70:1–32, 1994.

[20] I. Witten and E. Frank. *Data mining: Practical machine learning tools and techniques with Java implementations*. Morgan Kaufmann, San Francisco, 2000. Software available from http://www.cs.waikato.ac.nz/~ml/weka/.

[21] B. Zadrozny and C. Elkan. Learning and making decisions when costs and probabilities are both unknown. In *Proceedings of KDD-2001*, pages 204–213, Aug. 2001.

A Synchronization Based Algorithm for Discovering Ellipsoidal Clusters in Large Datasets

Hichem Frigui
Dept. of Electrical & Computer Eng.
University of Memphis
hfrigui@memphis.edu

Mohamed Ben Hadj Rhouma
Department of Mathematics
Georgia Institute of Technology
rhouma@math.gatech.edu

Abstract

This paper introduces a new scalable approach to clustering based on synchronization of pulse-coupled oscillators. Each data point is represented by an integrate-and-fire oscillator, and the interaction between oscillators is defined according to the relative similarity between the points. The set of oscillators will self-organize into stable phase-locked subgroups. Our approach proceeds by loading only a subset of the data and allowing it to self-organize. Groups of synchronized oscillators are then summarized and purged from memory. We show that our method is robust, scales linearly, and can determine the number of clusters. The proposed approach is empirically evaluated with several synthetic data sets and is used to segment large color images.

1. Introduction

Clustering is an effective technique for exploratory data analysis, and has been studied for several years. It has found applications in a wide variety of areas such as pattern recognition, data mining, and statistical data analysis. Most existing methods can be categorized into the following categories: partitioning methods, hierarchical methods, and locality-based methods. Partitional clusters generate a partition of the data such that objects in a cluster are more similar to each other than they are to objects in other clusters. The k-Means[25], EM[10], and k-medoids[19] are examples of partitional methods. Fuzzy partitional algorithms, such as the Fuzzy C-Means[3], generate a "fuzzy partition" where objects can belong to more than one cluster with different degrees. Hierarchical clustering procedures yield a nested sequence of partitions that corresponds to a graphical representation known as the dendrogram. Hierarchical procedures can be either agglomerative or divisive. Locality-based methods group objects based on local relationships. Some locality-based algorithms are density

based, while others assume a random distribution.

Recently, the advent of World Wide Web search engines, the problem of organizing massive multimedia databases, and the concept of "data mining" large databases has lead to renewal of interest in clustering and the development of new algorithms[17]. Some of these methods are evolutionary and introduce enhancements and combination of traditional methods, others are revolutionary and introduce new concepts. In this paper, we describe a new approach that can cluster very large data sets while operating within a limited memory (RAM) buffer. The proposed algorithm is based on the synchronization of pulse-coupled oscillators, and is an extension of our recently introduced clustering algorithm, called Self-Organization of Oscillators Network (SOON)[24], to efficiently cluster huge data sets.

The organization of the rest of the paper is as follows. In section 2, we briefly review related work. In section 3, we describe SOON, and in section 4, we instantiate it for the case of hype-ellipsoidal clusters. In section 5, we extend SOON to handle very large data sets. In section 6, we evaluate the performance of the proposed algorithm. Finally, section 7 contains the conclusions.

2. Related Work

Recently, few algorithms that can cluster large data sets have been proposed. In [19], Kaufman and Rousseeuw proposed CLARA, which is based on finding k representative objects that minimize the sum of the within-cluster dissimilarities. Ng and Han [23] proposed a variation of CLARA called CLARANS, that makes the search for the k medoids more efficient. CLARANS may require several passes over the database making the run time cost prohibitive for very large databases. The ScaleKM[4] and ScaleEM[5] are two other scalable partitional algorithms. These algorithms are based on loading only a subset of the data into the main memory, then using the K-Means [25] or EM [10] to partition it. Both ScaleKM and ScaleEM inherit the drawbacks of K-Means and EM algorithms, namely, sensitivity to noise and initial model parameters.

DBSCAN [12] is a density-based algorithm that was developed to identify arbitrarily shaped clusters. DBSCAN is not suitable for high dimensional data since the intrinsic structure of all clusters cannot be characterized by global density parameters. Moreover, because DBSCAN is density-based, random sampling may not be used to scale it. Other density-based algorithms include DBCLASD[32], which assumes that points within a cluster are uniformly distributed, STING[30], an enhancement of DBSCAN, WaveCluster[26], a method based on wavelets, and DENCLUE[16] which uses influence functions to model the points density.

CLIQUE[1] is a region-grouping algorithm that can find clusters embedded in subspaces of the original high dimensional data space. In the first step, CLIQUE identifies subspaces that contain clusters. Then, it identifies the clusters and generates their description. The clusters generated by CLIQUE depend on two parameters which are difficult to determine: the number of intervals in every dimension (ζ), and the threshold density in each unit (τ). Moreover, CLIQUE is scalable with respect to the number of records, but not with respect to the number of attributes. Finally, like most region growing approaches, CLIQUE cannot handle overlapping clusters.

BIRCH[33] and CURE[15] are two hierarchical algorithms that use region grouping techniques. BIRCH first performs a pre-clustering phase in which dense regions are identified and represented by compact summaries. Second, it treats each of the sub-cluster summaries as representative points and applies an agglomerative hierarchical clustering. Similar to CLARANS, BIRCH works satisfactory only when the clusters can be represented well by separated hyper-spheres of similar sizes, and when the clusters are spanned in the whole space. CURE represents each cluster by a given number of "well-scattered" points to capture its shape and extent. During the merging step, the chosen scattered points are "shrunk" towards the centroid of the cluster, and the clusters with the closest pair of representative points are merged. The multiple representative points allow CURE to recognize non-spherical clusters, and the shrinking process reduces the effect of outliers. To handle large databases, CURE employs a combination of random sampling and partitioning.

3. Synchronization of Coupled Oscillators

3.1. Background

Mutual synchronization of coupled oscillators is a widespread phenomenon that manifests itself in many fields [21, 22, 31]. One of the most cited examples is that of the southeastern fireflies that gather in large numbers on trees. First, these insects start flashing in random order. Then, they self organize and start flashing in total synchrony [7]. A characteristic feature of a population of biological oscillators is that they interact with each other by firing sudden impulses. For example, fireflies communicate through light flashes. The mathematical analysis of the details of such interactions is a complex task. An alternative approach is to neglect the details of the shape of the oscillations and model the population by a set of identical Integrate and Fire (IF) oscillators [2]. In this case, each oscillator is characterized by a state variable, which is assumed to be monotonically increasing toward a threshold. When this threshold is reached, the oscillator fires a pulse to the other oscillators, jumps back to a basal level, and a new period begins.

The dynamics of a population of N coupled oscillators has been investigated by several researchers. It has been shown that a population of N oscillators can exhibit a chaotic behavior, synchronize, or self-organize into phase-locked sub-groups. The interest in self-organization behavior has increased considerably since evidence that this technique is used by the visual cortex in the mammalian brain have been discovered [11]. Strogatz and Mirollo [22] proved that a population of N identical concave down IF oscillators with constant excitatory coupling synchronizes for almost all initial conditions. The effect of delay, inhibitory coupling, and local coupling on similar IF models have been examined by several authors[6, 29, 18].

In [24], we introduced a model that combines synchronization and clustering concepts and resulted in an efficient and robust clustering approach. In addition to helping the model self-organize into stable structured groups, the synergy between clustering and synchronization reduces the computational complexity significantly. This is because the number of competing oscillators shrinks progressively as synchronized oscillators get summarized by a single oscillator. A brief description of this model is presented in the following section.

3.2. Self-Organization of Oscillators Network

Let $\mathcal{Y} = \{\mathbf{y}_j | j = 1, \cdots, N\}$ be a set of N objects, where each object, $\mathbf{y}_j \in \mathbb{R}^p$. We represent each object ($\mathbf{y}_j$) by an oscillator (O_j) which is characterized by a phase variable ϕ_j and a state variable x_j, which evolves according to:

$$x_j = f(\phi_j) = \frac{1}{b} \ln \left[1 + (e^b - 1)\phi_j \right]. \quad (1)$$

In (1), b is a constant that measures the extent to which f is concave down. The function f plays the role of an amplitude function, while $\phi_i \in [0, 1]$ represents the phase, which in case of no coupling with other oscillators corresponds to the normalized time elapsed since the last firing of O_i. Whenever x_i reaches a threshold at $x_i = 1$, the ith oscillator fires (i.e., excites/inhibits other oscillators) and ϕ_i and

x_i are instantaneously reset to zero, after which the cycle repeats. As a consequence, the state variables of all other oscillators O_j ($j \neq i$) will change by an amount $\epsilon_i(\phi_j)$, i.e.,

$$x_j(t^+) = x_j(t) + \epsilon_i(\phi_j), \qquad (2)$$

where $\epsilon_i(\phi_j)$ is a coupling function that is positive if O_i and O_j are similar, and negative otherwise. We use

$$\epsilon_i(\phi_j) = \begin{cases} C_E\left[1 - d_{ij}^2/\delta_0\right] & \text{if} \quad d_{ij}^2 \leq \delta_0 \\ -C_I\left[\frac{d_{ij}^2 - \delta_0}{\delta_1 - \delta_0}\right] & \text{if} \quad \delta_0 < d_{ij}^2 \leq \delta_1 \\ -C_I & \text{otherwise} \end{cases} \qquad (3)$$

d_{ij} is the dissimilarity between O_i and O_j, C_E and C_I (typically $\in [0.01, 0.1]$) are the maximum excitatory and inhibitory coupling. Eq.(3) states that a firing oscillator pulls similar ones closer by an amount proportional to their degree of similarity, and pushes non-similar oscillators farther by an amount proportional to the degree of dissimilarity. δ_0 can be regarded as a resolution parameter, and δ_1 (typically $\delta_1 = 2 \times \delta_0$) is a constant that is used to indicate that if an oscillator is too far, then it should simply be maximally inhibited. The SOON algorithm is summarized below. The mathematical analysis and a proof of convergence for the case of two oscillators can be found in [24].

Self-Organization of Oscillators Network (SOON)

Select a dissimilarity measure d();
Initialize phases ϕ_i randomly for $i = 1, \cdots, N$;
Repeat
  Identify next oscillator to fire=$\{O_i : \phi_i = \max_{j=1}^N \phi_j\}$;
  Compute d_{ij} for $j = 1 \cdots N, j \neq i$;
  Bring ϕ_i to threshold, and adjust other phases:
    $\phi_j = \phi_j + (1 - \phi_i)$ for $j = 1, \cdots, N$;
  For *all oscillators O_j ($j \neq i$)* **Do**
    Compute state variable $x_j = f(\phi_j)$ using (1);
    Compute coupling $\epsilon_i(\phi_j)$ using (3);
    Adjust state variables using (2);
    Compute new phases using $\phi_j(t^+) = f^{-1}(x_j(t^+))$;
  Identify synchronized oscillators;
  Update the parameters of the synchronized group;
  Reset phases of oscillators that synchronized in this iteration;
Until *(Synchronized groups stabilize);*

Fig. 1 illustrates the evolution of the phases for the objects of a simple 2-D data set. The L_1 norm is used and δ_0 was set to 0.2 (the choice of δ_0 will be discussed later). Fig. 1(b) displays the initial random phases. Fig. 1(c), which displays the state of the system after 10 iterations, 5 groups have formed: $G_1 = \{y_{12}, y_{14}, y_{15}, y_{17}, y_{18}\}$, $G_2 = \{y_8, y_9\}$, $G_3 = \{y_{10}, y_{11}, y_{13}\}$, $G_4 = \{y_2, y_3, y_5\}$, and $G_5 = \{y_4, y_7\}$. Oscillators 1, 6, and 16 are not assigned to any group yet. As the system evolves further, new groups keep forming, and existing groups keep getting bigger by bringing other oscillators to threshold along with them, and

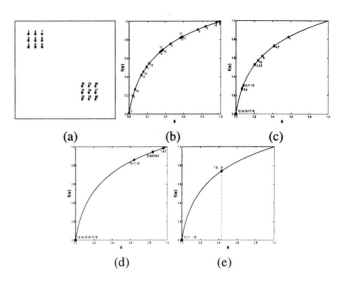

Figure 1. Evolution of SOON. (a)Objects in the feature space. (b)Initial phases. Phases after (b) 10, (c) 20, and (d) 25 iterations.

absorbing them. Moreover, a group can also bring another group to threshold, and the two groups will be merged into one. After a total of 25 iterations, only two groups (the 2 actual clusters) are present. The iteration process is stopped when the constant phase difference is detected.

3.3. Discussion

At first glance, SOON seems reminiscent of the standard Hierarchical Agglomerative Clustering (HAC) [27] and other neural networks based clustering algorithms such as VQ[14], SOM[20], and ART[8]. However, there are two major properties that distinguish SOON. First, SOON provides an efficient selection mechanism for candidate groups to be updated in every iteration. Most similar algorithms will either select all points in a sequential or in a random order. These simple selection schemes are inefficient since they do not consider the distribution of the data. The selection process in SOON is data driven and relies on the historical behavior (accumulated in the phase). For instance, objects that are similar and are expected to belong to the same cluster will excite each other often, and thus will be selected (i.e., reach the threshold and fire) more frequently. On the other hand, noise objects will get inhibited very often and will rarely reach the threshold.

The second property that distinguishes SOON is that the decision to merge objects is not based on a simple thresholding of the inter-point distances. In SOON, points are merged based on their phase values which are accumulated over several iterations (since $C_E \ll 1$). This property prevents the "bridging effect" which is a common drawback of hierarchical clustering. Fig. 2 illustrates this property. Let δ be the threshold used in HAC to decide if two points should be merged. If $d(x_1, x_2) < \delta$, then points from the two clusters can be lumped in the same cluster. On the other hand, if $\delta < d$, then no groups can form. SOON does not suffer from this drawback. This is because the decision to merge two points depends not only on the distance between them, but also on the behavior of the neighboring points in the previous iterations. For instance, if d is less than δ, then x_1 will receive excitatory pulses from x_2 and x_3, and inhibitory pulses from all the other points. On the other hand, x_2 will receive excitatory pulses from x_1 and most of the points in the left cluster. Thus, it is expected that after a few iterations the states of x_1, x_2 and x_3 will be different (even if they had similar initial values), and therefore, it is unlikely for these points to be lumped together.

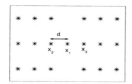

Figure 2. Bridging Effect of HAC

The SOON clustering framework is generic and can be used to cluster feature vectors composed of numerical as well as categorical attributes. Moreover, it can incorporate a multitude of similarity measures including subjective and non-metric ones. In this paper, we instantiate and numerically illustrate SOON for the case of hyper-ellipsoidal clusters. We also introduce an incremental version of SOON to cluster very large data that cannot be fully loaded into the main memory.

4. Identification of Hyper Ellipsoidal clusters

We assume that each cluster, k, has a multivariate normal distribution with mean $\mathbf{c}_k$ and covariance matrix $\mathbf{C}_k$. The synchronization process involves computing the distance between two oscillators, where each oscillator represents a cluster. We use a modified Mahalanobis distance:

$$d_{ij}^2 = min\{(\mathbf{c}_i - \mathbf{c}_j)^T \mathbf{C}_i^{-1}(\mathbf{c}_i - \mathbf{c}_j), (\mathbf{c}_i - \mathbf{c}_j)^T \mathbf{C}_j^{-1}(\mathbf{c}_i - \mathbf{c}_j)\},$$
(4)

where $\mathbf{c}_i, \mathbf{c}_j, \mathbf{C}_i, \mathbf{C}_j$ are the centers and covariance matrces of oscillators (clusters) O_i and O_j. By using a different covariance matrix for each cluster, the above distance can be used to detect ellipsoidal clusters of various shapes and orientations. The shape of each cluster k is generated by the eigenstructure of the matrix $\mathbf{C}_k$. If the clusters are assumed to come from a multivariate Gaussian distribution, then the

within-cluster distances have a χ^2 probability distribution with p (dimensionality of the data) degrees of freedom. This desirable feature will (i) automate the choice of δ_0; and (ii) make the neighborhood of the excitatory region dynamic and cluster dependent. We use $\delta_0 = \chi^2(\alpha, p)$, that is, the αth percentile of the χ^2 probability distribution. In other words, if the probability that a given point belongs to the firing cluster is greater than $(1 - \alpha)$, then its phase would be incremented. We use $\alpha = 95\%$.

Initially, each data point is represented by one oscillator and constitute a cluster by itself. The initial center of the oscillator (i.e., cluster) is the point itself, and the covariance matrix is initialized to $\epsilon \cdot \mathbf{I}_{p \times p}$, where $\mathbf{I}_{p \times p}$ is the identity matrix, and ϵ is a constant that depends on the dynamic range of the data. The center and the covariance matrix of each cluster will be updated using the features of the synchronized oscillators.

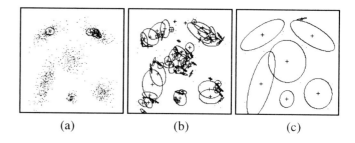

(a)   (b)   (c)

Figure 3. Detection of ellipsoidal clusters. Results at the end of (a) 5, (b) 500, and (c) 1200 iterations.

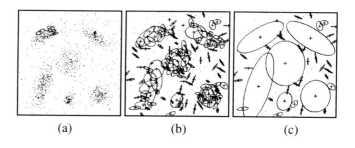

(a)   (b)   (c)

Figure 4. Detection of ellipsoidal clusters in a noisy data set. Results at the end of (a) 5, (b) 500, and (c) 1700 iterations.

Fig. 3 illustrates the evolution of SOON using a 2-D synthetic Gaussian mixture. Fig. 3(a) displays the results after 5 iterations where 4 small groups have formed. The center of each group is indicated by the "+" sign and the ellipses enclose points within the δ_0 neighborhood. The remaining points indicate oscillators that did not synchronize yet. Fig. 3(b) displays the results after 500 iterations, where most oscillators have synchronized and formed groups of various sizes. Fig. 3(c) shows the result after 1200 iterations where the remaining groups are phase locked. Fig. 4 illustrates the robustness of SOON to noise. As can be seen, noise points will either form very small clusters or will not synchronize at all. This is because noise points are located in non-dense regions and they get inhibited by most of the other points. Even if these points reach the threshold, they will excite a few if any other oscillators.

The previous two examples might indicate that SOON is not efficient since it takes more than 1500 iterations to obtain the final partition, and that a simple K-means or EM algorithm can converge in less than few hundred iterations. However, this is not the case. Unlike the K-means and EM which compute the distance between all points and all clusters in every iteration, SOON computes the distance to only one of the clusters (the one that fires) in every iteration. Thus, to provide a fair comparison, the number of iterations in SOON should be divided by the number of clusters. Moreover, K-means and EM would need many more iterations if the number of clusters is not known, and the computation in each iteration gets more complex for k-means type algorithms that are robust to noise [13].

To provide a quantitative indication of the efficiency of our approach, we compare the running time with two other algorithms. The first algorithm is the Fuzzy C-Means (FCM) [3] using the Mahalanobis distance which is similar to the EM algorithm. The FCM is very simple, however, it cannot handle noisy data, and requires the specification of the number of clusters. The second algorithm is the Robust Competitive Agglomeration (RCA) [13]. The RCA can cluster noisy data and find the optimal number of clusters. It only requires the specification of an over-specified number of clusters (C_{max}). Table 1 displays the average CPU time of the three algorithms over several runs using the data sets in Fig. 3 and Fig. 4. We should note here that the FCM is sensitive to the initial parameters, and that there are few instances were the small cluster was not detected. Both the RCA and SOON are not as sensitive because they start with a much larger number of initial prototypes. Notice that for the data in Fig. 4, the FCM cannot generate a meaningful partition, and thus the CPU time is not recorded.

Table 1. CPU time of 3 clustering algorithms

Image	Algorithm			
	FCM (C=6)	RCA (C_{max}=25)	RCA (C_{max}=50)	SOON
Fig. 3	2 Sec.	6 Sec.	10 Sec.	3 Sec.
Fig. 4	*****	7 Sec.	11 Sec.	4 Sec.

5 Incremental Clustering using SOON

During the evolution of SOON, once a group of oscillators synchronize, they will share the same center and covariance matrix. Thus, a group of synchronized oscillators can be treated as a single oscillator. Our goal is to exploit this fact, and design an algorithm that can efficiently cluster huge data sets while operating within a limited memory (RAM) buffer in one scan of the data set. Our approach, called ScaleSOON, is outlined as follows:

1. Get a sample from the data set, and fill the memory buffer.

2. Apply the algorithm to the data contents in the buffer.

3. Summarize each synchronized group by a single oscillator with equivalent sufficient statistics, and purge the synchronized oscillators from the buffer.

4. If there are any points that have not been previously loaded, go to step 1.

5.1. Data Compression and Sufficient Statistics

Let G be a group of synchronized oscillators. If the distance defined in (4) is used, then the sufficient statistics for G are the triplet $(N_G, \mathbf{S}_G, \mathbf{SS}_G)$, where N_G is the number of oscillators in group G, $\mathbf{S}_G = \sum_{\mathbf{y} \in G} \mathbf{y}$, and $\mathbf{SS}_G = \sum_{\mathbf{y} \in G} \mathbf{y}\mathbf{y}^T$. Note that $\mathbf{SS}_G$ is symmetric, and there is no need to store the entire matrix. Moreover, when the dimensionality of the feature space is large, it is common in practice to assume diagonal covariance matrices. In this case, the shape of $\mathbf{SS}_G$ reduces to a vector. Initially, each feature vector (or oscillator) $\mathbf{y}_j$ has its initial sufficient statistics, i.e., $(N_{y_j}, \mathbf{S}_{y_j}, \mathbf{SS}_{y_j}) = (1, \mathbf{y}_j, \mathbf{y}_j \mathbf{y}_j^T)$.

5.2. Purging and Filling the Memory Buffer

When the data set resident in the memory buffer reaches a stable state, each group of synchronized oscillators, G_k, will be compressed as follows:

1. **Summarization:** Add a new oscillator with sufficient statistics:

$$\begin{cases} N_{G_k} &= \sum_{\mathbf{y} \in G_k} N_y \\ \mathbf{S}_{G_k} &= \sum_{\mathbf{y} \in G_k} \mathbf{S}_y \\ \mathbf{SS}_{G_k} &= \sum_{\mathbf{y} \in G_k} \mathbf{SS}_y. \end{cases} \quad (5)$$

2. **Purging:** Purge the oscillators that belong to G_k from the memory buffer.

In (5), $\mathbf{y}$ can represent a single oscillator or a group of oscillators that have been synchronized and summarized in previous iterations. After summarizing and purging all of the synchronized groups, the memory buffer is filled with feature vectors that have not been previously loaded. Since the features of the purged oscillators are not available in the main memory, the center and covariance matrix should be updated using the sufficient statistics of the group they belong to. That is, we use

$$\mathbf{c}_k = \frac{1}{N_{G_k}} \mathbf{S}_{G_k} \quad \text{and} \quad \mathbf{C}_k = \frac{1}{N_{G_k}} \mathbf{SS}_{G_k} - \mathbf{c}_k \mathbf{c}_k^{\mathbf{T}}$$

6. Experimental Results

The performance of ScaleSOON is evaluated with several data sets. We demonstrate the scalability of Scale-SOON with respect to the number of records and the number of attributes using several synthetically generated data sets. All experiments were performed on an Ultra Sparc IIi 300 Mhz workstation with 256 MB RAM. Several data sets were generated by sampling from $k=10$ multivariate Gaussian distributions. Gaussian means and diagonal covariance matrices were chosen uniformly on $[0, 10]$, and $[0.8, 1.2]$ respectively. The number of attributes varied from 10 to 100, and the number of records varied from 10,000 to 1,000,000.

6.1. Effect of the Buffer Size

Initially, ScaleSOON was designed to cluster very large data sets that cannot be entirely loaded into the main memory, and we planned on setting the buffer size to be close to the size of the main memory. However, after running Scale-SOON on several data sets with different buffer sizes, we have discovered that it runs faster with smaller buffer sizes. Fig. 5 shows the running time for an increasing sequence of buffer sizes varying from 100 to 10,000. The data used in this experiment has 25 attributes and $100K$ records. There are two reasons that explain this behavior. First, the algorithm exhibits temporal locality and the frequency of cache misses would be minimized when the buffer size is less than the cache size. Second, we have noticed that ScaleSOON reaches a stable state in fewer iterations when the buffer size is smaller.

When the buffer size becomes very small, the running time does not decrease any further. This is probably due to the more frequent accesses to the secondary storage, and also because not all of the available cache memory is used. In addition to inefficient use of cache memory, very small buffer sizes cannot maintain a variety of sub-groups, and may lead to an unsatisfactory partition. Ideally, the buffer size should be much larger than the expected number of clusters to allow a smooth hierarchical agglomeration. In

the remainder of this section, we will assume that the number of clusters is always much smaller than 500, and let the buffer size be fixed to 500 oscillators.

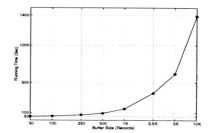

Figure 5. Effect of the buffer size.

6.2. Scalablity

To illustrate the scalability of ScaleSOON with respect to the number of records, we use data sets that have 25 attributes, 10 clusters, and 10K, 100K, 300K, 500K, and 1M records. For all data sets, ScaleSOON found 10 clusters and identified their parameters correctly. Fig. 6(a) displays the running time versus the number of records. As expected, ScaleSOON scales linearly. To illustrate the scalability with respect to the number of attributes, we use data sets that have 10 clusters, 500K records, and 10, 25, 50, and 100 attributes. For all data sets, ScaleSOON found 10 clusters and identified their parameters correctly. Fig. 6(b) displays the running time versus the number of records. As can be seen, ScaleSOON scales linearly with respect to the number of attributes.

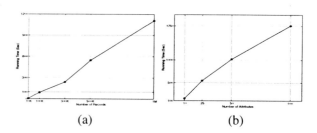

Figure 6. Scalability of ScaleSOON: (a) with respect to the number of records, and (b) with respect to the number of attributes.

6.3. Effect of the Initial Phases

ScaleSOON assigns a random number (initial phase) to each record when it gets loaded. To study the sensitivity of the algorithm with respect to these random phases, we ran ScaleSOON on the same data set with several different initial phases (using different seed values). The data used in this experiment has 25 attributes, 100K records, and 10 clusters. Fig. 7 (a) displays the total distance between the true Gaussian means and the means of the identified clusters for the 10 different initializations. As can be seen, the total distance does not exceed 0.11, which means that for all 10 initialization, ScaleSOON was able to identify the 10 correct clusters. Moreover, As shown in Fig. 7(b), the variation in the run time for these 10 different runs is small (less than 3%). This indicates that the total number of iterations required for the algorithm to reach a stable state is not sensitive to the initial phases.

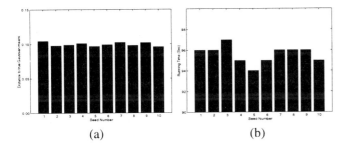

(a)   (b)

Figure 7. Effect of the Initial phases. (a) Total Euclidean distance from the true Gaussian means. (b) Running time.

6.4. Applications to Color Image Segmentation

ScaleSOON has been used to segment large color images. Each image contains 512×768 pixels, and each pixel is mapped to an 8-D vector consisting of 3 color, 3 texture, and 2 position features [9]. Typically, when using a clustering algorithm to segment large images, sampling is used to reduce the number of pixels. Unfortunately, sampling may result in the loss of small and/or thin objects. Fig. 8(a) shows 2 color images from the Corel image database. ScaleSOON was applied to each image (without sampling) to segment it into several homogeneous regions by clustering the feature vectors mapped from the image pixels. Fig. 8(b) shows the edges of the clustered objects.

7. Conclusions

We have introduced a scalable clustering framework by combining clustering techniques with the dynamics of simple and discrete Integrate-and-Fire oscillators. The proposed approach, ScaleSOON, associates one oscillator with each data point and defines the interaction between oscillators according to the relative similarity between the points. As a result, ScaleSOON reaches a stable state where similar oscillators synchronize and dissimilar ones phase-lock.

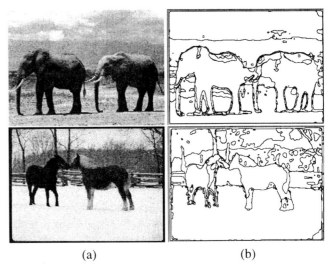

(a)   (b)

Figure 8. Color image segmentation. (a) Original images, (b) Edges of detected objects

ScaleSOON achieves scalability by loading only a subset of the data into main memory at a time, and allowing it to self-organize. Each group of oscillators is summarized by a single oscillators with sufficient statistics and are purged from memory. New data points are then loaded into memory and self-organize with the existing groups. Our empirical evaluation has shown that ScaleSOON scales linearly with respect to the number of records and the number of attributes. Our experiments have also indicated that even if large memory is available to hold the entire data, it is more efficient to process it incrementally. This is because the problem is much simpler when fewer oscillators are interacting, and also the cache memory is used more efficiently.

ScaleSOON does not require the specification of the actual number of clusters. This number is determined automatically depending on the resolution parameter δ_0. We have shown that using the Mahalanobis distance, δ_0 can be fixed by exploiting the χ^2 probability distribution of the distances in each cluster. Thus, each cluster can have its own adaptive resolution. The synchronization mechanism of ScaleSOON makes it robust to noise and outliers. Oscillators that represent noise points will synchronize with few if any other oscillators. Thus, they can be simply identified as those points that did not synchronize, or that belong to very small groups.

In this paper, we have instantiated our clustering framework using the Mahalanobis distance . This, however, does not constitute a limitation of our method. In fact, since ScaleSOON does not explicitly optimize an objective function, it can incorporate non-metric similarity measures. Moreover, it can be easily adapted to cluster discrete-valued measurements. This represents a very desirable features in many data mining applications where discrete data is very common and the most appropriate dissimilarity measures tend to be rather subjective, and thus non-metric.

Acknowledgment

Partial support of this research was provided by the Woodrow W. Everett, Jr. SCE EE Development Fund in cooperation with the Southeastern association of electrical engineering department heads.

References

[1] R. Agrawal, J. Gehrke, D. Gunopulos, and P. Raghavan. Automatic subspace clustering of high dimensional data for data mining aplications. In *Proc. of the ACM SIGMOD*, 1999.

[2] J. Bélair. Periodic pulsatile stimulation of a nonlinear oscillator. *J. Math. Biol*, 24:74–85, 1988.

[3] J. C. Bezdek. *Pattern Recognition with Fuzzy Objective Function Algorithms*. Plenum Press, New York, 1981.

[4] P. Bradley, U. Fayyad, and C. Reina. Scaling clustering algorithms to large databases. In *Proc. of the 4th Int. conf. on Knowledge Discovery and Data Mining*, 1998.

[5] P. Bradley, U. Fayyad, and C. Reina. Scaling EM (Expectation-Maximization) clustering to large databases. Technical Report MSR-TR-98-35, Microsoft Research, 1998.

[6] B. Bressloff and S. Coombes. Symmetry and phase-locking in a ring of pulse-coupled oscillators with distributed delays. *Physica D*, 126:99–122, 1999.

[7] J. Buck and E. Buck. Synchronous fireflies. *Scientific American*, 234:74–85, 1976.

[8] G. Carpenter and S. Grossberg. Adaptive resonance theory (art). In M. Arbib, editor, *Handbook of Brain Theory and Neural Networks*, pages 79–82. MIT Press, 1996.

[9] C. Carson, S. Belongie, H. Greenspan, and J. Malik. Color- and texture-based image segmentation usin em and its application to image querying and classification. Submitted to: IEEE Trans. on Pattern Analysis and Machine Intelligence.

[10] A. P. Dempster, N. M. Laird, and D. B. Rubin. Maximum likelihood from incomplete data via the EM algorithm. *Journal of the Royal Statistical Society Series B*, 39(1):1–38, 1977.

[11] R. Eckhorn, R. Bauer, W. Jordan, M. Brosch, W. Kruse, M. Munk, and H. J. Reitboeck. Coherent oscillations: a mechanism of feature linking in the visual cortex? *Biol. Cybern.*, 60:121–130, 1988.

[12] M. Ester, H. P. Kriegel, J. Sander, and X. Xu. A density-based algorithm for discovering clusters in large spatial databases with noise. In *Proc. of the 2nd international conf. on Knowledge Discovery and Data Mining (KDD96)*, Portland Oregon, 1996.

[13] H. Frigui and R. Krishnapuram. A robust competitive clustering algorithm with applications in computer vision. *IEEE Trans. Patt. Analysis Mach. Intell.*, 21(5):450–465, 1999.

[14] A. Gersho and R. M. Gray. *Vector Quantization and Signal Compression*. Kluwer Academic Publishers, 1992.

[15] S. Guha, R. Rastogi, and K. Shim. CURE: An efficient clustering algorithm for large data databases. In *Proc. of the ACM SIGMOD conference on Management of Data*, Seattle Washington, 1998.

[16] A. Hinneburg and D. Keim. An efficient approach to clustering in large multimedia databases with noise. In *Proc. of the 4th int. conf. on Knowledge Discovery and Data Mining*, pages 58–65, New York, NY, 1998.

[17] A. Hinneburg and D. Keim. Clustering techniques for large data sets: From the past to the future. In *Tutorial Notes for ACM SIGKDD int. conf. on Knowledge Discovery and Data Mining*, pages 58–65, New York, NY, 1999.

[18] D. Horn and I. Opher. Collective excitaion phenomena and their applications. In W. Maass and C. M. Bishop, editors, *Pulsed Neural Networks*, pages 297–320. MIT Press, 1999.

[19] L. Kaufman and P. J. Rousseeuw. *Finding Groups in Data: An Introduction to Cluster Analysis*. Addison Wesley, NEW York, 1990.

[20] T. Kohonen. *Self-Organization and Associative Memory*. Springer Verlag, 1989.

[21] Y. Kuramoto. *Chemical Oscillations, Waves and Turbulence*. Springer, Berlin, 1984.

[22] R. Mirollo and S. Strogatz. Synchronization of pulse coupled biological oscillators. *SIAM J. Appl. Math*, 50:1645–1662, 1990.

[23] R. T. Ng and J. Han. Efficient and effective clustering methods for spatial data mining. In *Proc. of the VLDB conference*, Santiago Chile, 1994.

[24] M. Rhouma and H. Frigui. Self-organization of a population of coupled oscillators with application to clustering. *IEEE Trans. Patt. Analysis Mach. Intell.*, 23(2), Feb. 2001.

[25] R.O.Duda and P. E. Hart. *Pattern Classification and Scene Analysis*. John Wiley and Sons, 1973.

[26] G. Sheikholeslami, S. Chatterjee, and A. Zhang. Wavecluster: A multi-resolution clustering approach for very large spatial databases. In *Proc. of the 24th Very Large Databases Conf.*, pages 428–439, New York, NY, 1998.

[27] P. H. A. Sneath and R. R. Sokal. *Numerical Taxonomy - The Principles and Practices of Numerical Classification*. W. H. Freeman, San Francisco, CA, 1973.

[28] D. Terman and D. Wang. Global competition and local cooperation in a network of neural oscillators. *Physica D.*, 81:148–176, 1995.

[29] W. Wei, J. Yang, and R. Muntz. Sting: A statistical infromation grid approach to spatial data mining. In *Proc. of the 23rd Very Large Databases Conf.*, pages 186–195, Athens, Greece, 1997.

[30] A. T. Winfree. Biological rhythms and the behavior of populations of coupled oscillators. *Journal Theoret. Biol.*, 16:15–42, 1967.

[31] X. Xiaowei, M. Ester, H. Kriegel, and J. Sander. A distribution-based clustering algorithm for mining in large spatial databases. In *Proc. of the 14th Int. Conf. on Data Engineering*, pages 324–331, Orlando, Florida, 1998.

[32] T. Zhang, R. Ramakrishnan, and M. Livny. BIRCH: An efficient data clustering method for very large databases. In *Proc. of the ACM SIGMOD conference on Management of Data*, Montreal Canada, 1996.

Functional Trees for Classification

João Gama
LIACC, FEP - University of Porto
Rua Campo Alegre 823, 4150 Porto, Portugal
jgama@liacc.up.pt

Abstract

The design of algorithms that explore multiple representation languages and explore different search spaces has an intuitive appeal. In the context of classification problems, algorithms that generate multivariate trees are able to explore multiple representation languages by using decision tests based on a combination of attributes. The same applies to model trees *algorithms, in regression domains, but using linear models at leaf nodes. In this paper we study* where *to use combinations of attributes in decision tree learning. We present an algorithm for multivariate tree learning that combines a univariate decision tree with a discriminant function by means of constructive induction. This algorithm is able to use decision nodes with multivariate tests, and leaf nodes that predict a class using a discriminant function. Multivariate decision nodes are built when growing the tree, while functional leaves are built when pruning the tree. Functional trees can be seen as a generalization of multivariate trees. Our algorithm was compared against to its components and two simplified versions using 30 benchmark datasets. The experimental evaluation shows that our algorithm has clear advantages with respect to the generalization ability and model sizes at statistically significant confidence levels.*

1. Introduction

The generalization capacity of a learning algorithm depends on the appropriateness of its representation language to express a generalization of the examples for the given task. Different learning algorithms employ different representations, search heuristics, evaluation functions, and search spaces. It is now commonly accept that each algorithm has its own selective superiority [4], each is best for some but not all tasks. The design of algorithms that explore multiple representation languages and explore different search spaces has an intuitive appeal.

In the context of supervised learning problems it is use-

ful to distinguish between classification problems and regression problems. In the former the target variable takes values in a finite and pre-defined set of un-ordered values, and the usual goal is to minimize a 0-1 loss function. In the latter the target variable is ordered and takes values in a subset of $\Re$. The usual goal is to minimize a squared error loss function. In the case of classification problems, a class of algorithms that explore multiple representation languages are the so called *multivariate trees* [3, 5, 14, 8, 13]. In this sort of algorithms decision nodes can contain tests based on a combination of attributes. The language bias of univariate decision trees (axis parallel splits) is relaxed allowing decision surfaces oblique with respect to the axis of the instance space. As in the case of classification problems, in regression problems some authors have studied the use of regression trees that explore multiple representation languages, here denominated *model trees* [3, 15, 20, 18]. But while in classification problems multivariate decisions appear in internal nodes, in regression problems multivariate decisions appear in leaf nodes.

The problem that we study in this paper is *where* to use decisions based on combinations of attributes. Should we restrict combinations of attributes to decision nodes? Should we restrict combinations of attributes to leaf nodes? Could we use combinations of attributes both at decision nodes and leaf nodes? We restrict this study, in this work, to classification problems. To study these problems we have developed our own multivariate decision tree. We near follow the method proposed in [10] where a multivariate tree is generated by combining a univariate decision tree with a discriminant function by means of constructive induction. The next Section briefly describes the method and the changes needed to allow functional leaves. In Section 3 we discuss the different variants of tree models using an illustrative example. In Section 4 we present related work both in the classification and regression settings. In Section 5 we evaluate our algorithm on 30 benchmark datasets. Last Section concludes the paper.

2. The Algorithm for Functional Trees

The standard algorithm to build univariate decision tree consists of two phases. In the first phase a large decision tree is constructed. In the second phase this tree is pruned back. The algorithm to grow the tree follows the standard divide-and-conquer approach. The most relevant aspects are: the splitting rule, the termination criterion, and the leaf assignment criterion. With respect to the last criterion, the usual rule consists of assigning a constant to a leaf node. This constant is usually the majority class of the examples that fall at this node. With respect to the splitting rule, each attribute value defines a possible partition of the dataset. We distinguish between nominal attributes and continuous ones. In the former the number of partitions is equal to the number of values of the attribute, in the latter a binary partition is obtained. To estimate the merit of the partition obtained by a given attribute we use the *gain ratio* heuristic. The attribute that maximizes the gain is chosen as test attribute at this node.

The pruning phase consists of traversing the tree in a depth-first fashion. At each non-leaf node two measures should be estimated. An estimate of the error of the subtree below this node, that is computed as a weighted sum of the estimated error for each leaf of the subtree, and the estimated error of the non-leaf node if it was pruned to a leaf. If the latter is lower than the former, the entire subtree is replaced to a leaf. To estimate the error at each leaf we assume a binomial distribution using a process similar to the *pessimistic error* of C4.5.

All of these aspects have several and important variants, see for example [3, 16]. Nevertheless all decision nodes contain conditions based on the values of one attribute.

2.1. Functional Trees

In this Section we present the general algorithm to construct a functional decision tree. Given a set of n examples of the form $\{\vec{x}_i, y_i\}$ and an attribute constructor, the main algorithm used to build a decision tree is presented in Figure 1. This algorithm is similar to many others, except in the constructive step (steps 2 and 3). Here a function is built and mapped to new attributes. In this paper, we restricted the constructor to the LINEARBAYES (LB) discriminant function [9]. There are some aspects of this algorithm that should be made explicit. In step 2, a model is built using the Constructor function. This is done using only the examples that fall at this node. Later, in step 3, the model is mapped to new attributes. The merit of each new attribute is evaluated using the merit-function of the decision tree, and in competition with the original attributes (step 4). The models built by our algorithm have two types of decision nodes: Those based on a test of one of the original

Function Tree(Dataset, Constructor)

1. If Stop_Criterion(DataSet)
   - Return a Leaf Node with a probability class distribution.

2. Construct a model Φ using Constructor

3. For each example $\vec{x} \in DataSet$
   - Obtain the probability class distribution given by $\Phi(\vec{x})$
   - Extend $\vec{x}$ with new attributes. Each new attribute is the probability that $\vec{x}$ belongs to one class.

4. Select the attribute from both original and all newly constructed attributes that maximizes the gain ratio criterion.

5. For each partition i of the DataSet using the selected attribute
   - Tree$_i$ = Tree(Dataset$_i$, Constructor)

6. Return a *Tree*, as a decision node based on the selected attribute, containing the Φ model, and descendents Tree$_i$.

End Function

Figure 1. Growing a Functional Tree.

attributes, and those based on the values of the constructor function. If the chosen attribute is one of the new attributes, then the decision surface is oblique with respect to the instance space defined by the original attributes. Once a tree has been constructed, it is pruned back. The general algorithm to prune the tree is presented in Figure 2. The error estimates needed in step 1 and 3 uses a process similar to the *pessimistic error* of C4.5 [16]. The pruning algorithm produces two different types of leaves: *Ordinary Leaves* that predict the mean of the target variable observed in the examples that fall at this node, and *Functional Leaves* that are leaves that predict the value of the constructor function learned (in the growing phase) at this node.

By simplifying our algorithm we obtain different conceptual models. Two interesting simplifications are described in the following sub-sections.

2.1.1 Bottom-Up Approach

We denote as *Bottom-Up Approach* to functional decision trees when the multivariate models are used exclusively at leaves. This is the strategy used for example in M5 [15, 20], and NBTree [12]. In our tree algorithm this is done by

Function Prune(Tree)

1. Estimate **Leaf_Error** as the error at this node.

2. If Tree is a leaf Return **Leaf_Error**.

3. Estimate **Constructor_Error** as the error of Φ^1.

4. For each descendent i

   - **Backed_Up_Error** += Prune(Tree$_i$)

5. If argmin
   (Leaf_Error,Constructor_Error,Backed_Up_Error)

   - Is Leaf_Error
     - Tree = Leaf
     - Tree_Error = Leaf_Error

   - Is Constructor_Error
     - Tree = Constructor Leaf
     - Tree_Error = Constructor_Error

   - Is Backed_Up_Error
     - Tree_Error = Backed_Up_Error

6. Return Tree_Error

End Function

[1] The Constructor model built in the growing phase at this node.

Figure 2. Pruning a Functional Tree.

restricting the selection of the test attribute (step 4 in the growing algorithm) to the original attributes. Nevertheless we still build, at each node, the discriminant function. The model built by the discriminant function is used and evaluated later in the pruning phase. In this way, all decision nodes are based in the original attributes. Leaf nodes could contain a constructor model. A leaf node contains a constructor model if and only if in the pruning algorithm the estimated error of the constructor model is lower than the *Backed-up-error* and the estimated error of the node if a leaf replaced it.

2.1.2 Top-Down Approach

We denote as *Top-Down Approach* to functional decision trees when the multivariate models are used exclusively at decision nodes (internal nodes). In our algorithm, restricting the pruning algorithm to choose only between the **Backed_Up_Error** and the **Leaf_Error** obtain this kind of models. In this case all leaves predict a constant value.

Our algorithm can be seen as a hybrid model that performs a tight combination of a decision tree and a discrim-

inant function. The components of the hybrid algorithm use different representation languages and search strategies. While the tree uses a divide-and-conquer method, the discriminant function performs a global minimization approach. While the former performs feature selection, the latter uses all (or almost all) the attributes to build a model. From the point of view of the bias-variance decomposition of the error [2] a decision tree is known to have low bias but high variance, while the discriminant function is known to have low variance but high bias. This is the desirable behavior for components of hybrid models.

2.1.3 Constructing New Attributes - The LinearBayes Classifier

Without loss of generality[1] we restrict in this work the attribute constructor to the LINEARBAYES classifier [9]. The LINEARBAYES classifier is a fusion of a linear discriminant with a naive Bayes. The basic idea consists of aggregating the attributes into two subsets: the first subset contains only continuous attributes, and the second subset contains all the other attributes. Assuming that both sets are conditionally independent given the class, Bayes theorem can be rewritten as follows:

$$P(C_i|\vec{x}) = \frac{P(C_i)P(\vec{x}_{1...j}|C_i)P(\vec{x}_{j+1...n}|C_i)}{P(\vec{x})} \quad (1)$$

where the attributes x_1 to x_j are continuous and the attributes x_{j+1} to x_n are nominal. Ignoring the term $P(\vec{x})$ that is the same for all the classes and applying logarithms, we obtain:

$$P(C_i|\vec{x}) \propto log(P(C_i)P(\vec{x}_{1...j}|C_i)) + log(P(\vec{x}_{j+1...n}|C_i))$$

To compute the joint probability of continuous attributes $log(P(C_i)P(\vec{x}_{1...j}|C_i))$ we assume a *multivariate normal distribution*[2]. Nominal attributes are assumed independent.

After some algebraic manipulations we obtain the equation of LINEARBAYES:

$$P(C_i|\vec{x}) \propto log(P(C_i)) - \frac{1}{2}\mu_i^T \Sigma^{-1}\mu_i + x^T\Sigma^{-1}\mu_i +$$

$$+ \sum_{k=j+1}^{n} log(P(\vec{x}_k|C_i))$$

When all the attributes are ordered, the LINEARBAYES classifier is a standard linear discriminant. When all the attributes are nominal the LINEARBAYES classifier is a standard naive Bayes. When there are mixed attribute types

---

[1] The actual implementation allows the use of several discriminant functions as attribute constructors. For example: naive Bayes, linear discriminant, and logistic discriminant.

[2] A standard naive Bayes will assume a normal distribution for each attribute.

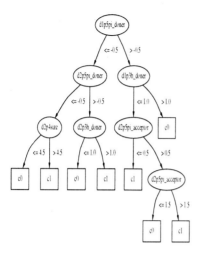

Figure 3. The Univariate Decision Tree.

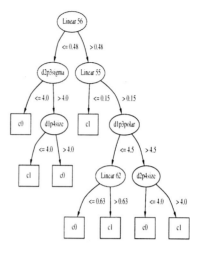

Figure 4. The Top-Down Functional Tree.

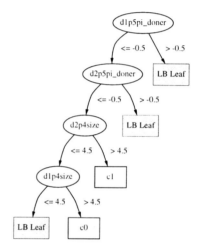

Figure 5. The Bottom-Up Functional Tree.

the fusion of the two classifiers will apply. Using distinct representations of the instance space, both approaches are combined using the previous equation. There is no need to discretize continuous attributes as it is done in standard implementations of naive Bayes. Moreover there is no need to binarize nominal attributes as it is done in standard implementations of linear discriminant function. The set of continuous attributes is treated as following a multivariate normal distribution. In this way we consider the interdependencies between the attributes. An extended analysis of the behavior of LinearBayes is presented in [9].

3. An Illustrative Example

In this section we use the UCI dataset *Learning Qualitative Structure Activity Relationships - QSARs pyrimidines.* to illustrate the different variants of tree models. This is a complex two classes problem defined by 54 continuous attributes. The attribute constructor used is the LINEAR-BAYES classifier. Figure 3 presents an univariate tree for the *QSARs* dataset. Decision Nodes only contain tests based on the original attributes. Leaf nodes predict the majority class taken from the examples that fall at this leaf.

In a top-down functional tree (Figure 4) decision nodes could contain (not necessarily) tests based on a linear combination of the original attributes. The tree contains a mixture of learned attributes, denoted as *Linear N*, and original attributes, *e.g. d2p3sigma, d1p4size.* Any of the linear attributes can be used both at the node where they have been created and at deeper nodes. For example, the attribute *Linear 55* has been created at the root. It is used as test attribute at the second level of the tree, due to the constructive ability of our system. Leaf nodes predict the majority class taken from the examples that fall at this leaf. In a bottom-up functional tree (Figure 5) decision nodes only contain tests

based on the original attributes. Leaf nodes could predict (not necessarily) values obtained by using a LINEARBAYES function built from the examples that fall at this node. This is the kind of multivariate trees that usually appears on the regression literature. For example, systems M5 [15, 20] and RT [18] generate this kind of models.

Figure 6 presents the full multivariate decision tree using both top-down and bottom-up multivariate approaches. In this case, decision nodes could contain (not necessarily) tests based on a linear combination of the original attributes, and leaf nodes could predict (not necessarily) values obtained by using a LINEARBAYES function built from the examples that fall at this node.

4. Related Work

In the context of classification problems, several algorithms have been presented that use at each decision

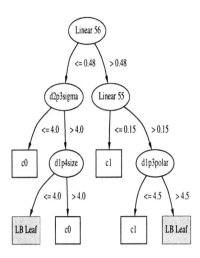

Figure 6. The Functional Tree.

node tests based on linear combination of the attributes [3, 14, 5, 8, 13]. The most comprehensive study on multivariate trees has been presented by Brodley and Utgoff in [5]. Brodley and Utgoff discusses several methods for constructing multivariate decision trees: representing a multivariate test, including symbolic and numeric features, learning the coefficients of a multivariate test, selecting the features to include in a test, and pruning of multivariate decision trees. Nevertheless, only multivariate tests at inner nodes in a tree are considered. In the context of classification problems few works consider functional tree leaves. One of the earliest work is the Percepton tree algorithm [19] where leaf nodes may implement a general linear discriminant function. Also Kohavi[12] has presented the naive Bayes tree that uses functional leaves. NBtree is a hybrid algorithm that generates a regular univariate decision tree, but the leaves contain a naive Bayes classifier built from the examples that fall at this node. The approach retains the interpretability of naive Bayes and decision trees, while resulting in classifiers that frequently outperform both constituents, especially in large datasets.

Gama [10] has presented *Cascade Generalization*, a method to combine classification algorithms by means of constructive induction. The work presented here near follows this method. The main difference is related to the pruning algorithm. In this work we consider functional leaves.

Breiman *et.al.* [3] presents the first extensive and in-depth study of the problem of constructing decision and regression trees. But, while in the case of decision trees they consider internal nodes with a test based on linear combination of attributes, in the case of regression trees internal nodes are always based on a single attribute and leaf nodes predict a constant.

Quinlan [15] (and later Witten and Frank [20]) has presented the system M5. It builds multivariate trees using lin-

ear models at the leaves. In the pruning phase for each leaf a linear model is built. Also Karalic [11] has studied the influence of using linear regression in the leaves of a regression tree. As in the work of Quinlan, Karalic shows that it leads to smaller models with increase of performance. Torgo [17] has presented an experimental study about functional models for regression tree leaves. Later, the same author [18] has presented the system RT. Using RT with linear models at the leaves, RT builds and prunes a regular univariate tree. Then at each leaf a linear model is built using the examples that fall at this leaf.

In a more general context, our work is also related to the problem of finding the appropriate bias for a given task. Here we only review the most relevant work for our approach. Wolpert [21] proposed *Stacked Generalization*, a technique that uses learning at two or more levels. A learning algorithm is used to determine how the outputs of the base classifiers should be combined. Brodley [4] have presented the *Model Class Selection - MCS system*, a hybrid algorithm that combines, in a single tree, nodes that are univariate tests, multivariate tests generated by *linear machines* and instance based learners. At each node MCS uses a set of *If-Then* rules to perform a heuristic best-first search for the best hypothesis for the given partition of the dataset. The set of rules incorporates knowledge of experts. *MCS* uses a dynamic search control strategy to perform an automatic model selection. *MCS* builds trees which can apply a different model in different regions of the instance space.

5. Experimental Evaluation

In this section we evaluate the proposed algorithm, its simplified variants, and its components on a set of 27 benchmark datasets from UCI repository [1]. The main goal in this experimental evaluation is to study the influence in terms of performance of the position inside a decision tree of the linear models. We evaluate three situations: 1)Trees that could use linear combinations at each internal node. 2) Trees that could use linear combinations at each leaf. 3) Trees that could use linear combinations both at each internal node and leaf node. All evaluated models are based on the same tree growing and pruning algorithm. That is, they use exactly the same splitting criteria, stopping criteria, and pruning mechanism. Moreover they share many minor heuristics that individually are too small to mention, but collectively can make difference. Doing so, the differences on the evaluation statistics are due to the differences in the conceptual model.

The evaluation methodology was designed as follows. To estimate the error rate of an algorithm on a given dataset we use 10 fold cross validation. To minimize the influence of the variability of the training set, we repeat this process ten times, each time using a different permutation of the dataset. The final estimate is the mean of the error obtained in each run of the cross validation. To apply pairwise comparisons we guarantee that, in all runs, all algorithms learn and test on the same partitions of the data.

The results in terms of error-rate and standard deviation are presented in Table 1. The first two columns refer to the results of the components of our system, the LINEARBAYES and the univariate tree. The next two columns refer to the lesioned versions of the algorithm, the Bottom-Up (FT-B) and Top-Down (FT-T). The fifth column refers to the full-proposed model (FT). The last column refers to the results of bagging FT. For each dataset, the algorithms are compared against the full multivariate tree using the *Wilcoxon signed rank-test*. The null hypothesis is that the difference between error rates has median value zero. A − (+) sign indicates that for this dataset the performance of the algorithm was worse (better) than the full model with a *p value* less than 0.01. It is interesting to note that the full model (FT) significantly improves over both components (LB and UT) in 6 datasets. Table 1 also presents a comparative summary of the results. The first two lines present the arithmetic and the geometric mean of the error rate across all datasets. The third line shows the average rank of all models, computed for each dataset by assigning rank 1 to the best algorithm, 2 to the second best and so on. The fourth line shows the average ratio of error rates. This is computed for each dataset as the ratio between the error rate of one algorithm and the error rate of the full Functional tree FT. The fifth line shows the number of significant differences using the *signed-rank test* taking the multivariate tree FT as reference. We use the *Wilcoxon Matched-Pairs Signed-Ranks Test* to compare the error rate of pairs of algorithms across datasets. The last line shows the *p values* associated with this test for the results on all datasets and taking FT as reference. All the evaluation statistics shows that any functional tree and in particular FT are competitive algorithms. In the next section we analyze in detail the performance of the functional trees variants.

When using more flexible representations the bias is reduced. We have tested this hypothesis. We have compared the bias-variance error decomposition of the univariate tree against the multivariate tree (FT). Using the decomposition suggested by Domingos [6] 87% of the error reduction is due to a reduction on the bias component. It is interesting to note that FT and FT-T have similar bias and variance reductions. FT-B shows a different behavior. In the case of FT-B we observe that the main error-reduction is due to a reduction in variance. Figure 7 shows the reduction in the error components of each functional tree with respect to the univariate tree. Several authors refer that there is a trade-off between the systematic error due to the representational language used by an algorithm (the *bias*) and the *variance* due to the dependence of the model to the training set [2]. One of the most attractive features of a univariate tree is that

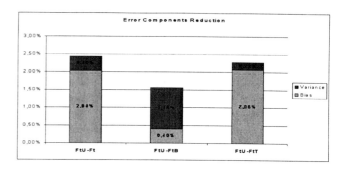

Figure 7. Reduction in Bias and Variance of Functional Trees Variants with respect to a Univariate tree.

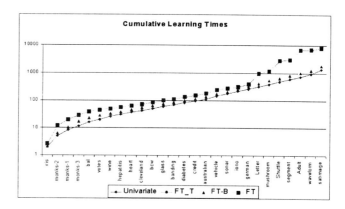

Figure 8. Cumulative Learning Times of Functional Trees Variants.

we can reduce its error by applying simple variance reduction methods. Does this feature apply to a multivariate tree? We have applied a standard variance reduction method, *bagging*, to our multivariate tree (FT). We report the results on the last column of table 1. On these datasets, bagging FT improves the overall error rate over FT. Moreover, it significantly improves on 3 datasets.

Another dimension of analysis is the size of the model. Here we consider the number of leaves. This measures the number of different regions into which the instance space is partitioned. On these datasets, the average number of leaves for the univariate tree is 70. Any multivariate tree generates smaller models. The average number of leaves of the full model is 50, for the bottom approach is 56, and for the top approach is 52. Nevertheless there is a computational cost associated with the increase in performance verified. To run all the experiments referred here, FT requires almost 1.7 more time than the univariate tree. Figure 8 shows, in a log scale, the accumulated learning time of all trees. This figure points out that FT-B is the faster functional tree. This is evidence that the most time-consuming operation in functional trees is not the construction of new attributes but the time needed to evaluate them. The new attributes are continuous and require a sort operation to estimate the merit of the attribute.

6. Conclusions

The design of algorithms that explore multiple representation languages and explore different search spaces has an intuitive appeal. In the context of classification problems, multivariate trees are able to explore multiple representation languages by using decision tests based on a combination of attributes. The same applies to *model trees*, in regression domains, but using linear models at leaf nodes. In this paper we have studied *where* to use decisions based on a combination of attributes. Instead of considering multivariate models restricted to leaves or decision nodes, we analyze and evaluate multivariate models both at leaves and internal nodes. Our experimental study provides evidence that *any* multivariate model is able to outperform both components. None of the three multivariate tree variants is a clear winner. It is interesting to note that FT and FT-T have similar behaviors under a bias and variance analysis, while FT-B shows a different behavior. In comparison to the univariate tree, the main error reduction is due to a reduction on bias component in the case of FT and FT-T and on the variance in the case of FT-B. On these datasets the full model (using LinearBayes *both* at decision nodes and leaves) shows some advantages with respect to accuracy and model complexity. We have observed that the most important factor to the reduction of the error observed is due to a reduction on the bias component. Moreover we can further improve our multivariate tree by applying a standard variance reduction method like bagging. Nowadays there are standard methods to reduce the variance of decision trees, namely bagging and boosting [7]. Why should we concern with bias reduction methods? We think that the research on bias reduction methods will have an increase of importance. The exponential increase of the size of the data naturally reduces the variance. For large datasets improvements should be possible mainly using bias reduction methods.

The increase on accuracy is accomplished with learning time costs. Using this criterion, FT-B presents clear advantages. FT-B shows learning times that are most similar to the univariate tree than to any other functional tree.

A natural extension of this work consists of applying the proposed methodology to regression problems. We have done this work using a standard linear regression function as attribute constructor. It is subject of another paper. The results on regression domain are consistent with the conclusions of this paper.

Acknowledgements: We would like to express our gratitude to the financial support given by the FEDER project, projects Metal, Sol-Eu-Net, and ALES, and the Plurianual support of LIACC.

References

[1] C. Blake, E. Keogh, and C. Merz. UCI repository of Machine Learning databases, 1999.

[2] L. Breiman. Arcing classifiers. *The Annals of Statistics*, 26(3):801–849, 1998.

[3] L. Breiman, J. Friedman, R. Olshen, and C. Stone. *Classification and Regression Trees*. Wadsworth International Group., 1984.

[4] C. E. Brodley. Recursive automatic bias selection for classifier construction. *Machine Learning*, 20:63–94, 1995.

[5] C. E. Brodley and P. E. Utgoff. Multivariate decision trees. *Machine Learning*, 19:45–77, 1995.

[6] P. Domingos. A unified bias-variance decomposition and its applications. In P. Langley, editor, *Machine Learning, Proceedings of the 17th International Conference*. Morgan Kaufmann, 2000.

[7] Y. Freund and R. E. Schapire. Experiments with a new boosting algorithm. In L. Saitta, editor, *Machine Learning, Proc. of the 13th International Conference*. Morgan Kaufmann, 1996.

[8] J. Gama. Probabilistic Linear Tree. In D. Fisher, editor, *Machine Learning, Proceedings of the 14th International Conference*. Morgan Kaufmann, 1997.

[9] J. Gama. A Linear-Bayes classifier. In C. Monard, editor, *Advances on Artificial Intelligence -SBIA2000*. LNAI 1952 Springer Verlag, 2000.

[10] J. Gama and P. Brazdil. Cascade Generalization. *Machine Learning*, 41:315–343, 2000.

[11] A. Karalic. Employing linear regression in regression tree leaves. In B. Neumann, editor, *European Conference on Artificial Intelligence*, 1992.

[12] R. Kohavi. Scaling up the accuracy of naive Bayes classifiers: a decision tree hybrid. In *Proceedings of the 2nd International Conference on Knowledge Discovery and Data Mining*. AAAI Press, 1996.

[13] W. Loh and Y. Shih. Split selection methods for classification trees. *Statistica Sinica*, 7:815–840, 1997.

[14] S. Murthy, S. Kasif, and S. Salzberg. A system for induction of oblique decision trees. *Journal of Artificial Intelligence Research*, 1994.

[15] R. Quinlan. Learning with continuous classes. In Adams and Sterling, editors, *Proceedings of AI'92*. World Scientific, 1992.

[16] R. Quinlan. *C4.5: Programs for Machine Learning*. Morgan Kaufmann Publishers, Inc., 1993.

[17] L. Torgo. Functional models for regression tree leaves. In D. Fisher, editor, *Machine Learning, Proceedings of the 14th International Conference*. Morgan Kaufmann, 1997.

[18] L. Torgo. *Inductive Learning of Tree-based Regression Models*. PhD thesis, University of Porto, 2000.

[19] P. Utgoff. Percepton trees - a case study in hybrid concept representation. In *Proceedings of the Seventh National Conference on Artificial Intelligence*. Morgan Kaufmann, 1988.

[20] I. Witten and E. Frank. *Data Mining: Practical Machine Learning Tools and Techniques with Java Implementations*. Morgan Kaufmann Publishers, 2000.

[21] D. Wolpert. Stacked generalization. In *Neural Networks*, volume 5, pages 241–260. Pergamon Press, 1992.

Dataset	LinBayes LB	Univ. Tree UT	Functional Trees Bottom	Top	FT	Bagging FT
Adult	− 17.012±0.5	14.178±0.5 −	14.307±0.4	13.800±0.4	13.830±0.4	13.583±0.4
Australian	13.498±0.3	14.750±1.0 −	14.343±0.4	13.928±0.6	13.638±0.6	13.351±5.6
Balance	− 13.355±0.3 −	22.467±1.1 −	10.445±0.6	7.313±0.9	7.313±0.9	5.748±2.8
Banding	23.681±1.0	23.512±1.8	23.512±1.8	23.762±2.2	23.762±2.2 +	19.337±5.4
Breast(W)	+ 2.862±0.1	− 5.123±0.2	− 4.337±0.1	3.346±0.4	3.346±0.4	3.561±2.9
Cleveland	16.134±0.4	20.995±1.4 +	15.952±0.5	17.369±0.9	16.675±0.8	16.514±6.3
Credit	+ 14.228±0.1	14.608±0.5	14.784±0.5	15.103±0.4	15.220±0.6	15.946±4.6
Diabetes	+ 22.709±0.2 −	25.348±1.0	23.998±1.0 −	25.206±0.9	23.658±1.0	22.787±2.7
German	24.520±0.2	28.240±0.7 +	23.630±0.5	24.870±0.5	24.330±0.7	24.100±4.0
Glass	− 36.647±0.8	32.150±2.3	32.150±2.3	32.509±3.3	32.509±3.3	27.919±12.8
Heart	17.704±0.2 −	23.074±1.7	17.037±0.6	17.333±1.4	17.185±0.8	17.037±4.7
Hepatitis	+ 15.481±0.7	17.135±1.3	17.135±1.3	17.135±1.3	17.135±1.3	16.701±6.0
Ionosphere	13.379±0.8	10.025±0.9	10.624±0.9	11.175±1.4	11.175±1.4	11.110±4.1
Iris	2.000±0.0	− 4.333±0.8	2.067±0.2	− 3.733±0.8	2.067±0.2	2.000±3.2
Letter	− 29.821±1.3	11.880±0.6	12.005±0.6	11.799±1.1	11.799±1.1 +	7.909±0.9
Monks-1	− 25.009±0.0	10.536±1.7	11.150±1.9	8.752±1.9	8.729±1.9	6.353±9.3
Monks-2	− 34.186±0.6 −	32.865±0.0 −	33.907±0.4	9.004±1.6	9.074±1.6	18.943±17.5
Monks-3	− 4.163±0.0	+ 1.572±0.4	3.511±0.9	2.884±0.4	2.998±0.4	3.933±4.2
Mushroom	− 3.109±0.0	+ 0.000±0.0	+ 0.062±0.0	0.112±0.0	0.112±0.0	0.148±0.2
Optdigits	− 4.687±0.1	− 9.476±0.3	− 4.732±0.1	3.295±0.1	3.300±0.1	3.437±0.8
Pendigits	− 12.425±0.0	− 3.559±0.1	− 3.099±0.1	2.890±0.1	2.890±0.1 +	2.202±0.5
Pyrimidines	− 9.846±0.1	+ 5.733±0.2	6.115±0.2	6.158±0.2	6.159±0.2	5.275±1.0
Satimage	− 16.011±0.1 −	12.894±0.2 −	12.894±0.2	11.776±0.3	11.776±0.3	11.763±3.0
Segment	− 8.407±0.1	3.381±0.2	3.381±0.2	3.190±0.2	3.190±0.2	2.771±0.9
Shuttle	− 5.629±0.3	0.028±0.0	0.028±0.0	0.036±0.0	0.036±0.0	0.033±0.0
Sonar	24.955±1.2	27.654±3.5	27.654±3.5	27.654±3.5	27.654±3.5	19.682±9.8
Vehicle	22.163±0.1 −	27.334±1.2 +	18.282±0.5	21.090±1.1	21.031±1.1	18.687±2.5
Votes	− 9.739±0.2	3.773±0.5	3.773±0.5	3.795±0.5	3.795±0.5	3.734±5.0
Waveform	+ 14.939±0.2 −	24.036±0.8 +	15.216±0.2 −	16.142±0.3	15.863±0.4	14.918±2.4
Wine	1.133±0.5	− 6.609±1.3	1.404±0.3	1.459±0.3	1.404±0.3	1.082±2.3

Summary of Results	LB	UT	FT-B	FT-T	FT	Bagg. FT
Average Mean	15.31	14.58	12.72	11.89	11.72	11.02
Geometric Mean	11.63	9.03	7.03	6.80	6.63	6.03
Average Rank	4.0	4.1	3.1	3.3	3.0	2.2
Average Ratio	7.545	1.41	1.12	1.032	1	0.97
Wins/Losses	11/19	9/19	13/13	6/10	−	24/6
Significant Wins/Losses	5/15	3/12	5/8	0/3	−	3/0
Wilcoxon Test	0.00	0.00	0.8	0.07	0.014	

Table 1. Results of Functional Trees (Error-rates).

A tight upper bound on the number of candidate patterns

Floris Geerts, Bart Goethals, and Jan Van den Bussche
Limburgs Universitair Centrum, Belgium

Abstract

In the context of mining for frequent patterns using the standard levelwise algorithm, the following question arises: given the current level and the current set of frequent patterns, what is the maximal number of candidate patterns that can be generated on the next level? We answer this question by providing a tight upper bound, derived from a combinatorial result from the sixties by Kruskal and Katona. Our result is useful to reduce the number of database scans.

1 Introduction

The frequent pattern mining problem [3] is by now well known. We are given a set of items $\mathcal{I}$ and a database $\mathcal{D}$ of subsets of $\mathcal{I}$ called transactions. A *pattern* is some set of items; its *support* in $\mathcal{D}$ is defined as the number of transactions in $\mathcal{D}$ that contain the pattern; and a pattern is called *frequent* in $\mathcal{D}$ if its support exceeds a given minimal support threshold. The goal is now to find all frequent patterns in $\mathcal{D}$.

The search space of this problem, all subsets of $\mathcal{I}$, is clearly huge. Instead of generating and counting the supports of all these patterns at once, several solutions have been proposed to perform a more directed search through all patterns. However, this directed search enforces several scans through the database, which brings up another great cost, because these databases tend to be very large, and hence they do not fit into main memory.

The standard Apriori algorithm [4] for solving this problem is based on its monotonicity property, that all subsets of a frequent pattern must be frequent. A pattern is thus considered potentially frequent, also called a *candidate* pattern, if its support is yet unknown, but all of its subsets are already known to be frequent. In every step of the algorithm, all candidate patterns are generated and their supports are then counted by performing a complete scan of the transaction database. This is repeated until no new candidate patterns can be generated. Hence, the number of scans through the database equals the maximal size of a candidate pattern. Several improvements on the Apriori algorithm try

to reduce the number of scans through the database by estimating the number of candidate patterns that can still be generated.

At the heart of all these techniques lies the following purely combinatorial problem, that must be solved first before we can seriously start applying them: *given the current set of frequent patterns at a certain pass of the algorithm, what is the maximal number of candidate patterns that can be generated in the passes yet to come?*

Our contribution is to solve this problem by providing a hard and tight combinatorial upper bound. By computing our upper bound after every pass of the algorithm, we have at all times a watertight guarantee on the size of what is still to come, on which we can then base various optimization decisions, depending on the specific algorithm that is used.

In the next Section, we will discuss existing techniques to reduce the number of database scans, and point out the dangers of using existing heuristics for this purpose. Using our upper bound, these techniques can be made watertight. In Section 3, we derive our upper bound, using a combinatorial result from the sixties by Kruskal and Katona. In Section 4, we show how to get even more out of this upper bound by applying it recursively. In Section 5, we discuss several issues concerning the implementation of the given upper bounds on top of Apriori-like algorithms. In Section 6, we give experimental results, showing the effectiveness of our result in estimating, far ahead, how much will still be generated in the future. Finally, we conclude the paper in Section 7.

Due to space limitations, the proofs of the theorems in this paper have been omitted.

2 Related Work

Nearly all frequent pattern mining algorithms developed after the proposal of the Apriori algorithm, rely on its levelwise candidate generation and pruning strategy. Most of them differ in how they generate and count candidate patterns.

One of the first optimizations was the DHP algorithm proposed by Park et al. [19]. This algorithm uses a hashing scheme to collect upper bounds on the frequencies of the candidate patterns for the following pass. Patterns of which it is already known they will turn up infrequent can then be eliminated from further consideration. The effectiveness of this technique only showed for the first few passes. Since our upper bound can be used to reduce the number of passes and hence after the first few passes, both techniques can be combined in the same algorithm.

Other strategies, discussed next, try to reduce the number of passes. However, such a reduction of passes often causes an increase in the number of candidate patterns that need to be explored during a single pass. This tradeoff between the reduction of passes and the number of candidate patterns is important since the time needed to process a transaction is dependent on the number of candidates that are covered in that transaction, which might blow up exponentially. Our upper bound can be used to predict whether or not this blowup will occur.

The Partition algorithm, proposed by Savasere et al. [20], reduces the number of database passes to two. Towards this end, the database is partitioned into parts small enough to be handled in main memory. The partitions are then considered one at a time and all frequent patterns for that partition are generated using an Apriori-like algorithm. At the end of the first pass, all these patterns are merged to generate a set of all potential frequent patterns, which can then be counted over the complete database. Although this method performs only two database passes, its performance is heavily dependent on the distribution of the data, and could generate much too many candidates.

The sampling algorithm proposed by Toivonen [22] performs at most two scans through the database by picking a random sample from the database, then finding all frequent patterns that probably hold in the whole database, and then verifying the results with the rest of the database. In the cases where the sampling method does not produce all frequent patterns, the missing patterns can be found by generating all remaining potentially frequent patterns and verifying their frequencies during a second pass through the database. The probability of such a failure can be kept small by decreasing the minimal support threshold. However, this can again cause a combinatorial explosion of the number of candidate patterns.

The DIC algorithm, proposed by Brin et al. [7], tries to reduce the number of passes over the database by dividing the database into intervals of a specific size. First, all candidate patterns of size 1 are generated. The frequencies of the candidate sets are then counted over the first interval of the database. Based on these relative frequencies, candidate patterns of size 2 are generated and are counted over the next interval together with the patterns of size 1. In general, after every interval k, candidate patterns of size $k + 1$ are generated and counted. The algorithm stops if no more candidates can be generated. Although this method drasti-

cally reduces the number of scans through the database, its performance is also heavily dependent on the the distribution of the data, and hence it could again generate too many candidates.

Recently, the first successful attempts to generate frequent patterns using a depth-first search were proposed by Agarwal et al. [1, 2] and by Han et al. [11]. Generating patterns in a depth-first manner implies that the monotonicity property cannot be exploited anymore. Hence, a lot more patterns will be generated and need to be counted, compared to the breadth-first algorithms. The FPgrowth algorithm from Han et al. solves this problem by loading a compressed form of the database in main memory using the proposed FPtree. This memory-resident FPtree benefits from a very fast counting mechanism of all generated patterns.[1] Obviously, it is not always possible to load the compressed form of the database into main memory.

Other strategies try to push certain constraints into the candidate pattern generation as deeply as possible to reduce the number of candidate patterns that must be generated [9, 15, 18, 21]. Still others try to find only the set of *maximal* frequent patterns, i.e. those frequent patterns that have no superset which is also frequent [6, 16, 23]. Of course, these techniques do not give us all frequencies of all frequent patterns as required by the general pattern mining problem we consider in this paper.

The first heuristic specifically proposed to estimate the number of candidate patterns that can still be generated was used in the AprioriHybrid algorithm [4, 5]. This algorithm uses Apriori in the initial passes and switches to AprioriTid if it expects it to run faster. This AprioriTid algorithm does not use the database at all for counting the support of candidate patterns. Rather, an encoding of the candidate patterns used in the previous pass is employed for this purpose. The AprioriHybrid algorithm switches to AprioriTid when it expects this encoding of the candidate patterns to be small enough to fit in main memory. The size of the encoding grows with the number of candidate patterns. Therefore, it calculates the size the encoding would have in the current pass. If this size is small enough and there were fewer candidate patterns in the current level than the previous pass, the heuristic decides to switch to AprioriTid.

This heuristic (like all heuristics) is not waterproof, however. Take, for example, two disjoint datasets. The first dataset consists of all subsets of a frequent pattern of size 20. The second dataset consists of all subsets of 1 000 disjoint frequent patterns of size 5. If we merge these two datasets, we get $\binom{20}{3} + 1\,000\binom{5}{3} = 11\,140$ patterns of size 3 and $\binom{20}{4} + 1\,000\binom{5}{4} = 9\,845$ patterns of size 4. If we have enough memory to store the encoding for all these patterns, then the heuristic decides to switch to AprioriTid. This de-

---

[1] Note that the patterns in the FPtree are represented in the so called header tables.

156

cision is premature, however, because the number of new patterns in each pass will start growing exponentially afterwards.

Another improvement of the Apriori algorithm, which is part of the folklore, tries to combine as many iterations as possible in the end, when only few candidate patterns can still be generated. The potential of such a combination technique was realized early on [4, 17], but the modalities under which it can be applied were never further examined. Our work does exactly that.

3 The basic upper bounds

In all that follows, L is some family of patterns of size k.

Definition 1. A *candidate pattern* for L is a pattern (of size larger than k) of which all k-subsets are in L. For a given $\ell > k$, we denote the set of all size-ℓ candidate patterns for L by $C_\ell(L)$.

For any $p \geq 1$, we will provide an upper bound on $|C_{k+p}(L)|$ in terms of $|L|$. The following lemma is central to our approach: (a simple proof was given by Katona [13])

Lemma 1. *Given n and k, there exists a unique representation*

$$n = \binom{m_k}{k} + \binom{m_{k-1}}{k-1} + \cdots + \binom{m_r}{r},$$

with $r \geq 1$, $m_k > m_{k-1} > \ldots > m_r$, and $m_i \geq i$ for $i = r, r+1, \ldots, k$.

This representation is called the *k-canonical representation of n* and can be computed as follows: The integer m_k satisfies $\binom{m_k}{k} \leq n < \binom{m_k+1}{k}$, the integer m_{k-1} satisfies $\binom{m_{k-1}}{k-1} \leq n - \binom{m_k}{k} < \binom{m_{k-1}+1}{k-1}$, and so on, until $n - \binom{m_k}{k} - \binom{m_{k-1}}{k-1} - \cdots - \binom{m_r}{r}$ is zero.

We now establish the following theorem. The proof is based on a combinatorial result of Kruskal and Katona [8, 13, 14].

Theorem 2. *If*

$$|L| = \binom{m_k}{k} + \binom{m_{k-1}}{k-1} + \cdots + \binom{m_r}{r}$$

in k-canonical representation, then

$$|C_{k+p}(L)| \leq \binom{m_k}{k+p} + \binom{m_{k-1}}{k-1+p}$$
$$+ \cdots + \binom{m_{s+1}}{s+p+1},$$

where s is the smallest integer such that $m_s < s + p$. If no such integer exists, we set $s = r - 1$.

Notation We will refer to the upper bound provided by the above theorem as $KK_k^{k+p}(|L|)$ (for Kruskal-Katona). The subscript k, the level at which we are predicting, is important, as the only parameter is the cardinality $|L|$ of L, not L itself. The superscript $k + p$ denotes the level we are predicting.

Proposition 3 (Tightness). *The upper bound provided by Theorem 2 is tight: for any given n and k there always exists an L with $|L| = n$ such that for any given p, $|C_{k+p}(L)| = KK_k^{k+p}(|L|)$.*

Analogous tightness properties hold for all upper bounds we will present in this paper, but we will no longer explicitly state this.

Example 1. Let L be the set of 13 patterns of size 3:

$$\{\{3, 2, 1\},$$
$$\{4, 2, 1\}, \{4, 3, 1\}, \{4, 3, 2\},$$
$$\{5, 2, 1\}, \{5, 3, 1\}, \{5, 3, 2\},$$
$$\{5, 4, 1\}, \{5, 4, 2\}, \{5, 4, 3\},$$
$$\{6, 2, 1\}, \{6, 3, 1\}, \{6, 3, 2\}\}.$$

The 3-canonical representation of 13 is $\binom{5}{3} + \binom{3}{2}$ and hence the maximum number of candidate patterns of size 4 is $KK_3^4(13) = \binom{5}{4} + \binom{3}{3} = 6$ and the maximum number of candidate patterns of size 5 is $KK_3^5(13) = \binom{5}{5} = 1$. This is tight indeed, because

$$C_4(L) = \{\{4, 3, 2, 1\}, \{5, 3, 2, 1\}, \{5, 4, 2, 1\},$$
$$\{5, 4, 3, 1\}, \{5, 4, 3, 2\}, \{6, 3, 2, 1\}\}$$

and

$$C_5(L) = \{\{5, 4, 3, 2, 1\}\}.$$

Estimating the number of levels The k-canonical representation of $|L|$ also yields an upper bound on the maximal size of a candidate pattern, denoted by maxsize(L). Recall that this size equals the number of iterations the standard Apriori algorithm will perform. Indeed, since $|L| < \binom{m_k+1}{k}$, there cannot be a candidate pattern of size $m_k + 1$ or higher, so:

Proposition 4. *If $\binom{m_k}{k}$ is the first term in the k-canonical representation of $|L|$, then maxsize(L) $\leq m_k$.*

We denote this number m_k by $\mu_k(|L|)$. From the form of KK_k^{k+p} as given by Theorem 2, it is immediate that μ also tells us the last level before which KK becomes zero. Formally:

Proposition 5. $\mu_k(|L|) = \min\{p \mid KK_k^{k+p}(|L|) = 0\} + k - 1$.

Estimating all levels As a result of the above, we can also bound, at any given level k, the *total* number of candidate patterns that can be generated, as follows:

Proposition 6. *The total number of candidate patterns that can be generated from a set L of k-patterns is at most*

$$KK_k^{\text{total}}(L) := \sum_{p=1}^{\mu_k(|L|)} KK_k^{k+p}(|L|).$$

4 Getting the most out of it

The upper bound KK on itself is neat and simple as it takes as parameters only two numbers: the current size k, and the number $|L|$ of current frequent patterns. However, in reality, when we have arrived at a certain level k, we do not merely have the cardinality: we have the actual set L of current k-patterns! For example, if the frequent patterns in the current pass are all disjoint, our current upper bound will still estimate their number to a certain non-zero figure. However, by the pairwise disjointness, it is clear that no further patterns will be possible at all. In sum, because we have richer information than a mere cardinality, we should be able to get a better upper bound.

To get inspiration, let us recall that the candidate generation process of the Apriori algorithm works in two steps. In the *join* step, we join L with itself to obtain a superset of C_{k+1}. The union $p \cup q$ of two patterns $p, q \in L$ is inserted in C_{k+1} if they share their $k-1$ smallest items:

insert into C_{k+1}
select $p[1], p[2], \ldots, p[k], q[k]$
from $L_k \ p, L_k \ q$
where $p[1] = q[1], \ldots, p[k-1] = q[k-1], p[k] < q[k]$

Next, in the *prune* step, we delete every pattern $c \in C_{k+1}$ such that some k-subset of c is not in L.

Let us now take a closer look at the join step from another point of view. Consider a family of all frequent patterns of size k that share their $k-1$ smallest items, and let its cardinality be n. If we now remove from each of these patterns all these shared $k-1$ smallest items, we get exactly n distinct single-item patterns. The number of pairs that can be formed from these single items, being $\binom{n}{2}$, is exactly the number of candidates the join step will generate for the family under consideration. We thus get an obvious upper bound on the total number of candidates by taking the sum of all $\binom{n_f}{2}$, for every possible family f.

This obvious upper bound on $|C_{k+1}|$, which we denote by $obvious_{k+1}(L)$, can be recursively computed in the following manner. Let I denote the set of items occurring in L. For an arbitrary item x, define the set L^x as

$$L^x = \{s - \{x\} \mid s \in L \text{ and } x = \min s\}.$$

Then

$$obvious_{k+1}(L) := \begin{cases} \binom{|L|}{2} & \text{if } k = 1; \\ \sum_{x \in I} obvious_k(L^x) & \text{if } k > 1. \end{cases}$$

This upper bound is much too crude, however, because it does not take the prune step into account, only the join step. The join step only checks two k-subsets of a potential candidate instead of all $k+1$ k-subsets.

However, we can generalize this method such that more subsets will be considered. Indeed, instead of taking a family of all frequent patterns sharing their $k-1$ smallest items, we can take all frequent patterns sharing only their k' smallest items, for some $k' \leq k-1$. If we then remove these k' shared items from each pattern in the family, we get a new set L' of n patterns of size $k-k'$. If we now consider the set C' of candidates (of size $k-k'+1$) for L', and add back to each of them the previously removed k' items, we obtain a pruned set of candidates of size $k+1$, where instead of just two (as in the join step), $k-k'+1$ of the k-subsets were checked in the pruning. Note that we can get the estimate $KK_{k-k'}^{k-k'+1}(|L'|)$ on the cardinality of C' from our upper bound Theorem 2.

Doing this for all possible values of k' yields an improved upper bound on $|C_{k+1}|$, which we denote by $improved_{k+1}(L)$, and which is computed by refining the recursive procedure for the obvious upper bound as follows:

$$improved_{k+1}(L) :=$$
$$\begin{cases} \binom{|L|}{2} & \text{if } k = 1; \\ \min\{KK_k^{k+1}(|L|), \sum_{x \in I} improved_k(L^x)\} & \text{if } k > 1. \end{cases}$$

Actually, as in the previous section, we can do this not only to estimate $|C_{k+1}|$, but also more generally to estimate $|C_{k+p}|$ for any $p \geq 1$. Henceforth we will denote our general improved upper bound by $KK_{k+p}^*(L)$. The general definition is as follows:

$$KK_{k+p}^*(L) :=$$
$$\begin{cases} \binom{|L|}{p+1} & \text{if } k = 1; \\ \min\{KK_k^{k+p}(|L|), \sum_{x \in I} KK_{k+p-1}^*(L^x)\} & \text{if } k > 1. \end{cases}$$

(For the base case, note that $\binom{|L|}{p+1}$, when $k = 1$, is nothing but $KK_k^{k+p}(|L|)$.)

By definition, KK_{k+p}^* is always smaller than KK_k^{k+p}. We can prove formally that it is still an upper bound on the number of candidate patterns of size $k + p$:

Theorem 7. $|C_{k+p}(L)| \leq KK_{k+p}^*(L)$.

158

A natural question is why we must take the minimum in the definition of KK^*. The answer is that the two terms of which we take the minimum are incomparable. The example of an L where all patterns are pairwise disjoint, already mentioned in the beginning of this section, shows that, for example, $KK_k^{k+1}(|L|)$ can be larger than the summation $\sum_{x \in I} KK_k^*(L^x)$. But the converse is also possible: consider $L = \{\{1,2\}, \{1,3\}\}$. Then $KK_2^3(L) = 0$, but the summation yields 1.

Example 2. Let L consist of all 19 3-subsets of $\{1,2,3,4,5\}$ and $\{3,4,5,6,7\}$ plus the sets $\{5,7,8\}$ and $\{5,8,9\}$. Because $21 = \binom{6}{3} + \binom{2}{2}$, we have $KK_3^4(21) = 15$, $KK_3^5(21) = 6$ and $KK_3^6(21) = 1$. On the other hand,

$$
\begin{aligned}
KK_4^*(L) &= KK_3^*(L^1) + KK_3^*(L^2) \\
&\quad + KK_3^*(L^3) + KK_3^*(L^4) \\
&\quad + KK_2^*((L^5)^6) + KK_2^*((L^5)^7) \\
&\quad + KK_2^*((L^5)^8) + KK_2^*((L^5)^9) \\
&\quad + KK_3^*(L^6) + KK_3^*(L^7) \\
&\quad + KK_3^*(L^8) + KK_3^*(L^9) \\
&= 4 + 1 + 4 + 1 + 0 + \cdots + 0 \\
&= 10
\end{aligned}
$$

and

$$
\begin{aligned}
KK_5^*(L) &= KK_4^*(L^1) + KK_4^*(L^2) \\
&\quad + KK_4^*(L^3) + KK_4^*(L^4) \\
&\quad + KK_3^*((L^5)^6) + KK_3^*((L^5)^7) \\
&\quad + KK_3^*((L^5)^8) + KK_3^*((L^5)^9) \\
&\quad + KK_4^*(L^6) + KK_4^*(L^7) \\
&\quad + KK_4^*(L^8) \\
&\quad + KK_4^*(L^9) \\
&= 1 + 0 + 1 + 0 + 0 + \cdots + 0 \\
&= 2.
\end{aligned}
$$

Indeed, we have 10 4-subsets of $\{1,2,3,4,5\}$ and $\{3,4,5,6,7\}$, and the two 5-sets themselves.

We can also improve the upper bound $\mu_k(|L|)$ on maxsize(L). Indeed, in analogy with Proposition 5, we define:

$$
\mu^*(L) := \min\{p \mid KK_{k+p}^*(L) = 0\} + k - 1.
$$

We then have:

Proposition 8. maxsize$(L) \leq \mu^*(L) \leq \mu(L)$.

We finally use Theorem 7 for improving the upper bound KK_k^{total} on the total number of candidate patterns. Indeed,

define:

$$
KK_{\text{total}}^*(L) = \sum_{p=1}^{\mu^*(L)} KK_{k+p}^*(L)
$$

Then we have:

Proposition 9. *The total number of candidate patterns that can be generated from a set L of k-patterns is bounded by $KK_{\text{total}}^*(L)$. Moreover, $KK_{\text{total}}^*(L) \leq KK_k^{\text{total}}(L)$.*

5 Efficient Implementation

To evaluate our upper bounds we implemented an optimized version of the Apriori algorithm using a trie data structure to store all generated patterns, similar to the one described by Brin et al. [7]. This trie structure makes it cheap and straightforward to implement the computation of all upper bounds. Indeed, a top-level subtrie (rooted at some singleton pattern $\{x\}$) represents exactly the set L^x we defined in Section 4. Every top-level subtrie of this subtrie (rooted at some two-element pattern $\{x,y\}$) then represents $(L^x)^y$, and so on. Hence, we can compute the recursive bounds while traversing the trie, after the frequencies of all candidate patterns are counted, and we have to traverse the trie once more to remove all candidate patterns that turned out to be infrequent. This can be done as follows.

Remember, at that point, we have the current set of frequent patterns of size k stored in the trie. For every node at depth d smaller than k, we compute the $k - d$-canonical representation of the number of descendants this node has at depth k, which can be used to compute μ_{k-d} (cf. Proposition 4), KK_{k-d}^ℓ for any $\ell \leq \mu_{k-d}$ (cf. Theorem 2) and hence also KK_{k-d}^{total} (cf. Proposition 6). For every node at depth $k - 1$, its KK^* and μ^* values are equal to its KK and μ values respectively. Then compute for every $p > 0$, the sum of the $KK_{k-d+p-1}^*$ values of all its children, and let KK_{k-d+p}^* be the smallest of this sum and KK_{k-d}^{k-d+p} until this minimum becomes zero, which also gives us the value of μ^*. Finally, we can compute KK_{total}^* for this node. If this is done for every node, traversed in a depth-first manner, then finally the root node will contain the upper bounds on the number of candidate patterns that can still be generated, and on the maximum size of any such pattern. The soundness and completeness of this method follows directly from the theorems and propositions of the previous sections.

We should also point out that, since the numbers involved can become exponentially large (in the number of items), an implementation should take care to use arbitrary-length integers such as provided by standard mathematical packages. Since the length of an integer is only logarithmic in its value, the lengths of the numbers involved will remain polynomially bounded.

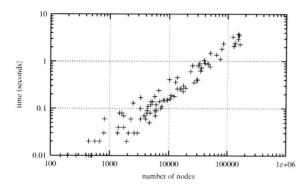

Figure 1. Time needed to compute upper bounds compared to the number of nodes.

The cost for the computation of the upper bounds is negligible compared to the cost of the complete algorithm. Indeed, the time T needed to calculate the upper bounds is largely dictated by the number n of nodes in the trie. We have shown experimentally that T scales linearly with n. Moreover, the constant factor in our implementation is very small (around 0.0025). We ran several experiments using two different datasets and varying minimal support thresholds. After every pass of the algorithm, we registered the number of nodes in the trie and the time spent to compute all upper bounds, resulting in 145 different datapoints. Figure 1 shows these results.

6 Experimental Evaluation

Data sets We have experimented using several synthetic datasets generated by the program provided by the Quest research group at IBM Almaden. For different settings of the parameters of the generator, the resulting figures were very analogous. We also experimented using a real market basket dataset from a Belgian retail store containing 41 373 transactions. The store carries 13 103 products. The results from this experiment were not immediately as good as the results from the synthetic datasets. The reason for this, however, turned out to be the bad ordering of the items, as explained next.

Reordering From the form of L^x, it can be seen that the order of the items can affect the recursive upper bounds. By computing the upper bound only for a subset of all frequent patterns, we win by incorporating the structure of the current collection of frequent patterns, but we also lose some information, because whenever we recursively restrict ourselves to a subtrie L^x, then for every candidate pattern s with $x = \min s$, we lose the information about exactly one subpattern in L, namely $s - x$, because all patterns in L^x

come from patterns in L that contain x. We therefore would like to make it likely that many of these excluded patterns are frequent. A good heuristic, which has already been used for several other optimizations in frequent pattern mining [2, 6, 7] is to reorder the single item patterns in increasing order of frequency, such that the excluded subpatterns have the highest probability of being frequent (under the assumption that the occurence of an event in a transaction is independent of the occurence of any other event in the transaction).

After reordering the items in the real life dataset, using this heuristic, the results became very analogous with the results using the synthetic datasets.

Results Figures 2(a), 2(b), and 2(c) show experimental results on the real life dataset.

- Figure 2(a) shows, after each level k, the computed upper bound KK and improved upper bound KK^* for the number of candidate patterns at the next level, as well as the actual number $|C_{k+1}|$ it turned out to be.

- Figure 2(b) shows the computed upper bounds μ and μ^* on the maximal size of a candidate pattern. In this experiment, this maximum turned out to be 11.

- Figure 2(c) shows the upper bounds on the total number of candidate patterns that could still be generated, compared to the actual number of candidate patterns, $|C_{\text{total}}|$, that effectively still were generated when we combined all further passes into a single one.

- Figures 2(d), 2(e) and 2(f) show the previous experiment, now performed over a synthetic dataset containing 100 000 transactions over 1 000 items, using a varying minimal support threshold of 0.025%, 0.075% and 0.125% respectively.

Discussion The results are pleasantly surprising:

- First, note that the improvement of KK^* over KK, and of μ^* over μ, anticipated by our theoretical discussion, is indeed dramatic.

- Second, comparing the computed upper bounds with the actual numbers, we observe the high accuracy of the estimations given by KK^*. Indeed, the estimations of KK^*_{k+1} match almost exactly the actual number of candidate patterns that has been generated at level $k + 1$.

- The upper bounds on the total number of candidate patterns are still very large when estimated in the first two passes, which is not surprising because at these initial stages, there is not much information yet. From the

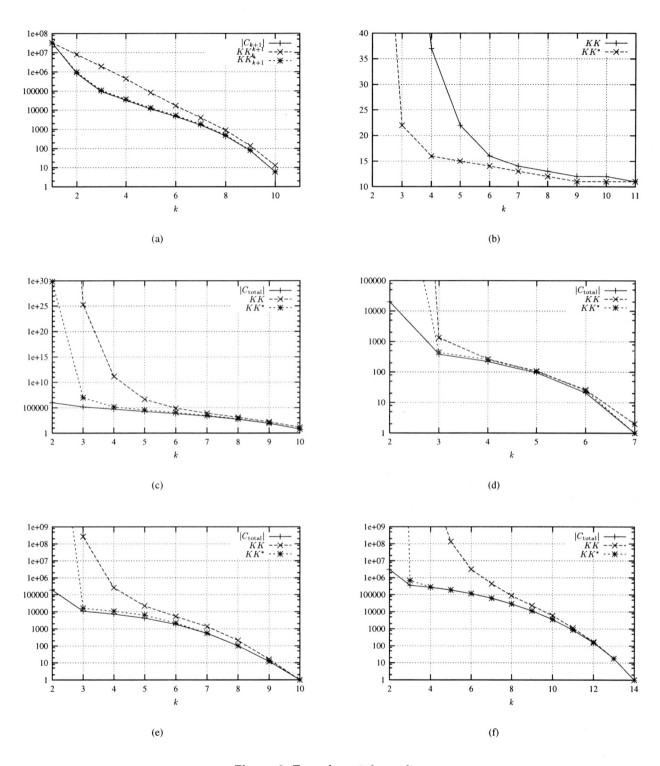

Figure 2. Experimental results

fourth pass on, however, when the frequent patterns of size 4 are known, the estimations become almost exact.

- Since the totals become manageable from there on, an optimizer using our estimates would decide to combine all iterations 5–11 in a single one, and would have generated at most 142 237 more candidate patterns.

- Entirely similar results are obtained when varying the minimal support thresholds.

References

[1] R. Agarwal, C. Aggarwal, and V. Prasad. Depth first generation of long patterns. In *Proceedings of the sixth ACM SIGKDD international conference on Knowledge discovery and data mining*. ACM Press, 2000.

[2] R. Agarwal, C. Aggarwal, and V. Prasad. A tree projection algorithm for generation of frequent itemsets. *Journal of Parallel and Distributed Computing*, 61(3):350–371, March 2001.

[3] R. Agrawal, T. Imielinski, and A. Swami. Mining association rules between sets of items in large databases. In *Proceedings of the 1993 ACM SIGMOD International Conference on Management of Data*, volume 22:2 of *SIGMOD Record*, pages 207–216. ACM Press, 1993.

[4] R. Agrawal, H. Mannila, R. Srikant, H. Toivonen, and A. Verkamo. Fast discovery of association rules. In U. Fayyad, G. Piatetsky-Shapiro, P. Smyth, and R. Uthurusamy, editors, *Advances in Knowledge Discovery and Data Mining*, pages 307–328. MIT Press, 1996.

[5] R. Agrawal and R. Srikant. Fast algorithms for mining association rules. IBM Research Report RJ9839, IBM Alamaden Research Center, San Jose, California, June 1994.

[6] R. Bayardo, Jr. Efficiently mining long patterns from databases. In Haas and Tiwary [10], pages 85–93.

[7] S. Brin, R. Motwani, J. Ullman, and S. Tsur. Dynamic itemset counting and implication rules for market basket data. In J. Peckham, editor, *Proceedings of the 1997 ACM SIGMOD International Conference on Management of Data*, volume 26:2 of *SIGMOD Record*, pages 255–264. ACM Press, 1997.

[8] P. Frankl. A new short proof for the Kruskal–Katona theorem. *Discrete Mathematics*, 48:327–329, 1984.

[9] B. Goethals and J. Van den Bussche. On supporting interactive association rule mining. In Y. Kambayashi, M. Mohania, and A. Tjoa, editors, *Data Warehousing and Knowledge Discovery*, volume 1874 of *Lecture Notes in Computer Science*, pages 307–316. Springer, 2000.

[10] L. Haas and A. Tiwary, editors. *Proceedings of the 1998 ACM SIGMOD International Conference on Management of Data*, volume 27:2 of *SIGMOD Record*. ACM Press, 1998.

[11] J. Han, J. Pei, and Y. Yin. Mining frequent patterns without candidate generation. In W. Chen, J. Naughton, and P. Bernstein, editors, *Proceedings of the 2000 ACM SIGMOD International Conference on Management of Data*, volume 29:2 of *SIGMOD Record*, pages 1–12. ACM Press, 2000.

[12] D. Heckerman, H. Mannila, and D. Pregibon, editors. *Proceedings of the Third International Conference on Knowledge Discovery & Data Mining*. AAAI Press, 1997.

[13] G. Katona. A theorem of finite sets. In *Theory Of Graphs*, pages 187–207. Akadémia Kiadó, 1968.

[14] J. Kruskal. The number of simplices in a complex. In *Mathematical Optimization Techniques*, pages 251–278. Univ. of California Press, 1963.

[15] L. Lakshmanan, R. Ng, J. Han, and A. Pang. Optimization of constrained frequent set queries with 2-variable constraints. In A. Delis, C. Faloutsos, and S. Ghandeharizadeh, editors, *Proceedings of the 1999 ACM SIGMOD International Conference on Management of Data*, volume 28:2 of *SIGMOD Record*, pages 157–168. ACM Press, 1999.

[16] D. Lin and Z. Kedem. Pincer-search: A new algorithm for discovering the maximum frequent set. In H.-J. Schek, F. Saltor, I. Ramos, and G. Alonso, editors, *Proceedings of the 6th International Conference on Extending Database Technology*, volume 1377 of *Lecture Notes in Computer Science*, pages 105–119. Springer, 1998.

[17] H. Mannila, H. Toivonen, and A. Verkamo. Efficient algorithms for discovering association rules. In R. U. U.M. Fayyad, editor, *Proceedings of the AAAI Workshop on Knowledge Discovery in Databases*, pages 181–192. AAAI Press, 1994.

[18] R. Ng, L. Lakshmanan, J. Han, and A. Pang. Exploratory mining and pruning optimizations of constrained association rules. In Haas and Tiwary [10], pages 13–24.

[19] J. Park, M.-S. Chen, and P. Yu. An effective hash based algorithm for mining association rules. In D. S. M.J. Carey, editor, *Proceedings of the 1995 ACM SIGMOD International Conference on Management of Data*, volume 24:2 of *SIGMOD Record*, pages 175–186. ACM Press, 1995.

[20] A. Savasere, E. Omiecinski, and S. Navathe. An efficient algorithm for mining association rules in large databases. In U. Dayal, P. Gray, and S. Nishio, editors, *Proceedings of the 21th International Conference on Very Large Data Bases*, pages 432–444. Morgan Kaufmann, 1995.

[21] R. Srikant, Q. Vu, and R. Agrawal. Mining association rules with item constraints. In Heckerman et al. [12], pages 66–73.

[22] H. Toivonen. Sampling large databases for association rules. In *Proceedings of the 22nd International Conference on Very Large Data Bases*, pages 134–145. Morgan Kaufmann, 1996.

[23] M. Zaki, S. Parthasarathy, M. Ogihara, and W. Li. New algorithms for fast discovery of association rules. In Heckerman et al. [12], pages 283–286.

Efficiently Mining Maximal Frequent Itemsets

Karam Gouda[†] and Mohammed J. Zaki[‡]
[†]Computer Science & Communication Engg. Dept., Kyushu University, Japan
[‡]Computer Science Dept., Rensselaer Polytechnic Institute, USA
Email: kgouda@csce.kyushu-u.ac.jp, zaki@cs.rpi.edu

Abstract

We present GenMax, a backtrack search based algorithm for mining maximal frequent itemsets. GenMax uses a number of optimizations to prune the search space. It uses a novel technique called progressive focusing *to perform maximality checking, and* diffset propagation *to perform fast frequency computation. Systematic experimental comparison with previous work indicates that different methods have varying strengths and weaknesses based on dataset characteristics. We found GenMax to be a highly efficient method to mine the exact set of maximal patterns.*

1 Introduction

Mining frequent itemsets is a fundamental and essential problem in many data mining applications such as the discovery of association rules, strong rules, correlations, multi-dimensional patterns, and many other important discovery tasks. The problem is formulated as follows: Given a large data base of set of items transactions, find all frequent itemsets, where a frequent itemset is one that occurs in at least a user-specified percentage of the data base.

Many of the proposed itemset mining algorithms are a variant of Apriori [2], which employs a bottom-up, breadth-first search that enumerates every single frequent itemset. In many applications (especially in dense data) with long frequent patterns enumerating all possible $2^m - 2$ subsets of a m length pattern (m can easily be 30 or 40 or longer) is computationally unfeasible. Thus, there has been recent interest in mining *maximal* frequent patterns in these "hard" dense databases. Another recent promising direction is to mine only closed sets [9, 11]; a set is closed if it has no superset with the same frequency. Nevertheless, for some of the dense datasets we consider in this paper, even the set of all closed patterns would grow to be too large. The only recourse is to mine the maximal patterns in such domains.

In this paper we introduce *GenMax*, a new algorithm that utilizes a backtracking search for efficiently enumerating all maximal patterns. GenMax uses a number of optimizations to quickly prune away a large portion of the subset search space. It uses a novel *progressive focusing* technique to eliminate non-maximal itemsets, and uses *diffset propagation* for fast frequency checking.

We conduct an extensive experimental characterization of GenMax against state-of-the-art maximal pattern mining methods like MaxMiner [3] and Mafia [4]. We found that the three methods have varying performance depending on the database characteristics (mainly the distribution of the maximal frequent patterns by length). We present a

systematic and realistic set of experiments showing under which conditions a method is likely to perform well and under what conditions it does not perform well. We conclude that while Mafia is the best method for mining a *superset* of all maximal patterns, GenMax is the current best method for enumerating the *exact* set of maximal patterns. We further observe that there is a type of data, where MaxMiner delivers the best performance.

2 Preliminaries and Related Work

The problem of mining maximal frequent patterns can be formally stated as follows: Let $\mathcal{I} = \{i_1, i_2, \ldots, i_m\}$ be a set of m distinct items. Let $\mathcal{D}$ denote a database of transactions, where each transaction has a unique identifier (*tid*) and contains a set of items. The set of all tids is denoted $\mathcal{T} = \{t_1, t_2, \ldots, t_n\}$. A set $X \subseteq \mathcal{I}$ is also called an *itemset*. An itemset with k items is called a k-itemset. The set $t(X) \subseteq \mathcal{T}$, consisting of all the transaction tids which contain X as a subset, is called the *tidset* of X. For convenience we write an itemset $\{A, C, W\}$ as ACW, and its tidset $\{1, 3, 4, 5\}$ as $t(X) = 1345$.

TID	Items	Frequent itemsets Min_Sup = 3 trans	Frequent itemsets Min_Sup = 2 trans	Itemset Size	Maximal itemsets Min_Sup=3 trans	Maximal itemsets Min_Sup = 2 trans
1	ACTW	A, C, D, T, W	A, C, D, T, W	1		
2	CDW	AC, AT, AW, CD, CT, CW, DW, TW	AC, AD, AT, AW, CD, CT, CW, DT, DW, TW	2		
3	ACTW					
4	ACDW					
5	ACDTW	ACT, ACW, ATW,CTW, CDW,	ACD, ACT, ACW, ADW, ATW, CDT, CDW, CTW	3	CDW	CDT
6	CDT					
		ACTW	ACDW, ACTW	4	ACTW	ACDW, ACTW

Figure 1. Mining Frequent Itemsets

The *support* of an itemset X, denoted $\sigma(X)$, is the number of transactions in which that itemset occurs as a subset. Thus $\sigma(X) = |t(X)|$. An itemset is *frequent* if its support is more than or equal to some threshold *minimum support* (*min_sup*) value, i.e., if $\sigma(X) \geq min\_sup$. We denote by F_k the set of frequent k-itemsets, and by **FI** the set of all frequent itemsets. A frequent itemset is called *maximal* if it is not a subset of any other frequent itemset. The set of all maximal frequent itemsets is denoted as **MFI**. Given a user specified *min_sup* value our goal is to efficiently enumerate all patterns in **MFI**.

Example 1 *Consider our example database in Figure 1. There are five different items,* $\mathcal{I} = \{A, C, D, T, W\}$ *and six transactions* $\mathcal{T} = \{1, 2, 3, 4, 5, 6\}$. *The figure also shows the frequent and maximal* k-itemsets *at two different* min_sup *values – 3 (50%) and 2 (30%) respectively.*

Backtracking Search GenMax uses backtracking search to enumerate the **MFI**. We first describe the backtracking paradigm in the context of enumerating all frequent patterns. We will subsequently modify this procedure to enumerate the **MFI**.

Backtracking algorithms are useful for many combinatorial problems where the solution can be represented as a set $I = \{i_0, i_1, ...\}$, where each i_j is chosen from a finite *possible set*, P_j. Initially I is empty; it is extended one item at a time, as the search space is traversed. The length of I is the same as the depth of the corresponding node in the search tree. Given a partial solution of length l, $I_l = \{i_0, i_1, ..., i_{l-1}\}$, the possible values for the next item i_l comes from a subset $C_l \subseteq P_l$ called the *combine set*. If $y \in P_l - C_l$, then nodes in the subtree with root node $I_l = \{i_0, i_1, ..., i_{l-1}, y\}$ will not be considered by the backtracking algorithm. Since such subtrees have been pruned away from the original search space, the determination of C_l is also called *pruning*.

```
// Invoke as FI-backtrack(∅, F₁, 0)
FI-backtrack(I_l, C_l, l)
1.    for each x ∈ C_l
2.        I_{l+1} = I ∪ {x} //also add I_{l+1} to FI
3.        P_{l+1} = {y : y ∈ C_l and y > x}
4.        C_{l+1} = FI-combine (I_{l+1}, P_{l+1})
5.        FI-backtrack(I_{l+1}, C_{l+1}, l + 1)

// Can I_{l+1} combine with other items in C_l?
FI-combine(I_{l+1}, P_{l+1})
1.    C = ∅
2.    for each y ∈ P_{l+1}
3.        if I_{l+1} ∪ {y} is frequent
4.            C = C ∪ {y}
5.    return C
```

Figure 2. Backtrack Algorithm for Mining FI

Consider the backtracking algorithm for mining all frequent patterns, shown in Figure 2. The main loop tries extending I_l with every item x in the current combine set C_l. The first step is to compute I_{l+1}, which is simply I_l extended with x. The second step is to extract the new possible set of extensions, P_{l+1}, which consists only of items y in C_l that follow x. The third step is to create a new combine set for the next pass, consisting of valid extensions. An extension is valid if the resulting itemset is frequent. The combine set, C_{l+1}, thus consists of those items in the possible set that produce a frequent itemset when used to extend I_{l+1}. Any item not in the combine set refers to a pruned subtree. The final step is to recursively call the backtrack routine for each extension. As presented, the backtrack method performs a depth-first traversal of the search space.

Example 2 *Consider the full subset search space shown in Figure 3. The backtrack search space can be considerably smaller than the full space. For example, we start with $I_0 = \emptyset$ and $C_0 = F_1 = \{A, C, D, T, W\}$. At level 1, each item in C_0 is added to I_0 in turn. For example, A is added to obtain $I_1 = \{A\}$. The possible set for A, $P_1 = \{C, D, T, W\}$ consists of all items that follow A in C_0. However, from Figure 1, we find that only AC, AT, and AW are frequent (at min_sup=3), giving $C_1 = \{C, T, W\}$. Thus the subtree corresponding to the node AD has been pruned.*

Related Work Methods for finding the maximal elements include All-MFS [5], which works by iteratively attempting to extend a working pattern until failure. A randomized version of the algorithm that uses vertical bit-vectors

was studied, but it does not guarantee every maximal pattern will be returned. The Pincer-Search [7] algorithm uses horizontal data format. It not only constructs the candidates in a bottom-up manner like Apriori, but also starts a top-down search at the same time, maintaining a candidate set of maximal patterns. This can help in reducing the number of database scans, by eliminating non-maximal sets early. The maximal candidate set is a superset of the maximal patterns, and in general, the overhead of maintaining it can be very high. In contrast GenMax maintains only the current known maximal patterns for pruning.

MaxMiner [3] is another algorithm for finding the maximal elements. It uses efficient pruning techniques to quickly narrow the search. MaxMiner employs a breadth-first traversal of the search space; it reduces database scanning by employing a lookahead pruning strategy, i.e., if a node with all its extensions can determined to be frequent, there is no need to further process that node. It also employs item (re)ordering heuristic to increase the effectiveness of superset-frequency pruning. Since MaxMiner uses the original horizontal database format, it can perform the same number of passes over a database as Apriori does.

DepthProject [1] finds long itemsets using a depth first search of a lexicographic tree of itemsets, and uses a counting method based on transaction projections along its branches. This projection is equivalent to a horizontal version of the tidsets at a given node in the search tree. DepthProject also uses the look-ahead pruning method with item reordering. It returns a superset of the **MFI** and would require post-pruning to eliminate non-maximal patterns. FP-growth [6] uses the novel frequent pattern tree (FP-tree) structure, which is a compressed representation of all the transactions in the database. It uses a recursive divide-and-conquer and database projection approach to mine long patterns. Nevertheless, since it enumerates all frequent patterns it is impractical when pattern length is long.

Mafia [4] is the most recent method for mining the **MFI**. Mafia uses three pruning strategies to remove non-maximal sets. The first is the look-ahead pruning first used in MaxMiner. The second is to check if a new set is subsumed by an existing maximal set. The last technique checks if $t(X) \subseteq t(Y)$. If so X is considered together with Y for extension. Mafia uses vertical bit-vector data format, and compression and projection of bitmaps to improve performance. Mafia mines a superset of the **MFI**, and requires a post-pruning step to eliminate non-maximal patterns. In contrast GenMax integrates pruning with mining and returns the exact **MFI**.

3 GenMax for efficient MFI Mining

There are two main ingredients to develop an efficient **MFI** algorithm. The first is the set of techniques used to remove entire branches of the search space, and the second is the representation used to perform fast frequency computations. We will describe below how GenMax extends the basic backtracking routine for **FI**, and then the progressive focusing and diffset propagation techniques it uses for fast maximality and frequency checking.

The basic **MFI** enumeration code used in GenMax is a straightforward extension of **FI-backtrack**. The main addition is the superset checking to eliminate non-maximal itemsets, as shown in Figure 4. In addition to the main steps

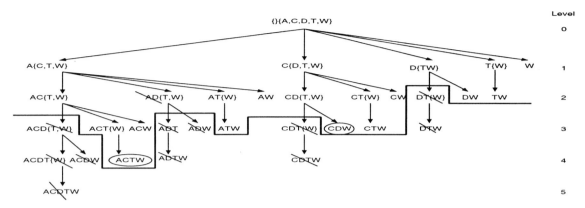

Figure 3. Subset/Backtrack Search Tree (*min_sup***= 3):** Circles indicate maximal sets and the infrequent sets have been crossed out. Due to the downward closure property of support (i.e., all subsets of a frequent itemset must be frequent) the frequent itemsets form a *border* (shown with the bold line), such that all frequent itemsets lie above the border, while all infrequent itemsets lie below it. Since **MFI** determine the border, it is straightforward to obtain **FI** in a single database scan of **MFI** is known.

```
// Invocation: MFI-backtrack(∅, F₁, 0)
MFI-backtrack(Iₗ, Cₗ, l)
1.     for each x ∈ Cₗ
2.         Iₗ₊₁ = I ∪ {x}
3.         Pₗ₊₁ = {y : y ∈ Cₗ and y > x}
4.*        if Iₗ₊₁ ∪ Pₗ₊₁ has a superset in MFI
5.*            return //all subsequent branches pruned!
6.         Cₗ₊₁ = FI-combine (Iₗ₊₁, Pₗ₊₁)
7.*        if Cₗ₊₁ is empty
8.*            if Iₗ₊₁ has no superset in MFI
9.*                MFI= MFI ∪ Iₗ₊₁
10.        else MFI-backtrack(Iₗ₊₁, Cₗ₊₁, l + 1)
```

Figure 4. Backtrack Algorithm for Mining MFI(* indicates a new line not in FI-backtrack)

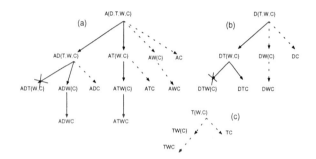

Figure 5. Backtracking Trees of Example 2

in **FI** enumeration, the new code adds a step (line 4) after the construction of the possible set to check if $I_{l+1} \cup P_{l+1}$ is subsumed by an existing maximal set. If so, the current and all subsequent items in C_l can be pruned away. After creating the new combine set, if it is empty and I_{l+1} is not a subset of any maximal pattern, it is added to the **MFI**. If the combine set is non-empty a recursive call is made to check further extensions.

Superset Checking Techniques: Checking to see if the given itemset I_{l+1} combined with the possible set P_{l+1} is subsumed by another maximal set was also proposed in Mafia [4] under the name HUTMFI. Further pruning is possible if one can determine based just on support of the combine sets if $I_{l+1} \cup P_{l+1}$ will be guaranteed to be frequent. In this case also one can avoid processing any more branches. This method was first introduced in MaxMiner [3], and was also used in Mafia under the name FHUT.

Reordering the Combine Set: Two general principles for efficient searching using backtracking are that: 1) It is more efficient to make the next choice of a subtree (branch) to explore to be the one whose combine set has the fewest items. This usually results in good performance, since it minimizes the number of frequency computations in FI-combine. 2) If we are able to remove a node as early as possible from the backtracking search tree we effectively prune many branches from consideration.

Reordering the elements in the current combine set to achieve the two goals is a very effective means of cutting

down the search space. The first heuristic is to reorder the combine set in increasing order of support. This is likely to produce small combine sets in the next level, since the items with lower frequency are less likely to produce frequent itemsets at the next level. This heuristic was first used in MaxMiner, and has been used in other methods since then [1, 4, 11].

In addition to sorting the initial combine set at level 0 in increasing order of support, GenMax uses another novel reordering heuristic based on a simple lemma

Lemma 1 *Let $IF(x) = \{y : y \in F_1, xy \text{ is not frequent}\}$, denote the set of infrequent 2-itemsets that contain an item $x \in F_1$, and let $M(x)$ be the longest maximal pattern containing x. Then $|M(x)| \leq |F_1| - |IF(x)|$.*

Assuming F_2 has been computed, reordering C_0 in decreasing order of $IF(x)$ (with $x \in C_0$) ensures that the smallest combine sets will be processed at the initial levels of the tree, which result in smaller backtracking search trees. GenMax thus initially sorts the items in decreasing order of $IF(x)$ and in increasing order of support.

Example 3 *For our database in Figure 1 with min_sup = 2, $IF(x)$ is the same of all items $x \in F_1$, and the sorted order (on support) is A, D, T, W, C. Figure 5 shows the backtracking search trees for maximal itemsets containing prefix items A and D. Under the search tree for A, Figure 5 (a), we try to extend the partial solution AD by adding to it item T from its combine set. We try another item W after itemset ADT turns out to be infrequent,* and so on. Since GenMax uses itemsets which are found earlier in the search to prune the combine sets of later branches, after finding the maximal set $ADWC$, GenMax skips ADC. After finding $ATWC$ all the remaining nodes with prefix A are pruned, and so on. The pruned branches are shown with dashed arrows, indicating that a large part of the search tree is pruned away

Theorem 1 *(Correctness) MFI-backtrack returns all and only the maximal frequent itemsets in the given database.*

3.1 Optimizing GenMax

Superset Checking Optimization

The main efficiency of GenMax stems from the fact that it eliminates branches that are subsumed by an already mined maximal pattern. Were it not for this pruning, GenMax would essentially default to a depth-first exploration of the search tree. Before creating the combine set for the next pass, in line 4 in Figure 4, GenMax check if $I_{l+1} \cup P_{l+1}$ is contained within a previously found maximal set. If yes, then the entire subtree rooted at I_{l+1} and including the elements of the possible set are pruned. If no, then a new extension is required. Another superset check is required at line 8, when I_{l+1} has no frequent extension, i.e., when the combine set C_{l+1} is empty. Even though I_{l+1} is a leaf node with no extensions it may be subsumed by some maximal set, and this case is not caught by the check in line 4 above.

The major challenge in the design of GenMax is how to perform this subset checking in the current set of maximal patterns in an efficient manner. If we were to naively implement and perform this search two times on an ever expanding set of maximal patterns **MFI**, and during each recursive call of backtracking, we would be spending a prohibitive amount of time just performing subset checks. Each search would take $O(|\textbf{MFI}|)$ time in the worst case, where **MFI** is the current, growing set of maximal patterns. Note that some of the best algorithms for dynamic subset testing run in amortized time $O(\sqrt{s} \log s)$ per operation in a sequence of s operations [8] (for us $s = O(\textbf{MFI})$). In dense domain we have thousands to millions of maximal frequent itemsets, and the number of subset checking operations performed would be at least that much. Can we do better?

The answer is, yes! Firstly, we observe that the two subset checks (one on line 4 and the other on line 8) can be easily reduced to only one check. Since $I_{l+1} \cup P_{l+1}$ is a superset of I_{l+1}, in our implementation we do superset check only for $I_{l+1} \cup P_{l+1}$. While testing this set, we store the maximum position, say p, at which an item in $I_{l+1} \cup P_{l+1}$ is not found in a maximal set $M \in \textbf{MFI}$. In other words, all items before p are subsumed by some maximal set. For the superset test for I_{l+1}, we check if $|I_{l+1}| < p$. If yes, I_{l+1} is non-maximal. If no, we add it to **MFI**.

The second observation is that performing superset checking during each recursive call can be redundant. For example, suppose that the cardinality of the possible set P_{l+1} is m. Then potentially, MFI-backtrack makes m redundant subset checks, if the current **MFI** has not changed during these m consecutive calls. To avoid such redundancy, a simple check_status flag is used. If the flag is false, no superset check is performed. Before each recursive call the flag is false; it becomes true whenever C_{l+1} is empty, which indicates that we have reached a leaf, and have to backtrack.

```
// Invocation: LMFI-backtrack(∅, F₁, ∅, 0)
// LMFIₗ is an output parameter
LMFI-backtrack(Iₗ, Cₗ, LMFIₗ, l)
1.    for each x ∈ Cₗ
2.        I_{l+1} = I ∪ {x}
3.        P_{l+1} = {y : y ∈ Cₗ and y > x}
4.        if I_{l+1} ∪ P_{l+1} has a superset in LMFIₗ
5.            return //subsequent branches pruned!
6. *        LMFI_{l+1} = ∅
7.        C_{l+1} = FI-combine (I_{l+1}, P_{l+1})
8.        if C_{l+1} is empty
9.            if I_{l+1} has no superset in LMFIₗ
10.               LMFIₗ = LMFIₗ ∪ I_{l+1}
11.*       else LMFI_{l+1} = {M ∈ LMFIₗ : x ∈ M}
12.           LMFI-backtrack(I_{l+1}, C_{l+1}, LMFI_{l+1}, l+1)
13.*      LMFIₗ = LMFIₗ ∪ LMFI_{l+1}
```

Figure 6. Mining MFI with Progressive Focusing (* indicates a new line not in MFI-backtrack)

The $O(\sqrt{s} \log s)$ time bounds reported in [8] for dynamic subset testing do not assume anything about the sequence of operations performed. In contrast, we have full knowledge of how GenMax generates maximal sets; we use this observation to substantially speed up the subset checking process. The main idea is to progressively narrow down the maximal itemsets of interest as recursive calls are made. In other words, we construct for each invocation of MFI-backtrack a list of *local maximal frequent itemsets*, $LMFI_l$. This list contains the maximal sets that can potentially be supersets of candidates that are to be generated from the itemset I_l. The only such maximal sets are those that contain all items in I_l. This way, instead of checking if $I_{l+1} \cup P_{l+1}$ is contained in the full current **MFI**, we check only in $LMFI_l$ – the local set of relevant maximal itemsets. This technique, that we call *progressive focusing*, is extremely powerful in narrowing the search to only the most relevant maximal itemsets, making superset checking practical on dense datasets.

Figure 6 shows the pseudo-code for GenMax that incorporates this optimization (the code for the first two optimizations is not show to avoid clutter). Before each invocation of LMFI-backtrack a new $LMFI_{l+1}$ is created, consisting of those maximal sets in the current $LMFI_l$ that contain the item x (see line 10). Any new maximal itemsets from a recursive call are incorporated in the current $LMFI_l$ at line 12.

Frequency Testing Optimization

So far GenMax, as described, is independent of the data format used. The techniques can be integrated into any of the existing methods for mining maximal patterns. We now present some data format specific optimizations for fast frequency computations.

GenMax uses a vertical database format, where we have available for each item its tidset, the set of all transaction tids where it occurs. The vertical representation has the following major advantages over the horizontal layout: Firstly, computing the support of itemsets is simpler and faster with the vertical layout since it involves only the intersections of tidsets (or compressed bit-vectors if the vertical format is stored as bitmaps [4]). Secondly, with the vertical layout, there is an automatic "reduction" of the database before each scan in that only those itemsets that are relevant to the following scan of the mining process are accessed from disk. Thirdly, the vertical format is more versatile in supporting various search strategies, including breadth-first, depth-first or some other hybrid search.

```
// Can I_{l+1} combine with other items in C_l?
FI-tidset-combine(I_{l+1}, P_{l+1})
  1.    C = ∅
  2.    for each y ∈ P_{l+1}
  3.*      y' = y
  4.*      t(y') = t(I_{l+1}) ∩ t(y)
  5.*      if |t(y')| ≥ min_sup
  6.          C = C ∪ {y'}
  7.    return C
```

Figure 7. FI-combine Using Tidset Intersections (* indicates a new line not in FI-combine)

Let's consider how the FI-combine (see Figure 2) routine works, where the frequency of an extension is tested. Each item x in C_l actually represents the itemset $I_l \cup \{x\}$ and stores the associated tidset for the itemset $I_l \cup \{x\}$. For the initial invocation, since I_l is empty, the tidset for each item x in C_l is identical to the tidset, $t(x)$, of item x. Before line 3 is called in FI-combine, we intersect the tidset of the element I_{l+1} (i.e., $t(I_l \cup \{x\})$) with the tidset of element y (i.e., $t(I_l \cup \{y\})$). If the cardinality of the resulting intersection is above minimum support, the extension with y is frequent, and y' the new intersection result, is added to the combine set for the next level. Figure 7 shows the pseudo-code for FI-tidset-combine using this tidset intersection based support counting.

In Charm [11] we first introduced two new properties of itemset-tidset pairs which can be used to further increase the performance. Consider the items x and y in C_l. If during intersection in line 4 in Figure 7, we discover that $t(x)$ – or equivalently $t(I_{l+1})$ – is a subset of or equal to $t(y)$, then we do not add y' to the combine set, since in this case, x always occurs along with y. Instead of adding y' to the combine set, we add it to I_{l+1}. This optimization was also used in Mafia [4] under the name PEP.

Diffsets Propagation Despite the many advantages of the vertical format, when the tidset cardinality gets very large (e.g., for very frequent items) the intersection time starts to become inordinately large. Furthermore, the size of intermediate tidsets generated for frequent patterns can also become very large to fit into main memory. GenMax uses a new format called diffsets [10] for fast frequency testing.

The main idea of diffsets is to avoid storing the entire tidset of each element in the combine set. Instead we keep track of only the differences between the tidset of itemset I_l and the tidset of an element x in the combine set (which actually denotes $I_l \cup \{x\}$). These differences in tids are stored in what we call the *diffset*, which is a difference of two tidsets at the root level or a difference of two diffsets at later levels. Furthermore, these differences are propagated all the way from a node to its children starting from the root. In an extensive study [10], we showed that diffsets are very short compared to their tidsets counterparts, and are highly effective in improving the running time of vertical methods.

We describe next how they are used in GenMax, with the help of an example. At level 0, we have available the tidsets for each item in F_1. When we invoke FI-combine at this level, we compute the diffset of y', denoted as $d(y')$ instead

```
// Can I_{l+1} combine with other items in C_l?
FI-diffset-combine(I_{l+1}, P_{l+1})
  1.    C = ∅
  2.    for each y ∈ P_{l+1}
  3.      y' = y
  4.      if level == 0 then d(y') = t(I_{l+1}) - t(y)
  5.      else d(y') = d(y) - d(I_{l+1})
  6.      if σ(y') ≥ min_sup
  7.          C = C ∪ {y'}
  8.    return C
```

Figure 8. FI-combine: Diffset Propagation

of computing the tidset of y as shown in line 4 in Figure 7. That is $d(y') = t(x) - t(y)$. The support of y' is now given as $\sigma(y') = \sigma(x) - |d(y')|$. At subsequent levels, we have available the diffsets for each element in the combine list. In this case $d(y') = d(y) - d(x)$, but the support is still given as $\sigma(y') = \sigma(x) - |d(y')|$. Figure 8 shows the pseudo-code for computing the combine sets using diffsets.

```
GenMax:
  1.    Compute F_1 and F_2
  3.    Compute IF(x) for each item x ∈ F_1
  4.    Sort F_1 (decreasing in IF(x), increasing in σ(x))
  5.    MFI = ∅
  6.    LMFI-backtrack(∅, F_1, MFI, 0) //use diffsets
  7.    return MFI
```

Figure 9. The GenMax Algorithm

Final GenMax Algorithm The complete GenMax algorithm is shown in Figure 9, which ties in all the optimizations mentioned above. GenMax assumes that the input dataset is in the vertical tidset format. First GenMax computes the set of frequent items and the frequent 2-itemsets, using a vertical-to-horizontal recovery method [10]. This information is used to reorder the items in the initial combine list to minimize the search tree size that is generated. GenMax uses the progressive focusing technique of LMFI-backtrack, combined with diffset propagation of FI-diffset-combine to produce the exact set of all maximal frequent itemsets, **MFI**.

4 Experimental Results

Past work has demonstrated that DepthProject [1] is faster than MaxMiner [3], and the latest paper shows that Mafia [4] consistently beats DepthProject. In out experimental study below, we retain MaxMiner for baseline comparison. At the same time, MaxMiner shows good performance on some datasets, which were not used in previous studies. We use Mafia as the current state-of-the-art method and show how GenMax compares against it.

All our experiments were performed on a 400MHz Pentium PC with 256MB of memory, running RedHat Linux 6.0. For comparison we used the original source or object code for MaxMiner [3] and MAFIA [4], provided to us by their authors. Timings in the figures are based on total wall-clock time, and include all preprocessing costs (such as horizontal-to-vertical conversion in GenMax and Mafia). The times reported also include the program output. We believe our setup reflects realistic testing conditions (as opposed to some previous studies which report only the CPU time or may not include output cost).

Benchmark Datasets: We chose several real and synthetic datasets for testing the performance of the the al-

Database	I	AL	R	MPL
chess	76	37	3,196	23 (20%)
connect	130	43	67,557	31 (2.5%)
mushroom	120	23	8,124	22 (0.025%)
pumsb*	7117	50	49,046	43 (2.5%)
pumsb	7117	74	49,046	27 (40%)
T10I4D100K	1000	10	100,000	13 (0.01%)
T40I10D100K	1000	40	100,000	25 (0.1%)

Figure 10. Database Characteristics: I denotes the number of items, AL the average length of a record, R the number of records, and MPL the maximum pattern length at the given *min_sup*.

gorithms, shown in Table 10. The real datasets have been used previously in the evaluation of maximal patterns [1, 3, 4]. Typically, these real datasets are very dense, i.e., they produce many long frequent itemsets even for high values of support. The table shows the length of the longest maximal pattern (at the lowest minimum support used in our experiments) for the different datasets. For example on pumsb*, the longest pattern was of length 43 (any method that mines all frequent patterns will be impractical for such long patterns). We also chose two synthetic datasets, which have been used as benchmarks for testing methods that mine all frequent patterns. Previous maximal set mining algorithms have not been tested on these datasets, which are sparser compared to the real sets. All these datasets are publicly available from IBM Almaden (www.almaden.ibm.com/cs/quest/demos.html).

While conducting experiments comparing the 3 different algorithms, we observed that the performance can vary significantly depending on the dataset characteristics. We were able to classify our benchmark datasets into four classes based on the distribution of the maximal frequent patterns.

Type I Datasets: Chess and Pumsb

Figure 11 shows the performance of the three algorithms on chess and pumsb. These Type I datasets are characterized by a symmetric distribution of the maximal frequent patterns (leftmost graph). Looking at the mean of the curve, we can observe that for these datasets most of the maximal patterns are relatively short (average length 11 for chess and 10 for pumsb). The **MFI** cardinality figures on top center and right, show that for the support values shown, the **MFI** is 2 orders of magnitude smaller than all frequent itemsets.

Compare the total execution time for the different algorithms on these datasets (center and rightmost graphs). We use two different variants of Mafia. The first one, labeled Mafia, does not return the exact maximal frequent set, rather it returns a superset of all maximal patterns. The second variant, labeled MafiaPP, uses an option to eliminate non-maximal sets in a post-processing (PP) step. Both GenMax and MaxMiner return the exact **MFI**.

On chess we find that Mafia (without PP) is the fastest if one is willing to live with a superset of the **MFI**. Mafia is about 10 times faster than MaxMiner. However, notice how the running time of MafiaPP grows if one tries to find the exact **MFI** in a post-pruning step. GenMax, though slower than Mafia is significantly faster than MafiaPP and is about 5 times better than MaxMiner. All methods, except MafiaPP, show an exponential growth in running time (since

the y-axis is in log-scale, this appears linear) faithfully following the growth of **MFI** with lowering minimum support, as shown in the top center and right figures. MafiaPP shows super-exponential growth and suffers from an approximately $O(|\mathbf{MFI}|^2)$ overhead in pruning non-maximal sets and thus becomes impractical when **MFI** becomes too large, i.e., at low supports.

On pumsb, we find that GenMax is the fastest, having a slight edge over Mafia. It is about 2 times faster than MafiaPP. We observed that the post-pruning routine in MafiaPP works well till around $O(10^4)$ maximal itemsets. Since at 60% min_sup we had around that many sets, the overhead of post-processing was not significant. With lower support the post-pruning cost becomes significant, so much so that we could not run MafiaPP beyond 50% minimum support. MaxMiner is significantly slower on pumsb; a factor of 10 times slower then both GenMax and Mafia.

Type I results substantiate the claim that GenMax is an highly efficient method to mine the exact **MFI**. It is as fast as Mafia on pumsb and within a factor of 2 on chess. Mafia, on the other hand is very effective in mining a superset of the **MFI**. Post-pruning, in general, is not a good idea, and GenMax beats MafiaPP with a wide margin (over 100 times better in some cases, e.g., chess at 20%). On Type I data MaxMiner is noncompetitive.

Type II Datasets: Connect and Pumsb*

Type II datasets, as shown in Figure 12 are characterized by a left-skewed distribution of the maximal frequent patterns, i.e., there is a relatively gradual increase with a sharp drop in the number of maximal patterns. The mean pattern length is also longer than in Type I datasets; it is around 16 or 17. The **MFI** cardinality is also drastically smaller than **FI** cardinality; by a factor of 10^4 or more (in contrast, for Type I data, the reduction was only 10^2).

The main performance trend for both Type II datasets is that Mafia is the best till the support is very low, at which point there is a cross-over and GenMax outperforms Mafia. MafiaPP continues to be favorable for higher supports, but once again beyond a point post-pruning costs start to dominate. MafiaPP could not be run beyond the plotted points. MaxMiner remains noncompetitive (about 10 times slower). The initial start-up time for Mafia for creating the bit-vectors is responsible for the high offset at 50% support on pumsb*. GenMax appears to exhibit a more graceful increase in running time than Mafia.

Type III Datasets: T10I4 and T40I10

As depicted in Figure 13, Type III datasets – the two synthetic ones – are characterized by an exponentially decaying distribution of the maximal frequent patterns. Except for a few maximal sets of size one, the vast majority of maximal patterns are of length two! After that the number of longer patterns drops exponentially. The mean pattern length is very short compared to Type I or Type II datasets; it is around 4-6. **MFI** cardinality is not much smaller than the cardinality of all frequent patterns. The difference is only a factor of 10 compared to a factor of 100 for Type I and a factor of 10,000 for Type II.

Comparing the running times we observe that MaxMiner is the best method for this type of data. The breadth-first or level-wise search strategy used in MaxMiner is ideal for

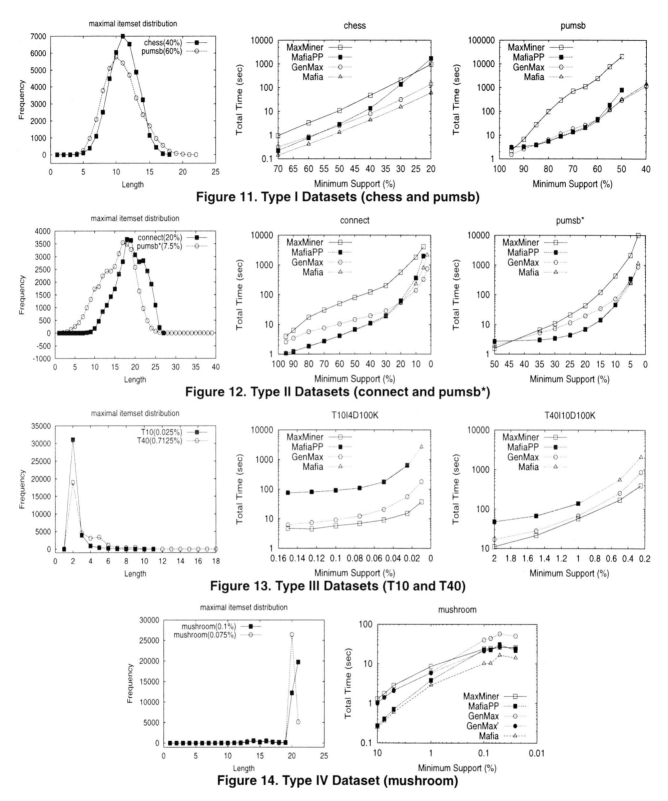

Figure 11. Type I Datasets (chess and pumsb)

Figure 12. Type II Datasets (connect and pumsb*)

Figure 13. Type III Datasets (T10 and T40)

Figure 14. Type IV Dataset (mushroom)

very bushy search trees, and when the average maximal pattern length is small. Horizontal methods are better equipped to cope with the quadratic blowup in the number of frequent 2-itemsets since one can use array based counting

to get their frequency. On the other hand vertical methods spend much time in performing intersections on long item tidsets or bit-vectors. GenMax gets around this problem by using the horizontal format for computing frequent

2-itemsets (denoted F_2), but it still has to spend time performing $O(|F_2|)$ pairwise tidset intersections.

Mafia on the other hand performs $O(|F_1|^2)$ intersections, where F_1 is the set of frequent items. The overhead cost is enough to render Mafia noncompetitive on Type III data. On T10 Mafia can be 20 or more times slower than MaxMiner. GenMax exhibits relatively good performance, and it is about 10 times better than Mafia and 2 to 3 times worse than MaxMiner. On T40, the gap between GenMax/Mafia and MaxMiner is smaller since there are longer maximal patterns. MaxMiner is 2 times better than GenMax and 5 times better than Mafia. Since the **MFI** cardinality is not too large MafiaPP has almost the time as Mafia for high supports. Once again MafiaPP could not be run for lower support values. It is clear that, in general, post-pruning is not a good idea; the overhead is too much to cope with.

Type IV Dataset: Mushroom

Mushroom exhibits a very unique **MFI** distribution. Plotting **MFI** cardinality by length, we observe in Figure 14 that the number of maximal patterns remains small until length 19. Then there is a sudden explosion of maximal patterns at length 20, followed by another sharp drop at length 21. The vast majority of maximal itemsets are of length 20. The average transaction length for mushroom is 23 (see Table 10), thus a maximal pattern spans almost a full transaction. The total **MFI** cardinality is about 1000 times smaller than all frequent itemsets.

On Type IV data, Mafia performs the best. MafiaPP and MaxMiner are comparable at lower supports. This data is the worst for GenMax, which is 2 times slower than MaxMiner and 4 times slower than Mafia. In Type IV data, a smaller itemset is part of many maximal itemsets (of length 20 in case of mushroom); this renders our progressive focusing technique less effective. To perform maximality checking one has to test against a large set of maximal itemsets; we found that GenMax spends half its time in maximality checking. Recognizing this helped us improve the progressive focusing using an optimized intersection-based method (as opposed to the original list based approach). This variant, labeled GenMax', was able to cut down the execution time by half. GenMax' runs in the same time as MaxMiner and MafiaPP.

5   Conclusions

This is one of the first papers to comprehensively compare recent maximal pattern mining algorithms under realistic assumptions. Our timings are based on wall-clock time, we included all pre-processing costs, and also cost of outputting all the maximal itemsets (written to a file). We were able to distinguish four different types of **MFI** distributions in our benchmark testbed. We believe these distributions to be fairly representative of what one might see in practice, since they span both real and synthetic datasets. Type I is a normal **MFI** distribution with not too long maximal patterns, Type II is a left-skewed distributions, with longer maximal patterns, Type III is an exponential decay distribution, with extremely short maximal patterns, and finally Type IV is an extreme left-skewed distribution, with very large average maximal pattern length.

We noted that different algorithms perform well under different distributions. We conclude that among the current

methods, MaxMiner is the best for mining Type III distributions. On the remaining types, Mafia is the best method if one is satisfied with a superset of the **MFI**. For very low supports on Type II data, Mafia loses its edge. Post-pruning non-maximal patterns typically has high overhead. It works only for high support values, and MafiaPP cannot be run beyond a certain minimum support value. GenMax integrates pruning of non-maximal itemsets in the process of mining using the novel progressive focusing technique, along with other optimizations for superset checking; GenMax is the best method for mining the exact **MFI**.

Our work opens up some important avenues of future work. The IBM synthetic dataset generator appears to be too restrictive. It produces Type III **MFI** distributions. We plan to develop a new generator that the users can use to produce various kinds of **MFI** distributions. This will help provide a common testbed against which new algorithms can be benchmarked. Knowing the conditions under which a method works well or does not work well is an important step in developing new solutions. In contrast to previous studies we were able to isolate these conditions for the different algorithms. For example, we were able to improve the performance of GenMax' to match MaxMiner on mushroom dataset. Another obvious avenue of improving GenMax and Mafia is to efficiently handle Type III data. It seems possible to combine the strengths of the three methods into a single hybrid algorithm that uses the horizontal format when required and uses bit-vectors/diffsets or perhaps bit-vectors of diffsets in other cases or in combination. We plan to investigate this in the future.

Acknowledgments We would like to thank Roberto Bayardo for providing us the MaxMiner algorithm and Johannes Gehrke for the MAFIA algorithm.

References

[1] R. Agrawal, C. Aggarwal, and V. Prasad. Depth First Generation of Long Patterns. In *ACM SIGKDD Conf.*, Aug. 2000.
[2] R. Agrawal, et al. Fast discovery of association rules. In *Advances in Knowledge Discovery and Data Mining*, AAAI Press, 1996.
[3] R. J. Bayardo. Efficiently mining long patterns from databases. In *ACM SIGMOD Conf.*, June 1998.
[4] D. Burdick, M. Calimlim, and J. Gehrke. MAFIA: a maximal frequent itemset algorithm for transactional databases. In *Intl. Conf. on Data Engineering*, Apr. 2001.
[5] D. Gunopulos, H. Mannila, and S. Saluja. Discovering all the most specific sentences by randomized algorithms. In *Intl. Conf. on Database Theory*, Jan. 1997.
[6] J. Han, J. Pei, and Y. Yin. Mining frequent patterns without candidate generation. In *ACM SIGMOD Conf.*, May 2000.
[7] D.-I. Lin and Z. M. Kedem. Pincer-search: A new algorithm for discovering the maximum frequent set. In *Intl. Conf. Extending Database Technology*, Mar. 1998.
[8] D. Yellin. An algorithm for dynamic subset and intersection testing. *Theoretical Computer Science*, 129:397–406, 1994.
[9] M. J. Zaki. Generating non-redundant association rules. In *ACM SIGKDD Conf.*, Aug. 2000.
[10] M. J. Zaki and K. Gouda. Fast vertical mining using Diffsets. TR 01-1, CS Dept., RPI, Mar. 2001.
[11] M. J. Zaki and C.-J. Hsiao. CHARM: An efficient algorithm for closed association rule mining. TR 99-10, CS Dept., RPI, Oct. 1999.

The DIAsDEM Framework for Converting Domain-Specific Texts into XML Documents with Data Mining Techniques

Henner Graubitz,* Myra Spiliopoulou and Karsten Winkler*
Leipzig Graduate School of Management (HHL)
Department of E-Business
Jahnallee 59, D-04109 Leipzig, Germany
{graubitz,myra,kwinkler}@ebusiness.hhl.de

Abstract

Modern organizations are accumulating huge volumes of textual documents. To turn archives into valuable knowledge sources, textual content must become explicit and queryable. Semantic tagging with markup languages such as XML satisfies both requirements. We thus introduce the DIAsDEM* framework for extracting semantics from structural text units (e.g., sentences), assigning XML tags to them and deriving a flat XML DTD for the archive. DIAsDEM focuses on archives characterized by a peculiar terminology and by an implicit structure such as court filings and company reports. In the knowledge discovery phase, text units are iteratively clustered by similarity of their content. Each iteration outputs clusters satisfying a set of quality criteria. Text units contained in these clusters are tagged with semi-automatically determined cluster labels and XML tags respectively. Additionally, extracted named entities (e.g., persons) serve as attributes of XML tags. We apply the framework in a case study on the German Commercial Register.

1. Introduction

Tan points out that up to 80% of a company's information is stored in unstructured textual documents [18]. Undoubtedly, they are a major source of organizational knowledge. Effective knowledge management thus requires techniques to extract actionable knowledge from text archives. Feldman and Dagan coined the phrase "knowledge discovery in textual databases" (KDT) that refers to the extraction of useful knowledge from unstructured text documents [6]. In this paper, we introduce the KDT approach pursued in the research project DIAsDEM for knowledge manage-

ment over application-specific documents. Our goal is the semantic tagging of textual content with meta-data to facilitate searching, querying and integration with associated texts and relational data. Hence, we aim at deriving an XML DTD that serves as a quasi-schema for the document collection and enables database-like queries on textual data.

DIAsDEM focuses on texts with domain-specific vocabulary and syntax. These application-specific collections contain rather homogeneous texts (e.g., police reports) with several particularities: Firstly, important and discriminating information is contained in fine-grained structural text components, although all texts deal with a limited set of subjects, e.g. the phases of crime investigation. Secondly, all texts adhere to a particular vocabulary as well as to a peculiar syntax and to linguistic conventions that may be far away from everyday language rules. Thirdly, these texts frequently share an inherent, though undocumented structure.

Our approach of converting texts into XML documents is based on clustering their structural components by semantics and making these semantics explicit as cluster labels. To this end, we propose an iterative clustering process: We progressively group text units (e.g., sentences) by similarity and identify concepts that describe the members of each group. For each semantic group, a cluster label is derived and subsequently used as an XML tag constituting meta-data for the corresponding text units. In addition, we identify named entities referenced in text units, e.g. names of persons and companies. Extracted named entities subsequently serve as attribute values of XML tags.

The rest of this paper is organized as follows: The next section discusses related work. Section 3 gives an overview of the proposed framework for semantic tagging, whereas section 4 describes its iterative KDT process in detail. Section 5 concisely describes the process of tagging text documents. Section 6 presents a case study that illustrates the application of the proposed framework. We conclude and present directions for future research in section 7.

*The research project DIAsDEM is funded by the German Research Society, DFG grant no. SP 572/4-1.

2. Related work

The related research can be categorized into knowledge discovery in textual databases, research on semi-structured data and projects pursuing similar objectives.

Tan briefly summarizes the current state of text mining and its future challenges [18]. He introduces a two-phase framework for text mining: In the text refining phase, unstructured texts are first transformed into an intermediary form that is later used to deduce knowledge in the knowledge distillation phase. This general approach is adopted in our proposed DIASDEM framework as well. We perform fine-grained semantic analysis and integrate domain knowledge that are open research problems according to Tan.

Nahm and Mooney propose the combination of methods from KDD and information extraction to perform text mining tasks [13]. They apply standard KDD techniques to a collection of structured records that contain previously extracted, application-specific features from texts. Feldman et al. propose text mining at the term level instead of focusing on linguistically tagged words [7]. The authors represent each document by a set of terms and construct a taxonomy of terms. The resulting dataset is input to KDD algorithms such as association rule discovery. Our framework adopts the idea of representing texts by terms and concepts. However, we aim at the semantic tagging of text units within the document according to a global DTD and not at the characterization of the entire document's content. Loh et al. suggest to extract concepts rather than individual words for subsequent use for KDD at the document level [9]. Similarly to our framework, the authors suggest to exploit existing vocabularies such as thesauri for concept extraction.

Our approach shares with this research thread the objective of extracting semantic concepts from texts. However, concepts to be extracted in DIAsDEM must be appropriate to serve as elements of an XML DTD. Among other implications, discovering a concept that is only peculiar to a single text unit is not sufficient for our purposes, although it may perfectly reflect its content. In order to derive a DTD, we need to discover groups of text units that share semantic concepts. Moreover, we concentrate on domain-specific texts, which significantly differ from average texts with respect to word frequency statistics. These collections can hardly be processed using standard text mining software because the integration of relevant domain knowledge is a prerequisite for successful knowledge discovery.

Semi-structured data is another topic of intensive research within the database community [3, 1]. A lot of effort has recently been put into methods inferring and representing structure in similar semi-structured documents [14, 19]. In order to transform existing content into XML documents, Sengupta and Purao propose a method that infers DTDs by using already tagged documents as input [17]. In contrast,

we propose a method that tags plain text documents and derives a DTD for them. Closer to our approach is the work of Lumera, who uses keywords and rules to semi-automatically convert legacy data into XML documents [10]. However, his approach relies on establishing a rule base that drives the conversion, while we employ a KDD methodology to reduce necessary human effort.

Bruder et al. introduce the search engine GETESS that supports query processing on texts by deriving and processing XML text abstracts [2]. These abstracts contain language-independent, content-weighted summaries of domain-specific texts. Instead of creating abstracts, we aim at tagging complete text documents. Decker et al. extract meta-data from Web documents using the ontology-based system ONTOBROKER [4]. Maedche and Staab introduce an architecture for semi-automatically learning ontologies from Web documents [11]. Embley et al. also apply ontologies to extract and to structure information contained in data-rich unstructured documents [5]. In DIAsDEM, we do not separate meta-data from original texts but rather provide a semantic annotation, keeping the texts intact for later processing or visualization. Given the aforementioned linguistic particularities of the application domains we investigate, a DTD characterizing the content of the documents is more appropriate than inferences on their content.

3. The DIAsDEM framework

Our framework pursues two objectives for an archive of text documents: All documents should be semantically tagged and an appropriate XML DTD should be derived for the archive. Rather than classifying entire documents or tagging single terms, the framework aims at annotating structural components of text documents that are referred to as text units. Table 1 illustrates this notion of semantic tagging: The semantics of text units (i.e. sentences) are made explicit by semantic XML tags containing further meta-data as (attribute, value)-pairs. Thus, the input to the DIAsDEM mining phase is the set of all text units and neither the set of documents nor the text units of a single document.

Text units are clustered by similarity of their content. The objectives of DIAsDEM are particularly challenging

```
(...)   <crime type="burglary" company="Miller's
Jewelers Inc.">A platinum diamond ring was stolen from
Miller's Jewelers Inc. on Saturday in one of several thefts reported
to police. </crime>   <arrest person="Bryan Ray
Owens"> The suspect Bryan Ray Owens was immediately arrested.
</arrest>   <value amountOfMoney="3300 USD">
The ring was valued at $3,300 </object>   (...)
```

Table 1. Semantically tagged police report

172

for the clustering methodology, because only semantically homogeneous clusters can be assigned a reasonable semantic tag. Additionally, a cluster should not be too specific, because a semantic tag comprised of many concepts such as <immediateArrestOfSuspect> can hardly be memorized and exploited during query formulation. Moreover, the cluster cardinality should not be too low, since lots of small clusters also imply many highly specialized tags.

Semantic tagging in DIAsDEM is a two-phase process. We have designed a KDT process that constitutes the first phase in order to build clusters according to the aforementioned requirements, to tag documents in XML according to the results and to derive an XML DTD describing the archive. This process is termed "iterative" because the clustering algorithm is invoked repeatedly. Our notion of iterative clustering should not be confused with the fact that most clustering algorithms perform multiple passes over the data before converging. Rather, in each iteration of the KDT process, we re-adjust cluster similarity parameters. This process is also "interactive", because a knowledge engineer is consulted during cluster selection that is performed at the end of each iteration. Phase 1 of the DIAsDEM framework results in a final set of clusters, whose labels serve as XML tags and DTD elements. Huge amounts of new documents can be converted into XML documents in the second, batch-oriented and productive phase of the DIAsDEM framework. In this phase, all text units contained in new documents are clustered by the previously built text unit clusterer and are subsequently tagged with the corresponding cluster labels.

4. The iterative KDT process

In this paper, we focus on the first phase of our framework whose iterative and interactive KDT process is depicted in Figure 1. Besides the text documents to be tagged, the following domain knowledge constitutes input to this knowledge discovery process: A thesaurus containing a domain-specific taxonomy of terms and concepts, a preliminary UML schema of the domain and descriptions of specific named entities of importance, e.g. persons and companies. The UML schema reflects the semantics of named entities and relationships among them, as they are initially conceived by application experts. This schema serves as a reference for the DTD to be derived from discovered semantic tags, but there is no guarantee that the final DTD will be contained in or will contain this preliminary schema.

Similarly to a conventional KDD process, our process starts with a preprocessing phase, in which a reduced feature space is established. All text units are mapped into vectors of this space. Additionally, named entities of interest are extracted from text units by a separate module. For instance, the surname and the forename of a named entity "Person" is recognized in the text. Discovered named

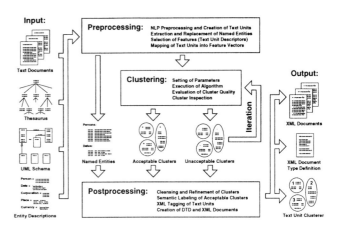

Figure 1. Iterative KDT process

entities and their values subsequently serve as attributes of XML tags. In the pattern discovery phase, text unit vectors are clustered based on similarity of their content. The objective is to discover dense and homogeneous text unit clusters. Clustering is performed in multiple iterations. Each iteration outputs a set of clusters which are partitioned into "acceptable" and "unacceptable" ones according to our quality criteria described in section 4.2. The postmining phase consists of a labeling step, in which "acceptable" clusters are semi-automatically assigned a label. Cluster labels are derived from feature space dimensions prevailing in the corresponding clusters. Cluster labels actually correspond to XML tags that are subsequently used to annotate cluster members. Finally, all original documents are tagged using valid XML tags. This phase is described in section 5.

4.1. Establishing the feature space

In the preprocessing phase, we first determine the text units to be clustered. Since the objective of DIAsDEM is the annotation of documents with semantic tags, a document is not a single entity but a collection of structural components whose semantics should be identified and mapped into tags. Currently, the level of granularity in our analysis is a sentence. A more elaborate approach using noun groups or sliding n-grams as text units is planned as future work.

After performing word stemming, we establish the feature space. In conventional text mining, the feature space is determined by an application-specific controlled vocabulary, including specific terminology and excluding stopwords. In DIAsDEM, the feature space is much smaller, not only to reduce the number of dimensions, but mainly to reach the ultimate goal of DIAsDEM, namely the derivation of a DTD that describes a document collection. Accordingly, the feature space is comprised of terms and concepts that (i) are not rare and (ii) belong to the specific terminology used in the collection of text documents to be tagged.

Requirement (i) excludes rare terms. Among them are named entities (e.g., persons) which have high selective power and are very important in other text mining applications. Nonetheless, named entity identification is important for the applications addressed in DIAsDEM, so that identifiers are detected in the preprocessing phase and incorporated into tags as attributes during the tagging phase.

Requirement (ii) excludes all general purpose terms. This reflects the purpose of the DTD to be derived: It should describe the documents in much the same way a database schema describes records. For example, in a database of police records, a burglary would be rather the value of an attribute "crime type" than an attribute itself. Some terms that are excluded due to this requirement are still taken into account during the tagging phase as attribute values. Currently, this is restricted to a predetermined set of named entities. Ultimately, requirement (ii) can only be satisfied by feature selection performed by a domain expert. In the DIAsDEM framework, we propose that the application domain is conceptually modeled. Terms appearing in this schema as names of entities, associations, attributes or high-level methods form the basis of the restricted feature space.

All terms and concepts remaining in the feature space after applying requirements (i) and (ii) on the vocabulary are frequent or very frequent. In conventional text mining applications, very frequent terms are also excluded because of their low descriptive power. In DIAsDEM, we only exclude words at the rightmost part of the word frequency curve but still retain many words of high frequency. The reason is that some frequent terms appear in combinations that characterize text units. For example, "crime" may be a very frequent term in police records, but it is necessary to characterize something as an "element of crime". Similarly to IR conventions, we only keep a very limited number of word combinations in the feature space [15]. Interesting combinations of terms are discovered during the clustering phase instead.

The feature space is established by the end of this phase. The number of its dimensions is much lower than implied by the cardinality of the controlled vocabulary. Our notion of a "text unit descriptor" or simply a "descriptor" might refer to a single term, a broader term that stands for other narrower terms or a concept reflected by various different terms. In our framework, each text unit descriptor is a dimension of the feature space. Each text unit is then mapped into a boolean text unit vector over this feature space. In particular, we assign an order upon the feature space D, so that each descriptor $d \in D$ obtains an ordinal number $i(d) \in \{1, \ldots, |D|\}$. The set of text units in all documents $\mathcal{T}$ is thereafter mapped into the boolean vector space $[0, 1]^{|D|}$ by a function m, so that for each $t \in \mathcal{T}$, $m(t)$ is a boolean vector v with $v[i(d)] = 1$ iff d appears in t and zero otherwise.

4.2. Iterative clustering of text unit vectors

Clustering of text unit vectors into groups of very similar content is the core of our proposed KDT process. This content is reflected by the set of text unit descriptors (i.e. feature space dimensions) that characterize each cluster. These prevailing descriptors are used in the next phase to derive cluster labels. Finally, these cluster labels are utilized to annotate the members of each cluster with XML tags.

The KDT process is based on a plug-in concept that allows the execution of different clustering algorithms within the DIAsDEM workbench. To group text unit vectors by similarity, we currently employ the so-called demographic clustering algorithm available in the IBM DB2 Intelligent Miner for Data [8] that maximizes the Condorcet criterion [12]. This criterion can be perceived as the difference between intra-cluster similarity and inter-cluster similarity. In particular, its value is the difference between the sum of all pair-similarities within the same cluster and the sum of all pair-similarities between vectors in and outside a cluster. This algorithm obtains as input an upper limit of clusters to be built and a similarity threshold value for assigning two vectors to the same cluster. We refer to the latter as the "intra-cluster similarity threshold".

We invoke the clustering algorithm iteratively. By the end of each iteration, a set of clusters is returned. These resulting clusters are evaluated against a set of DIAsDEM-specific cluster-quality criteria described below. If a cluster is found to be acceptable with respect to these criteria, a label is derived for it as described in section 5. Members of acceptable clusters are removed from the dataset, while the remaining text unit vectors are input to the clustering algorithm again. In each iteration, the intra-cluster similarity threshold value is stepwise decreased, so that acceptable clusters become progressively less specific in content. The iterative clustering approach reflects the objectives of XML tagging in DIAsDEM: It is desirable to derive a semantic tag reflecting the content of several text units as precisely as possible. If no precise content description can be found for a group of text units, a coarser one should be considered as well. If the number of text units sharing the same content description is too low, the intra-cluster similarity threshold should also be decreased. This again leads to coarser content descriptions.

In DIAsDEM, the quality of a cluster is high, i.e. the cluster is acceptable, if and only if it is (i) *homogeneous*, (ii) *large* and (iii) has its content described by a *small* number of text unit descriptors. The criterion of homogeneity is dealt with by the similarity-based clustering algorithm. As already noted, the homogeneity is progressively relaxed to allow for the maximization of the other two criteria.

The second criterion states that the cardinality of a cluster should be larger than a threshold lim_{size} provided by the knowledge engineer. The threshold lim_{size} should reflect the number of text units considered adequate to assign a tag to them, bearing in mind that this tag will be an element of the DTD to be derived.

The third criterion concerns the *cluster description*. A cluster c is described by its feature space dimensions, i.e. the text unit descriptors which appear among most of its members. Let $d \in D$ be a descriptor in the feature space D, let $i(d) \in \{1, \ldots, |D|\}$ be its ordinal number and let M_c be the collection of text units whose vectors are assigned to cluster c. Then, the normalized frequency of descriptor d in cluster c is the ratio of vectors containing d to all vectors in the cluster:

$$freq(d,c) = \frac{|\{\{t \in M_c | m(t)[i(d)] = 1\}\}|}{|M_c|}$$

where $\{\{\cdot\}\}$ denotes a multiset instead of a set, taking the fact into account that the collection of text units may contain duplicates. We denote the subcollection of M_c in the numerator as $M_c(d)$. Using this notion of frequency, the third criterion is decomposed into two constraints as follows:

- The ratio of the number of distinct descriptors in a cluster c to the total number of dimensions in the feature space D should be less than $lim_{dimensions}$.

$$\frac{|\{d \in D | M_c(d) \neq \emptyset\}|}{|D|} \leq lim_{dimensions}$$

- The frequencies of the descriptors within a cluster c are grouped into the intervals $HIGH$ $(0.8, 1.0]$, $MEDIUM$ $(0.6, 0.8]$ and LOW $(0, 0.6]$. The ratio of the number of distinct descriptors in the interval $HIGH$ to the total number of distinct descriptors in the cluster should be close to 1.

$$\frac{|\{d \in D | freq(d,c) \in HIGH\}|}{|\{d \in D | M_c(d) \neq \emptyset\}|} \geq 1 - \varepsilon$$

The first constraint excludes clusters characterized by a large number of descriptors, because such clusters are difficult to label in a precise way. The second constraint excludes clusters characterized by descriptors of modest frequency, because the homogeneity of these clusters is rather low. Hence, the third criterion of our quality scheme endeavors to find clusters, in which only a few descriptors appear in most members.

The reader might object that our quality criteria consider only descriptors within one cluster, without comparing them to the descriptors of other clusters. Indeed, a frequent descriptor in cluster c_1 might also be frequent in cluster c_2. This is partially alleviated by the clustering algorithm which maximizes cluster homogeneity and minimizes the similarity among clusters. We should not omit a descriptor that is frequent in more than one cluster altogether, since it may be part of *different* cluster labels. However, the feature space contains only a small number of term combinations, allowing for the free combinations of descriptors to formulate appropriate cluster descriptions and cluster labels.

5. Tagging of documents

The iterative KDT process outputs a set of clusters that satisfy our quality criteria. Each cluster is annotated with statistics calculated by the mining software and with a cluster description comprised of descriptors reflecting the cluster's content. Cluster descriptions and names of named entities are used to create tags for the semantic annotation of text units. XML tags are ultimately determined by the knowledge engineer. Nevertheless, DIAsDEM performs both a pre-selection and a ranking of candidate cluster labels for the expert to choose from. A cluster description consists of the feature space dimensions prevalent in the cluster, accompanied by their statistics. In order to label a cluster c, only descriptors $d \in D$ such that $freq(d,c) \in HIGH$ need to be considered. We distinguish between:

- Group-I descriptors that are considered frequent by the DIAsDEM workbench
- Group-II descriptors that are all other descriptors appearing in text units of a cluster and considered significant by the mining software

The descriptors in both groups determine the content of the corresponding cluster. With respect to the frequency intervals $HIGH$, $MEDIUM$ and LOW, a Group-II descriptor needs not belong to the $HIGH$ interval. For cluster labeling, the knowledge engineer is called to choose upon the Group-I descriptors, ordered by decreasing frequency. Group-II descriptors are also presented, because the expert may decide to concatenate the selected Group-I descriptor(s) with a member of Group-II. The visualization module of DIAsDEM aids in this procedure by presenting the text units assigned to the cluster. Thus, the knowledge engineer may cross-check the cluster's content against the descriptors and select a combination that is consistent with the linguistic style in the application domain.

For example, a cluster of text units from police reports might have the descriptor "location" categorized as a very frequent Group-I descriptor, while the descriptor "crime" is a member of Group-II. The knowledge engineer may check the cluster content and decide that "locationOfCrime" can be an appropriate label for this cluster.

During the preprocessing phase, named entities of interest are extracted by a special DIAsDEM workbench module. In the XML tagging phase, cluster labels are combined with (name, value)-pairs of named entities appearing in the text units to construct attributes of XML tags. In particular, all documents in the collection are tagged as follows:

1. Each document is decomposed into its text units.
2. Named entities appearing in each text unit are extracted and each named entity value is associated with its named entity name.
3. All text units are mapped into the feature space of text unit descriptors to create text unit vectors.
4. Iterative assignment of text unit vectors to clusters: In the ith iteration:
   (a) Consider only clusters built in the ith iteration of the original clustering process
   (b) For each text unit: If the corresponding vector can be assigned to one of the clusters under consideration, then tag the text unit with its label.
   (c) Remove all tagged text units from the dataset.
   (d) The remaining dataset is input to the next iteration.
5. The (name, value)-pairs of extracted named entities appearing in a tagged text unit are incorporated into the tag surrounding it.

DIAsDEM generates a set of tags for an archive that constitute a flat, unstructured XML DTD. This DTD reflects the content of documents and can thus serve as a preliminary database-like schema. If this quasi-schema is implemented in an DBMS, cluster labels correspond to table names, while names of named entities are attributes belonging to the tables. Text units and values of named entities constitute an instance of this schema. Discovering ordered or creating nested XML tags is part of our future work.

6. Case study

DIAsDEM is a general purpose framework. Its workbench can be coupled with application-specific thesauri, specific rule templates for named entity extraction and various clustering algorithms. In our case study, we applied the framework to a collection of German Commercial Register text documents. In Germany, each district court maintains a Commercial Register that contains important information about companies in the court's district. According to German law, company activities like the establishment of branch offices, changes in share capital, mergers and acquisitions must be reported. Knowledge of Commercial Register entries is indispensable for business transactions.

The availability of Commercial Register entries on the Web has a large potential for focused information acquisition. Indeed, due to the intense business demand for this commercial information, there are several information brokers offering both online and offline services to retrieve relevant knowledge from Commercial Registers. However, current services only encompass SQL queries to access relational data and full-text queries to search unstructured texts that contain most of the information.

HRB 12576 06.05.1999	Daniel Spiel-Center GmbH (Potsdamer Straße 94, 14513 Teltow).	publiziert am 19.05.1999

Der Betrieb von Spielhallen in Teltow und das Aufstellen von Geldspiel- und Unterhaltungsautomaten. Stammkapital: 25.000 EUR. Gesellschaft mit beschränkter Haftung. Der Gesellschaftsvertrag ist am 12. November 1998 abgeschlossen und am 19. April 1999 abgeändert. Ist nur ein Geschäftsführer bestellt, so vertritt er die Gesellschaft einzeln. Sind mehrere Geschäftsführer bestellt, so wird die Gesellschaft durch zwei Geschäftsführer oder durch einen Geschäftsführer in Gemeinschaft mit einem Prokuristen vertreten. Einzelvertretungsbefugnis kann erteilt werden. Pawel Balski, 14.04.1965, Berlin, ist zum Geschäftsführer bestellt. Er vertritt die Gesellschaft stets einzeln und ist befugt, Rechtsgeschäfte mit sich selbst oder mit sich als Vertreter Dritter abzuschließen. Nicht eingetragen: Die Bekanntmachungen der Gesellschaft erfolgen im Bundesanzeiger.

Table 2. German Commercial Register entry

Table 2 contains an exemplary German Commercial Register entry. Each entry consists of a structured part and an unstructured text. The former contains the company's registered name, its record number as an identifier, the business address and relevant dates of registration and publication. This information can easily be extracted using wrapper technologies. The unstructured section of each entry contains the registered text as recorded by the court's clerks. In this case study, we have used 1,145 documents published by the district court of Potsdam. These documents are foundation entries of new companies in 1999.

We have established a preliminary conceptual model that partly reflects the application domain. Its UML class diagrams serve as a reference, against which the derived DTD can be matched. This conceptual model also formed the basis for specifying a controlled vocabulary of the domain. We have used word frequency statistics and the DIAsDEM thesaurus editor to build a hierarchy of 70 descriptors and 109 non-descriptors pointing to valid descriptors. The final feature space consists of 85 descriptors, after adding some terms known to be of importance in this domain.

We have partitioned the documents into text units, whereby the level of granularity was set to a sentence. Afterwards, the multilingual part–of–speech tagger TreeTagger was applied to determine lemma forms of all words [16]. The number of unique word forms was reduced from 10,613 to approx. 5,400. Our Java-based named entity extractor was employed to identify instances of named entities such as "Person", "Company", "Date" and "AmountOfMoney".

In Table 3, we summarize the size of the dataset and parameter settings in each of three clustering iterations performed. The KDT process was stopped by the knowledge engineer after three iterations. Altogether, 73 acceptable clusters were identified. They represent approx. 85% of all text units in the collection. This high proportion of tagged sentences can be explained with the fact that Commercial Register entries are composed of rather regular German lan-

Clustering iteration of KDT process	1	2	3
Number of input text units	10,785	1,818	1,648
Intra-cluster similarity threshold	0.95	0.90	0.80
Maximum number of clusters	200	200	200
Visualization threshold (cluster size)	10	5	3
Number of output clusters	122	121	67
Global Condorcet value	0.8090	0.9147	0.8176
Number of acceptable clusters	42	12	19
Text units in acceptable clusters	8,969	168	74

Table 3. Summary of iterative clustering

```
<?xml version="1.0" encoding="ISO-8859-1"?>

<!ELEMENT CommercialRegisterEntry (#PCDATA |
BusinessPurpose | ShareCapital | FullyLiablePartner
| AppointmentManagingDirector | GeneralPartnership |
InitialShareholders | (...) | FoundationPartnership)* >

<!ELEMENT BusinessPurpose (#PCDATA)> (...)
<!ELEMENT FoundationPartnership (#PCDATA)>

<!ATTLIST BusinessPurpose NE CDATA #IMPLIED> (...)
<!ATTLIST FoundationPartnership NE CDATA #IMPLIED>
```

Table 5. Excerpt of the derived flat XML DTD

guage. In the future, the DIAsDEM framework will be evaluated against other archives such as company profiles and ad hoc news of publicly quoted companies.

In the last phase, labels of acceptable clusters were used to annotate sentences. In Table 4, the document of Table 2 is partly depicted after semantic tagging. The first sentence of this XML document is tagged as one referring to the business purpose of the new company. The second sentence refers to its share capital and contains a named entity, i.e. the amount of money invested in the company. Accordingly, the tag is extended to accommodate the named entity name "AmountOfMoney" and its value. The 5th tag refers to the manager appointed for the company: The named entity "Person" thus annotates this tag. Its value reflects the way persons are identified in many entries, i.e. by specifying surname, forename, current domicile and date of birth.

```
<?xml version="1.0" encoding="ISO-8859-1"?>
<!DOCTYPE CommercialRegisterEntry SYSTEM
'CommercialRegisterEntry.dtd'>

<CommercialRegisterEntry> <BusinessPurpose> Der
Betrieb von Spielhallen in Teltow und das Aufstellen von Geldspiel- und
Unterhaltungsautomaten. </BusinessPurpose> <ShareCapital
NE="AmoutOfMoney=[25000 EUR]"> Stammkapital: 25.000 EUR.
</ShareCapital> <LimitedLiabilityCompany> Gesellschaft
mit beschränkter Haftung. </LimitedLiabilityCompany>
<ConclusionArticles NE="Date=[12.11.1998], Date=
[19.04.1999]"> Der Gesellschaftsvertrag ist am 12. November 1998
abgeschlossen und am 19. April 1999 abgeändert. </Conclusion
Articles> (...) Einzelvertretungsbefugnis kann erteilt werden.
<AppointmentManagingDirector NE="Person=[Balski;
Pawel; Berlin; 14.04.1965]"> Pawel Balski, 14.04.1965, Berlin,
ist zum Geschäftsführer bestellt. </AppointmentManaging
Director> (...) <PublicationMedia> Nicht eingetragen: Die
Bekanntmachungen der Gesellschaft erfolgen im Bundesanzeiger.
</PublicationMedia> </CommercialRegisterEntry>
```

Table 4. Semantically tagged XML document

Table 5 contains an excerpt of the flat, unstructured XML DTD that was automatically derived from all discovered XML tags. It coarsely describes the semantic structure of the resulting XML collection. Currently, named entities are not fully evaluated. Named entities are denoted by the at-

tribute "NE" in the DTD, without taking the exact named entity name into account. As part of our future work, attributes will be assigned a semantic name as well.

In contrast to text classification, there are no pre-classified documents in our application domain, upon which the effectiveness of the DIAsDEM workbench could be measured. Instead, we have drawn a random sample containing approx. 5% of the 1,145 text units and asked a domain expert to detect tagging errors. We distinguish between two types of tagging errors, namely false positives and false negatives. A false positive occurs if the tag associated with a text unit does not entirely reflect its content. A false negative occurs when an un-tagged text unit conforms to a semantic concept that is part of the derived DTD.

Within the 5% sample, the false positive (false negative) error rate is 0.375% (3.565%). The percentage of false positives is very low. If a text unit is tagged, the tag is most likely to be correct. The percentage of false negatives is higher, indicating that some text units were not placed in the cluster they semantically belonged to. Our preliminary explanation for the comparatively high rate of false negatives is that these text units were characterized by terms that were not included in the feature space. The reader may recall that there was no thesaurus available for this case study, so that one had to be built from word statistics. A thesaurus contains several concepts, each of them expressed by many alternative terms. If some of these alternatives are less frequent than others, they may be ignored when building the thesaurus and deriving a feature space from it. Text units containing these infrequent words are thus mapped into vectors of poor quality.

The overall error rate in the 5% sample is 3.940%. With 0.95 confidence, the error rate in the entire dataset is in the interval [2.591%, 5.948%] which is a very promising result.

7. Conclusion

Collections of unstructured text documents contain information of great potential value. However, they can only be retrieved with full-text search in most cases. In this paper, we have presented a framework for semantic tagging and derivation of XML DTDs from domain-specific text archives. Our Java-based DIAsDEM workbench operates in two phases. An interactive and iterative KDT process groups all text units of all documents in the archive into a set of large, homogeneous clusters by their semantics, semi-automatically derives cluster labels that serve as XML tags and finally annotates text units with these tags, extended with information about named entities referenced in them.

We have tested our framework on a document collection from the German Commercial Register and shown that our approach is very successful, showing a very low error rate. This application area is particularly important for e-business, because Commercial Register entries contain indispensable information for business interactions among companies. While existing information brokers process these documents with conventional information retrieval techniques, DIAsDEM enables a more focused search through appropriate XML query languages that exploit XML tags and their associated attribute values.

Our future work includes the derivation of structured XML DTDs in contrast to the currently derived, rather unstructured and preliminary ones. We also intend to combine natural language processing techniques and n-gram clustering instead of sentence clustering. Additionally, further clustering algorithms and similarity metrics should be evaluated with respect to the objectives of our framework. Finally, we intend to reduce the human effort by (i) exploiting association rules during thesaurus construction and (ii) by extending the ranking mechanism that proposes cluster labels to the expert into a recommendation system that takes the preliminary schema into account.

8. Acknowledgments

We thank the German Research Society for funding the project DIAsDEM, the Bundesanzeiger Verlagsgesellschaft mbH for providing data and our project collaborators Evguenia Altareva and Stefan Conrad for helpful discussions. The IBM Intelligent Miner for Data is kindly provided by IBM in terms of the IBM DB2 Scholars Program.

References

[1] S. Abiteboul, P. Buneman, and D. Suciu. *Data on the Web: From Relations to Semistructured Data and XML*. Morgan Kaufman Publishers, San Francisco, 2000.

[2] I. Bruder, A. Düsterhöft, M. Becker, J. Bedersdorfer, and G. Neumann. GETESS: Constructing a linguistic search index for an Internet search engine. In *Proc. of the 5th Int'l Conf. on Applications of Natural Language to Information Systems*, pages 227–238, Versailles, France, June 2000.

[3] P. Buneman. Semistructured data. In *Proceedings of the Sixteenth ACM SIGACT-SIGMOD-SIGART Symposium on Principles of Database Systems*, pages 117–121, Tucson, AZ, USA, May 1997.

[4] S. Decker, M. Erdmann, D. Fensel, and R. Studer. ONTO-BROKER: Ontology based access to distributed and semi-structured information. In R. Meersman, editor, *Database Semantics: Semantic Issues in Multimedia Systems*, pages 351–369. Kluwer Academic Publisher, Boston, 1999.

[5] D. W. Embley, D. M. Campbell, R. D. Smith, and S. W. Liddle. Ontology-based extraction and structuring of information from data-rich unstructured documents. In *Proc. of the 1998 ACM 7th Int'l Conf. on Information and Knowledge Management*, pages 52–59, Bethesda, MD, USA, November 1998.

[6] R. Feldman and I. Dagan. Knowledge discovery in textual databases (KDT). In *Proc. of the First Int'l Conf. on Knowledge Discovery and Data Mining*, pages 112–117, Montreal, Canada, August 1995.

[7] R. Feldman, M. Fresko, Y. Kinar, Y. Lindell, O. Liphstat, M. Rajman, Y. Schler, and O. Zamir. Text mining at the term level. In *Proc. of the Second European Symposium on Principles of Data Mining and Knowledge Discovery*, pages 65–73, Nantes, France, September 1998.

[8] IBM DB2 Intelligent Miner for Data. http://www.ibm.com/software/data/iminer.

[9] S. Loh, L. K. Wives, and J. P. M. d. Oliveira. Concept-based knowledge discovery in texts extracted from the Web. *ACM SIGKDD Explorations*, 2(1):29–39, 2000.

[10] J. Lumera. Große Mengen an Altdaten stehen XML-Umstieg im Weg. *Computerwoche*, 27(16):52–53, 2000.

[11] A. Maedche and S. Staab. Learning ontologies for the Semantic Web. *IEEE Intelligent Systems*, 16(2):72–79, 2001.

[12] P. Michaud. Clustering techniques. *Future Generation Computer Systems*, 13(2–3):135–147, November 1997.

[13] U. Y. Nahm and R. J. Mooney. Using information extraction to aid the discovery of prediction rules from text. In *Proc. of the KDD-2000 Workshop on Text Mining*, pages 51–58, Boston, MA, USA, August 2000.

[14] S. Nestrov, S. Abiteboul, and R. Motwani. Inferring structure in semi-structured data. *SIGMOD Record*, 26(4):39–43, 1997.

[15] G. Salton and C. Buckley. Term weighting approaches in automatic text retrieval. *Information Processing and Management*, 24(5):513–523, 1988.

[16] H. Schmid. Probabilistic part–of–speech tagging using decision trees. In *Proc. of Int'l Conf. on New Methods in Language Processing*, pages 44–49, Manchester, UK, September 1994.

[17] A. Sengupta and S. Purao. Transitioning existing content: Inferring organization-spezific document structures. In *Tagungsband der 1. Deutschen Tagung XML 2000*, pages 130–135, Heidelberg, Germany, May 2000.

[18] A.-H. Tan. Text mining: The state of the art and the challenges. In *Proc. of the PAKDD 1999 Workshop on Knowledge Disocovery from Advanced Databases*, pages 65–70, Beijing, China, April 1999.

[19] K. Wang and H. Liu. Discovering structural association of semistructured data. *IEEE Transactions on Knowledge and Data Engineering*, 12(3):353–371, May/June 2000.

A Scalable Algorithm for Clustering Sequential Data *

Valerie Guralnik and George Karypis

University of Minnesota, Department of Computer Science and
Army HPC Research Center, Minneapolis, MN 55455

{guralnik,karypis}@cs.umn.edu

Abstract

In recent years, we have seen an enormous growth in the amount of available commercial and scientific data. Data from domains such as protein sequences, retail transactions, intrusion detection, and web-logs have an inherent sequential nature. Clustering of such data sets is useful for various purposes. For example, clustering of sequences from commercial data sets may help marketer identify different customer groups based upon their purchasing patterns. Grouping protein sequences that share similar structure helps in identifying sequences with similar functionality. Over the years, many methods have been developed for clustering objects according to their similarity. However these methods tend to have a computational complexity that is at least quadratic on the number of sequences. In this paper we present an entirely different approach to sequence clustering that does not require an all-against-all analysis and uses a near-linear complexity K-means based clustering algorithm. Our experiments using data sets derived from sequences of purchasing transactions and protein sequences show that this approach is scalable and leads to reasonably good clusters.

1 Introduction

In recent years, we have seen an enormous growth in the amount of available commercial and scientific data. Data from domains such as protein sequences, retail transactions, intrusion detection, and web-logs have an inherent sequential nature. Clustering of such data sets is useful for various purposes. For example, clustering of sequences from commercial data sets may help marketer identify different customer groups based upon their purchasing patterns. Grouping protein sequences that share similar structure helps in identifying sequences with similar functionality.

Over the years, many methods have been developed for clustering objects according to their similarity. These algorithms can be broadly classified into two categories: partitional and hierarchical. Partitional clustering algorithms, as typified by the K-medoid algorithm [9, 4], ob-

tain clusters of objects by selecting cluster representatives and assigning each object to the cluster with its representative closest to the object. On the other hand, hierarchical clustering algorithms, such as UPGMA or single-link [4], produce a nested sequence of clusters, with a single all-inclusive cluster at the top and single point clusters at the bottom. These clustering algorithms can be easily adapted to cluster sequential data sets, provided that the pairwise similarity between the sequences can be easily computed. However these methods tend to have a computational complexity that is at least quadratic on the number of sequences, as they need to compute the pairwise similarity between all the sequences. Thus, they are only applicable to small data sets. Moreover, computationally efficient schemes such as K-means cannot be directly applied as it is hard to compute sequence centroids.

In this paper we present an entirely different approach to sequence clustering that does not require an all-against-all analysis and uses a near-linear complexity K-means based clustering algorithm. The key idea of our approach is to find a set of features that capture the sequential nature of the various data-sequences, project each data-sequence into a new space whose dimensions are these features, and then use a traditional K-means based clustering algorithm to find the clusters of the data-sequences. Our approach was inspired by research in document clustering that showed that high quality clusters can be obtained when each document is represented using a "bag of words". Clustering the documents based solely on their similarity with respect to these words generates clustering solutions which are equally good to methods that try to take into account phrase, paragraph, and document structure. In light of this example, our algorithm can be thought of as first discovering the "words" (*i.e.*, features) of the sequences, and then clustering the sequences based on the words that they have. Our experiments using data sets derived from sequences of purchasing transactions and protein sequences show that this approach is scalable and leads to reasonably good clusters.

2 Background

Clustering is the task of grouping together the objects into meaningful subclasses. We focus on clustering sequential data in which each object is represented as a sequence of set of items, called *itemsets*. Such sequence is called *data-*

---

*This work was supported by NSF CCR-9972519, EIA-9986042, ACI-9982274, by Army Research Office contract DA/DAAG55-98-1-0441, by the DOE ASCI program, and by Army High Performance Computing Research Center contract number DAAH04-95-C-0008. Access to computing facilities was provided by the Minnesota Supercomputing Institute.

```
a   x   a   b   _   c   s
a   x   _   b   a   c   s
```

Figure 1: Example of string alignment

```
(a b)    (b d)    ()     (c f)    ()
(b f)    (b d g)  (h)    (f k)    (l m)
```

Figure 2: Example of sequence alignment

sequence. For sequential data sets, the problem of clustering becomes one of finding the groups of data-sequences similar to each other.

2.1 Measuring Similarity between Sequences

One of the key steps in all clustering algorithms is the method used to compute the similarity between the objects being clustered. Over the years, a number of different approaches have been developed for computing similarity between two sequences of symbols (*i.e.*, strings) based on sequence alignment [5]. The idea behind these approaches is to align two strings against each other so that to maximize the similarity between the portions of the strings that fall at the same location of the alignment. Figure 1 shows an example of such an alignment between two particular protein sequences. These string-based optimal alignment approaches can be extended to compute the similarity between two sequences of itemsets as follows. Let S_1 and S_2 be two sequences containing m and n itemsets, respectively. Let $S_1(i)$ be the ith itemset of S_1 and $S_2(j)$ be the jth itemset of S_2. Furthermore, let S_1' and S_2' be two sequences of length l obtained after aligning S_1 against S_2, by inserting empty itemsets at either inside, at the beginning, or at the ends of the two sequences, so that every itemset (including empty) in either sequence is opposite a unique itemset in the other sequences. An example of this type of alignment is shown in Figure 2. The score of such alignment A can be defined as

$$score(A) = \sum_{i=1}^{l} sim(S_1'(i), S_2'(i)).$$

The similarity between two itemsets $S_1'(i)$ and $S_2'(i)$ can be measured in various ways. One way is to count the number of items that are common between the two itemsets and scale the count so that the similarity is always a number between 0 and 1, resulting in the following measure:

$$sim(S_1'(i), S_2'(i)) = \frac{|S_1'(i) \bigcap S_2'(i)|}{\frac{|S_1'(i)| + |S_2'(i)|}{2}}.$$

Another way of measuring similarity is to represent itemsets using the vector-space model. In this model, each itemset is considered to be a vector in the item space. In its simplest form, each itemset is represented by the vector

$I = (i_1, i_2, \ldots, i_n)$, where i_j is an indicator whether the jth item is in the itemset. Given this representation, the cosine similarity measure is a natural way of computing the similarity, and is defined as

$$sim(S_1'(i), S_2'(i)) = \frac{S_1'(i) \bullet S_2'(i)}{\|S_1'(i)\| \|S_2'(i)\|}.$$

Given any scoring scheme (including the ones introduced above), the *optimal alignment* A^* of two sequences S_1 and S_2 is defined as an alignment that maximizes the total alignment score $score(A^*)$. The score of the optimal alignment can be used as the similarity measure of two sequences. Depending on the application domain, one might want to scale this value so that the similarity between sequences of different lengths are comparable. The following formulas achieve the desired result:

$$sim(S_1, S_2) = \frac{score(A^*)}{\frac{|S_1| + |S_2|}{2}} \text{ or } sim(S_1, S_2) = \frac{score(A^*)}{l}.$$

The similarity of two sequences S_1 and S_2, and the associated optimal alignment, can be computed via dynamic programming [5] with a complexity $O(|S_1| * |S_2|)$.

2.2 Clustering Algorithms

Agglomerative hierarchical clustering and K-means are two techniques that are commonly used for clustering. Hierarchical techniques produce a nested sequence of partitions, with a single all-inclusive cluster at the top and singleton clusters of individual points at the bottom. Each intermediate level can be viewed as combining two clusters from the next lower level (or splitting a cluster from the next higher level). Agglomerative hierarchical algorithms start with all the data points as a separate cluster. Each step of the algorithm involves merging two clusters that are most similar. After each merge, the total number of clusters decreases by one. These steps can be repeated until the desired number of clusters is obtained or the distance between two the closest clusters is above a certain threshold distance.

In contrast to hierarchical techniques, partitional clustering techniques create a one-level (un-nested) partitioning of the data points. Partitional clustering attempts to break a data set into K clusters such that the partition optimizes a given criterion. Centroid-based approaches, as typified by K-means try to assign objects to clusters such that the mean square distance of objects to the centroid of the assigned cluster is minimized. Centroid-based techniques are suitable only for data in metric spaces (e.g. Euclidean space) in which it is possible to compute centroid for a given set of points. Because it is computationally hard to compute centroids in the space of data-sequences, medoid-based approaches are better suited for clustering sequential data sets. Medoid-based methods work with similarity data, *i.e.*, data in arbitrary similarity space. These techniques try to find representative points (medoids) so as to minimize the sum of the distances of points from their closest medoid. It has been shown, that if the measure used to compute similarity satisfies the *triangle inequality*, then in each cluster of n data-sequences there exists a medoid S_m, such that $M = \sum_{i=1}^{n} score(S_m, S_i)$ is never less than $2 - 2/n$ times the $M_c = \sum_{i=1}^{n} score(S_c, S_i)$, where S_c is the centroid of the cluster [5].

2.3 Limitation of existing approaches

One limitation of using both hierarchical and medoid-based partitional clustering approaches is that when the dynamic programming algorithms are used to compute the similarity, their complexity is $O(n^2 m^2 + n^2 \log n)$ and $O(n^2 m^2 + ntk)$, respectively; where n is the number of data-sequences, m is the average length of each data-sequence, k is number of clusters and t number of iterations in the medoid-based approach. These high computational requirements make such approaches impractical for most applications that require clustering of moderate and large data sets.

3 Feature-based Clustering

The high computational requirements of both the hierarchical clustering algorithms and K-medoid approaches are due to the fact that (a) they need to compute the pairwise similarity between all the data-sequences and (b) the similarity computations have a complexity that is quadratic to the length of the data-sequences involved. To address these high computational requirements, we explore an alternate approach for clustering sequences that (i) does not use dynamic programming to compute the similarity, and (ii) it uses a K-means algorithm whose complexity is near-linear in the number of sequences.

The key idea of our approach is to find a set of features that capture the sequential nature of the various data-sequences, project each data-sequence into a new space whose dimensions are these features, and then use a traditional vector-space K-means clustering algorithm [14] to find the clusters of the data-sequences in this transformed space.

In the remaining of this section we describe the various algorithms and issues associated with each one of these three steps.

3.1 Finding the Feature Space

An essential part of the proposed approach is finding the set of features that will form the basis of the transformed space. In particular, these features must satisfy the following properties:

1. The features should capture the sequential relations between the different itemsets that are present in the data-sequences. This is particularly important, since the proposed clustering algorithm will cluster the data-sequences based solely on their similarity with respect to these features.

2. The features should be present in a nontrivial number of data-sequences. This is because rare features do

not improve the overall clustering, as they are useful only in defining affinity between a small set of data-sequences.

3. The feature space should be complete, in the sense that all such interesting features should be contained in the transformed space.

Our algorithm achieves these goals by using as features all the sequential patterns whose length is between l_{min} and l_{max} and satisfy a given minimum support constraint. A sequential pattern is a list itemsets with the support above a user-specified threshold, where the support of the pattern is the percentage of data-sequences that contain it. Given a sequential pattern $< s_1, s_2, \ldots, s_n >$, where s_i is an itemset, the length of the pattern is the number of items in all itemsets s_i of the pattern. The gap between itemsets i_1 and i_2 of the data-sequence supporting a particular pattern is defined $occurrence(i_1) - occurrence(i_2)$, where definition of the occurrence is domain specific. Depending on the application domain, one might impose minimum/maximum gap constraints on sequential patterns. These frequent sequential patterns, can be computed efficient using a variety of sequential pattern discovery algorithms [1, 13, 15, 8, 6].

3.2 Projecting in to the Feature Space

The critical step in our approach is that of representing each data-sequence in the newly discovered space of sequential features. If N is the dimensionality of the feature space, a straightforward way of achieving this is to represent each data-sequence as an N-dimensional vector of zeros and ones, with ones corresponding to all the features that are supported by that particular data-sequence.

Unfortunately, this representation can potentially lead to poor clustering results. This is because, the different features that are supported by a particular sequence may be highly dependent which can substantially distort the similarity measure that is used in the transformed space. For instance, if a particular sequential pattern w of length l, with $l > l_{min}$ is supported by a particular sequence, then all of its sub-patterns of length greater than l_{min} will also be supported as well. As a result, when we compare two sequences that both have w, their similarity will be distorted by the different sub-patterns of w that they also share. Similar problem occurs when two sequential patterns partially overlap as well. For example, consider the following scenario in context of protein clustering. Let's assume that we have the database of amino-acid sequences shown in Figure 3 together with all sequential patterns of consecutive amino-acids of lengths 3 and 4 that have support of 50%. Let's concentrate on the first two sequences S_1 and S_2 and the two discovered patterns AQVH and HKKS. Saying that both proteins subscribe to both patterns will mean that there are two similarity regions of length 4 between them, while if we computed the alignment of those proteins we would find that there is only one region of length 4 where both proteins align (either AQVH

181

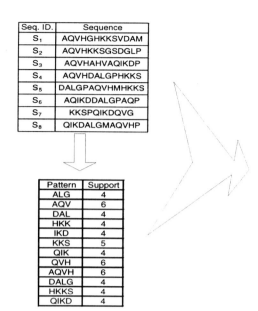

Seq. ID.	Sequence
S_1	AQVHGHKKSVDAM
S_2	AQVHKKSGSDGLP
S_3	AQVHAHVAQIKDP
S_4	AQVHDALGPHKKS
S_5	DALGPAQVHMHKKS
S_6	AQIKDDALGPAQP
S_7	KKSPQIKDQVG
S_8	QIKDALGMAQVHP

Pattern	Support
ALG	4
AQV	6
DAL	4
HKK	4
IKD	4
KKS	5
QIK	4
QVH	6
AQVH	6
DALG	4
HKKS	4
QIKD	4

Globally Selected Features

Seq.ID.	KKS	AQVH	DALG	QIKD
S_1	x	x		
S_2	x	x		
S_3		x		x
S_4	x	x	x	
S_5	x	x	x	
S_6			x	x
S_7	x			x
S_8		x	x	x

Locally Selected Features

Seq.ID.	ALG	KKS	AQVH	DALG	HKKS	QIKD
S_1			x		x	
S_2		x	x			
S_3			x			x
S_4			x	x	x	
S_5			x	x	x	
S_6				x		x
S_7		x				x
S_8	x		x			x

Figure 3: Feature Selection Example

or HKKS). Therefore, it is important to represent each sequence in a way such that the dimensions that they are using are as independent of each other as possible. We implemented two different approaches to address this problem, that are described in the rest of this section.

3.2.1 Global Approach

One way of addressing the above problem is to prune the feature space by selecting only a set of independent features prior to projection. In particular, we say that two sequential patterns are *dependent* if and only if (i) either one is the prefix of the other or one is a sub-pattern of the other, and (ii) the intersection of their respective supporting sets is non-trivial.

These conditions essentially call two patterns that draw support from the same region of the sequence to be dependent. Coming back to the example from Figure 3, let's assume that the intersection of two patterns supporting set is non-trivial if its cardinality is at least two thirds of smallest support of the pattern. Under this condition one possible set of independent patterns is KKS, AQVH, DALG, QIKD, as shown in Figure 3.

Using the definition of independence, we can then use a greedy algorithm to select a maximal set of independent features and restrict the space to only this set of features. Even though this approach ensures that the set of features that we select are independent, it has a number of potentially serious drawbacks. First, computation of the pairwise intersection of the supporting sets for each sequential pattern is computationally expensive. Second, the resulting space will either be over-pruned or under-pruned. Thus in our example, patterns AQVH and HKKS are found dependent (the number of proteins that support both of them is 4). As a result all the sequences supporting both of these patterns subscribe to only AQVH. However, almost all of the sequences that support both patterns have two regions

of similarity of length 4. Hence, we are presented with an over-pruned space. Ideally we would like for S_1 to subscribe to both patterns, and for S_2 to subscribe to only one of them. On the other hand, patterns DALG and QIKD are found independent (the number of proteins that support both of them is 2). As a result the sequences S_6 and S_8 have two regions of similarity of length 4 QIKD and DALG which is not correct. As we can see, over-pruning of the space contradicts the required property of completeness. Under-pruning doesn't solve the problem of having redundant features.

3.2.2 Local Approach

In order to correct the problem of the global approach, we developed a method for selecting a set of independent features that is done locally, on a per data-sequence basis. In this approach, for each data-sequence we first find the set of features that it supports, and from this set we select a maximal set of independent features. In this context, two features are considered to be *independent*, if they are supported by non-overlapping segments of the underlying data-sequence. The advantage of this approach is that it allows us to subscribe each data-sequence to as many independent features as possible (regardless of the features selected by other data-sequences), and at the same time, the process of feature selection is very fast.

One potential problem with this approach is that sequences that share a large number of sequential patterns, may actually end up having low similarity, because the independent sets they selected, had little overlap. Two address problem we select the locally independent features using the same greedy strategy, so that we increase the likelihood that if two data-sequences share a number of sequential patterns, then a considerable number of them will be selected by both of them—ensuring that if two data-sequences are similar in the original space, will also be similar in the transformed space. This can be done in a number of ways. One way to select a feature out of set of dependent patterns is to select a more frequent pattern, or pattern that has more items. An example of locally selected features is presented in Figure 3, in which the selection strategy gave preference to the longer pattern.

3.3 Clustering in the Feature Space

Once the data-sequences have been projected into the feature space, we use an efficient vector-space clustering algorithm based on K-means [14] to find k clusters. In this algorithm, each data-sequence is represented by a vector in the feature-space, and the similarity between two data-sequences is computed using the cosine similarity function, commonly used in the context of information retrieval [10]. Moreover, in some domains it is important to account for frequently occurring low complexity sequential patterns. To do this, we scale each of the features following the *inverse-document-frequency* methodology, again inspired by research in information retrieval. In this approach, if a particular feature appears in m out of n data-sequences, its weight is multiplied by $log(n/m)$. The effect of this scaling is that infrequently occurring features are given higher weight that features that occur in almost every data-sequence.

4 Experimental Evaluation

We experimentally evaluated our approach using datasets arising in two domains: retail and bioinformatics. All experiments were run on a Linux machine with 4GB of memory utilizing 550 MHz Pentium III CPU.

4.1 Evaluation of Cluster Quality

For clustering, two measures of cluster "goodness" or quality are used. One type of measure allows us to compare different sets of clusters without reference to external knowledge and is called an *internal quality* measure. One internal measure is weighted average similarity, which is based on the pairwise similarity of sequences in each cluster. The weighted average similarity is calculated as follows. Let CS be a clustering solution. For each cluster C_j, we first compute its average similarity

$$AS_j = \frac{\sum_{S \in C_j, S' \in C_j} sim(S, S')}{n_j(n_j - 1)},$$

where n_j is number of sequences in cluster C_j. The weighted average similarity for a set of clusters is calculated as the sum of the average similarities for each cluster weighed by the size of each cluster:

$$WAS_{cs} = \sum_{j=1}^{m} n_j * AS_j,$$

where n_j is the size of cluster C_j, and m is the number of clusters.

The other type of measures lets us evaluate how well the clustering is working by comparing the groups produced by the clustering techniques to known classes. This type of measure is called an *external quality* measure. One external measure is the *entropy* [12], that is calculated as follows. Let CS be a clustering solution. For each cluster C_j, we first compute the distribution of the data-sequences that it contains for each class i, *i.e.*, p_{ij} is equal to the probability a randomly drawn data-sequence from cluster C_j to be of class i. Then using this class distribution, the entropy of each cluster C_j is calculated using the formula

$$E_j = -\sum_i p_{ij} log(p_{ij}).$$

The total entropy for a set of clusters is calculated as the sum of the entropies for each cluster weighted by the size of each cluster:

$$E_{cs} = \sum_{j=1}^{m} \frac{n_j * E_j}{n},$$

where n_j is the size of cluster j, m is the number of clusters, and n is the total number of data-sequences in that data set. Note, that the entropy value 0 indicates a perfect clustering solution. The higher the entropy value the worse the clustering solution is.

4.2 Retail Data Set

The retail data set contained a history of store-branded credit-card purchases of 7451 customers of a major department store, such that each customer made 3 or more purchases. The total number of distinct products purchased was 222348. For this data set we found 2435 frequent sequential patterns of length 2 or more with minimum support equal to 0.1%. The maximum length of the pattern that was discovered was 9.

To subscribe data-sequences to discovered patterns we used both global and local methods with different feature selection approaches, namely selecting a longer pattern or a more frequent pattern, resulting in four test sets FB-GL (global selection of longer patterns), FB-GF (global selection of more frequent patterns), FB-LL (local selection of longer patterns) and FB-LF (local selection of more frequent patterns). After the independent patterns were selected, the FB-GL approach kept 255 patterns and subscribed 2061 data-sequences, the FB-GF approach selected 241 patterns and subscribed 2552 sequences, the FB-LL approach kept 707 frequent patterns and subscribed 3164 data-sequences, and the FB-LF kept 546 patterns and subscribed 3230 data-sequences. Note that schemes that give preference to the more frequent patterns resulted in spaces with fewer dimensions as frequent patterns are inherently more dependent. The sequences that didn't support any of the frequent patterns were not used for clustering.

The resulting clustering solutions were compared against solutions produced by similarity-based approaches

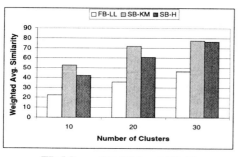

FB-LL vs. SB-KM and SB-H

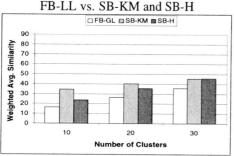

FB-GL vs. SB-KM and SB-H

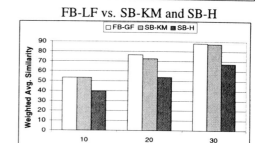

FB-LF vs. SB-KM and SB-H

FB-GF vs. SB-KM and SB-H

Figure 4: Comparison of Feature Based Clustering vs. Similarity Based Clustering

– hierarchical algorithm which optimizes group average similarity [4] (SB-H) and K-medoid (SB-KM). To ensure that the comparison were performed in an unbias way, only the data-sequences that could be projected on the feature space were clustered. This resulted in four different sets of experiments, one for each of the feature selection strategies. In the absence of class information, we used the weighted average similarity of the clusters in the sequence space, as a measure of quality of the clustering solution.

Figure 4 shows the weighted average similarity of 10, 20 and 30-way clustering solutions generated by the different algorithms. Note that high values of weighted average similarity represent better clustering solutions. From this figure it can be seen that both global and local approaches, which selected longer patterns, performed poorly. In analyzing the reason for this behavior, we discovered that the data-sequences in this data set are short and therefore supported only a small number of sequential patterns. As a result, by preferring longer sequential patterns the majority of data-sequences only subscribed to a small number of dimensions (usually one or two). Thus, if one sequence contained a long pattern and another contained its sub-pattern, those sequences mostly likely ended up in different clusters due to the fact that they contained different features. This resulted in un-similar data-sequences getting clustered in the same group. After examining frequent dimensions of the resulting clusters, we found for example that customers who bought home collection items were put in the same cluster as customers who bought hair-care products.

To overcome this problem, we ran the experiments FB-LF and FB-GF in which more frequent patterns were selected. In both cases the feature based approach outperformed the hierarchical algorithm, and showed comparable performance to K-medoid. Comparing the global se-

lection methods against those that select features that are locally independent in each data-sequence, we can see that the latter approach performs considerably better. Note, that as it was described in Section 3.2 the resulting global schemes became over-pruned. This is evident by cardinality of the transformed space in the global selection scheme which is about 3 times smaller. As a result global schemes were not able to cluster as many data-sequences as local ones.

Even though the feature-based approach didn't show significant improvement over similarity based algorithms, the proposed approach has number of advantages. First, by projecting only the data-sequences that support frequent patterns onto the feature space, our approach eliminates data-sequences that are outliers. This is because the sequences that do not contain frequent patterns are not similar to a lot of other sequences in the data set and thus are not relevant for clustering. Second, examining the dimensions which occur frequently in each cluster helps us to gain insight about its characteristics and thus interpret the clustering solution. The medoids of the K-medoid approach can serve as representatives of the clusters. However, since it is unknown what regions of the medoid sequence occur frequently in the cluster and what regions are unique to this particular medoid, it will be hard to use this sequence to describe the cluster. Examples of clusters found by our approach are group of customers who buy home collection products and group of people who buy clothes for teenagers.

4.3 Data Sets of Proteins

As another way to evaluate the performance of the proposed clustering algorithm we generated three different data sets, DS1, DS2, and DS3, containing protein se-

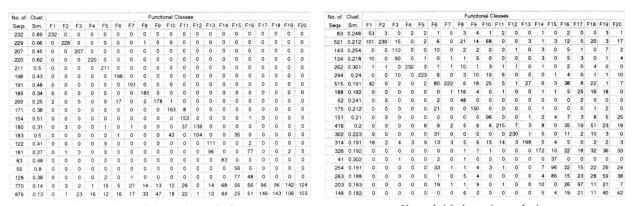

Feature-based clustering solution K-medoid clustering solution

Figure 5: Clustering solution for DS1

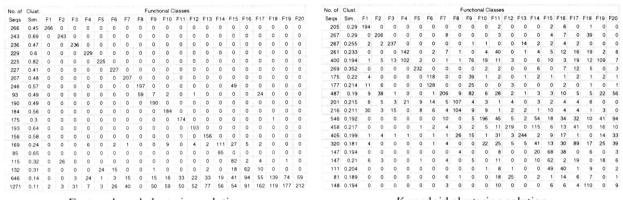

Feature-based clustering solution K-medoid clustering solution

Figure 6: Clustering solution for DS2

quences from the SWISS-PROT [2] public protein sequence database. Each one of the data sets contains proteins from 20 different protein families. DS1 contains 4,775 sequences, DS2 contains 5,288, and DS3 contains 43,569 sequences. For each of the data sets, we found frequent patterns of consecutive amino-acids, of length 3 through length 6. The minimum support used for each data set was equal to 25% of the size of the smallest class. In all of our experiments, we used the local scheme for selecting independent dimensions during projection, and these dimensions were selected by giving preference to the longest patterns. We also experimented with the global selection scheme, but the quality of the resulting solutions was quite poor. For this reason we do not report these experiments in this paper.

We evaluated the quality of the resulting clustering solution using the entropy measure.

Figure 5, 6, and 7 show the 20-way clustering solution produced by our algorithm on the DS1, DS2, and DS3 data sets, respectively. For DS1, a total of 13,331 frequent patterns of length 3–6 were discovered, out of which 11,780 were kept after independent patterns were selected locally. In the case of DS2, the initial and final number of patterns

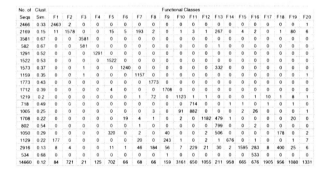

Figure 7: Feature-based clustering solution for DS3

were 19,129 and 14,139, respectively, and in the case of DS3 they were 22,672 and 21,223. Also, each sequence subscribed to an average of 71, 76, and 81 features for DS1, DS2, and DS3, respectively. The first two columns of each table show the number of proteins assigned to each cluster, and the average pairwise protein similarity between the proteins in each cluster, respectively. For each of the clusters, the remaining 20 columns of each row show the class distribution of the proteins that were assigned to that particular cluster.

Data Set	Feature-Based K-means	K-medoid
DS1	1.43	2.12
DS2	1.51	2.19

Table 1: Comparison of Entropy Measure

Looking at the various clustering solutions we can see that the proposed algorithm was able to produce clusters that primarily contained proteins from either one or two protein families. Furthermore, 14 functional classes are clearly distinguishable in both DS1 and DS2, and 13 are distinguishable in DS3. The members of the remaining functional classes were also mostly kept together, however they were clustered together with members of other functional classes. The overall quality of the clustering solution produced by our algorithm, as measured by entropy, was 1.43, 1.51, and 1.67, for DS1, DS2, and DS3, respectively.

A common characteristic of the clustering solutions for all three data sets was the fact that one or two of the clusters tend to be somewhat larger than the rest, and were both *loose* (as measured by the average pairwise similarity) and contained proteins from different families. In analyzing the reason for this behavior, we discovered that the proteins that were in these clusters contained patterns that were of length either 3 or 4, indicating that the proteins in them did not share some of the longer conserved patterns that the rest of the proteins did. One way of addressing this limitation of our approach is to use amino-acid substitution matrices or amino-acid similarity matrices to define equivalent classes of patterns [3, 11, 7].

The entropy measure of the clustering solution generated by our approach was compared against the entropy measure of clustering solution generated by K-medoid algorithm. Only two data sets DS1 and DS2 were used in this comparison, due to the need to compute all-against-all similarity matrix for each of the data sets. The computation of the matrix for each DS1 and DS2 took over three days. Because data set DS3 contained roughly ten times more data-sequences than either DS1 and DS2, the computation of the similarity matrix for this data set would have taken a prohibitively large amount of time.

Table 1 shows the comparison of entropy results for both data sets. From this table it can be observed that our algorithm outperformed the K-medoid. Figure 5 and 6 compares the 20-way clustering solutions produced by our approach and K-medoid algorithm on DS1 and DS2 respectively . A common characteristic of those clustering solutions is that the groups of proteins that could not be correctly clustered by our approach also did not cluster well by K-medoid. In addition, the functional classes which were clearly distinguishable in the feature based clustering solution were not clustered as well by K-medoid approach.

5 Conclusion

In this paper we presented a new approach to sequence clustering that uses a near-linear complexity K-means based clustering algorithm. Our approach is based on projecting the data-sequences onto space of frequent sequential patterns and using K-means based clustering algorithm to find clusters in that space. Our experimental evaluation in two domains shows that this approach appears promising and leads to reasonably good clusters. In addition, the feature based approach achieves comparable or better accuracy than similarity-based approaches.

References

[1] R. Aggrawal and R. Srikant. Mining sequential patterns. In *Proc. of the Int'l Conference on Data Engineering (ICDE)*, Taipei, Taiwan, 1996.

[2] A. Bairoch and B. Boeckmann. The swiss-prot protein sequence data bank. *Nucleic Acids Research*, 19:2247–2249, 1991.

[3] M. O. Dayhoff, R. M. Schwartz, and B. C. Orcutt. A model of evolutionary change in proteins. *Atlas of Protein Sequence and Structure*, 5:345–352, 1978.

[4] R.O. Duda and P.E. Hart. *Pattern Classification and Scene Analysis*. John Wiley & Sons, 1973.

[5] Dan Gusfield. *Algorithms on Strings, Trees, and Sequences*. Press Syndicate of the University of Cambridge, New Your, NY, 1997.

[6] J. Han, J. Pei, B. Mortazavi-Asl, Q. Chen, U. Dayal, and M.C. Hsu. Freespan: Frequent pattern-projected sequential pattern mining. In *Proc. 2000 Intl. Conference on KDD*, 2000.

[7] S. Henikoff and J. G. Henikoff. Amino acid substitution matrices from protein blocks. *Proc. Natl. Academy Science*, 89(10):915–919, 1992.

[8] Mahesh V. Joshi, George Karypis, and Vipin Kumar. Universal formulation of sequential patterns. Technical report, University of Minnesota, Department of Computer Science, Minneapolis, 1999.

[9] L. Kaufman and P.J. Rousseeuw. *Finding Groups in Data: an Introduction to Cluster Analysis*. John Wiley & Sons, 1990.

[10] G. Salton. *Automatic Text Processing: The Transformation, Analysis, and Retrieval of Information by Computer*. Addison-Wesley, 1989.

[11] R. M. Schwartz and M. O. Dayhoff. Matrices for detecting distant relationships. *Atlas of Protein Sequences*, pages 353–358, 1979.

[12] C. E. Shannon. A mathematical theory of communication. *Bell Systems Technical Journal*, 27:379–423, 1948.

[13] R. Srikant and R. Agrawal. Mining sequential patterns: Generalizations and performance improvements. In *Proc. of the Fifth Int'l Conference on Extending Database Technology*, Avignon, France, 1996.

[14] M. Steinbach, G. Karypis, and V. Kumar. A comparison of document clustering techniques. In *KDD Workshop on Text Mining*, 2000.

[15] M.J. Zaki. Efficient enumeration of frequent sequences. In *7th International Conference on Information and Knowledge Management*, 1998.

Clustering Validity Assessment: Finding the optimal partitioning of a data set

Maria Halkidi   Michalis Vazirgiannis
Dept of Informatics,
Athens University of Economics & Business
Email: {mhalk, mvazirg }@aueb.gr

Abstract

Clustering is a mostly unsupervised procedure and the majority of the clustering algorithms depend on certain assumptions in order to define the subgroups present in a data set. As a consequence, in most applications the resulting clustering scheme requires some sort of evaluation as regards its validity.

In this paper we present a clustering validity procedure, which evaluates the results of clustering algorithms on data sets. We define a validity index, S_Dbw, based on well-defined clustering criteria enabling the selection of the optimal input parameters' values for a clustering algorithm that result in the best partitioning of a data set. We evaluate the reliability of our index both theoretically and experimentally, considering three representative clustering algorithms ran on synthetic and real data sets. Also, we carried out an evaluation study to compare S_Dbw performance with other known validity indices. Our approach performed favorably in all cases, even in those that other indices failed to indicate the correct partitions in a data set.

1. Introduction and Motivation

In the literature a wide variety of algorithms have been proposed for different applications and sizes of data sets [14]. The application of an algorithm to a data set aims at, assuming that the data set offers such a tendency (clustering tendency), discovering its real partitions. This implies that i. all the points that naturally belong to the same cluster will eventually be attached to it by the algorithm, ii. no additional data set points (i.e., outliers or points of another cluster) will be attached to the cluster.

In most algorithms' experimental evaluations [1, 6, 10, 11, 12, 17], 2D-data sets are used in order the reader is able to visually verify the validity of the results (i.e., how well the clustering algorithm discovered the clusters of the data set). It is clear that visualization of the data set is a crucial verification of the clustering results. In the case of large multidimensional data sets (e.g. more than three dimensions) effective visualization of data can be difficult. Moreover the perception of clusters using available visualization tools is a difficult task for the humans that are not accustomed to higher dimensional spaces.

The various clustering algorithms behave in a different way depending on i)the features of the data set (geometry and density distribution of clusters), ii) the input parameters values.

Assuming that the data set includes distinct partitions (i.e., inherently supports clustering tendency), the second issue becomes very important. In Figure 1 we can see the way an algorithm (e.g. DBSCAN[6]) partition a data set having different input parameter values. It is clear that only some specific values for the algorithms' input parameters lead to optimal partitioning of the data set. As it is evident, if there is no visual perception of the clusters it is impossible to assess the validity of the partitioning. What is then needed is a visual-aids-free assessment of some objective criterion, indicating the validity of the results of a clustering algorithm application on a potentially high dimensional data set. In this paper we define and evaluate a cluster validity index (S_Dbw). Assuming a data set S, the index enables the selection of optimal input parameter values for a clustering algorithm that best partition S.

The rest of the paper is organized as follows. Section 2 surveys the related work. We motivate and define the validity index in Section 3, while in Section 4 we provide a theoretical and experimental evaluation of S_Dbw using different algorithms and data sets. Furthermore we compare our approach to other validity indices. In Section 5 we conclude by briefly presenting our contributions and indicate directions for further research.

2. Related Work

The fundamental clustering problem is to partition a given data set into groups (clusters), such that the data points in a cluster are more similar to each other than points in different clusters [10]. In the clustering process, there are no predefined classes and no examples that would show what kind of desirable relations should be valid among the data [2]. This is what distinguishes clustering from classification [7, 8].

There is a multitude of clustering methods available in the literature, which can be broadly classified into the following types [11, 14]: i) *Partitional clustering ii)Hierarchical clustering, iii) Density Based clustering, iv) Grid-based clustering.*

For each of these types there exists a wealth of subtypes and different algorithms [1, 11, 12, 13, 14, 17, 19, 22, 24] for finding the clusters. In general terms, the clustering algorithms are based on a criterion for judging the validity of a given partitioning. Moreover, they define a partitioning of a data set based on certain assumptions and *not* the optimal one that fits the data set.

Since clustering algorithms discover clusters, which are not known a priori, the final partition of a data set requires some sort of evaluation in most applications [18]. A

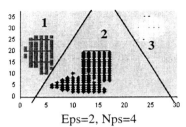 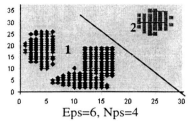

Eps=2, Nps=4   Eps=6, Nps=4

Figure 1: The different partitions resulting from running DBSCAN with different input parameter values.

particularly difficult problem, which is often ignored in clustering algorithms is "how many clusters are there in the data set?".

Previously described requirements for the evaluation of clustering results is well known in the research community and a number of efforts have been made especially in the area of pattern recognition [22]. However, the issue of cluster validity is rather under-addressed in the area of databases and data mining applications, even though recognized as important. In general terms, there are three approaches to investigate cluster validity [22]. The first is based on *external criteria*. This implies that we evaluate the results of a clustering algorithm based on a pre-specified structure, which is imposed on a data set and reflects our intuition about the clustering structure of the data set. The second approach is based on *internal criteria*. We may evaluate the results of a clustering algorithm in terms of quantities that involve the vectors of the data set themselves (e.g., proximity matrix). The third approach of clustering validity is based on *relative criteria*. Here the basic idea is the evaluation of a clustering structure by comparing it with other clustering schemes, resulting by the same algorithm but with different parameter values. A number of validity indices have been defined and proposed in the literature for each of above approaches [22]. A cluster validity index for crisp clustering proposed in [4], attempts to identify "compact and well-separated clusters". Other validity indices for crisp clustering have been proposed in [3] and [16]. The implementation of most of these indices is very computationally expensive, especially when the number of clusters and number of objects in the data set grows very large [25]. In [15], an evaluation study of thirty validity indices proposed in the literature is presented. The results of this study place Caliski and Harabasz(1974), Je(2)/Je(1) (1984), C-index (1976), Gamma and Beale among the six best indices. However, it is noted that although the results concerning these methods are encouraging they are likely to be data dependent. For fuzzy clustering [22], Bezdek proposed the partition coefficient (1974) and the classification entropy (1984). The limitations of these indices are [3]: i) their monotonous dependency on the number of clusters, and ii) the lack of direct connection to the geometry of the data. Other fuzzy validity indices are proposed in [9, 25, 18]. We should mention that the evaluation of proposed indices and the analysis of their reliability are limited.

Another approach for finding the best number of cluster of a data set proposed in [21]. It introduces a practical clustering algorithm based on Monte Carlo cross-validation. This approach differs significantly from the one we propose. While we evaluate clustering schemes based on widely recognized validity criteria of clustering, the evaluation approach proposed in [21] is based on density functions considered for the data set. Thus, it uses concepts related to probabilistic models in order to estimate the number of clusters, better fitting a data set, while we use concepts directly related to the data.

3. Validity index definition

In this research effort we focused on *relative* criteria where the algorithm is running repetitively using different input values and the resulting clusters are compared as for their validity.

The criteria widely accepted for partitioning a data set into a number of clusters are: i. the *separation* of the clusters, and ii. their *compactness*. However, the data set is falsely partitioned in most of the cases, whereas only specific values for the algorithms' input parameters lead to optimal partitioning of the data set. Here the term "optimal" implies parameters that lead to partitions that are as close as possible (in terms of similarity) to the real partitions of the data set.

Therefore our *objective* is the definition of a relative [22] algorithm-independent validity index, for assessing the quality of partitioning for each set of the input values. Such a validity index should be able to select for each algorithm under consideration the optimal set of input parameters with regard to a specific data set.

The criteria (i.e., compactness and separation) on which the proposed index is partially based are the fundamental criteria of clustering. However, the algorithms aim at satisfying these criteria based on initial assumptions (e.g. initial locations of the cluster centers) or input parameter values (e.g. the number of clusters, minimum diameter or number of points in a cluster). For instance the algorithm DBSCAN[6] defines clusters based on density variations, considering values for the cardinality and radius of an object's neighborhood. It finds the best partitions for the given input values but we don't know if the resulting partitions are the optimal or even the ones presented in the underlying data set.

The above motivated us to take in account density variations among clusters. We formalize our clustering validity index, S_Dbw, based on: i. clusters' compactness (in terms of intra-cluster variance), and ii.density between clusters (in terms of inter-cluster density).

Let D={v_i| i=1,...,c} a partitioning of a data set S into c convex clusters where v_i is the center of each cluster as it results from applying a clustering algorithm to S.

Let *stdev* be the average standard deviation of clusters defined as: $stdev = \frac{1}{c}\sqrt{\sum_{i=1}^{c}\|\sigma(v_i)\|}$.

Further the term ‖x‖ is defined as : $\|x\| = (x^T x)^{1/2}$, where x is a vector.

Then the overall inter-cluster density is defined as:

Definition 1. *Inter-cluster Density* (ID) - It evaluates the average density in the region among clusters in relation with the density of the clusters. The goal is the density among clusters to be significant low in comparison with the density in the considered clusters. Then, we can define inter-cluster density as follows:

$$Dens\_bw(c) = \frac{1}{c\cdot(c-1)}\sum_{i=1}^{c}\left(\sum_{\substack{j=1\\j\neq i}}^{c}\frac{density(u_{ij})}{\max\{density(v_i),density(v_j)\}}\right) \quad (1)$$

where v_i, v_j centers of clusters c_i, c_j, respectively and u_{ij} the middle point of the line segment defined by the clusters' centers v_i, v_j . The term density(u) defined in equation(2):

$$density(u) = \sum_{l=1}^{n_{ij}} f(x_l, u), \text{ where } n_{ij} = \text{number of tuples} \quad (2)$$

that belong to the clusters c_i and c_j, *i.e.*, $x_l \in c_i \cup c_j \subseteq S$

represents the number of points in the neighborhood of u. In our work, the neighborhood of a data point, u, is defined to be a hyper-sphere with center u and radius the average standard deviation of the clusters, *stdev*. More specifically, the function *f(x,u)* is defined as:

$$f(x,u) = \begin{cases} 0, & \text{if } d(x,u) > stdev \\ 1, & \text{otherwise} \end{cases} \quad (3)$$

It is obvious that a point belongs to the neighborhood of u if its distance from u is smaller than the average standard deviation of clusters. Here we assume that the data have been scaled to consider all dimensions (bringing them into comparable ranges) as equally important during the process of finding the neighbors of a multidimensional point [2].

Definition 2. *Intra-cluster variance* - Average scattering for clusters. The average scattering for clusters is defined as:

$$Scat(c) = \frac{1}{c}\sum_{i=1}^{c}\|\sigma(v_i)\|\Big/\|\sigma(S)\| \quad (4)$$

The term σ(S) is the variance of a data set; and its p_{th} dimension is defined as follows:

$$\sigma_x^p = \frac{1}{n}\sum_{k=1}^{n}\left(x_k^p - \overline{x}^p\right)^2 \quad (4a)$$

where $\overline{x}^p$ is the p_{th} dimension of

$$\overline{X} = \frac{1}{n}\sum_{k=1}^{n}x_k, \forall x_k \in S \quad (4b)$$

The term σ(v_i) is the variance of cluster c_i and its p_{th} dimension is given by

$$\sigma_{v_i}^p = \sum_{k=1}^{n_i}\left(x_k^p - v_i^p\right)^2\Big/n_i \quad (4c)$$

Then the validity index S_Dbw is defined as:

$$S\_Dbw(c) = Scat(c) + Dens\_bw(c) \quad (5)$$

The definition of S_Dbw indicates that both criteria of "good" clustering (i.e., compactness and separation) are properly combined, enabling reliable evaluation of clustering results. The first term of S_Dbw, *Scat(c)*, indicates the average scattering within c clusters. A small value of this term is an indication of compact clusters. *Dens_bw(c)* indicates the average number of points between the *c* clusters (i.e., an indication of inter-cluster density) in relation with density within clusters. A small *Dens_bw(c)* value indicates well-separated clusters. The number of clusters, *c*, that minimizes the above index can be considered as an optimal value for the number of clusters present in the data set.

4. Validity Index Evaluation

In this section we evaluate the proposed validity index S_Dbw both theoretically (at some points we offer intuitive proof sketches) and experimentally.

4.1 Theoretical Evaluation

Let a data set S containing convex clusters (as in Figure 2a) and various ways to partition it using different clustering algorithms (Figure 2b-e). Assume the optimal partitioning of data set S (as it is appeared in Figure 2a) in three clusters. The number of clusters as it emanates from the case of optimal partitioning is further called "correct number of clusters". We assume that the data set is evenly distributed, i.e., on average similar number of data points are found for each surface unit in the clusters.

Lemma 1: *Assume a data set S with convex clusters and a clustering algorithm A applied repetitively to S, each time with different input parameter values P_i, resulting in different partitions D_i of S. The value of S_Dbw is minimized when the correct number of clusters is found.*

Proof: Let *n* the correct number of clusters of the data set S corresponding to the partitioning D_1 (optimal partitioning of S): $D_1(n, S) = \{c_{D1i}\}$, i=1,...,n and *m* the number of clusters of another partitioning D_2 of the same data set: $D_2(m, S) = \{c_{D2j}\}$, j=1,...,m.

Let S_Dbw_{D1} and S_Dbw_{D2} be the values of the validity index for the respective partitioning schemes. Then, we consider the following cases:

i)   Assume D_2 to be a partitioning where more than the actual clusters are formed (i.e., m>n). Moreover, parts of the actual clusters (corresponding to D_1) are grouped into clusters of D_2 (as in Figure 2d). Let $fC_{D1}=\{fc_{D1p} \mid p=1, ..., nfr1$ $fc_{D1p} \subseteq c_{D1i}$, i=1,...,n\} a set of fractions of clusters in D_1. Similarly, we define $fC_{D2}=\{fc_{D2k} \mid k=1, ..., nfr2, fc_{D2k} \subseteq c_{D2j}$, j=1,..., m\}. Then:
a) $\exists\ c_{D2j}$: $c_{D2i} = \cup fc_{D1p}$, where $p=p_1,....,p_n$, $p_1 \geq 1$ and $p_n \leq nfr1$, nfr1 is the number of considered fractions of clusters in D_1, and b) $\exists\ c_{D1i}$: $c_{D1i} = \cup fc_{D2k}$, where $k=k_1,...., k_n$, $k_1 \geq 1$ and $k_n \leq nfr2$, where nfr2 is the number of considered fractions of clusters in D_2,

In this case, some of the clusters in D_2 include regions of low density (for instance cluster 3 in Figure 2d). Thus, the value of the first term of the index related to intra-cluster variance of D_2 increases as compared to the intra-cluster variance of D_1 (i.e., Scat(m) >Scat(n)). On the other hand,

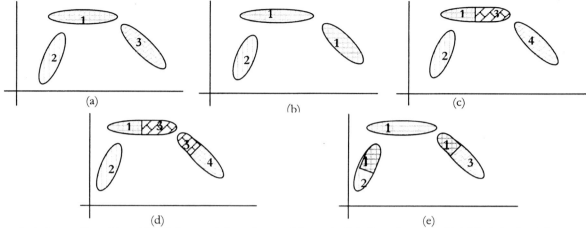

Figure 2: A data set S partitioned in (a) the actual three clusters, (b) two, (c,d) in four clusters and (e) falsely in three clusters

the second term (inter-cluster density) is also increasing as compared to the corresponding term of index for D_1 (i.e., Dens_bw(m)>Dens_bw(n)). This is because some of the clusters in D_1 are split and therefore there are border areas between clusters that are of high density (e.g., clusters 1 and 3 in Figure 3d). Then, since both S_Dbw terms regarding D_2 partitioning increase we conclude that $S\_Dbw_{D1} < S\_Dbw_{D2}$.

ii) Let D_2 be a partitioning where more clusters than in D_1 are formed (i.e., m>n). Also, we assume that at least one of the clusters in D_1 is split to more than one in D_2 while no parts of D_1 clusters are grouped into D_2 clusters (as in Figure 2c), i.e., $\exists c_{D1i} : c_{D1i} = \cup c_{D2j}$, j=k$_1$,..., k and k$_1$>=1, k<=m. In this case, the value of the first term of the index related to intra-cluster variance slightly decreases compared to the corresponding term of D_1 since the clusters in D_2 are more compact. As a consequence Scat(m)<=Scat(n). On the other hand, the second term (inter-cluster density) is increasing as some of the clusters in D_1 are split and therefore there are borders between clusters that are of high density (for instance clusters 1 and 3 in Figure 2c). Then Dens(m)>>Dens(n). Based on the above discussion and taking in account that the increase of inter-cluster density is significantly higher than the decrease of intra-cluster variance we may conclude that $S\_Dbw_{D1} < S\_Dbw_{D2}$.

iii)　　Let D_2 be a partitioning with less clusters than in D_1 (m<n) and two or more of the clusters in D_1 are grouped to a cluster in D_2 (as in Figure 2b.). Then, $\exists c_{D2j}$: $c_{D2j}=\cup c_{D1i}$, where i=p$_1$, ..., p and p$_1$>=1, p<=n. In this case, the value of the first term of the index related to intra-cluster variance increases as compared to the value of corresponding term of D_1 since the clusters in D_2 contain regions of low density. As a consequence, Scat(m)>>Scat(n). On the other hand, the second term of the index (inter-cluster density) is slightly decreasing or remains vaguely the same as compared to the corresponding term of D_1 (i.e., Dens_bw(n)≅Dens_bw(m)). This is because similarly to the case of the D_1 partitioning (Figure 3a) there are no borders between clusters in D_2 that are of high density. Then, based on the above discussion and considering that the increase of intra-cluster variance is significantly

higher than the decrease of inter-cluster density, we may conclude that $S\_Dbw_{D1} < S\_Dbw_{D2}$.

Lemma 2: *Assume a data set S containing convex clusters and a clustering algorithm A applied repetitively to S, each time with different parameter values P_i, resulting in different partitions D_i of S. For each D_i it is true that the correct number of clusters is found. The value S_Dbw is minimized when the optimal partitions are found for the correct number of clusters.*

Proof:. We consider D_2 to be a partitioning with the same number of clusters as the optimal one D_1 (Figure 3a), (i.e., m=n). Furthermore, we assume that one or more of the actual clusters corresponding to D_1 are split and their parts are grouped into different clusters in D_2 (as in Figure 2e). That is, if $fC_{D1} = \{fc_{D1p} | p=1, ..., nfr1$ $fc_{D1p} \subseteq c_{D1i}, i=1,...,n\}$ a set of clusters fractions in D_1 then $\exists c_{D2j}$: $c_{D2j} = \cup fc_{D1i}$, i=p$_1$, ..., p and p$_1$>=1, p<=n. In this case, the clusters in D_2 contain regions of low density and as a consequence the value of the first term of the index, intra-cluster variance, increases as compared to the corresponding term of D_1, i.e., Scat(m)>Scat(n). On the other hand, some of the clusters in D_2 are split and therefore there are border areas between clusters that are of high density (for instance clusters 1, 3 and 1, 2 in Figure 2e). Therefore, the second term (inter-cluster density) of D_2 is also increasing as compared to the one of D_1, i.e., Dens_bw(m)>Dens_bw(n). Based on the above discussion it is obvious that $S\_Dbw_{D1} < S\_Dbw_{D2}$.

4.2 Time Complexity

The complexity of the validity index S_Dbw, is based on the complexity of its two terms as defined in (1) and (4). Assuming d the number of attributes (data set dimension), c is the number of clusters; n is the number of database tuples. Then the intra-cluster variance complexity is O(ndc) while the complexity of inter-cluster density is O(ndc^2). Then S_Dbw complexity is O(ndc^2). Usually, c, $d << n$, therefore the complexity of our index for a specific clustering scheme is O(n). The graphs in Figure 3 show the results of an experimental study referring to the execution time of our approach. The considered datasets for these experiments are synthetically generated

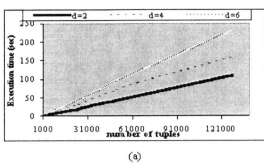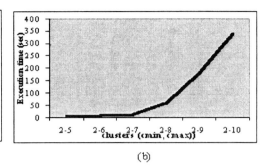

(a)   (b)

Figure 3: Execution time in seconds as function of (a) the number of points (b) the number of clusters

according to the normal distribution. Figure 3a demonstrates that the execution time is almost linear to the number of points as expected from the preceding complexity study. Furthermore, Figure 3b shows the execution time as function of the number of clusters. The execution time, as expected, is nearly quadratic with respect to the number of clusters but as c is usually a small integer, it creates no problem.

4.3 Experimental evaluation

In this section S_Dbw is experimentally tested using representative clustering algorithms of different categories: partitional, hierarchical and density-based.

We experiment with real and synthetic multidimensional data sets containing different number of clusters. In all cases our approach performs favorably selecting the best partitioning among these proposed by an algorithm. Additionally we compare S_Dbw to other validity indices found in the literature. In the sequel, due to lack of space, we present only some representative examples of our experimental study.

4.3.1. Selection of the optimal partitioning defined by a clustering algorithm. The goal of this experiment is to evaluate our index with regards to the selection of the optimal clustering scheme by a specific clustering

algorithm. More specifically, we consider a 2-dimensional data set consisting of four clusters (see Figure 4a). We define a number of different clustering schemes of our data set using the K-means algorithm, with its input parameters (number of clusters) ranging between 2 and 8. The behavior of S_Dbw is depicted in Figure 5. It is clear that the correct number of clusters is proposed (i.e., four), as at this value the index reaches its minimum.

Similarly, we assume the clustering schemes of DataSet3 (see Figure 4c) as defined by CURE when the number of clusters ranges between 2 and 8. Then, we evaluated the defined clustering schemes based on the S_Dbw index so as to find which of them best fits the underlying data. As Figure 6 shows the clustering scheme of seven clusters is proposed as the best partitioning of DataSet3.

A multidimensional data set. In the sequel, we demonstrate that our index works properly in multidimensional data sets. The validity of clustering results (i.e., that the set has been optimally partitioned) can be visually verified only in 2D or 3D cases. In higher dimensions it is difficult to verify the resulting clusters. The proposed index, S_Dbw, offers a solution to this problem giving an indication of the best clustering scheme without visualization of the data set. We consider a synthetic six-dimensional data set, containing two distinct clusters. This is also verified by S_Dbw. As Figure 7

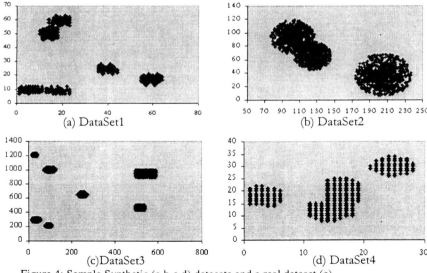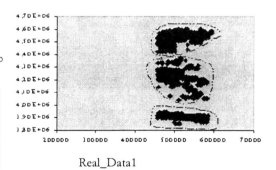

Figure 4: Sample Synthetic (a,b,c,d) datasets and a real dataset (e).

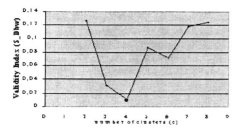

Figure 5:S_Dbw as a function of number of clusters for DataSet1.

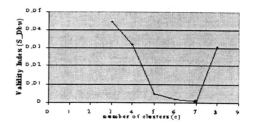

Figure 6: S_Dbw as a function of number of clusters for DataSet3.

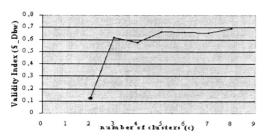

Figure 7:S_Dbw as a function of the number of clusters for a six-dimensional data set consisting of two clusters.

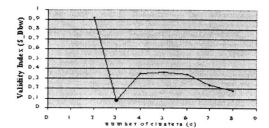

Figure 8: S_Dbw as a function of number of clusters for real data representing a part of Greek road network.

depicts, S_Dbw finds the correct number of clusters as it takes its minimum value when c=2.

Real data sets. Clustering spatial databases is an important problem and many applications require the management of spatial data. Therefore evaluate our approach using representative real spatial data sets [26]. One of the data sets, we studied, contains three parts of Greek roads network (Figure 4e). The roads are represented by their MBR approximations' vertices. The behavior of S_Dbw regarding the different clustering schemes (i.e., number of clusters) defined by K-means is depicted in Figure 8. It is clear that S_Dbw indicates the correct number of clusters (three) as the best partitioning for the data set.

4.3.2. The index is independent of clustering algorithm.
As mentioned in previous sections, different input values for clustering algorithms applied to a dataset result in different partitioning schemes. In the following we show that S_Dbw selects the optimal partitioning among those defined by a clustering algorithm independently of the algorithm used. We use three well-known algorithms, one from each of the popular algorithm categories: K-means (partitional), DBSCAN (density based) and CURE (hierarchical).
Table 1a and Table 1b present S_Dbw values for the resulting clustering schemes for DataSet1, and Real_Data1 (see Figure4a and Figure4e respectively) found by K-means, DBSCAN and CURE respectively. More specifically, we consider the clustering schemes revealed by the algorithms mentioned above while their input parameter values are depicted in Table 1. In the case of DataSet1, all three algorithms propose four clusters as the optimal clustering schemes (see Table 1a). Similarly, considering any of the three algorithms, the proposed validity index selects three clusters as the best partitioning for Real_Data1 (see Table1b).
In some cases, however, an algorithm may partition a data set into the correct number of clusters but in a wrong way. For instance, Figure 9(a) and (b) present the partitioning of

Dataset5 into three clusters by K-means and CURE respectively. Though the correct number of clusters is three (3), both algorithms partition it falsely. On the other hand, DBSCAN finds the correct three partitions of the data set (Figure 9(c)). Table 1c presents the behavior of S_Dbw in each of the above cases. If we consider the K-means clustering results, the index proposes four clusters as the best partitioning for our data set. Given the inability of K-means to handle skewed geometries, this result somehow makes sense. The results from running CURE can be interpreted in a similar way. In the case of DBSCAN the index finds the correct number of clusters that is three. The result is that S_Dbw selects the best partitioning among those proposed by different algorithms.

4.3.3. Comparison to other validity indices.
We consider the known validity indices proposed in the literature, such as RS-RMSSTD[20], DB[22] and the recent one SD[23]. RMSSTD and RS have to be taken into account simultaneously in order to find the correct number of clusters. The optimal values of the number of clusters are those for which a significant local change in values of RS and RMSSTD occurs. As regards DB, an indication of the optimal clustering scheme is the point at which it takes its minimum value. We carried an evaluation study comparing S_Dbw to the indices mentioned above. We used four synthetic two-dimensional data sets further referred to as DataSet1, DataSet2, DataSet3 and DataSet4 (see Figure 4a-d) and the real data set Real_Data1 (Figure 4e), which contains three clusters.
Table 2 summarizes the results of the validity indices (RS, RMSSDT, DB, SD and S_Dbw), for different clustering schemes of the above-mentioned data sets as resulting from a clustering algorithm. For our study, we use the results of the algorithms K-Means and CURE with their input value (number of clusters), ranging between 2 and 8. Indices RS, RMSSTD propose the partitioning of

192

Table 1: Optimal partitioning found by S_Dbw for each algorithm

No clusters	K-means		DBSCAN		CURE r=10, a=0.3)		
	Input	S_Dbw Value	Input	S_Dbw Value	Input	S_Dbw Value	
6	C=6	0.0712	Eps=2, MinC=8	0.087	C=6	0.082	(a) DataSet1
5	C=5	0.0866	Eps=2, MinC=4	0.0865	C=5	0.091	
4	**C=4**	**0.0104**	**Eps=10, MinC=15**	**0.0104**	**C=4**	**0.0104**	
3	C=3	0.0312	Eps=15, MinC=15	0.0312	C=3	0.031	
2	C=2	0.1262	Eps=20, MinC=15	0.1262	C=2	0.126	

No clusters	K-means		DBSCAN		CURE (r=10, a=0.3)		
	Input	S_Dbw Value	Input	S_Dbw Value	Input	S_Dbw Value	
6	C=6	0.3434	-	-	C=6	0.3434	(b) Real_Data1
5	C=5	0.367	-	-	C=5	0.3670	
4	C=4	0.35	Eps=20000, MinC =10	0.1925	C=4	0.3501	
3	**C=3**	**0.083**	**Eps=30000, MinC=10**	**0.084**	**C=3**	**0.0831**	
2	C=2	0.9189	Eps=50000, MinC=10	0.891	C=2	0.9188	

No clusters	K-Means		DBSCAN		CURE (r=10, a=0.3)		
	Input	S_Dbw Value	Input	S_Dbw Value	Input	S_Dbw Value	
6	C=6	0.1585	-	-	C=6	0.1767	(c) DataSet5
5	C=5	0.1354	–	–	C=5	0.1648	
4	**C=4**	**0.0329**	–		**C=4**	**0.0446**	
3	C=3	0.1094	Eps=2,MinC=4	0.0404	C=3	0.0597	
2	C=2	0.4374	Eps=5,MinC=4	1.7228	C=2	0.4096	

DataSet1 into three clusters while DB selects six clusters as the best partitioning. On the other hand, SD and S_Dbw select four clusters as the best partitioning for DataSet1, which is also the correct number of clusters fitting the underlying data. Moreover, the indices S_Dbw and DB select the correct number of clusters (i.e., seven) as the optimal partitioning for DataSet3 while RS, RMSSTD and SD select the clustering scheme of five and six clusters respectively. Also, all indices propose three clusters as the best partitioning for Real_Data1. In the case of DataSet2, DB and SD select three clusters as the optimal scheme, while RS-RMSSDT and S_Dbw select two clusters (i.e., the correct number of clusters fitting the data set).

Here, we have to mention that S_Dbw *is not a clustering algorithm itself* but a measure to evaluate the results of clustering algorithms and gives an indication of a partitioning that best fits a data set. The essence of clustering is not a totally resolved issue and depending on the application domain we may consider different aspects

as more significant. For instance, for a specific application it may be important to have well separated clusters while for another to consider more the compactness of the clusters. In this case, the relative importance of the two terms on which the S_Dbw definition is based can be adjusted. Having an indication of a good partitioning as proposed by the index, the domain experts may analyze further the validation procedure results. Thus, they could select some of the partitioning schemes proposed by S_Dbw, and select the one better fitting their demands for crisp or overlapping clusters. For instance DataSet2 can be considered as having three clusters with two of them slightly overlapping or having two well-separated clusters. In this case we observe that S_Dbw values for two and three clusters are not significantly different (0,12, 0,22 respectively). This is an indication that we may select either of the two partitioning schemes depending on the clustering interpretation. Then, we compare the values of *Scat* and *Dens_bw* terms for the cases of two and three clusters. We observe that the two clusters scheme

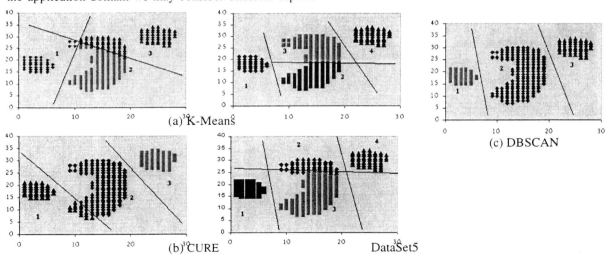

Figure 9: A 2D data set partitioned into (a) three and four clusters using K-Means, (b) three and four clusters using CURE and (c) three clusters using DBSCAN.

Table 2: Optimal number of clusters proposed by validity indices compared with S_Dbw

	DataSet1	DataSet2	DataSet3	DataSet4	RealData1
	Optimal number of clusters				
RS, RMSSTD	3	2	5	4	3
DB	6	3	7	4	3
SD	4	3	6	3	3
S_Dbw	4	2	7	3	3

corresponds to well-separated clusters (Dens_bw(2)= 0.09762<Dens_bw(3)=0.2154) while the three-clusters scheme contains more compact clusters (Scat(2)= 0.0215>Scat(3)= 0.0109).

Moreover, S_Dbw finds the correct number of clusters (three) for DataSet4, on the contrary to RS – RMSSTD and DB indices, which propose four clusters as the best partitioning. In all cases S_Dbw finds the correct number of clusters fitting a data set, while other validity indices fail in some cases.

5. Conclusions and Further Work

In this paper we addressed the important issue of assessing the validity of clustering algorithms' results. We have defined a new validity index (S_Dbw) for assessing the results of clustering algorithms. The index is optimized for data sets that include compact and well-separated clusters. The compactness of the data set is measured by the cluster variance whereas the separation by the density between clusters.

We have proved S_Dbw reliability and value i. theoretically, by illustrating the intuition behind it and ii.experimentally, using various data sets of non-standard (but in general non-convex) geometries covering also the multidimensional case. The index results, as indicated by experiments, are not dependent on the clustering algorithm used, and always indicate the optimal input parameters for the algorithm used in each case. It performs better than the most recent validity indices proposed in the literature as it was indicated by experimental evaluation.

Further work. As we mentioned earlier the validity assessment index we proposed in this paper does not work properly in the case of clusters of non-convex (i.e., rings) or extraordinarily curved geometry. We are going to work on this issue as the density and its continuity is not any more sufficient criteria. We plan to use sets of representative points, or even multidimensional curves rather than a single center point.

Acknowledgements

This work was supported by the General Secretariat for Research and Technology through the PENED ("99EΔ 85") project. We would like to thank Y. Batistakis for his help in the experimental study. We are also thankful to C. Rodopoulos and C. Amanatidis for the implementation of CURE algorithm as well as to Drs Joerg Sander and Eui-Hong (Sam) Han for providing information and the source code for DBSCAN and CURE algorithms respectively.

References

[1] Rakesh Agrawal, Johannes Gehrke, Dimitrios Gunopulos, Prabhakar Raghavan,"Automatic Subspace Clustering of High Dimensional Data for Data Mining Applications", *Proceedings of SIGMOD*, 1998.

[2] Michael J. A. Berry, Gordon Linoff. Data Mining Techniques For marketing, Sales and Customer Support. John Willey & Sons, Inc, 1996.

[3] Rajesh N. Dave. "Validating fuzzy partitions obtained through c-shells clustering", *Pattern Recognition Letters*, Vol .17, pp613-623, 1996

[4] J. C. Dunn. "Well separated clusters and optimal fuzzy partitions", *J. Cybern.* Vol.4, pp. 95-104, 1974

[5] Martin Ester, Hans-Peter Kriegel, Jorg Sander, Michael Wimmer, Xiaowei Xu. "Incremental Clustering for Mining in a Data Warehousing Environment", *Proceedings of 24th VLDB Conference*, New York, USA, 1998.

[6] Martin Ester, Hans-Peter Kriegel, Jorg Sander, Xiaowei Xu. "A Density-Based Algorithm for Discovering Clusters in Large Spatial Databases with Noise", *Proceedings of 2nd Int. Conf. On Knowledge Discovery and Data Mining*, Portland, OR, pp. 226-231, 1996.

[7] Usama M. Fayyad, Gregory Piatesky-Shapiro, Padhraic Smuth and Ramasamy Uthurusamy. *Advances in Knowledge Discovery and Data Mining*. AAAI Press 1996

[8] Usama Fayyad, Ramasamy Uthurusamy. "Data Mining and Knowledge Discovery in Databases", *Communications of the ACM*. Vol.39, No11, November 1996.

[9] I. Gath, B. Geva. "Unsupervised Optimal Fuzzy Clustering". *IEEE Transactions on Pattern Analysis and Machine Intelligence*, Vol 11, No7, July 1989.

[10] Sudipto Guha, Rajeev Rastogi, Kyueseok Shim. "CURE: An Efficient Clustering Algorithm for Large Databases", *Published in the Proceedings of the ACM SIGMOD Conference*, 1998.

[11] Sudipto Guha, Rajeev Rastogi, Kyueseok Shim. "ROCK: A Robust Clustering Algorithm for Categorical Attributes", *Published in the Proceedings of the IEEE Conference on Data Engineering*, 1999.

[12] Alexander Hinneburg, Daniel Keim. "An Efficient Approach to Clustering in Large Multimedia Databases with Noise". *Proceeding of KDD '98*, 1998.

[13] Zhexue Huang. "A Fast Clustering Algorithm to Cluster very Large Categorical Data Sets in Data Mining", *DMKD*, 1997

[14] A.K. Jain, M.N. Murty, P.J. Flyn. "Data Clustering: A Review", *ACM Computing Surveys*, Vol. 31, No3, September 1999.

[15] Milligan, G.W. and Cooper, M.C. (1985), "An Examination of Procedures for Determining the Number of Clusters in a Data Set", *Psychometrika*, 50, 159-179.

[16] Milligan G. W., Soon S.C., Sokol L. M. "The effect of cluster size. dimensionality and the number of clusters on recovery of true cluster structure". *IEEE Transactions on Pattern Analysis and Machine Intelligence*, Vol. 5, pp. 40-47, 1983

[17] Raymond Ng, Jiawei Han. "Efficient and Effective Clustering Methods for Spatial Data Mining". *Proceeding of the 20th VLDB Conference*, Santiago, Chile, 1994.

[18] Ramze Rezaee, B.P.F. Lelieveldt, J.H.C Reiber. "A new cluster validity index for the fuzzy c-mean", *Pattern Recognition Letters*, 19, pp237-246, 1998.

[19] C. Sheikholeslami, S. Chatterjee, A. Zhang. "WaveCluster: A MultiResolution Clustering Approach for Very Large Spatial Database". *Proceedings of 24th VLDB Conference, New York, USA*, 1998.

[20] Sharma S.C. *Applied Multivariate Techniques*. John Willwy & Sons, 1996.

[21] Padhraic Smyth. "Clustering using Monte Carlo Cross-Validation". *KDD 1996*, 126-133.

[22] S. Theodoridis, K. Koutroubas. *Pattern recognition*, Academic Press, 1999

[23] M. Halkidi, M. Vazirgiannis, Y. Batistakis. "Quality scheme assessment in the clustering process", *In Proceedings of PKDD*, Lyon, France, 2000.

[24] Tian Zhang, Raghu Ramakrishnman, Miron Linvy. "BIRCH: An Efficient Method for Very Large Databases", *ACM SIGMOD' 96*, Montreal, Canada, 1996.

[25] Xunali Lisa Xie, Genardo Beni. "A Validity measure for Fuzzy Clustering", *IEEE Transactions on Pattern Analysis and machine Intelligence*, Vol13, No4, August 1991.

[26] Spatial Datasets: an "unofficial" collection. http://dias.cti.gr/~ytheod/research/datasets/spatial.html

Automatic Topic Identification Using Webpage Clustering

Xiaofeng He[a,b], Chris H.Q. Ding[b], Hongyuan Zha[a], Horst D. Simon[b]

[a] Department of Computer Science and Engineering
The Pennsylvania State University, University Park, PA 16802

[b] NERSC Division, Lawrence Berkeley National Laboratory
University of California, Berkeley, CA 94720, USA
{xhe,zha}@cse.psu.edu, {chqding,hdsimon}@lbl.gov

Abstract

Grouping webpages into distinct topics is one way to organize the large amount of retrieved information on the web. In this paper, we report that based on similarity metric which incorporates textual information, hyperlink structure and co-citation relations, an unsupervised clustering method can automatically and effectively identify relevant topics, as shown in experiments on several retrieved sets of webpages. The clustering method is a state-of-art spectral graph partitioning method based on normalized cut criterion first developed for image segmentation.

1. Introduction

With the exponential growth of information on the World Wide Web, there is great demand for developing efficient and effective methods for organizing and retrieving the information available. Document clustering plays an important role in information retrieval and taxonomy management for the Web and remains an interesting and challenging problem.

A particular issue is how to effectively organize large amount of returned webpages for a user query on a search engine, according to their relevance. Since typical queries have only 1-3 words, ranking those webpages according to textual similarity between query words and webpage text content does not perform well.

Ranking webpages using the information contained in the hyperlinks between webpages currently is an active research area. Two popular ranking methods are PageRank of Brin and Page[2], and the HITS algorithm of Kleinberg [11, 9, 1].

In this paper we consider grouping returned webpages of a query into different topics which are automatically generated by the clustering methods exploring textual infor-mation, hyperlink structure and co-citation relations. For each topic or cluster, we rank the webpages according to the HITS algorithm and list those authoritative webpages only. The experimental results on several cases show that this is an effective way to represent the large number of webpages for a user query.

Document clustering has been studied by many people (see [18] and references there). Clustering retrieval results have been examined by Hearst and Paderson[10] based on textual information only, with emphasis on summarization. More recently this approach is taken in Grouper web interface[19]. Exploring web link structures in the information retrieval context to identify topical themes is examined by Larson[13], Pirolli, et al.[15]. Most recently, Text information is used together with the HITS algorithm by Chakrabarti et al.[4], in *topic distillation* by Bharat and Henzinger[1], and as the attribute vectors for clustering by Modha and Spengler[14].

The new thrust in our approach is (1) to comprehensively incorporate information from text, link structure and co-citation, (2) combine them in a new way, i.e., as weight matrix for graph partitioning. In our webpage clustering, the link structure is the dominant factor, and the textual similarity is used to modulate the strength of each hyperlink. The clustering problem is, in essence, partitioning a graph into connected subgraphs. The nodes of the graph are webpages and the edges of the graph are the hyperlinks between webpages. To further enhance the link structure, co-citation is also incorporated.

In this work, we use a new clustering method based on spectral graph partition. This method has been successfully used in image segmentation by Shi and Malik[17] who use the *normalized cut* as criterion to measure the goodness of the partitioning. This criterion lands itself immediately to the Rayleigh quotient which can be easily solved. The method recursively partition a graph into two subgraphs until a stopping condition is met.

It is important to note that our goal is "topic identification and extraction from a webpage collection". Exactly how many clusters or topics is not important as long as all main or significant topics are identified and extracted. The stopping condition is a measure of intra-cluster similarity vs inter-cluster dis-similarity, which essentially measures the significance of a cluster. Thus our recursive clustering method fits the goal well.

We gather three retrieved datasets, each corresponding to a one-word query: *amazon, star* and *apple* submitted to a search engine. Using a similarity metric that incorporates textual information, link structure and co-citation, we cluster each dataset using the normalized cut method. The results show that our method effectively distinguishes different topics mixed together in a dataset. This automatic topic clustering is rather difficult to achieve if we use text information only.

It is important to note that the goal of clustering webpages is to effectively *organize* the retrieved information. This is different from *topic distillation*[1] which attempts to find the most *relevant* webpages for a query. Given the large number of retrieved webpages and mixing of different topics therein, it is rather difficult to clearly define which webpage is most *relevant*. By grouping the webpages into different topics and listing the authoritative webpages in each topic, we let users determine which webpages are relevant. Very often, a user finds a webpage or a topic he/she had not anticipated, or may not be relevant in a strict sense; but the topic is related and interesting that the user will pursue further. This kind of *better-than-expected* webpages or topics could be missed in topic distillation process; however, they are enhanced in our approach as separate clusters, as the experimental results show.

2. Similarity metric

Clustering objects into groups is usually based on a similarity metric between objects, with the goal that objects within the same group are very similar, and objects between different groups are less similar. In clustering of a graph, similarity between nodes is represented as the weight of an edge.

In webpage clustering problem, we incorporate link structure, text information, and co-citation information into the similarity metric, which form the weight matrix W.

2.1 Hyperlink structure

The link information is obtained directly from the link graph. Given a link graph $G = (V, E)$, which is directed, we define the adjacency matrix A of the graph to be:

$$A_{ij} = \begin{cases} 1 & \text{if } e_{ij} \in E \quad \text{or} \quad e_{ji} \in E \\ 0 & \text{otherwise} \end{cases}$$

Link structure alone provides us with rich information on the topic. By exploring the link structure, we are able to extract useful information from the web[9, 5, 1, 8, 12]. One of the most popular algorithms to retrieve information from the link structure is Kleinberg's HITS algorithm[11], which will be briefly introduced later.

2.2 Textual information

The textual information is included to better cluster the webpages. Moreover, unlike printed literature, web text references each other more randomly. This is another reason that the text information is incorporated. One approach that textual information has been incorporated is to measure the similarity between user query and the anchor text (text between ⟨A HREF=...⟩ and ⟨/A⟩) as in [5, 1]. We experimented with this approach and found it did not work as effective in our datasets.

Here we use a new approach that (a) utilizes the entire text of a webpage, not just the anchored words; (b) measures the textual similarity S_{ij} between two webpages i, j, instead of between user query and the webpage; (c) uses S_{ij} as the strength of the hyperlink between webpages i, j. The key observation here is that if two webpages have very little text similarity, it is unlikely that they belong to the same topic, even though they are connected by a hyperlink. Therefore S_{ij} properly gauges the extent or the importance of an individual hyperlink.

We call each webpage a document. The content of a document is obtained using a web crawler written in *Perl*. To accommodate the vast differences in webpage lengths, we only use the first 500 words of each document. The rest of the document is discarded if it has more than 500 words.

After the text of all webpages are preprocessed, we represent each webpage by a vector in the vector space model of IR. For each element of the vector we use the standard tf.idf weighting: $tf(i, j) * idf(i)$. $tf(i, j)$ is the term frequency of word i in document j, representing the number of occurrence of word i in document j. $idf(i)$ is the Inverse Document Frequency for word i, computed as

$$idf(i) = log(\frac{\text{no. of total docs}}{\text{no. of docs containing word } i})$$

We compute the *similarity* (or *relevance*) between two webpages using the standard cosine similarity measure. If x and y are vectors of two documents j_1 and j_2, the similarity between j_1 and j_2 is:

$$S(j_1, j_2) = \frac{\sum_i x(i) * y(i)}{\|x\|_2 * \|y\|_2}$$

Note that this simple textual similarity is the starting point of our approach. More sophisticated forms of textual similarity can be used. For example, one may weight more on the words in webpage titles.

2.3 Co-citation

Co-citation is another metric to measure the relevance of two webpages. If there are many pages pointing to both of them, then these two pages are likely to address the similar issue. The co-citation $C(i,j)$ of pages i and j is the number of webpages pointing to both i and j. The co-citation matrix C is easily obtained from the link graph.

The overall similarity between two webpages is the combination of above three factors. In matrix form, it can be written as

$$W = \alpha \frac{A \otimes S}{\|A \otimes S\|_2} + (1 - \alpha) \frac{C}{\|C\|_2} \qquad (1)$$

where $(A \otimes S)_{ij} = A_{ij} S_{ij}$. W can also be viewed as the weight matrix of an *undirected* graph. Here α is a parameter and has value between 0 and 1. In all our experiments, we set α to be 0.5. Once W is computed, the problem of clustering webpages becomes the problem of graph partitioning using the weights given in W as the similarities between the nodes. Note that diagonal elements of W are all zeros.

3 Clustering algorithm

We solve the web graph partitioning problem by a spectral graph partitioning method which uses the Fiedler vector of the affinity matrix to separate two clusters, measured by the normalized cut criterion. We also used the K-means clustering method and found the results of spectral partitioning is usually much better.

3.1 Spectral graph partition using normalized cut

Normalized cut is an unbiased measure of partitioning the graph G into two subgraphs A, B. Shi and Malik [17] first use the normalized cut in image segmentation, taking the affinity matrix of an image as the weight matrix of an undirected graph. Using the similarity metric between webpages as the weight matrix on the web graph, the webpage clustering problem can use the same graph partitioning method as in the image segmentation problem.

Define the objective function for the normalized cut as:

$$J(A,B) = \frac{\text{cut}(A,B)}{\sum_{i \in A} d_i} + \frac{\text{cut}(A,B)}{\sum_{j \in B} d_j} \qquad (2)$$

where the weighted cutsize is defined as

$$\text{cut}(A,B) = \sum_{i \in A, j \in B} W(i,j),$$

and d_i is the degree of node i: $d_i = \sum_k W(i,k)$. The clustering problem is to find the partition of G that minimizes $J(A,B)$.

Let y be an indicator vector that determines the partition: each element y_i is an indicator variable for a node i,

$$y_i = \left\{ \begin{array}{ll} 1 & \text{if } i \in A \\ -b & \text{if } i \in B \end{array} \right.$$

Let $D = \text{Diag}(d_1, d_2, \cdots, d_n)$ be a diagonal matrix. The objective function (2) becomes

$$J(y) = \frac{y^T (D - W) y}{y^T D y} \qquad (3)$$

subject to the constraint

$$y^T D e = 0 \qquad (4)$$

where $e = (1, 1, \cdots, 1)^T$. Although solving this optimization problem for discrete variables y_i is rather difficult, one can *relax* y_i to continuous variables within $[-1, 1]$ and find the optimal solution.

Expression (3) is the Rayleigh quotient. It can be minimized by solving the generalized eigensystem:

$$(D - W)y = \lambda D y$$

One easily see that $y = e$ is the eigenvector corresponding to the smallest eigenvalue $\lambda_1 = 0$. Thus the eigenvector f corresponding to the second smallest eigenvalue is the solution to the minimization problem, since it automatically satisfies the constraint (4). f is usually called the *Fiedler vector* in recognition of M. Fiedler's work[6, 7].

Here we show the result on a simple example. Figure 1(a) shows the adjacency matrix randomly generated to denote an undirected graph with two main subgraphs, where the links between the subgraphs are very sparse (low density) and links within each subgraph are dense (highly connected). Figure 1(b) shows the Fiedler vector for partitioning the graph. In this example, each element of f is close to one of two discrete values (0.02 and -0.09), corresponding to $c(1, -b)$ where c is the normalization constant. The splitting point $f_s = 0$ clearly separates the graph into two distinct parts. An important property of the Fiedler vector is that if the original graph is simply connected and $f_i \neq 0$ for all i's, each subgraph is guaranteed to be simply connected. Without this property, the splitting of nodes could lead to disconnected subgraphs.

For general problems, f_i are continuous and there is no clear gap between two clear discrete values. We sort f_i and pickup a splitting point so that all nodes above it belong to one subgraph and all nodes below belong to the other subgraph. The cut point is chosen so that the objective function $J(y)$ is minimized. This can be done by checking N equally spaced splitting points, and then find the point with the smallest $J(f)$.

It is instructive to examine the objective function $J(A, B)$. If we minimize $\text{cut}(A, B)$ without restrictions

197

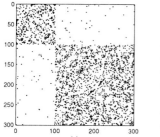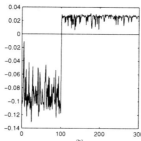

Figure 1. (a) The adjacency matrix of a random graph. The first and second diagonal blocks correspond to two subgraphs. They have high connectivity. Off-diagonal blocks represent sparse edges between the subgraphs. (b) Plot of the Fiedler vector.

on the sizes of two subgraphs, the optimal solution is often a very skew one, with one very small subgraph cut away from the original graph. If we minimize cut(A, B) requiring that the two subgraphs have the same number of nodes: $|A| = |B|$, this reduces to graph partitioning using spectral bisection[16]. In this case, the indicator variables have discrete values $y_i = \{-1, 1\}$ and the objective function becomes $J(y) = y^T(D - W)y/y^Ty$. The solution is the second smallest eigenvector of $(D - W)y = \lambda y$. The general situation is more interesting when the two subgraghs have different numbers of nodes (like our clustering problems). The objective function Eq.(2) allows the number of nodes to be determined as part of the solution, therefore is most appropriate for clustering.

3.2 Hierarchical divisive clustering

Once a webgraph is partitioned into two subgraphs, we can partition each of the subgraph using the same method. This recursive partitioning process is repeated until a stopping criterion is met. The value of the objective function in the normalized cut proves a natural stopping criterion. For a graph to be partitioned, we compute the Fiedler vector f, find the optimal cut, and obtain $\min J(f)$ value. If $\min J(f)$ value is above certain threshold J_{stop}, it means the cutsize between two partitions is relatively large, and the resulting two subgraphs would have relatively high connectivity between them, hence it is better not to partition the graph further and the recursive process stops. The threshold J_{stop} is set to 0.06 in all our experiments.

Note that in this method, exactly how many clusters or topics will results is not known *a priori*. This feature fits our goal of "topic identification and extraction" very well. We are only interested in extract main or significant topics.

In Web environment, documents (webpages) are created for many different reasons, and quality control is near zero. It is very likely that there are many webpages in a web collection that do not belong to any clear topics. Setting a K before hand and forcing all webpages into these K clusters will produce clusters of low quality.

The complete recursive clustering algorithm is:

1. $d = We$, where $e = (1, 1, \cdots, 1)^T$. $D = \text{Diag}(d)$.

2. Solve generalized eigensystem $(D - W)y = \lambda Dy$ for the second smallest eigenvector f.

3. Check N equally spaced splitting points of f, find the cut point with the smallest $J(A, B)$.

4. If the value of $J(A, B)$ is below the threshold, accept the partition and recursively partition the subgraphs. Otherwise, done.

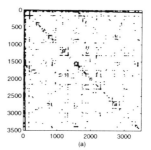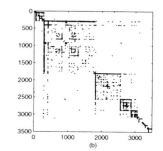

Figure 2. Clustering webpages related to user query *star*. (a) Weight matrix of the graph. (b) Clustering result. This corresponds to reordering the nodes such that nodes belonging to the same cluster are grouped together.

Here we illustrate the clustering result on a dataset retrieved from a query that contains one word *star* (Section 4.4). In Figure 2(a) we plot the weight matrix. All nonzero elements are shown as a dot. Figure 2(b) shows the reordered graph after clustering. Each diagonal block corresponds to a cluster. An off-diagonal block corresponds to a cut, i.e., all links between two clusters. One see that the clustering method effectively find the set of cut links that form a very sparse off-diagonal blocks.

4 Experiments

4.1 Datasets

A dataset is obtained in the following way [3, 11]. We first submit a query to the text-based search engine *hotbot*.

hotbot returns as query result a list of URLs with highest ranked webpages. We take top 120 of returned URLs which form the *root set*. Limiting the number of returned URLs to be 120, we can keep the overall dataset with a reasonable size. Then we expand the root set by including all webpages that point to a webpage in the root set and those pointed to by a webpage in the root set. This expanded *neighborhood set* of webpages is the dataset associated with a particular query. The hyperlinks between these webpages form a directed link graph, from which the adjacency matrix is computed. We run web crawler to get the text information of these webpages and compute the webpage-webpage textual similarity as described before. The co-citation matrix is calculated from the link graph.

We apply the clustering algorithm on the dataset. The threshold for stopping the recursive partitioning is set to .06. This leads to K clusters or topics. Since each cluster often has a large number of webpages, we choose only the most important webpages among a cluster. The most important or authoritative webpages are determined using Kleinberg's HITS algorithm.

4.2 HITS algorithm

The HITS algorithm makes use of the directionality, defining the *authorities* as the most relevant webpages for the topic, and the *hubs* as the webpages which link to many related authorities. Hubs implicitly represent an "endorsement" of the authorities they point to. The authority and hub information can be extracted based entirely on the link structure. Since good *authority* is pointed to by many good *hubs* and good *hub* points to many good authorities, such mutually reinforcing relationship can be represented as:

$$x_p = \sum_{q:e_{qp} \in E} y_q \qquad (5)$$

$$y_p = \sum_{q:e_{pq} \in E} x_q \qquad (6)$$

where x_p is the authority weight of webpage x and y_p is the hub weight. E is the set of links(edges). Final solutions are reached after iteratively updating the authority and hub weights of every webpage using Eqs.(5,6). Webpages with highest weights are the authorities and hubs of the topic.

We test our method on three datasets corresponding to three one-word queries: *amazon, star* and *apple*. The reason for using short query is to have multiple topics among the retrieved webpages, that can effectively test our clustering algorithm.

We first calculate the similarity matrix Eq.(1) for the web graph on the datasets, then run the spectral partitioning algorithm on the datasets to get clusters. Finally we apply the

HITS algorithm on each cluster obtained. The top authorities of each significant clusters are listed. By significant we mean the size of the cluster is not too small. The clusters with small size are not listed. Some small clusters exist because the nodes in them form highly connected components of the link graph. It shows that our algorithm is capable of finding these small but tightly connected clusters.

4.3 Dataset *amazon*

This dataset is retrieved for query *amazon* with total 2294 webpages (URLs). *amazon* has at least three meanings. One is related to amazon.com, one of the largest online shopping websites. Another is the famous rain forest in South America. And the third is the name of ancient female warriors from Alecto, a female ruled monarchy.

Applying the clustering algorithm, we obtain following significant clusters. (In the following, the order of the clusters has no special meanings. It is merely the sequence by which we process the clusters.)
Cluster 1:
www.amazon.com/
www.amazon.co.uk/
www.amazon.de

These three are the homepages of amazon.com, the largest online shopping company. The first website is located in USA, the second in UK and third, Germany. It is quite reassuring that our method clusters them together. We list only three authorities here because the rest ranked in the top 10 have very low authority weights compared with the first three. The reason is that those URLs have few in-coming links, and are not regarded as authorities, so we don't list them here.
Cluster 2:
www.amazoncity.com/
www.amazoncityradio.com/
www.amazoncity.com/spiderwoman/
www.wired.com/news/news/culture/story/6751.html

This cluster is about female issue.
Cluster 3:
www.amazon.org/
www.amazonfembks.com/
igc.apc.org/women/bookstores/
www.teleport.com/ rocky/queer.shtml
www.advocate.com/html/gaylinks/resources.html

The topic of this cluster is on female related issues: bisexuality and female books. That's a big surprise that we extract a cluster on bi-sexual topic. It's totally beyond our expectation.
Cluster 4:
sothebys.amazon.com/exec/varzea/tg/special-sales/
-/22822/-/8253/ref=gw_m_col_2/

*sothebys.amazon.com/exec/varzea/subst/home/sothebys.ht
ml/ref=gw_m_col_au_2/*
*sothebys.amazon.com/exec/varzea/tg/special-sales/
-/22822/-/8253/ref=gw_m_col_au_1/*
*s1.amazon.com/exec/varzea/subst/home/home.html/ref=
gw_auc_1/*
*sothebys.amazon.com/exec/varzea/subst/home/sothebys.ht
ml/ref=gw_m_ln_br_so_2/*

All five authorities listed here are webpages of a large on-line auction company formed by Sothebys and ama-zon.com. It is not clustered into Cluster 1 because there are only a few links between them.

Cluster 5:
www.swalliance.com/
timeline.echostation.com
www.echostation.com:8080/~1
downtime.echostation.com
rpg.echostation.com/

The topic of this cluster is about the movie *Star Wars*, sur-prisingly. But there are total 68 pages on this topic, most created by *Star Wars* fans. Some are on-line shopping com-panies selling goods related to the movie *star wars*.

There are two clusters, but for each of them, the web-pages are from the same site. These two clusters are:

Cluster 6:
misc.langenberg.com/
cooking.langenberg.com/
shipping.langenberg.com/
money.langenberg.com/
weather.langenberg.com/
and
Cluster 7:
www.latingrocer2.com
www.latingrocer.com
www.latingrocer.com/Pages/customer.html
www.latingrocer.com/Pages/privacy.html
www.latingrocer.com/Pages/contact.html

Cluster 8:
http://www.internext.com.br/ariau

This cluster has only one authority. All other web docu-ments in this cluster point to it. It is a website of a hotel in Amazon River valley.

Clusters 5, 6, 7 are not really relevant to the query *ama-zon*. Their presence in the dataset is mainly due to the root set expansion, since they have links to the webpages in the root set. This signals a problem with root set expansion: some high in-degree but not relevant nodes are included in the neighborhood set during the expansion. Once included, these high in-degree nodes will rank high and cause distrac-tion.

From the clusters we obtained, we find that no cluster has a focused topic on Amazon rain forest, unlike what we had expected. Checking the entire dataset, the 2294 URLs, we get only a couple of webpages that mention about the rain forest. They don't form a cluster with significant size. If we return to *hotbot* and enter the query *amazon*, the web-sites presented are dominantly related to amazon.com. The pages about rain forest are not in the top 120 list returned by *hotbot*, and thus is not included in the root set. This prob-ably indicated that on the web, the number of webpages on amazon rain forest is small.

As for the third meaning of amazon, although female warrior does not appear directly as a distinct topic in any cluster, some clusters focus on female issues, or even bi-sexual issue. By examining the content of these pages, we think that these issues are extension of the original mean-ing of amazon as female warriors. Especially, the cluster on the topic of bi-sexuality is beyond our expectation — our method can identify (from the web graph) topics even not aware of by us.

There are clusters with all authorities from the same websites, such as the clusters 6 and 7. They are explored as separate clusters because the webpages on the same site point to each other, raising the importance themselves. To avoid such situation to happen, before applying any cluster-ing algorithm, we can coarsen the link graph first, so that the webpages from the same site collapse to one node in the graph.

4.4 Dataset *star*

This dataset is retrieved for query *star*. There are 3504 webpages (URLs) in this dataset. For *star*, we can think about a planet, a movie star, a famous athlete, or the movie *Star Wars*.

We run our clustering algorithm on the dataset to get clusters automatically. The authorities of each cluster are listed below:
Cluster 1:
www.starwars.com/
www.lucasarts.com/
www.sirstevesguide.com/
www.jediknight.net/
www.surfthe.net/swma/

This cluster is focused on the movie *star wars*.
Cluster 2:
www.kcstar.com/
www.dailystarnews.com/
www.kansascity.com/
www.starbulletin.com/
www.trib.com/

This cluster includes the webpages of some news media with the word *star* as part of their names.

Cluster 3:

www.weatherpoint.com/starnews
www.starnews.com/digest/sports.html
www.starnews.com/digest/citystate.html
www.indy.com
speednet.starnews.com/

All the top authorities are webpages of starnews.com in this cluster.

Cluster 4:

www.state.mn.us/mainmenu.html
www.mda.state.mn.us/
www.doli.state.mn.us/
www.legalethics.com/pa/states/state/mn.htm
www.exploreminnesota.com

This cluster's topic is the state of Minnesota. The reason that Minnesota is a topic of the cluster under query *star* is because the official State of Minnesota website is called *North Star*, which is named second among all government websites.

Cluster 5:

www.star-telegram.com/
www.dfw.com/
www.virtualtexan.com/
marketplace.dfw.com
www.star-telegram.com/advertise/vshops/

This is a cluster of star-telegram.com located in Texas. It is interesting to note that clusters 2, 3, 5 are all webpages of news media. They are partitioned into different clusters since there is no link among the three clusters: they form separate communities.

Cluster 6:

www.starpages.net/

There is only one authority in this cluster. This website introduces stars in various fields, such as movie star, sport stars, model stars, etc. It is interesting to learn the existence of such a website.

Cluster 7:

www.aavso.org/
www.astro.wisc.edu/~dolan/constellations/
ourworld.compuserve.com/homepages/rawhide_home_page
adc.gsfc.nasa.gov/adc/adc_amateurs.html
heasarc.gsfc.nasa.gov/docs/www_info/webstars.html

This cluster talks about space and astronomy, as we had expected.

Overall, it appears that all topics related to *star* are automatically identified and extracted into separate clusters.

4.5 Dataset *apple*

In this dataset, there are 2757 URLs returned by the search engine. The authorities of each cluster found are listed below:

Cluster 1:

www.apple.com/
www.apple.com/support/
www.apple.com/education/
www.apple.com/quicktime/
www.apple.com/hotnews/

Here all top authorities are from the same website: *www.apple.com*. This cluster is dominant in this query. Most URLs belong to it. After running the HITS algorithm with the site information considered, that is, the URLs from the same website are collapsed to one node, we obtain different top authorities:

www.apple.com/powermac/server/
www.claris.com/
www.apple.ru/hardware/displays
www.cs.brandeis.edu/~xray/oldmac.html
www.next.com/

The second URL in this cluster is the website of a computer software company. It produces software used for the Macintosh. The other four URLs are all about the apple computer. This list of authorities provides more useful information than the previous one does.

Cluster 2:

www.yabloko.ru/
www.cityline.ru/politika/
www.russ.ru/
www.forum.msk.ru/
www.novayagazeta.ru

All web documents in this cluster are written in Russian.

Cluster 3:

www.michiganapples.com/

This cluster has only one authority. It is related to apple, the fruit.

The following cluster is formed in this query simply because its name happens to contain the query term *apple*:

Cluster 4:

www.ci.apple-valley.mn.us/

which is the website of the city of Apple Valley, MN.

Cluster 5:

www.valleyweb.com/

This is the website of Annapolis Valley in Canada where there is the Apple Blossom Festival in the spring celebrating the traditions and agricultural heritage.

There are not many clusters formed by the algorithm, nor do we find interesting topics which are beyond our original expectation.

5 Further discussion

By intuition, the links in the web graph can not be regarded as equally important, specifically many web links are created randomly. Text similarity between two webpages provides us with a useful metric to address this issue. Without the text similarity as the measure of the link strength, that is, if the weight matrix is formed as:

$$W = \alpha \frac{A}{\|A\|_2} + (1 - \alpha) \frac{C}{\|C\|_2},$$

this will unduly raise the strength of some links which connect two webpages with little in common. When applying our algorithm to the dataset *amazon*, we group Clusters 1, 3 and 4 into one single cluster, using the same threshold as the stopping criterion, namely 0.06 in our previous experiments. Cluster 3 addresses the female issues and Clusters 1 and 4 are related to *amazon.com*. Apparently this clustering result is not a good one. This result justifies our choice of incorporating text information into weight metric.

6 Concluding Remarks

In this paper, we present a method to automatically group webpages into distinct topics and list the most authoritative/informative webpages in each topic. This method of organizing retrieved information on the web is an effective way to help user to explore the vast amount of information on the web. The experimental results on several retrieved datasets indicate the effectiveness of the method.

Two key parts in our method are (1) the similarity metric incorporates comprehensive information of text, hyperlink structure and co-citation; and (2) the unsupervised clustering method based on spectral graph partitioning using the normalized cut.

In the future work, we will incorporate into our algorithm the modules to extract the text information summarizing the topic of each cluster. Thus users can easily pick up the right topic(s) they are interested in.

Acknowledgements. This work is supported by Office of Science, Office of Laboratory Policy and Infrastructure, of the U.S. Department of Energy under contract DE-AC03-76SF00098 through an LDRD grant in LBL, and by NSF grant CCR-9901986.

References

[1] K. Bharat and M. R. Henzinger. Improved algorithms for topic distillation in a hyperlinked environment. *ACM Conf. on Research and Development in Information Retrieval (SI-GIR'98)*, 1998.

[2] S. Brin and L. Page. The anatomy of a large-scale hypertextual web search engine. *Proc. of 7th WWW Conferece*, 1998.

[3] S. Carriere and R. Kazman. Webquery: Searching and visualizing the web through connectivity. *Computer Networks and ISDN Systems*, 29, 1997.

[4] S. Chakrabarti, B. E. Dom, and J. M. Kleinberg. Mining the link structure of the world wide web. Feb 1999.

[5] S. Chakrabarti, B. E. Dom, P. Raghavan, S. Rajagopalan, D. Gibson, and J. Kleinberg. Automatic resource compilation by analyzing hyperlink structure and associated text. *Computer Networks and ISDN Systems*, 30:65–74, 1998.

[6] M. Fiedler. Algebraic connectivity of graphs. *Czech. Math. J.*, 23:298–305, 1973.

[7] M. Fiedler. A property of eigenvectors of non-negative symmetric matrices and its application to graph theory. *Czech. Math. J.*, 25:619–633, 1975.

[8] G. W. Flake, S. Lawrence, and C. L. Giles. Efficient identification of web communities. *Proc. Int'l Conf. Knowledge Kiscovery and Data Mining (KDD)*, pages 150–159, 2000.

[9] D. Gibson, J. Kleinberg, and P. Raghavan. Inferring web communities from link topology. In *Proc. 9th ACM Conference on Hypertext and Hypermedia (HYPER-98)*, pages 225–234, 1998.

[10] M. A. Hearst and J. O. Paderson. Re-examining the cluster hypothesis: Scatter/gather on retrieval results. *Proc. SIGIR'96*, 1996.

[11] J. M. Kleinberg. Authoritative sources in a hyperlinked environment. *J. ACM*, 48:604–632, 1999.

[12] R. Kumar, P. Raghavan, S. Rajagopalan, and A. Tomkins. Extracting large-scale knowledge bases from the web. *Proc. of the 25th VLDB Conference*, 1999.

[13] R. R. Larson. Bibliometrics of the world wide web: an exploratory analysis of the intellectual structures of cyberspace. *Proc. SIGIR'96*, 1996.

[14] D. Modha and W. S. Spangler. Clustering hypertext with applications to web searching. In *Proc. ACM Conference on Hypertext and Hypermedia*, 2000.

[15] P. Pirolli, J. Pitkow, and R. Rao. Silk from a sow's ear: Extracting usable structures from the web. *Proc. SIGCHI'96*, 1996.

[16] A. Pothen, H. D. Simon, and K. P. Liou. Partitioning sparse matrices with egenvectors of graph. *SIAM Journal of Matrix Anal. Appl.*, 11:430–452, 1990.

[17] J. Shi and J. Malik. Normalized cuts and image segmentation. *IEEE. Trans. on Pattern Analysis and Machine Intelligence*, 2000.

[18] P. Willett. Recent trends in hierarchical document clustering. *Information Processing and Management*, 24, 1988.

[19] O. Zamir and O. Etzioni. Grouper: A dynamic clustering interface to web search results. *Proc. 8th World Wide Web Conference*, 1999.

Time series segmentation for context recognition in mobile devices

Johan Himberg   Kalle Korpiaho   Heikki Mannila   Johanna Tikanmäki
Hannu T.T. Toivonen

Nokia Research Center, Software Technology Laboratory
P.O. Box 407, FIN–00045 NOKIA GROUP, Finland
johan.himberg@nokia.com

Abstract

Recognizing the context of use is important in making mobile devices as simple to use as possible. Finding out what the user's situation is can help the device and underlying service in providing an adaptive and personalized user interface. The device can infer parts of the context of the user from sensor data: the mobile device can include sensors for acceleration, noise level, luminosity, humidity, etc. In this paper we consider context recognition by unsupervised segmentation of time series produced by sensors.

Dynamic programming can be used to find segments that minimize the intra-segment variances. While this method produces optimal solutions, it is too slow for long sequences of data. We present and analyze randomized variations of the algorithm. One of them, Global Iterative Replacement or GIR, gives approximately optimal results in a fraction of the time required by dynamic programming. We demonstrate the use of time series segmentation in context recognition for mobile phone applications.

1 Introduction

Succesful human communication is typically contextual. We discuss with each other in different ways depending on where we are, what time it is, who else is around, what has happened in the past, etc.: there is lots of context information that is implicitly being used in everyday life. Communication that is not aware of its context can be very cumbersome. The need for context-awareness is especially large in mobile communications, where the communication situations can vary a lot.

Information about the context of, say, a mobile phone can be used to improve the user interface. For example, if we know from the context information that the user is running, the font used in the display can be larger. Similarly, audio volume can be adjusted to compensate for higher levels of noise. Context awareness is currently studied in various aspects. Example of such studies include work on context sensitive applications, wearable computers and environmental audio signal processing, e.g., in [4, 5, 6, 9, 10, 14, 15, 17].

In this paper we discuss ways of achieving context-awareness in mobile devices such as mobile phone. A mobile device can infer useful context information from sensors for, e.g., acceleration, noise level, luminosity, and humidity. In general, figuring out what the user is actually doing is difficult, and we tackle one important subproblem. Specifically, we consider the problem of segmenting context data sequences into non-overlapping, internally homogeneous segments. The segments that are found may reflect certain states where the device, and eventually its user, are. Compact representations of the recognized segments can be used as templates against which the actions of the user (e.g., phone calls) are compared, so that for example prediction of future actions becomes possible. Formally, the segmentation problem is a special case of the general clustering problem, but the temporal structure of the data provides additional restrictions that can be used to speed up the computations.

The time series segmentation problem has been widely studied within various disciplines. A similar problem is the approximation of signals using line segments [1, 3, 7, 11, 13, 19]. The aim is often to compress or index the voluminous signal data [16, 18]. Computer graphics, cartography and pattern recognition utilize this reduction technique in simplifying or analyzing contour or boundary lines [12, 13]. Other applications range from phoneme recognition [14, 20] into paleoecological problems [2]. For an excellent review of time series segmentation, see [8] in this volume.

Our focus is on i) minimizing the cost function with a given number of segments, ii) cost functions that are sums of segmentwise costs, and iii) off-line segmentation, where all the data to be segmented is readily available.

Based on dynamic programming (e.g., [1]), optimal solutions to the time series segmentation problem can be found in time $O(kN^2)$ for sequences of length N and for k segments. However, for large values of N and k the algorithms are not efficient enough. Greedy algorithms can be used to solve the segmentation problem in time $O(kN)$ with very small constants (e.g., [8]). The algorithms provide solutions that in most cases are very close to the optimal ones. We describe experimental results showing the quality of context recognition in a test scenario.

2 Definition of k-segmentation

A *time series* s consists of N samples $\mathbf{x}(1), \mathbf{x}(2), \ldots, \mathbf{x}(N)$ from $\mathbf{R}^d$. We use the notation $s(a, b)$ to define a *segment* of the time series s, that is, the consecutive samples $\mathbf{x}(a), \mathbf{x}(a+1), \mathbf{x}(a+2), \ldots, \mathbf{x}(b)$ where $a \leq b$. If $s_1 = s(a, b)$ and $s_2 = s(b+1, c)$ are two segments, then $s_1 s_2 = s(a, c)$ denotes their concatenation.

A *k-segmentation* S of s is a sequence $s_1 s_2 \cdots s_k$ of k segments such that $s_1 s_2 \cdots s_k = s$ and each s_i is non-empty. In other words, there are segment boundaries $c_1, c_2, \ldots, c_{k-1}, 0 < c_1 < c_2 < \cdots < c_{k-1} < N$, where

$$s_1 = s(1, c_1), \; s_2 = s(c_1+1, c_2), \; \ldots, \; s_k = s(c_{k-1}+1, N).$$

For ease of notation, we define additionally $c_0 = 0$ and $c_k = N$.

We are interested in obtaining segmentations of s where the segments are internally homogeneous. In order to formalize this goal, we associate a cost function F with the internal heterogeneity of individual segments, and aim to minimize the overall cost of the segmentation. We make two assumptions on the overall cost. First, the cost $\text{cost}_F(s(a, b))$ of a single segment is a function of the data points and the number of data points $n = b - a + 1$,

$$\text{cost}_F(s(a, b)) = F(\mathbf{x}; n | \mathbf{x} \in s(a, b)). \tag{1}$$

Second, the *cost of a k-segmentation* $\text{Cost}_F(s_1 s_2 \cdots s_k)$ is the sum of the costs of its segments $s_1, s_2, \ldots, s_k$:

$$\text{Cost}_F(s_1 s_2 \cdots s_k) = \sum_{i=1}^{k} \text{cost}_F(s_k). \tag{2}$$

An optimal k-segmentation $S_F^{opt}(s; k)$ of time series s using cost function cost_F is such that $\text{Cost}_F(s_1 s_2 \cdots s_k)$ is minimal among all possible k-segmentations.

The cost function F in Eq. 1 can be an arbitrary function. We use the sum of the variances of the components of the segment:

$$V(s(a, b)) = \sum_{l=1}^{d} \left[\frac{1}{n} \sum_{i=a}^{b} x_l(i)^2 - \left(\frac{1}{n} \sum_{i=a}^{b} x_l(i) \right)^2 \right], \tag{3}$$

where $n = b - a + 1$ and d is the number dimensions. Thus the cost function for segmentations is simply

$$\text{Cost}_V(s_1 s_2 \cdots s_k) = \frac{1}{N} \sum_{i=1}^{k} n_i V(s_i), \tag{4}$$

where the segments have length $n_1, n_2, \ldots, n_k$, the length N of the sequence is $\sum_{i=1}^{k} n_k$, and $V(s_i)$ is defined as in Eq. 3.

By rewriting Eq. 4 we get

$$\text{Cost}_V = \frac{1}{N} \sum_{i=1}^{k} \sum_{j=c_{i-1}+1}^{c_i} \|\mathbf{x}(j) - \mu_i\|^2 \tag{5}$$

where μ_i is the mean vector of data vectors in segment $s_i = s(c_{i-1} + 1, c_i)$.

The problem we address is finding the segment boundaries c_i that minimize the cost. The problem is similar to clustering, but simpler. Eq. 5 is well comparable to a typical error measure of standard vector quantization (clustering), but in this case the clusters are limited to being contiguous segments of the time series instead of Voronoi regions in $\mathbf{R}^n$.

3 Algorithms

Dynamic programming The k-segmentation problem can be solved optimally by using dynamic programming [1]. The basic criteria for the applicability of dynamic programming to optimization problems is that the restriction of an optimal solution to a subsequence of the data has to be an optimal solution to that subsequence. For example, for our problem, given an optimal k-segmentation $s_1 s_2 \cdots s_k$, any subsegmentation $s_i \cdots s_j$ ($1 \leq i < j \leq k$) is an optimal $(j - i + 1)$-segmentation for the corresponding subsequence, so the condition obviously holds. The computational complexity of the dynamic programming is of order $O(kN^2)$ if the cost of a segmentation can be calculated in linear time.

The computational complexity of the dynamic programming algorithm is too high when there are large amounts of data. Greedy methods can take advantage of the simple fact that when the segmentation for a subsequence is changed, e.g., if a segment is divided further or a set of subsequent segments is redivided, the reduction in the total cost can be calculated efficiently within the subsequence.

A well-known and fast greedy heuristic for segmentation is the *top-down* approach or binary-split (e.g., [8]). This makes splits in hierarchical manner.

Top-down The method starts by splitting the time-series s optimally into two subsequences s_1 and s_2. Now assume that the algorithm has already segmented s into $m < k$ segments. Each of these segments $s_i, i = 1, 2, \ldots, m$ is split in turn optimally into two pieces s_{i_1} and s_{i_2} and the total cost of the segmentation $s_1 s_2 \ldots s_{i_1} s_{i_2} \ldots s_m$ is calculated. The split which reduces the total cost most is accepted. Now there are $m + 1$ segments and the procedure is carried on until there are k segments.

The top-down method never makes changes in the break points it has once set. The inflexibility of top-down is potentially a weak point, since it can turn out later in the process that the early decisions are far from optimal.

This problem can be assessed with dynamic procedures that first heuristically place all break points and then iteratively move one break point at a time using some decision rule that ensures convergence to some local optimum [11]. We next propose two greedy algorithms that move one breakpoint at a time straight into a local minimum.

Local iterative replacement (LIR) LIR is a simple greedy procedure where the new place for a break point is selected optimally between the neighboring two break points (including the beginning and ending of the time series). The approach is similar to [11] where break points are moved gradually towards better positions, rather than to the locally optimal ones.

1. Select the initial break points heuristically, e.g., by using evenly spaced or random initial locations, or with the top-down method.

2. Select a break point c_i, $1 \leq i \leq k - 1$, either in random or sequential order, remove it and concatenate the two consecutive segments that meet at c_i into $s(c_{i-1} + 1, c_{i+1})$.

3. Find a new, optimal location for the break point in the concatenated sequence: locate an optimal 2-segmentation break point c_i' for the concatenated segment. Replace break point c_i by c_i' in the solution.

4. Steps 2 and 3 are repeated until a stopping criterion is met. (Possible stopping criteria are discussed below.)

Global iterative replacement (GIR) Instead of relocating the break point c_i between its neighbors c_{i-1} and c_{i+1}, the best location is searched in the whole sequence. This includes clearly local iterative replacement but it may avoid some local minima. The approach bears some distant similarities with [13], where segments are also split and merged. The core idea of [13] is to split segments with large errors and merge ones with small errors until given error thresholds are met, whereas GIR makes one (at that time) optimal split–merge pair at a time and keeps the number of segments constant.

1. Set the initial segmentation $S_n = s_1 s_2 \cdots s_k$; $n = 0$, as in LIR.

2. Select a break point c_i, $1 \leq i \leq k-1$, either in random or sequential order, remove it and concatenate the two consecutive segments that meet at c_i into $\hat{s} = s(c_{i-1} + 1, c_{i+1})$.

3. Find a new optimal location for a break point anywhere in the sequence. For each segment s_j', $j = 1, 2, \ldots, k - 1$ in the new segmentation $S' = s_1 s_2 \cdots s_{i-1} \hat{s} s_{i+2} \cdots s_k :=$ (renumeration) $:= s'_1 s'_2 \cdots s'_{k-1}$, find the optimal 2-segmentation to s'_{j_1} and s'_{j_2}, and compute the respective (potential) savings $d_j = \mathrm{cost}_F(s_j') - (\mathrm{cost}_F(s'_{j_1}) + \mathrm{cost}_F(s'_{j_2}))$ in the segmentation cost.

4. Select the split with largest savings d_j, say s_l' with savings d_l, and set a break point at d_l. The new segmentation is $s'_1 s'_2 \cdots s'_{l_1} s'_{l_2} \cdots s'_{k-1}$.

5. Set $n := n + 1$ and renumerate the segments for the next round: $S_n = s_1 s_2 \cdots s_k$ (renumeration) $:= s'_1 s'_2 \cdots s'_{l_1} s'_{l_2} \cdots s'_{k-1}$.

6. Steps from 2 to 5 are repeated until a stopping criterion is met.

A natural stopping criterion for these algorithms is that the total cost cannot be decreased by any admissible move of a breakpoint. It is immediate that both LIR and GIR will stop in finite number of steps, since the cost decreases at each step and the number of points in the sequence is finite and discrete. A limit for the number of iterations is another simple stopping criterion.

The randomized iterative algorithms can be run a few times in order to reduce the chance of having an especially poor local minima.

The computational complexity of the greedy methods is linear in the size of the input data, if the cost of a segmentation can be calculated in linear time, as it can for the variance (cost function of Eq. 4). The complexity is of order $O(KN)$ where the factor K depends on the number of the break points k, on the number of iterations, and on the locations of the initial break points.

4 Experimental performance evaluation

The proposed iterative algorithms were benchmarked against the top-down algorithm. The optimal solution provided by the dynamic programming algorithm was used as a reference. The tested algorithms were

1. top-down approach

2. local iterative replacement (LIR)

3. global iterative replacement (GIR)

The cost function to be minimized was variance (Eq. 5). First, the algorithms were tested with a number of different artificial data sets.

4.1 Artificial data sets

The artificial data was generated as follows. First, the length $N \in \{100, 200, 300, 400, 500\}$ of the signal and the number $c \in \{6, 11, 16, 21\}$ of constant segments was fixed. Then the values and lengths for the constant segments were generated randomly, so that the $c - 1$ places for transitions (break points) were drawn randomly from $\{2, 3, \ldots, N-1\}$ with the restriction that the length of any segment had to be at least two. The value for each constant segment was randomly generated from a uniform distribution on $[0, 1]$.

Three different random prototype signals of this kind were generated for each combination of the number of segments and the length of signals, and three levels of gaussian *i.i.d.* noise was added to the signals. For the relative noise level (SNR; ratio of variance of signal to variance of noise) we used levels 10 and 1.0. For each prototype signal and for each combination for N, c and SNR level we generated 30 time series. Fig. 1 shows an example of two test signals ($N = 300$ and $c = 6$). Both are generated by adding different level of noise to the same prototype. Sample A has very low noise (SNR=100) while B has SNR=1.0. Each test signal was segmented once using the dynamic programming, top-down, LIR, and GIR algorithms. The number of segments k was set to c, the a priori number of the segments. We call this simply the "Test 1" data set.

For some larger experiments, another set of data was generated with the following procedure. One piecewise constant prototype was generated with $N = 500$ and $c = 16$, and fifty samples were generated by adding some gaussian *i.i.d* noise SNR=10. We call this the "Test 2" data set.

4.2 Comparison of partitionings

A random initial location for the break points was given for the iterative algorithms. Both LIR and GIR used the same initial segmentations. The iteration was stopped when the algorithms could not move the break points any more.

We compare the costs C of the segmentations achieved by top-down and proposed iterative methods LIR and GIR to the cost of the optimal solution C_{opt} achieved by dynamic programming. The comparison is made using a relative error measure since different signals and segmentations are compared:

$$ err_{rel}(C) = \frac{C - C_{opt}}{C_{opt}} $$

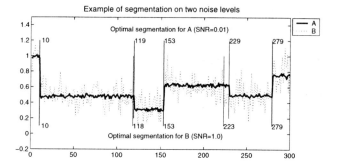

Figure 1. Two noise levels (SNR=100, SNR=1.0) added to an original signal of 6 constant segments, and their optimal segmentations.

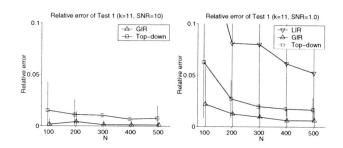

Figure 2. The average relative error of segmentation as a function of the length of the sequence (N), for low to high amounts of noise. Errorbars show one standard deviation. Local iterative replacement (LIR) is outside the visible area in the left panel.

This measure tends to increase without limit if C_{opt} goes to zero. However, since there was always noise present in the test signals C_{opt} is always greater than zero.

Experiments with simulated data (Test 1) and the "correct" amount of segments show that the relative errors of the partitionings produced by global iterative replacement are within a percent or two (Figs. 2 and 3). Local iteration performs badly, but the top-down method produces reasonable partitionings. The results indicate that for the purposes of the k-segmentation problem defined in 2 the top-down method and the global iterative method are sufficiently accurate.

More interesting results are obtained when the correct number of segments is not known. Of course, this is the situation in typical applications. Experiments with artificial data set "Test 2" show that GIR consistently outperforms the top-down approach, which in turn is superior to LIR. The better performance of GIR over the top-down method is probably explained by the fact that GIR can during the

206

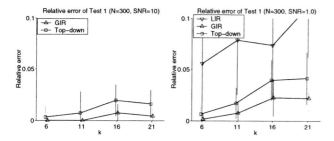

Figure 3. The average relative error of segmentation as a function of the number of segments (k), for low to high amounts of noise. Errorbars show one standard deviation. Local iterative replacement (LIR) is outside the visible area in the left panel.

operation change decisions made earlier, whereas the top-down method cannot.

4.3 Running times

As expected, the computational requirements of the top-down method and both local and global iterative replacements are linear in N, the length of the sequence, whereas the dynamic programming method is quadratic (Fig. 5).

For constant N, all methods behave roughly linearly in k (Figs. 6 and 7). However, dynamic programming has about two orders of magnitude larger consumption of computational resources (Fig. 7). Right panel of Fig. 7 allows a closer look at behavior in k. In average, both LIR and GIR behave in a similar fashion to the top-down algorithm.

Fig. 7 gives even an impression that, for this particular case, the tested greedy algorithms might behave sublinearly in k.

5 Context recognition

Real context data was collected with custom-built equipment. Sensor signals were logged from a certain user scenario where test subjects were told to perform different activities (Table 1).

5.1 Context data

The data were recorded using microphones and a sensor box that were attached to a mobile phone. The combination was hanging in users' neck in front of the chest. The data were logged by wire to a laptop that the user was carrying.

The raw signal was transformed to 19 variables, called *context atoms*, that indicate the amount of activation for an action or state: movement (running, walking fast, walking),

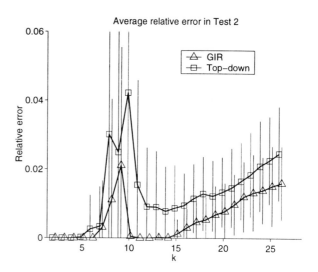

Figure 4. The average relative error of segmentation as a function of the number of segments (k), for an artificial sequence (Test 2: N=500, c=16) Local iterative replacement (LIR) is outside the visible area.

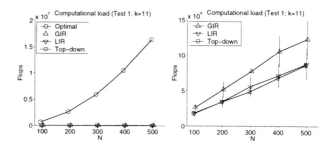

Figure 5. The average computational cost in floating point operations as a function of the length of the sequence (N). Both panels show the same data but on different scales. Errorbars show one standard deviation.

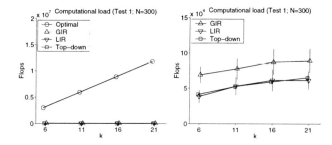

Figure 6. The computational cost in floating point operations as a function of the number of segments (k). Both panels show the same data but on different scales. Errorbars show one standard deviation.

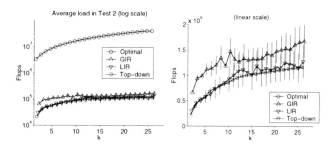

Figure 7. The average computational cost in floating point operations as a function of the number of segments (k), for an artificial sequence (Test 2: N=500, c=16). Errorbars show one standard deviation. Note that the scale on y-axis is logarithmic in the left panel and linear in the right one. The dynamic programming is out of the visible area in the right panel.

Table 1. Outline of activities in the user scenario

1.	user sits; device is on a table
2.	takes the device and puts it on
3.	stands up and starts to walk
4.	walks in a corridor
5.	walks down the stairs
6.	walks in a corridor
7.	walks outside
8.	walks in a porch
9.	walks in a lobby
10.	walks up the stairs
11.	walks in a corridor
12.	sits down
13.	puts the device on a table

sound pressure (loud, modest, silent), illumination conditions (total darkness, dark, normal, bright), touch (at hand), stability (unstable, stable), and device orientation (sideways left, sideways right, antenna up, antenna down, display up, display down). The pattern recognition algorithms for this transformation and the sensor box itself are outside the scope of this research, and we consider the context atom data as given.

The real context data set consisted of 44 time series arising from the same scenario. The lengths of the 19 dimensional time series varied between 223 and 267.

5.2 Performance on real context data

Each time series was segmented once to $2, \ldots, 21$ segments using the dynamic programming, top-down, LIR, and GIR algorithms. Results on relative error and running times (Fig. 8) confirm the observations made with the artificial data sets: GIR yields a small relative error with high computational efficiency.

5.3 Quality of context recognition

A study of the optimal $2, \ldots, 21$-segmentations for the real data shows that there is certain stability in the locations of the break points (Fig. 9A). Most of the break points occur in almost all segmentations after they occur the first time. This gives certain credibility for the break points.

Next, examine a time series from context atom data and its optimal 13-segmentation (Fig. 9B). An evaluation of the segmentation against a video recording of the test shows that segmentation can be very useful for context recognition. The segmentations seem to capture the most important changes when compared with the real situation: putting the equipment on and standing up, walking in stairs, being out, going through doors, stopping, and getting the equipment off. The 13 segments correspond practically one-to-one to the activities in the user scenario (Table 1). Furthermore, by comparing Figs. 9A and B one sees that the break points for phases "getting equipment on", "being out", and "getting equipment off" come up first. In this case, the order of the appearance of the break points and their (subjective) importance in real world seem to be consistent as well.

6 Conclusions

Context-awareness is becoming one of the major factors in mobile communications. We have studied a particular problem arising from mobile phones with sensors, the task of time series segmentation.

We outlined the dynamic programming algorithm for finding the optimal k-segmentation for a given cost function. However, dynamic programming is computationally

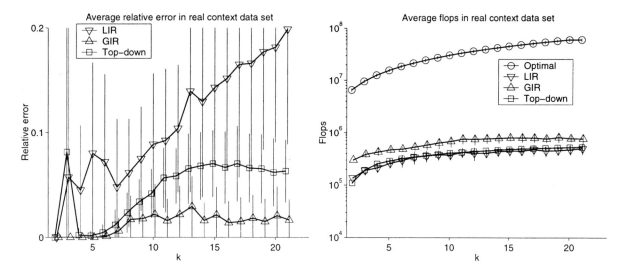

Figure 8. The average relative error (left) and computational cost in floating point operations (right) as functions of the number of segments (k), for real context data set. Errorbars show one standard deviation. Note that the scale on y-axis is logarithmic in the right panel.

too hard for long sequences, since the complexity of the algorithm is of order $O(kN^2)$ where N is the amount of data (assuming the cost of a single segment can be computed in linear time). For this reason, we proposed and analyzed fast greedy methods for time series segmentation. These iterative methods were tested against both the optimal segmentations and the top-down greedy segmentations. The proposed global iterative replacement method (GIR) outperformed other greedy methods in our empirical tests.

The cost function that was minimized in this work was the variance of the segment. This is just an example, and other cost functions might be considered. It is, however, advisable that the cost function could be calculated in linear time with respect to the amount of data, as is the case with the sample variance.

We applied the time series segmentation into sensor data that was collected using a sensor box in a mobile phone. The time series segmentation was used to capture interesting changes in the user's context. The experiment suggests that time series segmentation using a simple variance based cost function captures some essential phenomena in the context atom time series. The segmentations presented in Fig. 9 are optimal for the given data and cost function, but the reflections of this fact to the real world must be evaluated by an analyst. The analyst might be working using tools like visualization aids presented in Fig. 9, as well as video recordings of the tests to get an overview for some data in order to determine the usefulness of the emerged patterns.

For other analysis purposes, the segmentation gives an adaptive length window where the situation within window is more or less constant and the break points occur at places of changes. This can be useful in preprocessing the data for forming higher-level contexts.

Acknowledgments

The authors would like to thank Esa Alhoniemi, Jani Mäntyjärvi, and Jari Paloniemi for useful comments.

References

[1] R. Bellman. On the Approximation of Curves by Line Segments Using Dynamic Programming. *Communications of the ACM*, 4(6):284, 1961.

[2] K. D. Bennett. Determination of the Number of Zones in a Biostratigraphical Sequence. *New Phytol.*, 132:155–170, 1996.

[3] A. Cantoni. Optimal Curve Fitting with Piecewise Linear Functions. *IEEE Transactions on Computers*, C-20(1):59–67, 1971.

[4] B. Clarkson, K. Mase, and A. Pentland. Recognizing User Context via Wearable sensors. In *Digest of Papers of the Fourth International Symposium on Wearable Computers*, pages 69–76. IEEE, 2000.

[5] B. Clarkson and A. Pentland. Unsupervised Clustering of Ambulatory Audio and Video. In *Proceedings of the International Conference on Acoustics, Speech, and Signal Processing 1999*, volume 6, pages 3037–3040, 1999.

[6] S. Fels, Y. Sumi, T. Etani, N. Simonet, K. Kobayashi, and K. Mase. Progress of C-Map: a Context-Aware Mobile Assistant. In *Proceedings of AAAI 1998 Spring Symposium on Intelligent Environments*, pages 60–67, 1998.

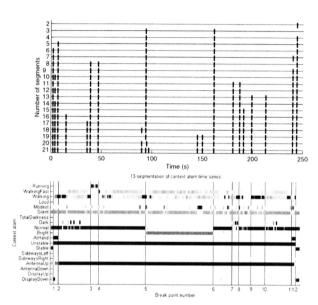

Figure 9. A. The optimal 2,...,21-segmentations of real data. The vertical line segments on each horizontal grid line of the y-axis presents one temporal segmentation. The x-axis shows time in seconds from the beginning of the test. **B. The context atom data and the optimal 13-segmentation.** The horizontal bars show the activation of the context atoms (labels on y-axis). Dark means high activation. The vertical lines that are numbered on x-axis show the places of break points. The segmentation here is the optimal 13-segmentation.

[7] H. Imai and M. Iri. An Optimal Algorithm for Approximating a Piecewise Linear Function. *Journal of Information Processing*, 9(3):159–162, 1986.

[8] E. Keogh, S. Chu, D. Hart, and M. Pazzani. An Online Algorithm for Segmenting Time Series. In *Proceedings of the First IEEE International Conference on Data Mining*, 2001. To appear.

[9] K. V. Laerhoven and O. Cakmakci. What Shall We Teach Our Pants? In *Digest of Papers of the Fourth International Symposium on Wearable Computers*, pages 77–83. IEEE, 2000.

[10] M. Lamming and M. Flynn. "Forget me not" Intimate Computing in Support of Human Memory. Technical Report EPC-1994-103, Rank Xerox Research Centre, Cambridge.

[11] T. Pavlidis. Waveform Segmentation Through Functional Approximation. *IEEE Transactions on Computers*, C-22(7):689–697, 1973.

[12] T. Pavlidis. Algorithms for Shape Analysis and Waveforms. *IEEE Transactions on Pattern Analysis and Machine Intelligence*, PAMI-2(4):301–312, 1980.

[13] T. Pavlidis and S. L. Horowitz. Segmentation of Plane Curves. *IEEE Transactions on Computers*, C-23(8):860–870, 1974.

[14] P. Prandoni, M. Goodwin, and M. Vetterli. Optimal Time Segmentation for Signal Modeling and Compression. In *Proceedings of IEEE International Conference on Acoustics, Speech and Signal Processing 1997*, volume 3, pages 2029–2032, 1997.

[15] A. Schmidt, K. Aidoo, A. Takaluoma, U. Tuomela, K. V. Laerhoven, and W. V. de Velde. Advanced Interaction in Context. In *Hand Held and Ubiquitous Computing*, number 1707 in Lecture Notes in Computer Science, pages 89–101. Springer-Verlag, 1999.

[16] H. Shatkay and S. B. Zdonik. Approximate queries and representations for large data sequences. In *Proceedings of the 12th International Conference on Data Engineering*, pages 536–545. IEEE, 1996.

[17] T. Starner, B. Schiele, and A. Pentland. Visual Contextual Awareness in Wearable Computing. In *Second International Symposium on Wearable Computers, Digest of Papers*, pages 50–57. IEEE, 1998.

[18] C. Wang and X. S. Wang. Supporting Content-based Searches on Time Series via Approximation. In *Proceedings of the 12th International Conference on Scientific and Statistical Database Management*, pages 69–81. IEEE, 2000.

[19] L.-D. Wu. A Piecewise Linear Approximation Based on a Statistical Model. *IEEE Transactions on Pattern Analysis and Machine Intelligence*, PAMI-6(1):41–45, 1984.

[20] Z. Xiong, C. Herly, K. Ramchandran, and M. T. Orchard. Flexible Time Segmentations for Time-Varying Wavelet Packets. In *IEEE Proc. Intl. Symp on Time-Frequency and Time-Scale Analysis*, pages 9–12, 1994.

Indiscernibility Degree of Objects for Evaluating Simplicity of Knowledge in the Clustering Procedure

Shoji Hirano and Shusaku Tsumoto

Department of Medical Informatics,
Shimane Medical University, School of Medicine
89–1 Enya-cho, Izumo 693–8501, Japan
E-mail: hirano@ieee.org, tsumoto@computer.org

Abstract

This paper presents a new, rough sets-based clustering method that enables evaluation of simplicity of classification knowledge during the clustering procedure. The method iteratively refines equivalence relations so that they become more simple set of relations that give adequately coarse classification to the objects. At each step of iteration, importance of the equivalence relation is evaluated on the basis of the newly introduced measure, indiscernibility degree. An indiscernibility degree is defined as a ratio of equivalence relations that classify the two objects into the same equivalence class. If an equivalence relation has ability to discern the two objects that have high indiscernibility degree, it is considered to perform too fine classification and then modified to regard them as indiscernible objects. The refinement is repeated decreasing the threshold level of indiscernibility degree, and finally simple clusters can be obtained. Experimental results on the artificial data showed that iterative refinement of equivalence relation lead to successful generation of coarse clusters that can be represented by simple knowledge.

1 Introduction

In recent years, clustering has been widely used as a powerful tool to reveal underlying structute in a database. Both partitional clustering techniques such as K-means [1] and fuzzy c-means [2], and hierarchial clustering techniqe [3] have produced excellent resluts in the analysis of reallife data. The more recent algotithms, for example BIRCH [4], CLIQUE [5] and CURE [6], have good scalability to the size of the data and can be applied to the analysis of large and high-dimensional numerical databases. Other types of algorithms such as ROCK [7] can be used for analysis of

the categorical data.

One of the main objective of database analysis is to discover some interesting knowledge that represents hidden characteristics of the data. This means that a clustering result would be further used to derive some classification rules. In order to generate reasonably small number of rules in high-dimensional data, the clustering result is required to be enough interpreteable. However, diverseness of attributes may cause to generate a lot of meaninglessly small clusters, especially in a complex database like a medical database. This primary due to the fact that a clustering system, especially unsupervised clustering system, should equally handle all attributes in the database to determine the best partition of the data. Although knowledge reduction techniques [8] can be used to eliminate meaningless rules, there remains some inconsistency between the derived rules and clustering result. To avoid such a problem, simplicity of classification knowledge should be evaluated in the clustering process, rather than in the process of rule generation.

This paper presents a knowledge-oriented clustering method based on rough set theory [9]. Our method evaluates simplicity of classification knowledge in the clustering process by the use of newly introduced concept, indiscernibility degree, which represents how many equivalence relations commonly regards the two objects as indiscernible. The two objects can be classified into the same class if they have high indiscernibility degree, even in presence of equivalence relations that assign different classes to these objects. Namely, objects are classified into the same class if most of the equivalence relations commonly regard them as indiscernible objects. This scheme enables to produce coarse clusters that can be represented by simple knowledge.

This paper is organized as follows. Section 2 briefly presents basic properties of rough sets that are related to this work. Section 3 describes our clustering method. Section 4 shows experimental results on the synthetic datasets and Section 5 concludes the technical results.

2   Preliminary

This section briefly describes some fundamental definitions of rough sets related to our work. Let $U \neq \phi$ be a universe of discourse and X be a subset of U. An equivalence relation, R, classifies U into a set of subsets $U/R = \{X_1, X_2, ...X_n\}$ in which following conditions are satisfied:

$$(1) X_i \subseteq U, X_i \neq \phi \qquad \text{for any } i,$$
$$(2) X_i \cap X_j = \phi \qquad \text{for any } i, j,$$
$$(3) \cup_{i=1,2,...n} X_i = U.$$

Any subset X_i, called a category, represents an equivalence class of R. A category in R containing an object $x \in U$ is denoted by $[x]_R$. For a family of equivalence relations $\mathbf{P} \subseteq \mathbf{R}$, an indiscernibility relation over $\mathbf{P}$ is denoted by $IND(\mathbf{P})$ and defined as follows

$$IND(\mathbf{P}) = \bigcap_{R \in \mathbf{P}} IND(R).$$

Approximation is used to represent roughness of the knowledge. Suppose we are given an equivalence relation R and a set of objects $X \in U$, the R-lower and R-upper approximations of X are defined as

$$\underline{R}X = \cup\{Y \in U/R \mid Y \subseteq X\},$$

$$\overline{R}X = \cup\{Y \in U/R \mid Y \cap X \neq \phi\}.$$

The lower approximation $\underline{R}X$ contains sets that are certainly included in X, and the upper approximation $\overline{R}X$ contains sets that are possibly included in X. Using $\underline{R}X$ and $\overline{R}X$, the accuracy measure of approximation can be defined as

$$\alpha_R(X) = |\underline{R}X| \, / \, |\overline{R}X|,$$

where $|Y|$ denotes cardinality of a set Y.

3   Clustering Method based on the Indiscernibility Degree of Objects

3.1   Overall Procedure

Likewise the other rough sets-based classification techniques, our method classifies objects according to the indiscernibility relation derived using a set of equivalence relations. The method consists of two stages: assignment of initial equivalence relations and iterative refinement of the initial equivalence relations. Each of the two stages captures *local* and *global* similarity of the objects, respectively.

In the first stage, we assign an initial equivalence relation to every object. An equivalence relation is defined on

the basis of relative similarity. The use of relative similarity makes it possible to handle nominal data, where the similarity cannot be represented on the ratio scale. An equivalence relation splits the entire set of objects into two equivalence classes: one containing similar objects and another containing dissimilar objects. Namely, each object independently gathers up similar objects with respect to the *local* similarity between itself and other objects.

The indiscernibility relation derived using these initial equivalence relations tends to split the objects into many equivalence classes, i.e., it gives very fine classification to the objects. This is because no global relationship among the initial equivalence relations is considered. Consequently, closely located objects may have slightly different equivalence relations which cause generation of meaninglessly small, fine classes. In the second stage, we refine such equivalence relations so that the resultant indiscernibility relation gives adequately coarse classification to the objects. The refinement is iteratively performed by evaluating the *indiscernibility degree* of objects, which reflects global relationships among equivalence relations. The indiscernibility degree represents a ratio of equivalence relations that commonly regard the two objects as indiscernible. An equivalence relation is considered to give too fine classification if it has ability to discern the two objects that have high indiscernibility degree. In such a case, the equivalence relation is modified to regard them as indiscernible objects. In this method, we associate roughness of the classification knowledge with the threshold level of the indiscernibility degree, and obtain coarsely classified objects by constantly decreasing the threshold level.

The procedure is summarized as follows.

1. Assign an initial equivalence relation to every object.

2. Iteratively refine the equivalence relations by constantly decreasing the threshold level T_h of the indiscernibility degree.

3.2   Assignment of Initial Equivalence Relations

First, we assign an initial equivalence relation to each object. Let $U = \{x_1, x_2, ..., x_n\}$ be the set of objects we are interested in, and assume that each object has p attributes represented by nominal or numerical values. Here we assign the following equivalence relation to every object.

[Definition 1] Initial Equivalence Relation
An equivalence relation R_i for object x_i is defined by

$$R_i = \{\{P_i\}, \{U - P_i\}\},$$

where

$$P_i = \{x_j \mid s(x_i, x_j) \geq S_i\}, \quad \forall x_j \in U.$$

$s(x_i, x_j)$ denotes similarity between objects x_i and x_j, and S_i denotes a threshold value of similarity for object x_i. Obviously, $R_i = \{\{[x_i]_{R_i}\}, \{\overline{[x_i]_{R_i}}\}\}$, $[x_i]_{R_i} \cap \overline{[x_i]_{R_i}} = \phi$ and $[x_i]_{R_i} \cup \overline{[x_i]_{R_i}} = U$ hold. The equivalence relation R_i classifies U into two categories: one containing objects similar to x_i and another containing objects dissimilar to x_i. When $s(x_i, x_j)$ is larger than S_i, object x_j is considered to be indiscernible to x_i. Similarity $s(x_i, x_j)$ is calculated as a weighted sum of the Mahalanobis distance $d_M(x_i, x_j)$ of numerical attributes and the Hamming distance $d_H(x_i, x_j)$ of nominal attributes as follows:

$$s(x_i, x_j) = \frac{p_c}{p}\left(1 - \frac{d_M(x_i, x_j)}{\max_{x_u, x_v \in U} d_M(x_u, x_v)}\right)$$
$$+ \frac{p_d}{p}\left(1 - \frac{d_H(x_i, x_j)}{\max_{x_u, x_v \in U} d_H(x_u, x_v)}\right),$$

where p_c and p_d denote the numbers of numerical and nominal attributes, respectively.

Similarity threshold S_i is automatically determined based on gradient the similarity curve. Assume that $s(x_i, x_j)$ is arranged in descendent order, and let $s'(x_i, x_j)$ denote first order derivative of $s(x_i, x_j)$. We derive $s'(x_i, x_j)$ as a convolution of $s(x_i, x_j)$ and first derivative of Gaussian function as follows.

$$s'(x_i, x_j) = \int_{-\infty}^{\infty} s(x_i, x_u) \frac{-(j-u)}{\sigma^3 \sqrt{2\pi}} e^{-(j-u)^2/2\sigma^2} du.$$

where $x_j = 1$ and $x_j = 0$ are used for $j < 0$ and $j > n$ respectively.

After calculating $s'(x_i, x_j)$ for all $j (1 \leq j \leq n)$, we calculate their mean and standard deviation, denoted respectively by $\mu_{s'}(i)$ and $\sigma_{s'}(i)$. Then we seek the minimal j^* that first satisfies

$$s'(x_i, x_{j^*}) \geq \mu_{s'}(i) + \sigma_{s'}(i)$$

and obtain j^* where similarity first delves largely. Finally, S_i is obtained as $S_i = s(x_i, x_{j^*})$.

[End of Definition]

[Example 1] Initial Equivalence Relation

Let $U = \{x_1, x_2, ..., x_9\}$ be the entire set of objects and $\mathbf{R} = \{R_1, R_2, ..., R_9\}$ be a set of equivalence relations over U. Suppose that each object has two numerical attributes (a_1 and a_2) and two nominal attributes (a_3 and a_4) as shown in Table 1. Similarity between objects x_1 and x_2, $s(x_1, x_2)$, is calculated as

$$s(x_1, x_2) = \frac{2}{4} \times (1.0 - \frac{0.629}{3.558}) + \frac{2}{4} \times (1.0 - \frac{0}{2}) = 0.912.$$

Table 2 tabulates similarity $s(x_1, x_j)$ and its gradient $s'(x_1, x_j)$ between x_1 and each of other objects. Note that in this example the order of similarity corresponds to that of object number. Mean and SD of $s'(x_1, x_j)$ are 0.0013

Table 1. Example objects.

Object	a_1	a_2	a_3	a_4
x_1	0.0	0.0	round	small
x_2	0.1	0.0	round	small
x_3	0.0	0.1	round	small
x_4	0.1	0.1	round	small
x_5	0.15	0.15	square	small
x_6	0.3	0.3	square	large
x_7	0.4	0.3	square	large
x_8	0.3	0.4	square	large
x_9	0.4	0.4	square	large

Table 2. Similarity s and its gradient s' between x_1 and other objects.

$s(x_1,x_1)$	$s(x_1,x_2)$	$s(x_1,x_3)$	$s(x_1,x_4)$	$s(x_1,x_5)$
1.000	0.912	0.912	0.875	0.563
$s'(x_1,x_1)$	$s'(x_1,x_2)$	$s'(x_1,x_3)$	$s'(x_1,x_4)$	$s'(x_1,x_5)$
0.0005	0.0005	0.0002	0.0021	0.0045
$s(x_1,x_6)$	$s(x_1,x_7)$	$s(x_1,x_8)$	$s(x_1,x_9)$	
0.125	0.058	0.058	0.000	
$s'(x_1,x_6)$	$s'(x_1,x_7)$	$s'(x_1,x_8)$	$s'(x_1,x_9)$	
0.0030	0.0004	0.0004	0.0004	

and 0.0015, respectively. In this case, similarity threshold S_1 for x_1 is determined as $S_1 = s(x_1, x_5) = 0.563$ because $s'(x_1, x_5)$ first satisfies $s'(x_1, x_5) = 0.0045 \geq 0.0013 + 0.0015 = 0.0028$. According to Definition 1, P_1 for x_1 determined as

$$P_1 = \{x_j | s(x_1, x_j) \geq 0.563\}, \forall x_j \in U.$$

Then we obtain classification of U by R_1 as follows.

$$U/R_1 = \{\{x_1, x_2, x_3, x_4, x_5\}, \{x_6, x_7, x_8, x_9\}\}.$$

Analogously, equivalence relations $R_2, R_3, ..., R_9$ are assigned to the corresponding objects. Consequently, we obtain classification of U as follows.

$$U/R_1, U/R_2, U/R_3, U/R_4 =$$
$$\{\{x_1, x_2, x_3, x_4, x_5\}, \{x_6, x_7, x_8, x_9\}\},$$
$$U/R_5 =$$
$$\{\{x_4, x_5\}, \{x_1, x_2, x_3, x_6, x_7, x_8, x_9\}\},$$
$$U/R_6, U/R_7, U/R_8, U/R_9 =$$
$$\{\{x_6, x_7, x_8, x_9\}, \{x_1, x_2, x_3, x_4, x_5\}\},$$
$$U/IND(\mathbf{R}) =$$
$$\{\{x_1, x_2, x_3\}, \{x_4, x_5\}, \{x_7, x_8, x_9\}\}.$$

As a result, objects are classified into three equivalence classes, namely clusters, by the initial equivalence relations.

[End of Example]

Rules that generate $U/IND(\mathbf{R})$ are derived by translating similarity back to the attribute domain. Since we use the Mahalanobis distance for numerical attribute and the Hamming distance for numerical attribute, range of the values and common values are used respectively for representing rules on these two attributes. For example, knowledge induced from $U/IND(\mathbf{R})$ of Example 1 can be represented by three rules below.

Rule 1:	IF	$(a_1 <= 0.1)$
	AND	$(a_2 <= 0.1)$
	AND	$(a_3 == round)$
	AND	$(a_4 == rmall)$
	THEN	Class 1
Rule 2:	IF	$(a_1 == 0.15)$
	AND	$(a_2 == 0.15)$
	AND	$(a_4 == small)$
	THEN	Class 2
Rule 3:	IF	$(0.3 <= a_1)$
	AND	$(0.3 <= a_2)$
	AND	$(a_3 == square)$
	AND	$(a_4 == large)$
	THEN	Class 3

3.3 Iterative Refinement of Initial Equivalence Relations

In the second stage, we perform refinement of the initial equivalence relations. Generally, objects should be classified into the same category when most of the equivalence relations commonly regard them as indiscernible. However, these similar objects will be classified into different categories if there exists at least one equivalence relation that has ability to discern the objects. In such a case, unpreferable clustering result containing small and fine categories will be obtained. An example can be found in Example 1. Here, an equivalence relation, R_5, makes slightly different classification compared to the others. R_5 classifies objects x_4 and x_5 into an independent category whereas all other relations regard x_5 as an indiscernible object to x_1, x_2, x_3 and x_4. Consequently, three small categories are obtained. The purpose of this stage is to refine such equivalence relations so that the resultant indiscernibility relation gives adequately coarse classification to the object.

First, we define an *indiscernibility degree*, $\gamma(x_i, x_j)$, of two objects x_i and x_j as follows.

[Definition 2] Indiscernibility Degree of Objects

$$\gamma(x_i, x_j) = \frac{1}{|U|} \sum_{k=1}^{|U|} \delta_k(x_i, x_j),$$

where

$$\delta_k(x_i, x_j) = \begin{cases} 1, & \text{if } [x_k]_{R_k} \cap ([x_i]_{R_k} \cap [x_j]_{R_k}) \neq \phi \\ 0, & \text{otherwise.} \end{cases}$$

[End of Definition]

[Example 2] Indiscernibility Degree of Objects

Let $U = \{x_1, x_2, x_3\}$ be the entire set of objects and let $\mathbf{R} = \{R_1, R_2, R_3\}$ be a family of equivalence relations over U. Suppose that R_1, R_2 and R_3 classify U as

$$\begin{aligned} U/R_1 &= \{\{x_1, x_2\}, \{x_3\}\}, \\ U/R_2 &= \{\{x_1, x_2\}, \{x_3\}\}, \\ U/R_3 &= \{\{x_2, x_3\}, \{x_1\}\}. \end{aligned}$$

An indiscernibility degree, $\gamma(x_1, x_2)$, between objects x_1 and x_2 is then calculated as

$$\begin{aligned} \gamma(x_1, x_2) &= \frac{1}{3} \sum_{k=1}^{3} \delta_k(x_1, x_2) \\ &= \frac{1}{3}\left(\delta_1(x_1, x_2) + \delta_2(x_1, x_2) + \delta_3(x_1, x_2)\right) \\ &= \frac{1}{3}(1 + 1 + 0) = \frac{2}{3}. \end{aligned}$$

This result $\gamma(x_1, x_2) = 2/3$ shows that objects x_1 and x_2 are regarded as indiscernible by 2/3 of the relations in $\mathbf{R}$.

[End of Example]

The higher $\gamma(x_i, x_j)$ represents that x_i and x_j are commonly regarded as indiscernible objects by large number of the equivalence relations. Therefore, if an equivalence relation discerns the objects that have high γ value, we consider that it gives excessively fine classification and refine it according to the following procedure.

[Definition 3] Refinement of Equivalence Relations

Let $R_i, R_j \in \mathbf{R}$ be initial equivalence relations and let $R_i', R_j' \in \mathbf{R}'$ be equivalence relations after refinement. For an initial equivalence relation R_i, a refined equivalence relation R_i' is defined as

$$R_i' = \{\{P_i'\}, \{U - P_i'\}\}$$

where P_i' denotes a subset of objects represented by

$$P_i' = \{x_j | \gamma(x_i, x_j) \geq T_h\}, \ \forall x_j \in U.$$

The value T_h denotes the lower threshold value of indiscernibility degree to regard x_i and x_j as the indiscernible objects.

[End of Definition]

[Example 3] Refinement of Equivalence Relations

Consider again the case of Example 1. According to Definition 2, an indiscernibility degree, $\gamma(x_5, x_1)$, between objects x_5 and x_1 is calculated as $\gamma(x_5, x_1) = 4/9$. Similarly,

$\gamma(x_5, x_2) = \gamma(x_5, x_3) = \gamma(x_5, x_4) = 4/9$, $\gamma(x_5, x_5) = 5/9$, $\gamma(x_5, x_6) = \gamma(x_5, x_7) = \gamma(x_5, x_8) = \gamma(x_5, x_9) = 0/9$ can be obtained. Now suppose that T_h is set to $4/9$. Objects x_5 and x_1 are considered to be indiscernible since $\gamma(x_5, x_1) = 4/9 \geq T_h = 4/9$ holds. From Definition 3, P_5' for R_5' is obtained as $P_5' = \{x_1, x_2, x_3, x_4, x_5\}$. Then R_5 is changed to R_5' as follows.

$$U/R_5' = \{\{x_1, x_2, x_3, x_4, x_5\}, \{x_6, x_7, x_8, x_9\}\}.$$

By applying this process to every equivalence relation, we obtain the refined set of equivalence relations $\mathbf{R}'$ for $T_h = 4/9$ as follows.

$$\begin{aligned}
U/R_1', U/R_2', U/R_3', U/R_4', U/R_5' = \\
\{\{x_1, x_2, x_3, x_4, x_5\}, \{x_6, x_7, x_8, x_9\}\} \\
U/R_6', U/R_7', U/R_8', U/R_9' = \\
\{\{x_6, x_7, x_8, x_9\}, \{x_1, x_2, x_3, x_4, x_5\}\} \\
U/IND(\mathbf{R}') = \\
\{\{x_1, x_2, x_3, x_4, x_5\}, \{x_6, x_7, x_8, x_9\}\}.
\end{aligned}$$

[End of Example]

In the above example, R_5 is modified to R_5' so that it classifies objects $x_{1,2,3,4,5}$, that are commonly regarded as indiscernible objects by other relations, into the same category. Types of relations are reduced from 3 to 2 and the number of generated categories are also reduced from 3 to 2.

From each category in $U/IND(\mathbf{R}')$, following new rules are obtained.

Rule 1:	IF	$(a_1 <= 0.15)$
	AND	$(a_2 <= 0.15)$
	AND	$(a_4 == small)$
	THEN	Class 1
Rule 2:	IF	$(0.3 <= a_1)$
	AND	$(0.3 <= a_2)$
	AND	$(a_3 == square)$
	AND	$(a_4 == large)$
	THEN	Class 2

The number of rules is also reduced from 3 to 2 because it corresponds to the number of categories. Rule 1 is generalization of rules 1 and 2, which were previously obtained without refinement. Small differences on attributes 1 and 2 are ignored and each becomes one rule that extends range of a_1 (or a_2) from $0.0 <= 0.1$ to 0.15. It is important that a_3 is completely ignored in the new rule 1. It means that objects in the first category may have different characteristics on a_3, however, they can be considered to be globally ignorable because they have many similar characteristics on the other attributes. In other words, classification is performed using more coarse knowledge.

We obtain the clustering result by iterating the refinement process. The value of T_h is constantly decreased at each iteration step. Since each refinement process is performed using the previously 'refined' set of equivalence relations, we can obtain adequately coarse clusters without disturbing local structure of the clusters formed at lower value of T_h.

4 Experimental Results

We first examined effect of refinement of initial equivalence relations. Two-dimensional numerical data were artificially created using Neyman-Scott method [10]. The number of clusters was set to 4. Each cluster contained approximately 50 objects, and total 185 objects were contained in the data. We evaluated validity of the clustering result based on the following measures.

- Accuracy $\mu_{\mathbf{R}}(C) = \frac{|X_{\mathbf{R}} \cap C|}{|X_{\mathbf{R}}|}$,

- Coverage $\nu_{\mathbf{R}}(C) = \frac{|X_{\mathbf{R}} \cap C|}{|C|}$,

- Validity $v_{\mathbf{R}}(C) = \min(\mu_{\mathbf{R}}(C), \mu_{\mathbf{R}}(C))$,

where $X_{\mathbf{R}}$ and C denote the cluster obtained by the proposed method and its expected cluster, respectively.

Figures 1 shows the clustering result obtained by our method. The refinement was performed up to five times, constantly decreasing T_h from 0.6 to 0.2. Without refinement, the method produced 67 small clusters as shown in Figure 1(A). Validity of the result was 0.181, which was the smallest of all. This was because small size of clusters produced very low coverage, namely, overlaps between the generated clusters and their corresponding expected clusters were very small compared with the size of the expected clusters. As the refinement proceeds, the small clusters became merged (B). Validity of the results kept increasing. Finally, 6 clusters were formed after fifth refinement as shown in Figure 1(C). Two small clusters (clusters 4 and 5) were not merged into any of the other large clusters. This primarily due to the fact that low indiscernibility degrees were assigned to these objects as a result of competition of the two large sets for including these objects into their clusters. The result demonstrates an interesting characteristic of the method that it produces some "boundary" clusters between two large clusters if they have significant overlaps of the distributions.

Figure 2 shows the relations between degree of refinement, number of generated clusters and cluster validity. We here used four numerical datasets containing different number of objects in order to examine how the number of objects affects performance of the refinement. In Figure 2, 'v #' denotes validity of the clustering result obtained on the dataset containing # objects. Analogously, 'nc #' denotes the number of clusters obtained on the dataset containing

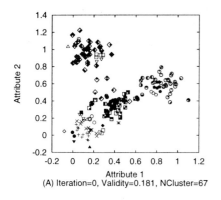 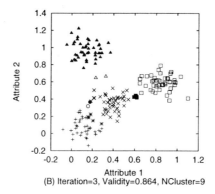 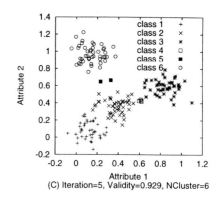

(A) Iteration=0, Validity=0.181, NCluster=67   (B) Iteration=3, Validity=0.864, NCluster=9   (C) Iteration=5, Validity=0.929, NCluster=6

Figure 1. Clustering result of the artificial data.

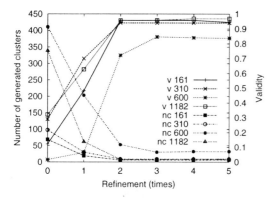

Figure 2. Relations between degree of refinement, number of generated clusters and cluster validity.

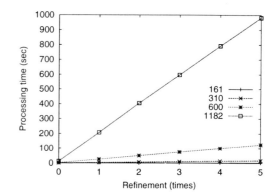

Figure 3. Relations between degree of refinement and processing time.

objects. In all datasets, validity increased following the number of refinement and saturated after five times of refinement. The inverse characteristic was observed in the curves of the number of generated clusters. These results show that refinement of equivalence relations contributed to successful generation of the expected clusters, regardless of the number of objects.

Figure 4 shows the relations between degree of refinement and processing time. The data was obtained using the same set as Figure 2. The processing time was measured on a workstation (SGI OCTANE2, R12000, 400MHz). It can be observed that the processing time increased proportional to the times of refinement in all cases. The figure also shows that the order of processing time of this method is almost n^3, where n denotes the number of objects.

5 Conclusions

In this paper, we have presented a rough sets-based clustering method with iterative refinement of equivalence relations. In it we introduced the concept of indiscernibility degree, represented by the number of equivalence relations that commonly regard objects as indiscernible, as a measure of global similarity between objects. By the use of indiscernibility degree, the system classified objects according to their global characteristics, regardless of small and local difference that might produce unpreferably fine categories. Experimental results on the artificially created numerical data showed that objects were classified into the expected clusters if refinement was performed, whereas they were classified into many small categories without refinement. This indicated that iterative refinement of equivalence relations based on indiscernibility degree well served for successful classification.

It remains as a future work to validate the method on large and complex databases such as medical databases.

References

[1] S. Z. Selim and M. A. Ismail, "K-means-type Algorithms: A Generalized Convergence Theorem and Characterization of Local Optimality," *IEEE Transactions on Pattern Analysis and Machine Intelligence*, vol. 6, no. 1, pp. 81–87, 1984.

[2] J. C. Bezdek, *Pattern Recognition with Fuzzy Objective Function Algorithm*, Plenum Press, New York, 1981.

[3] M. R. Anderberg, *Cluster Analysis for Applications*, Academic Press, New York, 1973.

[4] T. Zhang, R. Ramakrishnan, and M. Livny, "BIRCH: An Efficient Data Clustering Method for Very Large Databases," in *Proc. ACM SIGMOD Int. Conf. Manag. Data*, pp. 103–114, 1996.

[5] R. Agrawal, J. Gehrke, D. Gunopulos, and P. Raghavan, "Automatic Subspace Clustering of High Dimensional Data for Data Mining Applications," in *Proc. ACM SIGMOD Int. Conf. Manag. Data*, pp. 94–105, 1998.

[6] S. Guha, R. Rastogi, and K. Shim, "CURE: An Efficient Clustering Algorithm for Large Databases," in *Proc. ACM SIGMOD Int. Conf. Manag. Data*, pp. 73–84, 1998.

[7] S. Guha, R. Rastogi, and K. Shim, "ROCK: A Robust Clustering Algorithm for Categorical Attributes," in *Proc. IEEE the 15th Int. Conf. Data Eng.*, pp. 512–512, 1999.

[8] S. Tsumoto, "Automated Discovery of Positive and Negative Knowledge in Clinical Databases," *IEEE Engineering in Medicine and Biology Magazine*, vol. 19, no.4, pp. 56–62, 2000.

[9] Z. Pawlak, *Rough Sets, Theoretical Aspects of Reasoning about Data*, Kluwer Academic Publishers, Dordrecht, 1991.

[10] J. Neyman and E. L. Scott., "Statistical Approach to Problems of Cosmology," *Journal of the Royal Statistical Society*, Series B20, 1–43, 1958.

Mining Coverage-based Fuzzy Rules By Evolutional Computation

Tzung-Pei Hong
Department of Electrical Engineering
National University of Kaohsiung
tphong@nuk.edu.tw

Yeong-Chyi Lee
Graduate School of Information Engineering
I-Shou University
m883327m@isu.edu.tw

Abstract

In this paper, we propose a novel mining approach based on the genetic process and an evaluation mechanism to automatically construct an effective fuzzy rule base. The proposed approach consists of three phases: fuzzy-rule generating, fuzzy-rule encoding and fuzzy-rule evolution. In the fuzzy-rule generating phase, a number of fuzzy rules are randomly generated. In the fuzzy-rule encoding phase, all the rules generated are translated into fixed-length bit strings to form an initial population. In the fuzzy-rule evolution phase, genetic operations and credit assignment are applied at the rule level. The proposed mining approach chooses good individuals in the population for mating, gradually creating better offspring fuzzy rules. A concise and compact fuzzy rule base is thus constructed effectively without human expert intervention.

Keywords: data mining, machine learning, genetic algorithm, fuzzy set, rule base.

1. Introduction

Conventional approaches to knowledge base construction involve interaction and dialogue between knowledge engineers and domain experts. The cost is high and will become prohibitive as we attempt to build larger and larger systems [18]. Therefore, constructing and maintaining a knowledge base automatically becomes an interesting and challenging issue.

In the past, knowledge acquisition systems [1][6][14] based on the *Personal Constructs Psychology* (*PCP*) model [11] were successfully applied. Examples included ETS [2], AQUINAS [3], KSSO [6] and KITTEN [14]. In these systems, domain experts must however intervene during integration to resolve conflicts and contradictions, causing much time for knowledge acquisition.

Recently, genetic algorithms have been used to derive knowledge from training instances [4][5][8]. Two famous approaches commonly used by genetic algorithms as classifier systems are the Michigan approach and the Pittsburgh approach. The Michigan genetic classifier

system [8] operates at the level of individual rules and selects good parent rules for mating according to their strength values. The Pittsburgh approach [13] operates at the level of rule sets and selects good parent rule sets for mating based on their fitness values. Wang *et al.* proposed several GA-based knowledge-integration strategies that automatically integrated multiple rule sets in a distributed-knowledge environment [15][16][17][18]. Ishibuchi *et al.* proposed a GA-based classifier system to generate fuzzy rules based on the Michigan approach [9][10]. In their approach, the antecedent parts of fuzzy rules were first randomly generated, and the consequent class of each rule was then determined by a heuristic procedure. The fitness values of rules were obtained by the number of correctly classified and misclassified training patterns.

Most knowledge sources or actual instances in real-world applications contain fuzzy or ambiguous information. Especially in domains such as medical or control domains, the boundaries of a piece of information used may not be clearly defined. Expressions of domain knowledge by fuzzy descriptions are thus more and more commonly seen. In this paper, we thus propose a genetic fuzzy rule mining algorithm based on the Michigan approach to effectively construct a fuzzy rule base.

2. A GA-based fuzzy mining approach

In this paper, we propose a novel genetic fuzzy mining approach to effectively construct a fuzzy rule base. The proposed approach consists of three phases: fuzzy-rule generating, fuzzy-rule encoding and fuzzy-rule evolution, which are shown in Figure 1.

2.1 Fuzzy-rule generating phase

In the proposed algorithm, the initial N fuzzy rules are randomly generated. All possible values of an attribute in a rule are generated with the same probability. Restated, assume an attribute has m possible linguistic values, formed as its domain. The probability of each value is thus $1/(m+1)$, with a *"don't care"* value representing the

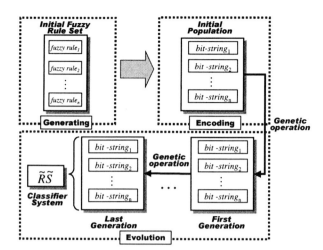

Figure 1. The three phases of the proposed approach

absence of this attribute in a rule. Numeric symbols (i.e. *1*, *2* and *3*...) are used here to represent the linguistic values of the attributes in the antecedent parts. For example, "*1*" is used to represent the linguistic term "*Small*". The symbol "***" is used to represent the "*don't care*" value of an attribute. Moreover, the alphabetic symbols (i.e. *A*, *B*, and *C*...) are used here to represent the possible consequent classes. For example, "*A*" is used to represent the Iris class "*Setosa*".

Example 1: Fisher's Iris data are used here to demonstrate the process of the proposed approach. In these data, the three species of Iris Flowers are *Setosa*, *Versicolor* and *Virginica*, respectively. Thus, a class domain D_{flower} is defined as D_{flower}={*Setosa*, *Versicolor*, *Virginica*}. The flowers are described by four attributes, *Sepal Length* (*S.L.*), *Sepal Width* (*S.W.*), *Petal Length* (*P.L.*), and *Petal Width* (*P.W.*). The possible linguistic values of each attribute are defined as:

$D_{S.L.}$ ={*Short, Medium, Long*},
$D_{S.W.}$ ={*Narrow, Medium, Wide*},
$D_{P.L.}$ ={*Short, Medium, Long*}, and
$D_{P.W.}$ ={*Narrow, Medium, Wide*}.

Three numeric symbols 1, 2 and 3 are used to represent the linguistic values {*Short, Medium, Long*} or {*Narrow, Medium, Wide*} of the attributes. The symbol "***" is used to represent the "*don't care*" condition. Three alphabetic symbols *A*, *B* and *C* are used to represent the three possible classes {*Setosa, Versicolor, Virginica*}.

Assume that *N* is set at 3. Three rules are thus randomly generated as follows:

$\tilde{r}_1$: **22B,
$\tilde{r}_2$: *23*C, and
$\tilde{r}_3$: 1*1*A.

The first rule $\tilde{r}_1$ is "**22B", which means "If (*P.L.=Medium*) and (*P.W.=Medium*), then *Class* is

Versicolor."

2.2 Fuzzy-rule encoding phase

It is important to encode each fuzzy rule as string representation for GAs to be applied. Several strategies for representing fuzzy knowledge structures in conceptual learning have been proposed in [10][12]. After the fuzzy rules are generated in the previous phase, each one is then encoded as a bit-string chromosome and handled as an individual. The encoding approach in this paper is stated as follows.

Let T_j^i be the test value of the *j*-th attribute in rule $\tilde{r}_i$, with m_j possible values. Each T_j^i of a fuzzy rule is then encoded into a fixed-length binary substring $s_{j1}^i...s_{jm_j}^i$, where s_{jk}^i represents the *k*-th possible value of T_j^i. For example, assume the set of possible linguistic values of attribute A_j is {a_{j1}, a_{j2}, a_{j3}}. Three bits are then used to represent this attribute. The bit string 100 would represent the test for attribute A_j being "a_{j1}".

Let φ_k^i be the *k*-th class. The consequent part of each rule is then encoded as a bit substring ($\varphi_1, \varphi_2, ..., \varphi_x$), where *x* is the number of possible classes. When the rule concludes to class *h*, φ_h is set at one and the others are set at zero. The *N* attribute tests and the one class pattern are then encoded and concatenated to represent as a fixed-length rule string, represented in Figure 2.

$$\tilde{r}_i : \underbrace{s_{11}^i...s_{1m_1}^i}_{T_1^i}...\underbrace{s_{N1}^i...s_{Nm_N}^i}_{T_N^i} \underbrace{\varphi_1^i...\varphi_x^i}_{Class}$$

Figure 2. The bit string representation of a fuzzy rule $\tilde{r}_i$

The representation is also flexible since disjunctive attribute tests can be easily described. For example, "110" is used to represent the disjunctive linguistic term "*Small* or *Medium*". Each rule is then encoded as a fixed-length bit string. The length of each rule is then:

$$Length\,(rule) = [\sum_{i=1}^{N} \text{number of possible values for}$$

$$Attribute\,(i)] + \text{number of Classes},$$

where *N* is the number of attributes. This representation allows genetic operators to easily manage fuzzy rules.

2.3 Fuzzy-rule evolution phase

After the fuzzy rules have been encoded as bit strings, they are collected to form the initial population. The genetic fuzzy-rule evolution phase then starts. In this phase, genetic operations and credit assignment are applied at the rule level. The proposed mining method chooses good individuals in the population for mating, gradually creating better offspring fuzzy rules. During evolution, a measurement process and a set of test objects are used to evaluate the fitness value of each offspring fuzzy rule. The population then undergoes recursive evolution until a really good fuzzy knowledge base has been produced. Thus, domain experts need not intervene in the process. After evolution, all the fuzzy rules in a population are then combined to form a resulting rule set.

3. The proposed genetic fuzzy mining algorithm

The proposed fuzzy mining method uses a genetic algorithm for optimization of fuzzy rules. Some characteristics are stated below.

3.1 Initial population

A genetic algorithm requires a population of feasible solutions to be initialized and updated during the evolution process. As mentioned above, the initial set of bit strings for fuzzy rules is randomly generated in our approach. Each individual within the population is a fuzzy rule, and is of fixed length.

3.2 Fitness

In order to develop a good fuzzy rule base from an initial population, the genetic algorithm selects parent rules with high fitness values for mating. An evaluation process and a set of training samples are used to qualify the rules. Three important factors including accuracy, utility, and coverage of the resulting rules are considered in the evaluation [19]. The evaluation process will be described in the next section.

3.3 Crossover and mutation operations

The crossover operation is the same as that in the simple genetic algorithm (SGA) proposed by Holland [7]. The mutation operation is also the same as that in the simple genetic algorithm proposed by Holland. It randomly changes some genes in a selected rule and leads to additional genetic diversity to help the process escape from local-optimum traps.

3.4 Fission operation

Here, a domain-specific operator, the fission operator, which emulates the chromosomal schizo-genesis in natural evolution, is introduced to solve the contradictive problem [17]. Two kinds of contradictions may occur

after the genetic operations are performed. The first kind of contradictions occurs when two rules with the same feature tests conclude to different classes. This kind of contradictions can be removed by the proposed evaluation process. The second kind of contradictions occurs when a rule concludes to two or more classes simultaneously. The fission operation is used here to split the rule into several ones, each concluding to only one class. The new rules generated by the fission operations will still contradict each other, but have been reduced to the first kind of contradictions, which can then be removed by the evaluation process. An example of a fission operation is given below.

Example 2: Assume a rule shown in Figure 3 is a contradictive rule.

Contradictive rule:	111	010	001	111	011
			↓		
New rule 1:	111	010	001	111	001
New rule 2:	111	010	001	111	010

Figure 3. A fission operation in Example 2

The two new rules generated by the fission operation are then:
New rule1: If (*S.W.=Medium*) and (*P.L.=Long*), then *Class* is *Virginica*.
New rule2: If (*S.W.=Medium*) and (*P.L.=Long*), then *Class* is *Versicolor*.

3.5 The mining algorithm

According to the above description, the proposed genetic fuzzy mining algorithm can be stated as follows.
Step 1: Randomly generate N rules as an initial rule set, where N is the population size.
Step 2: Encode each fuzzy rule generated in Step 1 into a bit string and combine them together to form an initial population.
Step 3: Evaluate the fitness values of each bit string by a set of training examples. The evaluation process will be described in the next section.
Step 4: Select appropriate individuals to perform crossover and mutation operations according to their fitness values.
Step 5: Perform the fission operations on contradictive offspring bit strings.
Step 6: Put the offspring bit strings together with the original bit strings.
Step 7: Evaluate the fitness values of each bit string in Step 6 by a set of training examples.

Step 8: Pick up *N* best bit strings according to the fitness values to form the next generation.

Step 9: When the number of evolution generations is reached, output the bit strings with their fitness values larger than zero and decode them into fuzzy rules; otherwise, go to Step 4 for next-generation evolution.

After Step 9, the output fuzzy rules are then gathered together to form the resulting fuzzy rule base.

4. The fitness evaluation process

In order to develop a good fuzzy rule base from an initial population, the genetic algorithm selects parent rules with high fitness values for mating. An evaluation process and a set of training examples are used to qualify the rules. Three important factors including accuracy, utility and coverage of the resulting rules are considered in the evaluation.

4.1. The accuracy measurement

The accuracy of a rule $\tilde{r}_i$ represents its correct classification capability on test objects. It is measured as:

$$Accuracy(\tilde{r}_i) = \frac{\varpi_i}{\varpi_i + \varepsilon_i}$$

where ϖ_i is the fuzzy correctness cardinality and ε_i is the fuzzy incorrectness cardinality of fuzzy rule $\tilde{r}_i$. Obviously, the higher the accuracy of a rule is, the better this rule is in correctly classifying the test objects.

4.2 The utility measurement

The utility of a rule $\tilde{r}_i$ represents its necessarily in classifying the objects. If an object is correctly predicted by only one rule, this rule is then necessary to classify the object, and its utility value equals 1. If an object $\tilde{e}$ is correctly classified by *m* rules, these rules then share the utility according to the ratios of their match degrees. The total utility of a rule is then the sum of its individual utility values for the set of objects. Obviously, the larger the utility of a rule is, the more inevitable the rule is in classifying the objects.

4.3 The coverage measurement

The coverage of a rule $\tilde{r}_i$ represents the amount of objects which $\tilde{r}_i$ can include. The degree for an object $\tilde{e}$ to be included in a rule $\tilde{r}_i$ can be measured by the match degree between $\tilde{e}$ and the conclusion part c_i of $\tilde{r}_i$. Also, a match degree is called effective coverage degree if it is above a coverage threshold γ. Thus the sum of the coverage degrees for all the objects can be used to measure the coverage capability of a rule.

4.4 The evaluation procedure for fitness values

The purpose of the proposed approach is to obtain a concise set of rules with high accuracy. Thus, we first sort the rules in descending order of their products of accuracy and utility. The rule with the largest product first calculates its coverage, and all the learning examples in the object set covered by this rule are removed from the object set. The same procedure is repeated for the next rule based on the remaining object set until the rules in the population are all evaluated or until the object set is empty. An object in the coverage set of a rule may be transferred to the coverage set of another rule if it has a larger match degree with the latter rule than with the former rule. By the removal of covered objects from the object set, a concise rule set can be easily obtained. The fitness values of the rules are then evaluated as the products of their accuracy, utility and coverage values. The simultaneous cooperation and competition of individual rules within the population is thus considered.

5. An example

An example is given below to illustrate the proposed genetic fuzzy mining algorithm. Assume that a set of twenty training examples shown in Table 1 is used to learn the rules.

Table 1. A set of twenty training examples

Case	S. L.	S. W.	P. L.	P. W.	Class
$\tilde{e}_1$	5.7	3.8	1.7	0.3	Setosa
$\tilde{e}_2$	5.5	3.5	1.3	0.2	Setosa
$\tilde{e}_3$	5.1	3.3	1.7	0.5	Setosa
$\tilde{e}_4$	5.2	3.5	1.5	0.2	Setosa
$\tilde{e}_5$	5	3.5	1.6	0.6	Setosa
$\tilde{e}_6$	5	2	3.5	1	Versicolor
$\tilde{e}_7$	6.5	2.8	4.6	1.5	Versicolor
$\tilde{e}_8$	5.6	3	4.5	1.5	Versicolor
$\tilde{e}_9$	5.5	2.5	4	1.3	Versicolor
$\tilde{e}_{10}$	7	3.2	4.7	1.4	Versicolor
$\tilde{e}_{11}$	5.6	2.8	4.9	2	Virginica
$\tilde{e}_{12}$	6	2.2	5	1.5	Virginica
$\tilde{e}_{13}$	7.2	3	5.8	1.6	Virginica
$\tilde{e}_{14}$	6.9	3.1	5.4	2.1	Virginica
$\tilde{e}_{15}$	5.9	3	5.1	1.8	Virginica
$\tilde{e}_{16}$	4.9	2.5	4.5	1.7	Virginica
$\tilde{e}_{17}$	5.7	4.4	1.5	0.4	Setosa
$\tilde{e}_{18}$	4.5	2.3	1.3	0.3	Setosa
$\tilde{e}_{19}$	4.9	2.4	3.3	1	Versicolor
$\tilde{e}_{20}$	6.4	2.9	4.3	1.3	Versicolor

Also assume that a set of membership functions shown in Figure 4 is given.

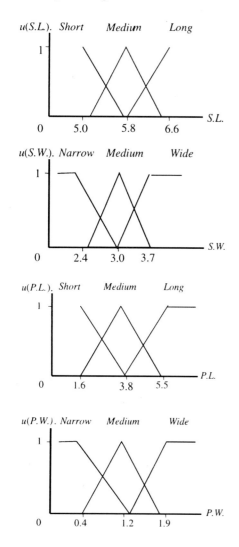

Figure 4. A set of membership functions for this example

Assume the population size is set at 15. Fifteen rules are randomly generated as an initial rule set. Since each attribute in a rule has three possible values: *Small*, *Medium* and *Large*, three numeric symbols *1*, *2* and *3* are used to represent them respectively. Moreover, since there are three classes, *Setosa*, *Versicolor* and *Virginica*, to be distinguished, three alphabetic symbols *A*, *B*, and *C* are used to represent them. Assume the fifteen initial rules randomly generated are encoded as shown in Table 2.

Each bit string in Table 2 is evaluated by the set of training examples shown in Table 1 using the three measurements: *accuracy*, *utility* and *coverage*. The resulting fitness values are shown in Table 3.

Table 2. The encoded bit strings for the fifteen fuzzy rules.

Rule	S.L S	M	L	S.W S	M	L	P.L S	M	L	P.W S	M	L	Class Se	Ve	Vi
$\tilde{r}_1$	1	0	0	1	1	1	0	0	1	1	1	1	0	1	0
$\tilde{r}_2$	1	1	1	1	0	0	1	1	1	0	1	0	0	0	1
$\tilde{r}_3$	1	0	0	1	1	1	0	0	1	0	0	1	0	1	0
$\tilde{r}_4$	0	1	0	1	1	1	1	1	1	0	0	1	0	0	1
$\tilde{r}_5$	0	0	1	1	0	0	1	1	1	0	1	0	0	1	0
$\tilde{r}_6$	1	1	1	1	1	1	0	0	1	0	1	0	0	1	0
$\tilde{r}_7$	1	1	1	0	1	0	1	1	1	0	1	0	0	0	1
$\tilde{r}_8$	1	1	1	0	0	1	1	1	1	1	1	1	1	0	0
$\tilde{r}_9$	1	0	0	0	0	1	1	1	1	1	1	1	1	0	0
$\tilde{r}_{10}$	1	1	1	1	1	1	0	1	0	0	1	0	0	1	0
$\tilde{r}_{11}$	1	0	0	1	1	1	1	0	0	1	1	1	1	0	0
$\tilde{r}_{12}$	1	1	1	0	0	1	1	0	0	1	1	1	1	0	0
$\tilde{r}_{13}$	1	1	1	0	1	0	0	0	1	0	0	1	0	0	1
$\tilde{r}_{14}$	1	0	0	1	0	0	0	1	0	1	0	0	0	1	0
$\tilde{r}_{15}$	0	0	1	1	0	0	0	1	0	1	1	1	0	0	1

Rules are then selected to perform crossover and mutation operations according to their fitness values. Assume that the new generated offspring bit strings are shown in Table 4.

Table 4. The new bit strings generated by crossover and mutation operations

Rule	SL S	M	L	SW S	M	L	PL S	M	L	PW S	M	L	Class Se	Ve	Vi
$\tilde{r}_1$	1	1	1	1	1	1	0	0	1	0	0	1	0	0	1
$\tilde{r}_2$	1	1	1	0	1	0	0	1	0	0	1	0	0	0	1
$\tilde{r}_3$	1	1	1	1	1	1	0	1	1	1	1	1	1	0	0
$\tilde{r}_4$	1	1	1	0	0	1	1	1	0	0	1	0	0	0	1
$\tilde{r}_5$	1	1	1	0	1	0	0	0	1	0	0	1	0	0	1
$\tilde{r}_6$	1	1	1	0	0	1	1	1	1	1	1	1	1	0	0
$\tilde{r}_7$	1	0	0	1	1	1	1	0	0	1	1	0	0	0	1
$\tilde{r}_8$	1	1	1	1	1	1	0	1	0	0	1	1	0	1	0
$\tilde{r}_9$	1	1	1	0	0	1	1	1	1	1	1	0	0	1	0
$\tilde{r}_{10}$	1	1	1	1	1	1	0	0	1	1	1	1	0	1	0
$\tilde{r}_{11}$	1	0	0	1	1	1	1	0	0	1	1	1	1	1	0
$\tilde{r}_{12}$	1	1	1	0	0	1	1	1	1	1	1	1	0	0	0

After crossover and mutation operations are performed, the fission operator is used to split the contradictive bit strings. In this example, new rule $\tilde{r}_{11}$ is generated by a mutation operation and has contradictive classes. It is then split as "100111100111010" and "100111100111100" respectively.

The fitness values of these newly generated rules are then evaluated, and Steps 4 to 8 are iteratively executed until the predefined number of generations is reached. When the number of evolution generations is reached, the bit strings with their fitness values larger than zero are output and decoded into fuzzy rules.

222

Table 3. The evaluation results of the fifteen rules

Rule	Accuracy	Utility	Coverage set C_i before object movement	Coverage set C_i after object movement	Coverage	Fitness	$U\text{-}C_i$
$\tilde{r}_{10}$	1	3.4074	{6, 7, 8, 9, 20}	{6, 7, 8, 9, 20}	3.157	10.757	{1, 2, 3, 4, 5, 10, 11, 12, 13, 14, 15, 16, 17, 18, 19}
$\tilde{r}_{13}$	0.8459	2.7123	{11 13 14 15 19}	{11, 13, 14, 15, 19}	3.245	7.445	{1, 2, 3, 4, 5, 10, 12, 16, 17, 18}
$\tilde{r}_{8}$	1	1.9276	{1, 2, 4 ,5, 17}	{1, 2, 4, 5, 17}	3.803	7.331	{3, 10, 12, 16, 18}
$\tilde{r}_{12}$	1	1.9276	{1, 2, 4, 5, 17}	ϕ	0	0	{3, 10, 12, 16, 18}
$\tilde{r}_{9}$	1	1.1776	{4, 5}	ϕ	0	0	{3, 10, 12, 16, 18}
$\tilde{r}_{11}$	1	1.0923	{3, 4, 5, 18}	{3, 18}	1.5	1.638	{10, 12, 16}
$\tilde{r}_{4}$	0.7507	1.3075	{11, 15, 19}	ϕ	0	0	{10, 12, 16}
$\tilde{r}_{6}$	0.5141	1.6403	{10, 12}	{10, 12}	1.029	0.868	{16}
$\tilde{r}_{2}$	0.3776	0.795	{6, 9, 12}	ϕ	0	0	{16}
$\tilde{r}_{1}$	0	0.3138	{16}	{16}	0.588	0	{16}
$\tilde{r}_{3}$	0	0.1771	{16}	ϕ	0	0	ϕ
$\tilde{r}_{5}$	0	0.4451	ϕ	ϕ	0	0	ϕ
$\tilde{r}_{7}$	0	0.679	{7, 8, 10, 20}	ϕ	0	0	ϕ
$\tilde{r}_{14}$	0	0.1479	ϕ	ϕ	0	0	ϕ
$\tilde{r}_{15}$	0	0.2308	ϕ	ϕ	0	0	ϕ

6. Conclusions and future works

In this paper, we have proposed a coverage-based genetic fuzzy-rule mining approach to construct an effective fuzzy rule base. The proposed approach consists of three phases: fuzzy-rule generating, fuzzy-rule encoding and fuzzy-rule evolution. Three criteria including accuracy, utility and coverage are used to evaluate each fuzzy rule in the population. The evolution process is iteratively executed until a predefined number of generations is reached. Finally, a concise and compact fuzzy rule base is derived.

Although the proposed approach can effectively generate fuzzy rule bases, there are still several issues to be explored. In the future, we will continuously focus on the following works.

1. The membership functions adopted here are given. Developing effective algorithms to simultaneously learn fuzzy rules and membership functions are desired.

2. The Michigan Approach and the Pittsburgh approach have their own advantages and disadvantages. Designing a hybrid genetic fuzzy-rule mining approach to utilize the advantages of both the two approaches is another topic to attempt.

References

[1] L. B. Booker, *Intelligent behavior as an adaptation to the task environment*, Doctoral Dissertation, University of Michigan, 1982.

[2] J. H. Boose, "A Knowledge acquisition program for expert systems based on personal construct psychology," *International Journal of Man-Machine Studies*, vol. 23, pp. 495-525, 1985.

[3] J. H. Boose and J. M. Bardshaw, "Expertise transfer and complex problems: using AQUINAS as a knowledge-acquisition workbench for knowledge-based systems," *International Journal of Man-Machine Studies*, vol. 26, pp. 3-28, 1987.

[4] B. Carse, T. C. Fogarty, and A. Munro, Evolving fuzzy rule based controllers using genetic algorithms, *Fuzzy Sets and Systems*, vol. 80, 273-293, 1996.

[5] K. A. DeJong, W. M. Spears, and D. F. Gordon, Using genetic algorithms for concept learning, *Machine Learning*, vol. 13, 161-188, 1993.

[6] B. R. Gaines and M. L. G. Shaw, "Eliciting knowledge and transferring it effectively to a knowledge-based system," *IEEE Transaction on Knowledge and Data Engineering*, vol. 5, no. 1, pp. 4-14, 1993.

[7] J. H. Holland. Adaptation in Natural and Artificial Systems, University of Michigan Press, 1975.

[8] J. H. Holland and J. S. Reitman, "Cognitive systems based on adaptive algorithms," Machine Learning: An Artificial Intelligence Approach, Morgan Kaufmann Publishers, Los Altos, CA, 1983.

[9] H. Ishibuchi, T. Nakashima, and T. Murata, "A fuzzy classifier system that generates fuzzy if–then rules for pattern classification problems," in Proc. 2nd IEEE Int.

Conf. Evolutionary Computation, Perth, Australia, Nov. 29–Dec. 1, 1995, pp. 759–764.

[10] H. Ishibuchi, T. Nakashima, and T. Kuroda, "A Hybrid Fuzzy Genetics-based Machine Learning Algorithm: Hybridization of Michigan and Pittsburgh Approach", IEEE SMC `99 conference proceeding, 1999.

[11] G. A. Kelly, The psychology of personal constructs, Norton, New York, 1955.

[12] O. K. Ngwenyama and N. Bryson, "A formal method for analyzing and integrating the rule sets of multiple experts," Information Systems, Vol. 17, No. 1, pp. 1-16, 1992.

[13] S. F. Smith, "A learning system based on genetic adaptive algorithms", Ph.D. Thesis, University of Pittsburgh, 1980.

[14] M. L. G. Shaw and B. R. Gaines, "KITTEN: Knowledge initiation and transfer tools for experts and novices," International Journal of Man-Machine Studies, vol. 27, pp. 251-280, 1987.

[15] C. H. Wang, T. P. Hong, and S. S. Tseng, Knowledge integration by genetic algorithms, accepted in the Seventh International Fuzzy Systems Association World Congress,1997.

[16] C. H. Wang, T. P. Hong and S. S. Tseng, "Integrating fuzzy knowledge by genetic algorithms," IEEE Transactions on Evolutionary Computation, Vol. 2, No.4, pp. 138-149, 1998.

[17] C. H. Wang, T. P. Hong, S. S. Tseng, and C. M. Liao, Automatically integrating multiple rule sets in a distributed-knowledge environment, accepted by IEEE Transactions on Systems, Man, and Cybernetics.

[18] C. H. Wang, T. P. Hong and S. S. Tseng, "Integrating membership functions and fuzzy rule sets from multiple knowledge sources," Fuzzy Sets and Systems, Vol. 112, pp. 141-154, 2000.

[19] Y. Yuan and M. J. Shaw, "Induction of fuzzy decision trees," Fuzzy Sets and Systems Vol. 69, pp. 125-139, 1995.

An Efficient Fuzzy C-Means Clustering Algorithm

Ming-Chuan Hung and Don-Lin Yang

Department of Information Engineering, Feng Chia University

100 Wenhwa Rd., Taichung, Taiwan 407

E-mail: mchong@fcu.edu.tw, dlyang@fcu.edu.tw

Abstract

The Fuzzy C-Means (FCM) algorithm is commonly used for clustering. The performance of the FCM algorithm depends on the selection of the initial cluster center and/or the initial membership value. If a good initial cluster center that is close to the actual final cluster center can be found, the FCM algorithm will converge very quickly and the processing time can be drastically reduced.

In this paper, we propose a novel algorithm for efficient clustering. This algorithm is a modified FCM called the psFCM algorithm, which significantly reduces the computation time required to partition a dataset into desired clusters. We find the actual cluster center by using a simplified set of the original complete dataset. It refines the initial value of the FCM algorithm to speed up the convergence time. Our experiments show that the proposed psFCM algorithm is on average four times faster than the original FCM algorithm. We also demonstrate that the quality of the proposed psFCM algorithm is the same as the FCM algorithm.

1. Introduction

Clustering is a process of partitioning or grouping a given set of unlabeled patterns into a number of clusters such that similar patterns are assigned to one cluster. There are two main approaches to clustering. One method is crisp clustering (or hard clustering), and the other one is fuzzy clustering. A characteristic of the crisp clustering method is that the boundary between clusters is fully defined. However, in many real cases, the boundaries between clusters cannot be clearly defined. Some patterns may belong to more than one cluster. In such cases, the fuzzy clustering method provides a better and more useful method to classify these patterns.

There are many fuzzy clustering methods being introduced [1]. The fuzzy C-means (FCM) algorithm is widely used. It is based on the concept of fuzzy C-partition, which was introduced by Ruspini [2], developed by Dunn [3], and generalized by Bezdek [4,5]. The FCM algorithm and its derivatives have been used very successfully in many applications, such as pattern recognition [6], classification [7], data mining [8], and image segmentation [9,10]. It has also been used for data analysis and modeling [11,12] etc.

Normally, the FCM algorithm consists of several execution steps. In the first step, the algorithm selects C initial cluster centers from the original dataset randomly. Then, in later steps, after several iterations of the algorithm, the final result converges to the actual cluster center. Therefore, choosing a good set of initial cluster centers is very important for an FCM algorithm. However, it is difficult to select a good set of initial cluster centers randomly. If a good set of initial cluster centers is chosen, the algorithm may take less iterations to find the actual cluster centers.

To show that selecting a set of initial cluster centers that approximates the actual cluster centers can reduce the number of iterations and improve the system performance, we use Figures 1 and 2 for illustration. Using the target tracking by initializing each iteration in the procedure with the clustering result from the previous one can speed up the convergence significantly. Since the number of iterations required in the FCM algorithm strongly depends on the initial cluster centers, the goal of our proposed method is to find a good set of initial cluster centers.

In [13], Cheng et al. propose the *multistage random sampling* FCM algorithm. It is based on the assumption that a small subset of a dataset of feature vectors can be used to approximate the cluster centers of the complete dataset. Under this assumption FCM is used to compute the cluster centers of an appropriate size subset of the original dataset. After obtaining the cluster centers of this small subset, the subset of data is merged with an additional small, randomly selected subset of the remaining unprocessed feature vectors to form a larger subset that is processed by FCM. The previously calculated cluster centers are used for the initialization of the fuzzy partition matrix of this newly formed set. The procedure above is repeated until the size of the feature vectors matrix used in calculations is large enough to approximate the actual cluster center of the full dataset. The resulting cluster centers are then used for the initialization of the fuzzy partition matrix used by FCM when it is applied to the original dataset. This results in a faster convergence for the FCM algorithm.

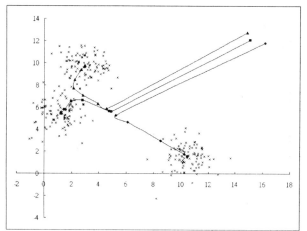

Figure 1. An example showing the convergence paths from three distant initial cluster centers to the final actual cluster centers after seven iterations by using the FCM algorithm.

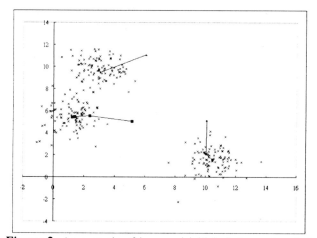

Figure 2. An example of improved initial cluster centers that are near the final cluster centers requiring only three FCM iterations.

The FCM algorithm and its derivatives have the iterative nature of an algorithm. In addition, their calculation often involves a huge number of membership matrices and candidate cluster centers matrices. It is a computationally intensive method. In our study, we mitigate the time problem by simplifying the computation and reducing the number of iterations required to converge. The idea of the proposed method is to simplify the dataset and find an initial candidate set of cluster

centers as close as possible to the actual cluster centers. This will reduce the number of iterations and improve the execution performance. The initial cluster center found by the proposed algorithm approximates the actual cluster center very well.

This efficient algorithm for improving the FCM is called the *partition simplification* FCM (psFCM). It is divided into two phases. In *Phase I*, we first partition the dataset into some small block cells using the *k-d tree* method [14] and reduce the original dataset into a *simplified dataset* with unit blocks as described in our previous work [15]. All patterns in a unit block are replaced by the *centroid* of these patterns. Then, the large number of patterns in the original dataset is drastically reduced to a small number of unit blocks' centroids, i.e., the simplified dataset. Secondly, we find the actual cluster center of this simplified dataset by the FCM algorithm. In *Phase II*, it is a standard process of the FCM with the cluster centers initialized by the final cluster centers from Phase I. The execution performance of the psFCM is much better than that of the FCM and its derivatives.

The rest of the paper is organized as follows. The review of the previously proposed approach for the FCM algorithm is in Section 2. In Section 3, we discuss the proposed algorithm. In Section 4, we show the experimental results and discuss the time complexity and accuracy issue. Finally, in Section 5, we conclude the paper.

2. Related Work

In this section, we briefly describe the Fuzzy C-means algorithm. Consider a set of unlabeled patterns $X=\{x_1,x_2,...,x_N\}$, $x_i \in R^f$, where N is the number of patterns and f is the dimension of *pattern vectors* (features). The FCM algorithm focuses on minimizing the value of an *objective function*. The objective function measures the quality of the partitioning that divides a dataset into C clusters.

The FCM algorithm measures the quality of the partitioning by comparing the distance from pattern x_i to the current candidate cluster center w_j with the distance from pattern x_i to other candidate cluster centers. The objective function is an optimization function that calculates the *weighted within-group sum of squared errors* (WGSS) as follows [5]:

$$\text{Minimize} \quad J_m(U,W) \equiv \sum_{j=1}^{C}\sum_{i=1}^{N}(\mu_{ij})^m d_{ij}^2 \qquad (1)$$

where:
  N: the number of patterns in X
  C: the number of clusters

U: the membership function matrix; the elements of U are μ_{ij}

μ_{ij}: the value of the membership function of the ith pattern belonging to the jth cluster

d_{ij}: the distance from x_i to w_j, viz., $d_{ij} = \left\| x_i - w_j^{(t)} \right\|$; where $w_j^{(t)}$ denotes the cluster center of the jth cluster for the tth iteration

W: the cluster center vector

m: the exponent on μ_{ij}; to control fuzziness or amount of clusters overlap

The FCM algorithm focuses on minimizing J_m, subject to the following constraints on U:

$$\mu_{ij} \in [0,1] \,,\, i = 1,...,N \,,\, \text{and } j = 1,...,C \qquad (2)$$

$$\sum_{j=1}^{C} \mu_{ij} = 1 \,,\, i = 1,...,N \qquad (3)$$

$$0 < \sum_{i=1}^{N} \mu_{ij} < N \,,\, j = 1,...,C \qquad (4)$$

Function (1) describes a constrained optimization problem, which can be converted to an unconstrained optimization problem by using the Lagrange multiplier technique.

$$\mu_{ij}^{(t)} = \frac{1}{\sum_{l=1}^{C} (\frac{d_{ij}}{d_{il}})^{\frac{2}{(m-1)}}} \,,\, i = 1,...,N \,,\, j,l = 1,...,C \qquad (5)$$

If $d_{ij} = 0$ then $\mu_{ij} = 1$ and $\mu_{ij} = 0$ for $l \neq j$ (6)

$$W_j^{(t)} = \frac{\sum_{i=1}^{N} (\mu_{ij}^{(t-1)})^m x_i}{\sum_{i=1}^{N} (\mu_{ij}^{(t-1)})^m} \,,\, j = 1,...,C \qquad (7)$$

The FCM algorithm starts with a set of *initial cluster centers* (or *arbitrary membership values*). Then, it iterates the two updating functions (5) and (7) at the tth iteration until the cluster centers are stable or the objective function in (1) converges to a local minimum. The complete algorithm consists of the following steps:

Step 1: Given a fixed number C, initialize the cluster center matrix $W^{(0)}$ by using a random generator from the original dataset. Record the cluster centers, set $t=0$, $m = 2$, and decide ε, where ε is a small positive constant.

Step 2: Initialize the membership matrix $U^{(0)}$ by using functions (5) and (6).

Step 3: Increase t by one. Compute the new cluster center matrix (candidate) $W^{(t)}$ by using (7).

Step 4: Compute the new membership matrix $U^{(t)}$ by using functions (5) and (6).

Step 5: If $\| U^{(t)} - U^{(t-1)} \| < \varepsilon$ then stop, otherwise go to step 3.

3. Our Proposed Algorithm

In this section, we propose a novel method for the clustering problem. The proposed psFCM algorithm can speed up the overall computation time and reduce the total number of calculations. The main idea of the proposed algorithm is to *refine the initial cluster centers* (initial prototypes). It finds a set of initial cluster centers that is very close to the actual cluster centers of the dataset.

First, we give an introductory explanation of the proposed algorithm followed by a formal description. The psFCM algorithm consists of two phases. Phase I is a sequence of processes that refines the initial cluster centers. In the first stage, we partition the dataset into several *unit blocks* by using the k-d tree method [14]. There must be at least one pattern in each unit block. Thus, the actual number of unit blocks depends on the size and pattern distribution of the dataset. For each unit block, we calculate the centroid of patterns in the unit block. The centroid of patterns will be used to represent all the patterns in this unit block. By doing so, a dataset X_N can be drastically reduced to a simplified dataset X_{ps} containing the centroids of the original patterns.

In the second stage, we apply the FCM algorithm to find the cluster centers of the simplified dataset $\overline{X}_{ps} = (\overline{x}_1, \overline{x}_2,...,\overline{x}_{ps})$, $\overline{x}_i \in R^f$. The number of centroids in the simplified dataset is N_{ps}. It is equivalent to the number of unit blocks N_{ub}. Since $N_{ps} << N$, we may reduce the number of calculations of the norm distance. This reduces the overall computation time.

The cluster centers found in Phase I are used in Phase II. In Phase II, we apply the FCM algorithm to find the actual cluster center of the dataset. That is, the cluster centers found in Phase I are the initial values of the fuzzy partition matrix used by the FCM algorithm in Phase II. The process in Phase II converges quickly because the initial cluster centers are near the location of the actual cluster centers.

Before we show details of the psFCM algorithm, there are several parameters that need to be defined. They are the number of clusters C, the *weight* exponent m, the number of *unit blocks* N_{ub} (the number of splits with the k-d tree method), and *the stopping conditions* ε_1 and ε_2 in Phases I and II, respectively. Here, we let the weight exponent m be 2. The number of unit blocks N_{ub} depends on the total number of patterns N and the distribution of the dataset. The value of ε_1 and ε_2 is decided from experiments as explained in Section 4.

The proposed psFCM algorithm consists of two phases as follows:

3.1. Phase I : Refine initial prototypes for fuzzy C-means clustering

Step1:

First, we partition the dataset into unit blocks by using the k-d tree method. The splitting priority depends on the scattered degree of data values for each dimension. If one dimension has a higher scattered degree, it has a higher priority to be split. The scattered degree is defined as the distribution range and the standard deviation of the feature. The formula of the scattered degree is as follows:

$$R_i = \frac{(X_{max} - X_{min})_i}{\sigma_i} \quad , \quad i = 1,..f \quad (8)$$

Where

R_i : the scattered degree for the ith feature (dimension)
X_{max} : the maximum value of pattern in the ith feature
X_{min} : the minimum value of pattern in the ith feature
σ_i : the standard deviation of all patterns in the ith feature
f : the number of features (dimensions)

The k-d tree is a kind of binary partition based on the difference between the maximum and minimum values of the partition dimension. Thus, we may easily acquire the range of each block in each dimension. If the number of splits is p, $N_{ub} \leq 2^p$.

After splitting the dataset into unit blocks, every unit block may contain some sample patterns. There must be at least one pattern in each unit block. If there is no sample pattern in a unit block, the unit block will then be discarded. We do not consider such a unit block in the following steps. Figure 3 gives an example where a two-dimension dataset is divided into several unit blocks. Here, we only have to scan the database twice to identify the location of each sample pattern.

Step 2:

After splitting the dataset into unit blocks, we calculate the centroid $\overline{X}_i$ for each unit block that contains some sample patterns. The centroid $\overline{X}_i$ represents all sample patterns in this unit block. Then, we use all of these centroids $\overline{X}_i$ to denote the original dataset. Figure 4 gives an example in which original patterns are represented by all the computed centroids $\overline{X}_i$.

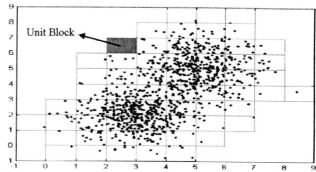

Figure 3. Partitioning the original dataset into several unit blocks.

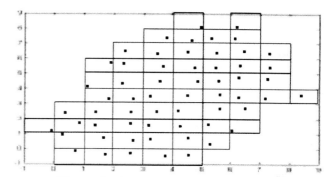

Figure 4. The simplified dataset of Figure 3.

In addition, each centroid contains statistical information of the patterns in each unit block. These include the number of patterns in a unit block (*WUB*) and the linear sum of all patterns in a unit block (*LSUB*). When we scan the database the second time, it also finds the statistics of each dimension. These statistics will be used when the algorithm calculates new candidate cluster centers, which improves the system performance.

The formula of calculating the centroid in the ith unit block is as follows:

$$\overline{X}_i = \frac{LSUB_i}{WUB_i} \quad (9)$$

The algorithm to split a dataset into unit blocks and to form the simplified dataset is shown in Figure 5.

Step 3:

Initialize the cluster center matrix $W^{(0)}$ by using a random generator from the dataset, record the cluster centers, and set $t=0$.

Step 4:

Initialize the membership matrix $U^{(0)}$ by using functions (5) and (6) with the simplified dataset $\overline{X}_{ps} = (\overline{x}_1, \overline{x}_2,..., \overline{x}_{ps})$ and $i = 1,..., N_{ps}$.

Proc partition_dataset (original dataset)
   for each dimension D_f of the dataset
     /* Find the range for dimension D_f */
     Range_Max[*f*] = the maximum value of dimension D_f
     Range_Min[*f*] = the minimum value of dimension D_f
     /* Calculate the interval of segment it would partition for dimension D_f */
     /* *Num_of_Split*[*f*] is the number of splits for dimension D_f */
     Interval_of_Seg[*f*] = (*Range_Max*[*f*] – *Range_Min*[*f*]) / *Num_of_Split*[*f*]
   for each pattern X_i
     /* Calculate the *UB* to which pattern X_i[*f*] belongs */
     for each dimension D_f of X_i, named X_i[*f*]
     Point_in_Dim[*f*] = (X_i[*f*] – *Range_Min*[*f*]) / *Interval_of_Seg*[*f*]
     /* Use the value of *Point_in_Dim*[*f*] to calculate the UB_i to which X_i[*f*] belongs, named *UB_Location* of X_i[*f*] */
     /* Calculate *LSUB* and *WUB* for each UB_i */
     *UB*_process (X_i[*f*], *UB_Location*)
     /* Compute $\bar{X}_i$: Centroid of Unit Block *i* */
$$\bar{X}_i = \frac{LSUB_i}{WUB_i}$$
End partition_dataset

Figure 5. The algorithm to partition the original dataset to form the simplified dataset.

Step 5:

Increase *t* (i.e., *t*=*t*+1); compute a new cluster center matrix (candidate) $W^{(t)}$ by using function (10).

$$W_j^{(t)} = \frac{\sum_{i=1}^{N_{ps}} (\mu_{ij}^{(t-1)})^m n_i \bar{x}_i}{\sum_{i=1}^{N_{ps}} (\mu_{ij}^{(t-1)})^m n_i}, \quad i = 1,...,N_{ps}, \quad j = 1,...,C \quad (10)$$

where n_i denotes the number of patterns of the ith unit block.

Step 6:

Compute the new membership matrix $U_{X_{ps}}^{(t)}$ by using functions (5) and (6) with the simplified dataset $\bar{X}_{ps} = (\bar{x}_1, \bar{x}_2,...,\bar{x}_{ps})$ and $i = 1,...,N_{ps}$.

Step 7:

If $\left\| U_{N_{ps}}^{(t)} - U_{N_{ps}}^{(t-1)} \right\| \geqq \varepsilon_1$, go to Step 5, otherwise go to

Phase II.

3.2. Phase II: Find the actual cluster centers for the dataset

Step1:
Initialize the fuzzy partition matrix $U^{(0)}$ by using the results of $W^{(t)}$ from Phase I with functions (5) and (6) for the dataset *X*.

Step 2:
Follow Step 3 to Step 5 of the FCM algorithm discussed in Section 2 using the stopping condition ε_2.

4. Experiments and Results

In this section, we discuss our experimental results, the time complexity of the proposed method, and its accuracy. The datasets used in the experiments are described in Section 4.1. Section 4.2 shows the experimental results. In Section 4.3, we discuss our findings.

4.1 Dataset Description

In this paper, we focus on improving the time complexity of the fuzzy C-means algorithm. To show that the result of our proposed algorithm is correct and more efficient than the other algorithms, we performed a series of experiments. Table 1 shows the datasets used in the experiments, where *N* is the number of patterns, *C* is the number of clusters, and *f* is the dimension of pattern vectors (features).

The datasets are generated by using the following criteria:
1) The datasets from D_1 to D_{10} are generated from a *normal distribution*. Here, we generate normally distributed data points (patterns) by using the *Marsaglia's Polar method* [17]. The *standard deviation* of these data points in each cluster is 1. We randomly select *C* data points from the range [0,4C]. These *C* data points may be treated as the mean value of the normal distribution of each cluster. Every cluster has the same number of data points *N/C* that is around a specific mean value, and *clusters can overlap*.
2) The datasets from R_1 to R_4 are generated from a *uniform distribution*. *Any two clusters cannot overlap.* The number of data points (patterns) in each cluster is the same, which is *N/C*.
3) The datasets from R_5 to R_{10} are also generated from a *uniform distribution*. However, *clusters can overlap*. The number of data points in each cluster is different. Each cluster has $N_i = i \times \dfrac{2N}{C(C+1)}$ data points, where $i = 1,2,...,C$.

Table 1. Description of the experiment datasets.

Dataset	Size (N)	Dimensionality (f)	No. of Clusters (C)	Characteristic (distribution)	Range
D_1	32k	2	8	Normal	[0,4C]
D_2	32k	2	16	Normal	[0,4C]
D_3	32k	2	32	Normal	[0,4C]
D_4	64K	2	8	Normal	[0,4C]
D_5	64k	2	16	Normal	[0,4C]
D_6	64k	2	32	Normal	[0,4C]
D_7	64k	2	64	Normal	[0,4C]
D_8	128k	2	8	Normal	[0,4C]
D_9	128k	2	16	Normal	[0,4C]
D_{10}	128k	2	32	Normal	[0,4C]
R_1	16k	2	4	Random	[0,1]
R_2	16k	2	8	Random	[0,1]
R_3	32k	2	4	Random	[0,1]
R_4	32k	2	8	Random	[0,1]
R_5	16k	2	4	Random	[0,1]
R_6	16k	2	8	Random	[0,1]
R_7	16k	2	16	Random	[0,1]
R_8	32k	2	4	Random	[0,1]
R_9	32k	2	8	Random	[0,1]
R_{10}	32k	2	16	Random	[0,1]

Table 2. The overall result of the normal distribution datasets D_1 to D_{10} where the number of splits for the k-d tree in the psFCM is 14.

Datasets	No. of Clusters	FCM		psFCM		FRT	FRD
		Total time (Seconds)	Distance calculation	Total time (Seconds)	Distance calculation		
D_1	8	295	5068800	55	1026346	5.4	4.94
D_2	16	680	10854400	167	2826976	4.07	3.84
D_3	32	1207	17408000	353	5368832	3.42	3.24
D_4	8	1091	7270400	210	2578333	5.2	4.61
D_5	16	2849	17817600	511	3560832	5.58	5.0
D_6	32	6586	38092800	2139	12958925	3.08	2.94
D_7	64	15033	97484800	5695	38018150	2.64	2.56
D_8	8	2283	14950400	348	2658806	6.56	5.62
D_9	16	5423	33587200	1153	7894640	4.7	4.2
D_{10}	32	12051	87654400	3038	23794278	3.97	3.68

Table 3. The overall result of the uniform distribution datasets R_1 to R_{10} where the number of splits for the k-d tree in the psFCM is 13.

Datasets	No. of Clusters	FCM		psFCM		FRT	FRD
		Total time (Seconds)	Distance calculation	Total time (Seconds)	Distance calculation		
R_1	4	59	614400	19	205760	3.11	2.99
R_2	8	186	1843200	63	655590	2.95	2.81
R_3	4	129	1331200	29	335872	4.45	3.96
R_4	8	332	3276800	65	720858	5.11	4.55
R_5	4	86	870400	23	240277	3.74	3.62
R_6	8	418	4069382	86	869598	4.86	4.68
R_7	16	1192	10848973	339	3106970	3.52	3.49
R_8	4	126	1305600	30	343549	4.2	3.8
R_9	8	631	6143232	86	929968	7.34	6.61
R_{10}	16	2277	20679629	395	3727757	5.76	5.55

4.2 Experimental Results

The experiment datasets ($D_1 \sim D_{10}$ and $R_1 \sim R_{10}$) are used to run on two personal computers. One is a *Pentium III* personal computer with the following specification: a clock rate of 800MHz and memory size of 512 Mbytes. The other is a *Celeron* personal computer with a clock rate of 433Hz and memory size of 64 Mbytes.

When we run the experiments using the FCM algorithm, different random initialization sets may result in different numbers of convergence iterations. Therefore, we run the proposed psFCM algorithm and the FCM algorithm with each dataset in ten trials. In each trial, the initial cluster centers are initialized in a random fashion. The same initial cluster centers are used by both the psFCM algorithm and the FCM algorithm.

The execution performance of the psFCM algorithm and the FCM algorithm is shown in Tables 2 and 3. Here, the comparison is based on the two factors: the factor reduction in overall time (FRT) and the factor reduction in distance calculations (FRD) [16]. From the results in Tables 2 and 3, the execution performance of the psFCM algorithm is approximately four times better than that of the FCM algorithm.

In the experiment of the psFCM algorithm, the stopping condition ε_1 of Phase I is set to 0.1. The number of convergence iterations may be reduced in Phase II if we let ε_1 have a smaller value. The stopping condition ε_2 for Phase II in the psFCM algorithm and the FCM algorithm is 0.4 for both.

To get the simplified dataset, the original dataset is divided into many equal size unit blocks by the psFCM algorithm. As mentioned in Section 3, all the patterns in one unit block are replaced by the centroid of the unit block. From the results of the experiments, we show that the proposed algorithm reduces a significant amount of time in Phase I.

To understand the relationship between the number of splits with the k-d tree method and the execution performance (speedup), we select some datasets (with different N or C) and compare the execution performance of these datasets by splitting them into a different number of unit blocks. Here, we measure the execution performance by using FRT. The results are shown in Figures 6 and 7. Figure 6 depicts the relationship between the number of splits and the speedup of execution time for datasets R2 and R4 whose sizes are 16k and 32k, respectively, while the number of clusters is the same (8 clusters). Figure 7 shows the relationship between the number of splits and the speedup of execution time for datasets R1 and R2 whose sizes are the same (16k) while the numbers of clusters are 4 and 8 clusters, respectively. We find the optimal number of splits is around 12. We also investigate the relationship between the number of clusters and the speedup of execution time. The experiment result is shown in Figure 8. The normal distribution dataset has a size of 64K, and the number of splits is 14. The decline of the speedup at 32 and 64 clusters can be rectified by increasing the number of splits. For example, when we adjust the number of splits to 16, the performance for the 64 clusters can be improved to a speedup of 3.81.

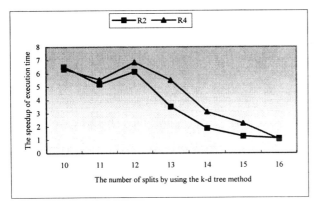

Figure 6. The relationship between the number of splits and the speedup of execution time for datasets *R2* and *R4*.

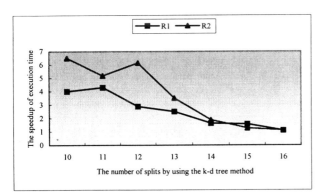

Figure 7. The relationship between the number of splits and the speedup of execution time for datasets *R1* and *R2*.

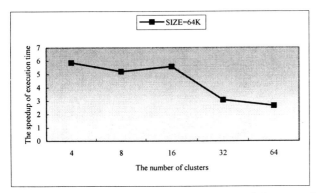

Figure 8. The relationship between the number of clusters and the speedup of execution time.

4.3 Discussions

From the experimental results described in the last section, the proposed psFCM algorithm has approximately the same speedup for the patterns of normal distribution as well as uniform distribution. In general, our method works well for most kinds of datasets.

In Phase I of the psFCM algorithm, the cluster centers found by using the simplified dataset is very close to the actual cluster centers. Phase II converges quickly if we use these cluster centers from Phase I as the initial cluster centers of Phase II. From the experiments, in most cases, Phase II converges in only a few iterations. For the psFCM algorithm, the system requires more iterations to converge if the stopping condition ε_1 is smaller. However, the number of patterns used in Phase I of the proposed algorithm is N_{ps}. The total number of norm distance calculations by the proposed algorithm is much smaller than the FCM algorithm because $N_{ps} << N$.

For the FCM algorithm, the system has to calculate the norm distance from each pattern to every candidate cluster center in each iteration. After calculating the norm distance, the system computes the membership matrix. Therefore, if the dimension of a dataset is f, the time complexity to calculate the distance is O(f). If there are N patterns and C clusters, the time complexity to calculate the membership matrix for each iteration is O(fNC). Thus, the time complexity is proportional to the number of patterns N and the number of clusters C. However, we have demonstrated that the time complexity to calculate the membership matrix for each iteration using the psFCM algorithm is O($fN_{ps}C$).

Here, we randomly select the initial cluster centers in Step 3 of the psFCM algorithm. Generally, the density of patterns near the cluster center is high. As mentioned in Section 3, the psFCM algorithm divides the dataset into unit blocks. The number of patterns in each unit block may be different. That is, the density of patterns in each unit block is different. We may randomly select C initial cluster centers $W_j(0)$ from the unit blocks with a higher pattern density. This will provide a better result.

The FCM algorithm does not guarantee that the cost function will converge to the local minimum, but it may converge to some saddle point.

5. Conclusions

In this paper, we proposed a novel method for efficient clustering that is better than the FCM algorithm. We reduce the computation cost and improve the performance by finding a good set of initial cluster centers.

The psFCM algorithm divides a dataset into several unit blocks. The centriods of unit blocks replace the patterns and form a new dataset, the simplified dataset. As mentioned in Section 4, the simplified dataset decreases the time complexity of computing the membership matrix from $O(fNC)$ to $O(fN_{ps}C)$ in every iteration. The number of iterations needed to converge in Phase II of the psFCM algorithm is also less than the number of convergence iterations of the FCM algorithm. From the experimental results, we have shown that the proposed algorithm improves the speedup in the execution time and the distance calculation. For large datasets, the psFCM algorithm improves the performance even more. We also demonstrate that the quality of our algorithm is the same as the FCM algorithm.

For a fair comparison, the initialization in Phase I of the psFCM algorithm and the FCM algorithm is determined randomly. We have also found in the psFCM algorithm that an initial cluster center selected from a unit block with a higher density is closer to the actual cluster center. This is a feature that cannot be found using the FCM algorithm and its derivatives. In future work, we will study this feature more thoroughly.

Reference

[1] F. Höppner, F. Klawonn, R. Kruse, and T. Runkler, *"Fuzzy cluster analysis,"* Wiley Press, New York, 1999.

[2] E. Ruspini, *"Numerical methods for fuzzy clustering,"* Information Sciences, Vol. 2, 1970, pp. 319-350.

[3] J.C. Dunn, *"A fuzzy relative of the ISODATA process and its use in detecting compact, well separated clusters,"* Cybernetics, Vol. 3, 1974, pp. 95-104.

[4] J.C. Bezdek, *"Cluster validity with fuzzy sets,"* Cybernetics, Vol. 3, 1974, pp. 58-73.

[5] J.C. Bezdek, *"Pattern recognition with fuzzy objective function algorithms,"* Plenum Press, New York, 1981.

[6] K.H. Chuang, M.J. Chiu, C.C. Lin, and J.H. Chen, *"Model-free functional MRI analysis using Kohonen clustering neural network and fuzzy C-means,"* IEEE Trans. On Medical Imaging, Vol. 18 (12), 1999, pp. 1117-1128.

[7] N.S. Iyer, A. Kandel, and M. Schneider, *"Feature-based fuzzy classification for interpretation of mammograms,"* Fuzzy Sets and Systems, Vol. 114, 2000, pp. 271-280.

[8] K. Hirota and W. Pedrycz, *"Fuzzy computing for data mining,"* Proceedings of the IEEE, Vol. 87(9), 1999, pp. 1575-1600.

[9] W.E. Phillips, R.P. Velthuizen, S. Phuphanich, L.O. Hall, L.P. Clark, and M.L. Silbiger, *"Application of fuzzy c-means segmentation technique for tissue differentiation in MR images of a hemorrhagic glioblastoma multifrome,"* Magnetic Resonance Imaging, Vol. 13(2), 1995, pp. 277-290.

[10] M.R. Rezaee, P.M.J. Zwet, B.P.E. Lelieveldt, R.J. Geest, and J.H.C. Reiber, *"A multiresolution image segmentation technique based on pyramidal segmentation and fuzzy clustering,"* IEEE Trans. On Image Processing, Vol. 97, 2000, pp. 1238-1248.

[11] P. Teppola, S.P. Mujunen, and P. Minkkinen, *"Adaptive fuzzy c-means clustering in process monitoring,"* Chemometrics and Intelligent Laboratory System, Vol. 45, 1999, pp. 22-38.

[12] X. Chang, W. Li, and J. Farrell, *"A C-means clustering based fuzzy modeling method,"* The Ninth IEEE International Conference on Fuzzy Systems, Vol. 2, 2000, pp. 937-940.

[13] T.W. Cheng, D.B. Goldgof, and L.O. Hall, *"Fast fuzzy clustering,"* Fuzzy Sets and Systems, Vol. 93, 1998, pp. 49-56.

[14] J.L. Bentley, *"Multidimensional binary search trees used for associative searching,"* Communications of the ACM, Vol. 18(9), 1975, pp. 509-517.

[15] D.L. Yang, J.H. Chang, M.C. Hung, and J.S. Liu, *"An efficient K-means-based clustering algorithm,"* Proceedings of The First Asia-Pacific Conference on Intelligent Agent Technology, Dec. 1999, pp. 269-273.

[16] K. Alsabti, S. Ranka, and V. Singh, *"An Efficient K-Means Clustering Algorithm,"* PPS/SPDP Workshop on High Performance Data Mining, 1997.

[17] G. Marsaglia, *"Random variables and computers,"* Information Theory Statistical Decision Functions Random Process, 1962, pp. 499-510.

Using Rough Sets Theory and Database Operations to Construct a Good Ensemble of Classifiers for Data Mining Applications

Xiaohua Hu
Vigilance Inc
270 Santa Ana Court
Sunnyvale, CA, USA
thu@vigilance.com

Abstract

In this paper we present a new approach to construct a good ensemble of classifiers using rough sets theory and database operations. Ensembles of classifiers is formulated precisely within the framework of rough sets theory and constructed very efficiently by using set-oriented database operations. Our method first computes a set of reducts which include all the indispensable attributes required for the decision categories. For each reduct, a reduct table is generated by removing those attributes which are not in the reduct. Next, a novel rule induction algorithm is used to compute the maximal generalized rules for each reduct table and a set of reduct classifiers is formed based on the corresponding reducts. The distinctive features of our method as compared to other methods of constructing ensembles of classifiers are: (1) present a theoretical model to explain the mechanism of constructing ensemble of classifiers, (2) each reduct is a minimum subset of attributes, has the same classification ability as the entire attributes, (3) each reduct classifier constructed from the corresponding reduct has a minimal set of classification rules, and is as accurate and complete as possible and at the same time as diverse as possible from the other classifiers, (4) the test indicates that the number of classifiers used to improve the accuracy is much less than other methods

1. Introduction

Ensemble of classifiers is to generate a set of classifiers instead of one classifier for the classification of new object, hoping that the combination of answers of multiple classifiers result in better performance. Ensemble of classifiers has been proved to be a very effective way to improve classification accuracy because uncorrelated errors made by the individual classifier can be removed by voting. A classifier which utilizes a single minimal set of classification rules to classify future examples may lead to mistakes. An ensemble of classifiers is a set of classifiers whose individual decisions are combined in some way to classify new example. Many research results illustrated that such multiple classifiers, if appropriately combined during classification, can improve the classification accuracy [3, 6, 2].

Many methods for constructing ensembles of classifiers have been developed, some are general and some are specific to particular algorithms [6]. The most popular way to construct multiple classifiers is to resample the training data set many times to get different subset of the original data set, typical examples of this method are bagging, boosting and cross-validation. The learning algorithm is run several times, each time with a different subset of the training examples. This technique works especially well for unstable learning algorithms, like decision trees, neural network. Another technique for generating multiple classifiers is to manipulate the set of input features available to the learning algorithms. Some other methods such as manipulating the output targets, injecting randomness, algorithm-specific methods for generating ensembles are also studied by some researchers [7]. Most study of such methods use a substantial ensemble of classifiers. For example, Bauer and Kohavi [3] use 25 classifiers, Freund and Schapire [9] use 100 classifiers, and in [23], it extends this to 1000.

However in many real data mining applications, it is infeasible to run an ensemble with many classifiers because it is too time consuming and takes a lot of cpu for huge data set, which is a typical characteristic of such applications. So we need to construct an ensemble of limited number but effective classifiers to improve the classification accuracy. In order to do that, some important questions in constructing such ensemble of classifiers, such as "how to generate classifiers less correlated to each other", "how many classifiers are good enough to improve the accuracy" need to be addressed. As we know, too many classifiers will hurt the comprehensibility and understanding ability of the rule sets and take too much cpu time and memory. Too few classifiers will not improve the classification accuracy. A similar phenomenon is also observed in [8, 20]. This also seems plausible in real life. Adding a novice to a team of experts is probably counterproductive and adding an expert whose knowledge is too similar to some other members only give more importance to the previous experts. The focus of this paper is to explore a theoretical model to explain the mechanism of multiple classifiers and efficiently construct a good ensemble of classifiers for data mining applications. In this paper, we propose a rough set approach to construct multiple classifiers by using database operations. Our approach manipulates the set of input features but with significant advantage over the previous methods. For example, PLAN-NETT [5] trained an ensemble of 32 neural netowrd based on 8 different subset of the 119 available input feature and 4 different network size. Each of the input feature subsets is human selected to group together. The ensemble of classifiers constructed in this way wasn't stable, even deleting a few of the input features degraded the performance of the individual classifiers and the voted ensemble did not perform very well. Our input feature to the learning algorithm is automatically chosen based on rough theory and each subset is a reduct, which is a minimum subset but with the same classification ability as the entire attribute of the training dataset.

In this paper, we introduce a method to construct a good ensemble of classifiers for data mining applications by using rough sets theory and set-oriented database operations. The rest of the paper is organized as follows: the basic notions of rough sets theory are reviewed and redefined in the database context in Section 2. We present a algorithm to find a set of reducts which consist of all the essential attributes of the data sets in Section 3. In Section 4, we discuss our novel algorithm to compute the maximal generalized rules for a reduct. In Section 5, we present the mechanism to form the ensemble of classifiers and the experimental results. Section 6 concludes with the concluding discussions.

2. Rough Sets

Assume we are given a set of examples with a class label to indicate the class to which each example belongs to. We call the class label the decision attribute, and rest of the attributes the condition attributes in this paper. Attributes are either numeric, coming from an ordered domain, or symbolic, coming from an unordered domain. (We don't consider numerical attributes in the paper because discretization of numerical attributes is considered as a preprocessing step in this research and there are a lot of discretization algorithms [14] which can convert the numeric attributes into

Door	Weight	Size	Cyl	mileage
2	Low	Camp	4	High
4	Low	Sub	6	Low
4	Med	Camp	4	High
2	High	Camp	6	Low
4	High	Camp	4	Low
4	Low	Camp	4	High
4	High	Sub	6	Low
2	Low	Sub	6	Low

Table 1. A Small Sample of Cars

discretized ones, the numeric attributes are treated as symbolic attributes after discretization). We also assume that our data set stored in a relational table has this form Table(condition-attributes decision-attribute). The table is called decision table, C is used to denote the condition attributes, D for decision attribute, t_j denotes the jth tuples. (It is trivial to rearrange the decision attribute to the last column in a relational table by using SELECT statement without changing the semantic meaning of the tuples in the table). It should be noted that a relational database does not make such distinction, it is only for our explanation purpose.

Rough sets introduced by Pawlak [21] is a powerful tool for data analysis and knowledge discovery from imprecise and ambiguous data and has been applied successfully in a lot of application domains such as machine learning and expert system [11]. Rough sets theory classifies all the attributes in the decision table into three categories according to their roles in the decision table: core attributes, reduct attributes, and superfluous attributes, which are very similar to the strong relevance, weak relevance and irrelevance defined by Kohavi based on Bayesian theory [12]. One of the drawbacks of rough sets theory is the inefficiency in computation, which limits its suitability in data mining applications. In considering of this and influenced by [15], we borrow some of the terms from rough sets theory and redefine them in the database context to utilize the very efficient set-oriented database operations. Almost all the operations in rough set computation used in our method can be performed using the database Count, Update and Projection operations (in the rest of this paper, we use Card to denote the Count operation, II for Projection operation) [21, 15]. Our definitions are self-content and do not rely on the knowledge of rough set theory.

Definition 1 An attribute $C_j \in C$ is superfluous in C with respect to D if the classification results of each tuple is not affected without using C_j.

This definition means that an attribute is superfluous if each tuple can be classified the same way no matter whether the attribute is present or not. We can check whether attribute C_j is superfluous by using some SQL operations. We only need to take two projections of the table: one on the attribute set $C - C_j + D$, and the other on $C - C_j$. If the cardinality of the two projection tables is the same, then it means no information is lost in removing attribute C_j, otherwise, it indicates that C_j is relevant and should be reinstated. Put it in a more formal way using database term, the cardinality of two projections being compared will be different iff there exist at least two tuples t_l, t_k such that for any $q \in C - C_j$, s.t. $t_l.q = t_k.q$, $t_l.C_j \neq t_k.C_j$ and $t_l.D \neq t_k.D$. In this case, a projection on $C - C_j$ will be one fewer row than the projection on $C - C_j + D$ because t_l, t_k being identical are being combined in this projection. However, in the projection $C - C_j + D$, t_l, t_k are still distingusable. Intuitively this means that some classification information is lost after C_j is eliminated. For example, Door is a superfluous attribute in Table 1, since $Card(\Pi(Weight, Size, Cyl)) = Card(\Pi(Weight, Size, Cyl, mileage)) = 6$

Definition 2 The subset of attributes $RED (RED \subseteq C)$ is a reduct of attributes C if it is a minimal subset of attributes which has the same classification power as the entire collection of condition attributes.

A decison table may have more than one reduct. For example, for Table 1, there are two reducts: {**Weight, Size**} and {**Weight, Cyl**} (in next section we will present the algorithm to find the reducts). Anyone of them can be used instead of the original table. None of the attributes of any reduct can be eliminated without affecting the classification accuracy. These minimal subsets can discern decision classes with the same discriminating power as the entire condition attributes. For each reduct, we can derive a reduct table from the original data set by removing those attributes which are not in the reduct. For example, Table 2 is a reduct table of Table 1, it can classify all the 8 tuples as Table 1. Table 3 is obtained by removing another attribute **Cyl** from Table 2, it cannot correctly distinguish between tuples 1, 6 and tuples 2, 8 because these tuples have the same **Weight** values but belongs to different classes which were distinguishable in the reduct table Table 2.

Definition 3 A attribute C_i is a core attribute if it satisfies the condition $Card(\Pi(C - C_i + D) \neq Card(\Pi(C - C_i))$.

A core attribute carries the essential information to make correct classification for the data set. Intuitively, for a core attribute C_i, there exist at least two tuples t_i, t_k with same values for all the attributes in C except C_i, and these two tuples are classified differently based on the value of attribute C_i. So eliminating attribute C_i will lose the ability to distinguish tuple t_i and t_k. For example, in Table 1, t_5, t_6 have the same values on all the condition attributes except **Weight**, the two tuples belong to different classes because they are different on their values on **Weight**. If Weight is eliminated, then t_5, t_6 are indistinguishable. So **Weight** is a core attribute for the table. All the core attributes are an indispensable part of every reduct. The following algorithm

tuple_id	Weight	Cyl	mileage
t1,t6	Low	4	High
t2,t8	Low	6	Low
t3	Medium	4	High
t4,t7	High	6	Low
t5	High	4	Low

Table 2. A Reduct Table

tuple_id	Weight	mileage
t1,t6	Low	High
t2,t8	Low	Low
t3	Medium	High
t4,t5, t7	High	Low

Table 3. A Reduced Table

obtains core attributes of a decision table.

Algorithm 1: (Core Attribute Algorithm)
Input: a decision table $T(C, D)$
Output: $CORE$ -the core attributes of T
1. Set CORE = $\emptyset$
2. For each attribute $Ci \in C$
    If $Card(\Pi(C - C_i + D)) \neq Card(\Pi(C - C_i))$ **Then**
        $CORE = CORE \cup C_i$
    Endfor

Definition 4 The *merit value* of an attribute C_j in C is defined as $Merit(C_j, C, D) = 1 - \frac{Card(\Pi(C - C_j + D)))}{Card(\Pi(C + D))}$

$Merit(C_j, C, D)$ reflects the degree of contribution made by the attribute C_j only between C and D. For example, in Table 1, $Card(\Pi(Door, Size, Cyl, mileage)) = 6$, $Card(\Pi(Door, Weight, Size, Cyl, mileage)) = 8$, so $Merit(C_j, C, D) = 1 - 6/8 = 0.25$.

Traditional techniques make use of feature merits based on either the information theoretic or statistical correlation between each attribute and the class, or the significant values based on rough sets theory [21]. These measures only consider the single attribute's effect on class distinguishability. However, in general, one attribute does not distinguish classes by itself; it does so in combination with other attributes. Therefore, it is desirable to obtain the attribute's correlation to the class in the context of other attributes. Most of the filter approaches using the traditional merit measure fails on parity data sets, where attributes have strong interactions. The following definition indicates that our feature merit measure ranks the attribute in the context of other attributes.

Definition 5 The degree of dependency $K(REDU, D)$ between the attributes $REDU \subseteq C$ and attributes D in decision table $T(C, D)$ is $K(REDU, D) = \frac{Card(\pi(REDU + D))}{Card(T)}$

The value $K(REDU, D)$ is the proportion of these tuples in the decision table which can be classified. It characterizes the ability to predict the class D and the complement concept $\rightarrow D$ from tuples in the decision table.

3. Generating Multiple Reducts

To utilize the power of ensemble to the maximum extent, it is essential to construct individual classifiers with error rate below 0.5 and whose errors are at least somewhat uncorrelated [6]. Empirical tests indicate that ensembles of classifiers are more helpful if they are as accurate and reliable as possible and at the same time as diversified as possible from the other classifiers. The multiple classifiers concept matches the concept of reducts in rough set theory. From a reduct, we can generate a reduct table, from a reduct table, we can construct a reduct classifier which consists of the corresponding decision rules. Finding all the reducts is a NP-complete problem [25]. Fortunately, it is usually not necessary to find all the reducts in practical applications including ours. A reduct uses a minimum number of attributes and represents a minimum and complete rules to classify objects in the decision table as perceived from "one angle". To classify unseen objects, it is desirable that (1) different reducts use different attributes as much as possible, (2) the union of the reduct attributes together include all the indispensable attributes, (3) the number of reducts used for classification is minimal. Here, we propose a greedy algorithm to compute a set of reducts which satisfy this optimal requirement partially. Our algorithm is sub-optimal because it cannot guarantee that the number of reducts is kept to minimum. (It may be conjured that this problem is computationally intractable to solve). Our algorithm starts with the core attribute (CORE). Then through backtracking, a set of reducts is constructed. A reduct is computed by using forward stepwise selection and backward stepwise elimination based on the merit values of the attributes and the dependency between conditions attributes and decision attributes. The algorithm terminates when the attributes in the union of the reducts include all the attributes required for the decision categories.

Algorithm 2: Computing Multiple Reducts
Input: A decision table $T(C, D)$
Output: A set of reducts $\cup REDU_i$ which includes all the attributes required for the decision categories
1. Apply Core Attribute Algorithm (Algorithm 1), obtain the core attributes $CORE$
2. $AR = C - CORE; REDU = CORE; 1 \rightarrow i$
3. Compute the merit value for each attribute $a \in AR$
4. Sort the set of attributes AR based on merit values
5. While the attributes in $\cup REDU_i$ do not include all the attributes required for the decision categories
/* backtrack to compute the next reduct */

(forward selection:)
/* Create a subset $REDU$ of attributes C by adding attributes */
    While $K(REDU, D) \neq K(C, D)$
        Select the next available attribute a_j in AR
        based on the merit value;
        $REDU = REDU \cup a_j, AR = AR - a_j$
        compute the degree of dependency $K(REDU, D)$;
    Endwhile
(backward elimination:)
    $\|REDU\| \rightarrow N$
/* create a reduct by dropping redundant attributes */
    For j= 0 to N-1 **Do**
        If a_j is not in $CORE$ **Then** remove it from $REDU_i$
        compute $K(REDU, D)$;
        If $K(REDU, D) \neq K(C, D)$ **Then**
            $REDU \cup a_i \rightarrow REDU$
    Endfor
    $REDU_i = REDU; i + 1 \rightarrow i;$
    delete the attribute with the smallest merit value
    from $REDU$
/* backtrack to compute the next reduct */
    Endwhile

Using Algorithm 2, we can find two reducts { {Weight Size}, {Weight, Cyl} } which together have all the three attributes required for decision table Table 1. The complexity of the algorithm cannot be determined exactly since it is highly dependent on the nature of the input data. The number of iterations really varies from data sets. From the experiment on the test data set from [17], it normally terminates after a few iterations. To compute a single reduct, it takes $O(AN + A\log A)$ in every iteration in the worst case for N objects with A attributes because computing the degree of dependency using a hashing technique is $O(N)$, computing attribute merit value is $O(AN)$, sorting the attributes based on the merit value $O(A\log A)$, creating the smaller subset of attributes using hash technology is $O(AN)$, and creating the reduct is $O(AN)$.

4. Maximal Generalized Rules: DBClass

A classification rule is a combination of values of some condition attributes such that the set of all examples matching it is contained in the set of examples labeled with the same class. A rule is denoted as an implication: $r : G_{i1} = v_{i1} \cap G_{i2} = V_{i2} \cap ... G_{ik} = V_{ik} \rightarrow D = d_i$. (Below, we use $cond(r)$ to denote the left hand and $deci(r)$ for the right hand of the rule r). Our aim is to produce rules in the learning process which are maximal generalized by removing the maximum number of condition attribute values without decreasing classification accuracy of the rule. Computing such rules is especially important in data mining applications since they represent the most general patterns existing in the data. Before describing our rule generation algorithm, we introduce two propositions: *rule redundancy* and *rule inconsistency*.

Rule redundancy: (1) if r_i and r_j are valid rules where $cond(r_i) = cond(r_j)$ and $dec(r_i) = dec(r_j)$, then r_i and r_j are logically equivalent rules. (2) if r_i and r_j are valid rules where $cond(r_j) \supset cond(r_i)$ and $dec(r_i) = dec(r_j)$, then r_j is logically included in r_i.

Rule inconsistency: if r_i and r_j are valid rules where $cond(r_j) \subseteq cond(r_i)$ and $dec(r_i) \neq dec(r_j)$, then r_i and r_j are inconsistent.

DBClass can find a set of maximal generalized rules from the reduct table. A reduct table can be considered as a set of specific rules RULES=$\{r_1, r_2, ..., r_n\}$. Each rule r_i corresponds to exact one tuple in the reduct table. Such rules can be generalized further by dropping conditions. The process by which the maximum number of condition attribute values are removed without losing essential information is called *attribute value reduction*, and the resulting rule is called a *maximal generalized rule*. The *maximal generalized rules* minimize the number of rule conditions and are optimal because their conditions are non-redundant. A condition is dropped from a rule r_i, and then rule r_i is checked for consistency with other rules in the rule set RULES. If rule r_i is inconsistent, then the dropped condition is restored. This step is repeated until every condition of the rule r_i has been tested. The resulting rules are a set of maximal generalized rules.

The order in which we process the attributes determines which *maximal generalized rule* is generated. Thus a *maximal generalized rule* may not turn out to be the best with respect to the conciseness or the coverage of the rule. Given a rule with a conditions, we could evaluate all $2^a - 1$ possible subsets of conditions on the database and select the best rule but this is, in general, impractical. For a near optimal solution, each condition of the rule is assigned a significance value by an evaluation function before dropping conditions process is started. The significant value indicates the relevance of this condition for this particular case. High significance values indicate more relevance. The process of dropping conditions should first drop the conditions with lower significance values, as described in [11]. The evaluation function for a condition $C_{ik} = V_{ik}$ is defined as $SIG(C_{ik} = V_{ik}) = P(C_{ik} = V_{ik})(P(D = d_i|C_{ik} = V_{ik}) - P(D = d_i))$, where $P(C_{ik} = V_{ik})$ is the probability of occurrence of the condition $C_{ik} = V_{ik}$; $P(D = d_i|C_{ik} = V_{ik})$ is the conditional probability of the class $D = d_i$ conditioned on the occurrence of the condition $C_{ik} = V_{ik}$; $p(D = d_i)$ is the proportion of the class $D = d_i$ in the database.

To avoid generating highly specific rules, DBClass uses Laplace test, a special case of the *m-probability-estimate* developed by Cestnik [4], to ensure that the distribution of examples among classes covered by the rule is significantly different from that which would occur by chance. In this way, many rules covering a few examples are eliminated, as the significance test believes their apparent high accuracy likely to simply due to chance. Laplace test avoids the undesirable "downward bias" of other measure and general rules tends to be favored. The Laplace measure is sufficient on its own to bias the search towards those general rules with higher predictive accuracy, tending to find rules of highest predictive accuracy (and thus also high significant). (the effect of Laplace to our methods is similar to the combined effect of minimum support and minimum confidence for association rule algorithm [1]).

$$Laplace = (n_c + l)/(n_{total} + k)$$

where k is the number of classes in the domain, n_c is the number of tuples in the predicted class c covered by the rule, n_{total} is the total number of tuples covered by rule.

For example, consider two rules r_1, r_2, where:
r_1 covers 450 tuples of class $High$ and 5 of Low
r_2 covers 5 tuples of class $High$ and 0 of Low
Here the algorithm should prefer r_l as its accuracy on new test data is likely the to be better. r_2 only covers a few tuples and its appear accuracy of 100% is not fully reflective of performance on new test data. For our example, the Laplace accuracy estimate for predicting the class with the most covered tuples are 98.7% for r_1, 85.7% for r_2.

Algorithm 3 DBClass: Maximal Generalized Rules for a Reduct

Input: a decision table $T(C, D)$, a reduct $REDUCT$
Output: A set of maximal generalized rules MG_Rules
1. Generate the reduct table RULES by projecting on REDUCT and D from T(C, D)
2. $MG\_Rules \leftarrow 0$
3. Compute the significance value SIG for each condition of the rules in $RULES$
4. Simplify each tuple in the reduct table $RULES$
    For each tuple r_i in $RULES$ **Do**
        Sort the set of conditions of the rule r_i based on the significant values
        For each condition value $(C_{ik} = V_{ik})$ in r_i **Do**
            Remove $(C_{ik} = V_{ik})$ from r_i
            If r_i is inconsistent with any rule r in $RULES$
            Then put $(C_{ik} = V_{ik})$ back to r_i
        Endfor
        Remove any rule $r' \in MG\_Rules$ that is logically included in rule r_i
        If rule r_i is not logically included in a rule $r' \in MG\_Rules$ **Then**
            $MG\_Rules \leftarrow r_i \cup MG\_Rules$
    Endfor
5. Calculate the Laplace measure for each tuple
6. Transform the tuples with Laplace measure greater than the threshold value into a classification rule

Suppose there are n tuples (rules) with a attributes. The computation of significance values of requires computation $0(an)$ and the processing of dropping conditions on rules requires $O(anlogn)$, so finding all maximal generalized rules for n tuples is $O(anlogn)$. The total cost of our algorithm DBClass is $0(anlogn)$.

5. Ensemble of Classifiers

Our approach uses reducts to construct an ensemble of classifiers. We first construct a set of reducts which contains all the essential attributes. Then using the novel induction method in Section 4, we construct a reduct classifier for each reduct from the corresponding reduct table. A reduct classifier is a set of maximal generalized classification rules without any redundant attributes and attribute values. A reduct classifier corresponding to a reduct is a minimal set of classification rules which is *fully covered* by the attributes of a reduct. The fully cover means that all the condition attributes used by the decision rules is also the attributes of the reduct table. Using different reducts of a decision table, we can derive different reduct classifiers, thus constructing an ensemble of classifiers. Below is the algorithm:

Algorithm 4: Computing Multiple Classifiers RedEnsemble
Input: A decision table T(C,D)
Output: An ensemble of reduct classifiers RedEnsemble
1. Apply Multiple Reduct Algorithm (Algorithm 2), obtain a set of reducts $REDUCTs$
2. For each $REDU_i \in REDUCTs$ **Do**
Apply Maximal Generalized Rule Algorithm (Algorithm 3) to construct a classifier for each $REDU_i$
   Endfor

For example, for Table 1, we have the set of reducts $RED = \{\{Weight, Size\}, \{Weight, Cyl\}\}$ with respect to decision attribute **mileage** (the reduct set consists of all the indispensable attributes of the dataset except the attribute **Door** because it is a superfluous attribute), so we can generate two reduct classifiers:
The reduct classifier for reduct "$Weight, Size$" is
$(Weight = Low)(Size = Comp) \rightarrow (mileage = High)$
$(Weight = Med) \rightarrow (mileage = High)$
$(Size = Sub) \rightarrow (mileage = Low)$
$(Weight = Heavy) \rightarrow (mileage = Low)$

The reduct classifier for reduct "$Weight, Cyl$" is
$(Weight = Low)(Cyl = 4) \rightarrow (mileage = High)$
$(Weight = Med) \rightarrow (mileage = High)$
$(Cyl = 6) \rightarrow (mileage = Low)$
$(Weight = Heavy) \rightarrow (mileage = Low)$

Currently, there are four strategies for combining multiple classifiers: (1) Sum of distribution, (2) Weighted or unweighted Voting, (3) Naive Baycsian combination [13], (4) Decision table method. A detailed discussion of these methods is in [10]. These four strategies are complementary to each other, each has its strong and weak point depending on the domain.

A deep analysis and comparison of these strategies can be find in [3,7, 10, 16]. A reduct classifier employs only the information necessary to represent the given data set without losing essential information. Our approach is to learn a reliable model for each classifier. We believe that each classifier has a particular sub domain for which it is most accurate, thus it is very hard to say which one is better than the others in the real applications. Depending on the subdomain, one reduct classifier can be more useful than another. In our test, the final classifier *RedEnsemble* is formed by using simple equal voting.

To evaluate the classification accuracy of *RedEnsemble*, we ran *RedEnsemble*, C4.5, Bagged C4.5, Boosted C4.5 on some data sets from the UCI machine learning reposi-tory [17]. (All the numeric attributes are discretized using algorithm DBChi2 [11]) If the number of reducts of a data set generated by using Algorithm 2 is greater than 10, we choose the first 10 reduct classifiers in our test. The results are shown in Table 4. 15 data sets from UCI repository databases were chosen and ten complete 10-fold cross-validation were carried out for each data set. Table 4 shows the results from the experiments described above. At the bottom of the table, each column's average is shown. *RedEnsemble* achieves a significant improvement on prediction accuracy over C4.5 and the accuracy is higher than bagged and boosted C4.5.

6. Concluding Discussion

Ensembles of classifiers are a very effective method to obtain highly accurate classifiers by combining less accurate one. In this paper, we present an alternative method to construct good ensemble of classifiers that does not rely on instability, our approach is based on rough sets theory and database operations. The concept of rough set offers a sound theoretical foundation for constructing ensemble of classifiers, the set-oriented database operations improve the efficiency greatly. Multiple classifier systems can be formulated precisely in the framework of rough set theory.

Our approach answers in some extent such questions as generating uncorrelated classifiers and control the number of classifiers needed to improve accuracy in the ensemble of classifiers. To make the classifiers less correlated to each other, our method uses the rough sets theory. Using rough sets theory, each reduct classifier is accurate and as diverse

Dataset	Data Size	#Concept	#Attribute	C4.5	Bagged C4.5	Boosted C4.5	RedEnsemble
credit-screening	690	2	15	85.05	85.90	84.36	86.18
breast (wisconsin)	699	2	9	94.10	95.82	96.41	96.98
diabetes	768	2	8	73.14	76.47	72.12	76.20
glass	214	6	9	68.50	71.98	77.05	77.66
hepatitis	155	2	19	80.40	82.48	83.12	84.12
horse colic	368	2	22	84.40	85.18	81.67	83.40
iris	150	3	4	95.33	94.82	93.72	94.00
letter	20000	26	16	89.11	92.58	95.48	94.36
lymph	148	4	18	79.03	80.09	82.46	84.04
phoneme	5438	47	7	79.46	81.41	83.67	84.49
segment	2310	7	19	96.01	97.70	98.23	97.42
sonar	208	2	60	75.10	76.18	81.40	81.23
soybean	683	19	35	92.07	92.41	93.06	92.24
splice	3190	3	62	94.26	94.45	94.61	94.15
vote	435	2	16	94.84	95.37	94.28	94.38
Average				85.39	86.86	87.44	88.08

Table 4. The Comparision on 15 Datasets

as possible from other reduct classifier because we tried to make the reduct attribute as different as we could during the generation phase of multiple reducts. Our method achieves a good tradeoff between accuracy and diversity. Each reduct generate a accurate reduct classifier, and each reduct classifier is different from the other as much as it can. In this way the errors made by one reduct classifier may be unrelated to the other reduct classifiers, thus the error could be corrected through voting. Another important problem, control the number of classifiers in an ensemble is also very important in data mining applications. While ensembles provide very accurate classifiers, too many classifiers in an ensemble may limit their practical application. To be feasible and competitive, it is important that the learning algorithms run in reasonable time. In our methods, we limit the number of reducts generated for the decision table, thus control the number of reduct classifiers. Based on our experience in data mining applications, we believe that an order of magnitude difference is reasonable but that two or three orders of magnitude is unreasonable in many practical applications. Boosting experiments with many trials (e.g., 1000 as in [22]) are not feasible in data mining applications, because ensembles with large number of classifiers can require large amount of memory to store and large amounts of cpu time to apply. This is a very serious problem in data mining applications because of the huge size of data set. Our approach in some level alleviate this problem because our methods avoid to generate high-correlated classifiers, and the number of classifiers generated in an ensemble is much less than other methods.

There are some other open problems in ensembles of classifiers, such as how to understand and interpreted the

decision by an ensemble of classifiers because an ensemble provides little insight into how it makes its decision. For learning task such as data mining applications, comprehensibility is crucial, voting methods normally results in incomprehensible classifiers that cannot easily understand by end-users. These are the research topics we are currently working on and hope to report our findings in the near future.

References

[1] Agrawal R. , Imielinski T., Swami A., *Mining Associations between Sets of Items in Massive Databases*, Proc. of ACM SIGMOD 1993

[2] Ali, K.M. and Pazziani, M.J., *Error Reduction through Learning Multiple Description* Machine Learning, 24(3), 173-202

[3] Bauer E., Kohavi R., *An Empirical Comparison of Voting Classification Algorithms: Bagging, Boosting, and Variants*, Machine Learning, 1998

[4] Cestnik B., *Estimating probabilities: A Crucial Task in Machine Learning*, Europe Conference in Artificial Intelligence, 1990

[5] Cherkauer, K.J, *Human Expert-Level Performance on a Scientific Image Analysis Task by A System Using Combined Artificial Neural Networks*, in Working Notes of the AAAI Workshop on Integrating Multiple Learned Models, 1996

[6] Dietterich T.G., *Machine Learning Research: Four Current Directions*, Artificial Intelligence Magazine, 18:4

[7] Dietterich T.G., *An Experimental Comparison of Three Methods for Constructing Ensembles of Decision Trees: Bagging, Boosting, and Randomization*, Machine Learning, 1998

[8] Elkan C., *Boosting and Naive Bayesian Learning*, Tech. Report CS97-557, Dept. of Computer Science, Univ. of California, San Diego

[9] Freund Y., and Schapire, R., *Experiments with a New Boosting Algorithms*, Proc of the International Conf. on Machine Learning, 1996

[10] Hu X., Cercone N., and Ziarko W., *Construction of Multiple Knowledge Bases from Data Using Rough Sets Theory*, Rough Sets and Data Mining: Analysis of Imprecise Data, Kluwer Academic Publishers, 1997

[11] Hu X., and Cercone N., *Data Mining via Generalization, Discretization and Rough Set Feature Selection*, Knowledge and Information System: An International Journal, Vol. 1 No. 1, 1999

[12] Kohavi R., John H., *Wrappers for Feature Subset Selection*, Artificial Intelligence Review, 2000

[13] Koppen M., Engerson, S., *Integrating Multiple Classifiers by Finding Their Area of Expertise*, in Working Notes of the AAAI Workshop on Integrating Multiple Learned Models, 1999

[14] Kohavi R., Sahami M., *Error-based and Entropy-based Discretization of Continuous Features*, Proc. of the 2nd International Conference on Knowledge Discovery and Data Mining, AAAI, 1996

[15] Kumar A., *New Techniques for Data Reduction in a Database System for Knowledge Discovery Applications*, Journal of Intelligent Information Systems, 10(3)

[16] Maclin,R. and Opitz, D, *An Empirical Evaluation of Bagging and Boosting*, Proc. of the International Conf. On Machine Learning, 1997

[17] Murphy P., Aha W., UCI repository of machine learning databases, http://www.ics.uci.edu/mlearn/MLRepository.html, 1996.

[18] Quinlan J. R., *C4.5: Program for Machine Learning*, Morgan Kaufmann, 1993.

[19] Quinlan J. R., *Bagging, Boosting and C4.5* Proc. of the America Association of Artificial Intelligence, 1996

[20] Quinlan J. R., *MiniBoosting Decision Tree*, Journal of Artificial Intelligence Research, 1998

[21] Pawlak Z., *Rough Sets*, International Journal of Information and Computer Science, Vol. 11(5), pp341-356, 1982

[22] Schpire, R.E. , Freund, Y. , *Boosting the Margin: A New Explanation for the Effective of Voting Methods*, Proc. of the International Conf. on Machine Learning, 1997

[23] Schapire, R.E, Freund y ., Bartlett, P., *Explanation for the Effectiveness of Voting Methods*, Machine Learning, 1998

[24] Ziarko, W., *Variable Precision Rough Set Model*, Journal of Computer and System Science, Vol 46. No.1 , 1993

Fuzzy Data Mining: Effect of Fuzzy Discretization

Hisao Ishibuchi, Takashi Yamamoto, and Tomoharu Nakashima
Department of Industrial Engineering, Osaka Prefecture University
Gakuen-cho 1-1, Sakai, Osaka 599-8531, JAPAN
{hisaoi, yama, nakashi}@ie.osakafu-u.ac.jp

Abstract

When we generate association rules, continuous attributes have to be discretized into intervals while our knowledge representation is not always based on such discretization. For example, we usually use some linguistic terms (e.g., young, middle age, and old) for dividing our ages into some fuzzy categories. In this paper, we describe the extraction of linguistic association rules and examine the performance of extracted rules. First we modify the definitions of the two basic measures (i.e., confidence and support) of association rules for extracting linguistic association rules. The main difference between standard and linguistic association rules is the discretization of continuous attributes. We divide the domain interval of each attribute into some fuzzy regions (i.e., linguistic terms) when we extract linguistic association rules. Next we compare fuzzy discretization with standard non-fuzzy discretization through computer simulations on a pattern classification problem with many continuous attributes. The classification performance of extracted rules on unseen test patterns is examined under various conditions. Simulation results show that linguistic association rules with rule weights have high generalization ability even when the domain of each continuous attribute is homogeneously partitioned.

1. Introduction

When our knowledge extraction task involves numerical data with continuous attributes, each attribute is usually discretized into several intervals [1,2]. The discretization into intervals is used in many machine learning techniques such as decision trees [3]. In some situations, human knowledge exactly corresponds to such discretization of continuous attributes. For example, the domain of our ages is divided into two intervals by the threshold age 20 in the following knowledge: *"People under 20 are not allowed to smoke"*. In other situations, the discretization into intervals is not appropriate for describing human knowledge. For example,

we may have the following knowledge: *"Tall people are not comfortable in small cars"*. We cannot appropriately represent this knowledge using the discretization of the domain of our height into intervals. This is because the linguistic term *"tall"* cannot be appropriately represented by an interval. A mathematical framework for representing linguistic terms is fuzzy logic. Fuzzy logic has been recognized as a convenient tool for handling continuous attributes by rule-based systems in a human understandable manner [4]. This recognition is supported by many successful applications of fuzzy control methods [5].

For function approximation problems with n inputs, we use linguistic rules of the following form:

$$\text{If } x_1 \text{ is } A_{q1} \text{ and } \ldots \text{ and } x_n \text{ is } A_{qn} \text{ then } y \text{ is } B_q, \quad (1)$$

where q is a rule index, $\mathbf{x} = (x_1, \ldots, x_n)$ is an n-dimensional input vector, A_{qi} is an antecedent linguistic term such as *"small"* and *"large"*, y is an output variable, and B_q is a consequent linguistic term. The above-mentioned linguistic knowledge on the comfortableness in small cars can be represented in the form of (1) as "If x is *tall* then y is *low*" where x is the height and y is the comfortableness. The linguistic rule in (1) can be viewed as an association rule $\mathbf{A}_q \Rightarrow B_q$ where $\mathbf{A}_q = (A_{q1}, \ldots, A_{qn})$. The main difference between our linguistic association rules and the standard formulation of association rules [6] is that the domain of each input (and output) variable is fuzzily divided into linguistic terms in our linguistic association rules. For example, one may divide the domain of our height into two linguistic terms *"tall"* and *"not tall"* as shown in Fig. 1. The vertical axis of this figure shows the extent to which a particular value of the height on the horizontal axis is compatible with each linguistic term. Of course, discretization into linguistic terms depends on the situation. When we talk about the height of professional basketball players, we implicitly assume different discretization from the case of the height of college students.

On the other hand, we use linguistic rules of the following form for pattern classification problems:

$$\text{If } x_1 \text{ is } A_{q1} \text{ and } \ldots \text{ and } x_n \text{ is } A_{qn} \text{ then Class } C_q, \quad (2)$$

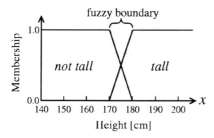

Figure 1. An example of fuzzy discretization.

where $\mathbf{x} = (x_1, \ldots, x_n)$ is an n-dimensional pattern vector and C_q is a class label. The above-mentioned linguistic knowledge on the comfortableness can be represented in the form of (2) as "If x is *tall* then Class 2" where x is the height and Class 2 is the class label corresponding to "not comfortable". This linguistic rule may be obtained from experimental results where a number of examinees are asked whether they feel comfortable or not in a small car. Suppose that we have responses in Table 1 from ten examinees on the comfortableness in the small car. From Fig. 1 and Table 1, we can extract two linguistic rules "If x is *not tall* then Class 1 (i.e., comfortable)" and "If x is *tall* then Class 2 (i.e., not comfortable)". These rules are much more intuitive than interval representation rules such as "If $x \leq 175$ then Class 1" and "If $x > 175$ then Class 2".

Table 1. Artificial data for illustration purpose.

Examinee (p)	Height (x_p)	Comfortableness
1	150	Comfortable
2	158	Comfortable
3	161	Comfortable
4	173	Not comfortable
5	174	Comfortable
6	176	Not comfortable
7	177	Comfortable
8	178	Not comfortable
9	185	Not comfortable
10	191	Not comfortable

The linguistic rules in (1) and (2) can be viewed as association rules $\mathbf{A}_q \Rightarrow B_q$ and $\mathbf{A}_q \Rightarrow C_q$, respectively. The confidence and the support of these association rules can be defined by extending their standard definitions [6] to the case of fuzzy discretization. Through computer simulations, we compare standard interval discretization with fuzzy discretization. We also examine three rule selection criteria (i.e., the confidence, the support, and their product) and two rule types (i.e., rules with/without rule weights).

2. Function Approximation

Let us assume that we have m input-output pairs $(\mathbf{x}_p, y_p)$, $p = 1, 2, \ldots, m$ where $\mathbf{x}_p$ is an n-dimensional input vector (i.e., $\mathbf{x}_p = (x_{p1}, \ldots, x_{pn})$) and y_p is the corresponding output value. Our data set D consists of these m input-output pairs (i.e., $|D| = m$). For calculating the confidence and the support of the linguistic association rule $\mathbf{A}_q \Rightarrow B_q$, we have to calculate the number of input-output pairs that are compatible with $\mathbf{A}_q$ and B_q. Such calculation is trivial for standard association rules with interval discretization. For example, when $\mathbf{A}_q$ is the inequality condition $x > 175$, we can see that five examinees in Table 1 are compatible with this condition.

In our rule extraction task, the compatibility grades of input-output pairs with $\mathbf{A}_q$ are different from each other. For example, each examinee in Table 1 has a different compatibility grade with the linguistic term *"tall"*. Such a compatibility grade is mathematically described by a membership function in fuzzy logic. The membership function of the linguistic term *"tall"* in Fig. 1 is written as

$$\mu_{tall}(x) = \begin{cases} 0, & \text{if } x \leq 170, \\ (x - 170)/10, & \text{if } 170 < x < 180, \\ 1, & \text{if } 180 \leq x. \end{cases} \quad (3)$$

A fuzzy set of examinees compatible with *"tall"* in Table 1 is explicitly written as

$$D(tall) = \left\{ \frac{\mu_{tall}(x_p)}{x_p} : p = 1, 2, \ldots, 10 \right\}$$
$$= \left\{ \frac{0.0}{150}, \frac{0.0}{158}, \frac{0.0}{161}, \ldots, \frac{0.8}{178}, \frac{1.0}{185}, \frac{1.0}{191} \right\}, \quad (4)$$

where the denominator shows the height of each examinee and the numerator shows its membership value. Each element in (4) should not be viewed as a fraction number but a pair of x_p and $\mu_{tall}(x_p)$. The total number of examinees compatible with *"tall"* is calculated from (4) as

$$|D(tall)| = \sum_{p=1}^{10} \mu_{tall}(x_p)$$
$$= 0.0 + 0.0 + 0.0 + 0.3 + \cdots + 1.0 = 4.8. \quad (5)$$

In general, a fuzzy set of input-output pairs compatible with $\mathbf{A}_q$ is written as

$$D(\mathbf{A}_q) = \left\{ \frac{\mu_{\mathbf{A}_q}(\mathbf{x}_1)}{\mathbf{x}_1}, \cdots, \frac{\mu_{\mathbf{A}_q}(\mathbf{x}_m)}{\mathbf{x}_m} \right\}, \quad (6)$$

where $\mu_{\mathbf{A}_q}(\cdot)$ is the membership function of $\mathbf{A}_q$, which is usually defined from the membership function of each linguistic term A_{qi} by the product operation as

$$\mu_{\mathbf{A}_q}(\mathbf{x}_p) = \mu_{A_{q1}}(x_{p1}) \times \cdots \times \mu_{A_{qn}}(x_{pn}). \quad (7)$$

The number of input-output pairs compatible with $\mathbf{A}_q$ (i.e., cardinality of $D(\mathbf{A}_q)$) is defined as

$$|D(\mathbf{A}_q)| = \sum_{p=1}^{m} \mu_{\mathbf{A}_q}(\mathbf{x}_p). \tag{8}$$

A fuzzy set of input-output pairs compatible with both $\mathbf{A}_q$ and B_q is defined as

$$D(\mathbf{A}_q) \cap D(B_q)$$
$$= \left\{ \frac{\mu_{\mathbf{A}_q}(\mathbf{x}_1) \times \mu_{B_q}(y_1)}{(\mathbf{x}_1, y_1)}, \ldots, \frac{\mu_{\mathbf{A}_q}(\mathbf{x}_m) \times \mu_{B_q}(y_m)}{(\mathbf{x}_m, y_m)} \right\}, \tag{9}$$

where $\mu_{B_q}(\cdot)$ is the membership function of B_q. The cardinality of $D(\mathbf{A}_q) \cap D(B_q)$ is defined as

$$|D(\mathbf{A}_q) \cap D(B_q)| = \sum_{p=1}^{m} \mu_{\mathbf{A}_q}(\mathbf{x}_p) \times \mu_{B_q}(y_p). \tag{10}$$

Now we can define the confidence and the support of the linguistic association rule $\mathbf{A}_q \Rightarrow B_q$ as follows:

$$
c(\mathbf{A}_q \Rightarrow B_q) = \frac{|D(\mathbf{A}_q) \cap D(B_q)|}{|D(\mathbf{A}_q)|}
$$
$$
= \frac{\sum_{p=1}^{m} \mu_{\mathbf{A}_q}(\mathbf{x}_p) \times \mu_{B_q}(y_p)}{\sum_{p=1}^{m} \mu_{\mathbf{A}_q}(\mathbf{x}_p)}, \tag{11}
$$

$$
s(\mathbf{A}_q \Rightarrow B_q) = \frac{|D(\mathbf{A}_q) \cap D(B_q)|}{|D|}
$$
$$
= \frac{\sum_{p=1}^{m} \mu_{\mathbf{A}_q}(\mathbf{x}_p) \times \mu_{B_q}(y_p)}{m}. \tag{12}
$$

3. Pattern Classification

Let us assume that we have m labeled patterns $(\mathbf{x}_p, t_p)$, $p = 1, 2, \ldots, m$ where $\mathbf{x}_p$ is an n-dimensional pattern vector (i.e., $\mathbf{x}_p = (x_{p1}, \ldots, x_{pn})$) and t_p is the class label of $\mathbf{x}_p$. Our data set D consists of these m labeled patterns. As in the previous section, we can define the confidence and the support of the association rule $\mathbf{A}_q \Rightarrow C_q$. The difference between $\mathbf{A}_q \Rightarrow B_q$ and $\mathbf{A}_q \Rightarrow C_q$ is that B_q is a linguistic term while C_q is a class label. Since C_q is a class label, the compatibility grade of t_p with C_q is 0 or 1:

$$
\mu_{C_q}(t_p) = \begin{cases} 1, & \text{if } t_p = C_q, \\ 0, & \text{otherwise.} \end{cases} \tag{13}
$$

Thus the cardinality of $D(\mathbf{A}_q) \cap D(C_q)$ is defined as

$$
|D(\mathbf{A}_q) \cap D(C_q)| = \sum_{p=1}^{m} \mu_{\mathbf{A}_q}(\mathbf{x}_p) \times \mu_{C_q}(t_p)
$$
$$
= \sum_{p \in \text{Class } C_q} \mu_{\mathbf{A}_q}(\mathbf{x}_p). \tag{14}
$$

The confidence $c(\mathbf{A}_q \Rightarrow C_q)$ and the support $s(\mathbf{A}_q \Rightarrow C_q)$ of the association rule $\mathbf{A}_q \Rightarrow C_q$ are calculated from (11)-(12) using $|D(\mathbf{A}_q) \cap D(C_q)|$ instead of $|D(\mathbf{A}_q) \cap D(B_q)|$.

As an example, let us calculate $c(tall \Rightarrow \text{Class 2})$ and $s(tall \Rightarrow \text{Class 2})$ from the ten training patterns in Table 1 where Class 2 corresponds to "not comfortable". Since the data set in Table 1 includes ten examinees, $|D| = 10$. As shown in the previous section, $|D(tall)|$ is calculated as $|D(tall)| = 4.8$. From Table 1 and (14), $|D(tall) \cap D(\text{Class 2})|$ is calculated as

$$|D(tall) \cap D(\text{Class 2})| = 0.3 + 0.6 + 0.8 + 1.0 + 1.0 = 3.7. \tag{15}$$

Thus the confidence and the support are calculated as

$$c(tall \Rightarrow \text{Class 2}) = 3.7/4.8 = 0.77. \tag{16}$$

$$s(tall \Rightarrow \text{Class 2}) = 3.7/10 = 0.37. \tag{17}$$

In the same manner, the confidence and the support of the linguistic rule "$tall \Rightarrow$ Class 1 (i.e., comfortable)" are calculated as

$$c(tall \Rightarrow \text{Class 1}) = 1.1/4.8 = 0.23. \tag{18}$$

$$s(tall \Rightarrow \text{Class 1}) = 1.1/10 = 0.11. \tag{19}$$

Thus we choose the linguistic association rule "$tall \Rightarrow$ Class 2" rather than "$tall \Rightarrow$ Class 1".

4. Computer Simulations

4.1. Rule Extraction and Pattern Classification

In our computer simulations, we used the wine recognition database in the UCI Machine Learning Repository (http://www.ics.uci.edu/~mlearn/MLSummary.html). The wine data set is a three-class pattern classification problem with 178 patterns and 13 continuous attributes. As a preprocessing procedure, we normalized each attribute value into a real number in the unit interval $[0, 1]$. The domain of each attribute was discretized into some linguistic terms. For example, five linguistic terms are shown in Fig. 2 (i.e., S: *small*, MS: *medium small*, M: *medium*, ML: *medium large*, and L: *large*). Using those linguistic terms, we generated linguistic association rules of the following type with two antecedent conditions:

If x_i is A_{qi} and x_j is A_{qj} then Class C_q with CF_q, (20)

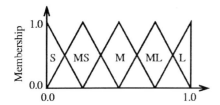

Figure 2. Five linguistic terms.

where CF_q is a rule weight (i.e., certainty factor).

For generating linguistic association rules of the form in (20), we examined all the combinations of two antecedent conditions: $_{13}C_2 \times 5^2$ combinations in the case of five linguistic terms. The consequent class C_q was specified for each combination $\mathbf{A}_q = (A_{qi}, A_{qj})$ as

$$c(\mathbf{A}_q \Rightarrow C_q) = \max\{c(\mathbf{A}_q \Rightarrow \text{Class 1}),$$
$$c(\mathbf{A}_q \Rightarrow \text{Class 2}),$$
$$c(\mathbf{A}_q \Rightarrow \text{Class 3})\}. \quad (21)$$

The confidence $c(\mathbf{A}_q \Rightarrow C_q)$ can be directly used as the rule weight CF_q:

$$CF_q = c(\mathbf{A}_q \Rightarrow C_q). \quad (22)$$

As shown by computer simulations, we obtained better results from the following definition:

$$CF_q = c(\mathbf{A}_q \Rightarrow C_q) - \bar{c}, \quad (23)$$

where $\bar{c}$ is the average confidence for the other two classes:

$$\bar{c} = \frac{1}{2}\left(\sum_{t=1}^{3} c(\mathbf{A}_q \Rightarrow \text{Class } t) - c(\mathbf{A}_q \Rightarrow C_q)\right). \quad (24)$$

In this manner, we generated a number of linguistic association rules of the form in (20). Let S be the set of the generated linguistic association rules. We used a single-winner-based classification method [7,8] for classifying a new pattern $\mathbf{x}_p = (x_{p1}, x_{p2}, \ldots, x_{pn})$ by the rule set S. The winner rule R_{q*} for the new pattern $\mathbf{x}_p$ was defined as

$$\mu_{A_{q*}}(\mathbf{x}_p) \cdot CF_{q*} = \max\{\mu_{A_q}(\mathbf{x}_p) \cdot CF_q : R_q \in S\}. \quad (25)$$

When multiple linguistic rules with different consequent classes had the same maximum value in (25), the classification of the new pattern $\mathbf{x}_p$ was rejected.

4.2. Effect of Fuzzy Partitions

Through computer simulations on the wine data set, we compared fuzzy partitions with interval partitions. First we

extracted linguistic association rules of the form in (20) using all the 178 patterns in the wine data set as training data. We used the two methods for specifying the rule weight CF_q of each rule. We also examined the case of no rule weight. This case was examined by assigning the same rule weight to all rules (i.e., $CF_q = 1.0$ for $\forall q$). Next the same 178 patterns were classified by the extracted linguistic association rules. In this manner, the classification rate on training data was examined. On the other hand, we used the leaving-one-out (LV1) technique for calculating the classification rate on test data. In the LV1 technique, 177 patterns were used for generating linguistic association rules, and the remaining single pattern was used for examining the classification ability of the generated rules. This procedure was iterated 178 times so that all the 178 patterns were chosen as test data. For comparing fuzzy partitions with interval partitions, we examined four fuzzy partitions in Fig. 3. We also examine the corresponding interval partitions. As shown in Fig. 3, each threshold value in the interval partitions was specified by the crossing point of the neighboring membership functions.

Simulation results are summarized in Table 2 ~ Table 5. Table 2 shows classification rates on training data when fuzzy partitions were used. Table 3 shows classification rates on test data. On the other hand, Table 4 and Table 5 show classification rates when interval partitions were used.

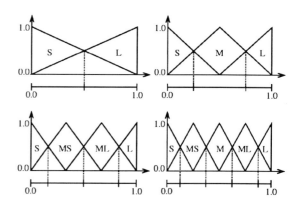

Figure 3. Four fuzzy and interval partitions.

Table 2. Results on training data (fuzzy).

# of linguistic terms	2	3	4	5
Direct use of confidence	90.4	94.9	96.6	94.4
Definition in (23)-(24)	94.9	96.6	97.2	97.2
No rule weight	84.8	70.2	71.9	74.7

From simulation results in Table 2 ~ Table 5, we can

Table 3. Results on test data (fuzzy).

# of linguistic terms	2	3	4	5
Direct use of confidence	90.4	93.3	93.3	89.9
Definition in (23)-(24)	92.7	95.5	94.9	93.3
No rule weight	80.3	68.0	68.5	69.1

Table 4. Results on training data (interval).

# of intervals	2	3	4	5
Direct use of confidence	90.4	93.8	99.4	99.4
Definition in (23)-(24)	90.4	93.8	99.4	99.4
No rule weight	0.0	0.0	1.7	0.6

Table 5. Results on test data (interval).

# of intervals	2	3	4	5
Direct use of confidence	84.8	75.3	74.7	61.2
Definition in (23)-(24)	84.8	75.3	74.7	61.2
No rule weight	0.0	0.0	1.7	0.0

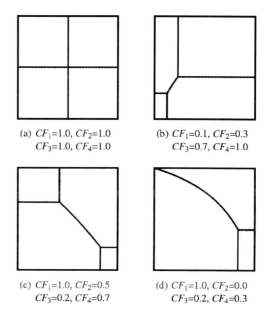

(a) CF_1=1.0, CF_2=1.0 CF_3=1.0, CF_4=1.0

(b) CF_1=0.1, CF_2=0.3 CF_3=0.7, CF_4=1.0

(c) CF_1=1.0, CF_2=0.5 CF_3=0.2, CF_4=0.7

(d) CF_1=1.0, CF_2=0.0 CF_3=0.2, CF_4=0.3

Figure 5. Classification boundaries.

observe the following:

(1) The use of rule weights improves the classification performance of extracted rules.

(2) The performance of standard association rules with no rule weights is terribly poor.

(3) While standard association rules have high classification performance on training data, their generalization ability is poor especially when the interval partitions are fine (i.e., when the number of intervals is large).

(4) The generalization ability of linguistic association rules is better than that of standard association rules.

We examine each of the above observations in detail. First let us consider the effect of rule weights [8]. In the case of fuzzy partitions, rule weights can adjust the classification boundary because we use the product of the compatibility and the rule weight for classifying new patterns (see (25)). For visually illustrating the effect of rule weights on the classification boundary, let us consider the four linguistic rules in Fig.4. Various classification boundaries can be generated from those four linguistic rules as shown in Fig. 5.

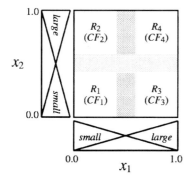

Figure 4. Four linguistic rules.

Next let us consider the classification with interval discretization. In Table 4 and Table 5, classification rates were very low when we used no rule weights. In this case, the classification of almost all patterns was rejected because they were compatible with many rules with different consequent classes. This situation is illustrated in Fig. 6 where the following two rules are depicted: "If x_1 is in the interval A then Class 1" and "If x_2 is in the interval B then Class 2". When these two rules have the same rule weight, we cannot classify any patterns in the overlapping area (i.e., the square in the center of Fig. 6). In our computer simulations, many rules overlap with each other in the 13-dimensional pattern space. Thus the classification of almost all patterns was rejected. When we used a different rule weight for each rule, such an undesirable situation was resolved.

Another interesting observation in Table 4 and Table 5 is that the same results were obtained from the two different specifications of rule weights. This is because the rule weight of each rule was used only for determining the winner rule in the case of interval discretization. On the contrary, rule weights modify classification boundaries in the

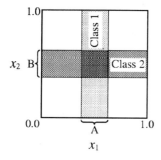

Figure 6. Two overlapping rules.

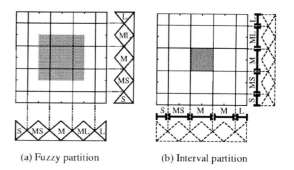

(a) Fuzzy partition   (b) Interval partition

Figure 7. Classifiable region by a single rule.

case of fuzzy discretization as shown in Fig. 5.

The poor generalization ability of association rules in the case of interval discretization (i.e., Table 5) is due to the following reasons:

(1) The discretization was not adjusted. The classification performance can be improved by appropriately partitioning the domain of each continuous attribute. This will be discussed in Section 5.

(2) All the association rules generated from training patterns were used for classifying test patterns. The relation between the number of rules and their generalization ability will be examined in the next subsection.

While the above two reasons also apply to the case of fuzzy discretization, the generalization ability of linguistic association rules is much higher than that of standard association rules. This is because the threshold values for discretization are not crisp but fuzzy. The classification boundaries can be adjusted by the use of rule weights as we have already shown in Fig. 5.

In Fig. 7, we compare the fuzzy discretization with the interval discretization from the viewpoint of the covered region by a single rule. In the case of the fuzzy discretization in Fig. 7 (a), the shaded region can be classified by a single linguistic rule located in the center of that region. On the other hand, the corresponding standard association rule can classify the much smaller shaded region in Fig. 7 (b). Thus the classification of much more new patterns may be rejected in the case of interval discretization than fuzzy discretization especially when the interval partitions are fine. The deterioration in the generalization ability by the use of fine partitions is not so severe in the case of fuzzy partitions because each linguistic association rule can cover a much larger region (compare Table 3 with Table 5).

4.3. Effect of Rule Selection

In our computer simulations in the previous subsections, we used all the extracted rules for classifying new patterns. In this section, we examine the relation between the number of rules and their generalization ability. We first divided

the extracted rules from training data into three groups according to their consequent classes. Then the rules in each group were sorted in a descending order of their confidence values. When multiple rules had the same confidence value, they were randomly sorted. For decreasing the effect of such randomization, we averaged simulation results over 20 independent runs. Finally we chose the first N rules from each group to classifying test data ($N = 1, 2, \ldots, 30$). As in the previous sections, we used the leaving-one-out (LV1) technique for evaluating the generalization ability of the extracted rules from training data. In addition to the confidence, we also examined two different rule selection criteria: the support and the product of the confidence and the support. In such computer simulations, we used (23)-(24) for specifying rule weights and the fuzzy partition by three linguistic terms. For comparison, we also used the interval partition by three intervals.

Simulation results are summarized in Fig. 8 ∼ Fig. 10. As we have already shown, higher classification rates on test data were obtained from linguistic association rules than standard association rules. We can see from those figures that the product of the confidence and the support is the best rule selection criterion among the examined three criteria. When we use the confidence as a rule selection criterion, we tend to select association rules with high confidence but low support. On the other hand, we tend to select association rules with high support but low confidence when we use the support as a rule selection criterion.

5. Inhomogeneous Partitions

In computer simulations in the previous section, we used homogeneous fuzzy partitions using symmetric triangular membership functions. While such partitions have been often used in many applications of fuzzy rule-based systems, those partitions are not optimal from the viewpoint of the classification performance of extracted linguistic rules. In the previous section, we also used interval partitions ob-

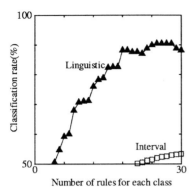

Figure 8. Results by the confidence.

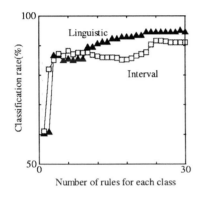

Figure 9. Results by the support.

tained from homogeneous fuzzy partitions. Such interval partitions are not optimal, either. In this section, we discretize the domain of each attribute into some intervals using the entropy measure (for details, see Quinlan [3]). The domain of each attribute was discretized independently of the other attributes. Let K be the number of intervals for each attribute. That is, the domain interval $[0, 1]$ was discretized into K intervals using $(K - 1)$ threshold values. The threshold values were selected from $(m-1)$ candidates, each of which is the mid-point of a pair of neighboring attribute values in the given m patterns. All the $_{m-1}C_{K-1}$ combinations for selecting $(K - 1)$ threshold values from $(m - 1)$ candidates were examined by calculating the corresponding entropy for each combination. The discretization with the minimum entropy was selected for each attribute. We performed this discretization as a preprocessing procedure before the rule extraction. For comparison, we specified the corresponding fuzzy partition from the interval partition as shown in Fig. 11. The specification of the fuzzy partition in Fig. 11 is based on the following two conditions: 1) The sum of neighboring membership functions is always 1, and 2) Crossing points of neighboring membership functions coincide with the threshold values in the interval partition.

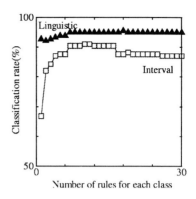

Figure 10. Results by the product.

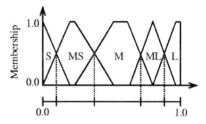

Figure 11. Inhomogeneous fuzzy partitions.

Using inhomogeneous partitions based on the entropy criterion, we compared fuzzy partition with interval partitions in the same manner as Subsection 4.2. Simulation results are summarized in Table 6 $\sim$ Table 9. From the comparison between the simulation results in this section and those in Subsection 4.2, we can see that the discretization based on the entropy measure improved the classification performance of standard association rules on training data (compare Table 4 with table 8). We can also observe from the comparison between Table 3 and Table 7 that the generalization ability of linguistic association rules does not strongly depend on the choice of a fuzzy partition.

Table 6. Results on training data (fuzzy).

# of linguistic terms	2	3	4	5
Direct use of confidence	93.7	93.3	97.2	98.3
Definition in (23)-(24)	97.8	94.9	97.2	98.3
No rule weight	68.0	50.0	45.5	28.7

In the same manner as in Subsection 4.3, we performed rule selection using the three criteria: the confidence, the support, and their product. We observed from simulation results that the generalization ability of standard association rules was drastically improved by the use of the entropy-based discretization and the rule selection. In Fig. 12, we

Table 7. Results on test data (fuzzy).

# of linguistic terms	2	3	4	5
Direct use of confidence	93.3	91.6	95.5	94.4
Definition in (23)-(24)	94.9	92.7	96.6	94.4
No rule weight	67.4	50.0	43.8	24.7

Table 8. Results on training data (interval).

# of intervals	2	3	4	5
Direct use of confidence	97.8	98.9	99.4	100
Definition in (23)-(24)	97.8	98.9	99.4	100
No rule weight	0.0	3.9	3.9	2.8

Table 9. Results on test data (interval).

# of intervals	2	3	4	5
Direct use of confidence	92.7	76.4	64.0	52.8
Definition in (23)-(24)	92.7	76.4	64.0	52.8
No rule weight	0.0	3.9	3.4	2.8

demonstrate the relation between the number of standard association rules and their generalization ability for several specifications of the interval discretization where K shows the number of intervals. From this figure, we can see that high generalization ability was obtained by appropriately choosing standard association rules.

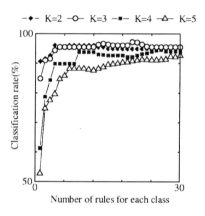

Figure 12. Results by the product (interval).

6. Concluding Remarks

In this paper, we extended the definitions of the two basic measures (i.e., confidence and support) of association rules to the case of linguistic rules. As we explained, linguistic rules are much more intuitive than the standard association rules in some situations. We demonstrated through computer simulations that the generalization ability of linguistic rules is less sensitive to the choice of a discretization method and the number of rules than that of standard association rules. Thus linguistic rules have two advantages over the standard association rules: intuitive interpretability and robust performance. Of course, the usefulness of linguis-

tic rules is problem-dependent. Linguistic rules are more intuitive in some situations, and standard association rules are more appropriate in other situations. We also demonstrated through computer simulations that we can obtain high generalization ability from standard association rules by appropriately specifying the discretization of continuous attributes and the number of rules.

References

[1] U. M. Fayyad and K. B. Irani, "Multi-interval discretization of continuous-valued attributes for classification learning," *Proc. of 13th International Joint Conference on Artificial Intelligence*, pp. 1022-1027, 1993.

[2] J. Dougherty, R. Kohavi, and M. Sahami, "Supervised and unsupervised discretization of continuous features," *Proc. of 12th International Conference on Machine Learning*, pp. 194-202, 1995.

[3] J. R. Quinlan, *C4.5: Programs for Machine Learning*, Morgan Kaufmann, 1993.

[4] S. J. Russell and P. Norvig, *Artificial Intelligence: A Modern Approach*, Prentice-Hall, 1995.

[5] C. T. Leondes (Ed.), *Fuzzy Theory Systems: Techniques and Applications*, Academic Press, 1999.

[6] R. Agrawal and R. Srikant, "Fast algorithms for mining association rules," *Proc. of 20th International Conference on Very Large Data Bases* (Santiago, Chile), pp. 487-499, September 1994. Expanded version is available as IBM Research Report RJ9839, June 1994.

[7] H. Ishibuchi, T. Nakashima and T. Morisawa, "Voting in fuzzy rule-based systems for pattern classification problems," *Fuzzy Sets and Systems*, vol.103, no.2, pp. 223-238, 1999.

[8] H. Ishibuchi and T. Nakashima, "Effect of rle weights in fuzzy rule-based classification systems," *IEEE Trans. on Fuzzy Systems*, vol. 9, no. 4, August 2001.

The Computational Complexity of High-Dimensional Correlation Search

Christopher Jermaine
Georgia Institute of Technology, College of Computing
jermaine@cc.gatech.edu

Abstract

There is a growing awareness that the popular support metric (often used to guide search in market-basket analysis) is not appropriate for use in every association mining application. Support measures only the frequency of co-occurrence of a set of events when determining which patterns to report back to the user. It incorporates no rigorous statistical notion of surprise or interest, and many of the patterns deemed interesting by the support metric are uninteresting to the user.

However, a positive aspect of support is that search using support is very efficient. The question we address in this paper is: can we retain this efficiency if we move beyond support, and to other, more rigorous metrics? We consider the computational implications of incorporating simple expectation into the data mining task. It turns out that many variations on the problem which incorporate more rigorous tests of dependence (or independence) result in NP-hard problem definitions.

1. Introduction

The technique of indirectly measuring the level of *correlation* or *interestingness* or *surprise* of a set of events by measuring the lack of independence of these events is well-accepted. One of the most straightforward applications of this strategy is the popular χ^2 test for independence [11] from statistics. An example of the application of this test is as follows. Say we want to check for correlation between the purchase of beer and the purchase of diapers at a supermarket. We first produce a contingency matrix for the four possible events, based on observations from the data:

	diapers	no diapers	$\sum$row
beer	1,734	4,589	6,323
no beer	3,474	45,722	49,196
$\sum$column	5,208	50,311	55,519

For example, in the above table, beer appeared without diapers 4,589 times, and beer appeared with diapers 1,734

times. We then compute a similar matrix of *expected* values, using an assumption of independence of the events:

	diapers	no diapers	$\sum$row
beer	593.1	5,729.9	6,323
no beer	4,614.9	44,581.1	49,196
$\sum$column	5,208	50,311	55,519

For example, the *expected* number of purchases of beer without diapers (given our assumption of independence) is $5729.9 = 6323 \times 50311 / 55519$; the expected number of purchases of beer with diapers is 593.1. Next, we compute the χ^2 statistic, which is a sum over the four different cells in the contingency matrix of observed values: $\chi^2 = \sum_{r \in matrix} \frac{(Obs(r) - Ex(r))^2}{Ex(r)}$. In our case, this sum is 2,732.8. Finally, by comparing with the χ^2 distribution, we obtain the probability that we would see such a large sum, were the events truly independent. In our case, this probability is nearly zero, rejecting the *NULL* hypothesis and testifying to the correlation between the purchase of beer and diapers.

In this paper, we consider the computational implications of integrating statistical expectation of this type into the data mining process. Specifically, we consider so-called *iceberg cube* queries [1], where we allow the function in the HAVING clause of the proposed SQL CUBE-BY query [6] to measure deviation from independence. The queries we consider are basically data cube queries of the form:

```
CREATE CUBE Iceberg AS
SELECT a_1, a_2, a_3,..., a_n
FROM SalesInfo
CUBE BY a_1, a_2, a_3,..., a_n
HAVING INTEREST(*) > k
```

where we will allow INTEREST to be some (potentially complex) statistical function that uses a notion of deviation from independence of attribute values to decide how inter-

Tuple	Items Purchased				Customer Age			Total $$ Spent			Purchase Year		
	#1	#2	#3	#4	0-20	21-40	41-80	0-20	21-30	31+	2000	2001	2002
1	1	0	1	1	1	0	0	0	0	1	1	0	0
2	0	1	0	0	0	1	0	1	0	0	1	0	0
3	1	0	0	0	0	1	0	1	0	0	1	0	0
4	1	0	0	1	1	0	0	0	1	0	0	1	0
5	0	1	1	0	1	0	0	0	1	0	0	1	0
6	1	1	1	1	1	0	0	0	0	1	0	0	1
7	1	1	0	0	0	0	1	0	1	0	0	0	1
8	1	0	0	1	0	0	1	0	1	0	0	0	1

Figure 1: A hypothetical, 13-attribute binary database.

esting the subcubes are. We remind the reader that the CUBE-BY operator essentially iterates over all combinations of the attributes in the CUBE-BY clause, and that p, the number of data dimensions, may be very large in practice: on the order of 10^5 or more (consider the case where each dimension corresponds to an item that may be purchased from a large supermarket or discount retailer).

Certain formulations of this type of problem have been studied previously. For example, if INTEREST is simply the COUNT(*) function, then the above query is equivalent to the frequent itemset problem from association rule mining and market-basket analysis [1].

Most relevant work considers simple aggregate functions, like COUNT (equivalent to *support* in market-basket analysis) and AVERAGE. While useful, researchers have commented on the limitations of such functions because they lack any notion of expectation [4]. Using support, for example, the level of correlation of two events is simply the fraction of times that they co-occur. As a metric, support facilitates fast search, but it has its drawbacks. For example, finding that values A and B occur together in 98% of the database tuples is uninteresting, if A and B both occur in 99% of the tuples when considered in isolation. This would be expected since $P(A) = P(A|B)$ and $P(B) = P(B|A)$. Most statistical tests over A and B (including the χ^2 statistic) would reflect this lack of true correlation of A and B, even though A and B together would have very high support.

In this work, we consider the computational implications of moving beyond simple aggregate functions like COUNT or AVERAGE, to more rigorous analysis. For example, one could imagine basing the INTEREST function on the χ^2 statistic, or on both the χ^2 statistic and the COUNT function, which would render the query basically equivalent to the problem addressed previously by Brin et al. [3] Such a query would clearly be useful, in that the user could choose a statistically meaningful correlation level, and receive back only the most significant subcubes. In this

paper, we will explore the computational implications of choosing different bases for the INTEREST function, in order to determine how practical it is to integrate expectation into this framework.

To give the reader a preview of our results, there are very few useful functions incorporating expectation that do not render the problem intractable. In particular, we show that by basing the INTEREST function on the *loglikelihood ratio* test from statistics [9], (which we will argue is far more appropriate for use here than the χ^2 test) we render the problem intractable. Given the growing awareness that support is not adequate for every situation, these results are significant in that they argue that moving beyond support and into the realm of more robust statistical measures will likely require a careful shift into the world of approximation. This is somewhat disappointing news, but is important for the data mining community to understand if we are to move beyond co-occurrence analysis and to more robust measures of correlation.

This paper is organized as follows. In Section 2, we present a bit of notation. In Sections 3 and 4, we consider the computational complexity of the use of some very simple INTEREST metrics based on expectation. In Section 5, we consider basing this metric on the loglikelihood ratio. In Section 6, we consider an alternative to the loglikelihood ratio which results in a problem definition that may be solved efficiently. We discuss future work in Section 7. The paper is concluded in Section 8.

2. Notation

We begin with a bit of notation.

We assume a database DB is composed of p attributes (n denotes the size, in tuples, of the database). We assume that each attribute is binary. This is not too restrictive since numerical attributes can be discretized (mapped into buckets) and encoded in binary; categorical attributes can be encoded as well. A database tuple is then a p-dimensional tuple over the database domain (or feature space) 2^p.

We define the notion of a *subcube*, which can be thought of as nothing more than an itemset from association rule mining, with the addition that we allow itemsets characterized by the *absence*, as well as presence, of items. A subcube can also be thought of as one of the subsets of attributes which are iterated over during the evaluation of a CUBE-BY query.

Definition 1: A *subcube* ς is any hyper-rectangle (or rectilinear region) from the binary data space 2^p. It is specified by a p-dimensional vector of items from the domain $\{0, 1, *\}$. "$*$" is a wild card matching any value. Then $Obs(\varsigma)$ is the number of tuples from DB falling in ς.

For example, consider the database of Figure 1. Let $\varsigma_1 = (1, *, *, *, 0, *, *, 0, *, *, 0, *, *)$. This subcube is a specification for all tuples where Item 1 was purchased by a customer more than 20 years old, more than 20 dollars was spent in total, and the purchase happened in the years 2000 or 2001. Since tuples 7 and 8 both fall in this subcube, $Obs(\varsigma_1) = 2$.

If we project the subcube along a dimension, we measure the observed support in that one dimension.

Definition 2: The projected support of a subcube ς along dimension i is defined as

$$P(\varsigma, i) = \frac{|\{t | t \in DB, t[i] = \varsigma[i]\}|}{n}.$$

For example, $P(\varsigma_1, 1) = 3/4$. That is, Item 1 was purchased in 3/4 of the tuples in the database. If we assume no relationships among attributes (as in the χ^2 test; this assumption is known as AVI, or attribute value independence), then the expected support of a subcube can be defined using the projected support.

Definition 3: The *expected support* or *probability* of a subcube ς is $P(\varsigma) = \prod_{i \in \{1...p\}} P(\varsigma, i)$.

In our example, $P(\varsigma_1) = \frac{3}{4} \times \frac{1}{2} \times \frac{3}{4} \times \frac{5}{8} = 0.176$. That is, given AVI, we expect this subcube to contain 17.6% of the tuples from the database.

Finally, we define our notion of a *correlation function*. This is a general class of functions whose purpose is to measure whether or not a subcube is considered dense.

Definition 4: A function $f(n, prob, L) \to \aleph$ is a *correlation function* if, given a database size n, and a subcube probability $P(\varsigma) = prob$:

(a) For fixed L, f is a continuous, non-decreasing function with respect to *prob*, and

(b) $f(n, prob, L_1) < f(n, prob, L_2)$ for $L_1 < L_2$.

This is meant to represent a very broad class of functions. Intuitively, a correlation function returns the minimum value for $Obs(\varsigma)$ for which a subcube is to be considered interesting at some level L. The higher the level L, the more interesting the subcube must be to satisfy the level, and the higher the required $Obs(\varsigma)$ value.

For example, the support function $f_{Sup}(n, prob, s) = s \times n$ is an example of a very simple correlation function; it is the correlation measure used in classical association rule (AR) mining. Why? In order to be accepted at correlation level s, a subcube must have an $Obs(\varsigma)$ value of larger than $s \times n$. In other words, more than $s\%$ of the database transactions must fall in ς; equivalently, the items required by ς must be present in more than $s\%$ of the database.

3. Use of the most obvious correlation function

Our purpose in this work is to explore for which correlation functions the following problem is tractable:

"Give me any subcube ς for which $Obs(\varsigma) \geq f(n, P(\varsigma), L)$ for correlation level L."

Note that this is essentially equivalent to the CUBE-BY query we described in the introduction, though it is a bit simpler since we are looking for only one subcube which has INTEREST at level L.

We begin at an obvious starting point. Perhaps the simplest correlation function that would take into account expectation is as follows. Let $f_{Rat}(n, prob, L) = (n \times prob \times L)$. f_{Rat} is very simple: using it in the above problem will find some subcube which contains more than L times as many tuples as expected. However, solving even this simple problem is not practical.

Theorem 1. Given a level L, the problem of finding a subcube where $Obs(\varsigma) \geq f_{Rat}(n, P(\varsigma), L)$ is NP-hard.

Proof. All proofs can be found in the full paper [8].

At first glance, this is an extraordinary result: simply determining whether there is any subcube (or itemset) which has fractionally more tuples than expected is not possible in polynomial time. Does this mean that any search through high-dimensional data for dense subcubes or itemsets based on expectation is impractical? Not necessarily.

The computational difficulty of this problem stems from having to identify subcubes which contain attribute values with high expected support. Not coincidentally, in traditional AR mining, such attributes have been ignored, or assumed not to exist. AR mining traditionally looks only for presence (and not absence) of items in market-baskets, and effectively assumes that a given item (or at least most

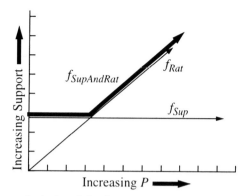

Figure 2: A plot of the $f_{SupAndRat}$ **correlation function.**

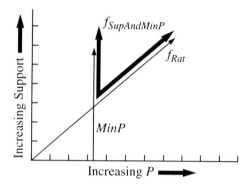

Figure 3: A plot of the $f_{SupAndMinP}$ **correlation function.**

items) is/are typically found in only a fraction of the total market-baskets.

What happens if we take a hint from traditional AR mining and restrict ourselves to look only for subcubes containing no attribute values with a projected probability of greater than α? This would be in-keeping with the spirit of traditional AR mining. We will call such subcubes α-*subcubes*. For example, the subcube (*, 1, 1, 1, *, *, *, 1, *, *, *, *, *), which corresponds to baskets purchased by youngsters that contain item 2, item 3, and item 4, is an α-subcube for an α value of 0.5. That is, attributes 2, 3, 4, and 8 all have positive values less than 50% of the time. If we restrict the problem in this way, then the computation of a solution is more reasonable:

Theorem 2. Given a level L, the problem of finding some α-subcube where $Obs(\varsigma) \geq f_{Rat}(n, P(\varsigma), L)$ is possible in $O\left(p \text{ choose } \left(\log_{1/\alpha}\left(\frac{n}{L}\right)\right)\right)$ time.

In subsequent sections, we will refer to those subcubes which are α-subcubes for an α value of 0.5 as being *well-formed*. A simple corollary to Theorem 2 is:

Corollary 2.1. Given a level L, the problem of finding a well-formed subcube where $Obs(\varsigma) \geq f_{Rat}(n, P(\varsigma), L)$ can be solved in polynomial time.

Thus, it *is* possible to search for regions judged interesting using f_{Rat} in an efficient manner, if we make some simple assumptions about what we are looking for.

Note that the algorithms suggested by Theorem 2 and Corollary 2.1 are essentially quadratic-time solutions. While this is clearly too slow for even a moderately-sized database, it does offer some hope. First, it is entirely possible that an asymptotically faster solution may exist. Second, we note that even a slow, quadratic solution is fast enough that the algorithm could be used over a rather large sample from the database (having tens or hundreds of thousands of tuples), which in turn could provide a good, approximate solution with certain probabilistic guarantees.

4. A More Reasonable Correlation Function

However, it turns out that f_{Rat} may be rather impractical to use in reality. The problem is that it will usually report back anomalies rather than significant trends in the data. Consider this: every tuple from the database is contained in a cell in the data space 2^p. That cell defines a subcube. But the correlation level corresponding to that tiny cell is usually incredibly high. For example, consider again Figure 1, and the subcube exactly enclosing tuple 1. The P value of this subcube is

$$\frac{5}{8} \times \frac{1}{2} \times \frac{3}{8} \times \frac{1}{2} \times \frac{1}{2} \times \frac{3}{4} \times \frac{3}{4} \times \frac{3}{4} \times \frac{1}{2} \times \frac{1}{4} \times \frac{3}{8} \times \frac{3}{4} \times \frac{5}{8} = 2.7 \times 10^{-4}.$$

Yet the f_{Rat} requirement is satisfied at a correlation level which is the inverse of this product, or 3682. This is clearly a very high correlation level; in fact, every tuple in the database will likely be considered interesting and surprising by this test, and the eight most interesting subcubes based on this metric correspond to single-tuple subcubes holding each of the eight tuples from the example database. But does it make sense to report back every tuple as an interesting subcube? We argue that it does not.

To fix this problem, we again consider the classical AR mining problem:

"Find all subcubes where $Obs(\varsigma) \geq f_{Sup}(n, P(\varsigma), s)$"

What if we combine f_{Sup} and f_{Rat}? That is, let:

$f_{SupAndRat}(n, P(\varsigma), (s, L)) =$
$\quad max\{f_{Sup}(n, P(\varsigma), s), f_{Rat}(n, P(\varsigma), L)\}$

The function is shown above in Figure 2. This would give us a simple variation on AR mining, where we integrate expectation into the definition. A subcube (or itemset) is interesting if it both attains a minimum support level, and has fractionally more tuples than expected. The minimum support level will help to discount statistically insignificant subcubes. However:

Theorem 3. Given a level L and a minimum support s, the problem of finding a well-formed subcube where $Obs(\varsigma) \geq f_{RatAndSup}(n, P(\varsigma), (s, L))$ is NP-hard.

In other words, simply adding a minimum support threshold to f_{Rat} to add a notion of statistical significance turns a tractable problem into an intractable one.

There is another way to ignore small subcubes. What if we attempt to discount uninteresting subcubes by adding a minimum subcube size, or P value? In other words, let:

$$f_{RatAndMinP}(n, P(\varsigma), (MinP, L)) = \infty \text{ if } P(\varsigma) < MinP; f_{Rat}(n, P(\varsigma), L) \text{ otherwise.}$$

This function is shown above in Figure 3. Again, the attempt here is to avoid reporting trivial subcubes. Still:

> *Theorem 4.* Given a level L and a minimum subcube probability $MinP$, the problem of finding a well-formed subcube where $Obs(\varsigma) \geq f_{RatAndMinP}(n, P(\varsigma), (MinP, L))$ is NP-hard.

Thus, both of these simple augmentations of f_{Rat} render the problem intractable.

5. The loglikelihood ratio test

While more practical than f_{Rat}, the correlation functions of the last section still leave something to be desired.

Consider two subcubes ς_1 and ς_2, where both subcubes have exactly twice the expected number of tuples. However, ς_1 contains 1,000,000 tuples, while ς_2 contains only 40 tuples. Since ς_2 is relatively small, it is quite possible that finding twice as many tuples as expected in ς_2 is purely a chance occurrence (we point out that there are an exponential number of subcubes in a given database; due to this large number, many smaller subcubes of somewhat surprising density are likely to occur purely by chance). However, the density of the much larger region ς_1 is surely not an accident: the probability of finding 1,000,000 tuples given that the true, underlying probability distribution would predict only 500,000 is extremely small. As such, it makes sense that we would prefer to report ς_1 over ς_2. However, if we use $f_{RatAndSup}$ and set s to be 40, *both* subcubes are reported back, or both are ignored. It is not acceptable to simply raise s in order to discount ς_2. Say that there were 10^{10} times as many tuples in ς_2 as expected (not unreasonable in correlated data). Would we want to lose such a dense subcube, simply because it contained only 40 tuples? Probably not.

Because of these limitations, in this section we describe a test from statistics that would take into account the issues raised above. We briefly consider (and dismiss) use of the popular χ^2 test in this domain, and settle instead on a test based on the *loglikelihood ratio* as an appropriate test. We show that unfortunately, the use of the likelihood ratio test to guide search through a data cube leads to an NP-hard problem definition. In response, in the next section we will introduce a relaxed variant on the likelihood ratio that produces a tractable problem definition.

5.1. The χ^2 test

The χ^2 test (many standard references on statistics contain good descriptions of this) is arguably the most popular statistical check for correlation, and the fact that it is specifically designed for use with binned, categorical data (the data we consider in this paper) makes it, at least superficially, an attractive possibility for integration into an association-mining algorithm. A now-classical work [3] did just that, though their framework was a bit different than the one presented here. However, this test's general applicability for checking for correlation within the itemset framework is doubtful.

The problem stems from the fact that a standard rule of thumb from statistics is that, for the classical χ^2 test of independence to be valid, *each possible event should expectedly occur at least five times* [11]. This requirement is simply unrealistic in many data mining domains.

For example, in market-basket (AR mining) applications, we can anticipate an upper limit of on the order of 10^5 items (or more) that may be purchased (consider a large discount retailer). Imagine a database recording market-baskets in this domain, where each basket averages 20 items in size. Say we want to apply the χ^2 test to an arbitrary, 3-itemset from this domain, specified by the subcube ς. In the best case (without a skewed distribution of item purchases), to ensure that we would *expect* to find at least one such 3-itemset in the database (that is, to ensure that $P(\varsigma) \times n \geq 1$), we would need a database with at least

$$\frac{((10^5)^3)}{20} \approx 10^{14}$$ transactions. That is, we would require

that every person on Earth purchase tens of thousands of baskets! In many other realistic situations, we would need an even larger database.

The result is that for the vast majority of items, we rarely see them, and hence would not expect them to be purchased together. The problem is that the χ^2 test is understood to be invalid under such conditions. The situation deteriorates quickly (exponentially) when we move beyond three-way correlations to four-way, five-way, and higher degree correlations. For the test to be valid on itemsets containing even a handful of items, we would effectively need a database containing billions *of* billions *of* billions of transactions.

This problem cannot simply be ignored. In an excellent paper from computational linguistics, Ted Dunning [5] shows how the application of the χ^2 test to the domain of co-occurrence analysis in text can produce poor results. This domain is closely related to the market-basket domain in that we have a relatively large number of possible "items" (words in the English language) and we lack enough data to validate the test. Using the χ^2 test on such data, Dunning shows how the test chooses a rather silly set of word co-occurrences as being among the most important bigrams in a small corpus when the assumptions underlying the test are not met (for example: "instance 280", "scanner cash", "maturity hovered" and so on). Similar problems are likely to result in the market-basket domain.

5.2. Likelihood ratio

For this reason, some statistical texts (for example, [11]) recommend the use of a parametric *likelihood ratio* test under such circumstances. Briefly, we describe how it can be used to define a correlation function, f_{Lik}. Our description of f_{Lik} is heavily influenced by a similar statistical test based on the loglikelihood ratio described by Dunning [5].

In general, a *likelihood function* is a function which is used to measure the goodness of fit of a statistical model to actual data. It can be written as:

$$H(p_1, p_2, ...; k_1, k_2, ...)$$

where the variables $p_1, p_2, ...$ describe the statistical model, and $k_1, k_2, ...$ describe the data. A famous example of the use of a likelihood function is the Gaussian EM clustering algorithm, where the statistical model is a multi-dimensional normal distribution, and the task is to maximize the value of the likelihood function by altering the model parameters to fit a specific data set.

The concept of a likelihood function can easily be used to statistically test a given hypothesis, by applying the *likelihood ratio* test. Essentially, we take the ratio of the greatest likelihood possible given our hypothesis, to the likelihood of the best "explanation" overall. The greater the value of the ratio, the stronger our hypothesis is said to be.

To apply the likelihood ratio test to our subcube/itemset domain to produce a correlation function, it is useful to consider the binomial probability distribution. This is a function of three variables:

$$\Pr_{bin}(prob, k, n) \rightarrow [0:1]$$

Intuitively, the binomial function models the following situation. Suppose we try n separate and independent times to toss a ball through a hoop, and each attempt has a probability of success *prob*. The probability of succeeding k times in those n trials is exactly $\Pr_{bin}(prob, k, n)$.

This is relevant to our problem definition, because we can consider a subcube ς as a "hoop" and tuple as a "ball". Then, a database of size n is n attempts to hit the subcube (hoop) with a tuple (ball). Given our assumption of independence of all attributes or items, we predict that each trial has a probability of success $P(\varsigma)$.

The correlation of ς can then be measured by quantifying to what extent our assumption of attribute value independence was violated in practice. To do this, we perform the likelihood ratio test, comparing the binomial likelihood of the fact that we observed $Obs(\varsigma)$ tuples in ς (when we thought the probability of ς was $P(\varsigma)$) with the best possible binomial explanation. The best possible explanation is that the probability of ς was *not* $P(\varsigma)$, but was instead simply $Obs(\varsigma) / n$.

Formally, the likelihood ratio in this case is

$$\frac{L(P(\varsigma), n, Obs(\varsigma))}{L\left(\frac{Obs(\varsigma)}{n}, n, Obs(\varsigma)\right)}$$

where L is derived from the formula for the binomial distribution, and is $L(p, n, k) = p^k (1-p)^{n-k}$. Commonly, this test is referred to as the *loglikelihood ratio* $(-2\log\lambda)$ and is computed as

$$-2\log\lambda = \log(L(P(\varsigma), n, Obs(\varsigma))) - \log\left(L\left(\frac{Obs(\varsigma)}{n}, n, Obs(\varsigma)\right)\right)$$

If we rewrite $-2\log\lambda$ (the level of correlation) as L_{Lik} to conform with the notation of this paper, and solve for $Obs(\varsigma)$, we obtain a mathematical expression for the function $f_{Lik}(n, P(\varsigma), L_{Lik})$.

We argue that given the severe limitations of the χ^2 test in such a setting, f_{Lik} is a far preferable statistical metric for use in this framework.

5.3. Computational complexity

In the preceding section, we wished to present an accepted statistical measure that could be used to measure the level of correlation of a subcube, to explore the computational complexity of the application of such a measure to the itemset framework. Given the results presented earlier in the paper, the following results are probably not surprising.

Theorem 5. Given a level L, the problem of finding a well-formed subcube where $Obs(\varsigma) \geq f_{Lik}(n, P(\varsigma), L_{Lik})$ is NP-hard.

Thus, according to Theorem 5, search based on a commonly accepted parametric statistical test is an intractable task in this setting.

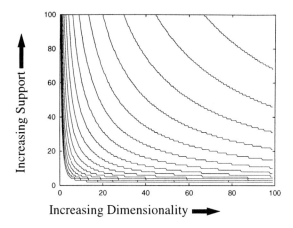

Figure 4: Plot of the f_{Lik} correlation function. Contours are shown with respect to increasing subcube dimensionality. For example, a subcube of dimensionality 75 and support 75 is accepted at the second highest contour (correlation level), but not the highest.

6. The support-biased correlation function

Can we do anything about this complexity? One solution is to develop some sort of approximation algorithm, which *attempts* to find subcubes of high likelihood ratio, and perhaps finds them within some probabilistic or approximation guarantees. However, finding and developing such approximations can be very difficult. A second solution is to somehow "tweak" the definition of the loglikelihood ratio correlation function, relaxing it somewhat (while trying to maintain many of its original characteristics) to arrive at a tractable problem definition. Once a useful problem has been found that has a tractable solution, then subsequent work might be undertaken with the goal of producing an asymptotically fast algorithm. We will explore this second option briefly in this section.

We first explore the nature of the f_{Lik} function. Consider the contours of the f_{Lik} function, for differing correlation levels. These contours are shown above in Figure 4, for a 100-tuple, 100-dimensional database. We show contours with respect to subcube observed support and subcube dimensionality. For simplicity, we assume that each of the 100 database dimensions has the same projected support.

Note that in the plot, with increasing dimensionality, the observed support required for a subcube to be accepted is always decreasing. However, the *rate* of decrease continually slows, and the required support never reaches zero. It is significant that the contours of the f_{Lik} function, when plotted in this way, resemble a set quadratic of curves governed by the equation $Obs(\varsigma) \times Dimensionality(\varsigma) = c$, where the constant c is a function of the correlation level L.

The quadratic nature of the f_{Lik} function when plotted in this way is the source of the computational complexity associated with the use of f_{Lik} in iceberg cube queries.

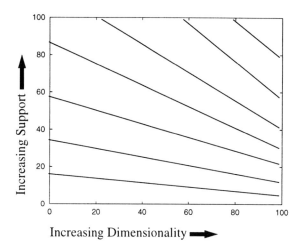

Figure 5: Contours of the support-biased correlation function, which provides a tractable approximation to the loglikelihood ratio-based search.

Were the curves linear and not quadratic, the problem would be tractable. This suggests a simple alternative to the loglikelihood-based correlation function. What if we alter it so that the contours are *linear* with respect to increasing subcube dimensionality? Consider the following:

Definition 5: The *support-biased correlation function* is $f_{SupBiased}(n, P(\varsigma), (L, \alpha)) = \alpha n - L_g^{-1} \log P(\varsigma)$.

When possible contours of the $f_{SupBiased}$ function are plotted in the same way as the plot of f_{Lik} in Figure 4, we can see the difference between the two metrics. The plot of the support-biased correlation function (Figure 5) is linear with respect to increasing subcube dimensionality. This clearly inhibits its value as an approximation of f_{Lik} at lower required levels of correlation, as the quadratic contours of f_{Lik} drop far below the linear contours of $f_{SupBiased}$. But at higher levels, the approximation is rather close. A particularly attractive characteristic of the support-biased correlation function is given in the following theorem:

Theorem 6. Given a correlation level (L, α) the problem of finding a well-formed subcube where $Obs(\varsigma) \geq f_{SupBiased}(n, P(\varsigma), (L, \alpha))$, is solvable in polynomial time.

Thus, by changing the definition of the problem (weakening the definition of f_{Lik} somewhat) we can arrive at a tractable problem definition. Especially in a real database where correlations are often numerous and strong, this may be an acceptable modification to the problem.

We again note briefly (as we did after Theorem 2) that the close-to quadratic complexity of the algorithm suggested by Theorem 6 is impractical for use with a large database. However, the polynomial-time solution offers some hope that such a relaxation may be useful.

7. Future work

This paper has been a work of theory, exploring the computational complexity of adding search for correlation (based on violation of expectation) to one formulation of the data mining problem. However, many practical questions remain.

- In practice, how useful and interesting are the features identified using $f_{SupBiased}$? How do they compare with the answers that would have been generated by f_{Lik}?

- It is possible to use $f_{SupBiased}$ in polynomial time. Is its use computationally practical for large databases?

- Would an approximation algorithm based directly on f_{Lik} be preferable to an exact but relaxed search based on $f_{SupBiased}$?

- Are there other robust, statistical measures based on violation of expectation (besides those explored here), that render a tractable search with good results?

- What practical problems are there with searches using these types of metrics in real data, for real, commercial users? How do the results compare with traditional market-basket analysis?

8. Conclusions

In this paper, we considered the computational implications of adding simple statistical expectation to the data mining paradigm. This is a natural extension for data mining, since defining statistical correlation in terms of violation of a simple expectation of attribute independence is a widely accepted technique (for example, the popular χ^2 test for independence does just that). Specifically, we considered the problem of adding an INTEREST check to *iceberg cube* queries of the form:

```
CREATE CUBE Iceberg AS
SELECT a_1, a_2, a_3,..., a_n
FROM SalesInfo
CUBE BY a_1, a_2, a_3,..., a_n
HAVING INTEREST (*) > k
```

We explored the type of expectation-based INTEREST functions for which this problem remains tractable. Perhaps the simplest such problem would be:

"Find me a subcube having 20 times as many tuples as expected."

Unfortunately, this problem is NP-hard, unless we restrict ourselves to well-formed subspaces (those that do not contain attribute values which are seen too frequently). Even for well-formed subspaces, adding some desired tweaks to the problem (such as a minimum support level)

renders the problem NP-hard once again. More unfortunately, basing our INTEREST function on the parametric loglikelihood ratio test from statistics (one of the most natural statistical tests for correlation or surprise in this domain) also renders the problem NP-hard. Given these results, we argue that adding robust statistics of surprise and interest to such CUBE-BY queries which take into account expectation will likely require a careful shift into the world of approximation. Along these lines, we have suggested a relaxation of the loglikelihood ratio test which allows a polynomial-time solution.

References

[1] Rakesh Agrawal, Ramakrishnan Srikant: Fast Algorithms for Mining Association Rules in Large Databases. *VLDB* 1994: 487-499

[2] Kevin S. Beyer, Raghu Ramakrishnan: Bottom-Up Computation of Sparse and Iceberg CUBEs. *SIGMOD Conference* 1999: 359-370

[3] Sergey Brin, Rajeev Motwani, Craig Silverstein: Beyond Market Baskets: Generalizing Association Rules to Correlations. *SIGMOD Conference* 1997: 265-276

[4] Edith Cohen, Mayur Datar, Shinji Fujiwara, Aristides Gionis, Piotr Indyk, Rajeev Motwani, Jeffrey D. Ullman, Cheng Yang: Finding Interesting Associations without Support Pruning. *ICDE* 2000: 489-499

[5] Ted Dunning: Accurate Methods for the Statistics of Surprise and Coincidence. *Computational Linguistics* 19(1), 1993

[6] Jim Gray, Adam Bosworth, Andrew Layman, Hamid Pirahesh: Data Cube: A Relational Aggregation Operator Generalizing Group-By, Cross-Tab, and Sub-Total. *ICDE* 1996: 152-159

[7] Min Fang, Narayanan Shivakumar, Hector Garcia-Molina, Rajeev Motwani, Jeffrey D. Ullman: Computing Iceberg Queries Efficiently. *VLDB* 1998: 299-310

[8] Christopher Jermaine. The Computational Complexity of High-Dimensional Correlation Search. *Georgia Institute of Technology Technical Report GIT-CC-01-23*

[9] A. M. Mood, F. A. Graybill, D. C. Boes. *Introduction to the Theory of Statistics*. McGraw Hill, 1974

[10] Rene Peters: The maximum edge biclique problem is NP-complete. *Tilburg University, Faculty of Economics and Business Administration Research Memorandum: RePEc:dgr:kubrem:2000789*

[11] David Sheskin: *Handbook of Parametric and Non-Parametric Statistical Procedures*. Chapman and Hall CRC, 2000

Evaluating Boosting Algorithms to Classify Rare Classes: Comparison and Improvements

Mahesh V. Joshi
IBM T. J. Watson Research Center
P.O.Box 704
Yorktown Heights, NY 10598, USA.
joshim@us.ibm.com

Vipin Kumar
Department of Computer Science
University of Minnesota
Minneapolis, MN 55455, USA.
kumar@cs.umn.edu

Ramesh C. Agarwal
IBM Almaden Research Center
650 Harry Road
San Jose, CA 95120, USA.
ragarwal@us.ibm.com

Abstract

Classification of rare events has many important data mining applications. Boosting is a promising meta-technique that improves the classification performance of any weak classifier. So far, no systematic study has been conducted to evaluate how boosting performs for the task of mining rare classes. In this paper, we evaluate three existing categories of boosting algorithms from the single viewpoint of how they update the example weights in each iteration, and discuss their possible effect on recall and precision of the rare class. We propose enhanced algorithms in two of the categories, and justify their choice of weight updating parameters theoretically. Using some specially designed synthetic datasets, we compare the capability of all the algorithms from the rare class perspective. The results support our qualitative analysis, and also indicate that our enhancements bring an extra capability for achieving better balance between recall and precision in mining rare classes.

1 Introduction and Motivation

Recent surge in volumes of data and relatively much smaller increase in the events of interest have brought critical importance to the problem of effectively mining rarely occurring events. One example of this is the click-stream data on the web. A popular e-commerce web site can receive millions of hits in a day, but very small proportion among these hits are of actual interest from the revenue generation point of view. Some work has started to emerge in building descriptive models for the rare events [1, 5]. Classification shows promise in achieving this task. In past few years, boosting has emerged as a competitive meta-technique that has a theoretically justified ability to improve the performance of any *weak* classification algorithm. Var-

ious different boosting algorithms have been proposed in the literature [7, 2, 10, 4]. They have been analyzed for their effectiveness [8], and they have been adapted to special tasks [9]. Despite of this abundant work on boosting, no work has dealt directly with evaluating boosting algorithms in the context of mining rare events.

Boosting algorithms work in iterations, each time learning a weak classifier model[1] on a different weighted distribution of training records. After each iteration, the weights of the examples are updated. The intention is to increase the weights of the incorrectly classified examples and decrease the weights of the correctly classified examples. This forces the classifier to focus more on the incorrectly classified examples in the next iteration. The algorithm stops after a pre-specified number of iterations, or based on some measured quality. While classifying a new example, all the models from all the iterations vote in proportion to their accuracy; the class with most votes wins.

The crucial step that we focus on in this paper is the weight update mechanism in each iteration. In the binary classification scenario, there are four kinds of examples after every iteration. From the perspective of rare class C (versus all the other classes clubbed into one class called NC), these can be categorized as follows:

	Predicted as C	Predicted as NC
Actually C	True Positives (TP)	False Negatives (FN)
Actually NC	False Positives (FP)	True Negatives (TN)

We evaluate boosting algorithms from three different categories: those making true or false decision for every example, those choosing to abstain from making any decision on some examples, and those that take misclassification costs into account. One of the contributions of this paper is that,

---

[1] A weak classifier is the algorithm that, given $\epsilon, \delta > 0$, can achieve at least slightly better error rate, ϵ, than random guessing ($\epsilon \geq 1/2 - \gamma$, where $\gamma > 0$), with a probability $(1 - \delta)$.

we bring out the differences in these algorithms with respect to how they modify the weights on four types of examples: TP, FP, TN, and FN. This insight allows us to qualitatively discuss the effects of their weight modifications on the recall and precision of the target class[2].

A classifier obtains high recall by learning better models for distinguishing FN from TN, and high precision by better distinguishing FP from TP. Recall and precision goals are often conflicting; hence, attacking them simultaneously may not work well, especially when one of the classes is rare. Thus, it is desirable to give different treatment to FPs and FNs. Based on this theme, we propose enhancements to two state-of-the-art algorithms, AdaBoost [7] and SLIP-PER [2]. We justify the weight update formulae theoretically.

The theme of applying different update factors to different types of examples is present in the boosting algorithms CSB1, CSB2 [10] and AdaCost [4]. These algorithms take into account different costs of making a false positive prediction versus a false negative prediction. Our study shows that AdaCost has the capability of controlling its emphasis on recall, while trying to focus on precision as well. This makes it a better algorithm in many datasets with rare classes. However, we also show that its over-emphasis on recall may sometimes lead to a much poorer precision.

We validate our qualitative study of weight update effects using some synthetic datasets specially designed for studying rare classes. We show that our proposed enhancements outperform their respective predecessors in achieving better recall-precision balance, and that they have the ability to even outperform the most competitive cost-sensitive algorithm, AdaCost, in some situations.

2 Boosting Algorithms that Do Not Abstain

In this section, we describe algorithms that make a true or false decision on *every* example.

The popular AdaBoost [7] learning algorithm is described in Figure 1. The weak model, h_t, must have an *accuracy* $> 50\%$, in order to increase weights of FP and FN decisions and decrease weights of TP and TN decisions, after each iteration. Note that the same update factor is used for all four types. The α_t value is chosen to minimize the sum of all the weights, Z_t, before the beginning of $(t+1)^{st}$ iteration, which is shown to minimize an upper bound on the training error. Also note that, α_t, voting power of h_t, is monotonic with the accuracy of h_t.

---

[2]Overall accuracy is not a good metric for evaluating rare class performance. Instead a balance between recall and precision, to be defined later, is desired.

Given: Training Set, $\mathcal{T} : \{(x_i, y_i)\}, i = 1 \cdots N$; $x_i \in \mathcal{X}, y_i \in \{-1, 1\}$; and number of trials, M.
Initialize weights $D_1(i) = 1/N$.
for $t = 1 \cdots M$

i. Learn weak model, h_t, using D_t.

ii. Compute importance weight, α_t:

$$r_t = \sum_{i=1}^{N} D_t(i) h_t(x_i) y_i; \quad \alpha_t = \frac{1}{2} ln \left(\frac{1 + r_t}{1 - r_t} \right) \quad (1)$$

iii. Update Weights:

$$D_{t+1}(i) = (D_t(i) exp(-\alpha_t y_i h_t(x_i))) / Z_t, \quad (2)$$

where Z_t is chosen such that $\sum D_{t+1}(i) = 1$.
endfor
Final Model:

$$H(x) = sign \left(\sum_{t=1}^{M} \alpha_t h_t(x) \right) \quad (3)$$

Figure 1. *AdaBoost Algorithm [7]*

2.1 Our Proposed Enhancement (RareBoost-1)

We propose an enhancement to AdaBoost, as described in Figure 2. The key observation to make is that we are giving a different treatment to positive and negative predictions. If each model makes every prediction (C or NC) with an accuracy of greater than 50%; i.e., if $TP_t > FP_t$ and $TN_t > FN_t$, then the algorithm will decrease (resp. increase) the weights of correct (resp. incorrect) predictions.

Proof for the choice of α_t^p and α_t^n:
We essentially modify the proof given in [7]. By recursively expanding the weight update rules 8 and 9, and using equation 10, the weights at the end of iteration M are

$$
\begin{aligned}
D_{M+1}(i) &= \frac{1}{N \prod_t Z_t} (exp(-(\sum_{t:h_t(x_i) \geq 0} \alpha_t^p y_i h_t(x_i) + \\
&\qquad \sum_{t:h_t(x_i) < 0} \alpha_t^n y_i h_t(x_i)))) \\
&= \frac{exp(-y_i g(x_i))}{N \prod_t Z_t}
\end{aligned}
$$

Following [7], training error can be minimized by greedily minimizing Z_t, which is the sum of weights after iteration t. $Z_t = Z_t^p + Z_t^n$ can in turn be minimized by minimizing each of its constituent terms. Using notation $u_i = y_i h_t(x_i)$, we have $Z_t^p = \sum_{i:h_t(x_i) \geq 0} D_t(i)exp(-\alpha_t^p u_i)$, and $Z_t^n = \sum_{i:h_t(x_i)<0} D_t(i)exp(-\alpha_t^n u_i)$. We now derive expressions for α_t^p by minimizing Z_t^p. Derivation for α_t^n is symmetric. Using the same linear upper bound as given in [7],

$$Z_t^p \leq \sum_{i:h_t(x_i) \geq 0} D_t(i)\left(\frac{1+u_i}{2}\right)exp(-\alpha_t^p) +$$
$$D_t(i)\left(\frac{1-u_i}{2}\right)exp(\alpha_t^p)$$

and minimizing it by differentiating it w.r.t. α_t^p, yields

$$\alpha_t^{p1} = \frac{1}{2}ln\left(\frac{1+\sum_{i:h_t(x_i) \geq 0} D_t(i)y_i h_t(x_i)}{1-\sum_{i:h_t(x_i) \geq 0} D_t(i)y_i h_t(x_i)}\right) \quad (4)$$
$$= \frac{1}{2}ln\left(\frac{1+TP_t-FP_t}{1-TP_t+FP_t}\right)$$

However, this is not a unique solution. It is just one possible solution for α_t^p obtained by minimizing the tightest *linear* upper bound. Here is another possible solution for α_t^p:

$$\alpha_t^{p2} = \frac{1}{2}ln\left(\frac{TP_t}{FP_t}\right). \quad (5)$$

This choice of α_t^{p2} simplifies the qualitative analysis that we present later. In fact, for the range of $h_t = \{-1, +1\}$; i.e., by ignoring confidence-rating of a decision, we can show that use of α_t^{p2} achieves smaller value of Z_t^p than use of α_t^{p1}. Using α_t^{p2}, we obtain $Z_t^{p2} = 2\sqrt{TP_t FP_t}$, since $u_i = -1$ or $+1$. Similarly, using α_t^{p1}, we obtain

$$Z_t^{p1} = TP_t\frac{\sqrt{\delta+2FP_t}}{\sqrt{\delta+2TP_t}} + FP_t\frac{\sqrt{\delta+2TP_t}}{\sqrt{\delta+2FP_t}};$$

where $\delta = (1-TP_t-FP_t) \geq 0$. The following expression can be easily derived using formulae for Z_t^{p1} and Z_t^{p2}.

$$Z_t^{p1} - Z_t^{p2} = \frac{\beta^2}{\sqrt{(\delta+2TP_t)(\delta+2FP_t)}} \geq 0$$

where

$$\beta = (\sqrt{\delta TP_t + 2TP_t FP_t} - \sqrt{\delta FP_t + 2TP_t FP_t})$$

Thus, $Z_t^{p2} \leq Z_t^{p1}$. Figure 2 uses $\alpha_t^p = \alpha_t^{p2}$. ♠

3 Boosting Algorithms that Abstain

In this section, we describe boosting algorithms using base classifiers that abstain from making any decision on some training examples. SLIPPER [2] is one such algorithm. It focuses on building single-rule model for only one of the classes in all the iterations. If a good model cannot be built, it uses default model for that iteration, which predicts everything to be of that class. In case of rare classes, its

---

Given: $\mathcal{T}$, M.
Initialize weights $D_1(i) = 1/N$.
for $t = 1 \cdots M$

   i. Learn weak model, h_t, using D_t.

  ii. Compute importance weight for positive predictions, α_t^p:

$$TP_t = \sum_{i:h_t(x_i) \geq 0, y_i > 0} D_t(i)h_t(x_i);$$
$$FP_t = \sum_{i:h_t(x_i) \geq 0, y_i < 0} D_t(i)h_t(x_i)$$
$$\alpha_t^p = 1/2\, ln\,(TP_t/FP_t) \quad (6)$$

  iii. Compute importance weight for negative predictions, α_t^n:

$$TN_t = \sum_{i:h_t(x_i) < 0, y_i < 0} D_t(i)h_t(x_i);$$
$$FN_t = \sum_{i:h_t(x_i) < 0, y_i > 0} D_t(i)h_t(x_i)$$
$$\alpha_t^n = 1/2\, ln\,(TN_t/FN_t) \quad (7)$$

  iv. Update weights: For positive predictions $(h_t(x_i) \geq 0)$,

$$D_{t+1}(i) = D_t(i)exp(-\alpha_t^p y_i h_t(x_i))/Z_t, \quad (8)$$

For negative predictions $(h_t(x_i) < 0)$,

$$D_{t+1}(i) = D_t(i)exp(-\alpha_t^n y_i h_t(x_i))/Z_t, \quad (9)$$

where Z_t is chosen such that $\sum D_{t+1}(i) = 1$.
endfor
Final Model:

$$H(x) = sgn(g(x)),$$

where

$$g(x) = \left(\sum_{t:h_t(x) \geq 0} \alpha_t^p h_t(x) + \sum_{t:h_t(x) < 0} \alpha_t^n h_t(x)\right) \quad (10)$$

Figure 2. *RareBoost-1 Algorithm: The difference from AdaBoost is the use of different importance weights for positive and negative predictions*

primary ability to achieve better recall stems from its use of default model. We explain later in section 5 as to why this is not a good strategy.

Our enhancement of SLIPPER, called RareBoost-2, is described in Figure 3. The primary difference is that we build models for both the classes in every iteration and do not use default model[3].

Due to space constraints, we refer reader to [6] for the derivation of the choice of α_t. It follows the guideline in SLIPPER's paper [2]. The key idea is again to choose α_t to minimize Z_t in every iteration, to minimize the training error. The choice between C's and NC's model is made based on whichever minimizes the corresponding Z_t value.

4 Cost-Sensitive Boosting Algorithms

The algorithms described so far use the same weight update factor for true and false predictions of a given kind. RareBoost-1 and RareBoost-2 enhance AdaBoost and SLIPPER to use different factors across positive and negative predictions. However, most generally, one can use different factors for each type: TP, FP, TN, and FN. Cost-sensitive algorithms take a step towards this. The AdaCost algorithm [4] modifies AdaBoost's weight update equation 2 to

$$D_{t+1}(i) = (D_t(i)exp(-\alpha_t y_i h_t(x_i)\beta_{sgn(h_t(x_i)y_i)}))/Z_t.$$

where $\alpha_t = 1/2\ ln((1 + r_t)/(1 - r_t))$ and $r_t = \sum_i D_t(i)exp(-y_i h_t(x_i)\beta_{sgn(h_t(x_i)y_i)})$. The AdaCost paper proves a general guideline for choosing the multiplying factors β_+ and β_-, that $0 \leq \beta_+ \leq \beta_- \leq 1$. We have chosen their recommended setting of $\beta_{TP} = 0.5 - 0.5\ cost(TP)/f = 0.5$, $\beta_{TN} = 0.5 - 0.5\ cost(TN)/f = 0.5$, $\beta_{FP} = 0.5 + 0.5\ cost(FP)/f = 0.5(f + 1)/f$, $\beta_{FN} = 0.5 + 0.5\ cost(FN)/f = 1.0$. f is an input parameter[4]. β_+ and β_- satisfy the required constraints, for $f \geq 1$. Using these values, the expanded weight update formulae look like

$$
\begin{aligned}
D_{t+1}(i) &= D_t(i)exp(-0.5\ \alpha_t h_t(x_i)), \text{for TP, TN} \\
&= D_t(i)exp(0.5\ \alpha_t h_t(x_i)(f + 1)/f), \text{for FP} \\
&= D_t(i)exp(\alpha_t h_t(x_i)), \text{for FN}
\end{aligned}
$$

Two other variations [10] of cost-sensitive algorithms are CSB1, that does not use any α_t factor (or

---

[3]Algorithm of Fig. 3 can be made equivalent to SLIPPER by replacing model for NC (resp. C) with a default model predicting all examples as C (resp. NC), when the focus is on class C (resp. NC). The values TN_t and FN_t (resp. TP_t and FP_t) will be replaced by $\sum_{i:y_i>0} D_t(i)$ and $\sum_{i:y_i<0} D_t(i)$ (resp. $\sum_{i:y_i<0} D_t(i)$ and $\sum_{i:y_i>0} D_t(i)$)

[4]The cost of true predictions (positive and negative) is assumed to be $cost(TP) = cost(TN) = 0$, cost of false positives is fixed at $cost(FP) = 1$, and cost of false negative is $cost(FN) = f$.

Given: $\mathcal{T}$, M.
Initialize weights $D_1(i) = 1/N$.
for $t = 1 \cdots M$

  i. Learn weak model for $y_i = +1$ (class C) examples, $h_t^{+1} : x_i \rightarrow \{+1, 0\}$, using D_t.

  ii. Learn weak model for $y_i = -1$ (class NC) examples, $h_t^{-1} : x_i \rightarrow \{-1, 0\}$, using D_t.

  iii. Evaluate C's model and NC's model:

$$TP_t = \sum_{i:y_i>0, h_t^{+1}(x_i)>0} D_t(i);$$

$$FP_t = \sum_{i:y_i<0, h_t^{+1}(x_i)>0} D_t(i)$$

$$TN_t = \sum_{i:y_i<0, h_t^{-1}(x_i)<0} D_t(i);$$

$$FN_t = \sum_{i:y_i>0, h_t^{-1}(x_i)<0} D_t(i)$$

  iv. Choose Model and Compute importance weight, α_t:
    if($(1 - (TP_t - FP_t)^2) < (1 - (TN_t - FN_t)^2)$) then,
    Choose C's Model, by setting $h_t = h_t^{+1}$:

$$\alpha_t = 0.5\ ln\,(TP_t/FP_t) \qquad (11)$$

    else Choose NC's Model by setting $h_t = h_t^{-1}$:

$$\alpha_t = -0.5\ ln\,(TN_t/FN_t) \qquad (12)$$

  endif

  v. Update Weights:

$$D_{t+1}(i) = D_t(i)exp(-\alpha_t y_i)/Z_t; h_t(x_i) \neq 0, \quad (13)$$

  where Z_t is chosen such that $\sum D_{t+1}(i) = 1$.

endfor
Final Model:

$$H(x) = sign\left(\sum_{t:x \text{ satisfies } h_t} \alpha_t\right)$$

Figure 3. *RareBoost-2 Algorithm: The difference from SLIPPER algorithm is the choice between C's model and NC's model, and absence of Default Model*

$\alpha_t = 1$), CSB2, that uses same α_t as computed by AdaBoost. The weight update formula for CSB1 is $D_{t+1}(i) = (D_t(i)C_{sgn(h_t(x_i)y_i)}exp(-y_ih_t(x_i))/Z_t$, and that for CSB2 is $D_{t+1}(i) = (D_t(i)C_{sgn(h_t(x_i)y_i)}exp(-\alpha_ty_ih_t(x_i))/Z_t$. The parameters C_+ and C_- are defined as $C_+ = 1$, and $C_- = cost(y_i, h_t(x_i)$. Using the same cost matrix as that for AdaCost, this is equivalent to $C_{TP} = 1$, $C_{TN} = 1$, $C_{FP} = 1$, and $C_{FN} = f$.

5 Comparing All Algorithms

In this section, we analyze all the described algorithms from the perspective of how they update the weights on four types of examples: TP, FP, FN, and FN. To simplify analysis, we assume, without loss of generality, that each model generates binary decision; i.e., we ignore confidence-rating of a prediction. It is in general difficult to assess how the weight of a given training example will change over all the iterations, because of the cumulative effect, and one example may switch its role among TP and FN or FP and TN from iteration to iteration. Using the fact that all the algorithms treat all examples of one kind equally (i.e. one TP is treated same as other TP) in an iteration, we decide to infer the effect by observing how aggregate weights of all example types change from iteration t to $t + 1$. Table 1 summarizes the effect for all algorithms.

Here is a brief reasoning of why the weight update factors are important. All algorithms try to concentrate on FP and FN examples by boosting their weights, and suppressing weights of TP and TN. In the next iteration, a model geared towards learning C will try to capture more FN and less FP examples. So the model tries to convert more FN's into TP's, thus increasing recall. However, if the weights of TN are reduced significantly (as compared to FN's), C's model may capture some of TN's, thus losing precision. Similarly, a model geared for NC will try to capture more FP and as little of FN as possible, thus trying to convert more FP's into TN's, thus improving precision. However, it might capture more TP's if weight on the TP's is reduced to low levels, thus losing recall.

AdaBoost vs. RareBoost-1:
AdaBoost gives equal importance to both types of false predictions. RareBoost-1 scales FP examples in proportion to how well they are distinguished in an iteration from TP examples, and FN in the proportion of how well they are distinguished from TN. The essential effect of weight update in AdaBoost is to stratify the sum of weights on *all* true predictions against *all* false predictions. RareBoost-1 stratifies true positives against false positives and true negatives against false negatives. Traditional weak learners learn effective models when the class proportion is balanced. The separate stratification of positive and negative predictions

gives the weak learner a better chance at distinguishing each type. Thus, we expect RareBoost-1 to achieve better recall and precision as compared to AdaBoost.

SLIPPER vs. RareBoost-2:
In rare class context, when it is difficult to build a good model for C, SLIPPER's primary ability to aim for recall comes due to its default model. From Table 1, with default model, effect of weight update is to equalize the weights on both classes. From our experience with rare classes in [5], such stratification usually improves recall at the cost of precision. If good models for C cannot be found to distinguish FP examples from TP examples, then the overall balance may suffer. Instead, RareBoost-2, at the cost of building models for both C and NC, specifically targets the weak learner to model either TP vs. FP, or TN vs. FN. This may help it achieve better performance than SLIPPER.

Cost-Sensitive vs. Cost-Insensitive Algorithms:
As shown in Table 1, unlike any of the cost-insensitive algorithms, AdaCost comes close to a generic strategy of updating weights of all four types of examples differently. For values of $f > 1$, it increases weights on FNs more than any other type of examples. The net effect is that the weak learner focuses on recall in the next iteration. The FPs also get boosted more than TPs are suppressed. This allows AdaCost to focus on precision as well. But, unlike other algorithms, TP and FP are not stratified (neither are TN and FN), so increasing precision might tend to lose recall by capturing more TP examples. Maybe for higher f values this loss in recall can be regained. Usually higher recall comes at a cost of lower precision. So, it will depend on the dataset whether the recall focus helps[5]. Like AdaCost, CSB1 and CSB2 focus on FN by varying f. However, this focus is not accompanied by focus on precision, which can result in high recall at a loss of precision.

6 Results on Synthetic Datasets

In this section, we validate our qualitative analysis using some specially designed synthetic datasets. Due to space constraints, we refer reader to [6] for more detailed experiment description. Briefly, we use RIPPER0 [3] as the weak learner. We evaluate the performance of each algorithm using $F1$-measure[6] after each iteration on the test data for 100 iterations, and report the best numbers[7]. We report best result of the two variants of RareBoost-1 formed by using α_t^{p1} and α_t^{p2}. For SLIPPER, we choose best result from two

---

[5]Note that unlike methods purely focusing on recall by an up-front oversampling of rare class, AdaCost can cater to precision also.

[6]F_1-measure is defined as $2*R*P)/(R+P)$, where recall R = TP/(TP+FN) and precision P = TP/(TP+FP).

[7]Test data is generated using the same model as training data. So, monitoring performance on it essentially is same as monitoring the generalization ability of the algorithm. For the purposes of our experiments, test data can be thought of as validation data.

AdaBoost	RareBoost-1
$TP_{t+1} = TP_t/\gamma$	$TP_{t+1} = TP_t/\gamma_1$
$FP_{t+1} = FP_t * \gamma$	$FP_{t+1} = FP_t * \gamma_1$
$TN_{t+1} = TN_t/\gamma$	$TN_{t+1} = TN_t/\gamma_2$
$FN_{t+1} = FN_t * \gamma$	$FN_{t+1} = FN_t * \gamma_2$
$\gamma = e^{\alpha_t} = \sqrt{(TP_t + TN_t)/(FP_t + FN_t)}$	$\gamma_1 = e^{\alpha_t^p} = \sqrt{TP_t/FP_t}, \gamma_2 = e^{\alpha_t^n} = \sqrt{TN_t/FN_t}$
Effect: $TP_{t+1} + TN_{t+1} = FP_{t+1} + FN_{t+1}$	Effect: $TP_{t+1} = FP_{t+1}$ & $TN_{t+1} = FN_{t+1}$

SLIPPER-C	SLIPPER-NC
If C's Model is chosen in t^{th} iteration,	If NC's Model is chosen in t^{th} iteration
$TP_{t+1} = TP_t/\gamma_1$	$TP_{t+1} = TP_t$
$FP_{t+1} = FP_t * \gamma_1$	$FP_{t+1} = FP_t$
$TN_{t+1} = TN_t$	$TN_{t+1} = TN_t/\gamma_2$
$FN_{t+1} = FN_t$	$FN_{t+1} = FN_t * \gamma_2$
$\gamma_1 = e^{\alpha_t} = \sqrt{TP_t/FP_t}$	$\gamma_2 = e^{\alpha_t} = \sqrt{TN_t/FN_t}$
Effect: $TP_{t+1} = FP_{t+1}$	Effect: $TN_{t+1} = FN_{t+1}$
OR	OR
If Default Model is chosen in t^{th} iteration,	If Default Model is chosen in t^{th} iteration
$TP_{t+1} = TP_t/\gamma_3$	$TP_{t+1} = TP_t/\gamma_3$
$FP_{t+1} = FP_t * \gamma_3$	$FP_{t+1} = FP_t * \gamma_3$
$TN_{t+1} = TN_t/\gamma_3$	$TN_{t+1} = TN_t/\gamma_3$
$FN_{t+1} = FN_t * \gamma_3$	$FN_{t+1} = FN_t * \gamma_3$
$\gamma_3 = e^{\alpha_t} = \sqrt{(TP_t + FP_t)/(TN_t + FN_t)}$	$\gamma_3 = e^{\alpha_t} = \sqrt{(TN_t + FN_t)/(TP_t + FP_t)}$
Effect: $TP_{t+1} + FN_{t+1} = TN_{t+1} + FP_{t+1}$	Effect: $TP_{t+1} + FN_{t+1} = TN_{t+1} + FP_{t+1}$

RareBoost-2	
If C's Model is chosen in t^{th} iteration OR	If NC's Model is chosen in t^{th} iteration
$TP_{t+1} = TP_t/\gamma_1$	$TP_{t+1} = TP_t$
$FP_{t+1} = FP_t * \gamma_1$	$FP_{t+1} = FP_t$
$TN_{t+1} = TN_t$	$TN_{t+1} = TN_t/\gamma_2$
$FN_{t+1} = FN_t$	$FN_{t+1} = FN_t * \gamma_2$
$\gamma_1 = e^{\alpha_t} = \sqrt{TP_t/FP_t}$	$\gamma_2 = e^{-\alpha_t} = \sqrt{TN_t/FN_t}$
Effect: $TP_{t+1} = FP_{t+1}$	Effect: $TN_{t+1} = FN_{t+1}$

AdaCost	CSB1 and CSB2
$TP_{t+1} = TP_t/\gamma$	$TP_{t+1} = TP_t/\gamma$
$FP_{t+1} = FP_t * \gamma^{(f+1)/f}$	$FP_{t+1} = FP_t * \gamma$
$TN_{t+1} = TN_t/\gamma$	$TN_{t+1} = TN_t/\gamma$
$FN_{t+1} = FN_t * \gamma^2$	$FN_{t+1} = FN_t * f * \gamma$
$\gamma = e^{0.5\alpha_t}$	$\gamma = e^1$ for CSB1, and $\gamma = e^{\alpha_t}$ for CSB2
Effect1: Increase weights of FN more than FP	
Effect2: Decrease weights of TP or TN by a smaller factor than FN or FP or both	

Table 1. *Comparing the effect of weight updates in each of the algorithms. This analysis assumes the range of h_t's prediction to be binary. The entities TP_t, etc. are aggregate weights of examples of that type.*

variants, one with focus on C and other with focus on NC. For CSB1 and AdaCost, we use $f=1, 2$, and 5, and report the best number. For $f=1$, CSB2 is equivalent to AdaBoost, so we report its best result among $f=2$ and $f=5$. Last point to note is that, we used only the binary valued models (i.e. ignored confidence-rated predictions). This is done so as to be consistent with our qualitative analysis assumptions[8].

Datasets Without Any Attributes Correlations :
The model has three types of attributes. The records of classes C and NC are divided into multiple subclasses. For each attribute, Figure 4 shows the histogram distribution of subclasses over the range of its values. Each attribute dis-

tinguishes one subclass of C and/or one subclass of NC. For example, C_a can be distinguished by a rule capturing the range of values in $ACOM_a$ where C_a peaks.

In our experiments, the proportion of the target class C with respect to NC was fixed at 5% in all these datasets. We varied four peak-width parameters, defined in Figure 4. These parameters let us control the recall and precision obtainable for a dataset.

All the algorithms perform equally well when all the peaks are very sharp (snc1). Even when the C_a and C_b peaks widen (snc2), all algorithms, except SLIPPER, are competitive, because good models for the majority class NC can still be learned. The reason for SLIPPER's performance deterioration can be attributed to its default model selection

---
[8]This assumption affects all but SLIPPER and RareBoost-2, where the confidence rating is embedded in the α_t factor.

mechanism. As the NC_b peaks are made wider (snc3), all the algorithms suffer a dramatic loss in F_1-measure. This can be attributed to the fact that NC_b is the majority sub-class of NC, and wider WNC_b makes it difficult to remove FPs due to it without removing TPs of C. And because of the rarity of C and the nature of the data model, it is difficult to learn a good model to regain true positives. RareBoost-1 is achieving higher precision while maintaining the recall at the level of AdaBoost. RareBoost-2 is significantly better than SLIPPER for both recall and precision. Although Ada-Cost is achieving the best F_1-measure on the basis of boosting false negatives significantly (best f is 5), in the process it suffers from a very poor precision (lowest precision). In fact, it can be claimed that recall and precision numbers of RareBoost-2 are better balanced. As the NC_a peaks are made wider (snc4), the loss in F_1-measure is not as dramatic as in snc3, because NC_a peaks are not captured when good signatures of C_a are learned. AdaCost again wins here on F_1-measure because of its emphasis on recall (again best f is 5). Its precision, however, is again much worse as compared to that of RareBoost-1. Here, RareBoost-1 can be said to achieve better balance. The last dataset (snc5) has a mixture of wide C_b peaks and wide NC_a peaks. This time AdaCost is able to capture good recall as well as good precision (for $f = 2$) among all. This dataset may be representing the scenario where the cost-sensitivity is required.

Datasets With Attribute Correlations:
We use the data generating model that was first used by us in [5]. It is described in detail therein. Briefly, it is similar to previous model, except for the correlations among signatures of attributes of type $ACOM_a$. It also has some categorical attributes of type ANC_b and AC_b. We believe that this model is fairly general and complex. The results on this generic model are given in Table 3. The dataset model is kept fixed (the parameters are $WC_a = WC_b = WNC_a = WNC_b = 2.0\%$), and only the target class proportion (Cfrc) in training (and test) data is varied. As Cfrc increases, it becomes easier to achieve better recall and precision. RareBoost-1 and RareBoost-2 outperform AdaBoost and SLIPPER in all cases. More importantly, the performance gap increases as Cfrc decreases. AdaCost is the most competitive cost-sensitive technique. For 2.9% and 5.7% datasets, it achieves its best numbers when $f = 2$. For these datasets, RareBoost variants are either closer in performance to AdaCost (2.9%) or they are better than Ada-Cost (5.7%). For higher Cfrc values, AdaCost achieves its best only for $f = 1$. RareBoost-2 beats it for 13.1% dataset. As f increases on these datasets, AdaCost's precision shows significant degradation [6]. These results indicate that over-emphasizing recall can result in a significant loss in precision. In fact, precisely in these kind of situations, cost-insensitive algorithms and our proposed RareBoost variants can perform better than cost-sensitive algorithms.

7 Concluding Remarks

The outcome of our study is a critical qualitative and empirical comparison of three representative categories of most popular boosting variants in the context of rare classes, and two enhanced versions of boosting algorithms that are shown to be better especially in certain situations involving rare classes. The guideline that emerges from this is that weight update mechanisms that resemble to those of RareBoost variants or AdaCost are required for handling rare classes using boosting algorithms. Further generalization of the weight update mechanisms should aim for theoretically arriving at different optimal update factors for four types of examples: true positives, false positives, true negatives, and false negatives.

References

[1] P. Chan and S. Stolfo. Towards scalable learning with non-uniform class and cost distributions: A case study in credit card fraud detection. In *Proc. of Fourth International Conference on Knowledge Discovery and Data Mining (KDD-98)*, pages 164–168, New York City, 1998.

[2] W. Cohen and Y. Singer. A simple, fast, and effective rule learner. In *Proc. of Annual Conference of American Association for Artificial Intelligence*, pages 335–342, 1999.

[3] W. W. Cohen. Fast effective rule induction. In *Proc. of Twelfth International Conference on Machine Learning*, Lake Tahoe, California, 1995.

[4] W. Fan, S. J. Stolfo, J. Zhang, and P. K. Chan. AdaCost: Misclassification cost-sensitive boosting. In *Proc. of Sixth International Conference on Machine Learning (ICML-99)*, Bled, Slovenia, 1999.

[5] M. V. Joshi, R. C. Agarwal, and V. Kumar. Mining needles in a haystack: Classifying rare classes via two-phase rule induction. In *Proc. of ACM SIGMOD Conference*, pages 91–102, Santa Barbara, CA, 2001.

[6] M. V. Joshi, V. Kumar, and R. C. Agarwal. Evaluating boosting algorithms to classify rare classes: Comparison and improvements. Technical Report RC-22147, IBM Research Division, August 2001.

[7] R. Schapire and Y. Singer. Improved boosting algorithms using confidence-rated predictions. *Machine Learning*, 37(3):297–336, 1999.

[8] R. E. Schapire. Theoretical views of boosting. In *Proc. 4th European Conference on Computational Learning Theory*, volume 1572, pages 1–10. Springer-Verlag, 1999.

[9] F. Sebastiani, A. Sperduti, and N. Valdambrini. An improved boosting algorithm and its application to text categorization. In *Proc. 9th International ACM Conf. on Information and Knowledge Management (CIKM-00)*, pages 78–85, New York, USA, 2000.

[10] K. M. Ting. A comparative study of cost-sensitive boosting algorithms. In *Proc. of 17th International Conf. on Machine Learning*, pages 983–990, Stanford University, CA, 2000.

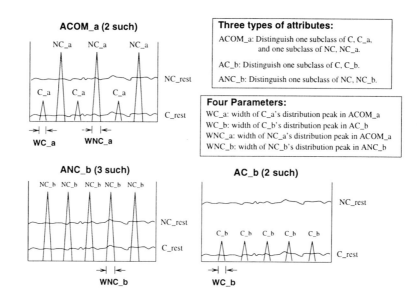

Figure 4. *Description of the model generating datasets with no correlations among attributes.*

Dataset	WC_a	WC_b	WNC_a	WNC_b
snc1	0.4	0.4	0.4	0.4
snc2	1.6	1.6	0.4	0.4
snc3	0.4	0.4	0.4	2.4
snc4	0.4	0.4	2.4	0.4
snc5	0.2	2.4	2.4	0.2

DSet		ABst	RB-1	SLIP	RB-2	CSB1	CSB2	ACst
snc1	R	77.04	77.04	81.13	74.93	77.04	77.04	77.04
	P	94.19	94.19	95.94	98.61	94.19	94.19	94.19
	F	84.76	84.76	87.92	85.16	84.76	84.76	84.76
snc2	R	76.78	76.78	69.39	76.78	76.78	76.78	77.31
	P	95.41	95.41	85.53	95.41	95.41	95.41	95.75
	F	85.09	85.09	76.62	85.09	85.09	85.09	85.55
snc3	R	41.03	41.16	35.09	49.21	43.14	43.14	79.02
	P	59.58	65.00	59.11	62.37	67.84	67.84	51.73
	F	48.59	51.10	44.04	55.01	52.74	52.74	62.53
snc4	R	54.75	58.71	47.63	56.99	52.64	38.13	69.53
	P	79.35	90.45	94.75	82.60	55.65	51.89	76.38
	F	64.79	71.20	63.39	67.45	54.10	43.95	72.79
snc5	R	47.23	51.58	43.14	53.96	56.46	55.67	63.19
	P	76.50	87.87	88.14	89.50	50.53	77.86	92.47
	F	58.40	65.00	57.93	67.33	53.33	64.92	75.08

Table 2. *Table on the Left: Specific Datasets Generated with model of Figure 4. Peak widths are given as a percentage of the total range of the attribute. Table on the Right: Results on datasets with no attribute correlations. Notation: R:recall for C (in %), P: precision for C (in %), F: F_1-measure (in %), ABst: AdaBoost, RB-1: RareBoost-1, SLIP: SLIPPER, RB-2: RareBoost-2, ACst: AdaCost.*

Cfrc		ABst	RB-1	SLIP	RB-2	CSB1	CSB2	ACst
2.9%	R	50.93	57.20	64.80	56.27	57.07	84.00	67.20
	P	71.27	81.25	57.51	82.10	60.03	44.74	68.39
	F	59.41	67.14	60.94	66.77	58.51	58.39	67.79
5.7%	R	63.20	68.67	63.60	73.20	67.07	84.13	76.00
	P	80.61	83.74	71.19	81.70	72.90	46.43	72.15
	F	70.85	75.46	67.18	77.22	69.86	59.84	74.03
13.1%	R	76.53	77.47	70.00	79.73	77.07	88.67	74.80
	P	80.62	83.36	78.59	86.04	72.70	58.18	85.65
	F	78.52	80.30	74.05	82.77	74.82	70.26	79.86
23.1%	R	78.27	84.40	80.80	80.80	86.13	96.13	85.07
	P	83.74	85.43	82.56	86.45	76.81	68.60	84.39
	F	80.91	84.91	81.67	83.53	81.21	80.07	84.73

Table 3. *Results on datasets correlations between attributes. Notation: Cfrc: Proportion of the target class C in the training dataset. R:recall for C (in %), P: precision for C (in %), F: F_1-measure (in %), ABst: AdaBoost, RB-1: RareBoost-1, SLIP: SLIPPER, RB-2: RareBoost-2, ACst: AdaCost.*

264

An Agglomerative Hierarchical Clustering using Partial Maximum Array and Incremental Similarity Computation Method.

SungYoung Jung, and Taek-Soo Kim
Machine Intelligence Group, LG Electronics Institute of Technology, Seoul, Korea
{syjung|tskim}@LG-Elite.com

Abstract

As the tractable amount of data is growing in computer science area, fast clustering algorithm is being required because traditional clustering algorithms are not so feasible for very large and high dimensional data. Many studies have been reported for clustering of large database, but most of them circumvent this problem by using the approximation method to result in the deterioration of accuracy. In this paper, we propose a new clustering algorithm by means of partial maximum array, which can realize the agglomerative hierarchical clustering with the same accuracy to the brute-force algorithm and has $O(N^2)$ time complexity. And we also present the incremental method of similarity computation which substitutes the scalar calculation for the time-consuming calculation of vector similarity. The experimental results show that clustering becomes significantly fast for large and high dimensional data.

1. Introduction

Most of the conventional clustering methods can be categorized into two classes. The first one is non-hierarchical clustering method. There are many clustering algorithms which belong to this category such as cover coefficient-based clustering [5], and K-Means algorithm which are based on an iterative manner. The traditional non-hierarchical algorithms are used in early work in which the number of cluster is small [8]. The other one is hierarchical clustering method that can be classified by the way of setting representative of each cluster for similarity computation. Single Link [16] and Minimum Spanning Tree [15] use the most similar pair of elements of different clusters. These methods have great advantages since the nearest cluster is not changed after the cluster merging step. Complete Link [8] and Group Average [17] require searching for nearest cluster for every cluster merging step. Minimum Variance method [14] [18] [19] merges two clusters which make the increment of variance smallest among all pairs of clusters after they are merged.

Many of these related studies are currently concentrated on making clustering method feasible for large data set. They are based on approximation method such as randomized searching [12] [20], partitioning [9] [12], and data sampling [6] [7] [9]. For considering the large database, 1-pass DB scanning is indispensable to avoid spending much time on reading database. Clustering for large database often means that it should manage large number of clusters more than 10^3.

The agglomerative hierarchical clustering with group average link and mean centroid method requires $O(N^3)$ time complexity given input data size N in general [8] [17]. In order to reduce the time complexity, there are some approaches to manage nearest neighbor for each cluster [8] [14] [17] [18]. They can reduce the time complexity to $O(N^2)$, however they can be inaccurate as compared with the brute-force method because they are based on the approximation mechanism that does not update nearest neighbor for each cluster when the cluster is not involved in merging clusters. We will show later in this paper the cases in which the Voorhees's nearest neighbor method [17] falls into incorrect result, and we propose a new method for the agglomerative hierarchical clustering by managing partial maximum array, which has the time complexity $O(N^2)$ and has the equivalent result to the brute-force algorithm.

High dimensionality is one of the important aspects to be considered in clustering large data. When the data are represented on high dimensional space, the calculation of the cluster similarity requires high cost of computational resource due to the vector manipulation itself. As the dimension of the data space increases, the computational time for cluster similarity becomes a critical factor. There are several well-known methods for the dimensional reduction, such as the singular value decomposition [11], the feature selection [2] [10], and the projected clustering [1]. In many cases, however, these are not so practical since they require high computational cost, sometimes the cost of the reduction in these approaches overwhelms that of the clustering itself. Even these approaches become infeasible when the principal features vary over time.

To cope with the problem of high dimensionality, we propose the method of incremental similarity computation which drastically reduces the amount of computation for high dimensional input data by substituting scalar calculation for time-consuming vector calculation in computing the cluster similarity by an incremental manner using geometrical properties to get such similarity measures as the squared distance, the cosine, and the inner product, even up to the minimum variance in the agglomerative hierarchical clustering with mean centroid method.

This paper is organized as follows: The next section explains why the Voorhees's nearest neighbor method can cause unexpected result because it is a kind of approximation. In the following section we describe the way to make it correct by fixing the problem of the nearest neighbor method using partial maximum similarity array. And then, we describe how the incremental clustering method can be applied in similarity computation for each similarity measure one by one. Subsequently, we will report on the experimental evaluation of the proposed method. Finally we will summarize our contributions.

2 Agglomerative Hierarchical Clustering with Mean Centroid method

2.1. Clustering with Nearest Neighbor

Most of the clustering methods manage similarity matrix for every two clusters in order to find most similar two clusters in cluster merging step. The most similar cluster pair should be found by rescanning the whole similarity matrix since it should be updated whenever the most similar cluster pair is merged. It makes the time complexity of hierarchical clustering to be $O(N^3)$ in general. This method is called as the brute-force algorithm.

Managing nearest neighbor for each cluster does not change the time complexity because all the nearest neighbors should be updated for every merging step. Voorhees [17] approximated it by making the nearest neighbor unchanged when neither the cluster nor its previous nearest neighbor is involved in merging clusters. Voorhees's method results in incorrect clustering as Figure 1 describes.

In Figure 1, the nearest neighbor of cluster **d** is cluster **e**, and the cluster **a** and **b** are merged to **c** which is the weighted average vector. Then all the information of cluster **a** and **b** are replaced with **c**. The similarity value between **d** and **b** is changed to that of **d** and **c**. Now, the nearest neighbor of **d** is not **e** any more. The nearest

neighbor of **d** should be changed to **c** since the cluster **c** is nearer than the previous nearest cluster **e** even though neither **d** nor **e** is involved in the merging clusters. It shows that the nearest neighbor should be updated even when neither the cluster nor its nearest neighbor is involved in the merging clusters. Therefore Voorhees' algorithm can cause unexpected results and it can be thought as an approximation. We instantiated it using distance similarity here. It is also valid for inner product and cosine similarity.

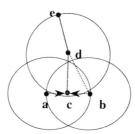

Figure 1: Inaccurate case of the Voorhees' method: It shows that the nearest neighbor should be updated even when neither of the cluster nor its nearest neighbor is involved in the merging clusters. **a**, **b** are the merging clusters which are the most similar pair in the system. **c** is the centroid of merged cluster. **e** is the nearest neighbor of **d**. Before merging, distance(**d**, **e**) < distance(**d**, **b**). After merging, distance(**d**, **e**) > distance(**d**, **c**). It shows that the nearest neighbor of **d** is not **e** any more after merging.

If the nearest neighbor is always updated for every merging step, it results in $O(N^3)$ time complexity. Now we will show in the next section how we make the clustering which has $O(N^2)$ time complexity with the same result of the brute-force method using the partial maximum array.

2.2. Clustering with the Partial Maximum Array

The similarity matrix has a 2-dimensional upper right triangular matrix which contains the similarity value for each cluster pair (Figure 2). The partial maximum array has the same size to the number of clusters. It contains the similarity value and its index of the cluster pair which has maximum value among the elements in the corresponding column of the similarity matrix.

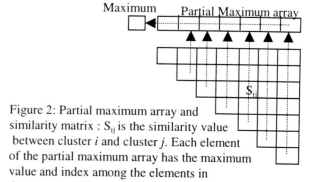

Figure 2: Partial maximum array and similarity matrix : S_{ij} is the similarity value between cluster i and cluster j. Each element of the partial maximum array has the maximum value and index among the elements in the corresponding column of similarity matrix.

New input data is entered in the first stage of clustering process, and then it is set to be a new cluster until the current number of cluster exceeds its predefined limit. When the number of cluster exceeds its limit, the most similar cluster pair is found and merged in order to keep the cluster limit. One of the two merged clusters is removed and the other is overwritten by the new cluster created by merging. Both of removal and overwriting are regarded as a kind of the update operation on the similarity matrix. After the merging step, each element of the similarity matrix and the partial maximum array should be updated appropriately for the newly created cluster. There are several different conditions for updating the similarity matrix.

Figure 3 describes the situation when cluster i is updated by removal or overwriting operation during cluster merging step. The left triangle area of i-th column in the similarity matrix and partial maximum array does not have to be changed since information in this area has nothing to do with the merged clusters. The i-th column and row constitute the "L" shaped area which contains the similarity value between the i-th cluster and all the other clusters. This area should be filled with the result of the cluster similarity computation since the cluster similarity for the current cluster between all the other clusters should be computed at least once.

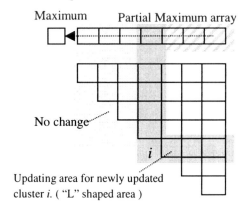

Maximum   Partial Maximum array

No change

i

Updating area for newly updated cluster i. ("L" shaped area)

Figure 3 : Partial maximum array and similarity matrix updating conditions :
Left triangle area of updating cluster
    : No change
Updating cluster area ("L"shape)
    :Updated by cluster similarity computation
Updating partial max array area (hatched box) :
  If new similarity value >= previous maximum
    : change to new value
  if new similarity value < previous maximum :
    - when previous maximum is related with updating
      cluster (i-th cluster)
      : rescan the corresponding column and find new
       maximum (=> very rare case !)
    - otherwise : no change.

During the i-th row in the "L" shaped area is being updated, the corresponding column of the partial maximum array (the hatched box area in Figure 3.) should be changed. There are three cases to consider. The first case is when the new similarity value is larger than or equal to the previous maximum value which is in the corresponding column of the partial maximum array. Then it should be changed to a new value because it means that the new cluster created by merging is more similar than the previous most similar cluster. The second case is when the new similarity value is less than the previous maximum and the previous maximum is related with updating cluster, i.e. i-th cluster here. Then the whole corresponding column should be rescanned and the new maximum value should be found because it means that the previous most similar cluster is changed to be less similar so that all the other clusters can be the candidate of nearest cluster. In the third case, there is no change otherwise. This algorithm does not have the problem described in the previous section with Figure 1 because it always check whether the similarity with the new cluster is larger than the previous partial maximum even when the current cluster is not related with merging clusters.

The most important fact to be emphasized here is that the column rescanning process occurs very rarely considering the number of clusters. It makes the time complexity of this method $O(N^2)$. We will examine the upper bound of the column rescanning in the next section, and confirm it later in this paper by experiment.

2.3. The Upper Bound of the Number of Column Rescanning.

Figure 4 shows an example of the case when the column rescanning is required. The cluster **d** has the nearest neighbor **a** which is one of the merging clusters. When the cluster **a** and **b** are merged to cluster **c**, and the cluster **c** is outside of the circle centered at **d**, the new nearest neighbor for cluster **d** should be found since it means the previous nearest neighbor is moved to be less similar and all the other clusters can be candidates of nearest neighbor. More specifically, the clusters inside the concentric circle (dotted line) can become the nearest neighbor of **d**. The column rescanning of similarity matrix is required in this situation.

Now, let us consider how many times this case can occur for one merging step. The important thing we should notice here is that there cannot be any other cluster center inside the circle in solid line centered at **d** which requires column rescanning. It drastically restricts the number of column rescanning. Consequently, the maximum number of column rescanning is constant given the vector dimension, for example it is 4 for 2-dimensional vector space and 12 for 3-dimensional vector space as it is illustrated in Figure 5.

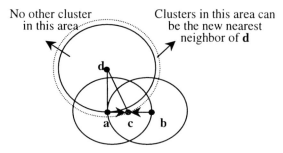

Figure 4: Column rescanning situation: **a** and **b** are the most similar clusters currently. **c** is the created cluster after merging. **d** is the cluster whose nearest neighbor is **a**. After the cluster merging, the nearest neighbor of **d** should be rescanned because the clusters in side of the concentric circle (dotted line) can become nearest neighbor

Now we can see that for the worst case all input data should be arranged in an equilateral triangle or a trigonal pyramid. That is a very rare and unrealistic case in real clustering problems.

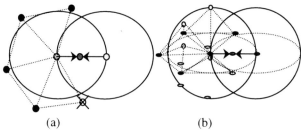

(a)   (b)

Figure 5: Maximum number of column rescanning in a merging step for each dimensional space: (a) For 2-dimensional space, maximum 4 clusters can be involved in nearest neighbor search. X marked cluster in bottom is excluded because the merged cluster is still the nearest cluster. (b) For 3-dimensional space, maximum 12 clusters can be involved the in nearest neighbor searching

2.4. Time Complexity

The memory requirement is $O(N^2)$ because of the similarity matrix. The time complexity of this algorithm is $O(2N*C*k)$, where N is the number of input data, C is the number of clusters, and k is the maximal number of column rescanning. The maximal number of column rescanning is determined by vector dimension, and it is not related to the number of data or clusters. So k is

constant given the vector dimension. Moreover, the actual number of column rescanning is so small that it is negligible for large data size, since the worst case of data arrangement mentioned before is very rare in real problems. Consequently, the time complexity can be reduced to $O(N^2)$. The experiments in this paper will confirm it with real data.

3. Incremental Computation Methods for Cluster Similarity.

Our approach for handling high dimensionality of input data is to deal with high dimensional vector very fast without any information loss. The main idea is to devise an incremental method for vector similarity computation since many part of vector similarity is computed after cluster merging in order to estimate the similarity of the cluster created by merging. Here, the similarities between the created cluster and the others can be inferred from the previous similarities related with two clusters which are merged to create new cluster. The important thing here is that it can be done without vector computation.

Now we will define general functional formation for the incremental computation of cluster similarity. As Figure 6 describes, the cluster **x** and **y** are going to be merged to cluster **n**. The target which must be computed is the similarity between cluster **n** and the other cluster **w**. The available information sources given are the similarities between cluster **w** and **x**, cluster **x** and **y**, cluster **w** and **y**, and the merged cluster element ratio which determines the relative position of **n** on $\overline{xy}$ line. The ratio is equivalent to $\overline{xn}/\overline{xy}$. Then the similarity between cluster **n** and **w** can be defined as equation (1).

This function should use only scalar calculation or triangular function without any vector operation. For the similarity of absolute or square of vector difference, the function can be easily derived based on geometrical property. We will describe about it next.

$$sim(\mathbf{w}, \mathbf{n}) = f(sim(\mathbf{w}, \mathbf{x}), sim(\mathbf{x}, \mathbf{y}), sim(\mathbf{w}, \mathbf{y}), \overline{xn}/\overline{xy}) \quad (1)$$

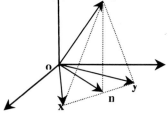

Figure 6: Formation for incremental cluster similarity computation: **x** and **y** are the merging cluster. **n** is the cluster created by merging. **w** is one of the other

cluster. Given values are sim(**w**,**x**), sim(**x**,**y**), sim(**w**,**y**), and $\overline{xn}/\overline{xy}$. The target is to derive sim(**w**,**n**) from similarities previously computed,

3.1. Incremental Vector Similarity Equation for Squared Geometrical Distance

The similarity for squared geometrical distance is defined as equation (2)

$$\text{sim}(\mathbf{p},\mathbf{q}) = |\mathbf{p}-\mathbf{q}|^2 \qquad (2)$$

The similarity between **w** and **n** becomes the squared length of the line $\overline{wn}$. The formula for the incremental similarity computation becomes the equation (3).

$$\text{sim}(\mathbf{w},\mathbf{n}) = \overline{wn}^2 = f\left(\overline{wx}^2, \overline{xy}^2, \overline{wy}^2, a\right) \qquad (3)$$

where $a = \overline{xn}/\overline{xy}$. It can be expressed with the edge line and the angle of the triangle $\triangle won$ as equation (4) by cosine theorem.

$$\overline{wn}^2 = \overline{xw}^2 + \overline{xn}^2 - 2\cdot\overline{xw}\cdot\overline{xn}\cdot\cos(\angle wxn) \qquad (4)$$

$$\overline{xn} = a\cdot\overline{xy}$$

The $\cos(\angle wxn)$ value is converted with the line length of triangle $\triangle wxy$ as equation (5)

$$\cos(\angle wxn) = \cos(\angle wxy)$$

$$= \frac{\overline{wx}^2 + \overline{xy}^2 - \overline{wy}^2}{2\cdot\overline{wx}\cdot\overline{wy}} \qquad (5)$$

Finally the similarity for vector **w** and **n** is derived with previously computed values by applying equation (5) to (4).

$$\therefore \overline{wn}^2 = \overline{xw}^2 + (a\cdot\overline{xy})^2 - a\cdot\frac{\overline{xy}}{\overline{wy}}\cdot\left(\overline{wx}^2 + \overline{xy}^2 - \overline{wy}^2\right) \qquad (6)$$

3.2. Incremental Vector Similarity Equation for Inner Product or Cosine Measure

The similarity for inner product is defined as equation (7).

$$\text{sim}(\mathbf{p},\mathbf{q}) = \mathbf{p}\bullet\mathbf{q} \qquad (7)$$

The corresponding formula for incremental similarity is defined as follows.

$$\text{sim}(\mathbf{w},\mathbf{n}) = \mathbf{w}\bullet\mathbf{n} = f(\mathbf{w}\bullet\mathbf{x}, \mathbf{x}\bullet\mathbf{y}, \mathbf{w}\bullet\mathbf{y}, a = \overline{xn}/\overline{xy}) \qquad (8)$$

The inner product can be replaced by the line component of triangle $\triangle won$ by cosine theorem

$$\mathbf{w}\bullet\mathbf{n} = |\mathbf{w}|\cdot|\mathbf{n}|\cdot\cos(\angle won)$$

$$= |\mathbf{w}|\cdot|\mathbf{n}|\cdot\frac{|\mathbf{w}|^2 + |\mathbf{n}|^2 - \overline{wn}^2}{2\cdot|\mathbf{w}|\cdot|\mathbf{n}|} = \frac{1}{2}(|\mathbf{w}|^2 + |\mathbf{n}|^2 - \overline{wn}^2) \qquad (9)$$

$\overline{wn}^2$ term can be replaced by known values such as line length and the input parameters in the function for incremental similarity (8)

$$\overline{wn}^2 = \overline{xw}^2 + \overline{xn}^2 - 2\cdot\overline{xw}\cdot\overline{xn}\cdot\cos(\angle wxn)$$

$$\overline{xw}^2 = \overline{ox}^2 + \overline{ow}^2 - 2\cdot\overline{ox}\cdot\overline{ow}\cdot\cos(\angle wox) = |\mathbf{x}|^2 + |\mathbf{w}|^2 - 2\cdot\mathbf{x}\bullet\mathbf{w}$$

$$\overline{xn} = a\cdot\overline{xy}$$

$$\overline{xy}^2 = |\mathbf{x}|^2 + |\mathbf{y}|^2 - 2\cdot\mathbf{x}\bullet\mathbf{y}$$

$$\overline{wy}^2 = |\mathbf{w}|^2 + |\mathbf{y}|^2 - 2\cdot\mathbf{w}\bullet\mathbf{y}$$

$$\cos(\angle wxn) = \cos(\angle wxy) = \frac{\overline{xw}^2 + \overline{xy}^2 - \overline{wy}^2}{2\cdot\overline{xw}\cdot\overline{xy}} = \frac{\left(|\mathbf{x}|^2 - \mathbf{x}\bullet\mathbf{w} - \mathbf{x}\bullet\mathbf{y} + \mathbf{w}\bullet\mathbf{y}\right)}{\overline{xw}\cdot\overline{xy}}$$

$$\therefore \overline{wn}^2 = |\mathbf{x}|^2 + |\mathbf{w}|^2 - 2\cdot\mathbf{x}\bullet\mathbf{w} + a^2\cdot\left(|\mathbf{x}|^2 + |\mathbf{y}|^2 - 2\cdot\mathbf{x}\bullet\mathbf{y}\right)$$
$$- 2a\cdot\left(|\mathbf{x}|^2 - \mathbf{x}\bullet\mathbf{w} - \mathbf{x}\bullet\mathbf{y} + \mathbf{w}\bullet\mathbf{y}\right) \qquad (10)$$

Consequently, the inner product similarity is deduced in the incremental similarity functional formation. Now the inner product similarity can be computed from the previous similarity values and squared absolute vector values in equation (11). Absolute value of the vector can be included in the input of the incremental method because its value is static for the given vector.

$$\therefore \mathbf{w}\bullet\mathbf{n} = \frac{1}{2}\left\{|\mathbf{n}|^2 - |\mathbf{x}|^2 + 2\cdot\mathbf{x}\bullet\mathbf{w} - a^2\cdot\left(|\mathbf{x}|^2 + |\mathbf{y}|^2 - 2\cdot\mathbf{x}\bullet\mathbf{y}\right) + 2a\cdot\left(|\mathbf{x}|^2 - \mathbf{x}\bullet\mathbf{w} - \mathbf{x}\bullet\mathbf{y} + \mathbf{w}\bullet\mathbf{y}\right)\right\} \qquad (11)$$

Now we can calculate the inner product similarity incrementally using equation (11). By the way, there is another way to get the inner product with equation (9). We already showed that the term $\overline{wn}^2$ can be replaced by line component in equation (6). Therefore, by managing squared distance similarity matrix as described in the previous section, inner product value can be directly computed with equation (9) and (6).

The cosine similarity can be directly computed from the inner product similarity which is computed incrementally

$$\cos(\angle won) = \frac{\mathbf{w}\bullet\mathbf{n}}{|\mathbf{w}|\cdot|\mathbf{n}|} \qquad (12)$$

3.3. Incremental Similarity Computation for Minimum Variance Clustering

The similarity value for minimum variance clustering [18] can be defined by the amount of variance increase when two clusters are merged. Among all the cluster pairs, the pair which has minimum increment of variance is selected to be merged for each step.

$$Sim(i, j) = \Delta E_{ij} = E_{ij} - (E_i + E_j)$$

$$E_i = \sum_{x_k \in c_i} |x_k - c_i|^2 = N_i \sigma_i^2 \qquad (13)$$

where E_i is the total amount of variance in cluster i, c_i is i-th cluster centroid, N_i is the number of element in cluster i. Then the similarity is defined by the increment of total amount of variance, ΔE_{ij}. σ_i^2 is the variance. c_{ij} is the merged cluster of c_i and c_j, and is determined by the center of gravity between two clusters.

$$\sigma_i^2 = \frac{1}{N_i} \sum_{x_k \in c_i} |x_k - c_i|^2 = \frac{1}{N_i} \sum_{x_k \in c_i} |x_k|^2 - |c_i|^2$$

$$c_{ij} = \frac{N_i c_i + N_j c_j}{N_i + N_j} \qquad (14)$$

In order to apply incremental computation method, the similarity equation is derived with the terms of cluster and number of element as follows.

$$\Delta E_{ij} = E_{ij} - (E_i + E_j) \qquad (15)$$

$$= N_{ij}\sigma_{ij}^2 - (N_i\sigma_i^2 + N_j\sigma_j^2)$$

$$= \sum_{x_k \in c_{ij}} |x_k|^2 - N_{ij}|c_{ij}|^2 - \sum_{x_k \in c_i} |x_k|^2 + N_i|c_i|^2 - \sum_{x_k \in c_j} |x_k|^2 + N_j|c_j|^2$$

$$= N_i|c_i|^2 + N_j|c_j|^2 - N_{ij}\left|\frac{N_i c_i + N_j c_j}{N_{ij}}\right|^2$$

$$= \frac{N_i N_j |c_i - c_j|^2}{N_i + N_j}$$

The equation (15) shows that the increment of variance can be computed by the squared distance of two clusters $|c_i - c_j|^2$, and their number of elements N_i and N_j. We showed before, the method of incremental computation for squared distance similarity in equation (6). Consequently, the similarity of minimum variance clustering, ΔE_{ij} can be computed in an incremental way by managing incremental squared distance similarity method, by applying the square distance equation (6) to equation (15) to get ΔE_{ij} value. It makes clustering drastically fast for high dimensional data space.

4 Experiments and Results

The clustering algorithm was applied to the collaborative filtering model using Pearson correlation measure [4] for a movie recommender system. The recommender system receives input data which is clustered by each clustering algorithm proposed in this paper. We regard the clustering result is better when the collaborative filtering result is more accurate. We adopted the precision as an accuracy measure. The precision is defined as the number of correct answers divided by the number of outputs of the system [8].

$$precision = \frac{\text{the number of correct answers}}{\text{the number of answers}} \qquad (16)$$

We used EachMovie data on public domain [13]. It consists of 2,811,983 transactions in which 72,916 users rated for 1,628 different movies during 18 months on the recommender service run by the DEC System Research Center. The hardware environment is Pentium III 500MHz, 256M RAM, MS Windows 2000.

Table 1 shows that experimental result of the brute force algorithm and the partial maximum search algorithm. We can see that there is no difference in the precision value between two algorithms. It confirms that partial maximum algorithm is the correct clustering method exactly same to the brute-force algorithm.

The factor k in the clustering time complexity $O(2N*C*k)$, which is the average number of columns scanned for a merging operation, has an important meaning for actual time complexity. From the experiment with 2,048 clusters, k is measured as 7.57. It confirms that the time complexity $O(2N*C*k)$ can be reduced to $O(N^2)$ since k is negligible comparing with the number of clusters, (7.57 << 2048).

The number of clusters	16	32	64	128	256	512	1024	2048
Precision	0.74	0.73	0.73	0.74	0.74	0.745	0.73	0.74
time (sec)	544	558	594	644	812	1197	1995	4452

(a)　Brute-force search for selecting closest clusters

The number of clusters	16	32	64	128	256	512	1024	2048
precision	0.74	0.73	0.73	0.74	0.74	0.75	0.73	0.74
time (sec)	525	533	572	630	746	973	1390	2040

(b) Partial maximum search for selecting closest clusters

Table 1: Comparison of precision and clustering time between (a) the brute force algorithm and (b) the partial maximum algorithm. Training data size: 20,000, test data size: 400, the number of minimum vote for test user : 10, the number of recommendation : 3

Figure 7 shows the clustering time of partial maximum algorithm. This Figure draws clustering time given the number of clusters instead of input data size N because the clustering time is mainly dominated by the predefined number of clusters and always linear to the input data size in an incremental clustering method. It shows that partial maximum algorithm becomes gradually faster than the brute-force algorithm as the number of cluster limit is increased. This graph is also consistent with that the partial maximum algorithm is of $O(N^2)$ time complexity.

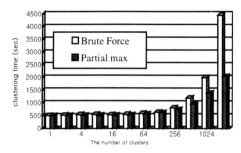

Figure 7: Clustering time comparison for the partial maximum array method.

Now, we made more experiments in order to estimate the actual improvement of the incremental similarity computation method in high dimensional data. The vector dimension of the input data used here is 1,628. So, it can be regarded as very high dimensional data.

Figure 8 shows the results of the incremental cluster similarity computation for inner product. The time spent for the inner product and the cosine similarity calculation is almost same since one of them can be directly computed from the other. It shows that the clustering time spent for the incremental method is less than non-incremental way as in Figure 8(a). We can also see that the precision does not be changed significantly. It means there is no significant difference in computational results between the incremental and the non-incremental method. The slight difference can be made by the inaccuracy of triangular functions.

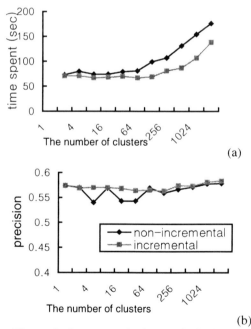

Figure 8: Incremental cluster similarity computation for inner product: (a) time spent, (b) precision for inner

product similarity. Training data size is 3000, test data size is 1000, and the number of recommendation : 10

Figure 9 shows the results for the squared distance similarity computation. The result of minimum variance can be directly inferred from squared distance similarity as equation (15). It shows that incremental method is significantly faster then non-incremental way, without accuracy degradation.

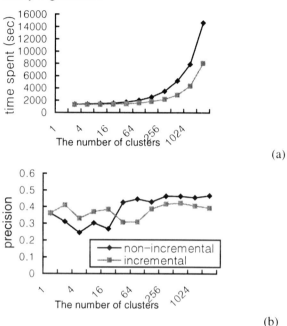

Figure 9: Incremental cluster similarity computation for square distance, or minimum variance similarity: (a) the spent time, (b) the precision for minimum variance clustering. Training data size is 50000, test data size is 5000, and the number of recommendation : 10

From these results, we can see that the incremental similarity computation method remarkably reduces the clustering time occurred in the similarity computation, and contribute to make clustering speed up in high dimensional data

5. Conclusions

The simplified nearest neighbor management is one of the well-known method to reduce the time complexity from $O(N^3)$ to $O(N^2)$ in agglomerative hierarchical clustering. But it is a sort of approximation, and it can cause unexpected clustering result. We showed that it is possible to reduce clustering in $O(N^2)$ time without approximation. We proposed a clustering algorithm using partial maximum array in agglomerative hierarchical clustering, which has the same accuracy to the brute-force algorithm and faster than it. We showed that the time complexity is $O(N^2)$ since the times of the column rescanning is constant given the vector dimension and is negligible relative to the number of clusters through experiments. The experimental results confirmed that our model produces the same result of the brute-force method and speed is improved.

For dealing with the problem of high dimensionality in clustering large data, well-known methods such as feature selection and projected clustering require very high computational cost and degrade the accuracy since they are based on approximation. We showed the method that is not based on approximation and results in accuracy intact. We proposed incremental similarity computation method for several similarity measures such as squared distance, inner product, cosine, and minimum variance in agglomerative hierarchical clustering. The incremental method replaces vector operation with scalar operation that results in computational speed up for high dimensional vector space. The experimental results show that incremental method is significantly faster than non-incremental way without accuracy degradation.

Most of current clustering algorithms that intend to make feasible on large data are based on approximation, such as random sampling, partitioning, and feature selection of which the accuracy degradation is unavoidable. We showed two methods that are not based on approximation. So it can contribute to making clustering more feasible for large and high dimensional data when combined with other approximating approaches. Beside the methods that we proposed here, there are remained many possibilities of non-approximated methods to speed up clustering and it should not be excluded in future work. Continuous efforts are required on this area.

Reference

[1] Aggarwal, C. C., and C. Procopiuc, "Fast Algorithms for Projected Clustering", ACM SIGMOD, 1999, Philadelphia, pp. 61-72.

[2] Blum, A. L., and P. Langley, "Selection of relevant features and examples in machine learning", Artificial Intelligence, 1997, pp. 245-271

[3] Boughettaya, A. "On-line Clustering", IEEE Transaction on Knowledge and Data Engineering, Vol. 8, No. 2, April 1996.

[4] Breese, J. S., D. Heckerman, and C. Kadie, "Empirical Analysis of Predictive Algorithms for Collaborative Filtering," in Proceedings of the Fourteenth Conference on Uncertainty in Artificial Intelligence, Madison, WI, July, 1998.

[5] Can, F., E. A. Ozkarahan, "Concepts of the cover coefficient-based clustering methodology". SIGIR 1985.

[6] Ester, M., et. al., "A Database Interface for Clustering in Large Spatial Databases", International Conference on Knowledge Discovery in Database and Data Mining, Montreol, Canada, August, 1995.

[7] Ester, M., et. al., "Incremental Clustering for Mining in a Data Warehousing Environment", Proceedings of the 24th VLDB Conference New York, USA, 1998.

[8] Frakes, W. B., Baeza-Yates, R., "Information Retrieval: Data Structures & Algorithms", Prentice-hall, 1992.

[9] Guha, S., et. al., "CURE: An Efficient Clustering Algorithm for Large Database", ACM SIGMOD conference 1998.

[10] Koller, D., and M. Sahami, "Toward Optimal Feature Selection", Machine Learning Proceedings of thirteenth International Conference, 1996, pp. 284-292

[11] Leon, S. J., "Linear Algerbra with applications", third edition, Macmillan Publishing Company, 1990.

[12] Ng, R. T. and J. Han, "Efficient and Effective Clustering Methods for Spatial Data Mining", Proceedings of the 20th VLDB Conference Santiago, Chile, 1994.

[13] McJones, P. "EachMovie collaborative filtering data set.", DEC Systems Research center. http://www.research.digital.com/SRC/eachmovie/.

[14] Murtagh, F. 1983. "A Survey of Recent Advance in Hierarchic Clustering Algorithms." Computer Journal, 26, pp. 354-59.

[15] Sohlf, F. J. "Single-Link Clustering Algorithms, " Classification, Pattern Recognition, and Reduction of Dimensionality, eds. P. R. Krishnaiah and J. N. Kanal, pp. 267-843 Amsterdam

[16] Sibson, R. "SLINK: an Optimally Efficient Algorithm for the Single-Link Cluster Method." Computer Journal, 16

[17] Voorhees, E. M. "Implementing Agglomerative Hierarchic Clustering Algorithms for use in Document Retireval", Information Processing & Management Vol. 22, No. 6, pp. 465-476, 1986

[18] Ward, J. H., "Hierarchical Grouping to Optimize an Objective Function", American Statistical Association, 58(301), pp. 235-244, 1963

[19] Ward, J. H., and E. H. Marion, "Application of an Hierarchical Grouping Procedure to a Problem of Grouping Profiles", Educational and Physiological Measurement, 1963.

[20] Zhang, T., et. al, "BIRCH: An Efficient Data Clustering Method for Very Large Database", ACM SIGMOD 1996.

Distance Measures for Effective Clustering of ARIMA Time-Series[1]

Konstantinos Kalpakis, Dhiral Gada, and Vasundhara Puttagunta
CSEE Department, UMBC, 1000 Hilltop Circle, Baltimore, MD 21250
{kalpakis, dgada1, vputta1}@csee.umbc.edu

Abstract

Many environmental and socioeconomic time–series data can be adequately modeled using Auto-Regressive Integrated Moving Average (ARIMA) models. We call such time–series ARIMA time–series. We consider the problem of clustering ARIMA time–series. We propose the use of the Linear Predictive Coding (LPC) cepstrum of time–series for clustering ARIMA time–series, by using the Euclidean distance between the LPC cepstra of two time–series as their dissimilarity measure. We demonstrate that LPC cepstral coefficients have the desired features for accurate clustering and efficient indexing of ARIMA time–series. For example, few LPC cepstral coefficients are sufficient in order to discriminate between time–series that are modeled by different ARIMA models. In fact this approach requires fewer coefficients than traditional approaches, such as DFT and DWT. The proposed distance measure can be used for measuring the similarity between different ARIMA models as well.

We cluster ARIMA time–series using the Partition Around Medoids method with various similarity measures. We present experimental results demonstrating that using the proposed measure we achieve significantly better clusterings of ARIMA time–series data as compared to clusterings obtained by using other traditional similarity measures, such as DFT, DWT, PCA, etc. Experiments were performed both on simulated as well as real data.

Keywords: time–series, similarity measures, clustering, ARIMA models, cepstral coefficients.

1 Introduction

Data–retrieval and data–mining applications in time–series databases have been gaining growing interest lately. Time–series form an important class of data objects that arise from various sources such as environmental and socioeconomic systems [4]. Typical applications on time–series deal with tasks like classification, clustering, similarity search, prediction, forecasting, outlier detection and noise removal. These applications rely heavily on the ability to measure the similarity or dissimilarity between time–series [1, 12]. The notion of similarity of complex objects such as time–series is specific to the application domain and also to the nature of the tasks [12]. Defining similarity is non–trivial. Simple equality or inequality is of little use. Also, time–series data tend to be very long because of which they suffer from the curse of dimensionality.

Previous Work. The problem of similarity search in time-series databases is extensively studied. Approaches differ mainly in their notion of similarity. Several different measures of pairwise similarity and dissimilarity have been proposed in the classification literature [11].

Agrawal et al [1] use the Euclidean distance between time–series of equal length as the measure of their similarity. They reduce sequences into points in low-dimensional space by using Discrete Fourier Transform (DFT). Parseval's theorem ensures that there are no false-dismissals in doing so. In addition, this approach improves upon the measurement of similarity between time-series since the effects of high frequency components in the DFT, which usually correspond to noise, are discarded. The idea has been generalized in [8] for subsequence matching. In a similar manner Struzit et al [17] use Discrete Wavelet Transform (DWT) and Gavrilov et al [10] use Principal Component Analysis (PCA) for measuring time–series similarity.

However there are many similarity queries where Euclidean distances between raw data elements fail to capture the notion of similarity (see [15] for examples). Agrawal et al [2] present a more intuitive idea that two series should be considered similar if they have enough non-overlapping time–ordered pairs of subsequences that are similar. The model allows translation and amplitude scaling. It also allows non-matching gaps in the matching subsequences. Rafiei et al [16] use moving window average for smoothening time–series and time-scaling (global stretching or shrinking of time axis). Yi et al [21] use time–warping distance as the similarity measure and look at the problem of indexing time–series when local time–warping transformations are allowed. Das et al [7] present a similarity model as follows: for a fixed set $\mathcal{F}$ of transformations (eg. the set of all linear transformations), two time–series X and Y are $\mathcal{F}$–similar if there exists a transformation f in $\mathcal{F}$ such that a long subsequence X' of X can be approximately mapped to a long subsequence Y' of Y using f.

Gavrilov et al [10] raise the question "Which (similarity)

[1]Supported in part by NASA under Contract NAS5–32337 and Cooperative Agreement NCC5–315. Please send all correspondence to Dr. Kalpakis.

measure is the best?" for mining stock market time–series. They observed that normalizing the time–series in any form always improved the quality of clustering. They conclude that piece–wise normalization and normalized derivatives results in highest quality clustering for stock–market data. But when they get the best clustering results, the time–series do not seem to be prone to dimensionality reduction.

Most existing approaches for mining time–series data do not appropriately take into account the stochastic properties of the time–series. A (1–dimensional) time–series is a sequence of observations of a particular variable. It consists of four components: a trend, a cycle, a stochastic persistence component, and a random element [4]. The stochastic component is present in almost all environmental and socio-economic time–series. Therefore, to accurately represent time–series and to define similarity between them, it is important to consider all four components of the time–series. These four components can be captured by modeling it by a Box-Jenkins seasonal model [20] (see Section 2). This model is also called an Auto-Regressive Integrated Moving Average (ARIMA) model. This model has been found very useful for describing a variety of seasonal environmental and socioeconomic time–series. It is further described in section 3. We call time–series that can be described or generated by ARIMA models *ARIMA time–series*.

Suppose we have a collection of time–series generated by different ARIMA models. In this paper, we attempt to answer the question "Which (similarity) measure is the best?" for such time–series. We propose to use the Euclidean distance between the LPC cepstra of time–series as a measure of their distance (dissimilarity). The most striking characteristics of this measure we propose are that it gives more accurate clusterings and achieves large dimensionality reduction. Since we use the estimated model of the time–series for clustering, we overcome problems that arise due to time–series of different lengths and time–series that are growing (as long as the model does not change).

Our Approach. Our notion of similarity is that two time–series are similar if the underlying physical models that generate them are the same or close. The intuition behind this notion of similarity is that, if the parameters of models fitted to the time–series are close, then the time–series behave in a similar manner (probabilistically). Two models are similar when one model can be fitted to a sequence generated by another model. Such a similarity measure can be used to more accurately cluster time–series. It enables us to draw inferences (extract knowledge) about a time–series from others belonging to the same cluster and improves our knowledge about the dynamics of the system being studied. For eg.(pg. 15 in [4]), the Keynesian macro-economic model based on Keynes's general theory of employment, explains the changes in the national income Y_t as $Y_t = a_1 Y_{t-1} - a_2 Y_{t-2} + b_0 U_t$, where Y_t and U_t are the national income and government spending at quarter t, and a_1, a_2, and b_0 are the parameters of the model. (Intuitively, these parameters depend on the rate of consumption, savings, and investment in an economy.) Considering a collection of national–income time–series, from various economies, how could one cluster those time–series so that series that are clustered together have similar spending, savings, and investment characteristics? Consider a case where two countries have the same values of parameters - a_1, a_2 and b_0 for the model fitted to their national income time series(Y_t). In such a case, we can make meaningful inferences about the economy of one country from the spending, savings, and investment characteristics of another country.

In using fitted ARIMA models for clustering time–series data, it is necessary to define an appropriate distance measure between ARIMA models and hence time–series. We define such a distance measure by using the Euclidean distance between the Linear Predictive Coding (LPC) cepstrum of two time–series (models). Our results show that the LPC cepstrum provides higher discriminatory power between time–series and superior clusterings than other widely used methods such as Euclidean distance between the DFT, DWT (with the S8 wavelet [14]), PCA, and DFT of the auto-correlation function (ACF) of two time–series. The LPC cepstrum retains high amount of information about the underlying time–series in very few coefficients. This property makes the LPC cepstrum a very effective similarity measure for clustering time–series data and models.

Organization. The organization of the rest of the paper is as follows. Preliminaries and definitions are given in Section 2. Properties of the LPC cepstrum of the time–series are given in Section 3. In Section 4 we present our results from clustering synthetic ARIMA time–series and real datasets. We conclude the paper in Section 5.

2 Preliminaries

We start with a brief description of various concepts and definitions used in this paper. Interested reader is referred to [4, 20, 22] for more details. A stationary time–series is one whose probability distribution is time-invariant. Note that a non-stationary time–series may have its mean μ_t or variance σ_t varying with time or have a trend. As mentioned earlier, a time–series has four components: a trend, a cycle, a stochastic persistence component, and a random element. These can be captured by modeling it by a Box-Jenkins seasonal model: $\Phi_P(B^s)\phi_p(B)(1 - B)^d(1 - B^s)^D X_t = \theta_q(B)\Theta_Q(B^s)\epsilon_t$. This model is also called ARIMA $(p, d, q) \times (P, D, Q)$ model. Here B is an operator such that $B^p X_t = X_{t-p}$, s is the seasonality (periodicity) of the time series, p and q are the orders of the autoregressive and moving average components respectively, P and Q are the orders of the seasonal autoregressive and moving average components respectively, d is the order of differencing and D is the order of seasonal differencing,(d=0 for a stationary time series, $d \geq 1$ for non-stationary time series), $\Phi_p(B^s) = (1 - \Phi_1 B^s - \ldots - \Phi_P B^{Ps})$ represents the correlation between the seasonal elements of the time–series, $\phi_p(B) = (1 - \phi_1 B - \ldots - \phi_p B^p)$ represents the correlation of X_t on its preceding values, $\Theta_q(B^s) = (1 - \Theta_1 B - \ldots - \Theta_q B^{Qs})$ represents the seasonal moving average component, $\theta_q(B) = (1 - \theta_1 B - \ldots - \theta_q B^q)$ represents the moving average component, ϵ_t is a sequence of uncorrelated random variables with constant mean and variance. Some special cases of the ARIMA $(p,d,q) \times (P,D,Q)$ model are as follows: AR(p) model is given as ARIMA $(1,0,0) \times (0,0,0)$; MA(q) model is given as ARIMA $(0,0,1) \times (0,0,0)$; ARMA(p,q) model is a combination of the stationary AR(p) and MA(q) models. For brevity, we refer to ARIMA $(p,d,q) \times (0,0,0)$ model as ARIMA (p,d,q) model.

We measure the dissimilarity between time–series using the Euclidean distance between their LPC cepstral coefficients. Cepstral analysis is a non–linear signal processing technique with a variety of applications in areas such as speech and image processing [9]. The cepstrum is defined as the inverse Fourier transform of the short-time logarithmic amplitude spectrum. One characteristic feature of the cepstrum is that it allows for the separate representation of the spectral envelope and fine structure. The real cepstrum is defined as the inverse Fourier transform of the real logarithm of the Fourier transform of the time–series. The complex cepstrum is defined as the inverse Fourier transform of the complex logarithm of the Fourier transform of the time–series. The cepstrum of an ARIMA time–series can be estimated using the parameters of an ARIMA model for that time–series. The cepstrum defined using the auto-regression coefficients is referred to as the LPC cepstrum, since it is derived through Linear Predictive Coding models (e.g. ARIMA) for the time–series. Hereafter, unless otherwise specified, we refer to the LPC cepstrum of a time–series simply as its cepstrum.

Consider a time–series X_t defined by an AR(p) model $X_t + \alpha_1 X_{t-1} + \ldots + \alpha_p X_{t-p} = \epsilon_t$ where $\alpha_1, \ldots, \alpha_p$ are the auto-regression coefficients and ϵ_t is white noise with mean 0 and certain non-zero variance. Note that for every ARIMA model there exists an equivalent AR model, that can be obtained from the ARIMA model by polynomial division. Hence, without loss of generality, for the remainder of this paper we focus on AR time–series.

The cepstral coefficients for an AR(p) time–series can be derived from the auto-regression coefficients [9]:

$$c_n = \begin{cases} -\alpha_1, & \text{if } n = 1 \\ -\alpha_n - \sum_{m=1}^{n-1}(1 - \frac{m}{n})\alpha_m c_{n-m}, & \text{if } 1 < n \leq p \quad (1) \\ -\sum_{m=1}^{p}(1 - \frac{m}{n})\alpha_m c_{n-m}, & \text{if } p < n \end{cases}$$

We use cepstral coefficients to extract the significant features of time–series and define distance between two time series as the Euclidean distance between their cepstra.

Given two clusterings $G = G_1, \ldots, G_k$ (say the "ground truth") and $A = A_1, \ldots, A_k$ (obtained using any feature extraction method, distance measure, or clustering method), the cluster similarity metric is defined as $Sim(G, A) = (\sum_i \max_j Sim(G_i, A_j))/k$, where, $Sim(G_i, A_j) = 2|G_i \bigcap A_j|/(|G_i| + |A_j|)$. Sim(G,A) can be used to evaluate the clustering results [10].

Silhouette width [14] is another measure for the quality of clustering. It lies between -1 and 1. For each object that is clustered, the silhouette width for that object can be interpreted as follows: if it is close to 1 then the object is well clustered (classified); if it is close to 0 then the object lies between two clusters; and if it is close to -1 then the object is badly clustered. The average silhouette width of all the clustered objects is another measure of quality of the clustering achieved. To evaluate our clustering experiments, we use both Sim(G,A) and silhouette width.

3 Properties of Cepstral coefficients

In this section we present some of our findings on the properties of cepstral coefficients of stationary time–series generated by different models. These observations justify our use of cepstral distance as an effective similarity measure and also as a good dimensionality reduction method for clustering purposes. A detailed discussion and experimental results can be found in [13].

3.1 Effective at distinguishing models.

There can be various ways of distinguishing different AR models. Suppose we have 3 models (M_1–M_3): $x_t = 0.3x_{t-1} + 0.2x_{t-2} + \epsilon_t$ (M_1), $x_t = 0.3x_{t-1} + 0.2x_{t-2} + 0.1x_{t-5} + \epsilon_t$ (M_2), and $x_t = 0.4x_{t-1} + 0.2x_{t-2} + \epsilon_t$ (M_3). The coefficients of M_1 and M_2 differ by 0.1. The coefficients of M_1 and M_3 also differ by 0.1. However, M_2 differs from M_1 in it's correlation with the 5th coefficient which is relatively less significant as compared to M_1 differing from M_3 in it's correlation with the 1st coefficient. According to our notion of similarity, M_1 is more similar to M_2 than it is to M_3. In essence, it means that for an AR(p) model, lower the order of the AR coefficient lower its importance.

In the above example it can be seen that simple Euclidean or Manhattan distances between the model parameters will not be of use. One might think of using some other distance measures such as the maximum distance between the model parameters or the distance between the principal components of the model parameters. Our experiments reveal that these too do not serve our purpose (see [13]). One could use weighted Euclidean distance, $\sum_{i=1}^{p} w_i(\alpha_i - \alpha_i')^2$. Here, α_i and α_i' are the ith AR coefficients of models 1 and 2 respectively, p is the order of the AR model. w_i is the weight for the ith AR coefficient set to $w_i = c^i/K$, where $K = \sum_{i=1}^{p} c^i$, for some constant $0 < c < 1$. The results of the weighted Euclidean method depend on the combination of the weights and the model parameters. We observe that when cepstral distance is used as the similarity measure, the distance between M_1 and M_2 is always lower than the distance between M_1 and M_3. The cepstral distance can be considered as a special case of the weighted Euclidean distance. Cepstral coefficients are effective as a similarity measure between models because they are sensitive to the position of the AR coefficients.

3.2 Decay rapidly to zero.

The cepstral coefficients decay rapidly to zero and thus, we need to retain only the first few coefficients to capture most of the information in the time–series. This property is important to overcome the curse of dimensionality. For an AR(1) model given as $X_t = \alpha_1 X_{t-1} + \epsilon_t$ it is easy prove this property from equation 1. Since we are considering stationary time–series, we have $|\alpha_1| < 1$, and thus $\lim_{n\to\infty} c_n = \lim_{n\to\infty} -\alpha_1^{n-1} c_1 / n = 0$, where c_n is the nth cepstral coefficient. We can prove this property for an AR(p) model using the Z-transform approach described in [19, pg. 212–213]. Also, the smaller the value of the AR parameters, the faster the cepstral coefficients will decay.

We performed experiments to find the effect of retaining only first few coefficients on the distances between two time–series. We generated AR(1) time–series of length 256. By fitting a model to the generated time–series the AR coefficients were estimated. Table 1 summarizes the results.

Table 1. Distances between two time–series by retaining k coefficients (in 10^{-3})

Measure	k				
	256	25	20	15	10
dist. between $AR(1)$ timeseries with $\hat\alpha_1 = 0.3$ and 0.34					
d_{CEP}	0.97	0.97	0.97	0.97	0.97
d_{DFT}	22.55	3.26	2.75	2.41	1.95
$d_{\mathrm{DFT(ACF)}}$	4.34	1.24	1.01	0.81	0.43
d_{DWT}	22.55	4.20	3.67	2.79	1.15
d_{PCA}&d_{MSE}	22.55	–	–	–	–
dist. between $AR(1)$ timeseries with $\hat\alpha_1 = 0.6$ and 0.64					
d_{CEP}	0.60	0.60	0.60	0.60	0.60
d_{DFT}	33.82	9.29	8.40	7.63	6.49
$d_{\mathrm{DFT(ACF)}}$	5.39	2.16	1.98	1.67	1.31
d_{DWT}	33.82	13.79	12.26	9.40	4.93
d_{PCA}&d_{MSE}	33.82	–	–	–	–

In this table, d_{CEP}, d_{DFT}, $d_{\mathrm{DFT(ACF)}}$, d_{DWT}, and d_{PCA} are the Euclidean distances between their Cepstral coefficients, their DFT coefficients, the DFT coefficients of their ACFs, their DWT coefficients, and their PCA coefficients respectively; d_{MSE} is the mean squared error between the time–series; k is the number of coefficients retained, and $\hat\alpha_1$ is the estimated auto-regression coefficient. In calculating d_{PCA}, we used only the first two principal components of the PCA since they are found to contain over 98% of the information in the time–series. cepstral coefficients are always computed using the estimated AR parameters.

From Table 1, we observe that when methods such as DFT or DWT are used, the distance between the two time–series reduces significantly as the number of coefficients retained is reduced. This could result in a lot of false positives when only a few coefficients are retained. Hence, a large overhead is required to remove the false positives. On the

other hand, retaining as few as only 10 cepstral coefficients are sufficient for distinguishing two time–series results with virtually no loss of information. Hence, only a few cepstral coefficients should be sufficient. This property of cepstral coefficients results in effectively reducing the dimensionality and is useful in indexing time–series data efficiently. An added benefit is that the number of cepstral coefficients to be retained does not depend on the length of the time–series.

3.3 High discriminatory power.

Discriminatory power of a feature is its ability to separate time–series generated by different models. Cepstral coefficients provide more discriminatory power than the other feature extraction methods.

We performed experiments to study the change in the distance obtained when the auto-regression parameter changes. We generate AR(1) time–series TS_1 and TS_2 with α_1=0.3 and 0.31 respectively. We then keep changing TS_2 time–series by generating AR(1) time–series with increasing values of α_1 and report the percentage increase in the distance between TS_1 and TS_2 w.r.t the first pair of time–series in table 2. We use the first 10 coefficients of the feature extraction methods to compute the distance. For MSE, all coefficients were used. From Table 2, we observe that

Table 2. Percentage increase in distances w.r.t. first row. TS_1 has $\hat\alpha_1 = 0.3$

$\hat\alpha_1$ of TS_2	% d_{CEP}	% d_{DFT}	% $d_{\mathrm{DFT(ACF)}}$	% d_{DWT}	% d_{PCA}	% d_{MSE}
0.31	–	–	–	–	–	–
0.33	23.272	0.44	0.87	0.38	0.38	0.38
0.34	106.64	3.28	7.94	2.68	2.41	2.41
0.39	286.51	4.76	12.89	3.69	3.58	3.58
0.43	551.07	1.92	28.45	-0.13	0.25	0.25
0.47	999.77	5.18	55.05	0.96	1.52	1.52
0.50	1345.7	10.93	70.56	4.67	5.08	5.08

the cepstral coefficients have higher percentage increase in the distance for small increase in the AR parameter of TS_2 than any other method. Therefore, the cepstral coefficients can distinguish between the two time-series much more accurately than the other feature extraction methods.

3.4 Invariant under basic transformations.

Amplitude Translation. By normalizing a time-series to have mean zero, and then computing the cepstrum we can achieve invariance of the cepstral distance to amplitude-translation. This property is useful to identify series that have similar patterns but fluctuate around different means.

Amplitude Scaling. Multiplying a time-series by a constant does not affect its cepstral coefficients. Consider two stocks which have the same price fluctuations, however one stock sells at twice the price of the other. This property is useful for identifying such patterns.

Time-Shifting. Translating (shifting) a time-series in time does not affect its cepstrum. Consider a time series monitoring the growth pattern of different bacteria. A particular bacteria could be triggered out of dormancy at a later time compared to another bacteria, however its growth pattern might follow that of the bacteria that got stimulated earlier.

3.5 Seasonal time-series.

For seasonal time–series, the cepstral coefficients have high values at the period of seasonality. The seasonal peaks show a decreasing trend and rapidly drop to zero in a manner similar to that of the cepstral coefficients in the case of AR time–series. We can think of the cepstrum of a seasonal time–series to be a superposition of two independent cepstra: the seasonal part which is formed using the coefficients at the peaks, and the non–seasonal part formed from the remaining coefficients. When comparing two seasonal models we find the distance between their seasonal parts and their non-seasonal parts.

Consider a seasonal ARIMA $(1,0,0) \times (1,0,0)$ model $(1-\alpha_1 B)(1-\Phi_1 B^s)X_t = \epsilon_t$, where α_1 is the auto-regression parameter, Φ_1 is the seasonal auto-regression parameter, and s is the period of seasonality. We conducted experiments by varying each one of these parameters while keeping the other two constant. We made the following observations: (a) when s is varied, the distance between the cepstra of the two time–series does not change. (b) when α_1 is varied, the distance between the non-seasonal cepstra is the most significant component of the distance between the cepstra of the two time-series. (c) when Φ_1 is varied, the distance between the seasonal cepstra is the most significant component. Due to observation (a), we can group time–series which differ only in the seasonality together. Observations (b) and (c) enable us to identify time–series which differ only in one of the two parameters – auto-regression parameter or seasonal auto-regression parameter.

3.6 Relationships between time–series.

Consider a filter with impulse response h_t applied to a time–series X_t to give a new time–series Y_t: $Y_t = h_t \star X_t$. The relationship between the cepstra of X_t and Y_t can be shown to be Cepstrum(Y_t) = Cepstrum(X_t) + Cepstrum(h_t), (see also [9, eqs. 4.18–4.20]). Therefore, given two time–series Y_t and X_t which are related to each other, the difference in the cepstra of the two time–series is equal to the cepstrum of h_t. Suppose we want to find all the series X_t which are related to Y_t through the filter function h_t. Considering the cepstra of time–series as a multi-dimensional point, this problem reduces to that of finding those "points" (cepstra of time series) that are within a small distance from the "point" Cepstrum(Y_t) − Cepstrum(h_t).

4 Clustering time–series.

We performed experiments to analyze the ability of cepstral coefficients to distinguish between ARIMA time series. We compared the clustering results obtained using cepstral coefficients with those obtained using other similarity measures such as DFT, DWT, PCA, DFT(ACF) and MSE. Experiments were conducted both on simulated as well as real datasets(collections). We used the Partitioning Around Medoids (PAM) clustering method [14] to cluster the time–series in each collection. To measure the accuracy and quality of clustering we use the similarity metric and silhouette width that are described in Section 2.

4.1 Clustering simulated datasets.

We perform clustering on a database of AR(1) time series and analyzed the results. We generate four groups (E, F, H, and I) each with 75 AR(1) time–series, with the α_1 parameter for the time–series in each group uniformly distributed in the ranges (0.3 ± 0.01), (0.34 ± 0.01), (0.6 ± 0.01), and (0.64 ± 0.01) respectively. The white noise ϵ_t used, had mean 0 and variance 0.01. We formed 10 collections from these time–series and ran clustering on each of the groups. Collections 1–5 were built by selecting 15 time–series each from groups E and F. Similarly, collections 6–10 were built from groups H and I.

Table 3. Clustering results of simulated datasets

Collection	Distance measure used					
	CEP	DFT	DFT(ACF)	DWT	PCA	MSE
Cluster results: Cluster Similarity Metric						
1	1	0.623	0.559	0.600	0.600	0.600
2	1	0.665	0.766	0.633	0.600	0.566
3	1	0.665	0.733	0.633	0.633	0.633
4	1	0.600	0.531	0.545	0.566	0.566
5	1	0.593	0.593	0.562	0.593	0.592
6	1	0.531	0.531	0.531	0.531	0.531
7	1	0.571	0.571	0.571	0.571	0.571
8	1	0.559	0.562	0.559	0.559	0.559
9	1	0.595	0.594	0.583	0.583	0.583
10	1	0.605	0.700	0.605	0.605	0.605
Cluster results: Average Silhouette Widths						
1	0.812	0.497	0.426	0.529	0.521	0.521
2	0.814	0.465	0.424	0.518	0.528	0.527
3	0.833	0.427	0.333	0.452	0.449	0.449
4	0.805	0.455	0.396	0.523	0.516	0.515
5	0.826	0.532	0.467	0.554	0.554	0.553
6	0.825	0.513	0.511	0.549	0.578	0.548
7	0.801	0.523	0.541	0.561	0.588	0.563
8	0.826	0.529	0.487	0.595	0.621	0.595
9	0.850	0.487	0.497	0.533	0.533	0.532
10	0.817	0.540	0.433	0.574	0.574	0.573

Table 3 shows the cluster similarity metric and silhouette width obtained when each of the collections was clustered using the different similarity measures. We get a perfect 1.0 for the cluster similarity metric when the cepstrum was used. Thus cepstral coefficients provide an accurate clustering for each of the collections. Also, the silhouette width obtained using the cepstrum is the highest and is always above 0.80. This indicates that the objects are clustered with a high confidence level.

The cluster plot [2] obtained using cepstral coefficients has a very low average dissimilarity within a cluster and a high dissimilarity between clusters. Hence the two clusters formed are well separated and it is a good clustering. The cluster plots obtained using the DFT and DWT coefficients have a high average dissimilarity within a cluster. Their dissimilarity within a cluster is higher than the dissimilarity between clusters and the two clusters overlap. Also, for some time–series, the individual silhouette width is close to zero and even negative. This indicates that the time–series were not clustered properly. The above results affirm that

---

[2]Omitted due to space limitation. See fig. 1 for an eg. cluster plot.

Euclidean distance between the cepstra is better than the other distance measures.

4.2 Clustering Real Data

We further performed experiments with four different real datasets: per capita personal income dataset; ECG recordings dataset; temperature dataset; and population dataset. The general methodology followed with each dataset consisted of identifying the different groups of time–series in the dataset, identifying the ARIMA model to be fitted, computing coefficients for each one of the methods, performing clustering using these coefficients and finally analyzing the clustering results obtained. The datasets were found to have non–stationarities in mean and/or variance, so there was a need for some preprocessing. Each step involved in the preprocessing and model identification for each of the datasets is explained in detail in [13]. Each of the datasets used had two groups of time–series. We performed the experiments on the normalized as well as the un-normalized time–series. Normalization is necessary to allow for differences in level and scale. In the experiments with DFT, DFT(ACF), PCA, DWT and CEP, we used the first 10 coefficients for clustering the time–series. For MSE, all the raw data values of the time–series were used. Due to space limitations we present only a few of the data and result plots. Interested readers are encouraged to see [13].

4.2.1 Personal Income Dataset

The personal income dataset [18] is a collection of time–series representing the per capita personal income from 1929-1999 in 25 states of the USA[3]. We define group 1 as the group of the east coast states, CA, and IL in which the personal income grows at a high rate. The mid-west states form a group in which the personal income grows at a low rate is called group 2.

The per capita income time–series are non-stationary in mean as well variance. To remove this non–stationarity, we do the following: (a) smoothen the original series by taking a window average over a window of size 2. This reduces the frequent variations and enables us to fit a lower–order model. (b) The non-stationarity in variance is dealt with by taking a logarithmic transform over the smoothened series. (c) after studying the ACF and PACF[4] of the resulting series, we decide the order of the ARIMA model to be fitted. We fitted ARIMA$(1, 1, 0)$ models to each of the series in the dataset after the preprocessing. We compute the cepstral coefficients using these ARIMA models (by converting the ARIMA model to an AR model through polynomial division). We performed the clustering experiments on the normalized as well as the un-normalized per capita personal income time–series. The results are summarized in Table 4. CEP gives the highest similarity metric and is

also the only method in which the separation between clusters is higher than the average dissimilarity within a cluster. The silhouette width is the highest in case of CEP. Thus, CEP produces the most accurate clustering of the per capita personal income dataset for both the normalized and un–normalized time–series. The MSE, DFT, PCA, and DWT perform worse in the case of the un–normalized time–series than they do in the case of the normalized time–series.

Table 4. Clustering the personal income dataset.

Method	Normalized		Unnormalized	
	Sim(G,A)	Sil. Width	Sim(G,A)	Sil. Width
CEP	0.844	0.752	0.844	0.752
DFT	0.750	0.391	0.679	0.596
DFT(ACF)	0.762	0.522	0.762	0.522
DWT	0.740	0.475	0.602	0.508
PCA	0.788	0.335	0.679	0.572
MSE	0.788	0.325	0.679	0.555

The high/low income growth rate is accurately captured in the AR models fitted to the personal income time–series. The cepstral coefficients are effective in distinguishing between these models. The other methods do not seem to be capable of that. For example, upon examining the cluster plots when clustering the normalized time–series using the cepstral coefficients and the PCA metric in two classes, we observe the following. When the cepstral metric is used, the low personal income growth states of ID, IA, NE, SD, and ND have been put in one cluster, while the other cluster consists mainly of the east coast states, CA and IL (high personal income growth states). On the other hand, when the PCA metric is used, the resulting clusters contain both low and high personal income growth states.

4.2.2 ECG Dataset

The ECG dataset was obtained from the ECG database at PhysioNet [3]. We use 3 groups of those ECG time–series in our experiments: Group 1 included 22 time–series representing the 2 sec ECG recordings of people having malignant ventricular arrhythmia; Group 2 included 13 time–series that are 2 sec ECG recordings of healthy people representing the normal sinus rhythm of the heart; Group 3 included 35 time–series representing the 2 sec ECG recordings of people having supraventricular arrhythmia.

The time–series in this dataset exhibit considerable periodicity. We fit an ARIMA$(2, 3, 0)$ model to each time–series in the dataset, after smoothening it by taking a window average over a window size of 3. We performed clustering on ECG time–series collection 1 (comprising time–series from groups 1 and 2) and collection 2 (comprising time–series from groups 2 and 3) Results of clustering normalized time–series from collection 1 can be seen in Table 5 and Fig. 1 shows the cluster and silhouette plots using DFT(ACF) and CEP. From table 5 we observe that DFT(ACF) gives the most accurate clustering, but gives the lowest silhouette width among all the methods. This is because many of the time–series have been clustered into a particular group with very low confidence level with the sil-

---

[3]The 25 states included were: CT, DC, DE, FL, MA, ME, MD, NC, NJ, NY, PA, RI, VA, VT, WV, CA, IL, ID, IA, IN, KS, ND, NE, OK, SD.

[4]Partial Auto–Correlation function. See [20] for definitions

houette width sometimes even negative (see Fig. 1(a)). This could be because the time–series lie between two clusters.

Table 5. Clustering normalized ECG collection 1.

Method	Sim(G,A)	Silhouette Width
CEP	0.771	0.502
DFT	0.629	0.539
DFT(ACF)	0.881	0.299
DWT	0.587	0.523
PCA	0.587	0.377
MSE	0.587	0.369

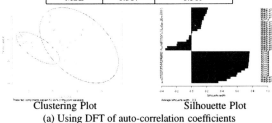

Clustering Plot   Silhouette Plot
(a) Using DFT of auto-correlation coefficients

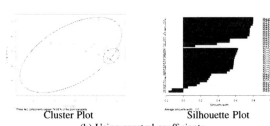

Cluster Plot   Silhouette Plot
(b) Using cepstral coefficients

Figure 1. Clustering ECG collection 1 with DFT(ACF) and CEP

The cepstral coefficients give the second best clustering for collection 1. Fig. 1(b) shows the results of clustering the ECG time–series using the cepstral coefficients. We observe from the silhouette plot in Fig. 1(b) that some of the "malignant" time–series have been clustered in the same group as "normal" time–series. Upon further inspection we observed that these series indeed looked more similar to the normal time–series than to the malignant arrhythmia time–series. This could be because the corresponding subjects are in the initial stages of arrhythmia and hence their ECG recordings are more close to "normal". In order to

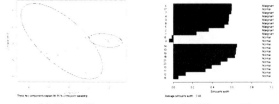

(a) Cluster Plot   (b) Silhouette Plot
Figure 2. Clustering ECG dataset using CEP

verify that the wrongly clustered time–series were indeed separable, we formed a collection consisting of the wrongly clustered time–series along with the normal sinus rhythm time-series. and clustered it using CEP. The results of this clustering are shown in Fig. 2. Sim(G,A) value of 0.87 was obtained and we observe that the malignant arrhythmia time–series have been well separated from the normal time–series. This is very interesting because it shows that CEP can distinguish efficiently between series which could

be difficult to separate. As can be seen in table 5, the remaining methods perform poorly.

Table 6 shows the results of clustering ECG collection 2 (both normalized and un-normalized). We observe that CEP gives the most accurate clustering for this collection.

Table 6. Clustering the ECG collection 2.

Method	Normalized		Unnormalized	
	Sim(G,A)	Sil. Width	Sim(G,A)	Sil. Width
CEP	0.779	0.519	0.779	0.519
DFT	0.579	0.649	0.639	0.972
DFT(ACF)	0.593	0.425	0.593	0.425
DWT	0.561	0.635	0.639	0.972
PCA	0.601	0.521	0.639	0.975
MSE	0.561	0.440	0.639	0.964

4.2.3 Temperature Dataset

This dataset, obtained from the National Climatic Data Center [6], is a collection of 30 time–series of the daily temperature in the year 2000 in various places in Florida, Tennessee and Cuba. It had temperature recordings from 10 places in Tennessee, 5 places in northern Florida, 9 places in southern Florida and 6 places in Cuba. Tennessee and northern Florida form group 1, because they are geographically close and their temperatures are known to be similar. Similarly, Cuba and southern Florida form group 2.

To fit a model, we first smoothen each of the time–series by taking a window average over a window size of 4, and then fit an ARIMA$(2, 1, 0)$ to the resulting time–series. We performed clustering experiments on both normalized and unnormalized time–series. Table 7 summarizes the results. MSE gives Sim(G,A) value of 0.933 with 366 data values. However, CEP gives the same accuracy with 10 coefficients. Thus, CEP gives the most accurate clustering on the normalized temperature time–series using very few coefficients. From Table 7, we observe that DFT, DWT, PCA and MSE

Table 7. Clustering the temperature dataset.

Method	Normalized		Unnormalized	
	Sim(G,A)	Sil. Width	Sim(G,A)	Sil. Width
CEP	0.933	0.531	0.933	0.531
DFT	0.828	0.533	1.000	0.700
DFT(ACF)	0.670	0.603	0.670	0.603
DWT	0.820	0.473	1.000	0.695
PCA	0.899	0.398	1.000	0.673
MSE	0.933	0.368	1.000	0.648

give accurate clustering for the unnormalized temperature data. This is not surprising because the temperature ranges of the two groups are distinctively different. Hence, MSE can clearly distinguish on the basis of these raw data values. This is also the reason for the success of DFT, DWT, and PCA in the un–normalized case. However, when we normalize the temperature time–series, the data values do not fall into a clearly defined separate range and therefore, DFT, DWT and PCA fail to give accurate clustering.

4.2.4 Population Dataset

The population dataset was a collection of time–series representing the population estimates from 1900-1999 in 20 states of the US [5]. Some of these time–series had an exponentially increasing trend while others had a stabilizing trend. The 20 states were partitioned into two groups based on their trends: group 1 consisted of CA, CO, FL, GA, MD, NC, SC, TN, TX, VA, and WA had the exponentially increasing trend while group 2 consisted of IL, MA, MI, NJ, NY, OK, PA, ND, and SD had a stabilizing trend. We followed the same steps of preprocessing as we did for the Personal Income Dataset and fitted an ARIMA$(1, 1, 0)$ model to each time–series in the dataset.

Table 8 summarizes the results of clustering the normalized and unnormalized time–series in this dataset. We observe that the MSE, DFT and PCA give the most accurate clustering for the normalized population dataset. MSE is based on the raw data values. The growth rate of the population time–series can be clearly distinguished from the normalized raw data values. This is because the group 1 time–series increase rapidly with time, hence at any instant the population estimate is only a small percentage of the total population in the year 1999. On the other hand, the group 2 time–series increase slowly with time, hence at any instant the population estimate is a large percentage of the total population in the year 1999. Thus, when we look at the normalized population time–series values, we observe that it is easy to separate the two groups based on the raw data values. This is the reason for the success of MSE, DFT and PCA on the normalized time–series.

We also observe that CEP gives the best results for the unnormalized population time–series. Comparing the results for the normalized and un–normalized datasets, we observe that normalization proves very beneficial for MSE, DFT, PCA and DWT on the population time–series. When the series are not normalized, the growth rates of the population time–series are difficult to separate by simply looking at the raw data values. Hence, MSE, DFT, PCA do not perform very well on the un-normalized time-series.

Table 8. Clustering the population dataset.

Method	Normalized		Unnormalized	
	Sim(G,A)	Sil. Width	Sim(G,A)	Sil. Width
CEP	0.744	0.687	0.744	0.687
DFT	1.000	0.651	0.596	0.652
DFT(ACF)	0.643	0.793	0.643	0.793
DWT	0.792	0.240	0.643	0.658
PCA	1.000	0.622	0.627	0.579
MSE	1.000	0.604	0.627	0.576

5 Conclusion

We consider the problem of defining an appropriate similarity measure for time–series that is crucial for data-mining applications in time–series databases (eg. similarity search and clustering).

We form a succinct representation of time–series using ARIMA models and then define a highly effective similarity measure for this representation. Representing a time–series as an ARIMA model captures the various important components of the time–series. We call two time–series similar when the same model fits the time–series. We propose a new distance measure using the LPC cepstral coefficients of the time–series for finding similarity between time–series models. We have demonstrated that the use of LPC cepstral coefficients for feature extraction helps in obtaining accurate clustering and also results in high dimensionality reduction both in the case of simulated as well as real data. Computing the feature vector from the model implies several desired features. The length of the time–series or differences in their lengths are no more a concern.

We compare the clustering results obtained using LPC cepstral coefficients with those obtained using other widely used methods such as DFT, DWT, PCA, and DFT of auto-correlation of the time–series. LPC cepstral coefficients clearly perform much better than

the other methods for clustering synthetic ARIMA time–series. Our method is competitive with the other approaches for clustering various real datasets and in many cases significantly better than the other methods.

Our approach is limited to time–series that can be modeled by ARIMA models. Future work includes: (a) extending this approach to non–ARIMA time–series, such as chaotic and other non–linear time–series, and (b) extending this approach to multi–variate ARIMA time–series.

References

[1] R. Agrawal, C. Faloutsos, and A. Swami. Efficient similarity search in sequence databases. *Proc. of FODO*, pg. 69–84, 1993.

[2] R. Agrawal, K. Lin, H. Sawhney, and K. Shim. Fast similarity search in the presence of noise, scaling, and translation in time–series databases. In *21st VLDB*, pg. 490–501, 1995.

[3] P. Archive. http://www.physionet.org/physiobank/database.

[4] R. Bennett. *Spatial Time Series*, Pion Limited, 1979.

[5] http://www.census.gov/population/www/estimates/st_stts.html.

[6] http://www.ncdc.noaa.gov/rcsg/datasets.html.

[7] G. Das, D. Gunopulos, and H. Mannila. Finding similar time series. In *Proc. of European Conf. on Principles of Data Mining and Knowledge Discovery*, pg. 88–100, 1997.

[8] C. Faloutsos, M. Ranganathan, and Y. Manolopoulos. Fast subsequence matching in time–series databases. In *Proc. of SIGMOD*, pg. 419–429, 1994.

[9] S. Furui. *Digital Speech Processing, Synthesis, and Recognition*. Marcel Deckker, Inc., New York, 1989.

[10] M. Gavrilov, D. Anguelov, P. Indyk, and R. Motwani. Mining the stock market: Which measure is best? In *Proc. of the KDD*, pg. 487–496, 2000.

[11] A. Gordon. *Classification*. Chapman and Hall, CRC, 1999.

[12] H. V. Jagadish, A. O. Mendelzon, and T. Milo. Similarity–based queries. In *Proc. of the 14th SIGACT-SIGMOD-SIGART Symp. of Database Systems*, pg. 36–45, 1995.

[13] K. Kalpakis, D. Gada, V. Puttagunta. Distance measures for effective clustering of ARIMA time–series. Technical Report TR–CS–01–14, CSEE, UMBC, 2001.

[14] Mathsoft, Inc. *SPlus–2000 guide to Statistics*.

[15] D. Rafiei. On similarity–based queries for time series data. In *Proc. of the 15th ICDE*, pg. 410–417, 1999.

[16] D. Rafiei and A. Mendelzon. Similarity–based queries for time series data. In *Proc. of SIGMOD*, pg. 13–24, 1997.

[17] Z. Struzik and A. Sibes. Measuring time series similarity through large singular features revealed with wavelet transformation. In *Proc. of the 10th Intl. Workshop on Database and Expert Systems Appl.*, pg. 162–166, 1999.

[18] http://www.bea.gov/bea/regional/spi.

[19] R. Vich. *Z Transform Theory and Applications*. D. Reidel, Holland, 1987.

[20] W. Wei. *Time Series Analysis*. Addison–Wesley, 1994.

[21] B. Yi, H. Jagadish, and C. Faloutsos. Efficient retrieval of similar time sequences under time warping. In *Proc. of 14th ICDE*, pg. 201–208, 1998.

[22] X. Zhongjie. *Case Studies in Time Series Analysis*. World Scientific, Singapore, 1993.

Mining Decision Trees from Data Streams in a Mobile Environment*

Hillol Kargupta and Byung-Hoon Park
Department of Computer Science and Electrical Engineering
1000 Hillltop Circle, University of Maryland Baltimore County
Baltimore, MD 21250, USA
{hillol, park1}@cs.umbc.edu

Abstract

This paper presents a novel Fourier analysis-based technique to aggregate, communicate, and visualize decision trees in a mobile environment. Fourier representation of a decision tree has several useful properties that are particularly useful for mining continuous data streams from small mobile computing devices. This paper presents algorithms to compute the Fourier spectrum of a decision tree and the vice versa. It offers a framework to aggregate decision trees in their Fourier representations. It also describes a touch-pad/ticker-based approach to visualize decision trees using their Fourier spectrum and an implementation for PDAs.

1. Introduction

Analyzing and monitoring time-critical data streams using mobile devices in a ubiquitous manner is important for many applications in finance, defense, process control and other domains. These applications demand the ability to quickly analyze large amount of data. Decision trees (e.g., CART[4], ID3[21], and C4.5 [22]) are fast, and scalable. So decision tree-based data mining is a natural candidate for monitoring data streams from ubiquitous devices like PDAs, palmtops, and wearable computers. However, there are several problems.

Mining time-critical data streams usually requires on-line learning that often produces a series of models [6, 8, 15, 23] like decision trees. From a data mining perspective it is important that these models are properly aggregated. This is because different data blocks observed at different time frames may generate different models that may actually belong to a single model which can be generated when all the data blocks are combined and mined together. Even for decision trees [5, 24] that are capable of incrementally modifying themselves based on new data, in many applications

(e.g., multiple data streams observed at different distributed locations) we end up with an ensemble of trees. Apart from better understanding of the model, communication of large number of trees over a wireless network also poses a major problem. We need on-line data mining algorithms that can easily aggregate and evolve models in an efficient representation.

Visualization of decision trees [1] in a small display is also a challenging task. Presenting a decision tree with even a moderate number of features in a small display screen is not easy. Since the number of nodes in a decision tree may grow exponentially with respect to the number of features defining the domain, drawing even a small tree in the display area of a palmtop device or a cell phone is a difficult thing to do. Reading an email in a cell phone is sometimes annoying; so imagine browsing over a large number of tree-diagrams in a small screen. It simply does not work. We need an alternate approach. We need to represent trees in such a way that they can be easily and intuitively presented to the user using a small mobile device.

This paper takes a small step toward that possibility. It considers manipulation and visualization of decision trees for mining data streams from small computing devices. It points out that Fourier basis offers an interesting representation of decision trees that can facilitate quick aggregation of a large number of decision trees [9, 18] and their visualization in a small screen using a novel "decision tree-ticker". The efficient representation of decision trees in Fourier representation also allows quicker communication of tree ensembles over low-bandwidth wireless networks. Although we present the material in the context of mobile devices, the approach is also useful for desktop applications.

Section 2 explains the relation between Fourier representation and decision trees. It also presents an algorithm to compute the Fourier spectrum of a decision tree. Section 3 considers aggregation of multiple trees in Fourier representation. Section 4 presents a decision tree visualization technique using a touch-pad and a ticker. Section 5 describes an application of this technology for mining stock

---

*Patent application pending

data streams. Finally, Section 6 concludes this paper.

2. Decision Trees as Numeric Functions

This paper adopts an algebraic perspective of decision trees. Note that a decision tree is a function that maps the domain members to a range of class labels. Sometimes, it is a symbolic function where features take symbolic (non-numeric) values. However, a symbolic function can be easily converted to a numeric function by simply replacing the symbols with numeric values in a consistent manner. See Figure 1 for an example. A numeric function-representation of a decision tree may be quite useful. For example, we may be able to aggregate a collection of trees (often produced by ensemble learning techniques) by simply performing basic arithmetic operations (e.g. adding two decision trees, weighted average) in their numeric representations. Later in this paper we will see that a numeric representation is also suitable for visualizing and aggregating decision trees.

Once the tree is converted to a numeric discrete function, we can also apply any appropriate analytical transformation that we want. Fourier transformation is one such possibility and it is an interesting one. Fourier basis offers an additively decomposable representation of a function. In other words, the Fourier representation of a function is a weighted linear combination of the Fourier basis functions. The weights are called Fourier coefficients. The coefficients completely define the representation. Each coefficient is associated with a Fourier basis function that depends on a certain subset of features defining the domain of the data set to be mined. The following section presents a brief review of Fourier representation.

2.1. A Brief Review of the Fourier Basis

Fourier bases are orthogonal functions that can be used to represent any function. Consider the function space over the set of all ℓ-bit Boolean feature vectors. The Fourier basis set that spans this space is comprised of 2^ℓ Fourier basis functions; for the time being let us consider only discrete Boolean Fourier basis. Each Fourier basis function is defined as $\psi_{\mathbf{j}}(\mathbf{x}) = (-1)^{(\mathbf{x} \cdot \mathbf{j})}$. Where $\mathbf{j}$ and $\mathbf{x}$ are binary strings of length ℓ. In other words $\mathbf{j} = (j_1, j_2, \cdots j_\ell)$, $\mathbf{x} = (x_1, x_2, \cdots x_\ell)$ and $\mathbf{j}, \mathbf{x} \in \{0, 1\}^\ell$; $\mathbf{x} \cdot \mathbf{j}$ denotes the inner product of $\mathbf{x}$ and $\mathbf{j}$. $\psi_{\mathbf{j}}(\mathbf{x})$ can either be equal to 1 or -1. The string $\mathbf{j}$ is called a *partition*. The *order* of a partition $\mathbf{j}$ is the number of 1-s in $\mathbf{j}$. A Fourier basis function depends on some x_i only when $j_i = 1$. Therefore, a partition can also be viewed as a representation of a certain subset of x_i-s; every unique partition corresponds to a unique subset of x_i-s. If a partition $\mathbf{j}$ has exactly α number of 1-s then we say the partition is of order α since the corresponding Fourier function depends on only those α number

of features corresponding to the 1-s in the partition $\mathbf{j}$. A function $f : \mathbf{X}^\ell \to \Re$, that maps an ℓ-dimensional space of binary strings to a real-valued range, can be written using the Fourier basis functions: $f(\mathbf{x}) = \sum_{\mathbf{j}} w_{\mathbf{j}} \psi_{\mathbf{j}}(\mathbf{x})$; where $w_{\mathbf{j}}$ is the Fourier coefficient corresponding to the partition $\mathbf{j}$; $w_{\mathbf{j}} = \frac{1}{2^\ell} \sum_{\mathbf{x}} f(\mathbf{x}) \psi_{\mathbf{j}}(\mathbf{x})$. The Fourier coefficient $w_{\mathbf{j}}$ can be viewed as the relative contribution of the partition $\mathbf{j}$ to the function value of $f(\mathbf{x})$. Therefore, the absolute value of $w_{\mathbf{j}}$ can be used as the "significance" of the corresponding partition $\mathbf{j}$. If the magnitude of some $w_{\mathbf{j}}$ is very small compared to other coefficients then we may consider the $\mathbf{j}$-th partition to be insignificant and neglect its contribution.

2.2. Fourier Analysis with Non-binary Features

The Fourier basis can be easily extended to the non-Boolean case. Consider a domain defined by ℓ possibly non-Boolean features where the i-th feature can take λ_i distinct values. Let $\overline{\lambda} = \lambda_1, \lambda_2 \cdots \lambda_\ell$. The generalized Fourier basis function over an $\overline{\lambda}$-ary feature space is defined as,

$$\psi_{\mathbf{j}}^{(\overline{\lambda})}(\mathbf{x}) = \Pi_{m=1}^l \exp^{\frac{2\pi i}{\lambda_m} x_m j_m} \qquad (1)$$

When $\lambda_1 = \lambda_2 = \cdots = \lambda_\ell = \lambda$ we can write, $\psi_{\mathbf{j}}^{(\lambda)}(\mathbf{x}) = \exp^{\frac{2\pi i}{\lambda}(\mathbf{x} \cdot \mathbf{j})}$. Where $\mathbf{j}$ and $\mathbf{x}$ are λ-ary strings of length ℓ.

The Fourier coefficients for non-Boolean domain can be defined as follows:

$$w_{\mathbf{j}} = \Pi_{i=1}^l \frac{1}{\lambda_i} \sum_{\mathbf{x}} f(\mathbf{x}) \overline{\psi}_{\mathbf{j}}^{(\overline{\lambda})}(\mathbf{x}) \qquad (2)$$

where $\overline{\psi}_{\mathbf{j}}^{(\overline{\lambda})}(\mathbf{x})$ is the complex conjugate of $\psi_{\mathbf{j}}^{(\overline{\lambda})}(\mathbf{x})$.

Since a decision tree is a function defined over a discrete space (inherently discrete or some discretization of a continuous space) we can compute its Fourier transformation. We shall discuss the techniques to compute the Fourier spectrum of a decision tree later. It turns out that the Fourier representation of a decision tree with bounded depth has some very interesting properties [12, 14]. These observations are discussed in the following section.

2.3. Fourier Spectrum of a Decision Tree: Why bother?

For almost all practical applications decision trees have bounded depths. The Fourier spectrum of a bounded depth decision tree has some interesting properties.

1. The Fourier representation of a bounded depth (say k) Boolean decision tree only has a polynomial number of non-zero coefficients; all coefficients corresponding to partitions involving more than k feature variables are zero. The proof is relatively straight forward.

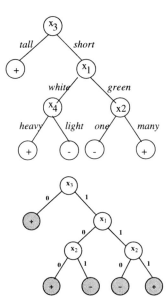

Figure 1. (Top) A symbolic decision tree and (Bottom) the numeric (Boolean) version that simply replaces the symbols by numbers.

2. If the order of a partition be its number of defining features then the magnitude of the Fourier coefficients decay exponentially with the order of the corresponding partition; in other words low order coefficients are exponentially more significant than the higher order coefficients. This was proved in [14] for Boolean decision trees. Its counterpart for trees with non-boolean features can be found elsewhere [18].

These observations suggest that the spectrum of the decision tree can be approximated by computing only a small number of low-order[1] coefficients. So Fourier basis offers an efficient numeric representation of a decision tree in the form of an algebraic function that can be easily stored, communicated, and manipulated.

2.4. From Fourier Coefficients to a Decision Tree

Fourier coefficients have important physical meanings. Recall that every coefficient is associated with a Fourier basis function. Any given basis function depends on a unique subset of features defining the domain. For an ℓ-bit Boolean domain there are 2^ℓ unique feature subsets. There are also 2^ℓ different Fourier basis functions and each of them is associated with a unique subset. The magnitude of a coefficient

[1]Order of a coefficient is the number of features defining the corresponding partition. Low-order coefficients are the ones for which the orders of the partitions are relatively small

represents the "strength" of the contribution of the corresponding subset of features to the overall function value. So if the magnitude of a coefficient is relatively large then the corresponding features together have strong influence on the function value. For example, consider a linear function of the form $f(\mathbf{x}) = \sum_i a_i x_i$. All terms in this function are linear; so the features together (in a multiplicative sense) do not make any contribution to the function value. This linearity is also reflected in its Fourier spectrum. It is easy to show that all Fourier coefficients of this function corresponding to basis functions that depend on more than one variable are zero. This connection between the structure of the function and its spectrum is a general property of the Fourier basis. The magnitudes of the Fourier coefficients expose the underlying structure of the function by identifying the dependencies and correlation among different features.

However, Fourier spectrum of a decision tree tells us more than the interactions among the features. This coefficients can also tell us about the distribution of class labels at any node of the decision tree. Recall that any node in the tree is associated with some feature x_i. A downward link from the node x_i is labeled with an attribute value of this i-th feature. As a result, a path from the root node to a successor node represents the subset of domain that satisfies the different feature values labeled along the path. These subsets are essentially similarity-based equivalence classes. In this paper we shall call them schemata (schema in singular form). If $\mathbf{h}$ is a schema in a Boolean domain, then $\mathbf{h} \in \{0, 1, *\}^\ell$, where $*$ denotes a wild-card that matches any value of the corresponding feature. For example, the path $\{(x_3 \xrightarrow{1} x_1, x_1 \xrightarrow{0} x_2\}$ in Figure 1(Bottom) represents the schema $0 * 1$, since all members of the data subset at the final node of this path take feature values 0 and 1 for x_1 and x_3 respectively.

The distribution of class labels in a schema is an important aspect since that identifies the utility of the schema as a decision rule. For example, if all the members of some schema $\mathbf{h}$ has a class label value of 1 then $\mathbf{h}$ can be used as an effective decision rule. On the other hand, if the proportion of label values 1 and 0 is almost equal then $\mathbf{h}$ cannot be used as an effective decision rule. In decision tree learning algorithms like ID3 and C4.5 this "skewedness" in the distribution for a given schema is measured by computing the *information-gain* defined in the following.

$$Gain(\mathbf{h}, x_i) = Entropy(\mathbf{h}) - \sum_{v \in Values(x_i)} \frac{|\mathbf{h}_v|}{|\mathbf{h}|} Entropy(\mathbf{h}_v)$$

where $Values(x_i)$ is the set of all possible values for attribute x_i, and $|\mathbf{h}_v|$ is the set of those members of $\mathbf{h}$ that have a value v for attribute x_i; if p and q are the proportions of the positive and negative instances in some $\mathbf{h}$, then $Entropy(\mathbf{h}) = -p \log p - q \log q$.

The gain computation clearly depends on the proportion of class labels in a schema which can be determined directly from the Fourier spectrum of the tree. For example consider a problem with Boolean class labels $\{0, 1\}$. The total number of members of schema $\mathbf{h}$ with class labels 1,

$$n_1(\mathbf{h}) = \sum_{\mathbf{j} \in \mathbf{J}(\mathbf{h})} w_{\mathbf{j}} \psi_{\mathbf{j}}(\beta(\mathbf{h})) \qquad (3)$$

where,

$$J_i(\mathbf{h}) = \begin{cases} 0 & \text{if } h_i = *; \\ * & \text{if } h_i = 0, 1; \end{cases}$$

$$\beta_i(\mathbf{h}) = \begin{cases} 0 & \text{if } h_i = 0, *; \\ 1 & \text{if } h_i = 1; \end{cases}$$

Let n_f be the total number of features that are set to specific values in order to define the schema and ℓ be the total number of features defining the entire domain. So the total number of members covered by the schema $\mathbf{h}$ is $2^{\ell - n_f}$. The total number of members in $\mathbf{h}$ with class label 0, $n_0 = 2^{\ell - n_f} - n_1$. Clearly, we can compute this distribution information for any given schema using the spectrum of the tree. In other words, we can construct the tree using the Fourier spectrum of the information gain. The following section presents a fast technique for computing the Fourier spectrum of a decision tree.

2.5. Computing the Fourier Transform of a Tree

The Fourier spectrum of a decision tree can be easily computed by traversing the leaf nodes in a systematic fashion. The proposed algorithm is extremely fast and the overhead of computing these coefficients is minimal compared to the load for learning the tree. Let Λ be the complete instance space. Let us also assume that there are n leaf nodes in the decision tree and the i-th leaf node covers a subset of Λ, denoted by S_{l_i}. Therefore, $\cup_{i=1}^{n} S_{l_i} = \Lambda$.

The $\mathbf{j}$-th coefficient of the spectrum can be computed as follows:

$$w_{\mathbf{j}} = \frac{1}{|\Lambda|} \sum_{\mathbf{x} \in \Lambda} f(\mathbf{x}) \psi_{\mathbf{j}}(\mathbf{x})$$

$$= \frac{1}{|\Lambda|} \sum_{\mathbf{x} \in S_{l_1}} f(\mathbf{x}) \psi_{\mathbf{j}}(\mathbf{x}) + \cdots + \frac{1}{|\Lambda|} \sum_{\mathbf{x} \in S_{l_n}} f(\mathbf{x}) \psi_{\mathbf{j}}(\mathbf{x})$$

Now note that both $f(\mathbf{x})$ and $\psi_{\mathbf{j}}(\mathbf{x})$ take a constant value for every member $\mathbf{x}$ in S_{l_i}. Since the path to a leaf node represents a schema, with some abuse of symbols we can write,

$$w_{\mathbf{j}} = \frac{|S_{l_1}|}{|\Lambda|} f(\mathbf{h_1}) \psi_{\mathbf{j}}(\mathbf{h_1}) + \cdots + \frac{|S_{l_n}|}{|\Lambda|} f(\mathbf{h_n}) \psi_{\mathbf{j}}(\mathbf{h_n})$$

Where $\mathbf{h_i}$ is a schema defined by a path to l_i respectively. Further details about this algorithm can be found elsewhere [18]. For each path from the root to a leaf node(schema $\mathbf{h}$), all non-zero Fourier coefficient are detected by enumerating all possible value for each attribute in $\mathbf{h}$. The running time of this algorithm is $O(n)$.

3. Aggregating Multiple Trees

The Fourier spectrum of a decision tree-ensemble classifier can also be computed using the algorithm described in the previous section. We first have to compute the Fourier spectrum of every tree and then aggregate them using the chosen scheme for constructing the ensemble. Let $f(\mathbf{x})$ be an ensemble of m different decision trees where the output is a weighted linear combination of the outputs of these trees.

$$\begin{aligned} f(\mathbf{x}) &= a_1 f_1(\mathbf{x}) + a_2 f_2(\mathbf{x}) + \dots + a_n f_m(\mathbf{x}) \\ &= a_1 \sum_{\mathbf{j} \in J_1} w_{\mathbf{j}}^{(1)} \overline{\psi_{\mathbf{j}}}(\mathbf{x}) + \dots + a_n \sum_{\mathbf{j} \in J_m} w_{\mathbf{j}}^{(m)} \overline{\psi_{\mathbf{j}}}(\mathbf{x}) \end{aligned}$$

where $f_i(\mathbf{x})$ and a_i are i^{th} decision tree and its weight respectively. J_i is set of non-zero Fourier coefficients that are detected by i^{th} decision tree and $w_{\mathbf{j}}^{(i)}$ is a Fourier coefficient in J_i. Now we can write,

$$f(\mathbf{x}) = \sum_{\mathbf{j} \in J} w_{\mathbf{j}} \overline{\psi_{\mathbf{j}}}(\mathbf{x}) \qquad (4)$$

where $w_{\mathbf{j}} = \sum_{i=1}^{m} a_i w_{\mathbf{j}}^{(i)}$ and $J = \cup_{i=1}^{m} J_i$.

Therefore Fourier spectrum of $f(\mathbf{x})$ (an ensemble classifier) is simply the weighted spectrum of each tree. The spectrum of the ensemble can be directly useful for at least two immediate purposes:

1. visualization of the ensemble through its Fourier spectrum,

2. minimizing the communication overhead,

3. understanding the ensemble classifier through its spectrum, and

4. construction of simpler and smaller ensemble (possibly a single concise tree) from the aggregated spectrum.

The following section considers the visualization aspect.

4. Visualization of the Fourier Representation

Fourier representation offers a unique way to visualize decision trees. This section presents a ticker and touchpad-based approach to visualize decision trees that are especially suitable for smaller displays like the ones that we get in palmtop devices. However, the approach is also suitable for desktop applications.

4.1. Fourier Spectrum-based Touch-pad and Ticker

Fourier coefficients of a function provide us a lot of useful information. As we noted earlier, individual coefficients tell us about strongly mutually interacting features that significantly contribute toward the overall function value. Moreover, different subsets of these coefficients can also provide us the distribution information (i.e. "information-gain" value used in ID3/C4.5) at any node. This section develops a novel approach for visualizing decision trees that exploits both of these properties of the Fourier spectrum. The approach is based on two primary components:

1. A *touch-pad* that presents a 2D density plot of all the significant coefficients and

2. a ticker that allows continuous monitoring of information-gain produced by a set of classifiers constructed by a certain group of features (possibly selected using the touch-pad). This is particularly important for time-critical applications.

Each of them is described in details next.

4.2. The Touch-pad

The *touch-pad* is a rectangular region that presents a graphical interface to interact with the distribution of Fourier coefficients. Let us consider any arbitrary set of coefficients. These coefficients can be viewed as a graph (V, E) where every node in V is associated with a unique coefficient; E is the set of edges where every edge between node v_i and v_j is associated with the "distance"($\rho(v_i, v_j)$) between their associated partitions. The distance metric (ρ) can be chosen in different ways. For example, if the domain is binary, partitions are also going to be binary strings. So we may choose hamming distance as the metric for defining the graph. For discrete non-binary partitions we may chose any of the widely known distance metrics. The choice of distance metric does not fundamentally change the proposed approach. Any reasonable distance metric that captures the distance between a pair of integer strings (i.e. partitions) should work fine with the proposed visualization approach.

Once the graph (V, E) is defined, our next task is to project it to a two dimensional space in such a way that "neighbors" in the original high dimensional space do remain "neighbors" in the projected space. In other words, we would like to have near isometric projections where $\frac{\rho(v_i, v_j)}{\rho(v_i', v_j')} = \alpha$ for all pairs i and j and constant value of α;

v_i' and v_j' are the projections of v_i and v_j respectively. This work makes use of existing off-the-shelf algorithms to construct this projection. It uses the widely known self organizing feature map (SOM) [10, 11, 13] for this purpose. The SOM takes the Fourier coefficients and maps them to a two dimensional grid where coefficients with similar partitions are located in neighboring positions. Although, this particular approach uses the SOM for the 2-D projection, any other technique (possibly greedy algorithms) should work fine as long as the relative distance between the nodes are reasonably preserved. The touch-pad is also color coded in order to properly convey the distribution of significant and insignificant coefficients. Figure 2 shows a screen shot of the implementations of the touch-pad in a HP Jornada palmtop device.

The touch-pad is also interactive. Since the display area is usually small our implementation of the touch-pad offers variable degrees of resolutions. The user can interactively zoom-in or zoom-out of a specific region. The user can also find out the subset of features defining a certain part of the touch-pad by interactively choosing a region from the screen. By marking a certain region of interest, the user will get a better understanding about interesting patterns among features residing and their finer and more detailed visualization. This interactive feature of the touch-pad also gives the user an opportunity to explore the dependencies among selected subset of features with the aid of a dynamically changing "ticker". The following section describes this in detail.

4.3. The Ticker

The ticker is provided to allow continuous monitoring of specific classifiers produced by the decision trees. This is particularly important for time-critical applications. The ticker shows the "strengths" (measures like information-gain used frequently in the decision tree literature) for a subset of "good" decision rules produced by the trees. Figure 2 shows screen shot of the ticker depicting the strengths of a set of classifiers at a particular time. As new data arrive the strengths are modified.

It is inherently designed to complement the touch-pad-based approach to visualize the spectrum of the decision tree. Recall that the information-gain (i.e. difference in the entropies) at a particular node of a decision tree is computed by using the distribution of the domain members that it covers. As we noted earlier, the information-gain can also be computed from the spectrum of the decision tree. User's selection of a certain region from the touch-pad identifies the current interest of the user to a certain subset of features. The user can invoke the ticker and instruct it to monitor all the decision rules that can be constructed using those features. The user can also interactively select the decision

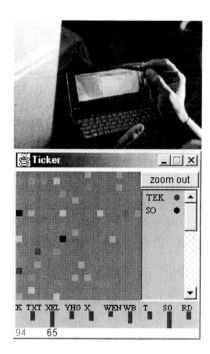

Figure 2. (Top) Fourier spectrum-based decision tree mining interface for HP Jornada. (Bottom) An enlarged view of the interface. The interface has three windows. The left-most window is the touch-pad. The bottom window shows the ticker. The right window is a small area to interactively construct and compute the accuracy of the classifiers.

rules that are comprised of different features. The ticker in turn collects the relevant Fourier coefficients and computes the information-gain associated with all the decision rules that can be constructed using those features and shows only the good ones.

5. Experiments with Financial Data Streams

This section presents the experimental performance of the proposed aggregation approach for combining multiple decision trees. It presents results using two ensemble learning techniques, namely Bagging and Arcing.

The ensemble learning literature considers different ways to compute the output of the ensemble. Averaging the outputs of the individual models with uniform weight is probably the simplest possibility. Perrone and Cooper [19][17] refer to this method as Basic Ensemble Method (BEM) or naive Bagging. Breiman proposed an Arcing method Arc-fx [2][3] for mining from large data set and stream data . It is fundamentally based on the idea of Arcing – adaptive re-sampling by giving higher weights to those

instances that are usually mis-classified. We consider both of these ensemble learning techniques to create an ensemble of decision trees from the data stream. These trees are however combined using the proposed Fourier spectrum-based approach which the regular ensemble learning techniques do not offer. We also performed experiments using an AdaBoost-based approach suggested elsewhere [7]. However, we choose not to report that since its performance appears to be considerably inferior to those of Bagging and Arcing for the data set we use.

Not all the models generated from different data blocks should always be aggregated together. Sometimes we may want to use a pruning algorithm [16, 20] for selecting the right subset of models. Sometimes a "windowing scheme" [7, 3] can be used where only W most recent classifiers are used for learning and classification.

Our experiments were performed using a semi-synthetic data stream with 174 Boolean attributes. The objective is to continuously evolve a decision tree-based predictive model for a Boolean attribute. The data-stream generator is essentially a C4.5 decision tree learned from three years of S&P100 and Nasdaq 100 stock quote data. The original data are pre-processed and transformed to discrete data by assigning discrete values for "increase" and "decrease" in stock quote between consecutive days (i.e. local gradient). Decision trees predict whether the Yahoo stock is likely to increase or decrease based on the attribute values of the 174 stocks.

We assume a non-stationary sampling strategy in order to generate the data. Every leaf in the decision tree-based data generator is associated with a certain probability value. Data samples are generated by choosing the leaves according to the assigned probability distribution. This distribution is changed several times during a single experiment. We also add white noise to the generator. Test data set is comprised of 10, 000 instances.

We implemented the naive Bagging and Arcing techniques and performed various tests over the validation data set as described below. Decision tree models are generated from every data block collected from the stream and their spectrums are combined using the BEM and Arcing. We studied the accuracy of each model with various sizes (N) of data block at each update. We use $N = 100, 200, 300, 400, 500$. We also studied the accuracy of each model generated using the "windowing" technique with various window sizes, $W = 50, 80, 100$. All the results are measured over 300 iterations where every iteration corresponds to a unique discrete time step.

Figure 3 plots the classification accuracies of Bagging and Arcing with various data block sizes. Bagging converges rapidly with all different block sizes before or around 50 iterations, while Arcing shows gradual increase throughout all iteration steps. Although we stopped at 300 itera-

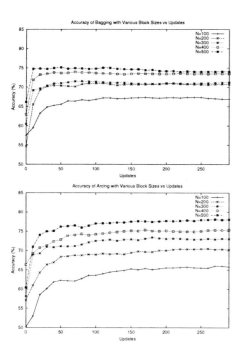

Figure 3. Accuracy vs. iterations with various data block sizes: (Top) Bagging (Bottom) Arcing.

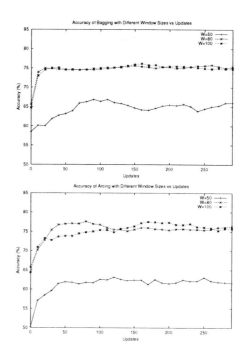

Figure 4. Accuracy vs. iterations with various window sizes: (Top) Bagging (Bottom) Arcing.

tions, the accuracy does not seem to reach its asymptotic value. Figure 4 plots the classification accuracies of Bagging and Arcing with various window size. With relatively large window size (80 and 100), we observed small decrease in accuracies in both cases. Figure 5 plots the classification accuracies of Bagging and Arcing using different significant fractions of the Fourier spectrum. It shows that only a small fraction of all the coefficients in the spectrum is sufficient for accurate classification. Further details about these and additional experiments studying the complexity of the Fourier representations of decision trees can be found elsewhere [18].

6. Conclusion

The emerging domain of wireless computing is alluding the possibility of making data mining ubiquitous. However, this new breed of applications is likely to have different expectations and they will have to work with different system resource requirements. This will demand dramatic changes in the current desktop technology for data mining. This paper considered a small but important aspect of this issue.

This paper presented a novel Fourier analysis-based approach to enhance interaction with decision trees in a mobile environment. It observed that a decision tree is a func-

tion and its numeric functional representation in Fourier basis has several utilities; the representation is efficient and easy to compute. It is also suitable for aggregation of multiple trees frequently generated by ensemble-based data stream mining techniques like boosting and bagging. This approach also offers a new way to visualize decision trees that is completely different from the traditional tree-based presentation used in most data mining software. The approach presented here is particularly suitable for portable applications with small display areas. The touch-pad and ticker-based approach is very intuitive and can be easily implemented on touch sensitive screen often used in small wireless devices. We are currently extending the ticker interface, introducing different additional application functionalities, and exploring related techniques to mine real-valued financial data online.

Acknowledgments

The authors acknowledge supports from the United States National Science Foundation CAREER award IIS-0093353 and NASA (NRA) NAS2-37143.

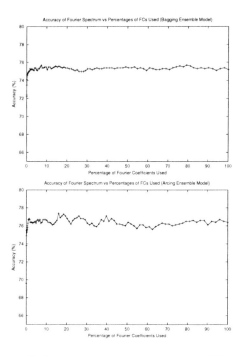

Figure 5. Accuracy vs. percentage of Fourier coefficients used for prediction: (Top) Bagging, (Bottom) Arcing.

References

[1] M. Ankerst, C. Elsen, M. Ester, and H. Kriegel. Visual classication: An interactive approach to decision tree construction. *Proceeding of the 5th International Conference on Knowledge Discovery and Data Mining*, pages 392–397, 1999.

[2] L. Breiman. Bias, variance and arcing classifiers. Technical Report 460, Statistics Department, University of California at Berkeley, 1996.

[3] L. Breiman. Pasting small votes for classification in large databases and on-line. *Machine Learning*, 36(1–2):85–103, 1999.

[4] L. Breiman, J. H. Freidman, R. A. Olshen, and C. J. Stone. Classification and regression trees.

[5] P. Domings and G. Hulten. Mining high-speed data streams. In *Sixth ACM SIGKDD International Conference on Knowledge Discovery and Data Mining*, Boston, MA, August, 2000.

[6] H. Drucker and C. Cortes. Boosting decision trees. *Advances in Neural Information Processing Systems*, 8:479–485, 1996.

[7] W. Fan, S. Stolfo, and J. Zhang. The application of AdaBoost for distributed, scalable and on-line learning. In *Fifth ACM SIGKDD International Conference on Knowledge Discovery and Data Mining*, San Diego, California, 1999.

[8] Y. Freund and R. E. Schapire. Experiments with a new boosting algorithm. In *Machine Learning: Proceedings of the Thirteenth International Conference*, Murray Hill, NJ, 1996.

[9] H. Kargupta, B. Park, D. Hershberger, and E. Johnson. Collective data mining: A new perspective toward distributed data mining. In H. Kargupta and P. Chan, editors, *Advances in Distributed and Parallel Knowledge Discovery*, pages 133–184. AAAI/ MIT Press, Menlo Park, California, USA, 2000.

[10] S. Kaski. Fast winner search for SOM-based monitoring and retrieval of high-dimensional data. In *Proceedings of ICANN99, Ninth International Conference on Artificial Neural Networks*, volume 2, pages 940–945. IEE, London, 1999.

[11] T. Kohonen. The self–organizing map. *Proceeding of the IEEE*, 78(9):1464–1479, 1990.

[12] S. Kushilevitz and Y. Mansour. Learning decision rees using fourier spectrum. In *Proc. 23rd Annual ACM Symp. on Theory of Computing*, pages 455–464, 1991.

[13] K. Lagus, T. Honkela, S. Kaski, and T. Kohonen. WEBSOM for textual data mining. *Artificial Intelligence Review*, 13(5/6):345–364, December 1999.

[14] N. Linial, Y. Mansour, and N. Nisan. Constant depth circuits, fourier transform, and learnability. *Journal of the ACM*, 40:607–620, 1993.

[15] R. Maclin and D. Opitz. An empirical evaluation of bagging and boosting. In *Proceedings of the Fourteenth International Conference on Artificial Intelligence*, pages 546–551, Cambridge, MA, 1997. AAAI Press / MIT Press.

[16] D. Margineantu and T. Dietterich. Pruning adaptive boosting. In *Proceedings, Fourteenth Intl. Conf. Machine Learning*, pages 211–218, 1997.

[17] C. J. Merz and M. J. Pazzani. A principal components approach to combining regression estimates. *Machine Learning*, 36(1–2):9–32, 1999.

[18] H. Park. Knowledge Discovery from Heterogeneous Data Streams Using Fourier Analysis of Decision Trees. PhD. Dissertation, School of Electrical Engineering and Computer Science, Washington State University, August, 2001.

[19] M. P. Perrone and L. N. Cooper. When networks disagree: Ensemble method for neural networks. In R. J. Mammone, editor, *Neural Networks for Speech and Image processing*. Chapman-Hall, 1993.

[20] A. L. Prodromidis and S. J. Stolfo. Mining databases with different schemas: Integrating incompatible classifiers. In R. e. a. Agrawal, editor, *The Fourth International Conference on Knowledge Discovery and Data Mining*, pages 314–318. AAAI Press, 1998.

[21] J. R. Quinlan. Induction of decision trees. *Machine Learning*, 1(1):81–106, 1986.

[22] J. R. Quinlan. *C4.5: Programs for Machine Learning*. Morgan Kauffman, 1993.

[23] J. R. Quinlan. Bagging, boosting and C4.5. In *Proceedings of AAAI'96 National Conference on Artificial Intelligence*, pages 725–730, 1996.

[24] P. Utgoff. Incremental induction of decision trees. *Machine Learning*, 4:161–186, 1989.

An Online Algorithm for Segmenting Time Series

Eamonn Keogh   Selina Chu   David Hart   Michael Pazzani

Department of Information and Computer Science
University of California, Irvine, California 92697 USA
{eamonn, selina, dhart, pazzani}@ics.uci.edu

Abstract

In recent years, there has been an explosion of interest in mining time series databases. As with most computer science problems, representation of the data is the key to efficient and effective solutions. One of the most commonly used representations is piecewise linear approximation. This representation has been used by various researchers to support clustering, classification, indexing and association rule mining of time series data. A variety of algorithms have been proposed to obtain this representation, with several algorithms having been independently rediscovered several times. In this paper, we undertake the first extensive review and empirical comparison of all proposed techniques. We show that all these algorithms have fatal flaws from a data mining perspective. We introduce a novel algorithm that we empirically show to be superior to all others in the literature.

1. Introduction

In recent years, there has been an explosion of interest in mining time series databases. As with most computer science problems, representation of the data is the key to efficient and effective solutions. Several high level representations of time series have been proposed, including Fourier Transforms [1,13], Wavelets [4], Symbolic Mappings [2, 5, 24] and Piecewise Linear Representation (PLR). In this work, we confine our attention to PLR, perhaps the most frequently used representation [8, 10, 12, 14, 15, 16, 17, 18, 20, 21, 22, 25, 27, 28, 30, 31].

Intuitively Piecewise Linear Representation refers to the approximation of a time series T, of length n, with K straight lines. Figure 1 contains two examples. Because K is typically much smaller that n, this representation makes the storage, transmission and computation of the data more efficient. Specifically, in the context of data mining, the piecewise linear representation has been used to:

- Support fast exact similarly search [13].
- Support novel distance measures for time series, including "fuzzy queries" [27, 28], weighted queries [15], multiresolution queries [31, 18], dynamic time warping [22] and relevance feedback [14].
- Support concurrent mining of text and time series [17].

- Support novel clustering and classification algorithms [15].
- Support change point detection [29, 8].

Surprisingly, in spite of the ubiquity of this representation, with the exception of [27], there has been little attempt to understand and compare the algorithms that produce it. Indeed, there does not even appear to be a consensus on what to call such an algorithm. For clarity, we will refer to these types of algorithm, which input a time series and return a piecewise linear representation, as segmentation algorithms.

The segmentation problem can be framed in several ways.

- Given a time series T, produce the best representation using only K segments.
- Given a time series T, produce the best representation such that the maximum error for any segment does not exceed some user-specified threshold, `max_error`.
- Given a time series T, produce the best representation such that the combined error of all segments is less than some user-specified threshold, `total_max_error`.

As we shall see in later sections, not all algorithms can support all these specifications.

Segmentation algorithms can also be classified as batch or online. This is an important distinction because many data mining problems are inherently dynamic [30, 12].

Data mining researchers, who needed to produce a piecewise linear approximation, have typically either independently rediscovered an algorithm or used an approach suggested in related literature. For example, from the fields of cartography or computer graphics [6, 9, 26].

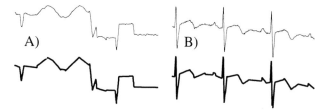

Figure 1. Two time series and their piecewise linear representation. A) Space Shuttle Telemetry. B) Electrocardiogram (ECG)

In this paper, we review the three major segmentation approaches in the literature and provide an extensive empirical evaluation on a very heterogeneous collection of datasets from finance, medicine, manufacturing and science. The major result of these experiments is that only online algorithm in the literature produces very poor approximations of the data, and that the only algorithm that consistently produces high quality results and scales linearly in the size of the data is a batch algorithm. These results motivated us to introduce a new online algorithm that scales linearly in the size of the data set, is online, and produces high quality approximations.

The rest of the paper is organized as follows. In Section 2, we provide an extensive review of the algorithms in the literature. We explain the basic approaches, and the various modifications and extensions by data miners. In Section 3, we provide a detailed empirical comparison of all the algorithms. We will show that the most popular algorithms used by data miners can in fact produce very poor approximations of the data. The results will be used to motivate the need for a new algorithm that we will introduce and validate in Section 4. Section 5 offers conclusions and directions for future work.

2. Background and Related Work

In this section, we describe the three major approaches to time series segmentation in detail. Almost all the algorithms have 2 and 3 dimensional analogues, which ironically seem to be better understood. A discussion of the higher dimensional cases is beyond the scope of this paper. We refer the interested reader to [9], which contains an excellent survey.

Although appearing under different names and with slightly different implementation details, most time series segmentation algorithms can be grouped into one of the following three categories.

- **Sliding Windows:** A segment is grown until it exceeds some error bound. The process repeats with the next data point not included in the newly approximated segment.
- **Top-Down:** The time series is recursively partitioned until some stopping criteria is met.
- **Bottom-Up:** Starting from the finest possible approximation, segments are merged until some stopping criteria is met.

Table 1. The notation used in this paper

T	A time series in the form $t_1, t_2, \ldots, t_n$
T[a:b]	The subsection of T from a to b, $t_a, t_{a+1}, \ldots, t_b$
Seg_TS	A piecewise linear approximation of a time series of length n with K segments. Individual segments can be addressed with Seg_TS(i).
create_segment(T)	A function which takes in a time series and returns a linear segment approximation of it.
calculate_error(T)	A function which takes in a time series and returns the approximation error of the linear segment approximation of it.

Given that we are going to approximate a time series with straight lines, there are at least two ways we can find the approximating line.

- **Linear Interpolation:** Here the approximating line for the subsequence T[a:b] is simply the line connecting t_a and t_b. This can be obtained in constant time.
- **Linear Regression:** Here the approximating line for the subsequence T[a:b] is taken to be the best fitting line in the least squares sense [27]. This can be obtained in time linear in the length of segment.

The two techniques are illustrated in Figure 2. Linear interpolation tends to closely align the endpoint of consecutive segments, giving the piecewise approximation a "smooth" look. In contrast, piecewise linear regression can produce a very disjointed look on some datasets. The aesthetic superiority of linear interpolation, together with its low computational complexity has made it the technique of choice in computer graphic applications [9]. However, the quality of the approximating line, in terms of Euclidean distance, is generally inferior to the regression approach.

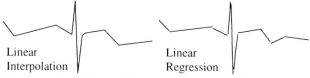

Linear Interpolation   Linear Regression

Figure 2. Two 10-segment approximations of electrocardiogram data. The approximation created using linear interpolation has a smooth aesthetically appealing appearance because all the endpoints of the segments are aligned. Linear regression, in contrast, produces a slightly disjointed appearance but a tighter approximation in terms of residual error

All segmentation algorithms also need some method to evaluate the quality of fit for a potential segment. A measure commonly used in conjunction with linear regression is the sum of squares, or the residual error. This is calculated by taking all the vertical differences between the best-fit line and the actual data points, squaring them and then summing them together. Another commonly used measure of goodness of fit is the distance between the best fit line and the data point furthest away in the vertical direction (i.e. the L_∞ norm between the line and the data). As before, we have kept our descriptions of the algorithms general enough to encompass any error measure. In particular, the pseudocode function calculate_error(T) can be imagined as using any sum of squares, furthest point, or any other measure.

2.1 The sliding window algorithm.

The Sliding Window algorithm works by anchoring the left point of a potential segment at the first data point of a time series, then attempting to approximate the data to the right with increasing longer segments. At some point i, the error for the potential segment is greater than the user-specified threshold, so the subsequence from the anchor to i-1 is transformed into a segment. The anchor is moved to location *i*, and the process repeats until the entire time series has been transformed into a piecewise linear approximation. The pseudocode for the algorithm is shown in Table 2.

Table 2. The generic Sliding Window algorithm

```
Algorithm Seg_TS = Sliding_Window(T , max_error)
anchor = 1;
while not finished segmenting time series
  i = 2;
  while  calculate_error(T[anchor: anchor + i ]) < max_error
    i = i + 1;
  end;
  Seg_TS =concat(Seg_TS,create_segment(T[anchor:anchor+(i-1)]);
  anchor = anchor + i;
end;
```

The Sliding Window algorithm is attractive because of its great simplicity, intuitiveness and particularly the fact that it is an online algorithm. Several variations and optimizations of the basic algorithm have been proposed. Koski et al. noted that on ECG data it is possible to speed up the algorithm by incrementing the variable *i* by "leaps of length *k*" instead of 1. For $k = 15$ (at 400Hz), the algorithm is 15 times faster with little effect on the output [12].

Depending on the error measure used, there may be other optimizations possible. Vullings et al. noted that since the residual error is monotonically non-decreasing with the addition of more data points, one does not have to test every value of *i* from 2 to the final chosen value [30]. They suggest initially setting *i* to *s*, where *s* is the mean length of the previous segments. If the guess was pessimistic (the measured error is still less than max_error) then the algorithm continues to increment *i* as in the classic algorithm. Otherwise they begin to decrement *i* until the measured error is less than max_error. This optimization can greatly speed up the algorithm if the mean length of segments is large in relation to the standard deviation of their length. The monotonically non-decreasing property of residual error also allows binary search for the length of the segment. Surprisingly, no one we are aware of has suggested this.

The Sliding Window algorithm can give pathologically poor results under some circumstances. Most researchers have not reported this [25, 31], perhaps because they tested the algorithm on stock market data, and its relative performance is best on noisy data. Shatkay (1995), in contrast, does notice the problem and gives elegant examples and explanations [27]. They consider three variants of the basic algorithm, each designed to be robust to a certain case, but they underline the difficulty of producing a single variant of the algorithm which is robust to arbitrary data sources.

Park et al. (2001) suggested modifying the algorithm to create "*monotonically changing*" segments [21]. That is, all segments consist of data points of the form of $t_1 \leq t_2 \leq \ldots \leq t_n$ or $t_1 \geq t_2 \geq \ldots \geq t_n$. This modification worked well on the smooth synthetic dataset it was demonstrated on.

But on real world datasets with any amount of noise, the approximation is greatly overfragmented.

Variations on the Sliding Window algorithm are particularly popular with the medical community (where it is known as FAN or SAPA), since patient monitoring is inherently an online task [11, 12, 19, 30].

2.2 The top-down algorithm.

The Top-Down algorithm works by considering every possible partitioning of the times series and splitting it at the best location. Both subsections are then tested to see if their approximation error is below some user-specified threshold. If not, the algorithm recursively continues to split the subsequences until all the segments have approximation errors below the threshold. The pseudocode for the algorithm is shown in Table 3.

Table 3. The generic Top-Down algorithm

```
Algorithm Seg_TS = Top_Down(T , max_error)
best_so_far = inf;
for i = 2 to length(T)- 2 // Find best place to divide.
improvement_in_approximation = improvement_splitting_here(T,i);
  if improvement_in_approximation < best_so_far
    breakpoint = i;
    best_so_far = improvement_in_approximation;
  end;
end;
        // Recursively split the left segment if necessary.
if calculate_error(T[1:breakpoint]) > max_error
  Seg_TS = Top_Down(T[1: breakpoint]);
end;
        // Recursively split the right segment if necessary.
if calculate_error( T[breakpoint + 1:length(T)] ) > max_error
  Seg_TS = Top_Down(T[breakpoint + 1: length(T)]);
end;
```

Variations on the Top-Down algorithm (including the 2-dimensional case) were independently introduced in several fields in the early 1970's. In cartography, it is known as the Douglas-Peucker algorithm [6]; in image processing, it is known as Ramers algorithm [26]. Most researchers in the machine learning/data mining community are introduced to the algorithm in the classic textbook by Duda and Harts, which calls it "Iterative End-Points Fits"[7].

In the data mining community, the algorithm has been used by [18] to support a framework for mining sequence databases at multiple abstraction levels. Shatkay and Zdonik use it (after considering alternatives such as Sliding Windows) to support approximate queries in time series databases [28].

Park et al. introduced a modification where they first perform a scan over the entire dataset marking every peak and valley [22]. These extreme points used to create an initial segmentation, and the Top-Down algorithm is applied to each of the segments (in case the error on an individual segment was still too high). They then use the segmentation to support a special case of dynamic time warping. This modification worked well on the smooth synthetic dataset it was demonstrated on. But on real world data sets with any amount of noise, the approximation is greatly overfragmented.

Lavrenko et al. uses the Top-Down algorithm to support the concurrent mining of text and time series [17]. They attempt to discover the influence of news stories on financial markets. Their algorithm contains some interesting modifications including a novel stopping criteria based on the t-test.

Finally Smyth and Ge use the algorithm to produce a representation which can support a Hidden Markov Model approach to both change point detection and pattern matching [8].

2.3 The bottom-up algorithm.

The Bottom-Up algorithm is the natural complement to the Top-Down algorithm. The algorithm begins by creating the finest possible approximation of the time series, so that $n/2$ segments are used to approximate the n-length time series. Next, the cost of merging each pair of adjacent segments is calculated, and the algorithm begins to iteratively merge the lowest cost pair until a stopping criteria is met. When the pair of adjacent segments i and $i+1$ are merged, the algorithm needs to perform some bookkeeping. First, the cost of merging the new segment with its right neighbor must be calculated. In addition, the cost of merging the $i-1$ segments with its new larger neighbor must be recalculated. The pseudocode for the algorithm is shown in Table 4.

Table 4. The generic Bottom-Up algorithm

```
Algorithm Seg_TS = Bottom_Up(T , max_error)

for i = 1 : 2 : length(T)      // Create initial fine approximation.

  Seg_TS = concat(Seg_TS, create_segment(T[i: i + 1 ]));

end;

for i = 1 : length(Seg_TS) - 1  // Find the cost of merging...

                                // ... each pair of segments.

  merge_cost(i)=calculate_error([merge(Seg_TS(i), Seg_TS(i+1))]);

end;

while min(merge_cost) < max_error  // While not finished.

  i = min(merge_cost);              // Find cheapest pair to merge.

  Seg_TS(i) = merge(Seg_TS(i), Seg_TS(i+1)); // Merge them.

  delete(Seg_TS(i+1));              // Update records.

  merge_cost(i)= calculate_error(merge(Seg_TS(i), Seg_TS(i+1)));

  merge_cost(i-1)= calculate_error(merge(Seg_TS(i-1), Seg_TS(i)));

end;
```

Two and three-dimensional analogues of this algorithm are common in the field of computer graphics where they are called *decimation* methods [9]. In data mining, the algorithm has been used extensively by two of the current authors to support a variety of time series data mining tasks [14, 15, 16]. In medicine, the algorithm was used by Hunter and McIntosh to provide the high level representation for their medical pattern matching system [10].

The properties of the various algorithms are summarized in Table 5.

Table 5. A feature summary for the 3 major algorithms.[1]KEY: E $\rightarrow$ Maximum error for a given segment, ME $\rightarrow$ Maximum error for a given segment for entire time series, K $\rightarrow$ Number of segments. [2]Possibly with modifications and/or extensions

Algorithm	User can specify[1]	Online	Complexity	Used by[2]
Top-Down	E, ME, K	No	$O(n^2K)$	6, 7, 8, 18, 22, 17
Bottom-Up	E, ME, K	No	$O(Ln)$	10, 14, 15 , 16
Sliding Window	E	Yes	$O(Ln)$	11, 12, 19, 25, 30, 31, 27

3. Empirical comparison of the major segmentation algorithms

In this section, we will provide an extensive empirical comparison of the three major algorithms. It is possible to create artificial datasets that allow one of the algorithms to achieve zero error (by any measure), but forces the other two approaches to produce arbitrarily poor approximations. In contrast, testing on purely random data forces the all algorithms to produce essentially the same results. To overcome the potential for biased results, we tested the algorithms on a very diverse collection of datasets. These datasets where chosen to represent the extremes along the following dimensions, stationary/non-stationary, noisy/smooth, cyclical/non-cyclical, symmetric/ asymmetric, etc. In addition, the data sets represent the diverse areas in which data miners apply their algorithms, including finance, medicine, manufacturing and science. Figure 3 illustrates the 10 datasets used in the experiments.

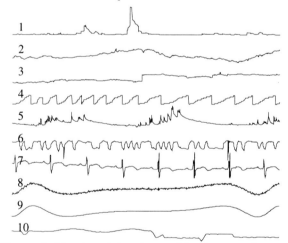

Figure 3. The ten datasets used in the experiments. 1) Radio Waves. 2) Exchange Rates. 3) Tickwise II. 4) Tickwise I. 5) Water Level. 6) Manufacturing. 7) ECG. 8) Noisy Sine Cubed. 9) Sine Cube. 10) Space Shuttle

3.1 Experimental methodology

For simplicity and brevity, we only include the linear regression versions of the algorithms in our study. Since linear regression minimizes the sum of squares error, it also minimizes the Euclidean distance (the Euclidean distance is just the square root of the sum of squares).

Euclidean distance, or some measure derived from it, is by far the most common metric used in data mining of time series [1, 2, 4, 5, 13, 14, 15, 16, 25, 31]. The linear interpolation versions of the algorithms, by definition, will always have a greater sum of squares error.

The performance of the algorithms depends on the value of `max_error`. As `max_error` goes to zero all the algorithms have the same performance, since they would produce $n/2$ segments with no error. At the opposite end, as `max_error` becomes very large, the algorithms once again will all have the same performance, since they all simply approximate T with a single best-fit line. Instead, we must test the relative performance for some reasonable value of `max_error`, a value that achieves a good trade off between compression and fidelity. Because this "reasonable value" is subjective and dependent on the data mining application and the data itself, we did the following. We chose what we considered a "reasonable value" of `max_error` for each dataset, then we bracketed it with 6 values separated by powers of two. The lowest of these values tends to produce an over-fragmented approximation, and the highest tends to produce a very coarse approximation. So in general, the performance in the mid-range of the 6 values should be consider most important. Figure 4 illustrates this idea.

Since we are only interested in the relative performance of the algorithms, for each setting of `max_error` on each data set, we normalized the performance of the 3 algorithms by dividing by the error of the worst performing approach.

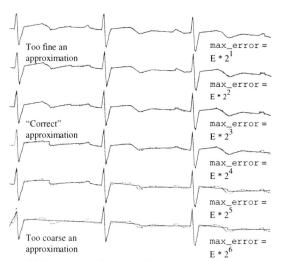

Figure 4. We are most interested in comparing the segmentation algorithms at the setting of the user-defined threshold max_error that produces an intuitively correct level of approximation. Since this setting is subjective we chose a value for E, such that max_error = E*2^i (i = 1 to 6), brackets the range of reasonable approximations

3.2 Experimental results

The experimental results are summarized in Figure 5. The most obvious result is the generally poor quality of the Sliding Windows algorithm. With a few exceptions, it is the worse performing algorithm, usually by a large amount.

Top-Down does occasionally beat Bottom-Up, but only by small amount. On the other hand Bottom-Up often significantly out performs Top-Down, especially on the ECG, Manufacturing and Water Level data sets.

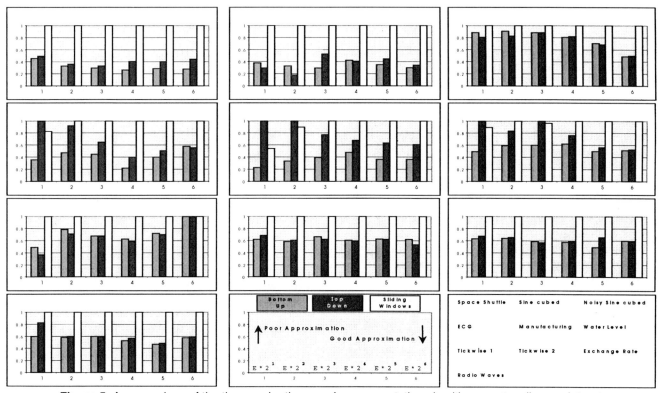

Figure 5. A comparison of the three major times series segmentation algorithms, on ten diverse datasets

4. A new approach

Given the noted shortcomings of the major segmentation algorithms, we investigated alternative techniques. The main problem with the Sliding Windows algorithm is its inability to look ahead, lacking the global view of its offline (batch) counterparts. The Bottom-Up and the Top-Down approaches produce better results, but are offline and require the scanning of the entire data set. This is impractical or may even be unfeasible in a data-mining context, where the data are in the order of terabytes or arrive in continuous streams. We therefore introduce a novel approach in which we capture the online nature of Sliding Windows and yet retain the superiority of Bottom-Up. We call our new algorithm SWAB (**S**liding **W**indow **a**nd **B**ottom-up).

4.1 The SWAB segmentation algorithm

The SWAB algorithm keeps a small buffer. The buffer size should initially be chosen so that there is enough data to create about 5 or 6 segments. Bottom-Up is applied to the data in the buffer and the leftmost segment is reported. The data corresponding to the reported segment is removed from the buffer and more datapoints are read in. The number of datapoints read in depends on the structure of the incoming data. This process is performed by the `Best_Line` function, which is basically just classic Sliding Windows. These points are incorporated into the buffer and Bottom-Up is applied again. This process of applying Bottom-Up to the buffer, reporting the leftmost segment, and reading in the next "best fit" subsequence is repeated as long as data arrives (potentially forever).

The intuition behind the algorithm is this. The `Best_Line` function finds data corresponding to a single segment using the (relatively poor) Sliding Windows and gives it to the buffer. As the data moves through the buffer the (relatively good) Bottom-Up algorithm is given a chance to refine the segmentation, because it has a "semi-global" view of the data. By the time the data is ejected from the buffer, the segmentation breakpoints are usually the same as the ones the batch version of Bottom-Up would have chosen. The pseudocode for the algorithm is shown in Table 6.

Using the buffer allows us to gain a "semi-global" view of the data set for Bottom-Up. However, it important to impose upper and lower bounds on the size of the window. A buffer that is allowed to grow arbitrarily large will revert our algorithm to pure Bottom-Up, but a small buffer will deteriorate it to Sliding Windows, allowing excessive fragmentation may occur. In our algorithm, we used an upper (and lower) bound of twice (and half) of the initial buffer.

Our algorithm can be seen as operating on a continuum between the two extremes of Sliding Windows and Bottom-Up. The surprising result (demonstrated below) is that by allowing the buffer to contain just 5 or 6 times the data normally contained by is a single segment, the algorithm produces essentially the same results as Bottom-Up, yet is able process a never-ending stream of data. Our new algorithm requires only a small, constant amount of memory, and the time complexity is a small constant factor worse than that of the standard Bottom-Up algorithm.

Table 6: The SWAB (Sliding Window and Bottom-up) algorithm

```
Algorithm Seg_TS = SWAB(max_error, seg_num)
          // seg_num is integer, about 5 or 6.


read in data points to fill w     // w is the buffer
          // Enough to approximate seg_num of segments.
lower_bound = (size of w) / 2;
upper_bound = 2 * (size of w);


while data at input
  T = Bottom_Up(w, max_error)
                 // Call the classic Bottom-Up algorithm.
  Seg_TS = CONCAT(SEG_TS, T(1));
                 // Sliding window to the right.
  w = TAKEOUT(w, w');
                 // Deletes w' points in T(1) from w.
  if data at input    // Add points from BEST_LINE() to w.
    w = CONCAT(w, BEST_LINE(max_error));
       // Check upper and lower bound, adjust if necessary.
  else  // Flush approximated segments from buffer.
       Seg_TS = CONCAT(SEG_TS, (T - T(1)))
  end;
end;


Function S = BEST_LINE(max_error) //returns S points.
  while error ≤ max_error         // next potential segment.
     read in one additional data point, d, into S
     S = CONCAT(S, d);
     error = approx_segment(S);
  end while;
return S;
```

4.2 Experimental Validation

We repeated the experiments in Section 3, this time comparing the new algorithm with pure (batch) Bottom-Up and classic Sliding Windows. The result, summarized in Figure 6, is that the new algorithm produces results that are essentiality identical to Bottom-Up.

5. Conclusions

We have carried out the first extensive review and empirical comparison of time series segmentation algorithms from a data mining perspective. We have shown the most popular approach, Sliding Windows, generally produces very poor results, and that while the second most popular approach, Top-Down, can produce reasonable results, it does not scale well. In contrast, the least well known, Bottom-Up, approach produces excellent results and scales linearly with the size of the dataset.

In addition, we have introduced SWAB, a new online algorithm, which scales linearly with the size of the dataset, requires only constant space and produces high quality approximations of the data.

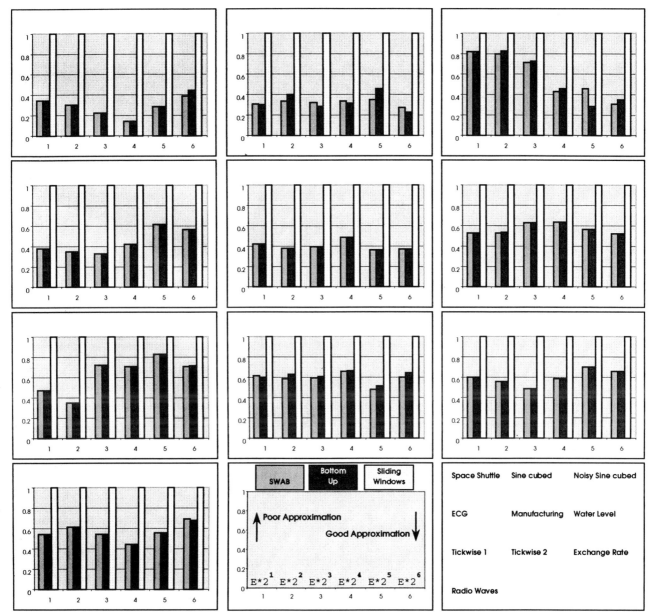

Figure 6. A comparison of the SWAB algorithm with pure (batch) Bottom-Up and classic Sliding Windows, on ten diverse datasets, over a range in parameters. Each experimental result (ie. a triplet of histogram bars) is normalized by dividing by the performance of the worst algorithm on that experiment

Reproducible Results Statement: In the interests of competitive scientific inquiry, all datasets and code used in this work are available, together with a spreadsheet detailing the original unnormalized results, by emailing the first author.

6. References

[1] Agrawal, R., Faloutsos, C., & Swami, A. (1993). Efficient similarity search in sequence databases. *Proceedings of the 4th Conference on Foundations of Data Organization and Algorithms.*

[2] Agrawal, R., Lin, K. I., Sawhney, H. S., & Shim, K. (1995). Fast similarity search in the presence of noise, scaling, and translation in times-series databases. *Proceedings of 21th International Conference on Very Large Data Bases.* pp 490-50.

[3] Agrawal, R., Psaila, G., Wimmers, E. L., & Zait, M. (1995). Querying shapes of histories. *Proceedings of the 21st International Conference on Very Large Databases.*

[4] Chan, K. & Fu, W. (1999). Efficient time series matching by wavelets. *Proceedings of the 15th IEEE International Conference on Data Engineering.*

[5] Das, G., Lin, K. Mannila. H., Renganathan, G., & Smyth, P. (1998). Rule discovery from time series. *Proceedings of*

the 3ʳᵈ International Conference of Knowledge Discovery and Data Mining. pp 16-22.

[6] Douglas, D. H. & Peucker, T. K.(1973). Algorithms for the Reduction of the Number of Points Required to Represent a Digitized Line or Its Caricature. *Canadian Cartographer*, Vol. 10, No. 2, December. pp. 112-122.

[7] Duda, R. O. and Hart, P. E. 1973. Pattern Classification and Scene Analysis. Wiley, New York.

[8] Ge, X. & Smyth P. (2001). Segmental Semi-Markov Models for Endpoint Detection in Plasma Etching. To appear in *IEEE Transactions on Semiconductor Engineering*.

[9] Heckbert, P. S. & Garland, M. (1997). Survey of polygonal surface simplification algorithms, Multiresolution Surface Modeling Course. *Proceedings of the 24ᵗʰ International Conference on Computer Graphics and Interactive Techniques*.

[10] Hunter, J. & McIntosh, N. (1999). Knowledge-based event detection in complex time series data. *Artificial Intelligence in Medicine*. pp. 271-280. Springer.

[11] Ishijima, M., et al. (1983). Scan-Along Polygonal Approximation for Data Compression of Electrocardiograms. *IEEE Transactions on Biomedical Engineering*. BME-30(11):723-729.

[12] Koski, A., Juhola, M. & Meriste, M. (1995). Syntactic Recognition of ECG Signals By Attributed Finite Automata. *Pattern Recognition*, 28 (12), pp. 1927-1940.

[13] Keogh, E,. Chakrabarti, K,. Pazzani, M. & Mehrotra (2000). Dimensionality reduction for fast similarity search in large time series databases. *Journal of Knowledge and Information Systems*.

[14] Keogh, E. & Pazzani, M. (1999). Relevance feedback retrieval of time series data. *Proceedings of the 22ᵗʰ Annual International ACM-SIGIR Conference on Research and Development in Information Retrieval*.

[15] Keogh, E., & Pazzani, M. (1998). An enhanced representation of time series which allows fast and accurate classification, clustering and relevance feedback. *Proceedings of the 4ᵗʰ International Conference of Knowledge Discovery and Data Mining*. pp 239-241, AAAI Press.

[16] Keogh, E., & Smyth, P. (1997). A probabilistic approach to fast pattern matching in time series databases. *Proceedings of the 3ʳᵈ International Conference of Knowledge Discovery and Data Mining*. pp 24-20.

[17] Lavrenko, V., Schmill, M., Lawrie, D., Ogilvie, P., Jensen, D., & Allan, J. (2000). Mining of Concurrent Text and Time Series. *Proceedings of the 6ᵗʰ International Conference on Knowledge Discovery and Data Mining*. pp. 37-44.

[18] Li, C,. Yu, P. & Castelli V.(1998). MALM: A framework for mining sequence database at multiple abstraction levels. *Proceedings of the 9ᵗʰ International Conference on Information and Knowledge Management*. pp 267-272.

[19] McKee, J.J., Evans, N.E., & Owens, F.J. (1994). Efficient implementation of the Fan/SAPA-2 algorithm using fixed point arithmetic. *Automedica*. Vol. 16, pp 109-117.

[20] Osaki, R., Shimada, M., & Uehara, K. (1999). Extraction of Primitive Motion for Human Motion Recognition. *The 2ⁿᵈ International Conference on Discovery Science*. pp.351-352.

[21] Park, S., Kim, S. W., & Chu, W. W. (2001). Segment-Based Approach for Subsequence Searches in Sequence Databases, To appear in *Proceedings of the 16ᵗʰ ACM Symposium on Applied Computing*.

[22] Park, S. & Lee, D., & Chu, W. W. (1999). Fast Retrieval of Similar Subsequences in Long Sequence Databases", *Proceedings of the 3ʳᵈ IEEE Knowledge and Data Engineering Exchange Workshop*.

[23] Pavlidis, T. (1976). Waveform segmentation through functional approximation. *IEEE Transactions on Computers*.

[24] Perng, C., Wang, H., Zhang, S., & Parker, S. (2000). Landmarks: a new model for similarity-based pattern querying in time series databases. *Proceedings of 16ᵗʰ International Conference on Data Engineering*.

[25] Qu, Y., Wang, C. & Wang, S. (1998). Supporting fast search in time series for movement patterns in multiples scales. *Proceedings of the 7ᵗʰ International Conference on Information and Knowledge Management*.

[26] Ramer, U. (1972). An iterative procedure for the polygonal approximation of planar curves. *Computer Graphics and Image Processing*. 1: pp. 244-256.

[27] Shatkay, H. (1995). Approximate Queries and Representations for Large Data Sequences. *Technical Report cs-95-03*, Department of Computer Science, Brown University.

[28] Shatkay, H., & Zdonik, S. (1996). Approximate queries and representations for large data sequences. *Proceedings of the 12ᵗʰ IEEE International Conference on Data Engineering*. pp 546-553.

[29] Sugiura, N. & Ogden, R. T. (1994). Testing Change-points with Linear Trend *Communications in Statistics B: Simulation and Computation*. 23: 287-322.

[30] Vullings, H.J.L.M., Verhaegen, M.H.G. & Verbruggen H.B. (1997). ECG Segmentation Using Time-Warping. *Proceedings of the 2ⁿᵈ International Symposium on Intelligent Data Analysis*.

[31] Wang, C. & Wang, S. (2000). Supporting content-based searches on time Series via approximation. *Proceedings of the 12th International Conference on Scientific and Statistical Database Management*.

AINE: An Immunological Approach to Data Mining

Thomas Knight and Jon Timmis
Computing Laboratory
University of Kent at Canterbury
Canterbury, Kent, CT2 7NF.
Tel: +44 (0)1227 764000
E-mail: {tpk1,jt6}@ukc.ac.uk
http://www.cs.ukc.ac.uk/people/rpg/tpk1

Abstract

An investigation has been undertaken to repeat previous work on an artificial immune system for data analysis called AINE (Artificial Immune Network). The previous work was limited to testing the algorithm on relatively small data sets. The aim of this investigation is two fold, firstly to corroborate the results presented in previous work and secondly, to test the algorithm on a larger and more complex data set. A new re-implementation of AINE is then described and differences in behaviour are identified and explained. It is argued that the behaviour seen in the new implementation is more accurate than that seen in previous work and an in-depth analysis of the algorithm structure is undertaken in order to confirm these observations. The algorithm is also tested on new data and the results of this are presented. Comparisons are draw with other similar techniques for data mining and it is argued that AINE is an effective data-mining algorithm.

1 Introduction

Using the immune system as a metaphor for machine learning has, in the last decade, become a more prominent part of computer science. This field of research is known as Artificial Immune Systems (AIS). When developing an AIS the concern is not to produce exact models of the immune system, but rather extract ideas or metaphors derived from components and processes of the immune system, which can then be applied to solving computational problems. These include, but are not limited to fault diagnostics [1], network intrusion detection [2], data mining [3] and scheduling [4].

The motivation for this work was driven by the desire to see AIS applied to larger scale, and more complex problem domains. It was the author's original intention to apply work in [5] to the area of document classification.

In order to achieve this, it was felt that is was pertinent to confirm the workings of the algorithm before proceeding to more complex areas. Through this undertaking, subtle differences emerged between the new implementation and the original proposed model. It was felt that this work should be reported, to show how the model now works and confirm that it is suitable and worthy of further investigation. The work in this paper is concerned with replicating that of [5], performing a detailed analysis of the algorithm and applying the algorithm to other data sets.

This paper details the re-implementation and testing of AINE (Artificial Immune NEtwork) described by [5], with the main details of the algorithm extracted from [6]. The re-implementation is then tested on the Fisher Iris data set [7] as in the previous work. This testing confirms many of the behavioural and functional aspects of the algorithm, but also highlighted a significant difference in the evolution of the networks over time. The nature of this evolution will be described and qualified.

This paper is organised in the following manner. Basic immunology is highlighted, and due to space, further readings cited for reference. The context of this work is then explained with reference to similar data mining techniques, followed by an outline of the work on which this paper is based. The new implementation of the algorithm is then discussed and analysed, showing that AINE will favour selection of the strongest patterns within the data. These results are of subtle difference to those presented in previous work and the reasons for this are highlighted and discussed. The results from the algorithm are then compared to two other techniques, Kohonen networks [8] and minimum distance clustering [9]. Further work using the Wisconsin Breast Cancer data set [10] is then described and comments made on future direction for the work.

2 Background

Over the last two decades understanding of the human immune system has significantly advanced. It defends our bodies from attack by foreign invaders (such as viruses and bacteria). The immune system has shown that it is capable of remembering previous encounters with these invaders and this knowledge has been harnessed to provide vaccines for a whole plethora of viruses and diseases. It also shows highly distributed detection and memory systems, diversity of detection ability across individuals, inexact matching strategies, and sensitivity to most new foreign patterns [11]. To computer scientists this ability to recognise and remember encounters with invaders over long periods of time is of great interest.

This section will provide the reader with an introduction to immunology and discuss related techniques to which work in this paper may be compared. This will place the work in a wider context and enable a sensible comparison of results.

2.1 Immunology

The function of the immune system is to identify and destroy foreign invaders or *antigens*. Antigens can be though of as bacteria, viruses and fungi that may cause disease. The immune system is composed of *lymphocytes*, which are white blood cells whose task it is to identify and destroy invading antigens [12]. There are two types of lymphocytes, B and T, however it is the behaviour of these B lymphocytes (B-cells) that AINE is based on, therefore these will be described here.

B-cells are produced and matured in the Bone-marrow. It is during this process that only those cells that can identify foreign invaders are released into our bodies. B-cells have Y shaped receptors (or antibodies) that surround the cell and are capable of recognising the proteins on the surface of an antigen. Idiotopes on the receptors are recognisable to other B-cells in the system. The receptors on any one B-cell are antigen specific and therefore can only identify proteins on a specific antigen. Jerne's idiotypic network theory [13] states that memory part of the immune system can be thought of as a dynamic feedback network of B-cells. Through stimulation and suppression of each other similar B-cells form networks that can recognise similar antigen. [14] supported this theory and also suggested that in order for the immune system to recognise all possible antigen it must have a complete repertoire of antibodies. If this were the case then we would be nothing but antibodies, however Perelson theorised that as B-cells rely on an imperfect matching strategy each B-cell antibody could match a given volume of antigen, and therefore reducing significantly reducing the number of B-cells required for a complete repertoire. This theory is known as Shape Space.

For brevity only a brief introduction to the relevant parts of immunology have been given, a more comprehensive description can be found in [15].

2.2 Related Data Mining Techniques

In order to place this work in context, it is necessary to mention related techniques that perform similar operations. As AINE is an unsupervised technique, this leads to the inevitable comparisons between techniques such as Kohonen networks [8], aiNet [16], which is an immune, inspired clustering technique, and traditional cluster analysis.

The Kohonen Network is an unsupervised neural network algorithm that is used commonly in data mining. The algorithm produces a feature map (series of connected nodes) that represents the key features of the data it is trying to map. Each node is a set of weights that represent the location of that node in data space. The node is activated by all data points that are near to that node in data space and on each iteration the node moves a proportion of the way to all of the nearby data points. The size of this proportion is governed by a learning rate. Each node is also connected to the other nodes around it and these also affect the position of the node in space. This affect is defined by the neighbourhood function. The learning process involves the training data being presented to the Kohonen network a number of times. On each iteration the neighbourhood function is decreased by a small amount to provide a dampening effect that prevents wild oscillations in the network and allows the structure of the map to be more accurately modelled. The trained Kohonen network can be considered to be topologically correct.

Work in [16] proposes an immune inspired clustering technique called aiNet. AiNet can be considered to be an edge-weighted graph, not necessarily fully connected, composed of a set of nodes, called cells and sets of node pairs called edges with a number assigned called weight, or connection strength, specified to each connected edge. Each node in the network is stimulated and suppressed by its neighbours as defined in Jernes' Immune Network theory. The nodes in the network also compete for *antigenic recognition* that leads to network activation and proliferation and therefore maintaining a presence in the network, while nodes that are not activated are removed from the network. The resulting networks represent the clusters within the data and also the structural organization. This work combines both immune inspired techniques and statistical tools for the final extraction of clusters, which is a different approach than that adopted in this paper.

For a simpler approach to identifying similar data items, cluster analysis may be used. Cluster analysis attempts to group together similar data items with the groupings representing relationships between the items; e.g. similarity of value or grouping such as a species of animal. Clustering is a useful first step in the data analysis process as it can act to direct the efforts of any further study that might be required [17]. There exist a wide variety of cluster analysis techniques [9] which may be used to separate data into groups or clusters, and are divided into two major types, *hierarchical* and *non-hierarchical* clustering. Hierarchical clustering includes *divisive* and *agglomerative* techniques. The divisive techniques start with all the data items in a single cluster and create *m* numbers of sub-clusters; i.e. until all data items are in a cluster of their own. Conversely, agglomerative techniques start with *m* different clusters and continue to merge together sub-clusters until all *m* data items are in the one cluster. The most frequently used clustering technique is the dendrogram, while quite effective for small sets of data, are very hard to use when data sets become large. The dendrogram is split over many pages, making interpretation very difficult. However, computing the dendrogram, or the similarity matrix that allows the dendrogram to be drawn, is not difficult and may be performed quickly, making this form of analysis effective for a quick *first look* at the data, to get a feel for the structure within the data set.

3 Immune inspired machine learning

There has been a limited body of work that has used the immune system metaphors for this problem domain of data mining and machine learning. Examples vary from fraud detection, [18] case-based reasoning, [19] pattern recognition, [20], [21], [22] and [5].

This section briefly outlines the previous work on which this paper is based. For brevity, only a simple explanation is given and the reader is directed to further reading for a more detailed explanation.

3.1 AINE

Work in [5] proposed an AIS called AINE to be used for pattern discovery and classification in data. A review the system can be seen in [15]. AINE employs a number of high-level metaphors drawn from the immune system. These are: A B-cell is capable of recognising pathogens (antigenic recognition); similar B-cells are linked together and these links form a network of B-cells (immune network theory); cloning and mutation operations are performed on B-cells (clonal selection and somatic hypermutation). A number of B-cells can be represented by an ARB given the theory of shape space [14]. In the natural immune system, pathogens produce antigens when invading a host. It is these antigens that are matched with the antibodies of the immune system. For the sake of simplicity in AINE, separate antigens are not created; rather the complete data items are considered to be representative of antigens rather than entire pathogens.

AINE evolves a network of ARBs that can be viewed via a specially developed tool aiVis [23]. AINE was successfully tested on a simulated data set and the Iris Data Set [7]. A detailed description of the results obtained is given in [5]. Although the results from AINE are positive there are a number of shortfalls in the work. The algorithm has only been tested on a two fairly simple data sets, although the iris data set is a standard benchmark for machine learning it is of low dimensionality and relatively small. To be of real use this algorithm should be tested on a more complex domain, with a greater number of variables and with larger data sets. As the work stands it is difficult to predict how this algorithm will perform on significantly larger data sets. The following section outlines a repeated study of this algorithm, which involved a complete re-implementation, testing on the same data, and a discussion of the issues arising from this investigation.

4 Recent Work

In order to take the work a stage further by applying it to a large scale real world problem, recent work has been undertaken to reproduce the results described in [5] and [24]. The AINE algorithm was re-implemented and tested using the same set of tests described in the latter paper. Due to space, a limited number of results are presented here, however a full description of results can be found in [25]. By comparing the performance of the original algorithm to that of the new version an error in the normalisation of the stimulation levels was identified. This has knock-on effects regarding the allocation of resources and the number of clones produced. On correcting these errors the behaviour altered slightly and it is this behaviour that is explained and justified in section 4.1

4.1 Analysis of the AINE algorithm

Extensive testing of the revised algorithm [25] confirms most of the results from the previous work but identified interesting new behaviour regarding the quality of network structure over time. It was shown that over a relatively short period of time (some 20 iterations) the network structure would change from being representative of the training data to only representing the strongest cluster (or clusters) within the training data. Figure 1 shows the evolution of the three clusters in the Iris data set over time.

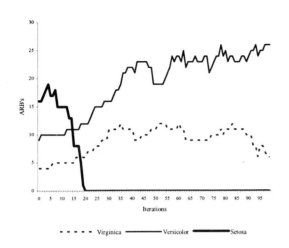

Figure 1 Changing representation in the network structure of the Iris data set over time

Each line represents the number of ARBs within the network that describes each class in the data set. It is evident that over a short period of time the representation of the Setosa class is removed. At 85 iterations the Virginia class also begins to decline leaving the Versicolor to dominate the network. It is this behaviour that was not seen in the previous work. Figure 2 shows the revised AINE algorithm, further details can be found in [25].

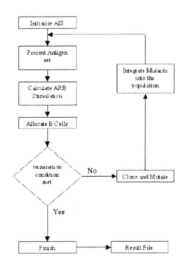

Figure 2 The revised AINE algorithm.

In order to take a detailed look at the nature of the algorithm, a simulated data set has been created for illustrative purposes. The initial population and training population are shown in Table 1 from which it can be seen that ARBs 001 and 002 form the first class, 003 and 004 forms the second class and 005 the third.

ID	d1	d2	d1	d2
001	0	0.1	0.1	0
002	0.1	0.1	0.1	0.2
003	0.5	0.6	0.2	0.1
004	0.6	0.5	0.5	0.6
005	1	0.9	0.7	0.9

Table 1 Initial population (left) and Training population (right).

Assuming that AINE has been initialised (Figure 3), the training set is then presented to the network and each cell in the network is stimulated depending on how close in data space, using Euclidean distance, it is to each training item. The first three training items are very close to ARBs 001 and 002, the fourth is close to ARB 003 and 004, and the fifth is close to ARB 005

Figure 3 The initial network structure

This would result in normalised stimulation levels shown in Table 2 where it is clear that ARBS 001 and 002 are the most stimulated. The stimulation levels are normalised because this allows a maximum number of resources per ARB, but also has a side effect that on every iteration at least one of the ARBs will have a stimulation level of zero and therefore have zero resources allocated to it. Consequently at the end of the iteration these zero-stimulated ARBs are going to be removed. The number of resources each ARB claims is simply the square of the stimulation level multiplied by a constant. Assuming that the maximum number of resources has been set to 19.3, on this iteration the network has claimed 19.403 and therefore the resource allocation mechanism executes and removes ARB 005.

ID	s	N
001	0.91685	8.406
002	1	10
003	0.2458	0.604
004	0.19815	0.393
005	0	0

Table 2 ARB stimulation after presenting the training data

The mutation mechanism is random, but biased toward those ARBs that are most stimulated. Three clones are produced from ARBs 002 and 003, two and one respectively. These are included in Table 3. The clones are then incorporated into the network and the training data is presented again. Resources are allocated (Table 3) and this time the network has 21.999 resources, which is greater than the maximum number allocated. Therefore according to the resource allocation mechanism node 005, 004, Clone1, Clone2 and Clone3 are removed from the network. 003 has its number of resources reduced to 0.488 and the network now is significantly different to the original (Figure 4).

ID	d1	d1	s	n
001	0	0.1	1	10
002	0.1	0.1	0.709	5.027
003	0.5	0.6	0.663	4.4
004	0.6	0.5	0.065	0.043
Clone1	0.5	0.301	0	0
Clone2	0.1	0.469	0.475	2.257
Clone3	0.313	0.1	0.165	0.272

Table 3 Stimulation and Resources including the new clones.

Figure 4 Network after two iterations.

On the next iteration there are no clones produced and because normalisation allocates ARB 003 zero resources, it is removed from the network and only ARBs 002 and 001 are left. Therefore it can be seen that the resource allocation strategy combined with the mutation mechanism naturally favour the most stimulated ARBs and therefore the behaviour that is seen in this paper and in [25] can be considered to be accurate. This however does not detract from the overall goals of AINE, which is to produce a clear representation of the key features of a data set and the relationships between individual items.

4.2 Results

The re-implementation of AINE was again tested on the simulated data and Iris data set to allow for comparison with the previous work. This paper only presents the results from the Iris data, other results for the simulated data can be found in [25]. Figure 5 and Figure 6 show two points in the evolution of the network for the iris data set, using the aiVis tool [23]. It can be seen that after 3 iterations the three-cluster pattern indicative to the data is clearly visible. However it can be seen that between iterations three and 20 something significant happens to the network. After 20 iterations the setosa class has completely disappeared from the network and now only the virginica and versicolor remain. This pattern of degradation is corroborated by Figure 1. These results are completely new to those in previous work and highlight the changes in behaviour of the algorithm. It should be noted, that the point of stability can be considered to be a termination condition for the algorithm. Therefore, once this period has been reached, it can be said that AINE has found a good representation of the data. However, one benefit of the new approach over the original is that if learning were to continue, the network would tend towards a stronger pattern. This could be highly beneficial in the data mining process, as not only is it possible to identify general patterns in the data, but also the strongest. It should be noted that the initial network size is critical in the performance of the algorithm. In these tests 75 items were used in the initial population, testing has shown that initial networks of greater than 100 significantly reduce the efficiency of the algorithm. However the size of the training population can be varied without significant effect.

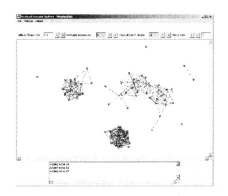

Figure 5 : Network after 3 iterations and the 1st point of stability (see Figure 18). Virginia; top-left, Versicolor; top-right, Setosa; bottom-middle.

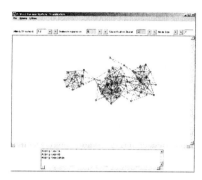

Figure 6 Network after 20 iterations. The Setosa class has completely disappeared from the network, and the Virginia and Versicolor classes are still connected.

It can be seen that the networks produced by AINE are significantly clearer in their topological structure and clearly show the relationships between each node in the network. Combined with the visualisation tool, exploration of these networks is made simpler and it takes less time to gain a good understanding of the structure present.

4.3 Learning using other techniques

As described in section 2.2 there are other techniques by which patterns can be learnt from data. In this section results are presented from two of those, Kohonen networks and simple cluster analysis. Figure 7 shows the results from analysis on the Iris data set using a Kohonen network (software obtained from [26]). It can be seen that the Kohonen has separated the Setosa class and some of the Virginia class but the area in the bottom right hand cluster contains clusters that include both the Virginia and Versicolor classes. The two main parameters, the learning rate and the neighbourhood function can be altered to help spread the clusters out, but do little to provide adequate separation of the clusters of both Virginia and Versicolor. It is also hard to gain any understanding between individual relationships between items in the data, information that can be extracted from AINE. The size of the grid is also an important parameter and increasing the number of rows and columns helps to produce more separation between individual classes, but this is at a cost. A larger grid size is more computationally expensive and also can produce too much separation in the data. Reducing the grid size has the opposite affect, computation is much quicker, but the results are more dense and difficult to interpret.

0	0	0	0	0
0	0	0	**21**	0
0	*22*	0	0	**6**
0	0	<u>18</u>	*10*	<u>23</u>
20	0	0	0	0

Figure 7 Result from a Kohonen net showing the iris data (Learning rate = 0.3; Neighbourhood function = 0.6; Epochs = 350).

Minimum distance clustering is the one of the other techniques described and this produces a dendrogram as shown in Figure 8. It can be clearly seen that there are two major clusters, one of which describes the Setosa class; the other is both Versicolor and Virginia. These two classes are eventually split, but that is after a number of reductions. Minimum distance clustering is capable of reducing the iris data set into its individual components but the results can be cluttered and confusing.

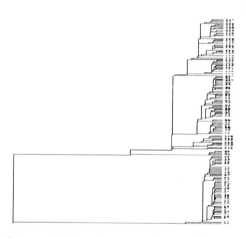

Figure 8 A Dendrogram from minimum distance clustering applied to the iris data set.

Further experiments were undertaken using the Wisconsin Breast Cancer Data set. This is a more complex data set in terms of size and dimensionality. The data itself was donated to the UCI repository [10] by Dr. William H. Wolberg from the University Of Wisconsin Hospitals, Madison [27]. There are 699 instances each with 11 numerical attributes (dimensions) two of which describe a unique patient identifier and a class type. There are two classes, benign and malignant, which have a distribution of 65.5% and 34.5% respectively. The 16 instances with null values were removed, as AINE at present does not handle null values. The raw data was divided into two sets, the initial set containing 76 instances and the training set containing 608 instances. AINE was run for 60 iterations.

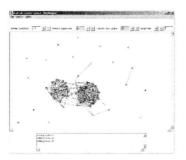

Figure 9 Network after 3 iterations. The large cluster in the middle represents the benign data and the single points represent the malignant data.

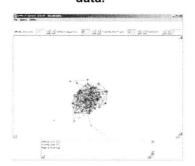

Figure 10 Network after 53 iterations and the malignant data items have been completely removed. Only the benign cluster remains

Figure 9 and Figure 10 show two visualisations of the output networks taken at periods of stability within the run. It is clear from the visualisations that AINE has been able to identify the pattern within the data. More interestingly is that it would appear that the benign data items are closer in data space than the malignant data items. There also exists the possibility of further investigating the reasons why ARBs are joined together. This information could potentially be useful for this example to enhance knowledge on breast cancer and what combinations of symptoms define benign or malignant cancer. These results are therefore potentially useful and could be used for classification either using aiVIS [23] as an exploratory tool on unseen data, or via the creation of a suitable rule set, using C4.5 [28]. Therefore it is reasonable to say that AINE is capable of analysing data of a higher dimensionality without significant cost to the algorithms ability to identify patterns. By measuring the time it takes for the algorithm to run it is possible to gain some idea of time complexity. The initial population for both data sets was 75 ARBs. For the Wisconsin breast cancer data the average time over five runs was 4.5 minutes for 100 iterations. The iris data set, using the same settings as for the cancer set took 30.35 seconds to execute 100 iterations, which is 9 times faster. Given that the breast cancer has a

training set of size 609 and the Iris set a training set of 75, which is 8 times larger it is possible to say that within a range of 0 – 1000 the algorithms time complexity is linear. The initial population size was 76 items because as mentioned in section 4.2 a population much larger than this would render the algorithm inefficient. This population contained the same proportions of benign and malignant ARBs sampled from the raw data set. The maximum number of resources used remained the same.

5 Conclusions

This work initial set out to apply work from [5] to a larger scale data mining problem domain. Before that was undertaken, corroboration of previous results were sought via the re-implementation of the algorithm and testing on benchmark data. Through this process a number of failings were identified with the original work and were corrected. The new version was then tested on a larger and more complex data set to understand issues surrounding the time complexity and pattern matching efficiency. The re-implementation of the work identified a different behavioural pattern not seen in the previous work that lead to a further investigation into the nature of the algorithm. The subsequent investigation discovered that the algorithm would naturally discover the strongest pattern within the data set that it was applied to. This new behaviour was deemed not to make a significant difference in the algorithms capability to discover patterns in data, but it is argued, enhances the usefulness of this algorithm.

This paper has argued that it is the combination of normalising the stimulation levels of ARBs in the network and the resource allocation mechanism that leads to this the biasing of AINE towards the strongest pattern in the data set to emerge. However, this is not considered to be a problem, in fact it can be considered to be an improvement on the original work. Tests have also shown that the algorithm performs well on larger and more complex data and has a linear time complexity for data sets within the range 0 – 1000 items in size. Foundations have now been laid for the application of this algorithm to larger scale, real world problems. This will inevitably result in the adaptation of the algorithm in certain areas, such as matching and mutation, but it is felt that the underlying model is now well-understood and suitable for adaptation.

6 Future Work

Now it is felt that the AINE model is well understood and problems ironed out, work can now proceed to a large scale problem domain. The initial idea was to use AINE for document classification, however focus has shifted to the application of large scale data mining on a corporate database provided by Sun© Microsystems . The data is time series event data on which it is hoped that event classification can be obtained using AINE.

Work is also being undertaken into the creation of a distributed version of this algorithm, which will help address some issues regarding scalability of the AINE algorithm to very large data sets.

7 Acknowledgements

The authors are grateful to Sun© Microsystems, USA for their continued sponsorship of Thomas Knight for his PhD studies.

8 References

[1] Y. Ishida, "Distributed and autonomous sensing based on the immune network," In Proceedings of Artificial Life and Robotics, Beppu, 1996.

[2] J. Kim and P. Bentley, "The human immune system and network intrusion detection.," In Proceedings of 7th European Congress on Intelligent Techniques - Soft Computing, Aachan, Germany, 1998.

[3] J. Timmis, M. Neal, and J. Hunt, "An Artificial Immune System for Data Analysis," *BioSystems*, vol. 55, pp. 143-150, 2000.

[4] T. Fukuda, K. Mori, and Tsukiyama, "Immune Networks using Genetic Algorithm for Adaptive Production Scheduling," In 15th IFAC World Congress, 1993.

[5] J. Timmis and M. Neal, "A resource limited artificial immune system for data analysis," *Knowledge Based Systems*, vol. 14(3-4), pp. 121-130, June 2001.

[6] J. Timmis, "Artificial immune systems: A novel data analysis technique inspired by the immune network theory," Department of Computer Science, University of Wales, Aberystwyth, Ceredigion. Wales, PhD Thesis, August 2000.

[7] R. A. Fisher, "The use of multiple measurements in taxonomic problems," *Annual Eugenics*, vol. 7, pp. 179-188, 1936.

[8] T. Kohonen, *Self-organising Maps*, 3rd Edition ed: Springer-Verlag Berlin and Heidelberg GmbH & Co, 2000.

[9] B. Everitt, *Cluster analysis*: Heinemann, 1974.

[10] C. L. Blake and C. J. Merz, "UCI Repository of machine learning databases," 1998.

[11] S. Forrest, S. A. Hofmeyr, and A. Somayaii, "Computer Immunology," *Communications of the ACM*, pp. 88-96,1996.

[12] G. J. V. Nossal, "Life, Death and the Immune System," in *Life, Death and the Immune System*: Scientific American Special Issue. W.H. Freeman and Company. NY, 1994.

[13] N. K. Jerne, "Towards a Network theory of the Immune System," *Annals of Immunology*, vol. 125C, pp. 373-389, 1974.

[14] A. Perelson, "Immune Network Theory," *Immunological review*, vol. 110, pp. 5-36, 1989.

[15] J. Timmis and T. Knight, "Artificial Immune Systems: Using the Immune System as Inspiration for Data Mining.," in *Data Mining: A Heuristic Approach*, R. A.

S. Hussein A. Abbass, and Charles S. Newton, Ed.: Idea Group Publishing, 2001, pp. 209-320.

[16] L. N. deCastro and F. J. Von_Zuben, "An Evolutionary Immune Network for Data Clustering," *Proceedings of the IEEE Computer Society Press, SBRN'00*, vol. 1, pp. 84-89, 2000.

[17] D. Hand, "Introduction to Intelligent Data Analysis," in *Intelligent Data Analysis*: Springer-Verlag, 1999, pp. 1-14.

[18] J. Hunt, C. King, and D. Cooke, "Immunising against fraud," *Proc. Knowledge Discovery and Data Mining. IEE Colloquim.IEE*, pp. 38-45, 1996.

[19] J. E. Hunt and A. Fellows, "Introducing an Immune response into a CBR system for Data Mining," *In BCS ESG'96 Conference and published in Research and Development in Expert Systems XIII*, 1996.

[20] D. E. Cooke and J. E. Hunt, *Recognising promoter sequences using an Artificial Immune System*: AAAI Press, 1995.

[21] J. E. Hunt and D. E. Cooke, "Learning using an artificial immune system," *Journal of Network and Computer Applications*, vol. 19, pp. 189-212, 1996.

[22] J. H. Carter, "The Immune System as a model for Pattern Recognition and Classification," *Journal of the American medical Informatics Association*, vol. 7, 28-41, 2000.

[23] J. Timmis, "aivis - artificial immune network visualisation," In Eurographics UK 2001 Conference Proceedings, University College London, pp. 61-69 April 2001. Eurographics.

[24] J. Timmis, "On parameter adjustment of the immune inspired machine learning algorithm AINE," Computing Laboratory, University of Kent at Canterbury, Canterbury Technical Report 12-00, 2000.

[25] T. Knight and J. Timmis, "Assessing the performance of the resource limited artificial immune system AINE," Computing Laboratory, University of Kent at Canterbury, UK Technical Report 3-01, 2001.

[26] neusciences, "aix Encoder," *http://www.neusciences.com/*, 2000.

[27] O. L. Mangasarian and W. H. Wolberg, "Cancer diagnosis via linear programming," *SIAM News*, vol. 23, pp. 1 & 18, 1990.

[28] J. R. Quinlan, *C4.5: Programs for Machine Learning*. San Mateo, CA: Morgan Kaufmann, 1993.

Concise Representation of Frequent Patterns based on Disjunction-free Generators

Marzena Kryszkiewicz
Institute of Computer Science
Warsaw University of Technology
Nowowiejska 15/19, 00-665 Warsaw, Poland
mkr@ii.pw.edu.pl

Abstract

Many data mining problems require the discovery of frequent patterns in order to be solved. Frequent itemsets are useful in the discovery of association rules, episode rules, sequential patterns and clusters. The number of frequent itemsets is usually huge. Therefore, it is important to work out concise representations of frequent itemsets. In the paper, we describe three basic lossless representations of frequent patterns in an uniform way and offer a new lossless representation of frequent patterns based on disjunction-free generators. The new representation is more concise than two of the basic representations and more efficiently computable than the third representation. We propose an algorithm for determining the new representation.

1. Introduction

Many data mining problems require the discovery of frequent patterns in order to be solved. Frequent itemsets are useful in the discovery of association rules, episode rules, sequential patterns and clusters etc. (see [6] for overview). Nevertheless, the number of frequent itemsets is usually huge. Therefore, it is important to work out concise, preferably lossless, representations of frequent itemsets. Recently, there have been investigated the following interesting subsets of frequent itemsets: closed itemsets (see e.g. [2,8-9]), generators (see e.g. [2,8]), and the representation based on disjunction-free sets [5]. Both frequent closed itemsets and the disjunction-free sets representation are lossless representations in the sense that they allow derivation and support determination of all frequent itemsets without accessing the database. The frequent generators themselves do not possess this property unless augmented by the set of minimal

infrequent generators. Applications of frequent closed itemsets and frequent generators have been demonstrated in the case of the discovery of association rules and their essential subsets (see e.g. [7-8,10-11]). In particular, in the case of representative association rules [7] and informative basis [8], the antecedent of any such rule is a generator, while the consequent is a closed itemset decreased by the items present in the rule's antecedent.

In this paper, we introduce yet another lossless representation of frequent itemsets that benefits both from the properties of generators and disjunction-free sets. We prove that the new representation constitutes a subset of the generators representation and the disjunction-free sets representation. On the other hand, the frequent closed itemsets representation may happen to be either more concise or less concise depending on particular data. Conciseness of the frequent closed itemsets representation has been proved experimentally (see e.g. [11]). The algorithms for computing this representation require the discovery of frequent generators first (see e.g. [2,8-9]). In [2,8], generators are treated as seeds of closed itemsets that are determined by intersecting database transactions. This makes the discovery of frequent closed itemsets inefficient. To the contrary, the new representation does not require such a computational overhead. In the paper, we propose an algorithm for determining the new representation.

The layout of the paper is as follows:

Section 2 introduces the notions and properties of frequent itemsets, closed itemsets and generators, as well as the representations based on closed itemsets, on generators, and on disjunction-free sets. In Section 3 we introduce the new representation based on disjunction-free generators and prove that all frequent itemsets and their supports can be derived from it. In Section 4 we prove that the new representation is not less concise than the ones based on generators and on disjunction-free sets. An algorithm for determining the new representation is presented in Section 5. Section 6 concludes the results.

2. Basic notions and properties

2.1. Itemsets, frequent itemsets

Let $I = \{i_1, i_2, ..., i_m\}$, $I \neq \emptyset$, be a set of distinct literals, called *items*. In the case of a transactional database, a notion of an item corresponds to a sold product, while in the case of a relational database an item will be an (*attribute,value*) pair. Any non-empty set of items is called an *itemset*. An itemset consisting of k items will be called *k-itemset*. Let D be a set of transactions (or tuples, respectively), where each transaction (tuple) T is a subset of I. (Without any loss of generality, we will restrict further considerations to transactional databases.) By I_D we will denote a subset of items in I that occurred in D at least once. *Support* of an itemset X is denoted by $sup(X)$ and defined as the number of transactions in D that contain X. The itemset X is called *frequent* if its support is greater than some user-defined threshold *minSup*. The set of all frequent itemsets will be denoted by F:

$$F = \{X \subseteq I \mid sup(X) > minSup\}.$$

Property 2.1.1 [1].
a) Let $X,Y \subseteq I$. If $X \subset Y$, then $sup(X) \geq sup(Y)$.
b) If $X \in F$, then $\forall Y \subset X$, $Y \in F$.

Property 2.1.2. Let $X,Y,V \subseteq I$. If $X \subset Y$ and $sup(X) = sup(Y)$, then $sup(X \cup V) = sup(Y \cup V)$.

2.2. Closures, closed itemsets and generators

Closure of an itemset X is denoted by $\gamma(X)$ and is defined as the greatest (w.r.t. set inclusion) itemset that occurs in all transactions in D in which X occurs.

Property 2.2.1. Let $X \subseteq I$.
a) $sup(\gamma(X)) = sup(X)$.
b) $\forall Y \subseteq I$, if $X \subset Y \subseteq \gamma(X)$, then $sup(Y) = sup(X)$.
Proof: Ad. a) Immediate by definition of a closure.
Ad. b). By Prop. 2.1.1a, $sup(X) \geq sup(Y) \geq sup(\gamma(X))$ and by Prop. 2.2.1a, $sup(\gamma(X)) = sup(X)$. Thus, $sup(Y) = sup(X)$. □

The itemset X is defined *closed* iff $\gamma(X) = X$. The set of all closed itemsets will be denoted by C, i.e.

$$C = \{X \subseteq I \mid \gamma(X) = X\}.$$

Let X be a closed itemset. A minimal itemset Y satisfying $\gamma(Y) = X$ is called a *generator* of X. By $G(X)$ we will denote the set of all generators of X. The union of generators of all closed itemsets will be denoted by G, i.e.

$$G = \cup \{G(X) \mid X \in C\}.$$

Example 2.2.1. Let D be the database from Table 1. The itemset $\{A,B,C,D,E\}$ is closed since $\gamma(\{A,B,C,D,E\}) =$

$\{A,B,C,D,E\}$. The itemsets $\{A,B,C\}$ and $\{A,B,C,D\}$ are not closed because $\gamma(\{A,B,C\}) = \{A,B,C,D,E\} \neq \{A,B,C\}$ and $\gamma(\{A,B,C,D\}) = \{A,B,C,D,E\} \neq \{A,B,C,D\}$, respectively. The support of $\{A,B,C\}$ and $\{A,B,C,D\}$ is the same as the support of their closure $\{A,B,C,D,E\}$, and is equal to 3. $\{A,B,C\}$ is a minimal subset the closure of which equals to $\{A,B,C,D,E\}$. Hence, $\{A,B,C\} \in G(\{A,B,C,D,E\})$. □

Id	Transaction
T_1	$\{A,B,C,D,E,G\}$
T_2	$\{A,B,C,D,E,F\}$
T_3	$\{A,B,C,D,E,H,I\}$,
T_4	$\{A,B,D,E\}$
T_5	$\{A,C,D,E,H,I\}$
T_6	$\{B,C,E\}$

Table 1. Example database D.

Property 2.2.2 [8]. Let $X \subseteq I$.

$$\gamma(X) = \cap\{T \in D \mid T \supseteq X\} = \cap\{Y \subseteq I \mid Y \in C \wedge Y \supseteq X\}.$$

Property 2.2.2 states that the closure of an itemset X can be computed: 1) as the intersection of the transactions in D that are supersets of X, or 2) as the intersection of the closed itemsets that are supersets of X.

Property 2.2.3 [2]. Let $X \subseteq I$.
$X \in G$ iff $sup(X) \neq \min\{sup(X \setminus \{A\}) \mid A \in X\}$.

Property 2.2.4. Let $X \subseteq I$. $X \in G$ iff $\forall Y \subset X$, $sup(X) \neq sup(Y)$.
Proof: By Property 2.2.3 and Property 2.1.1a. □

Lemma 2.2.1. Let $X,Y \subseteq I$. If $X \subset Y \subseteq \gamma(X)$ then $\forall Z \supseteq Y$, $Z \notin G$.
Proof (By contradiction): Let $X \subset Y \subseteq \gamma(X)$ and $Z \in G$, $Z = Y \cup V$, $Y \cap V = \emptyset$. Since $X \subset Y \subseteq \gamma(X)$, then $sup(Y) = sup(X)$ (by Property 2.2.1b) and $sup(Z) = sup(Y \cup V) = sup(X \cup V)$ (by Property 2.1.2). Hence, $X \cup V$, which is a proper subset of $Z = Y \cup V$, has the same support as Z. Then by Property 2.2.4, $Z \notin G$, which contradicts the assumption. □

Lemma 2.2.2. If $X \subset Y$ and $sup(Y) = sup(X)$, then $\gamma(Y) = \gamma(X)$.
Proof: Let $X \subset Y$ and $sup(Y) = sup(X)$. Then, the set of transactions in D in which X occurs, say D', equals to the set of transactions in which Y occurs. Thus, by definition of a closure, $\gamma(X)$ as well as $\gamma(Y)$ are the greatest itemset that occurs in all transactions in D'. Hence, $\gamma(Y) = \gamma(X)$. □

Theorem 2.2.1. Let $X \subseteq I$. If $X \in G$, then $\forall Y \subset X$, $Y \in G$.
Proof: (By contradiction): Let $X \in G$ and $Y \subset X$ such that $Y \notin G$. Then, by Property 2.2.4 there is some $Z \subset Y$ such that $sup(Z) = sup(Y)$. Hence, by Lemma 2.2.2, $\gamma(Z) = \gamma(Y)$ and thus $Z \subset Y \subseteq \gamma(Y) = \gamma(Z)$. By Lemma 2.2.1, we conclude that X, which is a superset of Y, is not a generator. This conclusion contradicts the assumption. □

Theorem 2.2.1 states that subsets of generators are generators (a different proof was provided in [2]).

Property 2.2.5. Let $X \subseteq I$.

a) $sup(X) = \max\{sup(Y)| \ Y \in C \wedge Y \supseteq X\}$.

b) $sup(X) = \min\{sup(Y)| \ Y \in G \wedge Y \subseteq X\}$.

Proof: Ad. a). Let $Z = \gamma(X)$. Then, $Z \supseteq X$ and $Z \in C$. Thus, $sup(X) = sup(Z)$ (by Prop. 2.2.1a) and $sup(X) \geq sup(Y)$ for every $Y \in C$ such that $Y \supseteq X$ (by Prop. 2.1.1a). Therefore, $sup(X) = \max\{sup(Y)| \ Y \in C \wedge Y \supseteq X\}$.

Ad. b). Let $Z \subseteq X$ such that $Z \in G(\gamma(X))$. Then, $Z \in G$ and $Z \subseteq X \subseteq \gamma(X) = \gamma(Z)$. Thus, $sup(X) = sup(Z)$ (by Prop. 2.2.1b) and $sup(X) \leq sup(Y)$ for every $Y \in G$, $Y \subseteq X$ (by Prop. 2.1.1a). Therefore, $sup(X) = \min\{sup(Y)| \ Y \in G \wedge Y \subseteq X\}$. □

Hence, in order to compute support of any itemset it is sufficient to know either supports of all closed itemsets or supports of all generators.

2.3. Closed itemsets representation

Most research on concise representations of frequent itemsets was devoted to closed itemsets. Here we will present this representation.

An itemset X is defined to be *frequent closed* iff X is closed and frequent. In the sequel, the set of all frequent closed itemsets will be denoted by FC, i.e.

$$FC = F \cap C.$$

Closed itemsets representation is defined as the set FC enriched by the information on support for each $X \in FC$.

The property below is an immediate consequence of Property 2.2.5a and shows how to determine if an itemset is frequent and if so, how to determine its support based on the closed itemsets representation.

Property 2.3.1. Let $X \subseteq I$.

- If there is $Z \in FC$, such that $Z \supseteq X$, then $X \in F$ and $sup(X) = \max(\{sup(Y)| \ Y \in FC \wedge Y \supseteq X\})$.
- Otherwise, $X \notin F$.

2.4. Generators representation

Generators are commonly used as an intermediate step for the discovery of closed itemsets. However, the generators themselves can constitute a concise lossless representation of frequent itemsets. Below we introduce such a generators representation:

Frequent generators, denoted by FG, are defined as:

$$FG = F \cap G.$$

Negative generators border, denoted by GBd^-, is defined as follows:

$$GBd^- = \{X \in G| \ X \notin F \wedge (\forall Y \subset X, Y \in FG)\}.$$

GBd^- consists of all minimal (w.r.t. set inclusion) infrequent generators.

Generators representation is defined as:

- the set FG enriched by the information on support for each $X \in FG$,
- the border set GBd^-,
- the set I_D of items that occurred in D.

It can be proved that the generators representation as introduced here is equivalent to the approximate δ-free sets representation [3-4] for $\delta = 0$, in which case the approximate representation becomes lossless.

The property below is an immediate consequence of Property 2.2.5b and shows how to determine if an itemset is frequent and if so, how to determine its support based on the generators representation.

Property 2.4.1. Let $X \subseteq I$.

- If $\neg(X \subseteq I_D)$ or $(\exists Z \in GBd^-, Z \subseteq X)$, then $X \notin F$.
- Otherwise, $X \in F$ and $sup(X) = \min(\{sup(Y)| \ Y \in FG \wedge Y \subseteq X\})$.

2.5. Disjunction-free sets representation

The notion of *disjunction-free sets* was introduced in [5]. Let us present this concept by means of an auxiliary notion called a *2-disjunctive rule*.

$X \Rightarrow A_1 \vee A_2$ is defined a *2-disjunctive rule* if $X \subseteq I$, $A_1, A_2 \in I$, $X \cap \{A_1, A_2\} = \varnothing$. Observe, that a 2-disjunctive rule $X \Rightarrow A_1 \vee A_2$ can have an empty antecedent ($X = \varnothing$) and its consequents can be equal ($A_1 = A_2$).

Support of $X \Rightarrow A_1 \vee A_2$, denoted by $sup(X \Rightarrow A_1 \vee A_2)$, is defined as the number of transactions in D in which X occurs together with A_1 or A_2, that is:

$$sup(X \Rightarrow A_1 \vee A_2) = sup(X \cup \{A_1\}) + sup(X \cup \{A_2\}) - sup(X \cup \{A_1, A_2\}).$$

Confidence of the rule $X \Rightarrow A_1 \vee A_2$, denoted by $conf(X \Rightarrow A_1 \vee A_2)$, is defined as follows:

$$conf(X \Rightarrow A_1 \vee A_2) = sup(X \Rightarrow A_1 \vee A_2)/sup(X).$$

$X \Rightarrow A_1 \vee A_2$ is defined a *certain rule* if $conf(X \Rightarrow A_1 \vee Y_2) = 1$. Thus, $X \Rightarrow A_1 \vee A_2$ is certain if each transaction containing X contains also A_1 or A_2.

Example 2.5.1. Let us consider the database D from Table 1. To make the notation brief, we will write itemsets without brackets and commas (e.g. AC instead of $\{A, C\}$).

Let us consider the 2-disjunctive rule $\varnothing \Rightarrow A \vee A$. The rule is not certain since there is a transaction (T_6) that contains $\varnothing$, and does not contain A. On the other hand, $\varnothing \Rightarrow A \vee C$ is a certain rule as each transaction in D contains A or C. Similarly, $C \Rightarrow D \vee E$ is a certain rule since each transaction containing C contains also D or E. □

Property 2.5.1 [5]. $X \Rightarrow A_1 \vee A_2$ is certain iff $sup(X) = sup(X \cup \{A_1\}) + sup(X \cup \{A_2\}) - sup(X \cup \{A_1, A_2\})$.

Property 2.5.2 [5]. If $X \Rightarrow A_1 \vee A_2$ is certain, then $\forall Z \supset X$, $Z \Rightarrow A_1 \vee A_2$ is also certain.

Example 2.5.2. Let us consider the database D from Table 1. The rule $C \Rightarrow D \vee E$ is certain, thus $AC \Rightarrow D \vee E$ and $ABC \Rightarrow D \vee E$ (and so forth) are also certain rules. □

An itemset X is defined *disjunctive* iff there are $A,B \in X$ such that $X \setminus \{A,B\} \Rightarrow A \vee B$ is a certain rule. Otherwise, the itemset is called *disjunction-free[1]*. The set of all disjunction-free sets will be denoted by *DFree*.

Example 2.5.3. Let us consider the database D from Table 1 and the itemset *DE*. The only 2-disjunctive rules involving all items in *DE* are: $\varnothing \Rightarrow D \vee E$, $D \Rightarrow E \vee E$, $E \Rightarrow D \vee D$. The rule $E \Rightarrow D \vee D$ is not certain, however $\varnothing \Rightarrow D \vee E$ and $D \Rightarrow E \vee E$ are certain, thus *DE* is a disjunctive set (i.e. $DE \notin DFree$). Now, since $\varnothing \Rightarrow D \vee E$ is certain in D, then by Property 2.5.2, $A \Rightarrow D \vee E$ is also certain. Hence $ADE \notin DFree$. Similarly, we can conclude $ACDE \notin DFree$ (and so forth). The property below generalizes this observation. □

Property 2.5.3 [5].
a) If $X \notin DFree$, then $\forall Y \supset X$, $Y \notin DFree$.
b) If $X \in DFree$, then $\forall Y \subset X$, $Y \in DFree$.

Frequent disjunction-free itemsets, denoted by *FDFree*, are defined as:

$$FDFree = DFree \cap F.$$

Negative border of FDFree is denoted by $DFreeBd^-$ and defined as:

$$DFreeBd^- = \{X \subseteq I \mid X \notin FDFree \wedge (\forall Y \subset X, Y \in FDFree)\}.$$

Disjunction-free sets representation is defined as:
- the set *FDFree* enriched by the information on support for each $X \in FDFree$,
- the border set $DFreeBd^-$ enriched by the information on support for each $X \in DFreeBd^-$,
- the set I_D of items that occurred in D.

The disjunction-free sets representation is sufficient to determine all frequent itemsets and their supports [5].

3. New representation of frequent itemsets based on disjunction-free generators

In this section we will introduce a new representation of frequent itemsets based on frequent generators that are disjunction-free sets. We will prove that the new representation is sufficient to derive all frequent itemsets.

Disjunction-free generators, denoted by *DFreeG*, are

defined as follows:

$$DFreeG = DFree \cap G.$$

Property 3.1. If $X \in DFreeG$, then $\forall Y \subset X$, $Y \in DFreeG$.
Proof: By Theorem 2.2.1 and Property 2.5.3b. □

Frequent disjunction-free generators, denoted by *FDFreeG*, are defined as:

$$FDFreeG = DFree \cap F \cap G.$$

Property 3.2. If $X \in FDFreeG$, then $\forall Y \subset X$, $Y \in FDFreeG$.
Proof: By Property 2.1.1b and Property 3.1. □

Negative infrequent generators border, denoted by $IDFreeGBd^-$, is defined as follows:

$$IDFreeGBd^- = \{X \in G \mid X \notin F \wedge (\forall Y \subset X, Y \in FDFreeG)\}.$$

$IDFreeGBd^-$ consists of all minimal (w.r.t. set inclusion) infrequent generators the subsets of which are disjunction-free generators.

Negative frequent generators border, denoted by $FDFreeGBd^-$, is defined as:

$$FDFreeGBd^- = \{X \in G \mid X \in F \wedge X \notin DFreeG \wedge (\forall Y \subset X, Y \in FDFreeG)\}.$$

$DFreeGBd^-$ consists of all minimal (w.r.t. set inclusion) frequent disjunctive generators.

Let us note that $IDFreeGBd^- \cap FDFreeGBd^- = \varnothing$.

Disjunction-free generators representation is defined as:
- the set *FDFreeG* enriched by the information on support for each $X \in FDFreeG$,
- the border set $FDFreeGBd^-$ enriched by the information on support for each $X \in FDFreeGBd^-$,
- the border set $IDFreeGBd^-$,
- the set I_D of items that occurred in D.

Theorem 3.1. The disjunction-free generators representation is sufficient to determine for any itemset if it is frequent and if so, to determine its support.
Proof (constructive): Any itemset X that is not a subset of I_D is infrequent. In the sequel of the proof, we assume $X \subseteq I_D$. The proof will be made by induction on $|X|$.
Induction hypothesis. For every itemset $V \subset X$, we can determine if it is frequent or not, and if V is frequent then we can determine its support.

One can distinguish the following five cases:
- If $X \in FDFreeG$, then $X \in F$ and $sup(X)$ is known.
- If $X \in FDFreeGBd^-$ then $X \in F$ and $sup(X)$ is known.
- If $\exists Y \in IDFreeGBd^-$, $Y \subseteq X$, then $X \notin F$.
- If $\neg \exists Z \in IDFreeGBd^-$, $Z \subset X$, and $\exists Y \in FDFreeGBd^-$, $Y \subset X$, then X is a disjunctive set as a superset of some disjunctive itemset in $FDFreeGBd^-$ (by Property 2.5.3a). Let $Y \in FDFreeGBd^-$ and $Y \subset X$. Hence, there are some items $A,B \in Y$ such that the

---
[1] For the original definition of a disjunction-free set see [5]. Based on Lemma 3 in [5], we propose an equivalent definition that is more suitable for further presentation.

rule $Y\backslash\{A,B\}\Rightarrow A\vee B$ is certain. Let A and B be such items. Then, by Property 2.5.2, $X\backslash\{A,B\}\Rightarrow A\vee B$ is also certain and $sup(X)=sup(X\backslash\{A\})+sup(X\backslash\{B\})-sup(X\backslash\{A,B\})$. By induction hypothesis, we can determine if $X\backslash\{A\}$, $X\backslash\{B\}$, and $X\backslash\{A,B\}$ are frequent, and if so, we can determine their supports. If any of these itemsets is not frequent, then $X\notin F$. Now, if all the three itemsets are frequent, then $sup(X)$ can be determined according to the formula above. If $sup(X)>minSup$, then $X\in F$; otherwise $X\notin F$.

- Let $X\notin FDFreeG$ and $\neg\exists Z\in FDFreeGBd^-\cup IDFreeGBd^-$, $Z\subseteq X$. Then no generator being a subset of X is a superset of any $Z\in FDFreeGBd^-\cup IDFreeGBd^-$. Hence, all generators being subsets of X are contained in $FDFreeG$. By Property 2.2.5b, $sup(X)=min(\{sup(Y)|\ Y\in G\ \wedge\ Y\subseteq X\})$. In our case, this equation is equivalent to: $sup(X)=min(\{sup(Y)|\ Y\in FDFreeG\ \wedge\ Y\subseteq X\})$. Clearly, $X\in F$ as $sup(X)$ is equal to the support of some frequent disjunction-free generator. $\square$

The proof of Theorem 3.1 can be treated as a naive algorithm for determining frequent itemsets and their supports.

Example 3.1. Given $minSup=1$, the following disjunction-free generators representation will be discovered in the database D from Table 1 (The information on supports of the itemsets is provided in the form of a subscript.):

- $FDFreeG = \{\varnothing_6, A_5, B_5, C_5, D_5, H_2, I_2\}$,
- $FDFreeGBd^- = \{AB_4, AC_4, BC_4, BD_4, CD_4\}$,
- $IDFreeGBd^- = \{F, G, BH, BI\}$,
- $I_D = ABCDEFGHI$.

Thus, the disjunction-free generators representation consists of 17 itemsets. Below we illustrate how to use this representation for evaluating the itemsets: $ACDF$ and ACD.

- The itemset $ACDF$ is infrequent, as it is a superset of the itemset F in $IDFreeGBd^-$;
- The itemset ACD is a superset of $AC\in FDFreeGBd^-$, so ACD is disjunctive. The following 2-disjunctive rule is certain for AC: $\varnothing\Rightarrow A\vee C$. Hence, $D\Rightarrow A\vee C$ is a certain 2-disjunctive rule for ACD. Thus, $sup(ACD)=sup(AD)+sup(CD)-sup(D)=sup(AD)+4-5$. We note that $AD\notin FDFreeG$ and there is no subset of AD in the border $FDFreeGBd^-\cup IDFreeGBd^-$. Hence, $sup(AD)=min(\{sup(Y)|\ Y\in FDFreeG\ \wedge\ Y\subseteq AD\})=min\{sup(\varnothing),sup(A),sup(D)\}=5$. Finally, $sup(ACD)=5+4-5=4$. $\square$

In the disjunction-free generators representation all infrequent items are kept in $IDFreeGBd^-$. An alternative more concise representation of frequent itemsets will not contain this information. Below, we specify such a *reduced disjunction-free generators representation*:

- $FDFreeG' = FDFreeG$,
- $FDFreeGBd^{-} = FDFreeGBd^-$,
- $IDFreeGBd^{-} = IDFreeGBd^- \setminus \{\{A\}|\ A\in I_D\ \wedge\ \{A\}\notin F\}$,
- $I_D' = I_D \setminus \{A\in I_D|\ \{A\}\notin F\}$.

We observe that only $IDFreeGBd^-$ and I_D are reduced in this representation. The reduced disjunction-free generators representation can be used for retrieving frequent itemsets the same way as the original one.

Example 3.2. Given $minSup=1$, the following reduced disjunction-free generators representation will be obtained for the database D from Table 1:

- $FDFreeG' = \{\varnothing_6, A_5, B_5, C_5, D_5, H_2, I_2\}$,
- $FDFreeGBd^{-} = \{AB_4, AC_4, BC_4, BD_4, CD_4\}$,
- $IDFreeGBd^{-} = \{BH, BI\}$,
- $I_D' = ABCDEHI$.

Let us note that the infrequent items F and G do not occur in the reduced representation. $\square$

4. Disjunction-free generators versus generators and disjunction-free sets

In this section we investigate the relationship between generators and disjunction-free sets and compare the disjunction-free generators representation with the generators and the disjunction-free sets representations.

Theorem 4.1. Let $X\subseteq I$.
a) If $X\notin G$, then $X\notin DFree$.
b) If $X\in DFree$, then $X\in G$.
c) $DFreeG = DFree$.

Proof: Ad. a) If $X\notin G$, then $\exists A\in X$, $sup(X\backslash\{A\})=sup(X)$ (by Property 2.2.3). Thus $X\backslash\{A\}\Rightarrow A\vee A$ is a certain disjunctive rule. So, $X\notin DisFree$.

Ad. b) By Theorem 4.1a: $X\notin G$ implies $X\notin DisFree$. Now, $X\notin G$ implies $X\notin DisFree$ iff $\neg X\notin G\vee X\notin DisFree$ iff $\neg X\in DisFree\vee X\in G$ iff $X\in DisFree$ implies $X\in G$.

Ad. c) Follows immediately from Theorem 4.1b. $\square$

Theorem 4.1 states an interesting fact that each disjunction-free set is a generator. The proposition below compares the disjunction-free generators representation with the generators representation.

Proposition 4.1.
a) $FDFreeG \cup FDFreeGBd^- \subseteq FG$,
b) $IDFreeGBd^- \subseteq GBd^-$,
c) $FDFreeG \cup FDFreeGBd^- \cup IDFreeGBd^- \cup \{I_D\} \subseteq FG \cup GBd^- \cup \{I_D\}$.

Proof: By definitions of the disjunction-free generators representation and the generators representation. $\square$

It follows from Proposition 4.1 that the disjunction-free generators representation constitutes a subset of the generators representation.

Example 4.1. Let us assume $minSup=1$. The following generators representation will be discovered in the database D from Table 1:

- $FG = \{\varnothing_6, A_5, B_5, C_5, D_5, H_2, I_2, AB_4, AC_4, BC_4, BD_4, CD_4, \underline{ABC}_3, \underline{BCD}_3\}$,
- $GBd^- = \{F, G, BH, BI\}$,
- $I_D = ABCDEFGHI$.

The generators representation consists of 19 itemsets. In comparison with the disjunction-free generators representation (see Example 3.1), the generators representation contains 2 more itemsets (the underlined ones). □

In order to compare the new representation with the disjunction-free sets one, below we specify properties of sets characteristic for these representations.

Lemma 4.1.
a) $IDFreeGBd^- = \{X\in G|\ X\notin F \wedge (\forall Y\subset X,\ Y\in FDFree)\}$,
b) $FDFreeGBd^- = \{X\in G|\ X\in F \wedge X\notin DFree \wedge (\forall Y\subset X, Y\in FDFree)\}$,
c) $DFreeBd^- \backslash F = \{X\subseteq I|\ X\notin F \wedge (\forall Y\subset X,\ Y\in FDFree)\}$,
d) $DFreeBd^- \cap F = \{X\subseteq I|\ X\in F \wedge X\notin DFree \wedge (\forall Y\subset X, Y\in FDFree)\}$.

Proof: Ad. a) By Theorem 2.2.1, if an itemset X is a generator, then all its subsets are generators. Thus, $\{X\in G|\ X\notin F \wedge (\forall Y\subset X,\ Y\in FDFree)\} =$ $\{X\in G|\ X\notin F \wedge (\forall Y\subset X,\ Y\in FDFreeG)\} = IDFreeGBd^-$.
Ad. b) Similar to that for the case a).
Ad. c, d) Immediate by definition of $DFreeBd^-$. □

Now, we are able to compare both representations:

Proposition 4.2.
a) $FDFreeG = FDFree$,
b) $FDFreeGBd^- \subseteq DFreeBd^- \cap F$,
c) $IDFreeGBd^- = DFreeBd^- \backslash F$,
d) $FDFreeG \cup FDFreeGBd^- \cup IDFreeGBd^- \cup\{I_D\} \subseteq FDFree \cup DFreeBd^- \cup \{I_D\}$.

Proof: Ad. a) Follows immediately from Theorem 4.1c.
Ad. b) Immediate from Lemma 4.1b, d.
Ad. c) We will prove that $IDFreeGBd^- = DFreeBd^-\backslash F$ by showing the equivalence of the following sets $\{X\in G|\ X\notin F \wedge (\forall Y\subset X,\ Y\in FDFree)\}$ and $\{X\subseteq I|\ X\notin F \wedge (\forall Y\subset X,\ Y\in FDFree)\}$ that are equal to $IDFreeGBd^-$ and $DFreeBd^-\backslash F$, respectively (by Lemma 4.1a,c).

Let X be an infrequent itemset whose all proper subsets are frequent. Then, $\forall Y\subset X,\ sup(Y)>sup(X)$. By Property 2.2.4, each such itemset X is a generator.

The set $\{X\subseteq I|\ X\notin F \wedge (\forall Y\subset X,\ Y\in FDFree)\}$ consists of infrequent itemsets whose proper subsets are frequent. Thus, each itemset in $\{X\subseteq I|\ X\notin F \wedge (\forall Y\subset X,\ Y\in FDFree)\}$

is a generator. Hence, $\{X\subseteq I|\ X\notin F \wedge (\forall Y\subset X,\ Y\in FDFree)\}$ $=\{X\in G|\ X\notin F \wedge (\forall Y\subset X,\ Y\in FDFree)\}$.
Ad. d) Immediate from Proposition 4.2a-c. □

As follows from Proposition 4.2, the disjunction-free generators representation constitutes a subset of the disjunction-free sets representation. Surprisingly, the both representations differ solely on the parts of the respective negative borders that contain frequent itemsets.

Example 4.2. Let us assume $minSup=1$. The following disjunction-free sets representation will be discovered in the database D from Table 1:

- $FG = \{\varnothing_6, A_5, B_5, C_5, D_5, H_2, I_2\}$,
- $DFreeBd^- \cap F = \{\underline{E}_6, AB_4, AC_4, \underline{AD}_5, \underline{AH}_2, \underline{AI}_2, BC_4, BD_4, CD_4, \underline{CH}_2, \underline{CI}_2, \underline{DH}_2, \underline{DI}_2, \underline{HI}_2\}$,
- $DFreeBd^- \backslash F = \{F, G, BH, BI\}$,
- $I_D = ABCDEFGHI$.

The disjunction-free sets representation consists of 26 itemsets. In comparison with the disjunction-free generators representation (see Example 3.1), the disjunction-free generators representation contains 9 more itemsets (the underlined ones). In accordance with Proposition 4.2, all the redundant itemsets belong to $DFreeBd^- \cap F$. □

5. Computing disjunction-free generators representation

5.1. Algorithmic properties of disjunction-free generators representation

In this subsection, we provide properties that will be used in the algorithm determining the disjunction-free generators representation.

Lemma 5.1.1. Let $X\subseteq I$. The following statements are equivalent.
- $\exists A\in X$ such that $X\backslash\{A\}\Rightarrow A\vee A$ is a certain rule.
- $\exists A\in X$ such that $sup(X) = sup(X\backslash\{A\})$.
- $X\notin G$.

Proof: $\exists A\in X$ such that $X\backslash\{A\}\Rightarrow A\vee A$ is a certain rule iff $sup(X)=sup(X\backslash\{A\})+sup(X\backslash\{A\})-sup(X\backslash\{A,A\})$ iff $sup(X)=sup(X\backslash\{A\})$ iff $X\notin G$ (by Property 2.2.3). □

Lemma 5.1.2.
a) $\varnothing\in DFree$.
b) $\varnothing\in G$.
c) Let $A\in I$. $\{A\}\in DFree$ iff $\{A\}\in G$.

Proof: Ad. a) There is no 2-disjunctive rule involving only $\varnothing$ and no more items. Hence, $X\in DFree$.
Ad. b) Immediate from Lemma 5.1.2a and Theorem 4.1b.
Ad. c) ($\Rightarrow$) Immediate from Theorem 4.1b.
($\Leftarrow$) If $\{A\}\in G$, then $\varnothing\Rightarrow A\vee A$, which is the only

2-disjunctive rule that can be built from $\{A\}$, is not certain (by Lemma 5.1.1). Thus $\{A\} \in DFree$. □

Lemma 5.1.3. Let $X \in G$. The following statements are equivalent.

- X is a disjunctive set.
- $\exists A, B \in X$ such that $A \neq B$ and $X \setminus \{A,B\} \Rightarrow A \vee B$ is a certain rule.
- $\exists A, B \in X$ such that $A \neq B$ and $sup(X) = sup(X \setminus \{A\}) + sup(X \setminus \{B\}) - sup(X \setminus \{A,B\})$.

Proof: Immediate by definition of a disjunctive set and Lemma 5.1.1. □

5.2. Algorithm for determining disjunction-free generators representation

The outline of the *DFreeGenApriori* algorithm we propose is similar to that of *Apriori* (see [1]). It differs from the original algorithm by additional constraints that guarantee the resultant set to be restricted to the frequent disjunction-free generators and their border instead of the whole set of frequent itemsets.

In the algorithm we use the following notation:

- $FDFreeG_k$, $FDFreeGBd^-_k$, $IDFreeGBd^-_k$, – k-itemsets in the respective components of the disjunction-free generators representation;
- C_k – candidate frequent disjunction-free k-generators.

The itemsets are assumed to be kept in an ascending order. With each itemset c there are associated the following fields:

- sup – support of c;
- $minSubSup$ – minimum of the supports of the proper subsets of c.

The *DFreeGenApriori* algorithm starts with checking if the number of transactions in D is greater than *minSup*. If so, then $\varnothing$ is frequent. By Lemma 5.1.2a-b, $\varnothing$ is a disjunction-free generator. Hence, $\varnothing$ is included in $FDFreeG_0$ provided $\varnothing$ is frequent. Next, all items in D are identified and stored as 1-candidates in C_1. Their union determines I_D. By Property 2.2.3, each itemset in C_1 is a generator if its support differs from $sup(\varnothing)$. In addition, Lemma 5.1.2c guarantees that each generator in C_1 is a disjunction-free set. Hence, each generator in C_1 is added to the set of frequent disjunction-free generators $FDFreeG_1$, if its support is sufficiently high. Otherwise, it is included in the negative infrequent generators border $IDFreeGBd^-_1$. Next, the 2-candidates C_2 are created from $FDFreeG_1$ by the *AprioriGGen* algorithm (see Subsection 5.3). Now, the following steps are performed level-wise for all k-candidates, for $k \geq 2$:

1. Supports for the candidate k-itemsets C_k are determined by a pass over the database (see proc. *SupportCount*)

2. The k-candidates C_k the support of which differs from the supports of their proper subsets ($c.sup \neq c.minSubSup$) are found generators (by Property 2.2.3).

3. Infrequent k-generators in C_k are added to the negative infrequent generators border $IDFreeGBd^-_k$. The *IsDis* function determines for each frequent k-generator if it is disjunctive (see Subsection 5.4). Frequent disjunctive k-generators are added to the negative frequent generators border $FDFreeGBd^-_k$. The remaining frequent k-generators are disjunction-free and hence, they are added to $DFreeG_k$.

4. The *AprioriGGen* function is called to generate the candidate $(k+1)$-itemsets C_{k+1} from the frequent disjunction free k-generators $FDFreeG_k$ and to initialize the *minSubSup* field for each new candidate (see Subsection 5.3). *AprioriGGen* follows Property 3.2 to guarantee that the $(k+1)$-candidates include all itemsets having all their subsets in $FDFreeG_k$.

The algorithm ends when there are no more candidates.

```
Algorithm DFreeGenApriori(var FDFreeG, FDFreeGBd⁻,
                                IDFreeGBd⁻, I_D);
FDFreeG = {}; FDFreeGBd⁻ = {}; IDFreeGBd⁻ = {}; I_D = ∅;
if |D| > minSup then begin
    ∅.sup = |D|; FDFreeG_0 = {∅};
    C_1 = {1-itemsets in D with minSubSup initialized to ∅.sup};
    I_D = ∪ C_1;
    forall candidates c ∈ C_1 do begin
        SupportCount(C_1);
        if c.sup ≠ ∅.sup then            // c is a generator
            if c.sup ≤ minSup then add c to IDFreeGBd⁻_1
/*or remove c from I_D if computing the reduced representation*/
            else add c to FDFreeG_1
            endif;
        endif;
    endfor;
    C_2 = AprioriGGen(FDFreeG_1);
    for (k = 2; C_k ≠ ∅; k++) do begin
        SupportCount(C_k);
        forall candidates c ∈ C_k do
            if c.sup ≠ c.minSubSup then       // c is a generator
                if c.sup ≤ minSup then add c to IDFreeGBd⁻_k
                elseif IsDis(c, FDFreeG_{k-1}, FDFreeG_{k-2}) then
                    add c to FDFreeGBd⁻_k
                else add c to FDFreeG_k
                endif;
            endif;
        endfor;
        C_{k+1} = AprioriGGen(FDFreeG_k);
    endfor;
    FDFreeG = ∪_k FDFreeG_k;
    FDFreeGBd⁻ = ∪_k FDFreeGBd⁻_k;
    IDFreeGBd⁻ = ∪_k IDFreeGBd⁻_k;
endif;
return <FDFreeG, FDFreeGBd⁻, IDFreeGBd⁻, I_D>;
```

```
procedure SupportCount(var C_k);
forall transactions t∈D do
    forall candidates c∈C_k do
        if c ⊆ t then c.count++;
        endif;
    endfor;
endfor;
endproc;
```

Let us observe that an algorithm for computing the reduced disjunction-free generators representation would differ only slightly from the presented *DFreeGenApriori* algorithm. The only change would occur for candidate infrequent 1-generators. Such candidates should be discarded from I_D instead of being added to *IDFreeGBd⁻₁*.

5.3. Generating candidates

The *AprioriGGen* function is similar to *AprioriGen* (see [1] for details). The difference consists in additional computing the value of *minSubSup* field. For each new candidate c, *minSubSup* is assigned the minimum from the supports of the proper subsets of c.

```
function AprioriGGen(G_k);
forall f, h ∈G_k do
    if f[1]=h[1] ∧ ... ∧ f[k-1]=h[k-1] ∧ f[k]<h[k] then begin
        c = f[1]•f[2]•...•f[k]•h[k];
        add c to C_{k+1}
    endif;
endfor;
/* Pruning */
forall c∈C_{k+1} do
    forall k-itemsets s ⊂ c do
        if s ∉ G_k then delete c from C_{k+1}
        else c.minSubSup = min(c.minSubSup, s.sup)
        endif;
    endfor;
endfor;
return C_{k+1};
```

5.4. Checking if generator is disjunctive

The *IsDis* function checks if an itemset c provided as the first argument is disjunctive or not. It is assumed that c is a frequent generator of the size $k≥2$. The second and third arguments: *FDFreeG_{k-1}*, *FDFreeG_{k-2}*, contain all frequent disjunction-free generators of the size $k-1$ and $k-2$, respectively. Let us note that for every pair (g_1, g_2) of different $(k-1)$-subsets of c, $g_1 \cap g_2$ is a $(k-2)$-subset of c. *IsDis* checks if there is a pair (g_1, g_2) of different $(k-1)$-subsets of c satisfying the equation: $sup(c)=sup(g_1)+sup(g_2)-sup(g_1 \cap g_2)$. If so, then by Lemma 5.1.3 the itemset c is disjunctive and the function returns **true**. Otherwise, c is not disjunctive and the function returns **false**.

```
function IsDis(k-itemset c, FDFreeG_{k-1}, FDFreeG_{k-2});
/* Assert: c is a frequent generator of the size k ≥ 2 */
forall (k-1)-itemsets g_1, g_2 ⊂ c such that g_1 ≠ g_2 do begin
    determine supports of g_1 and g_2 based on FDFreeG_{k-1};
    determine support of (g_1∩g_2) based on FDFreeG_{k-2};
    if c.sup = g_1.sup + g_2.sup − (g_1∩g_2).sup then return true;
    endif;
endfor;
return false;
```

6. Conclusions

An overview of concise lossless representations of frequent itemsets was provided. The new lossless disjunction-free generators representation was offered. It was proved that the new representation constitutes a subset of the generators representation and the disjunction-free sets representation. It was also proved that each disjunction-free set is a generator. The algorithm for determining the new representation was offered.

References

[1] R. Agrawal, H. Mannila, R. Srikant, H. Toivonen, A. I. Verkamo. Fast discovery of association rules. In *Advances in Knowledge Discovery and Data Mining*, pages 307-328. AAAI Press, Menlo Park, California, 1996.

[2] Y. Bastide, R. Taouil, N. Pasquier, G. Stumme, L. Lakhal. Mining frequent patterns with counting inference. *ACM SIGKDD Explorations*, Vol. 2(2):66-75, December 2000.

[3] J-F. Boulicaut, A. Bykowski, C. Rigotti. Approximation of frequency queries by means of free-sets. In *Proc. of PKDD '00*, pages 75-85, Springer, September 2000.

[4] J-F. Boulicaut, A. Bykowski, C. Rigotti. Free-Sets: a condensed representation of Boolean data for the approximation of frequency queries. Research Report, LISI, INSA-Lyon, June 2001.

[5] A. Bykowski, C. Rigotti. A condensed representation to find frequent patterns. In *Proc. of the 12th ACM SIGACT-SIGMOD-SIGART PODS' 01*, May 2001.

[6] J. Han, M. Kamber. *Data Mining: Concepts and Techniques*. Morgan Kaufmann Publishers, 2000.

[7] M. Kryszkiewicz. Closed set based discovery of representative association rules. In *Proc. of IDA '01*, Springer, September 2001.

[8] N. Pasquier. Data mining: Algorithmes d'extraction et de réduction des règles d'association dans les bases de données. Thèse de Doctorat, Université Blaise Pascal - Clermont-Ferrand II, January 2000.

[9] J. Pei, J. Han, R. Mao. CLOSET: An efficient algorithm for mining frequent closed itemsets. In *Proc. of the ACM-SIGMOD DMKD '00*, pages 21-30, Dallas, May 2000.

[10] J. Saquer, J. S. Deogun. Using closed itemsets for discovering representative association rules. In *Proc. of ISMIS '00*, pages 495-504, Springer, October 2000.

[11] M. J. Zaki. Generating non-redundant association rules. In *Proc. of the 6th ACM SIGKDD Intl Conf. on Knowledge Discovery and Data Mining*, pages 34-43, August 2000.

Frequent Subgraph Discovery*

Michihiro Kuramochi and George Karypis
Department of Computer Science/Army HPC Research Center
University of Minnesota
Minneapolis, MN 55455
{kuram, karypis}@cs.umn.edu

Abstract

As data mining techniques are being increasingly applied to non-traditional domains, existing approaches for finding frequent itemsets cannot be used as they cannot model the requirement of these domains. An alternate way of modeling the objects in these data sets is to use graphs. Within that model, the problem of finding frequent patterns becomes that of discovering subgraphs that occur frequently over the entire set of graphs. In this paper we present a computationally efficient algorithm for finding all frequent subgraphs in large graph databases. We evaluated the performance of the algorithm by experiments with synthetic datasets as well as a chemical compound dataset. The empirical results show that our algorithm scales linearly with the number of input transactions and it is able to discover frequent subgraphs from a set of graph transactions reasonably fast, even though we have to deal with computationally hard problems such as canonical labeling of graphs and subgraph isomorphism which are not necessary for traditional frequent itemset discovery.

1. Introduction

Efficient algorithms for finding frequent itemsets—both sequential and non-sequential—in very large transaction databases have been one of the key success stories of data mining research [2, 1, 22, 9, 3]. We can use these itemsets for discovering association rules, for extracting prevalent patterns that exist in the datasets, or for classification. Nevertheless, as data mining techniques have been increasingly applied to non-traditional domains, such as scientific, spatial and relational datasets, situations tend to occur on which we can not apply existing itemset discovery algorithms, because these problems are difficult to be adequately and correctly modeled with the traditional market-basket transaction approaches.

An alternate way of modeling the various objects is to use undirected labeled graphs to model each one of the object's entities—items in traditional frequent itemset discovery—and the relation between them. In particular, each vertex of the graph will correspond to an entity and each edge will correspond to a relation between two entities. In this model both vertices and edges may have labels associated with them which are not required to be unique. Using such a graph representation, the problem of finding frequent patterns then becomes that of discovering subgraphs which occur frequently enough over the entire set of graphs.

The key advantage of graph modeling is that it allows us to solve problems that we could not solve previously. For instance, consider a problem of mining chemical compounds to find recurrent substructures. We can achieve that using a graph-based pattern discovery algorithm by creating a graph for each one of the compounds whose vertices correspond to different atoms, and whose edges correspond to bonds between them. We can assign to each vertex a label corresponding to the atom involved (and potentially its charge), and assign to each edge a label corresponding to the type of the bond (and potentially information about their relative 3D orientation). Once these graphs have been created, recurrent substructures across different compounds become frequently occurring subgraphs.

Related Work Developing algorithms that discover all frequently occurring subgraphs in a large graph database is particularly challenging and computationally intensive, as graph and subgraph isomorphisms play a key role throughout the computations.

The power of using graphs to model complex datasets has been recognized by various researchers in chemical domain [18, 17, 5, 4], computer vision [12, 14], image and object retrieval [6], and machine learning [10, 20]. In particular, Dehaspe et al. [5] applied Inductive Logic Programming (ILP) to obtain frequent patterns in the toxicology evaluation problem [18]. ILP has been actively used for predicting

*This work was supported by NSF CCR-9972519, EIA-9986042, ACI-9982274, by Army Research Office contract DA/DAAG55-98-1-0441, by the DOE ASCI program, and by Army High Performance Computing Research Center contract number DAAH04-95-C-0008. Access to computing facilities was provided by the Minnesota Supercomputing Institute.

carcinogenesis [17], which is able to find all frequent patterns that satisfy a given criteria. It is not designed to scale to large graph databases, however, and they did not report any statistics regarding the amount of computation time required. Another approach that has been developed is using a greedy scheme [20, 10] to find some of the most prevalent subgraphs. These methods are not complete, as they may not obtain all frequent subgraphs, although they are faster than the ILP-based methods. Furthermore, these methods can also perform approximate matching when discovering frequent patterns, allowing them to recognize patterns that have slight variations.

Recently, Inokuchi et al. [11] presented a computationally efficient algorithm called AGM, that can be used to find all frequent *induced* subgraphs in a graph database that satisfy a certain minimum support constraint. A subgraph $G_s = (V_s, E_s)$ of $G = (V, E)$ is *induced* if E_s contains all the edges of E that connect vertices in V_s. AGM finds all frequent induced subgraphs using an approach similar to that used by Apriori [2], which extends subgraphs by adding one vertex at each step. Experiments reported in [11] show that AGM achieves good performance for synthetic dense datasets, and it required 40 minutes to 8 days to find all frequent induced subgraphs in a dataset containing 300 chemical compounds, as the minimum support threshold varied from 20% to 10%.

Our Contribution   In this paper we present a new algorithm, named FSG, for finding all connected subgraphs that appear frequently in a large graph database. Our algorithm finds frequent subgraphs using the same level-by-level expansion adopted in Apriori [2]. The key features of FSG are the following: (1) it uses a sparse graph representation which minimizes both storage and computation, (2) it increases the size of frequent subgraphs by adding one edge at a time, allowing to generate the candidates efficiently, (3) it uses simple algorithms of canonical labeling and graph isomorphism which work efficiently for small graphs, and (4) it incorporates various optimizations for candidate generation and counting which allow it to scale to large graph databases.

We experimentally evaluated FSG on a large number of synthetic graphs, that were generated using a framework similar to that used for market-basket transaction generation [2]. For problems in which a moderately large number of different types of entities and relations exist, FSG was able to achieve good performance and to scale linearly with the database size. In fact, FSG found all the frequent connected subgraphs in less than 500 seconds from a synthetic dataset consisting of 80000 graphs with a support threshold of 2%. For problems where the number of edge and vertex labels was small, the performance of FSG was worse, as the exponential complexity of graph isomorphism dominates the overall performance. We also evaluated the performance of FSG on the same chemical compound dataset used by AGM. Our results show that FSG is able to find all the frequent connected subgraphs using a 6.5% minimum support in 600 seconds.

2. Frequent Subgraph Discovery

In our problem setting, we have a dataset of transactions D. Each transaction $t \in D$ is a labeled undirected graph[1]. Edges and vertices have their labels. Given a minimum support $\sigma\%$, we would like to find all *connected* undirected subgraphs that occur in at least $\sigma|D|$ transactions. Table 1 shows the notation we use.

Table 1. Notation

Notation	Description
D	A dataset of graph transactions
t	A transaction of a graph in D
k-(sub)graph	A (sub)graph with k edges
g^k	A k-subgraph
C^k	A set of candidates with k edges
F^k	A set of frequent k-subgraphs
cl(g^k)	A canonical label of a k-graph g^k

The key restriction in our problem statement is that we are finding only subgraphs that are connected. This is motivated by the fact that the resulting frequent subgraphs will be encapsulating relations (or edges) between some of entities (or vertices) of various objects. Within this context, connectivity is a natural property of frequent patterns. An additional benefit of this restriction is that it reduces the complexity of the problem, as we do not need to consider disconnected combinations of frequent connected subgraphs.

In developing our frequent subgraph discovery algorithm, we decided to follow the structure of the algorithm Apriori used for finding frequent itemsets [2], because it achieves the most effective pruning compared with other algorithms such as *GenMax*, dEclat [22] and Tree Projection [1].

The high level structure of our algorithm FSG is shown in Algorithm 1. Edges in the algorithm correspond to items in traditional frequent itemset discovery. Namely, as these algorithms increase the size of frequent itemsets by adding a single item at a time, our algorithm increases the size of frequent subgraphs by adding an edge one by one. FSG initially enumerates all the frequent single and double edge graphs. Then, based on those two sets, it starts the main computational loop. During each iteration it first generates candidate subgraphs whose size is greater than the previous frequent ones by one edge (Line 5 of Algorithm 1). Next, it counts the frequency for each of these candidates, and

---

[1]The algorithm presented in this paper can be easily extended to directed graphs.

314

prunes subgraphs that do no satisfy the support constraint (Lines 7–11). Discovered frequent subgraphs satisfy the downward closure property of the support condition, which allows us to effectively prune the lattice of frequent subgraphs.

Algorithm 1 fsg(D, σ) (Frequent Subgraph)

1: $F^1 \leftarrow$ detect all frequent 1-subgraphs in D
2: $F^2 \leftarrow$ detect all frequent 2-subgraphs in D
3: $k \leftarrow 3$
4: **while** $F^{k-1} \neq \emptyset$ **do**
5:    $C^k \leftarrow$ fsg-gen(F^{k-1})
6:    **for each** candidate $g^k \in C^k$ **do**
7:       g^k.count $\leftarrow 0$
8:       **for each** transaction $t \in D$ **do**
9:          **if** candidate g^k is included in transaction t **then**
10:             g^k.count $\leftarrow g^k$.count $+ 1$
11:    $F^k \leftarrow \{g^k \in C^k \mid g^k.\text{count} \geq \sigma|D|\}$
12:    $k \leftarrow k + 1$
13: **return** $F^1, F^2, \ldots, F^{k-2}$

In Section 2.1, we briefly review some background issues regarding graphs. Section 2.2 contains details of candidate generation with pruning and Section 2.3 describes frequency counting in **FSG**.

2.1. Graph Representation, Canonical Labeling and Isomorphism

Sparse Graph Representation Our algorithm uses sparse graph representation to store input transactions, intermediate candidates and frequent subgraphs. Each one of the transactions, candidates and discovered frequent subgraphs is stored using adjacency-list representation, while our canonical labeling described in Section 2.1 is based on adjacency matrix representation. Thus, after determining canonical label for a subgraph, we convert its canonical adjacency matrix back into adjacency lists. This adjacency-list representation saves memory when input transaction graphs are sparse, and speeds up computation.

Canonical Labeling Because we deal with graphs, not itemsets, there are many differences between our algorithm and the traditional frequent itemset discovery. A difference appears when we try to sort frequent objects. In the traditional frequent itemset discovery, we can sort itemsets by lexicographic ordering. Clearly this is not applicable to graphs. To get total order of graphs we use canonical labeling. A canonical label is a unique *code* of a given graph [16, 7]. A graph can be represented in many different ways, depending on the order of its edges or vertices. Nevertheless, canonical labels should be always the same no matter how graphs are represented, as long as those graphs have the same topological structure and the same labeling of edges and vertices. By comparing canonical labels of graphs, we can sort them in a unique and deterministic way, regardless of the representation of input graphs. We denote a canonical label of a graph g by cl(g). It is easy to see that computing canonical labels is equivalent to determining isomorphism between graphs, because if two graphs are isomorphic with each other, their canonical labels must be identical. Both canonical labeling and determining graph isomorphism are not known to be either in P or in NP-complete [7].

We use a straightforward way of determining a canonical label. Using a *flattened* representation of the adjacency matrix of a graph, by concatenating rows or columns of an adjacency matrix one after another we construct a list of integers. Regarding this list of integers as a string, we can obtain total order of graphs by lexicographic ordering. To compute a canonical label of a graph, we try all the permutations of its vertices to see which ordering of vertices gives the minimum adjacency matrix. To narrow down the search space, we first partition the vertices by their degrees and labels, which is a well-known technique called vertex invariants [16]. Then, we try all the possible permutations of vertices inside each partition. Once we determine the caninical adjacency matrix, we convert our adjacency-list representation of the subgraph so that the ordering of vertices in the canonical adjacency matrix is reflected. All comparisons of subgraphs are done with the canonically reordered adjaceny-list representation. Further details can be found in [13].

Isomorphism In our algorithm, we need to solve both graph isomorphism and subgraph isomorphism. Graph isomorphism is a problem to determine whether given two graphs g_1 and g_2 are isomorphic, namely, to find a mapping from a set of vertices to another set. Automorphism is a special case of graph isomorphism where $g_1 = g_2$, which means to find a mapping from a graph to itself. Subgraph isomorphism is to find an isomorphism between g_1 and a subgraph of g_2. In other words, it is to determine if a graph is included in the other larger graph. A well-known algorithm for subgraph isomorphism is proposed in [19]. As suggested in [7], graph isomorphism can be directly solved in practice, although it is not known to be either in P or in NP-complete. On the other hand, subgraph isomorphism has been proved to be in NP-complete [8]. Thus, there is no scalable algorithm to solve it. When the size of graphs is small such as 10 vertices or less, however, it is also known that subgraph isomorphism can be feasible even with a simple exhaustive search [7, 19].

We solve graph isomorphism by a simple way, which is, starting from a single vertex in one graph, to try to find a mapping to one of the vertices in the other graph, that is consistent with the labeling. Then, we keep the same process by adding vertices one by one until either we find a complete mapping or we end up with exhausting the search space. When we seek for the next mapping, we have to be careful to keep the consistency of edge and vertex labels. We can reduce the search space more if there are more labels are assigned to edges and vertices, which leads to restriction against mapping. This approach can solve both graph and subgraph isomorphism.

2.2. Candidate Generation

In the candidate generation phase, we create a set of candidates of size $k + 1$, given frequent k-subgraphs. Candidate subgraphs of size $k + 1$ are generated by joining two frequent k-subgraphs. In order for two such frequent k-subgraphs to be eligible for joining they must contain the same $(k - 1)$-subgraph. We will refer to this common $(k - 1)$-subgraph among two k-frequent subgraphs as their *core*.

Unlike the joining of itemsets in which two frequent k-size itemsets lead to a unique $(k + 1)$-size itemset, the joining of two subgraphs of size k can lead to multiple subgraphs of size $k + 1$. This is due to three reasons. First, the resulting two $(k + 1)$-subgraphs produced by the joining may differ in a vertex that has the same label in both k-subgraphs. Figure 1(a) is such an example. This pair of graphs g_a^4 and g_b^4 generates two different candidates g_a^5 and g_b^5. The second reason is because a core itself may have multiple automorphisms and each automorphism can lead to a different $(k + 1)$-candidate. An example for this case is shown in Figure 1(b), in which the core—a square of 4 vertices labeled with v_0—has more than one automorphism which result in 3 different candidates of size 6. Finally, two frequent subgraphs may have multiple cores as depicted by Figure 1(c).

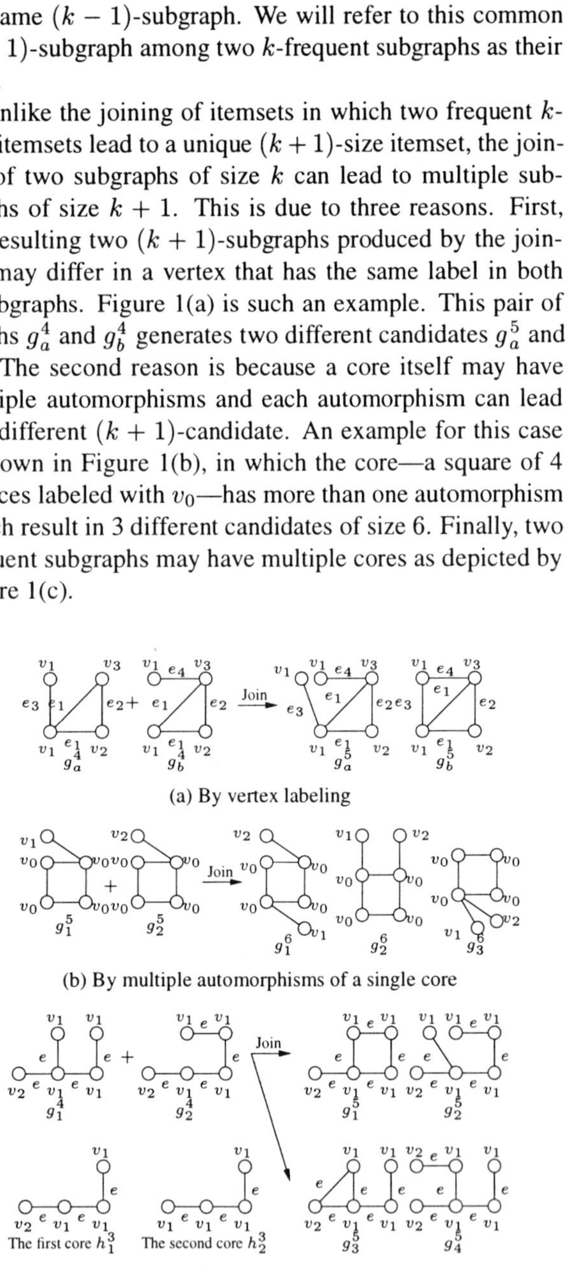

(a) By vertex labeling

(b) By multiple automorphisms of a single core

(c) By multiple cores

Figure 1. Three different cases of candidate joining

The overall algorithm for candidate generation is shown

in Algorithm 2. For each pair of frequent subgraphs that share the same core, the fsg-join is called at Line 6 to generate all possible candidates of size $k + 1$. For each of the candidates, the algorithm first checks if they are already in C^{k+1}. If they are not, then it verifies if all its k-subgraphs are frequent. If they are, fsg-join then inserts it into C^{k+1}, otherwise it discards the candidate (Lines 7–16). The algorithm uses canonical labeling to efficiently check if a particular subgraph is already in C^{k+1} or not.

The key computational steps in candidate generation are (1) core identification, (2) joining, and (3) using the downward closure property of a support condition to eliminate some of generated candidates. A straightforward way of implementing these tasks is to use subgraph isomorphism, graph automorphism and canonical labeling with binary search, respectively. The amount of computation required by the first step, however, can be substantially reduced by keeping some information from the lattice of frequent subgraphs. Particularly, if for each frequent k-subgraph we store the canonical labels of its frequent $(k - 1)$-subgraphs, then the cores between two frequent subgraphs can be determined by simply computing the intersection of these lists. Also to speed up the computation of the automorphism step during joining, we save previous automorphisms associated with each core and look them up instead of performing the same automorphism computation again. The saved list of automorphisms will be discarded once C^{k+1} has been generated.

Note we need to perform self join, that is, two graphs g_i^k and g_j^k in Algorithm 2 are identical. It is necessary because, for example, consider transactions without any labels, that is, each transaction in the input is an undirected and unlabeled graph. Then, we will have only one frequent 1-subgraph and one frequent 2-subgraph regardless of a support threshold, because those are the only allowed structures, and edges and vertices do not have labels assigned. From those F^1 and F^2 where $|F^1| = |F^2| = 1$, to generate larger graphs of C^k and F^k for $k \geq 3$, the only way is the self join.

2.3. Frequency Counting

Once candidate subgraphs have been generated, FSG computes their frequency. The simplest way of achieving this is for each subgraph to scan each one of the transaction graphs and determine if it is contained or not using subgraph isomorphism. Nonetheless, having to compute these isomorphisms is particularly expensive and this approach is not feasible for large datasets. In the context of frequent itemset discovery by Apriori, the frequency counting is performed substantially faster by building a hash-tree of candidate itemsets and scanning each transaction to determine which of the itemsets in the hash-tree it supports. Developing such an algorithm for frequent subgraphs, however, is

Algorithm 2 fsg-gen(F^k) (Candidate Generation)

$C^{k+1} \leftarrow \emptyset$;
for each pair of $g_i^k, g_j^k \in F^k, i \leq j$ such that $\mathrm{cl}(g_i^k) \leq \mathrm{cl}(g_j^k)$ **do**
  for each edge $e \in g_i^k$ **do** {create a $(k-1)$-subgraph of g_i^k by removing an edge e}
    $g_i^{k-1} \leftarrow g_i^k - e$
    if g_i^{k-1} is included in g_j^k **then** {g_i^k and g_j^k share the same core}
      $T^{k+1} \leftarrow$ fsg-join(g_i^k, g_j^k)
      for each $g_j^{k+1} \in T^{k+1}$ **do**
        {test if the downward closure property holds for g_j^{k+1}}
        flag $\leftarrow$ true
        for each edge $f_l \in g_j^{k+1}$ **do**
          $h_l^k \leftarrow g_j^{k+1} - f_l$
          if h_l^k is connected and $h_l^k \notin F^k$ **then**
            flag $\leftarrow$ false
            break
        if flag = true **then**
          $C^{k+1} \leftarrow C^{k+1} \cup \{g^{k+1}\}$
return C^{k+1}

challenging as there is no natural way to build the hash-tree for graphs. For this reason, FSG instead uses Transaction ID (TID) lists, proposed by [23, 21, 22]. In this approach for each frequent subgraph we keep a list of transaction identifiers that support it. Now when we need to compute the frequency of g^{k+1}, we first compute the intersection of the TID lists of its frequent k-subgraphs. If the size of the intersection is below the support, g^{k+1} is pruned, otherwise we compute the frequency of g^{k+1} using subgraph isomorphism by limiting our search only to the set of transactions in the intersection of the TID lists.

3. Experiments

We performed a set of experiments to evaluate the performance of FSG. There are two types of datasets we used. The first type was synthetically generated, and allowed us to study the performance of FSG under different conditions. The second type contains the molecular structures of chemical compounds, which is used to evaluate the performance of FSG for large graphs.

All experiments were done on 650MHz Intel Pentium III machines with 2GB main memory, running the Linux operating system.

3.1. Synthetic Datasets

For the performance evaluation, we generate synthetic datasets controlled by a set of parameters shown in Table 2. The basic idea behind our data generator is similar to the one used in [2], but simpler.

First, we generate a set of $|L|$ potentially frequent connected subgraphs whose size is determined by Poisson distribution with mean $|I|$. For each frequent connected subgraph, its topology as well as its edge and vertex labels are chosen randomly. It has a weight assigned, which becomes a probability that the subgraph is selected to be included

Table 2. Synthetic dataset parameters

Notation	Parameter
$|D|$	The total number of transactions
$|T|$	The average size of transactions (in terms of the number of edges)
$|I|$	The average size of potentially frequent subgraphs (in terms of the number of edges)
$|L|$	The number of potentially frequent subgraphs
N	The number of edge and vertex labels

in a transaction. The weights obey an exponential distribution with unit mean and the sum of the weights of all the frequent subgraphs is normalized to 1. We call this set of $|L|$ frequent subgraphs a *seed pool*. The number of distinct edge and vertex labels is controlled by the parameter N. In particular, N is both the number of distinct edge labels as well as the number of distinct vertex labels.

Next, we generate $|D|$ transactions. The size of each transaction is a Poisson random variable whose mean is equal to $|T|$. Then we select one of the frequent subgraphs already generated from the seed pool, by rolling an $|L|$-sided die. Each face of this die corresponds to the probability assigned to a potential frequent subgraph in the seed pool. If the size of the selected seed fits in a transaction, we add it. If the current size of a transaction does not reach its selected size, we keep selecting and putting another seed into it. When a selected seed exceeds the transaction size, we add it to the transaction for the half of the cases, and discard it and move onto the next transaction for the rest of the half. The way we put a seed into a transaction is to find a mapping so that the overlap between a seed and a transaction is maximized.

In the following experiments, we use the combinations of the parameters shown in Table 3.

Table 3. Parameter settings

Parameter	Values
$|D|$	10000
$|T|$	$5, 10, 20, 40$
$|I|$	$3, 5, 7, 10$
$|L|$	200
N	$3, 5, 10, 20, 40$

Table 4 shows the amount of time required by FSG to find all the frequent subgraphs for various datasets in which we changed N, $|I|$, $|T|$, and σ. In all of these experiments, the number of transactions $|D|$ was fixed to 10000 and the number of potential frequent subgraphs $|L|$ was set to 200. If the average transaction size $|T|$ is smaller than that of potential frequent subgraphs $|I|$, we omitted such combinations because we can not generate transactions. In some cases, we aborted computation because the running time was too long or because the main memory was exhausted, which are denoted by dashes in the table.

By looking at the table, we can observe a number of interesting points regarding the performance of FSG for different types of datasets. First, as the number of edge and vertex labels N increases, the amount of time required by FSG decreases. For example, when $\sigma = 2\%$, $N = 3$, $|I| = 3$ and $|T| = 10$, it takes 143 seconds, while the running time drops to 16 seconds for $N = 20$. This is because as the number of edge and vertex labels increases there are fewer automorphisms and subgraph isomorphisms, which leads to fast candidate generation and frequency counting. Also by having more edge and vertex labels, we can effectively prune the search space of isomorphism because they work as constraints when we seek for a mapping of vertices. Second, as the size of the average transaction $|T|$ increases the overall running time increases as well. The relative increase is higher when N is small than when N is large. For example, going from $|T| = 5$ to $|T| = 40$ under the setting of $N = 5$, $|I| = 3$ and $\sigma = 2\%$, the running time increases by a factor of 20, whereas for the same set of parameters when $N = 40$, the increase is only by a factor of 4. The reason for that is again having many edge and vertex labels effectively decreases the number of isomorphisms and the search space. With small N and large $|T|$, we can not narrow down efficiently the search space of subgraph isomorphism for frequency counting and the running time increases drastically. Third, as $|I|$ increases the overall running time also increases. Again the relative increase is smaller for larger values of N and smaller values of $|T|$ by the same reason described above.

To determine the scalability of FSG against the number of transactions we performed an experiment in which we used $|D| = 10000, 20000, 40000$ and 80000 with $|L| = 200$, $|I| = 5$ and $|T|$ ranging from 5 to 40. These results are shown in Figure 2. As we can see from the figure, FSG scales linearly with the number of transactions.

3.2. Chemical Compound Dataset

We obtained a chemical dataset from [15]. This was originally provided for the Predictive Toxicology Evaluation Challenge [18], which contains information on 340 chemical compounds in two separated files. The first file named `atoms.pl` contains definitions of atoms in compounds. For example, "atm$(d1, d1_1, c, 22, -0.133)$" means that a chemical compound $d1$ has an atom whose identifier is $d1_1$, of element carbon, of type 22 and with partial charge -0.133. The other file `bonds.pl` provides bonding information between atoms. A line in the file "bond$(d1, d1_1, d1_2, 7)$", for instance, states that in the compound $d1$ its atoms $d1_1$ and $d1_2$ are connected by a type 7 bond. There are 4 different types of bonds and 24 different

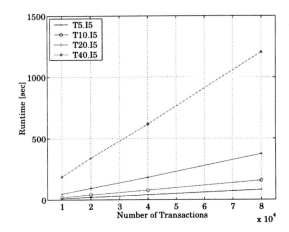

Figure 2. Scalability on the number of transaction

atoms, and there are 66 atom types.

We converted the data into graph transactions. Each compound becomes a transaction. Thus, there are 340 transactions in total. Each vertex corresponds to an atom, whose label is made of a pair of the atom element and the atom type. We did not include partial charge to vertex labels because those values were not discretized. Each edge is placed for every bond. Edge label directly corresponds to the bond type. By the conversion, there are 4 edge labels and 66 vertex labels produced in total. The average transaction size was 27.4 in terms of the number of edges, and 27.0 in terms of the number of vertices. Because the number of edges is very close to that of vertices, this dataset is sparse. There are 26 transactions that have more than 50 edges and vertices. The largest transaction contains 214 edges and 214 vertices.

The experimental results by FSG for finding frequent subgraphs are shown in Figure 3. Figure 3(a) shows the running time required for different values of support threshold and Figure 3(b) displays the number of discovered frequent subgraphs on those support levels. With $\sigma = 7\%$, the largest frequent subgraph discovered has 13 vertices.

With the support threshold σ below 10%, both the running time and the number of frequent subgraphs increase exponentially. FSG does well even for 7% support as it requires 600 seconds. AGM, a frequent *induced* subgraph discovery algorithm, required about 8 days for 10% and 40 minutes for 20% with almost the same dataset on 400MHz PC [11].

Comparing the performance of FSG on this dataset against those on the synthetic datasets, we can see that it requires more time for this chemical dataset, once we take into account of the difference in the number of transactions. This is because in the chemical dataset, edge and vertex labels have non-uniform distribution. As we decrease the minimum support, larger frequent subgraphs start to appear which generally contain only carbon and hydrogen and a

Table 4. Running times in seconds for synthetic data sets. We omitted parameter combinations where $|I| > |T|$, because transaction size is too small for potential frequent subgraphs. A dash in the table means we had to abort the computation for the set of parameters because of either memory exhaustion or taking too long time.

N	$|I|$	$|T|$	Running Time [sec]	
			$\sigma = 2\%$	$\sigma = 1\%$
2	3	5	18	24
		10	143	434
		20	—	—
		40	—	—
2	5	5	27	52
		10	251	2246
		20	—	—
		40	—	—
2	7	10	557	6203
		20	—	—
		40	—	—
2	10	10	—	—
		20	—	—

N	$|I|$	$|T|$	Running Time [sec]	
			$\sigma = 2\%$	$\sigma = 1\%$
3	3	5	12	22
		10	30	40
		20	112	390
		40	5817	—
3	5	5	18	32
		10	51	102
		20	189	736
		40	6110	—
3	7	10	66	4512
		20	1953	—
		40	—	—
3	10	10	8290	—
		20	—	—

N	$|I|$	$|T|$	Running Time [sec]	
			$\sigma = 2\%$	$\sigma = 1\%$
5	3	5	10	12
		10	20	25
		20	53	71
		40	196	279
5	5	5	24	44
		10	55	80
		20	124	174
		40	340	617
5	7	10	208	770
		20	772	1333
		40	2531	3143
5	10	10	10914	—
		20	—	—

N	$|I|$	$|T|$	Running Time [sec]	
			$\sigma = 2\%$	$\sigma = 1\%$
10	3	5	9	17
		10	16	25
		20	35	40
		40	87	98
10	5	5	10	18
		10	20	51
		20	47	119
		40	188	246
10	7	10	190	816
		20	866	1506
		40	2456	3199
10	10	10	10785	—
		20	—	—

N	$|I|$	$|T|$	Running Time [sec]	
			$\sigma = 2\%$	$\sigma = 1\%$
20	3	5	9	16
		10	16	28
		20	34	38
		40	78	85
20	5	5	10	19
		10	20	51
		20	48	117
		40	182	233
20	7	10	193	804
		20	884	1667
		40	2524	3271
20	10	10	10520	—
		20	—	—

N	$|I|$	$|T|$	Running Time [sec]	
			$\sigma = 2\%$	$\sigma = 1\%$
40	3	5	20	22
		10	27	44
		20	44	47
		40	84	89
40	5	5	20	28
		10	29	60
		20	55	131
		40	177	234
40	7	10	197	1236
		20	861	5273
		40	2456	9183
40	10	10	9687	—
		20	—	—

single bonding type. Essentially with $\sigma < 10\%$, this dataset becomes similar to the synthetic datasets where $N = 2$.

3.3. Summary of Discussions

We summarize the characteristics of FSG performance. First, FSG works better on graph datasets with more edge and vertex labels. During both candidate generation and frequency counting, what FSG essentially does is to solve graph or subgraph isomorphism. Without labels assigned, determining isomorphism of graphs is more difficult to solve, because we can not use labeling information as constraints to narrow down the search space of vertex mapping. We can confirm it by comparing the results in Table 4 with various values of the number of edge and vertex labels, N.

Second, the running time depends heavily on the size of frequent subgraphs to be discovered. If input transactions contain many large frequent patterns such as more than 10 edges, the situation corresponds to the parameter setting of $|I| = 10$, where FSG will not be likely to finish its computation in a reasonable amount of time. The same thing happened with the chemical dataset with a support threshold less than 10%. If we compare Figure 3(a) and Figure 3(b), we notice the running time increases at a higher rate than the number of discovered subgraphs does, as we decrease the minimum support. With a lower support criteria, we start getting larger frequent subgraphs and both candidate generation and frequency counting become much more expensive. On the other hand, as for the cases of $|I| \leq 5$ in

Table 4, FSG runs fast. The result of the chemical dataset is consistent with it. For example, if we use $\sigma = 10\%$ for the chemical dataset, FSG spends 28 seconds to get 882 frequent subgraphs in total. The largest frequent graphs among them have 11 edges, and there are only 10 such frequent 11-subgraphs discovered.

Another important factor is the size of a transaction. If the average size of transactions becomes large, frequency counting by subgraph isomorphism becomes expensive regardless of the size of candidate subgraphs. Traditional frequent itemset finding algorithms are free from this problem. They can perform frequency counting simply by taking the intersection of itemsets and transactions.

As of the number of transactions, FSG requires running time proportional to the size of inputs under the same set of parameters. This is the same as frequent itemset discovery algorithms.

4. Conclusion

In this paper we presented an algorithm, FSG, for finding frequently occurring subgraphs in large graph databases, that can be used to discover recurrent patterns in scientific, spatial, and relational datasets. Our experimental evaluation shows that FSG can scale reasonably well to very large graph databases provided that graphs contain a sufficiently many different labels of edges and vertices.

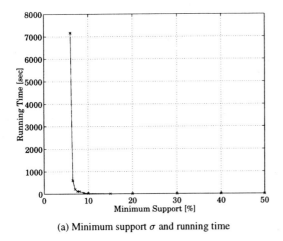
(a) Minimum support σ and running time

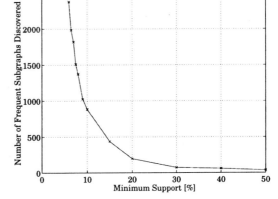
(b) Minimum support σ and the number of discovered frequent subgraphs

Figure 3. Performance with the chemical compound dataset

Acknowledgment

We deeply thank Professor Takashi Washio, Professor Hiroshi Motoda and their research group at the Institute of Scientific and Industrial Research, Osaka University, and Mr. Akihiro Inokuchi at Tokyo Research Laboratory, IBM Japan, Ltd. for providing the source code of AGM and useful comments.

References

[1] R. C. Agarwal, C. C. Aggarwal, V. V. V. Prasad, and V. Crestana. A tree projection algorithm for generation of large itemsets for association rules. IBM Research Report RC21341, 1998.

[2] R. Agrawal and R. Srikant. Fast algorithms for mining association rules. In *Proc. the 20th VLDB*, pages 487–499. Morgan Kaufmann, 1994.

[3] R. Agrawal and R. Srikant. Mining sequential patterns. In *Proc. the 11th ICDE*, pages 3–14. IEEE Press, 1995.

[4] R. N. Chittimoori, L. B. Holder, and D. J. Cook. Applying the SUBDUE substructure discovery system to the chemical toxicity domain. In *Proc. the 12th Int. Florida AI Research Society Conf.*, pages 90–94, 1999.

[5] L. Dehaspe, H. Toivonen, and R. D. King. Finding frequent substructures in chemical compounds. In *Proc. the 4th ACM SIGKDD KDD-98*, pages 30–36. AAAI Press, 1998.

[6] D. Dupplaw and P. H. Lewis. Content-based image retrieval with scale-spaced object trees. In *Proc. SPIE: Storage and Retrieval for Media Databases*, volume 3972, pages 253–261, 2000.

[7] S. Fortin. The graph isomorphism problem. Technical Report TR96-20, Department of Computing Science, University of Alberta, 1996.

[8] M. R. Garey and D. S. Johnson. *Computers and Intractability: A Guide to the Theory of NP-Completeness*. W. H. Freeman and Company, New York, 1979.

[9] J. Han, J. Pei, and Y. Yin. Mining frequent patterns without candidate generation. In *Proc. ACM SIGMOD*, 2000.

[10] L. Holder, D. Cook, and S. Djoko. Substructure discovery in the SUBDUE system. In *Proc. the Workshop on Knowledge Discovery in Databases*, pages 169–180, 1994.

[11] A. Inokuchi, T. Washio, and H. Motoda. An apriori-based algorithm for mining frequent substructures from graph data. In *Proc. PKDD'00*, pages 13–23, 2000.

[12] H. Kälviäinen and E. Oja. Comparisons of attributed graph matching algorithms for computer vision. In *Proc. STEP-90, Finnish Artificial Intelligence Symposium*, pages 354–368, 1990.

[13] M. Kuramochi and G. Karypis. Frequent subgraph discovery. Technical Report 01-028, Department of Computer Science, University of Minnesota, 2001.

[14] D. A. L. Piriyakumar and P. Levi. An efficient A* based algorithm for optimal graph matching applied to computer vision. In *GRWSIA-98*, 1998.

[15] http://oldwww.comlab.ox.ac.uk/oucl/groups/machlearn/PTE/.

[16] R. C. Read and D. G. Corneil. The graph isomorph disease. *Journal of Graph Theory*, 1:339–363, 1977.

[17] A. Srinivasan, R. D. King, S. Muggleton, and M. J. E. Sternberg. Carcinogenesis predictions using ILP. In *Proc. the 7th Int. Workshop on Inductive Logic Programming*, volume 1297, pages 273–287. Springer-Verlag, Berlin, 1997.

[18] A. Srinivasan, R. D. King, S. H. Muggleton, and M. Sternberg. The predictive toxicology evaluation challenge. In *Proc. the 15th IJCAI*, pages 1–6. Morgan-Kaufmann, 1997.

[19] J. R. Ullman. An algorithm for subgraph isomorphism. *Journal of the ACM*, 23(1):31–42, 1976.

[20] K. Yoshida and H. Motoda. CLIP: Concept learning from inference patterns. *Artificial Intelligence*, 75(1):63–92, 1995.

[21] M. J. Zaki. Scalable algorithms for association mining. *Knowledge and Data Engineering*, 12(2):372–390, 2000.

[22] M. J. Zaki and K. Gouda. Fast vertical mining using diffsets. Technical Report 01-1, Department of Computer Science, Rensselaer Polytechnic Institute, 2001.

[23] M. J. Zaki and C.-J. Hsiao. CHARM: An efficient algorithm for closed association rule mining,. Technical Report 99-10, Department of Computer Science, Rensselaer Polytechnic Institute, 1999.

Statistical Considerations in Learning from Data

Henry E. Kyburg, Jr.*
University of Rochester
Rochester, NY 14627
and
The Institute for Human and Machine Cognition
Pensacola, FLA 32501
hkyburg@ai.uwf.edu

Abstract

In this paper we focus on statistics. Classical statistics and Bayesian statistics are both employed in data mining. Both have advantages but both also have severe limitations in this context. We point out some of these limitations as well as some of the advantages. The fact that we may need to take account of evidence both internal and external to the data set presents a difficulty for classical statistics. The need to incorporate an objective measure of reliability creates a difficulty for Bayesian statistics.

We outline an approach to uncertainty that promises to capture the best of both worlds by incorporating both background knowledge and objectivity.

1 Introduction

Why do we want to learn from data? Unless we have strong antiquarian interests, It is because we wish to apply what we learn to the future, either directly (when we learn rules that we can apply directly) or indirectly (when we learn models or theories that help us understand how the world works). The connection between what we have encapsulated in our database, and what we need in order to have rational guidance for the future is provided by what is now often known as a *model*. These models may represent causal relations, in addition to statistical relations, but in every case they involve *at least* statistical relations. Induction is an implicit part of any data mining procedure. Our goal is almost always to use the past to improve our response to the challenges of the future. Uncertainty may be involved in two ways: First, the rules we obtain do not purport to yield certainties, and in fact may be expressed from the outset in

terms of probability distributions or statistical generalizations. Second, these rules are derived from past historical data, and therefore are themselves uncertain in their application to the future. The treatment of uncertainty in data mining is (appropriately) pragmatic. This leads, however, to a mixture of treatments of uncertainty that is not always consistent or coherent.

This relation is sometimes ignored, often in the interest of simplicity. For example in the fundamental paper [1] the "support" possessed by an association rule is represented by the fraction of the database in which its antecedent holds. From a statistical point of view, however, this fraction is irrelevant to inference (though it is of course relevant to the utility of what we uncover). A better indication of the *support* given to a rule is the absolute number of instances in which the antecedent is satisfied. Roughly speaking, if our mediating model is a sampling model, its accuracy is proportional to $1/\sqrt{n}$. Whether the relevant sample represents a large or a small fraction of the parent population is irrelevant.

You might think that we could avoid sampling altogether by examining the whole database. Not so. While the approach that descends from [1] is one in which the emphasis has been placed on speed and efficiency, with a view to processing the entire database, it is not the past that concerns us but the future. We want to *use* this data as a basis for prediction or for making decisions; we want to apply it to decisions about instances that are not (or not yet) part of our data base. In that case, what concerns us is not the body of data residing on our discs, not past data, but the data that will be generated in the future: the *next* million transactions. We can simply assume that "the future will be like the past" and we will usually be approximately right. But not always, and often the analysis of the data can give some idea of how usual and how approximate we may reasonably take our conjectures to be.

It is also true that as our databases get larger and larger,

---

*This material is based upon work supported by the National Science Foundation under Grants Nos. STS 9906128 and IIS 0082928.

it becomes more and more expensive to process them in their entirety. If we can get answers to some questions with a given level of certainty by sampling procedures, we can save a lot of time, at least with regard to those questions.

Getting a handle on the degrees of certainty and approximation involved requires paying attention to statistics, regardless of whether or not we process the entire data base. Even if we do process the whole database, it is not the dead past that concerns us, but the future, and what the past tells us about the future is both uncertain and approximate. The only connections we have to guide us are provided by statistics and probability. (There are other ways of representing and assessing uncertainty: the theory of belief functions [25], fuzzy logic [31], possibility theory [4], as well as hybrid mixtures of procedures. Nevertheless, when probabilities and statistical evidence are available, they seem to be preferred.)

But probability and statistics are controversial subjects. For many years, in the 1960's and 70's, the foundations of statistics came in for intense public debate, for example in [23, 14, 8]. This excitement, no doubt initiated by the initial controversy over the role of the subjective interpretation of probability in statistics, had begun to fade by 1980, at least in part because no definitive answers seemed to be forthcoming.

One reason for this cooling of interest in the foundations of statistics was the recognition that in actual practise, the mathematics and the design of experiments came to much the same thing, in many cases, regardless of the foundational viewpoint. Another reason was the emergence of "robust" and nonparametric statistical methods, under which precise prior distributions were no longer required. [9, 6] Finally there was the growing feeling (admittedly flattering to professional statisticians) that at root, good statistical practise relied on the professional judgement of the practising statistician, and that any attempt to replace this seasoned judgement with a mechanical adherence to rules was bound to fail. Not so flattering to the professional statistician, or to the logician, is the attitude that all we care about is whether a method "works", and that anybody can tell if something works.

It may now be time for another and closer look at the foundations of statistics. It can be argued that in data mining and knowledge discovery in databases, more is at stake that depends on the foundations of statistics than was at stake in the ordinary applications of statistics that were at issue in 1960. It is both trickier to detect the bias introduced by foundational assumptions, and more difficult to correct for that bias, when a large part of the process of statistical inference is automated.

We shall take a brief look first at "classical" statistics, then at "Bayesian" statistics. Classical statistics provides us with an objective approach to error, but only if a random sampling assumption is satisfied. Bayesian statistics has no problem with the "single case" nor with random sampling, but it does require an input of prior probabilities, which often seem arbitrary or subjective. Statistics appropriate to the inferential problems of data mining can be neither purely classical nor purely Bayesian. We shall then explore an approach that combines both the objectivity of the classical approach and the flexibility of the Bayesian approach.

2 Classical Statistics

Classical statistics, as developed by Fisher [5], Neyman [21], and others in the first decades of the last century, sought objectivity above all else. Probability was construed objectively in terms of long run relative frequencies. Particularly in the hands of Neyman and Pearson [22], and later Wald [27, 28] and Cramér [2], statisticians strove to develop methods that could be characterized by long run frequencies of error.

An example will make this clear. Suppose we want to test the hypothesis that the attribute a_1 is associated with the attribute b_1 with a higher frequency than f in a set D of transactions. We can express the hypothesis of interest this way: "$RF(b_1, a_1) > f$"; we are testing it against its alternative, "$RF(b_1, a_1) \leq f$". Since we want to apply this knowledge to future transactions, we must construe D as a *general* set of transactions, and not just those in the past. Of course what we have available is a set of past transactions — the ones recorded in our database.

Our conclusion goes beyond our observations, and is therefore risky. The classical approach to controlling and limiting this risk is to adopt a *method* that is characterized by certain long run properties. Let SD_N be the set of all subsets of D that contain N members, each of which has the attribute a_1. For a given value of $\alpha < 1$ it is straightforward to calculate a number d with the two properties: (1) IF "$RF(b_1, a_1) > f$" is true, THEN no more than a fraction α of SD_N will have a fraction smaller than $f - d$ instances of the attribute b_1, and (2) $f - d$ is the largest number of which this can be asserted. (For given N there is a trade-off between α and d; d can be made smaller at the cost of increasing α and vice versa.) This is just a statistical fact. We have yet to use it to construct a test of the hypothesis of interest.

From a classical point of view, we pass from this statistical fact to a *test* of a hypothesis by means of a *random sampling assumption*. This assumption says that each possible member of SD_N has the same chance of being selected as our sample, where *chance* is given a frequency interpretation: Our method of selecting samples is such that in the long run, each possible sample will be selected with equal frequency. This leads to the rule:

Obtain a random sample; if the relative frequency

322

of transactions with the attribute b_1 is greater than $f-d$, accept "$RF(b_1, a_1) > f$"; otherwise accept "$RF(b_1, a_1) \leq f$".

Some writers object to the use of the words "accept" and "reject" on the grounds that either may be undone by further evidence; let it be understood here that acceptance and rejection are nonmonotonic. This rule has the *demonstrable* property that in the long run, we will make the mistake of rejecting "$RF(b_1, a_1) > f$" when in fact it is true no more often than α; and at the same time we will minimize the frequency with which we make the opposite mistake of failing to reject "$RF(b_1, a_1) > f$" when it is false. Furthermore, α is a function of N, the cardinality of our sample size, alone. [18]

But from a data mining point of view, these nice properties just don't apply to what we do. The random sampling assumption does not hold: we are not "sampling" at all, but working with the data we have. The long run properties of the test depend completely on the random sampling assumption — that is where the probabilities or chances come from — and this assumption is just false.

Never mind that this is not the only application in which classical statistics gets along by making assumptions that are known to be flat out false. The methods by which samples are obtained is a bone of statistical contention in many studies; one can always ask was the sampling method truly random? But here we are not sampling at all! We are working with the data we have. (If we are sampling from the data, we are still taking that sample to be a sample of the whole set of transactions: future as well as historical.) The point is that this is exactly the circumstance in which we should be alert to bias; to make these classical assumptions is simply to assume ("presuppose") that this bias is absent.

It might be thought that one advantage of processing the entire database is that one would not have to worry about the randomness of one's sample. But as we pointed out earlier, our motivation is not merely antiquarian. Even if we process the whole data base, we need to bridge the gap between the past and the future: we need to consider the past as a sample of a universe to which the future also belongs. It is that universe of events, transactions, entities, that the data base provides us information about, and which, in turn provides us with information that guides our future choices and decisions.

The classical approach is tantalizing. That's exactly what we want: some objective measure of the reliability of our conclusions. But due to the falsity of the sampling assumption — it is not that it is merely an "ideal", it is not even applicable! — we cannot make the connection between these valuable long run frequencies and what we do.

Partly for this reason, but partly also, I'm afraid, for reasons of fashion, the most common statistical approach in data mining is Bayesian. Can the Bayesians help?

3 Bayesianism

The most pervasive objection to classical statistics in the world of real applications is that it does not yield long run frequency probabilities for particular cases. If we want to know how probable it is that an association rule will characterize a specific instance, or a specific class of instances, classical statistics will decline to answer: it makes no sense to talk about the frequency of error, or of accuracy, in a single case, which is typically what we are concerned with. This is true even if the single case is comprised of thousands of parts.

The foundation of a Bayesian approach to statistics is an interpretation of probability which takes it to apply to specific occurrences rather than arbitrarily large sequences of occurrences [24, 19, 20]. Probabilities, on this view, apply to just the right kinds of things: statements, hypotheses, events, specific objects. This first objection is met head on by Bayesianism. The Bayesian approach gives precise probabilities in every case.

Perhaps more serious than this "philosophical" motivation is the fact that while there are classical statistical methods for some problems, there are many problems that do not admit neatly of a classical solution, while Bayesian methods are truly universal. Suppose we want to evaluate the hypothesis H against the database D. We may simply write

$$
\begin{aligned}
Prob(H|D) &= \frac{Prob(H)Prob(D|H)}{Prob(D)} \\
&\propto Prob(H)Prob(D|H)
\end{aligned}
$$

There is nothing problematic about the *existence* of these probabilities, because the semantics for these probabilities is very weak and very idealized. Probabilities are relative to individuals (agents, knowers) and represent the degrees of belief of the individual. Ideally, perhaps, they represent the beliefs of experts.

But there is something problematic about the values of these probabilities. What probability should be assigned to a statistical hypothesis? That has always been a sticking point for the Bayesian approach. It has seemed to many that if we could just settle the question of how to evaluate $Prob(H)$, we'd be home free. To this end various proposals for the regimentation of prior probabilities have been made, for example in terms of information theory [10]. These proposals remain arbitrary, and are influenced by the subjective description of the problem at hand.

This is the downside of the Bayesian approach: that these methods are either subjective or arbitrary, and in either case divorced from the empirical domain. Recall that the long run performance of a classical statistical test is guaranteed: We will falsely reject the hypothesis under test, in the long run, no more than α of the time. In the Bayesian world there is no such guarantee. Worse than that, not only is there no guarantee about the future, probabilities do not even make claims about the future. Now of course we must not go off the deep end; frequency views give a guarantee, but it is a guarantee about the arbitrarily long run. That the limiting relative frequency of heads is a half guarantees that for any ϵ there exists an N such that the relative frequency of heads will not deviate by more than ϵ however much the sequence is extended beyond N. But this says nothing about the next toss, or the next ten tosses, or the next thousand tosses. So the guarantee provided by the frequency interpretation isn't very strong. But the Bayesian probability statement is compatible with whatever happens forever. This is true even of the regimented assignments made in accord with "objective" rules.

In practise, of course, subjective probabilities are influenced by frequencies. It is difficult to say *how* they are influenced, and by *what* frequencies. The opposite problem is also difficult: given that we know a lot of frequencies, which of these frequencies should influence our attitude or expectation regarding a specific instance. The latter problem is known as the problem of the choice of a reference class [17]. What we need is a way to understand this coy relation between frequency and applied probability.

4 Evidence and Background Knowledge

A pervasive problem within KDD is the problem of integrating background knowledge and evidence. This problem is a difficult one; it is merely mentioned and then dropped like a hot potato in a recent text [30, p. 38]; it is also mentioned as a problem in [26, p. 171], an early collection of papers on KDD.

To mention this problem is relevant here because it is one that calls for the integration of specific knowledge about the particular class of instances we face where the Bayesian approach seems capable of capturing what we want, and general knowledge about similar classes, which is the strong suit of the classical approach.

The general theme we keep encountering is that of combining knowledge of long run frequencies with knowledge about the specific instances we confront. It is the direct confrontation of this problem of combination that underlies Evidential Probability. [12]

The way in which probability is construed has a significant bearing on the issues with which we are concerned. To use an only slightly artificial example: if we are hidebound frequentists, we will feel obliged to accept as a basis for inference a statistically random sample of a population, however bizarre it may be. (For example, if it consists, as some properly random samples must, exclusively of plants from the northeast corner of the test plot.) On the other hand, if we are radical subjectivists, we may fail to see any reason at all for going to the trouble of obtaining a "random" sam-

ple of the population, since a carefully selected sample will allow us to avoid the waste of throwing away information.

The probability framework I will employ is that most recently adumbrated in *Uncertain Inference* [15], and earlier in [16, 11]. Since this is neither a frequentist nor a subjective interpretation of probability, it will be of value to provide a brief characterization here.

Mathematically, a *probability function* is a function that satisfies the well-known axioms of Kolmogorov. It is well known that finite relative frequencies satisfy these axioms. It is also possible to give a limiting relative frequency interpretation of these axioms. What we have in mind is not an interpretation of the function characterized by these axioms, but rather a *system* for applying known relative or limiting frequencies to particular instances.

In particular, we are concerned with the *logical* relation between what we know of a particular case and what we know of general frequencies — two relevant kinds of background knowledge — and what our rational attitude should be concerning a future (or as yet unknown) event. Put otherwise, we want to combine our knowledge of the particular and our knowledge of the general to obtain rational constraints on our expectations.

"Probability" is taken to be a two-place logical function, whose value is subinterval of $[0,1]$: $Prob(S, K) = [p, q]$. In this expression S represents a specific sentence (e.g., "The mean yield of variety V_{12b} is $y \pm \delta$ under conditions C"), and K represents the corpus of knowledge and evidence, including approximate knowledge of relative or limiting frequencies, relative to which the *probability* of this statement is determined (as a matter of logic) to be the interval $[p, q]$. The function $Prob(S, K)$ can be explicitly defined in a given language in terms of the expression S and the sentences comprising our general knowledge K [15]. The languages for which probability can be defined are general first-order languages, supplemented by variables and axioms for real numbers sufficient for the expression of statistical generalizations and distributions.

But an explicit definition is not to the point here; what we want is to evaluate instances of the probability function, which embodies both frequentist and specific elements. We offer instead of a formal definition, three algorithmic principles that together lie at the heart of the formal definition of probability, and which jointly suffice to rule out of consideration various possible candidates for a frequency-based probability of a given sentence S relative to given background knowledge and data K. The unique probability interval characterizing the sentence S, relative to the background knowledge and data K is the cover of the remaining intervals. With bad luck, this cover may be a large interval; in lucky cases it will be quite small, and sometimes will reflect a single item of statistical knowledge — when, as we might say, the subject of S is a *random member* of the reference class to which that item of statistical knowledge applies.

Our basic frequentist intuition is embodied in the stipulation that the probability interval $[p, q]$ be based on relative frequencies that are *known*, in the body of knowledge K, to hold in the real world. There are many such statements that we know. As is well known, there may be many ways in which the truth of the statement S can be tied to the occurrence of a relevant event; we will require (in a way to be made explicit below) that the relative frequencies of such relevant events be bounded by p and q.

The subjectivist (or better, epistemological) intuition is that the probability that matters to us is one that is based on what *we* know, and that what we know imposes bounds on the *rational* degree of belief we may have in the statement S. This intuition is captured informally by calling K our "body of knowledge," and thinking of K as the total *evidence*, both statistical and specific, bearing on S. Formally it is captured by providing a representation of the data and background knowledge that are to be taken into account in our inference, and defining probability relative to such a set of statements.

Just as there are many ways in which the truth of S can be tied to the occurrence of a relevant event, so there are an unlimited number of ways a statement S can be associated with a relative frequency given a body of knowledge K. "The next toss of coin c will land heads," for example, may be associated with the frequency with which coins land heads, or the frequency with which *this* coin lands heads, or the frequency with which I win bets, or the frequency with which a coin, launched under such and such precisely specified circumstances, will land face up.

There are three relatively simple and intuitive principles that suffice to allow us to ignore irrelevant bits of statistical information. These principles lie at the heart of the formal definition of probability. It is not to be expected that in all cases only one relevant item of statistical knowledge will fail to be ruled out, but in all cases there will be a unique interval that will *cover* all the relevant statistical knowledge we have bearing on S. In this sense these three principles suffice to pick out a probability interval to be associated with a sentence S based on our objective knowledge of relative frequencies.

Principle of Richness: If two statistical statements differ in the sense that they associate with S intervals neither of which is included in the other, and one is richer than the other in the sense that our knowledge K entails that the second is a marginalization of the first, then the second may be ignored: When conditionalization makes a difference, use it.

Example: Suppose an experiment in which urns are cho-sen with equal frequency, and balls are drawn randomly, can be represented by the table:

	Urn 1	Urn 2	Urn 3	total
black	9	9	100	118
white	1	1	900	902
	10	10	1000	1020

It would clearly be inappropriate to regard the probability of getting a black ball in such an experiment as 118/1020 (rather than 19/30) on the mistaken grounds that it is the outcome of an experiment involving 1020 balls of which 118 are black.

Principle of Specificity: If two statistical statements differ, and K entails that the reference class of the first is a subset of the reference class of the second, then the second may be ignored.

Example: Suppose that on a particular trial of this experiment, we know that Urn 2 was chosen, but not what color of ball was selected from the urn. Then only the numbers in the column under Urn 2 are relevant, and the probability that the ball is black is 9/10.

Principle of Precision: Consider the set of statistical statements relevant to S that cannot be eliminated by either of the first two principles. If an item of statistical knowledge associates an interval with S that is broader than the union of the intervals mentioned in the remainder of the statements, it may be ignored.

Example: Suppose that K contains the knowledge that the accident rate for 17 year-olds falls in the interval [0.015,0.025]; and that it is also known (on the basis of more limited evidence) that the accident rate for 17 year olds in Lyons, N.Y. lies between 0.0 and 0.10. The more specific knowledge about Lyons drivers does not *differ* from the more general knowledge, and so we take the more general (and more precise) knowledge as determining the probability.

In general we take the probability of the sentence S, relative to the body of knowledge K to be the cover of the intervals that survive the application of these three principles. To recapitulate: there may be many frequencies derivable from K that are germane to S, but leaner statistical claims give way to richer ones; less specific claims give way to more specific claims; and less precise knowledge gives way to more precise knowledge.

Note that this is *not* a Bayesian approach in the sense that the beliefs of the experimenter or the logic of the questions asked determines the probabilities. Such an approach to data mining and KDD seems fraught with peril. It is one thing when the conflicting opinions of a group of human investigators bias an investigation; it will all work out in the end; someone will point out the emperor's state of dress. But if bias or unwarranted assumptions undermine an automated system, it is not clear where correction can come from.

The two most important features of this treatment of probability are both tied to objectivity. First, it is established in [15] that if the probability of S is $[p, q]$, then *every* relevant long run frequency that can reasonably be associated with S lies within the bounds p and q. By "relevant" we mean "that cannot be ignored on the basis of the three principles mentioned above." There is a very strong connection between objective long run relative frequencies and probability.

Second, since this connection can be characterized formally, we assume that if agents can agree on what is probable, they can agree on what is in K. Given agreement on K, agreement on probability is objectively assured. It is assured because the relation between the set of sentences K, representing both background knowledge and data, the sentence S and the interval $[p, q]$ is defined explicitly. Every sentence S has exactly one (interval) probability relative to K.

An increasing number of authors have pursued interval-valued or "imprecise" probabilities, for example [7, 11, 3], and more recently Peter Walley [29] and contributors to the biennial symposium ISIPTA (International Symposium on Imprecise Probabilities and Their Applications).

We shall see how this approach leads to a knowledge representation structure that seems to allow us to find a satisfactory solution to a number of the problems of knowledge discovery and data mining.

5   A Modest Illustration

Consider a marketbasket domain, with possible items $A_1, \ldots, A_n$, and a set D of market baskets containing selections from among these items. Choose a level of "practical certainty" — say, 0.95. Suppose we wish to assess the association of A_2 with A_1, that is, we want a practically certain approximate statistical association of the form: between x and y of the time, a market basket with A_1 will also contain A_2.

A Bayesian statistician will have no trouble with this inference, provided he has the required prior probabilities. In particular, he needs the prior distribution of the association of A_2 with A_1. In lieu of a real distribution over this parameter, he might settle for a "flat" or "maximum entropy" distribution. Given a subjective or arbitrary prior distribution, we are still not quite through, since we must also assume a distribution for the evidence *given* value of the parameter. In general that isn't hard: we simply assume that the items of evidence — the marketbaskets — are probabilistically independent of one another, given the value of the parameter

of association.

It is clear that on this approach a number of assumptions are being made that may or may not be agreeable to all parties concerned. Much depends on intuition or agreeableness. To relativize solutions to assumptions may inhibit argument, but it does not necessarily lead to substantive agreement. We must escape from subjectivism.

A classical statistical approach, however, which we would hope would provide objectivity, simply is not properly applicable. If the set D of marketbaskets containing item A_1 were a *sample* of a well defined population of marketbaskets containing item A_1, we could construct a confidence interval inference: we could say that the 0.95 confidence interval determined by the sample assigns a value between x and y to the relative frequency with which A_2 accompanies A_1. This inference would be objective in a strong sense: In the arbitrarily long run, at least 95% of the time, the inference $[x, y]$ will include the true parameter.

The problem is that this objectivity depends on the randomness of the sample: we must assume that $D \cap A_1$ is chosen from the universe of all market baskets containing A_1 by some method that would, in the long run, choose each equinumerous subset of $D \cap A_1$ with equal frequency. But we haven't "chosen" this sample at all — it is just the sample we had given to us. It is not, properly speaking, a "sample" at all in the classical sense.

On the evidential approach, we can save the objectivity of the classical approach. The requirement of random sampling is replaced by the three criteria mentioned. We do know that the set $D \cap A_1$ is a member of the set of equinumerous subsets of the universe of *all* market baskets containing A_1. We do know that (at least) 95% of those sets are *representative* in the sense that they fall within the 0.95 confidence ellipse for that size of sample. If nothing undermined the inference that would allow us to say that we can be practically certain (i.e., that the probability is [0.95,1.0]) that the proportion of market baskets with A_1 that also contain A_2 is between x and y. The question is whether we can claim representativeness in this sense for that particular sample.

Does richness undermine this probability? Is this inference based on a marginalization of more complete data? That would be the case if we had objective knowledge of a prior distribution of the association parameter that led to a *conflicting* conclusion, but we do not generally have such knowledge. If we did, the inference would be undermined, but it would also be replaced by a conditional inference.

Does specificity undermine this probability? Is there a competing inference based on a more precise reference class? If so, we should not disregard that competing inference, but often there is no such competing inference.

Finally, is there a more precise statistical statement than the general confidence interval ellipse that can be used to obtain a probability for this conclusion? Again, this is unlikely, but possible.

If the answers to these questions are all negative, then the claim of an association parameter in $[x, y]$ can be regarded as "practically certain" at the 0.95 level.

It is easy enough to specify background knowledge that would lead to affirmative answers. For example, if we do have an objective prior distribution over the values of the association parameters (say, obtained from studies of similar problems) *and* that prior distribution led to a probability disagreeing with the confidence interval analysis, the confidence interval analysis would not apply.

Suppose that D consists of market baskets recorded during the spring months, and there are good sociological/psychological grounds for supposing that the association during the spring months is atypical of the full year. That would provide grounds for supposing that the sample comes from a set of subsets to which the 0.95 ellipse does not apply: we have reason to suppose that this particular subset is *not* practically certain to be representative in the sense determined by that ellipse.

The approach outlined is claimed to provide both objectivity and feasible sensitivity to background knowledge.

6 Conclusion

Data mining and knowledge discovery are, on the view adopted here, heavily dependent on statistical inference. Statistical inference, in turn, is dependent on probability. I claim that neither the classical approach to statistical inference — the Neyman-Pearson hypothesis testing approach — and the Bayesian approach, both of which live together rather uncomfortably in data mining applications, are able to deal with the basic problems of inference from fixed data, making use of actual background knowledge.

I have proposed an approach to statistical inference based on evidential probability. This approach embodies a semantics which firmly ties together the results of KDD and long run frequencies in the real world. Inferred *knowledge* is what we seek, and what we will use as a guide to decision in the future: the very same concept of probability, taking the body of inferred knowledge as evidence, will yield the probabilities and mathematical expectations we need as a guide to the future.

On the other hand, the knowledge that needs to be represented to implement this approach is rather limited in character: we need take into account sentences in a rather limited vocabulary that depends on the problem at hand. Even with a limited vocabulary, however, there may be many more possible rules than we can begin to think of testing. The treatment of probability and statistics that has been suggested is no panacea. The extent to which it provides a useful framework for the exploration of data bases remains to be seen. But I do claim that it has the virtue of objectivity, in two important senses.

First, and most important, probability, though it is applicable to specific instances, is objective in that it is derived from frequencies in the real world. In particular, the chances of error in particular inferences are characterized by long run error frequencies. When we infer an association rule to the effect that B accompanies A between 60% and 70% of the time, *what* we are concluding is that a frequency in this range characterizes the real world. What we make of that frequency is another matter. Under the right circumstances we may take the *probability* of finding an instance of B accompanying a given instance of A to be [0.6,0.7]. Probabilities are firmly tied to objective frequencies.

Second, through the explicit consideration of the body of knowledge relative to which probabilities are judged, the evaluation of probabilities is rendered *logically* objective. Anybody, including a computer, considering the statement S relative to the background knowledge and data K, will come to the same interval probability for S relative to K. This second sort of objectivity is particularly important computationally.

With regard to finding our way through the world, and using data as a guide to life [13] it is the first kind of objectivity that is of greatest importance. Suppose we must choose between two actions. We calculate the expected value of the possible outcomes attendant on each. The expected value of the outcomes consists of the sum of each possible outcome, multiplied by its probability. If that probability is a matter of belief or opinion, we have a conclusion that represents merely belief or opinion. If that probability is a matter of objective long run frequency, as it is in the framework proposed here, we have a guide that at least in the long run will be correct.

There are two further (negative) observations to be made. That a guide is in the long run correct doesn't mean that it will turn out to have led to the ideal choice today. The horse with the best statistics can still lose today's race. And it must also be noted that the framework suggested here does not lead, as does a subjectivistic framework, to clear cut decisions in almost every case. Since probabilities are interval valued, so are expectations; and if expectation intervals are nested or overlap, no clear decision is recommended.

References

[1] R. Agrawal, T. Imielinski, and A. Swami. Mining association rules between sets of items in large databases. In P. Buneman and S. Jajodia, editors, *ACM SIGMOD International Conference on Management of Data*, Washington, DC, 1993.

[2] H. Cramér. *Mathematical Methods of Statistics*. Princeton University Press, Princeton, 1951.

[3] A. P. Dempster. Upper and lower probabilities induced by a multivalued mapping. *Annals of Mathematical Statistics*, 38:325–339, 1967.

[4] D. Dubois and H. Prade. *Possibility Theory*. Plenum Presss, New York, 1985.

[5] R. A. Fisher. On the mathematical foundations of theoretical statistics. *Philosophical Transactions of the Royal Societ Series A*, 222:309–368, 1922.

[6] D. A. S. Frazer. *Nonparametric Methods in Statistics*. John Wiley and Sons, New York, 1957.

[7] I. J. Good. Subjective probability as a measure of a non-measurable set. In S. Nagel and Tarski, editors, *Logic, Methodology and Philosophy of Science*, pages 319–329. University of California Press, Berkeley, 1962.

[8] W. Harper and C. Hooker, editors. *Foundations of Probability Theory, Statistical Inference, and Statistical Theories of Science 3 Vols*. Reidel, Dordrecht, 1976.

[9] P. Huber. *Robust Statistical Procedures*. SIAM, Philadelphia, 1996.

[10] E. T. Jaynes. Probability theory in science and engineering. *Colloquium Lectures in Pure and Applied Science*, 4:152–187, 1958.

[11] H. E. Kyburg, Jr. *Probability and the Logic of Rational Belief*. Wesleyan University Press, Middletown, 1961.

[12] H. E. Kyburg, Jr. Combinatorial semantics: the semantics of frequent validity. *Computational Intelligence*, 13:215–257, 1997.

[13] H. E. Kyburg, Jr. Probability as a guide in life. *The Monist*, 84:135–152, 2001.

[14] H. E. Kyburg, Jr. and E. Nagel, editors. *Induction: Some Current Issues*. Wesleyan University Press, Middletown, 1962.

[15] H. E. Kyburg, Jr. and C. M. Teng. *Uncertain Inference*. Cambridge University Press, New York, 2001.

[16] H. E. J. Kyburg. *The Logical Foundations of Statistical Inference Reidel*. Reidel, Dordrecht, 1974.

[17] H. E. J. Kyburg. Randomness and the right reference class. *Journal of Philosophy*, 74:501–520., 1977.

[18] E. L. Lehman. *Testing Statistical Hypotheses*. John Wiley and Sons, New York, 1959.

[19] D. V. Lindley. *Introduction To Probability and Statistics Part I: Probabilty*. Cambridge University Press, Cambridge, 1965.

[20] D. V. Lindley. *Introduction To Probability and Statistics Part II. Inference*. Cambridge University Press, Cambridge, 1965.

[21] J. Neyman. Outline of a theory of statistical estimation based on the classical theory of probability. *Philosophical Transaction Of The Royal Society A*, pages 333–380, 1937.

[22] J. Neyman and E. Pearson. On the problem of the most efficient tests of statistical hypotheses. *Philosophical Transactions Of The Royal Soc.*, A 2311:289–337, 1933.

[23] G. V. P. and D. A. Sprott, editors. *Foundations of Statistical Inference*. Holt Rinehart and Winston of Canada, Toronto and Montreal, 1971.

[24] L. J. Savage. *The Foundations of Statistics*. John Wiley, New York, 1954.

[25] G. Shafer. *A Mathematical Theory of Evidence*. Wiley, New York, 1962.

[26] P. Smyth and R. M. Goodman. Rule induction using information theory. In G. Piatetsky-Shapiro and W. J. Frawley, editors, *Knowledge Discovery in Databases*, pages 159–176. AAAI Press/MIT Press, Menlo Park, 1991.

[27] A. Wald. *Sequential Analysis,*. John Wiley, New York, 1947.

[28] A. Wald. *Statistical Decision Functions*. Wiley, New York, 1950.

[29] P. Walley. *Statistical Reasoning with Imprecise Probabilities*. Chapman and Hall, London, 1991.

[30] I. H. Witten and E. Frank. *Data Mining*. Acadmic Press, San Diego, 2000.

[31] L. Zadeh. Fuzzy logic and approximate reasoning. *Synthese*, 30:407–428, 1975.

Subject Classification in the Oxford English Dictionary

Zarrin Langari   Frank Wm. Tompa

Department of Computer Science
University of Waterloo
Waterloo, ON
Canada
{zlangari, fwtompa}@db.uwaterloo.ca

Abstract

The Oxford English Dictionary is a valuable source of lexical information and a rich testing ground for mining highly structured text. Each entry is organized into a hierarchy of senses, which include definitions, labels and cited quotations. Subject labels distinguish the subject classification of a sense, for example they signal how a word may be used in Anthropology, Music or Computing. Unfortunately subject labeling in the dictionary is incomplete. To overcome this incompleteness, we attempt to classify the senses (i.e., definitions) in the dictionary by their subjects, using the citations as an information guide. We report on four different approaches: k Nearest Neighbors, a standard classification technique; Term Weighting, an information retrieval method dealing with text; Naive Bayes, a probabilistic method; and Expectation Maximization, an iterative probabilistic method. Experimental performance of these methods is compared based on standard classification metrics.

1 Introduction

Dictionaries encode rich semantic structures organized as a sequence of entries. Each entry for a word in a typical monolingual dictionary includes some main definitions and additional information about those words that helps readers to understand usage more easily. In the *Oxford English Dictionary* [22] (the OED) an *entry*, such as the one shown in Figure 1, contains various structural elements such as headword, pronunciation, part of speech, homonym number, usage labels, etymology and historical and current senses. Each *sense* contains a sense number, definition and cited quotations illustrating usage.

Some applications may need to distinguish those dictio-

vectoring ('vεktərɪŋ), *vbl. sb.* [f. VECTOR *sb.*, VECTOR *v.* + -ING¹.] 1. The action of VECTOR *v.*
   1956 W. A. HEFLIN *U.S. Air Force Dict.* 553/1 Vectoring is usually done from the ground, or from a mother aircraft. **2.** *Computers.* The provision or use of interrupt vectors.
   1977 E. E. KLINGMAN *Microprocessor Systems Design* xii. 352 These [lines] are for 'cascading' several 8214s if more than eight interrupting devices need vectoring. **1979** *Personal Computer World* Nov. 84/4 Software vectoring of interrupts to allow more than one interrupt driven peripheral at a time, and also multi-programming.

Figure 1. Simple entry from the OED [22]

nary senses related to a chosen discipline. For example, we may wish to extract a historical *computing* dictionary, containing only those senses from the OED pertaining to computing. Unfortunately the dictionary's editors did not include labels everywhere they apply, nor are labels abbreviated consistently. For example, although the entry for **recursive** has senses labeled *Math* and *Logic, Linguistics, Computing,* and *Phonetics,* the entry for **recursion** includes no explicit subject labels at all. Thus the user must rely on other means to select all subject-specific word senses.

In an attempt to mine this information, we exploit the observation that senses related to computing typically include illustrative citations from the computing literature, and this holds for other subjects as well. Our approach is inspired by the earlier work of Jonathan Spencer, who realized several years ago that the collections of citations for a word in *Anthropology* often includes works from anthropology, and who suggested finding other words or senses in the field by finding those that cite similar sources [2]. Citations include date, author, and source of each illustrative quotation, but there are no subject labels attached to citations. Thus we must rely on the information implicit in each citation paragraph or in our own experience to know which citations arise from which subject areas. We have investigated a *supervised* text classification task, in which we use the citations of other senses from the OED with an explicit subject label to induce a subject label for those senses without a label but with similar citations.

This paper summarizes our experience with extracting interesting lexical data from a 540 megabyte, highly structured text. Providing a data model for the dictionary senses, and considering the subjects as categories, we begin our categorization task by preprocessing the dictionary to make it more appropriate for our needs. Starting with the tagged dictionary, for example, we remove all unnecessary information from the entries. We also create suitable indexes over the labels and citation information to support our task. Thereafter we apply standard classification techniques and evaluate their effectiveness for this problem. We found that unlike many other categorization tasks, the problem size and the sparseness of the data were significant obstacles to address.

The remainder of this paper is organized as follows. In Section 2 we introduce the corpus (the OED) and our data model for classification. Section 3 gives a brief overview of the *k Nearest Neighbors*, *Term Frequency * Inverse Document Frequency, Naive Bayes,* and *Expectation Maximization* methods as they apply to our problem. Section 4 summarizes performance evaluation metrics, and Section 5 describes the experimental comparison of the classification methods for our task. In conclusion, we summarize our experience and describe anticipated future work.

2 Dictionary and Data Model

As mentioned in the introduction, the *Oxford English Dictionary,* like any other dictionary, has a specific structure to express the meanings of words [3]. In a typical OED entry a headword (i.e., the word being described by the entry) together with pronunciation, part of speech, and homonym number (if needed) forms a "headword group." Besides the headword group, three other main elements that appear for most entries are definitions, quotations and labels. *Definitions* appear in a hierarchical structure of numbered *senses* to express:

- grammatical and semantic subdivisions of the word,

- parallel meanings and usages of a word over time, and

- the chronological order of the uses of various meanings of a word.

As supporting evidence for each sense, *quotations* are provided to illustrate how the word being described has been used by various authors over time. Together with the quoted text, each citation typically contains the author's name, the

title of the work in which the quotation appeared, the publication date, and the location of the quotation within the work. *Labels* are related to various uses of a word, and they may appear in a headword group or with individual word senses. Among different types of labels, we are interested only in those that denote a subject. The entry for **vectoring** includes two senses, the first of which is unlabelled and has one supporting citation and the second of which is labelled *Computers* and has two citations.

Our model is based on extracted data from each entry, as illustrated for the entry for **lymphatic** in Figure 2.

lymphatic, *a. sb.*
A
 I
  1

BLOUNT, *Glossogr.*	SHAFTESB, *Charac.*
BAILEY	S. BURDER, *Orient. Lit.*

A
 II
  2
   a *Phys. Anat.*

EVELYN, *Mem.*	BOYLE, *Usef. Exp. Nat. Philos.*
ARBUTHNOT, *Rules of Diet.*	*Astruc's Fevers.*
ABERNETHY, *Surg. Obs.*	R. KNOX, *Beclard's Anat.*
ROLLESTON, *Anim. Life.*	*Allbutt's Syst. Med.*

A
 II
  2
   b *Bot.*

GREW, *Anat. Plants.*	LOUDON, *Encycl. Plants*

A
 II
  3

J. FORBES, *Laennec's Dis. Chest.*	
HAWTHORNE, *Fr. & It. Note-Bks.*	
G. MEREDITH, *R. Feverel.*	HUXLEY, *Physiol.*
Truth	

B
 1

SHAFTESBURY, *Charac.*	SHENSTONE, *Elegies*

B
 2

Phil. Trans.	FLOYER, *Physic. Pulse-Watch*
HEWSON, *Phil. Trans.*	GOOD, *Bk. Nat.*
MIVART, *Cat*	

Figure 2. Extracted information from the entry lymphatic.

From the headword group we extract the headword, part of speech, and homonym number and ignore any other components. For each sense in the hierarchy, we generate a sense locator based on the sense numbers (e.g. **A.I.1**). The other interesting information in each entry is contained in the labels, although not all labels denote subjects. For example, the subject label *Bot.* indicates that sense definition **A.II.2.b** pertains to botany. The final interesting elements for our classification task are citation components, namely author and title. For example, the title *Rules of Diet* in sense **A.II.2.a** appears for entry senses of **larynx** and **serus** that are also labelled *Anatomy*.

Our task is to classify the senses from the OED by choosing an appropriate label for each sense based on the evidence found in the corresponding citations' authors and titles. We restrict ourselves to *single-label* classification, in which only the top ranked category is assigned to each unlabeled document (so-called *1-per-doc* category assignment). We also apply *thresholding* [13], in which we assign a document to a category if its similarity or its probability of membership is above a user-defined amount.

After appropriate preprocessing the dictionary data can be considered as a pair of relations, one mapping sense identifiers to labels and the other mapping sense identifiers to cited authors and titles. These relations represent a *vector model* in which the authors and titles are the *terms* used as documents' features. The vector space is r-dimensional with one dimension for each possible term, and a specific document $\overline{d_j} = < f_{j1}, ..., f_{jr} >$ is a vector of *term frequencies* in which the value for each component in the vector is the number of occurrences of that term in the document.

With this model, we can apply a supervised classification method, which uses pre-labeled data (in our case the labeled senses) as a *training set* and builds a classifier by learning from this set. To categorize a new document, its characteristics are compared to those of the members of classified sets. For simplicity, we assume that an author or a title can be used individually as a term that may be associated with a label, that all the terms are independent of each other, and that authors or titles of the same name refer to the same entity. We believe that each of these assumptions, while generally invalid, reflect the state of the data closely enough that they will not be too detrimental to the performance of our classification strategies.

As an overview of the size of our data, we note that there are about 523,000 senses in the dictionary, of which only 63,000 are labeled with one of 128 unique subject labels that appear more than 45 times each. There are 300,000 unique references (cited authors or titles) that occur in 4.2 million instances overall, and on average each sense includes 8 to 10 references. Thus we must accommodate a very large data space, 523,000 documents × 300,000 terms, that is very sparsely populated.

3 Classification Methods

For our experiments, we investigated the performance of four techniques. The k Nearest Neighbors method (kNN) is a lazy learning method and a simple technique, often with high performance results. As a second approach, we investigated the tf*idf term weighting technique, which is com-

monly used in information retrieval applications. The last two techniques, Naive Bayes (NB) and Expectation Maximization (EM), are chosen from the probabilistic methods: both attempt to estimate the parameters of a generating model that creates documents in categories based on an unknown set of probabilities. More detailed descriptions of the methods can be found elsewhere [11].

3.1 k Nearest Neighbors

Using the kNN method [5, 15, 21, 23], for each unlabeled data vector, we find the k nearest training data vectors in the multi-dimensional vector space, judging proximity by the often-used *Cosine* similarity measure:

$$sim(\overline{d_x}, \overline{d_y}) = \frac{\sum_{t=1}^{r} f_{xt} f_{yt}}{\sqrt{\sum_{t=1}^{r} f_{xt}^2} \sqrt{\sum_{t=1}^{r} f_{yt}^2}} \quad (1)$$

where r is the number of dimensions, $\overline{d_x}$ is a labeled document vector, $\overline{d_y}$ is an unlabeled document vector, and f_{xt} and f_{yt} are the term frequencies of these two documents [10]. We assign to the new object the category of the majority of its neighbors.

As well as choosing a similarity function, specific applications of kNN require settings for various thresholds. The first is the value of k, indicating how many neighbors are to be considered for picking a category. This threshold is usually determined experimentally by a validation set. Other parameters are minimal thresholds for voting: how many neighbors must be in the chosen category, how similar must those neighbors be to the new object, and so forth.

3.2 Term Frequency * Inverse Document Frequency

Selection of tf*idf, first developed for information retrieval [1, 9, 19], as the second method is intended to overcome the weaknesses of depending on *one-to-one* comparisons for very small (sparse) documents. If each instance of unlabeled data is compared against a set of senses from the labeled data, we can find more common references and thus potentially improve the results.

To apply this approach to classification, we consider the concatenation of the training objects in each category to be the documents in our collection (i.e., one aggregated document per category) and the data object to be classified as a "query." In matching a query to candidate documents, the term weighting system gives higher value to a term that occurs often in a document if it occurs relatively *infrequently* in the document collection as a whole. Following Salton's suggestions [19], we must also account for differences in category size and query length. Specifically, the term weight for the tth term in category c_i is computed as:

$$w_{it} = \frac{f_{it} \log \frac{N}{n_t}}{\sqrt{\sum_{h=1}^{r}(f_{ih} \log \frac{N}{n_h})^2}} \qquad (2)$$

where again r is the number of terms, f_{it} is the frequency of term t in category i, N is the number of categories, and n_t is the number of categories containing at least one occurrence of term t. The term weight for the tth term in a data object to be classified (our "query") is computed as :

$$d'_{yt} = [0.5 + \frac{0.5 f_{yt}}{F_y}] \log \frac{N}{n_t} \qquad (3)$$

where f_{yt} is the frequency of term t in the query and F_y is the highest term frequency among all the query object's terms. With these definitions of weights, the similarity of a category c_i to an unlabeled document $\overline{d_y}$ is then calculated as $sim(c_i, \overline{d_y})$ using the Cosine measure in Equation 1 above, but with these term weights substituted for the simple term frequencies that are used in kNN. We finally classify the test data object by assigning it the label of the most similar category.

It is important to keep in mind that whereas kNN compares an unlabeled document to individual labeled documents, tf*idf compares an unlabeled document to the set of labeled documents in each category taken as a whole. Nevertheless, as for kNN, tf*idf requires settings for thresholds for choosing the appropriate category: how similar the closest category is to the new object and how much more similar it is than the other categories.

3.3 Naive Bayes

The idea underlying the last two classifiers is to use probabilities of categories and category-dependent joint probabilities of terms occurring in documents to find the probability of a category given a document [18]. The probabilistic model is "naive" in its assumption of term independence, i.e., the conditional probability of a term given a category is assumed to be independent of the conditional probabilities of other terms given that category [14, 16, 23]. Because citations are occasionally repeated within a single sense, we are interested in *multinomial* Bayesian classifiers, for which term frequencies, rather than merely presence or absence of terms, are used in computing the joint probabilities.

The metrics for these methods are based on $P(c_i|\overline{d_j})$, the probability of document $\overline{d_j}$ belonging to class c_i, for all the classes $i = 1..N$:

$$P(c_i|\overline{d_j}) = \frac{P(c_i) * \prod_{t=1}^{r} P(T_{jt}|c_i)^{f_{jt}}}{\sum_{q=1}^{N}(P(c_q) * \prod_{t=1}^{r} P(T_{jt}|c_q)^{f_{jt}})} \qquad (4)$$

where $\overline{d_j}$ is again a vector of term frequencies f_{jt}, $P(c_i)$ is the prior probability that a randomly picked document falls

within category c_i, $P(T_{jt}|c_i)$ is the probability of generating the tth term for document j if it is in the ith class, and r is again the number of distinct terms in the document space.

To calculate these probabilities, we need to estimate the probability of a term given a specific class. The maximum likelihood value is the total number of times that a term occurs in that class (for training data) divided by the total number of terms in that class:

$$P(T_{jt}|c_i) = \frac{\sum_{j=1}^{|D_l|} f_{jt} * B_{ji}}{\sum_{s=1}^{r} \sum_{j=1}^{|D_l|} f_{js} * B_{ji}} \qquad (5)$$

where B_{ji} is 1 if and only if document $\overline{d_j}$ belongs to category c_i and $|D_l|$ is the number of training documents. The class prior probability is also similarly estimated:

$$P(c_i) = \frac{\sum_{j=1}^{|D_l|} B_{ji}}{|D_l|} \qquad (6)$$

In practice, however, we need to account for the situation in which a term does not occur in some class in any of the training data but could appear in that class in some unseen data. In these situations, we must avoid assigning zero probability for that term given that class. Following best practices, we use *Simple Good-Turing* to "smooth" the probabilities by distributing a small portion of the probability mass from observed data to terms that do not appear in the training set [6].

In summary, with the NB method, we classify a document by first computing maximum likelihood values for the class prior probability $P(c_i)$ for all the classes and for the (smoothed) probability of document terms given each class $P(T_{jt}|c_i)$. We then calculate the posterior probability of each class given a document that comprises specific terms $P(c_i|\overline{d_j})$. We finally choose the class with the highest probability, subject once again to passing thresholds corresponding to those used in the other approaches.

3.4 Expectation Maximization

In his original approach to labeling OED senses based on citations, Spencer included iterative steps to incorporate additional evidence introduced as unlabeled senses were incrementally classified [2]. A similar iterative algorithm has also been shown to be useful in extracting author-title pairs from the World Wide Web [4]. Following these approaches, we decided to evaluate the performance of Expectation Maximization (EM), in which we use the terms that appear in unlabeled documents to strengthen the evidence of a term occurring in a class. The iterative behavior of the EM method provides a form of *many-to-many* basis of comparison, since all unlabeled senses are simultaneously compared to all labeled senses.

For the first step (expectation), we calculate $P(c_i|\overline{d_j})$ using the NB method described for each unlabeled document over all the classes. Then instead of using the labeled data only, in the next step (maximization), we use tentatively classified data as well as the labeled data to calculate revised probabilities $P(c_i)$ for each class and $P(T_{jt}|c_i)$ for each term:

$$P(T_{jt}|c_i) = \frac{\sum_{j=1}^{|D|} f_{jt} * P(c_i|\overline{d_j})}{\sum_{s=1}^{s=r} \sum_{j=1}^{|D|} f_{js} * P(c_i|\overline{d_j})} \quad (7)$$

$$P(c_i) = \frac{\sum_{j=1}^{|D|} P(c_i|\overline{d_j})}{|D|} \quad (8)$$

where $P(c_i|\overline{d_j})$ are the probabilities for all documents (and thus $P(c_i|\overline{d_j}) = B_{ji}$ for labeled documents). These are used in turn to revise the classification probabilities $P(c_i|\overline{d_j})$, and this cycle can be iterated until the probabilities $P(c_i|\overline{d_j})$ converge. At this stage, all the unlabeled data has been considered simultaneously, and all their probabilities for membership in each category have been estimated. Using these probabilities, we assign classes using the same thresholds we use for NB.

Experience has shown that EM improves over the NB method in applications where the assumptions are valid, i.e., the generative mixture model reflects the application as a whole and the probability models for each category adequately reflect the data objects, including the document length distribution and the assumption of term independence [18].

4 Evaluation

Before describing the details of the experiments, we need to determine how to measure the *effectiveness* of each method in classifying the dictionary senses. Recall and precision are two well-known metrics from information retrieval. In the context of text classification, they are defined as [8, 12]:

$$Pr = \frac{\# \, of \, documents \, correctly \, assigned \, to \, category \, i}{\# \, of \, documents \, assigned \, to \, category \, i}$$

$$Re = \frac{\# \, of \, documents \, correctly \, assigned \, to \, category \, i}{\# \, of \, documents \, that \, should \, be \, assigned \, to \, category \, i}$$

which show how to compute the precision and recall over one category. There are two approaches to compute the overall precision and recall:

- *macroaveraging*: Overall precision and recall are computed by averaging the results of the values for each category, which therefore gives equal weight to each category. If m is the number of categories then:

$$Pr = \frac{\sum_{i=1}^{m} Pr_i}{m} \quad Re = \frac{\sum_{i=1}^{m} Re_i}{m}$$

- *microaveraging*: First, for each category the number of correctly classified documents a_i, incorrectly classified ones b_i, and incorrectly rejected documents c_i are computed. Then, giving equal weight to each document, overall precision and recall is computed based on the totals of these values in all categories:

$$Pr = \frac{\sum_{i=1}^{m} a_i}{\sum_{i=1}^{m} (a_i + b_i)} \quad Re = \frac{\sum_{i=1}^{m} a_i}{\sum_{i=1}^{m} (a_i + c_i)}$$

Most researchers believe that for classification purposes microaveraging is a better indicator, because each categorization decision is weighted equally, but some prefer macroaveraging in which frequent categories are not weighted more heavily than infrequent ones [20]. Finally, in order to have a single measure of performance, we chose to use a simple *F-measure* that balances precision and recall [20]:

$$F = \frac{2 Pr Re}{(Pr + Re)}$$

5 Experiments

For our experiments we used the 63,000 senses that were labeled by any of the 128 labels occurring in the dictionary more than 45 times each. These senses served as both the training data and the test data, using *3-fold cross-validation*. We partitioned the whole set into three subsets of equal size, randomly assigning documents to subsets, to obtain three instances of training and test data with about $\frac{1}{3}$ of data in each training set and $\frac{2}{3}$ in each test set. After performing categorization with each of the four methods, two different thresholds were applied: the first one is a threshold to pick the best category (majority number for kNN, similarity for tf*idf, and probability for NB and EM methods) and the second is the threshold for the difference between the best and the second-best category. Threshold values were chosen to maximize the F-measures as explained above, yielding the results shown in Table 1.

	kNN	tf*idf	NB	EM
threshold for best	0	0.01	0.7	0.5
threshold for 2nd-best	1	0.01	10^{-8}	10^{-8}
Macro F-measure	0.28	0.41	0.43	0.41
Micro F-measure	0.48	0.49	0.57	0.54

Table 1. Maximal F-measures and corresponding thresholds for best and second-best categories

For the kNN method, the value chosen for k was 100 to achieve the best performance, although using any values of *k* between 15 and 200 produced very similar results. As seen in the table, the best result was achieved for kNN by not imposing a threshold to pick the nearest neighbor of an unlabeled sense, which means that at least one neighbor belonging to a class is enough to select the category. The other threshold, however, indicates that the class with the highest representation should have at least one more member than the class with the next highest value; when two different classes have the same number of representatives within the nearest *k* neighbors, we do not assign either one.

For tf*idf to pick the most similar category, the best performance was achieved using a threshold of 0.01 (that is, if the most similar category to the unlabeled document has a similarity measure less than 0.01, no category is assigned). Furthermore the most similar category should have a similarity measure that is at least 0.01 greater than the next closest one for it to be chosen. Interestingly, even though tf*idf uses consolidated information from all senses in a category to evaluate the similarity of a test sense, its F-measure based on microaveraging is comparable to that of kNN for this task.

NB and EM evaluate the fit of a test sense in terms of probabilities. Best performance was achieved for NB using 0.7 as the minimal probability for choosing a class for a given document. For EM best performance was achieved when the probability of a document to be assigned to a category was at least $\frac{1}{2}$. We found that for both probabilistic approaches, the most probable category and the next most probable one should have a difference in probability of at least 10^{-8} for best results.

Comparing the F-measures in Table 1, we note that Naive Bayes has the best performance results. We expected NB to outperform kNN since it uses consolidated information from all senses in a category, but we were surprised that it also outperformed EM. Apparently tuning the model through iterations causes it to diverge further from reality! The reason may be that the assumptions made for the probability model, primarily term independence, do not hold for our data. Perhaps the specific form of generating model may itself not match this data.

Table 2 shows the microaverage-based F-measures for each individual category, sorted by the best performance achieved across all four methods (shown in bold face in the table). The same data is presented graphically in Figures 3a, 3b, and 3c, which compare the performance of NB to each of the other three methods. For almost all classes NB outperforms the other methods. In 34 classes tf*idf performs slightly better than the others, and EM has somewhat better performance results in 25 classes. Notably kNN always underperforms the other methods, especially in some classes (for example, kNN has F-measure 0.01 for *Herb* whereas the other methods' performances are around 0.40); there are also five classes for which kNN has a zero F-measure (i.e.

no documents were correctly classified).

Interestingly the classes with highest F-measures have very different sizes and correspond to subjects covering a variety of disciplines. We conclude that kNN is not a good classification method when each document is very small and the number of common terms is very low. tf*idf and EM perform somewhat better, especially for some of the smaller classes, but for some classes they are also poor classifiers.

Unfortunately, we have not been able to detect a pattern that distinguishes in which classes any of the methods perform well. As shown in Figure 3d, the performances are slightly higher in very large categories, but the size of category alone is not a good criterion for predicting performance. We note that the dictionary was created by many people over a long period, but we know of no peculiarities in the methods of assigning labels or in choosing which works to cite that can explain the deviations in performance. For example, as can be seen in Table 2, there are three different *Law* categories with good F-measures, but *Civil Law* (with 50 documents) has maximal F-measure of 0.11; *Chemistry* and *Physics* could be well-classified, *Biology* and *Physical Chemistry* could not; *Cricket* and *Golf* worked well, but *Football* and *Racing* did not.

6 Conclusion

In this work we defined the subject classification problem for the *Oxford English Dictionary* and expressed the theory behind four different text classification methods to be used for this kind of data, namely *k* Nearest Neighbors, Term Frequency * Inverse Document Frequency, Naive Bayes and Expectation Maximization. We presented a data model for the senses in the OED that is suitable for classifying dictionary senses based on citation information. Our implementation of this model was designed to accommodate the vastness and sparseness of the data.

We evaluated the performance of the four methods experimentally, using the labeled senses of the dictionary for both training and test data. The evaluation metric we used to compare the above methods is the F-measure, a combination of precision and recall. The results show that the kNN method has the lowest results, which we attribute to the lack of common citations between two small "sense documents." With tf*idf microaverage-based F-measures were marginally improved, but still below .5; perhaps an alternative weighting system for "category documents" or a different similarity measure would improve performance. NB and EM, the two methods based on probability models, show higher results, but surprisingly EM is worse than NB. This reinforces the recent results from other researchers, who found that "Naive Bayes usually performs classification well despite violations of its assumptions...but (in EM)

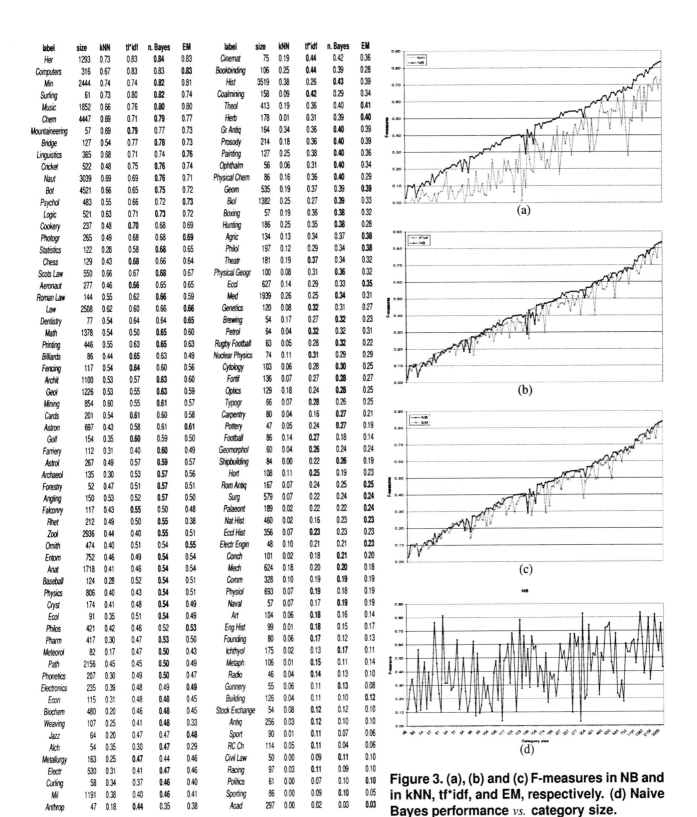

label	size	kNN	tf*idf	n. Bayes	EM		label	size	kNN	tf*idf	n. Bayes	EM
Her	1293	0.73	0.83	**0.84**	0.83		Cinemat	75	0.19	**0.44**	0.42	0.36
Computers	316	0.67	0.83	0.83	**0.83**		Bookbinding	106	0.25	**0.44**	0.39	0.28
Min	2444	0.74	0.74	**0.82**	0.81		Hist	3519	0.38	0.26	**0.43**	0.39
Surfing	61	0.73	0.80	**0.82**	0.74		Coalmining	158	0.09	**0.42**	0.29	0.34
Music	1852	0.66	0.76	**0.80**	0.80		Theol	413	0.19	0.36	0.40	**0.41**
Chem	4447	0.69	0.71	**0.79**	0.77		Herb	178	0.01	0.31	0.39	**0.40**
Mountaineering	57	0.69	**0.79**	0.77	0.73		Gr Antiq	164	0.34	0.36	**0.40**	0.39
Bridge	127	0.54	0.77	**0.78**	0.73		Prosody	214	0.18	0.36	**0.40**	0.39
Linguistics	365	0.68	0.71	0.74	**0.76**		Painting	127	0.25	0.38	**0.40**	0.36
Cricket	522	0.48	0.75	**0.76**	0.74		Ophthalm	56	0.06	0.31	**0.40**	0.34
Naut	3039	0.69	0.69	**0.76**	0.71		Physical Chem	86	0.16	0.36	**0.40**	0.29
Bot	4521	0.66	0.65	**0.75**	0.72		Geom	535	0.19	0.37	0.39	**0.39**
Psychol	483	0.55	0.66	0.72	**0.73**		Biol	1382	0.25	0.27	**0.39**	0.33
Logic	521	0.63	0.71	**0.73**	0.72		Boxing	57	0.19	0.36	**0.38**	0.32
Cookery	237	0.48	**0.70**	0.68	0.69		Hunting	186	0.25	0.35	**0.38**	0.28
Photogr	265	0.49	0.68	0.68	**0.69**		Agric	134	0.13	0.34	0.37	**0.38**
Statistics	122	0.28	0.58	**0.68**	0.65		Philol	197	0.12	0.29	0.34	**0.38**
Chess	129	0.43	**0.68**	0.66	0.64		Theatr	181	0.19	**0.37**	0.34	0.32
Scots Law	550	0.66	0.67	**0.68**	0.67		Physical Geogr	100	0.08	0.31	**0.36**	0.32
Aeronaut	277	0.46	**0.66**	0.65	0.65		Eccl	627	0.14	0.29	0.33	**0.35**
Roman Law	144	0.55	0.62	**0.66**	0.59		Med	1939	0.26	0.25	**0.34**	0.31
Law	2508	0.62	0.60	0.66	**0.66**		Genetics	120	0.08	**0.32**	0.31	0.27
Dentistry	77	0.54	0.64	0.64	**0.65**		Brewing	54	0.17	0.27	**0.32**	0.23
Math	1378	0.54	0.50	**0.65**	0.60		Petrol	64	0.04	**0.32**	0.32	0.31
Printing	446	0.55	0.63	**0.65**	0.63		Rugby Football	63	0.05	0.28	**0.32**	0.22
Billiards	86	0.44	**0.65**	0.63	0.49		Nuclear Physics	74	0.11	**0.31**	0.29	0.29
Fencing	117	0.54	**0.64**	0.60	0.56		Cytology	103	0.06	0.28	**0.30**	0.25
Archit	1100	0.53	0.57	**0.63**	0.60		Fortif	136	0.07	0.27	**0.28**	0.27
Geol	1226	0.53	0.55	**0.63**	0.59		Optics	129	0.18	0.24	**0.28**	0.25
Mining	854	0.60	0.55	**0.61**	0.57		Typogr	66	0.07	**0.28**	0.26	0.25
Cards	201	0.54	**0.61**	0.60	0.58		Carpentry	80	0.04	0.16	**0.27**	0.21
Astron	697	0.43	0.58	0.61	**0.61**		Pottery	47	0.05	0.24	**0.27**	0.19
Golf	154	0.35	**0.60**	0.59	0.50		Football	86	0.14	**0.27**	0.18	0.14
Farriery	112	0.31	0.40	**0.60**	0.49		Geomorphol	60	0.04	**0.26**	0.24	0.24
Astrol	267	0.49	0.57	**0.59**	0.57		Shipbuilding	84	0.00	0.22	**0.26**	0.19
Archaeol	135	0.30	0.53	**0.57**	0.56		Hort	108	0.11	**0.25**	0.19	0.23
Forestry	52	0.47	0.51	**0.57**	0.51		Rom Antiq	167	0.07	0.24	0.25	**0.25**
Angling	150	0.53	0.52	**0.57**	0.50		Surg	579	0.07	0.22	0.24	**0.24**
Falconry	117	0.43	**0.55**	0.50	0.48		Palaeont	189	0.02	0.22	0.22	**0.24**
Rhet	212	0.49	0.50	**0.55**	0.38		Nat Hist	460	0.02	0.16	0.23	**0.23**
Zool	2936	0.44	0.40	**0.55**	0.51		Eccl Hist	356	0.07	**0.23**	0.23	0.23
Ornith	474	0.40	0.51	0.54	**0.55**		Electr Engin	48	0.10	0.21	0.21	**0.23**
Entom	752	0.46	0.49	**0.54**	0.54		Conch	101	0.02	0.18	**0.21**	0.20
Anat	1718	0.41	0.46	**0.54**	0.54		Mech	624	0.18	0.20	**0.20**	0.18
Baseball	124	0.28	0.52	**0.54**	0.51		Comm	328	0.10	0.19	**0.19**	0.19
Physics	806	0.40	0.43	**0.54**	0.51		Physiol	693	0.07	**0.19**	0.18	0.19
Cryst	174	0.41	0.48	**0.54**	0.49		Naval	57	0.07	0.17	**0.19**	0.19
Ecol	91	0.35	0.51	**0.54**	0.49		Art	104	0.06	**0.18**	0.16	0.14
Philos	421	0.42	0.46	0.52	**0.53**		Eng Hist	99	0.01	**0.18**	0.15	0.17
Pharm	417	0.30	0.47	**0.53**	0.50		Founding	80	0.06	**0.17**	0.12	0.13
Meteorol	82	0.17	0.47	**0.50**	0.43		Ichthyol	175	0.02	0.13	**0.17**	0.11
Path	2156	0.45	0.45	**0.50**	0.49		Metaph	106	0.01	**0.15**	0.11	0.14
Phonetics	207	0.30	0.49	**0.50**	0.47		Radio	46	0.04	**0.14**	0.13	0.10
Electronics	235	0.39	0.48	0.49	**0.49**		Gunnery	55	0.06	0.11	**0.13**	0.08
Econ	115	0.31	0.48	**0.48**	0.45		Building	126	0.04	0.11	0.10	**0.12**
Biochem	480	0.20	0.46	**0.48**	0.45		Stock Exchange	54	0.08	**0.12**	0.12	0.10
Weaving	107	0.25	0.41	**0.48**	0.33		Antiq	256	0.03	**0.12**	0.10	0.10
Jazz	64	0.20	0.47	0.47	**0.48**		Sport	90	0.01	**0.11**	0.07	0.06
Alch	54	0.35	0.30	**0.47**	0.29		RC Ch	114	0.05	**0.11**	0.04	0.06
Metallurgy	163	0.25	**0.47**	0.44	0.46		Civil Law	50	0.00	0.09	**0.11**	0.06
Electr	530	0.31	0.41	**0.47**	0.46		Racing	97	0.03	**0.11**	0.09	0.10
Curling	58	0.34	0.37	**0.46**	0.40		Politics	61	0.00	0.07	**0.10**	0.10
Mil	1191	0.38	0.40	**0.46**	0.41		Sporting	86	0.00	0.09	**0.10**	0.05
Anthrop	47	0.18	**0.44**	0.35	0.38		Acad	297	0.00	0.02	0.03	**0.03**

Table 2. F-measures for all 128 categories

Figure 3. (a), (b) and (c) F-measures in NB and in kNN, tf*idf, and EM, respectively. (d) Naive Bayes performance *vs.* category size.

335

in some data sets, when there are a lot of labeled and a lot of unlabeled documents, this is not the case...and the incorporation of unlabeled data decreases, rather than increases, classification accuracy" [18]. Nevertheless, perhaps a better probability model for our data could improve performance [17].

The original purpose of classifying OED entries by subject is to provide the editors of the dictionary with a tool that can help them to improve the labeling of subject-specific senses. As a next step, then, we plan to carry out experiments that involve the unlabeled data, using the 63,000 labeled senses for training. More specifically, we need to evaluate whether our thresholds to choose *not* to categorize a sense can serve to identify the general vocabulary that should remain unlabeled. Furthermore, we should also evaluate multi-labeling techniques (i.e. *n-per-doc* category assignment), so as to provide editors with several ranked choices for selecting the right subject label for a sense; this will also support the few instances where one sense really should be assigned several subject labels. Finally we wish to measure the performance of the approaches based on citations against other schemes to create taxonomies based on natural language processing of the definition text (or of the cited quotation itself) [7]. We may also find that combining evidence from citations with evidence from the definitions yields even better results.

Acknowledgments

We are grateful to Dale Schuurmans, Reem Al-Halimi, Charlie Clarke, and Fuchun Peng for their many insights into approaches to addressing this research problem. Financial support was provided by grants from Bell Canada through Bell University Labs, the MITACS Centre of Excellence, the Natural Sciences and Engineering Research Council of Canada, and the University of Waterloo.

References

[1] R. BaezaYates and B. RibeiroNeto. *Modern Information Retrievel*. Addison-Wesley, ACM Press, 1999.

[2] D. L. Berg. The research potential of the electronic OED2 database at the University of Waterloo: A guide for scholars. Technical report, UW Centre for the New Oxford English Dictionary, 1989.

[3] D. L. Berg. *A Guide To The Oxford English Dictionary*. Oxford University Press, 1993.

[4] S. Brin. Extracting patterns and relations from the World Wide Web. In *Proceedings of WebDB Workshop at EDBT'98*, Valencia, Spain, March 1998.

[5] K. J. Cios, W. Pedrycz, and R. W. Swiniarski. *Data Mining Methods for Knowledge Discovery*. Kluwer Academic Publishers, 1998.

[6] W. A. Gale. Good-Turing smoothing without tears. Technical report, AT&T Bell Laboratories, 1994.

[7] N. Ide and J. Véronis. Knowledge extraction from machine-readable dictionaries: An evaluation. In *Machine Translation and the Lexicon*, pages 19–34. Springer-Verlag, 1994.

[8] M. Iwayama and T. Tokunaga. Cluster-based text categorization: A comparison of category search strategies. In *Proceedings of ACM SIGIR Conference (SIGIR)*, pages 273–280, Seattle, WA USA, 1995.

[9] T. Joachims. A probabilistic analysis of the Rocchio algorithm with TFIDF for text categorization. In *Proceedings of the 14th International Conference on Machine Learning ICML97*, 1997.

[10] R. Korfhage. *Information Storage and Retrieval*. Wiley Computer Publication, 1997.

[11] Z. Langari. Subject classifications in the Oxford English Dictionary. Master's thesis, University of Waterloo, Department of Computer Science, 2001.

[12] D. Lewis. Evaluating text categorization. In *Proceedings of speech and Natural Language Workshop*, pages 312–318, Asilomar, Feb. 1991.

[13] D. Lewis. An evaluation of phrasal and clustered representations on a text categorization task. In *Fifteenth Annual International ACM SIGIR Conference on Research and Development in Information Retrieval*, pages 37–50, 1992.

[14] D. Lewis. Naive (Bayes) at forty: The independence assumption in information retrieval. In *European Conference on Machine Learning*, 1998.

[15] C. D. Manning and H. Schütze. *Foundations of Statistical Natural Language Processing*. MIT Press, 1999.

[16] A. McCallum and K. Nigam. A comparison of event models for naive Bayes text classification. In *AAAI-98 Workshop on Learning for Text Categorization*, 1998.

[17] A. McCallum and K. Nigam. Text classification by bootstrapping with keywords, EM and shrinkage. In *ACL '99 Workshop for Unsupervised Learning in Natural Language Processing*, 1999.

[18] K. Nigam, A. McCallum, S. Thrun, and T. Mitchell. Text classification from labeled and unlabeled documents using EM. *Machine Learning*, 39(2/3):103–134, 2000.

[19] G. Salton and C. Buckley. Term weighting approaches in automatic text retrieval. *Information Processing & Management*, 24(5):513–523, 1988.

[20] F. Sebastiani. Machine learning in automated text categorization. Technical report, Istituto di Elaborazione dell'Informazione, 1999.

[21] T. Siedl and H. P. Kriegel. Optimal mnlti-step *k*-nearest neighbor search. In *Proceedings of ACM SIGMOD*, pages 154–165, June 1998.

[22] J. A. Simpson and E. S. C. Weiner, editors. *The Oxford English Dictionary*. Oxford University Press, second edition, 1989.

[23] Y. Yang and X. Liu. A re-examination of text categorization methods. In *Proceedings of ACM SIGIR Conference on Research and Development in Information Retrieval (SIGIR)*, pages 42–49, 1999.

On Mining General Temporal Association Rules in a Publication Database

Chang-Hung Lee, Cheng-Ru Lin, and Ming-Syan Chen
Department of Electrical Engineering
National Taiwan University
Taipei, Taiwan, ROC
E-mail: mschen@cc.ee.ntu.edu.tw, {chlee, owenlin}@arbor.ee.ntu.edu.tw

Abstract

In this paper, we explore a new problem of mining general temporal association rules in publication databases. In essence, a publication database is a set of transactions where each transaction T is a set of items of which each item contains an individual exhibition period. The current model of association rule mining is not able to handle the publication database due to the following fundamental problems, i.e., (1) lack of consideration of the exhibition period of each individual item; (2) lack of an equitable support counting basis for each item. To remedy this, we propose an innovative algorithm Progressive-Partition-Miner (abbreviatedly as PPM) to discover general temporal association rules in a publication database. The basic idea of PPM is to first partition the publication database in light of exhibition periods of items and then progressively accumulate the occurrence count of each candidate 2-itemset based on the intrinsic partitioning characteristics. Algorithm PPM is also designed to employ a filtering threshold in each partition to early prune out those cumulatively infrequent 2-itemsets. Explicitly, the execution time of PPM is, in orders of magnitude, smaller than those required by the schemes which are directly extended from existing methods.

1 Introduction

The discovery of association relationship among a huge database has been known to be useful in selective marketing, decision analysis, and business management [4, 9]. A popular area of applications is the market basket analysis, which studies the buying behaviors of customers by searching for sets of items that are frequently purchased together (or in sequence). For a given pair of confidence and support thresholds, the problem of mining association rules is to identify all association rules that have confidence and support greater than the corresponding minimum support

threshold (denoted as min_supp) and minimum confidence threshold (denoted as min_conf).

Since the early work in [1], several efficient algorithms to mine association rules have been developed in recent years. These studies cover a broad spectrum of topics including: (1) fast algorithms based on the level-wise Apriori framework [2, 13] and partitioning [11]; (2) FP-growth algorithms [8]; (3) incremental updating [6, 10]; (4) mining of generalized and multi-level rules [7, 14]; (5) mining of quantitative rules [15]; (6) mining of multi-dimensional rules [18]; (7) constraint-based rule mining [16] and multiple minimum supports issues [12, 17]; and (8) temporal association rule discovery [3, 5].

While these are important results toward enabling the integration of association mining and fast searching algorithms, e.g., BFS and DFS which are classified in [9], we note that these mining methods cannot effectively be applied to the mining of a *publication-like* database which is of increasing popularity recently. In essence, a publication database is a set of transactions where each transaction T is a set of items of which each item contains an individual exhibition period. The current model of association rule mining is not able to handle the publication database due to the following fundamental problems, i.e., (1) lack of consideration of the *exhibition period* of each individual item; (2) lack of an equitable support counting basis for each item. Note that the traditional mining process takes the same *task-relevant tuples*, i.e., the size of transaction set D, as a counting basis. Recall that the task of support specification is to specify the minimum transaction support for each itemset. However, since different items have different exhibition periods in a publication database, only considering the occurrence count of each item might not lead to a fair measurement. This problem can be further explained by the illustrative example below.

Example 1.1: In a bookstore transaction database as shown in Figure 1, the minimum transaction support and confidence are assumed to be $min\_supp = 30\%$ and $min\_conf = 75\%$, respectively. A set of time series

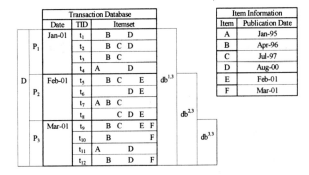

Figure 1. An illustrative transaction database and the corresponding item information

database indicates the transaction records from January 2001 to March 2001. The publication date of each transaction item is also given. Based on the traditional mining techniques, the *absolute support threshold* is denoted as $S^A = \lceil 12 * 0.3 \rceil = 4$ where 12 is the size of transaction set $\mathcal{D}$. It can be seen that only *{B, C, D, E, BC}* can be termed as frequent itemsets since the amounts of their occurrences in this transaction database are respectively larger than the absolute value of support threshold. Thus, only rule $C \implies B$ is termed as a frequent association rule with support $s = 41.67\%$ and confidence $c = 83.33\%$. However, some phenomena are observed when we take the "*item information*" in Figure 1 into consideration.

1. **An early publication intrinsically possesses a higher likelihood to be determined as a frequent itemset.** For example, the sales volume of an early product, such as A, B, C or D, is likely to be larger than that of a newly exhibited product, e.g., E or F, since an early product has a longer exhibition period. As a result, the association rules we usually get will be those with long-term products such as "milk and bread are frequently purchased together", which, while being correct by the definition, is of less interest to us in the association rule mining. In contrast, some more recent products, such as new books, which are really "frequent" and interesting in their exhibition periods are less likely to be identified as frequent ones if a traditional mining process is employed.

2. **Some discovered rules may be expired from users' interest.** Considering the generated rule $C \implies B$, both B and C were published from the very early dates of this mining transaction database. This information is very likely to have been explored in the previous mining database, such as the one from January 1996 to December 1997. Such mining results could be of less

interest to our on-going mining works. For example, most researchers tend to pay more attention to the latest published papers.

Note that one straightforward approach to addressing the above issues is to lower the value of the minimum support threshold required. However, this naive approach will cause another problem, i.e., those interesting rules with smaller supports may be overshadowed by lots of less important information with higher supports. As a consequence, we introduce the notion of *exhibition period* for each transaction item in this paper and develop an algorithm, *Progressive Partition Miner* (abbreviatedly as *PPM*), to address this problem. It is worth mentioning that the application domain of this study is not limited to the mining of a publication database. Other application domains include bookstore transaction databases, video and audio rental store records, stock market data, and transactions in electronic commerce, to name a few.

Explicitly, we explore in this paper the mining of *general temporal association rules*, i.e., $(X \implies Y)^{t,n}$, where t is the *latest-exhibition-start time* of both itemsets X and Y, and n denotes the *end* time of the publication database. In other words, (t, n) is the *maximal common exhibition period* of itemsets X and Y. An association rule $X \implies Y$ is termed to be a frequent general temporal association rule $(X \implies Y)^{t,n}$ if and only if its probability is larger than minimum support required, i.e., $P(X^{t,n} \cup Y^{t,n}) > min\_supp$, and the conditional probability $P(Y^{t,n}|X^{t,n})$ is larger than minimum confidence needed, i.e., $P(Y^{t,n}|X^{t,n}) > min\_conf$. Instead of using the *absolute support threshold* $S^A = \lceil |\mathcal{D}| * min\_supp \rceil$ as a minimum support threshold for each item in Figure 1, a *relative* minimum support, denoted by $S_X^R = \lceil |\mathcal{D}_X| * min\_supp \rceil$ where $|\mathcal{D}_X|$ indicates the amount of partial transactions in the exhibition period of itemset X, is given to deal with the mining of temporal association rules.

To deal with the mining of general temporal association rule $(X \implies Y)^{t,n}$, an efficient algorithm, *Progressive Partition Miner*, is devised. The basic idea of *PPM* is to first partition the publication database in light of exhibition periods of items and then progressively accumulate the occurrence count of each candidate 2-itemset based on the intrinsic partitioning characteristics. Algorithm *PPM* is also designed to employ a filtering threshold in each partition to early prune out those cumulatively infrequent 2-itemsets. The feature that the number of candidate 2-itemsets generated by *PPM* is very close to the number of frequent 2-itemsets allows us to employ the scan reduction technique by generating C_ks from C_2 directly to effectively reduce the number of database scan. Experimental results show that *PPM* produces a significantly smaller amount of candidate 2-itemsets than *Apriori*⁺, i.e., an extended version of *Apri-*

ori algorithm. In fact, the number of the candidate itemsets C_ks generated by *PPM* approaches to its theoretical minimum, i.e., the number of frequent k-itemsets, as the value of the minimal support increases. Explicitly, the execution time of *PPM* is, in orders of magnitude, smaller than those required by *Apriori*$^+$. Sensitivity analysis on various parameters of the database is also conducted to provide many insights into algorithm *PPM*. The advantage of *PPM* over *Apriori*$^+$ becomes even more prominent as the size of the database increases. This is indeed an important feature for *PPM* to be practically used for the mining of a time series database in the real world.

It is worth mentioning that the problem of mining *general* temporal association rules will be degenerated to the one of mining temporal association rules explored in prior works [3, 5] if the exhibition period (t, n) of association rule $(X \implies Y)^{t,n}$ is applied to a non-maximal exhibition period of $X \implies Y$, such as (j, n) where $j > t$. Consider for example the database in Figure 1 where $(C \implies B)^{1,3}$ and $(C \implies E)^{2,3}$ are two *general temporal* association rules in database $\mathcal{D}$ while the temporal subset of $(C \implies B)^{1,3}$, e.g., $(C \implies B)^{2,3}$, can also be a temporal association rule as defined in [3, 5], showing that the model we consider can be viewed as a general framework of prior studies. This is the reason we use the term "general temporal association rule" in this paper.

We mention in passing that the Frequent Pattern growth (FP-growth), which constructs a highly compact data structure (an FP-tree) to compress the original transaction database, is a method of mining frequent itemsets without candidate generation [8]. However, in our opinion, FP-growth algorithms do not have obvious extensions to deal with this publication database problem. Further, some methodologies were proposed to explore the problem of discovering temporal association relationship in the partial of database retrieved [3, 5], i.e., to determine association rules from a given subset of database specified by time. These works, however, do not consider the individual exhibition period of each transaction item, and are thus not applicable to solving the mining problems in a publication database. On the other hand, some techniques were devised to use multiple minimum supports for frequent itemsets generation [12, 17]. However, it remains unclear for how the techniques in [12, 17] to be coupled with the corresponding minimum confidence thresholds when general temporal association rules we consider in this paper in a publication database are being generated.

The rest of this paper is organized as follows. Problem description is given in Section 2. Algorithm *PPM* is described in Section 3. Performance studies on various schemes are conducted in Section 4. This paper concludes with Section 5.

2 Problem Description

Let n be the number of partitions with a time granularity, e.g., *business-week, month, quarter, year*, to name a few, in database $\mathcal{D}$. In the model considered, $db^{t,n}$ denotes the part of the transaction database formed by a continuous region from partition P_t to partition P_n, and $|db^{t,n}| = \sum_{h=t,n} |P_h|$ where $db^{t,n} \subseteq \mathcal{D}$. An item $x^{x.start,n}$ is termed as a *temporal item* of x, meaning that $P_{x.start}$ is the starting partition of x and n is the partition number of the last database partition retrieved.

Example 2.1: Consider the database in Figure 1. Since database $\mathcal{D}$ records the transaction data from January 2001 to March 2001, database $\mathcal{D}$ is intrinsically segmented into three partitions P_1, P_2 and P_3 in accordance with the "month" granularity. As a consequence, a partial database $db^{2,3} \subseteq \mathcal{D}$ consists of partitions P_2 and P_3. A temporal item $E^{2,3}$ denotes that the exhibition period of $E^{2,3}$ is from the beginning time of partition P_2 to the end time of partition P_3.

As such, we can define a maximal temporal itemset $X^{t,n}$ as follows.

Definition 1: An itemset $X^{t,n}$ is called a *maximal temporal itemset* in a partial database $db^{t,n}$ if t is the *latest starting partition number* of all items belonging to X in database $\mathcal{D}$ and n is the partition number of the last partition in $db^{t,n}$ retrieved.

For example, as shown in Figure 1, itemset $DE^{2,3}$ is deemed a maximal temporal itemset whereas $CD^{2,3}$ is not. In view of this, the exhibition period of an itemset is expressed in terms of *Maximal Common exhibition Period* (MCP) of the items that appear in the itemset. Let $MCP(x)$ denote the MCP value of item x. The MCP value of an itemset X is the shortest MCP among the items in itemset X. Consider three items C, E and F in Figure 1 for example. Their exhibition periods are as follows: $MCP(C) = (1, 3)$, $MCP(E) = (2, 3)$ and $MCP(F) = (3, 3)$. Since itemset CEF is termed to be $CEF^{3,n} = (CEF)^{3,n}$ with considering the exhibition of CEF, we have $MCP(CEF) = (3, 3)$.

In addition, $|db^{t,n}|$ is the number of transactions in the partial database $db^{t,n}$. The fraction of transaction T supporting an itemset X with respect to partial database $db^{t,n}$ is called the support of $X^{t,n}$, i.e., $supp(X^{MCP(X)}) = \frac{|\{T \in db^{MCP(X)} | X \subseteq T\}|}{|db^{MCP(X)}|}$. The support of a rule $(X \implies Y)^{MCP(XY)}$ is defined as $supp((X \implies Y)^{MCP(XY)}) = supp((X \bigcup Y)^{MCP(XY)})$. The confidence of this rule is defined as $conf((X \implies Y)^{MCP(XY)}) = \frac{supp((X \bigcup Y)^{MCP(XY)})}{supp(X^{MCP(XY)})}$. Consequently, a general temporal association rule $(X \implies Y)^{MCP(XY)}$

which holds in the transaction set D can be defined as follows.

Definition 2: An association rule $(X \implies Y)^{MCP(XY)}$ is called a *general temporal association rule* in the transaction set D with $conf((X \implies Y)^{MCP(XY)}) = c$ and $supp((X \implies Y)^{MCP(XY)}) = s$ if $c\%$ of transactions in $db^{MCP(XY)}$ that contain X also contain Y and $s\%$ of transactions in $db^{MCP(XY)}$ contain $X \bigcup Y$ while $X \bigcap Y = \phi$.

For a given pair of *min_conf* and *min_supp* as the minimum thresholds required in the maximal common exhibition period of each association rule, the problem of mining general temporal association rules is to determine all frequent general temporal association rules, e.g., $(X \implies Y)^{MCP(XY)} \in db^{MCP(XY)}$ which transaction itemsets X and Y have "relative" support and confidence greater than the corresponding thresholds. Thus, we have the following definition to identify the frequent general temporal association rules.

Definition 3: A general temporal association rule $(X \implies Y)^{MCP(XY)}$ is termed to be *frequent* if and only if $supp((X \implies Y)^{MCP(XY)}) > min\_supp$ and $conf((X \implies Y)^{MCP(XY)}) > min\_conf$.

Consequently, this rule mining of general temporal association can also be decomposed into to three steps:
(1) generate all frequent maximal temporal itemsets (TIs) with their support values.
(2) generate the support values of all corresponding temporal sub-itemsets (SIs) of frequent TIs.
(3) generate all temporal association rules that satisfy min_conf using the frequent TIs and/or SIs.

Example 2.2: Recall the illustrative general temporal association rules, e.g., $(C \implies E)^{2,3}$ with relative support 37.5% and confidence 75%, of the bookstore transaction database as shown in the Figure 1. In accordance with Definition 3, the implication $(C \implies E)^{2,3}$ is termed as a general temporal association rule if and only if $supp((C \implies E)^{2,3}) > min\_supp$ and $conf((C \implies E)^{2,3}) > min\_conf$. Consequently, we have to determine if $supp(CE^{2,3}) > min\_supp$ and $supp(C^{2,3}) > min\_supp$ for discovering the newly identified association rule $(C \implies E)^{2,3}$. It is worth mentioning that though $CE^{2,3}$ has to be a maximal temporal itemset, called TI, $C^{2,3}$ may not be a TI. We call $C^{2,3}$ is one of corresponding temporal sub-itemsets, i.e., SI, of itemset $CE^{2,3}$.

For better readability, a list of symbols used is given in Table 1. Then, the definition of a *frequent* maximal temporal itemset and the property of its corresponding sub-itemsets are given below.

Definition 4: A maximal temporal itemset $X^{MCP(X)}$ is termed to be frequent when the occurrence frequency of $X^{MCP(X)}$ is larger than the value of min_supp required, i.e., $supp(X^{MCP(X)}) > min\_supp$, in transaction set $db^{MCP(X)}$.

Property 1: When a maximal temporal k-itemset $X_k^{MCP(X_k)}$ is frequent in data set $db^{MCP(X_k)}$, each of its corresponding sub-itemset $X_i^{MCP(X_k)}$ ($1 \leq i < k$) is also frequent in $db^{MCP(X_k)}$.

$|db^{i,n}|$	Number of transactions in $db^{i,n}$
$X^{i,n}$	A temporal itemset in partial database $db^{i,n}$
TI	A maximal temporal itemset
SI	A corresponding temporal sub-itemset of TI

Table 1: Meanings of symbols used

Once, $\mathcal{F} = \{ X^{MCP(X)} \subseteq \mathcal{I} \mid X^{MCP(X)}$ is $frequent\}$, the set of all frequent TIs and SIs together with their support values is known, deriving the desired association rules is straightforward. For every $X^{MCP(X)} \in \mathcal{F}$, check the confidence of all rules $(X \implies Y)^{MCP(XY)}$ and drop those that do not satisfy $s(XY^{MCP(XY)})/s(X^{MCP(X)}) \geq min\_conf$. This problem can also be reduced to the problem of finding all frequent maximal temporal itemsets first and then generating their corresponding frequent sub-itemsets for the same support threshold. Therefore, in the rest of this paper we concentrate our discussion on the algorithms for mining frequent TIs and SIs. In fact, the process steps of generating frequent TIs and SIs can be further merged to one step in our proposed algorithm PPM.

As explained, we have to find all maximal temporal itemsets that satisfy min_supp first and then to calculate the occurrences of their corresponding sub-itemsets for producing all temporal association rules hidden in database $\mathcal{D}$. However, if we use an existing algorithm to find all frequent TIs for this new problem, the downward closure property, which Apriori-based algorithms are based on, no longer holds. In addition, the candidate generation process is not intuitive at all. Note that, even though itemset $X^{t,n}$ is not a frequent itemset, it does not imply that $X^{t+1,n}$, i.e., a temporal sub-itemset of $X^{t,n}$, is not a frequent itemset. In other words, even knowing $X^{t,n}$ is not frequent in $db^{t,n}$ where $MCP(X) = (t,n)$, we are not able to assert whether $XY^{t+1,n}$ is frequent or not when $MCP(Y) = (t+1,n)$. Specifically, to determine whether a general temporal association rule $(X \implies Y)^{t+1,n}$ is frequent, we have to find out the support values of $X^{t+1,n}$ and $XY^{t+1,n}$ where $MCP(XY) = MCP(Y) = (t+1,n)$.

Example 2.3: Consider $MCP(x_1) = (1,n)$, $MCP(x_2) = (2,n)$ and $MCP(x_3) = (3,n)$. If we find that item x_1 is not frequent at exhibition period $(1,n)$, then it does not satisfy min_supp requirement at level 1. Under a conventional

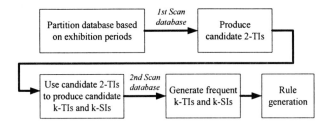

Figure 2. The flowchart of PPM

Apriori-based association rule mining algorithm, this itemset is discarded since it will not be frequent. The potentially frequent itemsets $x_1 x_2$ and $x_1 x_3$ will then not be generated at level 2 for consideration. Clearly, this disposition is incorrect in mining general temporal association rules since x_1 is still possible to be frequent at $(2, n)$ and $(3, n)$, indicating that the downward property is not valid in mining general temporal association rules.

It is worth mentioning that since the downward level-wise property, which holds for Apriori-like algorithms, is not valid in this general temporal association rule mining problem, the second method is to expand each transaction item to be its combination with different exhibition periods. For instance, all temporal sub-itemsets of $X_k^{t,n}$ at level k with different exhibition periods, i.e., $X_k^{t,n}$, $X_k^{t+1,n}$, $X_k^{t+2,n}$, ..., $X_k^{n,n}$, are taken as "*temporal candidate k-itemsets*" for producing any possible combination of general temporal association rules. Using this approach, the problem of mining temporal association rules can be implemented on an anti-monotone Apriori-like heuristic. As in most previous works, the essential idea is to iteratively generate the set of candidate itemsets of length $(k + 1)$, i.e., $X_{k+1}^{r,n}$, from the set of frequent itemsets of length k, i.e., $X_k^{r,n}$, (for $k \geq 1$), and to check their corresponding occurrence frequencies in the database $db^{r,n}$. This is the basic concept of an extended version of Apriori-based algorithm, called *Apriori+*, whose performance will be comparatively evaluated with algorithm *PPM* in our experimental studies later.

3 General Temporal Association Rules

An overview of progressive partition miner is given in Section 3.1. We present an illustrative example of algorithm *PPM* in Section 3.2.

3.1 An overview of Progressive Partition Miner

As explained above, a naive adoption of conventional methods to mine general temporal association rules will be

prohibitively expensive. To remedy this, by partitioning a transaction database into several partitions, algorithm *PPM* is devised to employ a filtering threshold in each partition to deal with the candidate itemset generation and process one partition at a time. For ease of exposition, the processing of a partition is termed a *phase* of processing. Explicitly, a progressive candidate set of itemsets is composed of the following two types of candidate itemsets, i.e., (1) the candidate itemsets that were carried over from the previous progressive candidate set in the previous phase and remain as candidate itemsets after the current partition is included into consideration (Such candidate itemsets are called type α candidate itemsets); and (2) the candidate itemsets that were not in the progressive candidate set in the previous phase but are newly selected after only taking the current data partition into account (Such candidate itemsets are called type β candidate itemsets). Under *PPM*, the cumulative information in the prior phases is selectively carried over toward the generation of candidate itemsets in the subsequent phases. After the processing of a phase, algorithm *PPM* outputs a *progressive screen*, denoted by PS, which consists of a progressive candidate set of itemsets, their occurrence counts and the corresponding partial supports required.

3.2 Algorithm of PPM

The operation of algorithm PPM can be best understood by an illustrative example described below and its corresponding flowchart is depicted in Figure 2. Recall the transaction database shown in Figure 1 where the transaction database $db^{1,3}$ is assumed to be segmented into three partitions P_1, P_2 and P_3, which correspond to the three time granularities from January 2001 to March 2001. Suppose that $min\_supp = 30\%$ and $min\_conf = 75\%$. Each partition is scanned sequentially for the generation of candidate 2-itemsets in the first scan of the database $db^{1,3}$. After scanning the first segment of 4 transactions, i.e., partition P_1, 2-itemsets $\{BD, BC, CD, AD\}$ are sequentially generated as shown in Figure 3. In addition, each potential candidate itemset $c \in C_2$ has two attributes: (1) $c.start$ which contains the partition number of the corresponding starting partition when c was added to C_2, and (2) $c.count$ which contains the number of occurrences of c since c was added to C_2. Since there are four transactions in P_1, the partial minimal support is $\lceil 4 * 0.3 \rceil = 2$. Such a partial minimal support is called the *filtering threshold* in this paper. Itemsets whose occurrence counts are below the filtering threshold are removed. Then, as shown in Figure 3, only $\{BD, BC\}$, marked by " $\bigcirc$ ", remain as candidate itemsets (of type β in this phase since they are newly generated) whose information is then carried over to the next phase P_2 of processing.

Similarly, after scanning partition P_2, the occurrence

P₁		
C₂	start	count
○ BD	1	2
○ BC	1	2
CD	1	1
AD	1	1

P₁ + P₂		
C₂	start	count
BD	1	2
○ BC	1	4
BE	2	1
○ CE	2	2
○ DE	?	2
AB	2	1
AC	2	1
CD	2	1

P₁ + P₂ + P₃		
C₂	start	count
○ BC	1	5
○ CE	2	3
DE	2	2
BE	3	1
○ BF	3	3
CF	3	1
EF	3	1
AD	3	1
BD	3	1
DF	3	1

After 1st scan database D, we have candidate itemsets (relative support = 30%) as follows:
$\{B^{1,3}\}, \{B^{3,3}\}, \{C^{1,3}\}, \{C^{2,3}\}, \{E^{2,3}\}, \{F^{3,3}\}, \{BC^{1,3}\}, \{BF^{3,3}\}, \{CE^{2,3}\}$

	Candidate Itemsets	count	S_X^R
C₁	$\{B^{1,3}\}$	8	4
	$\{B^{3,3}\}$	3	3
	$\{C^{1,3}\}$	6	4
	$\{C^{2,3}\}$	4	3
	$\{E^{2,3}\}$	4	3
	$\{F^{3,3}\}$	3	2
C₂	$\{BC^{1,3}\}$	5	4
	$\{BF^{1,3}\}$	3	2
	$\{CE^{2,3}\}$	3	3

Pruning →

	Freq. Itemsets	count
L₁	$\{B^{1,3}\}$	8
	$\{B^{3,3}\}$	3
	$\{C^{1,3}\}$	6
	$\{C^{2,3}\}$	4
	$\{E^{2,3}\}$	4
	$\{F^{3,3}\}$	3
L₂	$\{BC^{1,3}\}$	5
	$\{BF^{3,3}\}$	3
	$\{CE^{2,3}\}$	3

After 2nd scan database D, we have frequent itemsets (relative support = 30%) as follows:
$\{B^{1,3}\}, \{B^{3,3}\}, \{C^{1,3}\}, \{C^{2,3}\}, \{E^{2,3}\}, \{F^{3,3}\}, \{BC^{1,3}\}, \{BF^{3,3}\}, \{CE^{2,3}\}$

Rules	Supp.	Conf.
$(B \Rightarrow C)^{1,3}$	41.67%	62.50%
$(C \Rightarrow B)^{1,3}$	41.67%	83.33%
$(B \Rightarrow F)^{3,3}$	75.00%	100.00%
$(F \Rightarrow B)^{3,3}$	75.00%	100.00%
$(C \Rightarrow E)^{2,3}$	37.50%	75.00%
$(E \Rightarrow C)^{2,3}$	37.50%	75.00%

Pruning →

Rules	Supp.	Conf.
$(C \Rightarrow B)^{1,3}$	41.67%	83.33%
$(B \Rightarrow F)^{3,3}$	75.00%	100.00%
$(F \Rightarrow B)^{3,3}$	75.00%	100.00%
$(C \Rightarrow E)^{2,3}$	37.50%	75.00%
$(E \Rightarrow C)^{2,3}$	37.50%	75.00%

Figure 3. Frequent temporal itemsets generation for mining general temporal association rules by *PPM*

counts of potential candidate 2-itemsets are recorded (of type α and type β). From Figure 3, it is noted that since there are also 4 transactions in P_2, the filtering threshold of those itemsets carried out from the previous phase (that become type α candidate itemsets in this phase) is $\lceil (4+4) * 0.3 \rceil = 3$ and that of newly identified candidate itemsets (i.e., type β candidate itemsets) is $\lceil 4 * 0.3 \rceil = 2$. It can be seen that we have 3 candidate itemsets in C_2 after the processing of partition P_2, and one of them is of type α and two of them are of type β.

Finally, partition P_3 is processed by algorithm *PPM*. The resulting candidate 2-itemsets are $C_2 = \{BC, CE, BF\}$ as shown in Figure 3. Note that though appearing in the previous phase P_2, itemset $\{DE\}$ is removed from C_2 once P_3 is taken into account since its occurrence count does not meet the filtering threshold then, i.e., $2 < 3$. However, we do have one new itemset, i.e., BF, which joins the C_2 as a type β candidate itemset. Consequently, we have 3 candidate 2-itemsets generated by *PPM*, and two of them are of type α and one of them is of type β. Note that only 3 candidate 2-itemsets are generated by *PPM*.

After generating C_2 from the first scan of database $db^{1,3}$, we employ the scan reduction technique [13] and use C_2 to

generate C_k ($k = 2, 3, ..., m$), where C_m is the candidate *last*-itemsets. Instead of generating C_3 from $L_2 \star L_2$, a C_2 generated by *PPM* can be used to generate the candidate 3-itemsets and its sequential C'_{k-1} can be utilized to generate C'_k. Clearly, a C'_3 generated from $C_2 \star C_2$, instead of from $L_2 \star L_2$, will have a size greater than $|C_3|$ where C_3 is generated from $L_2 \star L_2$. However, since the $|C_2|$ generated by *PPM* is very close to the theoretical minimum, i.e., $|L_2|$, the $|C'_3|$ is not much larger than $|C_3|$. Similarly, the $|C'_k|$ is close to $|C_k|$. Since $C_2 = \{BC, CE, BF\}$, no candidate k-itemset is generated in this example where $k \geq 3$. Thus, $C'_k = \{BC, CE, BF\}$ and all C'_k can be stored in main memory. Then, we can find L_ks ($k = 1, 2, ..., m$) together when the second scan of the database $db^{1,3}$ is performed. Note that those generated itemsets $C'_k = \{BC, CE, BF\}$ are termed to be the candidate maximal temporal itemsets (TIs), i.e., $BC^{1,3}, CE^{2,3}$ and $BF^{3,3}$, with a maximal exhibition period of each candidate.

Before we process the second scan of the database $db^{1,3}$ to generate L_ks, all candidate SIs of candidate TIs can be propagated based on Property 1, and then added into C'_k. For instance, as shown in Figure 3, both candidate 1-itemsets $B^{1,3}$ and $C^{1,3}$ are derived from $BC^{1,3}$. Moreover, since $BC^{1,3}$, for example, is a candidate 2-itemset, its subsets, i.e., $B^{1,3}$ and $C^{1,3}$, should potentially be candidate itemsets. As a result, 9 candidate itemsets, i.e., $\{B^{1,3}, B^{3,3}, C^{1,3}, C^{2,3}, E^{2,3}, F^{3,3}, BC^{1,3}, BF^{3,3}, CE^{2,3}\}$ as shown in Figure 3, are generated. Note that since there is no candidate TI k-itemset ($k \geq 2$) containing A or D in this example, $A^{i,3}$ and $D^{i,3}$ ($1 \leq i \leq 3$) are not necessary to be taken as SI itemsets for generating general temporal association rules. In other words, we can skip them from the set of candidate itemsets C'_ks. Finally, all occurrence counts of C'_ks can be calculated by the second database scan. Note that itemsets $BC^{1,3}$, $BF^{3,3}$ and $CE^{2,3}$ are termed as frequent TIs, while $B^{1,3}, B^{3,3}, C^{1,3}, C^{2,3}, E^{2,3}$ and $F^{3,3}$ are frequent SIs in this example.

As shown in Figure 3, after all frequent TI and SI itemsets are identified, the corresponding general temporal association rules can be derived in a straightforward manner. Explicitly, the general temporal association rule of $(X \Rightarrow Y)^{MCP(XY)}$ holds if $conf((X \Rightarrow Y)^{MCP(XY)}) \geq min\_conf$.

4 Experimental Studies

To assess the performance of algorithm *PPM*, we performed several experiments on a computer with a CPU clock rate of 450 MHz and 512 MB of main memory. The methods used to generate synthetic data are described in Section 4.1. The performance comparison of *PPM* and $Apriori^+$ is presented in Section 4.2. Results on scaleup experiments are presented in Section 4.3.

4.1 Generation of synthetic workload

For obtaining reliable experimental results, the method to generate synthetic transactions we employed in this study is similar to the ones used in prior works [2, 13]. These transactions mimic the publication items in a publication database. Each database consists of $|D|$ transactions, and on the average, each transaction has $|T|$ items. To simulate the characteristic of the exhibition period in each item, transaction items are uniformly distributed into database $\mathcal{D}$ with a random selection. In accordance with the exhibition periods of items, database $\mathcal{D}$ is divided into n partitions. Table 2 summarizes the meanings of various parameters used in the experiments. The mean of the correlation level is set to 0.25 for our experiments. Without loss of generality, we use the notation $Tx - Iy - Dm$ to represent a database in which $D = m$ thousands, $|T| = x$, and $|I| = y$. We compare relative performance of $Apriori^+$ and PPM.

$|\mathcal{D}|$	Number of transactions in the database
$|T|$	Average size of the transactions
$|I|$	Average size of the maximal frequent itemsets
$|L|$	Number of maximal potentially frequent itemsets
N	Number of items
$|P_i|$	Number of transactions in the partition database P_i

Table 2: Meanings of various parameters

4.2 Relative performance

We first conducted several experiments to evaluate the relative performance of $Apriori^+$ and PPM. Since the experimental results are consistent for various values of n, $|L|$ and N, for interest of space, we only report the results on $|L| = 2000$ and $N = 10000$ in the following experiments. Figure 4 shows the relative execution times for both two algorithms as the minimum support threshold is decreased from 1% support to 0.1% support. When the support threshold is high, there are only a limited number of frequent itemsets produced. However, as the support threshold decreases, the performance difference becomes prominent in that PPM significantly outperforms $Apriori^+$. Explicitly, PPM is in orders of magnitude faster than $Apriori^+$, and the margin grows as the minimum support threshold decreases.

4.3 Scaleup performance

In this experiment, we examine the scaleup performance of algorithm PPM. The scale-up results for different selected datasets are obtained. Figure 5 shows the scaleup performance of algorithm PPM as the values of $|D|$ increase.

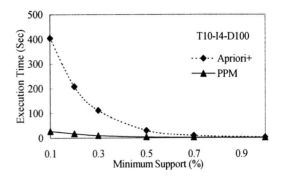

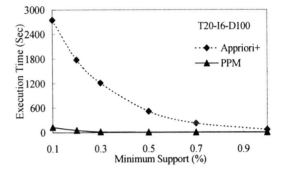

Figure 4. Relative performance studies

Three different minimum supports are considered. We obtained the results for the dataset $T10 - I4 - Dm$ when the number of customers increases from $100,000$ to one million. The execution times are normalized with respect to the times for the $100,000$ transactions dataset in the Figure 5. Note that, as shown in Figure 5 the execution time only slightly increases with the growth of the database size, showing good scalability of PPM.

5 Conclusion

In this paper, we not only explored a new model of mining general temporal association rules, i.e., $(X \Rightarrow Y)^{MCP(XY)}$, in a publication database but also developed algorithm PPM to generate the temporal association rules as well as conducted related performance studies. Under PPM, the cumulative information of mining previous partitions is selectively carried over toward the generation of candidate itemsets for the subsequent partitions. Algorithm PPM is particularly powerful for efficient mining for a publication-like transaction database, such as bookstore transaction databases, video rental store records, library-book rental records, and transactions in electronic commerce. One extension to our proposed model in this paper is to mine general temporal association rules with different

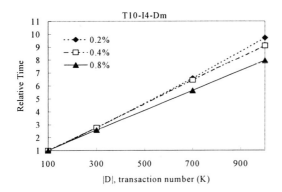

Figure 5. Scaleup performance of PPM

start and end points of items. This is an interesting yet challenging issue since the levelwise property does not hold in this situation, and will be a matter of future research.

6 Acknowledgment

The authors are supported in part by the Ministry of Education Project No. 89-E-FA06-2-4-7 and the National Science Council, Project No. NSC 89-2219-E-002-028 and NSC 89-2218-E-002-028, Taiwan, Republic of China.

References

[1] R. Agrawal, T. Imielinski, and A. Swami. Mining Association Rules between Sets of Items in Large Databases. *Proc. of ACM SIGMOD*, pages 207–216, May 1993.

[2] R. Agrawal and R. Srikant. Fast Algorithms for Mining Association Rules in Large Databases. *Proc. of the 20th International Conference on Very Large Data Bases*, pages 478–499, September 1994.

[3] J.M. Ale and G. Rossi. An Approach to Discovering Temporal Association Rules. *ACM Symposium on Applied Computing*, 2000.

[4] M.-S. Chen, J. Han, and P. S.Yu. Data Mining: An Overview from Database Perspective. *IEEE Transactions on Knowledge and Data Engineering*, 8(6):866–883, December 1996.

[5] X. Chen and I. Petr. Discovering Temporal Association Rules: Algorithms, Language and System. *Proc. of 2000 Int. Conf. on Data Engineering*, 2000.

[6] D. Cheung, J. Han, V. Ng, and C.Y. Wong. Maintenance of Discovered Association Rules in Large Databases: An Incremental Updating Technique.

Proc. of 1996 Int'l Conf. on Data Engineering, pages 106–114, February 1996.

[7] J. Han and Y. Fu. Discovery of Multiple-Level Association Rules from Large Databases. *Proc. of the 21th International Conference on Very Large Data Bases*, pages 420–431, September 1995.

[8] J. Han, J. Pei, and Y. Yin. Mining Frequent Patterns without Candidate Generation. *Proc. of 2000 ACM-SIGMOD Int. Conf. on Management of Data*, pages 486–493, May 2000.

[9] J. Hipp, U. Güntzer, and G. Nakhaeizadeh. Algorithms for association rule mining – a general survey and comparison. *SIGKDD Explorations*, 2(1):58–64, July 2000.

[10] C.-H. Lee, C.-R. Lin, and M.-S. Chen. Sliding-Window Filtering: An Efficient Algorithm for Incremental Mining. *Proc. of the ACM 10th Intern'l Conf. on Information and Knowledge Management*, November 2001.

[11] J.-L. Lin and M.H. Dunham. Mining Association Rules: Anti-Skew Algorithms. *Proc. of 1998 Int'l Conf. on Data Engineering*, pages 486–493, 1998.

[12] B. Liu, W. Hsu, and Y. Ma. Mining Association Rules with Multiple Minimum Supports. *Proc. of 1999 Int. Conf. on Knowledge Discovery and Data Mining*, August 1999.

[13] J.-S. Park, M.-S. Chen, and P. S. Yu. Using a Hash-Based Method with Transaction Trimming for Mining Association Rules. *IEEE Transactions on Knowledge and Data Engineering*, 9(5):813–825, October 1997.

[14] R. Srikant and R. Agrawal. Mining Generalized Association Rules. *Proc. of the 21th International Conference on Very Large Data Bases*, pages 407–419, September 1995.

[15] R. Srikant and R. Agrawal. Mining quantitative association rules in large relational tables. *Proc. of 1996 ACM-SIGMOD Conf. on Management of Data*, 1996.

[16] A. K. H. Tung, J. Han, L. V. S. Lakshmanan, and R. T. Ng. Constraint-Based Clustering in Large Databases. *Proc. of 2001 Int. Conf. on Database Theory*, January 2001.

[17] K. Wang, Y. He, and J. Han. Mining Frequent Itemsets Using Support Constraints. *Proc. of 2000 Int. Conf. on Very Large Data Bases*, September 2000.

[18] C. Yang, U. Fayyad, and P. Bradley. Efficient discovery of error-tolerant frequent itemsets in high dimensions. *The Seventh ACM SIGKDD International Conference on Knowledge Discovery and Data Mining*, 2001.

Preparations for Semantics-Based XML Mining

Jung-Won Lee
*Department of Computer
Science and Engineering
Ewha Institute of Science and
Technology
jungwony@ewha.ac.kr*

Kiho Lee
*Department of Computer
Science and Engineering
Ewha Institute of Science and
Technology
khlee@ewha.ac.kr*

Won Kim
*Cyber Databases Solutions
Austin, Texas
won.kim@cyberdb.com*

Abstract

XML allows users to define elements using arbitrary words and organize them in a nested structure. These features of XML offer both challenges and opportunities in information retrieval, document management, and data mining. In this paper, we propose a new methodology for preparing XML documents for quantitative determination of similarity between XML documents by taking account of XML semantics (i.e., meanings of the elements and nested structures of XML documents). Accurate quantitative determination of similarity between XML documents provides an important basis for a variety of applications of XML document mining and processing. Experiments with XML documents show that our methodology provides a 50-100% improvement in determining similarity, over the traditional vector-space model that considers only term-frequency and 100% accuracy in identifying the category of each document from an on-line bookstore.

1. Introduction

XML is a language for specifying semistructured data, and is rapidly emerging as the new standard for data representation and exchange on the Web. XML includes arbitrary tags for representing document elements, and allows the elements to be organized in a nested structure regardless of the existence of an explicitly specified Document Type Descriptor (DTD) or Schema. Automatic deduction of the structures of XML documents has been an active subject of research [1, 5, 13, 16]. XML allows users to define elements using arbitrary words instead of a predefined set of words. Therefore, an XML element may have meanings beyond the same words used in a flat or unstructured document. It can provide a hint for building an index structure for information retrieval or determining a schema for transferring data from the Web to a database.

We expect that many Web applications that process XML documents, such as grouping similar XML documents and searching for XML documents that match a sample XML document, will require techniques for clustering and classifying XML documents. It has been well-established in such fields as database management and information retrieval that the more semantics about data (e.g., metadata) are understood by a system, the more precise queries can become. It is intuitively obvious that if some of the rich semantics of XML can be taken into account, we should have a more powerful basis of supporting the clustering and classification of XML documents for a wide variety of XML applications. The following illustrates some of the aspects of the use words in XML documents that need to be taken into consideration in understanding the semantics of the documents.

First, synonyms, compound words, or abbreviations may be used for XML elements. Figure 1 shows parts of two sample XML documents about books obtained from two electronic commerce bookseller sites. In both only their elements are represented. The elements 'products' and 'goods', 'author' and 'writer', 'publisher' and 'publishing_company' and 'book' and 'bib' (as abbreviation of 'bibliography') are synonyms. It is clear that once apparently different sets of elements are "normalized", they may constitute rather similar documents.

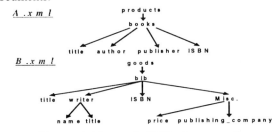

Figure 1. Example XML documents

Second, the context of a word often determines the meaning of a word in a document . In B.xml, the 'title' element next to the 'writer' element is the title (Mr., Ms., Dr., Sir) of a writer; and 'title' next to 'book' is the title of a book.

345

Third, the relevance of a word differs depending on whether the word appears as an element or in contents. A word used as an element has a greater relevance in representing a document than the same word that appears in contents. Therefore, we need to differentiate each word by assigning different weights to the word depending on whether it is used as an element or in contents.

Fourth, the elements in an XML document can collectively indicate the subject of the document. Both documents in Figure 1 consist of 'book', 'title', 'ISBN', and 'publisher' (or their synonyms). A collection of elements in an XML document can provide a hint for clustering and classifying documents.

In this paper, we propose a new methodology for computing similarity between XML documents by taking account of XML semantics (i.e., meanings of the elements and nested structures of XML documents) to prepare XML documents for XML mining. We create an extended-element vector for each element in an XML document, and a similarity matrix for comparing extended-element vectors. An extended-element vector is a list of synonyms, compound words, and abbreviations that are related to a given element. It forms a normalized basis for measuring similarity between elements belonging to different XML documents. We also compute a "minimal" hierarchical structure of an XML document using automata. We then adapt a sequential pattern mining algorithm to compute similarity between XML documents.

Accurate quantitative determination of similarity between XML documents provides an important basis for XML mining. Experiments with XML documents show that our methodology for preparation for semantics-based XML mining provides 50%-100% improvement in determining similarity, over the traditional vector-space model that considers only term-frequency. And it also provides 100% correctness in identifying categories of documents collected from on-line bookstore.

Our methodology has broad applicability. It may enable Web crawlers to collect documents that satisfy minimum similarity to a query document. Our method for minimizing the hierarchical structure of an XML document may be applied to building an index of XML documents for search engines and generating document summarizations in EDMS (Electronic Document Management System). Our method for finding maximal similar paths may be used for merging multiple XML documents.

2. Computing similarity between elements

In this section, we first describe the generation of extended-element vectors for the elements in an XML document. We then discuss the creation of a similarity matrix for computing similarity between two sets of extended-element vectors representing two XML documents.

2.1. Generating extended-element vectors

We generate extended-element vectors for an XML document as follows.

- Parse an XML document to extract elements and generate a DOM (Document Object Model) [17] tree.
- Sift meaningful tokens by filtering delimiters such as space, hyphen, and underscore.
- Delete tokens included in a stop-list.
- Extract stems or original form of the tokens through stemming process.
- Extend elements thus found, using the WordNet thesaurus and a user-defined word library, with synonyms, compound words, and abbreviations.

WordNet[6] is an electronic dictionary for natural language processing that we may use to find synonyms of elements. A user-defined word library is used to store and look up compound words and abbreviations. For example, the extended-element vector for a 'book' is book → (volume, record, recordbook, script, playscript, leger, ledger, book_info, textbook, booklist, bib). We formally define an extended-element vector as follows.

Definition 1. An extended-element vector
// SynVect_UDL and SynVect_WN: synonyms, abbreviation, or compound words that are found from user-defined library and WordNet
// MaxSize : maximum length of an extended-element vector
// <T> is an element, and t is a term in an extended-element vector

$Doc_i = (<T^i_1>, <T^i_2> ..., <T^i_m>)$, $T^i_m \rightarrow (t^i_{m1}, t^i_{m2}, ..., t^i_{ma})$
$Doc_j = (<T^j_1>, <T^j_2> ..., <T^j_n>)$, $T^j_n \rightarrow (t^j_{n1}, t^j_{n2}, ..., t^j_{nb})$
where $a, b \leq$ MaxSize, t^i_{ma} and $t^j_{nb} \in$ SynVect_UDL or SynVect_WN

2.2. Measure of element similarity

We now define measures of similarity between elements (i.e., extended-element vectors). The basis of the measures is the degree of match between original elements, between an original element and a term in the extended-element vector of another element. (In the measures below, Level 0 is the least similar and Level 6 is the most similar.)

Definition 2. Similarity measures between elements
- Level 6 : When two original elements completely match.
- Level 5 : When an original element completely matches a term in the extended-element vector of another element.
- Level 4 : When two terms in the extended-element vectors completely match.

- Level 3 : When two original elements partially match. (substring matching)
- Level 2 : When an original element partially matches a term in the extended-element vector of another element. (substring matching)
- Level 1 : When two terms in the extended-element vectors partially match. (substring matching)
- Level 0 : When there is no match.

2.3. Similarity matrix

We now show the construction of a similarity matrix for two sets of extended-element vectors representing two XML documents. One set of extended-element vectors forms the column, and another the row of the matrix. For convenience, the column will hold elements from a base document, and the row elements from a query document. Figure 2 shows a similarity matrix for books_catalogue.xml and books.xml. (In Figure 2, for illustrative simplicity, only the original elements are shown.) We can compute similarity between each pair of elements or terms in an extended-element vector on the basis of Definition 2. Empty row-column entries indicate Level 0 similarity (i.e., no match). If more than one value is applicable, the maximum value is selected.

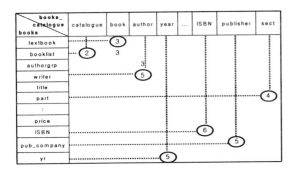

Figure 2. Similarity matrix between elements

3. Discovering and minimizing XML structure

Besides the extended-element vectors for the elements in XML documents, we need to determine the hierarchical structures of the documents in order to be able to compute similarity between XML structures. In this section we present a method for discovering and minimizing XML structures without loss of information using automata.

3.1. Formalizing an XML structure

There are several methods for formalizing the structure of semistructured data [1]. We have chosen to formalize

the structure of an XML document using NFA(Non-Deterministic Finite Automata). NFA is a natural means to represent the nesting of elements within an element in terms of state transitions between an element and elements nested in it [4]. By removing repeated state transitions, we can transform NFA to DFA (Deterministic Finite Automata). We can then apply a state minimization algorithm to DFA to minimize the number of states, i.e., a minimal XML structure. We can express an XML document about the bibliography as NFA-XML, which is shown in Figure 3.

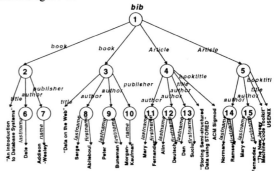

Figure 3. NFA-XML for bibliography.xml

Definition 3 formalizes NFA-XML.

Definition 3. NFA-XML M = (Q, D, Σ_N, Σ_T, δ, q0, F)

Q : a finite state set. If an element does not derive atomic data (contents), a new state is generated.

D : a finite data set (contents).

Σ_N : a finite element set, which does not derive atomic data and generates a new state.

Σ_T : a finite element set, which derives atomic data D.

δ : a transition function. If any element a $\in \Sigma_N$, $\delta(q,a)$ = p_1, p_2, ..., p_n (where p is a new state) and if any element a $\in \Sigma_T$, $\delta(q,a)$ = D_1, D_2, ..., D_n where a is an element.

q_0 : start state. The root element makes a transition to the start state.

F : final state. Only the element that has an atomic data ($\in \Sigma_T$) makes a transition to the final state.

3.2. Minimizing an XML structure

We must delete repeated elements to minimize such a structure, that is, transform an NFA-XML to a DFA-XML in which an input symbol (i.e., an element) causes a unique state transition. Figure 4(b) shows the DFA-XML that results from the NFA-XML, and Figure 4(a) the state transition table that drives the conversion. From the start state [1], reached by the root element, transitions are made to new states by subsequent elements ($\Sigma_N \cup \Sigma_T$). State transition reaches the final state (indicated by the symbol '⊥') when atomic data is found.

We may obtain a simplified structure by treating a set of equivalent states as a single state, that is by removing all but one of the states from each set of equivalent states. If we name the states in the left column of Figure 4(a) 'A'~'F' and the final state 'G', we obtain the DFA-XML of Figure 4(b). We may simplify the resulting DFA-XML by further discovering and merging equivalent states. Figure 4(b) reveals that states D and F are equivalent. Figure 4(c) shows a minimized DFA-XML obtained by merging equivalent states using a state minimization algorithm for DFA [4].

δ	book	article	title	author	publisher	booktitle	lastname	name	firstname
[1]	[2,3]	[4,5]	φ	φ	φ	φ	φ	φ	φ
[2,3]	φ	φ	⊥	[6, 8, 9]	[7,10]	φ	φ	φ	φ
[4,5]	φ	φ	⊥	[11,12,13,14,15]	φ	⊥	φ	φ	φ
[6,8,9]	φ	φ	φ	φ	φ	φ	⊥	φ	⊥
[7,10]	φ	φ	φ	φ	φ	φ	φ	⊥	φ
[11,12,13,14,15]	φ	φ	φ	φ	φ	φ	⊥	φ	⊥

⊥ : atomic data

[1] → A,   [2,3] → B,   [4,5] → C,
[6,8,9] → D,   [7,10] → E,   [11,12, 13, 14, 15] → F

(a) State transition table

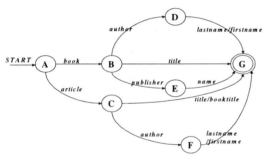

(b) DFA-XML

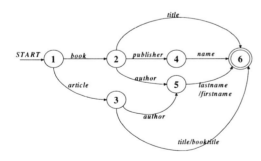

(c) Minimized DFA-XML

Figure 4. Minimized DFA-XML for bibliography.xml

The minimized DFA-XML of Figure 4(c) consists of the following full paths: (bib, book, title, ⊥), (bib, book, publisher, name, ⊥) and so on. The paths can be used to infer similarity between XML structures. The more similar paths they share, the more similar two documents may be regarded. Specifically, applying a sequential pattern mining algorithm[15] to the paths in a minimized DFA-XML, we may find maximal similar paths by regarding an XML element as a transaction. A sequential pattern mining algorithm, unlike association rule [3] which considers only occurrences of transactions, considers the sequence of transactions.

4. Similarity between XML structures

We are now ready to propose a method for computing similarity between XML structures by making use of the similarity matrix developed in Section 2 and the minimized DFA-XML structure developed in Section 3. We compute similarity between XML documents by determining the number of paths that are common and similar between the hierarchical structures for the documents. We need to be able to determine similar paths regardless of the level of the hierarchy for an element or the number of branches of an element.

In this section we propose an adapted sequential pattern mining algorithm for finding maximal similar paths between XML structures. A sequential pattern mining algorithm finds maximal sequences among transaction sequences that satisfy user-defined minimum support [15]. Transaction sequences which the original sequential pattern mining algorithms deal with are random sequences of goods purchased by customers, such as 'beer', 'diaper' and 'milk'. Maximal sequences that satisfy some minimum support among large transaction sequences are found. Similar sequences in our adapted sequential pattern mining algorithm have semantic relationships among transactions, namely, nested XML elements on a path. However, in the concept of minimum support needs to be viewed from a different perspective. In particular, minimum support for finding maximal similar paths between the base and query document must be 100%. It is reasonable to presume that XML documents are more similar when they have more identical sequences in their structures.

4.1. Adapted sequential pattern mining algorithm for XML

First we minimize the DFA-XML (obtained in Section 3.2) by removing repeated paths. Then we sort elements on path by tree levels. By traversing elements from the root element to elements with atomic data, we obtain large 1-paths, large 2-paths, and so on, until large n-paths. We can determine similar elements from two documents by referencing the similarity matrix (obtained in Section 2.3) between XML elements.

There are 5 phases to mining sequential patterns – sort, litemset, transformation, sequence, and maximal phase. We adapt sequential pattern mining algorithms to find maximal similar sequences between XML structures. Changes in each of the phases are shown in Table 1.

Table 1. Adapted sequential pattern mining algorithm for XML

Phase	Adapted one for XML
Sort	XML document is converted to DFA-XML. Path expressions are extracted from minimized DFA-XML and are sorted by level.
Litemset	All large 1-paths are found considering element similarity.
Transformation	All extracted elements of path expressions are replaced with integers.
Sequence	Large 1, 2,..n paths are found with similarity.
Maximal	Maximal similar paths are found among the set of large paths.
Computing	Similarity between XML structures is computed as the ratio between the maximal similar paths of the query document and the total paths of the base document.

An extra phase, computing phase, has been added, in which similarity between XML structures is quantified finally. For the purpose of computing similarity between XML structures, user-defined minimum support is necessarily 100% because similar paths must be in both structures.

The simplest measure of similarity between structures is the ratio of maximal similar paths to total paths. One XML structure is the base document, and the other is the query document for the purpose of comparing two structures. Similarity between the two structures is the ratio between the maximal similar paths of the query document and the total paths of the base document.

< Example 1 >

Figure 5 shows minimized DFA-XMLs of two XML documents on books. These are based on result pages obtained by searching for "professional WAP" in online bookstores amazon.com and barnes&noble.com. We assume that amazon.xml is the base document B and b&n.xml is a query document Q_1. For simplicity we show only one query document. We extract path expressions from the minimized DFA-XML of each XML document. And we map similar elements on a path by replacing the elements with same integer corresponding to the elements in the element similarity matrix as following Table 2.

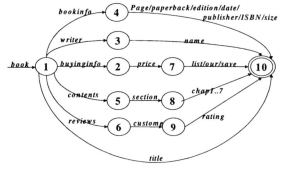

(a) amazon.xml

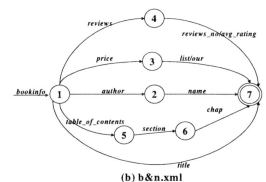

(b) b&n.xml

Figure 5. Minimized DFA-XMLs

Table 2. Path transformation

Doc.	Original paths	Transformed paths
amazon. xml	book.title.⊥	<{1}{2}>
	book.bookinfo.page.⊥	<{1}{3}{4}>
	book.bookinfo.paperback.⊥	<{1}{3}{5}>
	book.bookinfo.edition.⊥	<{1}{3}{6}>
	book.bookinfo.date.⊥	<{1}{3}{7}>
	book.bookinfo.publisher.⊥	<{1}{3}{8}>
	book.bookinfo.ISBN.⊥	<{1}{3}{9}>
	book.bookinfo.size.⊥	<{1}{3}{10}>
	book.buyinginfo.price.list.⊥	<{1}{11}{12}{13}>
	book.buyinginfo.price.our.⊥	<{1}{11}{12}{14}>
	book.buyinginfo.price.save.⊥	<{1}{11}{12}{15}>
	book.contents.section.chap.⊥	<{1}{16}{17}{18}>
	book.reviews.customer.rating.⊥	<{1}{19}{20}{21}>
	book.writer.name.⊥	<{1}{22}{23}>
b&n.xml	bookinfo.title.⊥	<{3}{2}>
	bookinfo.price.list.⊥	<{3}{12}{13}>
	bookinfo.price.our.⊥	<{3}{12}{14}>
	bookinfo.author.name.⊥	<{3}{22}{23}>
	bookinfo.tableofcontents.section.chap.⊥	<{3}{16}{17}{18}>
	bookinfo.reviews.reviews_no. ⊥	<{3}{19}{24}>
	bookinfo.reviews.avg_rating.⊥	<{3}{19}{21}>

Table 3 shows the process of finding maximal similar paths from the transformed paths through the sequence and maximal phase.

Table 3. Finding maximal similar paths

Large 1-paths	Large 2-paths	Large 3-paths
<u><{2}></u>, <u><{3}></u>, <{12}>,<{13}>, <{14}>, <{16}>, <{17}>, <{18}>, <{19}>,<{21}>, <{22}>, <{23}>	<u><{12} {13}></u> <u><{12} {14}></u> <{16} {17}> <{16} {18}> <{17} {18}> <u><{19} {21}></u> <u><{22} {23}></u>	<u><{16} {17} {18}></u>

In Table 3 the underlined paths are maximal similar paths. We can see that two sample XML documents are very similar because their paths are nearly covered by maximal similar paths.

4.2. Computing similarity between XML structures

We can obtain all maximal large paths in the base document and query documents by performing the phases from sort to maximal. To quantify similarity between XML structures, we add the computing phase.

After we generate nested path expressions of the base document(NPE_B) of transformed path expressions of the base document(PE_B), we compute similarity between two structures as the ratio between the maximal similar paths of the query document and the total paths of the base document. To reduce potentially excessive effect of the root element in computing similarity, we treat the root element as an element on the 1st level of the tree.

< Example 2 >

We convert transformed paths (PE_B) of Table 2 to nested path expressions NPE^B as follows { <1>, <u><2></u>, <u><3</u>, (4, 5, 6, 7, 8, 9, 10)>, <11, <u>12</u>, (<u>13</u>, <u>14</u>, 15)>, <u><16, 17, 18></u>, <u><19</u>, 20, <u>21</u>>, <u><22, 23></u> }. NPE holds information about the nested structure. Between the maximal similar paths of query document (PE_Q) and all paths of NPE^B, underlined paths are common. Detailed process is shown in Table 4.

Table 4. Computing similarity between PE^B and PE^{Q1}

NPE^B	Paths	Ratio
NPE^B_1	<1>	$1/7 * (1/1 * (0))$
NPE^B_2	<u><2></u>	$1/7 * (1/1 * (1))$
NPE^B_3	<u><3</u>, (4, 5, 6, 7, 8, 9, 10)>	$1/7 * (1/2 * (1 + 1/7 * (0 + 0 + 0 + 0 + 0 + 0 + 0)))$
NPE^B_4	<11, <u>12</u>, (<u>13</u>, <u>14</u>, 15)>	$1/7 * (1/3 * (0 + 1 + 1/3 * (1 + 1 + 0)))$
NPE^B_5	<u><16, 17, 18></u>	$1/7 * (1/3 * (1 + 1 + 1))$
NPE^B_6	<u><19</u>, 20, <u>21</u>>	$1/7 * (1/3 * (1 + 0 + 1))$
NPE^B_7	<u><22, 23></u>	$1/7 * (1/2 * (1 + 1))$
length(NPE^B) $\sum_{k=1}$ the ratio of NPE_k^B		**0.833**

We find 83.3% as similarity between amazon.xml and b&n.xml. (We may use different methods for computing the ratio.) This computing measure is formalized as follows. $V(E_k)$ is a recursive function because of nested lists of NPE such as <3, (4, 5, 6, 7, 8, 9, 10)>.

$$\sum_{k=1}^{L(NPE)} \frac{1}{S(n)} \times V(E_k)$$

$S(n)$ is a number of siblings of 1st level, $L( )$ is length function

$$V(E_k) = \begin{cases} 1, & \text{if } E_k \text{ is a atomic and selected} \\ 0, & \text{if } E_k \text{ is a atomic and not selected} \\ \frac{1}{L(E_k)} \sum_{i=1}^{L(E_k)} V(E_i), & \text{if } E_k \text{ is a list} \end{cases}$$

5. Experimental results

XML documents with various structures are needed to validate effectiveness of our proposed methodology. Due to difficulty in obtaining large XML documents with various structures, we chose to translate HTML documents to equivalent XML documents.

Our experiments have two purposes. The first is to measure effectiveness of our methodology relative to the general vector-space document model[14] that only considers term-frequency (experiment1 and 2). In the traditional vector-space model, terms that are not included in an index set are represented by '0's because they cannot be recognized as similar elements if they are expressed with different words. It also does not have a method considering XML structures. The second purpose of our experiments (experiment 3) is to show that similarity between XML structures may be an important hint for classifying and clustering documents.

5.1. Experiment 1. documents of the same type of object

• **Traditional vector-space model considering only term frequency :** we used two similar XML documents amazon.xml and b&n.xml shown in Figure 5. They have some different elements and different structures. We use amazon.xml as the base document and b&n.xml as the query document. Elements of the base document form the index set in a vector-space model. We express each sample XML document in vector-space model by computing the weight of each index word in the document. We then use the widely used cosine coefficient[14] to compute similarity between the two vector-space models. The weights of elements in b&n.xml are the term-frequencies. The following are the vector-space models for the two documents. T is the index set and X and Y are the document models.

T = (Book, Title, BuyingInfo, Price, List, Our, Save, Writer, Name, BookInfo, Page, Paperback, Edition, Date, Publisher, ISBN, Size, Contents, Section, Chap1, Chap2, Chap3, Chap4, Chap5, Chap6, Chap7, Reviews, Customer, Rating)
X= (1,1,1,1,1,1,1,1,1,1,1,1,1,1,1,1,1,1,1,1,1,1,1,1,1,1,1,1,1)
Y=(0,1,0,1,0,1,1,0,1,1,0,0,0,0,1,1,0,0,0,0,0,0,0,0,0,0,1,0,0)

Using cosine coefficient [14], we obtain a 55.7% similarity. Intuitively, the traditional vector-space model considering only term-frequency cannot identify similar elements and similar structures, and is necessarily inferior to a method that takes into account similarity in elements and structure of documents.

• **Proposed model using an adapted sequential pattern mining algorithm :** in section 4, we presented structure similarity between amazon.xml and b&n.xml and described the detail process for computing similarity between two documents. Table 5 shows a summary of the results. Our proposed method takes into account both the element similarity and structure similarity. The second method is clearly superior to the first.

Table 5. Result of experiment 1

	Traditional model	Proposed model
amazon.xml	100 %	100 %
b&n.xml	55.7 %	83.3 %

5.2. Experiment 2. documents of different types of object

We did another experiment with sample documents of different types of object sold by a "composite" electronic commerce shop. These documents have different elements but somewhat similar structures. To compare similarity among more than two documents, we need to use a centroid document as the base document. We use goods.xml as the base document, and compare it against the other two documents.

Table 6. Result of experiment 2

	Traditional model	Proposed model
goods.xml	100 %	100 %
electronics.xml	49.66 %	85.71 %
clothes.xml	49.65 %	52.38 %

Using the proposed model, we obtain a 52.38% similarity between clothes.xml and goods.xml. The reason is that the root element of clothes.xml had an unduly large effect on similarity measure. To reduce this, we may change the formula to reduce the effect of the root at the computing phase of an adapted sequential pattern mining. However, the root element should rightly be given a bigger weight than any other element.

5.3. Experiment 3. categorical documents

We collected HTML pages from amazon.com site. There are 4 categories: music, book, electronics, and videos. We selected 20 HTML pages from the collection and translated them to XML documents with meaningful elements, such as <title>, <price>, <buying_info>, <record_company> and so on. We present the results of similarity computation among all documents in Figure 6.

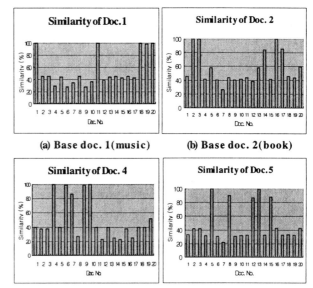

(a) Base doc. 1(music)   (b) Base doc. 2(book)

(c) Base doc.4(electronics)   (d) Base doc. 5(videos)

Figure 6. Document similarity according to each category

We show the results using representative documents - 1 (Music), 2(Book), 4 (Electronics), 5 (Video). Top 4 similar documents of base document 1, 2, 4, and 5 (except itself) are as follows. Doc.1 (music) : {11, 18, 20 (100%), 19 (98.21%)}, Doc.2 (book) : {3, 16 (100%), 17 (85.71%), 14 (84.82%)}, Doc.4 (electronics) : {10 (100%), 6 (98.96%), 9 (98.96%), 7 (86.46%)}, and Doc.5 (videos) : {13 (99.24%), 8 (90.15%), 15 (88.26%), 12 (86.74%)}. Our proposed methodology correctly identified all 20 documents.

6. Related work

[18] proposes an approach to mining semistructured documents. It proposes a classification model that considers document structure. Its goal is to classify documents with regular structures and works well with documents from one database or the same site. If documents have various structures, it may not work well.

[11, 12] consider both structure and contents in database or text. However their purpose is to query and build an index. As more XML documents are used, we

need to analyze similarity between XML documents for clustering or classifying.

Some research has been done to discover structures from semistructured data. [5] proposes a schema-generation algorithm to use relational database systems for storing, querying, and managing semistructured data. Its focus is on optimizing the storage and query cost in mapping given semistructured data instances to a relational database. [13] presents an algorithm for approximate typing of semistructured data. Typing problems result in extracting a schema from semistructured data.

[16] determines paths of a tree with a maximum frequency using association rules. The work considered links of multiple hierarchical documents and assumes that a hierarchical structure within a document has already been determined. [2] discovers a structure semi-automatically through training. If a user partitions one file into regions of interest hierarchically, it can compute a structure using the partition information through a training process.

Tree pattern-matching algorithms have long been a subject of research [7, 8, 9, 10]. However, they are difficult to use, without some alteration and adaptation, for comparing XML structures. The goal of tree pattern matching algorithm is to replace sub-expressions for optimization, or to find common structure using edit operations. Among tree pattern matching problems, we may use solutions for unordered tree inclusion and unordered path inclusion problems to find maximal similar paths between XML structures [9]. However tree inclusion problem is NP-complete and path inclusion problem has no systematic process for preparing data structure for XML.

7. Conclusions and future work

In this paper, we proposed a new methodology for preparing XML documents for quantitative determination of similarity between XML documents by taking account of XML semantics. We extracted maximal similar paths between state-minimized XML structures using an adapted sequential pattern mining algorithm. We presented a method for finding a state-minimized XML structure using automata. To provide a basis for computing similarity between XML elements, we also presented a method to generate an extended-element vector and build a similarity matrix. Experiments showed that our methodology provides over 50% improvement in determining similarity between XML documents over the traditional vector-space model that considers only term-frequency and 100% accuracy in identifying the category of each document from an on-line bookstore.

We need further research to adapt the current proposed methodology to mixing both contents and structures of XML documents, for use in XML mining operations, namely, clustering or classification.

References

[1] Abiteboul, Buneman, and Suciu. *Data on the web : from relations to semistructured data and XML*, Morgan-Kaufmann, 2000.

[2] Brad Adelberg. NoDoSE - A Tool for Semi-Automatically Extracting Structured and Semistructured Data from Text Documents, In *Proc. of SIGMOD*, pages 283-294, 1998.

[3] R. Agrawal, R. Srikant. Fast Algorithms for Mining Association Rules, In *Proc. of the 20th Int'l Conference on VLDB*, Santiago, Chile, Sept. 1994.

[4] A.V.Aho, R.Sethi and J.D.Ullman. *Compilers:Principles, Techniques, and Tools*, Addison Wesley, 1986.

[5] Deutsch, Fernandez and Suciu. Storing Semistructured DAta with STORED, *In Proc. of SIGMOD*, pages 431-442, 1999.

[6] C.Fellbaum. *WordNet : An Electronic Lexical Database*, Cambridge:MIT Press. 1998.

[7] Bunke H., Shearer K. A Graph Distance Metric Based on the Maximal Common Subgraph, *Pattern Recognition Letters*, (19)3-4:pages 255-259, Elsevier Science, 1998.

[8] Wang J.T.L., Shapiro B.A., Shasha D., Zhang K., Currey K.M. An Algorithm for Finding the Largest Approximately Common Substructures of Two Trees, *IEEE Transactions on Pattern Analysis and Machine Intelligence (PAMI)* 20(8), pages 889-895, 1998.

[9] P.Kilpelainen and H.Mannila. The Tree Inclusion Problem, *In Proc. of the International Joint Conference on the Theory and Practice of Software Development*, Vol. 1:Colloqium on Trees in Algebra and Programming (CAAP '91), pages 202-214, Springer-Verlag, 1991

[10] Christoph M. Hoffmann and Michael J. O'Donnell. Pattern Matching in Trees, *Journal of ACM* 29, 1, pages 68 – 95, Jan. 1982.

[11] Myaeng et al. A Flexible Model for Retrieval of SGML Documents, *In Proc. of SIGIR*, pages 138-145, 1998.

[12] Navaro and Baeza-Yates. A Language for Queries on the Structure and Contents of Structured Documents, *In Proc. of SIGIR*, pages 93-101, 1995.

[13] Nestorov, Abiteboul, Motwani. Extracting Schema from Semistructured Data, *In Proc. of SIGMOD*, pages 295-306, 1998.

[14] Gerard Salton and Michael J. McGill. *Introduction to Modern Information Retrieval*, McGraw-Hill, 1983.

[15] R. Srikant and R. Agrawal. Mining Sequential Patterns:Generalizations and Performance Improvements, In *Proc. of the Fifth Int'l Conf. on Extending Database Technology (EDBT)*, Mar. 1996.

[16] Ke Wang and Huiqing Liu. Discovering Typical Structures of Documents: a Road Map Approach, In *Proc. of SIGIR*, pages 146-154, 1998.

[17] http://www.w3.org/DOM/

[18] Jeonghee Yi, Neel Sundaresan. A Classifier for Semi-Structured Documents, In *Proc. of SIGKDD*, pages 340-344, 2000.

Mining Image Features for Efficient Query Processing

Beitao Li, Wei-Cheng Lai, Edward Chang and Kwang-Ting Cheng
Electrical & Computer Engineering
University of California, Santa Barbara
echang@ece.ucsb.edu

Abstract

The number of features required to depict an image can be very large. Using all features simultaneously to measure image similarity and to learn image query-concepts can suffer from the problem of dimensionality curse, *which degrades both search accuracy and search speed. Regarding search accuracy, the presence of irrelevant features with respect to a query can contaminate similarity measurement, and hence decrease both the recall and precision of that query. To remedy this problem, we present a mining method that learns online users' query concepts and identifies important features quickly. Regarding search speed, the presence of a large number of features can slow down query-concept learning and indexing performance. We propose a divide-and-conquer method that divides the concept-learning task into G subtasks to achieve speedup. We notice that a task must be divided carefully, or search accuracy may suffer. We thus propose a genetic-based mining algorithm to discover good feature groupings. Through analysis and mining results, we observe that organizing image features in a multi-resolution manner, and minimizing intra-group feature correlation, can speed up query-concept learning substantially while maintaining high search accuracy.*

Keywords: data mining, query concept, relevance feedback.

1 Introduction

We explore two multimedia data mining problems in this paper. The first problem is to mine a user's query concept. A user who searches for multimedia content often encounters difficulty articulating his/her query concept. We present an intelligent mining method that can grasp the target concept quickly with a small number of labeled instances. The second mining problem that we tackle is to discover the optimal grouping of multimedia features (attributes) to achieve learning speedup while maintaining high search accuracy.

Mining a user's query concept is critical for online mul-timedia search such as looking up an e-commerce product or finding a desired image. In these applications, a query concept is difficult to articulate, and articulation can be subjective. For instance, a user may find it difficult to depict an image in low-level features, and different people may describe and interpret the same image differently. To remedy this query articulation difficulty, many search engines [5, 10, 13, 14, 15] require users to provide examples to seed a query. (For example, providing sunset images as examples in order to search for sunset pictures.) However, finding good examples is the job of a search engine itself, and this circular requirement leaves the core problem—understanding users' query concepts—unsolved.

We would like to use mining techniques that not only can learn users' query concepts, but also can grasp the concepts quickly. Unfortunately, traditional data mining algorithms and techniques are not suitable for this task for at least two reasons:

1. *Time and sample constraints.* Traditional learning methods such as decision trees and neural networks require a large number of training instances and can take a long time (more than a few seconds) to learn a concept in a high-dimensional feature space. But, online users are often too impatient to wait around or to provide a great deal of feedback.

2. *Limited room for preprocessing.* Traditional mining techniques such as user profiling and feature reduction may not be helpful for online query-concept learning. First, a user's query concept may be independent of his/her past queries. Profiling users, or using their past query patterns to predict future query concepts, can be counter-productive. In addition, performing feature reduction is infeasible in this online learning setting, since not all query concepts can be known in advance. (Performing feature reduction requires knowing all possible concepts, i.e., instance labels.)

In this paper, we first review a query-concept learner, MEGA, that we proposed in [2, 9] to learn a concept through an intelligent sampling process. MEGA models query concepts in k-CNF [7], which can model virtually all practical query concepts[1]. Learning a k-CNF, however, can be time consuming. For instance, when the number of features is larger, a k-CNF concept with a moderate k can have millions of terms. The focus of this paper thus aims to reduce learning time of MEGA by dividing the learning task into G subtasks (to achieve a speedup of $O(G^{k-1})$ folds). At first sight, dividing features seems to be straightforward. For instance, many systems divide image features into color, texture, and shape sets. Our empirical study, however, shows that this "natural" division can often yield poor search precision. We employ a genetic-based algorithm to discover good feature groupings that yield good precision. Our study using a diversified image dataset with 144-dimension features shows that the groupings that achieve high precision tend to have low intra-group feature correlation. As a part of our study, we also discovered k-CNF expressions for various image categories. We present and compare some selective learned concepts and discuss how concept-feature associations can be used for enhancing image search and similarity measurement.

The rest of this paper is organized into four sections. Section 2 defines notations and briefly reviews MEGA. Section 3 depicts the feature-division problem and presents the genetic-based algorithm for mining the optimal grouping. Section 4 presents our experimental results. Finally, we offer our conclusions in Section 5.

2 Query-Concept Learning

To provide the context, this section defines notations and reviews MEGA—a concept learning algorithm that we present in [2]. In MEGA, we use Valiant's learning algorithm [7] as the starting point, and further extend it to handle fuzzy membership functions. We also employ an intelligent sampling process to expedite the learning process.

2.1 Definitions and Notations

Our learner models query concepts in k-CNF and uses k-DNF to bound the uncertain region for sampling.

Definition 1: k-**CNF**: For constant k, the representation class k-CNF consists of Boolean formulae of the form $c_1 \wedge \cdots \wedge c_\theta$, where each c_i is a disjunction of at most k literals over the Boolean variables $x_1, \ldots, x_n$. No prior bound is placed on θ.

Definition 2: k-**DNF**: For constant k, the representation class k-DNF consists of Boolean formulae of the form $d_1 \vee \cdots \vee d_\theta$, where each d_i is a conjunction of at most k literals over the Boolean variables $x_1, \ldots, x_n$. No prior bound is placed on θ.

---

[1]k-CNF is more expressive than k-term DNF, and it has both polynomial sample complexity and time complexity [8, 11].

In our retrieval system, queries are boolean expressions consisting of predicates connected by the boolean operators $\vee$ (or) and $\wedge$ (and). A predicate on feature x_k in our system is in the form of P_{x_k}. Note that the membership function [3] of P_{x_k} can be either crispy or fuzzy. A database system consists of a number of predicates. Our goal is to find the proper operators to combine individual predicates to form the query concept. We choose k-CNF to model query concepts, since it can express most practical queries and can be learned via positive-labeled instances in polynomial time [7, 11]. In addition, we use non-positive-labeled instances to reduce our sampling space (bounded by k-DNF), which we will discuss in detail in Section 2.2. A k-CNF has three characteristics:

1: The terms (or literals) are combined by the $\wedge$ operator.

2: The predicates in a term are combined by the $\vee$ operator.

3: A term can have at most k predicates.

Suppose we have three predicates P_{x_1}, P_{x_2} and P_{x_3}. The 2-CNF of these predicates is

$$P_{x_1} \wedge P_{x_2} \wedge P_{x_3} \wedge (P_{x_1} \vee P_{x_2}) \wedge (P_{x_1} \vee P_{x_3}) \wedge (P_{x_2} \vee P_{x_3}).$$

Suppose a dataset contains N objects, denoted as O_i, where $i = 1 \ldots N$. Suppose each object can be depicted by M features, each of which is denoted by x_k, where $k = 1 \ldots M$. To find objects that best satisfy a k-CNF concept, we need to compute the membership value of an object with respect to the concept. We first compute the membership values at predicate level and then aggregate them into the membership value at concept level. At the predicate level, suppose $F_{x_k}(O_i)$ is the value of object i on feature x_k. We transform $F_{x_k}(O_i)$ to the predicate level membership value using a membership function μ: $F_{x_k}(O_i) \rightarrow [0, 1]$. Let $P_{x_k}(O_i)$ denote the predicate level membership value of object i for predicate P_{x_k}. When $P_{x_k}(O_i) = 1$, it means that object i fully satisfies predicate P_{x_k}. When $P_{x_k}(O_i) = 0$, it means that object i does not satisfy predicate P_{x_k} at all, and when $0 < P_{x_k}(O_i) < 1$, it means that object i satisfies predicate P_{x_k} to a degree. For example, people's heights can vary from 3 feet to 9 feet. If we want to grasp the fuzzy predicate of "tall", we use a membership function to transform each height value between 3 feet and 9 feet to a membership value between 0 and 1. If we consider people over 7 feet to be definitely tall, then we map heights over 7 feet to 1.0. If we consider people under 5 feet definitely not tall, then we map heights under 5 feet to 0.0. Heights between 5 and 7 feet are considered tall to a degree, and we map them to membership values between 0 and 1.

At the concept level, we use the standard fuzzy rules, as defined by Zadeh [4, 16], to aggregate membership values on individual predicates. To combine M predicate level membership values into one concept level membership value, we need an *M-ary* aggregation function that maps $[0, 1]^M$ to $[0, 1]$. The rules are as follows:

$$P_{x_1 \wedge x_2 \wedge \ldots \wedge x_M}(O_i) = \min\{P_{x_1}(O_i), P_{x_2}(O_i), \ldots P_{x_M}(O_i)\}$$
$$P_{x_1 \vee x_2 \vee \ldots \vee x_M}(O_i) = \max\{P_{x_1}(O_i), P_{x_2}(O_i), \ldots P_{x_M}(O_i)\}$$

The objects that best satisfy a concept have the largest aggregated membership values.

2.2 The MEGA Algorithm

MEGA models query concepts in k-CNF, which can model virtually all practical query concepts. MEGA consists of two major parts:

- Refinement: Refine the query concept based on positive-labeled instances. The refinement step is carefully designed to tolerate noisy data.

- Sampling: Refine the sampling space based on negative-labeled instances and select samples judiciously for expediting the learning process.

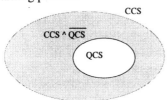

Figure 1. Sampling Space: $CCS \wedge \overline{QCS}$.

MEGA initializes the query concept space (QCS) as a k-CNF and the candidate concept space (CCS) as a k-DNF. The QCS starts as the most specific concept and the CCS as the most general concept. The target concept that MEGA learns is more general than the initial QCS and more specific than the initial CCS. MEGA learns the QCS, while at the same time refining the CCS to delimit the boundary of the sampling space. (The shaded area in Figure 1 shows the sampling space between the QCS and the CCS). To ensure that target concepts can be learned quickly and with a small number of samples, MEGA judiciously selects samples that can collect maximum information from users to refine k-CNF and k-DNF. MEGA removes irrelevant terms from the query-concept (i.e., a k-CNF), and at the same time, refines the sampling boundary (i.e., a k-DNF) so that the most informative samples can be selected in its subsequent iteration. MEGA uses refinement and sampling in a complementary way to achieve fast convergence to target concepts.

Note that MEGA does not require seeding a query. MEGA presents randomly selected images as the first round of examples. Even if all of the images generated in the first round are irrelevant, MEGA uses the negative images to reduce the set of potentially relevant images substantially (the k-DNF that bounds the sampling space can be shrunk substantially by the negative images). Thus, the probability is high that a relevant image will be generated in the next round. For the detailed description of MEGA, please refer to [2].

3 Mining Optimal Feature Groupings

The MEGA scheme described so far is not yet concerned with scalability in regard to M (the number of features for depicting an object). In this section, we describe a mining method for tackling the *dimensionality-curse* problem.

The number of disjunctions in a k-CNF (and, likewise, the conjunctives in a k-DNF) can be written as

$$\sum_{i=1}^{k} \binom{M}{i}.$$

When M is large, a moderate k can result in a large number of disjunctive terms in a k-CNF, which causes high space and time complexity for learning. For instance, an image database that we have built [1] characterizes each image with 144 features ($M = 144$). The initial number of disjunctions in a 3-CNF is half a million, and in a 4-CNF is eighteen million.

To reduce the number of terms in a k-CNF, we divide a learning task into G sub-tasks, each of which is to learn a subset of the features. Dividing a feature space into G subspaces reduces both space and time complexity by a factor of $O(G^{k-1})$. For instance, setting $G = 12$ in our image database reduces both space and time complexity for learning a 3-CNF by 140 times (the number of terms is reduced to $3,576$), and for learning a 4-CNF by $1,850$ times (the number of terms is reduced to $9,516$). The savings is enormous in both space and learning time. (The wall-clock time is less than half a second for one learning iteration for a 4-CNF concept on a Pentium-III processor.)

This divide-and-conquer approach may trade precision for speed, since some terms that involve features from more than one feature subset can no longer be included in a concept. For instance, if we divide features a, b, c, and d into two groups $\{a, b\}$ and $\{c, d\}$, a 2-CNF can no longer have the following four terms: $a \vee c$, $a \vee d$, $b \vee c$, and $b \vee d$. Missing terms may or may not hurt search accuracy. If a query concept does not contain the missing terms, its search accuracy is not affected; conversely, its accuracy decreases. If we know a term is not relevant to any search concept, we can comfortably separate its variables into different groups.

In the remainder of this section, we propose using a genetic-based algorithm to mine the best feature groupings so that the missing terms have a minimum effect on search accuracy.

3.1 The Genetic Algorithm for Mining Grouping

We apply genetic algorithms (GAs) [6] to search the best feature grouping. GAs are search algorithms based on an analogy to biological evolution. The simple GAs involve three operations: *selection*, *crossover*, and *mutation*. By applying these operations, GAs repeatedly update the current population. On each iteration, each individual of the population is evaluated according to a *fitness function*, which depends on the application. The objective of the simple GAs is to evolve a population of individuals having high fitness values.

In this section, we present our genetic-based algorithm for searching the best feature groupings. To use GAs, we need to address three issues.

1. Choosing an encoding scheme to translate a hypothesis in the solution space to an individual in GAs, and vice versa.

2. Determining the appropriate genetic operators that meet our objectives.

3. Selecting a good fitness function, since the results of GAs depend on the chosen fitness function.

Suppose there are M image features that we would like to divide into G groups. We further limit the search space by forcing the proposition that a valid grouping solution contains exactly M features and no feature is replicated. An individual is defined as such a collection of M features. Therefore, each individual represents a feature-grouping solution. Here, we do not require features inside groups to be ordered. Given an individual, an offspring can be generated by applying *selection*, *crossover*, and *mutation* operations. We define these genetic operators as follows:

- *Selection.* A portion of the next population is generated by selection within the current population. Selection is biased toward individuals with higher fitness values. We apply the tournament selection without placement as the selection process [12]. It separates the current population into two groups, a "better" group and a "worse" group. This selection scheme repeatedly picks two individuals from the pool and puts the one with higher fitness into the better group and the other one into the worse group until the pool is empty. The selection process is repeated once more. The new population is obtained after putting together the two better groups. This selection technique guarantees that the individual with the highest fitness value will be selected twice, and the individual with the lowest fitness value will not be selected at all.

- *Crossover.* The crossover operator produces a new offspring from a parent by exchanging features between feature groups of the parent. Given a parent, the crossover operator randomly selects two feature groups of the parent, randomly determines the number of features to be exchanged, randomly selects the features to be exchanged, and then exchanges those features between two selected groups. The other $G-2$ feature groups remain unchanged. After the crossover operation, the new offspring still contains exactly M features, and only two feature groups are updated from the parent. This operator allows GAs to explore different feature combinations inside a feature group.

- *Mutation.* The mutation operator perturbs the genes of an individual, with a very small probability. Usually, the mutation operator is applied after the crossover operator. Given an individual, the mutation operator decides if the individual is going to be mutated based on the mutation probability. If yes, the mutation operator randomly chooses a feature from a feature group and moves it to another feature group. This operator allows GAs to explore different grouping sizes.

Since a better feature grouping should yield higher search accuracy, we define the fitness function of a feature grouping as its search accuracy. We can estimate a grouping's search accuracy through simulation using training data. For instance, we use an image dataset consisting of $51,000$ images of 18 categories. We treat each category as a query concept. MEGA learns each of these 18 query concepts and returns the top-K images which best match each learned concept. The learned concept may be different from the actual concept. We measure search accuracy as the fraction of the top-K images retrieved based on the learned concept actually belonging to the real concept (category). For example, a bear query returns top-20 images that meet the bear concept learned by MEGA. The percentage of these 20 images that actually belong to the bear category represents the precision, and thus the fitness, of the query. We estimate fitness of a grouping by taking the average precision of the top-K retrieval (using the concepts learned based on that grouping) over 18 categories.

We apply the genetic algorithm to discover the optimal groupings as follows: In the initialization phase, the algorithm randomly creates a population with N individuals (i.e., groupings). In the evolution phase, we first compute the fitness value for each grouping by running extensive simulations on the image dataset. The best grouping is assigned as the grouping with the highest fitness value. In the next step, we apply tournament selection without replacement to generate some offspring groupings. The other offspring groupings are created using a crossover operator. Mutation operation is then applied to a certain fraction (e.g., 0.1 in our experiments) of the offspring. We then update the population with the offspring and repeat the same process until it reaches the desired number of generations. At the end, the genetic algorithm reports the best grouping(s) it found during the evolution process. We present our discovery of the optimal feature grouping in Section 4.

4 Experiments

In this section we report our experimental results. The main goals of our experiments were to

1: Study the tradeoff between learning time and learning accuracy (Sections 4.1 and 4.2).

2: Find ways to group features so that high retrieval precision can be achieved within a few iterations (Section 4.3).

3: Examine which features are important for different query concepts (Section 4.4).

We conducted experiments on a 51,000-image dataset collected from Corel image CDs and the Internet. Each image was characterized by a 144-dimension feature vector, which contained information about color histograms, color moments, textures, etc [2].

Each of the query concepts we tested belongs to one of the eighteen image categories: *architecture, bears, big cities, clouds, elephants, fabrics, fireworks, flowers, food, landscapes, people, objectionable images, stars, textures, tigers, tools,* and *waves*. Many categories were added to make the learning task challenging. For instance, the *big cities* and *architecture* categories both have buildings. Three animal categories —*bears, elephants,* and *tigers*— all have landscape background which makes the discernment of these categories difficult. The *fireworks* and *stars* categories both share the same dark sky background. *Clouds* and *waves* can appear very similar to each other, as can *flowers* and *fabrics*. Finally, various texture images and randomly crawled Internet images were added to raise the learning difficuly for all categories.

We used *precisions* of the top-10 and top-20 retrievals to measure performance. Since in the online image query scenario, 10 and 20 are practical numbers of images to present to a user, and the ratio of these images fitting the user's target concept is of major concern. We tallied precision for up to only five iterations, since we deemed it unrealistic to expect an interactive user to conduct more than five rounds of relevance feedback. To be objective, we ran each experiment ten times.

4.1 The Effect of Negations in Boolean Formulae

As previously stated, each of our images was characterized by a 144-dimension vector. Each feature has a corresponding predicate. We further expanded the method to include negations of these predicates. In other words, the boolean variables in a Boolean formula not only can be of form P_{x_i}'s, but also can be their negations, ($\neg P_{x_i}$'s). We first ran experiments without including negations of predicates and then included them with all other conditions fixed. The average top-10 and top-20 retrieval precisions are compared in Figure 2.

The figure shows that the precisions of both top-10 and top-20 retrievals are significantly increased when negations are included. This is because many query concepts can be expressed only with negations. For instance, an *elephant* image usually does not involve red color. The negation of the predicate "red high" can be useful for distinguishing an elephant image from, say, a flower image that may satisfy

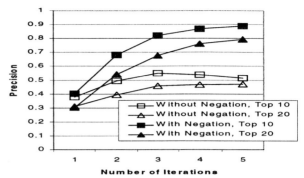

Figure 2. The Effect of Negations.

the "red high" predicate. Since including negations can substantially improve retrieval precision, we employ negations in our system.

4.2 The Effect of k and G

We model query concepts as k-CNF. The larger the value of k, the more complex concepts we can model. However, learning a more complex concept requires higher space and computational complexity. We should find a k that can adequately capture the query concepts for our applications, and can also be learned in a reasonable amount of space and time.

We experimented with different values of k, from $k = 1$ to $k = 4$. Figure 3 shows the average precisions of top-10 and top-20 retrievals. Figure 4 shows the running time for employing different k's. (We set $G = 20$ in this experiment. We explain shortly how the value of G is selected.)

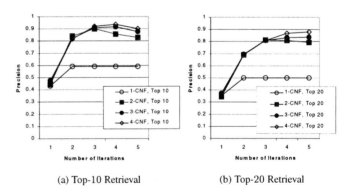

(a) Top-10 Retrieval   (b) Top-20 Retrieval

Figure 3. The Effect of k on Precision.

Since the trends of the top-10 and top-20 retrievals are similar, we discuss only the top-10 results. For 1-CNF, although the learning time is very short, the achieved search precision is under 60%. After we increased k to two, precision reached 90% after just three iterations. The learning time increased to about 0.1 second, which is satisfactory. When we further increased k to three, the precision improved, and the learning time (0.4 second) remained low.

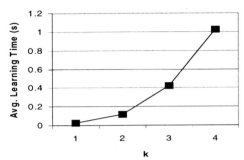

Figure 4. The Effect of k on Learning Time.

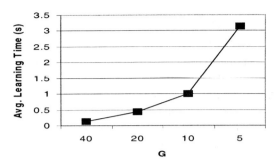

Figure 6. The Effect of G on Learning Time.

Further increasing k to four would not be productive, since the precision gain is marginal but the learning time increases substantially. For this image dataset, it is thus sufficient to model query concepts in 3-CNF.

Next, we examine the effect of G. In section 3 we discussed dividing features into G groups to speed up learning time. We experimented on different G values: 40, 20, 10 and 5.

Figures 5 and 6 show that tradeoffs exist between running time and search accuracy. When G is large ($G = 40$), the average running time is short (0.2 second), but the achieved precision can be dismal (around 80% for top-10 retrieval). At the other extreme, when we set $G = 5$, the precision is good but the running time is unacceptably high. When features are divided into too many groups, we are left with fewer terms to represent some query concepts. When features are divided into too few groups, the number of terms can be very large and hence would require lengthy learning time. Setting G to between 10 and 20 seems to give us a reasonable tradeoff between precision and running time. In the remainder of our experiments, we thus divided features into $G = 20$ groups.

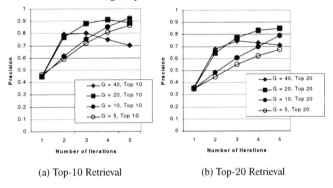

(a) Top-10 Retrieval   (b) Top-20 Retrieval

Figure 5. The Effect of G on Precision.

4.3 Discovering Optimal Groupings

Based on the above experimental results, we set G to 20 and model query concepts in 3-CNF. In this subsection, we

are interested in finding how features should be divided into $G = 20$ groups.

We used the genetic algorithm presented in Section 3 to learn the optimal groupings. We started with 40 randomly generated groupings. We ran experiments on each of them. Based on their results (fitness), we generated the next generation of groupings. We ran the experiment up to 120 generations. Figure 7 plots the precision that can be achieved in those 120 generations.

Figure 7. Average of the Highest Precisions.

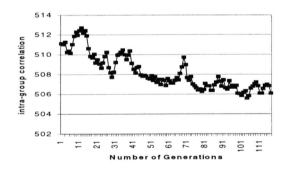

Figure 8. Average of Intra-group correlations.

From Figure 7, we can see that the genetic algorithm increases the precision from 89% to 92%, which is not an insignificant boost. To understand the factors for achieving that improvement, we also studied the average intra-group feature correlation of each generation, which is presented in Figure 8. From both Figures 7 and 8 we can identify a pattern: that having a low intra-group correlation tends to lead toward a higher search precision. To verify that our observation was valid, we conducted extensive experiments on precision achieved by different intra-group correlations. Figure 9 shows that the low intra-group correlation grouping can achieve a 92% precision, whereas the high intra-group correlation grouping can achieve only 85% precision.

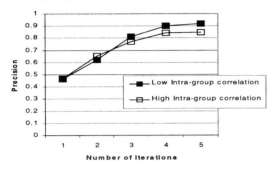

Figure 9. Precision of Top-10 Retrieval.

Remarks

We have shown that the loss of precision can be reduced by organizing a feature space intelligently. The terms *feature resolution* and *feature correlation* (a weak form of feature resolution) defined below can help us understand the reasons.

Definition 3: **Feature resolution**: Feature P_i is said to have higher resolution than feature P_j if the presence of P_i implies the presence of P_j (or the absence of P_j implies the absence of P_i). Let $P_i \in P_j$ denote that P_i has higher resolution than P_j. We say that $P_i \in P_j$ if and only if the conditional probability $P(P_j|P_i) = 1$.

Definition 4: **Feature correlation**: A feature P_i is said to have high correlation with feature P_j if the presence of P_i implies the presence of P_j (and vice versa) with high probability. We say that $P_i \sim P_j$ if and only if the conditional probability $P(P_j|P_i)/P(P_j) = P(P_i|P_j)/P(P_i) \geq \delta$.

We believe that the following three grouping heuristics can achieve fast and accurate learning.

1. Inter-group multi-resolution features. If features can be divided into groups of different resolutions, we need not be concerned with terms that involve inter-group features. This is because any inter-group terms can be subsumed by intra-group terms. Formally, if P_i and P_j belong to two feature groups and $P(P_i|P_j) = 1$, then $P_1 \vee P_2 = P_2$ and $P_1 \wedge P_2 = P_1$.

2. Intra-group multi-resolution features. Within a feature group, the more predicates involved in a disjunctive term, the lower the resolution of the term. Conversely, the greater the number of predicates involved in a conjunctive term, the higher the resolution of that term. For instance, in a 2-CNF that has two predicates P_1 and P_2, term P_1 and

term P_2 have a higher resolution than the disjunctive term $P_1 \vee P_2$ and a lower resolution than the conjunctive term $P_1 \wedge P_2$. The presence of P_1 or P_2 makes the presence of $P_1 \vee P_2$ useless. Base on this heuristic, MEGA examines a term only when all terms with higher resolution have been eliminated.

3. Minimizing intra-group feature correlation. After exploring feature resolution, we can explore the weak form of resolution: feature correlation. According to our empirical study, minimizing intra-group feature correlation tends to improve search accuracy.

4.4 Concepts Learned

In previous subsections we explored how to enhance the retrieval performance by including negations of predicates, selecting appropriate values for k and G, and carefully dividing features into groups. In this subsection, we examine the query concepts we learned for several representative categories: *architecture, bears, clouds, elephants,* and *fabrics*.

	Channels	Ar'	Be'	Cl'	El'	Fa'
Colors	Red color	−	−	−	−	+
	Yellow color	−	+	−	+	−
	Blue color	+	−	+	−	−
	Brown color	−	−	−	+	−
Textures	Vertical coarse		−	−	−	+
	Horizontal coarse	+	+	−	+	+
	Diagonal coarse	+	−	−	+	+
	Vertical medium	+	−	−	+	+
	Horizontal medium	+	−	−	+	
	Vertical fine	+	−	−	+	+
	Horizontal fine	+	−	−	−	−
	Diagonal fine	+	−	−	−	+

Table 1. Summary of the Five Categories.

Table 1 highlights key feature-concept associations of the five concepts (categories). A plus sign in a cell indicates the feature on that row and the concept on that column has a strong association. A negative sign indicates that the feature on that row and the concept on that column has a strong negative association. For example, in the color channels, the blue color has a strong association with architecture and clouds but has a strong negative association with the rest of the concepts. Since most architecture and all cloud images in our dataset have blue sky in the background, this association makes sense. In the texture channels, almost all features are strongly associated with architecture, but are negatively associated with cloud images. It is interesting to examine the feature-concept associations of bears and elephants, since they share similar landscape backgrounds. In the color channels, these two categories are similar except in the brown channel. Brown is strongly associated with elephants but not with bears. The major difference between elephants and bears comes from the textures: The elephant category is associated with various textures, whereas the bear category is strongly associated with only the horizontal coarse texture channel.

4.5 Observations

We make the following observations from our image-concept mining results:

1. *Including negations.* It is critical to include both predicates and their negations in a boolean formula. Including negations helps to express complex concepts more accurately and hence enhance search accuracy.

2. *Setting k to achieve good search accuracy and time tradeoff.* For our dataset, it is sufficient to model query concepts in 3-CNF to achieve high precision at low search cost. In general, we need to choose a proper k through empirical study in order to adequately model query concepts while keeping the computational cost low.

3. *Choosing G to achieve good search accuracy and space/time complexity tradeoff.* For our dataset, it is desirable to divide features into 20 groups. We need to choose a proper G to speed up learning time while maintaining high search accuracy.

4. Organizing features to minimize intra-group correlation for maintaining high search accuracy. The genetic algorithm is effective in finding feature groupings that yield better search accuracy. The groupings with smaller intra-group correlation tend to yield higher search accuracy.

5. Understanding feature-concept associations for measuring similarity. From concept mining, we can identify what features are important for an image concept. This information can be used for measuring image similarity. For instance, if we know that the search concept is clouds, we can weight the blue channel and texture negation predicates more heavily to achieve better search results.

5 Conclusion

In this paper, we have presented two mining problems: learning users' query concepts and discovering optimal feature groupings. Our mining results showed that when parameters k and G are properly selected, our learning algorithm (MEGA) can fuzzily capture a k-CNF query concept usually in two to three feedback iterations and can comprehend a target concept very well in three to five iterations.

To speed up learning and to reduce the learning space requirement, we proposed a divide-and-conquer method that divides the concept-learning task into G subtasks. We noticed that a task must be divided carefully, or search accuracy may suffer. We used a genetic-based mining algorithm to discover good feature groupings. Through analysis and mining results, we observed that organizing image features in a multi-resolution manner, and maximizing inter-group feature correlation (or minimizing intra-group correlation), can speed up query-concept learning by $O(G^{k-1})$ folds, while maintaining high search accuracy. We also presented the discovered k-CNF expressions for various image categories. We believe that the concept-feature associations learned can be used for enhancing image search accuracy.

References

[1] E. Chang and T. Cheng. Perception-based image retrieval. *ACM Sigmod (Demo)*, May 2001.

[2] E. Chang and B. Li. Mega — the maximizing expected generalization algorithm for learning complex query concepts (extended version). *Technical Report http://www-db.stanford.edu/~echang/mega.ps*, November 2000.

[3] C. Chen. *Fuzzy Logic and Neural Network Handbook.* McGraw-Hill, 1996.

[4] R. Fagin. Fuzzy queries in multimedia database systems. *ACM Sigacr-Sigmod-Sigart Symposium on Principles of Database Systems*, 1998.

[5] C. Faloutsos, R. Barber, M. Flickner, J. Hafner, W. Niblack, D. Petkovic, and W. Equitz. Efficient and effective querying by image content. *Journal of Intelligent Information System: Integerating Artificial Intelligence and Database Technologies*, 3(3-4), 1994.

[6] D. E. Goldberg and R. Burch. *Genetic Algorithms in Search, Optimization, and Machine Learning, Reading.* Addison-Wesley, 1989.

[7] M. Kearns, M. Li, and L. Valiant. Learning boolean formulae. *Journal of ACM*, 41(6):1298–1328, 1994.

[8] M. Kearns and U. Vazirani. *An Introduction to Computational Learning Theory.* MIT Press, 1994.

[9] B. Li, E. Chang, and C.-S. Li. Learning image query concepts via intelligent sampling. *Proceedings of IEEE Multimedia*, August 2001.

[10] J. Li, J. Z. Wang, and G. Wiederhold. Irm: Integrated region matching for image retrieval. *ACM Multimedia*, 2001.

[11] T. Michell. *Machine Learning.* McGraw Hill, 1997.

[12] B. L. Miller and D. E. Goldberg. Genetic algorithms, tournament selection, and the effects of noise. *Complex Systems*, pages 193–212, 1995.

[13] A. Natsev, R. Rastogi, and K. Shim. Walrus: A similarity retrieval algorithm for image databases. *SIGMOD*, 1999.

[14] Y. Rui, T. S. Huang, and S.-F. Chang. Image retrieval: Current techniques, promising directions and open issues. *Journal of Visual Communication and Image Representation*, March 1999.

[15] J. Smith and S.-F. Chang. An image and video search engine for the world-wide web. *Storage and Retrieval for Image and Video Databases V, Proc SPIE 3022*, 1997.

[16] L. A. Zadeh. Fuzzy sets. *Information and Control*, pages 338–353, 1965.

Mining the smallest association rule set for predictions

Jiuyong Li, Hong Shen and Rodney Topor
School of Computing and Information Technology
Griffith University
Brisbane, Australia, QLQ 4111
{jiuyong, hong, rwt}@cit.gu.edu.au

Abstract

Mining transaction databases for association rules usually generates a large number of rules, most of which are unnecessary when used for subsequent prediction. In this paper we define a rule set for a given transaction database that is much smaller than the association rule set but makes the same predictions as the association rule set by the confidence priority. We call this subset the informative rule set. The informative rule set is not constrained to particular target items; and it is smaller than the non-redundant association rule set. We present an algorithm to directly generate the informative rule set, i.e., without generating all frequent itemsets first, and that accesses the database less often than other unconstrained direct methods. We show experimentally that the informative rule set is much smaller than both the association rule set and the non-redundant association rule set, and that it can be generated more efficiently.

1 Introduction

The rapidly growing volume and complexity of modern databases makes the need for technologies to describe and summarise the information they contain increasingly important. The general term to describe this process is data mining. Association rule mining is the process of generating associations or, more specifically, association rules, in transaction databases. Association rule mining is an important subfield of data mining and has wide application in many fields. Two key problems with association rule mining are the high cost of generating association rules and the large number of rules that are normally generated. Much work has been done to address the first problem. Methods for reducing the number of rules generated depend on the application, because a rule may be useful in one application but not another.

In this paper, we are particularly concerned with generating rules for prediction. For example, given a set of as-

sociation rules that describe the shopping behavior of the customers in a store over time, and some purchases made by a particular customer, we wish to predict what other purchases will be made by that customer.

The association rule set [1] can be used for prediction if the high cost of finding and applying the rule set is not a concern. The constrained and optimality association sets [4, 3] can not be used for this prediction because their rules do not have all possible items to be consequences. The non-redundant association rule set [17] can be used, after some extension, but can be large as well.

We propose the use of a particular rule set, called the informative (association) rule set, that is smaller than the association rule set and that makes the same predictions under natural assumptions described below.

The general method of generating association rules by first generating frequent itemsets can be unnecessarily expensive, as many frequent itemsets do not lead to useful association rules. We present a direct method for generating the informative rule set that does not involve generating the frequent itemsets first. Unlike other algorithms that generate rules directly, our method does not constrain the consequences of generated rules as in [3, 4] and accesses the database less often than other unconstrained methods [16].

We show experimentally, using standard synthetic data, that the informative rule set is much smaller than both the association rule set and the non-redundant rule set, and that it can be generated more efficiently.

2 Related work

Association rule mining was first studied in [1]. Most research work has been on how to mine frequent itemsets efficiently. Apriori [2] is a widely accepted approach, and there have been many enhancements to it [6, 7, 9, 11, 13]. In addition, other approaches have been proposed [5, 14, 18], mainly by using more memory to save time. For example, the algorithm presented in [5] organizes a database into a condensed structure to avoid repeated database accesses, and algorithms in [14, 18] use the vertical layout of databases.

Some direct algorithms for generating association rules without generating frequent itemsets first have previously been proposed [4, 3, 16]. Algorithms presented in [4, 3] focused only on one fixed consequence and hence is not efficient for mining all association rules. The algorithm presented in [16] needs to scan a database as many times as the number of all possible antecedents of rules. As a result, it may not be efficient when a database cannot be retained in the memory.

There are also two types of algorithms to simplify the association rule set, direct and indirect. Most indirect algorithms simplify the set by post-pruning and reorganization, as in [15, 8, 10], which can obtain an association rule set as simple as a user would like but does not improve efficiency of the rule mining process. There are some attempts to simplify the association rule set directly. The algorithm for mining constraint rule sets is one such attempt [4]. It produces a small rule set and improves mining efficiency since it prunes unwanted rules in the processing of rule mining. However, a constraint rule set contains only rules with some specific items as consequences, as do the optimality rule sets [3]. They are not suitable for association prediction where all items may be consequences. The most significant work in this direction is to mine the non-redundant rule set because it simplifies the association rule set and retains the information intact [17]. However, the non-redundant rule set is still too large for prediction.

3 The informative rule set

3.1 Association rules and related definitions

Let $I = \{1, 2, \ldots, m\}$ be a set of *items*, and $T \subseteq I$ be a *transaction* containing a set of items. An *itemset* is defined to be a set of items, and a k-itemset is an itemset containing k items. A database D is a collection of transactions. The *support* of an itemset (e.g. X) is the ratio of the number of transactions containing the itemset to the number of all transactions in a database, denoted by $sup(X)$. Given two itemsets X and Y where $X \cap Y = \emptyset$, an association rule is defined to be $X \Rightarrow Y$ where $sup(X \cup Y)$ and $sup(X \cup Y)/sup(X)$ are not less than user specified thresholds respectively. $sup(X \cup Y)/sup(X)$ is called the *confidence* of the rule, denoted by $conf(X \Rightarrow Y)$. The two thresholds are called the *minimum support* and the *minimum confidence* respectively. For convenience, we abbreviate $X \cup Y$ by XY and use the terms rule and association rule interchangeably in the rest of this paper.

Suppose that every transaction is given a unique identifier. A set of identifiers is called a *tidset*. Let mapping $t(X)$ be the set of identifiers of transactions containing the itemset X. It is clear that $sup(X) = |t(X)|/|D|$. In the following, we list some basic relationships between itemsets and tidsets.

1. $X \subseteq Y \Rightarrow t(X) \supseteq t(Y)$,

2. $t(X) \subseteq t(Y) \Rightarrow t(XZ) \subseteq t(YZ)$ for any Z, and

3. $t(XY) = t(X) \cap t(Y)$.

We say that rule $X \Rightarrow Y$ is *more general* than rule $X' \Rightarrow Y$ if $X \subset X'$, and we denoted this by $X \Rightarrow Y \subset X' \Rightarrow Y$. Conversely, $X' \Rightarrow Y$ is *more specific* than $X \Rightarrow Y$. We define the *covered set* of a rule to be the tidset of its antecedent. We say that rule $X \Rightarrow Y$ *identifies* transaction T if $XY \subset T$. We use Xz to represent $X \cup \{z\}$ and $sup(X \neg Z)$ for $sup(X) - sup(XZ)$.

3.2 The informative rule set

Let us consider how a user uses the set of association rules to make predictions. Given an input itemset and the association rule set. Initiate the prediction set to be an emptyset. Select a matched rule with the highest conference from the rule set, and then put the consequence of the rule into prediction set. We say that a rule matches a transaction if its antecedent is a subset of the transaction. To avoid repeatedly predicting on the same item(s), remove those rules whose consequences are included in the prediction set. Repeat selecting the next highest confidence matched rule from the remaining rule set until the user is satisfied or there is not rule to select.

We have noticed that some rules in the association rule set will never been selected in the above prediction procedure, so we will remove those rules from the association rule set and form a new rule set. This new rule set will predict exactly the same as the association rule set, the same set of prediction items in the same generated order. Here, we consider the order because a user may stop selection at any time, and we will guarantee to obtain the same prediction items in this case.

Formally, given an association rule set R and an itemset P, we say that the *predictions* for P from R is a sequence of items Q. The sequence of Q is generated by using the rules in R in descending order of confidence. For each rule r that matches P (i.e., for each rule whose antecedent is a subset of P), each consequent of r is added to Q. After adding a consequence to Q, all rules whose consequences are in Q are removed from R.

To exclude those rules that never been used in the prediction, we present the following definition.

Definition 1 *Let R_A be an association rule set and R_A^1 the set of single-target rules in R_A. A set R_I is informative over R_A if (1) $R_I \subset R_A^1$; (2) $\forall r \in R_I \nexists r' \in R_I$ such that $r' \subset r$ and $conf(r') \geq conf(r)$; and (3) $\forall r'' \in R_A^1 - R_I$, $\exists r \in R_I$ such that $r'' \supset r$ and $conf(r'') \leq conf(r)$.*

The following result follows immediately.

Lemma 1 *There exists a unique informative rule set for any given rule set.*

We give two examples to illustrate this definition.

Example 1 *Consider the following small transaction database:* $\{1 : \{a,b,c\}, 2 : \{a,b,c\}, 3 : \{a,b,c\}, 4 : \{a,b,d\}, 5 : \{a,c,d\}, 6 : \{b,c,d\}\}$. *Suppose the minimum support is 0.5 and the minimum confidence is 0.5. There are 12 association rules (that exceed the support and confidence threshholds). They are* $\{a \Rightarrow b(0.67,0.8), a \Rightarrow c(0.67,0.8), b \Rightarrow c(0.67,0.8), b \Rightarrow a(0.67,0.8), c \Rightarrow a(0.67,0.8), c \Rightarrow b(0.67,0.8), ab \Rightarrow c(0.50,0.75), ac \Rightarrow b(0.50,0.75), bc \Rightarrow a(0.50,0.75), a \Rightarrow bc(0.50,0.60), b \Rightarrow ac(0.50,0.60), c \Rightarrow ab(0.50,0.60)\}$, *where the numbers in parentheses are the support and confidence respectively. Every transaction identified by the rule $ab \Rightarrow c$ is also identified by rule $a \Rightarrow c$ or $b \Rightarrow c$ with higher confidence. So $ab \Rightarrow c$ can be omitted from the informative rule set without losing predictive capability. Rule $a \Rightarrow b$ and $a \Rightarrow c$ provide predictions b and c with higher confidence than rule $a \Rightarrow bc$, so rule $a \Rightarrow bc$ can be omitted from the informative rule set. Other rules can be omitted similarly, leaving the informative rule set containing the 6 rules* $\{a \Rightarrow b(0.67,0.8), a \Rightarrow c(0.67,0.8), b \Rightarrow c(0.67,0.8), b \Rightarrow a(0.67,0.8), c \Rightarrow a(0.67,0.8), c \Rightarrow b(0.67,0.8)\}$.

Example 2 *Consider the rule set* $\{a \Rightarrow b(0.25,1.0), a \Rightarrow c(0.2,0.7), ab \Rightarrow c(0.2,0.7), b \Rightarrow d(0.3,1.0), a \Rightarrow d(0.25,1.0)\}$. *Rule $ab \Rightarrow c$ may be omitted from the informative rule set as the more general rule $a \Rightarrow c$ has equal confidence. Rule $a \Rightarrow d$, must be included in the informative rule set even though it can be derived by transitivity from rules $a \Rightarrow b$ and $b \Rightarrow d$. Otherwise, if it were omitted, item d could not be predicted from the itemset $\{a\}$, as the definition of prediction does not provide for reasoning by transitivity.*

Now we present the main property of the informative rule set.

Theorem 1 *Let R_A be an association rule set. Then the informative rule set R_I over R_A is the smallest subset of R_A such that, for any itemset P, the prediction sequence for P from R_I equals the prediction sequence for P from R_A.*

Proof We will prove this theorem from two aspects. Firstly, a rule omitted by R_I does not affect prediction from R_A for any P. Secondly, a rule set omitted one rule from R_I cannot present the same prediction sequences as R_A for any P.

Firstly, we will prove that a rule omitted by R_I do not affect prediction from R_A for any P.

Consider a single-target rule r' omitted by R_I, there must be another rule r in both R_I and R_A such that the $r \subset r'$ and $conf(r) \geq conf(r')$. When r' matches P, r does. If both rules have the same confidence, omitting r' does not affect prediction from R_A. If $conf(r) > conf(r')$, r' must be automatically omitted from R_A after r is selected and the consequence of r is included in the prediction sequenc. So, omitting r' does not affect prediction from R_A.

Consider a multiple-target rule in R_A, e.g. $A \Rightarrow bc$, there must be two rules $A' \Rightarrow b$ and $A' \Rightarrow c$ in both R_I and R_A for $A' \subseteq A$ such that $conf(A' \Rightarrow b) \geq conf(A \Rightarrow bc)$ and $conf(A' \Rightarrow c) \geq conf(A \Rightarrow c)$. When rule $A \Rightarrow bc$ matches P, $A' \Rightarrow b$ and $A' \Rightarrow c$ do. It is clear that if $conf(A' \Rightarrow b) = conf(A' \Rightarrow c) = conf(A \Rightarrow bc)$, then omitting $A \Rightarrow bc$ does not affect prediction from R_A. If $conf(A' \Rightarrow b) > conf(A \Rightarrow bc)$ and $conf(A' \Rightarrow c) > conf(A \Rightarrow bc)$, rule $A \Rightarrow bc$ must be automatically omitted from R_A after $A' \Rightarrow b$ and $A' \Rightarrow c$ are selected and item b and c are included in the prediction sequence. Similarly, we can prove that omitting $A \Rightarrow bc$ from R_A does not affect prediction when $conf(A' \Rightarrow b) > conf(A' \Rightarrow c) = conf(A \Rightarrow bc)$ or $conf(A' \Rightarrow c) > conf(A' \Rightarrow b) = conf(A \Rightarrow bc)$. So omitting $A \Rightarrow bc$ from R_A does affect prediction. Similarly, we can conclude that a multiple-target rule in R_A does not affect its prediction sequence.

Thus a rule omitted by R_I does not affect prediction from R_A.

Secondly, we will prove the minimum property. Suppose we omit one rule $X \Rightarrow c$ from the R_I. Let $P = X$, there must be a position for c in the prediction sequence from R_A determined by $X \Rightarrow c$ because there is not other rule $X' \Rightarrow c$ such that $X' \subset X$ and $conf(X' \Rightarrow c) \geq conf(X \Rightarrow c)$. When $X \Rightarrow c$ is omitted from R_I, there may be two possible results for the prediction sequence from R_I. One is that item c does not occur in the sequence. The other is that item c is in the sequence but its position is determined by another rule $X' \Rightarrow c$ for $X' \subset X$ with smaller confidence than $X \Rightarrow c$. As a result, the two prediction sequences would not be the same.

Hence, the informative rule set is the smallest subset of R_A that provides the same predictions for any itemset P.

Consequently, the theorem is proved. □

Finally, we describe a property that characterises some rules to be omitted from the informative rule set.

We can divide the tidset of an itemset X into two parts on an itemset (consequence), $t(X) = t(XZ) \cup t(X \neg Z)$. If the second part is an empty set, then the rule $X \Rightarrow Z$ has 100% confidence. Usually, the smaller is $|t(X \neg Z)|$, the higher is the confidence of the rule. Hence, $|t(X \neg Z)|$ is very important in determining the confidence of a rule.

Lemma 2 *If $t(X \neg Z) \subseteq t(Y \neg Z)$, then rule $XY \Rightarrow Z$ does not belong to the informative rule set.*

Proof Let us consider two rules, $XY \Rightarrow Z$ and $X \Rightarrow Z$.

We know that $conf(XY \Rightarrow Z) = s_1/(s_1 + r_1)$, where $s_1 = |t(XYZ)|$ and $r_1 = |t(XY\neg Z)|$, and $conf(X \Rightarrow Z) = s_2/(s_2 + r_2)$, where $s_2 = |t(XZ)|$ and $r_2 = |t(X\neg Z)|$.

$r_1 = |t(XY\neg Z)| = |t(X\neg Z) \cap t(Y\neg Z)| = |t(X\neg Z)| = r_2$.

$s_1 = |t(XYZ)| \leq |t(XZ)| = s_2$.

As a result, $conf(XY \Rightarrow Z) \leq conf(X \Rightarrow Z)$. Hence rule $XY \Rightarrow Z$ must be excluded by the informative rule set. $\square$

This is an important property for the informative rule set, since it enables us to predict rules that cannot be included in the informative rule set in the early stage of association rule mining. We will discuss this in detail in the next section.

4 Upward closed properties for generating informative rule sets

Most efficient association rule mining algorithms use the upward closed property of infrequency of itemset: if an itemset is infrequent, so are all its super itemsets. Hence, many infrequent itemsets are prevented from being generated in association rule mining, and this is the essence of Apriori. If we have similar properties of the rules excluded by the informative rule set, then we can prevent generation of many rules excluded by the informative rule set. As a result, algorithm based on the properties will be more efficient.

First of all, we discuss a property that will facilitate the following discussions. It is convenient to compare support of itemsets in order to find subset relationships among their tidsets. This is because we always have support information when mining association rules. We have a relationship for this purpose.

Lemma 3 $t(X) \subseteq t(Y)$ *if and only if* $sup(X) = sup(XY)$.

We have two upward closed properties for mining the informative association rule set. In the following two lemmas, we use a description that is easy to use in algorithm design but may not be very good in terms of mathematical simplicity

As a direct result of Lemma 2 and 3, we have

Lemma 4 *If* $sup(X\neg Z) = sup(XY\neg Z)$, *then rule* $XY \Rightarrow Z$ *and all more specific rules do not occur in the informative rule set.*

The following special case is useful in practice.

Lemma 5 *If* $sup(X) = sup(XY)$, *then for any* Z, *rule* $XY \Rightarrow Z$ *and all more specific rules do not occur in the informative rule set.*

These two lemmas enable us to prune unwanted rules in a "forward" fashion before they are actually generated. In fact we can prune a set of rules when we prune each rule not in the informative rule set in the early stages of the computation. This allows us to construct efficient algorithms to generate the informative rule set.

5 Algorithm

5.1 Basic idea and storage structure

We proposed a direct algorithm to mine the informative rule set. Instead of first finding all frequent itemsets and then forming rules, the proposed algorithm generates informative rule set directly. An advantage is that it avoids generating many frequent itemsets that produce rules excluded by the informative rule set.

The proposed algorithm is a level wise algorithm, which searches for rules from antecedent of 1-itemset to antecedent of l-itemset level by level. In every level, we select qualified rules, which could be included in the informative rule set, and prune those unqualified rules. The efficiency of the proposed algorithm is based on the fact that a number of rules excluded by the informative rule set are prevented from being generated once a more general rule is pruned by Lemma 4 or 5. Consequently, searching space is reduced after every level's pruning. The number of phases of scanning a database is bounded by the length of the longest rule in the informative rule set.

In the proposed algorithm, we extend a set enumeration tree [12] as the storage structure, called *candidate tree*. A simplified candidate tree is illustrated in Figure 1. The tree in Figure 1 is completely expanded, but in practice only a small part is expanded. We note that every set in the tree is unique and is used to identified the node, called *identity set*. We also note that labels are locally distinct with each other under a parent node in a layer, and labels along a path from the root to the node form exactly the identity set of the node. This is very convenient for retrieving the itemset and counting its frequency. In our algorithm a node is used to store a set of rule candidates.

5.2 Algorithm for mining the informative rule set

The set of all items is used to build a candidate tree. A node in the candidate tree stores two sets $\{A, Z\}$. A is an itemset, the identity set of the node, and Z is a subset of the identity itemset, called potential target set where every item can be the consequence of an association rule. For example, $\{\{abc\}, \{ab\}\}$ is a set of candidates of two rules, namely, $bc \Rightarrow a$ and $ac \Rightarrow b$. It is clear that the potential target set is initialized by the itemset itself. When there is a case satisfying Lemma 4, for example, $sup(a\neg c) = sup(ab\neg c)$, then

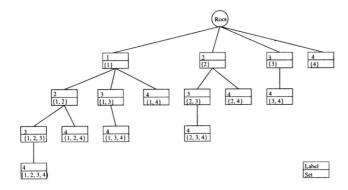

Figure 1. A fully expanded candidate tree over the set of items $\{1, 2, 3, 4\}$

we remove c from the potential target set, and accordingly all rules such as $abX \rightarrow c$ cannot be generated afterwards.

We firstly illustrate how to generate a new candidate node. For example, we have two sibling nodes $\{\{abc\}, \{ab\}\}$ and $\{\{abd\}, \{ad\}\}$, then the new candidate is $\{\{abcd\}, \{ad\}\}$, where $\{ad\} = (\{ab\} \cup \{d\}) \cap (\{ad\} \cup \{c\})$. Hence the only two candidate rules that could be included in the informative rule set in this case are $bcd \Rightarrow a$ and $abc \Rightarrow d$ given $abcd$ is frequent.

We then show how to remove unqualified candidates. One way is by the frequency requirement, for example, if $sup(abcd) < \sigma$ then we remove the node whose identity set is $abcd$, simply called node $abcd$. Please note here that a node in the candidate tree contains a set of candidate rules. Another method is by the properties of the informative rule set, and again consists of two cases. Firstly, given a candidate node $\{A^l, Z\}$ where A^l means that A^l is a l-itemset. For an item $z \in Z$, when there is $sup((A^l \backslash z) \neg z) = sup((A^{l-1} \backslash z) \neg z)$ for $(A^l \backslash z) \supset (A^{l-1} \backslash z)$, then remove the z from Z by Lemma 4. Secondly, we say node $\{A^l, Z\}$ is *restricted* when there is $sup(A^l) = sup(A^{l-1})$ for $A^l \supset A^{l-1}$. A restricted node does not extend its potential target set and keeps it as that of node $\{A^{l-1}, Z\}$. The reason is that all rules $A^{l-1}X \Rightarrow c$ for any X and c are excluded from the informative rule set by Lemma 5, so we need not generate such candidates. This potential target set is removable by Lemma 4, and a restricted node is *dead* when its potential target set is empty. All super sets of the itemset of a dead node are unqualified candidates, so we need not generate them.

We give the top level of the informative rule mining algorithm as the following.

Algorithm: The informative rule miner

Input: Database D, the minimum support σ and the minimum confidence ψ.

Output: The informative rule set R.

(1)　　Set the informative rule set $R = \emptyset$
(2)　　Count support of 1-itemsets
(3)　　Initialize candidate tree T
(4)　　Generate new candidates as leaves of T
(5)　　While (new candidate set is non-empty)
(6)　　　Count support of the new candidates
(7)　　　Prune the new candidate set
(8)　　　Include qualified rules from T to R
(9)　　　Generate new candidates as leaves of T
(10)　Return rule set R

The first 3 lines are general description, and we do not explain them here. We will emphasize on two functions, Candidate generator in line 4 and 9 and Pruning in line 6. They are listed as follows.

We begin with introducing notations in the functions. n_i is a candidate node in the candidate tree. It is labeled by an item i_{n_i} and it consists of an identity itemset A_{n_i} and a potential target set Z_{n_i}. T_l is the l-th level of candidate tree. $\mathcal{P}^l(A)$ is the set of all l-subsets of A. n_A is a node whose identity itemset is A. The set of items are ordered lexically.

Function: Rule candidate generator
(1)　for each node $n_i \in T_l$
(2)　　for each sibling node n_j $(i_{n_j} > i_{n_i})$
(3)　　　generate a new candidate node n_k as a son of n_i such that
　　　　//Combining
(4)　　　$A_{n_k} = A_{n_i} \cup A_{n_j}$
(5)　　　$Z_{n_k} = (Z_{n_i} \cup i_{n_j}) \cap (Z_{n_j} \cup i_{n_i})$
　　　　//Pruning
(6)　　　if $\exists A \in \mathcal{P}^l(A_{n_k})$ but $n_A \notin T_l$ then remove n_k
(7)　　　else if n_A is restricted then mark n_k restricted and let $Z_{n_k} = Z_{n_A} \cap Z_{n_k}$
(8)　　　else $Z_{n_k} = (Z_{n_A} \cup (A_{n_k} \backslash A)) \cap Z_{n_k}$
(9)　　　if n_k is restricted and $Z_{n_k} = \emptyset$, remove node n_k

We generate the $(l + 1)$-layer candidates from the l layer nodes. Firstly, we combine a pair of sibling nodes and insert their combination as a new node in the next layer. Secondly, if any of its l-sub itemset cannot get enough support then we remove the node. If an item is not qualified to be the target of a rule included in the informative rule set, then we remove the target from the potential target set.

Please note that in line 6, not only a super set of an infrequent itemset is removed, but also a super set of a frequent itemset of a dead node is removed. The former case is common in association rule mining, and the latter case is unique for the informative rule mining. A dead node is removed in line 9. Accordingly, in the informative rule mining, we need not to generate all frequent itemsets.

Function: Pruning

(1)   for each $n_i \in T_{l+1}$

(2)   if $sup(A_{n_i}) < \sigma$, remove node n_i and return

(3)   if n_i is not restricted node, do

(4)   if $\exists n_j \in T_l$ for $A_{n_j} \subset A_{n_i}$ such that $sup(A_{n_j}) = sup(A_{n_i})$

                then mark n_i restricted and let $Z_{n_i} = Z_{n_i} \cap Z_{n_j}$ // Lemma 4

(5)   for each $z \in Z_{n_i}$

(6)   if $\exists n_j \in T_l$ for $(A_{n_j} \backslash z) \subset (A_{n_i} \backslash z)$ such that $sup((A_{n_j} \backslash z) \cup \neg z) = sup((A_{n_i} \backslash z) \cup \neg z)$

                then $Z_i = Z_i \backslash z$.   // Lemma 5

(7)   if n_i is restricted and $Z_{n_i} = \emptyset$, remove node n_i

We prune a rule candidate from two aspects, the frequency requirement for association rules and the qualification requirement for the informative rule set. The method for pruning infrequent rules is the same as that of a general association rule mining algorithm. As for the method in pruning unqualified candidates for the informative rule set, we restrict the possible targets in the potential target set of a node (a possible target is equivalent to a rule candidate) and remove a restricted node when its potential target set is empty.

5.3 Correctness and efficiency

Lemma 6 *The algorithm generates the informative rule set properly.*

It is very hard to give a closed form of efficiency for the algorithm. However, we expect certain improvements over other association rule mining algorithms based on the following reasons. Firstly, it does not generate all frequent itemsets, because some frequent itemsets cannot contain rules being included in the informative rule set. Secondly, it does not test all possible rules in every generated frequent itemset because some items in an itemset are not qualified as consequences for rules being included in the informative rule set.

The phases of scanning a database is bounded by the length of longest rule in the informative rule set.

6 Experimental results

In this section, we show that the informative rule set is much smaller than both the association rule set and the non-redundant association rule set. We further show that it can be generated more efficiently with less number of interactions with a database. Finally, we show that the efficiency improvement gains from the fact that the proposed algorithm for the informative rule set accesses the database

fewer times and generates fewer candidates than Apriori for the association rule set.

Since the informative rule set contains only single target rules, for a fair comparison, the association rule set and the non-redundant rule set in this section contain only single target rules as well. The reason for the comparison with the non-redundant rule set is that the non-redundant rule set can make the same predictions the association rule set.

The two testing transaction databases, T10.I6.D100K.N2K and T20.I6.D100K.N2K, are generated by the synthetic data generator from QUEST of IBM Almaden research center. Both databases have 1000 items and contain 100,000 transactions. We chose the minimum support in the range such that 70% to 80% of all items are frequent, and fixed the minimum confidence as 0.5.

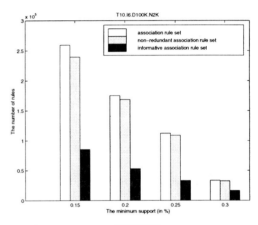

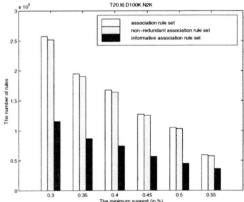

Figure 2. Sizes of different rule sets

Sizes of different rule sets are listed in Figure 2. It is clear that the informative rule set is much smaller than both the association rule set and the non-redundant rule set. The size difference between an informative rule set and an association rule set becomes more evident when the minimum support decreases, and as does the size difference between an informative rule set and a non-redundant rule set. This is because the length of rules becomes longer when the minimum support decreases, and long rules are more likely to be excluded by the informative rule set than short rules. There is little difference in size between an association rule set and a non-redundant rule set. So, in the following comparisons, we only compare the informative rule set with the association rule set.

Now, we will compare generating efficiency of the informative rule set and the association rule set. We implemented Apriori on the same data structure as the proposed algorithm and generated only single target association rules. Our experiments were conducted on a Sun server with two 200 MHz UltraSPARC CPUs.

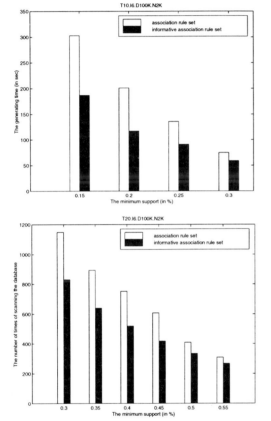

Figure 3. Generating time for different rule sets

The generating time for association rule sets and informative rule sets is listed in the Figure 3. We can see that mining an informative rule set is more efficient than mining a single target association rule set. This is because the informative rule miner does not generate all frequent itemsets, and does not test all items as targets in a frequent itemset. The improvement of efficiency becomes more evident when the minimum support decreases. This is consistent with the deduction of rules being excluded from an association rule

set as shown in Figure 2.

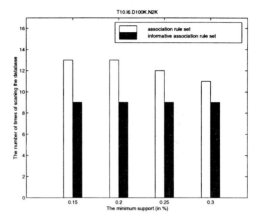

Figure 4. The number of times for scanning the database

Further, the number of times of scanning a database for generating an informative rule set is smaller than that for an association rule set, as showed in Figure 4. This is because the proposed algorithm avoids generating many long frequent itemsets that contain no rules included in an informative rule set. From the results, we also know that long rules are easier to be excluded by an informative rule set than short rules. Clearly, this number is significantly smaller than the number of different antecedents in the generated rule set which are needed to scan a database in aother direct algorithm.

To better understand of improvement of efficiency of the algorithm for mining the informative rule set over that for the association rule set, we list the number of nodes in a candidate tree for both rule sets in Figure 5. They are all frequent itemsets for the association rule set and partial frequent itemsets searched by mining the informative rule set. We can see that in mining the informative rule set, the searched itemsets is less than all frequent itemsets for forming association rules. So, this is the reason for efficiency improvement and reduction in number of scanning a database.

7 Conclusions

We have defined a new, informative, rule set that generates prediction sequences equal to those generated by the association rule set by the confidence priority. The informative rule set is significantly smaller than the association rule set, especially when the minimum support is small. We have studied the upward closed properties of informative rule set for omission of unnecessary rules from the set, and presented a direct algorithm to efficiently mine the informative rule set without generating all frequent itemsets first.

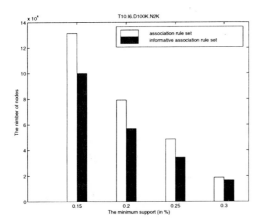

Figure 5. The number of candidate nodes

The experimental results confirm that the informative rule set is significantly smaller than both the association rule set and the non-redundant association rule set, that can be generated more efficiently than the association rule set. The experimental results also show that this efficiency improvement results from that the generation of the informative rule set needs fewer candidates and database accesses than that of the association rule set. The number of database accesses of the proposed algorithm is much smaller than other direct methods for generating unconstrained association rule sets.

Although the informative rule set provides the same prediction sequence as the association rule set, there may exist other definitions of "interesting" in different applications. How to use the informative rule set to make predictions under such different criteria remains a subject of future work.

References

[1] R. Agrawal, T. Imielinski, and A. Swami. Mining associations between sets of items in massive databases. In *Proc. of the ACM SIGMOD Int'l Conference on Management of Data*, 1993.

[2] R. Agrawal and R. Srikant. Fast algorithms for mining association rules in large databases. In *Proceedings of the Twentieth International Conference on Very Large Databases*, pages 487–499, Santiago, Chile, 1994.

[3] R. Bayardo and R. Agrawal. Mining the most interesting rules. In S. Chaudhuri and D. Madigan, editors, *Proceedings of the Fifth ACM SIGKDD International Conference on Knowledge Discovery and Data Mining*, pages 145–154, N.Y., Aug. 15–18 1999. ACM Press.

[4] R. Bayardo, R. Agrawal, and D. Gunopulos. Constraint-based rule mining in large, dense database. In *Proc. of the 15th Int'l Conf. on Data Engineering*, pages 188–197, 1999.

[5] J. Han, J. Pei, and Y. Yin. Mining frequent patterns without candidate generation. In *Proc. 2000 ACM-SIGMOD Int. Conf. on Management of Data (SIGMOD'00)*, pages 1 – 12, May, 2000.

[6] M. Holsheimer, M. Kersten, H. Mannila, and Toivonen. A perspective on databases and data mining. In *1st Intl. Conf. Knowledge Discovery and Data Mining*, Aug. 1995.

[7] M. Houtsma and A. Swami. Set-oriented mining of association rules in relational databases. In *11th Intl. Conf. data Engineering*, 1995.

[8] B. Liu, W. Hsu, and Y. Ma. Pruning and summarizing the discovered associations. In *SIGKDD 99*, 1999.

[9] H. Mannila, H. Toivonen, and I. Verkamo. Efficient algorithms for discovering association rules. In *AAAI Wkshp. Knowledge Discovery in Databases*, July 1994.

[10] R. Ng, L. Lakshmanan, J. Han, and A. Pang. Exploratory mining and pruning optimizations of constrained associations rules. In *Proceedings of the ACM SIGMOD International Conference on Management of Data (SIGMOD-98)*, volume 27 of *ACM SIGMOD Record*, pages 13–24, New York, June 1–4 1998. ACM Press.

[11] J. S. Park, M. Chen, and P. S. Yu. An effective hash based algorithm for mining association rules. In *ACM SIGMOD Intl. Conf. Management of Data*, May 1995.

[12] R. Rymon. Search through systematic set enumeration. In W. Nebel, Bernhard; Rich, Charles; Swartout, editor, *Proceedings of the 3rd International Conference on Principles of Knowledge Representation and Reasoning*, pages 539–552, Cambridge, MA, oct 1992. Morgan Kaufmann.

[13] A. Savasere, R. Omiecinski, and S. Navathe. An efficient algorithm for mining association rules in large databases. In *21st VLDB Conf.*, 1995.

[14] P. Shenoy, J. R. Haritsa, S. Sudarshan, G. Bhalotia, M. Bawa, and D. Shah. Turbo-charging vertical mining of large databases. In *Proceedings of the ACM SIGMOD International Conference on Management of Data (SIGMOD-99)*, pages 22–33.

[15] H. Toivonene, M. Klemettinen, P. RonKainen, K. Hatonen, and H. Mannila. Pruning and grouping discovered association rules. Technical report, Department of Computer Science, University of Helsinki, Finland, 1998.

[16] G. I. Webb. Efficient search for association rules. In R. Ramakrishnan, S. Stolfo, R. Bayardo, and I. Parsa, editors, *Proceedinmgs of the 6th ACM SIGKDD International Conference on Knowledge Discovery and Data Mining (KDD-00)*, pages 99–107, N. Y., Aug. 20–23 2000. ACM Press.

[17] M. J. Zaki. Generating non-redundant association rules. In *6th ACM SIGKDD International Conference on Knowledge Discovery and Data Mining*, pages 34 – 43, August 2000.

[18] M. J. Zaki, S. Parthasarathy, M. Ogihara, and W. Li. New algorithms for fast discovery of association rules. In D. Heckerman, H. Mannila, D. Pregibon, and R. Uthurusamy, editors, *Proceedings of the Third International Conference on Knowledge Discovery and Data Mining (KDD-97)*, page 283. AAAI Press, 1997.

CMAR: Accurate and Efficient Classification Based on Multiple Class-Association Rules *

Wenmin Li   Jiawei Han   Jian Pei
School of Computing Science, Simon Fraser University
Burnaby, B.C., Canada V5A 1S6
E-mail: {wli, han, peijian}@cs.sfu.ca

Abstract

Previous studies propose that associative classification has high classification accuracy and strong flexibility at handling unstructured data. However, it still suffers from the huge set of mined rules and sometimes biased classification or overfitting since the classification is based on only single high-confidence rule.

In this study, we propose a new associative classification method, CMAR, i.e., Classification based on Multiple Association Rules. The method extends an efficient frequent pattern mining method, FP-growth, constructs a class distribution-associated FP-tree, and mines large database efficiently. Moreover, it applies a CR-tree structure to store and retrieve mined association rules efficiently, and prunes rules effectively based on confidence, correlation and database coverage. The classification is performed based on a weighted χ^2 analysis using multiple strong association rules. Our extensive experiments on 26 databases from UCI machine learning database repository show that CMAR is consistent, highly effective at classification of various kinds of databases and has better average classification accuracy in comparison with CBA and C4.5. Moreover, our performance study shows that the method is highly efficient and scalable in comparison with other reported associative classification methods.

1 Introduction

Building accurate and efficient classifiers for large databases is one of the essential tasks of data mining and machine learning research. Given a set of cases with class labels as a *training set*, *classification* is to build a model (called *classifier*) to predict future data objects for which the class label is unknown.

Previous studies have developed heuristic/greedy search techniques for building classifiers, such as decision trees [10], rule learning [2], naïve-Bayes classification [4], and statistical approaches [8]. These techniques induces a representative subset of rules (e.g., a decision tree or a set of rules) from training data sets for quality prediction.

Recent studies propose the extraction of a set of high quality association rules from the training data set which satisfy certain user-specified frequency and confidence thresholds. Effective and efficient classifiers have been built by careful selection of rules, e.g., CBA [9], CAEP [3], and ADT [11]. Such a method takes the most effective rule(s) from among all the rules mined for classification. Since association rules explore highly confident associations among multiple variables, it may overcome some constraints introduced by a decision-tree induction method which examines one variable at a time. Extensive performance studies [6, 9, 3, 11] show that association-based classification may have better accuracy in general. However, this approach may also suffer some weakness as shown below.

On one hand, *it is not easy to identify the most effective rule at classifying a new case.* Some method, such as [9, 3, 11], simply selects a rule with a maximal user-defined measure, such as confidence. As we will see later, such a selection may not always be the right choice in many cases. Such a simple pick may affect the classification accuracy.

On the other hand, *a training data set often generates a huge set of rules. It is challenging to store, retrieve, prune, and sort a large number of rules efficiently for classification.* Many studies [1, 5] have indicated the inherent nature of a combinatorial explosive number of frequent patterns and hence association rules that could be generated when the support threshold is small (i.e., when rare cases are also be included in the consideration). To achieve high accuracy, a classifier may have to handle a large set of rules, including storing those generated by association mining methods, retrieving the related rules, and pruning and sorting a large number of rules.

Can we solve the above two problems? To solve the first problem, that is, to predict a new case accurately, instead of applying only a single rule, one may consider a small subset of the most related, highly confident rules and make a collective and all-around decision. Intuitively, that

---

*The work was supported in part by the Natural Sciences and Engineering Research Council of Canada (grant NSERC-A3723), and the Networks of Centres of Excellence of Canada (grant NCE/IRIS-3).

would help us avoid bias, exceptions, and overfitting of too small data sets. To overcome the second problem, the efficiency and scalability problem of association-based classification, one needs to develop efficient methods for storing and retrieving rules. This may help improve efficiency as well as the accuracy of classification since more rules can be stored and considered. This is the motivation of this research.

In this paper, we develop a new technique, *CMAR*, for accurate and efficient classification and make the following contributions.

First, *instead of relying on a single rule for classification*, CMAR *determines the class label by a set of rules*. Given a new case for prediction, *CMAR* selects a small set of high confidence, highly related rules and analyzes the correlation among those rules. To avoid bias, we develop a new technique, called *weighted* χ^2, which derives a good measure on how strong the rule is under both conditional support and class distribution. An extensive performance study shows that *CMAR* in general has higher prediction accuracy than CBA [9] and C4.5 [10].

Second, *to improve both accuracy and efficiency*, CMAR *employs a novel data structure*, CR-tree, *to compactly store and efficiently retrieve a large number of rules for classification*. *CR-tree* is a prefix tree structure to explore the sharing among rules, which achieves substantial compactness. *CR-tree* itself is also an index structure for rules and serves rule retrieval efficiently.

Third, *to speed up the mining of complete set of rules*, CMAR *adopts a variant of recently developed* FP-growth *method*. *FP-growth* is much faster than *Apriori*-like methods used in previous association-based classification, such as [9, 3, 11], especially when there exist a huge number of rules, large training data sets, and long pattern rules.

The remaining of the paper is arranged as follows. Section 2 revisits the general idea of associative classification. Section 3 devotes to the generation of rules for classification. Section 4 discusses how to classify a new data object using the generated rules. The experimental results on classification accuracy and the performance study on efficiency and scalability are reported in Section 5. The paper is concluded in Section 6.

2 Associative Classification

Suppose a data object $obj = (a_1, \ldots, a_n)$ follows the schema $(A_1, \ldots, A_n)$, where A_1, ..., A_n are called *attributes*. Attributes can be categorical or continuous. For a categorical attribute, we assume that all the possible values are mapped to a set of consecutive positive integers. For a continuous attribute, we assume that its value range is discretized into intervals, and the intervals are also mapped to consecutive positive integers. By doing so, all the attributes are treated uniformly in this study.

Let $C = \{c_1, \ldots, c_m\}$ be a finite set of *class labels*. A *training data set* is a set of data objects such that, for each object obj, there exists a class label $c_{obj} \in C$ associated with it. A *classifier* $\mathcal{C}$ is a function from $(A_1, \ldots, A_n)$ to C. Given a data object obj, $\mathcal{C}(obj) \in C$ returns a class label.

In general, given a training data set, the task of **classification** is to build a classifier from the training data set such that it can be used to predict class labels of unknown objects with high accuracy.

Besides many different approach for classification, such as decision tree approach, naive Bayesian approach, k-nearest neighbors approach, neural network approach, a new approach is to explore association relationships between object conditions and class labels [9]. The idea is natural since it utilizes frequent patterns and association relationships between cases and class labels in training data set to do classification. If strong associations among some frequent patterns and class labels can be observed in training data set, the future object of similar patterns can be classified.

In general, a **pattern** $P = a_{i_1} \ldots a_{i_k}$ is a set of attribute-values such that for $(1 \leq j \leq k)$, $a_{i_j} \in A_{i_j}$, and $i_j \neq i_{j'}$ for $j' \neq j$. A data object obj is said to **match** pattern $P = a_{i_1} \ldots a_{i_k}$ if and only if for $(1 \leq j \leq k)$, obj has value a_{i_j} in attribute A_{i_j}.

Given a training data set T, let c be a class label. For rule $R : P \rightarrow c$, the number of data objects in T matching pattern P and having class label c is called the **support** of R, denoted as $sup(R)$. The ratio of the number of objects matching pattern P and having class label c versus the total number of objects matching pattern P is called the **confidence** of R, denoted as $conf(R)$.

For example, if 95% of customers who have no job cannot get a credit limit more than \$3000, i.e., the confidence of rule $R : no\_job \rightarrow credit\_limit\_less\_than\_3000$ is 95%, then we can use rule R to classify future data objects. To avoid noise, a rule is used for classification only if it has enough support. Given a support threshold and a confidence threshold, **associative classification** method finds the complete set of class-association rules (CAR) passing the thresholds. When a new (unknown) object comes, the classifier selects the rule which matches the data object and has the highest confidence and uses it to predict the class label of the new object.

Recent studies show that associative classification is intuitive and effective and has good classification accuracy in many cases. In most existing associative classification methods [9, 3, 11], the rule with the highest confidence is used for classification. However, such a decision may not always be the correct one.

For example, suppose we want to determine the credit limit of a customer with attribute values (*no_job*, *investment_immigrant*, oversea_asset$\geq 500k$). The top-3 most confident rules matching the customer are as follows.

- Rule R_1: *no_job* $\rightarrow$ *credit_limit_3000$^-$* (support: 3000, confidence: 95%);

- Rule R_2: $investment\_immigrant \rightarrow$ $credit\_limit\_3000^+$ (support: 5000, confidence: 93%); and

- Rule R_3: $oversea\_asset \geq 500k \rightarrow$ $credit\_limit\_3000^+$ (support: 8000, confidence: 91%).

So, given such a customer, what class label should we predict?

A conventional associative classification method, like CBA, may predict $credit\_limit\_3000^-$ according to rule R_1 only, since it has the highest confidence. However, a closer look at rules R_2 and R_3 may suggest that we reconsider the decision seriously. The three rules have very similar confidence, but R_2 and R_3 have stronger support. The decision based on rules R_2 and R_3 seems to be more reliable.

The above example indicates that to make a reliable and accurate prediction, the most confident rule may not always be the best choice, and a thorough, detailed, and all-around measure analysis based on multiple rules may lead to better quality prediction.

3 Generating Rules for Classification

In this section, we develop a new associative-classification method, called *CMAR*, which performs **C**lassification based on **M**ultiple **A**ssociation **R**ules.

CMAR consists of two phases: *rule generation* and *classification*.

In the first phase, *rule generation*, *CMAR* computes the *complete* set of rules in the form of $R : P \rightarrow c$, where P is a pattern in the training data set, and c is a class label such that $sup(R)$ and $conf(R)$ pass the given support and confidence thresholds, respectively. Furthermore, *CMAR* prunes some rules and only selects a subset of high quality rules for classification.

In the second phase, *classification*, for a given data object *obj*, *CMAR* extracts a subset of rules matching the object and predicts the class label of the object by analyzing this subset of rules.

In this section, we develop methods to generate rules for classification. The second phase, classification, will be discussed in Section 4.

3.1 Mining Class-Association Rules Passing Support and Confidence Thresholds

To find rules for classification, *CMAR* first mines the training data set to find the complete set of rules passing certain support and confidence thresholds. This is a typical frequent pattern or association rule mining task [1]. To make mining highly scalable and efficient, *CMAR* adopts a variant of *FP-growth* method [5]. *FP-growth* is a frequent pattern mining algorithm which is faster than conventional *Apriori*-like methods, especially in the situations where

there exist large data sets, low support threshold, and/or long patterns. The general idea of mining rules in *CMAR* is shown in the following example.

Example 1 (Mining class-association rules) Given a training data set T as shown in Table 1. Let the support threshold is 2 and confidence threshold is 50%. *CMAR* mines class-association rules as follows.

Row-id	A	B	C	D	Class label
1	a_1	b_1	c_1	d_1	A
2	a_1	b_2	c_1	d_2	B
3	a_2	b_3	c_2	d_3	A
4	a_1	b_2	c_3	d_3	C
5	a_1	b_2	c_1	d_3	C

Table 1. A training data set.

First, *CMAR* scans the training data set T once, find the set of attribute values happening at least twice in T. The set is $F = \{a_1, b_2, c_1, d_3\}$ and is called *frequent item set*. All other attribute values, which fail the support threshold, cannot play any role in the class-association rules, and thus can be pruned.

Then, *CMAR* sorts attribute values in F in support descending order, i.e., *F-list* $= a_1 - b_2 - c_1 - d_3$. Then, *CMAR* scans the training data set again to construct an *FP-tree*, as shown in Figure 1(a).

FP-tree is a prefix tree w.r.t. *F-list*. For each tuple in the training data set, attributes values appearing in *F-list* are extracted and sorted according to *F-list*. For example, for the first tuple, (a_1, c_1) are extracted and inserted in the tree as the left-most branch in the tree. the class label is attached to the last node in the path.

Tuples in the training data set share prefixes. For example, the second tuple carries attribute values (a_1, b_2, c_1) in *F-list* and shares a common prefix a_1 with the first tuple. So, it also shares the a_1 sub-path with the left-most branch.

All nodes with same attribute value are linked together as a queue started from the *header table*.

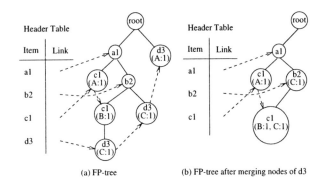

(a) FP-tree   (b) FP-tree after merging nodes of d3

Figure 1. *FP-tree* in Example 1.

Third, based on *F-list*, the set of class-association rules can be divided into 4 subsets without overlap: (1) the ones having d_3; (2) the ones having c_1 but no d_3; (3) the ones having b_2 but no d_3 nor c_1; and (4) the ones having only a_1. CMAR finds these subsets one by one.

Fourth, to find the subset of rules having d_3, CMAR traverses nodes having attribute value d_3 and look "upward" to collect a d_3-projected database, which contains three tuples: $(a_1, b_2, c_1, d_3) : C$, $(a_1, b_2, d_3) : C$ and $d_3 : A$. It contains all the tuples having d_3. The problem of finding all frequent patterns having d_3 in the whole training set can be reduced to mine frequent patterns in d_3-projected database.

Recursively, in d_3-projected database, a_1 and b_2 are the frequent attribute values, i.e., they pass support threshold. (In d_3-projected database, d_3 happens in every tuple and thus is trivially frequent. We do not count d_3 as a local frequent attribute value.) We can mine the projected database recursively by constructing FP-trees and projected databases. Please see [5] for more details.

It happens that, in d_3-projected database, a_1 and b_2 always happen together and thus $a_1 b_2$ is a frequent pattern. a_1 and b_2 are two subpatterns of $a_1 b_2$ and have same support count as $a_1 b_2$. To avoid triviality, we only adopt frequent pattern $a_1 b_2 d_3$. Based on the class label distribution information, we generate rule $a_1 b_2 d_3 \rightarrow C$ with support 2 and confidence 100%.

After search for rules having d_3, all nodes of d_3 are merged into their parent nodes, respectively. That is, the class label information registered in a d_3 node is registered in its parent node. The FP-tree is shrunk as shown in Figure 1(b). Please note that this tree-shrinking operation is done at the same scan of collecting the d_3-projected database.

The remaining subsets of rules can be mined similarly.

There are two major differences in the rule mining in CMAR and the standard FP-growth algorithm.

On one hand, CMAR *finds frequent patterns and generates rules in one step.*

Conventionally, association rules must be mined in two steps [1]. This is also the case for traditional associative classification methods [9]. First, all the frequent patterns (i.e., patterns passing support threshold) are found. Then, all the association rules satisfying the confidence threshold are generated based on the mined frequent patterns.

The difference of CMAR from other associative classification methods is that for every pattern, CMAR maintains the distribution of various class labels among data objects matching the pattern. This is done without any overhead in the procedure of counting (conditional) databases. Thus, once a frequent pattern (i.e., pattern passing support threshold) is found, rules about the pattern can be generated immediately. Therefore, CMAR has no separated rule generation step.

On the other hand, CMAR *uses class label distribution to prune.*

For any frequent pattern P, let c be the most dominant class in the set of data objects matching P. If the number of objects having class label c and matching P is less than the support threshold, there is no need to search any superpattern (superset) P' of P since any rule in the form of $P' \rightarrow c$ cannot satisfy the support threshold either.

3.2 Storing Rules in *CR-tree*

Once a rule is generated, it is stored in a *CR-tree*, which is a prefix tree structure. We demonstrate the general idea of *CR-tree* in the following example.

Example 2 (*CR-tree*) After mining a training data set, four rules are found as shown in Table 2.

Rule-id	Rule	Support	Confidence
1	$abc \rightarrow A$	80	80%
2	$abcd \rightarrow A$	63	90%
3	$abe \rightarrow B$	36	60%
4	$bcd \rightarrow C$	210	70%

Table 2. Rules found in a training data set.

A *CR-tree* is built for the set of rules, as shown in Figure 2, while the construction process is explained as follows.

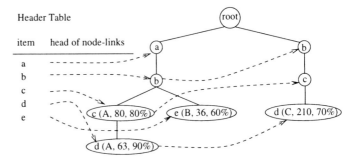

Figure 2. A *CR-tree* for rules in Example 2.

A *CR-tree* has a *root node*. All the attribute values appearing at the left hand side of rules are sorted according to their frequency, i.e., the most frequently appearing attribute value goes first.

The first rule, $abc \rightarrow A$ is inserted into the tree as a path from root node. The class label as well as the support and confidence of the rule, denoted as $(A, 80, 80\%)$, are registered at the last node in the path, i.e., node c for this rule.

The second rule, $abcd \rightarrow A$, shares a *prefix abc* with the first rule. Thus, it is inserted into the tree by extending a new node d to the path formed by the first rule. Again, the class label, support and confidence of the rule are registered at the last node, i.e., d.

The third and fourth rules can be inserted similarly. All the nodes with the same attribute value are linked together by *node-link* to a queue. The head of each queue is stored in a *Header table*.

To store the original rule set, 13 cells are needed for the left hand sides of the rules. Using *CR-tree*, only 9 nodes are needed.

As can be seen from the above example, the *CR-tree* structure has some advantages as follows.

CR-tree is a compact structure. It explores potential sharing among rules and thus can save a lot of space on storing rules. Our experimental results show that, in many cases, about $50 - 60\%$ of space can be saved using *CR-tree*.

CR-tree itself is an index for rules. For example, if we want to retrieve all the rules having attribute value b and d in the set of rules in Example 2, we only need to traverse node-links of d, which starts at the header table, and keep looking upward for b.

Once a *CR-tree* is built, rule retrieval becomes efficient. That facilitates the pruning of rules and using rules for classification dramatically.

3.3 Pruning Rules

The number of rules generated by class-association rule mining can be huge. To make the classification effective and also efficient, we need to prune rules to delete redundant and noisy information.

According to the facility of rules on classification, a global order of rules is composed. Given two rules R_1 and R_2, R_1 is said **having higher rank** than R_2, denoted as $R_1 > R_2$, if and only if (1) $conf(R_1) > conf(R_2)$; (2) $conf(R_1) = conf(R_2)$ but $sup(R_1) > sup(R_2)$; or (3) $conf(R_1) = conf(R_2)$, $sup(R_1) = sup(R_2)$ but R_1 has fewer attribute values in its left hand side than R_2 does. In addition, a rule $R_1 : P \rightarrow c$ is said a **general rule** w.r.t. rule $R_2 : P' \rightarrow c'$, if and only if P is a subset of P'.

CMAR employs the following methods for rule pruning.

First, *using general and high-confidence rule to prune more specific and lower confidence ones.* Given two rules R_1 and R_2, where R_1 is a general rule w.r.t. R_2. *CMAR* prunes R_2 if R_1 also has higher rank than R_2. The rationale is that we only need to consider general rules with high confidence, and thus more specific rules with low confidence should be pruned.

This pruning is pursued when the rule is inserted into the *CR-tree*. When a rule is inserted into the tree, retrieval over the tree is triggered to check if the rule can be pruned or it can prune other rules that are already inserted. Our experimental results show that this pruning is effective.

Second, *selecting only positively correlated rules.* For each rule $R : P \rightarrow c$, we test whether P is positively correlated with c by χ^2 testing. Only the rules that are positively correlated, i.e., those with χ^2 value passing a significance level threshold, are used for later classification. All the other rules are pruned.

Algorithm 1 (Selecting rules based on database coverage)

Input: a set of rules and a coverage threshold δ

Output: a subset of rules for classification

Method:

1. Sort rules in the rank descending order;
2. For each data object in the training data set, set its cover-count to 0;
3. While both the training data set and rule set are not empty, for each rule R in rank descending order, find all data objects matching rule R. If R can correctly classify at least one object then select R and increase the cover-count of those objects matching R by 1. A data object is removed if its cover-count passes coverage threshold δ;

Figure 3. Selecting rules based on database coverage.

The rationale of this pruning is that we use the rules reflecting strong implications to do classification. By removing those rules not positively correlated, we prune noise.

This pruning happens when a rule is found. Since the distribution of class labels w.r.t. frequent patterns is kept track during the rule mining, the χ^2 testing is done almost for free.

Third, *pruning rules based on database coverage.* *CMAR* selects a subset of high quality rules for classification. That is achieved by pruning rules based on database coverage. *CMAR* uses a *coverage threshold* [7] to select database coverage, as shown in Figure 3.

The database coverage method used in *CMAR* is similar to that in CBA. The major difference is that, instead of removing one data object from the training data set immediately after it is covered by some selected rule, we let it stay there until it is covered by at least δ rules. That allows more selected rules. When classifying a new data object, it may have more rules to consult and may have better chance to be accurately predicted.

This pruning is pursued when the rule mining process finishes. It is the last pruning of rules.

4 Classification Based on Multiple Rules

After a set of rules is selected for classification, as discussed in Section 3, *CMAR* is ready to classify new objects. Given a new data object, *CMAR* collects the subset of rules matching the new object from the set of rules for classification. In this section, we discuss how to determine the class label based on the subset of rules.

Trivially, if all the rules matching the new object have the same class label, *CMAR* just simply assigns that label to the new object.

If the rules are not consistent in class labels, *CMAR* divides the rules into groups according to class labels. All rules in a group share the same class label and each group has a distinct label. *CMAR* compares the effects of the groups and yields to the strongest group.

To compare the strength of groups, we need to measure the "*combined effect*" of each group. Intuitively, if the rules in a group are highly positively correlated and have good support, the group should have strong effect.

There are many possible ways to measure the combined effect of a group of rules. For example, one can use the strongest rule as a representative. That is, the rule with highest χ^2 value is selected. However, simply choosing the rule with highest χ^2 value may be favorable to minority classes, as illustrated in the following example.

Example 3 In a credit card application approval case, there are two rules.

R_1 : $job = no \rightarrow rejected(support = , confidence = 60\%)$, and

R_2 : $education = university \rightarrow approved(sup = 200, confidence = 99.5\%)$

The observed and expected contingencies are shown in Figure 4.

R_1	approved	rejected	total
job=yes	438	32	470
job=no	12	18	30
total	450	50	500

The observed contingency of rule R_1.

R_2	approved	rejected	total
ed=univ	199	1	200
ed≠univ	251	49	300
total	450	50	500

The observed contingency of rule R_2.

R_1	approved	rejected	total
job=yes	423	47	470
job=no	27	3	30
total	450	50	500

The expected contingency of rule R_1.

R_2	approved	rejected	total
ed=univ	180	20	200
ed≠univ	270	30	300
total	450	50	500

The expected contingency of rule R_2.

Figure 4. Observed and expected contingencies for rules.

Based on the observed and expected values, the χ^2 values for R_1 and R_2 are 88.4 and 33.6, respectively. For a customer having no job and with university education, we may predict her application would be rejected using rule R_1, if the choice of rules is based on only χ^2 values.

However, rule R_2 is intuitively much better than R_1 since R_2 has much higher support and confidence.

Another alternative is to use the compound of correlation of rules as measure. For example, we can sum up χ^2 values in a group as the measure of the group. However, this method suffers from the same problem that it may favors minority too much.

A better way is to integrate both information of correlation and popularity into the measure. After empirical verification, *CMAR* adopts a *weighted* χ^2 measure [7] as follows.

For each rule $R : P \rightarrow c$, let $sup(c)$ be the number of data objects in training data set that associated with class label c and $|T|$ the number of data objects in the training data set. We define $max\chi^2$ for rule R as follows.

$$max\chi^2 = (min\{sup(P), sup(c)\} - \frac{sup(P)sup(c)}{|T|})^2 |T| e$$

where

$$e = \frac{1}{sup(P)sup(c)} + \frac{1}{sup(P)(|T|-sup(c))} + \frac{1}{(|T|-sup(P))sup(c)} + \frac{1}{(|T|-sup(P))(|T|-sup(c))}$$

$max\chi^2$ computes the upper bound of χ^2 value of the rule w.r.t. other settings are fixed. Then, for each group of rules, the *weighted* χ^2 measure of the group is defined as $\sum \frac{\chi^2 \chi^2}{max\chi^2}$.

As can be seen, we use the ratio of χ^2 value against its upper bound (i.e., $max\chi^2$) to overcome the bias of χ^2 value favoring minority class. Please note that, theoretically, it is hard to verify the soundness or effect of measures on strength of groups of rules. Instead, we explore the effect of measures empirically, and according to our experimental results, weighted χ^2 value is the best from among a good set of candidate measure formulas that can be worked out by us.

5 Experimental Results and Performance Study

To evaluate the accuracy, efficiency and scalability of *CMAR*, we have performed an extensive performance study. In this section, we report our experimental results on comparing *CMAR* against two popular classification methods: CBA [9] and C4.5 [10]. It shows that *CMAR* outperforms both CBA and C4.5 in terms of average accuracy, efficiency and scalability.

All the experiments are performed on a 600MHz Pentium PC with 128M main memory, running Microsoft Windows/NT. CBA and C4.5 were implemented by their authors, respectively. In the experiments, the parameters of the three methods are set as follows.

All C4.5 parameters are default values. We test both C4.5 decision tree method and rule method. Since the rule method has better accuracy, we only report the accuracy for rule method.

For CBA, we set support threshold to 1% and confidence threshold to 50% and disable the limit on number of rules. Other parameters remain default.

For *CMAR*, the support and confidence thresholds are set as same as CBA. The database coverage threshold is set to 4 and the confidence difference threshold to 20%.

All reports of the runtime include both CPU time and I/O time.

We test 26 data sets from UCI Machine Learning Repository. We use C4.5's *shuffle* utility to shuffle the data sets. Also, we adopt the same method used by CBA to discretize continuous attributes.

Data set	# attr	# cls	# rec	C4.5	CBA	CMAR
Anneal	38	6	898	94.8	97.9	97.3
Austral	14	2	690	84.7	84.9	86.1
Auto	25	7	205	80.1	78.3	78.1
Breast	10	2	699	95	96.3	96.4
Cleve	13	2	303	78.2	82.8	82.2
Crx	15	2	690	84.9	84.7	84.9
Diabetes	8	2	768	74.2	74.5	75.8
German	20	2	1000	72.3	73.4	74.9
Glass	9	7	214	68.7	73.9	70.1
Heart	13	2	270	80.8	81.9	82.2
Hepatic	19	2	155	80.6	81.8	80.5
Horse	22	2	368	82.6	82.1	82.6
Hypo	25	2	3163	99.2	98.9	98.4
Iono	34	2	351	90	92.3	91.5
Iris	4	3	150	95.3	94.7	94
Labor	16	2	57	79.3	86.3	89.7
Led7	7	10	3200	73.5	71.9	72.5
Lymph	18	4	148	73.5	77.8	83.1
Pima	8	2	768	75.5	72.9	75.1
Sick	29	2	2800	98.5	97	97.5
Sonar	60	2	208	70.2	77.5	79.4
Tic-tac	9	2	958	99.4	99.6	99.2
Vehicle	18	4	846	72.6	68.7	68.8
Waveform	21	3	5000	78.1	80	83.2
Wine	13	3	178	92.7	95	95
Zoo	16	7	101	92.2	96.8	97.1
Average				83.34	84.69	85.22

Table 3. The comparison of C4.5, CBA and *CMAR* on accuracy.

As can be seen from the table, *CMAR* outperforms both C4.5 and CBA on accuracy. Furthermore, out of the 26 data sets, *CMAR* achieves the best accuracy in 13 ones. In another word, *CMAR* wins in 50% of test data sets. In some data sets, e.g. Lymph, *CMAR* wins the second place over 5% in accuracy.

There are two important parameters, *database coverage threshold* and *confidence difference threshold*, in *CMAR*.

As discussed before, these two thresholds control the number of rules selected for classification.

In general, if the set of rules is too small, some effective rules may be missed. On the other hand, if the rule set is too large, the training data set may be overfit. Thus, we need to test the sensitivities of the two thresholds w.r.t. classification accuracy.

As an example, we test different database coverage threshold values on the *Sonar* data set from UCI Machine Learning Database Repository. The results are shown in Figure 5, where the confidence difference threshold is set to 0. On the other hand, we test different confidence difference threshold values on the *Sonar* data set. The results are shown in Figure 6, where the database coverage threshold is set to 1.

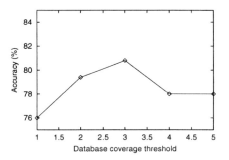

Figure 5. The effect of coverage threshold on accuracy.

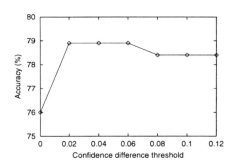

Figure 6. The effect of confidence difference threshold on accuracy.

From the figures, one can see that the peaks of accuracy are achieved at the middle of both curves. That is, there are optimal settings for both thresholds. However, according to our experimental results, there seems no way to pre-determine the best threshold values. Fortunately, both curves are quite plain. That means the accuracy is not very sensitive to the two thresholds values.

CR-tree is a compact structure to store rules. To test the effectiveness of *CR-tree*, we compare the main memory usage of CBA and *CMAR* on large test data sets. The results are shown in Table 4.

Dataset	# attr	# cls	# rec	CBA mem (M)	CMAR mem (M)	saving (%)
Auto	25	7	205	488	101	79.30%
Hypo	25	2	3163	330	90	72.73%
Iono	34	2	351	334	86	74.25%
Sick	29	2	2800	321	85	73.52%
Sonar	60	2	208	590	88	85.09%
Vehicle	18	4	846	590	88	85.09%
Average				393.33	90	77.12%

Table 4. The comparison of CBA and *CMAR* on main memory usage.

Please note that, in this experiment, we disable the limitation of number of rules in CBA. In such a setting, CBA and *CMAR* generate all the rules necessary for classification and thus are compared in a fair base. From the table, one can see that, on average, *CMAR* achieves 77.12% saving on main memory usage.

The saving in main memory usage can be explained from two apsects.

First, *CMAR* uses *CR-tree*. The compactness of *CR-tree* brings significant gain in storing a large set of rules where many items in the rules can be shared.

On the other hand, *CR-tree* is also an index structure of rules. Before a rule is inserted into a *CR-tree*, *CMAR* checks if there is a general rule or some more specific rules in the tree. If so, related pruning is pursued immediately. Such a pruning techique also contributes to the saving of main memory.

To test the scalability of *CMAR*, we compare the runtime of CBA and *CMAR* on six data sets. The results are shown in Figure 5. Again, we disable the limit on number of rules in CBA. In the experiments, CBA spends a large portion of runtime on I/O.

Dataset	# attr	# cls	# rec	CBA runtime	CMAR runtime
Auto	25	7	205	612s	408s
Hypo	25	2	3163	92s	19s
Iono	34	2	351	150s	89s
Sick	29	2	2800	74s	13s
Sonar	60	2	208	226s	145s
Vehicle	18	4	846	284s	192s

Table 5. The runtime of CBA and *CMAR*.

As can be seen from the table, *CMAR* is faster than CBA in many cases. Please be note that the machine we use for testing is with relatively small size of main memory (128M). Both CBA and *CMAR* can be expected running significantly faster if more main memory is available.

6 Conclusions

In this paper, we examined two major challenges in associative classification: (1) efficiency at handling huge number of mined association rules, and (2) effectiveness at predicting new class labels with high classification accuracy. We proposed a novel associative classification method, *CMAR*, i.e., **C**lassification based on **M**ultiple **A**ssociation **R**ules. The method has several distinguished features: (1) its classification is performed based on a weighted χ^2 analysis enforced on multiple association rules, which leads to better overall classification accuracy, (2) it prunes rules effectively based on confidence, correlation and database coverage, and (3) its efficiency is achieved by extension of an efficient frequent pattern mining method, *FP-growth*, construction of a class distribution-associated *FP-tree*, and applying a *CR-tree* structure to store and retrieve mined association rules efficiently.

Our experiments on 26 databases in UCI machine learning database repository show that *CMAR* is consistent, highly effective at classification of various kinds of databases and has better average classification accuracy in comparison with CBA and C4.5, and is more efficient and scalable than other associative classification methods.

References

[1] R. Agrawal and R. Srikant. Fast algorithms for mining association rules. In *VLDB'94*, Chile, Sept. 1994.

[2] P. Clark and T. Niblett. The CN2 induction algorithm. *Machine Learning*, 3:261–283, 1989.

[3] G. Dong, X. Zhang, L. Wong, and J. Li. Caep: Classification by aggregating emerging patterns. In *DS'99 (LNCS 1721)*, Japan, Dec. 1999.

[4] R. Duda and P. Hart. *Pattern Classification and Scene Analysis*. John Wiley & Sons, 1973.

[5] J. Han, J. Pei, and Y. Yin. Mining frequent patterns without candidate generation. In *SIGMOD'00*, Dallas, TX, May 2000.

[6] B. Lent, A. Swami, and J. Widom. Clustering association rules. In *ICDE'97*, England, April 1997.

[7] W. Li. Classification based on multiple association rules. *M.Sc. Thesis*, Simon Fraser University, April 2001.

[8] T.-S. Lim, W.-Y. Loh, and Y.-S. Shih. A comparison of prediction accuracy, complexity, and training time of thirty-three old and new classification algorithms. *Machine Learning*, 39, 2000.

[9] B. Liu, W. Hsu, and Y. Ma. Integrating classification and association rule mining. In *KDD'98*, New York, NY, Aug. 1998.

[10] J. R. Quinlan. *C4.5: Programs for Machine Learning*. Morgan Kaufmann, 1993.

[11] K. Wang, S. Zhou, and Y. He. Growing decision tree on support-less association rules. In *KDD'00*, Boston, MA, Aug. 2000.

Analyzing the Interestingness of Association Rules from the Temporal Dimension

Bing Liu, Yiming Ma

School of Computing
National University of Singapore
3 Science Drive 2, Singapore 117543
{liub, maym}@comp.nus.edu.sg

Ronnie Lee

Department of Statistics and Applied Probability
National University of Singapore
3 Science Drive 2
Singapore 117543

Abstract

Rule discovery is one of the central tasks of data mining. Existing research has produced many algorithms for the purpose. These algorithms, however, often generate too many rules. In the past few years, rule interestingness techniques were proposed to help the user find interesting rules. These techniques typically employ the dataset as a whole to mine rules, and then filter and/or rank the discovered rules in various ways. In this paper, we argue that this is insufficient. These techniques are unable to answer a question that is of critical importance to the application of rules, i.e., can the rules be trusted? In practice, the users are always concerned with the question. They want to know whether the rules indeed represent some true and stable (or reliable) underlying relationships in the domain. If a rule is not stable, does it show any systematic pattern such as a trend? Before any rule can be used, these questions must be answered. This paper proposes a technique to use statistical methods to analyze rules from the temporal dimension to answer these questions. Experimental results show that the proposed technique is very effective.

6. Introduction

The objective of data mining is to find interesting/useful knowledge for the user. Rules are an important form of knowledge. Existing research has produced many algorithms for rule mining. These techniques, however, often generate too many rules, and most of the rules are of no use to the user [22, 23, 15]. In the past few years, a number of rule interestingness techniques were proposed to deal with the problem [12, 13, 14, 15, 21, 22, 23, 4, 16, 24, 25, 28]. They typically use the whole dataset to mine rules and then filter and/or rank the discovered rules in various ways to help the user identify interesting/useful ones. These techniques, however, have a major shortcoming. They are unable to answer a question that is crucial to the application of rules, i.e., can the rules be trusted or will the rules hold in the future? A rule has no use if it does not hold in the future or is not predictive.

In this paper, we argue that an important aspect of the rules has not been studied, i.e., the temporal aspect. Analyzing rules from the temporal dimension is important

for real-life applications. In the past few years, we used a number of interestingness techniques to help our users find interesting rules [13, 14, 15]. Although these techniques helped a great deal, our users often still felt uncomfortable. The reason is that the users are concerned with the reliability of the rules. They want to know whether the rules will hold in the future, i.e., whether the rules indeed represent some stable (or reliable) underlying relationships in the domain. If a rule is not stable, does it show any systematic trend? The inability of the existing approaches to answer these questions lies with the fact that they do not study the dynamic behavior of rules. In this research, we analyze the interestingness of rules from the temporal dimension to solve the problem. This approach makes sense as most datasets are collected over time and represent the behaviors of the application domains in different time periods.

In this research, we focus on analyzing association rules. Association rule mining is commonly stated as follows [3]: Let $I = \{i_1, ..., i_n\}$ be a set of *items*, and D be a set of data tuples (records). Each data tuple consists of a subset of items in I. An *association rule* is an implication of the form $X \rightarrow Y$, where $X \subset I$, $Y \subset I$, and $X \cap Y = \emptyset$. The rule $X \rightarrow Y$ holds in D with confidence c if $c\%$ of data tuples in D that support X also support Y. The rule has support s in D if $s\%$ of data tuples in D contains $X \cup Y$. Given a set of data tuples D (the database), the problem of mining association rules is to discover all rules that have support and confidence greater than or equal to the user-specified minimum support (called *minsup*) and minimum confidence (called *minconf*).

This paper presents a set of statistical methods to analyze the behavior of rules over time. The basic idea is as follows: The dataset is first partitioned into a few blocks or sub-datasets corresponding to the time periods (e.g., years, months or weeks) in which they were collected. The granularity of the time period is application dependent. We then mine rules from each block. Since the amount of data available is usually large, the partitioning does not lose significance of the rules discovered. After all the rules are found, we analyze the supports and confidences of the rules in these time periods, which allow us to answer the above questions and to find various types of important rules, e.g.,

- Stable rules: These rules do not change a great deal over time. Stable rules are more reliable and can be trusted. That is, they can be safely used in real-world performance tasks.
- Trend rules: These rules indicate some underlying systematic trends. If the trend rules are known, the user can take necessary actions to exploit desirable trends, and to reverse/delay undesirable trends.

Our experiments and practical applications show that the proposed technique is very effective. Testing on unseen future data confirms that the stable rules and the trend rules identified by our method are indeed reliable. Our experiments also indicate that although the number of rules generated from the data can be large, the number of stable rules and those rules that show some trends is actually quite small. It is possible to manually inspect them to identify those truly useful/actionable ones.

2. Related Work

Existing research on rule interestingness focuses on a few directions, namely, template matching, unexpected rule identification, rule summarization and organization. We discuss them below in turn.

[12] proposes a template-based approach for finding interesting rules. This approach first asks the user to specify what rules he/she wants. The system then finds those matching rules.

[15, 23, 21] propose to used user expectations or beliefs to help him/her find unexpected rules. In this approach, the user first input his/her existing knowledge about the domain, and the system then finds those conforming and unexpected rules.

[14] presents a technique to summarize the discovered association rules using a small subset of the rules. [13] presents a technique to organize the discovered rules in such a way that they can be easily browsed by the user.

[4, 25, 18, 10] report a number of methods for ranking the discovered rules using some statistical interestingness measures.

All these techniques are different from our work as none of them analyzes rules over time. Thus, they are unable to answer the rule stability or reliability question.

[2] proposes to mine and to monitor rules in different time periods. The discovered rules from different time periods are collected into a rule base. Ups and downs in support or confidence over time (called history) are represented and defined using shape operators. The user can then query the rule base by specifying some history specifications. This is related to our work. However, there is a major difference. We analyze rules generated over different time periods using statistical tests rather than simply matching user specifications. By using statistical tests, we can formally analyze the significance of ups and downs of support and confidence. User specifications lack statistical foundation. One will not know whether the changes are significant and worth investigating.

[6] presents a framework for measuring changes in two models. The difference between the two models (e.g., two sets of itemsets, one generated from dataset D_1 and one generated from dataset D_2) is quantified as the amount of work (e.g., difference in supports) required to transform one model into the other. In a related work, [5] finds the support differences of association rules mined from two datasets and uses the differences to detect emerging patterns. These are different from our work as we analyze rules over a number of time periods, while [6, 5] only compare the supports/confidences of rules from two periods. Our method uses statistical methods to identify significant changes, trends and stable rules. Both [6, 5] do not perform these tasks.

3. Basic Steps of the Proposed Approach

This section gives an overview of the proposed approach, which consists of 3 steps:

1. **Partitioning the dataset**: The original dataset D is first partitioned vertically into a number of blocks (or sub-datasets) D_1, D_2, ..., D_q according to the time periods, T_1, T_2, ..., T_q, in which they were collected, e.g., years or months.

2. **Mining rules from sub-datasets**: We then mine rules from each sub-dataset D_i. Let the set of rules mined from D_i be R_i. The set R of rules that will be analyzed in the third step below is defined as follows:

$$R = \{r \mid r \in (R_1 \cup R_2 \ldots \cup R_q)\}$$

This means that if a rule appears in any rule set R_i it is considered a potentially interesting rule. The reason that we consider all such rules will be clear later.

Clearly, a rule r in R may appear in R_i but not in R_j ($i \neq j$) because r may not satisfy minsup and/or minconf in D_j. For our analysis later, we need the supports and confidences of every rule in R in all time periods (or all D_i). Thus, the missing support and confidence information in certain time periods for each rule needs to be obtained. This can be done quite easily. We can first mine rules from each sub-dataset D_i to produce R. We then scan the data D once to obtain all the missing supports and confidences.

Note that in rule mining, pruning is also performed to remove those insignificant rules. We use the technique given in [14].

3. **Analyzing rules over time:** After all the necessary information about supports and confidences of each rule r in R in all time periods is obtained, we analyze

the rules to give the user different types of interesting rules. A number of rankings of rules according to different statistical measures are performed to enable the user to view those most interesting rules first.

In the next section, we discuss step 3, which is the focus of this paper. Step 1 and 2 will not be discussed further as they are fairly straightforward.

4. Analyzing Rules Over Time

We now present a number of statistical tests to analyze the discovered rules in R from different perspectives. We assume that the confidence value (denoted by $conf_i$) and the support value (denoted by sup_i) of each rule in R in each time period T_i has been obtained by a mining algorithm. Our analysis aims to identify:

- semi-stable rules
- stable rules
- rules that exhibit trends.

Note that the statistical tests presented here are by no means the only tests that can be performed on rules. In fact, many other tests may also be used for various purposes. We also point out that the kinds of datasets, and the problems, dealt with here are different from time series data. In the latter, a given population is tracked over time. For our case, although the behavior of rules over time is of interest, each time period typically corresponds to a different population.

4.1 Semi-stable rules

Intuitively, a rule r in R is a *semi-stable rule* if none of its confidences (or supports) in the time periods, T_1, T_2, ..., T_q, is statistically below minconf (or minsup). If some observed confidence $conf_i$ (or support sup_i) of the rule is less than minconf (or minsup), it may be due to chance. Semi-stable rules are in contrast with *stable rules* which have more stringent conditions (see the next sub-section).

Definition (semi-stable confidence rules): Let minsup and minconf be the minimum support and the minimum confidence, $conf_D$ and sup_D be the actual support and the actual confidence of a rule r obtained from the whole dataset D, $conf_i$ be the actual confidence of the rule in the time period T_i, and α be a specified significance level. The rule r is a *semi-stable confidence rule* over the time periods, T_1, T_2, ..., T_q, if the following two conditions are met:

1. $sup_D \geq$ minsup and $conf_D \geq$ minconf.
2. For each time period (or sub-dataset), we fail to reject the following null hypothesis at the significance level α:

$$H_0: conf_i \geq \text{minconf}$$

Note that the first condition is to ensure that the rule r satisfies the user specified minsup and minconf thresholds

in the whole dataset. To test the hypothesis in the second condition, we can use the statistical test on a single proportion [26, 17].

Test statistic

Consider testing the following null hypothesis (H_0) against the alternative hypothesis (H_1):

$$H_0: p \geq p_0$$
$$H_1: p < p_0$$

where p_0 is the given proportion. The *test statistic* z (with standard normal distribution) for the sample proportion, $\hat{p}$, is:

$$z = \frac{\hat{p} - p_0}{\sigma_{\hat{p}}} \qquad \sigma_{\hat{p}} = \sqrt{\frac{p_0(1 - p_0)}{n}}$$

where n is the sample size. If z is less than its critical value at the significance level α, we reject the null hypothesis. In our case, p_0 is minconf and $\hat{p}$ is $conf_i$.

Example 1: Assume in a mining session we set minconf to 50%. There is a time period T_i in which the confidence $conf_i$ of a rule, $A \rightarrow B$, is 45%. There are 300 data tuples that satisfy the condition A, and out of these 300 tuples 135 tuples also satisfy the consequent B (i.e., $conf_i = 135/300 = 45\%$). The question is whether $conf_i$ is statistically below 50%.

We solve the problem as follows: From the problem description, we obtain the population size $n = 300$, $\hat{p} = 45\%$ and $p_0 = 50\%$. We use $\alpha = 5\%$. The null and alternative hypotheses are:

$$H_0: p \geq 0.50$$
$$H_1: p < 0.50$$

The critical value for z is -1.65 at $\alpha = 5\%$, which can be obtained from statistical tables. Let us compute z,

$$\sigma_{\hat{p}} = \sqrt{\frac{p_0(1 - p_0)}{n}} = \sqrt{\frac{0.5 * 0.5}{300}} = 0.0288675$$

$$z = \frac{\hat{p} - p_0}{\sigma_{\hat{p}}} = \frac{0.45 - 0.5}{0.0288675} = -1.73$$

The observed value of the test statistic $z = -1.73$, which is less than the critical value of $z = -1.65$. Therefore, we reject H_0, and accept the alternative hypothesis H_1. In other words, the difference between the sample proportion and the hypothesized value of the population proportion is large and this difference is unlikely to have occurred due to chance alone.

We now define *semi-stable support rules*.

Definition (semi-stable support rules): Let minsup and minconf be the minimum support and the minimum confidence, $conf_D$ and sup_D be the actual support and the actual confidence of a rule r obtained from the whole dataset D, sup_i be the actual support of the rule in the time period T_i, and α be a specified significance level. The rule r is a *semi-stable support rule* over the time periods, T_1, T_2, ..., T_q, if the following two conditions are met.

1. $sup_D \geq$ minsup and $conf_D \geq$ minconf.
2. For each time period (or sub-dataset), we fail to reject the following null hypothesis at the significance level α:

$$H_0: \; sup_i \geq \text{minsup}$$

Here, again we can use the statistical test on a single proportion to test the null hypothesis.

Computation complexity: Let the number of rules in R be $|R|$, and the number of time periods be q. The complexity of semi-stability test is $O(q|R|)$. Since q is normally very small, and $|R|$ is very large (in thousands or more), the computation is thus linear in $|R|$.

4.2 Stable rules

A semi-stable rule only requires that its confidences (or supports) over time are not statistically below minconf (or minsup). However, the confidences (or supports) of the rule may vary a great deal. Hence, the behavior can be unpredictable. In practice, the user often wants rules that are stable over time, i.e., with predictable behaviors. We call such rules *stable rules*. Intuitively, a stable rule is a semi-stable rule and its confidences (or supports) over time do not vary a great deal, i.e., they are homogeneous.

Since both confidence and support are population proportions, we need a statistical test for population proportions. The Chi-square test [26, 17] is a popular choice for testing homogeneity of multiple proportions.

Definition (stable confidence rules): Let minsup and minconf be the minimum support and minimum confidence, $conf_i$ be the actual confidence of a rule in the time period T_i, and α be a specified significance level. The rule r in R is a *stable confidence rule* over the time periods, T_1, T_2, ..., T_q, if the following two conditions are met:

1. r is a semi-stable confidence rule.
2. We fail to reject the following hypothesis at the significance level α:

$$H_0: \; conf_1 = conf_2 = ... = conf_q$$

Test of homogeneity: A test of homogeneity involves testing the null hypothesis (H_0) that the proportions, p_1, p_2, ..., p_k, in two or more different populations are the same against the alternative hypothesis (H_1) that these proportions are not the same. That is,

$$H_0: p_1 = p_2 = ... = p_k$$

H_1: the population proportions are not all equal.

We assume that the data consists of independent random samples of size n_1, n_2, ..., n_k from k populations. The data is arranged in a $2 \times k$ contingency table (Figure 1). The numbers x_1, x_2, ..., x_k, n_1-x_1, n_2-x_2, ..., n_k-x_k listed inside

	Sample			
	1	2	...	k
Successes	x_1	x_2	...	x_k
Failures	n_1-x_1	n_1-x_2	...	n_1-x_k

Figure 1: A $2 \times k$ contingency table

the $2k$ cells are called *observed frequencies* of the respective cells.

Let O be an observed frequency, and E be an expected or theoretical frequency for a cell in the above table. The statistic defined as

$$\chi^2 = \sum \frac{(O - E)^2}{E}$$

has a χ^2 distribution with

$$df = (Row - 1)(Column - 1)$$

degrees of freedom, where *Row* and *Column* are the number of rows and the number of columns, respectively, in the given contingency table.

Under the null hypothesis in a test of homogeneity, we would expect the frequency E (expected frequency) for a cell to be as follows [26, 17]:

$$E = \frac{(\text{Row total})(\text{Column total})}{\text{Sample size}}$$

Thus, χ^2 represents a normalized deviation from expectation. If all values were really homogeneous, the χ^2 value would be 0. If it is higher than a threshold value (5.99, at the 5% significant level and two degrees of freedom) we reject H_0. Note that the threshold value for any given significance level can be obtained from widely available tables for Chi-square distribution.

Example 2: In an application, we have three years of data with 30000 tuples. The data is partitioned into three sub-datasets according to years. We want to analyze a particular rule r, $A \rightarrow B$, found in the dataset. The confidences of r in different time periods are:

T_1 (year 1): confidence$_1$ = 70% (= 450/680)
T_2 (year 2): confidence$_2$ = 80% (= 400/500)
T_3 (year 3): confidence$_3$ = 58% (= 420/720)

Note that the confidence of r in D_i is computed using the support counts of A and $A \wedge B$ in D_i. These support counts are given in parentheses next to each confidence value. We want to test the null hypothesis that the confidences of r over the 3 time periods are the same using the significance level $\alpha = 5\%$.

The confidence information (using the support counts) can be presented in a 2x3 contingency table (Figure 2) containing 6 cells. The expected frequencies are included in parentheses next to the observed frequencies within the corresponding cells.

For the values in the table of Figure 2, the value for the

	T_1	T_2	T_3	Col. Total
satisfy $A \wedge B$	**450** (454.5)	**400** (334.2)	**420** (481.3)	1270
satisfy $A \wedge \neg B$	**230** (225.5)	**100** (165.8)	**300** (238.7)	630
Row total (satisfy A)	680	500	720	1900

Figure 2: The 2x3 contingency table of confidences

test statistic χ^2 is 62.7 [1]. If we use the significance level of 5%, the critical value for χ^2 is 5.99 with 2 degree of freedom (df = (2-1)(3-1) = 2). The observed χ^2 value is much larger than the critical value. Thus, we reject the null hypothesis, and conclude that the confidences of the rule over the three time periods are significantly different.

The above example tests the homogeneity of confidences of a rule over time. We can also use the same method to test the supports of a rule.

Definition (stable support rules): Let minsup and minconf be the minimum support and minimum confidence, sup_i be the actual support of a rule r in R in the time period T_i, and α be a specified significance level. The rule r is a *stable support rule* over the time periods, T_1, T_2, ..., T_q, if the following two conditions are met:

1. r is a semi-stable support rule.
2. We fail to reject the following hypothesis at the significance level α:
   H_0: $sup_1 = sup_2 = ... = sup_q$

After a set of stable (confidence or support) rules are found, ranking can be performed according to the mean confidence or the mean support of each rule over time. This ranking allows the user to see rules that have higher average confidences or supports first.

Computation complexity (without considering the final ranking): Since the number of cells in a contingency table is $2q$, the computation complexity of stability test is $O(q|R|)$. Since q is small and $|R|$ is very large, the computation is linear in $|R|$.

4.3 Rules that exhibit trends

In many applications, users are interested in knowing whether changes in support or confidence of a rule over time are random or there is an underlying trend. A statistical test called the *run test* [11] is often used to test whether a sequence of data is from a random process or exhibits trend. Below, we give a brief description of the run test in our application context.

Assume we have a rule that has the following confidences for T_1, ..., T_6.

Time	confidence	change	
T_1	70%		
T_2	75%	+	⎫
T_3	79%	+	⎬ Run 1
T_4	82%	+	⎭
T_5	78%	-	⎬ Run 2
T_6	81%	+	⎬ Run 3

The direction of change in successive observations is shown by plus and minus signs. A *run* is a succession of plus or minus signs, surrounded by the opposite sign. If we read from top to bottom, we would say that we have a *run* of three +s, followed by a *run* of one -, and followed by a *run* of one +. In our example, there are 3 runs: one run of length three and two runs of length one.

The above sequence may suggest a trend toward increasing values of confidence. That is, these values of confidence may not reasonably be looked upon as being the items of a random sample.

The exact run test for trends is based on the probability density function (p.d.f) of W, the number of runs in a combined ordered sample consisting of two types of items, X and Y, say. Let m be the number of X items, and n be the number of Y items. Then as shown in [11], the p.d.f of W is given by:

when W is odd:

$$\Pr(W = 2k+1) = \left\{ \binom{m-1}{k}\binom{n-1}{k-1} + \binom{m-1}{k-1}\binom{n-1}{k} \right\} \bigg/ \binom{m+n}{m}$$

when W is even:

$$\Pr(W = 2k) = \binom{m-1}{k-1}\binom{n-1}{k-1} \bigg/ \binom{m+n}{m}$$

where $2k$ and $2k+1$ are elements that belong to the space of W, and k is a positive integer. When $k = 0$ (i.e., $W = 1$), we need special treatment. There are two cases:

1. If $m = 0$ or $n = 0$, $\Pr(W = 1) = 1$. That is, if $m = 0$ or $n = 0$, one run is the only possibility. This case clearly indicates a trend.
2. If $m \neq 0$ and $n \neq 0$, $\Pr(W = 1) = 0$. That is, if $m \neq 0$ and $n \neq 0$, it is not possible to be one run.

We are interested in testing:

H_0: sequence generated by a random process
H_1: sequence exhibits trend

The critical region of this test is of the form $W \leq v$. v is determined by computing $\alpha = \Pr(W \leq v; H_0)$, where α is the significance level (normally 5% or 10%). Let W_0 denote the observed number of runs (e.g., in our above

---

[1] One of the main assumptions of the χ^2 test is that the expected frequencies are not be too small [8]. The rule of thumb is that the χ^2 test is appropriate only when no expected frequency is less than 5. This seldom happens in our case as we normally deal with large datasets. When an expected frequency is below 5, extensions of the Fisher's exact test may be used, which, however, is quite cumbersome and not popular [8]. In our application, we find that for stability test the user is willing to give a range such that if the confidences or supports are within the range, the rule is considered stable.

381

example, $W_0 = 3$). If W_0 is greater than v, we fail to reject the null hypothesis. In the computation, we do not need to find the value of v. We can simply do the following: We compute $P = \Pr(W = 1) + \Pr(W = 2) + \ldots + \Pr(W = W_0)$. If $P \leq \alpha$, we reject H_0, and accept the alternative hypothesis H_1: *sequence exhibits trend*.

When m and n are small, it is easy to compute the probability. When they are large, the distribution of W can be approximated by a normal distribution [11] with mean

$$\mu = 2\frac{mn}{m+n} + 1$$

and variance $\sigma^2 = \frac{(\mu-1)(\mu-2)}{m+n-1}$

We can then use the standard normal approximation to test our hypothesis:

$$z = \frac{W - \mu}{\sigma}$$

The run test above finds those rules that exhibit trends. However, it does not tell the types of trends. We rank the rules according to the number of +s in each of them to show whether a rule is more likely to have an upward or a downward trend. Thus, the rules on the top are more likely to show upward trends, while the rules at the bottom are more likely to show downward trends.

Computation complexity (without considering the final ranking): Since "m (or n) choose k" and finding the numbers m and n can be done in linear time (in q), the complexity of the trend analysis is $O(qW_0|R|)$. Since both q and W_0 ($W_0 \leq q$) are small, the whole computation is linear in $|R|$. When q is large (more than 20 [11]), we can use the normal approximation. Then, the complexity becomes $O(q|R|)$ as z can be computed in $O(1)$.

5. Evaluation

We now report our experiment results. The objective is to show the effectiveness and efficiency of the proposed technique. We used 4 real life datasets, one from a vehicle insurance company, one from an education institution, and two from another education institution. We did not use public domain datasets such as those in UCI machine learning repository [19] because most of these datasets are not time or sequence related. For those datasets that have sequence, we do not understand them and thus do not know how to partition them meaningfully.

a. Finding different types of rules

Table 1 (next page) shows the datasets and the results of rule generation and statistical tests. Column 1 gives the name of each dataset. Column 2 gives the number of tuples in each dataset. Column 3 shows the number of partitions of each dataset. In our case, each partition contains one year of data. Column 4 gives the number of

rules generated from all partitions or blocks, i.e., the size of R. Column 5 gives the number of rules generated from the original dataset D. Note that the minsup and minconf values were suggested by our users.

From column 4 and 5, we can see that the number of rules generated from each dataset is very large. Column 6 gives the number of rules left after pruning from all partitions or blocks. Column 7 gives the number of rules after pruning for the whole dataset D (we used the pruning method in [14]). From column 6 and 7, we observe that the number of rules after pruning is substantially smaller for each data. Column 8 gives the execution time (in seconds) for rule generation. Column 9 gives the execution time for statistical tests (running on Pentium II 350 with 128MB RAM). We see that statistical tests can be done very efficiently.

The following two tables (Table 2 and 3) show the statistical test results [2]. We used the significance level of 5% (a commonly used level [26, 17]) in all our statistical tests. In column 2 of both Table 2 and Table 3, we reproduce the number of rules to be analyzed for each dataset, which is shown in column 6 of Table 1. Table 2 gives the results of the analysis on rule confidence. We observe that although the number of discovered rules from each dataset is large, the number of stable confidence rules (column 3) and the number of rules that exhibit trends (column 5) are actually quite small. Column 4 gives the number of semi-stable rules (which does not include the stable rules). We observe that the education domains are quite stable as most of the rules are either stable or semi-stable. The insurance domain is, however, much more volatile. A large majority of rules are unstable. Rule support analysis given in Table 3 shows similar results. Since the number of stable rules and trend rules are not that large, manual analysis is possible.

5.2 Accuracy tests

The main aim of our technique is to find rules that can be trusted and used in the future. Thus, we need to see whether the stable rules identified will still be stable and trend rules will still maintain their trends in the future. For these experiments, we make use of unseen test sets. Since we partition each dataset into q blocks, we use the first q-1 blocks to find stable rules, semi-stable rules and trend rules. We then test them on the unseen qth block.

For comparison, we use mean squared error and mean absolute error to evaluate stable rules, semi-stable rules and the rest of the rules (called *unstable rules*). We will use the mean (expected) confidence (or support) of each

---

[2] In Chi-square test, it is assumed that the populations are independent. For the 3 education datasets, this is true as the data from different years represent different student populations. In the insurance case, the dataset records those insurers who had accidents and made claims. It is also reasonable to assume that the data from different years are independent.

Table 1: Application datasets and the generated rules

	1	2	3	4	5	6	7	8	9
		tuples	blocks	rules in all blocks	rules in D	rules in all blocks (aft. prn)	rules in D (aft. prn.)	rule gen. (sec.)	analysis (sec.)
Insur	158151	7	81463	20177	5026	3797	80.52	9.34
Edu1	4780	5	46428	21516	2743	2743	7.28	7.36
Edu2-1	6540	5	4606	2776	1075	1057	2.74	0.61
Edu2-2	5320	5	11722	8531	1177	1174	5.76	1.43

Table 2: Analysis on rule confidences

	1	2	3	4	5
CONF	all rules	stable	semi-stable	trend
Insur	5026	252	132	213
Edu1	2743	209	1919	35
Edu2-1	1075	215	603	52
Edu2-2	1177	433	626	10

Table 3: Analysis on rule supports

	1	2	3	4	5
SUP	all rules	stable	semi-stable	trend
Insur	5026	20	20	223
Edu1	2743	494	782	166
Edu2-1	1075	314	239	86
Edu2-2	1177	257	241	62

rule over the q-1 time periods as the predicted confidence (or support) of the rule in the new (qth block) data. We want to see the error produced by each type of rules on the test data. Mean squared error (MSE) and mean absolute error (MAE) are commonly used in statistics to evaluate model accuracy. They are defined as follows:

$$MSE = \frac{\sum (Y_i - \hat{Y}_i)^2}{S} \qquad MAE = \frac{\sum |Y_i - \hat{Y}_i|}{S}$$

where Y_i is the confidence (or support) of a rule in the new data, and $\hat{Y}_i$ is the estimated confidence (or support) of the rule, which is the mean value of the confidences (or supports) of the rule in the q-1 blocks. S is the total number of rules tested.

Table 4 and 5 show the accuracy results on confidence and support respectively. We discuss Table 4 first. Column 2 of Table 4 gives the percentage of stable confidence rules that remain stable after considering the qth block (the final year) of data. That is, our statistical tests now consider one more year. In the case of insurance data, 96.4% of stable rules remain stable. 2.4% of the

stable rules become semi-stable. For the other three datasets, the percentages of stable rules remaining stable are slightly smaller, but are still very large. We believe the reason is that these datasets are smaller and thus tend to have bigger variations over time. However, the remaining rules are almost all semi-stable. Column 4 shows that almost all semi-stable confidence rules are still semi-stable after the qth block is considered (note that the semi-stable rules here do not include stable rules). Column 5 shows that most trend rules still exhibit trends. The proportions are slightly less than those for stable rules and semi-stable rules because the number (q) of time periods in our experiments is small and thus the trend test is less stable. Column 6, 7 and 8 show the mean squared errors for each dataset when we use the mean confidences of stable rules, semi-stable rules and unstable rules to predict the confidences of these rules on the qth data block respectively. Column 9, 10, and 11 give the respective mean absolute errors for each dataset. We can see that stable rules commit least error. The error of unstable rules can be very large. For example, in the case of Edu1, for

Table 4: Accuracy results on confidence analysis

	1	2	3	4	5	6	7	8	9	10	11
		stable		semi stable	trend	MSE			MAE		
CONF	stable	semi-stable	semi-stable	trend	stable	semi-stable	unstable	stable	semi-stable	unstable
Insur	96.4%	2.4%	91.15%	73.7%	0.0004	0.00060	0.00684	0.008	0.015	0.062
Edu1	67.0%	33.0%	98.68%	54.2%	0.0021	0.00641	0.04273	0.035	0.059	0.168
Edu2-1	72.6%	26.1%	91.69%	61.2%	0.0162	0.03490	0.06423	0.064	0.119	0.177
Edu2-2	69.5%	29.8%	96.60%	88.6%	0.0071	0.00770	0.02102	0.066	0.067	0.096

Table 5: Accuracy results on support analysis

	1	2	3	4	5	6	7	8	9	10	11
		stable		semi stable	trend	MSE			MAE		
SUP	stable	semi-stable	semi-stable	trend	stable	semi-stable	unstable	stable	semi-stable	unstable
Insur	100.0%	0.0%	100.0%	84.1%	0.00000	0.00000	0.00002	0.0001	0.0002	0.002
Edu1	99.0%	0.2%	86.4%	50.8%	0.00011	0.00089	0.00236	0.0080	0.0230	0.039
Edu2-1	99.7%	0.3%	84.4%	62.3%	0.00006	0.00017	0.00011	0.0060	0.0100	0.011
Edu2-2	98.1%	0.8%	79.5%	51.8%	0.00011	0.00020	0.00028	0.0080	0.0110	0.012

unstable confidence rules, the error in confidence on the qth block is 16.8% on average, while the error in confidence for stable confidence rules is only 3.5%. The errors with the insurance data are smaller because this dataset is large and thus the variance is small. Note that the MSE and MAE values are not computed for trend rules, as it is not reasonable to use the mean confidence as the predicted confidence in the next time period due to the trend. Our trend test is mainly to give the user an indication that trends exist rather than predict the confidence of the rule in the future, for which we need a larger sample (large q) and further statistical analysis.

Table 5 gives the corresponding results on the analysis of supports. From column 2 and 3, we see that almost all stable support rules are still stable. A large majority of semi-stable support rules are also still semi-stable (column 4). Column 5 shows that most trend rules still exhibit trends. From column 6-11, we observe that the stable support rules commit least error. The results from both Table 4 and 5 confirm that stable rules and trend rules identified by our technique are indeed reliable, and can be trusted in the future.

6. Conclusions

Association mining is an important data mining task. Its application is, however, hampered by the fact that it often generates a large number of rules. In this paper, we argue that the large number of rules is only part of the problem. Lack of systematic analysis procedures to help the user understand the behavior of rules is also a major issue. Without understanding the behavior of a rule over time, the rule cannot be used in practice. This paper presented a number of statistical tests to analyze the behavior of rules. Using these tests, we are able to identify stable rules and trend rules, and at the same time remove those unreliable (unstable) rules. Experiment results showed that the proposed technique is very effective and efficient.

References

[1]. Aggarwal, C., and Yu, P. "Online generation of association rules." *ICDE-98*, 402-411.

[2]. Agrawal, R. and Psaila, G. "Active data mining." *KDD-95*, 1995.

[3]. Agrawal, R. and Srikant, R. "Fast algorithms for mining association rules." *VLDB-94*, 1994.

[4]. Bayardo, R. and Agrawal, R. "Mining the most interesting rules" *KDD-99*, 1999.

[5]. Dong, G. and J. Li. "Efficient mining of emerging patterns: discovering trends and differences." *KDD-99*, 1999.

[6]. Ganti, V., Gehrke, J., and Ramakrishnan, R. "A framework for measuring changes in data characteristics" *POPS-99*.

[7]. Ganti, V. Gehrke, J. and Ramakrishnan, R.
"DEMON: Mining and Monitoring Evolving Data." *ICDE-2000*.

[8]. Hamilton, L. C. *Modern data analysis: a first course in applied statistics*, Brooks/Cole, 1990.

[9]. Han, J. and Fu, Y. "Discovery of multiple-level association rules from large databases." *VLDB-95*.

[10]. Hilderman, R. and Hamilton, H. "Principles for Mining Summaries Using Objective Measures of Interestingness." *ICTAI-00*, 2000.

[11]. Hogg, R. & Craig, A. *Introduction to mathematical statistics*. Macmillan Publishing, 1970.

[12]. Klemetinen, M., Mannila, H., Ronkainen, P., Toivonen, H., and Verkamo, A.I. "Finding interesting rules from large sets of discovered association rules." *CIKM-94*, 1994.

[13]. Liu, B., Hu, M. and Hsu, W. "Multi-level organization and summarization of the discovered rules." *KDD-2000*.

[14]. Liu, B. Hsu, W. and Ma, Y. "Pruning and summarizing the discovered associations." *KDD-99*.

[15]. Liu, B., Hsu, W. Mun, L. and Lee, H. "Finding interesting patterns using user expectations." *IEEE Trans. on Knowl. & Data Eng*, vol: 11(6), 1999.

[16]. Liu, H., Lu, H., Feng, F and Hussain, F. "Efficient search of reliable exceptions." *PAKDD-99*, 1999.

[17]. Mann, P. S. *Introductory statistics*. John Wiley & Sons, 1998.

[18]. Megiddo, M. and Srikant, R. "Discovering predictive association rules." *KDD-98*, 1998.

[19]. Merz, C. J, and Murphy, P. UCI repository of machine learning databases, 1996. [http://www.cs.uci.edu/~mlearn/MLRepository.html].

[20]. Ng, R., Lakshmanan, L. Han, J. "Exploratory mining and pruning optimizations of constrained association rules." *SIGMOD-98*, 1998.

[21]. Padmanabhan, B., and Tuzhilin, A. "A belief-driven method for discovering unexpected patterns." *KDD-98*, 1998.

[22]. Piatesky-Shapiro, G., and Matheus, C. "The interestingness of deviations." *KDD-94*, 1994.

[23]. Silberschatz, A., and Tuzhilin, A. "What makes patterns interesting in knowledge discovery systems." *IEEE Trans. on Know. and Data Eng.* 8(6), 1996, pp. 970-974.

[24]. Suzuki, E. "Autonomous discovery of reliable exception rules." *KDD-97*, 1997.

[25]. Tan, P-N. and Kumar, V. "Interestingness measures for association patterns: a perspective." *KDD-2000 Workshop on Post-processing in Machine Learning and Data Mining*, 2000.

[26]. Walpole, R & Myers, R. *Probability and statistics for engineers and scientists*. Prentice Hall, 1993.

[27]. Zaki, M. "Generating non-redundant association rules." *KDD-2000*, 2000.

[28]. Zhong, N., Ohshima, M., & Ohsuga, S. "Peculiarity Oriented Mining and Its Application for Knowledge Discovery in Amino-acid Data." *PAKDD-2001*.

Closing the Loop: an Agenda- and Justification-Based Framework for Selecting the Next Discovery Task to Perform

Gary R. Livingston
University of Pittsburgh
gary@cs.pitt.edu

John M. Rosenberg
University of Pittsburgh
jmr@jmr3.xtal.pitt.edu

Bruce G. Buchanan
University of Pittsburgh
buchanan@cs.pitt.edu

Abstract

We propose and evaluate an agenda- and justification-based architecture for discovery systems that selects the next tasks to perform. This framework has many desirable properties: (1) it facilitates the encoding of general discovery strategies using a variety of background knowledge, (2) it reasons about the appropriateness of the tasks being considered, and (3) it tailors its behavior toward a user's interests. A prototype discovery program called HAMB demonstrates that both reasons and estimates of interestingness contribute to performance in the domains of protein crystallization and patient rehabilitation.

1. Introduction

The rapid growth of data available for knowledge discovery argues for fully autonomous machine learning and knowledge discovery in databases (KDD) systems. However, most current machine learning systems require manual assistance, making numerous runs while adjusting one or more parameters and manually inspecting the discoveries to identify the interesting ones. Autonomous discovery systems will save much of this time, eliminate human error, and examine orders-of-magnitude more hypotheses in the search for interesting discoveries. When using larger datasets, with more attributes to investigate, using an autonomous discovery system becomes even more desirable.

Moreover, autonomous discovery systems can be much more powerful, because they can flexibly use multiple strategies, rather than be limited to a single discovery strategy. However, because the space of possible hypotheses is immense, an autonomous discovery system must have strong heuristics to focus on tasks and goals that are more likely to be interesting [1].

One necessary capability of an autonomous discovery system is the ability to choose the next task to perform. The research presented here evaluates an agenda- and justification-based framework for implementing autonomous discovery programs and its mechanism for deciding which task to perform next.

1.1. The framework

The agenda- and justification-based framework, derived from that of AM [2], consists of an agenda of tasks prioritized by their *plausibility*. Plausibility is calculated using a function of *strengths* of *reasons* given for performing a task and estimates of the *interestingness* of the items the task operates upon. An *item* is an instance of the space being searched for discoveries (e.g., rules or subsets of the data). Each task is an operation upon zero or more items. Reasons are qualitative representations of the theoretical support and fit of the tasks to the discovery problem, and strengths are corresponding quantitative representations. By making this theoretical support and fit explicit, the framework facilitates reasoning about the appropriateness of tasks.

Tasks are performed using heuristics that create new items for further exploration and that place new tasks on the agenda. When putting a new task on the agenda, a heuristic must also provide reasons and corresponding strengths for performing the task. New reasons given for performing a task already on the agenda are attached to the existing task, thus increasing its plausibility.

Figure 1 sketches the framework's top-level control.

1.2. Plausibility function

The plausibility function we used is: $Plausibility(T) = (\Sigma R_T) * (\Sigma Interestingness(I_T))$, where $\{R_T\}$ is the set of the strengths of T's reasons, and $\{Interestingness(I_T)\}$ represents the estimated interestingness of T's items.

This function has three properties that may be necessary for appropriate task selection [2]:

- The plausibility of a task is a monotonically increasing function of each of its reasons' strengths. If a new supporting reason is found, the task's value is increased. The better that new reason, the bigger the increase.
- If an already known supporting reason is re-proposed, the plausibility of the associated task is not increased.
- The plausibiliy of a task involving an item C should be a monotonically increasing function of the esti-

0. Initialize the agenda
1. Compute the plausibilities of the tasks on the agenda using the strengths of the reasons given for performing them and the interestingness of the items involved in the tasks.
2. Select and remove from the agenda the task with the greatest plausibility.
3. Perform the task using heuristics, involving one or more of:
   - Proposing new tasks
   - Evaluating items
   - Creating new items
   - Examining relationships among the items
4. Check the stopping criterion, and if it is met, stop the discovery process. Otherwise, loop back to Step 1.

Figure 1. Top-level control of the framework.

mated interestingness of C. Two similar tasks dealing with two different concepts, each supported by the same list of reasons and strengths of reasons, should be ordered by the interestingness of those two concepts.

1.3. Evaluation

We evaluated the framework and its plausibility function by implementing them in a prototype, HAMB (pronounced HamBEE), and using HAMB to make discoveries from data taken from two domains: macromolecule crystallization and patient rehabilitation. Our evaluations suggest that HAMB is a general and capable discovery program and that using reasons and interestingness to select tasks is better than using either alone.

To conserve space and because HAMB is not the primary focus of this paper, we only summarize the implementation of HAMB. For more details of the heuristics used in HAMB and their evaluation, the reader is directed to [3] and to [4].

2. An example

Figure 2 presents an example designed to show the basic operation of the framework and how the framework's use of the strengths of reasons for performing tasks may be used to tailor its behavior to fit the data and discovery problem. To keep the example simple, it is concocted rather than taken from an actual trace of HAMB, but it is closely patterned after actual traces generated by HAMB. *Predictivity* between two attributes is the ratio of the reduction in entropy of the second attribute's values when using the first attribute to partition the cases to the entropy of the first attribute's values (c.f., Quinlan's information-gain [5]).

3. The HAMB program

HAMB uses rule induction as its primary method for discovering patterns and uses the rule-induction program

RL [6], a descendant of Meta-DENDRAL [7]. RL is efficient, flexible, robust with respect to incomplete or noisy data, and uses a variety of domain knowledge.

Because HAMB uses rule induction to perform empirical discovery, HAMB's items are attributes, examples, rule-conjuncts, and rules, plus sets of any of these. HAMB's discoveries are items with interesting properties or relationships.

HAMB estimates the interestingness of its items and discoveries using a hierarchical weighted sum of their properties, with the weights forming a simple model of the user's interestingness function. Interested readers are directed to [4] for details of HAMB's estimation of interestingness.

HAMB's stopping condition is: (1) the agenda is empty, (2) the plausibility of all tasks on the agenda falls below a user-specified threshold (i.e., no task is interesting enough), or (3) the number of completed discovery cycles exceeds a user-defined threshold.

HAMB's input is a database of cases from which discoveries are to be made, an optional testing database of cases, and a domain-theory which contains domain specific information, such as known relationships among the attributes.

HAMB reports as discoveries those items with interesting relationships or properties. A property or relationship is interesting if its value exceeds a threshold provided for each relationship or property. HAMB creates a report for each relationship or property, where the items having values for that property or relationship greater than or equal to the threshold are listed in decreasing order.

Table 1 presents an overview of HAMB's task-types and heuristics. Although most of the task-types have only one heuristic, the framework allows for more than one heuristic per task-type.

4. Evaluation

Several experiments with HAMB using data taken from the domain of macromolecule crystallization were performed. Those related to task selection are reported here. The other experiments are presented in [3] and [4]. The studies presented in this paper are:

- *Evaluation of HAMB's behavior* to see if, as hypothesized, it is able to adapt its behavior to the data.
- *Evaluation of HAMB's discoveries* to study HAMB's efficacy.
- *Evaluation of the plausibility function.* We used a lesion study to determine if using the plausibility function to select the next task to perform is more helpful than randomly selecting tasks from the agenda or using the strengths assigned to the reasons or interestingness alone.

DISCOVERY CYCLE 101
Agenda:
Task–100 *Examine-relationship (age, pneumonia, predictivity)*   Item interestingness: 70, 100   Plausibility: 17,000
  Reason: Need to examine age's predictivity of pneumonia   Strength: 100
Task–30: Examine-item (weight)   Item interestingness: 120   Plausibility: 9,600
  Reason: Never been examined   Strength: 80
Task–40: Induce-rule-set (pneumonia)   Item interestingness: 100   Plausibility: 5,000
  Reason: Pneumonia is a target-attribute   Strength: 50

Performing Task–100: examine-relationship (age, pneumonia, predictivity)   Plausibility: 17,000
  Reasons:
    Haven't examined age's predictivity of pneumonia   Strength: 100

  Applicable heuristics: general-examine-relationship
  Performing general-examine-item heuristic:
    Calculating predictivity of age for pneumonia
    Predictivity (age, pneumonia) is 0.306; age may be a predictor of pneumonia

  Proposing new task: Induce-rule-set (pneumonia)
    Age may be a predictor of pneumonia (predictivity: 0.306)   Strength: 61
  Proposing new task: Examine-item (age)
    Predictivity (age, pneumonia) has changed from NIL to 0.8   Strength: 40
  Proposing new task: Examine-item (pneumonia)
    Predictivity (age, pneumonia) has changed from NIL to 0.8   Strength: 40

DISCOVERY CYCLE 102
Agenda:
Task–40: Induce-rule-set (pneumonia)   Item interestingness: 100   Plausibility: 11,100
  Reason: Pneumonia is a target-attribute   Strength: 50
  Reason: Age may be a predictor of pneumonia (predictivity: 0.306)   Strength: 61
Task–30: Examine-item (weight)   Item interestingness: 120   Plausibility: 10,200
  Reason: Never been examined   Strength: 85
Task–131: Examine-item (pneumonia)   Item interestingness: 100   Plausibility: 4,000
  Reason: Predictivity (age, pneumonia) has changed from NIL to 0.8   Strength: 40
Task–132: Examine-item (age)   Item interestingness: 70   Plausibility: 2,800
  Reason: Predictivity (age, pneumonia) has changed from NIL to 0.8   Strength: 40

Figure 2. An artificial example illustrating the use of reasons to prioritize tasks and the effects of performing a task. Task–40 is reproposed during the execution of Task–100, and since it was already on the agenda for another reason, the new reason given for performing the task is attached to Task–40, causing its plausibility to be increased proportionally to the strength of the new reason.

- *Evaluation of HAMB's assignment of strengths to the reasons given for performing tasks* to see if the strengths can be used to direct HAMB toward a desired behavior.
- *Evaluation of HAMB's generality.*

4.1. Macromolecule crystallization data

This dataset consists of reports of experiments for growing crystals of proteins, nucleic acids, or larger complexes, such as proteins bound to DNA, for X-ray diffraction and subsequent determination of three-dimensional structure [8]. These data have been problematic machine-learning and clustering techniques for a variety of reasons: no clear target attribute, a high level of redundancy in the data, heterogeneous data (e.g., nucleic acids crystallize under a very different set of conditions than proteins), and a high degree of noisy and incomplete data.

The database consists of 2,225 examples of crystallization experiments, each with 225 attributes. The attributes include:

- macromolecular properties—macromolecule name, macromolecule-class name, and molecular weight;
- experimental conditions—pH, temperature, crystallization method, macromolecular concentration, and concentrations of chemical additives in the growth medium;
- characteristics of the grown crystal (if any)—descriptors of the crystal's shape (e.g., CRFORM, and SPGRPS-DESC) and its diffraction-limit, which measures how well the crystal diffracts.

4.2. Evaluation of HAMB's behavior

We evaluated HAMB's ability to respond opportunistically to the data by examining traces showing its choices. In particular we asked about the program's abilities to (a) propose new tasks, (b) reason about the appropriateness of the tasks, and (c) direct its behavior toward tasks more likely to produce interesting discoveries.

Figure 3 presents narrative descriptions of four excerpts from a run of HAMB upon the data that illustrate HAMB's ability to tailor its tasks to the data. The first

Table 1. An overview of HAMB's task-types and heuristics. *Tasks* indicates the type of task, *Summary of heuristics* provides a summary of how the tasks are performed by heuristics, and *Calls* indicates which other types of tasks are proposed while performing the current type of task. Examine-item tasks are proposed during initialization to examine a given dataset and the attributes used to describe its cases.

Tasks	Summary of heuristics	Calls
Tasks examining items		
examine-item (*item*)	Check *item's* membership in item-groups, evaluate *item's* properties, and estimate its interestingness.	examine-relationships-with select-training-set
examine-relationships-with (*item*)	For each type of relationship *R* defined to hold with *item*, propose an examine-relationships-with task.	examine-r-relationships
examine-r-relationships (*item, R*)	For each possible relationship of type R that could hold with *item*, if the relationship may be evaluated quickly then do so. Otherwise propose a task for examining that relationship.	examine-relationship examine-item select-training-set
examine-relationship (*item₁, item₂, ... itemₙ, R*)	Evaluate the *R* relationship among *item₁, item₂, ... itemₙ*.	examine-item
Tasks creating new items		
select-training-set (*target attribute*)	Select a training set from which rules predicting *target attribute* will be induced.	select-feature-set
select-feature-set (*target attribute, training set*)	Select a feature set from which rules predicting *target attribute* will be formed.	select-bias
select-bias (*target attribute, training set, feature set*)	Select a bias for inducing rules predicting *target attribute* using hill-climbing. Use cross-validation upon *training set* to evaluate the biases.	examine-item induce-rule-set
induce-rule-set (*target attribute, training set, feature set, bias*)	Induce a rule set predicting *target attribute* using the selected *training set, feature set,* and *bias*.	examine-item create-exception-set
create-exception-set (*rule set, training set*)	Create an exception set for *rule set*.	examine-item select-feature-set

excerpt, shown at discovery cycle 5, illustrates a heuristic opportunistically identifying a potential rule-induction target. The second excerpt, shown at cycle 1,029, shows HAMB assigning low strengths to a task its heuristics suggest would not lead to a promising line of investigation: Finally, the excerpt at cycle 1,202, shows HAMB selecting a training set for predicting values for the attribute ADD-IRON-[II]-CITRATE (the concentration of the additive iron-[II]-citrate) because it has determined that ADD-IRON-[II]-CITRATE may be an "easy" rule-induction target (not shown are the many reasons HAMB found for doing so).

4.3. Evaluation of HAMB's discoveries

After semi-manual removal of redundant discoveries HAMB made from the crystal-growing database, 431 discoveries were presented to one of the authors (JMR, a crystallographer) for categorization of their significance and novelty. His categorizations are presented in Table 2. The redundant rules removed during the semi-manual filtering (approximately 144) are counted as Category 0 discoveries (uninteresting) in the table.[1] One Category II discovery that caught Dr. Rosenberg's interest is an *improving-rule-specialization* relationship between two rules in which the first rule is specialized by the second and the positive predictive value (PPV) of the specialization is greater than that of the first rule. The first rule

matches 63 examples correctly and 97 examples incorrectly (PPV= 0.39):

> *Rule 1: An organic amine is present ⇒ the macromolecule being crystallized is a nucleic acid.*

The second rule of the relationship intensionally specializes the first:

> *Rule 2: An organic amine is present AND ammonium is not present ⇒ the macromolecule being crystallized is a nucleic acid,*

refining the general domain knowledge represented by Rule 1. This rule matches 62 examples correctly and 25 examples incorrectly (PPV= 0.71).

Rule 1 captures the general but imprecise domain knowledge that "Organic amines tend to promote the growth of nucleic acid crystals but are less likely to be of use in the crystallization of proteins." Rule 2 refines this general knowledge by adding the condition "ammonium is not present," which eliminated 72 incorrect predictions of the first rule while eliminating only one correct prediction.

4.4. Evaluation of the plausibility function

Given an expert's assessment (JMR's) of the degree of interest of over 400 discoveries, we performed lesion studies to further evaluate the plausibility function. To perform this experiment, we used HAMB and three variations:

* *Random-HAMB*, which selects the next task to perform randomly from the tasks on the agenda

---

[1] Future research will involve the automation of the method used to remove the redundant discoveries.

Cycle 5: HAMB examines predictivity relationships involving the attribute CRFORM before the other attributes because it has a higher estimated interestingness at this point in the discovery cycle
- Discovers two strong predictors of CRFORM and that CRFORM is highly predictive of several others.
- One of HAMB's heuristics suggests that it is easier to induce good rules for a target attribute with many good predictors, causing HAMB to propose a task to select a training set for inducing rules predicting CRFORM each time HAMB discovers a good predictor of CRFORM.
- Similarly, each time HAMB discovers that CRFORM is a good predictor of another attribute, HAMB proposes a task to select a training set for that attribute.

This excerpt illustrates a heuristic opportunistically identifying a potential rule-induction target.

Cycle 1,029: HAMB selects a training set for inducing rules predicting CRFORM's values before doing so for other attributes primarily because CRFORM has the greatest a priori interest to the user, but also because HAMB has discovered many good predictors of CRFORM
- HAMB creates the training set from the discovery-database's examples that do not have uninformative values for CRFORM (e.g., missing values, or "miscellaneous"), avoiding the induction of many uninteresting rules.
- The selected training set is small, containing only 164 out of 1,482 possible examples.
- Proposes the next step of inducing rules predicting CRFORM's values—selecting a feature set.
- Because HAMB believes that it is harder to induce good rules using a small training set, HAMB assigns very low strengths to the reasons it provides for selecting a feature set for CRFORM, causing HAMB to postpone performing the newly proposed task until cycle 11,172.
- When HAMB finally does induce a rule set for CRFORM, the accuracy of the induced rule set on the testing-database is 0.02.

This excerpt shows HAMB assigning low strengths to a task its heuristics suggest would not lead to a promising line of investigation.

Cycle: 1,123: HAMB selects a training set for inducing rules to predict the attribute SPGRPS-DESC
- The selected training set is fairly large, containing 1,305 examples.
- Once again, HAMB uses domain-knowledge to exclude examples that would cause the induction of uninformative rules and then proposes a task for selecting a feature set from which rules predicting SPGRPS-DESC may be induced.

Cycle 1,202: HAMB selects a training set for inducing rules predicting the attribute ADD-IRON-[II]-CITRATE
- HAMB selects a training set for ADD-IRON-[II]-CITRATE before most of the attributes not because it has a high estimated interestingness, but because HAMB found many reasons for performing this task.
- The selected training set contains 1,482 out of 1,482 possible examples.

This excerpt depicts HAMB performing a task because it has determined that ADD-IRON-[II]-CITRATE may be an "easy" rule-induction target (not shown are the many reasons HAMB found for doing so), not because its ADD-IRON-[II]-CITRATE is especially interesting to the user.

Figure 3. Excerpts taken from a run of HAMB upon the macromolecule crystal-growing data illustrating HAMB's ability to be opportunistic as well as to postpone less-promising tasks in favor of more-promising ones.

- *Reasons-Only-HAMB*, which computes the plausibility of a task as the sum of the strengths of the task's reasons
- *Interestingness-Only-HAMB*, which computes a task's plausibility as the sum of the estimates of the interestingness of the items involved in the task

Figure 4 presents a graph of the sum of the interestingness of the discoveries reported by the three versions of HAMB during periodic reports of their discoveries versus the discovery cycle that followed the generation of the reports.

When comparing the graphs for HAMB and Random-HAMB in Figure 4, note that for the first approximately 1,500 discovery cycles, Random-HAMB's total interestingness is greater than HAMB's, after which HAMB's scores equal or exceed Random-HAMB's. We attribute this difference to preliminary investigations HAMB performs of the attributes and their relationships before inducing rule sets. The additional time HAMB spends examining the attributes is useful in reducing the redundancy of its discoveries. The plot shown in Figure 4 only reports the total interestingness of the reported discoveries, not their redundancy; but another study showed that HAMB is able to use this discovered knowledge to reduce the redundancy in its induced rule sets by 19% [3].

The difference between the two plots for HAMB and Random-HAMB after 1,500 discovery cycles is statistically significant (p-value is 0.007).[2] Differences are significant between HAMB and Reasons-Only-HAMB (p-value is 0.003) and between HAMB and Interestingness-Only-HAMB (p-value is 0.049).

We also compared the average interestingness of the discoveries made by the four versions of HAMB and found that the plot for Random-HAMB was slightly better, and the p-value of the difference between these two plots is 0.015.

Random-HAMB's selection of tasks is not truly random. The tasks are randomly selected from the agenda, not from the space of all possible tasks; therefore, Random-HAMB's behavior is aided by the heuristics which propose the tasks, biasing its task selection toward more appropriate tasks. If Random-HAMB's tasks were selected from the space of all possible tasks rather than the space of tasks chosen by the heuristics, Random-HAMB's performance would probably be much worse.

Moreover, to conserve time, the complexity of many of the tasks was reduced: for example, HAMB uses an

---

[2] A paired t-test was used to evaluate the statistical differences of the plots; significance level for rejecting H_0 is $p \leq 0.05$. The p-value of the difference between the entire plots for Random-HAMB and HAMB is 0.158.

Table 2. Categories used by an expert to assess the interestingness of 531 discoveries made by HAMB from the macromolecule crystallization domain. The redundant rules removed during the semi-manual filtering (approximately 144) are counted as Category 0 discoveries.

Category	Significance	Number	Percent
IV	Individually, these discoveries could be the basis of a publication in the crystallography literature, being both novel and extremely significant to the crystallography literature	0 / 575	0
III	In groups of about a dozen, these discoveries could form the core of research papers in the crystallography literature	92 / 575	16
II	These discoveries are about as significant as Category III, but are not novel	192 / 575	33
I	These discoveries are not as interesting as Category II or III, but still are of some interest	51 / 575	9
0	These discoveries are any discoveries that are not Category I, II, III, or IV	240/ 575	42

iterative cross-validation process to select a bias to be given to the rule-induction program. For this study, only a few bias points were examined using two-fold cross-validation. In addition, the size of the database given to HAMB was reduced to 500 cases. When more complex tasks are added or the size of the database is increased, we expect that the improvement in HAMB's performance over that of the other versions will increase.

Note that HAMB often uses the results of tasks performed earlier when performing the current task; therefore, *the order in which the tasks are performed is important;* for example, HAMB's aforementioned use of its discoveries to reduce its redundant discoveries.

4.5. Evaluation of HAMB's assignment of reasons and strengths to tasks

HAMB's heuristics use the results of performing one phase of inducing a rule set, such as selecting a training set, to assign reasons and corresponding strengths to the task for the next phase, such as selecting a feature set. By doing so, the reasons and their strengths should help HAMB to tailor its behavior to the data and induce rule sets for target attributes that may have better test accuracies. (We preferred this behavior because we reasoned that more accurate rule sets would yield more interesting discoveries.)

To evaluate the effectiveness of the heuristics in assigning reasons and corresponding strengths, we examined the strengths of the reasons at three points in the process of inducing a rule set (to conserve space, plots of the data, which are referred to in the following paragraphs, are not shown; these plots may be found in [4]):

- *before performing* select-training-set *tasks, when the strengths of reasons given for selecting a training set reflect the predictiveness of attributes toward target attributes.* Regressing a line between the strengths of the reasons given for performing the tasks and the accuracy of the induced rule sets on the test database revealed little correlation (a coefficient of determination of 0.02). However, visual examination of a plot of the data indicates that there are two groups of datapoints: those for which the strengths of the reasons are suggestive of the test accuracy of the induced rule set and those for which the test accuracy is zero. If those da-

tapoints with a test accuracy of zero are removed, the coefficient of determination goes up to 0.37.

- *after selecting a training set, when the strengths have been adjusted to account for the size of the selected training set.* A plot of the sizes of the training sets to the test accuracy of the induced rule sets shows little correlation with a coefficient of determination of 0.02. However, very few rule sets induced from smaller training sets (containing fewer than approximately 300 examples) had accuracies on the test database greater than 0.3. Therefore, while large training set size may be insufficient for predicting a high accuracy for an induced rule set, small training set size may be useful for predicting low accuracy on the test database, allowing HAMB to identify less-promising rule-induction tasks.

- *after selecting the parametric bias.* A plot of the strengths of the reasons given for the last task performed when inducing rule sets—the actual induction of the rule set—to the accuracies of the induced rule sets on the test database indicates a strong correlation, with a coefficient of determination of 0.86.

These results and the results of the lesion study demonstrate HAMB's ability to use its heuristics to assign reasons and corresponding strengths to the tasks, allowing HAMB to adapt its behavior to fit the data, in this case allowing HAMB to achieve the desired behavior of inducing rules with greater test accuracies first.

4.6. Evaluation of generality

To evaluate the generality of the system, we used HAMB to perform discovery from a second database: 930 cases of patients in rehabilitation after a medical disability, such as stroke or amputation. There are 11 attributes in the database, ranging from demographic data to admission and discharge scores of the patients' functional independence. Thus, this database represents a domain that is dissimilar to the macromolecule crystallization domain. After running HAMB upon this data, we presented HAMB's discoveries to the physician who provided us with the data, Dr. Louis Penrod of the University of Pittsburgh Medical Center. His examination of the discoveries revealed that there were 26 (9%) Category III discoveries, of which 2 were bordering on Cate-

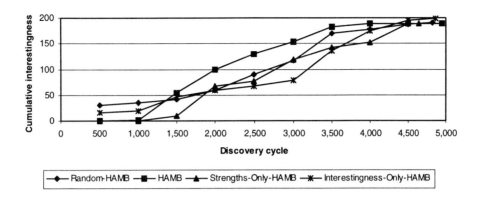

Figure 4. Plot of the total interestingness of reported discoveries versus the discovery cycle for each of the four versions of HAMB. Interestingness is the sum of the category numbers assigned by Dr. Rosenberg to the discoveries reported by the four versions of HAMB. Discovery cycle is the discovery cycle before which the discoveries are reported.

gory IV (revolutionary), 5 (2%) were Category II discoveries, 53 were (18%) Category I discoveries (marginally interesting), and 215 (71%) were uninteresting. Because of the smaller number of attributes, we were able to represent almost all of the known relationships among the attributes, which HAMB's heuristics were able to use to greatly reduced the number of Category II (non-novel, but significant) discoveries.

5. Discussion

HAMB demonstrated that it is able to tailor its tasks to the data, being opportunistic by identifying better rule-induction targets and postponing less-promising lines of investigation in favor of more-promising ones. HAMB also demonstrated that it considers the user's interests when deciding which task to perform. Finally, HAMB demonstrated that it uses knowledge about performing discovery, which is contained in HAMB's heuristics, to propose tasks and to provide reasons and corresponding strengths for performing those tasks. We also used HAMB to make discoveries from a second domain, suggesting that HAMB and the proposed framework are general, thus easily adapted to make discoveries from data taken from new domains.

5.1. Related work

The agenda- and justification-based framework presented in this paper was adapted from the framework used in Lenat's AM and EURISKO discovery programs [2]. AM is recognized as one of the best-known artificial intelligence programs of the 1970s [9] and discovers concepts in the domain of number theory. Because discovery in an empirical science is different, HAMB uses new sets of concepts, tasks, and heuristics. The modifications made to AM's framework are:

- Tasks may operate upon zero or more items, not strictly upon a specific slot of one item as with AM.
- The slots used to represent items may vary with item-type, instead of being fixed as they are in AM.
- The manipulated and discovered items are *instances* and sets of instances of the meta-concepts (e.g., the attribute CRFORM) used in the type of discovery being performed, not the meta-concepts themselves (e.g., the concept *of an attribute*), as they are in AM. Using the proposed framework, as long as the heuristics are domain-independent and modify only *instances* and sets of instances of the meta-concepts, not the meta-concepts themselves, the heuristics will remain applicable, rather than suffer from losing their applicability, as with AM.
- The function for computing a task's plausibility is a simplification of AM's priority function.

No published system completely combines all phases of the empirical discovery process, although KDD planning systems, such as the framework presented in [10], perform sequences of tasks for a discovery goal *provided by a user*. Similarly, multistrategy systems such as [11] perform multiple discovery operations; but again, the discovery goals are provided by a user. Evaluation of the discovered patterns is also left to the user. Therefore, while these systems have an increase in autonomy over traditional KDD systems, they do not run autonomously.

When viewed along the spectrum of autonomy, "single-shot" learning programs, such as linear regression, neural networks, or rule learning systems, have the least autonomy, followed by programs that automatically select their bias, such as COMBS and CLIMBS [12] and multistrategy and KDD-planning systems that may perform more than one task but require a user to examine their results and select new discovery goals. Then come intelligent assistant programs, such as Shen's assistant for defining metapatterns [13], AIDE [14], and IDEA [15], which propose new tasks but still require a user to choose the next task and to select top-level goals. Toward the end of this spectrum lies HAMB, which autonomously performs the entire discovery process (after the datasets have been collected and verified).

5.2. Scaling up and future work

The overhead incurred by the framework is small compared to the complexity of the performed tasks. The complexity of computing plausibility and selecting the task with the greatest plausibility is $O(n)$, where n is the number of tasks on the agenda. The complexity of the RL induction program in the inner loop is $O(n*m)$ where n is the number of cases and m is the number of attributes. RL takes about 20 seconds to find rules in a dataset of 1,000 cases and 100 attributes.

Future work involves devising more heuristics for autonomous discovery. HAMB's heuristics, [3,4], form solutions for periodically examining the items' relationships and properties and demonstrate that the use of heuristics seems to facilitate the use of domain knowledge. Additional heuristics are needed that can better take advantage of an autonomous discovery system's ability to perform more than one task, such as being able to use more than one task to evaluate its discoveries or to examine patterns that may be found by examining the results of more than one task, such as a group of cases that unexplicably behave differently for a variety of tasks.

6. Conclusions

Our results suggest that the proposed agenda- and justification-based framework may provide a sufficient mechanism for selecting the next task to perform for implementing fully autonomous discovery systems and that heuristics may be appropriate vehicles for proposing new tasks and providing justifications for performing them. Our experiments also suggest that both the strengths of *reasons* for performing tasks and the estimates of the *interestingness* of the tasks' items are useful in selecting the next task to perform. In addition, we have demonstrated the framework's and HAMB's generality by using HAMB to make significant discoveries from data taken from two dissimilar scientific domains.

7. Acknowledgments

We thank John Aronis, Tom Fawcett, David Jensen, Foster Provost, and anonymous reviewers for their numerous discussions and suggestions. This work was funded in part by grants from the National Library of Medicine (1 G08 LM006625-01, the National Center for Research Resources (RR14477–2), and the National Science Foundation (9412549).

References

[1] Zytkow, J. M. 1993. Introduction: Cognitive Autonomy in Machine Discovery. *Machine Learning 12*: 7-16.

[2] Lenat, D. 1982. AM: Discovery in Mathematics as Heuristic Search. In Davis, R. and Lenat, D., Eds., *Knowledge-Based Systems in Artificial Intelligence*, 3-225. New York: McGraw-Hill.

[3] Livingston, G. R., Rosenberg, J. M., and Buchanan, B. G. 2001. Closing the Loop: Heuristics for Autonomous Discovery. To appear in *Proc. of the 2001 IEEE Intl. Conf. on Data Mining*, San Jose, CA, Nov. 29–Dec. 2. IEEE Computer Society Press.

[4] Livingston, G. R. 2001. *A Framework for Autonomous Knowledge Discovery from Databases*. Ph.D. Diss., Dept. of Computer Science, Univ. of Pittsburgh, Pittsburgh, PA.

[5] Quinlan, J. R. 1993. *C4.5: Programs for Machine Learning*. San Francisco, CA: Morgan Kaufmann.

[6] Provost, F. J. and Buchanan, B. G. 1995. Inductive Policy: The Pragmatics of Bias Selection. *Machine Learning 20*(1): 35-61.

[7] Buchanan, B. G. and Mitchell, T. 1978. Model-Directed Learning of Production Rules. In Waterman, D. A. and Hayes-Roth, F., Eds., *Pattern Directed Inference Systems*, 297-312. New York, NY: Academic Press.

[8] Hennessy, D., Buchanan, B., Subramanian, D., Wilkosz, P., and Rosenberg, J. 2000. Statistical Methods for the Objective Design of Screening Procedures for Macromolecule Crystallization. *Acta Crystallographica Section D*: 817-827.

[9] Dietterich, T. G. and Shavlik, J. W. 1990. Discovery. In Shavlik, J. W. and Dietterich, T. G., Eds., *Readings in Machine Learning*, 337-340. San Mateo, CA: Morgan Kaufmann Publishers.

[10] Engels, R. 1996. Planning Tasks for Knowledge Discovery in Databases; Performing Task-Oriented User-Guidance. In *Proc. of the Second Intl. Conf. on Knowledge Discovery and Data Mining*, 170-175, Portland, OR, Aug. 2-4. Menlo Park, CA: AAAI Press.

[11] Klosgen, W. 1996. Explora: A Multipattern and Multistrategy Discovery Assistant. In Fayyad, U., Piatetsky-Shapiro, G., Smyth, P., and Uthurusamy, R., Eds., *Advances in Knowledge Discovery and Data Mining*, 249-271. Menlo Park, CA: AAAI Press.

[12] Provost, F. J. 1992. *Policies for the Selection of Bias in Inductive Machine Learning*. Ph.D. Diss., Dept. of Computer Science, Univ. of Pittsburgh, Pittsburgh, PA.

[13] Shen, W.-M. and Leng, B. 1996. A Metapattern-Based Automated Discovery Loop for Integrated Data Mining. *IEEE Trans. on Knowledge and Data Engineering 8*(6): 898-910.

[14] Amant, R. S. and Cohen, P. R. 1997a. Evaluation of a Semi-Autonomous Assistant for Exploratory Data Analysis. In *Proc. of the First Intl. Conf. on Autonomous Agents*, 355-362, Marina Del Rey, CA, February 5-8. ACM Press.

[15] Bernstein, A. and Provost, F. 2001. An Intelligent Assistant for the Knowledge Discovery Process. In *Proc. of the IJCAI-01 Workshop on Wrappers for Performance Enhancement in KDD*, Seattle, WA, Aug. 4. Morgan Kaufmann.

Closing the Loop: Heuristics for Autonomous Discovery

Gary R. Livingston
202 Mineral Industries Building
Univ. of Pittsburgh
Pittsburgh, PA 15260
gary@cs.pitt.edu

John M. Rosenberg
312 Clapp Hall
Univ. of Pittsburgh
Pittsburgh, PA 15260
jmr@jmr3.xtal.pitt.edu

Bruce G. Buchanan
206 Mineral Industries Building
Univ. of Pittsburgh
Pittsburgh, PA 15260
buchanan@cs.pitt.edu

Abstract

Autonomous discovery systems will be able to peruse very large databases more thoroughly than people can. In a companion paper [1], we describe a general framework for autonomous systems. We present and evaluate heuristics for use in this framework. Although these heuristics were designed for a prototype system, we believe they provide good initial solutions to problems encountered when implementing fully autonomous discovery systems. As such, these heuristics may be used as the starting point for future research into fully autonomous discovery systems.

1. Introduction

Autonomous discovery systems will be able to peruse very large databases more thoroughly than people can, will be able to free a considerable amount of a data-miner's time, and may be more easily used. In a companion paper [1], we describe a general agenda- and justification-based framework for implementing autonomous systems. Because the space of possible hypotheses is immense, an autonomous discovery system must have strong heuristics to focus on tasks and goals that are more likely to be interesting [2].

The research presented here evaluates domain-independent heuristics for use in autonomous discovery systems implementing the agenda- and justification-based framework. These heuristics (1) keep an item's properties and relationships sufficiently up-to-date, allowing a discovery system to select appropriate tasks without needlessly re-examining these properties and relationships after every task, (2) select rule-induction targets and other goals worth pursuing, and (3) use domain-specific knowledge to improve the quality of reported discoveries.

1.1. The agenda- and justification-based framework

The framework, discussed in [1], consists of an agenda of tasks prioritized by their plausibility, where a task's plausibility is calculated as a function of *strengths* of justifications (called *reasons*) given for performing the task and estimates of the *interestingness* of the items it operates upon. An item is an instance of the space being searched for discoveries (e.g., rules or subsets of the data). Each task is an operation upon zero or more items.

Tasks are performed using heuristics that create new items for further exploration and that place new tasks on the agenda. When proposing a new task to be put onto the agenda, a heuristic must also provide reasons and corresponding strengths for performing the task. New reasons given for performing a task already on the agenda are attached to the existing task, thus increasing its plausibility.

1.2. Evaluation

We evaluated our heuristics by implementing them in a prototype, HAMB (pronounced HamBEE), and using it to make discoveries from data taken from two domains: macromolecule crystallization and patient rehabilitation. Our evaluations suggest that the heuristics are useful in guiding the discovery process and in using background knowledge. A study of HAMB's generality shows that the heuristics are domain-independent.

Because the results of our experiments with HAMB provide support for both the agenda- and justification-based framework and our heuristics, we use many of them in [1] to support the framework and in this report to support our heuristics. We also present in this report the results of a study not reported in [1].

2. An example

Figure 1 presents an example designed to show the basic operation of the framework and its use of heuristics both to propose new tasks and to provide strengths of reasons for performing tasks (which are used to tailor a discovery system's behavior to the data). To keep the example simple, it is concocted rather than taken from an actual trace of HAMB, but it is closely patterned after actual traces generated by HAMB.

DISCOVERY CYCLE 101
Agenda:
Task–100 *Examine-relationship (age, pneumonia, predictivity)*   Item interestingness: 70, 100   Plausibility: 17,000
   Reason: Need to examine age's predictivity of pneumonia   Strength: 100
Task–30: Examine-item (weight)   Item interestingness: 120   Plausibility: 9,600
   Reason: Never been examined   Strength: 80
Task–40: Induce-rule-set (pneumonia)   Item interestingness: 100   Plausibility: 5,000
   Reason: Pneumonia is a target attribute   Strength: 50

Performing Task–100: examine-relationship (age, pneumonia, predictivity)   Plausibility: 17,000
   Reasons:
     Haven't examined age's predictivity of pneumonia   Strength: 100

   Applicable heuristics: general-examine-relationship
   Performing general-examine-item heuristic:
     Calculating predictivity of age for pneumonia
     Predictivity (age, pneumonia) is 0.306; age may be a predictor of pneumonia
     Proposing new task: Induce-rule-set (pneumonia)
       Age may be a predictor of pneumonia (predictivity: 0.306)   Strength: 61
     Proposing new task: Examine-item (age)
       Predictivity (age, pneumonia) has changed from NIL to 0.8   Strength: 40
     Proposing new task: Examine-item (pneumonia)
       Predictivity (age, pneumonia) has changed from NIL to 0.8   Strength: 40

DISCOVERY CYCLE 102
Agenda:
Task–40: Induce-rule-set (pneumonia)   Item interestingness: 100   Plausibility: 11,100
   Reason: Pneumonia is a target attribute   Strength: 50
   Reason: Age may be a predictor of pneumonia (predictivity: 0.306)   Strength: 61
Task–30: Examine-item (weight)   Item interestingness: 120   Plausibility: 10,200
   Reason: Never been examined   Strength: 85
Task–131: Examine-item (pneumonia)   Item interestingness: 100   Plausibility: 4,000
   Reason: Predictivity (age, pneumonia) has changed from NIL to 0.8   Strength: 40
Task–132: Examine-item (age)   Item interestingness: 70   Plausibility: 2,800
   Reason: Predictivity (age, pneumonia) has changed from NIL to 0.8   Strength: 40

Figure 1. An artificial example illustrating the use of reasons to prioritize tasks and the effects of performing a task. Each task is put on the agenda by a heuristic. Task-100 is to examine a predictive relationship from age to pneumonia and was suggested because predictivity is an interesting relationship and both the variables age and pneumonia are interesting. Examine-item tasks are proposed to examine *age* and *pneumonia* in cycle 102 because the value of their predictivity relationship has changed.

3. The HAMB program

As described in [1], HAMB uses rule induction as its primary method for discovering patterns and uses the rule-induction program RL [3], derived from Meta-DENDRAL [4]. Because HAMB mainly uses rule induction to perform discovery, HAMB's items are attributes, examples, rule-conjuncts, and rules, plus sets of these. HAMB's discoveries are items with interesting properties or relationships.

HAMB estimates the interestingness of its items and discoveries using a hierarchical weighted sum of their properties, with the weights forming a simple model of the user's interestingness function. Interested readers are directed to [5] for details of HAMB's estimation of interestingness.

HAMB's stopping condition is: (1) the agenda is empty, (2) the plausibility of all tasks on the agenda falls below a user-specified threshold (i.e., no task is interesting enough), or (3) the number of completed discovery cycles exceeds a user-defined threshold.

HAMB's input is a database of cases from which discoveries are to be made, an optional testing database of cases, and a *domain-theory* which contains domain-specific information, such as known relationships among the attributes.

HAMB reports as discoveries those items with interesting relationships or properties. A property or relationship is interesting if its value exceeds a threshold provided for each relationship or property. HAMB creates a report for each relationship or property, where the items having values for that property or relationship greater than or equal to the threshold are listed in decreasing order.

The types of tasks HAMB performs and its heuristics for performing them are presented in Table 1, and they are divided into two groups based upon function: those examining items and those creating new items. The task-types and heuristics for creating items may be further divided into two subgroups, those creating new items using rule induction and those creating new items using a deductive heuristic (creating exception sets). Due to space limitations, we could only briefly discuss these

394

Table 1. An overview of HAMB's task-types and heuristics. *Tasks* indicates the type of task and *summary of heuristics* provides a brief description of the heuristics performing the tasks. Not shown is that examine-item tasks are proposed during initialization.

Tasks	Summary of heuristics
Tasks examining items	
Examine-item (*item*)	Check *item's* membership in item-groups, evaluate item's properties, and estimate its interestingness. Propose *examine-relationships-with* (*item*) If *item* is an attribute and this is the first time *item* has been examined, then propose *select-training-set* (*item*)

Examine-relationships-with (*item*)	For each type of relationship R defined to hold with *item*:
	  Propose an *examine-relationships-with* task to examine all possible R relationships involving *item*
	    Assign a strength to the reason given for the task that is proportional to the utility of the relationship

Examine-r-relationships (*item, R*)	For each possible relationship of type R that could hold with *item*:
	  If the relationship may be evaluated quickly, then do so using a function given in the definition of R for evaluating R relationships[1]
	    Propose *examine-item* tasks to examine any items in relationships whose values have changed
	      Assign strengths to the reasons given for performing the tasks which are proportional to the change in the relationships' values
	  Otherwise propose an *examine-relationship* task to examine that relationship
	    Assign a strength to the reason given for performing the task that is proportional to the utility of the relationship

Examine-relationship (*item$_1$, item$_2$, ... item$_n$, R*)	Evaluate the R relationship among *item$_1$, item$_2$, ... item$_n$*[1] If the relationship's value has changed, propose *examine-item* tasks for *item$_1$, item$_2$, ... item$_n$* Assign strengths to the reasons given for performing the tasks which are proportional to the change in the relationships' values
Tasks creating new items	
Select-training-set (*target attribute*)	Select a training set from which rules predicting *target attribute* will be induced. Omit from the training set cases with missing values for *target attribute* Propose a select-feature-set task for *target attribute* Assign a strength to the reason given for performing the task that is proportional to the size of the selected training set

Select-feature-set (*target attribute, training set*)	Select a feature set from which rules predicting *target attribute* will be formed
	  Omit from the feature set the following attributes:
	    Attributes which are known or discovered to be a synonym to the target attribute
	    Attributes which are known to be or are definitionally related to *target attribute*
	    Attributes that have information-gains with the *target attribute* which are in the lower n percentile
	  If the feature set is not empty, propose a select-bias task for *target-attribute*
	    Assign to the newly proposed task the reasons and strengths associated with the current task

Select-bias (*target attribute, training set, feature set*)	Select a bias for inducing rules predicting *target attribute* using hill-climbing. Use cross-validation upon *training set* to evaluate the biases
	  Propose an *examine-item* task for each newly induced rule set
	  Propose an *examine-item* task for each newly induced rule
	  Propose an *examine-item* task for each attribute, rule-conjunct, or rule used in a newly induced rule set
	  Propose an *induce-rule-set* task for *target attribute*
	    Assign a strength to the reason given for performing the newly proposed *induce-rule-set* task that is proportional to the score of the selected bias

Induce-rule-set (*target attribute, training set, feature set, bias*)	Induce a rule set predicting *target attribute* using the selected *training set, feature set,* and *bias*
	  Propose an *examine-item* task for the induced rule set
	  Propose an *examine-item* task for each newly induced rule
	  Propose an *examine-item* task for each attribute, rule-conjunct, or rule used in the induced rule set
	Propose a *create-exception-set* task to create an exception set for the induced rule set
	  Assign a strength to the reason given for performing the newly proposed *create-exception-set* that is proportional to the test-accuracy of the induced rule set

Create-exception-set (*rule set, training set*)	Create an exception set for *rule set*. If the exception set is smaller than *training set*, then propose a *select-feature-set* task to begin the process of inducing a rule set from the exception set to "fill in the gaps" of the theory encoded in the rule set Assign a strength to the reason given for performing the task that is proportional to the size of the exception set and the test-accuracy of the rule set

---

[1] The function given for examining predictivity relationships contains a heuristic that proposes a select-training-set task for a target attribute whenever a predictor is found for that attribute. The strength of the reason given for the newly proposed task is proportional to the strength of the predictivity relationship.

heuristics in this paper. Readers are directed to [5] for full details of these heuristics.

3.1. Heuristics for examining items

Heuristics for examining items create tasks on the agenda that, essentially, look at what is known (given in the domain-theory or discovered by HAMB) about the named item(s) and determine whether some properties or relationships are interesting.

HAMB's heuristics for examining items solve a novel problem for fully autonomous discovery systems: keeping the values of an item's properties, relationships, and interestingness up-to-date without recalculating their values after every discovery cycle. HAMB's heuristics use satisficing to solve this problem: whenever a heuristic indicates that some aspect (property, relationship, or interestingness) of an item may have changed, a task is (re)proposed for reexamining the item. As HAMB's heuristics notice that more and more aspects of the item may have changed, more and more reasons accumulate for the task of examining the item, eventually causing the sum of the strengths of those reasons to become great enough to cause HAMB to examine the item.

3.2. Heuristics for inducing rule sets

When HAMB determines that an attribute of a set of objects might make an interesting target variable, heuristics propose a task for inducing rules predicting the value of that variable.

We decomposed the induction of rule sets into four subtasks: selecting a training set, selecting a feature set, selecting a parametric bias, and calling an induction program (RL) with the selected training set, feature set, and bias to actually induce the rule set. Each of these subtasks corresponds to one of HAMB's task-types: *select-training-set*, *select-feature-set*, *select-bias*, and *induce-rule-set*, respectively. After the completion of one of these tasks, the next task in the sequence is proposed, ensuring that HAMB performs the tasks in the order given above.

When proposing the next task in the sequence, the results of the current task are often used to determine the strengths of the reason given for performing the next task, allowing HAMB to factor the results of the current task into its decision about when to perform the next task in the sequence, if at all. For example, the heuristic for selecting a training set proposes a task for selecting a feature set, with the strengths of the reasons given for the proposed task being proportional to the size of the training set (encoding the rule of thumb that inducing a rule set from a small training set may result in a rule set with poor performance on future cases).

HAMB proposes *select-training-set* tasks, the first in the series of tasks given above, when it examines an at-

tribute that is a possible target attribute or when it discovers a potentially good predictor of a possible target attribute (i.e., detecting opportunities for inducing rule sets).

3.3. Heuristics for creating exception sets

HAMB creates exception sets for rule sets in order to induce rule sets from these exception sets, hopefully filling in the gaps of the "theory" formed by the initial rule set. An exception set is created for a rule set by selecting the rule set's counter-examples from the training set. After creating the exception set, HAMB proposes an *examine-item* task to examine the set and a *select-feature-set* task which will begin the process of inducing rules from the exception set.

4. Evaluation

Several experiments with HAMB using data taken from the domain of macromolecule crystallization were performed. We report here the results of our evaluations of HAMB's heuristics. The reader is directed to [1] and [5] for details of our examination of the framework's task selection mechanism.

The studies presented in this paper are:

- *Evaluation of HAMB's behavior* to see if the heuristics allow it to adapt its behavior to the data.
- *Evaluation of HAMB's discoveries* to study the efficacy of the heuristics.
- *Evaluation of the heuristics' assignment of reasons and strengths.*
- *Evaluation of the ability of the heuristics—which are domain independent—to use domain-specific knowledge,* allowing HAMB to achieve domain-specific behavior using domain-independent heuristics.
- *Evaluation of HAMB's generality* to determine the generality of the heuristics.

4.1. Macromolecule crystallization data

The macromolecule crystallization dataset consists of reports of experiments for growing crystals of proteins, nucleic acids, or larger complexes, such as proteins bound to DNA, for X-ray diffraction and subsequent determination of three-dimensional structure [6]. As described in [1] this dataset is a good test for autonomous discovery because it is relatively unexplored.

The database consists of 2,225 examples of crystallization experiments, each with 225 attributes. The attributes include:

- macromolecular properties—macromolecule name, macromolecule-class name, and molecular weight;
- experimental conditions—pH, temperature, crystallization method, macromolecular concentration, and

Cycle 5: HAMB examines the predictivity of other attributes toward CRFORM, discovering two predictors of CRFORM, and also examines CRFORM's predictivity of the other attributes, discovering that CRFORM is predictive of several others. One of HAMB's heuristics suggests that it is easier to induce good rules for a target attribute with many good predictors, causing HAMB to propose a task to select a training set for inducing rules predicting CRFORM each time HAMB discovers a good predictor of CRFORM. And each time HAMB discovers that CRFORM is a good predictor of another attribute, HAMB proposes a task to select a training set for the attribute. HAMB's identification of "easier" rule-induction targets illustrates how heuristics may be used to identify opportunities and propose tasks accordingly.

...

Cycle 1,029: Primarily because CRFORM has the greatest a priori interest to the user, but also because HAMB has discovered many good predictors of CRFORM, HAMB selects a training set for inducing rules predicting CRFORM before doing so for other attributes. HAMB creates the training set from the discovery-database's examples that do not have uninformative values for CRFORM (e.g., missing values, or "miscellaneous"), avoiding the induction of many uninteresting rules. After selecting the training set, HAMB notices that the selected training set is small, containing only 164 out of 1,482 possible examples. Because HAMB believes that it is harder to induce good rules using a small training set, HAMB postpones performing the next step of inducing rules for CRFORM—selecting a feature set—until task 11,172. Note that when HAMB finally does induce a rule set for CRFORM the accuracy of the induced rule set on the testing-database is 0.02.

...

Cycle: 1,123: HAMB selects a training set for inducing rules to predict the attribute SPGRPS-DESC, again using domain-knowledge to exclude examples that would cause the induction of uninformative rules, and then proposes a task for selecting a feature set from which rules predicting SPGRPS-DESC may be induced. The selected training set is fairly large, containing 1,305 examples.

...

Cycle 1,202: HAMB selects a training set for inducing rules predicting ADD-IRON-[II]-CITRATE, not because ADD-IRON-[II]-CITRATE is especially interesting, but because HAMB found many reasons for performing this task. The selected training set contains 1,482 out of 1,482 possible examples.

...

Figure 2. Excerpts taken from a run of HAMB with the macromolecule crystal-growing data illustrating HAMB's ability to be opportunistic as well as to postpone less-promising tasks. After 33,204 discovery cycles HAMB finished its discovery process, at which time HAMB reported approximately 575 discoveries it considered interesting.

concentrations of chemical additives in the growth medium;

- characteristics of the grown crystal (if any)—descriptors of the crystal's shape (e.g., crform, and spgrps-desc) and its diffraction-limit, which measures how well the crystal diffracts.

4.2. Evaluation of HAMB's behavior

We evaluated HAMB's ability to respond opportunistically to the data by examining traces showing its choices. In particular we asked about the program's abilities to (a) propose new tasks, (b) reason about the appropriateness of the tasks, and (c) direct its behavior toward tasks more likely to produce interesting discoveries.

Figure 2 presents narrative descriptions of four excerpts from a run of HAMB upon the data that illustrate HAMB's ability to tailor its tasks to the data. The first excerpt, shown at discovery cycle 5, illustrates a heuristic opportunistically identifying a potential rule-induction target. The second excerpt, shown at cycle 1,029, shows HAMB assigning low strengths to a task its heuristics suggest would not lead to a promising line of investigation: When a selected training set's size is small, HAMB's heuristics, encoding the rule of thumb that inducing a "good" rule set is more likely with larger training sets, cause HAMB to assign low strengths to the reasons given for selecting a feature set for the attribute *crform*. Finally, the excerpt at cycle 1,202 shows HAMB performing a task because it has determined that *add-iron-[II]-citrate* may be an "easy" rule-induction target

(not shown are the many reasons HAMB found for doing so), not because it had reason to believe that *add-iron-[II]-citrate* is especially interesting to the user.

4.3. Evaluation of HAMB's discoveries

After semi-manual removal of redundant discoveries HAMB made from the crystal-growing database, 431 discoveries were presented to one of the authors (JMR, a crystallographer) for categorization of their significance and novelty. His categorizations are presented in Table 2. The redundant rules removed during the semi-manual filtering (approximately 144) are counted as Category 0 discoveries (uninteresting) in the table. One Category II discovery that caught Dr. Rosenberg's interest is an *improving-rule-specialization* relationship between two rules in which the first rule is specialized by the second and the positive predictive value (PPV) of the specialization is greater than that of the first. The first rule matches 63 examples correctly and 97 examples incorrectly (PPV = 0.39):

Rule 1: An organic amine is present $\Rightarrow$ the macromolecule being crystallized is a nucleic acid.

The second rule of the relationship intensionally specializes the first:

Rule 2: An organic amine is present AND ammonium is not present $\Rightarrow$ the macromolecule being crystallized is a nucleic acid,

refining the general domain knowledge represented by Rule 1. This rule matches 62 examples correctly and 25 examples incorrectly (PPV = 0.71).

Table 2. Categories used by an expert to assess the interestingness of 531 discoveries made by HAMB from the macromolecule crystallization domain. The redundant rules removed during the semi-manual filtering (approximately 144) are counted as Category 0 discoveries.

Category	Significance	Number	Percent
IV	Individually, these discoveries could be the basis of a publication in the crystallography literature, being both novel and extremely significant to the crystallography literature	0 / 575	0
III	In groups of about a dozen, these discoveries could form the core of research papers in the crystallography literature	92 / 575	16
II	These discoveries are about as significant as Category III, but are not novel	192 / 575	33
I	These discoveries are not as interesting as Category II or III, but still are of some interest	51 / 575	9
0	These discoveries are any discoveries that are not Category I, II, III, or IV	240/ 575	42

Rule 1 captures the general but imprecise domain knowledge that "Organic amines tend to promote the growth of nucleic acid crystals but are less likely to be of use in the crystallization of proteins." Rule 2 refines this general knowledge by adding the condition "ammonium is not present," which eliminated 72 incorrect predictions of the first rule while eliminating only one correct prediction.

4.4. Evaluation of HAMB's assignment of reasons and strengths to tasks inducing rule sets

HAMB's heuristics use the results of performing one phase of inducing a rule set, such as selecting a training set, to assign reasons and corresponding strengths to the task for the next phase, such as selecting a feature set. By doing so, the reasons and their strengths should help HAMB tailor its behavior to the data and induce rule sets for target attributes that may have better test accuracies. (We preferred this behavior because we reasoned that more accurate rule sets would yield more interesting discoveries.)

To evaluate the effectiveness of the heuristics in assigning reasons and corresponding strengths, we examined the strengths of the reasons at three points in the process of inducing a rule set (to conserve space, plots of the data, which are referred to in the following paragraphs, are not shown; these plots may be found in [5]):

- *before performing* select-training-set *tasks, when the strengths of reasons given for selecting a training set reflect the predictiveness of attributes toward target attributes.* Regressing a line between the strengths of the reasons given for performing the tasks and the accuracy of the induced rule sets on the test database revealed little correlation (a coefficient of determination of 0.02). However, visual examination of a plot of the data indicates that there are two groups of datapoints: those for which the strengths of the reasons are suggestive of the test accuracy of the induced rule set and those for which the test accuracy is zero. If those datapoints with a test accuracy of zero are removed, the coefficient of determination goes up to 0.37.
- *after selecting a training set, when the strengths have been adjusted to account for the size of the selected*

training set. A plot of the sizes of the training sets to the test accuracy of the induced rule sets shows little correlation with a coefficient of determination of 0.02. However, very few rule sets induced from smaller training sets (containing fewer than approximately 300 examples) had accuracies on the test database greater than 0.3. Therefore, while large training set size may be insufficient for predicting a high accuracy for an induced rule set, small training set size may be useful for predicting low accuracy on the test database, allowing HAMB to identify less-promising rule-induction tasks.

- *after selecting the parametric bias.* A plot of the strengths of the reasons given for the last task performed when inducing rule sets—the actual induction of the rule set—to the accuracies of the induced rule sets on the test database indicates a strong correlation, with a coefficient of determination of 0.86.

These results demonstrate how HAMB's heuristics allow it to assign reasons and corresponding strengths and to adapt its behavior to fit the data, in this case allowing HAMB to achieve the desired behavior of inducing rules with greater test accuracies first.

4.5. Evaluation of HAMB's use of domain-specific knowledge

We performed a lesion study to evaluate the effectiveness of some of HAMB's heuristics that use domain-specific knowledge. To perform this study, we used 500 cases randomly selected from the macromolecule crystallization data.

The unmodified version of HAMB with the complete domain-theory was also run on this set of cases, as was a version of HAMB which used no domain knowledge. In the study described below, the latter version is called *no-domain-knowledge.*

The heuristics tested during this study are:

- *heuristics reducing redundancy by eliminating synonyms.* If an attribute is found in the feature set that is synonymous (as either discovered by HAMB or stated in the domain-theory) with another attribute in the feature set, the attribute with the lesser estimated interestingness is removed from the feature set. A baseline version of HAMB omitted these heuristics and did not eliminate synonyms. It allowed the creation of 40 (19%) more redundant rules than did HAMB. This was surprising, because the data contain many similar attributes. However, HAMB's definition of redundancy is very strict, requiring either intensional or extensional equivalence; therefore only a few pairs of attributes met its strict criterion of similarity.

- *heuristics reducing the number of uninteresting discoveries.* The domain-theory may contain knowledge about attributes and values which are uninteresting or meaningless to the user. HAMB's heuristics use this knowledge to avoid inducing rules containing (either in the left-hand side or right-hand side of a rule) uninteresting features. A baseline version of HAMB omitted this heuristic and allowed the generation of 300 (141%) additional uninteresting rules.

- *heuristics reducing the number of non-novel discoveries.* HAMB uses domain knowledge to remove attributes that are known to be associated (by causation, definition, association, etc.) with the current target attribute. It also removes attributes that are discovered to be extensionally equivalent to the target attribute. The baseline version of HAMB used to test these heuristics omitted this use of domain knowledge and allowed the generation of *2,897 (1,367%)* additional non-novel rules.

The regular version of HAMB induced 212 rules, whereas the baseline *no-domain-knowledge* version induced 3,936 rules, most of them uninteresting. Thus, HAMB was able to use domain knowledge to avoid the creation of 3,724 uninteresting rules. In addition HAMB only required 5,030 discovery cycles to finish, while the baseline *no-domain-knowledge* version required approximately 45,000 cycles.

4.6. Evaluation of generality

To evaluate the generality of the system, we used HAMB to perform discovery from a second database: 930 cases of patients in rehabilitation after a medical disability, such as stroke or amputation. There are 11 attributes in the database, ranging from demographic data to admission and discharge scores of the patients' functional independence. Thus, this database represents a domain that is dissimilar to the macromolecule crystallization domain.

After running HAMB with these data, we presented HAMB's discoveries to the physician who provided us with the data, Dr. Louis Penrod of the University of Pittsburgh Medical Center. He decided that there were 26 (9%) Category III discoveries (novel and significant), of which 2 were bordering on Category IV (revolutionary), 5 (2%) were Category II discoveries (non-novel, but significant), 53 (18%) were Category I

discoveries (novel and marginally interesting), and 215 (71%) were uninteresting. Note that because of the smaller number of attributes, we were able to represent almost all of the known relationships among the attributes, which HAMB's heuristics were able to use to greatly reduce the number of Category II (non-novel, but significant) discoveries.

Our conclusion from this study is that the heuristics are general enough to make significant discoveries from two dissimilar domains.

5. Discussion

Our experiments with HAMB demonstrate that the heuristics allowed HAMB to tailor its tasks to the data, such as being opportunistic by identifying better rule-induction targets and postponing less-promising lines of investigation in favor of more-promising ones. The heuristics allowed HAMB to perform significantly better than randomly selecting tasks from the agenda. We also showed that our heuristics for inducing rule sets were able to use a variety of domain-specific knowledge to avoid reporting a large proportion of uninteresting discoveries. Our evaluation of the generality of HAMB suggests that our heuristics are general.

5.1. Related work

When viewed along the spectrum of autonomy, "single-shot" learning programs, such as linear regression, neural networks, or rule-learning systems, have the least autonomy, followed by programs that automatically select their bias, such as COMBS and CLIMBS [7], and multistrategy and KDD-planning systems that may perform more than one task but require a user to examine their results and select new discovery goals. Then come intelligent assistant programs, such as Shen's assistant for defining metapatterns [8], AIDE [9], and IDEA [10], which propose new tasks but still require a user to choose the next task and to select top-level goals. Toward the end of this spectrum lies HAMB, which autonomously performs the entire discovery process (after the datasets have been collected and verified).

5.2. Scaling up and future work

Future work involves devising more heuristics for autonomous discovery. Additional heuristics are needed to better take advantage of an autonomous discovery system's ability to perform more than one task, such as being able to use more than one task to evaluate its discoveries or to identify patterns that may be found by examining the results of more than one task, such as a group of cases that unexplicably behave differently for a variety of tasks. Sources of heuristics may be found in the KDD and machine learning literature, and additional sources may be found in the writings of philosophers of science, such as [11], who have studied discovery for hundreds of years.

6. Conclusions

Our experiments suggest that heuristics are sufficiently powerful and flexible for suggesting new tasks to perform and for providing reasons and the strengths of those reasons for performing them.

We presented heuristics for keeping the values of the properties and relationships of the items sufficiently up-to-date and heuristics for choosing rule-induction targets; these heuristics allow the identification of targets for which rule sets with better or worse generalization scores on a test database may be induced. We also presented heuristics for use in fully autonomous discovery programs for proposing the next task to perform and providing justifications for performing those tasks. Finally, we presented heuristics for inducing rule sets which are able to use a variety of domain-specific knowledge to avoid inducing a large proportion of uninteresting rules. Our evaluations of these heuristics suggest that they are valid and general. We believe that these heuristics may be used as the starting point for further research into heuristics for autonomous discovery systems.

7. Acknowledgments

We thank John Aronis, Tom Fawcett, David Jensen, Foster Provost, and anonymous reviewers for their numerous discussions and suggestions. This work was funded in part by grants from the National Library of Medicine (1 G08 LM006625-01, the National Center for Research Resources (RR14477–2), and the National Science Foundation (9412549).

References

[1] Livingston, G. R., Rosenberg, J. M., and Buchanan, B. G. 2001. Closing the Loop: An Agenda- and Justification-Based Framework for Selecting the Next Discovery Task to Perform. To appear in *Proc. of the 2001 IEEE Intl. Conf. on Data Mining*, San Jose, CA. IEEE Computer Society Press.

[2] Zytkow, J. M. 1993. Introduction: Cognitive Autonomy in Machine Discovery. Machine Learning 12: 7-16.

[3] Provost, F. J. and Buchanan, B. G. 1995. Inductive Policy: The Pragmatics of Bias Selection. *Machine Learning 20*(1): 35-61.

[4] Buchanan, B. G. and Mitchell, T. 1978. Model-Directed Learning of Production Rules. In Waterman, D. A. and Hayes-Roth, F., Eds., *Pattern Directed In-ference Systems*, 297-312. New York, NY: Academic Press.

[5] Livingston, G. R. 2001. *A Framework for Autonomous Knowledge Discovery from Databases.* Ph.D. Diss., Dept. of Computer Science, Univ. of Pittsburgh, Pittsburgh, PA.

[6] Hennessy, D., Buchanan, B., Subramanian, D., Wilkosz, P., and Rosenberg, J. 2000. Statistical Methods for the Objective Design of Screening Procedures for Macromolecule Crystallization. *Acta Crystallographica Section D*: 817-827.

[7] Provost, F. J. 1992. *Policies for the Selection of Bias in Inductive Machine Learning.* Ph.D. Diss., Dept. of Computer Science, Univ. of Pittsburgh, Pittsburgh, PA.

[8] Shen, W.-M. and Leng, B. 1996. A Metapattern-Based Automated Discovery Loop for Integrated Data Mining. *IEEE Trans. on Knowledge and Data Engineering 8*(6): 898-910.

[9] Amant, R. S. and Cohen, P. R. 1997a. Evaluation of a Semi-Autonomous Assistant for Exploratory Data Analysis. In *Proc. of the First Intl. Conf. on Autonomous Agents*, 355-362, Marina Del Rey, CA, Feb. 5-8. ACM Press.

[10] Bernstein, A. and Provost, F. 2001. An Intelligent Assistant for the Knowledge Discovery Process. In *Proc. of the IJCAI-01 Workshop on Wrappers for Performance Enhancement in KDD*, Seattle, WA, Aug. 4. Morgan Kaufmann.

[11] Darden, L. 1991. *Theory Change in Science.* Oxford: Oxford Univ. Press.

Anchor Text Mining for Translation of Web Queries

Wen-Hsiang Lu

Department of CSIE,
National Chiao Tung University;
Institute of Information Science,
Academia Sinica,
Taiwan, Republic of China
whlu@csie.nctu.edu.tw

Lee-Feng Chien

Institute of Information Science,
Academia Sinica,
Taiwan, Republic of China
lfchien@iis.sinica.edu.tw

Hsi-Jian Lee

Department of CSIE,
National Chiao Tung University,
Taiwan, Republic of China
hjlee@csie.nctu.edu.tw

Abstract

This paper presents an approach to automatically extracting translations of Web query terms through mining of Web anchor texts and link structures. One of the existing difficulties in cross-language information retrieval (CLIR) and Web search is the lack of the appropriate translations of new terminology and proper names. Such a difficult problem can be effectively alleviated by our proposed approach, and the resource of anchor texts in the Web is proven a valuable corpus for this kind of term translation.

1. Introduction

Most efforts on data mining research have focused on knowledge discovery in structured databases [1]. Text mining is a relatively new research area of data mining [2], and much interests have been focused on automatic extractions of terms or phrases [3], the discovery of information extraction patterns or rules [4, 5], and ontology construction [6, 7]. In our research we are interested in discovering knowledge for the translations of new terminology and proper names from the Web.

A number of recent works have explored authoritative Web pages based on their link structures and associated *anchor texts* [8, 9, 10]. The purpose of this paper is to present an approach that allows the bilingual translations of many Web users' query terms can be automatically extracted through mining of Web anchor texts. This is a part of our research related to cross-language information retrieval (CLIR) and Web search [11, 12].

In fact, there are a number of ways Web users can query in one language and search documents that are written or indexed in another language. Our analysis on a query log of a commercial Chinese search engine in Taiwan, namely, Dreamer, showed that 19.2% of Chinese

users' query terms are input using English or English letters [12]. It was found that some Chinese users used English query terms to express search concepts related to foreign affairs, e.g., "Microsoft", "Nokia", "Yahoo", "PDA", "Stanford", etc. However, these concepts might be expressed in Chinese in the requested documents. Although research on CLIR has been advancing in recent years [13, 14], its application to practical Web search services has not lived up to expectations. In terms of Web search, one of the bottlenecks of CLIR is the lack of up-to-date bilingual lexicons that contain real effective translations for popular queries, such as names of foreign movie stars, international company names, recent worldwide events, etc [15]. For the translations of Web query terms, manual compilation of a bilingual lexicon is very time-consuming and inapplicable.

Related researches on machine translation often used statistical techniques to automatically extract word translations from domain-specific, parallel or comparable bilingual texts, such as bilingual newspapers [16, 17, 18, 19]. Unfortunately, since Web query terms are often diverse and dynamic, only a certain set of the translations can be extracted through such corpora with limited domains. Different from the previous works, Nie [14] developed a feasible method for extracting parallel text corpora from bilingual Web sites instantly, based on use of the Web's multilingual natures and wide range of hypertext resources to collect live bilingual corpora.

An initial idea on mining anchor texts for query translation has been reported in our previous work [20]. This paper is an extended study on developing an effective probabilistic model to make use of Web links and the associated anchor texts for the determination of correct query translations. In an experiment on 109,416 Web pages and a set of 622 English query terms selected from among popular query terms, it was found that 57% of the test query terms can obtain effective Chinese translations in the extracted top-1 translation candidates, and 91% of query terms could obtain the results in the top-10 candidates. Importantly, most of the extracted translations

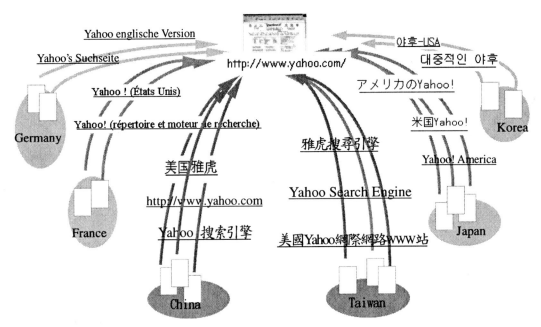

Fig. 1. An illustration showing various anchor texts in multiple languages linking to the Yahoo! site from all over the world.

cannot be found out in general-purpose translation dictionaries.

2. Anchor Text Mining

2.1. Characteristics of Anchor Texts

An anchor text is the descriptive part of an out-link of a Web page. It represents a brief description of the linked Web page and is often used by commercial Web search engines to index linked pages. We use a triple form $<U_j, U_i, D_k>$ to indicate that page U_j points to page U_i with description text D_k. For a Web page (or URL) U_i, its anchor-text set $AT(U_i)$ is defined as all of the anchor texts of the links pointing to U_i, i.e., U_i's in-links. In general, $AT(U_i)$ records U_i's alternative concepts and textual expressions, such as titles and headings, which are cited by other Web pages. With different preferences, conventions and levels of language competence, $AT(U_i)$ could be multilingual phrases, short texts, acronyms, or even U_i's URL. For a query term appearing in $AT(U_i)$, it is likely that its corresponding translations also appear together. The anchor-text sets can be considered a potential comparable corpus of translated texts, from the viewpoint of translation extraction. On the other hand, from the viewpoint of database management, a collection of anchor-text sets can be considered a Web-based concept database. Discovering knowledge from such a special database is a challenge. In this paper, our major goal is to investigate the feasibility of mining anchor texts for translations of query terms.

2.2. Observation

A typical example of an anchor-text set is illustrated in Fig.1, in which there are a variety of anchor texts in multiple languages linking to the URL at http://www.yahoo.com/ from all over the world. It is not hard to see that most of Yahoo's regional aliases can be obtained from the anchor-text set of the Yahoo! site. We carried out a simple analysis on a collection of 109,416 Web pages containing both English and Chinese texts in their in-links. It is interesting that we found 45 different pages whose anchor-text sets contained both Yahoo and Yahoo's Chinese aliases. This level of correlation between translated terms pairs seems to reveal the potential for extraction of term translation.

Note that anchor-text sets constitute a live multilingual source that is contributed by a huge amount of Web volunteers daily. It is crucial that a feasible way is found to utilize this live source. Our initial task was to extract English-Chinese translation pairs for popular queries used in the Chinese communities. In the future, we hope to develop a universal approach to extracting the translations for most of the major languages in the world.

2.3. Considered Problem and Challenge

For each query term expressed in the source language, the question examined in this paper is whether it is possible to extract translations in the target language from anchor-text sets containing the query term. To deal with this problem, the first step is to extract the translation candidates that frequently co-occur with the source query term (or source query for simplicity in the following discussion, since most of the Web user's queries contain only single terms) in the same anchor-text sets. However, determining of correct translations is not a straightforward task. The co-occurred terms may contain many irrelevant and noise terms. For example, in our analysis of a set of 283 Web pages containing the English term "Yahoo" in their anchor-text sets, we found 768 co-occurring Chinese terms in which only one term was a correct translation (as shown in Table 1). The determination of correct translations is challenging.

Table 1. Some terms which frequently co-occur with "Yahoo" in the anchor-text.

Co-occurred Traditional-Chinese Terms:
搜尋/雅虎/中文/網站/引擎/索引/網路/資源/
台灣/資訊/新聞/查詢/美國/日本/……

3. The Proposed Approach

3.1. The Idea

According to the phenomenon described above, we can reasonably assume that anchor texts linking to the same pages may contain terms with similar semantics, and that some of them may be written in different languages. Therefore, a candidate term has a higher chance of being effectively translated if it is written in the target language and frequently co-occurs with the source query term in the same anchor-text sets (in the anchor texts linking to the same pages). In the field of Web research, it has been proven that link structures can be used effectively to examine the authority of Web pages [10]. Our approach further assumes that translation candidates in the anchor-text sets of the pages with higher authority may have more supports in confidence level.

3.2. The Probabilistic Inference Model

Since the advent of statistical machine translation [21], many studies on term translation have used parallel text corpora to build probabilistic translation models, by means of which we are able to determine the most probable target translation T_t for source term T_s using the probability distribution $P(T_t|T_s)$:

$$P(T_t \mid T_s) = \frac{P(T_s \cap T_t)}{P(T_s)}. \tag{1}$$

In our research, we call this model the *similarity estimation model*. A similar application can be found in rule-based knowledge discovery systems, where the conditional probability $P(T_t|T_s)$ is used to measure the strength of the inductive rule "if T_s then T_t". This rule provides a plausible measure of confidence in proposition T_t given evidence T_s, i.e., $P(T_s{\rightarrow}T_t)$. In fact, the estimation is an asymmetric measure; i.e., the degree to which T_s implies T_t may not necessarily be the same as the degree to which T_t implies T_s. The asymmetric model may encounter the drawback that $P(T_t|T_s)$ is high when T_t frequently occurs and is highly correlated with T_s. This will cause some incorrect translations to be extracted; e.g., some common terms may, therefore, become the best translations.

To enhance the confidence quality of the similarity estimation, we have developed another model. If T_s and T_t form a translation pair, i.e., they are equivalent to each other, then the inductive rules "if T_s then T_t," and "if T_t then T_s," must exist simultaneously. Our proposed approach, therefore, employs a symmetric similarity estimation function, which is based on the probabilistic inference model [22] defined below:

$$P(T_s \leftrightarrow T_t) = \frac{P(T_s \cap T_t)}{P(T_s \cup T_t)}. \tag{2}$$

This measure is adopted to estimate the degree of similarity between a source term and each translation candidate that co-occurs in the same anchor-text sets. For each source term T_s, the proposed approach extracts the most probable translation T_t that maximizes the estimation.

The above measure is then estimated by considering the link structures and concept space of Web pages. Let $U=(U_1,U_2,...,U_n)$ be a concept space (Web page space), consisting of a set of pair-wised disjoint basic concepts (Web pages), i.e., $U_i \cap U_j = \phi$ for $i \neq j$. On the basis of the Web page space, we can rewrite Eq. (2) as

$$P(T_s \leftrightarrow T_t) = \frac{P(T_s \cap T_t)}{P(T_s \cup T_t)} = \frac{\sum_{i=1}^{n} P(T_s \cap T_t \cap U_i)}{\sum_{i=1}^{n} P((T_s \cup T_t) \cap U_i)}$$

$$\approx \frac{\sum_{i=1}^{n} P(T_s \cap T_t \mid U_i)P(U_i)}{\sum_{i=1}^{n} P(T_s \cup T_t \mid U_i)P(U_i)}. \tag{3}$$

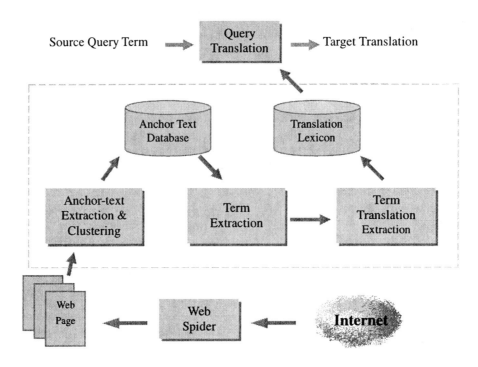

Fig.2. Computational modules of the query translation system.

Here, the probability $P(U_i)$ is used to measure the authority of page U_i. Currently, we estimate this parameter with the probability of U_i being linked, and its estimation is defined as follows:

$$P(U_i) = \frac{L(U_i)}{\sum_{j=1}^{n} L(U_j)}. \quad (4)$$

where $L(U_j)$ = the number of in-links of pages U_j. The above estimation is simplified from the authority estimation of Web pages used in HITS algorithm [10].

In addition, we assume that T_s and T_t are independent given U_i; then, the joint probability $P(T_s \cap T_t | U_i)$ is equal to the product of $P(T_s|U_i)$ and $P(T_t|U_i)$, and the similarity measure becomes

$$P(T_s \leftrightarrow T_t) \approx$$

$$\frac{\sum_{i=1}^{n} P(T_s | U_i)P(T_t | U_i)P(U_i)}{\sum_{i=1}^{n}[P(T_s | U_i) + P(T_t | U_i) - P(T_s | U_i)P(T_t | U_i)]P(U_i)}. \quad (5)$$

The values of $P(T_s|U_i)$ and $P(T_t|U_i)$ can be estimated by calculating the fractions of the numbers of U_i's in-links containing T_s and T_t in their anchor texts over $L(U_i)$,

respectively.

Different from conventional statistical translation models or rule induction used in data mining, the above estimation approach considers the link information and the degree of authority among Web pages.

4. The Query Translation System

A query translation system was, therefore, designed based on the above approach to extracting term translations through mining of real-world anchor-text sets. This system integrates the three major computational modules shown in Fig. 2.

• *Anchor-text Extraction and Clustering:* This process was constructed by using a Web spider to collect pages from the Web and extract all of the composed links and anchor texts to build up a database of anchor-text sets. Anchor texts linking to the same pages are grouped together as an anchor-text set. The anchor-text sets containing texts in both target and source languages will be collected in the database for further processing. The process is started whenever up-to-date information is required.

• *Term Extraction:* Considering that an anchor text

might be a short text, heading, phrase, or URL, the term extraction process needs to extract key terms as translation candidates from the anchor-text database. The extracted candidate terms are indexed to provide quick access for retrieval of all the related parameters. For English anchor texts, a Part-Of-Speech (POS) tagger is used to extract possible uncommon terms or noun phrases [23]. On the other hand, we use three different methods to extract Chinese terms:

1. *PAT-Tree-Based:* The PAT-tree-based keyword extraction method is an efficient statistics-based approach that includes n-gram modeling and significance analysis of semantics [11]. It can extract many significant terms and phrases without a dictionary.

2. *Query-Set-Based:* This method uses users' queries from real-world search engines as vocabulary sets to segment key terms.

3. *Tagger-Based:* This method uses CKIP's tagger, a representative Chinese POS tagger [24] to segment Chinese texts into meaningful words and to extract unknown words, such as proper nouns and new terms. The method different from the PAT-tree-based method is that it is more linguistics-based. It relies much on the dictionary and linguistic rules used.

• *Term Translation Extraction:* Based on the similarity estimation model presented in the previous section, the process extracts all the possible translation candidates for each source query term. The candidates are ranked according to the similarity.

5. The Experiments

5.1. Experimental Environment

We collected 1,980,816 Chinese Web pages in Taiwan using a Web spider. From these pages, we extracted 13,188,199 links and 2,521,165 unique anchor texts. Among these pages, 109,416 pages whose anchor-text sets contained both Chinese and English terms were taken as the training corpus to construct the anchor text database in our initial research. The corpus contained a total 2,177,622 in-links and 322,524 unique anchor texts. Each page, therefore, had 19.9 in-links (2,177,622/109,416) and 2.95 (322,524/109,416) associated anchor texts on average. There are 2.8 MB Chinese text and 3.1 MB English text in this corpus.

We also collected popular query terms with the logs from two real-world Chinese search engines, i.e., Dreamer

and GAIS[*]. The Dreamer log contained 228,566 unique query terms from a period of over 3 months in 1998, and the GAIS log contained 114,182 unique query terms from a period of two weeks in 1999. We selected 9,709 most popular query terms as so-called *core terms*, whose frequencies were above 10 in both of the logs. These query terms were taken as the major test set in our analysis of extraction of term translation. There were 1,230 English terms among these core terms. We filtered out the terms which had no corresponding Chinese translations in the anchor text database, and picked up 622 terms as *the source query set*. In order to determine the effectiveness of our approach in translating these test query terms, several experiments were conducted and will be introduced later.

5.2. Evaluation Metric

To evaluate the achieved performance of query translation, we used the *average top-n inclusion rate* as a metric. For a set of test query terms, its top-n inclusion rate is defined as the percentage of the query terms whose effective translation(s) can be found in the top n extracted translations. The determination of whether or not the extracted translations are effective is based on whether the translations can be used to perform similar search requests in the target language, which needs to be judged manually.

In terms of Web search, there is a major difference between query-term translation and common-term translation. Query terms usually indicate certain information requests. Their translated terms should be effective for the same requests. Direct translation by looking up terms in bilingual lexicons may not be suitable in many cases. A typical example is translation of Chinese query term "kafe" (coffee in Chinese). The English translation, "Internet Café", is found to be more effective than "coffee" in Web search applications. That is because the query "kafe" in Chinese is usually used to express the request for Internet café sites. Such a translation is quite special and can not be obtained by looking up terms in general-purpose bilingual dictionaries.

5.3. Experimental Results

In this section, the obtained experimental results will be presented. To compare the effects under different conditions, such as different similarity estimation models and term extraction methods, extensive experiments were performed. The obtained results are categorized into three different classes: effects of similarity estimation models,

---

* These two search engines are second-tier portals in Taiwan, whose logs have certain representatives in the Chinese communities, and whose URL's are as follows: http://www.dreamer.com.tw/ and http://gais.cs.cu.edu.tw/.

effects of term extraction methods, and effects of query-set sizes.

- **Performance with Different Similarity Estimation Models**

To observe the effects of using the symmetric inference model and link structure information, four different models as follows were tested:

1. M_A, Asymmetric model as in Eq. (1);
2. M_{AL}, Asymmetric model with link information:

$$P(T_t \mid T_s) \approx \frac{\sum_{i=1}^{n} P(T_s \mid U_i) P(T_t \mid U_i) P(U_i)}{\sum_{i=1}^{n} P(T_s \mid U_i) P(U_i)};$$

3. M_S, Symmetric model as in Eq. (2);
4. M_{SL}, Symmetric model with link information as in Eq. (5) (the proposed model).

The test query set was the source query set with the 622 English query terms, and the method used to segment translation candidates was based on the query-set-based method, using the 9709 core terms as the vocabulary set. As shown in Table 2, the symmetric model with link information actually achieved the best performance for both inclusion rates of top-1 and top-10. Both the symmetric inference model and the link structure information were found to improve the translation quality. However, the inclusion rate of top-1 still exists improvable room. The main errors observed mostly resulted from interference of noise terms, especially when the frequencies of the test terms were low in the collected anchor-text sets. In this case, the probability estimations were unreliable.

Table 2. Top-n inclusion rates obtained with four different models.

Type of Model	Top-1	Top-10
M_A	41%	81%
M_{AL}	44%	83%
M_S	51%	84%
M_{SL}	53%	85%

- **Performance with Different Term Extraction Methods**

To determine the effects of using different term extraction methods, we also carried out an experiment and tested the three different Chinese term extraction methods mentioned in Section 4. The similarity estimation model adopted was the proposed symmetric inference model with link information. The obtained results are shown in Table 3. We observed that the method based on the users' query set achieved better performance. The main reason was the interference caused by common terms in the PAT-tree- and tagger-based methods. However, the two

methods achieved better inclusion rates when the number of the extracted candidates was larger.

Table 3. Top-n inclusion rates obtained with different term extraction methods.

Type of Extraction	Top-1	Top-10
PAT-Tree-Based	49%	94%
Query-Set-Based	53%	85%
Tagger-Based	49%	94%

- **Performance with Different Query-Set Sizes**

To determine the effects of using different query sets, an additional experiment was performed. We tested three sets of query terms: 9,709 core terms, the top 19,124 terms (occupy 80% query requests in the Dreamer log) and the total set of 228,566 unique terms. Table 4 shows the obtained results. It is interesting that the medium size of query set achieve the best performance. In our observation, larger query sets could provide more translation candidates and achieve higher top-n inclusion rates, but may cause more noises.

Table 4. Top-n inclusion rates obtained with query sets of different sizes.

Size of Query Set	Top-1	Top-10
#9,709	53%	85%
#19,124	57%	91%
#228,566	53%	94%

5.4. Discussion

Examining the top-1 effective translations obtained using the proposed approach (the set shown in the third row and the second column of Table 4), it was found that 58.7% of them could not be found in Oxford Advanced Learner's English-Chinese Dictionary (which contains 57,100 entries, and was published in 1995). The achieved performance surpassed our expectations. In fact, the proposed approach is language-independent and can be extended to deal with different language pairs, e.g., German-Japanese.

Based on this observation, we also collected 2,179,171 Simplified Chinese[*] Web pages published in China (The pages we used in Section 5 were in Traditional Chinese.) From these pages, we extracted 157,786 pages whose anchor-text sets contain both English and Simplified Chinese terms. After performing initial experiments, we found that the obtained results were similar to our previous results. Table 5 shows some of the obtained translation pairs.

---

[*] Simplified Chinese is used in China and Singapore, and Traditional Chinese in Taiwan, Hong Kong and Macau.

6. Conclusion

In this paper, we have proposed a new and effective approach to mining Web link structures and anchor texts for translation of Web query terms. The proposed approach successfully exploits the anchor-text resources and partially solves the existing difficulties involved in term translation. There are further possible directions of research, for example, combining more in-depth linguistic knowledge and using it to remove noise terms or stop words.

Reference

[1] Deogun, J. S., Raghavan V. V., Server, H., *Data Mining: Research Trends, Challenges, and Applications, Rough Sets and Data Mining: Analysis of Imprecise Data*, Kluwer Academic Publishers, 1997, pp. 9-45.

[2] Hearst, M., "Untangling Text Data Mining", *Proceedings of the 37th Annual Meeting of the Association for Computational Linguistics*, 1999.

[3] Feldman, R. and Dagan, I., "KDT - Knowledge Discovery in Texts", *Proceedings of the 1st International Conference on Knowledge Discovery and Data Mining*, 1995.

[4] Huffman, S. B., "Learning Information Extraction Patterns from Examples" *Proceedings of IJCAI 1995 Workshop on New Approaches to Learning for Natural Language Processing*.

[5] Soderland, S., "Learning to Extract Text-based Information from the World Wide Web", *Proceedings of the 3rd International Conference on Knowledge Discovery and Data Mining*, 1997.

[6] Agirre, E., Ansa, O., Hovy E., and Martinez D., "Enriching Very Large Ontologies Using the WWW", *Proceedings of ECAI 2000 Workshop on Ontology Learning*.

[7] Maedche, A., Staab, S., "Mining Ontologies from Text", *Proceedings of the 12th International Conference on Knowledge Engineering and Knowledge Management*, 2000.

[8] Brin, S., Page, L., "The Anatomy of a Large-scale Hypertextual Web Search Engine", *Proceedings of the 7th International World Wide Web Conference*, 1998, pp 107-117.

[9] Chakrabarti, S., Dom, B., Gibson, D., Kleinberg, J., Raghavan, P., Rajagopalan, S., "Automatic Resource List Compilation by Analysing Hyperlink Structure and Associated Text", *Proceedings of the 7th International World Wide Web Conference*, 1998.

[10] Kleinberg, J., "Authoritative Sources in a Hyperlinked Environment", *Proceedings of the 9th ACM SIAM Symposium on Discrete Algorithms*, 1998.

[11] Chien, L. F., "PAT-tree-based Keyword Extraction for Chinese Information Retrieval", *Proceedings of the 20th ACM*

Table 5. Selected term translations in English, Traditional Chinese and Simplified Chinese, which were extracted by our system.

English	Traditional Chinese	Simplified Chinese
Yahoo	雅虎	雅虎
Dell	戴爾	德尔
HP	惠普	惠普
Nokia	諾基亞	诺基亚
Ericsson	易利信	爱立信
Sony	新力	索尼
Stanford	史丹佛	斯坦福
internet	網際網路	互联网
online	線上	在线
download	下載	下载
computer	電腦	计算机
database	資料庫	数据库
information	資訊	信息
game	遊戲	游戏
movie	電影	电影
video	影視	录像

SIGIR Conference, 1997, pp. 50-59.

[12] Pu, H. T., Chuang, S. L., Yang, C. , "Exploration of Web Users' Search Interests through Automatic Subject Categorization of Query terms", *Proceedings of American Society for Information Science and Technology Annual Meeting*, 2001.

[13] Dumais, S. T., Landauer, T. K., Littman, M. L., "Automatic Crosslinguistic Information Retrieval Using Latent Semantic Indexing", *Proceedings of ACM SIGIR 1996 Workshop on Cross-Linguistic Information Retrieval*, pp. 16-24.

[14] Nie, J. Y., Isabelle, P., Simard, M., and Durand, R., "Cross-language Information Retrieval Based on Parallel Texts and Automatic Mining of Parallel Texts from the Web", *Proceedings of the 22nd ACM SIGIR Conference*, 1999.

[15] Kwok, K. L., "NTCIR-2 Chinese, Cross Language Retrieval Experiments Using PIRCS", *Proceedings of NTCIR Workshop Meeting*, 2001.

[16] Dagan, I., Church, K. W., Gale, W. A, "Robust Bilingual Word Alignment for Machine Aided Translation", *Proceedings of ACL 1993 Workshop on Very Large Corpora*, pp. 1-8.

[17] Smadja, F., McKeown, K., Hatzivassiloglou, V., "Translating Collocations for Bilingual Lexicons: A statistical approach", *Computational Linguistics*, 22(1), 1996, pp. 1-38.

[18] Fung, P. and Yee, L. Y., "An IR Approach for Translating New Words from Nonparallel, Comparable Texts", *Proceedings of the 36th Annual Meeting of the Association for Computational Linguistics*, 1998, pp. 414-420.

[19] Rapp, R., "Automatic Identification of Word Translations from Unrelated English and German Corpora", *Proceedings of the 37th Annual Meeting of the Association for Computational Linguistics*, 1999.

[20] Lu, W. H., Chien, L. F., Lee, H. J., "Anchor-text Mining for Translation Extraction of Query Terms", *Proceedings of the 24th ACM SIGIR Conference*, 2001.

[21] Brown, P., Cocke, J., Della Pietra, S. A. Della Pietra, V. J., Jelinek, F., Lafferty, J. D., Mercer, R. L., Rossin, P. S., "A Statistical Approach to Machine Translation", *Computational Linguistics*, 16(2), 1990, pp. 79-85

[22] Wong, S. K. M., Yao Y. Y., "On Modeling Information Retrieval with Probabilistic Inference", *ACM transactions on Information Systems*, Vol.13, 1995, pp. 38-68.

[23] Brill, E., "Some Advance in Transformation Based Part of Speech Tagging", *Proceedings of the 12th National Conference on Artificial Intelligence*, 1994.

[24] Liu, S. H., Chen, K. J., Chang, L. P., Chin, Y. H., "Automatic Part-of-Speech Tagging for Chinese Corpora", *Computer Processing of Chinese and Oriental Languages*, Vol. 9, No. 1, 1995, pp. 31-47.

Mining Mutually Dependent Patterns

Sheng Ma and Joseph L. Hellerstein
IBM T.J. Watson Research Center
Hawthorne, NY 10532

Abstract—In some domains, such as isolating problems in computer networks and discovering stock market irregularities, there is more interest in patterns consisting of infrequent, but highly correlated items rather than patterns that occur frequently (as defined by $minsup$, the minimum support level). Herein, we describe the m-pattern, a new pattern that is defined in terms of $minp$, the minimum probability of mutual dependence of items in the pattern. We show that all infrequent m-pattern can be discovered by an efficient algorithm that makes use of: (a) a linear algorithm to qualify an m-pattern; (b) an effective technique for candidate pruning based on a necessary condition for the presence of an m-pattern; and (c) a level-wise search for m-pattern discovery (which is possible because m-patterns are downward closed). Further, we consider frequent m-patterns, which are defined in terms of both $minp$ and $minsup$. Using synthetic data, we study the scalability of our algorithm. Then, we apply our algorithm to data from a production computer network both to show the m-patterns present and to contrast with frequent patterns. We show that when $minp= 0$, our algorithm is equivalent to finding frequent patterns. However, with a larger *minp*, our algorithm yields a modest number of highly correlated items, which makes it possible to mine for infrequent but highly correlated itemsets. To date, many actionable m-patterns have been discovered in production systems.

I. INTRODUCTION

Data mining aims to discover useful patterns in large data sets. To date, much emphasis has been placed on finding frequent patterns in the setting of the market basket data[2][3]. Market basket data consists of transactions, each of which is a set of items purchased together. An association rule relates two itemsets, E_1 and E_2. Such a rule indicates that E_1 is strongly dependent on E_2, which is denoted by $E_1 \Rightarrow E_2$. Directly discovering all such rules is computationally intractable because the large number of possible itemsets. To avoid this difficulty, Agrawal et.al.[2] proposed finding all *frequent* association rules. Here, "frequent" places an additional requirement, and enables the two-step algorithm [2][4] for discovering all frequent itemsets followed by (exhaustively) computing association rules of the frequent itemsets. The efficiency gain is achieved by exploring the downward closeness property of the frequent itemsets. However, this diminishes quickly when searching for infrequent itemsets, in which the minimum support $minsup$ has to be set very low.

Some real world applications requires the discovery of *infrequent*, but highly correlated patterns. Cohen[8] discussed this and analyzed pair-wise patterns for news articles and web logs. Other such applications include problem detection in computer networks, intrusion detection in computer systems, and fraud detection in financial systems. In these applications, normal behavior dominates; abnormal behavior, such as failures and intrusions, is rare. Thus, it is interesting in discovering *infrequent* patterns that relate to problem situations. Consider the example in [10] in which the following events are generated from a router: network interface card failure, unreachable destination, and "cold start" trap. The last event indicates that the router has failed and restarted. If these events commonly occur together, then the first two events may provide advance warning of when

the third will occur.

One naive approach to mining for infrequent patterns is to discover all frequent patterns (e.g., using A-priori) with very low minimum support ($minsup$), and then use post-processing to discover significant patterns. However, this is impractical. Specifically, to find infrequent patterns, the minimum support in A-priori must be set very low, which in turn results in long processing time as well as many irrelevant patterns that must be examined. Irrelevant patterns (i.e. pattern occurring simply by chances) are particularly problematic in real applications with a wide disparity in the frequency of items. As an example in event data, some events have a very high probability of occurrence, such as the "connection closed" events issued by network hubs that support the dynamic host configuration protocol (DHCP). As a result, there are a large number of patterns that have "connection closed" in them even though this event has little correlation with the rest of events.

The foregoing motivates us to develop the m-pattern. An m-pattern is an itemset for which any two subsets are strongly dependent with each other characterized by a minimum dependence probability of at least $minp$ (a user-specified parameter), where $0 \leq minp \leq 1$. That is, if some items in an m-pattern occurs, then it is very likely that the other items in the itemset occur as well. Here, $minp$ plays a similar role to that of $minconf$, but requires for any two subsets.

An m-pattern differs from a frequent association rule[2][4][3] and the correlated pattern[7] in three major aspects.

- An m-pattern requires mutual dependence. An association rule only requires one-way dependence. For example, an association rule might specify either $diaper \Rightarrow beer$ or $beer \Rightarrow diaper$; while an m-pattern is present only if $diaper \Leftrightarrow beer$. A correlated pattern refers to an itemset whose items are not independent determined by a statistical test. Thus, it is a much "weaker" correlation compared to both association rules and m-patterns. However, because of this, it is not feasible to discover infrequent patterns. We note that our m-pattern definition excludes the situation that some two subset pairs, but not all, of an itemset are strongly dependent. This strong dependence requirement provides many nice properties that enables us to efficiently discover all m-patterns, even if their supports are very low.

- An m-pattern requires that any two subsets of the itemset be mutually dependent. Neither an association rule nor a correlated pattern has such a property. As we will show later, such a property enables directly, efficiently discovering all m-patterns.

- An m-pattern does not have a condition of minimum support (although this can be added). This makes it possible to find all infrequent m-patterns. In contrast, only frequent association rules and correlated rules can be efficiently discovered in practice.

To provide more insight into m-patterns and how they differ

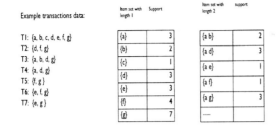

Example transactions data:	Item set with length 1	Support	Item set with length 2	support
T1: {a, b, c, d, e, f, g}	{a}	3	{a b}	2
T2: {d, f, g}	{b}	2	{a d}	3
T3: {a, b, d, g}	{c}	1	{a e}	1
T4: {a, d, g}	{d}	3	{a f}	1
T5: {f, g}	{e}	3	{a g}	3
T6: {e, f, g}	{f}	4	......	
T7: {e, g}	{g}	7		

Fig. 1. Illustrative transaction data

from frequent associations, an example is presented. Figure 1 displays data for transactions that are listed in the left side of the figure. The i-th transaction is denoted by T_i, and symbols a through g represent items. Also, there is a table that displays support levels for patterns of length one and another table for patterns of length two. For example, the support level for $\{a, b\}$ is 2, since a and b are contained in T_1 and T_3. Frequent itemsets have a number of occurrences that exceeds $minsup$. For example, let $minsup = 3$. Then, $\{a, d\}$ and $\{a, g\}$ are frequent itemsets since both have a support level of 3. In contrast, m-patterns are defined by mutual dependence using the threshold $minp$. As we show later, if $minp = 0.5$, then $\{a, b\}$ is an m-pattern, but $\{a, g\}$ is not. Intuitively, since g occurs in every transaction, $g \not\Rightarrow a$, although $\{a, g\}$ occurs frequently and $a \Rightarrow g$.

How can we use m-patterns? As we will show in Section 5, m-patterns are common in event data as a result of the extensive interdependencies introduced by logical and physical interconnections of network elements. These dependencies manifest themselves as a set of correlated events (or alarms) when a problem arises. For example, when a link of a local area network (LAN) goes down, all hosts connected to the link generates "lost connection" events. Clearly, it is important to quickly pinpoint problem causes before there are wide spread service disruptions. Discovering an m-pattern may provide a way to characterize or anticipate problem situations. We refer to [10] for more detailed explanations.

To efficiently discover **all** m-patterns for given $minp$, we need to resolve two non-trivial issues. First, the definition of m-pattern requires any two subsets of an itemset to be mutually dependent. On the surface, checking whether an itemset is a valid m-pattern requires exponential computational complexity in respect to the size of pattern. This makes it very inefficient. Second, the search space is exponentially large in respect to the number of distinct items. Examining and qualifying each of the candidate is computationally intractable. This is the same issue as that of discovering all frequent itemset.

Herein, we resolve these efficiency issues by exploiting special properties of m-patterns. We demonstrate analytically that examining a small number of two subset pairs is sufficient for qualifying an itemset as a m-pattern. This results in a simple linear algorithm. Further, we show that an m-pattern has the downward closure property, and thus it can be searched effi-

ciently through a level-wise search strategy. Last, we establish a necessary condition for qualifying m-patterns. This necessary condition provides an upper bound that can be used to further prune candidates effectively.

To explore the relationship with frequent patterns, we define frequent m-patterns in terms of both $minp$ and $minsup$. We show that when $minp = 0$, frequent m-patterns reduce to frequent patterns; While, with a larger $minp$, our algorithm yields a modest number of highly correlated items, which makes it possible to mine for relatively infrequent but highly correlated itemsets. Consequently, we can explore the tradeoff between the strength of mutual dependence and the occurrence frequency of patterns.

A. Related work

Much prior work is relevant to this paper. Agrawal et.al.[2][4][3] developed an elegant algorithm called Apriori that finds all frequent patterns in a level-wise manner. Since then, many techniques have been proposed to improve the algorithm's efficiency by minimizing the number of data scans needed, memory required, etc [1][6][18]. In this paper, we propose mutual dependence patterns. We demonstrate that m-patterns can be discovered, even if they occur infrequently.

Much work has been done for finding different types of patterns (e.g., [16], [11], [5], [12]). However, most these efforts require that frequent itemsets be discovered first; rules are derived in a separate post-processing step. As discussed before, this approach cannot find infrequent patterns without examining a huge number of candidates.

Closely related to our work, Cohen et al.[8] discussed the needs for discovering infrequent, but highly correlated itemsets. However, they defined a symetric similarity measure of two items and their algorithm can only discover itemsets containing only two items. Herein, we define the mutual depedency of an itemset with any length. We develop an efficient level-wise algorithm that discovers all infrequent, but highly correlated patterns with any length. Brin et.al.[7] defined correlated patterns, i.e. itemsets that are not independent based on a chi-squared test. The condition used for a correlated pattern is rather weak in that correlated patterns are upward closed. That is, any super set of a correlated pattern is a correlated pattern. To avoid a potential explosion of patterns, the authors focus on frequent, correlated patterns, as specified by $minsup$. In contrast, m-patterns capture mutual dependency without using $minsup$ by using $minp$. As we show later, m-patterns are downward closed, which allows for the efficient discovery of infrequent m-patterns.

B. Our contributions

Our main contributions can be summarized in the following. *(1)* We define a new type of patterns called m-pattern that captures the mutual dependence of items. We demonstrate that the major advantage of m-pattern is its ability to discover infrequent, but mutually dependent patterns. We demonstrate empirically the significance (e.g. actionable, interesting, unexpected) of m-patterns in system management applications *(2)* We develop an efficient algorithm that can check whether an itemset is a qualified m-pattern in a linear time. This is not obvious because the definition of m-patterns requires that any two subset pairs are dependent with each other. This leads to exponential computational complexity in respect to the size of a patterns.

(3) We derive an upper bound property of an m-pattern. This can be used to effectively eliminate the search space.

(4) We derive an algorithm for efficiently discovering all m-patterns. Our algorithm integrates (2) and (3) above with the well-known level-wise search strategy.

(5) We show that the m-pattern condition defined by *minp* can be used together with the occurrence frequence defined by *minsup*. This allows to explore the tradeoff between the strength of mutual dependence and the occurrence frequency of patterns.

C. Organization of this paper

The remainder of this paper is organized as follows. Section 2 defines m-patterns and related concepts. Section 3 presents our algorithm for finding m-patterns. Section 4 discusses extensions to the basic algorithm to handle frequent m-patterns. Section 5 provides empirical assessments of our algorithms. Our conclusions are contained in Section 6.

II. DEFINITIONS OF M-PATTERNS AND RELATED CONCEPTS

This section formalizes m-patterns and related concepts. We begin by generalizing the notion of a qualified pattern, a concept that is usually associated with support levels. We then specify what is meant by mutual dependence, a concept that we formalize in terms of the empirical distribution of the transaction data to be mined. With this background, we then define m-patterns.

We begin by generalizing what is meant by a qualified pattern. Let I be a collection of distinct items, and let the itemset E be a non-empty subset of I. As usual, the transaction data, $D = \{D_i\}_{i=1}^N$, is a collection of N transactions, where the i-th transaction $D_i \subset I$.

We define a **qualification function** $f_D(E)$ to be $f_D : E \rightarrow \{true, false\}$, where $f_D(E) = true$ iff E is a qualified f−pattern in D. For example, let f_D be the qualification function for a frequent pattern with minimum support level $minsup$. Then, the qualification for frequent pattern:

$$f_D(E) = true \text{ iff } support_D(E) \geq minsup, \quad (1)$$

where $support_D(E) = |\{D_i \in D | E \subseteq D_i\}|$ is the number of occurrences of E in data D. $|s|$ represents the cardinality of a set s.

Now we formalize what is meant by dependence (known as rule confidence in association rules) and mutual dependence. Let E_1 and E_2 be two itemsets. $E_1 + E_2$ is the union of E_1 and E_2. The empirical probability of the occurrence of E is defined by

$$P_D(E) = support_D(E)/N, \quad (2)$$

where N is a normalization constant. For the market basket data, N is the number of transactions in D. Under a mild assumption, the empirical probability $P_D(.)$ approaches the real probability $P(.)$ as the number of observations becomes large.

The dependence of itemset E_1 on itemset E_2 is quantified by the empirical conditional probability. Denoted by $P_D(E_1|E_2)$, the empirical conditional probability is computed by

$$P_D(E1|E2) = P_D(E_1 + E_2)/P_D(E_2). \quad (3)$$

Using Equation 2, we can further obtain

$$P_D(E_1|E_2) = support_D(E_1 + E_2)/support_D(E_2). \quad (4)$$

The above equation provides another interpretation of the conditional probability: the ratio of the number of transactions in which E_1 *and* E_2 occur together to the number of transactions in which E_2 occurs. Clearly, a large $P_D(E_1|E_2)$ indicates that E_1 depends more strongly on E_2. In an extreme case, $P_D(E_1|E_2) = 1$ implies that whenever E_2 occurs, E_1 also occurs. Note that $P_D(E_1|E_2)$ characterizes a one-way dependence. In order to have a mutual dependence, we must also examine $P_D(E_2|E_1)$.

Definition 1: Two non-empty itemsets E_1, E_2 are **significantly mutually dependent** for a given D and a minimum dependence threshold $0 \leq minp \leq 1$, iff $P_D(E_1|E_2) \geq minp$ and $P_D(E_2|E_1) \geq minp$.

With this background, we define an m-pattern to be an itemset for which any subset is significantly mutually dependent on all other subsets. That is, if any subset of an m-pattern is present, the remaining items occur with high probability. This is formalized as follows:

Definition 2: A nonempty itemset E is an **m-pattern** with minimum mutual dependence threshold $minp$, iff

$$P_D(E_1|E_2) \geq minp \quad (5)$$

holds for any non-empty two subsets E_1 and E_2 of E, where $0 \leq minp \leq 1$.

Note that this definition does not refer to a support level. Thus, unlike frequent associations, m-patterns will be discovered regardless of the frequency of their occurrences. However, as we note later, it is quite reasonable to consider frequent m-patterns that use both $minp$ and $minsup$.

We now return to the example in Figure 1 to illustrate why $\{a, d\}$ is an m-pattern but $\{a, g\}$ is not assuming $minp = 0.5$. M-patterns are defined by mutual dependence, which requires that all pairs of subsets be significantly mutually dependent above the $minp$ threshold. For the itemset $E = \{a, b\}$, we compute two conditional probabilities: $P_D(\{a\}|\{b\}) = support_D(\{a, b\})/support_D(\{a\}) = 2/3$ and $P_D(\{b\}|\{a\}) = 2/2$. Therefore, $\{a, b\}$ is a m-pattern with $minp = 0.5$. However, $\{a, g\}$ is not an m-pattern since $P_D(\{a\}|\{g\}) = 3/7 < 0.5$.

III. ALGORITHM FOR MINING M-PATTERNS

This section develops an efficient algorithm for discovering all m-patterns. Efficiency is obtained by addressing three issues: (1) how to test (qualify) that an itemset is an m-pattern; (2) how to exploit a level-wise search; and (3) how to prune the search space using a necessary condition for the presence of an m-pattern.

A. Efficiently Qualifying an M-Pattern

The definition of m-patterns (Equation 5) can be used to test whether an itemset is an m-pattern. However, doing so means computing the pairwise conditional probability of all subsets of a candidate m-pattern. Assuming that E_1, E_2 are disjoint and observing that these sets are chosen so that an item is in at most one, then the number of conditional probabilities that must be computed is $O(3^k)$, where k is the length of E. (If E_1, E_2 are not disjoint, the computational complexity is $O(4^k)$.) This means that the direct application of the definition to qualify an m-pattern is computationally intractable even for modest sized values of k.

To qualify an m-pattern efficiently, we derive the following equivalent definition of a m-pattern. Roughly speaking, it shows that we just need to compute a linear number of conditional probabilities rather than to compute all pairwise conditional probabilities of m-pattern subsets.

Property 1: (Equivalent definition of m-patterns) An itemset E is an m-pattern as in Definition 2, iff

$$P_D(E - \{a\}|\{a\}) \geq minp \qquad (6)$$

for every item a in E.

Proof: We first prove the necessary condition. That is, we must show that if E is an m-pattern, then $P_D(E - \{a\}|\{a\}) \geq minp$ for any item $a \in E$. But this follows by letting $E_1 = E - \{a\}$, $E_2 = \{a\}$, and using Definition 2.

Now, we prove that if $P_D(E - \{a\}|\{a\}) \geq minp$ for any $a \in E$, then E is m-pattern. Let E_1 and E_2 represent any two non-empty subsets of E. Let $a \in E_2$. Since $support_D(\{a\}) \geq support_D(E_2)$, we obtain $P_D(\{a\}) \geq P_D(E_2)$ by using Equation 2. Similarly, since $E_1 + E_2$ is a subset of E, $P_D(E_1 + E_2) \geq P_D(E)$. Therefore, we obtain

$$
\begin{aligned}
P_D(E_1 + E_2)/P_D(E_2) &\geq P_D(E)/P_D(\{a\}) \qquad (7) \\
&= P_D(E - \{a\}|\{a\}) \geq minp.
\end{aligned}
$$

Since E_1 and E_2 are any two subsets of E, we have proven that E is an m-pattern by Definition 2. □

The above property allows us to qualify an m-pattern in linear time $O(k)$. The specifics are described in the algorithm below:

Algorithm: **isMPattern**
Input: itemset E, the supports for E, the support for each item in E, and $minp$
Output: $\{true, false\}$
(1) For each item a in E;
(2) If $Support_D(E)/Support_D(\{a\}) < minp$
(3)   Return false
(4) End for
(5) Return true

B. Level-Wise Searching

Now, we develop an efficient algorithm for discovering all m-patterns. Similar to frequent itemset discovery, the number of all potential m-patterns is huge, on the order of n^k, where n is the number of distinct items, and k is the maximum length of an itemset. It is not uncommon that n can to be 1,000 or more. Thus, it is computationally intractable even for modest sized k.

We note that a downward closure (See [7] for more discussion of downward closure.) can lead to an efficient search algorithm. Now, we demonstrate that m-patterns have such a property.

Definition 3: An itemset E is said to be downward closed under a qualification function $f_D(.)$ if the following is true: if the qualification condition $f_D(E)$ holds, then $f_D(E')$ holds for any $E' \subset E$.

Put differently, if $f_D(E')$ does not hold for a subset E', then $f_D(E)$ cannot be true. With the downward closure, we can greatly reduce the number of itemsets that must be examined. For example, frequent itemsets are downward closed since $support_D(E) \leq support_D(E')$. By taking advantage of this property, Agrawal et.al.[2][3] devised a level-wise algorithm called A-priori that discovers all frequent itemsets with a support of at least $minsup$. In specific, starting with $k = 1$, A-priori explores the candidate space iteratively in level wise by first finding all frequent itemsets of size k, and then using this knowledge to construct the candidates of size $k + 1$ based on the downward closure property. Since then, much work has been developed to improve the algorithm by exploring different search strategies (see [1][6][9], and references therein). All these work is built on the downward closure property of frequent itemsets.

Herein, we first show the downward closure property of m-patterns. We then focus on the level-wise algorithm, although all other algorithms can be applied equivalently.

Property 2: (**Downward closure property**) M-patterns are downward closed.

Proof: let E be an itemset and E' be a subset of E. We need to prove that if E is an m-pattern, then E' must be an m-pattern. Let E_1 and E_2 be any two non-empty subsets of E'. Clearly, E_1 and E_2 are also subsets of E because $E' \subset E$. Since E is an m-pattern, we obtain $P_D(E_1|E_2) \geq minp$ (Equation 5). Therefore, E' is an m-pattern. □

Since m-patterns are downward closed, we use a level-wise algorithm for discovering all m-patterns.

Algorithm: **DiscoverMPatterns**
Input: $minp$ and data D
Output: all qualified m-patterns $\{L_k\}$
(1) $L_1 = \{\{a\}|a \in I\}$; $C_2 = \{\{a,b\}|a, b \in I\}$
(2) Scan D to count the occurrences of each pattern in L_1 and C_2
(3) $k = 2$
(4) Compute the qualified candidate set: $L_k = \{v \in C_k|isMPattern(v) = true\}$
(5) Compute the new candidate set C_{k+1} based on L_k
(6) If C_{k+1} is empty, output $\{L_k\}$ and terminate
(7) Scan D and count the occurrence of each pattern $v \in C_{k+1}$
(8) $k = k + 1$; go back to (4)

We note that all itemsets with size 1 are qualified m-patterns by our definition. The set of candidate itemsets of size 2 are thus the set of all combinations of two items. Steps 1 and 2 treat this special situation. Then, the algorithm iteratively searches the candidate space in a level-wise manner. Step 4 finds all m-patterns of length k by using **isMPattern**. Step 5 constructs C_{k+1}, the candidate itemsets for level $k + 1$, based on L_k, the qualified m-patterns found in level k. This can be accomplished by the join operation followed by the pruning done in the A-priori algorithm [2]. If no more candidates can be generated, step 6 terminates and outputs all m-patterns found. Otherwise, Step 7 scans the data to count the occurrences of each candidate in C_{k+1}. Steps 4 through 8 are repeated until no more qualified candidates are found.

Implementing this algorithm requires keeping a counter for each candidate pattern in C_k. As each market basket in D is examined, the counter is increased by one if the candidate is a subset of the transaction. We refer to [2] for further implementation details.

This algorithm needs k-1 data scans. The complexity of this algorithm is linearly dependent on the length of data, but is exponentially dependent on the size of the longest m-pattern. In practice, the algorithm converges quickly, especially when patterns are not very long.

C. Pruning Candidate M-Patterns

The most time-consuming step in the above algorithm is counting the occurrences of candidates. Clearly, the smaller C_k, the faster the algorithm. Therefore, we should prune candidates as much as possible before scanning the data and counting. Below, we show how this can be done by making use of a necessary condition for the presence of an m-pattern.

Property 3: **(Upper bound property)** Let E' be a non-empty subset of E. Let an item $a \in E'$. Then,
(1) $P_D(E - \{a\}|\{a\}) \leq P_D(E - \{a\})/P_D(\{a\})$.
(2) $P_D(E - \{a\})/P_D(\{a\}) \leq P_D(E - E')/P_D(E')$.
Proof: Recall that $P_D(E - \{a\}|\{a\}) = P_D(E)/P_D(\{a\})$ (Equation 3). Since $P_D(E) \leq P_D(E-\{a\})$, the first conclusion holds. Further, since $a \in E'$, $P_D(E - \{a\}) \leq P_D(E - E')$ and $P_D(\{a\}) \geq P_D(E')$, the second inequality holds as well. $\square$

The above property provides an upper-bound for the empirical conditional probability $P_D(E - \{a\}|\{a\})$. Moreover, it also proves that $P_D(E - \{a\})/P_D(\{a\})$ is the tightest upper bound among possible upper bounds.

Using Property 3, we easily obtain a necessary condition for qualifying an m-pattern.

Property 4: **Necessary condition** If E is an m-pattern with $minp$, then

$$support_D(E - \{a\})/support_D(\{a\}) \geq minp, \text{ for any item } a \tag{8}$$

Proof: This follows by combining Equation 5, 4, and Property 3. $\square$

We note that the above necessary condition only depends on the support of patterns found at level 1 and level $k - 1$ (this is different from Property 1 which is dependent on $support_D(E)$ computed by an additional data scan.). Thus, this condition can be used to prune candidates in Step 5, thereby reducing the number of candidates for which counting is done in Step 7. We summarize the pruning algorithm as follows.

Algorithm: **Pruning**
Input: a set of candidate patterns C_k
Output: a set of pruned candidate patterns
(1) For each pattern E in C_k
(2)   For each item a in E
(3)   If $support_D(E - \{a\})/support_D(\{a\}) < minp$
(4) $C_k = C_k - E$
(5)   Goto (7)

(6)   End for
(7) End for
(8) Return C_k

D. Algorithm for Mining M-Patterns

Putting the above described algorithms together, we obtain
Algorithm: **DiscoverMPatternsWithPruning**
Input: $minp$ and data D
Output: all qualified m-patterns $\{L_k\}$
(1) $L_1 = \{\{a\}|a \in I\}$; $C_2 = \{\{a,b\}|a, b \in I\}$
(2) Scan D to count the occurrences of each pattern in L_1 and C_2
(3) $k = 2$
(4) Compute the qualified candidate set: $L_k = \{v \in C_k | \text{isMPattern}(v) = \text{true}\}$
(5a) Construct the new candidate set C_{k+1} based on L_k by the downward closure property
(5b) Prune C_{k+1} based on Property 4 using the **Pruning** algorithm.
(6) if C_{k+1} is empty, output $\{L_k\}$ and terminate
(7) Scan D and count the occurrence of each pattern $v \in C_{k+1}$
(8) $k = k + 1$; go back to (4)

We note that the level-wise algorithm for m-patterns and that for the frequent association have two common steps: constructing the next level candidate patterns based on the previously qualified patterns (Step 5a) and counting occurrences of candidates (Step 7). However, these algorithms differ in several ways. In particular, our algorithm for m-pattern discovery: (a) requires a different treatment for the first and the second levels (Steps 1 to 3); (b) takes advantage of an extra pruning step (Step 5b); and (c) employs a different algorithm to qualify a candidate pattern (Step 4)

E. Extensions

Here, we consider a couple of extensions to our algorithm for discovering m-patterns.

First, note that the definitions and results thus far presented make no assumption about how transactions in D are obtained. Thus, if items have a timestamp (e.g. temporal event data. See [15][14] for the detailed definition), transactions can be constructed using windowing schemes as in[15]. Doing so allows us to discover temporal m-patterns[1].

Second, we show how further performance gain can be obtained by partitioning items. We note that Property 3 can be used to partition the search space. To illustrate this, consider $E = \{a, b\}$. By the property 3, E may be an m-pattern, if both $P_D(\{a\})/P_D(\{b\}) \geq minp$ and $P_D(\{b\})/P_D(\{a\}) \geq minp$. By Equation 2, we obtain

$$support_D(\{b\}) * minp \leq support_D(\{a\}) \leq support_D(\{b\})/minp. \tag{9}$$

Extending this to other items, we can partition items so that the above equation will not hold for items in two different partitions. In this way, a potential m-pattern can only be a subset of items in one and only one partition. Consequently, the original problem is divided into several sub-problems, each of which relates to

---

[1]Some cares are needed to deal with the overlapped windows. We refer to [15] for more implementation details.

one partition of items. This reduces the search space as we only need to consider candidates within a partition. Further, we can solve these sub-problems in parallel.

IV. FREQUENT M-PATTERNS

This section shows that the concepts of frequent itemsets and m-patterns can be combined to develop an algorithm that discovers **frequent m-patterns**. A frequent m-pattern is defined in terms of both $minp$ and $minsup$. That is, a frequent m-pattern is significantly mutually dependent with the dependence threshold $minp$ and has support threshold $minsup$.

How do frequent m-patterns compare with frequent association rules? A frequent association rule with the form $E_1 \Rightarrow E_2$ requires two conditions: (1) $support_D(E_1 + E_2) \geq minsup$; and (2) $P_D(E_2|E_1) \geq minconf$. We note that the second condition does not have the closure property, and thus it is computationally intractable to consider (2) alone. In contrast, m-patterns can be discovered efficiently since downward closure holds. However, mutual dependency, which is required by m-patterns, is a stronger condition than association, as required by association rules.

We now formalize the notion of frequent m-patterns.

Definition 4: E is said to be a frequent m-pattern with $minsup$ and $minp$, iff E is an m-pattern with $minp$, and the number of occurrences of E is no less than $minsup$.

We note that the frequent m-pattern is a more general pattern than the frequent itemset and the m-pattern. In that, when $minsup = 0$, the frequent m-pattern reduces to the m-pattern. When $minp = 0$, the frequent m-pattern becomes the frequent itemsets.

We can mine all frequent m-patterns efficiently. The key insight is that frequent m-patterns are downward closed. We demonstrate this by showing a much stronger result. ([17] discusses this in a slightly different form).

Property 5: (**Conjunction and disjunction of downward closure properties**) Let boolean functions $f_1(.)$ and $f_2(.)$ be two qualification functions of an item set such that $f_1(.)$ and $f_2(.)$ are both downward closed. Then, the qualification function $f_1(E) \wedge f_2(E)$ is downward closed, where "$\wedge$" represents the "and" operation. And $f_1(E) \vee f_2(E)$ is also downward closed, $\vee$ is the "or" operation.

Proof: Let E be a nonempty itemset, $E' \subset E$. Assume that $f_1(E) \wedge f_2(E)$ holds. Since $f_1(E)$ and $f_2(E)$ both hold, we know that both $f_1(E')$ and $f_2(E')$ are true since f_1 and f_2 are downward closed. Therefore, we obtain $f_1(E') \wedge f_2(E')$ is true. Similarly, assume that $f_1(E) \vee f_2(E)$ holds. Then, at least one of $f_1(E)$ and $f_2(E)$ is true and so $f_1(E') \vee f_2(E')$ is true. $\square$

The foregoing allows us to construct a level-wise algorithms for frequent m-patterns by modifying Step 7 of the m-pattern mining algorithms. For a frequent m-pattern, the qualified patterns at level k is $L_k = \{v \in C_k | \mathbf{isMPattern(v)} = \mathbf{true}$ and $support_D(v) \geq minsup\}$. The remaining steps of the algorithm are unchanged.

V. EXPERIMENTAL RESULTS

This section assesses our algorithms for discovering m-patterns. Two kinds of assessments are presented. The first evaluates the performance of our algorithm using synthetic trans-

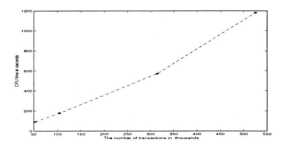

Fig. 2. Average run time in second vs. the number of transactions in 1,000.

action data. The second studies our algorithm using real data collected from a production computer network.

A. Synthetic data

We begin by using synthetic data to study the scalability and efficiency of our algorithm for discovering m-patterns. The synthetic data are constructed by first generating items randomly and uniformly, and then adding instances of patterns into randomly selected transactions. Thus, the synthetic data are specified by the following parameters: the number of transactions, the number of distinct items, the average number of random items per transaction, the number of patterns and their length, and the noise to single ratio (NSR). Here, the NSR for an item in a pattern is defined by the ratio between the number of random instances to the number of the item instances in the pattern. Throughout, the number of distinct items is 1000; the number of patterns is 10 with length 5; the average number of random items in a transaction is 20; and the NSR is 5.

We assess scalability by varying the number of transactions. We compare the level-wise algorithm for mining frequent pattern itemsets with our **DiscoverMPatternsWithPruning** algorithm for mining m-patterns. The values we choose for $minsup$ for frequent patterns and $minp$ for m-pattern are set[2] so that there is no false positive above level 2. An experiment consists of 5 runs done with different random seeds. Figure 2 plots the average CPU time against the total number of transactions (in ten thousands). The results for frequent itemsets are designated by the '*' markers and those for m-patterns by the '+' marker. We see that the two curves are almost indistinguishable, although the curve for frequent patterns is just below that for m-patterns. It is somewhat surprising that m-pattern discovery is so efficient since qualifying an m-pattern requires k comparisons where as frequent itemset only requires one comparison. This suggests that a linear algorithm for qualifying m-patterns is sufficiently fast. Indeed, we see that both algorithms scale linearly as the number of transactions increases.

Now, we study the effect of $minp$ and the benefits provided by the **Pruning** algorithm. Here, the number of transaction is fixed at 50,000. The results are plotted in Figure 3. The x-axis is $minp$, and the y-axis is the CPU seconds required to discover m-patterns. The line with the '+' markers are the results for **DiscoverMPatterns**, and the line with the '*' markers is for **DiscoverMPatternsWithPruning**. Note that for larger values

---

[2]Our results are not sensitive to the specific values used for $minsup$ and $minp$.

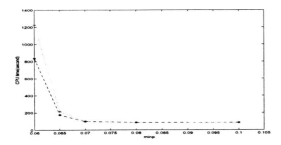

Fig. 3. Average run time vs. $minp$

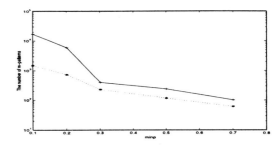

Fig. 4. M-patterns of the first data set. "–": the number of m-patterns in the log scale; "..": the number of border m-patterns in the log scale; x-axis is $minp$

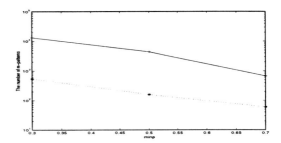

Fig. 5. M-patterns of the second data set. "–": the number of m-patterns in the log scale; "..": the number of border m-patterns in the log scale; x-axis is $minp$

of $minp$ (e.g., $minp > 7\%$), there is little impact on CPU consumption. This is because $minp$ is sufficiently large compared to the fraction of "noise" transactions. However, when $minp$ is small, pruning provides significant benefits. In fact, when $minp$ is 6.5%, a typical run generates about 3730 candidates at the third level. With pruning, the number of candidates reduces to 2550.

B. Production Data

This section applies our algorithms for discovering m-patterns in data from a production computer network. Here, our evaluation criteria are more subjective than the last section in that we must rely on the operations staff to detect whether we have false positives or false negatives.

Two temporal data sets are considered. The first was collected from an insurance company that has events from over two thousand network elements (e.g., routers, hubs, and servers). The second was obtained from an outsourcing center that supports multiple application servers across a large geographical region. Events in the second data set are mostly server-oriented (e.g. the cpu utilization of a server is above a threshold), and those in the first relate largely to network events (e.g. "link down" events). Each data set consists of a series of records describing events received by a network console. An event has three attributes of interest here: host name, which is the source of the event; alarm type, which specifies what happened (e.g., a connection was lost, port up); and the time when the event message was received at the network console. We preprocess these data to convert events into items, where an item is a distinct pair of host and alarm type. The first data set contains approximately 70,000 events for which there are over 2,000 distinct items during a two-week period. The second data set contains over 100,000 events for which there are over 3,000 distinct items across three weeks.

We apply our algorithm for m-pattern discovery to both data sets, and compare the results to those for mining frequent itemsets. We fix $minsup$ to be 3 so as to eliminate a pattern with only one or two instances, and we vary $minp$. Our results are reported in Figures 4 and 5 for data sets 1 and 2, respectively. These figures plot the total number of m-patterns (the solid line) and the number of border m-patterns (the dashed line) against $minp$. Here, a border pattern refers to a pattern that is not a subset of any other pattern. The x-axis is $minp$, and the y-axis is the number of m-patterns discovered on a log scale. Clearly, $minp$ provides a very effective way to select the strongest patterns in that the number of m-patters discovered drops dramatically as

$minp$ increases. Many of these patterns have very low support levels. For example, we found 59 border m-patterns with length from 2 to 5 in the first data set when $minp = 0.7$. Half of these patterns have support levels below 10.

To compare with frequent patterns, it suffices to set $minp = 0$ since the algorithm reduces to mining frequent patterns. Figure 6 reports frequent patterns found in the first data. Here the x-axis is $minsup$, and the y-axis is the log of the number of patterns found. Note that the number of frequent patterns is huge–in excess of 1,000–even when when $minsup$ is 20. Examining the frequent patterns closely, we find that most are related to items that occur frequently, not necessarily items that are causally related. This is not surprise since the marginal distribution of items in our data is highly skewed. Indeed, a small set of items account for over 50% of total events, and consequently, these items tend to appear in many frequent patterns.

Beyond the quality of the results produced by mining for fre-

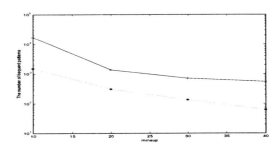

Fig. 6. Frequent patterns of the first data set. "–": the number of frequent patterns in the log scale; "..": the number of border frequent patterns in the log scale; x-axis is $minp$

quent itemsets, there is an issue with scalability as well. In Figures 4 and 5, $minp \geq 0.1$ and $minsup = 3$. Suppose we have $minp = 0$ and $minsup = 3$ so that we are mining for frequent itemsets, but with a very low support threshold. When we attempt to run this case, more than 30k candidates are generated at the third level. Not only does this result in very large computation time, we ultimately run out of memory and so are unable to process the data.

We reviewed the m-pattern found with the operations staff. Many patterns are related to installation errors (e.g. a wrong parameter setting of a monitoring agent) and redundant events (e.g. 11 events are generated to signal a single problem). In addition, a couple of correlations were discovered that are being studied for incorporating into event correlation rules for the real-time monitoring. We emphasize that over half of the m-patterns discovered have very low support levels.

Why are m-patterns common in these data? One reason is a result of physical dependence that manifests itself as a set of events when a problem arises. For example, when a local area network (LAN) fails, all hosts connected to the LAN generate "lost connection" events. Further, the same hosts generate these events if the same failure occurs. This results in the mutual dependence of these events. This observation suggests that m-patterns can be used to construct signatures for problematic situations.

A second cause of m-patterns is redundant information. For example, a device may generate an event to report a problem it detects. However, there may also be several management agents that monitor the same device and report the same problem. This results in an m-pattern consisting of redundant events. Identifying such m-patterns can aid in constructing filtering rules that remove redundant events. More details and insights can be found in [13][10].

VI. CONCLUSION

Motivated by the need to discover infrequent, but strongly correlated patterns, we propose a new pattern, a mutual dependence pattern or a **m-pattern.** M-patterns are defined in terms of $minp$, the minimum probability of mutual occurrence of items in the pattern. In contrast to one-way dependence as in association rules, an m-pattern is characterized by a strong mutual dependency between any two of its subsets. That is, if any part of an itemset occurs, the other part is very likely to occur as well. Our results suggest that such strong mutual dependencies are common in computer networks, such as due to interrelated components that are impacted by the same failure.

We develop an efficient algorithm for discovering m-patterns. This is accomplished in three steps. First, we develop a linear algorithm to qualify an m-pattern based on an equivalence we prove. Second, we show that a level-wise search can be used for m-pattern discovery, a technique that is possible since we prove that m-patterns are downward closed. Last, we develop an effective technique for candidate pruning by establishing a necessary condition for the presence of an m-pattern. A significant impact of the resulting algorithm is that it discovers strongly correlated itemsets that may occur with low support levels, something that is difficult to do with existing mining algorithms.

Using synthetic data, we demonstrate that our algorithm scales well as the data set increases in size. We also show that the pruning algorithm provides considerable benefit, especially for small values of $minp$.

We apply our algorithm to data collected from two production computer networks. The results show that there are many m-patterns, many of which of have very low support levels (e.g., fewer than 10 occurrences). Attempting to discover these patterns using A-priori requires a very small value for support levels, which results in an explosion of candidates that overruns the memory of the computer we used.

We further develop frequent m-patterns that are defined in terms of both $minsup$ and $minp$. We show that this is a more general pattern. That is, when $minp = 0$, this pattern is equivalent to frequent itemsets, and when $minsup = 0$, frequent m-patterns become m-patterns.

ACKNOWLEDGMENT

The authors would like to thank Chang-shing Perng for helpful discussions.

REFERENCES

[1] C. Aggarwal, C. Aggarwal, and V.V.V Parsad. Depth first generation of long patterns. In *Int'l Conf. on Knowledge Discovery and Data Mining*, 2000.
[2] R. Agrawal, T. Imielinski, and A. Swami. Mining association rules between sets of items in large databases. In *Proc. of VLDB*, pages 207–216, 1993.
[3] R. Agrawal and R. Srikant. Fast algorithms for mining association rules. In *Proc. of VLDB*, 1994.
[4] R. Agrawal and R. Srikant. Mining sequential patterns. In *Proc. of the 11th Int'l Conference on Data Engineering, Taipei, Taiwan*, 1995.
[5] R. Bayardo, R. Agrawal, and D. Gunopulos. Constraint-based rule mining in large, dense database. In *ICDE*, 1999.
[6] R.J. Bayardo. Efficiently mining long patterns from database. In *SIGMOD*, pages 85–93, 1998.
[7] S. Brin, R. Motiwani, and C. Silverstein. Beyond market baskets: Generalizing association rules to correlations. *Data Mining and Knowledge Discovery*, pages 39–68, 1998.
[8] Edith Cohen, Mayur Datar, Shinji Fujiwara, Aristides Gionis, Piotr Indyk, Rajeev Motwani, Jeffrey D. Ullman, and Cheng Yang. Finding interesting associations without support pruning. In *ICDE*, pages 489–499, 2000.
[9] J. Han, J. Pei, and Y. Yin. Mining frequent patterns without candidate generation (pdf). In *Proc. 2000 ACM-SIGMOD Int. Conf. on Management of Data (SIGMOD'00), Dallas, TX*, 2000.
[10] J.L. Hellerstein and S. Ma. Mining event data for actionable patterns. In *International Conference for the resource management & performance evaluation of enterprive computing systems*, 2000.
[11] B. Liu and W. Hsu. Post-analysis of learned rules. In *AAAI-96*, pages 828–834, 1996.
[12] Bing Liu, Wynne Hsu, and Yiming Ma. Pruning and summarizing the discovered associations. In *Proceedings of the ACM SIGKDD International Conference on Knowledge Discovery & Data Mining*, pages 15–18, 1999.
[13] S. Ma and J.L. Hellerstein. Eventbrowser: A flexible tool for scalable analysis of event data. In *DSOM'99*, 1999.
[14] S. Ma and J.L. Hellerstein. Mining partially periodic event patterns. In *ICDE*, pages 205–214, 2001.
[15] H. Mannila, H. Toivonen, and A. Verkamo. Discovery of frequent episodes in event sequences. *Data Mining and Knowledge Discovery*, 1(3), 1997.
[16] B. Padmanabhan and A. Tuzhilin. A belief-driven method for discovering unexpected patterns. In *KDD-98*, 1998.
[17] J. Pei and J. Han. Can we push more constraints into frequent pattern mining? In *Conf. on Knowledge Discovery and Data Mining (KDD'00), Boston, MA,*, 2000.
[18] H. Toivonen. Discovery of frequent patterns in large data collections, 1996. Technical Report A-1996-5, Department of Computer Science, University of Helsinki.

The EQ Framework for Learning Equivalence Classes of Bayesian Networks

Paul Munteanu*   Mohamed Bendou
Centre de Recherche du Groupe ESIEA
38 rue des Docteurs Calmette et Guérin
53 000 Laval, France
munteanu@esiea-ouest.fr, bendou@esiea-ouest.fr

Abstract

This paper proposes a theoretical and an algorithmic framework for the analysis and the design of efficient learning algorithms which explore the space of equivalence classes of Bayesian network structures.

This framework is composed of a generic learning model which uses essential graphs and more general partially directed graphs in order to represent the equivalence classes evaluated during search, operational characterizations of these graphs, processing procedures and formulas for directly calculating their score.

The experimental results of the algorithms designed within this framework show that the space of equivalence classes may be explored efficiently and with better results than the classical search in the space of Bayesian network structures.

1 Introduction

Learning Bayesian networks from data is one of the most ambitious approaches to Knowledge Discovery in Databases. Unlike most other data mining techniques, it does not focus its search on a particular kind of knowledge but aims at finding all the (probabilistic) relations which hold between the considered variables.

From a statistical viewpoint, a Bayesian network efficiently encodes the joint probability distribution of the variables describing an application domain. This kind of knowledge allows making rational decisions involving any arbitrary subset of these variables on the basis of the available knowledge about another arbitrary subset of variables.

Moreover, Bayesian networks may be represented in a graphical annotated form which seems quite natural to human experts for a large variety of applications. The nodes of a Bayesian network correspond to domain variables and the edges which connect the nodes correspond to direct probabilistic relations between these variables. Under certain assumptions [6], these relations have causal semantics (a directed edge $A \rightarrow B$ may be interpreted as *A is a direct cause of B*), while most other data mining approaches deal exclusively with correlation.

There are two main approaches to learning Bayesian networks with unknown structure. The first one is to build the network according to the conditional independence relations found in data (*e.g.*, [6]). Traditionally, these methods aim at discovering causal relations between the variables and, therefore, emphasize the structural fidelity of the Bayesian networks they learn. However, they suffer from the lack of reliability of high-dimensional conditional independence tests.

The other approach to learning Bayesian networks is to define an evaluation function (or score) which accounts for the quality of candidate networks with respect to the available data and to use some kind of search algorithm in order to find, in a "reasonable" amount of time, a network with an "acceptable" score (we use the terms "reasonable" and "acceptable" because this learning task has been proven to be NP-hard for the evaluation functions mentioned in the following section). These algorithms are less sensitive to the quality of the available data and their results can be successfully used in various decision making tasks.

However, as we will see in the following section, the exploration of the space of Bayesian network structures by a greedy search algorithm may end with a structure which fails to reveal some independence relations between the variables and, therefore, may be rather different from the true one. The space of equivalence classes of Bayesian network structures seems to be better suited for this kind of search. Learning algorithms which explore this space have already been proposed by some authors, as described in section 3. Unfortunately, these algorithms are considerably slower than classical ones, mainly because they have to build instances of the equivalence classes in order to check their consistency and in order to calculate their score.

---

* Also with Bayesia S.A., 6 rue Léonard de Vinci, 53 000 Laval, France

417

Section 4 proposes a new framework for designing more efficient learning algorithms which explore the space of equivalence classes of Bayesian networks. This framework relies on some theoretical results and algorithms presented in section 5 and on the definition of transformation operators that can be directly applied and evaluated on essential graphs, which are presented in section 6. The experimental results presented in section 7 confirm the fact that the algorithms designed within this framework are able to efficiently produce better results than classical greedy and tabu search in the space of Bayesian networks.

2 Heuristic search in the space of Bayesian networks

Like in many other machine learning approaches, the quality of a Bayesian network with respect to the available data is evaluated on the basis of a score issued from the information theory or from Bayesian inference. Some of these scores, like MDL [3] and BDe [4] have been proven to be asymptotically correct and have some nice mathematical properties that can be exploited by the search algorithms:

- the score of a Bayesian network may be expressed as a sum of local scores involving only a node and its parents;

- the Bayesian networks belonging to the same equivalence class (*i.e.*, representing the same conditional independence relations) have the same score.

Since the unconstrained learning of Bayesian networks is NP-hard, most authors propose the use of heuristic search algorithms, which explore the space of Bayesian network structures. The transformation operators are the addition, the suppression, and the reversal of edges, submitted to the constraint that the resulting network contains no cycle (on the basis of score decomposability, these operators ensure that no more than two local scores have to be re-evaluated in order to evaluate the resulting network). The search strategy is based on some general-purpose method (greedy search, simulated annealing or tabu search).

Unfortunately, there are many local optima in the space of Bayesian networks and heuristic search algorithms may easily be trapped in one of them. The main reason for this difficulty is the equality of the score of equivalent networks. We illustrate this statement by a learning task which is very simple but nevertheless confusing for greedy search (fig. 1). In this example, we have three variables distributed according to the Bayesian network 1a (which is the only instance of its equivalence class). Let us consider that there is enough data, such as the evaluation function we use (which is asymptotically correct) assigns the best score to the network 1a, among all possible network structures.

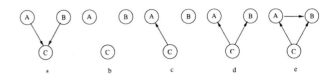

Figure 1. Greedy search

Suppose the search starts with the totally unconnected network of fig. 1b. Hopefully, the search algorithm will immediately find that adding edges between A and C and between B and C improves the score of the network. Suppose, for instance, that the addition of an edge between A and C produces the greatest improvement of the score. Since the structures $(A \rightarrow C \quad B)$ and $(A \leftarrow C \quad B)$ belong to the same equivalence class (as described in the next section), the addition of the edge $A \rightarrow C$ and the addition of the edge $A \leftarrow C$ have the same impact on score at the beginning of the search. Therefore, there is a 50 % chance[1] that the search algorithm adds the first edge in the wrong direction $(A \leftarrow C)$. If it does so, the direction of the edge between B and C also becomes indifferent from the score viewpoint, as the structures $(A \leftarrow C \rightarrow B)$ and $(A \leftarrow C \leftarrow B)$ belong to the same equivalence class. Globally, there is a 25 % chance that the network found after the second iteration is $(A \leftarrow C \rightarrow B)$. In this case, since A and B become dependent when C is known (as shown by fig. 1a), an edge will be added between these nodes (e.g. $A \rightarrow B$). This makes the search stop in an incorrect state, because no further single edge reversal or removal can improve the score. In larger networks, this kind of early wrong decisions are very probable and their effects can cumulate and make the final network very different from the ideal one.

3 Heuristic search in the space of equivalence classes of Bayesian network structures

Bayesian networks that represent the same conditional independence relations form an equivalence class. All Bayesian networks belonging to the same equivalence class have the same *skeleton* (undirected graph resulting from ignoring the directionality of edges) and the same *v-structures* (triples of nodes A, B, C such that A and B are not adjacent and are connected to C by the edges $A \rightarrow C \leftarrow B$ (as in fig. 1a) [7].

---

[1]From our experience with publicly available software, it appears that most programmers seem to neglect this issue and simply apply the first best operator found. Since the order of evaluation of edge additions generally depends on node order and publicly available networks often declare nodes in their topological order, the results of these programs on "gold-standard" benchmarks are over-optimistic. Reversing the order of nodes declarations can lead to serious degradations of their performance.

Equivalence classes are generally represented as partially directed graphs (*essential graphs, completed pdags* or *patterns*) in which edges that may appear in either direction in networks belonging to the same equivalence class are represented as undirected edges and the other edges are represented as directed edges. These conditions define a unique representation for equivalence classes but do not ensure that the equivalence classes represented this way are legal (e.g. can be instantiated).

In order to overcome the difficulties presented in the previous section, we can realize the search in the space of equivalence classes. Intuitively, this approach consists in allowing the addition of undirected edges when no direction is preferred by the score. Edge orientation is delayed until the interactions between edges make possible the choice of a direction on the basis of the score. As the obtained partially directed graphs may be interpreted as equivalence classes, this solution consists in a modification of the search space: the search algorithm explores the space of equivalence classes of Bayesian networks instead of the space of Bayesian networks.

This kind of solution has already been studied in [2]. The conclusion of this work was that the search in the space of equivalence classes generally provides better results than the search in the space of Bayesian networks but, unfortunately, it is much more time consuming.

One of the difficulties Chickering met in his work was the evaluation of equivalence classes. As available evaluation functions have been designed to score Bayesian networks (and not equivalence classes), his solution consists in the generation of an arbitrary instance of the equivalence class to be evaluated and the evaluation of this instance according to classical formulas. Additionally, Chickering's algorithm relies on this procedure in order to prevent the construction of illegal equivalence classes (without instances).

This procedure is much more time-consuming than the evaluation of a Bayesian network because it needs some additional time to generate an instance from the equivalence class and because more than two local scores may have to be evaluated in order to evaluate the generated instance.

4   Overview of the EQ framework

Essential graphs which represent similar equivalence classes (*i.e.*, equivalence classes which are close in terms of the conditional independence relations they assert) may be rather different in terms of structure (directed and undirected edges). For this reason, it is not possible to design simple transformation operators which allow the exploration of this search space by directly moving from an essential graph to a similar essential graph.

We use instead transformation operators that realize tiny modifications of the current essential graph and produce

partially directed graphs which are generally not essential graphs. An arbitrary partially directed graph G may be interpreted as representing the set of DAGs ("instances") which have the same skeleton and the same v-structures as G and contain all the directed edges of G.

Obviously, we are interested in producing partially directed graphs which represent non-empty sets of instances, which we call *instantiable graphs*. It follows that all essential graphs are instantiable graphs. The set of instances represented by an essential graph forms an equivalence class but, generally, an instantiable graph only represents a subset (possibly empty) of an equivalence class. The following section gives an algorithmic characterization of instantiable graphs. This characterization allows the elaboration of constraints on the applicability of transformation operators which ensure that the transformed graphs are instantiable. The verification of these constraints is more efficient than the instantiation algorithm used by Chickering for the same reason.

The applicability of transformation operators is also constrained in order to keep transformations tiny. There are two main reasons for doing this. On one hand, great steps in the search space are not suitable for greedy search strategies (each iteration have to carefully inspect the neighborhood of the current search state). On the other hand, we are able to evaluate tiny transformations more efficiently than greater ones.

We propose the following definition for tiny transformations: Let G be the current essential graph and G' the instantiable graph obtained by the application of a transformation operator on G. The transformation is tiny if there exist an instance I of G and an instance I' of G' such that I' may be obtained from I by the addition or the suppression of a single edge $X \rightarrow Y$.

Since equivalent DAGs have equal scores and all instances represented by a partially directed graph belong to a single equivalence class, we can define the score of an instantiable partially directed graph as being the score of any of its instances. In the following, $S(G)$ denotes the score of the (directed or partially directed) graph G. $Pa_G(X)$ ("parents" of X in G) denotes the set of nodes Y such that $X \leftarrow Y$ belongs to graph G (the subscript G will be omitted when it is obvious from context). $S(X \mid \mathcal{P})$ denotes the score of node X with the set of nodes $\mathcal{P}$ as parents (remember the score of a Bayesian network is decomposable on nodes).

The quality of a tiny transformation is therefore given by the following formula:

$$\Delta S(G', G) = S(G') - S(G) = S(I') - S(I) = S(Y \mid Pa_{I'}(Y)) - S(Y \mid Pa_I(Y))$$

We will see in the following sections that we can identify $Pa'_I(Y)$ et $Pa_I(Y)$ without instantiating G and G', and, therefore, the quality of the transformation can be directly evaluated by computing only two local scores.

Once the best transformation identified, the learning algorithm has to elaborate the essential graph corresponding to the winning instantiable graph. As we will see in section 5.2, this conversion consists in orienting some previously undirected edges and removing the orientation of some previously directed edges, in order to "propagate" the effects of the transformation through the entire graph.

This theoretical framework extends our previous work on the EQ1 algorithm presented in [5], which restricts intermediate representations to instantiable chain graphs (instantiable graphs without partially directed cycles). It allows the relaxation of some of the contraints on the transformation operators used by EQ1 and facilitates the definition of new transformation operators (*i.e.*, suppression of edges).

5 Algorithmic characterizations of some classes of partially directed graphs

5.1 Instantiable graphs

The characterization of instantiable graphs we propose relies on a constructive approach. The following definitions provide the rules for orienting undirected edges (*pseudo directed edges* and *pseudo directed paths*) and characterize the substructures of a partially directed graph that cannot be instantiated (*minimal undirected cycles, pseudo directed cycles* and *colliding minimal chains*).

Definition 1 (Pseudo directed edges) *We say that an undirected edge $X - Y$ of a graph G is a pseudo directed edge from X to Y, and we note $X \overset{\rightarrow}{-} Y$, if $X - Y$ occurs in at least one of the three configurations of fig.2 as an induced subgraph of G.*

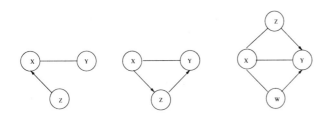

Figure 2. Possible configurations for pseudo directed edges

The orientation of pseudo directed edges is directly imposed by the neighboring directed edges in order to prevent directed cycles or spurious v-structures.

Definition 2 (Minimal chain) *A succession of undirected edges $X_1, \ldots, X_n$ is called a minimal chain if X_i, X_{i+2} are not adjacent for any $i \leq N - 2$.*

Figure 3. Minimal chain

All edges belonging to the same minimal chain have to be oriented in the same direction in order to avoid the introduction of spurious v-structures.

Definition 3 (Minimal undirected cycle) *A minimal chain $X_1, \ldots, X_n$ is called a minimal undirected cycle if $X_{N-1} = X_1$ and $X_n = X_2$.*

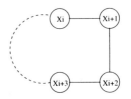

Figure 4. Minimal undirected cycle

Alternatively, an undirected cycle is minimal if it is not chordal (chords may be directed). Since all edges of a minimal undirected cycle have to be oriented in the same direction, this kind of substructure cannot be instantiated.

Definition 4 (Pseudo directed path) *We say that a minimal chain $X_1, \ldots, X_n$ is a pseudo directed path, and we note $X_1, \overset{\rightarrow}{\ldots}, X_n$ if $X_1 \overset{\rightarrow}{-} X_2$.*

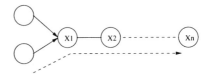

Figure 5. Pseudo directed path

The orientation of the pseudo directed edges have to be propagated through the graph along the pseudo directed paths.

Definition 5 (Pseudo directed cycle) *A partially directed cycle is called a pseudo directed cycle if all the undirected edges of the cycle belong to pseudo directed paths oriented in the same direction as the cycle.*

420

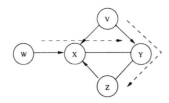

Figure 6. Example of a pseudo directed cycle

Since all its undirected edges have to be oriented in the same direction, a pseudo directed cycle cannot be instantiated.

Definition 6 (Colliding minimal chain) *A minimal chain* $X_1, \ldots, X_N$ *is called a colliding minimal chain if and only if* $X_1, \overset{..}{\rightarrow}., X_N$ *and* $X_1, \overset{..}{\leftarrow}. X_N$.

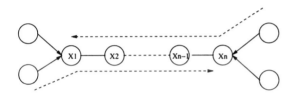

Figure 7. Colliding minimal chain

This kind of substructure cannot be instantiated without introducing spurious v-structures.

The following quasi algorithmic theorem characterizes instantiable graphs.

Theorem 1 *A partially oriented graph, G, is instantiable if and only if :*

1. *G does not contain any directed cycle;*

2. *G does not contain any pseudo directed cycle;*

3. *G does not contain any minimal undirected cycle;*

4. *G does not contain any colliding minimal chain.*

5.2 Essential graphs

Since the class of instantiable graphs is larger than the class of essential graphs, the previous characterization must be completed with further constraints in order to apply to essential graphs.

First of all, it is obvious that an essential graph may not contain any pseudo directed edge (because the pseudo directed edges of an instantiable graph are oriented in the same direction for all its instances, which is contradictory with the role of undirected edges in essential graphs).

As we have seen earlier, an instantiable graph represents only a subsets of an equivalence class. The reason is that some edges of the uncovered instances, which correspond to some directed edges of the instantiable graph, can be oriented in the opposite direction. The neighborhood of a directed edge allows us to recursively detect such superfluous directed edges on the basis of the following definition:

Definition 7 (Pseudo undirected edges) *We say that a directed edge* $X \rightarrow Y$ *of a graph G is a pseudo undirected edge, and we note* $X \overset{\rightarrow}{-} Y$, *if and only if* $Pa_G(X) = Pa_G(Y) \setminus X$ *or* $Pa_G(X) \subset Pa_G(Y)$ *and* $Pa_G(Y) \setminus Pa_G(X)$ *is a proper complete set* [2] *of G.*

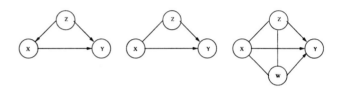

Figure 8. Examples of possible configurations for pseudo undirected edges

The following theorem characterizes essential graphs in relation to instantiable graphs (see [1] for a characterization of essential graphs in relation to chain graphs).

Theorem 2 (Characterization of essential graphs) *An instantiable graph G is an essential graph if and only if it does not contain any pseudo directed or pseudo undirected edge.*

Remark 1 *If G is an essential graph,* $Pa_G(X) = Pa_G(Y)$ *for all undirected edges* $X - Y$ *of G (X and Y are "brothers").*

If G is an instantiable graph, the following algorithm will produce the essential graph corresponding to the instances of G:

Algorithm 1 ("Propagation" algorithm)
Do

    While there exists at least an edge $X \overset{\rightarrow}{\rightarrow} Y$ *do*
        Remove the orientation of $X \rightarrow Y$
    While there exists at least an edge $X \overset{\rightarrow}{-} Y$ *do*
        Orient $X - Y$ *as* $X \rightarrow Y$
Until no more pseudo edges are left in G.

---

[2] A proper complete set of a graph is a set of two or more nodes which are all interconnected by edges.

6 Transformation operators

Let G be the current essential graph and G' the transformed graph. Remember G' has to be instantiable and the transformation has to be tiny.

The following subsections present four operators which respect these conditions. In order to improve the efficiency of the search algorithm we consider here two different operators for the addition of directed and undirected edges, although the addition of directed edges together with the propagation phase are able to emulate the addition of undirected edges.

6.1 Operator 1: Addition of an undirected edge

6.1.1 Definition

$$G' = Op1(G, X, Y) = G \cup \{X - Y\}$$

6.1.2 Constraints

We will consider this "shortcut" operator only when $Pa_G(X) = Pa_G(Y)$. In these cases, we are sure that the added edge will remain undirected (no pseudo directed edge is generated by the transformation).

Clearly, the addition of an undirected edge cannot violate condition 1 of theorem 1. Conditions 2 and 4 are also trivially verified since *Operator 1* does not introduce pseudo directed edges.

Since G is an essential graph and $Pa_G(X) = Pa_G(Y)$, condition 3 may be expressed in a simpler form: if $X - Y$ introduces an undirected cycle in G', then X and Y must have at least a common "brother" (a node Z such that $X - Z$ and $Y - Z$ belong to G).

6.1.3 Score

Remember we can efficiently evaluate transformations if we are able to (imaginarily) build two instances I of G and I' of G' which differ only in a single edge.

It can be easily verified that the following orientations result in instantiable graphs:

- $X - Y$ is oriented as $X \to Y$ in G';

- all edges $Y - W$, where W is a brother of X, are oriented as $Y \leftarrow W$ in G and G' (in order to have the same parents for X and W in both graphs);

- all other undirected edges adjacent to Y in G, $Y - W$, are oriented as $Y \to W$ in G and G'.

Furthermore, after these orientations, the two graphs have the same pseudo directed edges and, therefore, there exists two instances I and I' of each of these graphs which differ only in the edge $X \to Y$.

We have therefore:

$$\Delta S(G', G) = S(Y \mid Pa(Y), Br(X, Y), X) - S(Y \mid Pa(Y), Br(X, Y))$$

where $Pa(Y)$ is the set of parents of Y in G and $Br(X, Y)$ ("common brothers" of X and Y) denotes the set of nodes Z such that $X - Z$ and $Y - Z$ belong to G.

6.2 Operator 2: Addition of a directed edge

6.2.1 Definition

$$G' = Op2(G, X, Y) = G \cup \{X \to Y\}$$

6.2.2 Constraints

First of all, we will consider the application of this operator only when $Pa_G(X) \neq Pa_G(Y)$, since in the other cases we directly try to apply *Operator 1*.

Condition 3 of theorem 1 is trivially verified for this operator.

Since G is an essential graph, the only pseudo directed edges in G' are those possibly introduced by $X \to Y$, which are all adjacent to Y. Therefore, condition 4 of the theorem is also trivially verified.

On the basis of conditions 1 and 2 of theorem 1 we have to verify that $X \to Y$ does not introduce any directed or pseudo directed cycles in G'. Since all possible pseudo directed paths of G' start with an edge adjacent to Y, the verification of the absence of pseudo directed cycles can be made efficiently.

6.2.3 Score

The formula for calculating the score of this operator is based on the following orientations:

- all edges $Y - W$, where W is a parent of X, are oriented as $Y \leftarrow W$ in G and G' (pseudo directed edges of type 2 in G');

- all other undirected edges adjacent to Y in G, $Y - W$, are oriented as $Y \to W$ in G and G'.

$$\Delta S(G', G) = S(Y \mid Pa(Y), Br(Y) \cap Pa(X), X) - S(Y \mid Pa(Y), Br(Y) \cap Pa(X))$$

6.3 Operator 3: Addition of v-structure

6.3.1 Definition

$$G' = Op3(G, X, Y, Z) = (G \setminus \{Y - Z\}) \cup \{X \to Y\} \cup \{Y \leftarrow Z\}$$

This operator realizes the addition of a directed edge together with the orientation of a previously undirected edge.

6.3.2 Constraints

Conditions 3 and 4 of theorem 1 are trivially verified, as for the previous operator. Condition 1 and 2 must be explicitly verified.

As for the previous operator, pseudo directed cycles can be efficiently detected by following the pseudo directed paths which starts with pseudo directed edges adjacent to Y.

Unlike the other operators presented here, operator 3 may propose transformations which are not tiny in the sense of our definition. For instance, the transformation depicted in figure 9 produces an instantiable graph but its evaluation need more than two computations of local scores. A simple modification of the procedure which detects pseudo directed cycles can explicitly forbid these transformations.

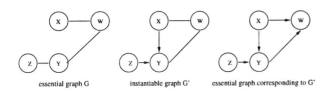

essential graph G   instantiable graph G'   essential graph corresponding to G'

Figure 9. Transformation prohibited by operator 3

6.3.3 Score

If the transformations proposed by this operator are tiny, we can calculate their score on the basis of the following orientations:

- $Y - Z$ is oriented as $Y \leftarrow Z$ in both G and G';

- all edges $Y - W$, where W is a parent of X, are oriented as $Y \leftarrow W$ in G and G' (pseudo directed edges of type 2 in G');

- all edges $Y - W$, where W is a brother of X and Z, are oriented as $Y \leftarrow W$ in G and G' (pseudo directed edges of type 3 in G');

- all other undirected edges adjacent to Y in G, $Y - W$, are oriented as $Y \rightarrow W$ in G and G'.

$\Delta S(G', G) =$
$S(Y \mid Pa(Y), Z, Br(Y) \cap Pa(X), Br(X, Y, Z), X) -$
$S(Y \mid Pa(Y), Z, Br(Y) \cap Pa(X), Br(X, Y, Z))$

6.4 Operator 4: Suppression of an undirected edge

6.4.1 Definition

$$G' = Op4(G, X, Y) = G \setminus \{X - Y\}$$

6.4.2 Constraints

The suppression of an undirected edge clearly cannot violate conditions 1, 2 and 4 of theorem 1. In order to satisfy condition 3, the common brothers of X and Y have to form a complete set.

6.4.3 Score

The formula for calculating the score of this operator is based on the following orientations:

- $X - Y$ is oriented as $X \rightarrow Y$ in G;

- all edges $Y - W$, where W is a common brother of X and Y, are oriented as $Y \leftarrow W$ in G and G' (in order to have the same parents for X and W in both graphs);

- all other undirected edges adjacent to Y in G, $Y - W$, are oriented as $Y \rightarrow W$ in G and G'.

$$\Delta S(G', G) = S(Y \mid Pa(Y), Br(X, Y)) - S(Y \mid Pa(Y), Br(X, Y), X)$$

6.5 Operator 5: Suppression of a directed edge

6.5.1 Definition

$$G' = Op5(G, X, Y) = G \setminus \{X \rightarrow Y\}$$

6.5.2 Constraints

The suppression of a directed edge clearly cannot violate conditions 1, 2 and 3 of theorem 1. In order to satisfy condition 4, the brothers of Y have to form a complete set.

6.5.3 Score

The formula for calculating the score of this operator is based on the following orientations:

- all edges $Y - W$ are oriented as $Y \leftarrow W$ in G and G' (pseudo directed edges of type 1 in G').

$$\Delta S(G', G) = S(Y \mid Pa(Y) \setminus X, Br(Y)) - S(Y \mid Pa(Y), Br(Y))$$

7 Experimental results

Two versions of a learning algorithm have been implemented in the proposed framework:

- EQ2 which uses *Operators 1, 2* and *3* (no suppression of edges is allowed);

- EQ3 which uses all the transformation operators presented in this paper.

In order to evaluate their performances we have compared them experimentally to classical greedy search and tabu search in the space of Bayesian networks.

Tabu search uses a tabu list of 10 states and stops after 10 consecutive iterations without score improvement. All algorithms use the MDL score, as defined in [3].

The comparison has been realized on learning tasks involving seven publicly available Bayesian networks of various sizes: *Seismometer* (1): 4 nodes, 4 edges, *Cancer* (2): 5 nodes, 5 edges, *Asia* (3): 8 nodes, 8 edges, *Year2000* (4): 8 nodes, 11 edges, *CarStarts* (5): 18 nodes, 17 edges, *Alarm* (6): 37 nodes, 46 edges, and *Hailfinder* (7): 56 nodes, 66 edges.

In order to improve the statistical significance of the experimental results, we have compared the algorithms on thirty different data sets for each network (1,000 examples for the small networks *Seismometer*, *Cancer*, *Asia*, *Year2000*, and 10,000 for the others, generated according to the probability distributions modeled by the networks).

Table 1 presents the means of the score of the compared algorithms (the MDL score has to be *minimized*). The best results are presented in bold face.

N	GreedyBN	TabuBN	EQ2	EQ3
1	1854,81	**1847,77**	1879,29	1853,80
2	3266.29	3262.61	**3261.57**	**3261.57**
3	3343.20	3336.69	**3335.82**	**3335.82**
4	82042,58	81513,59	81513,12	**81132,48**
5	33563.80	33553.79	**33517.19**	**33517.19**
6	139719.52	139558.87	139196,04	**139116,70**
7	720712.31	720383.23	**720038.42**	**720038.42**

Table 1. Scores

Table 2 presents the comparison of the average execution times of the three algorithms. They are all programmed in Java, using the same base classes, the same methods for computing scores and the same caching schemas. The tabu list of TabuBN is implemented as a hash table. The comparison has been realized on a PIII 500Mhz CPU. The results are given in seconds.

These results clearly show that EQ algorithms are systematically more successful than GreedyBN, and even

N	GreedyBN	TabuBN	EQ2	EQ3
1	**0,17**	0,18	**0,17**	0,19
2	0,20	0,25	**0,19**	0,20
3	0,48	0,55	**0,47**	**0,47**
4	**4,35**	5,16	4,84	5,11
5	16,76	19,23	**15,86**	15,94
6	**103,62**	162,18	107,92	108,43
7	**223,02**	502,92	246,53	246,95

Table 2. Execution times

TabuBN on non-trival tasks, for execution times comparable to those of GreedyBN and smaller than those of TabuBN. The experimental results also show that the edge suppression operators used by EQ3 allow a better exploration of the search space and have a rather reduced impact on the duration of the search.

8 Conclusion

This paper shows that it is possible to learn equivalence classes of Bayesian networks by handling only partially directed graphs which represent sets of network structures.

The EQ framework provides the means for the verification of the consistency of these partially directed graphs and for the computation of their score without instantiation. It allows the design of efficient and successful learning algorithms well adapted to the characteristics of their search space.

References

[1] S. Andersson, D. Madigan, and M. Perlman. A characterization of markov equivalence classes for acyclic digraphs. *Annals of Statistics*, 25:505–541, 1997.

[2] D. Chickering. Learning equivalence classes of bayesian-network structures. In *Proc. of the 12th Conf. on Uncertainty in Artificial Intelligence*. Morgan Kaufmann, 1996.

[3] N. Friedman and M. Goldszmidt. Learning bayesian networks with local structure. In *Proc. of the 12th Conf. on Uncertainty in Artificial Intelligence*. Morgan Kaufmann, 1996.

[4] D. Heckerman, D. Geiger, and D. Chickering. Learning bayesian networks: The combination of knowledge and statistical data. *Machine Learning*, 20:197–243, 1995.

[5] P. Munteanu and D. Cau. Efficient learning of equivalence classes of bayesian networks. In *Proc. of the 4th European Conf. on Principles and Practice of Knowledge Discovery in Databases*. Springer-Verlag, 2000.

[6] P. Spirtes, C. Glymour, and R. Scheines. *Causation, Prediction and Search*. Springer-Verlag, 1993.

[7] T. Verma and J. Pearl. Equivalence and synthesis of causal models. In *Proc. of the 6th Conf. on Uncertainty in Artificial Intelligence*. Elsevier, 1990.

Visualizing Association Mining Results through Hierarchical Clusters

Steven Noel
Center for Secure Information Systems
George Mason University
snoel@gmu.edu

Vijay Raghavan and C.-H. Henry Chu
Center for Advanced Computer Studies
University of Louisiana at Lafayette
[raghavan,cice]@cacs.louisiana.edu

Abstract

We propose a new methodology for visualizing association mining results. Inter-item distances are computed from combinations of itemset supports. The new distances retain a simple pairwise structure, and are consistent with important frequently occurring itemsets. Thus standard tools of visualization, e.g. hierarchical clustering dendrograms can still be applied, while the distance information upon which they are based is richer. Our approach is applicable to general association mining applications, as well as applications involving information spaces modeled by directed graphs, e.g. the Web. In the context of collections of hypertext documents, the inter-document distances capture the information inherent in a collection's link structure, a form of link mining. We demonstrate our methodology with document sets extracted from the Science Citation Index, applying a metric that measures consistency between clusters and frequent itemsets.

1. Introduction

In some respect, the World Wide Web is like a vast library without an index system. Search engines are thus critical in finding Web pages of interest. Traditionally, search engines rank their results according to how well pages match keywords in the user query. In contrast, more innovative search engines such as Google [1] first perform a keyword search, and use results from prior analyses of the structure of Web hyperlinks to generate page ranks, independent of user queries for the selected pages. However, the results for these link-based search engines are still displayed as ranked lists, just as for traditional search engines.

Simple linear lists cannot adequately capture many of the complex hyperlink relationships among Web pages. Techniques from the field of information visualization can help in this regard, making complex relationships more readily understandable. Visualization augments serial language processing with eye/brain parallel processing. Thus, the goal of visualization techniques is to enable users to recognize patterns in Web link structure, thus helping to alleviate cyberspace information overload.

Previous approaches in this area have typically analyzed Web hyperlinks directly to determine page relationships [2], or have relied on measures of similarity that only consider joint referencing of pairs of pages. The approach proposed in this work relies instead on measures of similarity that exploit sets of pages of arbitrary cardinality. In particular, the similarity among a set of pages is based on the number of other pages that jointly link to them.

The proposed similarity measures are inspired by the concept of co-citations, introduced in classical information retrieval in the context of citations appearing in published literature [3]. Co-citations reduce complex citation or hyperlink graphs to simple scalar similarities between documents or Web pages. Co-citation based similarities allow the direct application of standard tools developed in other areas of science, such as cluster analysis [4].

Similarity among objects by common reference has recently received some attention in the form of association mining [5]. While they are not usually recognized as such, what are defined as itemsets in association mining can be interpreted as generalized co-citations. Similarities between pairs of documents in co-citation analysis can be generalized to reflect the impact of sets of documents of arbitrary, larger cardinality that are jointly cited. Thus, itemsets are interpreted as higher-order co-citations.

This work is the first known application of association mining to the visualization of link structures. Important (frequently occurring) higher-order itemsets are often obscured by the mere pairwise treatment of traditional co-citation analysis. The approach we take here involves the discovery of frequently occurring itemsets of arbitrary cardinalities, and the assigning of importance to them according to their support frequencies.

In a collection of itemsets, pairs of itemsets can overlap, so that there is a combinatorial explosion in the numbers of sets the user has to potentially deal with. We propose a novel approach to the problem of presenting results of association mining to users, which involves embedding higher-order co-citations (itemset supports) into pairwise document similarities. This hybrid of pairwise and higher-order similarities greatly reduces the complexity of user interaction, while being significantly more consistent with higher-order co-citations than standard pairwise similarities. It also admits the application of fast algorithms developed for data mining, which are empirically known to scale linearly with problem size [6].

The next section introduces our higher-order generalization of co-citations, and describes how they can be included in inter-document distances. Section 3 then proposes the augmented dendrogram clustering visualization for information retrieval, and demonstrates the effects of our new distances on the dendrogram. In Section 4, we define a metric that measures consistency between clusters and frequently occurring itemsets, and apply the metric to a number of test cases with real-world data extracted from a literature citation database. Section 5 then summarizes our work and highlights its conclusions.

2. Distances from Itemset Supports

Hyperlink systems, e.g. the World Wide Web or science citations, can in general be modeled as directed graphs. A graph edge from one document to another indicates a link from first to second. It is convenient to apply a matrix formulation for the development of link-based document distances. In fact, for actual implementation this leads to the direct application of matrix data structures and operations usually found in programming languages.

In the matrix formulation, a binary adjacency matrix is formed that corresponds to the linkage graph. We take the convention that adjacency matrix rows are for citing documents and columns are for cited documents. Thus for adjacency matrix $\mathbf{A}$, element $a_{i,j} = 1$ indicates that document i cites document j, and $a_{i,j} = 0$ is the lack of citation.

A co-citation between two documents is the citing (or hypertext linking) of the two documents by another one [3]. A measure of similarity between a pair of documents is the number of documents that co-cite the pair. This is known as citation count. Taken over all pairs of documents, the co-citation count similarity serves as a compact representation of citation graph structure.

A central component in classical citation analysis is clustering based on co-citations as a measure of similarity. In the case of co-citations, an association is made between two documents according to the number of times they are co-referenced, i.e. through hypertext links or literature citations. The purpose of clustering is to form larger sets of documents that are more strongly

associated with one another than they are to documents outside the cluster.

Traditional citation analysis typically applies single-linkage clustering, because of its lower computational complexity [7]. But because of its very weak clustering criterion, single-linkage can have problems unless the data are inherently well clustered. Given the improved performance of modern computing machines, it becomes feasible to apply stronger clustering criteria in citation analysis.

For the stronger clustering criterion of complete linkage, *all* similarities for the three pairs need to exceed the threshold before the documents constitute a single cluster. But it is still possible to construct cases in which there is not even one document that cites all of the clustered documents simultaneously. The complete-linkage criterion is a necessary but not sufficient condition for the simultaneous citing of all documents in a cluster.

We propose a generalization of the co-citation similarity in which sets of cardinality above two are considered for co-citation. That is, we defin e a similarity among a set of cited documents that is based on the number of times all the members of the set are simultaneously cited. Because the similarity is among more than two documents, we consider it to be higher order than pairwise.

In our matrix formulation, itemset supports are computed for sets of columns (cited documents) of the adjacency matrix, just as they are computed for pairs of columns in computing co-citation counts. For itemset I of cardinality $|I|$, whose member documents correspond to columns $j_1, j_2, ..., j_{|I|}$, its scalar support $\zeta(I)$ is

$$\zeta(I) = \sum_i a_{i,j_1} a_{i,j_2} \cdots a_{i,j_{|I|}} = \sum_i \prod_{\alpha=1}^{|I|} a_{i,j_\alpha} ,$$

where i indexes rows (citing documents). Just as for pairwise co-citations, the term $a_{i,j_1} a_{i,j_2} \cdots a_{i,j_{|I|}}$ represents single co-citation occurrences, which are now generalized to higher orders. The summation then counts the individual higher-order co-citation occurrences.

A central problem in data mining is the discovery of frequent itemsets. In the context of hypertext systems, such frequent itemsets represent groups of highly similar documents based on higher-order co-citations. But managing and interacting with itemsets for information retrieval is problematic. Because of the combinatorially exploding numbers of itemsets and their overlap, user interaction becomes unwieldy.

Also, standard tools of analysis and visualization such as clustering assume an input matrix of pairwise distances. Mathematically, distances for all document pairs correspond to a fully connected distance graph. But the generalization to higher-order distances means that the distance graph edges are generalized to *hyperedges*, that is, edges that are incident upon more than two vertices. It is difficult to generalize clustering algorithms to such distance hypergraphs.

Our approach to this problem is to apply standard clustering algorithms, but with pairwise distances that include higher-order co-citation similarities. The new distances we propose are thus a hybrid between standard pairwise distances and higher-order distances. For information retrieval visualization, users need only deal with disjoint sets of items, rather than combinatorial explosions of non-disjoint itemsets. The approach is designed such that member documents of frequent itemsets are more likely to appear together in clusters.

We extend the standard model by computing document similarities from higher-order support features by summing supports over all itemsets that contain the document pair in question. More formally, the itemset support feature summation is

$$s_{j,k} = \sum_{\{I|j,k\in I\}} \zeta(I).$$

This yields the similarity $s_{j,k}$ between documents j and k, where $\zeta(I)$ is the support of itemset I.

We then introduce a nonlinear transformation $T[\zeta(I)]$ to be applied to the itemset supports $\zeta(I)$ before summation. The transformation T is super-linear (asymptotically increasing more quickly than linearly), so as to favor large itemset supports. The hybrid similarity $s_{j,k}$ then becomes

$$s_{j,k} = \sum_{\{I|j,k\in I\}} T[\zeta(I)]. \qquad (1)$$

A straightforward approach for reducing computational complexity for hybrid pairwise/higher-order distances is to exclude itemsets whose supports fall below some threshold value, denoted *minsup*. The worst-case complexity of the problem of finding all frequent itemsets is exponential. But algorithms have been proposed that empirically scale linearly with respect to both the number of transactions and the transaction size [6]. We then simply exclude from the summation in (1) all itemsets with supports $\zeta(I)$ below *minsup* = m, i.e.

$$s_{j,k} = \sum_{\{I|j,k\in I, \zeta(I)\geq m\}} T[\zeta(I)]. \qquad (2)$$

It is convenient to normalize the similarity $s_{j,k}$ through the linear transformation

$$\hat{s}_{j,k} = \frac{s_{j,k} - \min(s_{j,k})}{\max(s_{j,k}) - \min(s_{j,k})}, \qquad (3)$$

yielding the normalized similarity $\hat{s}_{j,k} \in [0,1]$. Standard clustering algorithms assume *dissimilarities* rather than similarities. We convert the normalized similarity $\hat{s}_{j,k}$ to a dissimilarity (distance) through additive inversion, i.e.

$$d_{j,k} = 1 - \hat{s}_{j,k}. \qquad (4)$$

This results in distance $d_{j,k}$ between documents j and k, normalized to $d_{j,k} \in [0,1]$.

We have derived a theoretical guarantee for the nonlinear transformation of itemset-support features in the similarity computation. In the discussion below, we provide a sketch of this theoretical result. It begins with a proof that the most frequent itemset can always be made a cluster, given a large enough degree of nonlinearity in the transformation. The proof relies on the fact that for a super-linear transformation $T = T_p = T(\zeta; p)$ of itemset supports ζ in (1) or (2), as the degree of nonlinearity p increases, $T_p(\zeta)$ with a larger ζ is asymptotically bounded from below by $T_p(\zeta)$ with a smaller ζ. Since the term with largest ζ asymptotically dominates the distance summation, the result is that documents in the most frequent itemset are asymptotically closer to one another than to any other documents, thus forming a cluster.

We then generalize the proof to cover the clustering of arbitrary itemsets in terms of their relative supports and document overlap. The result is that more frequent itemsets asymptotically form clusters at the expense of less frequent itemsets that overlap them. If there is no overlapping itemset with more support, then a given itemset will form a cluster for a sufficiently large value of the nonlinearity parameter p. For overlapping itemsets with equal support, the itemset members not in common asymptotically form clusters, and each of the members in common are asymptotically in one of those clusters, though there is no guarantee for exactly which of them.

This theoretical guarantee provides no upper bound on the necessary degree of nonlinearity of p to ensure itemset clustering for a given data set. But empirically, we have found that the transformation

$$T(\zeta) = \zeta^p \qquad (5)$$

with $p = 4$ usually results in the most frequent itemsets appearing together in clusters.

In this section, we proposed a new class of co-citation based inter-document distances. These are a hybrid between pairwise distances and higher-order distances. The new hybrid distances retain a simple pairwise structure, but are better able to match higher cardinality itemsets than are standard pairwise distances. The next section applies these hybrid distances to hierarchical clustering visualizations, in support of information retrieval tasks.

3. Hierarchical Clusters with Higher-Order Co-Citations

Clustering plays a central role in information retrieval. In classical work, clustering based on co-citation similarity is known to correspond well to individual fields of knowledge [7]. For information retrieval, results from simple keyword queries can be clustered into more refined topics. Co-citation-based clustering provides a narrowing of search results, by allowing the user to focus on documents in pertinent clusters only. This helps alleviate the potentially tedious task of manually reviewing large lists of search results. Also, co-citation analysis can broaden search results by providing alternative documents linked by co-citation.

Three important heuristics for clustering are *single-linkage*, *average-linkage*, and *complete-linkage*. These heuristics are agglomerative, at each step merging clusters that have the closest distance between them. Arguments have been given for all three heuristics in terms of desirable clustering characteristics.

For our experiments with real-world document collections, clusters resulting from the 3 criteria are generally significantly different. This suggests that the documents are not inherently distributed as well-separated clusters. In particular, we have seen ample real-world examples of single-linkage "chaining." This is in direct contrast to the classical notion that typical document collections have well defined clusters, so that single-linkage is adequate [7]. However, at least one author has suggested that single-linkage clustering may be inadequate for citation analysis [8].

The *dendrogram* is a tree visualization of a hierarchical clustering. Leaves of the dendrogram tree are individual documents, at the lowest level of the hierarchy. Non-leaf nodes represent the merging of two or more clusters, at increasing levels of the hierarchy. A node is drawn as a horizontal line that spans over its children, with the line drawn at the vertical position corresponding to the merge threshold distance.

We now demonstrate our approach to itemset-based clustering, in which we compare frequent itemsets to graph-theoretic clustering. The demonstration employs data extracted from a literature citation database, the Institute for Scientific Information's Science Citation Index (SCI). We do the itemset/clustering comparison by a novel augmentation of the dendrogram with members of frequent itemsets, which allows an easy visual assessment of our proposed itemset-matching metric. For the example, we do an SCI query with keyword "wavelet*" for the year 1999. The first 100 documents returned by the query cite 1755 documents. We filter these cited documents by citation count, retaining only those cited three or more times, resulting in a set of 34 highly cited documents.

We then compute complete-linkage, average-linkage, and single-linkage clusters for the set of 34 highly cited documents. Here we first apply the standard pairwise method of computing co-citation based distances. The resulting augmented dendrogram is shown in Figure 1. The dendrogram is augmented by the addition of graphical symbols for members of frequent 4-itemsets, added at the corresponding tree leaves.

In this example, the most frequently occurring 4-itemset is {2, 17, 19, 20}▲. For complete linkage, documents 17, 19, and 20 of this itemset are a possible cluster. These documents apply wavelets to problems in the field of chemistry, and are well separated from the rest of the collection, both thematically and in terms of co-citations. But including document 2 (a foundational wavelet paper by wavelet pioneer Mallat) in this cluster would require the inclusion of documents 12, 15, and 25, which are not in the itemset. These three additional documents are another foundational wavelet paper by Mallat, and two foundational papers by fellow pioneer Daubechies.

For single linkage, there is even less cluster/itemset consistency. The itemset {2, 17, 19, 20}▲ is possible within a cluster only by including 8 other documents. We interpret this as being largely caused by single linkage chaining. In general, the application of clustering to mere pairwise co-citation similarities is insufficient for ensuring that itemsets of larger cardinality appear as clusters, even with complete-linkage.

As a comparison with standard pairwise distances, Figure 2 shows complete-linkage clusters computed with our hybrid pairwise/higher-order distances. It considers three separate cases, each case being taken over multiple values of itemset cardinality χ. The three cases are $\chi = 2,3$; $\chi = 2,3,4$; $\chi = 3,4$. Here the itemset supports $\zeta(I)$ are nonlinearly transformed by $T[\zeta(I)] = [\zeta(I)]^4$, with distances computed via (1), (3), and (4).

Consistency between clusters and frequent itemsets is considerably improved with our hybrid distances. The most frequent itemset {2,17,19,20}▲ forms a cluster for the two cases $\chi = 2,3,4$ and $\chi = 3,4$. However, the case $\chi = 2,3$ has inconsistency for the most frequent itemset. It is apparent that the lowest-order (pairwise) supports are the source of the disagreement. Lower order supports are generally larger than higher-order supports, and thus tend to dominate the summation in (1).

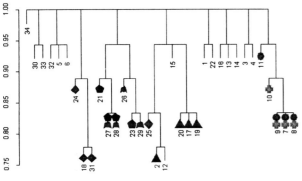

Complete linkage

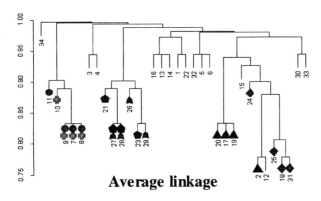

Average linkage

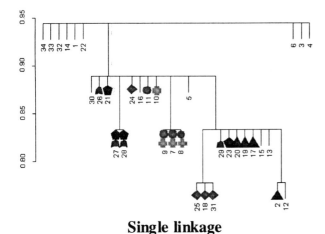

Single linkage

Figure 1. For standard co-citation document distances, there is considerable inconsistency between clusters and frequent itemsets.

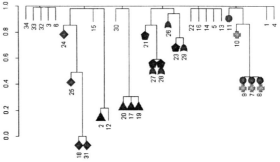

(Cardinality 2)^4 + (Cardinality 3)^4

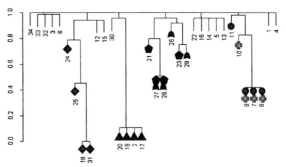

(Cardinality 2)^4 + (Cardinality 3)^4 + (Cardinality 4)^4

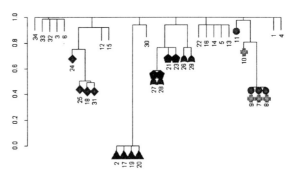

(Cardinality 3)^4 + (Cardinality 4)^4

Figure 2. Distances that include higher-order co-citations yield much improved consistency between clusters and frequent itemsets.

We suggest that clustering dendrograms such as Figure 2 can provide greatly enhanced understanding of document sets resulting from information retrieval keyword searches. Augmentation with symbols for frequent itemset members allows direct identification of these important itemset. The visualized clusters and itemsets are computed from distances based on citation (link) information, thus complementing text-based analysis. As retrieval output, the user would be presented with a modified form of the dendrogram shown here, which has been rotated clockwise by 90° and augmented with text corresponding to each document.

429

The augmented dendrogram we propose can help guide the navigation of retrieval results. For example, small representative samples can be examined from a number of separate clusters, allowing the user to more quickly identify documents of potential interest. Once a promising cluster is identified, the user can then focus solely on documents within it.

4. Experimental Results

This paper proposes new methods of visualizing hypertext document clusters for information retrieval. The methodology employs a new class of inter-document distances that is a hybrid between standard pairwise and higher-order distances. These higher-order distances are analogous to itemset supports in association mining.

In this section, we apply our proposed hybrid document distances to real-world hypertext. In particular, we apply them to data sets from the Institute for Scientific Information's Science Citation Index (SCI). Science citations are a classical form of hypertext, and are of significant general interest. The assumption that links imply some form of content influence also holds reasonably well for citations. This is in contrast to Web hypertext, in which links could be for more general purposes, such as navigation.

The SCI data sets we employ are described in Table 1. For each data set, the table gives the SCI query keyword and publication year(s), the number of citing documents resulting from the query, and the number of documents they cite after filtering by citation count. For the data sets 1, 5, and 9, results are included for both co-citations and bibliographic coupling, yielding data sets 2, 6, and 10 (respectively), for a total of 10 SCI data sets.

Our empirical tests apply a metric that compares clustering to frequent itemsets, determining whether given itemsets form clusters comprised only of the itemset members. In other words, we determine the minimal-cardinality cluster that contains all the members of a given itemset, and compare that cluster cardinality to the itemset cardinality. This is then averaged over a number of itemsets, to yield an overall itemset-matching metric for a clustering.

More formally, let $\pi = \{\pi_1, \pi_2, \ldots, \pi_{k_1}\}$ be a partition of items consistent with the hierarchical clustering merge tree. Furthermore, let $I = \{I_1, I_2, \ldots, I_{k_2}\}$ be a set of itemsets. Then for each itemset $I_i \in I$, there is some block of the partition $\pi_j \in \pi$ such that $|\pi_j|$ is minimized, subject to the constraint that $I_i \subseteq \pi_j$. We call this π_j the minimal cluster containing the itemset.

Table 1. Details for SCI data sets.

Data Sets	Query Keyword	Years	Citing Docs	Cited Docs
1, 2	adaptive optics	2000	89	60
3	collagen	1975	494	53
4	genetic algorithm* and neural network*	2000	136	57
5,6	quantum gravity AND string*	1999-2000	114	50
7	wavelet*	1999	100	34
8	wavelet*	1999	472	54
9,10	wavelet* AND brownian	1973-2000	99	59

Once a minimal (cardinality) cluster π_j is found for an itemset, a metric can be defined for measuring the extent to which the itemset is consistent with the cluster. This metric $M(\pi, I_i)$ is simply the portion of the cluster occupied by the itemset, or in terms of set cardinalities,

$$M(\pi, I_i) = \frac{|I_i|}{|\pi_j|}.$$

The metric $M(\pi, I)$ is defined for a set of itemsets I by averaging $M(\pi, I_i)$ over $I_i \in I$, that is,

$$M(\pi, I) = \frac{1}{|I|} \sum_{I_i \in I} M(\pi, I_i) = \frac{1}{|I|} \sum_{I_i \in I} \left(\frac{|I_i|}{|\pi_j|} \right). \quad (6)$$

The itemset-matching metric $M(\pi, I)$ takes its maximum value of unity when $I_i = \pi_j$, indicating the best possible match between itemsets and clusters, and its minimum value $M(\pi, I) = |I_i|/n$, indicating the poorest possible match. Figure 3 illustrates the itemset-matching clustering metric $M(\pi, I)$.

Table 2 shows how hybrid pairwise/higher-order distances are computed for the experiments with SCI data sets. The table shows the itemset cardinalities $|I|$ that are applied in the distance formula (1), and the itemset support nonlinearity parameters p for itemset nonlinearity $T(\zeta) = \zeta^p$. For each hybrid distance formula, we compare metric values to those for standard pairwise distances, applying the same cardinalities in (6) as in (1).

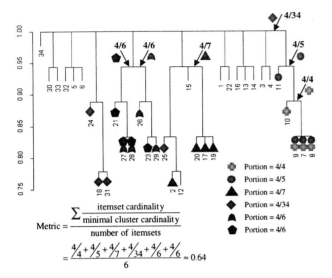

$$\text{Metric} = \frac{\sum \frac{\text{itemset cardinality}}{\text{minimal cluster cardinality}}}{\text{number of itemsets}}$$

$$= \frac{\frac{4}{4} + \frac{4}{5} + \frac{4}{7} + \frac{4}{34} + \frac{4}{6} + \frac{4}{6}}{6} \approx 0.64$$

Figure 3. Itemset-matching clustering metric is the average portion occupied by an itemset within the minimal cluster containing it.

The comparisons are done for each combination of complete-linkage, average-linkage, and single-linkage clustering. We also compare for each combination of the most frequent itemset, the 5 most frequent itemsets, and the 10 most frequent itemsets in (6). For test cases in which nonlinearity parameter value $p = 4$ yields relatively low metric values, we include additional test cases with $p = 6$. Since there are 25 different combinations of itemset cardinalities and support nonlinearities, each with $3 \times 3 = 9$ different combinations of clustering criteria and sets of most frequent itemsets, there are $9 \times 25 = 225$ total test cases.

Table 2. Itemset cardinalities and support nonlinearities for hybrid pairwise/higher-order distances.

Data Sets	[Itemset Cardinality, Support Nonlinearity]
1	[3,4], [3,6], [4,4], [4,6]
2,6	[3,4], [4,4], [4,6]
3,5,7,8,9,10	[3,4], [4,4]
4	[3,4], [3,6], [4,4]

Table 3 compares clustering metric values for the test cases in Table 2. The table classifies cases as having metric values for hybrid distances equal to, greater than, or less than metric values for standard pairwise distances. Higher metric values correspond to clusters being more consistent with frequent itemsets. For most test cases (169 of 225 versus 27 of 225), the new hybrid pairwise/higher-order distances result in better

consistency with frequent itemsets in comparison to standard pairwise distances. For a relatively small number of cases (29 of 225), the metric values are equal.

Table 3. Clustering metric comparisons for standard pairwise (P.W.) versus higher-order (H.O.) distances.

Data set	H.O.=P.W.	H.O.>P.W.	H.O.<P.W.	Cases
1	6	16	14	36
2	7	15	5	27
3	0	18	0	18
4	1	24	2	27
5	3	13	2	18
6	2	22	3	27
7	2	16	0	18
8	5	13	0	18
9	3	14	1	18
10	0	18	0	18
Totals	29	169	27	225

For the 20 combinations of 10 data sets and 2 itemset cardinalities, we find that itemset support nonlinearities with $p=4$ are usually sufficient (15 of 20) for a good match to frequent itemsets. Otherwise nonlinearities with $p=6$ in (5) are sufficient, in all but one of the 20 combinations. Here we consider a clustering metric value greater than about 0.7 to be a good match. This corresponds to a frequent itemset comprising on average about 70% of a cluster that contains all its members.

Table 4. Clustering metrics for hybrid distances with full computational complexity (*minsup* 0) versus hybrid distances with reduced complexity (*minsup* 2).

Data set	(*minsup* 2) = (*minsup* 0)	(*minsup* 2) > (*minsup* 0)	(*minsup* 2) < (*minsup* 0)	Cases
3	18	0	0	18
5	18	0	0	18
8	18	0	0	18
9	18	0	0	18
10	11	0	7	18
Totals	83	0	7	90

For data sets 3, 5, 8, 9, and 10, we compute itemset-matching clustering metrics resulting from the complexity reduction technique in (2), and compare metric values to the full-complexity method in (1). The clustering metric results of the 90 cases from the five extracted data sets are summarized in Table 4. The

431

results show that excluding itemset supports below *minsup* generally has little effect on clustering results, particular for smaller values of *minsup*. However, there is some degradation in metric values for higher levels of *minsup*. Here "degradation" means that metric values are smaller when some itemset supports are excluded, corresponding to a poorer clustering match to frequent itemsets.

We offer the following interpretation for the *minsup*-dependent degradation in clustering metric. Members of frequent itemsets are typically frequently cited documents overall. Such frequently cited documents are likely to appear in many itemsets, even less frequent itemsets. Thus there are likely to be many itemsets below *minsup* that contain these frequently cited documents. Excluding itemsets below *minsup* then removes the supports that these itemsets contribute to the summations in computing hybrid distances.

5. Summary and Conclusions

We have proposed a new methodology for visualizing association mining results. A central component in the methodology is a new class of inter-item distances computed directly from itemset supports. While the distances are computed from supports of itemsets of arbitrary cardinality, they still retain a simple pairwise structure. These hybrid pairwise/higher-cardinality distances thus allow the direct application of standard visualization tools such as clustering dendrograms. However, they require much less complex user interaction compared to that of working directly with all frequent itemsets. The hybrid distances are computationally feasible via fast algorithms for computing frequent itemsets. We provided a theoretical guarantee that under the new hybrid distances, consistency between clusters and frequent itemsets is attainable independent of the clustering criterion.

We proposed the application of the hierarchical clustering dendrogram for association mining visualization, which enables quick comprehension of complex distance relationships among items. We also introduced new augmentations of the dendrogram to support the visual mining process by adding item-descriptive text, and graphical symbols for members of frequent itemsets.

We tested the effects of our new hybrid distances on hierarchical clustering dendrograms, for large numbers of test cases with data extracted from the Science Citation Index. In particular, we compared dendrograms between a variety of hybrid distance formulas and standard pairwise distances, in terms of a metric that measures consistency between clusters and frequent itemsets. For the majority of the test cases, metric values were higher for our hybrid distances, indicating better consistency between clusters and frequent itemsets. We also conducted experiments showing that excluding itemset supports below some minimum value has relatively little effect on itemset/cluster consistency, so that it is reasonable to apply fast algorithms for computing the frequent itemsets needed for the hybrid distances.

This is the first known application of clustering for the visualizing association mining results. The pairwise structure of the new hybrid inter-item distances allows the visualization of frequent itemsets of arbitrary cardinalities. The nonlinear transformation of itemset supports helps ensure consistency between clusters and important frequent itemsets, making frequent itemsets less likely to be obscured during visualization. As a more basic contribution, this work represents a first step towards the unification of association mining and clustering visualization.

6. References

[1] M. Henzinger, "Link Analysis in Web Information Retrieval," *Bulletin of the Technical Committee on Data Engineering*, 23, special issue on Next-Generation Web Search, pp. 3-8, September 2000.

[2] J. Kleinberg, "Authoritative Sources in a Hyperlinked Environment," in *Proceedings of the ACM-SIAM Symposium on Discrete Algorithms*, January 1998, pp. 668-677.

[3] H. Small, "Co-citation in the Scientific Literature: A New Measure of the Relationship Between Two Documents," *Journal of the American Society of Information Science*, 24, pp. 265-269, 1973.

[4] J. Hartigan, *Clustering Algorithms*, John Wiley & Sons, New York, 1975.

[5] R. Agrawal, T. Imielinski, A. Swami, "Mining Association Rules between Sets of Items in Large Databases," in *Proceedings of the 1993 International Conference on the Management of Data*, Washington, DC, May 1993, pp. 207-216.

[6] R. Agrawal, R. Srikant, "Fast Algorithms for Mining Association Rules," in *Proceedings of the 20th International Conference on Very Large Databases*, Santiago, Chile, September 1994, pp. 487-499.

[7] E. Garfield, *Citation Index: Its Theory and Application in Science, Technology, and Humanities*, John Wiley & Sons, New York, 1979.

[8] H. Small, "Macro-Level Changes in the Structure of Co-Citation Clusters: 1983-1989," *Scientometrics*, 26, pp. 5-20, 1993.

Mining Constrained Association Rules to Predict Heart Disease *

Carlos Ordonez[1], Edward Omiecinski[1], Levien de Braal[1],
Cesar A. Santana[2], Norberto Ezquerra[1], Jose A. Taboada[3],
David Cooke[2], Elizabeth Krawczynska[2], Ernest V. Garcia[2]

[1]College of Computing
Georgia Institute
of Technology

[2]Radiology Department
Emory University
Hospital

[3]Departamento de Computacion
Universidad de Santiago
Compostela

Abstract

This work describes our experiences on discovering association rules in medical data to predict heart disease. We focus on two aspects in this work: mapping medical data to a transaction format suitable for mining association rules and identifying useful constraints. Based on these aspects we introduce an improved algorithm to discover constrained association rules. We present an experimental section explaining several interesting discovered rules.

1. Introduction

Data Mining is an active research area. One of the most popular approaches to do data mining is discovering association rules [1, 2]. Association rules are generally used with basket, census or financial data. On the other hand, medical data is generally analyzed with classifier trees, clustering, or regression, but rarely with association rules. A survey on these techniques is found in [10].

In this work we analyze the idea of discovering constrained association rules in medical records that include numeric, categorical, time and image data. This work is based on a long time joint research effort by Georgia Tech and Emory University to discover knowledge in medical data to predict coronary heart disease [6, 5, 7, 13, 14]. In [5] association rules are proposed and preliminary results are justified from the medical point of view. In [7] neural networks are used to predict reversibility images based on stress and myocardial thickening images. In [14] we explore the idea of constraining association rules in binary data and report preliminary findings from a data mining perspective.

One of the most important features of association rules

is that they are combinatorial in nature. This is particularly useful to discover patterns that appear in subsets of all the attributes. However, most patterns discovered by algorithms that do not constrain associations are not useful because they may contain redundant information, may be irrelevant or describe trivial knowledge. The goal is then to find those rules that are medically significant or interesting, but which also have minimum support and confidence.

In our research project the discovered rules have two main purposes: validating rules used by an expert system to aid in diagnosing coronary heart disease (PERFEX [9, 6]) and discovering new rules that relate patient data to heart disease and thus can enrich the expert system knowledge base. At the moment all rules used by our expert system were discovered and validated by a group of domain experts, as described in detail in [9]. Since PERFEX is essentially a production rule system (i.e., composed of IF-THEN rules) used in conjunction with temporal and uncertainty reasoning models, the discovery of knowledge resulting from association rule mining would represent a potentially powerful and innovative way to validate and acquire knowledge to enhance the knowledge base. Importantly, the methods proposed herein are capable of inferring medical knowledge from a vast array of data that includes image and alphanumeric data that represent highly relevant, patient-specific clinical data (such as electrocardiographic information, patient history, symptoms and the results of clinical tests). Hence the methods described in this paper may provide a more efficient knowledge acquisition technique than classical approaches.

Throughout the paper we try to provide a general framework for understanding the approach underlying our research. We believe many of the problems we are facing (small data size, richness of content, high dimensionality, missing information, etc) are likely to appear in other domains. As such, this work tries to isolate those problems that we consider will be of greatest interest to the data mining

*This work was supported by grant LM 06726 from the National Library of Medicine

community.

1.1. Contributions and paper outline

Our main contributions are the following. First, a justification is given for the use of association rules in the medical domain. We explain why mining medical data for association rules is an interesting and hard problem and we present the problem in an abstract manner so that this work can be applied to other domains. We introduce a simple mapping algorithm that transforms medical records into a binary format suitable to mine constrained association rules. We identify important constraints to make association rules useful for the medical domain and propose an algorithm to discover constrained association rules with very low support and relatively high confidence. Finally, we identify open problems that require further research.

This is an outline of the rest of the paper. Section 2 states the definition of association rules and describes our medical data. We use a small example to motivate the use of association rules in the medical field and explain the kind of rules that are sought. Section 3 addresses the problem of mapping medical data to binary attributes to be treated as items, emphasizes the main difficulties encountered using association rules, and introduces useful constraints for a customized A-priori type algorithm. Experimental results with medical data sets are described in Section 4. Finally, section 5 contains the conclusions of this article and directions for future research.

2. Definitions, data mapping and interesting rules

2.1. Association rules

The standard definition of association rules [1] is the following. Let $D = \{T_1, T_2, \ldots, T_n\}$ be a set of n transactions and let $\mathcal{I}$ be a set of items, $\mathcal{I} = \{i_1, i_2 \ldots i_m\}$. Each transaction is a set of items, i.e. $T_i \subseteq \mathcal{I}$. An *association rule* is an implication of the form $X \Rightarrow Y$, where $X, Y \subset \mathcal{I}$, and $X \cap Y = \emptyset$. X is called the antecedent and Y is called the consequent of the rule. In general, a set of items, such as the antecedent or the consequent of a rule, is called an *itemset*. Each itemset has an associated measure of statistical significance called *support*. For an itemset $X \subset \mathcal{I}$, $support(X)$ is the fraction of transactions $T_i \in D$ such that $X \subseteq T_i$. The support of a rule is defined as $support(X \Rightarrow Y) = support(X \cup Y)$. The rule has a measure of strength called *confidence* defined as the ratio $confidence(X \Rightarrow Y) = support(X \cup Y)/support(X)$. The standard problem of mining association rules is to generate all rules that have support and confidence greater or equal than some prespecified minimum support and minimum confidence thresholds [2].

2.2. Brief literature review

Literature on association rules has become extensive since their introduction in the seminal paper [1]. Our work shares some similarities with [4, 11, 17]. In [17] the authors propose a few algorithms that can incorporate constraints to include or exclude certain items in the association generation phase; they focus only in two types of constraints: items constrained by a certain hierarchy [15] or associations which include certain items. This approach is limited for our purposes since we do not use hierarchies and excluding/including items is not enough to mine medically meaningful rules. The work which addresses the constraining problem in the most general way is [11]. Their approach based on succinctness and 2-var constraints is different as it is more query oriented and does not deal with rule semantics, mapping, rule size or noisy data. Bayardo et. al. [3] show that support and confidence are fundamental interestingness metrics.

2.3. General description of our medical data

The medical data set we are mining describes the profiles of patients being treated for coronary heart disease. All medical information is put in one file having several records. Each record corresponds to the most relevant information of one patient. This profile contains personal information such as age, race, smoking habits and other relevant information. Measurements on the patient such as weight, heart rate, blood pressure and information regarding the preexistence or existence of certain diseases are also stored. The diagnostics made by a clinician or technician are included as well. Time attributes mainly involve medical history dates. Then we have a complex set of measurements that estimate the degree of disease in certain regions of the heart, how healthy certain regions remain, and quality numbers that summarize the patient's heart effort under stress and relaxed conditions. Finally, imaging (perfusion) information from several regions of the myocardium (heart muscle) is stored as boolean data.

Table 1 shows the 25 medical fields that will be used throughout this paper. For each attribute we give its usual abbreviation in the medical domain, its data type (DT), what type of medical information (MI) it contains and a complete description. Attributes are classified into three types according to the medical information they contain. 'P' attributes correspond to perfusion measurements on specific regions of the heart, 'R' attributes correspond to risk factors and 'D' attributes correspond to heart disease measurements. The goal is to relate perfusion measurements and risk factors to

No	Name	DT	MI	Description
1	Age	N	R	Age of patient
2	LM	N	D	Left Main artery
3	LAD	N	D	Latero Anterior Desc.
4	LCX	N	D	Left CircumfleX
5	RCA	N	D	Right Coronary Art.
6	AL	N	P	Antero-Lateral
7	AS	N	P	Antero-Septal
8	SA	N	P	Septo-Anterior
9	SI	N	P	Septo-Inferior
10	IS	N	P	Infero-Septal
11	IL	N	P	Infero-Lateral
12	LI	N	P	Latero-Inferior
13	LA	N	P	Latero-Anterior
14	AP	N	P	Apical
15	Sex	C	R	Gender
16	HTA	C	R	Hyper-tension
17	Diab	C	R	Diabetes
18	HYPLD	C	R	Hyperlipidemia
19	FHCAD	C	R	Fam. hist. of disease
20	Smoke	C	R	Smoking habits
21	Claudi	C	R	Claudication
22	PAngio	C	R	Previous angina
23	PStroke	C	R	Prior stroke
24	PCarSur	C	R	Prior carotid surgery
25	Chol	N	R	Cholesterol level

Table 1. Attributes

disease measurements. The image data represents the local degree of blood distribution (perfusion) in the heart muscle (myocardium). There are some fields that are commonly selected in data mining experiments. These fields include 4 fields that store the percentage of heart disease caused by a specific artery of the heart (LM, LAD, LCX, and RCA) and 9 fields that store a perfusion measurement which is a value in the range $[-1, 1]$. Closer to 1 indicates a more severe perfusion defect. Closer to -1 indicates absence of a perfusion defect. Each of the artery fields has a value between 0 and 100, and each heart region has a value between -1 and 1.

2.4. Alternative approaches

Here we explain why other data mining techniques are inadequate to solve our problem. Decision trees [10] produce rules to classify records from a data set minimizing classification error. This approach assumes there is a target variable indicating the class to which each record belongs. In our case it would have to be a categorical variable indicating if the patient is healthy or sick. However, patients cannot be classified in such a simple way because they have a degree of sickness. It could be argued that there could be several classes indicating the degree of sickness, but this

would have to be done for each artery making many runs and significant analysis effort mandatory. Besides this does not cover the case that the patient has combinations of diseased arteries. There is even another worse drawback about decision trees: they automatically split numerical variables. The medical community has standard cutoffs used to understand numerical variables and these cutoffs are widely accepted (high blood pressure, high cholesterol, male overweight, etc). Therefore, the split points chosen by the decision tree may be of little use if they are different from the standard ones; experimental results interpretation becomes more difficult.

Clustering [8, 10, 12] is another potential technique. In our case it was useful to have a global understanding of the data set. However, it was not adequate to produce rules relating a subset of all the variables. A constrained version of clustering focusing on projections of the data could be useful but that is an aspect that deserves further research.

3. Mining constrained association rules

In this section we introduce our most important contributions. First, we analyze the problem of mapping information from categorical and numerical attribute values to items. Second, we identify useful constraints on attributes and items to get interesting association rules.

3.1. Mapping attributes

The medical data records have to be transformed into a transaction format suitable to discover association rules. As noted above, there are categorical, numerical, time and image attributes. To make the problem simpler all attributes are uniformly treated as categorical or numerical. In numerical attributes there is a natural order among values as opposed to categorical attributes where there does not exist such order.

Let $A_1, A_2, \ldots A_p$ be all the attributes, let $R = \{r_1, r_2, \ldots r_n\}$ be a relation with n tuples whose values are taken from $dom(A_1) \times dom(A_2) \times \ldots \times dom(A_p)$, where $dom(A_i)$ is either a categorical or numerical domain. The data set size is n and its dimensionality is p. Let $D = \{T_1, T_2, \ldots, T_n\}$ be a set of n transactions containing subsets of m items, resulting from the mapping process. Items are identified by consecutive integers starting in one, i.e. $1, 2, \ldots, m$.

The following mapping algorithm discretizes medical data records transforming numerical and categorical values into binary data. The mapping process is divided in two phases. In the first phase a mapping table M is constructed based on user's requirements. In the second phase attribute values in each tuple r_j are mapped to items based on M. Each tuple r_j becomes a transaction T_j, suitable for association rule mining. For a categorical attribute A_i each categorical value is mapped to one item. If negation is desired for categorical attribute A_i then each negated value is mapped to an item. The domain expert specifies k cut-off points for each numerical attribute A_i producing $k+1$ intervals. Then each interval is mapped to one item. If negation is desired then $k+1$ additional items are created corresponding to each negated interval. In general negation significantly increases the potential number of associations. Therefore, it must be used on a per attribute basis after careful consideration. Once the M mapping table has been constructed the second phase is straightforward.

3.2. Constraining association rules

This is a summary of the main difficulties faced when trying to discover interesting association rules in medical data. For each problem we propose a solution that is generally in the form of a constraint. Problems are described in an abstract manner.

Association size. Associations and rules that involve many items are hard to interpret and can potentially generate a very high number of rules. And further, they slow down the interactive process by the user. Therefore, there should be a default threshold for association size. Most approaches are exhaustive in the sense that they find *all* rules above the user-specified thresholds but in our domain that produces a huge amount of rules. The biggest size of discovered associations is a practical bottleneck for algorithm performance. In our case even $k > 5$ produces too many rules rendering the results useless. Another reason to limit size is that if there are two rules $X_1 \Rightarrow Y$ and $X_2 \Rightarrow Y$ s.t. $X_1 \subset X_2$ the *first* rule is more interesting because it is simpler and it is more likely to have higher support. Or if $Y_1 \subset Y_2$ and $X \Rightarrow Y_1$ and $X \Rightarrow Y_2$ then the 2nd rule is likely to have higher confidence but lower support.

Items restricted to appear only in the antecedent, only in the consequent or in either place. Remember that by rule definition an item appears only once in a rule and therefore it appears either in the antecedent or in the consequent of the rule. Note that given the interesting rule $X \Rightarrow Y$ no matter where an item appears the association $X \cup Y$ must be a frequent itemset because this association is precisely the rule support, but where the item appears prunes out many uninteresting rules that have useless combinations of items. In other words, support is still needed to prune uninteresting associations but confidence is not enough to prune out uninteresting rules because there may be many rules having high confidence containing forbidden items in the antecedent or in the consequent. Therefore items need to be constrained to appear in a specific part of the rule.

Associations having uninteresting combinations of items. This is the case where certain combinations are known to

be trivial or have such a high support that do not really say anything new about the data set. Consider items i_j and $i_{j'}$. If the association $X_1 = \{i_j, i_{j'}\}$ is not interesting then any other association X_2 s.t. $X_1 \subset X_2$ will not be interesting. Therefore, many of the items (if not all) can be grouped by the domain expert to discard uninteresting associations. If no grouping is done then item i_j is always relevant no matter which other items $i_{j'}$ appear together with it. We assume small groups can be identified either automatically by running a straight association rules algorithm or by previous knowledge.

Low support. It has been shown that support is the performance bottleneck for association rules [11]. It is desirable to run the algorithm once with a very low support avoiding repeated runs with decreasing supports. We are interested in rules involving at least two transactions; this is a very low minimum support level.

High support. Even though the algorithm may prune out many rules by the above criteria, since we are working with high dimensional data there may still be lots of rules involving a few items having a high support. This problem is duly identified in [16] for quantitative association rules, and it basically appears because of the high number of combinations of partitioned intervals. So this idea is helpful: the algorithm should have a maximum support threshold.

Important constraints

Based on the difficulties outlined above we introduce the following improvements. Extend items with two fields indicating constraints. Let $\mathcal{I} = \{i_1, i_2, \ldots i_m\}$ be the set of items to be mined obtained by the mapping process from the attributes $A_1, \ldots, A_p$.

Let $\mathcal{C} = \{c_1, c_2, \ldots c_p\}$ be a set antecedent and consequent constraints for each attribute A_j. Note that constraints are specified on attributes and not on items. Each constraint c_j can have one out of 3 values: 1 if item A_j can only appear in the antecedent of a rule, 2 if it can only appear in the consequent and 0 if it can appear in either. We define the function antecedent/consequent $ac : \mathcal{R} \to \mathcal{C}$ as $ac(A_j) = c_j$ to make reference to one such constraint.

Let $\mathcal{G} = \{g_1, g_2, \ldots g_p\}$ be a set of group constraints for each attribute A_j; g_i is a positive integer if A_j is constrained to belong to some group or 0 if A_j is not group constrained at all. We define the function $group : \mathcal{R} \to \mathcal{G}$ as $group(A_j) = g_j$. Since each attribute belongs to one group then the group numbers induce a partition on the attributes. This will induce a partition on the attributes. Attributes belonging to some group and attributes not constrained to belong to any group. Note that if the group is > 0 then there must be two or more attributes with the same group value, otherwise, the attribute would appear as not constrained.

Let $X = \{i_1, i_2, \ldots, i_k\}$ be a k-itemset. X is said to be antecedent-interesting if $\forall i_j \in X$ $ac(i_j) \neq 2$. X is said to be consequent-interesting if $\forall i_j \in X$ $ac(attribute(i_j)) \neq 1$. X is said to be group-interesting if $\forall i_j \forall i_{j'} \in X$ $i_j \neq i'_j \Rightarrow group(attribute(i_j)) \neq group(attribute(i_{j'}))$. We will use $group(i)$ and $ac(i)$ for item i to simplify notation.

Lemma 1 Itemset interestingness has the downward closure property in both $ac(i)$ and $group(i)$ constraints.
Proof: this is straightforward to prove since these properties are defined on sets. □

Lemma 2 The $ac(i)$ constraint cannot be used to prune away associations because of the rule generation phase.
Proof: Assume we have a rule $X \Rightarrow Y$. X and Y must respect the ac constraint for each of their items, but $X \cup Y$ will not. $ac(i)$ is an antimonotic constraint, but it cannot be used to discard $X \cup Y$ because the support for the rule is computed on $X \cup Y$. □

Lemma 3 Let X be a frequent k-dimensional itemset. Assume $\kappa < k$ then there are $2^k - \binom{k}{\kappa}2^\kappa$ pruned associations.
Proof: We just need to substract the number of itemsets of size κ, which is the right term, from the powerset on k items. □

Lemma 4 Let $X \Rightarrow Y$ be a valid rule where all items are $ac(i)$ constrained. Then there are $O(2^{|X|+|Y|})$ discarded rules.
Proof: Consider the powersets of X and Y. Every union of X and one or more elements of Y is invalid. Every union of Y and one or more elements of X is invalid. Counting all these cases gives the stated bound. □

Lemma 1 is used to prune out associations based on the $group(i)$ constraint. Lemma 2 states that the algorithm cannot take advantage of $ac(i)$ constraints in Phase 1. Lemma 3 states that the number of pruned associations is big when the maximal frequent itemset is large. In our case this produces significant speedup to make computation more interactive. Lemma 4 gives an idea about the number of discarded rules.

3.3. Algorithm to mine constrained association rules

We propose the following algorithm based on the well-known A-priori algorithm [2]. All the basic notation and definitions are taken from section 2. Let κ be the maximum number of items appearing in one rule. Let $X_1, X_2 \ldots X_M$ be all frequent itemsets obtained in phase 1. We require a minimum support allowing us to mine associations referring to only two transactions. This number will be fixed. Pruning will be based mostly on constraints. Minimum confidence will vary from run to run.

1. Mapping algorithm

   - Construct mapping table M
   - For each tuple $r_1, r_2, \ldots, r_n$ do the following. Map attribute values of $A_1, A_2, \ldots, A_p$ to items $1, 2, \ldots, m$

based on M producing transactions $T_1, T_2, \ldots, T_n$ (section 3.1).

2. Constrained association rule algorithm

   - Phase 1:

     Generate all 1-itemsets as candidates and make one pass over $t_1, t_2, \ldots, t_n$ to compute their supports.

     for $k = 2$ to κ do

     Extend frequent $(k-1)$-itemsets by one item belonging to any frequent $(k-1)$-itemset. Let $X = \{i_1, i_2, \ldots, i_k\}$ be a k-itemset. If $group(attribute(i_j)) \neq group(attribute(i_{j'}))$ and $group(attribute(i_j)) * group(attribute(i_{j'})) > 0$ for $j \neq j' \wedge 1 \leq j, j' \leq k$ then X is a candidate. Check support for all candidate k-itemsets making one pass over the transactions. If there is no frequent itemset stop (sooner) this phase.

   - Phase 2:

     for $j = 1$ to M do for $k = 1$ to M do

     Let $X = X_j, Y = X_k$,

     if $X \cap Y = \emptyset$ and $minsupport \leq support(X \cup Y) \leq maxsupport$ and $(ac(attribute(i)) \neq 2 \; \forall i \in X)$ and $(ac(attribute(i)) \neq 1 \; \forall i \in Y)$ and $(minconfidence \leq support(X \cup Y)/support(X))$ then $X \Rightarrow Y$ is a valid rule.

4. Experimental evaluation

In this section we present important association rules discovered by our algorithm. Our experiments were run on a Sun computer. Our algorithm implementation was done in the C language.

4.1. Medical data set used

All our experiments were based on a real data set obtained from a hospital. The data set consisted of 655 patients having 113 attributes. We selected the 25 most important medical attributes for mining listed in table 1. So $p = 25$ and $n = 655$. These attributes include perfusion measurements for 9 regions of the heart and heart vessel disease for 4 vessels and attributes relating high risk factors for heart disease. The perfusion measurements quantify the deviation each heart region has from the corresponding region of a normal heart. The normal values for the 9 regions are taken as the means from which deviations are computed. Each of the LM, LAD, LCX, and RCA numerical attributes refer to vessel measurements.

4.2. Setting program parameters

To automatically map attributes to items we did the following. The LAD, RCA, LCX and LM numbers represent the percentage of vessel narrowing and they are split into ranges as follows. LAD, LCX and RCA were partitioned by cutoff points 50% and 70%. The 70% value indicates significant coronary disease. The 50% value indicates borderline disease. Less than 50% means the patient is considered healthy. The most common cutoff value used by the cardiology community is 50%. LM was partitioned by cutoff points at 30% and 50%. Both the LAD and the LCX arteries branch from the LM artery and then a defect in it is more likely to cause a larger diseased heart region. That is why its cutoff values are set lower. The 9 heart regions (AL, IL, IS, AS, SI, SA, LI, LA, AP) were partitioned into 2 ranges at a cutoff point of 0.2. CHOL was partitioned with cutoff points 200 (warning) and 250 (high). These values correspond to known medical settings. Since the clinicians were interested in getting rules involving healthy and sick patients these 4 attributes were chosen for negation. Missing values were assigned one item but were ignored for rule generation.

In general we are interested in rules that involve at least two patients. Obviously rules that refer to only one patient are not reliable and some of those may have 100% confidence. Then the minimum support was always fixed at $2/n \approx 0.2\%$. Note that this is in fact the lowest support discarding rules for one transaction. The minimum confidence was set at 70%. The maximum support was set at 30%.

In the past we attempted using association rules without constraints [14], but results were useless. The number of rules went over 1 million, and most of them involved the same medical variables. So, a post-processing approach did not work. That is, mining association rules with minimum support and confidence and then filtering out unwanted rules was not practical. This made constraints a required ingredient both from a performance point of view and from a practical standpoint. Note that we require a very low support allowing us to mine associations referring to only two transactions.

Now we explain what constraints were set for association rule finding. This set of constraints is by no means definitive or optimal, but it represents what our experience has shown to be most useful. Please refer to table 1 to understand the attribute meanings. The constraints for the association rule mining program were set as follows. The 4 main coronary arteries LM, LAD, LCX, and RCA were constrained to appear in the consequent of the rule, that is, ac(i) = 2. All the other attributes were constrained to appear in the antecedent, i.e. ac(i) = 1. In other, words R (Risk factors) and P (Perfusion Measurements) should appear in the antecedent, whereas D (disease) medical fields should appear in the consequent of a rule.

The 9 regions of the heart (AL, IS, SA, AP, AS, SI, LI, IL, LA) were constrained to be in the same group. Sex, HTA, HYPLPD, FHCAD, Smoke and Chol were constrained to be in the same group. Claudi, PANGIO, PSTROKE, PCAR-SUR were constrained to be in the same group. Age, Sex, LAD, LCX, RCA were not group constrained. Remember that combinations of items in the same group are not considered interesting.

4.3. Medical significance of association rules

The goal of the experiment was to relate perfusion measurements and risk factors to vessel disease (also known as stenosis) to validate and improve actual diagnosis rules used by an expert system [9]. Some rules were expected, confirming valid medical knowledge, and some rules were surprising, having the potential to enrich the expert system knowledge base. This is an analysis of our most interesting results.

There are two main measurements to quantify the quality of medical findings: sensitivity and specificity. Sensitivity refers to the probability of correctly identifying patients with disease. Specificity is the probability of correctly identifying healthy individuals. These measures rely on a gold standard, that is, a measurement that tells with very high accuracy if the person is sick or not. Getting such ideal measurement may involve doing invasive medical procedures on the patient. In the context of this paper the gold standard was catheterization. In a few cases a clinician reading was taken, but in general it was not available.

The data mining algorithm produced a total of 2987 rules, almost all having a medical significance of some sort. All of them could be used in answering medical questions. Most, however, were addressing issues that were not being examined at this time. Reducing the number of rules found to the point where the results can be easily interpreted by a clinician was done in two steps.

The first step reduced the total number of rules to 850. This was achieved by removing rules that are, in whole or in part, counter-intuitive to medical knowledge. These rules can be useful in confirming, disproving, and further quantifying what is already considered established fact. Although interesting in their own right, these investigations fall outside the scope of our present research. Doing this requires filtering out combinations for specific values of the variables combined in the rules. Although our extensions to the association rules algorithm allow filtering out combinations of fields, this does not extend to combinations of specific values.

The second step reduced the number left for further examination down to 73. To achieve this, rules were further subdivided into categories. Examples of these categories are 'relating Age to CAD', 'relating smoking habits to CAD', and 'predicting CAD from image data'. In each category, only the rules with the highest support and/or confidence were selected to represent the results in that category.

The 73 rules were analyzed by a domain expert (clinician). In the following paragraphs we will discuss the most interesting rules. The discovered rules were classified into 2 groups: First, those that express that if there no risk factor then there is no heart disease. Second, those that express that if there exists a risk factor then there is heart disease. It is important to observe that the rules below involve several attributes in the antecedent or in the consequent, negation and attributes being in different ranges.

Rules predicting no heart disease

In this case new medical fields not previously included in the expert system are mined for association rules. All these rules have the potential to improve the expert system. In this example we can see there is less incidence of coronary disease in the patients who do not smoke, and in those who have lower cholesterol. The second rule has very high support, compared to the other rules. It states that non smokers have a lower chance of having a diseased RCA artery; note that there is the chance that some of these patients are in the 50-70% range, i.e. being borderline cases. The fourth rule is particularly interesting as it involves two arteries in the consequent. Basically if a person is young (regardless of sex) and does not smoke the risk for heart disease is low. There are more complex rules relating two heart arteries. The last two rules say that an adult female patient with no diabetes is very likely to be healthy, that is, having no heart disease.

1. $[Sex = F] \Rightarrow ([0.0 <= LCX < 50.0])\ s = 0.229, c = 0.728$
2. $[Smoke = n] \Rightarrow [not(70.0 <= RCA < 100.1)]\ s = 0.290, c = 0.714$
3. $[0.0 <= CHOL < 200.0] \Rightarrow [not(70.0 <= LAD < 100.1)])\ s = 0.078, c = 0.708$
4. $[0.0 <= Age < 40.0][Smoke = n] \Rightarrow [0.0 <= LCX < 50.0][0.0 <= RCA < 50.0]\ s = 0.008, c = 0.714$
5. $[0.0 <= Age < 40.0][Diab = n] \Rightarrow [0.0 <= LAD < 50.0]\ s = 0.027, c = 0.818$
6. $[0.0 <= Age < 40.0][Diab = n] \Rightarrow [0.0 <= LAD < 50.0]\ s = 0.027, c = 0.818$
7. $[40.0 <= Age < 60.0]and[Sex = F][Diab = n] \Rightarrow [0.0 <= LCX < 50.0]\ s = 0.084, c = 0.917$
8. $[40.0 <= Age < 60.0]and[Sex = F][Diab = n] \Rightarrow [0.0 <= RCA < 50.0]\ s = 0.073, c = 0.800$

Rules predicting heart disease

These rules relate risk factors to heart disease. Heart disease can be detected by tomography or coronary catheterization. Tomography corresponds to myocardial perfusion studies. Catheterization involves inserting a tube into the coronary artery and injecting a substance to measure which regions are not well irrigated. These rules characterize the patient with coronary disease. There are three basic elements for analysis: perfusion defect, coronary stenosis and risk factors.

Most of the rules below refer to older patients with localized perfusion defects in specific heart regions. Rule 1 says that if the patient has a perfusion defect and had a previous carotid surgery then he has a high probability of having heart disease. The number of patients for this rule is low, but when conditions hold the disease probability will be high. These rules relate more information such as age, smoking habits, cholesterol levels. Rules 4,5,6 are outstanding as they confirm medical knowledge for very high risk of heart disease with high accuracy. Basically if a person is old, has high cholesterol levels and has a perfusion defect then it is almost sure that person has a serious heart condition. All these aspects have an impact on the risk for heart disease. Rules 5 and 6 state that high cholesterol levels and age are determinant factors to have a diseased RCA artery; these rules have 100% confidence. Rule 11 has relatively high support and very high confidence; it relates a specific defect in a heart region (SA) with a chance of having a diseased LAD artery. We conclude observing that according to medical knowledge the LAD artery has a higher chance of being diseased than the other arteries [5]. As can be seen the rules that involve the LAD artery confirm this fact since they have higher support and almost 100% confidence.

1. $[0.2 <= AP < 1.1][PCARSUR = y] \Rightarrow [not(0.0 <= LAD < 50.0)][not(0.0 <= RCA < 50.0)])\ s = 0.012, c = 0.800$
2. $[60.0 <= Age < 100.0][0.2 <= AP < 1.1][Smoke = y] \Rightarrow [not(0.0 <= LAD < 50.0)])\ s = 0.107, c = 0.833$
3. $[0.2 <= LA < 1.1][Sex = M]and[250.0 <= CHOL < 500.1] \Rightarrow [not(0.0 <= LCX < 50.0)])s = 0.014, c = 0.750$
4. $[60.0 <= Age < 100.0][0.2 <= IL < 1.1][250.0 <= CHOL < 500.1] \Rightarrow [not(0.0 <= RCA < 50.0)])\ s = 0.017, c = 0.917$
5. $[60.0 <= Age < 100.0][0.2 <= IS < 1.0][250.0 <= CHOL < 500.1] \Rightarrow [not(0.0 <= RCA < 50.0)])\ s = 0.015, c = 1.000$
6. $[60.0 <= Age < 100.0][0.2 <= IS < 1.0][250.0 <= CHOL < 500.1] \Rightarrow [not(0.0 <= RCA < 50.0)])\ s = 0.015, c = 1.000$
7. $[60.0 <= Age < 100.0][0.2 <= SA < 1.0][FHCAD = y] \Rightarrow [not(0.0 <= LAD < 50.0)])s = 0.015, c = 1.000$
8. $[0.2 <= SA < 1.0]and[PANGIO = y] \Rightarrow [not(0.0 <= LAD < 50.0)])s = 0.023, c = 0.938$
9. $[60.0 <= Age < 100.0][0.2 <= AP < 1.1][Sex = F] \Rightarrow [not(0.0 <= LAD < 50.0)])s = 0.049, c = 0.941$
10. $[60.0 <= Age < 100.0][0.2 <= SA < 1.0][Claudi = y] \Rightarrow [not(0.0 <= LAD < 50.0)])s = 0.029, c = 0.950$
11. $[60.0 <= Age < 100.0][0.2 <= SA < 1.0][HYPLPD = y] \Rightarrow [not(0.0 <= LAD < 50.0)])s = 0.070, c = 0.939$

5. Conclusions

This article presented our experiences mining association rules from medical data to predict heart disease. We explained the motivation and validity of using association rules on medical data. Association rules are useful for our purpose given their combinatorial nature. We described all information contained in medical records. We introduced a simple mapping algorithm to transform medical records to a transaction format. We then presented an improved algorithm to mine constrained association rules. Medical data records contain numerical, categorical, time and image attributes. The mapping algorithm uniformly treats attributes as numerical or categorical. Numerical attributes are split into intervals. Negation is used on a per attribute basis to avoid an explosion in the number of associations. A mapping table is constructed and based on this table attribute values are mapped to items. The algorithm to mine association rules uses several important constraints to reduce the number of rules and speed up the mining process. It uses a constraint to exclude combinations of attributes eliminating trivial or useless associations. Certain attributes are constrained to appear only in the antecedent, only in the consequent or in both to get medically meaningful rules. Rules are constrained to include a maximum number of items to make them simpler and more general. Maximum support is a constraint used to eliminate trivial rules. These constraints allowed us to mine medical records at a minimum support involving only two transactions. The experimental section discussed several important association rules predicting absence or presence of heart disease.

This is a summary of issues for future research. We would like to examine problems with missing information more closely. We want to identify other useful constraints besides grouping and antecedent/consequent. We want to compare the discovered association rules with classification rules obtained by a decision tree algorithm. We plan to process the data with a clustering algorithm [12] to explain why certain rules have low confidence and to find high confidence rules in subsets of medical records. Finally, we want to assess the impact on performance of each constraint.

References

[1] Rakesh Agrawal, Tomasz Imielinski, and Arun Swami. Mining association rules between sets of items in large databases. In *ACM SIGMOD Conference*, pages 207–216, 1993.

[2] Rakesh Agrawal and Ramakrishnan Srikant. Fast algorithms for mining association rules in large databases. In *VLDB Conference*, 1994.

[3] Roberto Bayardo and Rakesh Agrawal. Mining the most interesting rules. In *ACM KDD Conference*, 1999.

[4] Roberto Bayardo, Rakesh Agrawal, and D. Gounopolos. Constraint-based rule mining in large, dense databases. In *IEEE ICDE Conference*, 1999.

[5] David Cooke, Carlos Ordonez, Ernest V. Garcia, Edward Omiecinski, Elyzabeth Krawczynska, Russell Folks, Cesar Santana, Levien de Braal, and Norberto Ezquerra. Data mining of large myocardial perfusion spect (mps) databases to improve diagnostic decision making. *Journal of Nuclear Medicine*, 40(5), 1999.

[6] David Cooke, Cesar Santana, Tahia Morris, Levien de Braal, Carlos Ordonez, Edward Omiecinski, Norberto Ezquerra, and Ernest V. Garcia. Validating expert system rule confidences using data mining of myocardial perfusion spect databases. In *Computers in Cardiology Conference*, 2000.

[7] Levien de Braal, Norberto Ezquerra, E. Schwartz, and Ernest V. Garcia. Analyzing and predicting images through a neural network approach. In *Proc. of Visualization in Biomedical Computing*, 1996.

[8] Richard Duda and Peter Hart. *Pattern Classification and Scene Analysis*, pages 10–45. John Wiley and Sons, 1973.

[9] Norberto Ezquerra and Rakesh Mullick. Perfex: An expert system for interpreting myocardial perfusion. *Expert Systems with Applications*, 6:455–468, 1993.

[10] Usama Fayyad and G. Piateski-Shapiro. *From Data Mining to Knowledge Discovery*. MIT Press, 1995.

[11] Raymond Ng, Laks Lakshmanan, and Jiawei Han. Exploratory mining and pruning optimizations of constrained association rules. In *ACM SIGMOD Conference*, 1998.

[12] Carlos Ordonez and Paul Cereghini. SQLEM: Fast clustering in SQL using the EM algorithm. In *ACM SIGMOD Conference*, pages 559–570, 2000.

[13] Carlos Ordonez and Edward Omiecinski. Discovering association rules based on image content. In *IEEE Advances in Digital Libraries Conference (ADL'99)*, pages 38–49, 1999.

[14] Carlos Ordonez, Cesar A. Santana, and Levien de Braal. Discovering interesting association rules in medical data. In *ACM SIGMOD Workshop on Research Issues on Data Mining and Knowledge Discovery (DMKD 2000)*, pages 78–85, 2000.

[15] Ramakrishnan Srikant and Rakesh Agrawal. Mining generalized association rules. In *VLDB Conference*, 1995.

[16] Ramakrishnan Srikant and Rakesh Agrawal. Mining quantitative association rules in large relational tables. In *ACM SIGMOD Conference*, 1996.

[17] Ramakrishnan Srikant, Q. Vu, and Rakesh Agrawal. Mining association rules with item constraints. In *ACM KDD Conference*, 1993.

H-Mine: Hyper-Structure Mining of Frequent Patterns in Large Databases

Jian Pei[†‡], Jiawei Han[‡], Hongjun Lu[*], Shojiro Nishio[§], Shiwei Tang[†], Dongqing Yang[†]

[†] Peking University, Beijing, China (pei@db.pku.edu.cn, {tsw, dqyang}@pku.edu.cn)
[‡] Simon Fraser University, B.C., Canada ({peijian, han}@cs.sfu.ca)
[*] Hong Kong University of Science and Technology, Hong Kong (luhj@cs.ust.hk)
[§] Osaka University, Osaka, Japan (nishio@ise.eng.osaka-u.ac.jp)

Abstract

Methods for efficient mining of frequent patterns have been studied extensively by many researchers. However, the previously proposed methods still encounter some performance bottlenecks when mining databases with different data characteristics, such as dense vs. sparse, long vs. short patterns, memory-based vs. disk-based, etc.

In this study, we propose a simple and novel hyper-linked data structure, H-struct, *and a new mining algorithm,* H-mine, *which takes advantage of this data structure and dynamically adjusts links in the mining process. A distinct feature of this method is that it has very limited and precisely predictable space overhead and runs really fast in memory-based setting. Moreover, it can be scaled up to very large databases by database partitioning, and when the data set becomes dense, (conditional) FP-trees can be constructed dynamically as part of the mining process. Our study shows that* H-mine *has high performance in various kinds of data, outperforms the previously developed algorithms in different settings, and is highly scalable in mining large databases. This study also proposes a new data mining methodology,* space-preserving mining, *which may have strong impact in the future development of efficient and scalable data mining methods.*

1 Introduction

As an important data mining problem, frequent pattern mining plays an essential role in many data mining tasks, such as mining associations [3, 8], sequential patterns [15, 12], max-patterns and frequent closed patterns [4, 11, 17], classification [7, 16], and clustering [2].

There have been many algorithms developed for fast mining of frequent patterns, which can be classified into two categories. The first category, *candidate generation-and-test approach*, such as Apriori [3] as well as many subsequent studies, are directly based on an anti-monotone *Apriori* property [3]: *if a pattern with k items is not frequent, any of its super-pattern with $(k + 1)$ or more items can never be frequent.* A candidate-generation-and-test approach iteratively generates the set of candidate patterns of length $(k + 1)$ from the set of frequent patterns of length k $(k \geq 1)$, and check their corresponding occurrence fre-

quencies in the database.

The *Apriori* algorithm achieves good reduction on the size of candidate sets. However, when there exist a large number of frequent patterns and/or long patterns, candidate-generation-and-test methods may still suffer from generating huge numbers of candidates and taking many scans of large databases for frequency checking.

Recently, another category of methods, *pattern-growth methods*, such as *FP-growth* [6] and *TreeProjection* [1], have been proposed. A pattern-growth method uses the *Apriori* property. However, instead of generating candidate sets, it recursively partitions the database into sub-databases according to the frequent patterns found and searches for local frequent patterns to assemble longer global ones.

Nevertheless, these proposed approaches may still encounter some difficulties in different cases.

First, *huge space is required to serve the mining*. An *Apriori*-like algorithm generates a huge number of candidates for *long or dense* patterns. To find a frequent pattern of size 100, such as $\{a_1, \ldots, a_{100}\}$, up to $50 \times \binom{100}{50}$ units of space is needed to store candidates. *FP-growth* [6] avoids candidate generation by compressing the transaction database into an *FP-tree* and pursuing partition-based mining recursively. However, if the database is *huge and sparse*, the *FP-tree* will be large and the space requirement for recursion is a challenge. None is superior in all the cases.

Second, *real databases contain all the cases*. Real data sets can be sparse and/or dense in different applications. For example, for telecommunication data analysis, calling patterns for home users vs. business users could be very different: some are frequent and dense (e.g., to family members and close friends), but some are huge and sparse. Similar situations arise for market basket analysis, census data analysis, classification and predictive modeling, etc. It is hard to select an appropriate mining method on the fly if no algorithm fits all.

Third, *large applications need more scalability*. Many existing methods are efficient when the data set is not very large. Otherwise, their core data structures (such as *FP-tree*) or the intermediate results (e.g., the set of candidates in *Apriori* or the recursively generated conditional databases in *FP-growth*) may not fit in main memory and easily cause thrashing.

441

This poses a new challenge: *"Can we work out a better method which is (1) efficient in all occasions (dense vs. sparse, huge vs. memory-based data sets), and (2) space requirement is small, even for very large databases?"*

In this paper, we propose a new data structure, H-struct, and a new mining method, H-mine, to overcome these difficulties, with the following progress.

First, a memory-based, efficient pattern-growth algorithm, H-mine(Mem), is proposed for mining frequent patterns for the data sets that can fit in (main) memory. A simple, memory-based hyper-structure, H-struct, is designed for fast mining. H-mine(Mem) has polynomial space complexity and is thus more space efficient than pattern-growth methods like *FP-growth* and *TreeProjection* when mining sparse data sets, and also more efficient than *Apriori*-based methods which generate a large number of candidates. Experimental results show that, in many cases, H-mine has very limited and exactly predictable space overhead and is faster than memory-based *Apriori* and *FP-growth*.

Then, based on H-mine(Mem), we propose H-mine, a scalable algorithm for mining large databases by first partitioning the database, mining each partition in memory using H-mine(Mem), and then consolidating global frequent patterns.

Third, for dense data sets, H-mine is integrated with *FP-growth* dynamically by detecting the swapping condition and constructing FP-trees for efficient mining.

Such efforts ensure that H-mine is scalable in both large and medium sized databases and in both sparse and dense data sets. Our comprehensive performance study confirms that H-mine is highly scalable and is faster than *Apriori* and *FP-growth* in all the occasions.

The remaining of the paper is organized as follows. Section 2 is devoted to H-mine(Mem), an efficient algorithm for memory-based frequent pattern mining. In Section 3, H-mine(Mem) is extended to huge, disk-based databases, together with some further optimizations techniques. Our performance study is reported in Section 4. We discuss related issues and conclude our study in Section 5.

2 H-mine(Mem): Memory-Based Hyper-Structure Mining

In this section, H-mine(Mem) (memory-based hyper-structure mining of frequent patterns) is developed, and in Section 3, the method is extended to handle large and/or dense databases.

We first define the problem of frequent pattern mining.

Definition 2.1 Let $I = \{x_1, \ldots, x_n\}$ be a set of **items**. An **itemset** X is a subset of items, i.e., $X \subseteq I$. For the sake of brevity, an itemset $X = \{x_1, x_2, \ldots, x_m\}$ is also denoted as $X = x_1 x_2 \cdots x_m$. A **transaction** $T = (tid, X)$ is a 2-tuple, where tid is a transaction-id and X an itemset. A transaction $T = (tid, X)$ is said to **contain** itemset Y if and only if $Y \subseteq X$. A **transaction database** TDB is a set of transactions. The number of transactions in TDB containing itemset X is called the **support** of X, denoted as $sup(X)$. Given a transaction database TDB and a **support threshold** min_sup, an itemset X is a **frequent pattern**, or a **pattern** in short, if and only if $sup(X) \geq min\_sup$.

The **problem of frequent pattern mining** is to *find the complete set of frequent patterns in a given transaction database with respect to a given support threshold.*

Our general idea of H-mine(Mem) is illustrated in the following example.

Example 1 Let the first two columns of Table 1 be our running transaction database TDB. Let the minimum support threshold be $min\_sup = 2$.

Trans ID	Items	Frequent-item projection
100	c, d, e, f, g, i	c, d, e, g
200	a, c, d, e, m	a, c, d, e
300	a, b, d, e, g, k	a, d, e, g
400	a, c, d, h	a, c, d

Table 1. The transaction database TDB as our running example.

Following the *Apriori* property [3], only frequent items play roles in frequent patterns. By scanning TDB once, the complete set of frequent items $\{a : 3, c : 3, d : 4, e : 3, g : 2\}$ can be found and output, where the notation $a : 3$ means item a's support (occurrence frequency) is 3. Let $freq(X)$ (the *frequent-item projection* of X) be the set of frequent items in itemset X. For the ease of explanation, the frequent-item projections of all the transactions of Table 1 are shown in the third column of the table.

Following the alphabetical order of frequent items[1] (called *F-list*): a-c-d-e-g, the complete set of frequent patterns can be partitioned into 5 subsets as follows: (1) those containing item a; (2) those containing item c but no item a; (3) those containing item d but no item a nor c; (4) those containing item e but no item a nor c nor d; and (5) those containing only item g.

If the frequent-item projections of transactions in the database can be held in main memory, they can be organized as shown in Figure 1. All items in frequent-item projections are sorted according to the *F-list*. For example, the frequent-item projection of transaction 100 is listed as $cdeg$. Every occurrence of a frequent item is stored in an entry with two fields: an *item-id* and a *hyper-link*.

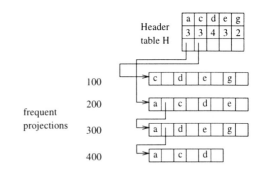

Figure 1. H-struct.

---

[1]As you may aware, any ordering should work, and the alphabetical ordering is just for the convenience of explanation.

A *header table* H is created, where each frequent item entry has three fields: an *item-id*, a *support count*, and a *hyper-link*. When the frequent-item projections are loaded into memory, those with the same first item (in the order of *F-list*) are linked together by the hyper-links as a queue, and the entries in header table H act as the heads of the queues. For example, the entry of item a in the header table H is the head of a-queue, which links frequent-item projections of transactions 200, 300, and 400. These three projections all have item a as their first frequent item (in the order of *F-list*). Similarly, frequent-item projection of transaction 100 is linked as *c-queue*, headed by item c in H. The d-, e- and g-queues are empty since there is no frequent-item projection that begins with any of these items.

Clearly, it takes one scan (the second scan) of the transaction database TDB to build such a memory structure (called H-struct). Then the remaining of the mining can be performed on the H-struct only, without referencing any information in the original database. After that, the five subsets of frequent patterns can be mined one by one as follows.

First, let us consider how to find the set of frequent patterns in the first subset, i.e., all the frequent patterns containing item a. This requires to search all the frequent-item projections containing item a, i.e., the *a-projected database*[2], denoted as $TDB|_a$. Interestingly, the frequent-item projections in the a-projected database are already linked in the a-queue, which can be traversed efficiently.

To mine the a-projected database, an *a-header table H_a* is created, as shown in Figure 2. In H_a, every frequent item, except for a itself, has an entry with the same three fields as H, i.e., *item-id, support count* and *hyper-link*. The support count in H_a records the support of the corresponding item in the a-projected database. For example, item c appears twice in a-projected database (i.e., frequent-item projections in the a-queue), thus the support count in the entry c of H_a is 2.

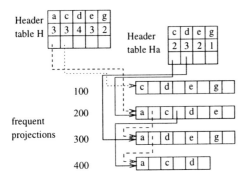

Figure 2. Header table H_a and ac-queue.

By traversing the a-queue once, the set of locally frequent items, i.e., the items appearing at least 2 times, in the a-projected database is found, which is $\{c : 2, d : 3, e : 2\}$ (Note: $g : 1$ is not locally frequent and thus will not be considered further.) This scan outputs frequent patterns $\{ac : 2, ad : 3, ae : 2\}$ and builds up links for H_a header as shown in Figure 2.

---

[2]The a-projected database consists of all the frequent-item projections containing item a, but these are all "virtual" projections since no physical projections are performed to create a new database.

Similarly, the process continues for the ac-projected database by examining the c-queue in H_a, which creates an *ac-header table H_{ac}*, as shown in Figure 3.

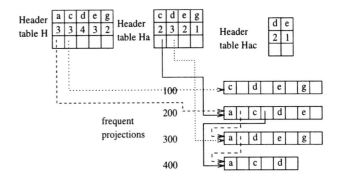

Figure 3. Header table H_{ac}.

Since only item $d : 2$ is locally frequent item in the ac-projected database, only $acd : 2$ is output, and the search along this path completes.

Then the recursion backtracks to find patterns containing a and d but no c. Since the queue started from d in the header table H_a, i.e., the ad-queue, links all frequent-item projections containing items a and d (but excluding item c in the projection), one can get the complete ad-projected database by inserting frequent-item projections having item d in the ac-queue into the ad-queue. This involves one more traversal of the ac-queue. Each frequent-item projection in the ac-queue is appended to the queue of the next frequent item in the projection according to *F-list*. Since all the frequent-item projections in the ac-queue have item d, they are all inserted into the ad-queue, as shown in Figure 4.

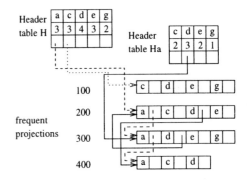

Figure 4. Header table H_a and ad-queue.

It can be seen that, after the adjustment, the ad-queue collects the complete set of frequent-item projections containing items a and d. Thus, the set of frequent patterns containing items a and d can be mined recursively. Please note that, even though item c appears in frequent-item projections of ad-projected database, we do not consider it as a locally frequent item in any recursive projected database since it has been considered in the mining of the ac-queue. This mining generates only one pattern $ade : 2$. Notice also the third level header table H_{ad} can use the table H_{ac} since the search for H_{ac} was done in the previous round. Thus we only need one header table at the third level. Later we can see that only one header table is needed for each level in the whole mining process.

For the search in the ae-projected database, since e contains no child links, the search terminates, with no patterns generated.

After the frequent patterns containing item a are found, the a-projected database, i.e., a-queue, is no longer needed in the remaining of mining. Since the c-queue includes all frequent-item projections containing item c except for those projections containing both items a and c, which are in the a-queue. To mine all the frequent patterns containing item c but no a, and other subsets of frequent patterns, we need to insert all the projections in the a-queue to the proper queues.

We traverse the a-queue once more. Each frequent-item projection in the queue is appended to the queue of the next item in the projection following a in the *F-list*, as shown in Figure 5. For example, frequent-item projection $acde$ is inserted into c-queue and $adeg$ is inserted into d-queue.

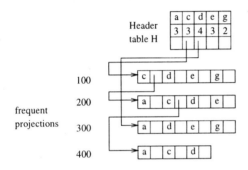

Figure 5. Adjusted hyper-links after mining a-projected database.

By mining the c-projected database recursively (with shared header table at each level), we can find the set of frequent patterns containing item c but no a. Notice item a will not be included in the c-projected database since all the frequent patterns having a have already been found.

Similarly, the mining goes on. It is easy to see that the above mining process finds the complete set of frequent patterns without duplication. The remaining mining process is left as an exercise to interested readers.

Notice also that the depth-first search for mining the first set of frequent patterns at any depth can be done in one database scan by constructing the header tables at all levels simultaneously.

The general idea of H-mine(Mem) is shown in the above example. Limited by space, we omit a formal presentation of H-mine(Mem) as well as a complexity analysis of the algorithm. Comparing with other frequent pattern mining methods, the efficiency of H-mine(Mem) comes from the following aspects.

First, H-mine(Mem) avoids candidate generation and test by adopting a frequent-pattern growth methodology, a more efficient method shown in previous studies [6, 1]. H-mine(Mem) absorbs the advantages of pattern growth.

Second, H-mine(Mem) confines its search in a dedicated space. Unlike other frequent pattern growth meth-

ods, such as *FP-growth* [6], it does not need to physically construct memory structures of projected databases. It fully utilizes the information well organized in the H-struct, and collects information about projected databases using header tables, which are light-weight structures. That also saves a lot of efforts on managing space.

Third, H-mine(Mem) does not need to store any frequent patterns in memory. Once a frequent pattern is found, it is output to disk. In contrast, the candidate-generation-and-test method has to save and use the frequent patterns found in the current round to generate candidates for the next round.

The above analysis is verified by our extensive performance study, as presented in Section 4.

3 From H-mine(Mem) to H-mine: Efficient Mining in Different Occasions

In this section, we first extend our algorithm H-mine(Mem) to H-mine, which mines frequent-patterns in large data sets that cannot fit in main memory. Then, we explore how to integrate *FP-growth* when the data sets being mined become very dense.

3.1 H-mine: Mining in Large Databases

H-mine(Mem) is efficient when the frequent-item projections of a transaction database plus a set of header tables can fit in main memory. However, we cannot expect this is always the case. When they cannot fit in memory, a database partitioning technique can be developed as follows.

Let TDB be the transaction database with n transactions and min_sup be the support threshold. By scanning TDB once, one can find L, the set of frequent items.

Then, TDB can be partitioned into k parts, TDB_1, ..., TDB_k, such that, for each TDB_i $(1 \leq i \leq k)$, the frequent-item projections of transactions in TDB_i can be held in main memory, where TDB_i has n_i transactions, and $\sum_{i=1}^{k} n_i = n$. We can apply H-mine(Mem) to TDB_i to find frequent patterns in TDB_i with the minimum support threshold $min\_sup_i = \lfloor min\_sup \times \frac{n_i}{n} \rfloor$ (i.e., each partitioned database keeps the same relative minimum support as the global database).

Let F_i $(1 \leq i \leq k)$ be the set of (locally) frequent patterns in TDB_i. Based on the property of partition-based mining [13], P cannot be a (globally) frequent pattern in TDB with respect to the support threshold min_sup if there exists no i $(1 \leq i \leq k)$ such that P is in F_i. Therefore, after mining frequent patterns in TDB_i's, we can gather the patterns in F_i's and collect their (global) support in TDB by scanning the transaction database TDB one more time.

Based on the above observation, we can extend H-mine(Mem) to H-mine.

Note that our partition-based mining share some similarities with a *partitioned Apriori* method proposed in [13] in which a transaction database is first partitioned, every partition is mined using *Apriori*, then all the locally frequent patterns are gathered to form globally frequent candidate patterns before counting their global support by one more scan of the transaction database. However, there are two essential differences between these two methods.

As also indicated in [13], it is not easy to get a good partition scheme using the *partitioned Apriori* [13] since it is hard to predict the space requirement of *Apriori*. In contrast, it is straightforward for H-mine to partition the transaction database, since the space overhead is very small and predictable during mining.

On the other hand, H-mine first finds globally frequent items. When mining partitions of a database, H-mine examines only those items which are globally frequent. In skewed partitions, many globally infrequent items can be locally frequent in some partitions, H-mine does not spend any effort to check them but the *partitioned Apriori* [13] does.

Furthermore, we can do better in consolidating globally frequent patterns from local ones, as illustrated in the following example.

Example 2 A large transaction database TDB is partitioned into four parts, P_1, P_2, P_3 and P_4. Let the support threshold be 100. The four parts are mined respectively using H-mine(Mem). The locally frequent patterns as well as the partition-ids where they are frequent are shown in Table 2. The accumulated support count for a pattern is the sum of support counts from partitions where the pattern is locally frequent.

Local freq. pat.	Partitions	Accumulated sup. cnt
ab	P_1, P_2, P_3, P_4	280
ac	P_1, P_2, P_3, P_4	320
ad	P_1, P_2, P_3, P_4	260
abc	P_1, P_3, P_4	120
$abcd$	P_1, P_4	40
$\cdots$	$\cdots$	$\cdots$

Table 2. Local frequent patterns in partitions.

Pattern ab is frequent in all the partitions. Therefore, it is globally frequent. Its global support count is its accumulated support count, i.e., 280. So do patterns ac and ad.

Pattern abc is frequent in all partitions except in P_2. The accumulated support count of abc covers the occurrences of the pattern in partitions P_1, P_3 and P_4. Thus, the pattern should be checked only in P_2. The global support count of abc is its accumulated count plus its support count in P_2. Similarly, pattern $abcd$ need to be checked in only partitions P_2 and P_3.

In the third scan of H-mine, after scanning partition P_2, suppose the support count of pattern $abcd$ in partition P_2 is 20. Since $abcd$ is not frequent in partition P_3, its support count in P_3 must be less than the local support threshold. If the local support threshold is 30, we do not need to check pattern $abcd$ in partition P_3, since $abcd$ has no hope to be globally frequent.

As can be seen from the example, we have the following optimization methods on consolidating globally frequent patterns.

First, accumulate the global support count from local ones for the patterns frequent in every partition.

Second, only check the patterns against those partitions where they are infrequent.

Third, use local support thresholds to derive the upper bounds for the global support counts of locally frequent patterns. Only check those patterns whose upper bound pass the global support threshold.

With the above optimization, the number of patterns to be consolidated can be reduced dramatically. As shown in our experiments, when the data set is relatively evenly distributed, only up to 20% of locally frequent patterns have to be checked in the third scan of H-mine.

In general, the following factors contribute to the scalability and efficiency of H-mine.

As shown in Section 2, H-mine(Mem) has small space overhead and is efficient in mining partitions which can be held in main memory. With the current memory technology, it is likely that many medium-sized databases can be mined efficiently by this memory-based frequent-pattern mining mechanism.

No matter how large the database is, it can be mined by at most three scans of the database: the first scan finds globally frequent items; the second mines partitioned database using H-mine(Mem); and the third verifies globally frequent patterns. Since every partition is mined efficiently using H-mine(Mem), the mining of the whole database is highly scalable.

One may wonder that, since the *partitioned Apriori* [13] takes two scans of TDB, whereas H-mine takes three scans, how can H-mine outperform the one proposed in [13]? Notice that the major cost in this process is the mining of each partitioned database. The last scan of TDB for collecting supports and generating globally frequent patterns is fast because the set of locally frequent patterns can be inserted into one compact structure, such as a hashing tree. Since H-mine generates less partitions and mines each partition very fast, it has better overall performance than the Apriori-based partition mining algorithm. This is also demonstrated in our performance study.

3.2 Handling dense data sets: Dynamic integration of H-struct and *FP-tree*-based mining

As indicated in several studies [5, 6, 11], finding frequent patterns in dense databases is a challenging task since it may generate dense and long patterns which may lead to the generation of very large (and even exponential) number of candidate sets if an *Apriori*-like algorithm is used. The *FP-growth* method proposed in our recent study [6] works well in dense databases with a large number of long patterns due to the effective compression of shared prefix paths in mining.

In comparison with *FP-growth*, H-mine does not generate physical projected databases and conditional *FP-trees* and thus saves space as well as time in many cases. However, *FP-tree*-based mining has its advantages over mining on H-struct since *FP-tree* shares common prefix paths among different transactions, which may lead to space and time savings as well. As one may expect, the situation under which one method outperforms the other depends on the characteristics of the data sets: if data sharing is rare such as in sparse databases, the compression factor could be small and *FP-tree* may not outperform mining on H-struct. On the other hand, there are many dense data sets in practice. Even though the data sets might not be dense originally, as mining progresses, the projected databases become smaller, and data often becomes denser as the relative support goes up when the number of transactions in a projected database reduces substantially. In such cases, it is beneficial to swap the data structure from H-struct to FP-tree since FP-tree's compression by common prefix path sharing and then mining on the compressed structures will overweigh the benefits brought by H-struct.

The question becomes what should be the appropriate situations that one structure is more preferable over the other and how to determine when such a structure/algorithm swapping should happen. A dynamic pattern density analysis technique is suggested as follows.

In the context of frequent pattern mining, a (projected) database is *dense* if the frequent items in it have *high relative support*. The *relative support* can be computed as the ratio of absolute support against number of transactions (or frequent-item projections) in the (projected) database. When the relative support is high, such as 10% or over, i.e., the projected database is dense, and the number of (locally) frequent items is not large (so that the resulting FP-tree is not bushy), then FP-tree should be constructed to explore the sharing of common prefix paths and database compression. On the other hand, when the relative support of frequent items is low, such as far below 1%, it is sparse, and H-struct should be constructed for efficient H-mine. However, in the middle lies the gray area, and which structure and method should be used will depend on the size of the frequent-item projection database, the size of the main memory and other performance factors.

4 Performance Study

To evaluate the efficiency and scalability of H-mine, we have performed an extensive performance study. In this section, we report our experimental results on the performance of H-mine in comparison with Apriori and FP-growth. It shows that H-mine outperforms Apriori and FP-growth and is efficient and highly scalable for mining very large databases.[3]

All the experiments are performed on a 466MHz Pentium PC machine with 128 megabytes main memory and 20G hard disk, running Microsoft Windows/NT. H-mine and FP-growth are implemented by us using Visual C++6.0, while the version of Apriori that we used is a well-known version, "GNU Lesser General Public License", available at http://fuzzy.cs.uni-magdeburg.de/~borgelt/. All reports of the runtime of H-mine include both the time of constructing H-struct and mining frequent-patterns. They also include both CPU time and I/O time.

We have tested various data sets, with consistent results. Limited by space, only the results on some typical data sets are reported here.

---

[3]A prototype of H-mine is also tested by a third party in US (a commercial company) on business data. Their results are consistent with ours. They observed that H-mine is more than 10 times faster than Apriori and other participating methods in their test when the support threshold is low.

4.1 Mining in main memory

In this sub-section, we report results on mining transaction databases which can be held in main memory. H-mine is implemented as stated in Section 2. For FP-growth, the FP-trees can be held in main memory in the tests reported in this sub-section. We modified the source code for Apriori so that the transactions are loaded into main memory and the multiple scans of database are pursued in main memory.

Data set Gazelle is a sparse data set. It is a web store visit (clickstream) data set from Gazelle.com. It contains 59, 602 transactions, while there are up to 267 item per transaction.

Figure 6 shows the run time of H-mine, Apriori and FP-growth on this data set. Clearly, H-mine wins the other two algorithms, and the gaps (in term of seconds) become larger as the support threshold goes lower.

Apriori works well in such sparse data sets since most of the candidates that Apriori generates turn out to be frequent patterns. However, it has to construct a hashing tree for the candidates and match them in the tree and update their counts each time when scanning a transaction that contains the candidates. That is the major cost for Apriori.

FP-growth has a similar performance as Apriori and sometime is even slightly worse. This is because when the database is sparse, FP-tree cannot compress data as effectively as what it does on dense data sets. Constructing FP-trees over sparse data sets recursively has its overhead.

Figure 7 plots the high water mark of space usage of H-mine, Apriori and FP-growth in the mining procedure. To make the comparison clear, the space usage (axis Y) is in logarithmic scale. From the figure, we can see that H-mine and FP-growth use similar space and are very scalable in term of space usage with respect to support threshold. Even when the support threshold reduces to very low, the memory usage is still stable and moderate.

The memory usage of Apriori does not scale well as the support threshold goes down. Apriori has to store level-wise frequent patterns and generate next level candidates. When the support threshold is low, the number of frequent patterns as well as that of candidates are non-trivial. In contrast, pattern-growth methods, including H-mine and FP-growth, do not need to store any frequent patterns or candidates. Once a pattern is found, it is output immediately and never read back.

What are the performance of these algorithms over dense data sets? We use the synthetic data set generator described in [3] to generate a data set $T25I15D10k$, which contains 10, 000 transactions and each transaction has up to 25 items. There are 1, 000 items in the data set and the average longest potentially frequent itemset is with 15 items. It is a relatively dense data set.

Figure 8 shows the runtime of the three algorithms on this data set. When the support threshold is high, most patterns are of short lengths, Apriori and FP-growth have similar performance. When the support threshold becomes low, most items (more than 90%) are frequent. Then, FP-growth is much faster than Apriori. In all cases, H-mine is the fastest one. It is more than 10 times faster than Apriori and 4-5 times faster than FP-growth.

Figure 9 shows the high water mark of space usage of the three algorithms in mining this data set. Again, the space usage is drawn in logarithmic scale. As the number of pat-

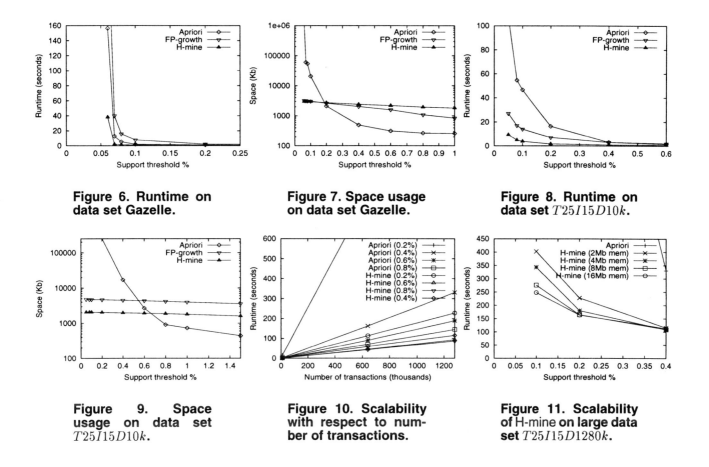

Figure 6. Runtime on data set Gazelle.

Figure 7. Space usage on data set Gazelle.

Figure 8. Runtime on data set $T25I15D10k$.

Figure 9. Space usage on data set $T25I15D10k$.

Figure 10. Scalability with respect to number of transactions.

Figure 11. Scalability of H-mine on large data set $T25I15D1280k$.

terns goes up dramatically as support threshold goes down, *Apriori* requires an exponential amount of space. H-mine and *FP-growth* use stable amount of space. In dense data set, an *FP-tree* is smaller than the set of all frequent-item projections of the data set. However, long patterns means more recursions and more recursive *FP-trees*. That makes *FP-growth* require more space than H-mine in this case. On the other hand, since the number of frequent items is large in this data set, an *FP-tree*, though compressing the database, still has many branches in various levels and becomes bushy. That also introduces non-trivial tree browsing cost.

In very dense data set, such as *Connect-4* (from UC-Irvine: (www.ics.uci.edu/~mlearn/MLRepository.html), and *pumsb* (from IBM Almaden Research Center: www.almaden.ibm.com/cs/quest/demos.html), H-mine builds *FP-trees* since the numbers of frequent items are very small. Thus it has the same performance as *FP-growth*. Previous studies, e.g., [4], show that *Apriori* is incapable of mining such data sets.

4.2 Mining very large databases

To test the efficiency and scalability of the algorithms on mining very large databases, we generate data set $T25I15D1280k$ using the synthetic data generator. It has $1,280,000$ transactions with similar statistic features as the data set $T25I15D10k$.

We enforce memory constraints on H-mine so that the total memory available is limited to 2, 4, 8 and 16 megabytes, respectively. The memory covers the space for H-struct and all the header tables, as well as the related mechanisms. Since the *FP-tree* built for the data set is too big to fit in main memory, we do not report the performance of *FP-growth* on this data set. We do not explicitly compose any memory constraint on *Apriori*.

Figure 10 shows the scalability of both H-mine (with main memory size constraint 2 megabytes) and *Apriori* with respect to number of transactions in the database. Various support threshold settings are tested. Both algorithms have linear scalability and H-mine is a clear winner. From the figure, we can see that H-mine is more efficient and scalable at mining very large databases.

To study the effect of memory size constraint on the mining efficiency and scalability of H-mine in large databases, we plot Figure 11. The figure shows the scalability of H-mine w.r.t. support threshold with various memory constraints, i.e., 2, 4, 8 and 16 megabytes, respectively. As shown in the figure, the runtime is not sensitive to the memory limitation when support threshold is high. When the support threshold goes down, as available space increases, performance gets better.

Our experimental results also show that H-mine has a very light workload in its third scan to consolidate global

447

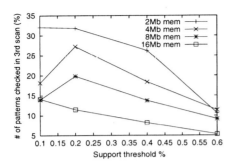

Figure 12. The ratio of patterns to be checked by H-mine **in the 3-rd scan.**

ically switches its data structure from H-struct to *FP-tree* and its mining algorithm from mining on H-struct to *FP-growth* when the data set becomes dense and the number of frequent items becomes small.

H-mine can be scaled-up to very large databases due to its small and precisely predictable run-time memory overhead and its database partitioned mining technique.

Based on the above analysis, one can see that H-mine represents a new, highly efficient and scalable mining method. Its *structure- and space-preserving mining* methodology may have strong impact on the development of new, efficient and scalable data mining methods for mining other kinds of patterns, such as closed-itemsets [11], max-patterns [4], sequential patterns [14, 12], constraint-based mining [9, 10], etc. This should be an interesting direction for further study.

frequent patterns. We consider the ratio of the number of patterns to be checked in the third scan over that of all distinct locally frequent patterns, where a locally frequent pattern is to be checked in the third scan if it is not frequent in every partition. Figure 12 shows the ratio numbers. In general, as the support threshold goes down, the ratio goes up. That means mining with low support threshold may lead to more patterns frequent in some partitions. On the other hand, less memory (small partition) leads to more partitions and also increase the ratio.

As shown in the figure, only a limited portion of locally frequent patterns, e.g., less than 35% in our test case, needs to be tested in the third scan. This leads to a low cost of the third scan in our partition-based mining.

In summary, our experimental results and performance study verify our analysis and support our claim that H-mine is an efficient algorithm for mining frequent patterns. It is highly scalable in mining very large databases.

5 Discussion and Conclusions

In this paper, we have proposed a simple and novel hyper-linked data structure, H-struct, and a new frequent pattern mining algorithm, H-mine, which takes advantage of H-struct data structure and dynamically adjusts links in the mining process. As shown in our performance study, H-mine has high performance and is scalable in all kinds of data, with very limited and predictable space overhead, and outperforms the previously developed algorithms with various settings.

A major distinction of H-mine from the previously proposed methods is that H-mine re-adjusts the links at mining different "projected" databases and has very small space overhead, even counting temporary working space. H-mine absorbs the nice features of *FP-growth*. It is essentially a frequent-pattern growth approach since it partitions its search space according to both patterns to be searched for and the data set to be searched on, by a divide-and-conquer methodology, without generating and testing candidate patterns. However, unlike *FP-growth*, H-mine does not create any physical projected databases nor constructing conditional (local) *FP-trees*. H-mine is not confined itself to H-struct only. Instead, it watches carefully the changes of data characteristics during mining and dynam-

References

[1] R. Agarwal, C. Aggarwal, and V. V. V. Prasad. A tree projection algorithm for generation of frequent itemsets. In *J. of Parallel and Distributed Computing (Special Issue on High Performance Data Mining)*, 2000.

[2] R. Agrawal, J. Gehrke, D. Gunopulos, and P. Raghavan. Automatic subspace clustering of high dimensional data for data mining applications. In *SIGMOD'98*, pages 94–105.

[3] R. Agrawal and R. Srikant. Fast algorithms for mining association rules. In *VLDB'94*, pages 487–499.

[4] R. J. Bayardo. Efficiently mining long patterns from databases. In *SIGMOD'98*, pages 85–93.

[5] R. J. Bayardo, R. Agrawal, and D. Gunopulos. Constraint-based rule mining on large, dense data sets. In *ICDE'99*.

[6] J. Han, J. Pei, and Y. Yin. Mining frequent patterns without candidate generation. In *SIGMOD'00*, pages 1–12.

[7] B. Liu, W. Hsu, and Y. Ma. Integrating classification and association rule mining. In *KDD'98*, pages 80–86.

[8] H. Mannila, H. Toivonen, and A. I. Verkamo. Efficient algorithms for discovering association rules. In *KDD'94*, pages 181–192.

[9] R. Ng, L. V. S. Lakshmanan, J. Han, and A. Pang. Exploratory mining and pruning optimizations of constrained associations rules. In *SIGMOD'98*, pages 13–24.

[10] J. Pei, J. Han, and L. V. S. Lakshmanan. Mining frequent itemsets with convertible constraints. In *ICDE'01*, pages 433–332.

[11] J. Pei, J. Han, and R. Mao. CLOSET: An efficient algorithm for mining frequent closed itemsets. In *Proc. 2000 ACM-SIGMOD Int. Workshop Data Mining and Knowledge Discovery (DMKD'00)*, pages 11–20.

[12] J. Pei, J. Han, B. Mortazavi-Asl, H. Pinto, Q. Chen, U. Dayal, and M.-C. Hsu. PrefixSpan: Mining sequential patterns efficiently by prefix-projected pattern growth. In *ICDE'01*, pages 215–224.

[13] A. Savasere, E. Omiecinski, and S. Navathe. An efficient algorithm for mining association rules in large databases. In *VLDB'95*, pages 432–443.

[14] R. Srikant and R. Agrawal. Mining quantitative association rules in large relational tables. In *SIGMOD'96*, pages 1–12.

[15] R. Srikant and R. Agrawal. Mining sequential patterns: Generalizations and performance improvements. In *EDBT'96*, pages 3–17.

[16] K. Wang, S. Zhou, and S. C. Liew. Building hierarchical classifiers using class proximity. In *VLDB'99*, pages 363–374.

[17] M. Zaki. Generating non-redundant association rules. In *KDD'00*, pages 34–43.

FARM: A Framework for Exploring Mining Spaces with Multiple Attributes

Chang-Shing Perng   Haixun Wang   Sheng Ma   Joseph L. Hellerstein

{perng,haixun,shengma,hellers}@us.ibm.com

IBM Thomas J. Watson Research Center

Hawthorne, NY 10532

Abstract

Mining for frequent itemsets typically involves a pre-processing step in which data with multiple attributes are grouped into transactions, and items are defined based on attribute values. We have observed that such fixed attribute mining can severely constrain the patterns that are discovered. Herein, we introduce mining spaces, a new framework for mining multi-attribute data that includes the discovery of transaction and item definitions (with the exploitation of taxonomies and functional dependencies if they are available). We prove that special downward closure properties (or anti-monotonic property) hold for mining spaces, a result that allows us to construct efficient algorithms for mining patterns without the constraints of fixed attribute mining. We apply our algorithms to real world data collected from a production computer network. The results show that by exploiting the special kinds of downward closure in mining spaces, execution times for mining can be reduced by a factor of three to four.

1. Introduction

Mining for frequent itemsets has been studied extensively because of the potential for actionable insights. Typically, mining involves a preprocessing step in which data with multiple attributes are grouped into transactions and items are defined based on attribute values. For example in supermarket data, the market basket attribute might be used to group data into transactions and the product-type attribute (with values such as diapers, beer) to define items.

We have observed that fixing the attributes used to define transactions and items can severely constrain the patterns that are discovered. For example, by having items characterized in terms of product type, we may fail to discover relationships between baby items in general (e.g., diapers, formula, rattles) and adult beverages (e.g., beer and wine). And, by having transactions be market baskets, we may fail to note relationships between items purchased by the same family in a single day.

To go beyond the limits of fixed attribute mining, we introduce *FARM*, a new mining framework that uses mining spaces to discover frequent patterns for transactions and items that are defined in terms of data attributes. Here a "transaction" is a general term for a group of records. Our framework exploits taxonomies and functional dependencies but does not depend on such information. We prove that downward closure holds for a class of mining spaces. This results provide for the implementation of efficient mining algorithms. We apply our algorithms to event data collected from a production computer network and show that our approach is considerably faster than simply employing apriori-like algorithms on each choice of attributes for defining transactions and items.

(Rec)	Date	Time	Interval	EventType	Host	Severity
(1)	08/21/00	2:12am	2:10am	TcpCnnctClose	3	harmless
(2)	08/21/00	2:13am	2:10am	InterfaceDown	45	severe
(3)	08/21/00	2:14am	2:10am	InterfaceDown	23	severe
(4)	08/21/00	2:14am	2:10am	InterfaceDown	5	severe
(5)	08/21/00	2:15am	2:10am	InterfaceDown	24	severe
(6)	08/21/00	2:16am	2:15am	CiscoLinkUp	16	harmless
(7)	08/21/00	3:16am	3:15am	NetworkManagerUp	16	harmless
(8)	08/21/00	3:16am	3:15am	RouterLinkUp	16	harmless
(9)	08/21/00	3:33am	3:30am	InterfaceDown	45	severe
(10)	08/21/00	3:34am	3:30am	CiscoLinkUp	16	harmless
(11)	08/21/00	3:51am	3:50am	InterfaceDown	23	severe
(12)	08/21/00	4:06am	4:05am	NetworkManagerUp	19	harmless
(13)	08/21/00	4:06am	4:05am	RouterLinkUp	19	harmless
(14)	08/21/00	4:10am	4:10am	InterfaceDown	45	severe
(15)	08/21/00	4:11am	4:10am	InterfaceDown	23	severe
(16)	08/21/00	4:13am	4:10am	network down	32	severe
(17)	08/21/00	4:14am	4:10am	CiscoLinkUp	16	harmless
(18)	08/21/00	5:18am	5:15am	NetworkManagerUp	19	harmless
(19)	08/21/00	5:18am	5:15am	RouterLinkUp	19	harmless
(20)	08/21/00	6:15am	6:15am	InterfaceDown	23	severe
(21)	09/15/00	3:53am	3:50am	NetworkManagerUp	12	harmless
(22)	09/15/00	3:53am	3:50am	InterfaceDown	45	severe
(23)	09/15/00	3:53am	3:50am	RouterLinkUp	12	harmless
(24)	09/15/00	3:55am	2:55am	CiscoLinkUp	16	harmless
(25)	09/15/00	4:35am	4:35am	InterfaceDown	23	severe
(26)	09/15/00	5:15am	5:15am	InterfaceDown	24	severe
(27)	09/15/00	5:18am	5:15am	InterfaceDown	45	severe
(28)	09/15/00	5:19am	5:15am	SegmentDown	32	severe
(29)	09/15/00	5:12pm	5:10pm	RouterLinkDown	46	fatal
(30)	09/15/00	5:18pm	5:15pm	DBServerDown	73	fatal
(31)	09/15/00	5:21pm	5:20pm	CiscoLinkUp	16	harmless

Figure 1. System Management Events.

To better motivate the problem, consider the domain of event management for complex networks. Events are messages that are generated when a special condition arises. The relationship between events often provides actionable insights into the cause of existing network problems as well as advanced warnings of future problem occurrences. Figure 1 illustrates event data we obtained from a production network at a large financial institution. The attributes of the data are: date, Time, Interval (five minute interval), Event-Type, Host from which the event originated, and Severity. Observe the following:

1. Host 23 generated a large number of InterfaceDown events on 8/21. Such situations may indicate a problem with that host.

2. When Host 45 generates an InterfaceDown event, Host 16 generates a CiscoLinkUp (failure recovery) event within the same five minute interval. Thus, a Host 45 InterfaceDown event may provide a way to anticipate the failure of Host 16.

3. The event types NetworkManagerUp and Router-LinkUp tend to be generated from same Host and within the same minute. This means that when a Cisco router recovers a link, it will discover that its mid-level manager is accessible.

4. Host 24 and Host 32 tend to generate events with same severity in the same day. This suggests a close linkage between these hosts. If this linkage is unexpected, it should be investigated to avoid having problems with one host cause problems with the other host.

These patterns have been proven to be very useful in system management. However, three challenges emerge as one tries to build a system to discover these patterns. First, what is the language that has enough expressive power to express the mining goals that produce the above patterns but is not too expressive hence becomes computationally infeasible. We need such a language to define a problem space so we can *explore* the problem space to find all significant patterns. We can see that it is not very difficult to write programs to discover or verify each individual statement. However, it is less clear how to discover all these patterns in a systematic process. Second, what is the structure of the problem. As the field of frequent itemset mining is mostly based on the *apriori* property[2, 3], what are the similar properties in this new problem that we can utilize to speed up the mining process. Third, in many cases, prior knowledge (taxonomies, functional dependencies, etc) is available, how can the exploring process apply this knowledge to improve mining performance and avoid producing meaningless patterns.

Herein, we extend the mining problem to include the manner in which data attributes are used to define transactions and items. One way to approach this **extended data mining problem** is to iteratively preprocess the data to form different items and transaction groupings and then apply current mining algorithms. However, this scales poorly. Another approach is to mine for multi-level associations (e.g., [6] and [11]). Unfortunately, this requires specifying hierarchies. Since many such hierarchies are possible, considerable iteration may be necessary. Further, these approaches do not address how to group data into transactions.

1.1. Related Work

Agrawal et.al.[2, 3] identified the association rule problem and developed the level-wise search algorithm. Since then, many algorithms have been proposed to make mining more efficient (e.g. [1, 4, 7, 8]). Our work builds on these efforts but broadens the scope of the mining problem.

Srikant et.al.[11] and Han et.al.[6] consider multi-level association rules based on item taxonomies, and [9] and [12] provide further extensions to handle more general constraints. All of these efforts assume that items occupy a fixed position in the hierarchy and that the hierarchies are known in advance. Further, none of these efforts considers different ways of grouping records into transactions. In contrast, our framework enables the discovery of patterns without either fixing the way in which transactions are defined or prespecifying an item hierarchy.

More recently, Grahne et.al.[5] proposed dual mining to mine situations in which a given itemset is frequent. The similarities to our work are that (a) they consider multiple attributes (when describing items and circumstances); (b) they use a lattice to show relationships (between circumstances); and (c) they employ downward closure on attributes used in item construction, which we do as well. However, their very different problem means that they do not address factors that are central to our problem on two aspects. First, the choice of transaction identifier is central to the mining problem that we address, whereas it is not considered in their problem. Second, we are interested in all itemsets in which items are define by any set of attributes of data. In some sense, dual mining is a special case of FARM by considering items as the combination of items and situations. Put differently, FARM considers items and situations in a unified way. Thus, FARM is a more general framework.

2. The *FARM* Framework

This section describes the elements of the *FARM* framework for mining data with multiple attributes. Section 2.1 provides key definitions. Section 2.2 establishes the conditions for three types of downward closure for mining within our framework. Section 2.3 extends our framework to include taxonomies and functional dependencies.

2.1. Problem Statement

The *FARM* framework goes beyond fixed attribute mining to mine directly from multi-attribute data. We are given data D with attributes $A = \{A_1, \cdots, A_k\}$. Thus, each record in D is a k tuple. For a given pattern, a subset of these attributes is used to define how transactions are grouped and another (disjoint) subset of attributes determines the items. The former are called the **grouping attributes**, and the latter are the **itemizing attributes**.

We begin with an example based on Figure 1. Here, $k = 6$. For pattern 3, the grouping attributes are $Host$ and $Time$; the itemizing attribute is $EventType$. The pattern has length two, which means that a pattern instance has two records. The items specified by these records are determined by the value of the $EventType$ attribute. That is, one record must have $EventType = NetworkManagerUp$ and the other has $EventType = RouterLinkUp$. Further, these records must have the same value for their $Host$ and $Time$ attributes. Records 7 and 8 form an instance of pattern 3 with $Host = 16$ and $Time = 3 : 16am$. Note that items may be formed from multiple attributes. For example, pattern 2 has the itemizing attributes $Host$ and $EventType$.

We use the term **mining camp** to provide the context in which patterns are discovered. Context includes pattern length (as in existing approaches), grouping attributes, and itemizing attributes. For example, pattern 3 has the mining camp $(2, \{Host, Time\}, \{EventType\})$.

Definition 1 *A **mining camp** is a triple (n, G, S) where n is number of records in a pattern, G is a set of grouping attributes, and S is the set of itemizing attributes. A mining camp is **well formed** if $G \bigcap S = \emptyset$. A mining camp is **minable** if $S \neq \emptyset$.*

We demand that $G \bigcap S = \emptyset$ to avoid interactions between the manner in which groupings are done and items are defined. We require that $S \neq \emptyset$ since there must be items to count (even if there is only one group).

Next, we formalize the notion of a pattern. There are several parts to this. First, note that two records occur in the same grouping if their G attributes have the same value. Let $r \in D$. We use the notation $\pi_G(r)$ to indicate the values of r that correspond to the attributes of G.

Definition 2 *Given a set of attribute G, two records r_1 and r_2 are **G-equivalent** if and only if $\pi_G(r_1) = \pi_G(r_2)$.*

In Figure 1, records 7 and 8 are G equivalent, where $G = \{Host, Time\}$.

In *FARM*, items are determined by the combinations of values of the attributes of S. Consider pattern 2 for which we require one record with $EventType =$

$InterfaceDown$, $Host = 45$ and a second for which $EventType = CiscoLinkUp$, $Host = 16$. Thus, $(InterfaceDown, 45)$ is one component (or item) of the pattern and $(CiscoLinkUp, 16)$ is the other component.

Definition 3 *Given a mining camp (n, G, S) where $S = \{S_1, \cdots, S_m\}$. A **pattern component or item** is a sequence of attribute values $sv = \langle s_1, \cdots, s_m \rangle$ where $s_i \in S_i$ for $1 \leq i \leq m$. $p = \{sv_1, \cdots, sv_n\}$ is a **pattern** of length n for this mining camp if each sv_i is a pattern component for S.*

An instance of a pattern is a set of records that are in the same grouping and whose itemizing attributes match those in the pattern.

Definition 4 *Let $p = \{sv_1, \cdots, sv_n\}$ be a pattern in mining camp (n, G, S) and let D be a set of records. An **instance** of pattern p is a set of n records $R = \{r_1, \cdots, r_n\}$ such that $r_i \in D$ and $\pi_S(r_i) = sv_i$ for $1 \leq i \leq n$, and r_i and r_j are G-equivalent for all $r_i, r_j \in R$.*

We now consider the support for a pattern. A G-equivalent class may have a large number of records. A decision has to be made about whether multiple instances in a G-equivalent class should provide more support than one instance. Early work [2, 3] assumes at most one pattern instance can be found in one transaction. We believe that this decision is domain dependent. So, we isolate this decision to the choice of an **aggregating function** $f : Z_+ \longrightarrow Z_+$. Two common choices of f are:

Existence Function: $f(x) = \begin{cases} 0 & \text{if } x = 0 \\ 1 & \text{otherwise} \end{cases}$

Identity Function: $f(x) = x$

Now we can define the concept of support in the *FARM* framework.

Definition 5 *Given an aggregating function f, a mining camp (n, G, S) and a set of records D that can be divided to G-equivalent classes $GEC_1, \cdots, GEC_w$, the **f-support** of a pattern p is defined as $f(|GEC_1|_p) + \cdots, + f(|GEC_w|_p)$ where $|GEC_i|_p$ is the number of disjoint instances of p in GEC_i for $1 \leq i \leq w$.*

We now have in place all of the definitions necessary to discuss mining in the *FARM* framework. First, note that if G and S are fixed, then we have the traditional fixed attribute data mining problem. Here, downward closure of the pattern length is used to look for those patterns in $(n+1, G, S)$ for which there is sufficient support in (n, G, S).

In *FARM*, G and S need not be fixed. Consider the attributes T, A, B for which we require that $T \in G$. Figure 2 displays one way to search these mining camps. In essence, a separate search is done for each combination of G, S. This

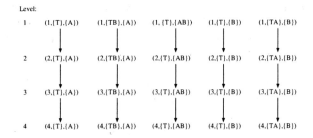

Figure 2. A Simple Search Space

scales poorly. In particular, the number of permitted combinations of G and S is $3^k - 2^k$, where k is the number of attributes (which follows from observing that A_i may be in G, S, or neither and eliminating the 2^k cases for which $S = \emptyset$).

We propose the following definitions for connecting mining camps.

Definition 6 *Given a mining camp $c = (n, G, S)$ and an attribute $A_i \notin G \cup S$ then*

1. $(n + 1, G, S)$ *is the **type-1** successor of c.*

2. $(n, G \cup \{A_i\}, S)$ *is a **type-2** successor of c.*

3. $(n, G, S \cup \{A_i\})$ *is a **type-3** successor of c.*

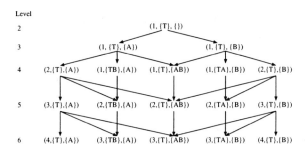

Figure 3. Search Space $MS(1, \{T\}, \{\})$ for attribute set $\{T, A, B\}$

Figure 3 depicts the predecessor/successor relationships present in Figure 2. The root precedes all other mining camps. (In this case, it is not a real camp since $S = \emptyset$.) The level of mining camp (n, G, S) is defined as $n + |G| + |S|$. Since n is at least 1 and S is nonempty, a minable mining camp has level no less than 2. We structure the mining camps so that the successor relationships only exist between mining camps at different levels. This imposes a partial order. Figure 3 is an example of a mining space. More formally,

Definition 7 *A **mining space** $MS(c)$ is a partially ordered set (poset) of mining camps containing c and all of its successors.*

To make the notation more readable, we use $MS(n, G, S)$ to denote $MS((n, G, S))$.

Figure 4. Example of a Taxonomy

In some situations, taxonomies (*is-a* hierarchies) are available. For example, Figure 4 shows a taxonomy of geographical information with three levels: *zip code*, *city* and *state*. A reasonable database design is to store only the lowest level attribute, e.g. *zip code*, in the main table, keep the taxonomies in a separate table, and create a logical view that contains all attributes for data ming.

Since the value of a lower level attribute uniquely determines the value of attributes in higher level, taxonomies are special cases of functional dependencies. So it is sufficient to discuss functional dependencies. Assume the values of an attribute set U uniquely determine the values of attribute set V, we denote the functional dependency as $U \longrightarrow V$.

The objective of the *FARM* framework is now clear

Definition 8 *A FARM problem is a quadruple $(MS(c), FD, f, \theta)$ where FD is a set of functional dependencies, f is an aggregating function and θ is the threshold. The solution of a FARM problem in dataset D is all patterns of every mining camp in $MS(c)$ with f-support greater than θ.*

2.2. Downward Closure Properties

This section shows that several types of downward closure can be present in the *FARM* framework. Exploiting these properties provides considerable benefit in terms of efficiency. We begin by defining properties of the aggregating function.

Definition 9 *Assume f is an aggregating function, then*

1. *f is type-1 and type-3 downward closed if f is nondecreasing.*

2. *f is type-2 downward closed if f is monotonic increasing and for any two G-equivalent classes GEC_1 and GEC_2 and a given pattern p, $f(|GEC_1|_p) + f(|GEC_2|_p) \le f(|GEC_1 \cup GEC_2|_p)$.*

Our main result is that downward closure is possible for n, G, and S.

Theorem 1 *Given a mining camp $c = (n, G, S)$ and an aggregating function f such that the f-support of a pattern $p = \{sv_1, \cdots, sv_n\}$ is less than θ.*

1. *If f is type-1 downward closed then for any type-1 successor of c, any pattern that is a superset of p has f-support less than θ.*

2. *If f is type-2 downward closed then the f-support of p in any of type-2 successor of c is less than θ.*

3. *If f is type-3 downward closed then the f-support of pattern $p' = \{sv'_1, \cdots, sv'_n\}$ of any type-3 successor of c is less then θ if $sv_i \subset sv'_i$ for all $1 \leq i \leq n$.*

Proof:

1. This is the a priori property proved in [3].

2. For A_i not in $G \cup S$, let $G' = G \cup \{A_i\}$ and consider $c' = (n, G', S)$, a type-2 successor of c. Let $GEC_1, \cdots, GEC_m$ be the G-equivalent classes in c, and $GEC'_1, \cdots, GEC'_{m'}$ be the G'-equivalent classes in c'. Note that for all $1 \leq j \leq m$, there is a set $Z_j \subset \{GEC'_1, \cdots, GEC'_{m'}\}$ and $GEC_j = \bigcup_{V \in Z_j} V$. Now, consider a pattern p. Its support in G is θ_p and its support in G' is θ'_p. Observe that

$$\theta_p = \sum_{j=1}^{m} f(|GEC_j|p) = \sum_{j=1}^{m} f(|\bigcup_{V \in Z_j} V|p)$$

$$\geq \sum_{j=1}^{m} \sum_{V \in Z_j} f(|V|p) = \theta'_p$$

The inequality holds because of f being type-2 downward closed.

3. Suppose $c' = (n, G, S')$ is a type-3 successor of c. The G-equivalent classes of c remain in tact in c'. It is obvious that for every pattern instance $inst' = \{sv'_1, \cdots, sv'_n\}$, its projection to S, $inst = \{\pi_S(sv'_1), \cdots, \pi_S(sv'_n)\}$ is a pattern instance of c. But not every pattern instance of c can expand to a pattern instance of c'. So the f-support of $inst'$ is lower than that of $inst$.

Downward closure properties are the foundation of *MAM* as they are in traditional (fixed attribute) mining for frequent itemsets. The more downward properties the chosen aggregating function has, the greater the efficiencies that can be realized in mining. Note that the identity function has all three downward closure properties. However, the existence function is type-1 and type-3 downward closed but not type-2 downward closed.

2.3. Taxonomies and Functional Dependency

As previously stated, the number of mining camps grows exponentially with the number of attributes. There is definitely no need to discover that "houses located in the same zip code tend to be in the same city". The following theorem shows how to avoid such unnecessary computation.

Theorem 2 *Suppose U, V, G and S are attribute sets and U uniquely determine V.*

1. *The output of $(n, U \cup V \cup G, S)$ and $(n, U \cup G, S)$ are identical.*

2. *The output of $(n, G, S \cup U \cup V)$ can be derived from the output of $(n, G, S \cup U)$ by looking up the taxonomy.*

3. *For $n > 1$, $(n, U \cup G, V)$ has no pattern.*

Proof:

1. In each $U \cup G$-equivalent class, every record is also V-equivalent. That is, $U \cup G$-equivalent classes are exactly $U \cup V \cup G$-equivalent classes. So the two camps have the same grouping and labeling hence produce identical result.

2. trivial.

3. Let $G' = G \bigcup U$, and $c' = (n, G', V)$. Now consider r_1 and r_2 in a G'-equivalent class. Clearly, $\pi_U(r_1) = \pi_U(r_2)$. But since U determines V, we have $\pi_V(r_1) = \pi_V(r_2)$. Thus, there can be at most one distinct item in each G'-equivalent class.

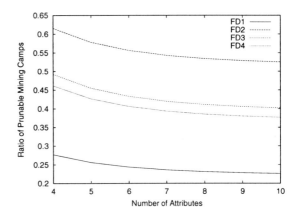

Figure 5. Ratio of prunable mining camps

By studying some typical functional dependency set, it is easy to see that the effect of Theorem 2. Assume the attribute set is $\{A_1, \cdots, A_l\}$. We study the following four functional dependency sets: $FD1 = \{\{A_1\} \longrightarrow \{A_2\}\}$, $FD2 = \{\{A_1\} \longrightarrow \{A_2\}, \{A_2\} \longrightarrow \{A_3\}\}$, $FD3 = \{\{A_1\} \longrightarrow \{A_2\}, \{A_3\} \longrightarrow \{A_4\}\}$ and $FD4 = \{\{A_1\} \longrightarrow \{A_2, A_3\}\}$. The ratios of *prunable* mining camps corresponding to the functional dependency set and number of attributes are shown in Figure 5. As we can see a two-level taxonomy like the one in Figure 4(equivalent to $FD2$) can prune more than half of the mining camps on each level.

3. Algorithm

This section describes the **multiple attribute mining** (*MAM*) algorithm for mining *FARM* problems. *MAM* exploits the downward closure properties in Theorem 1 to improve the efficiency of mining.

The extended mining problem we address raises some difficult scaling issues as a result of discovering mining camps with different grouping attributes (G). Existing mining algorithms assume that data are sorted by transaction identifier so that locality can be exploited in counting pattern instances. Such locality can be imposed on *FARM* problems as well if there is an attribute T, called the **ordering attribute** such that: (1) T is required to be in G, (2) data records are sorted by T, and (3) all of the records in a T-equivalent class fit in main memory. Possible ordering attributes include those that deal with time (e.g., day) and place (e.g., zip code). However, even if locality is not present, other techniques can be used to improve efficiency. We assume there is an ordering attribute T, and we address the mining problem $(MS(1, \{T\}, \emptyset), f, \theta)$.

We describe *MAM* in an object-oriented fashion. The core data structure is the *Camp* class.

```
class Camp
{
    n:      Integer                 // number of items
    G:      Sequence of Attributes  // grouping attributes
    S:      Sequence of Attributes  // surrogate attributes
    pred1:  Camp                    // type 1 predecessor
    pred2:  Set of Camp             // type 2 predecessors
    pred3:  Set of Camp             // type 3 predecessors
    ptrns:  Set of Pattern          // candidates and patterns }
```

The *Pattern* class is defined as:

```
class Pattern
{
    svalue:  Set of Sequences of Attribute Values See Definition 3
    support: Real                   // f-support }
```

The *MAM* algorithm adapts to the choice of the aggregating functions. If the aggregating function has all three downward closure properties, the mining space looks like Figure 3, and the lowest level containing minable camps is level 3, e.g. $(1, \{T\}, \{A_i\})$. Otherwise, the mining space looks like Figure 2.

We structure the *MAM* algorithm into seven routines. Due to the space limit, we only show the pseudo codes of the first four. Readers can refer to [10] for full description of the seven routines. Algorithm 1, the top level routine, is very similar to the classical apriori algorithm. However, Algorithm 1 sets levels based on the kinds of downward closure present, and the algorithm operates on mining camps, not candidate patterns.

Algorithm 2, CampGen, is called by Algorithm 1 to generate mining camps. Note that type-2 downward closure is used to make camp generation more efficient.

Algorithm 3, SetPredAndCandiGen, determines the predecessor to use when extending the set of patterns. Type-2 downward closure is exploited here as well.

Algorithm 1 MAIN(AttributeSet: A, Ordering-Attribute: T, Dataset: D, MinSupport: θ)

Input: $A = \{A_1, \cdots, A_k\}$: set of attributes.
      T: a special ordering attribute
      D: a dataset with $k + 1$ attributes ($A \cup \{T\}$), sorted by attribute T.
      θ: minsupport threshold
Output: frequent itemsets of all the mining camps

```
if f is type-2 downward closed then
    l ← 3
else
    l ← 1
end if
camps_l ← CampGen(l, A)
for each camp ∈ camps_l do
    camp.ptrns ← { frequent 1-itemsets }
end for
while exist camp ∈ camps_l, camp.ptrns ≠ ∅ do
    Evaluate(D, camps_l)
    for each camp ∈ camps_l do
        eliminate patterns with support lower than θ in camp.ptrns;
    end for
    l ← l + 1
    camps_l ← CampGen(l, A)
    camps_l.SetPredAndCandiGen()
end while
return {camp.ptrn|camp ∈ camps_l, l ≥ 3}
```

Algorithm 2 CampGen(Level: l, AttributeSet: A, Ordering-Attribute: T)

```
if f is type-2 downward closed then
    camps ← {(n, {T} ∪ G, S)|1 ≤ n ≤ l − 2, G ⊂ A, |G| ≤ l − n − 2, S ⊆
             A − G, |S| = l − n − |G| − 1}
else
    camps ← {(l, {T} ∪ G, S)|G ⊂ A, S ⊆ A − G, S ≠ ∅}
end if
return camps
```

Algorithm 3 SetPredAndCandiGen(CampSet: *camps*)

```
for each camp = (n, G, S) ∈ camps do
    if n > 1 then
        camp.pred1 ← (n − 1, G, S)
    end if
    if |S| > 1 then
        camp.pred3 ← {(n, G, S − {A_y})|A_y ∈ S}
    end if
    if (f is type-2 downward closed) and (|G| > 1) then
        camp.pred2 ← {(n, G − {A_x}, S)|A_x ∈ G, A_x ≠ T}
    end if
    CandiGen(camp)
end for
```

454

Algorithm 4, CandiGen, applies the extended downward closure properties. There are two issues here: how to generate candidates and how to filter out impossible candidates. The initial candidate set can be generated from the pattern sets of any of type of predecessors. But in general, the most efficient candidate generation is to start from patterns of type-2 predecessors. This is because patterns of type-2 predecessors have the same n and S as their successors. Thus, successor patterns are computed by refining the G-equivalent classes of the predecessor. This is done by taking intersections, a computation that can be done in linear time (if patterns are sorted). In contrast, both type-1 and type-3 require a "join" operation. Not not only is this more computationally intensive, the number of candidates generated tends to be very large. The algorithm tries to generate candidates from the pattern sets of its type-2 predecessors and then uses pattern sets of other types to further filter candidates. If there is no type-2 predecessor, the type-1 predecessor is used instead. If there is no type-1 predecessor, type-3 predecessors are used.

Algorithm 4 CandiGen(Camp: $camp$)

---

if $camp.pred2 \neq \emptyset$ then
  $camp.ptrns \leftarrow \bigcap_{c \in camp.pred2} c.ptrns$
  Type1Filter($camp.ptrns, camp.pred1$)
  Type3Filter($camp, camp.pred3$)
else if $camp.pred1 \neq \emptyset$ then
  $camp.ptrns \leftarrow \{p = p_1 \cup p_2 | \{p_1, p_2\} \subset camp.pred1.ptrns, |p| = n\}$
  Type1Filter($camp.ptrns, camp.pred1$)
  Type3Filter($camp, camp.pred3$)
else
  $c_1 \leftarrow$ the camp with the least number of patterns in $camp.pred3$
  $c_2 \leftarrow$ the camp with the least number of patterns in $camp.pred3 - \{c_1\}$
  $camp.ptrns \leftarrow \{\langle s_1, \cdots, s_n\rangle | (\pi_{c_1.S}(s_1), \cdots, \pi_{c_1.S}(s_n)) \in c1.ptrns,$
    $(\pi_{c_2.S}(s_1), \cdots, \pi_{c_2.S}(s_n)) \in c2.ptrns$ and $|s_i| = |S|$, for $1 \leq$
    $i \leq n\}$
  Type3Filter($camp, camp.pred3 - \{c_1, c_2\}$)
end if
return

SUBROUTINE Type1Filter($ptrns, camp$)
if $camp \neq null$ then
  for each $p \in ptrns$ do
    for each $p' \subset p, |p'| = n - 1$ do
      eliminate p from $ptrns$ if $p' \notin camp.ptrns$
    end for
  end for
end if

SUBROUTINE Type3Filter($thiscamp, camps$)
if $camps \neq \emptyset$ then
  for each $p \in thiscamp.ptrns$ do
    for each $S' \subset thiscamp.S$ where $|S'| = |S| - 1$ do
      eliminate p from $ptrns$ if there exists $c \in camps$ such that $c.S = S'$ and $\pi_{S'}(p) \notin c.ptrns$
    end for
  end for
end if

The pesudo codes of the rest three algorithms are not included in this paper but interested reader can find them in [10]. Algorithm *Evaluate* computes the support level of candidate patterns. Each pattern component is checked in turn. The resulting support level is the minimum of f applied to the minimum of the count of each pattern component. Algorithm *AttrHash* provides a hash table to the counting routines. Algorithm *PatternComponentCount* builds the count matrix for each pattern component.

4. Performance

This section assesses the performance of the *MAM* algorithm. First we detail the data used in our assessments. Then we compare the *MAM* algorithm with one that does not exploit downward closure for G (type 2) or S (type 3). The results show that *MAM* provides considerable efficiencies, reducing execution times by a factor of three to four.

Two sets of event data are used in our study. The first are taken from a production computer network at a financial service company. One data set (NETVIEW) has six attributes: $Hour$, $EventType$, $Host$, $Severity$, $Interestingness$, $DayofWeek$; $Hour$ is used as the ordering attribute. There are 241 values of $EventType$, 2526 for $Host$, 5 levels of $Severity$, and 5 for $Interestingness$. The second data set (TEC) has the attributes $Hour$, $EventType$, $Source$, $Severity$, $Host$ and $DayOfYear$. Again, $Hour$ is used as the ordering attribute. There are 75 values of $EventType$, 16 types of $Source$, 2718 $Host$ values, and 7 $Severity$ levels.

To our best knowledge, there is no existing algorithm that solves the mining problem proposed in this paper. A naive approach is to preprocess the data to obtain every possible combination of G and S. Clearly, this has poor efficiency since it requires many data scans.

A more insightful study is to compare *MAM* with an approach that only uses downward closure based on pattern length and ignores the type-2 and type-3 downward closure. We refer to this as the *Single Attribute Mining* algorithm or *SAM*. *SAM* is a degenerate case of *MAM* in which the aggregating function is not type-2 nor type-3 downward closed. Put differently, we show the performance gain obtained by exploiting type-2 and type-3 downward closure.

Figure 6 compares *MAM* and *SAM* in terms of the number of candidates generated and execution time. The rationale for doing so is that *MAM* and *SAM* require about same number of data scans. So, the reduced execution time achieved by *MAM* is entirely due to having far fewer candidates. In our experiments, *SAM* generates several orders of magnitude more candidates than *MAM*. As a result, *SAM* execution times are often a factor of three to five greater than *MAM* execution times.

A closer look at this figure reveals that the *MAM* provides the greatest speedup over *SAM* when there is the *smallest* difference in the number of candidates generated. This occurs when the support threshold is smallest. To understand why, we must dig deeper. The overhead at the first level of the algorithms does not depend on the support threshold. For *SAM*, the overhead is proportional to the number of distinct records; for *MAM*, the overhead is proportional to the sum of number of distinct values of each attribute.

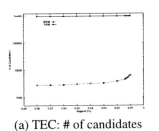
(a) TEC: # of candidates

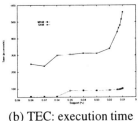
(b) TEC: execution time

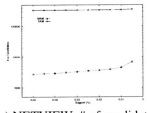
(c) NETVIEW: # of candidates

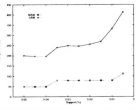
(d) NETVIEW: execution time

Figure 6. Performance Comparison

In both cases, the number of candidates considered is fixed. But at low support thresholds, processing at the first level dominates the overall execution time.

In Figure 7, we show that the execution times of *MAM* and *SAM* are roughly linear to the number of records, although execution times do increase as the support threshold decreases. However, *SAM* execution times increase at a considerably faster rate than those for *MAM*.

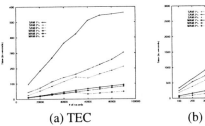
(a) TEC

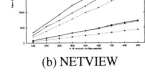
(b) NETVIEW

Figure 7. Effect of the Number of Records at Different Support Levels

5. Conclusion and Future Work

Mining typically involves a preprocessing step in which data with multiple attributes are grouped into transactions, and items are defined based on attribute values. Unfortunately, fixing the attributes used to define transactions and items can severely constrain the patterns that are discovered.

This has motivated us to introduce *FARM*, a new framework for mining multi-attribute data. In *FARM*, mining is done directly from multi-attribute data without prespecifying the attributes used to group records into transactions or the attributes used to define items. The framework is based on the concept of a mining camp: (n, G, S), where n is the pattern length (the number of items), G is the set of attributes used to group data into transactions, and S are the attributes used to define items. We identify (and prove) two new kinds of downward closure related to searching mining camps for patterns based on the relationship between the G and S. These results are incorporated into the multi-attribute mining *MAM* algorithm. Empirical studies with

real world data show a factor of three to four reduction in execution time by using the new kinds of downward closure that we identify.

References

[1] C. Aggarwal, C. Aggarwal, and V. Parsad. Depth first generation of long patterns. In *Int'l Conf. on Knowledge Discovery and Data Mining (SIGKDD)*, 2000.

[2] R. Agrawal, T. Imielinski, and A. Swami. Mining association rules between sets of items in large databases. In *Proc. of Very Large Database (VLDB)*, pages 207–216, 1993.

[3] R. Agrawal and R. Srikant. Fast algorithms for mining association rules. In *Proc. of Very Large Database (VLDB)*, 1994.

[4] R. Bayardo. Efficiently mining long patterns from database. In *SIGMOD*, pages 85–93, 1998.

[5] G. Grahne, L. Lakshmanan, X. Wang, and M. Xie. On dual mining: From patterns to circumstances, and back. In *Int. Conf. Data Engineering (ICDE)*, pages 195–204, 2001.

[6] J. Han and Y. Fu. Discovery of multiple-level association rules from large databases. In *Proc. of Very Large Database (VLDB)*, 1995.

[7] J. Han, J. Pei, and Y. Yin. Mining frequent patterns without candidate generation. In *Int. Conf. Management of Data (SIGMOD)*, 2000.

[8] J. Hipp, A. Myka, R. Wirth, and U. Guntzer. A new algorithm for faster mining of generalized association rules. In *Proc. 2nd PKKD, 1998.*, 1998.

[9] R. Ng, L. Lakshmanan, J. Han, and A. Pang. Exploratory mining and pruning optimizations of constrained associations rules. In *Int. Conf. Management of Data (SIGMOD)*, pages 13–24, 1998.

[10] C.-S. Perng, H. Wang, S. Ma, and J. L. Hellerstein. Farm: A framework for exploring mining spaces with multiple attributes. Technical Report RC 21990, IBM Research, March 2001.

[11] R. Srikant and R. Agrawal. Mining generalized association rules. In *Proc. of Very Large Database (VLDB)*, pages 407–419, 1995.

[12] R. Srikant, Q. Vu, and R. Agrawal. Mining association rules with item constraints. In *Int'l Conf. on Knowledge Discovery and Data Mining (SIGKDD)*, pages 67–93, 1997.

Neural Analysis of Mobile Radio Access Network

Kimmo Raivio
Helsinki University of Technology
Laboratory of Computer and Information Science
P.O. Box 5400, FIN-02015 HUT, Finland
Kimmo.Raivio@hut.fi

Olli Simula
Helsinki University of Technology
Laboratory of Computer and Information Science
P.O. Box 5400, FIN-02015 HUT, Finland

Jaana Laiho
Nokia Networks
P.O.Box 301, FIN-00045 Nokia Group
Finland

Abstract

The Self-Organizing Map (SOM) is an efficient tool for visualization and clustering of multidimensional data. It transforms the input vectors on two-dimensional grid of prototype vectors and orders them. The ordered prototype vectors are easier to visualize and explore than the original data. Mobile networks produce a huge amount of spatio-temporal data. The data consists of parameters of base stations (BS) and quality information of calls. There are two alternatives in starting the data analysis. We can build either a general one-cell-model trained using state vectors from all cells, or a model of the network using state vectors with parameters from all mobile cells. In both methods, further analysis is needed to understand the reasons for various operational states of the entire network.

1 Introduction

Data mining and exploration is an expanding new area of research in artificial intelligence and information management. The objective of data mining is to extract relevant information from databases containing large amounts of information. Typical data mining and analysis tasks include classification, regression, and clustering of data, determining parameter dependencies, and finding various anomalies from the data. In many engineering applications, the dimension of complex data is too large for human observation. Therefore, extracting relevant information from the data calls for intelligent and adaptive computational methods. Artificial Neural Networks (ANNs) have successfully been used in various intelligent data engineering applications.

The Self-Organizing Map (SOM) is a widely used neural network algorithm [8]. It has several beneficial features making it a useful tool in data mining and exploration. The SOM forms a nonlinear, topology-preserving mapping from the input to the output space. The SOM follows the probability density function of the underlying data and functions, thus, as an efficient clustering and data reduction algorithm. The SOM is readily explainable, simple and - perhaps most importantly - highly visual. SOM based methods have been applied in the analysis of process data, e.g., in steel and forest industry [9]. In addition, the SOM has been used in analysis and monitoring of telecommunications systems. Applications include novel equalizer structures for discrete-signal detection and adaptive resource allocation in telecommunications networks. In the current research, the goal is to develop efficient adaptive methods for monitoring the mobile network behavior and performance. Special interest is on finding clusters of mobile cells, which can be configured using similar parameters.

The SOM algorithm is able to perform both data clustering and visualization. The benefit of using SOM is in visualization of interesting parts of data. The algorithm moves the nodes of the map towards the areas of higher density of mapped input vectors. As a result, the SOM efficiently visualizes the clusters. In this work, a batch variate of the original SOM algorithm is used. The samples collected from a fixed time interval are first averaged over the topological neighborhoods of the respective winner cells in the map. After that the node vectors are updated in one step using these averaged values, as in the classical K-means algorithm [10].

The data used in this work has been generated using wideband code division multiple access (WCDMA) radio network simulator [7]. The WCDMA radio networks used in this study have been planned to provide 64-kbps service with 95% coverage probability, and with reasonable (2%) blocking. The microcellular scenario depicted in Fig. 1 is capable of providing 2 to 3 fold (depending on service mix) the capacity of the macrocellular solution. The propagation model in the macrocellular case has been standard Okumura-Hata [1] [4] [11], in the microcellular case ray tracing has been utilized [6] [12].

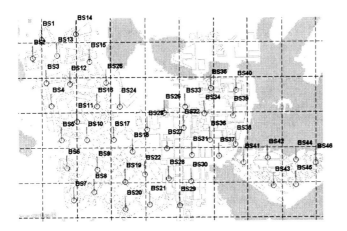

Figure 1. Helsinki city area with microcell scenario. The map area is approximately 8.6 km^2.

The network configurations studied in this paper were macrocellular with 32 cells (11 base station sites) and microcellular with 46 omnidirectional cells. The macrocellular sites were sectored and equipped with 65-degree antennas, except one site was equipped with omnidirectional antenna. The network configurations were planned to cover the same area in Helsinki City. During the simulation the users of the network were circuit-switched, with 64-kbps, and the admission control was parameterized so that uplink interference had no impact on the admission process. Macrocell scenario is used to test the applicability of SOM clustering in general, and furthermore, to see whether same clustering techniques can be applied to different cell types.

The state of the network is characterized by 17 parameters of each base station. These parameters are stored every 100ms. The parameters include the number of users connected to BS, uplink noise raise in dBs, average frame error rate (FER) and the real number of users, which are used in this study. During a call each mobile user keeps a list of possible BSs. Here, the maximum length of list is three. The user is connected to all of them, but uses only one of them at a time for the call. For the rest of the BSs on the list the user is in softhandover. So, the first number of users variable (noOfUsers) includes users in softhandover. A logarithmic scale with 10^{-2} as minimum is used for the error rate.

2 Classification of cells using class frequencies

Here, a method for classification of mobile cells will be presented. Preliminary results are also included. The method utilizes the SOM algorithm twice. A block diagram of the method is shown in Fig. 2.

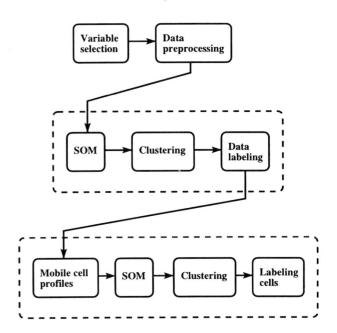

Figure 2. Classification of mobile cells using a general one cell model.

Analysis of the network starts with selection of variables and data preprocessing. The method is designed to handle any number of variables, but it gives more benefit if the number of variables is large. After preprocessing, the algorithm consists of two main steps.

At first, a general model of one mobile cell is built using the SOM. The model is an average of all used cells. Clusters of the SOM node vectors can be found manually using U-matrix presentation [14] of the vectors or some other clustering method can be used.

The second step of the algorithm builds a model of the network using cluster histograms of the data as profiles of mobile cells. Histograms for each mobile cell can be computed using the clusters as bins. Class frequencies are the data, which is used to train the second SOM and to find the best-matching units (BMU) of each cell.

2.1 General mobile cell model

In Fig. 3a the SOM component planes of the general mobile cell model of microcell network scenario are shown.

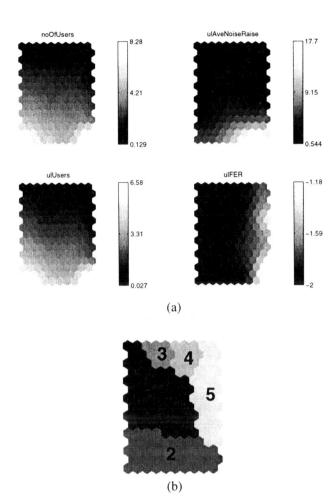

(a)

(b)

Figure 3. The component planes of SOM with denormalized colorbars (a) and five clusters of SOM node vectors given by Ward clustering (b).

The topology of the map is 2D 10 x 15 hexagonal grid. Clusters of the general model are searched using hierarchical clustering methods [3]. Hierarchical clustering techniques are either agglomerative, where at each round two smaller groups of samples are added together to form larger groups, or divisive, where the data vectors are separated in finer groupings.

In this paper, five agglomerative clustering techniques are used to find out the clusters of SOM codebook. The tested methods are Ward, centroid, and single, average and complete linkage clustering. Hierarchical clustering of SOM codebook has been considered in [16] and [13]. The computational complexity of hierarchical clustering of SOM codebook vectors is much lower than clustering directly the data.

The search for clusters of SOM node vectors is started

by finding local minimas of the codebook. Different sets of local minimas are found depending on how large area around each node is verified until a node is decided to be local minima. The search area is limited by the maximum topological distance or the radius of a neuron. The distance to the nearest neuron equals one.

The local minimas are selected as the first centroids of the base clusters. The rest of the neurons are added to the base clusters using the selected clustering method. A Davies-Bouldin (DB) validity index [2] is computed for each clustering. For each clustering method the optimal number of clusters minimizes

$$\frac{1}{C}\sum_{k=1}^{C}\max_{l\neq k}\{\frac{S_c(Q_k)+S_c(Q_l)}{d_{ce}(Q_k,Q_l)}\} \qquad (1)$$

where C is the number of clusters, S_c within-cluster distance and d_{ce} between clusters distance, Q_k and Q_l are the clusters. The studied clustering methods differ in the definition of between clusters distance.

Table 1. Optimal base clusters of the first level SOM. Radius of local minima search defines the base clusters and the one corresponding the lowest DB index is selected. The best methods are marked with *.

Microcell scenario			
Method	Radius	DB	C
Ward	2.7	0.99	5*
centroid	2.7	1.00	5
complete	3.1	1.49	3
single	3.1	1.11	3
average	3.1	1.17	3
Macrocell scenario			
Method	Radius	DB	C
Ward	3.7	1.01	2
centroid	3.7	0.99	2
complete	3.7	0.75	2*
single	3.7	0.78	2
average	3.7	0.84	2

In Table 1 the results of the search for the best base clusters are shown. The base clusters are found by quantizing the SOM codebook vectors to the local minimas of the codebook. Different base cluster sets are found using different radius for the search of local minimas. The radii giving the clustering with lowest DB indexes are shown. Because the studied clustering techniques are hierarchical, optimal clustering can be found by testing the clusterings found from the dendrograms against the validity index. However, this is not done at this level, because it is desirable for further studies to have more states. There are small variations in the the performance of the methods, but only complete linkage method has some difficulties in finding reasonable base clusters from microcell scenario data. For the microcell scenario Ward clustering gives the best results with lowest values of Davies-Bouldin index. Five base clusters or states of mobile cells minimize the validity index. The clustering result is shown in Fig. 3b where the state 2 represents the higher load state, state 5 higher FER state and the others normal state.

2.2 SOM of class frequencies

The BMUs of data vectors give the state or the class of the cell. From a sequence of states we can compute the class frequencies of mobile cells. Using these frequency vectors as data to a second level SOM we get a SOM of frequency vectors or class histograms. The topology of the new SOM is 2D rectangular grid. Grid of size 9 x 9 nodes has been used for microcell scenario and grid of size 8 x 8 nodes has been used for macrocell scenario. The BMU search and the training of the map use Kullback-Leibler distance [5]. The Kullback-Leibler distance or relative entropy between two probability distributions $p_X(x)$ and $q_X(x)$ is defined by

$$D_{p||q} = \sum_{x \in \mathcal{X}} p_X(x) \log(\frac{p_X(x)}{q_X(x)}) \qquad (2)$$

where the sum is over all states of the system (i.e., the alphabet $\mathcal{X}$ of the discrete random variable X). In Fig. 4 the second level SOM of histograms has been shown.

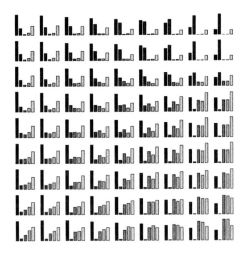

Figure 4. 9 x 9 SOM of class frequency histograms.

The same hierarchical clustering methods as in the first level SOM have been used to find clusters of the second level SOM except now the optimal clustering is also searched from dendrograms. From the results of Table 2 it can be seen that Ward clustering gives the best base clusters of mobile cells in microcell scenario. For both scenarios clustering with lower DB index can be found from the dendrograms as can be seen from Table 3. The dendrograms built on optimal base clusters and on first guess base clusters (radius equals one) are searched. For microcell scenario centroid and single linkage clustering give the lowest values of the validity index. All methods give two or three clusters. The results are usually quite similar, but sometimes a method may fail to find reasonable clustering. So, more than one method should always be used.

Table 2. The best base clusters for the SOM of histograms. Radius of local minima search defines the base clusters and the one corresponding the lowest DB index is the best (marked with *).

Microcell scenario			
Method	Radius	DB	C
Ward	4.1	0.73	2*
centroid	4.1	0.73	2
complete	4.1	0.73	2
single	4.1	0.74	2
average	4.1	0.73	2
Macrocell scenario			
Method	Radius	DB	C
Ward	1.0	4.19	5
centroid	1.0	4.19	5
complete	3.1	0.73	4*
single	3.1	0.73	4
average	3.1	0.73	4

The clusters given by centroid algorithm and the BMUs of mobile cells are shown in Fig. 5. The BMUs of the original data have been printed using subscript 1 and the BMUs of the new data set with subscript 2 ($c44_1$ means cell 44 with original data). In the original data set the admission control was turned off, which means that all users have access to the network all the time. Thus, the probability for lower call qualities should have been larger. In the new data set of the microcell network scenario, the admission control was turned on. Old first level clusters (Fig. 3b) were used to label the new data and compute new histograms.

The method divides the cells in two classes. By comparing Fig. 5 with Fig. 4 and Fig. 3b, we can see that the cells in lower right corner are characterized by higher FER and

460

Table 3. Optimal clusters of the SOM of histograms given by dendrogram search. Radius for local minima search defines the base clusters for each method. The best methods are marked with *.

Microcell scenario			
Method	Radius	DB	C
Ward	1.0	0.90	2
	4.1	0.73	2
centroid	1.0	0.31	2*
	4.1	0.73	2
complete	1.0	0.63	2
	4.1	0.73	2
single	1.0	0.31	2
	4.1	0.74	2
average	1.0	0.73	3
	4.1	0.73	2

Macrocell scenario			
Method	Radius	DB	C
Ward	1.0	0.31	2*
centroid	1.0	0.39	2
complete	1.0	0.50	3
	3.1	0.49	3
single	1.0	0.32	2
	3.1	0.31	2
average	1.0	0.31	2
	3.1	0.31	2

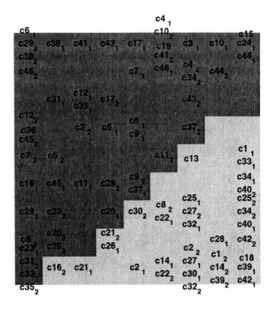

Figure 5. Clusters of mobile cells are found using class frequencies of the SOM, which is trained by number of connected users, uplink noise raise, real number of users and FER of each cell.

lower number of users. All the cells at this location suffer from same problems.

Such a clustering is beneficial in the radio network optimization process. It is reasonable to assume that the configuration parameters for cells in one cluster within one optimized radio resource management function (admission control, handover control, etc.) are the same. Furthermore, on radio network "performance map" cells having close topographical location suffer from the same problem and can be, with high probability, fixed with the same solution.

The method described above classifies cells using class frequencies as models of cell behavior. The distributions describe how much a particular cell differs from a general cell model, which has been built using as much data as possible. The data which is used to build the lower level SOM in this method should be selected carefully so that it represents well all the possible states of the cells. If it does not, the lower level SOM should be trained again using new set of data. When SOM and hierarchical clustering are used twice on the same algorithm, it is not so clear how the first clustering should be done to obtain reasonable results on the

final level.

3 Classification of cells using correlations of SOM component planes

In this section, another method for clustering mobile cells on the basis of covariance matrixes of SOM component planes is presented. Also this method uses two level SOMs. In the previous method, the data was used to build a model of one base station. The same data can also be used to build models of the network. A block diagram of the method is shown in Fig. 6.

At first SOMs of one variable are built. Each of these SOMs is a model of the network. Next, the component planes of the SOMs are processed. In this paper, the covariance matrixes of the component planes are computed. Covariances of one or more variables are concatenated to be used as profiles of mobile cells. These profiles are the data to a second level SOM. The outputs of the second SOM are the clusters of mobile cells.

3.1 SOM of one variable

Data of each cell is masked so that one variable of each mobile cell is analyzed with the corresponding ones of the other cells. The data to be analyzed has been normalized

461

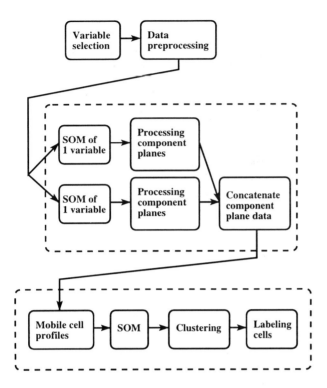

Figure 6. Classification of mobile cells using one variable SOMs as models of the network.

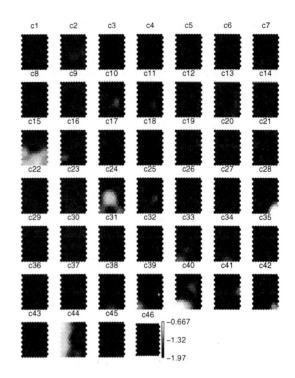

Figure 7. SOM component planes of the FERs. Minimum FER is fixed to 10^{-2}.

to zero mean and unit variance as one data vector over all the cells. Here the number of connected users, uplink noise raise, real number of users and uplink FER of each cell have been analyzed using the SOM. Hexagonal 2D neighborhood grid of 10 x 15 nodes is used. Fig. 7 shows the SOM component planes when the FER is studied. There is one component plane per each mobile cell. The parameter values of the network state at one moment can be read from similar locations on component planes. For example, upper left corner gives one possible combination of network error rates.

The component planes are visualized using a common color axis. This makes it possible to see the real error rates, but it also hides the smaller variations inside the cells. In the figure only some of the cells seem to differ from the common behavior. Cells 15, 24 and 44 have a lot higher FER than all the others.

3.2 Correlation of SOM component planes

If we are interested in, for example, to find out which mobile cells have similar FER distribution, the task of human analyzer can be made easier by further processing the component planes of SOM [15]. This kind of postprocessing is more important if the number of component planes is high.

The component planes are considered as separate figures. Covariance matrix of the figures is computed by first converting the figure dot values c_{ij}^n to vectors a^n, where i and j are the coordinates on the map and n is the mobile cell number. The length of each vector a^n is the product of the dimensions of SOM topology.

The covariance matrix C of the planes a^n is the new data, which will be used on later studies. This data has one row for each mobile cell. A new second level SOM is trained using the covariance matrix. The topology of the new SOM is 2D rectangular grid. When 46 component planes are analyzed grid of size 9 x 9 nodes is used. For macrocell scenario network map of size 8 x 8 nodes is used. The covariance matrix row of each cell is mapped on the second level SOM and the BMU for each mobile cell is found. The map nodes are labeled using the results of BMU search. The SOM component planes have been reordered so that the similar ones locate near each other.

3.3 Classification using several variables

Several SOMs for different variables can be built and reorganized using the methods of Sections 3.1 and 3.2. The covariance matrixes C_k of all first level SOMs can be combined so that we get a new data matrix $C = [C_1 \ldots C_k]$,

Table 4. Optimal base clusters of the second level SOM. Radius of local minima search defines the base clusters and the on corresponding to the lowest DB index is the best. The best methods are marked with *.

Microcell scenario			
Method	Radius	DB	C
Ward	1.0	0.94	8*
centroid	1.0	0.95	8
complete	1.0	1.16	8
single	1.6	1.21	6
average	1.6	1.14	6
Macrocell scenario			
Method	Radius	DB	C
Ward	3.7	0.95	3
centroid	3.7	0.92	3
complete	3.7	0.89	3
single	3.7	0.81	3*
average	3.7	0.89	3

Table 5. Optimal clusters of SOM given by a search through dendrograms. Radius defines the base clusters for each method. The best methods are marked with *.

Microcell scenario			
Method	Radius	DB	C
Ward	1.0	0.65	3
centroid	1.0	0.53	2
complete	1.0	0.72	3
single	1.0	0.40	2*
	1.6	0.40	2
average	1.0	0.40	2
	1.6	0.40	2
Macrocell scenario			
Method	Radius	DB	C
Ward	1.0	0.90	2
	3.7	0.95	3
centroid	1.0	0.89	3
	3.7	0.92	3
complete	1.0	0.90	2
	3.7	0.89	3
single	1.0	0.90	2
	3.7	0.81	3*
average	1.0	0.90	2
	3.7	0.89	3

$k = 1, 2, \ldots$. Matrix C has a row C^n for each cell n. The row is a concatenated vector of cell correlations of used variables.

When the SOM is trained using this new data, the cells appear in a new order. The second level SOM can now be analyzed using the same hierarchical clustering methods as in Section 2 to find clusters of mobile cells. Now, Euclidean distance measure has been used. The base clusters are found by quantization of SOM codebook vectors to the local minimas of the codebook. Several sets of base clusters are found using different radius for local minima search. The radii giving best base clusters are shown in Table 4. The final clustering results are shown in Table 5. Ward and single linkage clustering give the best base clusters, but the DB indexes of all studied methods are about the same. However, for microcells scenario better clusterings can be found by analyzing the dendrograms. The clusters of the microcell scenario and the BMUs of the original data are shown in Fig. 8. Cells 15, 24 and 44 form one cluster and the rest of the cells form another cluster.

If new data is analyzed from a new cell or from a cell which has been analyzed before component plane representation of this data has to be constructed. The easiest way to do this is training the SOM again. When the SOM is trained the new data can be used in the BMU search or it can be masked out. If the new data is masked out in the BMU search, but used when the neurons are updated we can obtain similar SOM as before, but in addition we get the component planes for the new data. From the component planes new covariance matrices can be computed, new clusters can be found and the BMUs of the new and the old data can be found.

The method described above classifies mobile cells on basis of correlations of selected variables. A model of mobile network which describes the relations between mobile cells has been built.

4 Conclusion

In this paper, two new methods to find clusters of mobile cells in two radio access network scenarios have been presented. In the first method, a lower level SOM, which represents general mobile cell model is built. Histograms of the states of the base stations are built using clusters of lower level SOM. The same clusters can be used later to find out histograms of new data. Thus, the operational mode of each cell and the whole network can be monitored. In the second method, lower level SOMs of one variable are first build. Covariance matrices of the component planes of these SOMs are then used to train another map, which reorders the mobile cells.

States of one mobile cell and groups of similar mobile

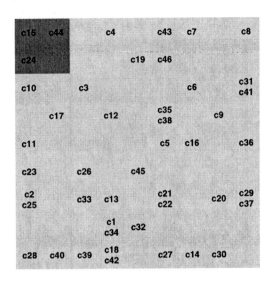

Figure 8. Clusters of mobile cells are found using correlations of all four one variable SOM component planes.

cells are found using agglomerative hierarchical clustering techniques on SOM codebook vectors. Usually, all the tested methods gave reasonable clusters with about the same validity index, but sometimes some method may fail to find clusters. Thus, more than one method should always be tested. However, a search through dendrograms built using both the first guess and optimal base clusters gave often better clusters when tested against Davies-Bouldin index.

The performance of clustering methods vary depending on selected set of variables and performed preprocessing like definition of outliers. The algorithms process data on multiple successive levels. Thus, a minor lower level change like organization of the SOM on another way might affect on final clustering. Usually, these changes are small, but it is also possible that a clustering method fails due to lower level reconfiguration. The algorithms should be tested more using real data in several real networks to obtain more reliable results.

Furthermore, in this paper it has been demonstrated that the SOM provides powerful means to move from time consuming and ineffective per cell optimization to cell cluster optimization. It has also been shown that the same methods can be used with a network of any type of cells.

Acknowledgment

The study has been financed by Nokia Networks, Nokia Mobile Phones and the Technology Development Centre Finland (TEKES) which is gratefully acknowledged. Furthermore, the authors wish to thank Jukka Henriksson, Ari Hämäläinen and other colleagues from Nokia Research Center for valuable comments during the work.

References

[1] Urban transmission loss models for mobile radio in the 900 and 1800 MHz bands, September 1991. COST 231, TD(91)73.

[2] D. L. Davies and D. W. Bouldin. A cluster separation measure. *IEEE Transactions on Pattern Analysis and Machine Intelligence*, 1(2):224–227, April 1979.

[3] B. S. Everitt. *Cluster Analysis*. Arnold, 1993.

[4] M. Hata. Empirical formula for propagation loss in land mobile radio services. *IEEE Transactions on Vehicular Technology*, 29(3):317–325, August 1980.

[5] S. Haykin. *Neural Networks, a Comprehensive Foundation*. Macmillan, 1999.

[6] K. Heiska and A. Kangas. Microcell propagation model for network planning. In *Personal, Indoor and Mobile Radio Communications*, volume 1, pages 148–152, 1996.

[7] S. Hämäläinen, H. Holma, and K. Sipilä. Advanced WCDMA radio network simulator. In *Personal, Indoor and Mobile Radio Communications*, volume 2, pages 951–955, Osaka, Japan, September 12-15 1999.

[8] T. Kohonen. *Self-Organizing Maps*. Springer-Verlag, Berlin, 1995.

[9] T. Kohonen, E. Oja, O. Simula, A. Visa, and J. Kangas. Engineering applications of the self-organizing map. *Proceedings of the IEEE*, 84(10):1358–1384, October 1996.

[10] Y. Linde, A. Buzo, and R. Gray. An algorithm for vector quantizer design. *IEEE Transactions on Communications*, 28(1):84–95, January 1980.

[11] Y. Okumura, E. Ohmori, T. Kawano, and K. Fukuda. Field strength and its variability in the VHF and UHF land mobile service. *Review Electronic Communication Lab.*, 16(9-10):825–873, 1968.

[12] J. Rajala, K. Sipilä, and K. Heiska. Predicting in-building coverage for microcells and small macrocells. In *IEEE Vehicular Technology Conference*, volume 1, pages 180–184, 1999.

[13] M. Siponen, J. Vesanto, O. Simula, and P. Vasara. An approach to automated interpretation of SOM. In N. Allinson, H. Yin, L. Allinson, and J. Slack, editors, *Advances in Self-Organizing Maps*, pages 89–94. Springer, 2001.

[14] A. Ultsch and H. P. Siemon. Kohonen's self organizing feature maps for exploratory data analysis. In *Proceedings of the International Neural Network Conference*, pages 305–308, Dordrecht, Netherlands, 1990.

[15] J. Vesanto. SOM-based data visualization methods. *Intelligent Data Analysis*, 3(2):111–126, 1999.

[16] J. Vesanto and E. Alhoniemi. Clustering of the self-organizing map. *IEEE Transactions on Neural Networks*, 11(3):586–600, May 2000.

Discovery of Association Rules in Tabular Data

G Richards and V J Rayward-Smith

School of Information Systems, University of East Anglia, Norwich, NR4 7TJ, UK.
Graeme.Richards@uea.ac.uk, vjrs@sys.uea.ac.uk

Abstract

In this paper we address the problem of finding all association rules in tabular data. An Algorithm, ARA, for finding rules, that satisfy clearly specified constraints, in tabular data is presented. ARA is based on the Dense Miner algorithm but includes an additional constraint and an improved method of calculating support. ARA is tested and compared with our implementation of Dense Miner; it is concluded that ARA is usually more efficient than Dense Miner and is often considerably more so.

We also consider the potential for modifying the constraints used in ARA in order to find more general rules.

1. Introduction

The problem of mining association rules was introduced by Agrawal et al. in 1993 [1] in the context of the analysis of transaction data (often referred to as market basket data). A transaction database comprises a set of transactions where each transaction comprises a set of items. The set of all items in the database is U.

Association rules were presented as expressions of the form $antecedent \Rightarrow consequent$ where $antecedent \subset U$, $consequent \subset U$ and $antecedent \cap consequent = \phi$, they express an association between the antecedent and consequent. We refer to rules of this type as "market basket association rules" or mb-rules.

Several algorithms have been developed to find mb-rules in transaction data. The most well known of these is Apriori [2], others include AIS [3] and SETM [4].

However, association rules can be considered to be much more general, particularly when applied to tabular data. A tabular database comprises a set of records. A record specifies values for each attribute in a set of attributes.

The antecedent and consequent may each then describe *any* subset of records in a database. They could, for example, include feature constructions, conjunctions, disjunctions, negations, equality and inequality tests etc. An example of a general association rule is;

$(\textbf{weight} < \textbf{height}^2) \wedge (\textbf{colour} = \text{green} \vee \textbf{colour} = \text{red}) \Rightarrow \textbf{wheels} > 6 \vee (\textbf{Engine} \neq \text{diesel}).$

We refer to rules of this type as "general association rules" or simply as "rules". The problem with generalisation is that the search space is often very large. In order to limit the search space constraints may be imposed on rules.

mb-rules in tabular data may be defined by constraining general association rules so that the antecedent and consequent are conjunctions of attribute tests (ATs) where each AT is an equality test of the form "attribute = value" and ATs can be formed for each attribute / value pair. ATs are then synonymous with items in mb-rules. An example of this type of rule is:

$$\textbf{model} = \text{sports} \wedge \textbf{colour} = \text{red} \Rightarrow \textbf{risk} = \text{high}.$$

When mb-rules are expressed in this format the constraints are clearly defined and it is also clear how they can be modified. The consequences of this are discussed further in section 3.

Algorithm ARA (All Rules Algorithm), for finding mb-rules in tabular data is presented in section 2.

Section 2.9 describes the evaluation of ARA. The final section describes ways in which ARA may be developed.

2. All Rules Algorithm

ARA is based on Dense Miner [5 and 6] but applies directly to tabular data, includes additional pruning functions and collects more support information to enable the calculation of tighter bounds for pruning. Dense Miner is described in greater detail in [5] and ARA in [7].

2.1. Notation

The *antecedent* of a rule, r, is designated $r - c$ where c is the consequent of the rule.

Operations on conjunctions of ATs $\bigwedge M$ and $\bigwedge P$ are defined in terms of the equivalent operations on the associated sets of ATs M and P as follows.

$$\bigwedge M \subseteq \bigwedge P \text{ iff } M \subseteq P,$$
$$\bigwedge M \subset \bigwedge P \text{ iff } M \subset P,$$
$$\left| \bigwedge M \right| = |M| \text{ and } \bigwedge M = \phi \text{ iff } M = \phi.$$

A rule, r', is a subrule of a rule, r, if the *consequents* of the two rules are identical, c, and $r' - c \subset r - c$.

The *support* of a conjunction of ATs or a single AT, M, $sup(M)$, is the number of records in the database for which M holds.

2.2. Constraints

The constraints imposed by ARA are described below.

2.2.1. Rule Structure Constraints. U is the set of all ATs that can be formed from attribute / value pairs in the database.

- **Consequent constraint:** A single AT, c, from U is designated as the consequent for all rules in a single search. This reduces considerably the number of valid rules. The justification for incorporating the consequent constraint is that often there is a single target class of interest.

- **Antecedent Constraint:** I' is the subset of ATs in U with the same attribute as the consequent. $I = U - I'$. The antecedent of a rule is a conjunction of ATs drawn from I.

- *MaxATs* **Constraint:** A user-defined value, *maxATs*, sets the maximum number of ATs that can be used in the antecedent of a rule. Introducing this constraint can considerably reduce the search space and also improve the bounds used for pruning. The justification for using it is that, when the rules are required for gaining insight into data, shorter rules are generally preferable.

2.2.2. Rule Value Constraints. Three parameters, *minSup, minConf* and *minImp*, are specified by the user.

- **Support constraint:** The support for a rule, r, $sup(r)$, is defined as $sup(r\text{-}c \wedge c)$. Rule r satisfies the support constraint iff $sup(r) \geq min Sup$. This constraint ensures that rules have generality.

- **Confidence constraint:** The *confidence* of a rule, r, $conf(r)$, is defined as $\dfrac{sup(r)}{sup(r-c)}$. Rule r satisfies the confidence constraint iff $conf(r) \geq min Conf$. This constraint ensures the predictive value of rules.

- **Improvement constraint:** The improvement of a rule, r, $imp(r)$, was introduced in [5] and is defined as $conf(r) - conf(r')$, where r' is the subrule of r with the greatest confidence.

Rule r satisfies the improvement constraint iff $imp(r) \geq minImp$. This constraint ensures that all ATs in a rule add significantly to its value.

2.3. Search Strategy

Dense Miner and ARA are constraint based searches. The search space of rules is explored by use of a set enumeration tree (SE-Tree) as described in [8].

Each node in the SE-Tree is represented by a structure called a group. A group, g, has a head $H(g)$ and a tail $T(g)$, $g = H(g) \| T(g)$.

The head is a conjunction of ATs that represents the antecedent of a rule. The tail is a set of ATs that can be added to the head to form a new antecedent. A total order, $\underset{g}{\geq}$ is defined on the tail ATs of a group, g. In practice the tail ATs are stored in a vector that is sorted according to the ordering.

The head and tail of the group at the root of the SE-Tree are $H(root) = \phi$ and $T(root) = I$, where I is defined in section 2.2.1.

A group, g, is expanded to create a set of groups in the next level of the SE-Tree by producing one child for each of the ATs in $T(g)$.

For each child, h, of group, g, $H(h)$ is a conjunction of the head of the parent and a single AT, v, from the tail of the parent. $T(h)$ consists of each of the tail ATs in g that follow v in the ordering.

$$H(h) = H(g) \wedge v \text{ for some } v \in T(g)$$
$$\text{and then } T(h) = \{w | \ w \in T(g) \text{ and } w >_g v \}.$$

Tail ordering determines the order of expansion of groups. It thus leads to more effective pruning by concentrating unpromising groups in one part of the tree. Tail ordering is carried out within each group by sorting the tail vector of ATs according to some heuristic; it is discussed in more detail in section 2.8.

Figure 2-1 shows an SE-Tree for the set of ATs {A, B, C}, the ordering of tail ATs is indicated by their positions in the tails. An arbitrary reordering of the tail ATs has been carried out at each level to demonstrate that the completeness of the tree is not compromised but no pruning is carried out, i.e. the tree is complete. It can be seen that the antecedent of every possible rule that can be constructed from the ATs is enumerated in the heads of the groups.

A group, h, is **derivable** from a group, g, iff $H(h) \wedge (\bigwedge T(h)) \subseteq H(g) \wedge (\bigwedge T(g))$ and $H(g) \subseteq H(h)$ i.e. a group is derivable from itself. g is an **ancestor** of h iff h is derivable from g.

A rule, r, is **derivable** from a group, g, iff
$r\text{-}c \subseteq H(g) \wedge \left(\bigwedge T(g) \right)$ and $H(g) \subset r - c$.

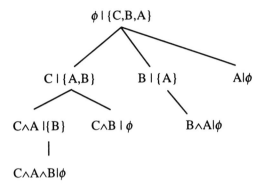

Figure 2-1. SE-Tree for the set {A, B, C}.

2.4. Top level of algorithm

Database D
group $root \leftarrow create\_root\_group(D)$
set of groups $G \leftarrow \{root\}$
set of rules $R \leftarrow \phi$
while ($G \neq \phi$ and $headLength < maxATs$)
$\quad G \leftarrow tail\_sort(G)$
$\quad G \leftarrow evaluate(G, D)$
$\quad R \leftarrow extract\_rules(G, R)$
$\quad G \leftarrow prune(G)$
$\quad G \leftarrow split(G)$
$\quad G \leftarrow prune(G)$
$R \leftarrow post\_process(R, D)$

Figure 2-2. Top Level of Algorithm

The algorithm enumerates the antecedents of all rules that potentially satisfy the constraints by expanding an SE-Tree. The *create_root_group* function creates the group at the root of the SE-Tree as described in section 2.3. A set of groups, G, is defined; initially this comprises the single group, *root*. The set of rules, R, is used to return the set of all rules that satisfy the constraints.

The main loop of the algorithm executes until either all groups have been pruned from G or the maximum length of antecedent has been reached.

The order of the ATs in the tails of each group in G are redefined using the *tail_sort* function *before* G is evaluated. The necessity for ordering *before* evaluation is described in section 2.5.

The *evaluate* function collects support information for each group in G for the purpose of calculating rule support and confidence and for use in the pruning function. The function, *extract_rules*, adds rules that potentially satisfy the constraints to R.

The *split* function takes the set of groups, G, and expands each $g \in G$ as described in section 2.3, the children of g replace g in G, forming the next level of the SE-Tree. The *prune* function is applied both before and after the *split* function. It removes some groups from G and is described in section 2.7.

The *post_process* function removes any rules that do not satisfy the constraints from R. It is the same as described in [5] and is not repeated here.

2.5. Evaluate Function

A *candidate set* of conjunctions is defined for each group. The evaluation function computes the support for each of the conjunctions in the candidate set of each group in G. A group is described as an *evaluated* group when the supports for all the conjunctions in its candidate set have been computed.

The candidate set used in Dense Miner for each group, g, is:

$H(g)$ and $H(g) \wedge c$,

$H(g) \wedge \left(\bigwedge T(g) \right)$ and $H(g) \wedge \left(\bigwedge T(g) \right) \wedge c$,

and, for each $t \in T(g)$, $H(g) \wedge t$ and $H(g) \wedge t \wedge c$.

The candidate set used in ARA is:

$H(g)$ and $H(g) \wedge c$,

and for each $t \in T(g)$, $H(g) \wedge t$, $H(g) \wedge t \wedge c$

and $H(g) \wedge \left(\bigwedge \{w | w \in T(g) \text{ and } w \underset{g}{\geq} t \} \right) \wedge \neg c$.

Thus, ARA collects more support information for each group. This requires additional time to collect and more storage but means that tighter bounds can be calculated for use in the pruning functions, as described in section 2.7. Also note that $\underset{g}{\geq}$ must be defined *before* g is evaluated.

Each group has a counter associated with each conjunction in its candidate set. As in Dense Miner, each record is considered in turn. A trie is used to find all groups in G for which the antecedent of the rule represented by the head of a group holds for the record. For each group, g, that is found, the counter for $H(g)$ is incremented and, if the conclusion holds for the record, the counter for $H(g) \wedge c$ is incremented. Then, for each group that is found, the tail ATs are considered in reverse order. If a tail AT, t, holds for the record then the counter for $H(g) \wedge t$ is incremented, if the conclusion also holds for the record then the counter for $H(g) \wedge t \wedge c$ is incremented, if the conclusion does not hold for the record and every previously considered AT in $T(g)$ held for the record then the counter associated with

467

$$H(g) \wedge \left(\bigwedge \{w | w \in T(g) \text{ and } w \geq_g t\} \right) \wedge \neg c$$

is incremented.

Thus, after considering all of the records in the database, the supports for all of the conjunctions in the candidate sets of each of the groups in G have been computed. The purpose of collecting this support information is to maximise the pruning opportunities, as described in section 2.7.

2.6. Extract Function

Extract_rules extracts, from the set of *evaluated* groups, rules that can potentially satisfy the constraints; these rules are added to the set of rules, R. For each $g \in G$ the rules that are considered are $H(g) \wedge t \Rightarrow c \; \forall \, t \in T(g)$.

A rule can potentially satisfy the constraints and is added to R iff

$$sup(H(g) \wedge t \Rightarrow c) = sup(H(g) \wedge t \wedge c) \geq min \, Sup$$

AND

$$conf(H(g) \wedge t \Rightarrow c) = \frac{sup(H(g) \wedge t \wedge c)}{sup(H(g) \wedge t)} \geq min \, Conf$$

AND

$$conf(H(g) \wedge t \Rightarrow c) - C \, max(g) \geq minImp \,,$$

where $C \, max(g)$ is the maximum confidence of any rule represented by the head of an ancestor of g or g itself.

The *minImp* constraint is fully enforced in the post processing stage, as described in [5].

2.7. Prune Function

The pruning function is applied to a set of groups after evaluation and after a new level of the SE-Tree has been created.

A group, g, is said to be *pruneable* if it can be determined that no rule *derivable* from g can satisfy the constraints. If g is pruneable and is a member of G then g can be removed from G. If a group, g, is not pruneable it may be possible to remove some ATs from its tail. A new group, g', can be formed from g by moving a single AT, v, from the tail into the head. If g' is *pruneable* then no rule derivable from g that includes v can satisfy the constraints and v can be removed from the tail of g. If some ATs are removed from the tail of g then tighter bounds for pruning can be achieved. Therefore, the pruning function is re-applied until either the whole group is pruned or no tail ATs are removed.

2.7.1 Pruning based on support. If $sup(H(g) \wedge c) < min \, Sup$ then no rule derivable from g can meet the *minSup* constraint and g is pruneable. The

value, $sup(H(g) \wedge c)$, is available from the candidate set of g^e, where g^e is the last evaluated ancestor of g.

2.7.2 Pruning based on confidence. Let r be the rule with maximum confidence that is derivable from a group, g. The maximum confidence of any rule derivable from g is $max \, Conf(g) = conf(r)$. If $max \, Conf(g) < min \, Conf$ then g is pruneable.

$max \, Conf(g)$ can be expressed as $max \, Conf(g) = \dfrac{x}{x + y}$

where $x = sup(r)$ and $y = sup(r - c) - sup(r)$.

$max \, Conf(g)$ is monotonically increasing in x and monotonically decreasing in y. Therefore, x may be replaced with an upper bound x' and y with a lower bound y', then $max \, Conf(g) \leq \dfrac{x'}{x' + y'}$.

When attempting to prune an *evaluated* group Dense Miner uses the bounds $x' = sup(H(g) \wedge c)$ and $y' = y_1$ where $y_1 = sup(H(g) \wedge (\bigwedge T(g)) \wedge \neg c)$. ARA, however, uses the *maxATs* constraint. It is then possible to calculate another lower bound on y, y_2.

Lemma 1
y_2 is a lower bound on $y = sup(r - c) - sup(r)$

where $y_2 = sup(H(g) \wedge \neg c) - \sum_{t \in S} sup(H(g) \wedge \neg t \wedge \neg c)$,

where S comprises the n tail ATs, t, of $T(g)$ with the highest values of $sup(H(g) \wedge \neg t \wedge \neg c)$ and $n = min(max \, ATs - |H(g)|, |T(g)|)$.

Proof
The proof is initially given for the general case $y_2 \leq sup(u - c) - sup(u)$ where u is *any* rule derivable from a group, g, as this is required for improvement pruning, and then for the particular case $y_2 \leq sup(r - c) - sup(r)$.

Rule, u, may be written as, $H(g) \wedge M \Rightarrow c$, where M is a conjunction of ATs from $T(g)$.
Then,

$$\begin{aligned} &sup(u - c) - sup(u) \\ &= sup(H(g) \wedge M) - sup(H(g) \wedge M \wedge c) \\ &= sup(H(g) \wedge M \wedge \neg c) \\ &= sup(H(g) \wedge \neg c) - sup(H(g) \wedge \neg M \wedge \neg c) \end{aligned}$$

Now, $M = (m_1 \wedge m_2 \wedge \ldots \wedge m_p)$
and $\neg M = \neg(m_1 \wedge m_2 \wedge \ldots \wedge m_p)$
$$= (\neg m_1 \vee \neg m_2 \vee \ldots \vee \neg m_p)$$

Since $sup(a \vee b) = sup(a) + sup(b) - sup(a \wedge b)$
$$\leq sup(a) + sup(b)$$
it follows that
$$\sum_{t \in M} sup(H(g) \wedge \neg t \wedge \neg c) \geq sup(H(g) \wedge \neg M \wedge \neg c)$$

In the presence of *maxATs*,
$$|M| \leq min(maxATs - |H(g)|, |T(g)|) = n = |S|.$$

Given that S comprises the n tail ATs with the highest values of $sup(H(g) \wedge \neg t \wedge \neg c)$ and $|S| \geq |M|$ it follows that
$$\sum_{t \in S} sup(H(g) \wedge \neg t \wedge \neg c) \geq \sum_{t \in M} sup(H(g) \wedge \neg t \wedge \neg c)$$

Therefore,
$$sup(H(g) \wedge \neg c) - \sum_{t \in S} sup(H(g) \wedge \neg t \wedge \neg c)$$
$$\leq sup(H(g) \wedge \neg c) - sup(H(g) \wedge \neg M \wedge \neg c)$$
Hence,
$$sup(H(g) \wedge \neg c) - \sum_{t \in S} sup(H(g) \wedge \neg t \wedge \neg c)$$
$$\leq sup(u - c) - sup(u)$$
and $y_2 \leq sup(u - c) - sup(u)$.

Therefore, since r is a rule derivable from g, $y_2 \leq sup(r - c) - sup(r) = y$.

When attempting to prune an evaluated group the supports are available to calculate x' and both y_1 and y_2; y' may then be set to $max\{y_1, y_2\}$ for use in the pruning function. However, when considering a group, g, that is not evaluated it may not be possible to calculate x' or y_1 or y_2. Then, since x' is an upper bound, it may be set to $sup(H(h) \wedge c)$, where h is the last ancestor of g to have this value available in its candidate set, since $sup(H(h) \wedge c) \leq sup(H(g) \wedge c)$. It is also possible to calculate values y'_1 and y'_2 such that $y'_1 \leq y_1$ and $y'_2 \leq y_2$. The values y_1 and y_2 are lower bounds on y, therefore, so are y'_1 and y'_2 and so y' may be set to $max\{y'_1, y'_2\}$.

When y_1 cannot be calculated, Dense Miner calculates
$$y'_1 = max \begin{cases} sup(H(g^p) \wedge (\bigwedge T(g^p)) \wedge \neg c) \\ sup(H(g) \wedge \neg c) - \sum_{t \in T(g)} sup(H(g^p) \wedge \neg t \wedge \neg c) \end{cases}$$

where g^p is the parent of g in the SE-Tree. Both of these values are less than or equal to y_1 and can be calculated from the supports of the conjunctions in the candidate set of g^p.

ARA, with its larger candidate set, can often find a higher value for y'_1 and also a value for y'_2.

Let g be a group that is derived from an evaluated group g^e. Two cases are considered; case 1, when $H(g) = H(g^e)$ i.e. some ATs have been removed from the tail of g^e to create g, and case 2, when $H(g) = H(g^e) \wedge v$ where v is a single AT from $T(g^e)$, i.e. g is either a group created for the purpose of tail pruning or g is in the next level of the SE-Tree from g^e.

Case 1, $H(g) = H(g^e)$.

If the supports are not available to calculate $y_1 = sup(H(g) \wedge (\bigwedge T(g)) \wedge \neg c)$ then ARA calculates $y'_1 = sup(H(g^e) \wedge (\bigwedge \{w \mid w \in T(g^e) \text{ and } w \geq_{g^e} p\}) \wedge \neg c)$, where p is the minimal AT in $T(g)$ under the ordering $\geq_g$. Provided that the ordering of g is the same as g^e y'_1 is less than or equal to y_1. The issue of tail ordering, and how the ordering can be maintained, is discussed in section 2.8.

$sup(H(g^e) \wedge (\bigwedge \{w \mid w \in T(g^e) \text{ and } w \geq_{g^e} t\}) \wedge \neg c)$ is available for every $t \in T(g)$, since these conjuncts are members of the candidate set of g^e, and is therefore available for the minimal AT, p.

The supports necessary to calculate
$$y_2 = sup(H(g) \wedge \neg c) - \sum_{t \in S} sup(H(g) \wedge \neg t \wedge \neg c) \text{ are}$$

available from the candidate set of $H(g^e)$, since $H(g) = H(g^e)$.

Case 2. $H(g) = H(g^e) \wedge v$.

Again it may not be possible to calculate $y_1 = sup(H(g) \wedge (\bigwedge T(g)) \wedge \neg c)$. Then ARA calculates $y'_1 = sup(H(g^e) \wedge (\bigwedge \{w \mid w \in T(g^e) \text{ and } w \geq_{g^e} u\}) \wedge \neg c)$ where u is the minimal AT in $T(g) \cup \{v\}$ under the ordering $\geq_g$. y'_1 is less than or equal to y_1 (provided that the ordering of g is the same as g^e).

$sup(H(g^e) \wedge (\bigwedge \{w \mid w \in T(g^e) \text{ and } w \geq_{g^e} t\}) \wedge \neg c)$ is available for every $t \in T(g) \cup \{v\}$, since these conjuncts are members of the candidate set of g^e, and is therefore available for the AT, u.

It may also not be possible to calculate $y_2 = sup(H(g) \wedge \neg c) - \sum_{t \in S} sup(H(g) \wedge \neg t \wedge \neg c)$.

However, $sup(H(g) \wedge \neg c) = sup(H(g^e) \wedge v \wedge \neg c)$ and for every $t \in T(g^e)$

$$sup(H(g^e) \wedge \neg t \wedge \neg c) \geq sup(H(g) \wedge \neg t \wedge \neg c).$$

Therefore,

$$sup(H(g^e) \wedge v \wedge \neg c) - \sum_{t \in S'} sup(H(g^e) \wedge \neg t \wedge \neg c)$$

$$\leq sup(H(g) \wedge \neg c) - \sum_{t \in S} sup(H(g) \wedge \neg t \wedge \neg c) = y_2$$

where S' consists of the $|S|$ tail ATs of g with the maximum values of $sup(H(g^e) \wedge \neg t \wedge \neg c)$. ARA therefore calculates

$$y_2' = sup(H(g^e) \wedge v \wedge \neg c) - \sum_{t \in S'} sup(H(g^e) \wedge \neg t \wedge \neg c).$$

The support values necessary to calculate y_2' are available from the candidate set of g^e.

2.7.3 Pruning based on improvement. Let r be the rule derivable from a group, g, with the maximum improvement. Then $imp(r) = maxImp(g)$. If $maxImp(g) \leq minImp$ then g is pruneable.

In order to find an upper bound on $maxImp(g)$ the same methods as Dense Miner are used. However, because the value of y' calculated for confidence pruning is re-used and may be higher in ARA than in Dense Miner, the upper bound on $maxImp(g)$ may be lower. The methods are presented below without proofs. These can be found in [5] or [7].

Method 1. $maxImp(g) \leq maxConf(g) - conf(r')$ where r' is the highest confidence rule enumerated in any ancestor group of g.

Method 2. $maxImp(g) \leq \dfrac{x'}{x' + y'} - \dfrac{x'}{x' + y' + \beta'}$

where

$x' = max\left(minSup, min\left(sup(H(g) \wedge c), \sqrt{y'^2 + y'\beta'}\right)\right)$, y' is defined above and $\beta' \leq sup((H(g) - z) \wedge \neg z \wedge \neg c)$ where z is the AT in $H(g)$ that minimises this expression.

In order to be used in improvement pruning, y' must be a lower bound on $sup(r - c) - sup(r)$ where r is the rule derivable from g with the maximum improvement. It was shown in lemma 1 that $y' \leq sup(u - c) - sup(u)$ where u is *any* rule derivable from g. Therefore, y' is a lower bound on $sup(r - c) - sup(r)$.

Example of pruning. Let $A|\{B, C, D, E, F, G, H\}$ be an evaluated group, g^e. Assume that g^e is not pruneable, therefore try to remove some tail ATs. To do this we form a group, $g' = A \wedge B|\{C, D, E, F, G, H\}$. It is found that no rule derivable from g' can satisfy the constraints, i.e. g' is pruneable, and so B can be removed from the tail of g^e. After considering each of the tail ATs in the same way it is found that ATs B and D may be removed from the tail of g^e. We form a new group, $g_1 = A|\{C, E, F, G, H\}$, which replaces g^e in the SE-Tree. Now, because some ATs have been removed from the tail and tighter bounds may be available for y an attempt is made to prune g_1. When attempting to prune g_1 (and when attempting to prune ATs from the tail of g_1) ARA will use the value $sup(A \wedge C \wedge D \wedge E \wedge F \wedge G \wedge H \wedge \neg c)$ as a value for

$$y_1' \leq y_1 = sup(A \wedge C \wedge E \wedge F \wedge G \wedge H \wedge \neg c)$$

which is potentially higher than $sup(A \wedge B \wedge C \wedge D \wedge E \wedge F \wedge G \wedge H \wedge \neg c)$ as used in Dense Miner. Also, y_2 is greater than or equal to the other value used in Dense Miner,

$$sup(H(g) \wedge \neg c) - \sum_{t \in T(g)} sup(H(g^p) \wedge \neg t \wedge \neg c).$$

Assume it is found that g_1 is not pruneable and no ATs can be removed from its tail. A new set of groups in the next level of the SE-Tree are created which replace g_1. Amongst these is the group $h = A \wedge F|\{G, H\}$. Now, in determining if h is pruneable ARA has available and will use $y_1 = sup(A \wedge F \wedge G \wedge H \wedge \neg c)$. Dense Miner will use $sup(A \wedge B \wedge C \wedge D \wedge E \wedge F \wedge G \wedge H \wedge \neg c)$, which is likely to be lower. Again y_2 is greater than or equal to the other value used in Dense Miner,

$$sup(H(g) \wedge \neg c) - \sum_{t \in T(g)} sup(H(g^p) \wedge \neg t \wedge \neg c).$$

This example shows how tighter bounds can be achieved for pruning using the additional support information collected by ARA. If the *maxATs* constraint is specified even tighter bounds can be achieved.

2.8. Tail ordering

As described in [5] tail ordering is essential for efficient algorithm performance. ARA requires that the tail of a group, g, is ordered before evaluation and the order maintained in groups derived from g until pruning is complete. Therefore, the vector of tail ATs is sorted *before* a group is evaluated. The ordering used to sort the vector of tail ATs of a group, g, is descending value of $sup(H(g^e) \wedge \neg t \wedge \neg c)$ where g^e is the last evaluated ancestor of g. An initial evaluation is carried out as the basis for sorting the tail of the root group. For clarity this has not been shown in Figure 2-2.

2.9. Results

ARA was evaluated on two databases; the connect 4 database [9] and a census database [10]. Due to limitations of space only the results of the connect 4 tests are reported here. The results achieved using the census data base were similar and are presented in [7]. Connect 4 has 65,577 records and 42 predictive attributes each of which is categorical with 3 possible values, the consequent was defined as "result = draw" of which there are 6,449 records.

The algorithm was evaluated according to the following measures.

1. Execution Time. Times are for the search phase only, post processing time is not included.
2. Number of groups evaluated. This represents the size of the search tree.
3. Number of tail ATs evaluated. This is required because a small number of groups with large tails may be more time consuming to evaluate than a large number of groups with small tails.

In order to compare ARA with Dense Miner a version of Dense Miner was implemented in accordance with the description given in [5], this version of Dense Miner is referred to as ARA-Dense. ARA-Dense is identical to ARA in all respects except for the support information collected and the pruning functions; any variation in performance can thus be attributed to these differences alone. The execution times for ARA-Dense were compared with the times for Dense Miner reported in [5] and found to be slower by a factor of 1.5 - 1.8. This variation may be attributable to hardware or compiler differences or the detail of implementation.

All tests were carried out on a Dell Dimension XPS PIII 450 with 128MB memory.

2.10. Commentary on test results

When *minConf* was set to zero it was found that there was no significant difference in the execution times of the two algorithms over a wide range of tests; indicating that the advantage of a smaller search tree was offset by the overhead for collecting more information. Figure 2.1 shows the effect of using confidence for pruning by varying the values specified for *minConf*. The size of tree searched by ARA was smaller than ARA-Dense by a factor of 1.2 to 2.5, the higher the setting of *minConf* the greater the reduction in tree size. The number of tail items evaluated varied by a similar order. Execution time also varied in proportion to the size of the search tree; indicating that the overhead for collecting the additional support information was outweighed by the benefit of a smaller tree when confidence was used for pruning.

The second set of tests, reported in figure 2.2, shows the effect of introducing the *maxATs* constraint.

In order to demonstrate the effect of the *maxATs* constraint a further algorithm, ARA-Part was implemented. This is identical to ARA but does not include the additional pruning functionality based on the *maxATs* constraint.

ARA-Dense and ARA-Part simply stop searching when the number of ATs in the consequent of extracted rules is equal to *maxATs*. The improvement of ARA-Part over ARA-Dense is thus attributable to the additional support information collected. The improvement of ARA over ARA-Part is attributable to the additional pruning using the *maxATs* constraint.

When *maxATs* is lower than 11 (the maximum antecedent length of any rule that satisfies the other constraints) there are considerable benefits to using the constraint. For example, with *maxATs* set to 6 the execution times for ARA and ARA-Part were 149 and 493 seconds respectively; a saving of over 5 minutes. The time for ARA-Dense was 818 seconds which is over 5 times or 11 minutes longer.

It is concluded that when *minConf* is specified ARA generally outperforms ARA-Dense. When the *maxATs* constraint is specified further significant gains in performance can be achieved.

3. Future Work

An attribute test in ARA is a 3 tuple [attribute, operator, value] where operator is "=". However, it is straightforward to construct ATs with different operators. For example an AT could be "*age* < 50" or "*colour* ≠ red" allowing a richer variety of rules to be constructed.

A problem with increasing the variety of ATs is that the search space and the number of discovered rules may be vastly increased. To counteract this, additional constraints may be necessary. However, these could be problem specific rather than algorithm specific. For example, one possible constraint is to define which ATs (or combinations of ATs) are of interest (or conversely which are not of interest) before the search is undertaken. As a result some generality of the search will be lost but the search can be targeted at areas of interest, thus making the problem more tractable and avoiding rules that are not likely to be interesting.

One of the problems of finding all rules is specifying suitable values for *minCov* and *minConf*. In this research we have experimented with the use of the heuristic search techniques in the DataLamp package developed by the University of East Anglia and the Lanner Group [11]. DataLamp has been used to find a good rule according to its fitness function, then ARA used to find all rules with coverage and confidence greater than that rule.

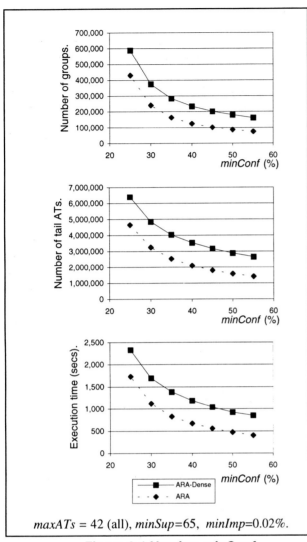

$maxATs$ = 42 (all), $minSup$=65, $minImp$=0.02%.

Figure 2-1 Varying *minConf*

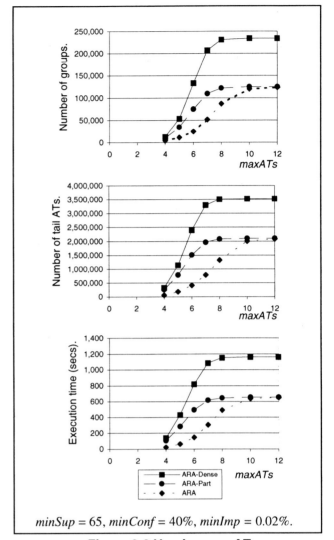

$minSup$ = 65, $minConf$ = 40%, $minImp$ = 0.02%.

Figure 2-2 Varying *maxATs*

4. References

[1] Agrawal R, Imielinski T, Swami A. Mining association rules between sets of items in large databases. *Proceedings of the ACM SIGMOD International Conference on Management of Data,* May 1993, pp 207 – 216. ACM Press, 1993.

[2] Agrawal R, Srikant R. Fast Algorithms for Mining Association Rules. *Proceedings of the 20th International Conference on VLDB,* September 1994, pp 487 - 499, Morgan Kaufmann, 1994.

[3] Agrawal R, Imielinski T, Swami A. Mining association rules between sets of items in large databases. *Proceedings of the ACM SIGMOD International Conference on Management of Data,* May 1993, pp 207 – 216. ACM Press, 1993.

[4] Houtsma M, Swami A. Set Oriented Mining of Association Rules in Relational Databases. *Proceedings of the Eleventh International Conference on Data Engineering,* March 1995, pp 25 - 33. IEEE, 1995.

[5] Bayardo R, Agrawal R, Gunopulos D. Constraint-Based Rule Mining in Large, Dense Databases. *Proc. of the 15th*

International Conf. on Data Engineering, March 1999, pp 188 - 197. IEEE, 1999.

[6] Bayardo R, Agrawal R. Mining the Most Interesting Rules. *Proceedings of the 5th International Conference on Knowledge Discovery and Data Mining,* (KDD 99), August 1999, pp 145 - 153. AAAI Press, 1999.

[7] Richards G. Mining All Rules. *University of East Anglia Technical report.* SYS-C00-10.

[8] Rymon R. Search Through Systematic Set Enumeration. *Proceedings of the 3rd International Conference on Principles of Knowledge Representation and Reasoning,* (KR 92), October 1992, pp 539 - 550. Morgan Kaufmann, 1992.

[9] Connect 4 data base. http://www.ics.uci.edu/ ~mlearn/MLSummary.html

[10] Census data base. http://kdd.ics.uci.edu/ databases/census-income/census-income.html

[11] Lanner Web Site. http://www.lanner.com/ solutions/datamining.html

Theory and Applications of Attribute Decomposition

Lior Rokach
Department of Industrial Engineering
Tel-Aviv University
Ramat Aviv, Tel Aviv 69978, Israel
liorr@eng.tau.ac.il

Oded Mainon
Department of Industrial Engineering
Tel-Aviv University
Ramat Aviv, Tel Aviv 69978, Israel
maimon@eng.tau.ac.il

Abstract

This paper examines the Attribute Decomposition Approach with simple Bayesian combination for dealing with classi£cation problems that contain high number of attributes and moderate numbers of records. According to the Attribute Decomposition Approach, the set of input attributes is automatically decomposed into several subsets. A classi£cation model is built for each subset, then all the models are combined using simple Bayesian combination. This paper presents theoretical and practical foundation for the Attribute Decomposition Approach. A greedy procedure, called D-IFN, is developed to decompose the input attributes set into subsets and build a classi£cation model for each subset separately. The results achieved in the empirical comparison testing with well-known classi£cation methods (like C4.5) indicate the superiority of the decomposition approach.

1. Introduction

Classi£cation modeling is one of the most important techniques for data mining. In classi£cation problem the induction algorithm is given a set of training instances and the corresponding class labels and outputs a classi£cation model. The classi£cation model takes an unlabeled instance and predicts its class.

Fayyad *et al.* [8] claim that the explicit challenges for the KDD research community is to develop methods that facilitate the use of data mining algorithms for real-world databases. One of the characteristics of a real world databases is high dimensionality. High Dimensionality increases the size of the search space in an exponential manner, and thus increases the chance that the algorithm will £nd spurious models that are not valid in general. Elder and Pregibon [7] de£ne this phenomenon as the "curse of dimensionality". Techniques that are ef£cient in low dimensions fail to provide meaningful results when the number of dimensions goes beyond a 'modest' size of 10 attributes. Furthermore smaller data mining models, involving less attributes, are much more understandable by humans. Smaller models are also more appropriate for user-driven data mining, based on visualization techniques.

Most of the methods for dealing with high dimensionality focus on *Feature Selection* techniques, i.e. selecting some subset of attributes upon which the induction algorithm will run, while ignoring the rest. In the last decade, *Feature Selection* has enjoyed increased interest by the data mining community. Consequently many *Feature Selection* algorithms have been proposed, some of which have reported remarkable accuracy improvement. The literature on this subject is too wide to survey here, however, we recommend [12] on this topic.

Despite its popularity, using *Feature Selection* methodology for overcoming the high dimensionality obstacles has several shortcomings:

- The assumption that a large set of input attributes can be reduced to a small subset of relevant attributes is not always true; in some cases the target attribute is actually affected by most of the input attributes, and removing attributes will cause a signi£cant loss of important information.

- The outcome of many algorithms for *Feature Selection* is strongly dependent on the training set size. That is, if the training set is small the size of the reduced subset will be small as well.

- In some cases, even after eliminating a set of irrelevant attributes, the researcher is left with relatively large numbers of relevant attributes.

- The backward elimination strategy, used by some methods, is extremely inef£cient for working with large-scale databases, where the number of original attributes is large.

A number of linear dimension reducers have been developed over the years. The linear methods of dimensionality reduction include projection pursuit [9], factor analysis [10], and principal components analysis [6]. These methods are not aimed directly at eliminating irrelevant and redundant attributes, but are rather concerned with transforming the observed variables into a small number of "projections" or "dimensions". The underlying assumptions are that the variables are numeric and the dimensions can be expressed as linear combinations of the observed variables. Each discovered dimension is assumed to represent an unobserved factor and thus provide a new way of understanding the data.

The linear dimension reducers have been enhanced constructive induction systems that use a set of existing attributes and a set of predefined constructive operators to derive new attributes [17]. Zupan *et al.* [24] presented a general-purpose function decomposition approach for machine learning. According to this approach, attributes are transformed into new concepts in an iterative manner and create a hierarchy of concepts. These methods are effective for high dimensionality applications only if the original domain size of the input attribute can be in fact decreased dramatically.

One way to deal with the aforementioned disadvantages is to use a very large training set (which should grows in an exponential manner as the number of input attributes increases). However, the researcher rarely enjoys this privilege, and even if it does happen, the researcher will probably encounter the aforementioned difficulties derived from high number of records.

The rest of the paper is organized into three parts. In the first part we introduce the Attribute Decomposition Approach literally and theoretically. In the second part we develop a heuristic algorithm for implementing the decomposition approach. In the third part we examine the algorithm on several artificial data and real applications.

2. Attribute Decomposition Approach

The purpose of decomposition is to break down a complex problem into several manageable problems.

Problem decomposition's benefts include: conceptual simplification of the problem, making the problem more feasible by reducing its dimensionality, achieving clearer results, reducing run time by solving smaller problems and by using parallel computation, and allowing different solution techniques for individual sub problems.

The decomposition approach is frequently used for operation research and engineering design, however, as Buntine [3] states, it has not attracted as much attention in KDD and machine learning.

In this paper we present the attribute decomposition approach where the original attribute set is decomposed to mutually exclusive subsets by an algorithm. A learning algorithm is run upon the training data for each subset independently and then the generated models are combined in order to classify new instances. This method facilitates the creation of a classification model for high dimensionality databases.

Variety of methods (like boosting or bagging), which also provide an improvement in classification performance by combining several simple classifers produced by the same method, can be found in the literature. However, the resulting predictions are usually inscrutable to end-users [19].

Other methods that deals directly with high dimensional data like support vector machines also suffer from inscrutability. The method proposed here improves classification performance, without jeopardizing the model's comprehensibility.

The problem of decomposing the input attributes set is that of finding the best decomposition, such that if a specific induction algorithm is run on each attribute subset data, then the combination of the generated classifers will have the highest possible accuracy.

In this paper we focus on simple Bayesian combination, which is an extension of the *Simple Bayesian* classifer. The *Simple Bayesian* classifer uses Bayes rule to compute the probability of each possible value of the target attribute given the instance, assuming the input attributes are conditionally independent given the target attribute. The predicted value of the target attribute is the one, which maximizes the calculated probability. Due to the attribute independence assumption, this method is also known as "naive" Bayesian. However, a variety of empirical research shows surprisingly that the simple Bayesian classifer can perform quite well compared to other methods even in domains where clear attribute dependencies exist. Furthermore, simple Bayesian classifers are also very simple and easy to understand.

In the attribute decomposition approach with simple Bayesian combination we use a similar idea, namely the prediction of a new instance s_q is based on the product of the conditional probability of the target attribute, given the values of the input attributes in each subset. Mathematically it can be formulated as follows:

$$v_{MAP} = \underset{v_{y,j} \in V_y}{\text{argmax}} \frac{\prod\limits_{k=1}^{\omega} \hat{P}_I(y=v_{y,j}|a_i=x_{q,i}\ i \in R_k)}{\hat{P}_I(y=v_{y,j})^{\omega-1}}$$

Where $x_{q,i}$ denotes the value of attribute i in an observation q. V_y represents the domain of the target attribute. R_k denotes the indexes of the attributes that belong to subset k. y represents the class variable or the target attribute.

In fact extending the simple Bayesian classifer by joining attributes is not new. Kononenko [11] used a conditional independence test to join attributes. Domingos and Pazzani [4] used estimated accuracy (as determined by leave one out cross validation on the training set). In both cases, the suggested algorithm £nds the single best pair of attributes to join by considering all possible joins. However these methods have not noticeably improved accuracy. The reasons for the moderate results are two-fold. First both algorithms used a limited criterion for joining attributes. Second and more importantly, attributes are joined by creating a new attribute, whose values are the Cartesian product of its ingredients' values, speci£cally the number of attributes that can be joined together is restricted to a small number. Furthermore the problem have not been formally de£ned and explored.

Duda and Hart [5] showed that Bayesian classi£er has highest possible accuracy (i.e. Bayesian classi£er predicts the most probable class of a given instance based on the complete distribution). However in practical learning scenarios, where the training set is very small compared to the whole space, the complete distribution can hardly be estimated directly.

According to the decomposition concept the complete distribution is estimated by combining several partial distributions. Bear in mind that it is easier to build a simpler model from limited number of training instances because it has less parameters. This makes classi£cation problems with many input attributes more feasible.

This problem can be related to the bias-variance tradeoff. The bias of a learning algorithm for a given learning problem is the persistent or systematic error that the learning algorithm is expected to make. A concept closely related to bias is variance. The variance captures random variation in the algorithm from one training set to another. This variation can result from variation in the training sample, from random noise in the training data, or from random behavior in the learning algorithm itself. The smaller each subset is, the less probabilities we have to estimate and potentially less variance in the estimation of each one of them. On the other hand, when there are more subsets, we expect that the approximation of the full distribution using the partial distributions is less accurate (i.e. higher bias error). Formally the problem can be phrased as follows:

Given a learning method I, and a training set S with input attribute set $A = \{a_1, a_2, ..., a_n\}$ and target attribute y from a distribution D over the labeled instance space, the goal is to £nd an optimal decomposition Z_{opt} of the input attribute set A into ω subsets $G_k = \{a_{k,j(i)} | j = 1, ..., l_k\}$ $k = 1, ..., \omega$ fulfilling $(\bigcup_{k=1}^{\omega} G_k) \subseteq A$ and $G_i \cap G_j = \emptyset; i, j = 1, ..., \omega; i \neq j$ such that the generalization error of the simple Bayesian combination of the induced classi£ers will be minimized over the distribution D.

It should be noted that the optimal is not necessarily unique. Furthermore the problem can be treated as an extension of the feature subset selection problem, i.e. £nding the optimal decomposition of the form $Z_{opt} = \{G_1\}$, as the non-relevant features are in fact $A - G_1$. Moreover, the Naive Bayes method can be treated as speci£c decomposition where each subset contains a single attribute.

De£nition 1 (Complete Equivalence) *The decomposition $Z = \{G_1, ...G_k..., G_\omega\}$ is said to be completely equivalent if for each instance with positive probability ($\forall x_q \in X; P(x_q) > 0$), the following is satis£ed:*

$$\underset{v_{y,j} \in V_y}{\arg\max} \frac{\prod_{k=1}^{\omega} P(y=v_{y,j}|a_i=x_{q,i} \; i \in R_k)}{P(y=v_{y,j})^{\omega-1}} = \underset{v_{y,j} \in V_y}{\arg\max} P(y=v_{y,j}|a_i=x_{q,i} \; \forall a_i \in A)$$

Since Duda and Hart showed that the right term of the equation is optimal, it follows that a completely equivalent decomposition is optimal as well. The importance of £nding a completely equivalent decomposition is derived from the fact that in real problems with limited training sets, we can only estimate the probability and it is easier to approximate probabilities with lower dimensions.

It can be shown that the number of possible decompositions (i.e. the size of the search space) increases in a strong exponential manner as the number of input attributes grows [14], i.e. an exhaustive search is not practical for high number of input attributes.

Hereby we present three Lemmas that will shed light on the suggested problem. The proof of the following Lemmas is straightforward.

Lemma 2 (Suf£cient condition) *Let Z be a decomposition, which satis£es $G_k, k = 1, ..., \omega$ and $NR = A - \bigcup_{k=1}^{\omega} G_k$ are conditionally independent given y and that NR and y are independent, then Z is completely equivalent.*

The above Lemma represents a suf£cient condition for complete equivalence. However it is important to note that it does not represent a necessary condition, the following Lemma illustrates this statement.

Lemma 3 *Let $A = \{a_1, ..., a_l, ..., a_n\}$ be a group of n independent input binary attributes and let $Z = \{G_1, ..., G_\omega\}$ be a decomposition, then if the target attribute follows the function:*

$$y = f_1(a_i, i \in R_1) \vee f_2(a_i, i \in R_2) \vee ... \vee f_\omega(a_i, i \in R_\omega)$$

or

$$y = f_1(a_i, i \in R_1) \wedge f_2(a_i, i \in R_2) \wedge ... \wedge f_\omega(a_i, i \in R_\omega)$$

Where $f_1, ..., f_\omega$ are Boolean functions and $R_1, ..., R_\omega$ are mutually exclusive then Z is completely equivalent.

The above Lemma illustrates that although the conditionally independent requirement is not fulfilled we still find a completely equivalent decomposition.

Lemma 4 (XOR Problem) *Let* $A = \{a_1, ..., a_i, ..., a_n\}$ *be a group of* n *input binary attributes, if the target attribute behave as* $y = a_1 \oplus a_2 \oplus ... \oplus a_n$ *then there is no decomposition beside* $Z = \{A\}$ *which is completely equivalent.*

The last Lemma shows that there are problems that no completely equivalent decomposition can be found, beside the obvious one.

3. D-IFN Algorithm

Maimon and Last [13] present a *Multi-Layer Info-Fuzzy Network (IFN)* aimed at finding the minimum number of input attributes required for predicting a target attribute. Each vertical layer is uniquely associated with an input attribute by representing the interaction of that attribute and the input attributes of the previous layers. The first layer includes only the root node and is not associated with any input attribute. This structure is also known as *Oblivious Decision Trees*. The multi-layer network can also be used to predict values of target attributes in a disjunctive manner, similar to the decision tree. The principal difference between the structure of a multi-layer network and a decision-tree structure is the *constant ordering* of input attributes at every predicting node of the multi-layer network, the property which is necessary for minimizing the overall subset of input attributes (resulting in dimensionality reduction).

Figure 1 represents a typical IFN with three input attributes: glucose level, age and blood pressure of a certain patient and the Boolean target attribute representing whether that patient suffer from diabetes. The arcs that connect the terminal nodes and the nodes of the target layer are labeled with the number of records that fit this path. For instance there are twelve patients in the training set whose their glucose level is less than 107 but who still suffer from diabetes. The in-depth description of the IFN Methodology can be found in a new book by Maimon and Last (2000).

As the IFN method was found to be effective in discovering the relevant attributes and their relations to the target attribute, we further extended it aiming to approach the optimal decomposition. For our purpose each subset is represented by a different network, while each attribute in this subset is located in a different layer. Attributes in the same network should be dependent, namely independent attributes should be in different networks as the independence assumption suggests. However it does not mean that attributes in different networks are necessarily independent. In some cases assigning dependent attributes into different groups contributes to the overall prediction accuracy.

Obviously we can construct up to n networks (in the extreme case where each network may represent one input attribute) and up to n attributes in each network (in the case where we have one network that include all input attributes).

For creating the multiple networks we use a greedy depth-first algorithm, called D-IFN. The D-IFN learning algorithm starts with a single network with a single node (the root node), representing an empty subset of input attributes. In each iteration the algorithm decides which attribute should be added to the current network as a new layer, and to what nodes on the previous layer it will be connected (the splitted nodes). The nodes of a new layer are defined as all Cartesian product combinations of the splitted nodes with the values of the new input attribute, which have at least one observation associated with it.

The selection of the a new input attribute is made according the following criteria:

- The selected attribute should maximize the total significant decrease in the conditional entropy, as a result of adding it as a new layer. In order to calculate the total significant decrease in the conditional entropy, we estimate for each node in the last layer, the decrease in the conditional entropy as a result of splitting that node according the candidate attribute values. Furthermore the decrease in the conditional entropy is tested for significance by a likelihood-ratio test [2]. The null hypothesis (H_0) is that a candidate input attribute and a target attribute are conditionally independent, given the node (implying that their conditional mutual information is zero). If H_0 holds, the test statistic is distributed as χ^2 with degrees of freedom equal to the number of independent proportions estimated from the observations associated with this node. Finally all significant decreases of specific nodes are summed up to achieve the total significant decrease.

- The attribute is conditionally dependent on the splitted nodes given the target attribute. For testing the conditional independency we use a standard test [23]. The null hypothesis (H_0) is that a candidate input attribute and all splitted nodes are conditionally independent, given the target attribute.

- Adding the attribute to the current network should decrease the generalization error bound of the combined networks so far. The bound is discussed in the following section. In this case there are two purposes for using it; First of all as adding a new attribute to the current network increases its complexity. Under the Occam's-razor assumption that simplicity is a virtue in conflict with training accuracy, we verify whether the decrease in the entropy worth the addition in the complexity; Moreover we check whether the addition of the attribute to the current network, contributes to the performance of the combined networks structure as a whole.

If no input attribute was selected an attempt is made to construct a new network (a new subset) with the input attributes that were not used by previous networks. This procedure continues until there is no more unused attributes or until the last network is left empty. Figure 2 presents the main £owchart of the algorithm.

The networks constructed by D-IFN algorithm, can be used for classi£cation of unlabeled instances, by performing the following steps:

- For each network:

  - Locate the relevant node (£nal or unsplitted) that satis£es the unseen instance.

  - Extract the frequency vector (how many instances relate to each possible value of the target attribute.)

  - Transform the frequency vector to probability vector. Using the frequency as is will typically over-estimate the probability so we use the Laplace correction to avoid this phenomenon [4].

- Combine the probability vectors using Naive Bayesian combination.

- Select the target value maximizing the Naive Bayesian combination.

The complexity of the proposed algorithm can be bounded by: $O(n^2 \cdot m \cdot d_y \cdot \max(d_i))$

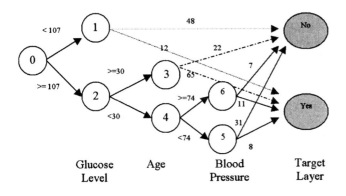

Figure 1. Illustration of IFN.

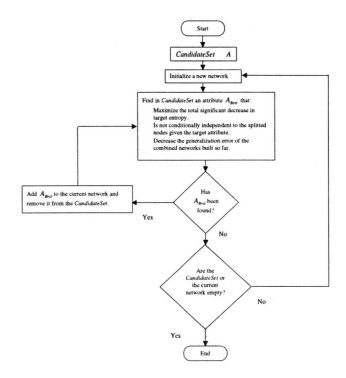

Figure 2. Flowchart of D-IFN Algorithm

4. Generalization Error Bound for D-IFN

Over-£tting and under-£tting are well known problems in learning. A conventional approach to overcome these problems is to use a generalization error bound in terms of the training error and concept size.

As stated before, a IFN can be considered as restricted decision tree, for that reason we might use one of the generalization error bound that were developed for decision trees in the literature [15]. However there are several reasons to develop a speci£c bound. First, we can utilize the fact that the considered structure is more restricted, in order to develop a tighter bound. Second we are required to extend the bound for several networks using simple Bayesian combination.

Due to the fact that we use probabilistic classi£ers (represented by real value weights on the terminal nodes), the hypothesis space is in£nite. A typical bound for in£nite hypothesis space, which makes use of VC dimension, and holds with probability at least $1 - \delta$, has the following form [21]:

$$|\varepsilon(h) - \hat{\varepsilon}(h)| \leq \sqrt{\frac{d \cdot (\ln \frac{2m}{d} + 1) - \ln \frac{\delta}{4}}{m}} \quad \begin{array}{l} \forall h \in H \\ \forall \delta > 0 \end{array}$$

Where d is the VC-Dimension of hypothesis class H, $\hat{\varepsilon}(h)$ is the error of h on training set of cardinality m.

The VC dimension for a set of indicator functions is defined as the maximum number of data points that can be shattered by the set of admissible functions. By definition, a set of m points is shattered by a concept class if there are functions in the class that split the points into two classes in all of the 2^m possible ways. The VC dimension might be difficult to compute accurately. Hereby we introduce an upper and lower bound of the VC dimension.

Theorem 5 *The VC-Dimension of ω mutually exclusive IFNs on n binary input attributes that are combined using simple Bayesian combination and that have $\vec{L} = (l_1, \ldots, l_\omega)$ layers and $\vec{T} = (t_1, \ldots, t_\omega)$ terminal nodes is not greater than:*

$$\begin{cases} F + \log U & \omega = 1 \\ 2(F+1)\log(2e) + 2\log U & \omega > 1 \end{cases}$$

and at least:

$$F - \omega + 1$$

where:

$$U = \frac{n!}{(n - \sum\limits_{i=1}^{\omega} l_i)!} \cdot \prod_{i=1}^{\omega} \frac{(2t_i - 4)!}{(t_i - 2)! \cdot (t_i - 2)!} \; ; \; F = \sum_{i=1}^{\omega} t_i$$

For proofing the theorem we first consider two Lemmas:

Lemma 6 *The VC dimension of IFN on n binary input attributes with l layers and t terminal nodes is not greater than:*

$$t + \log_2\left(\frac{n!}{(n-l)!} \cdot \frac{(2t-4)!}{(t-2)! \cdot (t-2)!}\right)$$

Proof: Any IFN can be converted to a suitable classification tree with leafs labeled $\{0,1\}$ according to the highest weight of each of the terminal node in the original network. Because the IFN and its corresponded classification tree shattered the same subsets, their VC dimensions are identical.

The hypothesis space size of an IFN with l layers, t terminal nodes and n input attributes to choose from is not greater than:

$$\frac{n!}{(n-l)!} \cdot 2^t \cdot \frac{(2t-4)!}{(t-2)! \cdot (t-2)!}$$

The first multiplier indicates the number of combinations for selecting with order l attributes from n. The second multiplier corresponds to the different classification options of the terminal nodes. The third multiplier represents the number of different binary tree structures that contains t leaves. The last multiplier is calculated using standard tree structure [22].

Based on the familiar relation $VC(H) \leq \log_2(|H|)$ for finite H, we proved the Lemma.

Lemma 7 *Consider ω mutually exclusive IFNs that are combined with simple Bayesian and that have a fixed structure containing $\vec{T} = (t_1, \ldots, t_\omega)$ terminal nodes. The number of dichotomies it induces on a set of cardinality m is at most:*

$$2\left(em \middle/ (1+F)\right)^{1+F}$$

Proof: For proving the Lemma, we use a similar Lemma introduced by Schmitt [20] for the number of dichotomies that a higher order threshold neuron with k monomials induces on a set of cardinality.

Multiple IFNs which are combined with simple Bayesian, can be converted to a higher order threshold neuron, where the set of terminal nodes constitutes the neuron's monomials and the log-odds in favor of $y = 1$ in each terminal node is the corresponded neuron's weight. Furthermore to be able to use the sign activation function we use a threshold that equals to the sum of all other monomials.

Proof of Theorem 5: We first discuss the upper bound. For a single IFN we can use Lemma 6 directly. For the multiple IFNs we first bound the number of dichotomies induced by ω mutually exclusive IFNs on an arbitrary set of cardinality m. Because the biggest shattered set follows this bound as well, we derive the statement of theorem.

There are at most:

$$U = \frac{n!}{(n - \sum\limits_{i=1}^{\omega} l_i)!} \cdot \prod_{i=1}^{\omega} \frac{(2t_i - 4)!}{(t_i - 2)! \cdot (t_i - 2)!}$$

different structures for ω mutually exclusive IFNs. Combining the last result with Lemma 7 we derive that there are at most:

$$U \cdot 2\left(\frac{em}{F+1}\right)^{F+1}$$

dichotomies on a given set of cardinality m that are induce by the class considered. If the above class shatters the given set, we must have:

$$2^m \leq U \cdot 2\left(\frac{em}{F+1}\right)^{F+1}$$

However the last inequality will not be true if we choose $m \geq 2(F+1)\log(2e) + 2\log U$. This concludes our proof.

The lower bound is true due to the fact that any set of ωtrees with fixed structure has the above VC dimension. The result can be achieved by setting in each tree (beside one) a neutralized terminal node (i.e. a terminal node with posteriori probabilities that are equal to the apriority probabilities).

Our preliminary experiments have shown that estimating the generalization error by using the lower bound of the VC Dimension provides a better performance.

5. Empirical Test

In order to validate the D-IFN algorithm and to illustrate the usefulness of the decomposition approach in classi£cation problems, we apply our method to various domains and compare the results to other methods. In this paper we decided to compare the D-IFN algorithm to the following algorithms: IFN, Naive Bayes and C4.5. We have special interest in both IFN and Naive Bayes as they represent speci£c points in the search space of the D-IFN algorithm. We also compare the D-IFN to C4.5, because its similarity to IFN (in the model structure) and due to its popularity in many other studies.

The D-IFN approach has been applied to 15 public domain dataset from the UCI Machine learning [16].

Table 1 shows the average accuracy and sample standard deviation obtained by using 10-fold-cross-validation. One tailed paired t-test with con£dence level of 95% was used in order to verify whether the differences in accuracy are statistically signi£cant. The superscript "+" or "-" indicates that the accuracy rate of D-IFN was signi£cantly higher or lower than the corresponding algorithm. The results of our experimental study are very encouraging. In fact there was no signi£cant case where Naive Bayes or IFN were more accurate than D-IFN, on the other hand D-IFN was more accurate than Naive Bayes and IFN in 8 databases. and 7 databases respectively. Furthermore D-IFN was signi£cantly more accurate than C4.5 in 8 databases, and less accurate in only 2 databases.

In order to understand when the suggested approach introduces considerable performance enhancement, we checked the correlation between error reduction and the problem complexity.

There are two obvious alternatives for measuring the error reduction achieved by using Attribute Decomposition approach: measuring the error difference between IFN and D-IFN or measuring the error ratio (i.e. the error of D-IFN divided by the error of single IFN). Following [1] we use error ration because it manifests the fact that it becomes gradually harder to achieve error reduction as the error of single IFN converge to zero.

In order to estimate the problem complexity we used the following ratio: the log of the hypothesis space size divided by the training set size.

The estimated linear correlation coef£cient (r) is 0.9. This result is quite encouraging as it evidently indicates when should we potentially use attribute decomposition.

6. Summary and Future Work

In this paper we presented a new concept of attribute decomposition for classi£cation problems and proposed the

Table 1. Summary of experimental results

Database	Naive Bayes	C4.5	IFN	D-IFN
Aust	84.93±2.7	85.36±5.1	84.49±5.1	84.49±2.9
Bcan	97.29±1.6	+92.43±3.5	+94.39±3.5	97.29±1.6
LED17	+63.18±8.7	+59.09±6.9	+55.55±6.3	73.64±5.5
LETTER	+73.29±1	+74.96±0.8	+69.56±0.7	79.07±0.9
Monks1	+73.39±6.7	+75.81±8.2	+75.00±10.7	92.74±11
Monks2	+56.21±6.1	+52.07±8.6	63.87±6.4	62.13±6.4
Monks3	93.44±3.7	93.44±3.7	92.38±3.3	92.62±3.3
MUSH	+95.48±0.9	100±0	100±0	100±0
Nurse	+65.39±24	−97.65±0.4	92.47±0.5	92.67±0.6
OPTIC	91.73±1.3	+62.42±2	+48.90±2.5	91.73±1.4
Sonar	75.48±7.3	69.71±5.4	76.48±6.8	77.12±8.7
SPI	+94.2±0.9	+91.2±1.9	+87.00±2.6	95.8±0.9
TTT	+69.27±3.2	−85.31±2.7	73.19±3.9	73.33±4
Wine	96.63±3.9	+85.96±6.9	+91.45±5	96.63±3.9
Zoo	89.11±7	93.07±5.8	90.89±9.7	92.71±7.3

D-IFN algorithm for discovering the appropriate decomposition. The algorithm has been implemented on variety of datasets, and has generated models with higher classi£cation accuracy than other comparable methods.

Finally, the issues to be further studied include: considering other search methods for the problem de£ned, examining how the attribute decomposition concept can be implemented using other classi£cation methods like Neural Networks, examining other techniques to combine the generated classi£ers, and exploring different decomposition paradigms other than attribute decomposition.

Along with performing more empirical, we hope to better understand when it will be appropriate to use attributes decomposition.

References

[1] K. M. Ali and M. J. Pazzani. Error reduction through learning multiple descriptions. *Machine Learning*, 24(3):173–202, 1996.

[2] F. Attneave. *Applications of Information Theory to Psychology*. Holt, Rinehart and Winston, New York, 1959.

[3] W. Buntine. Graphical Models for Discovering Knowledge, in U. Fayyad, G. Piatetsky-Shapiro, P. Smyth, and R. Uthurusamy, editors, *Advances in Knowledge Discovery and Data Mining*, pp 59-82. AAAI/MIT Press, 1996.

[4] P. Domingos and M. J. Pazzani. On the the optimality of the simple Bayesian classi£er under zero-one loss. *Machine Learning*, 29(2-3):103–130, 1997.

[5] R. Duda and P. Hart. *Pattern Classi£cation and Scene Analysis*, New-York, NY: Wiley, 1973.

[6] G. Dunteman. *Principal Components Analysis*, Sage Publications, 1989.

[7] J. Elder IV and D. Pregibon. A Statistical Perspective on Knowledge Discovery in Databases, in U. Fayyad, G. Piatetsky-Shapiro, P. Smyth, and R. Uthurusamy, editors, *Advances in Knowledge Discovery and Data Mining*, pp 83-113. AAAI/MIT Press, 1996.

[8] U. Fayyad, G. Piatesky-Shapiro, and P. Smyth. From Data Minig to Knowledge Discovery: An Overview, in U. Fayyad, G. Piatetsky-Shapiro, P. Smyth, and R. Uthurusamy, editors, *Advances in Knowledge Discovery and Data Mining*, pp 1-30, AAAI/MIT Press, 1996.

[9] J. Friedman and J. Tukey. A Projection Pursuit Algorithm for Exploratory Data Analysis, *IEEE Transactions on Computers*, 23 (9): 881-889, 1974.

[10] J. Kim and C. Mueller. *Factor Analysis: Statistical Methods and Practical Issues*. Sage Publications, 1978.

[11] I. Kononenko. Semi-naive bayesian classifer. *Proceedings of the Sixth European Working Session on Learning*, pages 206–219, 1991.

[12] Liu and Motoda. *Feature Selection for Knowledge Discovery and Data Mining*, Kluwer Academic Publishers, 1998.

[13] O. Maimon and M. Last. *Knowledge Discovery and Data Mining: The Info-Fuzzy network (IFN) methodology*, Kluwer Academic Publishers, 2000.

[14] O. Maimon and L. Rokach. Data Mining by Attribute Decomposition with semiconductors manufacturing case study in D. Bracha, Editor, *Data Mining for Design and Manufacturing: Methods and Applications*, Kluwer Academic Publishers, 2001.

[15] Y. Mansour and D. McAllester. Generalization Bounds for Decision Trees, *COLT 2000*: 220-224.

[16] C. Merz and P. Murphy. UCI Repository of machine learning databases. Irvine, CA: University of California, Department of Information and Computer Science, 1998.

[17] B. Pfahringer. Controlling constructive induction in CiPF, *Proceedings of the European Conference on Machine Learning*, Springer-Verlag, pp. 242-256. 1994.

[18] J. Quinlan. *C4.5: Programs for Machine Learning*, Morgan Kaufmann, 1993.

[19] G. Ridgeway, D. Madigan, T. Richardson, and J. O'Kane. Interpretable Boosted Naive Bayes Classifcation, *Proceedings of the Fourth International Conference on Knowledge Discovery and Data Mining*, pp 101-104, 1998.

[20] M. Schmitt. On the complexity of computing and learning with multiplicative neural networks, to appear in Neural Computation, 2001.

[21] V. Vapnik. *The Nature of Statistical Learning Theory*. Springer-Verlag, New York, 1995.

[22] C. Wallace. MML Inference of Predictive Trees, Graphs and Nets, *Computational Learning and Probabilitic Reasoning*, A. , Gammerman (ed), Wiley, pp 43-66, 1996.

[23] R. Walpole and R. Myers. *Probability and Statistics for Engineers and Scientists*, pp. 268-272, 1986.

[24] B. Zupan, M. Bohanec, J. Demsar, and I. Bratko. Feature transformation by function decomposition, *IEEE intelligent systems & their applications*, 13: 38-43, 1998.

FlExPat: Flexible Extraction of Sequential Patterns

Pierre-Yves ROLLAND

Laboratoire d'Informatique de Paris 6 (LIP6)
and Atelier de Modélisation et de Prévision, Université d'Aix-Marseille III,
15/19 allée Claude Forbin, 13627 Aix en Provence cedex 1, France
P_Y_Rolland@yahoo.com

Abstract

This paper addresses sequential data mining, *a sub-area of data mining where the data to be analyzed is organized in sequences. In many problem domains a natural ordering exists over data. Examples of* sequential databases *(SDBs) include: (a) collections of temporal data sequences, such as chronological series of daily stock indices or multimedia data (sound, music, video...); and (b) macromolecule banks, where aminoacid or proteic sequences are represented as strings.*

In a SDB it is often valuable to detect regularities *through one or several sequences. In particular, finding exact or approximate repetitions of segments can be utilized directly (e.g. for determining the biochemical activity of a protein region) or indirectly, e.g. for prediction in finance. To this end, we present concepts and an algorithm for automatically extracting sequential patterns from a sequential database. Such a pattern is defined as a group of significantly similar segments from one or several sequences. Appropriate functions for measuring similarity between sequence segments are proposed, generalizing the edit distance framework. There is a trade off here between flexibility, particularly in sequence data representation and in associated similarity metrics, and computational efficiency. We designed the FlExPat algorithm to satisfactorily cope with this trade-off. FlExPat's complexity is in practice lesser than quadratic in the total length of the SDB analyzed, while allowing high flexibility. Some experimental results obtained with FlExPat on music data are presented and commented.*

1 Introduction and Motivation

This paper addresses the sub-area of data mining where data is organized in sequences. In this case, there is a natural ordering (often time) over data, and a database — called *sequential database* — is made of one or several *sequences*. A sequence is an ordered collection of individual data structures (possibly mere numbers or strings) called the sequence's *elements*. There are many areas in which data presents itself in the form of sequences, including: (a) temporal data, for instance in multimedia (sound, speech, music, video, etc.), finance or telecom-munications [4]; and (b) molecular biology and genomics/genetics.

1.1 Mining Sequence Data

We are concerned with the automated extraction of *sequential patterns* [1], which roughly corresponds to the intuitive notions of regularity and recurrence in sequences. Although precise definitions will be given later on, we can for the moment give the following informal definition. A *sequential pattern* is a set of segments from the sequential database which share a significant degree of resemblance: for pairs of segments in the pattern, the similarity between the two segments can be measured numerically and is above a given threshold. Each segment is called an *occurrence* of the pattern. A pattern is characterized *extensionaly* by a list of segments as was just introduced. It can also be characterized *intensionaly* by a *prototype*: a structure that is representative of the set of segments it 'summarizes'. We will focus here on the case where prototypes are sequential structures of the same form as the pattern's segments. In many application contexts, the prototype is in fact one of these segments.

1.2 Applications

The extraction of regularities in sequences is a very general problem appearing in diverse application contexts, often with great scientific or economic stake. In molecular biology and genomics/genetics, regularities are sought in sets of macromolecular sequences, either nucleic acids or proteic/peptidic chains. In particular, finding similar regions in several different such sequences yields important information on the latters' common biochemical activities or tri-dimensional structures. In finance, extracted regularities can be used to predict the evolution of time-ordered sequences (time series) such as interest rates or stock prices. Applications of sequential pattern extraction to music data [3] will be given particular emphasis in this paper. Musical pattern mining, and more specifically the extraction of melodic or harmonic (sequential) patterns in given sets of composed or improvised works has many different applications. These range from musical analysis to music generating systems [6] to the more recent applications in content-based music information retrieval [8]. In music analysis, understanding and characterizing style is the core motivation of *melodic pattern-based analysis*, where the uncovering of recurring structures and of their organization in works offers a way to gain insights into the style or techniques of composers and improvisers. For instance, in a very large study [5] musicologist T. Owens characterized the techniques and style of Charlie Parker through the nature and organization of recurrent melodic patterns ('formulae') in the jazz saxophone player's improvised playing. He extracted a hierarchically classified lexicon of 193 such formulae from a corpus of about 250 Parker solos (examples appear in Figure 9). Many studies such as Owens' have been carried out on corpuses of both improvised music, e.g. Davis, Coltrane, and composed music, e.g. Debussy. These studies often take years for a human analist to carry out, as s/he must deal manually with the large combinatorics (see next section) inherent to the sequential pattern extraction process. Hence, in melodic pattern-oriented music analysis, just like for other sequential pattern extraction (SPE) contexts, there is a strong motivation in seeking to automate the process.

1.3 Motivation and Underlying Features of the FlExPat Approach

SPE is an inherently combinatorial problem ; in fact, the notion of sequential pattern as we define it relies on the measurement of similarity between sequence segments. Not only is there a combinatorial set of possible segment pairs (for instance, the number of possible pairs of segments from a L-element sequence and a L'-element sequence is of order $L^2 \times L'^2$). But, further, measuring the similarity between two sequence segments is itself a combinatorial problem as soon as flexible matching schemes, such as the edit distance, are used.

1.3.1 Data and Knowledge Representation.
In most situations there are several possible ways to represent sequences and their elements. Additionally, many application domains are knowledge-intensive, meaning that artificial systems must possess vast amounts of domain-specific knowledge to achieve satisfactory performance. Music is among these domains [13], which we have found out to imply that representing music for SPE (typically: melodic sequences of notes and rests) should not be limited to usual basic descriptions such as absolute pitch (e.g. "D# 4") and relative duration (e.g. "eight-note"). Based on music theory and music psychology works at large, and on empirical experimentation, we have proposed an effective and flexible framework for representing musical sequences based on multiple simultaneous descriptions. These descriptions are organized according to their level of abstraction, as illustrated in Figure 1. We have designed and implemented algorithms for incrementally computing all chosen descriptions based on the initial, basic representation of notes and rests. Part of the concepts in this general framework (see e.g. [7]) apply directly to domains other than music.

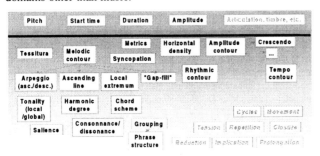

Figure 1. Some musical descriptions, from more abstract (bottom) to more concrete (top)

1.3.2 Similarity Measurement.
The very principle of sequential pattern extraction implies that similarity measurement plays a critical role in the process. The computational schemes for measuring the similarity between candidate pairs of segments have a major influence on SPE algorithms. In fact, as will be seen there is a trade-off between computational efficiency and the richness of the similarity notion captured by the system — which is intrinsically related to the computational schemes for similarity measurement. Among the simplest of these schemes are boolean ones: the segments compared are determined either identical ('True') or different ('False'). With such

a notion of similarity, very efficient SPE algorithms (with linear complexity) have been proposed based on specialized data structures such as suffix trees/arrays (see e.g. [12]). However it has been widely recognized that such algorithms, which find *exactly* repeating segments, are completely inappropriate for many application contexts. In these contexts, e.g. music, repetitions are hardly ever exact, because of, e.g., mutation and evolution in molecular biology, or variation and ornamentation in music.At the other end of the spectrum, very rich models of sequential similarity have been designed based on generalizations of the edit distance [2][9] framework. The important idea is that, to measure the similarity between two segments, one should find the best *correspondence structure* between them, i.e. between their elements. Among these models is the multi-description valued edit model (<u>MVEM</u>) we have designed. Only the main features of MVEM will briefly be presented in this paper. In MVEM the edit distance has been reformulated in the more flexible *pairings* paradigm. An *alignment* between segments s and s' is a series of pairings corresponding to one possible correspondence structure between s and s' (see example in Figure 2). A pairing π materializes the putting in correspondence between a small group of consecutive elements of S with a small group of consecutive elements of S'. One or both groups may be empty (denoted by "λ"). There are different types of pairings; for instance, the alignment in Figure 2 is a series of *replacement, insertion*, replacement, *deletion, fragmentation, multideletion*, and *generalized substitution*. MVEM's main parameter is the *allowed pairing type set* <u>APTS</u>. In classic edit distance, the set of pairing types allowed is $\underline{APTS_{standard}}$={Replacement, Insertion, Deletion}. Choosing an appropriate APTS depends on the application context. For instance, using all of the above types, the very frequent phenomena of variation and ornamentation in music can be neatly dealt with.

$$\binom{s[1]}{t[1]}, \binom{\lambda}{t[2]}, \binom{s[2]}{t[3]}, \binom{s[3]}{\lambda}, \binom{s[4]}{t[4]t[5]}, \binom{s[5]s[6]}{\lambda}, \binom{s[7]s[8]s[9]}{t[6]t[7]}$$

Figure 2. An example alignment between segments s and t. Top: trace diagram; Bottom: corresponding list of pairings

The V ("valued") in "MVEM" means that a numerical *contribution* Contrib(π) is associated to each pairing π. A contribution function Contrib — which correspond to a cost function in the edit distance framework — allows to quantify the contribution of each pairing to the similarity (positive contribution) or dissimilarity (negative contribution) between the two segments compared. The value of an alignment A is computed as in Équation 1 (left), and the similarity between two segments is defined as being the greatest value of all possible alignments between the two segments. The initial M ("multi-description") means that MVEM has been designed to be able to deal with representations of sequences and elements that use multiple simultaneous descriptions. In fact, in MVEM contribution functions are weighted sums of terms each relating to a single description, see Équation 1 (right). The user or calling program can adjust the weight attributed to each description, allowing them in particular to take different *viewpoints* over the data. For instance, on musical data, by giving greater weights to temporal descriptions — durations, metrics, etc.— than to frequential descriptions — pitches, intervals, etc.—, rhythmic patterns, rather than melodic patterns, will be extracted.

$$Value(A) = \sum_{p \in A} contrib(p) \qquad contrib(p) = \sum_{D \in R} w_D \times contrib_D(p)$$

Équation 1

1.3.3 Discussion. To close this section: our motivation in designing of FlExPat has been to satisfactorily cope with the trade-off between computational efficiency and flexibility. As will be seen, the flexibility offered by FlExPat lies particularly in the fact that it uses an extremely rich and flexible similarity model, MVEM. And this model is itself based on a rich and flexible data/knowledge representation framework allowing multiple simultaneous descriptions for (elements of) sequences.

2 Formalization

2.1 Sequences and Segments

In the area of string algorithms design (also called stringology), sequences' elements are symbols belonging to a domain (i.e. set of possible values) called an alphabet. The notion of alphabet is extended here to the case of non-symbol elements. In the simpler cases, the alphabet contains tuplets of scalar values, for instance the set of all possible couples (Φ, Ψ) of dihedral angle values for peptidic chains. In more advanced cases, the alphabet contains complex structures such as (software) objects.

Definition 1. A **sequence** S is an ordered collection of individual data structures $S[i]$ called the sequence's **elements**: $S = S[1]S[2] \ldots S[L]$. L is the sequence's **length**, also noted $|S|$. A sequence is constructed over an **alphabet** Σ, the set of all possible elements. A **sequential database** is a set of sequences over the same alphabet.

Definition 2. A sequence **segment** is a contiguous part of a sequence: $S[i]S[i+1]\ldots S[i+m-1]$ is the segment of S with length m and starting at **position** i. (In stringology segments are often called 'factors', ambiguously, 'subsequences')

2.2 Similarity and Equipollence

Definition 3. Given an alphabet Σ, a **similarity function over** Σ^* is a function $(\Sigma^* \times \Sigma^*) \to \mathbf{R}$, where $\underline{\Sigma^*}$ denotes the set of all possible sequences over Σ. A **normalized** similarity function has values in [0;1].

Given a sequential database **SDB** over alphabet Σ, a similarity function *Simil* over Σ^* can thus be used to measure the similarity between any two segments s_1 and s_2 of any two sequences of SDB: $Simil(s_1, s_2)$.

Definition 4. Two sequence segments s_1 and s_2 are said to be **equipollent** iff their similarity is greater or equal to a given threshold. An **equipollence function over** Σ^* is a boolean function *Equip* over $(\Sigma^* \times \Sigma^*)$ defined trivially by: "For any segment pair s_1, s_2, $Equip(s_1, s_2)$=True iff s_1 and s_2 are equipollent"

The term 'equipollent' is used rather than 'equivalence', to avoid implying that we are dealing with equivalence relations here. In fact, the definition of an equivalence relation implies a number of properties, such as transitivity. In practice, similarity models that appropriately mimic human similarity assessment often do not possess these properties (see e.g. [11]).

2.3 Sequential Patterns

Definition 5. A sequential pattern P is defined **extensionaly** as a constrained set of sequence segments from the sequential database, called the pattern's **occurrences**. This set is named the pattern's **extension** and is noted $\underline{Ext(P)}$. The constraint takes the form of the imposed equipollence between pairs of segments of the set. Depending on the particular type of sequential pattern under consideration, the equipollence constraint may apply to all segment pairs or only to some of them. For instance, for a *star-type* pattern (see Definition 8) one of the segments must be equipollent to all the others. *Note:* Sequential patterns will often be simply called « pattern » when there is no ambiguity

Definition 6. A **prototype** is the **intensional** characterization of a pattern. It is a sequence, noted $\underline{Proto(P)}$, over the same alphabet. For simplicity it will be assumed in this paper that a pattern can only have one prototype.

Definition 7. Let P be a sequential pattern from sequential database *SDB*. The **quorum** of P is the number of different sequences of *SDB* that contain occurrences of P.

Definition 8. A **star-type pattern** is a sequential pattern P whose extension $Ext(P) = \{s_1, s_2 \ldots, s_p\}$ possesses both of the following properties:

♦ $Ext(P)$ contains P's prototype, i.e. $\exists i, s_i = Proto(P)$.
♦ Every other occurrence of P is equipollent to the prototype, i.e.: $\forall j \in \{1, ..., p\}, j \neq i, Equip(s_i, s_j)$=True.

In Figure 3, the sequential database is made of sequences Seq_1 through Seq_6. Star-type pattern P has 5 occurrences (its quorum is 4): one occurrence s_0 in Seq_2, which is P's prototype; one occurrence in Seq_1; two in Seq_2; and one in Seq_5. Arrows denote equipollence links. Star-type patterns are among pertinent pattern types that can be defined, inspired by molecular biology work.

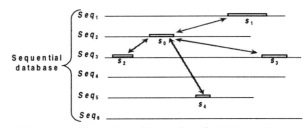

Figure 3. An illustration of the notion of star-type pattern

2.4 Sequential Pattern Extraction

Definition 9. Given a sequential database over an alphabet Σ, a similarity function over Σ^* and an equipollence threshold, **sequential pattern extraction** or **SPE** consists of finding <u>all</u>

sequential patterns that exist in the database. Every extracted pattern is characterized extentionaly, intensionaly, or both.

Additional constraints over the patterns to be extracted may be imposed. Basic examples are a minimum and/or maximum pattern cardinalities, or minimum and maximum lengths of segments in any pattern. Another example is a *quorum threshold*, which imposes a minimum value for the number of different sequences in the databases in which the pattern has occurrences. In the case of additional constraints, only a part of all possible sequential patterns are extracted from the database.

3 FlExPat Overview

3.1 I/O and Parameters

FlExPat's **input** is a sequential database SDB. FlExPat's main **parameters**, which are set by the user or by the calling program, are:

♦ The similarity threshold defining equipollence
♦ All the parameters of the MVEM-based similarity function.
♦ Other parameters, either numbers or functions, each of which allows to enforce an optional constraint. These parameters include:
  1. The minimum and maximum possible length for candidate segments (i.e. potential pattern occurrences)
  2. The maximum possible length difference between segments to be compared
  3. The maximum length of overlap between two candidate segments
  4. A quorum threshold (see Definition 7)

Each of the constraints in categories 1, 2 and 3 above filters out either a part of the candidate segments or a part of the candidate segment pairs. This induces a reduction in computation time and/or memory. A candidate segment is a segment from one of the database's sequences that can potentially be an occurrence of one or several extracted pattern(s). A candidate segment pair is a pair of segments (s,s') that can potentially become a pair of equipollent occurrences in one or several extracted pattern(s). The similarity between s and s' should thus be computed, in order to then *equipollence-test* the pair, i.e. determine if *Simil(s,s')* is greater or equal to the similarity threshold. The constraint of category 1 leads to the filtering out of candidate segments, while those of categories 2 and 3 eliminate candidate segment pairs. Finally, constraint 4 leads to the filtering out of part of the patterns extracted.

In practice, it is very useful, if not indispensable, to impose constraints of categories 1, 2 and 3. For instance, too short patterns (i.e., patterns with too short occurrences) and too long patterns are seldom meaningful. In the music application domain, whether one deals with composed music (such as baroque or classical) or impovised music (such as bebop jazz), one could propose 3 and 30, respectively, as reasonable values for minimum and maximum lengths. By definition (see 2.4), and as a function of possible constraints set by the user or by the calling program over the patterns looked for, FlExPat's **output** is the set of

♦ all sequential patterns that exist in *SDB*, or only those satisfying the constraints,
♦ each characterized extentionaly, intensionaly, or both.

3.2 A Two-Phase Algorithm

FlExPat is structured in two main algorithmic phases (see Figure 4):

I) The *equipollence graph construction* phase identifies in a computationally-economic fashion all equipollent segment couples. An intermediate structure, which we name *equipollence graph*, is incrementally produced in which:
♦ Every vertex corresponds to (i.e. points to) a distinct sequence segment of one of the database's sequences
♦ Every edge denotes an equipollence relation between two segments. In other words, assuming v corresponds to segment s and v' corresponds to segment s', there is an edge (v,v') iff s and s' are equipollent.

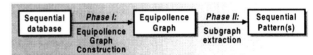

Figure 4. FlExPat's overall algorithmic scheme

Note that the equipollence graph *EG* is connex, so every vertex is connected to at least one other vertex. In other words, a segment s has a corresponding vertice in *EG* only if s is equipollent to at least one other segment. *EG* is undirected, provided *Simil* is a symmetric function (which in turn induces the symmetry of the equipollence relation). *EG* is normally weighted, as depicted in Figure 5: every edge (v,v'), corresponding to segment pair (s, s'), is labeled with *Simil(s,s')*. That value is computed online.

II) The *subgraph extraction* phase extracts the actual patterns from the equipollence graph. As a function of the type of sequential patterns requested by the user (or application) appropriate subgraphs are extracted, and in each such subgraph the set of vertices points to a corresponding set of segments which in turn is interpreted as the extension of a pattern. Connex subgraphs, for instance star-shaped ones such as the one in Figure 5, appear to make more sense, although FlExPat does not impose any obligation with that respect. In the case of star-type patterns, an efficient subgraph extraction algorithm will be presented in the next section which not only yields extension of every pattern but also its prototype. In the general case, when the user (or application) requires a prototype for every extracted pattern, the prototype has to be computed in a postprocessing phase after the subgraph extraction phase itself.

4 FlExPat in Greater Detail

For the sake of clarity it will be assumed in this section that the sequential database, i.e. FlExPat's input, has in fact only **one** sequence, over an alphabet Σ. We also will assume that the set of allowed pairing types is APTS$_{standard}$={Replacement, Insertion, Deletion}. Generalizations to the cases of several sequences and to different pairing type sets will be made in 4.4.

4.1 Parameters (Mandatory or Optional)

♦ A similarity threshold *ST* defining equipollence between segments. Typical appropriate thresholds when using a normalized similarity function are 0.75 or 0.8.

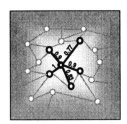

Figure 5. Example star-type pattern _P_ extracted from the Equipollence graph. The central vertex points to _P_'s prototype, peripheral vertices point to _P_'s other occurrences

♦ All the parameters of the MVEM-based similarity function **_Simil_** over Σ^*.

♦ Integers $m_{min} \in \{1;...;|S|\}$ and $m_{max} \in \{m_{min};..;|S|\}$ controlling the minimum (resp. maximum) length of pattern segments (i.e. occurrences). These parameters can be neutralized by setting $m_{min}=1$ and $m_{max}=|S|$.

♦ A boolean function over $\Sigma^* \times \Sigma^*$, **_ExcessLengthDiff_**, that prevents two segments to be equipollence-tested when their length difference is too great. In fact _ExcessLengthDiff_ is defined using an integer function over **N**, **_MaxLengthDiff_**

$S[[i',m']]$ will be equipollence-tested with $S[[i,m]]$ only if

$$|m'-m| < \text{MaxLengthDiff}(m)$$

It is generally appropriate to define _MaxLengthDiff_ an increasing function of m, for instance:

$$MaxLenghDiff(m) = \left\lfloor \frac{m}{3} \right\rfloor$$

In that case, a segment of length 10 may only be equipollence-tested to segments whose length is comprised between 7 and 13. The action of _ExcessLengthDiff_ can be canceled by setting $MaxLengthDiff \equiv \infty$.

♦ A boolean function over $\Sigma^* \times \Sigma^*$, **_ExcessOverlap_**, that prevents two segments to be equipollence-tested when they overlap too much. ExcessOverap is defined using an integer function over **N**, **_MaxOverlap_**, similar to _MaxLengthDiff_ In fact, two segments are all the more likely to be similar as they strongly overlap, but equipollence links between such strongly overlapping segments are hardly ever of any practical interest in SPE. The action of _ExcessOverlap_ can nevertheless be canceled by setting $MaxOverlap \equiv \infty$.

4.2 Equipollence Graph Construction

4.2.1 Traversal of Segment Pair Space. The equipollence graph is initially empty. The space of all legal segment pairs is traversed in a specific order, viz. increasing segment positions combined with increasing segment lengths, as explained below. A segment pair (s,s') is said to be _legal_ when neither s nor s' nor the pair itself are _de facto_ filtered out by optional constraints imposed by the user or by the calling program. For each legal pair of segments (s,s'), the similarity between s and s' is computed and compared to the threshold _ST_. **If _Simil_(s,s') is greater or equal to _ST_ then:**
1) If no vertex corresponding to _s_ yet exists in the equipollence graph then it is created. Same for _s'_.
2) **an edge is created** between the vertices corresponding to _s_

and _s'_ in the equipollence graph. It is labeled with the value _Simil(s,s')_.

Any segment of S is uniquely identified by its **(position, length)** couple. We denote by <u>_S[[i,m]]_</u> the segment of _S_ starting at position _i_ and with length _m_. The list of segments that will be processed is given in Figure 6, in processing order. _Processing_ segment S[[i,m]] means comparing it with a specific list of segments in a specific order. _Comparing_ two segments means here: computing their similarity and then testing their equipollence. The segments S[[i',m']] that will be compared to S[[i,m]] verify the following property:

$$(i',m')<(i,m),$$

which means ("$\leq$" denotes lexicographic ordering):

$$\{i'<i\} \text{ or } \{i'=i \text{ and } m'<m\}$$

$S[[1,m_{min}]], S[[1,m_{min}+1]],...,S[[1,m_{max}]],$

$S[[2,m_{min}]],...,S[[2,m_{max}]],$

...

$S[[|S|-m_{max}+1,m_{min}]],...,S[[|S|-m_{max}+1,m_{max}]].$

Figure 6. Ordered list of segments _S[[i,m]]_ to be processed

Remark that this guarantees, among others, that no two segments may be compared more than once. For clarity let us initially not take into account the optionnal _ExcessLengthDiff_ and _ExcessOverlap_ constraints. In that case the list of segments S[[i',m']] given in Figure 7 get compared to S[[i,m]], in order. Taking into account _ExcessLengthDiff_ and _ExcessOverlap_ constraints leads to a smaller list of target segments.

$S[[1,m_{min}]], S[[1,m_{min}+1]], ... S[[1,m_{max}]],$

...

$S[[i-1,m_{min}]], ... , S[[i-1,m_{max}]],$

$S[[i, m_{min}]],... , S[[i,m-1]]$

Figure 7. Ordered list of segments to compare to _S[[i,m]]_

4.2.2 Similarity Computation. Computing each similarity $Simil(S[[i,m]], S[[i',m']])$ normally takes time proportional to $m.m'$ (see e.g. [10]). Instead, we propose a different approach allowing to compute each similarity $Simil(S[[i,m]], S[[i',m']])$ in <u>constant time</u>. This yields a strong reduction in the sequential pattern extraction process's overall computation time. Unfortunately space limitations imposed to this paper prevent the following lemmas' complete proofs to be given. These proofs are partly based on classic results in stringology (see e.g. [10]).

Lemma 1 For any segments s=S[[i,m]] and s'= S[[i',m']], _Simil_(s,s') can be computed in constant time if the similarities $Simil(S[[i,m-1]], S[[i',m'-1]])$, $Simil(S[[i,m-1]], S[[i',m']])$ and $Simil(S[[i,m]], S[[i',m'-1]])$ are already known. ("Constant time" means: independent from s and s'.)
Proof: the proof follows directly from the classical recurrence relation of Équation 2. □

Lemma 2 In the traversal of segment pair space as specified in 4.2.1, for each legal segment pair (s,s') the computation of _Simil_(s,s') takes constant time.

Lemma 3 The processing of all legal segment pairs (i.e., similarity computation then equipollence testing) can be carried out in time $O(m_{max}^2.|S|^2)$.

485

$$Simil(S[[i,m]],S[[i',m']]) = \max \left\{ \begin{array}{l} contrib \left(\begin{array}{l} S[i+m-1] \\ S[i'+m'-1] \end{array} \right) + Simil(S[[i,m-1]],S[[i',m'-1]]) \\ contrib \left(\begin{array}{l} S[i+m-1] \\ \lambda \end{array} \right) + Simil(S[[i,m-1]],S[[i',m']]) \\ contrib \left(\begin{array}{l} \lambda \\ S[i'+m'-1] \end{array} \right) + Simil(S[[i,m]],S[[i',m'-1]]) \end{array} \right.$$

Équation 2

Proof: Basing on Lemma 2, to prove Lemma 3 all we need is prove that the number NSP of segment pairs to be processed (similarity computation + equipollence-test) is upper bounded by $m_{max}^2.|S|^2$. By examining the segment lists in Figure 6 and Figure 7 we have for NSP the expression in Équation 3, obviously loosely upper bounded by $m_{max}^2.|S|^2$. □

$$NSP = \frac{1}{2}(|S| - m_{max} + 1)$$
$$\times \left[(m_{max} - m_{min})(m_{max} - m_{min} + 1)(|S| - m_{max}) + m_{max}(m_{max} - 1) - m_{min}(m_{min} - 1) \right]$$

Équation 3

4.2.3 Initialization and Preprocessing. As was seen, equipollence tests only need to be performed on legal segment pairs after computing their similarity. Additional similarity computations, without equipollence tests, need to be carried out on a number of illegal segment pairs. In fact, due to Équation 2 situations occur when the computation of the similarity of a legal segment pair requires knowing the similarity values of one or more illegal segment pairs. These illegal segment pairs include in particular pairs whose segments' lengths are lesser than m_{min}, due to border cases. Another possible source of illegal segments pairs needing to be similarity-assessed is overlap constraints. These computations are performed in a preprocessing phase, just before the main equipollence graph construction phase. Dealing with border cases encountered during preprocessing in turn demands that pairs of segments $(S[[i,m]], S[[i',m']])$ where m'=0 should also be similarity-assessed. These are in fact similarities $(S[[i,m]], \lambda)$ between a segment $S[[i,m]]$ and the empty segment λ. All these computations are carried out in an initialization phase.

Theorem 1: The equipollence graph can be constructed in time $O(m_{max}^2.|S|^2)$. This construction includes initialization, preprocessing and actual equipollence graph construction phases.

Proof: compared to the conditions of Lemma 3, including initialization and preprocessing is equivalent — running time wise — to setting $m_{min}=0$ in Équation 3. Clearly, NSP is still upper-bounded by $O(m_{max}^2.|S|^2)$, hence the proof. □

4.3 Subgraph Extraction

4.3.1 Introduction. The algorithm for the subgraph extraction phase directly depends on the characteristics of subgraphs to be extracted, e.g. star-shaped subgraphs. These characteristics in turn directly correspond to the type of patterns sought. An algorithm will now be presented for extracting star-subgraphs, as in Figure 5, from the equipollence graph. This algorithm, called StarEx, is far simpler than the algorithms proposed above for equipollence graph construction. Correlatively, as will be seen its time complexity is also significantly smaller. Some preliminary notions need to be formalized: The equipollence graph output from FlExPat's first phase is denoted $EG=(V,E)$ where V is EG's set of vertices and E its set of edges.

Definition 10. A **star-subgraph** is a subgraph SG of EG that:

♦ comprises p vertices $v_1, v_2, ... v_p$ and $p-1$ edges (p being an integer, not necessarily equal to 6 as in Figure 5), and:

♦ there exists $c \in \{1,2,...,p\}$ such that v_c is the **central vertex** of SG, i.e. there is an edge between v_c and v_i for all $i \in \{1,2,...,p\}-\{c\}$

Definition 11. Let v be a vertex of EG. The **total neighbor similarity** of v, denoted *TotalNeighborSimil (v)*, is the sum of the weights of all edges adjacent to v

Let v be a vertex of EG. The **average neighbor similarity** of v, denoted *AvgNeighborSimil (v)*, is the average weight of all edges adjacent to v.

4.3.2 Basic Star-Subgraph Extraction Algorithm. This algorithm, shown in Figure 8, extracts all star-subgraphs SSG such that $Simil(SSG)$ is greater or equal to a threshold.

Algorithm ***BasicStarEx(EG, T)***

Input: equipollence graph EG, numerical threshold T
Output: an ordered list L of star-subgraphs.

Step 0. Create empty star-subgraph list L.
Step 1 (Edge set Traversal). For each v in EG:
    Step 1.1 Compute TotalNeighborSimil(v)
    Step 1.2 If TotalNeighborSimil(v) ⃞ T then add to list L the largest star subgraph whose central vertex is v.
Step 2 (Ordering output). Order list L according to decreasing TotalNeighborSimil values of central vertices. Return L.

Figure 8. Algorithm BasicStarEx

4.3.3 Variants. Several variants of BasicStarEx can usefully be used. Only one, named StarEx-Avg, will be presented. It consists of replacing function *TotalNeighborSimil* by the **average** neighbor similarity. BasicStarEx privileges star-subgraphs of high order (number of vertices) while StarEx-Avg privileges star-subgraphs — even small ones — having a *high average similarity*. Hence, BasicStarEx often identifies short music patterns that are not very characteristic of the composer or improviser in question but are used very extensively by him/her. Conversely, Variant 2 extracts *themes*, which are much longer passages appearing only a few times in a work (with some variation at each repetition).

4.4 Extensions and Generalizations

4.4.1 Database Contains Several Sequences. Moving from a database one sequence to N induces in fact only minor changes to the algorithms presented above. Equipollence graph construction starts with the *concatenation* of $S_1, S_2...S_N$ into a *global sequence S*. The algorithm proceeds on S with the main exception that all segments of S that are spread over the boundary between two sequences are illegal and are thus (easily) removed from the lists of Figure 6 and Figure 7. In subgraph extraction no change occurs.

4.4.2 The Set of Allowed Pairing Types is Different. If the user or calling program decides to use a different *APTS*, the (still constant) number of operations carried out upon the processing of a legal segment pair changes, but not the number of legal segment pairs.

4.5 Complexity

4.5.1 Time. Given Lemma 2, Theorem 1 and 4.4, even in the more general cases equipollence graph construction takes at most time $O(m_{max}^2 \cdot |S|^2)$. The running time of BasicStarEx or any of its proposed variants can be upper-bounded by $O(Size(EG))$, because every edge (v,v') in EG appears exactly twice in the algorithm: once when computing $TotalNeighborSimil(v)$ and once when computing $TotalNeighborSimil(v')$. $Size(EG)$ is trivially upper-bounded by the number of all pairs of segments from S with length between m_{min} and m_{max}. This number is clearly upper-bounded by $O(m_{max}^2 \cdot |S|^2)$. As a total, **FlExPat's time complexity is (loosely) upper-bounded by $O(m_{max}^2 \cdot |S|^2)$.**

4.5.2 Space. The main two terms here are :
- The memory for storing computed similarity values to be used later during equipollence graph construction.
- The memory for storing EG until patterns (subgraphs) are finally extracted, which is upper bounded by $O(m_{max}^2 \cdot |S|^2)$: $O(m_{max}^2 \cdot |S|^2)$) for edges, $O(m_{max}^2 \cdot |S|^2)$ for vertices (see 4.5.1).

We designed techniques allowing that, at any moment, only m_{max}^2 similarity values at most need to be kept in memory. Consequently, similarities storage is a negligible term w.r.t. EG storage. Similarly, pairing contributions are cached to avoid their repeated computation, but this uses negligible memory compared to EG storage. As a total, **FlExPat's space complexity is (loosely) upper-bounded by $O(m_{max}^2 \cdot |S|^2)$.**

4.5.3 Concluding Remarks. *In practice*, as previously mentioned m_{max} is very small compared to $|S|$; thus **both complexity bounds can legitimately be rewritten as $O(|S|^2)$.** Further, as confirmed experimentally (see section 5 and particularly Tableau 1) the order and size of EG are drastically smaller than the theoretical maximum values used above, so actual time and space complexities are much smaller.

5 Experimental Results and Discussion

FlExPat was implemented and validated in our music data manipulation system Imprology. Material from the aforementioned study [5] was used: a corpus of transcribed Parker solos and Owens' lexicon of extracted formulae. Note that in our formalization, what the lexicon contains is pattern **prototypes**. We converted about 150 solos into a substantial music sequence database *MSDB*: about 60,000 notes (or rests).

5.1 Example Results Obtained

To mimic Owens' analysis method, SPE was carried out on specific sub-corpuses according to key and harmonic structure. We will focus on one such sub-database: $MSDB_1$ corresponds to 10 Parker solos in the 'C major - Blues' category: 3 *takes* on "Cool Blues",(S_1, S_2, S_3), 3 takes on "Relaxin' at Camarillo" (S_4, S_5, S_6) and 4 takes on "Perhaps" (S_7, S_8, S_9, S_{10}). Each take is a different recording, i.e. a different improvisation, of the same tune — e.g. Cool Blues — during the same studio session. $|MSDB_1|$ is about 2,000 (precisely: 1,967). All solos (except one) comprise between 25 and 40 bars and between 130 and 250 notes. A typical multi-description representation of music,

which will not be detailed here, is used. FlExPat main parameter values are:
- $m_{min}=3$; $m_{max}=27$;
- Equipollence threshold: **0.7** (normalized similarity values);
- $MaxLenghDiff(m) = \left\lfloor \dfrac{m}{3} \right\rfloor$
- Main parameter of MVEM: $APTS=APTS_{standard}$ (contribution functions and weights will not be detailed)

A summary of numerical results is given in the following table. The maximum possible quorum, 10, is reached by 58 patterns. These have at most length 4 and at most 21 occurrences.

EG order	EG size	Largest star	Longuest prototype
11,734 vertices	39,228 edges	35 segments (prototype + 34 occurrences)	$\|Proto(P)\|=27$

FlExPat satisfactorily 're-discovered' from $MSDB_1$ several patterns of Owens' lexicon, Figure 9 shows three such examples. Figure 10 (a) shows the prototype of another pattern extracted from $MSDB_1$ by FlExPat: P_1 is the best length-26 pattern, i.e. with the greatest TotalNeighborSimil (quorum=3). Using the usual <bar No.>:<beat No.> notation, Proto(P) is the [19:3-23:1[segment of S_6 sequence (solo). Also shown are 2 of its 3 occurrences: *(b)* 1st occurrence of P_1: [7:4-11:1[segment of S_6; and *(c)* 2nd occurrence of P_1: [32:1.75-35:1[segment of S_9. Respective similarity values with $Proto(P_1)$ are 0.93 and 0.76. P_1 clearly makes musical sense, and illustrates the way FlExPat neatly succeeds in dealing with non-trivial variation/ornamentation. Further, P_1 was effectively **'discovered'** by the system as it was not signaled by Owens.

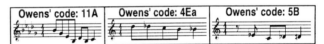

Figure 9. Examples of motives from Owens' lexicon 'rediscovered' by FlExPat

5.2 General Results

Overall, the validation of the FlExPat approach on Owens' material is successful. Additionally, using FlExPat on different music databases has yielded a number of musicological findings, including new Parker formulae or characterizations of the influence of music representation on patterns extracted.

Figure 10. Prototype & 2 occurrences of pattern P_1

5.2.1 Statistical summaries. Following are some typical statistical summaries of results obtained on music data with varying database lengths. FlExPat main parameter values are those of 5.1. Tableau 1 concerns the EGC phase. Showing running times of the EGC phase would not be significant. In fact, Imprology is written in an interpreted object-oriented language (Smalltalk-80). To directly reuse Imprology's rich features (complete music representation- and automated redescription platform, graphical music editors...) FlExPat has also been implemented in Smalltalk. The fact that Smalltalk is interpreted enormously increases EGC running times, which may for instance be as long as several minutes for |S|=1000. Algorithm re-implementation in a compiled language has been started. Tableau 2 concerns the Subgraph Extraction Phase. Durations were measured using an Intel Pentium III 733 MHz processor and 256 MB RAM.

Total sequential database length $|S|$	50	500	5000
order(EG)	27	2,194	73,454
size(EG)	53	4,212	247,133

Tableau 1. Experimental measurements for EGC phase...

Total sequential database length $|S|$	50	500	5000
Basic StarEx's running time (seconds)	4.10^{-4}	3.10^{-3}	0.1
Largest star size (total occurrences number)	3 segments	10 segments	98 segments
Final number of star-type patterns extracted	2	23	245

Tableau 2. ...and for subgraph extraction phase

5.2.2 **Other Findings.** The star-subgraph approach offers several advantages. First, It naturally and directly yields a prototype for every pattern: the prototype plays an explicit role in the extraction of a pattern, as opposed to approaches where prototypes are computed 'offline', involving additional computing, after extracting pattern extensions. Second, a quantitative strength / prominence evaluation, TotalNeighborSimil, is obtained for every pattern, again without any additional computation. Finally, Its complexity (see 4.5.1) is satisfactory in theory and even more in practice, compared to other naturally appropriate approaches for extracting subgraphs from EG. For instance, finding [maximal] cliques is a classical NP-complete problem. Last but not least, the division of FlExPat in two algorithmic phases appears a very strong feature. Indeed, given the very short running times of star-subgraph extraction algorithms (see Tableau 2), the user can experiment **interactively,** typically in real time, with different algorithm variants and/or parameter settings once EG has been output by the more computationally-expensive EGC phase.

5.3 Conclusion

FlExPat allows using a rich and flexible similarity model while maintaining reasonable time and space complexities (lesser than quadratic in practice). To our knowledge no general SPE algorithm other than FlExPat allows the use of a valued edit model with non-constant contribution functions. Even algorithms allowing only valued edit models with **constant** contribution functions have intractable space and complexities in application contexts such as music. For instance, LeMoivre [9] is among the most elaborate and efficient of these general algorithms. Its time complexity grows exponentially with the maximum total number e of insertions, deletions and substitutions allowed in alignments. For $e=10$, a typical value e.g. for music data, LeMoivre's complexity is $O(|S|^{12} \times m_{max}^{21})$!

6 Future Work

One direction for future work is the integration of FlExPat within a music information retrieval system such as Melodiscov [8]. Melodiscov implements the content-based retrieval paradigm which we dubbed WYHIWIG (What You Hum Is What You Get). With Melodiscov users query a music database (at large, e.g. a collection of mp3 files on the web) by humming, singing (with lyrics) or whistling a few notes into a microphone. For every sequential pattern P found by FlExPat in the database (and there are, in practice, huge numbers of such patterns in e.g. pop/rock databases), it can be sufficient to compare the query once to $Proto(P)$ instead of comparing it to all of its occurrences. Tremendous efficiency enhancements w.r.t. existing WYHIWYG algorithms could be obtained via such a preprocessing of the database.

7 References

[1] Agrawal, R. and R. Srikant. 1995. Mining sequential patterns. Proc. Int'l Conf. on Data Engineering (ICDE), 3-14.

[2] Levenshtein, V.I. 1965. Binary codes capable of correcting deletions, insertions and reversals. Cybernetics and Control Theory 10(8): 707-710.

[3] Liu, C.C., J.L. Hsu and A.L.P. Chen. 1999. "Efficient Theme and Non-Trivial Repeating Pattern Discovering in Music Databases". Proc. IEEE Int'l Conf. on Data Engineering (ICDE).

[4] Mannila, H., Toivonen, H. and Verkamo, A.I. 1997. Discovery of Frequent Episodes in Event Sequences. Report C-1997-15, Dept. of Computer Science, University of Helsinki.

[5] Owens, T. 1974. Charlie Parker: Techniques of Improvisation. Ph.D. Thesis, Dept. of Music, UCLA.

[6] Ramalho, G., Rolland, P.Y., and Ganascia, J.G., 1999. An Artificially Intelligent Jazz Performer. Journal of New Music Research 28:2.

[7] Rolland, P.Y., Ganascia, J.G. 1996. Automated Identification of Prominent Motives in Jazz Solo Corpuses. Proceedings 4th International Conference on Music Perception and Cognition (ICMPC'96, Montreal).

[8] Rolland, P.Y., Raskinis, G., Ganascia, J.G. 1999. Musical Content-Based Retrieval: an Overview of the Melodiscov Approach & System. 7th ACM International Multimedia Conf.

[9] Sagot, M.F., Escalier, V.; Viari, A., Soldano, H. 1995. Searching for repeated words in a text allowing for mismatches and gaps. 2nd South American Workshop on String Processing.

[10] Sankoff, D. & Kruskal, J. (eds.). 1983. Time Warps, String Edits and Macromolecules. The Theory and Practice of Sequence Comparison. Addison Wesley.

[11] Tversky, A., and I. Gati. (1982). Similarity, separability, and the triangle inequality. Psychological Review 89:123-154.

[12] Ukkonen, E. 1992. Constructing suffix trees on-line in linear time. IFIP'92, pp. 484-492.

[13] Widmer, G. 1994. The Synergy of Music Theory and AI: Learning Multi-Level Expressive Interpretation. Extended version of paper appearing in Proc. AAAI'94 (11th NCAI)

Interestingness PreProcessing

Sigal Sahar
Tel-Aviv University
gales@post.tau.ac.il

Abstract

As the size of databases increases, the number of rules mined from them also increases, often to an extent that overwhelms users. To address this problem, an important part of the KDD process is dedicated to determining which of these patterns is interesting. In this paper we define the Interestingness PreProcessing Step, and introduce a new framework for interestingness analysis. In a similar fashion to data-preprocessing, this preprocessing should always be applied prior to interestingness processing. A strict requirement, and the biggest challenge, in defining Interestingness PreProcessing techniques is that the preprocessing will not eliminate any potentially interesting patterns. That is, the preprocessing methods must be domain-, task- and user-independent. This property differentiates the preprocessing methods from existing interestingness criteria, and, since they can be applied automatically, makes them very useful. This generic nature also makes them rare: PreProcessing methods are very challenging to define.

We also define in this paper the first two preprocessing techniques, and present the empirical results of applying them to six databases. The results indicate that Interestingness PreProcessing Step is very powerful: in most cases, an average of half the rules mined were eliminated by the application of the two Interestingness PreProcessing techniques. These results are particularly significant since no user-interaction is required to achieve them.

1 Introduction

Builders of Knowledge Discovery in Databases (KDD) systems face the challenge of extracting interesting patterns from large masses of data [7]. Much attention has been dedicated to the development of data mining algorithms to efficiently mine patterns from databases, for example, [3]. As the size of the databases increases, the number of patterns mined from them also increases. This number can easily increase to an extent it overwhelms users of the KDD process. For the KDD process to successfully meet users' expectations, an important part of it must be dedicated to determining which patterns are interesting to its users.

Characterizing what is interesting is a difficult problem. Numerous attempts have been made to formulate the qualities that define what is interesting; they range from evidence and simplicity to novelty and usefulness, as in [11, 18, 10, 27, 1, 4, 17, 15, 8, 22].

Many distinct interestingness criteria (see Section 3) are available to process mined patterns to determine which ones are interesting. Determining interestingness according to different criteria can result in different sets of patterns marked as interesting. This dependence — of the patterns marked as interesting on the domain knowledge — is clear when domain or prior knowledge is used explicitly (as in [10, 27, 12, 19, 16], etc.). When prior and domain knowledge are applied implicitly in the interestingness criteria this dependence is not as clear, but still imposes a bias on the type of rules that will be outputted as interesting (see Section 3). This dependence should not be ignored.

1.1 Contributions

In this paper we introduce the Interestingness PreProcessing Step and show through an empirical evaluation the powerful results of its application. Interestingness PreProcessing is applied to the list of mined association rules (see the interestingness analysis framework in Figure 1) in order to reduce the size of the problem: the number of potentially interesting rules that need to subsequently be processed for interestingness.

The Interestingness PreProcessing criteria eliminate uninteresting rules independently of: (1) the data used in the mining process, (2) the domain of the problem, (3) the task addressed, and, (4) the specific interests and prior knowledge of the user. Thus, Interestingness PreProcessing methods can be deployed automatically, without any human intervention. This generic nature of the Interestingness PreProcessing criteria differentiates them from the existing interestingness criteria, the Processing Step (as in Section 3).

In this paper we also define the first two Interestingness PreProcessing techniques. Since Interestingness PreProcessing methods do not impose any bias on the rules they mark as potentially interesting, they can be run sequentially. This generic nature makes Interestingness PreProcessing techniques rare. To demonstrate the power of these techniques, we provide an empirical evaluation of the results of the application of the two Interestingness PreProcessing techniques on six databases. These results are very encouraging, yielding, in almost all cases, an average deletion of more than half of the mined rules.

We stress that the Interestingness PreProcessing Criteria are meant to complement the existing types of interestingness process criteria and not to replace them. The Interestingness PreProcessing Step is the first step towards the comprehensive solution to determining which rules are interesting, independently of the domain, task and user, by eliminating some of the rules that are not interesting.

The rest of the paper is organized as follows: in Section 2 we provide needed definitions. We review the available interestingness criteria in Section 3, and show the explicit and/or implicit dependencies of these methods on domain or prior knowledge. We define PreProcessing in the interestingness analysis framework in Section 4. We introduce the first two Interestingness PreProcessing techniques in Section 5, and present the powerful empirical results of their application on six different databases in Section 6. We end with our conclusions and future work in Section 7.

2 Definitions and Preliminaries

2.1 Attributes and Association Rules

Let Λ be a set of literals over the boolean domain. An **attribute** is any one of these literals. A **set of attributes** is a set, A, such that $A \subseteq \Lambda$.

An association rule is a specific kind of pattern that is very popular due to its many practical applications. Let A and B be sets of attributes such that $A, B \subseteq \Lambda$ and $A \cap B = \emptyset$. Let D be a set of transactions over Λ. A transaction is a subset of attributes of Λ that have the boolean value of TRUE. The **association rule** $A \to B$ is defined [3] to have **support** $s\%$ and **confidence** $c\%$ if $s\%$ of the transactions contain $A \wedge B$, and $c\%$ of the transactions that contain A also contain B. Given a support and a confidence threshold, [3]'s algorithm outputs the exhaustive list of all association rules that have at least those support and confidence levels. For convenience we refer to A as the **assumption** of the rule $A \to B$, and to B as the **consequent** of the rule.

2.2 Interestingness: Problem Definition

Definition 1 *Let Ω be the set of association rules outputted by a mining algorithm run with support and confidence thresholds of s and c. Find $\widehat{\Omega} \subseteq \Omega$, the set of "interesting rules"*.

Definition 1 describes the general problem we are addressing: finding the set of interesting rules. Our goal is not to infer from rules in Ω rules that have not been mined, i.e.,

---

* We do not attempt to formally define which rules are "interesting".

that do not appear in Ω, that could be of interest to the user. This is the only supposition we make of a user's interests, a standard one often made implicitly.

Definition 1 is stated as a post-processing problem, a methodology with many benefits thoroughly discussed in [23]. Innovative approaches such as [4] and [24] incorporate the interestingness measures into the mining process, but to achieve that, make assumptions on what attributes (or consequents) are interesting. In this work we introduce the first step towards the solution of the general problem of determining interestingness, as defined in Definition 1.

3 Existing Interestingness Criteria and Dependencies on Domain Knowledge

To determine which patterns are interesting, one needs to determine which interestingness criterion to use. User preferences to particular types of rules are implied by a user's selection of an interestingness criterion, a selection often performed without considering the bias it imposes on the types of rules outputted as interesting. The task of choosing the subjectively "right" interestingness criteria for a specific KDD process is far from trivial. Table 1 summarizes the use of explicit and implicit knowledge used to perform this task for different types of existing interestingness criteria. The details follow in this section.

3.1 Explicit Use of Domain Knowledge

The KDD literature offers three main approaches to explicit use of domain knowledge. The first, and most popular, approach proposes to have a domain expert or advanced user to formally (even if vaguely) express on demand, using a predefined grammar, what he or she finds (not) interesting or what a domain user already knows. For example, [10] define templates of patterns that describe the structure of interesting rules, [12] define generalized templates that permit the expression of imprecise domain knowledge and [24] introduces user constraints. [1] determine interestingness according to user defined actionability and [27, 16] use user beliefs. The success of these strategies is conditioned upon the availability of a domain expert willing to go through the often significant effort of completing this task.

The second approach, taken in [25], constructs the knowledge base by having users classify every single rule. This approach requires very intensive user interaction, this time of a mundane nature, and, as the author says, "may be argued [to be] ... tedious". In some cases, the sheer amount of work involved in this approach may render it infeasible.

The third approach, presented in [19], is to eliminate a substantial portion of the un-interesting rules by having the user classify only a few simple rules. This technique requires very low-intensity user interaction. Since its output

Interestingness Method Used		Results affected by		
		criterion selection	initialization	explicit user interests
Explicit methods (Section 3.1)		Yes	Yes	Yes
Implicit Methods (Section 3.2)	Ranking Patterns	Yes	No	No
	Pruning & Constraints	Yes	Yes	No
	Summarization	Yes	No	For analysis of results
PreProcessing methods		No	No	No

Table 1. Dependency of Interestingness Methods on User Preference

is a superset of the list of interesting rules, it is used as a first step in incorporating subjective interestingness.

3.2 Implicit Use of Domain Knowledge

Approaches that use domain knowledge implicitly do not compel users to specify directly what is interesting to them, but require information that only a domain user can provide: how to select the interestingness criterion to be used, how to initialize parameters used by these criteria, etc.

3.2.1 Ranking Patterns

In order to rank association rules according to their interestingness, a mapping, f, is introduced from the mined rules, Ω, to the domain of real numbers, $f : \Omega \to \Re$. The number an association rules is mapped to is an indication of how interesting the association is; the larger the number a rule is mapped to, the more interesting the rule is assumed to be. For example, $interest(A \to B) = confidence(A \to B)/\mathbf{Pr}[B]$ (defined in [6]) ranks highly association rules with high confidence and low a-priori probability of the consequent. This characteristic is not unique to the *interest* criterion. $AddedValue(A \to B) = confidence(A \to B) - \mathbf{Pr}[B]$ (defined in [20]) shares this property. And yet, there is a significant difference between the order these two criteria impose on the rules they rank. One difference is derived from the *interest* criterion's indiscrimination to the same differences in orders of magnitude in the values of the confidence and that a-priori probability of the consequent[†]. This indifference to orders of magnitude may be exactly what a user is looking for. However, a user unaware of this property may fail to choose the subjectively beneficial objective interestingness criterion in his/her particular case. The same applies to other differences between the two criteria, such as *interest*'s symmetrical treatment of the assumption and consequent. [9] described principles ranking criteria should satisfy and lists 13 criteria. More ranking criteria are listed in [20, 4].

3.2.2 Pruning and Application of Constraints

The mappings defined in Section 3.2.1 can also be used as pruning techniques. Using a user-defined threshold, all patterns mapped to an interest score lower than the predefined threshold are pruned or filtered out as not interesting.

Additional methods can be used to prune patterns that do not require the interest mapping criteria. Statistical tests, such as the χ^2 test, used are used to prune in [6, 13]. These tests have associates parameters (significance, confidence, etc.) that need to be initialized.

A collection of instrumental pruning methods is detailed in [21]. These methods require the initialization, by a user, of several parameters (error, strength, etc.).

[4] present a novel algorithm that includes, in addition to the two usual constraints of minimum support and confidence thresholds, two new constraints: a user-specified consequent, and the second, unprecedented, constraint of a user specified minimum confidence improvement threshold.

Initialization of thresholds (improvement [4], type-I error for the χ^2 test, etc.), implicitly requires users to use domain knowledge. Defaulting to commonly used values, for example, 95% significance level for the χ^2 test, and even the choice to use the χ^2 test for pruning [6, 13] (as opposed to another method), are decisions that affect which rules will be outputted as interesting. As explained in [6], the use of the χ^2 test requires conditions that do not always hold, and thus, cannot be used in all cases. There is also the acute problem of multiplicity: when performing a series of tests at a given significance level, the *overall* probability of making at least one type-I error can be much higher than the predetermined level. When using the χ^2 tests, one should also be aware of the type-II errors, since only a minute fraction of the rules is expected to be interesting.

3.2.3 Summarization of Patterns

Several distinct methods fall under the summarization approach. [2] suggest a redundancy measure that summarizes all the rules at the *given* levels of support and confidence very compactly using the more "complex" rules[‡]. Under the

---

[†]For example, for $A \to B$ and $C \to D$ such that $confidence(A \to B) = 0.5$, $\mathbf{Pr}[B] = 0.2$ and $confidence(C \to D) = 0.05$, $\mathbf{Pr}[D] = 0.02$, $interest(A \to B) = 0.5/0.2 = 0.05/0.02 = interest(C \to D)$. However, $AddedValue(A \to B) = 0.5 - 0.2 = 0.3 > 0.03 = 0.05 - 0.02 = AddedValue(C \to D)$.

[‡]The preference to complex rules is formally defined as: given rules $A \to B$ and $C \to D$, $C \to D$ is redundant with respect to $A \to B$ if (1) $A \wedge B = C \wedge D$, and $A \subset C$, or (2) if $C \wedge D \subset A \wedge B$ and $A \subseteq C$.

assumption that the user has no preference to higher support and confidence levels than those specified, this summary includes a relatively small number of rules that summarizes the entire list of rules without losing any information at all.

[13]'s summary of association rules with a single attributed consequent includes "direction-setting" rules. The direction is calculated using the χ^2 test, which is also used to prune the mined outputted. This technique favors "less-complex" rules. [14] provides an intuitive summary that simplifies the discovered rules by providing an overall picture of the relationships in the data and their exceptions.

[26] suggest clustering rules "that make statements about the same database rows [...]", using a simple distance metric. [26] also introduce an algorithm to compute rule covers as short descriptions of large sets of rules. For this approach to work without losing any information, [26] makes a monotonicity assumption on the databases on which the algorithm can be applied, making this method domain independent but not task independent.

When a user decides to use summarization (a subjective decision in itself), further consideration needs to be given to what kind of summary is preferred. Are the "more complex" rules suggested in [2] to be favored over a summary such as the one suggested by [4] or [13]?

4 Interestingness PreProcessing

The **Interestingness PreProcessing Step** preprocesses the mined patterns in order to eliminate patterns that can be determined to be not interesting independently of the domain, user and task. No information or user interaction is required by the Interestingness PreProcessing Step to perform this analysis, other than the problem definition (Definition 1). The Interestingness PreProcessing Step therefore precedes the Interestingness Processing, and follows directly after the data-mining process as depicted in the interestingness framework outlined in Figure 1. The Interestingness PreProcessing methods do not impose bias on the rules they output as potentially interesting, or on the nature of "interestingness" in Definition 1.

The Interestingness PreProcessing Step has several benefits: (**1**) First, and most pragmatically, users can apply the Interestingness PreProcessing Step *automatically*, directly after the mining process, to all problem that conform to Definition 1. This enables a significant reduction to every case of the interestingness analysis problem. (**2**) Running the Interestingness PreProcessing comes with zero cost to users since these techniques do not require user interaction. (**3**) The output of the Interestingness PreProcessing Step (rules that were not filtered out during this step) does not require appraisal by users, as it is in other approaches, e.g., summarization. (**4**) The output of the filtering of the Interestingness PreProcessing Step can be used as the input for interesting-

ness processing methods, such as ranking, summarization, etc. (**5**) The Interestingness PreProcessing Step circumvents the pitfall of a precise definition of what is interesting.

5 Interestingness PreProcessing Techniques

5.1 Interestingness PreProcessing 1: Overfitting

The first Interestingness PreProcessing technique we introduce filters out overfitting by capitalizing on the basic characteristic of association rules: the implication as captured by the *confidence* of the association. The confidence value of an association rule is not the best predictor for the interestingness of the rule; *confidence* does not take into account the a-priori probability of the consequent. A rule may have a high confidence level, but this confidence value may be equal to the a-priori probability of the consequent, rendering the association rule meaningless. Yet, the confidence criterion captures an inherent property of association rules that may be exploited in some cases as detailed below.

Let the task to whose solution we are trying to approach be as defined in Definition 1.

Interestingness PreProcessing Method 1 *The application of the first preprocessing technique to Ω consists of the deletion of any rule $r = C \to D \in \Omega$ if there exists a rule $\hat{r} = A \to B \in \Omega$ such that: (1) $A \subset C$, (2) $B = D$, and (3) confidence($\hat{r}$) $\geq$ confidence(r). Of course, support($\hat{r}$) > support(r).*

Verification: To show that the method above is an Interestingness PreProcessing method, we need to show that any rule that this method eliminates from Ω is an un-interesting rule (as in Section 2.2): a rule that does not provide any more information than rules that already exist in Ω. This follows directly from the definition of when rules are deleted according to this method. We examine two rules, $r_1, r_2 \in \Omega$ such that $r_1 = C \to D$, $r_2 = A \to B$ where $A \subset C$ (that is, $A \neq C$), $B = D$, and confidence(r_2) $\geq$ confidence(r_1). In the general case, given rules with the same consequent and assumptions that strictly contain each other, not much can be concluded without making stronger assumptions. However, **when** confidence($A \to B$) $\geq$ confidence($C \to D$), the rule $C \to D$ does not provide more information than $A \to B$ since we are adding more attributes to the assumption, A, to form a larger assumption, C, and diminishing the predictive power (confidence). In this case, given $A \to B$, we can delete $C \to D$, as we wanted to show. •

Example 1 *Given $r = \langle milk \wedge shoes \rangle \to \langle cereal \rangle$ and $\hat{r} = \langle milk \rangle \to \langle cereal \rangle$ such that $\boldsymbol{Pr}[milk] = 0.8$, $\boldsymbol{Pr}[cereal] = 0.6$, $\boldsymbol{Pr}[shoes] = 0.5$, $\boldsymbol{Pr}[milk \wedge cereal] = 0.4$, $\boldsymbol{Pr}[milk \wedge shoes] = 0.4$, $\boldsymbol{Pr}[cereal \wedge shoes] = 0.3$, and $\boldsymbol{Pr}[milk \wedge cereal \wedge shoes] = 0.2$, r can be deleted by the*

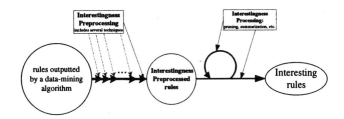

Figure 1. Framework for Determining interestingness.

first Interestingness PreProcessing method, as it provides no more information than r̂ (and both rules have the same confidence level 0.5).

Note that Interestingness PreProcessing Method 1 does *not* eliminate $r_1 = C \rightarrow D$, $r_2 = A \rightarrow B$ where $A = C$, $B \subset D$ ($B \neq D$). In this case, $confidence(A \rightarrow B) = \mathbf{Pr}[A \wedge B]/\mathbf{Pr}[A] > \mathbf{Pr}[A \wedge D]/\mathbf{Pr}[A] = confidence(C \rightarrow D)$. The relationship between the respective confidence values and the a-priori probabilities of the consequents can be measured in many ways (for example, *interest* and *AddedValue* as in Section 3). A possible scenario is that the a-priori probability of B is so large compared to that of D, that the rule $A \rightarrow B$ does not give significantly more information than $\rightarrow B$, while $A \rightarrow D = C \rightarrow D$ does. To remain generic, i.e., an Interestingness PreProcessing method, this technique does *not* eliminate either rule, r_1 or r_2. Following the same reasoning, for $r_1 = C \rightarrow D$, $r_2 = A \rightarrow B$ such that $A \subset C$ and $B \subset D$, no deletions are performed by this Interestingness PreProcessing method in order to avoid, in the general case, the elimination potentially interesting associations.

5.2 Interestingness PreProcessing 2: Transition

Interestingness PreProcessing Method 2 *The application of the second preprocessing technique consists of the deletion of any rule r, $r = A \rightarrow C \in \Omega$, for which $\exists r_2, r_3 \in \Omega$ such that (1) $r_2 = A \rightarrow C \wedge D$, and (2) $r_3 = C \rightarrow D$ where $confidence(r_3) = 1$.*

Verification: To show that the technique above is an Interestingness PreProcessing technique, we need to show that any rule that this technique eliminates from Ω is an un-interesting rule (as in Section 2.2): a rule that does not provide any more information than rules that already exist in Ω. This follows directly from the definition of when rules are eliminated according to this technique: from $r_3 = C \rightarrow D : confidence(r_3) = 1$ we get that $\mathbf{Pr}[C \wedge D] = \mathbf{Pr}[C]$. Hence, for $r_2 = A \rightarrow C \wedge D$ we have $confidence(A \rightarrow C) = confidence(r_2)$, and we have $support(A \rightarrow C) = support(r_2)$, indicating that the rule

$r = A \rightarrow C$ does not contain any more information than the rule r_2. Since according to the definition we have that $r_2, r_3 \in \Omega$, we have easily proven our claim. •

Example 2 *Given $r = \langle raisins \rangle \rightarrow \langle cereal \rangle$, $r_2 = \langle raisins \rangle \rightarrow \langle milk \wedge cereal \rangle$, and $r_3 = \langle cereal \rangle \rightarrow \langle milk \rangle$ such that $Pr[milk] = 0.8$, $Pr[cereal] = 0.6$, $Pr[raisins] = 0.3$, $Pr[milk \wedge cereal] = 0.6$, $Pr[milk \wedge raisins] = 0.2$, $Pr[cereal \wedge raisins] = 0.1$, and $Pr[milk \wedge cereal \wedge raisins] = 0.1$. We get that $confidence(r_3) = 1$, indicating that the Interestingness PreProcessing 2 method would delete the rule r. We note that $support(r) = support(r_2)$ and that $confidence(r) = confidence(r_2)$. This preprocessing method does not delete r_3, available for users interested in a relationship between milk and cereal.*

Note that given four rules, $r = A \rightarrow C \wedge D$, $r_2 = A \rightarrow C$, $r_3 = C \rightarrow D$ such that $confidence(r_3) = 1$, and, $r_4 = A \rightarrow D$, r_4 cannot be deleted in the general case without risking losing a potentially interesting rule. In Example 2, r_4 corresponds to the rule $\langle milk \rangle \rightarrow \langle raisins \rangle$. Now, $confidence(r_4) = 0.25$, and users interested in the relationship between customers who purchase milk and customers who purchase raisins may find the higher confidence level of r_4 interesting.

6 Experiments With Real Data

To determine the effectiveness of the Interestingness PreProcessing techniques we introduced in Section 5, we present the results of their application on six databases.

6.1 Data Description

In this section, we describe the different databases we used in this empirical analysis. We procured the WWW Database and the Grocery Database from independent sources. The other four databases were compiled from the UCI repository [5].

WWW Proxy Logs Database: This database was complied from the logs of a World Wide Web (WWW) proxy server. Each transaction in the database specifies the categories of sites (for example, NEWS, PORNOGRAPHIC, etc.) a particular user browsed. The database represents the accesses of the 2,336 heaviest users to 15 site categories.

Grocery Database: We obtained this real-life dataset from an Israeli commercial company that sells groceries via telephone, fax, and the Internet. The company has a list of approximately 95,000 items, not all of which are available at all times. In order to make the dataset more manageable, we chose to work on the 1,728 items that cover 80% of the gross income of the store. We translated each transaction in the original dataset to one containing 1,757 boolean attributes: 1,728 attributes describe the items purchased, another 19 attributes are used to indicate different distribution centers in the country, and 10 attributes to indicate the range of money spent on a single shopping basket. Thus, the processed database contains 67,470 transactions, each describing a single shopping basket: its contents, how much money was spent on it and where in the country the order was made. Note the very large number of attributes compared to the number of transactions in this database.

Adult Database: The Adult dataset contains 15 attributes, 6 continuous and 9 nominal, which we discretisized into 171 boolean attributes. We used the 45,222 entries in the original dataset from [5] that had no missing attributes as the basis for the compiled database we used.

Mushroom Database: The Mushroom dataset contains 23 nominal attributes (one of these attributes was an indicator of whether or not the mushroom is poisonous) which we converted to 113 boolean variables. We discarded the eleventh nominal attribute that contained missing values. Thus we were able to use all 8,124 instances.

Nursery Database: The Nursery dataset was derived from a hierarchical decision model originally developed to rank applications for nursery schools. It contains 8 nominal attributes which we turned into 32 boolean ones. There were no missing values for any of the attributes and we were able to use all 12,960 instances of the dataset.

Chess Database: This dataset, King and Rook (white) versus King and Pawn (the pawn is one square away from queening on a7), has 3,196 instances and 37 nominal attributes. Each instance describes a single board position.

6.2 The Data Mining Process

We implemented the association rule discovery algorithm (`aprioriTid` and the rule generation algorithm) in [3]. The algorithm outputs all the association rules in the dataset that have at least the given support and confidence levels. We ran this algorithm on each of the databases described above with the most permissive thresholds that the limited computational resources available to us permitted. These support and confidence thresholds were as follows: for the Grocery database, 3.5% thresholds were used, yielding 3,046 rules; for the WWW database, 6% thresholds,

yielding 9,206 rules; for the Nursery database, 3% thresholds, yielding 8,314 rules; for the Chess database, 10% threshold, yielding 8,292 rules; for the Adult database, 20% thresholds, yielding 13,906 rules; and for the Mushroom database, 35% thresholds, yielding 6,356 rules.

6.3 Experimental Results

6.3.1 Results: Interestingness PreProcessing Tech. 1

As explained in Section 5.1, the first Interestingness PreProcessing method relies on relative values of the confidence, the predictability value, of the association rules in order to perform rule deletion. To demonstrate that this reliance does not translate into a functional dependence of the criterion on a particular choice of confidence mining thresholds, we applied this preprocessing method to the outputs of mining the databases using different confidence thresholds. That is, we mined each of the datasets using several different confidence thresholds and the most permissive (lowest) support threshold our computational resources allowed us, as detailed in Section 6.2.

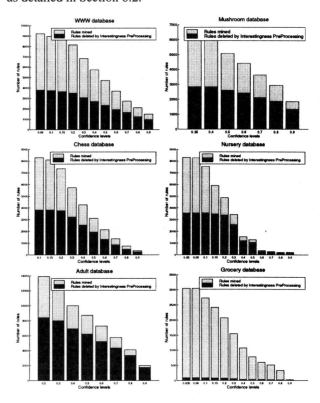

Figure 2. Results of the application of the first Interestingness PreProcessing technique.

For each of the six databases, we applied the first Interestingness PreProcessing technique to the list of rules outputted by mining the database with the given support thresh-

494

old (as in Section 6.2) and increasing confidence thresholds. For example, the WWW database was mined with confidence thresholds of 0.06, 0.1, 0.2, 0.3, 0.4, 0.5, 0.6, 0.7, 0.8, and 0.9 using a 0.06 support threshold in all cases. The results of the application of this preprocessing technique on the association rules outputted by these ten mining processes of the WWW database are summarized in the upper left hand histogram of Figure 2. Each gray bar indicates the number of rules mined using a specific confidence threshold. For example, the first (leftmost) gray bar in the WWW histogram depicts the 9,206 association rules that were mined with 0.06 confidence level. The black bar superimposed on it indicates the number of rules deleted as a result of the application of this preprocessing technique on the respective list of rules, 3,793 in this case. That is, over 41% of the rules mined by from the WWW database using 0.06 support and confidence thresholds were deleted by Interestingness PreProcessing technique 1. This deletion is very significant considering that no information of any sort was required to perform it. This Interestingness Preprocessing technique performed even better on the output of mining the WWW database using increasingly higher confidence levels, deleting as much as 65% of the rules mined with 0.9 confidence levels, as indicated by the rightmost bar in the WWW database histogram: out of the 1,503 rules mined (the rightmost gray bar), 977 rules (the superimposed black bar) rules were deleted. The other five histograms in Figure 2 summarize the results of applying the first Interestingness PreProcessing technique to the other five databases.

The average deletion brought about by the application of the first Interestingness PreProcessing technique are 49.3% ± 7.9% for the WWW database, 55.2% ± 9.8% for the Mushroom database, 69.4% ± 18.0% for the Nursery database, 57.7% ± 7.3% for the Chess database, 72.6% ± 8.6% for the Adult database, and 3.7% ± 1.5% for the Grocery database. These results are extremely encouraging: a significant number, in most cases, an average of over *half* the rules outputted by the mining algorithm are deleted by the application of this preprocessing technique. This is a significant result not only because of the large number of rules that is deleted, but also because this deletion requires *no* information of any kind from a user of the KDD process.

6.3.2 Results: Interestingness PreProcessing Tech. 2

The results of the application of the Interestingness PreProcessing 2 technique (Section 5.2) to the six databases were more modest than those of the application of the first technique. Even these modest results are very significant: a reduction even of a small percentage of the rules is both effective and important when these results are achieved automatically, without any interaction with any users. The average elimination brought about by the second prepro-

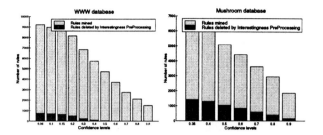

Figure 3. Results of the application of Interestingness PreProcessing 2 technique

cessing technique was as follows: 3.3% ± 3.4% for the WWW database, 17.4% ± 5% for the Mushroom database, 2.5% ± 2.7% for the Nursery database, 3.1% ± 1.8% for the Chess database, 1% ± 1.9% for the Adult database. We present the detailed results in a graphical representation in Figure 3. for the first two databases.

6.3.3 Results: Sequential Application of Interestingness PreProcessing Techniques

As depicted in Figure 1, the Interestingness PreProcessing techniques can and *should* be applied sequentially. We proceeded to do so, applying the two preprocessing techniques we introduced in this paper sequentially. The results of this sequential application are depicted in Figure 4.

7 Conclusions and Future Work

In this work we defined an Interestingness PreProcessing Step, as part of the interestingness analysis framework, that eliminates association rules that can be determined to be not interesting in a user-, domain-, and task-independent manner. The generic nature of the preprocessing differentiates it from the interestingness processing that do impose a bias on the type of rules outputted as interesting.

In this work we also introduced the first Interestingness PreProcessing techniques. The deletion of un-interesting rules by these techniques is very significant since it is achieved without requiring a user to provide *any* information. Our empirical results indicate that these are powerful techniques: in most cases, more than half the rules were eliminated by their application. It is important to note that any filtering power, however weak, of any preprocessing technique is significant since *all* the PreProcessing methods are deployed sequentially immediately following the mining process on any set of mined rules, and these results add up. We hope that this work will encourage the development of more preprocessing techniques by the KDD community.

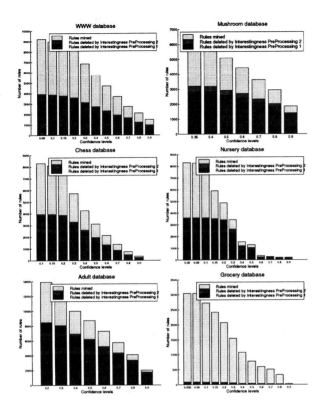

Figure 4. Results of sequential application of Interestingness PreProcessing

Our future work includes the development of other Interestingness PreProcessing methodologies. We are also working on the incorporation of the preprocessing methods into the mining process and of running them in parallel.

References

[1] G. Adomavicius and A. Tuzhilin. Discovery of actionable patterns in databases: The action hierarchy approach. In *SIGKDD*, pages 111–114, 1997.

[2] C. C. Aggarwal and P. S. Yu. A new approach to online generation of association rules. Technical Report Research Report RC 20899, IBM T J Watson Research Center, 1998.

[3] R. Agrawal, H. Mannila, R. Srikant, H. Toivonen, and A. I. Verkamo. *Advances in Knowledge Discovery and Data Mining*, chapter 12: *Fast Discovery of Association Rules*, pages 307–328. 1996.

[4] R. J. Bayardo Jr., R. Agrawal, and G. D. Constraint-based rule mining in large, dense databases. In *ICDE*, pages 188–197, 1999.

[5] C. Blake, E. Keogh, and C. Merz. UCI repository of machine learning databases http://www.ics.uci.edu/~mlearn/mlrepository.html.

[6] S. Brin, R. Motwani, and C. Silverstein. Beyond market baskets: generalizing association rules to correlations. In *SIGMOD*, pages 265–276, 1997.

[7] U. M. Fayyad, G. Piatetsky-Shapiro, and P. Smyth. *Advances in Knowledge Discovery and Data Mining*, chapter 1:

From Data Mining to Knowledge Discovery: An Overview, pages 1–34. 1996.

[8] A. A. Freitas. A multi-criteria approach for the evaluation of rule interestingness. In *ICDM*, pages 7–20, 1998.

[9] R. Hilderman and H. Hamilton. Evaluation of interestingness measures for ranking discovered knowledge. In *PAKDD*, pages 247–259, 2001.

[10] M. Klemettinen, H. Mannila, P. Ronkainen, H. Toivonen, and A. I. Verkam. Finding interesting rules from large sets of discovered association rules. In *CIKM*, pages 401–407, 1994.

[11] W. Klosgen. *Advances in Knowledge Discovery and Data Mining*, chapter 10: *Explora: a Multipattern and Multistrategy Discovery Assistant*, pages 249–271. 1996.

[12] B. Liu, W. Hsu, and S. Chen. Using general impressions to analyze discovered classification rules. In *SIGKDD*, pages 31–36, 1997.

[13] B. Liu, W. Hsu, and Y. M. Pruning and summarizing the discovered associations. In *SIGKDD*, pages 125–134, 1999.

[14] B. Liu, M. Hu, and W. Hsu. Multi-level organization and summariztion of the discovered rules. In *SIGKDD*, pages 208–217, 2000.

[15] C. J. Matheus, G. Piatetsky-Shapiro, and D. McNeill. *Advances in Knowledge Discovery and Data Mining*, chapter 20: *Selecting and Reporting What Is Interesting*, pages 495–515. 1996.

[16] B. Padmanabhan and A. Tuzhilin. Small is beautiful: Discovering the mimimal set of unexpected patterns. In *SIGKDD*, pages 54–63, 2000.

[17] G. Piatetsky-Shapiro and B. Masand. Estimating campaign benefits and modeling lift. In *SIGKDD*, pages 185–193, 1999.

[18] F. Provost and D. Jensen. Evaluating knowledge discovery and data mining. In *Tutorial T7: SIGKDD*, 1998.

[19] S. Sahar. Interestingness via what is not interesting. In *SIGKDD*, pages 332–336, 1999.

[20] S. Sahar and Y. Mansour. An empirical evaluation of objective interestingness criteria. In *SPIE Conf. on Data Mining and Knowledge Discovery*, pages 63–74, 1999.

[21] D. Shah, L. V. S. Lakshmanan, K. Ramamritham, and S. Sudarshan. Interestingness and pruning of mined patterns. In *SIGMOD Workshop DMKD*, 1999.

[22] A. Silberschatz and A. Tuzhilin. What makes patterns interesting in knowledge discovery systems. *IEEE Trans. Knowledge Discovery and Data Engineering*, 8(6):970–974, 1996.

[23] M. Spiliopoulou and J. F. Roddick. Higher order mining: Modelling and mining the results of knowledge discovery. In *Conf. on Data Mining Methods and Databases*, 2000.

[24] R. Srikant, Q. Vu, and R. Agrawal. Mining association rules with item constraints. In *SIGKDD*, pages 67–73, 1997.

[25] R. Subramonian. Defining diff as a data mining primitive. In *SIGKDD*, pages 334–338, 1998.

[26] H. Toivonen, M. Klemettinen, P. Ronkainen, K. Hätönen, and H. Mannila. Pruning and grouping discovered association rules. In *MLnet Familiarization Workshop on Statistics, Machine Learning and KDD*, pages 47–52, 1995.

[27] A. Tuzhilin and A. Silberschatz. A belief-driven discovery framework based on data monitoring and triggering. Technical Report IS-96-26, Stern School of Business, New York University, 1996.

Data Analysis and Mining in Ordered Information Tables

Ying Sai, Y.Y. Yao
Department of Computer Science
University of Regina
Regina, Saskatchewan, Canada S4S 0A2
E-mail: yyao@cs.uregina.ca

Ning Zhong
Department of Information Engineering
Maebashi Institute of Technology
460-1, Kamisadori-Cho, Maebashi 371, Japan
E-mail: zhong@maebashi-it.ac.jp

Abstract

Many real world problems deal with ordering objects instead of classifying objects, although majority of research in machine learning and data mining has been focused on the latter. For modeling ordering problems, we generalize the notion of information tables to ordered information tables by adding order relations on attribute values. The problem of mining ordering rules is formulated as finding association between orderings of attribute values and the overall ordering of objects. An ordering rules may state that "if the value of an object x on an attribute a is ordered ahead of the value of another object y on the same attribute, then x is ordered ahead of y". For mining ordering rules, we first transform an ordered information table into a binary information, and then apply any standard machine learning and data mining algorithms. As an illustration, we analyze in detail Maclean's universities ranking for the year 2000.

1 Introduction

In real world situations, we may be faced with many problems that are not simply classification [1, 7]. One such type of problems is the ordering of objects. Two familiar examples are the ranking of universities and the ranking of consumer products produced by different manufacturers. In both examples, we have a set of attributes that are used to describe the objects under consideration. Consider the example of ranking consumer products. Attributes may be the price, warranty, and other information. The values of a particular attribute, say the price, naturally induce an ordering of objects. The overall ranking of products may be produced by their market shares of different manufacturers. The orderings of objects by attribute values may not necessarily be the same as the overall ordering of objects. In this setting, a number of important issues arise. It would be interesting to know which attributes play more important roles in determining the overall ordering, and which attributes do

not contribute at all to the overall ordering. It would also be useful to know which subset of attributes would be sufficient to determine the overall ordering. The dependency information of attributes may also be valuable.

In this paper, we study the problem of data analysis with ordered information in general, and mining ordering rules in particular, based on our earlier results on this topic [12, 14, 15]. The problem of mining ordering rules can be described as follows. There is a set of objects described by a set of attributes. There is an ordering on values of each attribute, and there is also an overall ordering of objects. The overall ordering may be given by experts or obtained from other information, either dependent or independent of the orderings of objects according to their attribute values. We are interested in mining the association between the overall ordering and the individual orderings induced by different attributes. More specifically, we want to derive ordering rules exemplified by the statement that "if the value of an object x on an attribute a is ordered ahead of the value of another object y on the same attribute, then x is ordered ahead of y".

The notion of ordered information tables is introduced as a generalization of information tables. As a starting point, we focus on the dependency of attributes. The notions of reducts and core, which have been studied extensively in the literature of rough sets [6], are derivable from the dependency of attributes and play an important role in mining ordering rules. In mining ordering rules, we first transform an ordered information table into a binary information, and then apply any standard machine learning and data mining algorithms.

Ordered information tables are related to ordinal information systems proposed and studied by Iwinski [4]. Orderings induced by attribute values in information tables were also considered by Greco, Matarazzo and Slowinski [2, 3]. They addressed the problem of finding ordering rules by approximating preference relations through dominance relations. They also discussed approach of transforming an ordered information table into a binary table and mining the corresponding binary table. However, they suggested that the method is not very suitable in some situations for decision making. Instead, they proposed a method based on the approximation of a preference relation by dominance relations, in which certain parameters must be determined by experiments. Although their method may be more general, it does not provide a pure qualitative framework, which may be important for the analysis of ordered information tables. Furthermore, one may gain more insights by studying a less general model.

2 Ordered Information Tables

In many information processing systems, objects are typically represented by their values on a finite set of attributes. Such information may be conveniently described in a tabular form [6]. The rows of the table correspond to objects of the universe, the columns correspond to a set of attributes, and each cell gives the value of an object with respect to an attribute.

Definition 1 *An information table is a quadruple:*

$$IT = (U, At, \{V_a \mid a \in At\}, \{I_a \mid a \in At\}),$$

where

U *is a finite nonempty set of objects,*

At *is a finite nonempty set of attributes,*

V_a *is a nonempty set of values for $a \in At$,*

$I_a : U \to V_a$ *is an information function.*

For simplicity, we have considered only information tables characterized by a finite set of objects and a finite set of attributes. Each information function I_a is a total function that maps an object of U to exactly one value in V_a. An information table represents all available information and knowledge about the objects under consideration. Objects are only perceived, observed, or measured by using a finite number of properties.

An information table does not consider any semantic relationships between distinct values of a particular attribute. By incorporating semantics information, we may obtain different generalizations of information tables [12]. Generalized information tables may be viewed as information tables with added semantics. In this paper, we introduce order relations on attribute values.

Definition 2 *Let U be a nonempty set and $\succ$ be a binary relation on U. The relation $\succ$ is a weak order if it satisfies the two properties:*

Asymmetry :

$$x \succ y \Longrightarrow \neg(y \succ x),$$

Negative transitivity :

$$(\neg(x \succ y), \neg(y \succ z)) \Longrightarrow \neg(x \succ z).$$

An important implication of a weak order is that the following relation,

$$x \sim y \Longleftrightarrow (\neg(x \succ y), \neg(y \succ x)), \qquad (1)$$

is an equivalence relation. For two elements, if $x \sim y$ we say x and y are indiscernible by $\succ$. The equivalence relation $\sim$ induces a partition $U/\sim$ on U, and an order relation $\succ^*$ on $U/\sim$ can be defined by:

$$[x]_\sim \succ^* [y]_\sim \Longleftrightarrow x \succ y, \qquad (2)$$

where $[x]_\sim$ is the equivalence class containing x. Moreover, $\succ^*$ is a linear order. Any two distinct equivalence classes of $U/\sim$ can be compared. It is therefore possible to arrange the objects into levels, with each level consisting of indiscernible elements defined by $\succ$. For a weak order, $\neg(x \succ y)$ can be written as $y \succeq x$ or $x \preceq y$, which means $y \succ x$ or $y \sim x$. For any two elements x and y, we have either $x \succ y$ or $y \succeq x$, but not both.

Definition 3 *An ordered information table is a pair:*

$$OIT = (IT, \{\succ_a \mid a \in At\}),$$

where IT is a standard information table and $\succ_a$ is a weak order on V_a.

An ordering of values of a particular attribute a naturally induces an ordering of objects, namely, for $x, y \in U$:

$$x \succ_{\{a\}} y \Longleftrightarrow I_a(x) \succ_a I_a(y), \qquad (3)$$

where $\succ_{\{a\}}$ denotes an order relation on U induced by the attribute a. An object x is ranked ahead of another object y if and only if the value of x on the attribute a is ranked ahead of the value of y on a. The relation $\succ_{\{a\}}$ has exactly the same properties as that of $\succ_a$. For a subset of attributes $A \subseteq At$, we define:

$$
\begin{aligned}
x \succ_A y &\Longleftrightarrow \forall a \in A[I_a(x) \succ_a I_a(y)] \\
&\Longleftrightarrow \bigwedge_{a \in A} I_a(x) \succ_a I_a(y) \\
&\Longleftrightarrow \bigcap_{a \in A} \succ_{\{a\}} . \qquad (4)
\end{aligned}
$$

That is, x is ranked ahead of y if and only if x is ranked ahead of y according to all attributes in A. The above definition is a straightforward generalization of the standard definition of equivalence relations in rough set theory, where the equality relation $=$ is used [6]. Mining ordering rules based on order relations is a concrete example of applications of our earlier studies on generalizations of rough set model with non-equivalence relations [11, 13].

For simplicity, we also assume that there is a special attribute, called the decision attribute. The ordering of objects by the decision attribute is denoted by $\succ_{\{o\}}$ and is called the overall ordering of objects.

498

	a	b	c	d	o
p_1	middle	3 years	\$200	heavy	1
p_2	large	3 years	\$300	very heavy	3
p_3	small	3 years	\$300	light	3
p_4	small	3 years	\$250	very light	2
p_5	small	2 years	\$200	very light	3

$\succ_a$:   small $\succ_a$ middle $\succ_a$ large,

$\succ_b$:   3 years $\succ_b$ 2 years,

$\succ_c$:   \$200 $\succ_c$ \$250 $\succ_c$ \$300,

$\succ_d$:   very light $\succ_d$ light $\succ_d$ heavy $\succ_d$ very heavy,

$\succ_o$:   1 $\succ_o$ 2 $\succ_o$ 3.

Table 1. An ordered information table

Example 1 *Suppose we have an ordered information table of a group of products produced by five manufacturers as shown in Table 1. In this table, a, b, c, d, and o stand for size, warranty, price, weight, and overall ordering on a set of products, respectively. Based on orderings of attribute values, we obtain the following orderings of products:*

$$\succ_{\{a\}}^* \quad : \quad [p_3, p_4, p_5] \succ_{\{a\}}^* [p_1] \succ_{\{a\}}^* [p_2],$$

$$\succ_{\{b\}}^* \quad : \quad [p_1, p_2, p_3, p_4] \succ_{\{b\}}^* [p_5],$$

$$\succ_{\{c\}}^* \quad : \quad [p_1, p_5] \succ_{\{c\}}^* [p_4] \succ_{\{c\}}^* [p_2, p_3],$$

$$\succ_{\{d\}}^* \quad : \quad [p_4, p_5] \succ_{\{d\}}^* [p_3] \succ_{\{d\}}^* [p_1] \succ_{\{d\}}^* [p_2],$$

$$\succ_{\{o\}}^* \quad : \quad [p_1] \succ_{\{o\}}^* [p_4] \succ_{\{o\}}^* [p_2, p_3, p_5].$$

For subsets $\{a, b\}$ and $\{c, d\}$, we have:

$$\succ_{\{a,b\}} \quad : \quad \emptyset,$$

$$\succ_{\{c,d\}} \quad : \quad p_1 \succ_{\{c,d\}} p_2, \quad p_4 \succ_{\{c,d\}} p_2,$$

$$p_5 \succ_{\{c,d\}} p_2, \quad p_4 \succ_{\{c,d\}} p_3,$$

$$p_5 \succ_{\{c,d\}} p_3.$$

By combining attributes a and b, all objects are put into the same class. It is interesting to note that $\succ_{\{c,d\}}$ is not a weak order. That is, the intersection of two weak orders may not produce a weak order. This suggests that rules using simple condition $\bigwedge_{a \in A} I_a(x) \succ_a I_a(y)$ might not be very useful.

3 Analyzing Ordered Information Tables

In an ordered information table OIT, an atomic expression over a single attribute a is defined as either $(a, \succ)$ or $(a, \preceq)$. For a set of attributes $A \subseteq At$, an expression over A in OIT is defined by $\bigwedge_{a \in A} e(a)$, where $e(a)$ is an atomic expression over a. The set of all expressions over A in an ordered information table OIT is denoted by $E(A)$. In general, we may also consider expressions connected by other

logic connectives such as $\neg$ and $\vee$. For simplicity, we restrict our discussion to only $\wedge$.

In an ordered information table, we deals with pairs of objects. We will not consider the object pairs (x, x). The universal set is thus given by $(U \times U)^+ = U \times U - \{(x, x) \mid x \in U\} = \{(x, y) \mid x, y \in U, x \neq y\}$. The meanings of the expressions are given as follows:

$$m(a, \succ) = \{(x, y) \in (U \times U)^+ \mid I_a(x) \succ_a I_a(y)\},$$

$$m(a, \preceq) = \{(x, y) \in (U \times U)^+ \mid I_a(x) \preceq_a I_a(y)\},$$

$$m(\bigwedge_{a \in A} e(a)) = \bigcap_{a \in A} m(e(a)).$$

An object pair (x, y) satisfies an expression ϕ, written $(x, y) \models \phi$, if the order as specified by the expression ϕ is (x, y). The set $m(\phi)$ consists of all object pairs that satisfy the expressed ϕ.

For the set of expressions $E(A)$, the family $\{m(\phi) \neq \emptyset \mid \phi \in E(A)\}$ forms a partition of $(U \times U)^+$, denoted by $P(A)$. Each object pair satisfies one and only one expression from $E(A)$.

Definition 4 *An attribute set B depends on another attribute set A, or A determines B, written $A \rightarrow B$, if and only if $P(A)$ is a finer partition of $P(B)$, namely, for each equivalence class $X \in P(A)$, there exist an equivalence class $Y \in P(B)$ such that $X \subseteq Y$.*

Suppose B depends on A. For any expression $\phi \in E(A)$, if an object pair $(x, y) \in (U \times U)^+$ satisfies ϕ, i.e., $(x, y) \models \phi$, then there exists a corresponding expression $\psi \in E(B)$, such that $(x, y) \models \psi$. The ordering of objects by A determines the ordering of objects by B.

Definition 5 *Two attribute sets $A, B \subseteq At$ are equivalent if and only if $P(A) = P(B)$.*

Two sets of attributes A and B are equivalent, if and only if A depends on B and B depends on A. The ordering of objects by A determines the ordering of objects by B, and vice versa. Regarding the ordering of objects, A and B contain exactly the same information.

Definition 6 *An attribute $a \in A$ is dispensable in A if and only if A and $A - \{a\}$ are equivalent; otherwise a is indispensable in A.*

Definition 7 *An attribute set A is an independent set if and only if every $a \in A$ is indispensable; otherwise A is a dependent set.*

Each attribute in an independent attribute set contributes to the ordering of objects.

Definition 8 *A subset $B \subseteq A$ is a reduct of A if and only if B is an independent set and is equivalent to A.*

A reduct $B \subseteq A$ is a minimal subset of A, in the sense that it does not contain any dispensable attributes, and produces the ordering of objects as given by A. Typically, a set of attributes may have many reducts. The set of all reducts of an attribute set A is denoted by $RED(A)$.

Definition 9 *The set of all indispensable elements of A is called the core of A and is denoted by $CORE(A)$.*

An attribute in the core must be in every reduct. Thus, we have:

$$CORE(A) = \bigcap RED(A). \qquad (5)$$

The set of attributes $CORE(A)$ are so essential that they can not be eliminated without losing the ordering information provided by A. The core may be empty.

Definition 10 *An attribute $a \in A$ is absolutely dispensable in A if it does not belong to any reduct, namely, $a \in A - \bigcup RED(A)$.*

An absolutely dispensable attribute does not contribute at all to ordering of objects based on A.

Example 2 *Let $U = \{x, y, z\}$ and $A = \{a, b, c\}$. Consider the order relations induced by the three attributes:*

$$\succ_{\{a\}}^*: \quad [x] \succ_{\{a\}}^* [y] \succ_{\{a\}}^* [z],$$
$$\succ_{\{b\}}^*: \quad [z] \succ_{\{b\}}^* [x, y],$$
$$\succ_{\{c\}}^*: \quad [z] \succ_{\{c\}}^* [y] \succ_{\{c\}}^* [x].$$

For the entire set of attributes, we have:

$$\begin{aligned}
E(\{a, b, c\}) = \quad &\{(a, \succ) \wedge (b, \preceq) \wedge (c, \preceq), \\
&(a, \preceq) \wedge (b, \preceq) \wedge (c, \succ), \\
&(a, \preceq) \wedge (b, \succ) \wedge (c, \succ), \ldots\}.
\end{aligned}$$

For clarity, we only explicitly give the expressions whose meanings are nonempty sets of object pairs. The corresponding partition, $P(\{a, b, c\})$, is given by:

$$m((a, \succ) \wedge (b, \preceq) \wedge (c, \preceq)) = \{(x, y), (x, z), (y, z)\},$$
$$m((a, \preceq) \wedge (b, \preceq) \wedge (c, \succ)) = \{(y, x)\},$$
$$m((a, \preceq) \wedge (b, \succ) \wedge (c, \succ)) = \{(z, x), (z, y)\}.$$

For the subset of attributes $\{a, b\}$, we have:

$$\begin{aligned}
E(\{a, b\}) = \quad &\{(a, \succ) \wedge (b, \preceq), (a, \preceq) \wedge (b, \preceq), \\
&(a, \preceq) \wedge (b, \succ), \ldots\},
\end{aligned}$$

which induces the partition $P(\{a, b\})$:

$$m((a, \succ) \wedge (b, \preceq)) = \{(x, y), (x, z), (y, z)\},$$
$$m((a, \preceq) \wedge (b, \preceq)) = \{(y, x)\},$$
$$m((a, \preceq) \wedge (b, \succ)) = \{(z, x), (z, y)\}.$$

Since $P(\{a, b, c\}) = P(\{a, b\})$, the attribute sets $\{a, b, c\}$ and $\{a, b\}$ are equivalent. It can be easily verified that $P(\{a, b\}) \neq P(\{a\})$ and $P(\{a, b\}) \neq P(\{b\})$. Thus, the attribute set $\{a, b\}$ is an independent set and is a reduct of A. Another reduct is given by $\{b, c\}$. We have $RED(A) = \{\{a, b\}, \{b, c\}\}$ and $CORE(A) = \{b\}$. There is no absolute dispensable attribute.

The concepts of dependency, dispensable attributes and reduct capture the connections between attributes with respect to ordering produced by a set A. They provide us with a basis for analyzing and simplifying an ordered information table by removing certain attribute without loss of information. In some situations, it is necessary to study relationship between attributes relative to the overall ordering of objects. In what follows, we consider an ordered information table with a decision attribute o, i.e., the overall ordering of objects. All the concepts developed so far can be easily extended.

Definition 11 *Let $A \subseteq At$ be an attribute set. For an expression $\phi \in E(A)$, we say o ϕ-depends on A, denoted by $A \rightarrow_\phi o$, if and only if $m(\phi) \subseteq m(o, \succ)$ or $m(\phi) \subseteq m(o, \preceq)$.*

While dependency of attributes show global connection between attributes, ϕ-dependency shows local connection. Assume o ϕ-depends on A. If any two objects satisfy the particular orderings specified by ϕ on A, one can tell their ordering by o.

Definition 12 *Let $A, B \subseteq At$. Two attributes sets A and B are equivalent with respect to o, if and only if*

$$\bigcup_{\phi \in E(A)} M_o(\phi) = \bigcup_{\phi' \in E(B)} M_o(\phi'), \qquad (6)$$

where $M_o(\phi)$ is defined by:

$$M_o(\phi) = \begin{cases} m(\phi), & A \rightarrow_\phi o, \\ \emptyset, & otherwise. \end{cases} \qquad (7)$$

If A and B are equivalent with respect to o, any two objects that can be properly ordered on o according to A must be properly ordered according to B, and vice versa.

Definition 13 *An attribute $a \in A$ is dispensable with respect to o, if and only if A and $A - \{a\}$ are equivalent with respect to o; otherwise a is indispensable with respect to o.*

Definition 14 *An attribute set A is an independent set with respect to o, if and only if there is no dispensable attribute in A with respect to o.*

Definition 15 *A subset $B \subseteq A$ is a reduct of A with respect to o, if and only if B is an independent set and equivalent to A with respect to o.*

A reduct $B \subseteq A$ with respect to o is sometimes called a relative reduct of A with respect to o. It consists of a minimal subset of attributes of A that provides the same ordering of objects on o as A itself. A set of attributes may have more than one relative reduct. The set of all relative reducts of an attribute set A is denoted by $RED_o(A)$.

Definition 16 *The set of all indispensable elements of A with respect to o is called the core of A with respect to o and is denoted by $CORE_o(A)$.*

Similarly, the core of A with respect to o is called a relative core. The relative core of A is the intersection of all its relative reducts:

$$CORE_o(A) = \bigcap RED_o(A). \tag{8}$$

A relative core may be empty. Attributes in a nonempty relative core play essential roles in describing the overall ordering induced by o.

Example 3 *Let $U = \{x, y, z\}$, $A = \{a, b, c\}$, and $At = A \cup \{o\}$. Consider order relations induced by attributes given by:*

$$\succ_{\{a\}}^*: \quad [x] \succ_{\{a\}}^* [y, z],$$
$$\succ_{\{b\}}^*: \quad [x, y] \succ_{\{b\}}^* [z],$$
$$\succ_{\{c\}}^*: \quad [z] \succ_{\{c\}}^* [y] \succ_{\{c\}}^* [x],$$
$$\succ_{\{o\}}^*: \quad [x] \succ_{\{o\}}^* [y] \succ_{\{o\}}^* [z].$$

For the set $\{a, b, c\}$, we have:

$$
\begin{aligned}
E(\{a, b, c\}) = \quad & \{(a, \succ) \wedge (b, \preceq) \wedge (c, \preceq), \\
& (a, \succ) \wedge (b, \succ) \wedge (c, \preceq), \\
& (a, \preceq) \wedge (b, \preceq) \wedge (c, \succ), \\
& (a, \preceq) \wedge (b, \succ) \wedge (c, \preceq), \dots\} \\
= \quad & \{\phi_1, \phi_2, \phi_3, \phi_4, \dots\}.
\end{aligned}
$$

The relationships between orderings induced by a, b, c and o can be seen as follows:

$$
\begin{aligned}
m(o, \succ) &= \{(x, y), (x, z), (y, z)\}, \\
m(o, \preceq) &= \{(y, x), (z, x), (z, y)\}, \\
m(\phi_1) &= \{(x, y)\} \subseteq m(o, \succ), \\
m(\phi_2) &= \{(x, z)\} \subseteq m(o, \succ), \\
m(\phi_3) &= \{(y, x), (z, x), (z, y)\} \subseteq m(o, \preceq), \\
m(\phi_4) &= \{(y, z)\} \subseteq m(o, \succ).
\end{aligned}
$$

We have:

$$\bigcup_{\phi \in E(A)} M_o(\phi) = (U \times U)^+.$$

For the subset $\{a, b\}$, we obtain:

$$
\begin{aligned}
E(\{a, b\}) &= \{(a, \succ) \wedge (b, \preceq), (a, \succ) \wedge (b, \succ), \\
& \quad (a, \preceq) \wedge (b, \preceq), (a, \preceq) \wedge (b, \succ)\} \\
&= \{\phi_1', \phi_2', \phi_3', \phi_4'\}.
\end{aligned}
$$

We have:

$$
\begin{aligned}
m(\phi_1') &= \{(x, y)\} &\subseteq m(o, \succ), \\
m(\phi_2') &= \{(x, z)\} &\subseteq m(o, \succ), \\
m(\phi_3') &= \{(y, x), (z, x), (z, y)\} &\subseteq m(o, \preceq), \\
m(\phi_4') &= \{(y, z)\} &\subseteq m(o, \succ),
\end{aligned}
$$

and

$$\bigcup_{\phi' \in E(\{a, b\})} M_o(\phi') = (U \times U)^+.$$

Since $\bigcup_{\phi \in E(A)} M_o(\phi) = \bigcup_{\phi' \in E(\{a, b\})} M_o(\phi')$, attribute sets $\{a, b, c\}$ and $\{a, b\}$ are equivalent with respect to o. It is easy to check that $\{a\}$ and $\{b\}$ are not equivalent to A, i.e., the attribute set $\{a, b\}$ is an independent set, and is is a relative reduct. One can also show that $\{c\}$ is the other relative reduct of A. Hence we have $RED_o(A) = \{\{a, b\}, \{c\}\}$ and $CORE_o(A) = \emptyset$.

4 Mining Ordering Rules

Data mining in an ordered information table may be formulated as finding association between orderings induced by attributes. One is interested in finding associations between two arbitrary subsets of attributes A and B.

Definition 17 *Consider two subsets of attributes $A, B \subseteq At$. For two expressions $\phi \in E(A)$ and $\psi \in E(B)$, an ordering rule is read "if ϕ then ψ" and denoted by $\phi \Rightarrow \psi$. The expression ϕ is called the rule's antecedent, while the expression ψ is called the rule's consequent.*

An ordering rule states how orderings of objects by attributes in A determines orderings of objects by attributes in B. For example, an ordering rule,

$$(a, \succ) \wedge (b, \preceq) \Rightarrow (c, \succ),$$

can be re-expressed as,

$$x \succ_{\{a\}} y \wedge x \preceq_{\{b\}} y \Rightarrow x \succ_{\{c\}} y.$$

That is, for two arbitrary objects x and y, if x is ranked ahead of y by attribute a, and at the same time, x is not ranked ahead of y by attribute b, then x is ranked ahead of y by attribute c. We adopt conditional probabilistic interpretations for ordering rules. A systematic analysis of probability related quantities associated with rules was given by Yao and Zhong [16]. We choose to use two measures called accuracy and coverage [10].

Definition 18 *The accuracy and coverage of an ordering rule, $\phi \Rightarrow \psi$, are defined, respectively, by:*

$$accuracy(\phi \Rightarrow \psi) = \frac{|m(\phi \wedge \psi)|}{|m(\phi)|},$$

$$coverage(\phi \Rightarrow \psi) = \frac{|m(\phi \wedge \psi)|}{|m(\psi)|}, \qquad (9)$$

where $|\cdot|$ denotes the cardinality of a set.

The quantity $accuracy(\phi \Rightarrow \psi)$ gives a measure of the correctness of the rule, and $coverage(\phi \Rightarrow \psi)$ gives a measure of the applicability of the rule. In the extreme case, if $accuracy = 1$, the ordering by ϕ would determine the ordering by ψ. If $coverage = 1$, the rule states something about the entire ordering by ψ. The accuracy and coverage are not independent of each other, as both are related to the quantity $|m(\phi \wedge \psi)|$. It is desirable for a rule to be accurate as well as to have a high degree of coverage. In general, one may observe a trade-off between accuracy and coverage. A rule with higher coverage may have a lower accuracy, while a rule with higher accuracy may have a lower coverage.

Example 4 *From the data in Example 1, we can get, for example, two ordering rules:*

$$(b, \preceq) \wedge (c, \preceq) \Rightarrow (o, \preceq),$$
$$accuracy = 1.0, \quad coverage = 0.615,$$
$$(c, \succ) \Rightarrow (o, \succ),$$
$$accuracy = 0.625, \quad coverage = 0.714.$$

To mine ordering rules from an ordered information table, we transform an ordered information table into a binary information. Any standard data mining algorithms can be immediately applied. In the binary information table, we consider object pairs $(x, y) \in (U \times U)^+$. The information function is defined by:

$$I_a(x, y) = \begin{cases} 1, & x \succ_{\{a\}} y, \\ 0, & x \preceq_{\{a\}} y. \end{cases} \qquad (10)$$

Statements in an ordered information table can be translated into equivalent statements in the binary information table. For example, $x \succ_{\{a\}} y$ can be translated into $I_a(x, y) = 1$. In the translation process, we will not consider object pairs of the form (x, x), as we are not interested in them.

In our approach, the interpretation of an ordered information table and the translation to a binary information table are crucial. Once we obtain the binary information table, any existing data mining algorithm can be used to mine ordering rules. For example, using Rosetta, a rough set toolkit for analyzing data, one can obtain a set of minimal ordering rules from reducts with certain properties [9]. A well known machine learning system C4.5 can also be used to learn ordering rules [8].

Object	a	b	c	d	o
$(1,2)$	1	0	1	1	1
$(1,3)$	0	0	1	0	1
$(1,4)$	0	0	1	0	1
$(1,5)$	0	1	0	0	1
$(2,1)$	0	0	0	0	0
$(2,3)$	0	0	0	0	0
$(2,4)$	0	0	0	0	0
$(2,5)$	0	1	0	0	0
$(3,1)$	1	0	0	1	0
$(3,2)$	1	0	0	1	0
$(3,4)$	0	0	0	0	0
$(3,5)$	0	1	0	0	0
$(4,1)$	1	0	0	1	0
$(4,2)$	1	0	1	1	1
$(4,3)$	0	0	1	1	1
$(4,5)$	0	1	0	0	1
$(5,1)$	1	0	0	1	0
$(5,2)$	1	0	1	1	0
$(5,3)$	0	0	1	1	0
$(5,4)$	0	0	1	0	0

Table 2. A binary information table derived from an ordered information table

Example 5 *Consider the ordered information table in Example 1. It can be transformed into the binary information table, given by Table 2. For this table, we obtain a reduct consisting of $\{b, c\}$. Examples of rules are given by:*

$R_1:$ $(b, \preceq) \wedge (c, \preceq) \Rightarrow (o, \preceq),$
$$accuracy = 1, \quad coverage = 0.615;$$

$R_2:$ $(c, \succ) \Rightarrow (o, \succ),$
$$accuracy = 0.625, \quad coverage = 0.714;$$

$R_3:$ $(b, \succ) \Rightarrow (o, \succ),$
$$accuracy = 0.5, \quad coverage = 0.286.$$

For R_2, it can be paraphrazed as saying that if $x \succ_{\{c\}} y$ then $x \succ_{\{o\}} y$ with accuracy 0.625 and coverage 0.714.

One may use other types of translation methods. For example, we may consider two strict order relations $\succ$ and $\prec$, instead of $\succ$ and $\preceq$. Alternatively, one may translate an ordered information table into a three-valued information table, corresponding to $\succ$, $\prec$, and $\sim$. Greco, Matarazzo and Slowinski used graded preference relations which produce a multi-valued information table [3]. By translating an ordered information table into a multi-valued information table, one may consider magnitudes of attribute values. Unfortunately, it may be difficult to interpret these magnitudes. They must be obtained from either experts or experiments.

For this reason, we focus on the binary information table approach. It is important to realize that the framework presented in this paper can be easily applied with very simple modification.

5 A Real World Example

To demonstrate the usefulness and effectiveness of the proposed model, we analyze the data from the Maclean's universities 2000 ranking [5]. The Maclean's ranking compared universities with similar structures and mandates. All universities in Canada are classified into one of three categories: Medical/Doctoral universities, Comprehensive universities, and Primarily Undergraduate universities. Maclean's ranked 15 Medical/Doctoral universities based on 22 performance measure that are divided into six groupings, namely, Student Body (22%), Classes (17%), Faculty (17%), Finances (12%), Library (12 %), and Reputation (20%), where the weights in the parentheses indicate the contributions of the measures to the overall ranking. Table 3 summarizes the ranking measures.

The 22 performance measures produce 22 individual rankings and an overall ranking suggested by Maclean's. The details can be found in the November issue of Maclean's [5]. Using data analysis and data mining method introduced earlier, we can find reduct(s) and the core of the ordered information table. We can also induce ordering rules which state association between the overall ranking and the rankings by 22 performance measures.

For our experiment, we used the Rosetta, a rough set toolkit for analyzing data [9]. We found that there are several reducts for this information table. One reduct with the minimal set length for explanation is $\{c1, f3, fi3, l4, r1, s2, s5\}$. This suggests that one can use seven measures to provides the same overall ranking of universities as given by Maclean's. The total weight of the seven measures is only 30.8%. In addition, measures in this reduct do not necessarily have the highest weights among performance measures. The number of measures in the reduct and the total weight are less than 1/3 of the ones used in the entire table. We also find that the core is empty, which means that there does not exist a measure that is absolutely essential for producing the overall ranking. These observations are interesting, as they indicate that some measures used by Maclean's may not be necessary, and moreover the weights may not necessarily reflect the importance of measures in producing the overall ranking. Another interesting observation of the the reduct $\{c1, f3, fi3, l4, r1, s2, s5\}$ is that it contains at least one measure from each of the six categories.

Many ordering rules were found by using Rosetta. As examples, we list some rules with accuracy 1 and the highest degrees of coverage:

$$R_1 : (f4, \succ) \wedge (fi3, \succ) \wedge (s2, \succ) \Rightarrow (o, \succ),$$

$$coverage = 0.6,$$
$$R_2 : (f2, \succ) \wedge (fi3, \succ) \wedge (r1, \succ) \Rightarrow (o, \succ),$$
$$coverage = 0.590476,$$
$$R_3 : (fi3, \succ) \wedge (r1, \succ) \wedge (s2, \succ) \Rightarrow (o, \succ),$$
$$coverage = 0.590476,$$
$$R_4 : (f1, \succ) \wedge (fi3, \succ) \wedge (s1, \succ) \Rightarrow (o, \succ),$$
$$coverage = 0.580952,$$
$$R_5 : (f4, \succ) \wedge (r2, \succ) \wedge (s2, \succ) \Rightarrow (o, \succ),$$
$$coverage = 0.580952,$$
$$R_6 : (f4, \succ) \wedge (fi3, \succ) \wedge (s1, \succ) \Rightarrow (o, \succ),$$
$$coverage = 0.571429.$$

All the rules use only three performance measures. Even using such a small number of measures, one can correctly state close to 60% of the overall ranking.

Although the preliminary results obtained from the Maclean's university ranking may need further study, in-depth analysis, and careful interpretation, they at least present another point of view to look at the important issue of university ranking. An added advantage is that our method is of qualitative nature, without considering any quantitative information.

6 Conclusions

Ordering of objects is a fundamental issue in human decision making and may play a significant role in the design of intelligent information systems. This problem is considered from the perspective of data mining. The commonly used attribute value approaches are extended by introducing order relations on attribute values. A data analysis model is thus proposed to describe properties of ordered information tables. Mining ordering rules is formulated as the process of finding associations between orderings on attribute values and the overall ordering of objects. These ordering rules tell us, or explain, how objects should be ranked according to orderings on their attribute values.

The proposed solution for mining ordering rules is simple. Our main contribution is the formulation of the problem, and the translation of the problem to existing data mining problem. Consequently, one can directly apply any existing data mining algorithms for mining ordering rules. The application of the proposed model to a real world example demonstrates its usefulness and effectiveness. Depending on the specific problems, one may use different translation methods.

References

[1] Cohen, W.W., Schapire, R.E., and Singer, Y., Learning to order things, *Advances in Neural Information*

measure	meaning	weight
s1	incoming students' average high-school grades	12%
s2	proportion of those with averages of 75 per cent or more	3%
s3	proportion of out-of-province first-year undergraduate students	1%
s4	percentage of international students at the graduate level	1%
s5	graduation rates	2%
s6	proportion of winning national academic awards	3%
c1	class sizes at the first- and second-year levels	7%
c2	class sizes at the third- and fourth-year levels	7%
c3	percentage of first-year classes taught by tenured/tenure-track professors	3%
f1	percentage of those with PhDs	3%
f2	the number who win national awards	3%
f3	social sciences and humanities grants, Canada Council grants last year	5.5%
f4	medical/science grants last year	5.5%
fi1	the amount of money for current expenses per weighted full-time-equivalent student	3.3%
fi2	percentage of the budget spent on student services	4.3%
fi3	scholarships and bursaries	4.3%
l1	the number of volumes and volume equivalents per total number of students	3%
l2	total holdings	1%
l3	percentage of a university's operating budget that was allocated to library services	4%
l4	percentage of the actual library budget that was spent on updating the collection	4%
r1	alumni support	5%
r2	reputational survey	15%

Table 3. Maclean's performance measures for universities ranking, 2000

Processing Systems, **10**, 1998.

[2] Greco, S., Matarazzo, B., and Slowinski, R., The use of rough sets and fuzzy sets in MCDM, In: *Advances in Multiple Criteria Decision Making*, Gal, T., Hanne, T., and Stewart, T. (Eds.) Kluwer Academic Publishers, Boston, pp. 14.1-14.59, 1999.

[3] Greco, S., Matarazzo, B., and Slowinski, R., Rough approximation of a preference relation by dominance relations, *European Journal of Operational Research* **117**, 63-83, 1999.

[4] Iwinski, T.B., Ordinal information system, I, *Bulletin of the Polish Academy of Sciences, Mathematics*, **36**, 467-475, 1988.

[5] Maclean's Universities 2000, *Macleans*, November 20, 2000.

[6] Pawlak, Z., *Rough Sets, Theoretical Aspects of Reasoning about Data*, Kluwer Academic Publishers, Dordrecht, 1991.

[7] Pawlak, Z. and Slowinski, R., Rough set approach to multi-attribute decision analysis. *European Journal of Operational Research*, **72**, 443-359, 1994.

[8] Quinlan, J.R., *C4.5: Program for Machine Learning*, Morgan Kaufmann Publishers, San Marteo, 1993.

[9] Rosetta, a rough set toolkit for analyzing data, *http://www.idi.ntnu.no/ aleks/rosetta/*.

[10] Tsumoto, S., Modelling medical diagnostic rules based on rough sets, *Rough Sets and Current Trends in Computing, Lecture Notes in Artificial Intelligence, 1424*, Springer-Verlag, Berlin, pp. 475-482, 1998.

[11] Yao, Y.Y., Generalized rough set models, in: *Rough Sets in Knowledge Discovery*, Polkowski, L. and Skowron, A. (Eds.), Physica-Verlag, Heidelberg, pp. 286-318, 1998.

[12] Yao, Y.Y., Information tables with neighborhood semantics, in: *Data Mining and Knowledge Discovery: Theory, Tools, and Technology II*, Dasarathy, B.V. (Ed.), Society for Optical Engineering, Bellingham, Washington, pp. 108-116, 2000.

[13] Yao, Y.Y. and Lin, T.Y., Generalization of rough sets using modal logic, *Intelligent Automation and Soft Computing, An International Journal*, **2**, 103-120, 1996.

[14] Yao, Y.Y. and Sai, Y., Mining ordering rules using rough set theory, *Bulletin of International Rough Set Society*, **5**, 99-106, 2001.

[15] Yao, Y.Y. and Sai, Y., On mining ordering rules, manuscript, 2001.

[16] Yao, Y.Y. and Zhong, N., An analysis of quantitative measures associated with rules, *Proceedings of PAKDD'99*, 479-488, 1999.

LPMiner: An Algorithm for Finding Frequent Itemsets Using Length-Decreasing Support Constraint*

Masakazu Seno and George Karypis
Department of Computer Science and Engineering, Army HPC Research Center
University of Minnesota
4-192 EE/CS Building, 200 Union Street SE, Minneapolis, MN 55455
Fax: (612) 625-0572
{seno, karypis}@cs.umn.edu

Abstract

Over the years, a variety of algorithms for finding frequent itemsets in very large transaction databases have been developed. The key feature in most of these algorithms is that they use a constant support constraint to control the inherently exponential complexity of the problem. In general, itemsets that contain only a few items will tend to be interesting if they have a high support, whereas long itemsets can still be interesting even if their support is relatively small. Ideally, we desire to have an algorithm that finds all the frequent itemsets whose support decreases as a function of their length. In this paper we present an algorithm called LPMiner, that finds all itemsets that satisfy a length-decreasing support constraint. Our experimental evaluation shows that LPMiner is up to two orders of magnitude faster than the FP-growth algorithm for finding itemsets at a constant support constraint, and that its runtime increases gradually as the average length of the transactions (and the discovered itemsets) increases.

1 Introduction

Data mining research during the last eight years has led to the development of a variety of algorithms for finding frequent itemsets in very large transaction databases [2, 1, 4, 8]. These itemsets can be used to find association rules or extract prevalent patterns that exist in the transactions, and have been effectively used in many different domains and applications.

The key feature in most of these algorithms is that they control the inherently exponential complexity of the problem by finding only the itemsets that occur in a sufficiently large fraction of the transactions, called the *support*. A limitation of this paradigm for generating frequent itemsets is that it uses a constant value of support, irrespective of the length of the discovered itemsets. In general, itemsets that contain only a few items will tend to be interesting if they have a high support, whereas long itemsets can still be interesting even if their support is relatively small. Unfortunately, if constant-support-based frequent itemset discovery algorithms are used to find some of the longer but infrequent itemsets, they will end up generating an exponentially large number of short itemsets. Maximal frequent itemset discovery algorithms [8] can potentially be used to find some of these longer itemsets, but these algorithms can still generate a very large number of short infrequent itemsets if these itemsets are maximal. Ideally, we desire to have an algorithm that finds all the frequent itemsets whose support decreases as a function of their length. Developing such an algorithm is particularly challenging because the downward closure property of the constant support constraint cannot be used to prune short infrequent itemsets.

In this paper we present another property, called *smallest valid extension* (SVE), that can be used to prune the search space of potential itemsets in the case where the support decreases as a function of the itemset length. Using this property, we developed an algorithm called LPMiner, that finds all itemsets that satisfy a length-decreasing support constraint. LPMiner uses the recently proposed FP-tree [4] data structure to compactly store the database transactions in main memory, and the SVE property to prune certain portions of the conditional FP-trees, that are being generated during itemset discovery. Our experimental evaluation shows that LPMiner is up to two orders of magnitude faster than the FP-growth algorithm for finding itemsets at a constant support constraint, and that its runtime increases

---
*This work was supported by NSF CCR-9972519, EIA-9986042, ACI-9982274, by Army Research Office contract DA/DAAG55-98-1-0441, by the DOE ASCI program, and by Army High Performance Computing Research Center contract number DAAH04-95-C-0008. Access to computing facilities was provided by the Minnesota Supercomputing Institute.

gradually as the average length of the transactions (and the discovered itemsets) increases.

The rest of this paper is organized as follows. Section 2 provides some background information and related research work. Section 3 describes the FP-growth algorithm [4], on which LPMiner is based. In Section 4, we describe how the length-decreasing support constraint can be exploited to prune the search space of frequent itemsets. The experimental results of our algorithm are shown in Section 5, followed by the conclusion in Section 6.

2 Background and related works

The problem of finding frequent itemsets is formally defined as follows: Given a set of transactions T, each containing a set of items from the set I, and a support σ, we want to find all subsets of items that occur in at least $\sigma|T|$ transactions. These subsets are called *frequent itemsets*.

Over the years a number of algorithms have been developed for finding all frequent itemsets. The first computationally efficient algorithm for finding itemsets in large databases was Apriori [2], which finds frequent itemsets of length l based on previously generated $(l-1)$-length frequent itemsets. The key idea of Apriori is to use the downward closure property of the support constraint to prune the space of frequent itemsets. The FP-growth algorithm [4] finds frequent itemsets by using a data structure called FP-tree that can compactly store in memory the transactions of the original database, thus eliminating the need to access the disks more than twice. Another efficient way to represent transaction database is to use *vertical tid-list database* format. The vertical database format associates each item with all the transactions that include the item. Eclat in [7] uses this data format to find all frequent itemsets.

Even though to our knowledge no work has been published for finding frequent itemsets in which the support decreases as a function of the length of the itemset, there has been some work in developing itemset discovery algorithms that use multiple support constraints. Liu *et al.* [5] presented an algorithm in which each item has its own minimum item support (or MIS). The minimum support of an itemset is the lowest MIS among those items in the itemset. By sorting items in ascending order of their MIS values, the minimum support of the itemset never decreases as the length of itemset grows, making the support of itemsets downward closed. Thus an Apriori-based algorithm can be applied. Wang *et al.* [6] allow a set of more general support constraints. In particular, they associate a support constraint for each one of the itemsets. By introducing a new function called Pminsup that has "Apriori-like" property, they proposed an Apriori-based algorithm for finding the frequent itemsets. It is possible to represent a length-decreasing support constraint by using the formulation in [6]. However, the "*pushed*" minimum support of each itemset is forced to

be equal to the support value corresponding to the longest itemset. Thus, it cannot prune the search space. Finally, Cohen *et al.* [3] adopt a different approach in that they do not use any support constraint. Instead, they search for similar itemsets using probabilistic algorithms, that do not guarantee that all frequent itemsets can be found.

3 FP-growth algorithm

In this section, we describe how the FP-growth algorithm works because our approach is based on this algorithm. The description here is based on [4].

The key idea behind FP-growth is to use a data structure called FP-tree to obtain a compact representation of the original transactions so that they can fit into the main memory. As a result, any subsequent operations that are required to find the frequent itemsets can be performed quickly, without having to access the disks. The FP-growth algorithm achieves that by performing just two passes over the transactions. Figure 1 shows how the FP-tree generation algorithm works given an input transaction database that has five transactions with a total of six different items. First, it scans the transaction database to count how many times each item occurs in the database to get an "Item Support Table" (step (a)). The "Item Support Table" has a set of (item-name, support) pairs. For example, item A occurs twice in the database, namely in a transaction with tid 1 and another one with tid 5; therefore its support is $2/5 = 40\%$. In step (b), those items in the Item Support Table are sorted according to their support. The result is stored in item-name field of Node-Link header table NL. Notice that item F is not included in NL because the support of item F is less than the minimum support constraint 40%. In step (c), items in each transaction in the input transaction database are sorted in the same order as items in the Node-Link header table NL. While transaction tid 5 is sorted, item F is discarded because the item is infrequent and has no need of consideration. In step (d), the FP-tree is generated by inserting those sorted transactions one by one. The initial FP-tree has only its root. When the first transaction is inserted, nodes that represent item B, C, E, A, and D are generated, forming a path from the root in this order. The count of each node is set to 1 because each node represents only one transaction (tid 1) so far. Next, when the second transaction is inserted, a node representing item B is *not* generated. Instead, the node already generated is reused. In this case, because the root node has a child that represents item B, the count of the node is incremented by one. As for item E, since there is no child representing item E under the current node, a new node with item-name E is generated as a child of the current node. Similar processes are repeated until all the sorted transactions are inserted into the FP-tree.

Once an FP-tree is generated from the input transaction database, the algorithm mines frequent itemsets from the

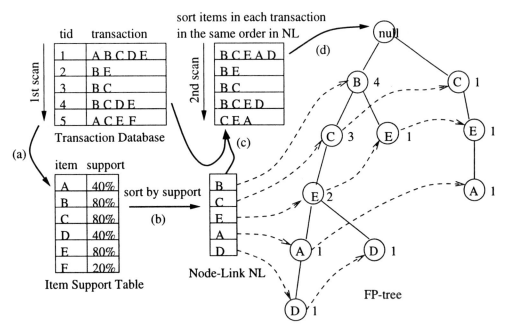

Figure 1. Flow of FP-tree generation.

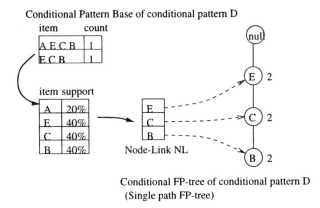

Conditional Pattern Base of conditional pattern D

Conditional FP-tree of conditional pattern D
(Single path FP-tree)

Figure 2. Conditional FP-tree.

FP-tree. The algorithm generates itemsets from shorter to longer ones adding items one-by-one to those itemsets already generated. It divides mining the FP-tree into mining smaller FP-trees, each of which is based on an item on the Node-Link header table in Figure 1. Let us choose item D as an example. For item D, we generate a new transaction database called *conditional pattern base*. Each transaction in the conditional pattern base consists of items on the paths from parent nodes whose child nodes have item-name D to the root node. The conditional pattern base for item D is shown in Figure 2. Each transaction in the conditional pattern base also has its count of occurrence corresponding to the count of the node with item-name D in the original FP-tree. Note that item D itself is a frequent itemset consisting of one item. Let us call this frequent itemset "D" a *conditional pattern*. A conditional pattern base is a set of transactions each of which includes the conditional

pattern. What we do next is to forget the original FP-tree in Figure 1 for a while and then focus on the conditional pattern base we got just now to generate frequent itemsets that include this conditional pattern "D". For this purpose, we generate a smaller FP-tree than the original one, based on the conditional pattern "D". This new FP-tree, called *conditional FP-tree*, is generated from the conditional pattern base using the FP-tree generation algorithm again. If the conditional FP-tree is not a single path tree, we divide mining this conditional FP-tree to mining even smaller conditional FP-trees recursively. This is repeated until we obtain a conditional FP-tree with only a single path. During those recursively repeated processes, all selected items are added to the conditional pattern. Once we obtain a single path conditional FP-tree like the one in Figure 2, we generate all possible combinations of items along the path and combine each of these sets of items to the conditional pattern. For example, from those three nodes in the conditional FP-tree in Figure 2, we have $2^3 = 8$ combinations of item B, C, and E: " " (no item), "B", "C", "E", "BC", "CE", "EB", and "BCE". Then we obtain frequent itemsets based on conditional pattern base "D": "D", "DB", "DC", "DE", "DBC", "DCE", "DEB", and "DBCE".

4 LPMiner algorithm

LPMiner is an itemset discovery algorithm, based on the FP-growth algorithm, which finds all the itemsets that satisfy a particular length-decreasing support constraint $f(l)$; where l is the length of the itemset. More precisely, $f(l)$ satisfies $f(l_a) \geq f(l_b)$ for any l_a, l_b such that $l_a < l_b$. The idea of introducing this kind of support constraint is that by using a support that decreases with the length of the itemset, we may be able to find long itemsets, that may be of interest, without generating an exponentially large number of shorter itemsets. Figure 3 shows a typical length-decreasing support constraint. In this example, the support constraint decreases linearly to the minimum value and then stays the same for itemsets of longer length. Our problem is restated as finding those itemsets located above the curve determined by length-decreasing support constraint $f(l)$.

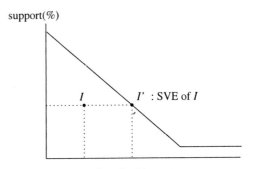

support(%)

I I' : SVE of I

length of itemset
Figure 4. Smallest valid extension (SVE).

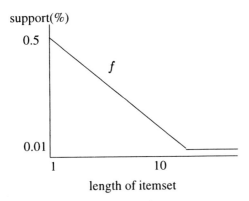

support(%)

0.5

f

0.01

1   10

length of itemset

Figure 3. An example of typical length-decreasing support constraint.

A simple way of finding such itemsets is to use any of the traditional constant-support frequent itemset discovery algorithms, in which the support was set to $\min_{l>0} f(l)$, and then discard the itemsets that do not satisfy the length-decreasing support constraint. This approach, however, does not reduce the number of infrequent itemsets being discovered, and as our experiments will show, requires a large amount of time.

As discussed in the introduction, finding the complete set of itemsets that satisfy a length-decreasing support function is particularly challenging because we cannot use the downward closure property of the constant support frequent itemsets. This property states that in order for an itemset of length l to be frequent, all of its subsets have to be frequent as well. As a result, once we find that an itemset of length l is infrequent, we know that any longer itemsets that include this particular itemset cannot be frequent, and thus eliminate such itemsets from further consideration. However, because in our problem the support of an itemset decreases as its length increases, an itemset *can* be frequent even if its subsets are infrequent.

A key property, regarding the itemset whose support decreases as a function of their length, is the following. Given a particular itemset I with a support of σ_I, such that $\sigma_I < f(|I|)$, then $f^{-1}(\sigma_I) = \min(\{l|f(l) = \sigma_I\})$ is the minimum length that an itemset I' such that $I' \supset I$ must have before it can potentially become frequent. Figure 4

illustrates this relation graphically. The length of I' is nothing more than the point at which a line parallel to the x-axis at $y = \sigma_I$ intersects the support curve; here, we essentially assume the best case in which I' exists and it is supported by the same set of transactions as its subset I. We will refer to this property as the *smallest valid extension* property or *SVE* for short.

LPMiner uses this property as much as it can to prune the conditional FP-trees, that are generated during the itemset discovery phase. In particular, it uses three different pruning methods that, when combined, substantially reduce the search space and the overall runtime. These methods are described in the rest of this section.

4.1 Transaction pruning, TP

The first pruning scheme implemented in LPMiner uses the smallest valid extension property to eliminate entire candidate transactions of a conditional pattern base. Recall from Section 3 that, during frequent itemset generation, the FP-growth algorithm builds a separate FP-tree for all the transactions that contain the conditional pattern currently under consideration. Let CP be that conditional pattern, $|CP|$ be its length, and $\sigma(CP)$ be its support. If CP is infrequent, we know from the SVE property that in order for this conditional pattern to grow to something indeed frequent, it must have a length of at least $f^{-1}(\sigma(CP))$. Using this requirement, before building the FP-tree corresponding to this conditional pattern, we can eliminate any transactions whose length is shorter than $f^{-1}(\sigma(CP)) - |CP|$, as these transactions cannot contribute to a valid frequent itemset in which CP is part of it. We will refer to this as the *transaction pruning* method and denote it by *TP*.

We evaluated the complexity of this method in comparison with the complexity of inserting a transaction to a conditional pattern base. There are three parameters we have to know to prune a transaction: the length of each transaction being inserted, $f^{-1}(\sigma(CP))$, and $|CP|$. The length of each transaction is calculated in a constant time because we can count each item when the transaction is actually being generated. As $f^{-1}(\sigma(CP))$ and $|CP|$ are common values for all transactions in a conditional pattern base, these values need to be calculated only once for the conditional pattern base. It takes a constant time added to the original FP-growth algorithm to calculate $|CP|$. As for $f^{-1}(\sigma(CP))$, evaluating f^{-1} takes $O(\log(|I|))$ to execute binary search on the support table determined by $f(l)$. Let cpb be the conditional pattern base and $m = \sum_{tran \in cpb} |tran|$. The complexity per inserting a transaction is $O(\log(|I|)/m)$. Under an assumption that all items in I are contained in cpb, this value is nothing more than $O(1)$. Thus, the complexity of this method is just a constant time per inserting a transaction.

4.2   Node pruning, NP

The second pruning method focuses on pruning certain nodes of a conditional FP-tree, on which the next conditional pattern base is about to be generated. Let us consider a node v of the FP-tree. Let $I(v)$ be the item stored at this node, $\sigma(I(v))$ be the support of the item in the conditional pattern base, and $h(v)$ be the height of the longest path from the root through v to a leaf node. From the SVE property we know that the node v will contribute to a valid frequent itemset only if

$$h(v) + |CP| \geq f^{-1}(\sigma(I(v))) \tag{1}$$

where $|CP|$ is the length of conditional pattern of the current conditional FP-tree. The reason that equation (1) is correct is because, among the transactions that go through node v, the longest itemset that $I(v)$ can participate in has a length of $h(v)$. Now, if the support of $I(v)$ is small such that it requires an itemset whose length $f^{-1}(\sigma(I(v)))$ is greater than $h(v) + |CP|$, then that itemset cannot be supported by any of the transactions that go through node v. Thus, if equation (1) does not hold, node v can be pruned from the FP-tree. Once node v is pruned, then $\sigma(I(v))$ will decrease as well as the height of the nodes through v, possibly allowing further pruning. We will refer to this as the *node pruning* method, or *NP* for short.

A key observation to make is that both the TP and NP methods can be used together as each one of them prunes portions of the FP-tree that the other one does not. In particular, the NP methods can prune a node in a path that is longer than $f^{-1}(\sigma(CP)) - |CP|$, because the item of that node has lower support than CP. On the other hand, TP reduces the frequency of some itemsets in the FP-tree by removing entire short transactions. For example, consider two transactions; (A, B, C, D) and (A, B). Let's assume that $f^{-1}(\sigma(CP)) - |CP| = 4$, and each one of the items A,B,C,D has a support equal to that of CP. In that case, the NP will not remove any nodes, whereas TP will eliminate the second transaction.

In order to perform the node pruning, we need to compute the height of each node and then traverse each node v

to see if it violates equation (1). If it does, then the node v can be pruned. The height of all the nodes whose longest path goes through v must be decremented by one, and the support of $I(v)$ needs to be decremented to take account of the removal of v. Every time we make such changes in the tree, nodes that could not have been pruned before may now become eligible for pruning. In particular, all the rest of the nodes that have the same item $I(v)$ needs to be rechecked, as well as all the nodes whose height was decremented upon the removal of v. Our initial experiments with such an implementation showed that the cost of performing the pruning was often quite higher than the saving we achieved when used in conjunction with the TP scheme. For this reason we implemented an approximate but fast version of this scheme that achieves a comparable degree of pruning.

Our approximate NP algorithm initially sorts the transactions of the conditional pattern base in decreasing transaction length, then traverses each transaction in that order, and tries to insert them in the FP-tree. Let t be one such transaction and $l(t)$ be its length. When t is inserted into the FP-tree it may share a prefix with some transactions already in the FP-tree. However, as soon as the insertion of t results in a new node being created, we check to see if we can prune it using equation (1). In particular, if v is that newly created node, then $h(v) = l(t)$, because the transactions are inserted into the FP-tree in decreasing length. Thus v can be pruned if

$$l(t) + |CP| < f^{-1}(\sigma(I(v))) \ . \tag{2}$$

If that can be done, the new node is eliminated and the insertion of t continues to the next item. Now if one of the next items inserts a new node u, then that one may be pruned using equation (2). In equation (2), we use the original length of the transaction $l(t)$, not the length after the removal of the item previously pruned. The reason is that $l(t)$ is the correct upper bound of $h(u)$, because one of the transactions inserted later may have a length of at most $l(t)$, the same as the length of the current transaction, and can modify its height.

The above approach is approximate because (i) the elimination of a node affects only the nodes that can be eliminated in the subsequent transactions, not the nodes already in the tree; (ii) we use pessimistic bounds on the height of a node (as discussed in the previous paragraph). This approximate approach, however, does not increase the complexity of generating the conditional FP-tree, beyond the sorting of the transactions in the conditional pattern base. Since the length of the transaction falls within a small range, they can be sorted in linear time using bucket sort.

4.3 Path pruning, PP

Once the tree becomes a single path, the original FP-growth algorithm generates all possible combinations of items along the path and concatenates each of those combinations with its conditional pattern. If the path contains k items, there exist a total of 2^k such combinations. However, using the SVE property we can limit the number of combinations that we may need to consider.

Let $\{i_1, i_2, \ldots, i_k\}$ be the k items such that $\sigma(i_j) \geq \sigma(i_{j+1})$. One way of generating all possible 2^k combinations is to grow them incrementally as follows. First, we create two sets, one that contains i_1, and the other that does not. Next, for each of these sets, we generate two new sets such that, in each pair of them, one contains i_2 and the other does not, leading to four different sets. By continuing this process a total of k times, we will obtain all possible 2^k combinations of items. This approach essentially builds a binary tree with k levels of edges, in which the nodes correspond to the possible combinations. One such binary tree for $k = 4$ is shown in Figure 5.

To see how the SVE property can be used to prune certain subgraphs of this tree (and hence combinations to be explored), consider a particular internal node v of that tree. Let $h(v)$ be the height of the node (root has a height of zero), and let $\beta(v)$ be the number of edges that were one on the path from the root to v. In other words, $\beta(v)$ is the number of items that have been included so far in the set. Using the SVE property we can stop expanding the tree under node v if and only if

$$\beta(v) + (k - h(v)) + |CP| < f^{-1}(\sigma(I_{h(v)})) \ .$$

Essentially, the above formula states that, based on the frequency of the current item, the set must have a sufficiently large number of items before it can be frequent. If the number of items that were already inserted in the set ($\beta(v)$) plus the number of items that are left for possible insertion ($k - h(v)$) is not sufficiently large, then no frequent itemsets can be generated from this branch of the tree, and hence it can be pruned. We will refer to this method as *path pruning* or *PP* for short.

The complexity of PP per one binary tree is $k \log |I|$ because we need to evaluate f^{-1} for k items. On the other hand, the original FP-growth algorithm has the complexity of $O(2^k)$ for one binary tree. The former is much smaller for large k. For small k, this analysis tells that PP may cost more than the saving. Our experimental result, however, suggests that the effect of pruning is bigger than the cost.

5 Experimental results

We experimentally evaluated the various search space pruning methods of LPMiner using a variety of datasets generated by the synthetic transaction generator that is provided

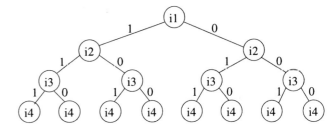

Figure 5. Binary tree when $k = 4$.

by the IBM Quest group and was used in evaluating the Apriori algorithm [2]. All of our experiments were performed on Intel-based Linux workstations with Pentium III at 600MHz and 1GB of main memory. All the reported runtimes are in seconds.

We used two classes of datasets DS1 and DS2. Both of them contained 100K transactions. For each of the two classes we generated different problem instances in which we varied the average size of the transactions from 3 items to 35 items for DS1, obtaining a total of 33 different datasets, DS1.3, ..., DS1.35, and from 3 items to 30 items for DS2, obtaining DS2.3, ..., DS2.30. For each problem instance in both of DS1.x and DS2.x, we set the average size of the maximal long itemset to be $x/2$, so as x increases, the dataset contains longer frequent itemsets. The difference between DS1.x and DS2.x is that each problem instance DS1.x consists of 1K items, whereas each problem instance DS2.x consists of 5K items. The characteristics of these datasets are summarized in Table 1.

Table 1. Parameters for datasets used in our tests ($|D|$: Number of transactions, $|T|$: Average size of the transactions, $|I|$: Average size of the maximal potentially long itemsets, $|L|$: Number of maximal potentially large itemsets, N: Number of items).

parameter	DS1	DS2
$|D|$	100K	100K
$|T|$	3 to 35	3 to 30
$|I|$	$|T|/2$	$|T|/2$
$|L|$	10000	10000
N	1000	5000

In all of our experiments, we used minimum support constraint that decreases linearly with the length of the frequent itemsets. In particular, for each of the DS1.x datasets, the initial value of support was set to 0.5 and it was decreased linearly down to 0.01 for itemsets up to length x. For the rest of the itemsets, the support was kept fixed at 0.01. The left graph of Figure 6 shows the shape of the support curve for DS1.20. In the case of the DS2 class of datasets, we used a similar approach to generate the constraint, however instead of using 0.01 as the minimum support, we used 0.005.

The right graph of Figure 6 shows the shape of the support curve for DS2.20.

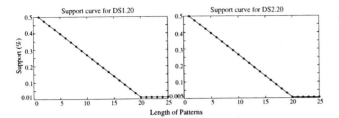

Figure 6. Support curve for DS1.20 and DS2.20.

5.1 Results

Tables 2 and 3 show the experimental results that we obtained for the DS1 and DS2 datasets, respectively. Each row of the tables shows the results obtained for a different DS1.x or DS2.x dataset, specified on the first column. The remaining columns show the amount of time required by different itemset discovery algorithms. The column labeled "FP-growth" shows the amount of time taken by the original FP-growth algorithm using a constant support constraint that corresponds to the smallest support of the support curve, 0.01 for DS1, and 0.005 for DS2. The columns under the heading "LPMiner" show the amount of time required by the proposed itemset discovery algorithm that uses the decreasing support curve to prune the search space. A total of seven different variations of the LPMiner algorithm are presented that use different combinations of the pruning methods described in Section 4. For example, the column label "NP" corresponds to the scheme that uses only node pruning (Section 4.2), whereas the column labeled "NP+TP+PP" corresponds to the scheme that uses all the three different schemes described in Section 4. Note that values with a "-" correspond to experiments that were aborted because they were taking too long time.

A number of interesting observations can be made from the results in these tables. First, either one of the LPMiner methods performs better than the FP-growth algorithm. In particular, the LPMiner that uses all three pruning methods does the best, requiring substantially smaller time than the FP-growth algorithm. For DS1, it is about 2.2 times faster for DS1.10, 8.2 times faster for DS1.20, 33.4 times faster for DS1.30, and 115 times faster for DS1.35. Similar trends can be observed for DS2, in which the performance of LPMiner is 4.2 times faster for DS2.10, 21.0 times faster for DS2.20, and 55.6 times faster for DS2.27.

Second, the performance gap between FP-growth and LPMiner increases as the length of the discovered frequent itemset increases (recall that, for both DS1.x and DS2.x, the length of the frequent itemsets increases with x). This is due to the fact that the overall itemset space that LPMiner can prune becomes larger, leading to improved relative performance.

Third, comparing the different pruning methods in isolation, we can see that NP and TP lead to the largest runtime reduction and PP achieves the smallest reduction. This is not surprising as PP can only prune itemsets during the late stages of itemset generation.

Finally, the runtime with three pruning methods increases gradually as the average length of the transactions (and the discovered itemsets) increases, whereas the runtime of the original FP-growth algorithm increases exponentially.

6 Conclusion

In this paper we presented an algorithm that can efficiently find all frequent itemsets that satisfy a length-decreasing support constraint. The key insight that enabled us to achieve high performance was the smallest valid extension property of the length decreasing support curve.

So far, we have dealt with a common length-decreasing support for all the items. However, the proposed algorithm can be easily extended to allow different length-decreasing support constraint to be specified for each item or itemset.

References

[1] R. Agarwal, C. Aggarwal, V. Prasad, and V. Crestana. A tree projection algorithm for generation of large itemsets for association rules. *IBM Research Report*, RC21341, November 1998.

[2] R. Agrawal and R. Srikant. Fast algorithms for mining association rules. In *Proc. of the 20th Int'l Conference on Very Large Databases*, Santiago, Chile, September 1994.

[3] E. Cohen, M. Datar, S. Fujiwara, A. Gionis, P. Indyk, R. Motwani, J. D. Ullman, and C. Yang. Finding interesting associations without support pruning. In *ICDE*, pages 489–499, 2000.

[4] J. Han, J. Pei, and Y. Yin. Mining frequent patterns without candidate generation. In *Proc. 2000 ACM-SIGMOD Int. Conf. Management of Data (SIGMOD'00)*, pages 1–12, Dallas, TX, May 2000.

[5] B. Liu, W. Hsu, and Y. Ma. Mining association rules with multiple minimum supports. In *SIGKDD 1999*, 1999.

[6] K. Wang, Y. He, and J. Han. Mining frequent itemsets using support constraints. In *The VLDB Journal*, pages 43–52, 2000.

[7] M. J. Zaki. Scalable algorithms for association mining. *IEEE Transactions on Knowledge and Data Engineering*, 12(3):372–390, May/June 2000.

[8] M. J. Zaki and K. Gouda. Fast vertical mining using diffsets. Technical Report 01-1, RPI, 2001.

Table 2. Comparison of pruning methods using DS1.

Dataset	FP-growth	LPMiner						
		NP	TP	PP	NP+TP	NP+PP	TP+PP	NP+TP+PP
DS1.3	3.664	3.559	3.695	3.672	3.614	3.598	3.706	3.572
DS1.4	4.837	3.816	4.423	4.828	3.764	3.871	4.407	3.775
DS1.5	7.454	5.035	6.361	7.467	4.904	4.993	6.369	4.865
DS1.6	11.164	6.813	8.810	11.149	6.324	6.829	8.813	6.421
DS1.7	15.316	8.778	11.827	15.329	8.065	8.798	11.842	8.051
DS1.8	22.079	12.153	15.666	22.065	10.701	12.155	15.630	10.667
DS1.9	28.122	15.260	19.676	28.025	13.519	15.245	19.695	13.559
DS1.10	40.427	21.369	25.035	40.387	18.322	21.291	25.038	18.342
DS1.11	49.420	25.276	29.291	49.583	22.320	25.767	29.805	22.178
DS1.12	71.091	32.806	35.726	70.920	27.886	32.648	35.595	27.874
DS1.13	86.639	38.489	41.226	86.282	32.921	38.271	41.203	32.805
DS1.14	130.604	47.867	48.314	125.701	40.552	47.590	48.261	40.389
DS1.15	155.171	54.868	54.903	154.612	46.734	54.727	54.839	47.934
DS1.16	255.528	67.794	68.522	253.890	56.468	67.161	64.066	60.442
DS1.17	289.600	73.841	70.428	285.373	63.333	77.307	70.126	61.611
DS1.18	409.961	85.851	80.079	404.513	71.296	84.641	79.170	71.043
DS1.19	488.898	95.666	89.101	483.596	79.276	94.794	88.480	78.827
DS1.20	730.399	113.983	105.252	711.947	93.823	110.499	101.096	89.358
DS1.21	856.614	125.378	117.470	837.304	102.944	122.580	114.886	100.077
DS1.22	1224.417	145.259	141.530	1180.976	117.607	137.180	133.186	109.376
DS1.23	1430.478	153.676	156.277	1385.205	124.548	150.661	151.419	121.270
DS1.24	1840.375	183.516	191.363	1739.318	142.728	174.060	184.608	134.174
DS1.25	2147.452	199.894	219.430	2038.823	155.002	193.338	210.911	148.172
DS1.26	3465.201	287.813	306.509	3134.160	212.427	226.667	259.939	166.956
DS1.27	3811.978	296.645	336.420	3479.318	217.086	253.775	302.121	185.205
DS1.28	7512.347	2142.169	1911.442	4646.935	1733.971	300.822	362.577	210.955
DS1.29	8150.431	1748.402	1552.467	5271.311	1288.414	337.896	412.495	233.016
DS1.30	8884.682	431.021	534.117	7370.503	338.811	397.331	489.129	266.111
DS1.31	9744.785	489.858	604.189	8073.919	347.581	447.265	568.864	302.462
DS1.32	31063.532	11001.177	8289.842	12143.147	7943.063	547.121	676.441	361.113
DS1.33	29965.612	4750.367	1789.832	14037.153	1423.910	615.470	760.411	408.505
DS1.34	51420.519	16214.516	10990.934	18027.933	10446.444	751.236	905.894	487.831
DS1.35	64473.916	11282.476	6828.611	21458.692	6426.131	856.127	1024.330	561.449

Table 3. Comparison of pruning methods using DS2.

Dataset	FP-growth	LPMiner						
		NP	TP	PP	NP+TP	NP+PP	TP+PP	NP+TP+PP
DS2.3	11.698	11.436	12.708	12.680	13.392	11.579	11.354	11.277
DS2.4	16.238	15.178	15.060	16.558	15.768	14.762	15.219	14.243
DS2.5	20.230	16.781	17.701	20.406	16.627	16.712	17.516	17.004
DS2.6	33.859	21.293	22.972	33.719	20.705	21.411	23.700	20.691
DS2.7	42.712	23.419	27.253	43.554	22.864	23.583	26.654	23.009
DS2.8	71.215	29.089	33.553	70.947	26.878	28.848	33.619	26.846
DS2.9	90.909	30.675	38.187	89.857	29.446	30.496	38.669	29.732
DS2.10	146.919	37.372	47.848	147.161	34.559	37.153	47.757	35.100
DS2.11	181.040	40.243	54.862	182.041	38.316	39.713	55.119	37.986
DS2.12	275.834	47.299	66.480	274.819	43.653	46.978	66.040	43.281
DS2.13	329.967	49.697	75.979	329.018	47.775	49.714	76.343	47.594
DS2.14	475.752	58.445	90.502	471.671	53.758	56.396	88.981	52.975
DS2.15	542.815	62.627	104.307	539.249	60.567	61.607	103.873	60.503
DS2.16	812.486	80.111	125.099	798.523	72.078	77.162	122.502	70.391
DS2.17	936.694	85.838	142.994	926.153	80.798	84.775	140.097	78.362
DS2.18	1280.641	100.254	165.018	1252.841	93.058	91.616	160.608	86.791
DS2.19	1437.460	106.910	183.748	1409.567	99.812	101.294	181.314	97.464
DS2.20	2359.507	143.242	223.244	2282.950	125.456	116.602	207.559	112.240
DS2.21	2563.249	154.079	249.584	2483.045	135.950	130.427	234.743	125.072
DS2.22	3592.047	229.332	315.034	3388.120	186.411	150.000	267.465	139.401
DS2.23	3935.333	236.802	336.882	3725.836	191.559	166.241	300.465	156.602
DS2.24	5137.134	313.264	373.711	4676.638	208.681	186.624	336.514	173.389
DS2.25	5898.104	293.610	392.530	5424.018	208.909	208.689	375.901	194.778
DS2.26	12974.804	2297.732	2094.524	10022.341	1884.838	241.356	426.627	221.592
DS2.27	13411.080	2351.364	2053.704	10314.877	1823.076	263.164	466.550	241.366
DS2.28	-	8431.519	7149.525	-	6977.563	328.289	551.046	296.884
DS2.29	-	7980.772	6288.037	-	6050.794	334.178	581.189	299.912
DS2.30	-	4564.717	2243.066	-	1905.217	367.330	639.672	322.922

Document Clustering and Cluster Topic Extraction in Multilingual Corpora

Joaquim Silva
FCT / Universidade Nova de Lisboa
2725 Monte da Caparica, Portugal
jfs@di.fct.unl.pt

João Mexia
FCT / Universidade Nova de Lisboa
2725 Monte da Caparica, Portugal

Agra Coelho
ISA / Universidade Técnica de Lisboa
Tapada da Ajuda, Portugal
coelho@madpet.isa.utl.pt

Gabriel Lopes
FCT / Universidade Nova de Lisboa
2725 Monte da Caparica, Portugal
gpl@di.fct.unl.pt

Abstract

A statistics-based approach for clustering documents and for extracting cluster topics is described. Relevant (meaningful) Expressions (REs) automatically extracted from corpora are used as clustering base features. These features are transformed and its number is strongly reduced in order to obtain a small set of document classification features. This is achieved on the basis of Principal Components Analysis. Model-Based Clustering Analysis finds the best number of clusters. Then, the most important REs are extracted from each cluster and taken as document cluster topics.

1. Introduction

We aimed at developing a computational approach for automatically organizing documents from multilingual corpora into clusters. We required no prior knowledge about document subject matters or language. So, we cleaned every keyword that might influence the behavior of our algorithm. Since we want a language independent system, no morpho-syntactic information is used. Moreover, we also want to extract the documents main topics of each cluster.

Available software for clustering, usually needs a matrix of objects characterized by a set of features. So we need to evaluate the documents according to features / subjects. In order to obtain those features, we used the LocalMaxs algorithm [6] to automatically extract Multiword Lexical Units or Relevant Expressions (REs) from corpora, i.e. meaningful expressions denoting important concepts such as *Common agriculture policy*, *Common Customs*, *produits agricoles*, etc.. Since these REs provide important information about the content of the documents, we use them as *base*

features for clustering. The most informative REs correspond to cluster topics, as we will show. This paper is organized as follows: features extraction is explained in section 2; clustering and summarization in sections 3 and 4; section 5 discusses the results obtained; related work and limitations are presented in section 6 and conclusions are drawn in section 7.

2. Extracting multiword features from corpora

Three tools working together, are used for extracting REs from any corpus: the LocalMaxs algorithm, the Symmetric Conditional Probability (SCP) statistical measure and the Fair Dispersion Point Normalization (FDPN). A full explanation of these tools is given in [6]. However, a brief description is presented here.

Thus, let us consider that an n-gram is a sequence of words in text[1]. For example the word *president* is an 1-gram; the sequence *President of the Republic* is a 4-gram. LocalMaxs is based on the idea that each n-gram has a kind of "glue" or cohesion sticking the words together within the n-gram. Different n-grams usually have different cohesion values. One can intuitively accept that there is a strong cohesion within the n-gram (*Giscard, d'Estaing*) i.e. between the words *Giscard* and *d'Estaing*. However, one cannot say that there is a strong cohesion within the n-gram (*or, uninterrupted*) or within the (*of, two*). So, the $SCP(.)$ cohesion value of a generic bigram (x, y) is obtained by

$$SCP((x,y)) = p(x|y).p(y|x) = \frac{p(x,y)^2}{p(x).p(y)} \quad (1)$$

where $p(x,y)$, $p(x)$ and $p(y)$ are the probabilities of occurrence of bigram (x, y) and unigrams x and y in the cor-

---

[1] We use the notation $(w_1 \ldots w_n)$ or $w_1 \ldots w_n$ to refer an n-gram of length n.

pus; $p(x|y)$ stands for the conditional probability of occurrence of x in the first (left) position of a bigram, given that y appears in the second (right) position of the same bigram. Similarly $p(y|x)$ stands for the probability of occurrence of y in the second (right) position of a bigram, given that x appears in the first (left) position of the same bigram.

However, in order to measure the cohesion value of each n-gram of any size in the corpus, the FDPN concept is applied to the $SCP(.)$ measure and a new cohesion measure, $SCP\_f(.)$, is obtained.

$$SCP\_f((w_1 \ldots w_n)) = \frac{p((w_1 \ldots w_n))^2}{F} \quad (2)$$

where $\quad F = \frac{1}{n-1} \sum_{i=1}^{n-1} p(w_1 \ldots w_i).p(w_{i+1} \ldots w_n) \quad (3)$

where $p((w_1 \ldots w_n))$ is the probability of the n-gram $w_1 \ldots w_n$ in the corpus. So, any n-gram of any length is "transformed" into a pseudo-bigram[2] that reflects the *average cohesion* between each two adjacent contiguous sub-n-grams of the original n-gram. Then, LocalMaxs algorithm elects every n-gram whose $SCP\_f(.)$[3] cohesion value is a salient one (a local maximum), i.e., the cohesion of the n-gram is greater or equal than the cohesion of any of its contiguous sub-$n-1$-grams, and greater than the cohesion of any $n+1$-gram of which it is a sub-sequence of words (see [6] for details). See some examples of elected n-grams, i.e., REs: *Human Rights, Human Rights in East Timor, common agricultural policy, economia energética* and *publication au Jounal officiell des Communautés*.

2.1. The number of features

Since we want to cluster documents, we must build a matrix of documents "classified" in accordance with the smallest possible set of variables and convey that matrix to clustering software. In order to test our approach, we used a multilingual 872,795 words corpus with 324 documents[4]. LocalMaxs algorithm extracted 25,838 REs from that corpus. Although, we do not use such a high number of features for distinguishing such a small number of objects (324 documents) — in the worst case we would need no more than $324 - 1$ *discriminants* to do it (see [4, pages 517-524] for details). However, these REs (base features) provide the basis for building a new and reduced set of features.

---

[2]Roughly we can say that known statistical cohesion / association measures such as $MI(.)$, χ^2, etc. seem to be "tailored" just for 2-grams. However, by applying FDPN to those measures, it is possible to use them for measuring the cohesion values of n-grams for any value of n [6].

[3]LocalMaxs has been used in other applications with other statistical measures, as it is shown in [6]. However, for Information Retrieval (IR) purposes, very interesting results were obtained by using $SCP\_f(.)$, in comparison with other measures [7].

[4]This is part of the European Legislation in Force (sub-ELIF) corpus: htp://europa.eu.int/eur-lex.

2.2. Principal Components analysis. Reducing the number of features

Let us take the following extracted REs containing the word *agricultural*: *agricultural products, processing of agricultural products, agricultural products receiving refunds* and *common agricultural policy*.

For document clustering purpose, there is redundancy in these REs, since, for example, whenever *processing of agricultural products* is in a document, *agricultural products* is also in the same document and it may happen that, *common agricultural policy* is also in that document. Let us show how these redundancies can be used to reduce the number of features. According to Principal Components analysis, often the original m correlated random variables (features) $X_1, X_2, \ldots, X_m$ can be "replaced" by a subset $Y_1, Y_2, \ldots, Y_k$ of the m new *uncorrelated* variables (components) $Y_1, Y_2, \ldots, Y_m$, each one being a linear combination of the m original variables, i.e., those k *principal components* provide most of the information of the original m variables [4, pages 340-350]. The original data set, consisting of l measurements of m variables, is reduced to another one consisting of l measurements of k principal components. Principal components depends solely on the covariance matrix Σ (or the correlation matrix ρ) of the original random variables $X_1, X_2, \ldots, X_m$. Now we state $RE_1, RE_2, \ldots, RE_p$ as being the original p variables (REs) of the sub-ELIF corpus. Then, for a reduced set of new variables (principal components) we would have to estimate the associated covariance matrix of the variables $RE_1, \ldots, RE_p$. So, let the sample covariance[5] matrix S be the estimator of Σ.

$$S = \begin{bmatrix} S_{1,1} & S_{1,2} & \cdots & S_{1,p} \\ S_{1,2} & S_{2,2} & \cdots & S_{2,p} \\ \vdots & \vdots & \ddots & \vdots \\ S_{1,p} & S_{2,p} & \cdots & S_{p,p} \end{bmatrix} \quad (4)$$

where $S_{i,k}$[6] is the estimator of the covariance $Cov(RE_i, RE_k)$. S can be seen as a matrix of "similarities" between REs. Unfortunately, it is impracticable to obtain principal components from this matrix using available software, due to the computational effort associated to its huge size ($25,838 \times 25,838$). Furthermore it seems unlikely that Principal Components analysis could achieve the strong reduction we need: from $25,838$ original features to $k < 324$ (the number of documents) new features (principal components).

---

[5]When we say covariance matrix, we mean variance-covariance matrix, since $Cov(RE_i, RE_k) = Var(RE_i)$ for $k = i$.

[6]In this paper, we use $S_{.,.}$ to denote the estimator of the covariance between two random variables.

2.3. Geometrical representations

We can associate to the jth document, the vector $d_j^T = [x_{1,j}, \ldots, x_{p,j}]^7$ whose components are the original (or transformed) numbers of occurrences of the REs in the jth document. Now we have a smaller (324×324) covariance matrix

$$S = \begin{bmatrix} S_{1,1} & S_{1,2} & \ldots & S_{1,n} \\ S_{1,2} & S_{2,2} & \ldots & S_{2,n} \\ \vdots & \vdots & \ddots & \vdots \\ S_{1,n} & S_{2,n} & \ldots & S_{n,n} \end{bmatrix} \quad (5)$$

where the generic element in matrix S is given by

$$S_{j,l} = \frac{1}{p-1} \sum_{i=1}^{i=p} (x_{i,j} - x_{\cdot,j})(x_{i,l} - x_{\cdot,l}) \quad (6)$$

and $x_{\cdot,j}$, meaning the average number of occurrences per RE in the jth document, is given by[8]

$$x_{\cdot,j} = \frac{1}{p} \sum_{i=1}^{i=p} x_{i,j} \quad . \quad (7)$$

Then S will be a matrix of similarities between documents.

Escoufier and L'Hermier [2] proposed an approach, based on Principal Components analysis, to derive geometrical representations from similarity matrices. Since S is symmetric we have $S = PAP^T$, with P orthogonal ($P = [e_1, \ldots, e_n]$, the matrix of normalized eigenvectors of S) and A diagonal. The principal elements of A are the eigenvalues $\lambda_1, \ldots, \lambda_n$ of S and $\lambda_1 \geq \lambda_2 \cdots \geq \lambda_n \geq 0$. Thus $S = QQ^T$ with

$$Q = PA^{1/2} \quad . \quad (8)$$

The elements of the ith line of Q will be the coordinates of the point associated with the ith document. When there are leading eigenvalues we may consider only the corresponding coordinates since the remaining are near 0. Then, to assess how much of the total information is carried out by the first k components, i.e. the first k columns of Q, we may use

$$PTV(k)^9 = \frac{\sum_{j=1}^{j=k} \lambda_j}{\sum_{j=1}^{j=n} \lambda_j} \quad . \quad (9)$$

So, by taking the first k columns of matrix Q such that $PTV(k)$ equals, say .80 or more (depending on the criterion used), we can reduce the initial large number of features to $k < n$ new features (components). However, considering the 324 documents of the sub-ELIF corpus, if we

[7] From now on we will use p for the number of REs of the corpus and n for the number of documents.

[8] When we replace an index by a dot, a mean value has been obtained.

[9] PTV are initials for cumulative Proportion of the Total Variance.

use the original number of occurrences of the ith RE in the jth document ($x_{i,j}$) to obtain "similarities" (see (6)), we need the first 123 components to provide 0.85 of the total information, i.e. $PTV(123) = 0.85$. Although it corresponds to 0.4% of the initial 25,838 features, this means we have 123 components for distinguishing 324 documents. Besides, to minimize computational effort of the clustering process, it is important to avoid large number of components. So, this number must be reduced without much loss of information. Thus, in order to "stimulate" similarities between documents, the original occurrences of the REs in documents will be transformed.

2.4. Transformed occurrences

As referred above, the geometrical representation may be obtained from transformed occurrences. The technique we used has four phases. In the first phase we standardize in order to correct document heterogeneity. This heterogeneity is measured by the variation between the occurrence numbers of the different REs inside each document. With $x_{i,j}$ the number of times that the ith RE occurs in the jth document, this variation may be assessed by

$$V(D_j) = \frac{1}{p-1} \sum_{i=1}^{i=p} (x_{i,j} - x_{\cdot,j})^2 \quad j = 1, \ldots, n \quad (10)$$

where $x_{\cdot,j}$ is given by (7). The standardized values will be

$$z_{i,j} = \frac{x_{i,j} - x_{\cdot,j}}{\sqrt{V(D_j)}} \quad i = 1, \ldots, p; \quad j = 1, \ldots, n \quad . \quad (11)$$

In the second phase we evaluate the variation between documents for each RE. It is important to evaluate this variation as if the documents had the same size, i.e. each RE associated variation must reflect how much the RE occurrences vary in different documents, due to document content, not due to document size. Therefore we use normalized values to calculate this variation:

$$V(RE_i) = \frac{1}{n-1} \sum_{j=1}^{j=n} (z_{i,j} - z_{i,\cdot})^2 \quad i = 1, \ldots, p \quad . \quad (12)$$

These values are important since we found that, generally, the higher $V(RE_i)$, the more information is carried out by the ith RE. On the other hand, it was observed that REs constituted by long words, usually are more informative from the IR / Text Mining point of view (e.g. *agricultural products* or *communauté economique européenne* are more informative than *same way*, *plus au moins* or *reach the level*). Thus, in a third phase we define *weighted occurrences* as

$$x_{i,j}^* = x_{i,j} \cdot V(RE_i) \cdot AL(RE_i) \quad (13)$$

515

where $i = 1, \ldots, p$, $j = 1, \ldots, n$ and $AL(RE_i)$ is the average length of the words in the ith RE. This is measured by the number of characters of the words. Lastly, in the fourth phase we carry out a second standardization considering the *weighted occurrences*. This is for correcting document size heterogeneity, since we do not want that the document size affects its relative importance. Thus

$$z_{i,j}^* = \frac{x_{i,j}^* - x_{\cdot,j}^*}{\sqrt{V(D_j^*)}} \qquad i = 1, \ldots, p; \quad j = 1, \ldots, n \quad (14)$$

$$V(D_j^*) = \frac{1}{p-1} \sum_{i=1}^{i=p} (x_{i,j}^* - x_{\cdot,j}^*)^2 \quad j = 1, \ldots, n \ . \quad (15)$$

These standardizations are *transformed occurrences* and are used to obtain the matrix of similarities between documents. In this matrix, the generic element, $S_{j,l}$, where $j = 1, \ldots, n$ and $l = 1, \ldots, n$, is given by

$$S_{j,l} = \frac{1}{p-1} \sum_{i=1}^{i=p} (z_{i,j}^* - z_{\cdot,j}^*)(z_{i,l}^* - z_{\cdot,l}^*) \qquad (16)$$

2.5. Non-informative REs

Some high-frequency REs appearing in most documents written in the same language are not informative from a IR / Text Mining point of view, e.g., locutions such as *Considérant que* (*having regard*), *tendo em conta* (*having regard*), *and in particular*, or other expressions which cannot be considered correct REs, such as *of the* or *dans les* (*in the*). Although these expressions are useless to identify document topics, they are informative for distinguishing different languages. As a matter of fact they occur in most documents of the same language, and their associated variation (see (12)) is usually high or very high, i.e., they are relevant to "approximate" documents of the same language for calculating similarities between documents (see (13), (14) and (16)).

So, it seems that either they should be removed to distinguish topics in documents written in the same language, or they should be kept for distinguishing documents of different languages. To solve this problem, we use the following criterion: the REs having at least one extremity (the leftmost or the rightmost word) that exists in at least 90 % of the documents we are working with, are removed from the initial set of REs. We follow that criterion since these expressions usually begin or end with words occurring in most documents of the same language, e.g., *of*, *les*, *que*, etc.. As we will see in Subsect. 3.3, the documents and REs with which the system is working, depends on the node of the clustering tree.

To summarize, in this section we obtained a matrix where a small set of components classifies a group of documents, which will be given as input to the clustering software. For this purpose, the matrix of similarities between

documents (S) was previously calculated (see (5)), and the generic element of this matrix was given by (16). Then, from S, Q was obtained by (8) and the first k columns of Q was taken, such that $PTV(k) \geq 0.80$. Finally, the latter matrix will be taken as input to clustering software.

Considering the initial $25,838$ REs for the 324 documents of the sub-ELIF corpus, we obtained $PTV(3) = .848$; $PTV(5) = .932$ and $PTV(8) = .955$.

3. Clustering documents

We need to split documents into meaningful subgroups. However we do not know how many subgroups (clusters) should be obtained. Furthermore, though we have obtained k features (components) to evaluate the documents, we do not know neither the composition of each cluster, nor its volume, shape and orientation in the k-axes space.

3.1. The Model-Based Cluster Analysis

Considering the problem of determining the structure of clustered data, without prior knowledge of the number of clusters or any other information about their composition, Fraley and Raftery [3] developed the Model-Based Clustering Analysis (MBCA). By this approach, data are represented by a mixture model where each element corresponds to a different cluster. Models with varying geometric properties are obtained through different Gaussian parameterizations and cross-cluster constraints. Partitions (clusters) are determined by the EM (expectation-maximization) algorithm for maximum likelihood, with initial agglomerative hierarchical clustering (see [3] for details). This clustering methodology is based on multivariate normal (Gaussian) mixtures. So the density function associated to cluster c has the form

$$f_c(\boldsymbol{x}_i | \boldsymbol{\mu}_c, \boldsymbol{\Sigma}_c) = \frac{exp\{-\frac{1}{2}(\boldsymbol{x}_i - \boldsymbol{\mu}_c)^T \boldsymbol{\Sigma}_c^{-1}(\boldsymbol{x}_i - \boldsymbol{\mu}_c)\}}{(2\pi)^{\frac{p}{2}} |\boldsymbol{\Sigma}_c|^{\frac{1}{2}}} \ . \quad (17)$$

Clusters are ellipsoidal, centered at the means $\boldsymbol{\mu}_c$; element $\boldsymbol{x}_i$ belongs to cluster c. The covariance matrix $\boldsymbol{\Sigma}_c$ determines other geometric characteristics. This clustering methodology is based on the parameterization of the covariance matrix in terms of eigenvalue decomposition in the form $\boldsymbol{\Sigma}_c = \lambda_c \boldsymbol{D}_c \boldsymbol{A}_c \boldsymbol{D}_c^T$, where $\boldsymbol{D}_c$ is the orthogonal matrix of eigenvectors, determining the orientation of the principal components of $\boldsymbol{\Sigma}_c$. $\boldsymbol{A}_c$ is the diagonal matrix whose elements are proportional to the eigenvalues of $\boldsymbol{\Sigma}_c$, determining the shape of the ellipsoid. The volume of the ellipsoid is specified by the scalar λ_c. Characteristics (orientation, shape and volume) of distributions are estimated from the input data, and can be allowed to vary between clusters, or constrained to be the same for all clusters. Considering

Table 1. Parameterizations of the covariance matrix Σ_c in the Gaussian model and their geometric interpretation.

Σ_c	Distrib.	Volume	Shape	Orient.
λI	Spher.	Equal	Equal	
$\lambda_c I$	Spher.	Vari.	Equal	
$\lambda D A D^T$	Ellips.	Equal	Equal	Equal
$\lambda_c D_c A_c D_c^T$	Ellips.	Vari.	Vari.	Vari.
$\lambda D_c A D_c^T$	Ellips.	Equal	Equal	Vari.
$\lambda_c D_c A D_c^T$	Ellips.	Vari.	Equal	Vari.

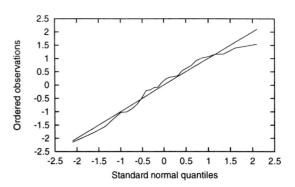

Figure 1. QQ-plot for assessing normality of data for cluster 1.2 on 2th component.

our application, input data is given by the k components "classifying" n documents, corresponding to the k columns of matrix Q (see (8) and (9)).

In Table 1, *Distrib.*, *Orient.*, *Spher.*, *Ellips.* and *Vari.* abbreviate *Distribution, Orientation, Spherical, Ellipsoidal* and *Variable.* MBCA subsumes the approach with $\Sigma_c = \lambda I$, long known as *k-means*, where sum of squares criterion is used, based on the assumption that all clusters are spherical and have the same volume (see Table 1). However, in the case of *k-means*, the number of clusters has to be specified in advance, and considering many applications, real clusters are far from spherical in shape. Therefore we have chosen MBCA for clustering documents. Then, function `emclust` has been used with `S-PLUS` package, which is available for `Windows` and `Linux`.

During the cluster analysis, `emclust` shows the Bayesian Information Criterion (BIC), a measure of evidence of clustering, for each "pair" *model-number of clusters*. These "pairs" are compared using BIC: the bigger the BIC, the stronger the evidence of clustering. The problem of determining the number of clusters is solved by choosing the *best model*. Table 1 shows the different models used during the calculation of the *best model*. Models must be specified as a parameter of the function `emclust`. However, usually there is no prior knowledge about the model to choose. Then, by specifying all models, `emclust` gives us BIC values for each pair *model-number of clusters* and proposes the *best model* which indicates what cluster must be assigned to each object (document).

3.2. Assessing normality of data

MBCA works based on the assumption of normality of data. Then, Gaussian distribution must be checked for the marginal distributions of the documents on each component. Thus, a QQ-plot is made for each component. So, each of the first k columns of matrix Q (see (8)) is standardized, ordered and put on y axis of the QQ-plot. Then, standardized normal quantiles are generated and put on x

axis of the QQ-plot (see [4, pages 146-162] for details).

Fig. 1 represents the QQ-plot for the 2th component, assessing the normality of data of *cluster 1.2*[10]. We consider this QQ-plot representative, since most of the components for other clusters produced similar QQ-plots. Although the straightness of this QQ-plot is not perfect, as it should be for a high certainty of normality, it is close enough to encourage us to use MBCA as an adequate approach for clustering this kind of data.

3.3. Sub-clusters

As we will see in Sect. 5, our approach organizes sub-ELIF corpus in 3 main clusters: English, Portuguese and French documents. However, we can distinguish different subjects in different documents of the same cluster. So, a hierarchical tree of clusters is built as follows: let us consider that every cluster in the tree is a node. For every node, non-informative REs are removed (see Subsect. 2.5) from the set of REs contained in the documents of that node (a subset of the original REs), in order to obtain a new matrix of similarities between documents (see (16)). Then, the first k columns of the new matrix Q are taken (see (8) and (9)), and new clusters are proposed by MBCA.

3.4. Choosing the best number of clusters

As has been said, MBCA calculates the *best model* based on the k first columns of matrix Q (k components). A large number of components means no significant information loss, which is important for a correct clustering (*best model*) to be proposed by MBCA. On the other hand, a large number of components must be avoided, since it takes MBCA

---

[10]In Sect. 5 we will deal with specific clusters.

to estimate large covariance matrices — during the internal computation for different models — which can be judged to be close to singularity (see [3]). Therefore, we use the following criterion: the first k components are chosen in such a way that $PTV(k) \geq 0.80$ (see (9)).

Then, based on those k components, MBCA produces a list of BIC values for each model: *VVV (Variable volume, Variable shape, Variable orientation), EEV,* etc. (see Table 1). Each list may have several local maxima. The largest local maximum over all models is usually proposed as the *best model*. However, a heuristic that works well in practice (for further discussion, see [3]) — and has been followed by us — chooses the number of clusters corresponding to the first decisive local maximum over all the models considered.

4. Summarization

Summarizing a document and summarizing a cluster of documents are different tasks. As a matter of fact, documents of the same cluster have common relevant expressions such as *Community agricultural Regulations* or *Common agricultural policy*, rather than long sentences which are likely to occur in just one or two documents. Then, summarizing topics seems adequate to disclose the core content of each cluster.

Cluster topics correspond to the most important REs in the cluster. Let the cluster from where we want to extract its topics be the "target cluster". In order to extract it, first the REs of the *parent node* of the target cluster are ordered according to the following criterion: the value given by $Score(RE_i)$ is assigned to the ith RE of the parent node, where

$$Score(RE_i) = V(RE_i) \cdot AL(RE_i) \cdot Thr(RE_i) \ . \quad (18)$$

$V(RE_i)$ and $AL(RE_i)$ have the same meaning as in (13); $Thr(RE_i)$ is given by

$$Thr(RE_i) = \left\{ \begin{array}{ll} 1 & SCP\_f(RE_i) \geq threshold \\ 0 & \text{otherwise} \end{array} \right. . \quad (19)$$

Thus, $Thr(\cdot)$ corresponds to a filter that "eliminates" REs whose $SCP\_f(\cdot)$ cohesion value (see Sect. 2) is lower than *threshold*. These REs, e.g., *Considérant que, and in particular,* etc., are not informative for IR / Text Mining[11]. Most of the times, these REs are previously eliminated, when selecting the informative REs for calculating the covariance matrix; however it may not happen in case of a multilingual set of documents (see Subsect. 2.5).

So, the largest $Score(RE_i)$ corresponds to the most important RE. For example, according with this criterion, the 15 most important REs of the initial cluster (the

one containing all documents) are the following: *Nomenclatura Combinada (Combined Nomenclature), nomenclature combinée, Member States, combined nomenclature, États membres (Member states), Council Regulation, produtos agrícolas (agricultural products), produits agricoles, utilização racional (rational use), nomenclature tarifaire (tariff nomenclature), autoridades aduaneiras (customs authorities), estância aduaneira (customs office), Common Customs, indicados na coluna (indicated in column)* and *agricultural products.*

Now, considering for instance the "French documents" as the target cluster, whose parent is the "initial cluster", we cannot "guarantee" that *produits agricoles* will be a topic, since not every French document content is about *produits agricoles.* On the other hand, the same topic often appears in different documents, written in different forms, (e.g. *produits agricoles* and *Produits Agricoles*). Hence, according to $Score(\cdot)$, the 15 most important REs of the target cluster occurring in at least 50 % of its documents are put in a list. From this list, the REs with $Score(\cdot)$ value not lower than 1 / 50 of the maximum $Score(\cdot)$ value obtained from that list, are considered topics.

5. Results

Sub-ELIF is a multilingual *corpus* with 108 documents per language (English, Portuguese and French). For each document there are two other documents which are translations to the other languages. From Table 2 we can see the hierarchical tree of clusters obtained by this approach. Custer 0 indicates the "initial cluster" containing all documents of the corpus. Now we present the topics extracted from each cluster.

Cluster 1: *European Communities, Member States, EUROPEAN COMMUNITIES, Council Regulation, Having regard to Council Regulation, Having regard to Council* and *Official Journal.*

Cluster 2: *Comunidade Europeia (European Community), Nomenclatura Combinada, COMUNIDADES EUROPEIAS* and *directamente aplicável (directly applicable).*

Cluster 3: *Communauté européenne, nomenclature combinée, États membres, COMMUNAUTÉS EUROPÉENNES* and *directement applicable.*

Cluster 1.1: *rational use of energy, energy consumption* and *rational use.*

Cluster 1.2: *agricultural products, Official Journal, detailed rules, Official Journal of the European Communities, proposal from the Commission, publication in the Official Journal* and *entirely and directly.*

Cluster 1.3: *combined nomenclature, Common Customs, customs authorities, No 2658/87, goods described, general rules, appropriate CN, Having regard to Council Regulation, tariff and statistical* and *Customs Code.*

---

[11] The empirically defined value for *threshold* was 0.015.

Table 2. Evaluation of the clusters.

Cluster	Main topic	Correct #	Total #	Act. corr. #	Prec. (%)	Rec. (%)
1	european communities	108	108	108	100	100
2	Comunidade Europeia	108	107	107	100	99.1
3	Communauté européenne	108	109	108	99.1	100
1.1	rational use of energy	23	23	20	86.9	86.9
1.2	agricultural products	27	27	21	77.8	77.8
1.3	combined nomenclature	58	58	51	87.9	87.9
2.1	economia de energia	23	26	21	80.8	91.3
2.2	produtos agrícolas	27	25	21	84	77.8
2.3	Nomenclatura Combinada	58	56	52	92.9	89.7
3.1	politique énergétique	23	26	22	84.6	95.7
3.2	produits agricoles	27	27	21	77.8	77.8
3.3	nomenclature combinée	58	56	53	94.6	91.4

Cluster 2.1: *economia de energia (energy saving), utilização racional, racional da energia (rational of energy)* and *consumo de energia (energy consuming)*.

Cluster 2.2: *produtos agrícolas, Comunidades Europeias, Jornal Oficial (Official Journal), directamente aplicável, COMUNIDADES EUROPEIAS, Jornal Oficial das Comunidades (Official Journal of the Communities), directamente aplicável em todos os Estados-membros (directly applicable to all Member States), publicação no Jornal Oficial (publication in the Official Journal), publicação no Jornal Oficial das Comunidades* and *Parlamento Europeu (European Parliament)*.

Cluster 2.3: *Nomenclatura Combinada, autoridades aduaneiras, indicados na coluna, mercadorias descritas (goods described), informações pautais vinculativas (binding tariff informations), Aduaneira Comum (Common Customs), regras gerais (general rules), códigos NC (NC codes)* and *COMUNIDADES EUROPEIAS*.

Cluster 3.1: *politique énergétique (energy policy), rationnelle de énergie* and *l'utilization rationnelle*.

Cluster 3.2: *produits agricoles, organisation commune (common organization), organisation commune des marchés (common organization of the markets), directment applicable, Journal officiel, Journal officiel des Communautés* and *COMMUNAUTÉS EUROPÉENNES*.

Cluster 3.3: *nomenclature combinée, autorités douanières (customs authorities), nomenclature tarifaire, No 2658/87, marchandises décrites (goods described), tarifaire et statistique (tariff and statistical)* and *COMMUNAUTÉS EUROPÉENNES*.

5.1. Discussion

Clusters 1, 2 and 3 were proposed by MBCA (function `mclust`) considering EEV model (*Equal volume, Equal shape, Variable orientation*) the *best model*, (see Table 1). EEV model was also considered *best model* when the sub-clusters of clusters 1, 2 and 3 were calculated.

In Table 2, column *Main topic* means the most relevant topic according to (18) obtained for the cluster indicated by column *Cluster*; by *Correct #* we mean the correct number of documents in the corpus for the topic in *Main topic*; *Total #* is the number of documents considered to belong to the cluster by our approach; *Act. corr. #* is the number of documents correctly assigned to the cluster; *Prec. (%)* and *Rec. (%)* are Precision and Recall.

Although the original texts of the sub-ELIF corpus are classified by main topic areas, e.g., Agriculture, Energy — Rational use, etc., we have removed that information from the documents before extracting the REs using LocalMaxs algorithm, as we wanted to test our approach for clustering usual documents. Although, the topics shown in the previous lists capture the core content of each cluster. However, each cluster is not a perfect "translation" of the "corresponding" clusters in the other languages. Some reasons may help to explain why. Thus, because in Portuguese we write *Estado-Membro* (just one word) for *Member State*, this concept is not extracted in Portuguese since Local-Maxs does not extract unigrams. Then, *Estado-Membro* is not in cluster 2. On the other hand, not every RE has the same number of occurrences of the corresponding RE in the other languages. For example, there are 55 occurrences of *Nomenclatura Combinada*, 54 of *nomenclature combinée*, 45 of *combined nomenclature* and 10 of *Combined Nomenclature*. Then, under the criterion used for extracting topics (see Sect. 4), 45 occurrences is less than 50% of the 108 documents of the cluster 1. Therefore *combined nomenclature* is not considered a topic in cluster 1.

As we keep the original words in text, the same topic may be shown in different forms, e.g., *EUROPEAN*

COMMUNITIES and *European Communities* in cluster 1. Though some REs are not topics or just weakly informative expressions, such as *Journal officiel* or *general rules*, we think that about 80% of these REs can be considered topics/subtopics, exposing the core content of the clusters.

Since our approach is not oriented for any specific language, we believe that different occurrences for the same concept in the three different languages, are the main reason for different Precision and Recall scores comparing "corresponding" clusters. Precision and Recall values for clusters 1.2, 2.2 and 3.2 are relatively low. However, we believe that using larger corpora, better results will be obtained.

As has been said in Sect. 3.1, the bigger the BIC value, the stronger the evidence of clustering. Then BIC can be used to decide whether to "explore" sub-clusters or not. However we did not work on a criterion to decide that yet.

6. Related work

Some known approaches for extracting topics and relevant information from documents use morpho-syntactic information, e.g., TIPSTER [8]. So, these approaches would need specific morpho-syntactic information in order to extract topics from documents in other languages, and that information might not be available. In [1], a topic detection system is presented and Natural Language Processing techniques are also used to identify key entities.

In [5], a multi-document summarizer, called MEAD is presented. It generates summaries using cluster topic detection and tracking system. However, in this approach, topics are unigrams. Though many uniwords have precise meanings, multiword topics are usually more informative and specific than unigrams. For example, *human* is too generic and vague, but *human rights* is much more precise.

Joe Zhou [9] suggests automatic topic-oriented two-word terms, based on mutual information scores for adjacent words. For multiword terms, mutual information score is calculated for non-adjacent words. A threshold is set to decide if terms are important or not. We prefer to avoid thresholds in this phase, by using LocalMaxs approach, since there are relevant terms with lower mutual information scores than other terms and then, a threshold may reject a relevant term and elect a non-relevant one.

In our approach, the size of the covariance matrix for calculating the principal components, depends on the number of documents to cluster. This may be a limitation. We will work on this problem.

7. Conclusions

This paper presents an unsupervised statistics-based and language independent approach for document clustering and topic extraction. We applied it to multilingual corpus, using just information extracted from it. No pre-defined topics, features or descriptors were used. Thousands of REs were extracted by LocalMaxs algorithm. They were then transformed and aggregated into a small set of new features (components), which — according to the results obtained — showed good document *classification* power. The best number of clusters was automatically calculated by Model-Based Cluster Analysis and the results obtained led to a rather precise clustering of the documents. Thus, the number of clusters was not left to the user choice, as it might correspond to an *unnatural* clustering. Although we tested this approach on a small corpus (872,795 words), the results are encouraging, since about 80% of the clusters REs are sufficiently informative for being taken as topics of documents in the obtained document clusters. This lead us to believe that topics, rather than long sentences belonging to just one or two documents, are adequate to define clusters core content. In future work, we want to include informative unigrams in order to enrich the base feature set and therefore obtain better results.

References

[1] C. Clifton and R. Cooley. Topcat: Data mining for topic identification in a text corpus. In *Principles of Data Mining and Knowledge Discovery*, pages 174–183, 1999.

[2] Y. Escoufier and H. L'Hermier. A propos de la comparaison graphique des matrices de variance. *Biometrischc Zeitschrift*, 20(5):477–483, 1978.

[3] C. Fraley and A. E. Raftery. How many clusters? which clustering method? - answers via model-based clustering analysis. *The computer Journal*, 41:578–588, 1998.

[4] R. A. Johnson and D. W. Wichern. *Applied Multivariate Statistical Analysis*. Prentice-Hall International, second edition edition, 1988.

[5] D. R. Radev, J. Hongyan, and B. Makgorzata. Centroid-based summarization of multiple documents: sentence extraction, utility-based evaluation, and user studies. In *Proceedings of the ANLP/NAACL Workshop on Summarization*, 2000.

[6] J. F. Silva, G. Dias, S. Guilloré, and G. P. Lopes. Using LocalMaxs algorithm for the extraction of contiguous and non-contiguous multiword lexical units. In *Progress in Artificial Intelligence*, volume 1695 of *Lecture Notes in Artificial Intelligence*, pages 113–132. Springer-Verlag, 1999.

[7] J. F. Silva and G. P. Lopes. A local maxima method and a fair dispersion normalization for extracting multiword units. In *Proceedings of the 6th Meeting on the Mathematics of Language*, pages 369–381, Orlando, July 1999.

[8] Y. Wilks and R. Gaizauskas. Lasie junps the gate. In *Natural Language Information Retrieval*, pages 200–214. Kluwer Academic Publishers, 1999.

[9] J. Zhou. Phrasal terms in real-world ir applications. In *Natural Language Information Retrieval*, pages 225–259. Kluwer Academic Publishers, 1999.

Hierarchical Text Classification and Evaluation

Aixin Sun and Ee-Peng Lim
Center for Advanced Information Systems
Nanyang Technological University
Nanyang Avenue, Singapore 639798, Singapore
sunaixin@pmail.ntu.edu.sg   aseplim@ntu.edu.sg

Abstract

Hierarchical Classification refers to assigning of one or more suitable categories from a hierarchical category space to a document. While previous work in hierarchical classification focused on virtual category trees where documents are assigned only to the leaf categories, we propose a top-down level-based classification method that' can classify documents to both leaf and internal categories. As the standard performance measures assume independence between categories, they have not considered the documents incorrectly classified into categories that are similar or not far from the correct ones in the category tree. We therefore propose the Category-Similarity Measures and Distance-Based Measures to consider the degree of misclassification in measuring the classification performance. An experiment has been carried out to measure the performance of our proposed hierarchical classification method. The results showed that our method performs well for Reuters text collection when enough training documents are given and the new measures have indeed considered the contributions of misclassified documents.

1. Introduction

Text classification (TC) or text categorization is the process of automatically assigning one or more predefined categories to text documents. In TC research, most of the studies have focused on *flat classification* where the predefined categories are treated in isolation and there is no structure defining the relationships among them [1, 19]. Such categories are also known as *flat categories*. However, when the number of categories grows to a significantly large number, it will become much more difficult to browse and search the categories. One way to solve this problem is to organize the categories into a hierarchy like the one developed by Yahoo! [18].

Hierarchical classification allows us to address a large classification problem using a divide-and-conquer approach. At the root level in the category hierarchy, a document can be first classified into one or more sub-categories using some flat classification method(s). The classification can be repeated on the document in each of the sub-categories until the document reaches some leaf categories or cannot be further classified into any sub-categories. A few hierarchical classification methods have been proposed recently [1, 2, 10, 13, 15, 17]. In most of the hierarchical classification methods, the categories are organized in tree-like structures. On the whole, we can identify four distinct category structures for text classification. They are:

1. *Virtual category tree:* In this category structure, categories are organized as a tree. Each category can belong to at most one parent category and documents can *only* be assigned to the leaf categories [2].

2. *Category tree:* This is an extension of the virtual category tree that allows documents to be assigned into both internal and leaf categories [15].

3. *Virtual directed acyclic category graph:* In this category structure, categories are organized as a Directed Acyclic Graph (DAG). Similar to the virtual category tree, documents can only be assigned to leaf categories.

4. *Directed acyclic category graph:* This is perhaps the most commonly-used structure in the popular web directory services such as Yahoo! [18] and Open Directory Project [11]. Documents can be assigned to both internal and leaf categories.

In this paper, we will only focus on hierarchical classification that involves category trees.

To compare different hierarchical classification methods, experiments involving training and test data sets have to be conducted, and some performance measures are used to determine the effectiveness of the methods. In flat classification, performance measures such as *precision* and *recall* have been widely used [14, 19]. The same performance measures have also been used to measure the performance of hierarchical classification methods. In this paper, we argue that these performance measures are not adequate as they have largely ignored the parent-child and sibling relationships between categories in a hierarchy. By not considering the "closeness" of categories, the performance of hierarchical classification may not be accurately captured. In general, the categories from the same subtree share more domain knowledge than the ones from different subtrees, that is, the categories from the same subtree are semantically closer to one another. With the standard precision and recall measures, all these relationships among categories are not accounted for. In this paper, we will present several performance measures applicable to hierarchical classification. Among them are the *category similarity measures* and *distance-based measures*.

In this paper, we aim to establish a framework to evaluate the performance of hierarchical classification. There are two main contributions:

1. We define a new set of performance measures that consider the semantic relationships and parent-child relationships among categories in a hierarchy. The intuition is that when a document is wrongly classified, one has to examine how different is the incorrect category from the correct category.

2. We develop a top-down level-based hierarchical classification method for category tree using Support Vector Machine (SVM) classifiers. By conducting experiments using the Reuters text collection and the new performance measures, we illustrate how the performance of hierarchical classification can be more accurately determined.

This paper is organized as follows. We first give an overview of the related hierarchical classification work in Section 2. In Section 3, we present several new performance measures for hierarchical classification. The experiment on our proposed hierarchical classification method will be described in Section 5. The results of both standard performance measures and the new performance measures are presented in this section. Finally, we conclude our work in Section 6.

2. Related work

The existing hierarchical classification methods have mostly assumed a *virtual category tree* structure [2, 13]. Furthermore, these methods have often been evaluated using the performance measures developed for flat classification. There are basically two approaches adopted by the existing hierarchical classification methods, namely, the *big-bang approach* and the *top-down level-based approach*.

In the big-bang approach, only a single classifier is used in the classification process. Given a document, the classifier assigns it to one or more categories in the category tree. The assigned categories can be internal or leaf categories depending on the category structure supported by the methods. The big-bang approach has been achieved with Rocchio-like classifier [7], rule-based classifier [13] and methods built upon association rule mining [15]. The performance measures used in these experiments have been very much based on simple empirical observations of the number of correctly classified documents or the percentage of incorrectly classified documents.

In the top-down level-based approach, one or more classifiers are constructed at each level of the category tree and each classifier works as a flat classifier at that level. A document will first be classified by the classifier at the root level into one or more lower level categories. It will then be further classified by the classifier(s) of the lower level category(ies) until it reaches a final category which could be a leaf category or an internal category. The top-down level-based classification has been implemented with ACTION (for Automatic Classification for Full-Text Documents) algorithm in [1], multiple Bayesian classifiers in [6] and Support Vector Machine classifiers in [2]. Three performance measures, i.e., precision, recall and F-measure have been used in these experiments.

Compared to the top-down level-based approach, the big-bang approach can only use the information carried by the category structure during the training phase but not the classification phase. As discriminative features (e.g., terms) at a parent category may not be discriminative at the child categories, it is usually very difficult for a classification method using big-bang approach to exploit different sets of features at different category levels. Another issue in the big-bang approach is that the classifier constructed may not be flexible enough to cater for changes to the category structure. The classifier needs to be retrained once the category structure is changed.

On the other hand, the top-down level-based classification approach is not problem-free. One of its obvious problems is that a misclassification at a parent (ancestor) category may force a document to be excluded from the child categories before it could be examined by the classifiers of the child categories. Classification methods based on top-down approach also require more training examples since multiple classifiers have to be constructed and each requires a different training set. Without adequate training examples, the performance of these classifiers may suffer.

3. Performance measures

To evaluate a hierarchical classification method, one can directly apply the standard precision and recall for flat clas-

Category		Expert Judgments	
C_i		YES	NO
Classifier	YES	TP_i	FP_i
Judgments	NO	FN_i	TN_i

Table 1. Contingency table for category C_i

sification on each category of the entire category space.

Most hierarchical classification methods that involve virtual category trees often exclude the internal categories from the performance measurement as they are virtual categories and there are no documents under them. In a category tree, however, all categories have to be considered. In addition, categories are connected with *parent-child* and *sibling* relationships. Two categories can be similar when they share many common documents. For example, the *Programming* and *Software Engineering* categories may have several common features allowing documents to be classified under both of them. Therefore, if a document is not classified to the correct category, one should consider the degree of wrong classification. In other words, wrongly classifying a document into a parent or child category is considered better than classifying it into categories that are far away from the correct category.

3.1. Measures for flat classification

The performance of text classification methods can be measured in several ways. In this paper, we are interested in measuring the accuracy of the final classification results, i.e., the correctness of assigning categories to a set of documents. According to the text classification survey by Sebastiani [14], the most commonly used performance measures in flat classification are the classic information retrieval (IR) notions of *Precision* and *Recall*. Precision for a category C_i, denoted as Pr_i, measures the percentage of correct assignments among all the documents assigned to C_i. The Recall Re_i gives the percentage of correct assignments in C_i among all the documents that should be assigned to C_i. Pr_i and Re_i are also known as the standard precision and recall for C_i in this paper. The contingency table for a particular category C_i from the category space $\{C_1, \ldots, C_m\}$ is shown in Table 1. Let TP_i be the set of documents correctly classified into category C_i; FP_i be the set of documents wrongly classified; FN_i be the set of documents wrongly rejected and TN_i be the set of documents correctly rejected. The standard precision and recall are defined as follows[1]:

$$Pr_i \quad = \quad \frac{|TP_i|}{|TP_i| + |FP_i|} \quad (1)$$

---

[1] In all the formulas presented in this paper, $|S|$ gives the number of elements in set S.

$$Re_i \quad = \quad \frac{|TP_i|}{|TP_i| + |FN_i|} \quad (2)$$

Based on the standard precision and recall for each category, the overall precision and recall for the whole category space, i.e., $\{C_1, \ldots, C_m\}$, can be obtained in two ways, namely, *Micro-Average* and *Macro-Average*. Micro-Average gives equal importance to each document, while Macro-Average gives equal importance to each category [19]:

1. *Micro-Average*:

$$\hat{Pr}^\mu \quad = \quad \frac{\sum_{i=1}^m |TP_i|}{\sum_{i=1}^m (|TP_i| + |FP_i|)} \quad (3)$$

$$\hat{Re}^\mu \quad = \quad \frac{\sum_{i=1}^m |TP_i|}{\sum_{i=1}^m (|TP_i| + |FN_i|)} \quad (4)$$

2. *Macro-Average*:

$$\hat{Pr}^M \quad = \quad \frac{\sum_{i=1}^m Pr_i}{m} \quad (5)$$

$$\hat{Re}^M \quad = \quad \frac{\sum_{i=1}^m Re_r}{m} \quad (6)$$

Neither precision nor recall can effectively measure classification performance in isolation [14]. Therefore, the performance of the text classification has often been measured by the combination of the two measures. The popular combinations are listed below:

1. *Break-Even Point*(BEP): BEP, proposed by Lewis [8], defines the point at which precision and recall are equal. However, in some cases, BEP can never be obtained. For example, if there are only a few positive test documents compared to a large number of negative ones, the recall value can be so high that the precision can never reach.

2. *F_β Measure*: F_β measure was proposed by Rijsbergen [12]. It is a single score computed from precision and recall values according to the user-defined importance (i.e., β) of precision and recall. Normally, $\beta = 1$ is used [19]. The formula is:

$$F_\beta \quad = \quad \frac{(\beta^2 + 1) \cdot P_r \cdot R_e}{\beta^2 \cdot P_r + R_e} \quad \text{where } \beta \in [0, \infty)(7)$$

3. *Average 11-Point Precision*: The precision values are interpolated at 11 points at which the recall values are $0.0, 0.1, \ldots, 1.0$. This measure is mostly used in the situation when the classification method ranks documents according to their appropriateness to a category or similarly ranks categories to a document [14].

Besides precision and recall, other commonly-used performance measures include *Accuracy* and *Error* [14, 6], denoted by Ac_i and Er_i for category C_i respectively.

$$Ac_i = \frac{|TP_i| + |TN_i|}{|TP_i| + |TN_i| + |FP_i| + |FN_i|} \quad (8)$$

$$Er_i = \frac{|FP_i| + |FN_i|}{|TP_i| + |TN_i| + |FP_i| + |FN_i|}$$

$$= 1 - Ac_i \quad (9)$$

3.2. Measures based on category similarity

Intuitively, if a classification method A misclassifies documents into categories similar to the correct categories, it is considered better than another method, say B, that misclassifies the documents into totally unrelated categories. We therefore extend the standard precision and recall definitions to distinguish the performance of A and B.

The *Category Similarity* between two categories C_i and C_k, denoted by $CS(C_i, C_k)$, can be computed in several ways. In our work, we have chosen to adopt cosine distance between the feature vectors of two categories. It is suggested that the feature vector for a category should be derived by summation of the feature vectors of all training documents under it. The feature vectors of documents are the ones used to build the classifiers. From the category similarities, one can define the *Average Category Similarity* (*ACS*). The formulas for CS and ACS are:

$$C_i = \{w_1 t_1, w_2 t_2, \ldots, w_N t_N\}$$
$$C_k = \{v_1 t_1, v_2 t_2, \ldots, v_N t_N\}$$

$$CS(C_i, C_k) = \frac{\sum_{n=1}^{N}(w_n \times v_n)}{\sqrt{\sum_{n=1}^{N} w_n^2 \times \sum_{n=1}^{N} v_n^2}} \quad (10)$$

$$ACS = \frac{2 \times \sum_{i=1}^{m} \sum_{k=i+1}^{m} CS(C_i, C_k)}{m \times (m-1)} \quad (11)$$

where t_n's are index terms, w_n's and v_n's are the corresponding term weights.

Based on the category similarity, we can now measure the degree of correctness of the assigned categories $d_j.agd$ of document d_j while its labelled categories are $d_j.lbd$. In the simplest case where d_j is assigned to C_i correctly, i.e., $d_j \in TP_i$, d_j is counted as 1 in computation of precision and recall for C_i, similar to flat classification. However, if d_j is wrongly assigned to C_i (i.e., $d_j \in FP_i$), we should consider whether the d_j's labelled categories are similar to C_i; that is, how much d_j can *contribute* to C_i when we compute the precision and recall values for C_i. In this case, the *contribution* of d_j to C_i, denoted by $Con(d_j, C_i)$ is defined as follows:

$$Con(d_j, C_i) = \frac{\sum_{C' \in d_j.lbd}(CS(C', C_i) - ACS)}{1 - ACS} \quad (12)$$

Similarly, if d_j is wrongly rejected from C_i, say, $d_j \in FN_i$ the *contribution* of d_j to C_i depends on the category similarities between C_i and the assigned categories of d_j.

$$Con(d_j, C_i) = \frac{\sum_{C' \in d_j.agd}(CS(C', C_i) - ACS)}{1 - ACS} \quad (13)$$

The contribution of a document can be positive or negative depending on how similar its labelled and assigned categories are in comparison with the average category similarity ACS. Note that a document can belong to or be assigned to more than one category. To prevent one document from being over-shined or over-punished, the *contribution* of each document d_j to category C_i should be restricted to the range of $[-1, 1]$. Therefore, the *Refined − Contribution*, denoted by $RCon(d_j, C_i)$ is defined as follows:

$$RCon(d_j, C_i) = \min(1, \max(-1, Con(d_j, C_i))) \quad (14)$$

For all the documents that belong to FP_i, the total contributions $FpCon_i$ will be:

$$FpCon_i = \sum_{d_j \in FP_i} RCon(d_j, C_i) \quad (15)$$

and similarly, the total contributions $FnCon_i$ is:

$$FnCon_i = \sum_{d_j \in FN_i} RCon(d_j, C_i) \quad (16)$$

The extended *Precision* Pr_i^{CS} and *Recall* Re_i^{CS} for category C_i based on category similarity are defined as follows:

$$Pr_i^{CS} = \frac{\max(0, |TP_i| + FpCon_i + FnCon_i)}{|TP_i| + |FP_i| + FnCon_i} \quad (17)$$

$$Re_i^{CS} = \frac{\max(0, |TP_i| + FpCon_i + FnCon_i)}{|TP_i| + |FN_i| + FpCon_i} \quad (18)$$

Since both $FpCon_i$ and $FnCon_i$ can be negative, $|TP_i| + FpCon_i + FnCon_i$ can be negative. Therefore, a *max* function is applied to the numerator to make it not less than 0. As $FpCon_i \leq |FP_i|$, when $|TP_i| + |FP_i| + FnCon_i \leq 0$, the numerator $\max(0, |TP_i| + FpCon_i + FnCon_i) = 0$ and Pr_i^{CS} can be treated as 0 in this case. The same rule is applicable to Re_i^{CS}.

The *Micro-Average* and *Macro-Average* can be extended to consider category similarity. We give the extended definitions as follows:

Micro-Average:

$$\hat{Pr}^{\mu CS} = \frac{\sum_{i=1}^{m}(\max(0, |TP_i| + FpCon_i + FnCon_i))}{\sum_{i=1}^{m}(|TP_i| + |FP_i| + FnCon_i)} \quad (19)$$

$$\hat{Re}^{\mu CS} = \frac{\sum_{i=1}^{m}(\max(0, |TP_i| + FpCon_i + FnCon_i))}{\sum_{i=1}^{m}(|TP_i| + |FN_i| + FpCon_i)} \quad (20)$$

Macro-Average:

$$\hat{Pr}^{Mcs} = \frac{\sum_{i=1}^{m} Pr_i^{CS}}{m} \qquad (21)$$

$$\hat{Re}^{Mcs} = \frac{\sum_{i=1}^{m} Re_r^{CS}}{m} \qquad (22)$$

Similar to the extended precision and recall, the extended *accuracy* and *error* for category C_i can be defined based on document contribution:

$$Ac_i^{CS} = \frac{|TP_i| + |TN_i| + FpCon_i + FnCon_i}{|TP_i| + |TN_i| + |FP_i| + |FN_i|} \qquad (23)$$

$$Er_i^{CS} = \frac{|FP_i| + |FN_i| - FpCon_i - FnCon_i}{|TP_i| + |TN_i| + |FP_i| + |FN_i|} \qquad (24)$$

Note that the sum of extended accuracy and error is 1 which is the same as the original definitions.

As we have discussed in Section 3.1, it is not sufficient to evaluate a classification method using only precision or recall. Instead, they have to be considered together. The performance measures that combine both precision and recall are the Break-Even Point (BEP), F_β and Average 11-Point Precision. Among them, F_β can be easily computed using the extended precision and recall. BEP can be applied to classification methods that can rank documents for each category. In hierarchical classification using the big-bang approach, BEP and Average 11-Point Precision can be computed for classification methods that can rank *all* documents in the test set for each category. On the other hand, for those classification methods using top-down level-based approach, the test documents available for classification at a level are determined by the parent classifier as the latter may reject documents before they reach the child classifier(s). With such restriction, it is difficult to compute the BEP and Average 11-Point Precision for each category. Hence, we argue that the above two performance measures are less applicable to the hierarchical classification methods.

3.3. Measures based on category distance

Instead of using category similarity, we can define performance measures based on the distances between categories in a category tree. The distance between two categories C_i and C_k, denoted by $Dis(C_i, C_k)$, is defined to be the number of the links between C_i and C_k. Intuitively, the shorter the length, the closer the two categories.

The distance between categories was first proposed to measure misclassification in [16]. Nevertheless, the work did not define performance measures based on category distance. To define the *contribution* of misclassified documents, an *acceptable distance*, denoted as Dis_θ, must first be specified by the user. Dis_θ must be greater than 0. For example, if $Dis_\theta = 1$, a misclassification of document that

involves the labelled and assigned categories at more than 1 link apart will yield negative contribution, but zero contribution at 1 link apart. Formally, the *contribution* of a document d_j to category C_i based on category distance is defined as follows:

- If $d_j \in FP_i$:

$$Con(d_j, C_i) = \sum_{C' \in d_j.lbd} \left(1.0 - \frac{Dis(C', Ci)}{Dis_\theta}\right) \quad (25)$$

- If $d_j \in FN_i$:

$$Con(d_j, C_i) = \sum_{C' \in d_j.agd} \left(1.0 - \frac{Dis(C', Ci)}{Dis_\theta}\right) \quad (26)$$

For the same reason, the *contribution* needs to be refined to be in the range of $[-1, 1]$. With this new definition for *contribution*, the extended precision and recall based on category distance, denoted by Pr_i^{DB} and Re_i^{DB}, can be defined using the formulae (17) and (18) respectively. Similarly, *Micro-Average*, *Macro-Average*, F_β, *accuracy* and *error* can be extended.

4. Hierarchical classification method

In this section, we propose a hierarchical classification method for *category tree* structure based on top-down level-based approach. All the classifiers involved in this method are binary classifiers. Binary classifiers normally need to be trained with both positive and negative training documents. In the hierarchical classification method, a binary classifier is built for each category. These classifiers that determine whether a document should belong to the corresponding categories are known as the *local-classifiers*. However, an additional binary classifier is built for each internal category to determine whether a document should be given to the classifiers of its sub-categories. This special classifier is known as the *subtree-classifier* since it decides whether a document should belong to a subtree. This separation of local and subtree classifiers distinguishes our method from that proposed by Dumais and Chen [2]. To build binary classifiers in hierarchical classification, special consideration must be given to the selection of training documents for each classifier.

The *Coverage* of a category C_i in a given category tree, denoted by $Coverage(C_i)$ is the set of categories that belongs to the subtree rooted at C_i including C_i. For example, in the hierarchy shown in Figure 1 Tree (a), $Coverage(grain) = \{wheat, corn, grain\}$. For any document d_j, $d_j \in C_i$ is true if and only if d_j belongs to category C_i; $d_j \in Coverage(C_i)$ is true if and only if d_j belongs to any of the categories in $Coverage(C_i)$.

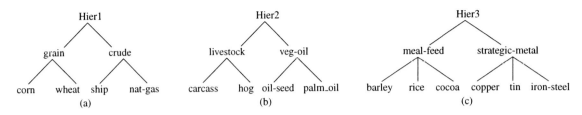

Figure 1. Category trees from Reuters collection

$Parent(C_i)$ returns the parent category of category C_i. Let $\{d_1, \ldots, d_m\}$ denote a set of training documents. The positive and negative training documents are selected differently for each type of classifier given below[2] where +ve and -ve refer to positive and negative training documents respectively and $d_j \in \{d_1, \ldots, d_m\}$.

- Subtree-classifier of a root category C_{root}:

  - +ve: All d_j such that $d_j \in Coverage(C_{root})$.

  - -ve: All d_j or Equal number (to positive documents) of random selected d_j such that $d_j \notin Coverage(C_{root})$. The number of d_j selected and the method of selection are classification methods dependent for this subtree-classifier.

- Subtree-classifier of an internal category C_i:

  - +ve: All d_j such that $d_j \in Coverage(C_i)$.

  - -ve: All d_j such that $d_j \notin Coverage(C_i)$ and $d_j \in Coverage(Parent(C_i))$.

- Local-classifier of an internal category C_i:

  - +ve: All d_j such that $d_j \in C_i$.

  - -ve: All d_j such that $d_j \notin C_i$ and $d_j \in Coverage(C_i)$.

- Local-classifier of a leaf category C_l:

  - +ve: All d_j such that $d_j \in C_l$.

  - -ve: All d_j such that $d_j \notin C_l$ and $d_j \in Coverage(Parent(C_l))$.

5. Experiments with SVM classifier

Support Vector Machine (SVM) classifiers have been shown to be fast and effective in text classification [3, 5]. Dumais and Chen have shown that SVM works well for virtual category tree but they did not consider category tree in their work [2]. The purpose of this experiment is to explore the use of SVM classifiers in classifying documents into a category tree. In the experiments, we compared the classification performance indicated by both the standard and extended precision and recall. The SVM classifier used in our experiment is *SVM* ^{light} Version 3.50 implemented by Joachims [4].

In our experiment, Reuters-21578 collection[3] was used. To conduct our experiment, category trees need to be manually derived from the 135 categories. Kohler and Sahami extracted three category trees from the Reuters-22173 collection by identifying the category labels that suggest parent-child relationships [6]. Three slightly different category trees are derived from the Reuters-21578 collection using a similar approach (see Figure 1). Note that the roots of the three category trees are virtual categories.

Almost all documents in Reuters collection come with title, dateline and text body. We obtained the index terms from only the title and text body after stopword removal and stemming. The stopwords and the stemming algorithms have been taken directly from the BOW library [9]. A binary term vector is obtained for each document without applying any feature selection. In our experiment, we used *Lewis Split* provided by Reuters collection to obtain training documents and test documents.

All the test documents that belong to one or more category in a category tree are used as its positive test documents. The same number of test documents that do not belong to the category tree are randomly selected to be the negative test documents. The statistics about our training and test documents are shown in Table 2. For Category C_i, C_i:s and C_i:l refer to the subtree-classifier and local-classifier for C_i respectively. In the table, $+Tr$, $-Tr$ and $+Te$ refer to number of positive training, negative training and positive test documents respectively. The category similarity matrix for Tree(a) is shown in Table 3. As $CS(C_i, C_k) = CS(C_k, C_i)$, only the lower half of the matrix is shown. The ones for Tree(b) and Tree (c) can be computed in a similar way.

The results of our experiment are shown in Tables 4, 5 and 6 for the three category trees. We computed the standard *Precision Pr* and *Recall Re*, the precision Pr^{CS} and recall Re^{CS} based on category similarity; and the precision Pr^{DB} and recall Re^{DB} based on category distance for

---

[2]As normally there is no document directly under the root category, the local-classifier for the root category is not constructed.

Tree (a)				Tree (b)				Tree (c)			
Category	+Tr	-Tr	+Te	Category	+Tr	-Tr	+Te	Category	+Tr	-Tr	+Te
Hier1	981	981	394	Hier2	270	270	104	Hier3	271	271	123
crude:s	574	435	-	livestock:s	83	188	-	meal-feed:s	153	119	-
crude:l	391	183	189	livestock:l	75	8	24	meal-feed:l	30	123	19
grain:s	437	544	-	veg-oil:s	191	81	-	str-metal:s	119	153	-
grain:l	434	3	149	veg-oil:l	87	104	37	str-metal:l	16	103	11
nat-gas	75	499	30	carcass	50	33	18	barley	37	116	14
ship	198	376	89	hog	16	67	6	rice	55	98	18
corn	182	255	56	oil-seed	124	67	47	cocoa	35	118	24
wheat	212	225	71	palm-oil	30	161	10	copper	47	72	18
-	-	-	-	-	-	-	-	iron-steel	40	79	14
-	-	-	-	-	-	-	-	tin	18	101	12

Table 2. Number of training and test documents for Trees

Category	crude	grain	nat-gas	ship	corn	wheat
crude	1.000	-	-	-	-	-
grain	0.523	1.000	-	-	-	-
nat-gas	0.602	0.453	1.000	-	-	-
ship	0.574	0.556	0.432	1.000	-	-
corn	0.487	0.791	0.463	0.510	1.000	-
wheat	0.497	0.815	0.472	0.513	0.699	1.000
Average Category Similarity			0.559			

Table 3. Category similarity matrix for Tree (a)

Category	Pr	Re	Pr^{CS}	Re^{CS}	Pr^{DB}	Re^{DB}
crude	0.846	0.962	0.849	0.963	0.890	0.964
grain	0.869	0.939	0.869	0.938	0.868	0.932
nat-gas	0.818	0.600	0.833	0.614	0.900	0.714
ship	0.879	0.820	0.879	0.821	0.888	0.843
corn	0.888	0.857	0.944	0.939	0.929	0.913
wheat	0.886	0.986	0.976	0.993	0.942	0.980
Micro-Ave	0.864	0.909	0.883	0.919	0.892	0.922
Macro-Ave	0.864	0.860	0.892	0.878	0.903	0.891

Table 4. Testing results for Tree (a)

Category	Pr	Re	Pr^{CS}	Re^{CS}	Pr^{DB}	Re^{DB}
livestock	0.629	0.708	0.816	0.771	0.734	0.654
veg-oil	0.878	0.783	0.906	0.845	0.904	0.880
carcass	0.611	0.611	0.778	0.734	0.600	0.473
hog	1.000	0.333	1.000	0.287	1.000	0.416
oil-seed	0.646	0.893	0.688	0.919	0.625	0.901
palm-oil	1.000	0.700	1.000	0.799	1.000	0.918
Micro-Ave	0.710	0.760	0.789	0.815	0.734	0.769
Macro-Ave	0.794	0.671	0.864	0.726	0.810	0.695

Table 5. Testing results for Tree (b)

Category	Pr	Re	Pr^{CS}	Re^{CS}	Pr^{DB}	Re^{DB}
meal-feed	1.000	0.315	1.000	0.332	1.000	0.368
str-metal	0.000	0.000	0.000	0.000	0.000	0.000
barley	0.923	0.857	0.923	0.857	0.923	0.857
rice	1.000	0.833	1.000	0.833	1.000	0.833
cocoa	1.000	0.500	1.000	0.505	1.000	0.520
copper	0.937	0.833	0.937	0.833	0.937	0.833
iron-steel	0.500	0.428	0.500	0.428	0.500	0.428
tin	1.000	0.250	1.000	0.249	1.000	0.166
Micro-Ave	0.896	0.530	0.896	0.534	0.896	0.534
Macro-Ave	0.795	0.502	0.795	0.505	0.795	0.501

Table 6. Testing results for Tree (c)

each category. The Pr^{DB} and Re^{DB} are computed with $Dis_\theta = 2$. We also computed the Micro-Averages and Macro-Averages for the three definitions of precision and recall.

From Table 2, Tree (a) receives the largest number of training and test documents. Most of the precision and recall (both the standard and extended) values for Tree (a) are good. This is consistent with the experimental results given by Koller and Sahami in [6] although slightly different collections are used. The extended precision and recall based on category similarity are better than the standard ones in most cases (i.e., except the category *grain*). From the category similarity matrix shown in Table 3, we observe that the categories within one subtree are more similar to each other compared to the categories across the two subtrees. In top-down level-based approach, most of the misclassification will occur in the subtrees, unless the document is wrongly rejected at the level *grain* and *crude*. Therefore,

the documents misclassified within the subtrees should contribute positively to the extended precision and recall based on category similarity. Therefore, it is reasonable for our extended precision and recall to be better than the standard ones.

The same observation holds for the extended precision and recall based on category distance, i.e., most of the extended precision and recall values are higher than the standard ones. Since the acceptable error distance is 2, the documents misclassified within the subtrees contributed positively to the extended precision and recall.

For Trees (b) and (c), there are several categories (i.e., *hog*, *tin* and *strategic-metal*) trained with documents fewer than 20. Since SVM classifiers require about 20 training documents to yield stable performance [2], the performance result may not be representative enough for analysis. Although the extended precision and recall based on either category similarity or category distance give different values compared to the standard precision and recall, it is not clear enough to conclude the performance of our method for Tree(b) and (c).

In summary, our method performed reasonably well for the Reuters collection when given enough training documents. The extended measures have indeed considered contributions of wrongly classified documents.

6. Conclusions

In this paper, we give an overview of hierarchical classification problem and its solutions. While the commonly-used performance measures are the ones for flat classification, the relationships among the categories in category tree are not accounted for. We propose some novel approaches to include the contributions of wrongly classified documents towards performance measures. We have also developed a top-down level-based classification method using binary classifiers (such as SVM) and evaluated the method using the Reuters collection. The results show that our method works well and the extended precision and recall can be feasibly implemented.

In our future work, we are going to evaluate the hierarchical classification method using classifiers other than SVM to compare their performance using the extended measures. Since we use category similarity and distance to measure the classification results, we plan to design a new hierarchical classification method that makes use of such information. In the top-down level-based approach, the error made at the parent category is not recoverable at the child category. We will also try to design a more tolerant hierarchical classification method with which the child classifiers are able to recover the errors made by the parent classifier(s).

References

[1] S. D'Alessio, K. Murray, R. Schiaffino, and A. Kershenbaum. The effect of using hierarchical classifiers in text categorization. In *Proc. of the 6th Int. Conf. "Recherche d'Information Assistee par Ordinateur"*, pages 302–313, Paris, FR, 2000.

[2] S. Dumais and H. Chen. Hierarchical classification of Web content. In *Proc. of the 23rd ACM Int. Conf. on Research and Development in Information Retrieval*, pages 256–263, Athens, GR, 2000.

[3] S. Dumais, J. Platt, D. Heckerman, and M. Sahami. Inductive learning algorithms and representations for text categorization. In *Proc. of the 7th Int. Conf. on Information and Knowledge Management*, pages 148–155, 1998.

[4] T. Joachims. SVM^{light}, an implementation of Support Vector Machines (SVMs) in C. http://ais.gmd.de/~thorsten/svm_light/.

[5] T. Joachims. Text categorization with support vector machines: learning with many relevant features. In *Proc. of the 10th European Conf. on Machine Learning*, pages 137–142, Chemnitz, DE, 1998.

[6] D. Koller and M. Sahami. Hierarchically classifying documents using very few words. In *Proc. of the 14th Int. Conf. on Machine Learning*, 1997.

[7] Y. Labrou and T. W. Finin. Yahoo! as an ontology: Using Yahoo! categories to describe documents. In *Proc. of the 8th Int. Conf. on Information Knowledge Management*, pages 180–187, Kansas City, MO, 1999.

[8] D. D. Lewis. An evaluation of phrasal and clustered representations on a text categorization task. In *Proc. of the 15th Annual Int. ACM SIGIR Conf. on Research and Development in Information Retrieval*, pages 37–50, 1992.

[9] A. K. McCallum. Bow: A toolkit for statistical language modeling, text retrieval, classification and clustering. http://www.cs.cmu.edu/~mccallum/bow, 1996.

[10] D. Mladenic. Turning yahoo to automatic web-page classifier. In *Proc. of the European Conf. on Artificial Intelligence*, pages 473–474, 1998.

[11] ODP - Open Directory Project. http://dmoz.org/.

[12] C. J. V. Rijsbergen. *Information Retrievel*. London: Butterworths, 2nd edition, 1979.

[13] M. Sasaki and K. Kita. Rule-based text categorization using hierarchical categories. In *Proc. of the IEEE Int. Conf. on Systems, Man, and Cybernetics*, pages 2827–2830, La Jolla, US, 1998.

[14] F. Sebastiani. Machine learning in automated text categorisation: a survey. Technical Report IEI-B4-31-1999, Istituto di Elaborazione dell'Informazione, Consiglio Nazionale delle Ricerche, Pisa, IT, 1999. Revised version, 2001.

[15] K. Wang, S. Zhou, and Y. He. Hierarchical classification of real life documents. In *Proc. of the 1st SIAM Int. Conf. on Data Mining*, Chicago, 2001.

[16] K. Wang, S. Zhou, and S. C. Liew. Building hierarchical classifiers using class proximity. In *Proc. of the 25th Int. Conf. on Very Large Data Bases*, pages 363–374, Edinburgh, UK, 1999.

[17] A. S. Weigend, E. D. Wiener, and J. O. Pedersen. Exploiting hierarchy in text categorization. *Information Retrieval*, 1(3):193–216, 1999.

[18] Yahoo! http://www.yahoo.com.

[19] Y. Yang. An evaluation of statistical approaches to text categorization. *Information Retrieval*, 1(1-2):69–90, 1999.

Web Cartography for Online Site Promotion:
An Algorithm for Clustering Web Resources

François Velin[1,2], Pascale Kuntz[2], and Henri Briand[2]

[1] Lnet Multimedia, Saint-Herblain, France
fvelin@Lnet.fr

[2] Ecole polytechnique de l'université de Nantes, France
{fvelin, pkuntz, hbriand}@ireste.fr

Abstract

This paper presents an approach of Web cartography to be used in the context of online site promotion. The overall objective is to provide users with handy maps offering information about candidate sites for the creation of hyperlinks that enable a large flow of targeted visitors. Two main types of data must be considered: texts and hyperlinks. We propose to exploit the latter to construct a relevant corpus on which semantic as well as graph analyses can be applied. The stress is put on the clustering of Web resources based on the link network, which makes it possible to highlight groups of strongly connected sites which are of the utmost interest for our application. To tackle the site graph partitioning problem, we turn to a promising iterative approach initially developed in the context of computer-aided design. It uses spectral decomposition of the Laplacian matrix to embed the considered graph in a geometric space where efficient methods can be applied. An algorithm that was adapted from an existing one implements the method. Experiments were conducted on a real application case concerning the promotion of a site dealing with Cognac. We present the obtained map as well as leads to exploit it.

1. Introduction

Competitive intelligence (CI) aims at studying an economic environment in order to have all the information that is necessary for making strategic choices [19]. CI can use the Web as a worldwide medium that makes classical techniques more effective. In addition, the Web contains a lot of information about people and organizations that can be exploited by CI, whose "action" part then consists in creating new digital resources [8]. One particular application of CI on the Web deals with the important problem of online site promotion. Beside the usual process of page indexing on search engines, it is necessary to ask for the creation of incoming hyperlinks on popular pages dealing with given topics, so as to attract as many visitors as possible. In this context, one must do an in-depth examination of existing sites and pages to extract valuable information that should be presented in a synthetic and intelligible form to decision-makers. The ultimate objective is to provide them with a map representing a set of sites related to a given domain, which will facilitate the choice of sites to contact for link creation.

On the Web, one generally has to consider two types of data: page contents, which include texts, images or sounds, and the logical organization of documents, which is implemented essentially with hyperlinks (e.g. [24]). The latter form a graph that can be analyzed with specific methods so as to find macroscopic features in great amounts of data, while the former are typically handled with text or multimedia mining techniques. This dual approach is often used for two main applications on the Web: information retrieval and exploration (or navigation). The effectiveness of a search engine is measured by its ability to find pages that contain the information a user needs. Today, the most efficient engines take hyperlinks into account to find the most popular pages –a popular page being a page pointed at by many popular pages (recursive definition) [7] [9]. Visualization is often more specifically used for navigational purposes [14] [16]. In this case, one needs overviews of Web resources that help find one's way when wandering from page to page using links or exploring the sections of a site or the organization of semantic contents.

Our approach of Web cartography is strongly linked to the particular application it will be used for, just as the characteristics of the corpus to be analyzed. Like [25] or [6], we find it relevant to consider the Web site rather than the Web page as the basic unit of analysis. The corpus must represent the digital environment where the considered site could be efficiently integrated; it is a site set which can be viewed as a graph whose vertices are sites and whose edges are deduced from hyperlinks, and also an amount of textual data. Taking both aspects into consideration, our main goal is to get an automatic evaluation of some proximity or similarity (partnership or similar topic) between sites, in order to provide the user with means to easily comprehend how the environment is laid out. To facilitate the handling of extracted information, we propose to implement a tool capable of generating Web-based interactive software maps restituting this knowledge.

In this paper, we focus on the evaluation and representation of proximities between sites based on combinatorial relationships deducible from hyperlinks. Those relationships are of the highest importance for the promotion issue, since they make it possible to understand the topology of the studied network and to put forth hypotheses as to the efficiency of a choice in terms of expected visitor flows. Indeed, relying on combinatorial information makes it possible to deal with the lack of data concerning the actual inter-site flows, which are considered strategic and are therefore often kept secret. Thus, we aim at discovering classes of strongly connected sites, assuming that the creation of a link on one of the sites of such a class increases the probability of being accessed *via* another site of the class.

We show that our problem comes down to a graph partitioning problem for which spectral approaches have been recently developed notably in CAD (Computer-Aided Design) and have proved promising [1]. We here develop an iterative approach that makes it possible to highlight the inner structure of classes. The process is illustrated with a real corpus containing sites dealing with Cognac and other related topics.

2. Our approach of Web cartography

2.1. Corpus construction

The initial corpus must contain a "sufficient" number of sites that deal with the main topic characterizing the site to promote, or with other related topics; that makes it possible to have candidate sites dealing with a broad enough range of themes and thus not to miss potentially interesting ones. To achieve this goal, we first propose to rely on the index and search capabilities of existing search engines to find sites talking about a given subject. To be effective, this step must involve efficient services (e.g. Google [7]) and be conducted by an expert in information retrieval [22]. To complete the site list, we use outgoing hyperlinks found in the first set to identify new related resources. In addition, we also retain sites that link to an element of the initial set, by using appropriate search engine features. It must be noticed that those complementary resources will probably deal with diverse topics, while the first ones deal only with the main topic. In order to automate as many tasks as possible, we

implemented functionalities using standard technologies and tools: Sun's Java 2 SDK and Java API for XML Processing (JAXP), D. Raggett's HTML Tidy utility (used to transform retrieved HTML pages into valid XML documents), Apache's Xalan C++ (used to manipulate XML data by applying XSL Transformations), and Maxim Klimov's WebCopier (used to retrieve site contents)[1]. Experiments have shown that the size of the corpus is often about a few hundred sites.

At this step, one often encounters classical practical limits due to possible network deficiencies which can make servers temporarily unreachable, or due to the rapid evolution of Web contents which can quickly make pages obsolete. As a result, a number of documents are certainly missing while a few others contain somehow outdated data. Nevertheless, it is possible to compute a corpus that contains enough information to be considered sufficiently reliable for our purpose.

2.2. Components of our Web maps

When promoting a Web site online, one has to create hyperlinks that will allow a large and targeted flow of visitors. One necessary task to perform is to submit the address of the site to the most popular generic search engines and directories as well as to thematic portals, which can be found using efficient search services in a clever manner. In addition, a more specific analysis can be conducted exploiting our corpus: its aim is to discover groups of strongly connected sites, on which the creation of a link will allow a great number of net surfers to reach the considered site, either directly or *via* one of the numerous sites in its "neighborhood". One very appropriate way to do that is to partition the graph determined by sites and links between pages on these sites, in order to find clusters of practicable sizes that ensure both the quality of local cohesion within all clusters (abundance of intra-class edges) and the quality of dislocation of clusters (rarity of inter-cluster edges). More precisely, the site network is modeled as a graph $G = (V, E)$ with a set of n vertices $V = \{v_1, v_2, ..., v_n\}$ representing sites and a set of edges E representing the existence of at least one hyperlink from one site towards another. A k-way partitioning $P^k = \{V_1, V_2, ..., V_k\}$ is a set of k non-empty clusters $V_1, V_2, ..., V_k$ of V so that $V_1 \cup V_2 \cup ... \cup V_k = V$.

The overall structure of our maps is then based on a k-partitioning of the site graph: a disc is divided into colored

---

[1] Information about these tools may be found respectively at the following addresses:
 – http://www.w3.org/People/Raggett/tidy/
 – http://xml.apache.org/xalan-c/
 – http://www.maximumsoft.com/

sectors corresponding to clusters with at least two sites; singletons are aggregated to form one big virtual cluster (figure 1). There exists a wide variety of more or less sophisticated cyberspace maps used for many different purposes [12]. Circular representations are often used for numerous applications so much so that users usually find them easy to interpret.

Moreover, one has to know about the topic, contents, and services offered by candidate sites. So information about the characteristics of each site must be provided. We propose to rely on a semantic analysis of textual contents to construct, for each initial cluster, a typology of sites based on their themes (we refer to [26] for details). On a map, each sector is then divided into subsectors of the same color representing these complementary classes.

3. Site graph partitioning

Generally speaking, the most common objective for graph partitioning consists in minimizing the number of edges $c(P^k) = \sum_{i=1}^{k} | E(V_i) |$ that go across two or more clusters, where $E(V_i) = \{(v_l, v_m) \in E; v_l \in V_i \text{ and } v_m \notin V_i\}$. Depending on the technological constraints, other formulations have been proposed. In order to integrate cut size and cluster size balance within a single objective, we here focus on the Scaled Cost criterion proposed in [10]: minimizing

$$c'(P^k) = \frac{1}{n(k-1)} \sum_{i=1}^{k} \frac{|E(V_i)|}{|V_i|}.$$

We here propose to tackle the site graph partitioning problem by adapting a method that was recently developed for the processing of integrated circuits. The latter are generally described as netlists, which can be easily modeled as hypergraphs. Our graphs offer an analogy with those hypergraphs in terms of the number of nodes they have (several hundreds to a few thousands). Moreover, hyperedges could be used to model more sophisticated links between sites, and notably extended links, which are introduced by the XML Linking Language (XLink) to associate several resources at one go. Since then, we can envisage exploiting many existing netlist partitioning methods for our application. In the following, we will restrict ourselves to a simple graph modeling, which is sufficient to take a large majority of present cases into account.

3.1. Spectral methods

Numerous heuristics have been proposed to deal with netlist partitioning. Further to seminal works by Kernighan and Lin in the 1960's [23], a lot of them are based upon iterative approaches employing node exchanges. However, these last few years, geometric ways

have been investigated and proved to give very interesting results. The basic underlying idea is to transform the graph G into a geometric object by constructing a one-to-one mapping between the module set and a point set in a d-dimensional geometric space, which transfers the connectivity properties of the graph components onto the new geometric object. This makes clustering algorithms accessible which would have been impossible to apply on the initial abstract graph.

Geometric representations based on spectral decomposition of the discrete Laplacian have known an increasing development in the last decade for multi-way partitioning. Let $A = (a_{ij})_{ij}$ be the $n \times n$ adjacency matrix of G where $a_{ij} = 1$ if there exists an edge between v_i and v_j and $a_{ij} = 0$ otherwise, and $D = (\sum_{j=1}^{n} a_{ij})_{ii}$ be its diagonal degree matrix. Generally speaking, the first eigenvectors of the $n \times n$ Laplacian matrix $Q = D - A$ provide guidance for the search of a k-partitioning.

3.2. Interpretation of eigenvectors

The interpretation of the first embedding axes in terms of connectivity relationships is originally based on an analogy between partitioning and placement problems [15] and is motivated by a well-established relationship between the second eigenvector of the Laplacian and the bipartitioning ($k = 2$) problem[2]. An extension to the k-way weighted quadratic placement $Min \frac{1}{2} \sum_{i=1}^{n} \sum_{j=1}^{n} \sum_{h=1}^{k} a_{ij} (x_{ih} - x_{jh})^2$, $X^t X = I^k$ with $X = (x_{ih})$ is given by Fan's theorem [13] and detailed in [10]: the matrix which minimizes the quadratic form is the $n \times k$ matrix composed of the k eigenvectors of Q associated with the k smallest eigenvalues. It is also possible to resort to another −very close− algebraic characterization based on Rayleigh's principle developed in variational theory (e.g. [17]) and used in spectral graph theory [11].

These characterizations show that the first axes define an "elastic surface" that tends to bring adjacent vertices with strong connections closer. Consequently, the first dimensions allow distinguishing between the main structures −in terms of density of connections− in the graph.

---

[2] By introducing a binary vector $x = (x_i)_i$ describing a bipartition P^2 such that $x_i = 1$ if vertex v_i belongs to V_1 and $x_i = 0$ otherwise, it is easy to show that the bipartitioning objective is $Min\ c(P^2) = x^t Q x$. It follows that Q is positive semi-definite and that its eigenvalues $\lambda_1 < \lambda_2 < ... < \lambda_n$ are positive. When x is real and $x^t x = 1$ (to avoid trivial solutions), a solution of the problem given by a classical Lagrangian relaxation is the second eigenvector μ_2 of Q. A heuristic for the bipartitioning problem consists in computing the binary solution closest to μ_2 by sorting μ_2 coordinates.

3.3. Partitioning in a geometrical space

Once the graph is embedded in a d-dimensional space, we have to find a convenient clustering method to define a k-way partitioning. A comparison of various traditional classification criteria (diameter,...) has showed that due to poor correlation with the initial objective –minimizing the Scaled Cost–, the classical clustering algorithms could lead to debased results [2]. Alpert and Kahng have consequently developed an approach that integrates both the spectral embedding and the hypergraph structure. This approach is inspired by a well-known heuristic proposed for the traveling salesman problem [20]: it generates, from the geometric point set in the d-dimensional space, a linear ordering $\pi^d: \{1, ..., n\} \rightarrow \{1, ..., n\}$. The ordering in the d-dimensional space is generated by the spacefilling curve heuristic of Bartholdi and Platzman [4], which uses the recursive construction of Sierpinski. Then, the objective is to find an optimal k-partitioning such that consecutive vertices on the tour tend to remain in the same class. Alpert and Kahng have developed a dynamic programming algorithm to solve this restricted problem [2] [3].

3.4. A new iterative algorithm

The appropriate dimension d of the embedding obviously depends on the structure of the netlist and also on the number of clusters k. Numerical experiments show that the best d may be quite large especially for large k's [2].

Instead of embedding the graph once and for all in a large d-dimensional space as usually done in the literature, we here adapt a recent algorithm which looks for the main "vertex groups" iteratively in small d-dimensional spaces [21]. Each class V_i of a k-partitioning is embedded in a small d-dimensional space and the $(k+1)$-partitioning is deduced from a bipartitioning of a class V_i. We have showed that when k increases, this approach discriminates relevant classes with better precision than one with a unique embedding of G.

Recursive bipartitioning has often been criticized as it can lead to poor results for multi-way partitioning, according to the choices of the first bipartitions. To overcome this difficulty, we propose to guide the successive bipartitionings by embedding the different subgraphs induced by the vertex classes at each step. From paragraph 3.2, the first axes of the spectral decomposition of Q make it possible to discriminate groups of strongly linked vertices which must be gathered in the same class in the first bipartition. Then, to find the best partition in three classes, we must detect among vertex groups of previously defined classes V_1 and V_2 the ones that separate off the most distinctly from the others.

With the same argument as previously, they can be highlighted by a spectral decomposition of the subgraph of G associated with V_1 and of the subgraph of G associated with V_2.

More generally, let $P^k = \{V_1, V_2, ..., V_k\}$ be the k-partitioning obtained at step k. A $(k+1)$-partitioning P^{k+1} is deduced from P^k by embedding each subgraph G^i of G associated with each V_i, $i = 1, ..., k$, in a small d-dimensional space and by finding the bipartition $V_i = V_i^1 \cup V_i^2$, $i = 1, ..., k$, which leads to the best $(k+1)$-partitioning.

For G^i bipartitioning, we adapt the approach presented in the previous paragraph. As we only compute a bipartitioning, we do not need to resort to dynamic programming as for k-way partitioning. We simply evaluate all bipartitions made up of consecutive vertices on the ordering π_i^d. Each index pair (a, b) so that $1 \le a \le b \le n_i$ and $a \ne 1$ or $b \ne n_i$, determines two complementary clusters denoted as $V_{[a, b]}$ and $V_{[\mathrm{succ}(b), \mathrm{pred}(a)]}$, where $\mathrm{succ}(b)$ is the successor of b and $\mathrm{pred}(a)$ is the predecessor of a on the tour. Therefore $\{V_{[a, b]}, V_{[\mathrm{succ}(b), \mathrm{pred}(a)]}\}$ is a bipartition of V_i and $\{V_1, V_2, ..., V_{[a, b]}, V_{[\mathrm{succ}(b), \mathrm{pred}(a)]}, ..., V_k\}$ is a $(k+1)$-partitioning of G. To find the best $(k+1)$-partitioning, we have to test every possible values for a and b, and consider the ones which give the best (lowest) cost.

4. Application case study

We here present a study we conducted on the case of a Cognac producer and seller who wants to promote his Web site (www._____.com) online.

4.1. Construction of the map

We first used the Google search engine to find a reference site in the field of Cognac. "le-cognac.com" appeared to be the most convenient one and was chosen as a starting point for the corpus construction. The initial set of sites then contained "le-cognac.com" and 112 other sites –identified by the URL (Uniform Resource Locator) of their home pages– linking to or linked to by it. These include notably sites dealing with Cognac, and also sites dealing with gastronomy or cigars, sites owned by companies specialized in new technologies, or search engines. The resulting graph we considered has 113 vertices v_i –one for each site– and 366 edges (v_i, v_j) –one for existence of at least one hyperlink between v_i and v_j.

The partitioning algorithm was applied on these data with different values for the number of classes k. We retained a value for k corresponding to a negligible Scaled Cost variation, i.e. when there is little change in the structure. We obtained 56 heterogeneous classes: 1 with

50 sites, 2 with 3 sites, 4 with 2 sites, and 49 singletons.

The second step of the process consisted in determining site categories from the contents. This work was done by an expert (table 1).

The resulting map is presented in figure 1.

Table 1. Site categories determined according to inner contents

Category	Corresponding sites
Catering	Official sites of restaurants or bars, and other sites dealing with catering
Cigars	Sites dealing with cigars
Cinema	Official sites of film companies, and other sites dealing with cinema
New technologies	Official sites of companies specialized in new technologies
Food – Gastronomy	Sites dealing with food and/or gastronomy
Internet	Sites talking about Internet and/or the World Wide Web
Internet: audience measurement, advertising	Web resources providing audience measurement or advertising services
Pleasures of life – Leisure	Sites dealing with leisure and pleasures of life in general
Site directory – Hosting	Site directories and/or sites hosting pages dealing with various topics
French socio-economic life	Sites dealing with French companies, organizations or local authorities
Wines, spirits, and other drinks	Sites dealing with wines, spirits, or drinks in general
Miscellaneous	Sites that do not fall into any other category

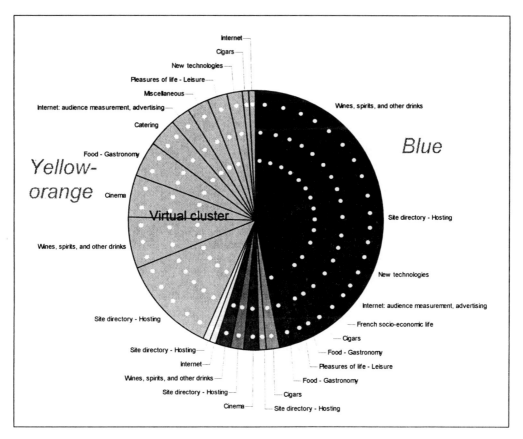

Figure 1. Map providing a view on the set of candidate sites for the creation of hyperlinks toward www._____.com. Sites are represented by white dots.

4.2. Exploitation of the map

When looking for a site dealing with Cognac, a net surfer will probably first search for popular resources on this topic, i.e. thematic portals. The latter include "le-cognac.com" as well as a small number of other sites. Since those sites constitute a highly connected logical network, we can say that the "Wines, spirits, and other drinks" class in the blue cluster will probably include most of them. The class with the same label in the yellow-orange cluster must contain sites that also deal with the considered topic but are lesser popular. The smallest "Wines..." class must contain two sites that are very close –from the point of view of hyperlinks– but separated from the others. Two main conclusions may be drawn from this primary analysis. First, links should be created on sites in the blue "Wines..." class. Notice that when the number k of clusters increases, this class still contains the most popular Cognac sites and is therefore always of high interest for link creation. Second, the smallest "Wines..." class should be further examined to find out if it is worth creating a link on one of its sites.

A number of classes correspond to other themes related to Cognac: "Food – Gastronomy", "Catering", "Pleasures of life – Leisure", "Cigars", "French socio-economic life" and "Cinema" (Cognac is not only a French brandy but also the name of a town where a film festival takes place once a year). Sites in these classes should be handled the same way as those in "Wines..." classes.

The remaining classes, with the exception of "Miscellaneous", are related to the infrastructure of the network resources that are involved: "New technologies", "Internet", "Site directory – Hosting", and "Internet: audience measurement, advertising". Sites in those classes will probably appear in many cartographies, independently of the considered topic; and because of the absence of a thematic bound, it is unlikely that surfers will visit them if they have already found an interesting site. Nevertheless, let us notice that there are probably relevant sites in "Site directory – Hosting"; but these can normally be taken into account by using more traditional Web site promotion techniques.

Finally, "Miscellaneous" sites should be examined individually so that their interest can be evaluated.

5. Conclusions and future works

In this paper, we have described an approach to construct maps usable in the context of online site promotion whose aim is to create numerous hyperlinks on well-chosen pages in order to draw a large and targeted flow of visitors. The objective is to provide users with an interface enabling them to have all the information they need to decide what sites are interesting for link creation. We focused on highlighting relevant characteristics in the organization of candidate sites dealing with given topics. In particular, we proposed to rely on the graph structure of the Web to try and identify big enough groups of strongly connected sites in which the traffic is dense and that are therefore of high interest for our application. To tackle this problem, we turned to a novel iterative algorithm for graph partitioning that we had initially developed in the context of integrated circuits. This algorithm is based on a method that was adapted from existing researches on geometric approaches using spectral decomposition of the Laplacian matrix. The analogy between those circuits and our networks allowed us to obtain valuable results for Web cartography. To furnish further details about the contents of sites, we proposed to resort to a semantic analysis of texts that helps construct a complementary thematic classification. Experiments on a real case were presented, with an example of map integrating both aspects.

A number of enhancements can be brought at different steps of the process. These include refinements in the corpus construction and possible changes in the values given to the algorithm parameters. In addition, the actual creation of interactive software maps will have to be automated: we consider using SVG (Scalable Vector Graphics), a language for describing two-dimensional graphics in XML, to generate such interfaces.

More fundamentally, the particular characteristics of the considered graph structure could be better taken into account to help make the partitioning more relevant. We notably intend to integrate the fact that hyperlinks are oriented by considering a directed graph rather than an undirected one [18].

Furthermore, we will investigate ways to take better advantage of the clustering. First, a pre-order induced by the partitioning –two sites can be either *close* or *distant*– could be used in the context of non-metric (ordinal) multidimensional scaling methods to find a "good" planar representation of the actual proximity between sites (e.g. [5]). That would provide a more precise and richer view of information, since the two available dimensions would be fully exploited. Secondly, instead of considering only independent classes at the end of the process, we are thinking of using the successive steps of the algorithm itself to deduce a relevant distance metric between sites. The way groups of sites are progressively detached from one another should provide information about the relationships between the involved sites. For example, when a cluster A is divided into two clusters A_1 and A_2, we could say that the distance $d(a_1, a_2)$, with a_1 in A_1 and a_2 in A_2, is a function of the corresponding induced cost. In this case, metric multidimensional scaling methods could be used to obtain corresponding bidimensional representations.

6. References

[1] C.J. Alpert and A.B. Kahng, "Recent Directions in Netlist Partitioning: A Survey", *Integration: the VLSI Journal*, Vol. 19, No. 1-2, 1995, pp. 1-81.

[2] C.J. Alpert and A.B. Kahng, "Multi-Way Partitioning Via Geometric Embeddings, Orderings and Dynamic Programming", *IEEE Transactions on Computer-Aided Design*, Vol. 14, No. 11, Nov. 1995, pp. 1342-1358.

[3] C.J. Alpert and A.B. Kahng, "Splitting Orderings into Multi-Way Partitionings to Minimize the Maximum Diameter", *Journal of Classification*, Vol. 14, 1997, pp. 51-74.

[4] J.J. Bartholdi and L.K. Platzman, "Heuristics Based on Spacefilling Curves for Combinatorial Problems in Euclidean Space", *Management Science*, Vol. 34, No. 3, March 1988, pp. 291-305.

[5] I. Borg and P.J.F. Groenen, *Modern Multidimensional Scaling*, Springer-Verlag, 1997.

[6] T. Bray, "Measuring the Web", *Proceedings of the Fifth International World Wide Web Conference, Computer Networks and ISDN Systems*, Vol. 28, No. 7-11, May 1996, pp. 993-1005.

[7] S. Brin and L. Page, "The Anatomy of a Large-Scale Hypertextual Web Search Engine", *Proceedings of the Seventh World Wide Web Conference, Computer Networks*, Vol. 30, No. 1-7, April 1998, pp. 107-117.

[8] H. Burwell, C.R. Ernst, and M. Sankey, *Online Competitive Intelligence: Increase Your Profits Using Cyber-Intelligence*, Facts on Demand Press, 1999.

[9] S. Chakrabarti, B.E. Dom, S. Kumar, P. Raghavan, S. Rajagopalan, A. Tomkins, D. Gibson, and J. Kleinberg, "Mining the Web's Link Structure", *IEEE Computer*, Vol. 32, No. 8, August 1999, pp. 60-67.

[10] P.K. Chan, M.D.F. Schlag, and J.Y. Zien, "Spectral K-Way Ratio-Cut Partitioning and Clustering", *IEEE Transactions on Computer-Aided Design*, Vol. 13, No. 9, September 1994, pp. 1088-1096.

[11] F.R.K. Chung, "Spectral Graph Theory", *American Mathematical Society*, Regional Conference Series in Mathematics, No. 92, Providence, RI, 1997.

[12] M. Dodge and R. Kitchin, *Mapping Cyberspace*, Routledge, 2000.

[13] K. Fan, "On a Theorem of Weyl Concerning Eigenvalues of Linear Transformations", *Proc. National Academy of Sc. of the USA*, Vol. 35, 1949, pp. 652-655.

[14] N. Gershon and S.G. Eick (Eds.), "Information Visualization", *IEEE Computer Graphics and Applications*, Vol. 17, No. 4, July/Aug. 1997, pp. 29-78.

[15] K.M. Hall, "An r-Dimensional Quadratic Placement Algorithm", *Management Science*, Vol. 17, No. 3, November 1970, pp. 219-229.

[16] I. Herman, G. Melançon, and M.S. Marshall, "Graph Visualization and Navigation in Information Visualization: A Survey", *IEEE Transactions on Visualization and Computer Graphics*, Vol. 6, No. 1, January-March 2000, pp. 24-43.

[17] R.A. Horn and C.R. Johnson, *Matrix Analysis*, Cambridge University Press, 1985.

[18] B. Jouve, "Multiplicity of cortex visual areas: an approach by graph theory" (in French), Ph.D Thesis, Ecole des Hautes Etudes en Sciences sociales, 1999.

[19] L. Kahaner, *Competitive Intelligence: How to Gather, Analyze, and Use Information to Move Your Business to the Top*, Touchstone, 1998.

[20] R.M. Karp, "Probabilistic Analysis of Partitioning Algorithms for the Traveling Salesman Problem in the Plane", *Mathematics of Operations Research*, Vol. 2, No. 3, August 1977, pp. 209-224.

[21] P. Kuntz, F. Velin, and H. Briand, "Iterative geometric representations for multi-way partitioning", *Electrical and Computer Engineering International Reference Book Series*, WSES Press, 2001 (to appear).

[22] P. Lenca and P. Picouet, "Why include human-centered processes in a data mining process?", *Proceedings of EURO XVIII – The European Operational Research Conference*, 2001 (to appear).

[23] S. Lin and B.W. Kernighan, "An Effective Heuristic Algorithm for the Traveling-Salesman Problem", *Operations Research*, Vol. 21, No. 2, March/April 1973, pp. 498-516.

[24] P. Pirolli, J. Pitkow, and R. Rao, "Silk from a Sow's Ear: Extracting Usable Structures from the Web", *Proc. of the CHI'96 Conference on Human Factors in Computing Systems*, ACM, 1996, pp. 118-125.

[25] L.G. Terveen, W.C. Hill, and B. Amento, "Constructing, Organizing, and Visualizing Collections of Topically Related Web Resources", *ACM Transactions on Computer-Human Interaction*, Vol. 6, No. 1, March 1999, pp. 67-94.

[26] F. Velin, P. Peter, and C. Belleil, "Exploitation of textual data in the context of Web mining" (in French), *Proceedings of the EGC'2001 Conference on KDD and Knowledge Management*, Revue ECA, Vol. 1, No. 1-2, Hermes Science, 2001, pp. 251-256.

Maintenance of Sequential Patterns for Record Deletion

Ching-Yao Wang[1], Tzung-Pei Hong[2] and Shian-Shyong Tseng[1]

[1]*National Chiao-Tung University, Taiwan*
{cywang, sstseng}@cis.nctu.edu.tw
[2]*National University of Kaohsiung, Taiwan*
tphong@nuk.edu.tw

Abstract

In the past, we proposed an incremental mining algorithm for maintenance of sequential patterns based on the concept of pre-large sequences as new records were inserted. In this paper, we attempt to apply the concept of pre-large sequences to maintain sequential patterns as records are deleted. Pre-large sequences are defined by a lower support threshold and an upper support threshold. They act as buffers to avoid the movements of sequential patterns directly from large to small and vice-versa. Our proposed algorithm does not require rescanning original databases until the accumulative amount of deleted customer sequences exceeds a safety bound, which depends on database size. As databases grow larger, the numbers of deleted customer sequences allowed before database rescanning is required also grow. The proposed approach is thus efficient for a large database.

Keywords: data mining, incremental mining, record deletion, maintenance, sequential pattern.

1. Introduction

Mining useful information and helpful knowledge from large databases has evolved into an important research area [1][3]. Among them, finding sequential patterns in temporal transaction databases is important since it allows modeling of customer behavior [2][8][10].

Mining sequential patterns was first proposed by Agrawal *et al.* in 1995 [2], and is a non-trivial task. It attempts to find customer purchase sequences and to predict whether there is a high probability that when customers buy some products, they will buy some other products in later transactions. Note that the transaction sequences need not be consecutive.

Although customer behavior models can be efficiently extracted by Agrawal and Srikant's mining algorithm [2] to assist managers in making correct and effective decisions, the sequential patterns discovered may become invalid or inappropriate when databases are updated. Conventional approaches may re-mine entire databases to get correct sequential patterns for maintenance.

In the past, some approaches have been proposed to improve rule-maintenance performance with previously mined information, such as the FUP algorithm proposed by Cheung *et al.* [4][5], the adaptive algorithm proposed by Sarda and Srinivas [9], the incremental mining algorithm based on pre-large concept proposed by Hong *et al.* [6][7] and the FASTUP algorithm proposed by Lin and Lee [8]. The common idea is that previously mined information should be utilized as much as possible to reduce maintenance costs.

In [7], we proposed an efficient incremental mining algorithm capable of updating sequential patterns based on the concept of pre-large sequences when new records were inserted. In addition to record insertion, record deletion is also commonly seen in real-world applications. Developing efficient maintenance algorithms to update sequential patterns for record deletion is also necessary. In this paper, we attempt to apply the concept of pre-large sequences to solve this issue. The proposed algorithm doesn't need to rescan the original database until a number of original customer sequences have been deleted. If the database is large, then the number of deleted customer sequences allowed will be large too.

2. Rule maintenance for record deletion

When records are deleted from databases, the original sequential patterns may become invalid, or new implicitly valid patterns may appear in the resulting updated databases. For example, assume a database has three attributes, *Cust_id*, *Trans_time* and *Trans_content*. *Cust_id* records the unique identification of a customer, *Trans_time* stores the time a transaction occurs, and *Trans_content* stores what items were purchased in a transaction. Also assume that it consists of the sixteen records, sorted first by *Cust_id* and then by *Trans_time*, as shown in Table 1.

Table 1. The sixteen records sorted first by Cust_id and then by Trans_time

Cust_id	Trans_time	Trans_content
1	1998/01/01	A
1	1998/01/20	B
2	1998/01/11	C, D
2	1998/02/02	A
2	1998/02/11	E, F, G
3	1998/01/07	A, H, G
4	1998/02/09	A
4	1998/02/19	E, G
4	1998/02/23	B
5	1998/01/05	B
5	1998/01/12	C
6	1998/01/05	A
6	1998/01/13	B, C
7	1998/01/01	A
7	1998/01/17	B, C, D
8	1998/01/23	E, G

Let a *sequence* be an ordered list of itemsets and a *customer sequence* be a sequence of all transactions for a customer in order of transaction times. Note that each transaction in a customer sequence corresponds to an itemset. A sequence A is contained in a sequence B if the former is a sub-sequence of the latter. Take the data in Table 1 as an example. These records in Table 1 are transformed into customer sequences as shown in Table 2.

Table 2. The customer sequences transformed from the records in Table 1

Cust_id	Customer sequence
1	<(A)(B)>
2	<(C, D)(A)(E, F, G)>
3	<(A, H, G)>
4	<(A)(E, G)(B)>
5	<(B)(C)>
6	<(A)(B, C)>
7	<(A)(B, C, D)>
8	<(E, G)>

Assume the minimum support is set at 50% (i.e., four customer sequences for this example). All the large sequences mined from the customer sequences in Table 2 by Agrawal and Srikant's AprioriAll approach [2] are presented in Table 3.

Table 3. All large sequences mined from the customer sequences in Table 2

Large sequences			
1-sequence	Count	2-sequence	Count
<(A)>	6	<(A)(B)>	4
<(B)>	5		
<(C)>	4		
<(G)>	4		

If the two records, Cust_id = 2 with Trans_time =

1998/01/11 and Cust_id = 8 with Trans_time = 1998/01/23, are deleted from Table 1, the large sequences in Table 3 will be modified as those shown in Table 4.

Table 4. The large sequences after record deletion.

Large sequences			
1-sequence	Count	2-sequence	Count
<(A)>	6	<(A)(B)>	4
<(B)>	5		

The originally large sequences <(C)> and <(G)> become small after the two records are deleted. Conventional batch-mining algorithms must re-process the entire updated database to find the updated sequential patterns for managing these situations.

3. The concept of pre-large sequences

In [7], we proposed the concept of pre-large sequences capable of further reducing the amount of rescanning original databases in mining sequential patterns when new records are inserted. A pre-large sequence is not truly large, but promises to be large in the future. A lower support threshold and an upper support threshold are used to realize this concept. The upper support threshold is the same as the minimum support used in conventional mining algorithms. The support ratio of a sequence must be larger than the upper support threshold in order to be considered large. On the other hand, the lower support threshold defines the lowest support ratio for a sequence to be treated as pre-large. A sequence with a support ratio below the lower threshold is thought of as a small sequence.

Processing record deletion is different from processing record insertion. When records are deleted from a database, the following two cases may occur.

1. All of the records by some old customers are deleted. This will also delete the corresponding customer sequences. The number of customer sequences thus decreases.
2. Parts of the records by some old customers are deleted. This will not change the number of customer sequences. Some itemsets are however removed from the existing customer sequences, thus decreasing the counts of some sequential patterns.

The deleted records for the same customers are first grouped into deleted customer sequences. For example, assume the original records and customer sequences are shown in Tables 1 and 2. When the two records shown in Table 5 are deleted, the corresponding deleted customer sequences are shown in Table 6

Table 5. The two deleted records in this example

Cust_id	Trans_time	Trans_content
2	1998/01/11	C, D
8	1998/01/23	E, G

Table 6. The two deleted customer sequences transformed from Table 5

Cust_id	Customer sequence
2	<(C, D)>
8	<(E, G)>

The candidate sequences can then be formed from the deleted customer sequences and the corresponding old customer sequences. Each candidate sequence must contain a subsequence in the deleted customer sequences and must exist in the corresponding old customer sequences. It is easily seen that the itemsets in deleted customer sequences will be removed from the corresponding old customer sequences. The count of a sequential pattern containing itemsets in the transactions deleted may thus remain the same or decrease. The counts of the candidate sequences derived from the deleted customer sequences are then defined by their count decrements due to the deletion of old transactions. Let k-sequences be the sequences with k itemsets. The candidate 1-sequences for the deleted customer sequences in Table 6 are shown in Table 7. Their counts are also shown there.

Table 7. The candidate 1-sequences with their counts

Candidate 1-sequences	
1-sequence	Count
<(C)>	1
<(D)>	1
<(E)>	1
<(G)>	1
<(C, D)>	1
<(E, G)>	1

Note that in this example, the customer sequence with Cust_id = 8 is empty after the deletion operations. The number of the customer sequences thus decreases by 1.

Considering the old customer sequences in terms of the two support thresholds, the candidate sequences from the deleted customer sequences may fall into the following three cases illustrated in Figure 1.

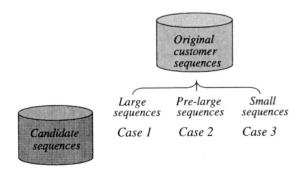

Large sequences   Pre-large sequences   Small sequences

Case 1   Case 2   Case 3

Figure 1. Three cases arising from deleting transactions from existing databases

Case 1 may remove existing large sequences, and cases 2 and 3 may add new large sequences (due to the decrease of the customer number). If we retain all large and pre-large sequences with their counts in the original database, then cases 1 and 2 can be easily handled. Also, in the maintenance phase, the ratio of deleted customer sequences to original customer sequences is usually very small. This is more apparent for a larger database. A sequence in case 3 cannot possibly be large for the entire updated database as long as the number of deleted customer sequences is small when compared to the number of customer sequences in the original database. This point is proven below.

4. Notation

The notation used in this paper is defined below.

D: the set of original customer sequences;

T: the set of deleted customer sequences transformed from the deleted records;

U: the entire updated customer sequences;

d: the number of customer sequences in D;

t: the number of deleted customer sequences in T;

q: the number of deleted customers from T;

S_u: the upper support threshold for large sequences;

S_l: the lower support threshold for pre-large sequences, $S_l < S_u$;

L_k^D: the set of large k-sequences from D;

L_k^T: the set of large k-sequences from T;

L_k^U: the set of large k-sequences from U;

P_k^D: the set of pre-large k-sequences from D;

P_k^T: the set of pre-large k-sequences from T;

P_k^U: the set of pre-large k-sequences from U;

C_k: the set of all candidate k-sequences from T;

I: a sequence;

$S^D(I)$: the number of occurrences of I in D;

$S^T(I)$: the number of occurrence decrements of I due to T;

$S^U(I)$: the number of occurrences of I in U.

5. Theoretical foundation

In this section, we will show that if the number of deleted customer sequences is small when compared with the number of original customer sequences, a sequence that is small (neither large nor pre-large) in the original database cannot possibly be large for the entire updated database. Two definitions are first given below.

Definition 1: For two customer sequences $A=<a_1, a_2, ..., a_n>$ and $B=<b_1, b_2, ..., b_m>$, where each element is an itemset, sequence A is *contained* in sequence B if there exist integers $i_1 < i_2 <...< i_n$ such that $a_1 \subseteq b_{i1}, a_2 \subseteq b_{i2}, ..., a_n \subseteq b_{in}$.

Definition 2: For two customer sequences $A=<a_1,$

$a_2...a_n>$ and $B=<b_1, b_2...b_n>$, sequence A is *equal* to sequence B if A is *contained* in B and B is *contained* in A.

The following theorem is then derived as the foundation for the proposed algorithm.

Theorem 1: Let S_l and S_u be, respectively, the lower and the upper support thresholds, d be the number of original customer sequences, t be the number of deleted customer sequences, and q be the number of deleted customers (i.e. the number of deleted customer sequences which are *equal* to the corresponding original customer sequences), $q \le t$. If $q \le \frac{(S_u - S_l)d}{S_u}$, then a sequence that is small (neither large nor pre-large) in the original database is not large for the entire updated database.

Proof: The following derivation can be obtained from $q \le \frac{(S_u - S_l)d}{S_u}$:

$$q \le \frac{(S_u - S_l)d}{S_u} \qquad (1)$$

$$\Rightarrow \quad qS_u \le (S_u - S_l)d$$

$$\Rightarrow \quad qS_u \le dS_u - dS_l$$

$$\Rightarrow \quad dS_l \le S_u(d-q)$$

$$\Rightarrow \quad \frac{dS_l}{d-q} \le S_u.$$

If a sequence I is small (neither large nor pre-large) in D, then its count $S^D(I)$ must be less than $S_l * d$. Therefore, $S^D(I) < dS_l$.

Since the number of deleted customer sequences is t, the count decrement (called count) of I in T is at most t. Thus:

$$t \ge S^T(I) \ge 0.$$

The entire support ratio of I in U is $\frac{S^U(I)}{d-q}$, which can be further expanded to:

$$\frac{S^U(I)}{d-q} = \frac{S^D(I) - S^T(I)}{d-q}$$

$$< \frac{dS_l}{d-q}$$

$$\le S_u.$$

I is thus not large for U. This completes the proof. $\square$

Example 1: Assume $d=100$, $S_l=50\%$ and $S_u=60\%$. The allowed number q of deleted customers within which the original database need not be re-scanned for maintenance of sequential patterns is:

$$\frac{(S_u - S_l)d}{S_u} = \frac{(0.6-0.5)100}{0.6} = 16.6.$$

If the number of deleted customers is equal to or less than 16, then an originally small sequence cannot be large for the entire updated database.

From Theorem 1, the bound of deleted customers is determined by S_l, S_u and d. It is easily seen from Formula 1 that if d grows larger, then q will grow larger too.

Therefore, as the database grows, our proposed approach thus becomes increasingly efficient.

6. The proposed maintenance algorithm for record deletion

In the proposed algorithm, the original large and pre-large sequences with their counts from preceding runs are retained for later use in maintenance. As records are deleted, they are first transformed into deleted customer sequences. The number of deleted customers is also found and accumulated. The deleted customer sequences are then scanned to generate candidate 1-sequences. These candidate sequences are then compared to the large and pre-large 1-sequences which were previously retained. They are thus divided into three parts according to whether they are large, pre-large or small in the original database. If a candidate 1-sequence is also among the previously retained large or pre-large 1-sequences, its new total count for the entire updated database can easily be calculated from its current count (decrement) and previous count, since all previous large and pre-large sequences with their counts have been retained. Whether an original large or pre-large sequence is still large or pre-large after records are deleted is then determined from its new support ratio, which is derived from its updated count over the number of customer sequences in the updated database. On the contrary, if a candidate 1-sequence does not exist among the previously retained large or pre-large 1-sequences, then the sequence is absolutely not large for the entire updated database as long as the number of deleted customers is within the safety bound derived from Theorem 1. In this situation, no action is needed. When records are gradually deleted and the total number of deleted customers exceeds the safety bound, the updated database must be re-scanned to find correct large and pre-large sequences. The proposed algorithm can thus find all large 1-sequences for the entire updated database. After that, candidate 2-sequences from the deleted customer sequences are formed, and the same procedure is used to find all large 2-sequences. This procedure is repeated until all large sequences have been found. The details of the proposed maintenance algorithm are described below. The global variable, c, is used to accumulate the number of deleted customers since the last re-scan of the entire updated database. The details of the proposed maintenance algorithm are described below.

The proposed maintenance algorithm for record deletion:

INPUT: A lower support threshold S_l, an upper support threshold S_u, a set of large and pre-large sequences in the original database D consisting of $(d-c)$ customer sequences, and a set of t deleted customer sequences transformed from deleted records.

OUTPUT: A set of sequential patterns for the updated database.

STEP 1: Calculate the safety bound according to Formula 1 as:

$$f = \frac{(S_u - S_l)d}{S_u}.$$

STEP 2: Count the number q of deleted customer sequences that are equal to the corresponding old customer sequences.

STEP 3: If $c + q \leq f$, then do the next step; otherwise, rescan the original database to determine large or pre-large sequences, set $d = d - c - q$ and $c = 0$, and exit the algorithm.

STEP 4: Find all candidate 1-sequences C_1 and their count decrements from the deleted customer sequences T and the corresponding original customer sequences.

STEP 5: Set $k = 1$, where k is used to record the number of itemsets in the sequences currently being processed.

STEP 6: Divide the candidate k-sequences into three parts according to whether they are large, pre-large or small in the original database.

STEP 7: Do the following substeps for each k-sequence I in the original large k-sequences L_k^D:

Substep 7-1: Set the new count $S^U(I) = S^D(I) - S^T(I)$.

Substep 7-2: If $S^U(I)/(d-c-q) \geq S_u$, then assign I as a large sequence, set $S^D(I) = S^U(I)$ and keep I with $S^D(I)$;

otherwise, if $S^U(I)/(d-c-q) \geq S_l$, then assign I as a pre-large sequence, set $S^D(I) = S^U(I)$ and keep I with $S^D(I)$;

otherwise, remove I.

STEP 8: Do the following substeps for each k-sequence I in the original pre-large k-sequences P_k^D:

Substep 8-1: Set the new count $S^U(I) = S^D(I) - S^T(I)$.

Substep 8-2: If $S^U(I)/(d-c-q) \geq S_u$, then assign I as a large sequence, set $S^D(I) = S^U(I)$ and keep I with $S^D(I)$;

otherwise, if $S^U(I)/(d-c-q) \geq S_l$, then assign I as a pre-large sequence, set $S^D(I) = S^U(I)$ and keep I with $S^D(I)$;

otherwise, remove I.

STEP 9: Select candidate $(k+1)$-sequences C_{k+1} from the originally large and pre-large $(k+1)$-sequences ($L_{k+1}^D \bigcup P_{k+1}^D$), each of which must contain a subsequence in the deleted customer sequences and must exist in the corresponding old customer sequences. Calculate their count decrements.

STEP 10: Set $k = k+1$.

STEP 11: Repeat STEPs 6 to 10 until no large or pre-large sequences are found.

STEP 12: Modify the maximal large sequence patterns according to the modified large sequences.

STEP 13: Set $c = c + q$.

After Step 13, the finally maximal large sequences for the updated database can be determined.

7. An Example

In this section, an example is given to illustrate the proposed maintenance algorithm for record deletion. Assume that the initial customer sequences are the same as those shown in Table 2. Also assume S_l is set at 30% and S_u is set at 50%. The sets of large and pre-large sequences for the given data are shown in Tables 8 and 9, respectively.

Table 8. The large sequences for the customer sequences in Table 2

Large sequences			
1-sequence	Count	2-sequence	Count
<(A)>	6	<(A)(B)>	4
<(B)>	5		
<(C)>	4		
<(G)>	4		

Table 9. The pre-large sequences for the customer sequences in Table 2

Pre-large sequences			
1-sequence	Count	2-sequence	Count
<(E)>	3		
<(E, G)>	3		

Assume the two records shown in Table 10 are deleted from Table 1.

Table 10. The two records deleted from Table 1

Cust_id	Trans_time	Trans_content
2	1998/01/11	C, D
8	1998/01/23	E, G

The deleted customer sequences transformed from Table 10 are presented in Table 11.

Table 11. The two deleted customer sequences transformed form Table 10

Cust_id	Customer sequence
2	<(C, D)>
8	<(E, G)>

The global variable c is initially set at 0. The safety bound f is calculated as:

$$f = \frac{(S_u - S_l)d}{S_u} = \frac{(0.5 - 0.3)8}{0.5} = 3.2.$$

540

Since the customer with Cust_id = 8 is deleted, $q = 1$. All candidate 1-sequences C_1 with their counts from the two deleted customer sequences are shown in Table 12.

Table 12. All candidate 1-sequences from the two deleted customer sequences

Candidate 1-sequences	Count
<(C)>	1
<(D)>	1
<(E)>	1
<(G)>	1
<(C, D)>	1
<(E, G)>	1

All the candidate 1-sequences in Table 12 are divided into three parts according to whether they are large, pre-large or small in the original database. The new count of each originally large 1-sequence is shown in Table 13.

Table 13. The new counts of the originally large 1-sequences

1-sequence	Count
<(A)>	6
<(B)>	5
<(C)>	3
<(G)>	3

<(C)> and <(G)> thus become pre-large sequences. The new count of each originally pre-large 1-sequence is shown in Table 14.

Table 14. The new counts of the originally pre-large 1-sequences

1-sequence	Count
<(E)>	2
<(E, G)>	2

<(E)> and <(E, G)> thus become small sequences. STEPs 6 to 10 are repeated until no large or pre-large sequences are found. The 2-sequence <(A)(B)> is still large after the transaction deletion. The maximally large sequence derived from the large 2-sequence <(A)(B)> is:

$$A \rightarrow B \ (Confidence=4/6).$$

After Step 13, the maximally large sequence for the updated database has been found, and c is 1. The new value c will be used for processing next deleted records.

8. Conclusions

In this paper, we have proposed a novel efficient maintenance algorithm to sequential patterns for record deletion. The concept of pre-large sequences is used to reduce the need for rescanning original databases and to save maintenance costs. The safety bound for not rescanning original databases is derived and proven. If the size of the database grows larger, then the number of deleted records allowed will be larger. This characteristic is especially useful for real-world applications.

References

[1] R. Agrawal, T. Imielinksi and A. Swami, "Database mining: a performance perspective," *IEEE Transactions on Knowledge and Data Engineering,* Vol. 5, No. 6, pp. 914-925, 1993.

[2] R. Agrawal and R. Srikant, "Mining sequential patterns," *The Eleventh IEEE International Conference on Data Engineering,* pp. 3-14, 1995.

[3] M. S. Chen, J. Han and P. S. Yu, "Data mining: An overview from a database perspective," *IEEE Transactions on Knowledge and Data Engineering,* Vol. 8, No. 6, pp. 866-883, 1996.

[4] D. W. Cheung, J. Han, V. T. Ng and C. Y. Wong, "Maintenance of discovered association rules in large databases: An incremental updating approach," *The Twelfth IEEE International Conference on Data Engineering,* pp. 106-114, 1996.

[5] D. W. Cheung, S. D. Lee and B. Kao, "A general incremental technique for maintaining discovered association rules," *In Proceedings of Database Systems for Advanced Applications,* pp. 185-194, Melbourne, Australia, 1997.

[6] T. P. Hong, C. Y. Wang and Y. H. Tao, "A new incremental data mining algorithm using pre-large itemsets," *Intelligent Data Analysis,* Vol. 5, No. 2, pp. 111-129, 2001.

[7] T. P. Hong, C. Y. Wang and S. S. Tseng "Incremental data mining for sequential patterns using pre-large sequences," *The Fifth World Multi- Conference on Systemics, Cybernetics and Informatics,* Orlando, Florida, U.S.A, 2001.

[8] M. Y. Lin and S. Y. Lee, "Incremental update on sequential patterns in large databases," *The Tenth IEEE International Conference on Tools with Artificial Intelligence,* pp. 24-31, 1998.

[9] N. L. Sarda and N. V. Srinivas, "An adaptive algorithm for incremental mining of association rules," *The Ninth International Workshop on Database and Expert Systems,* pp. 240-245, 1998.

[10] R. Srikant and R. Agrawal, "Mining sequential patterns: generalizations and performance improvements," *The Fifth International Conference on Knowledge Discovery and Data Mining (KDD'95),* pp. 269-274, 1995.

SSDT: A Scalable Subspace-Splitting Classifier for Biased Data

Haixun Wang
IBM T. J. Watson Research Center
Yorktown Heights, NY 10598
haixun@us.ibm.com

Philip S. Yu
IBM T. J. Watson Research Center
Yorktown Heights, NY 10598
psyu@us.ibm.com

Abstract

Decision trees are one of the most extensively used data mining models. Recently, a number of efficient, scalable algorithms for constructing decision trees on large disk-resident dataset have been introduced. In this paper, we study the problem of learning scalable decision trees from datasets with biased class distribution. Our objective is to build decision trees that are more concise and more interpretable while maintaining the scalability of the model. To achieve this, our approach searches for subspace clusters of data cases of the biased class to enable multivariate splittings based on weighted distances to such clusters. In order to build concise and interpretable models, other approaches including multivariate decision trees and association rules, often introduce scalability and performance issues. The SSDT algorithm we present achieves the objective without loss in efficiency, scalability, and accuracy.

1 Introduction

Decision trees are one of the most extensively used data mining models. Decision tree induction is a greedy algorithm that partitions the data in a top-down, divide-and-conquer manner. Decision trees are especially attractive in mining large datasets because i) the decision tree model is easier to interpret [5] and, ii) the induction process is more efficient compared to other methods [12, 8]. Recently, a number of efficient, scalable algorithms for constructing univariate decision trees from large disk-resident data have been introduced [12, 8, 7, 14].

Our work focuses on the scenario where the training data has a highly imbalanced class distribution, i.e., we assume there are only 2 class labels, positive and negative, and the positive (target) class accounts for a small fraction (say between 0.1% and 5%) of the entire dataset. This situation arises frequently in the data mining environment, such as in fraud detection, network intrusion detection, and etc. In this paper, we first discuss several limitations of the deci-

sion tree induction process under this scenario. Then, we introduce a new technique, SSDT, which aims at overcoming these problems while preserving the efficiency of the decision tree algorithms.

Representational limitations of univariate decision trees
The decision tree induction process has several deficiencies. Consider the training set in Figure 1(a), where `Play?` is the class label. The C4.5 decision tree is shown in Figure 1(b), which has only one node. Obviously, it misses the pattern of (`hot`, `high`) that has a strong support of `No`. The difficulty is largely due to univariate tests at each node and it is also compounded by the use of categorical attributes.

Applying multivariate decision tree algorithms, such as OC1 [11] and LMDT [6], to such datasets may reveal patterns univariate decision tree can not discover. However, it is computationally expensive to gauge the value of a linear combination of many variables per node, and is practically infeasible to use on large disk-resident datasets.

Biased data distribution Training sets of certain data mining tasks have a very biased data distribution, inasmuch as the target class accounts for an extremely tiny fraction (say 0.5%) of the data. Most learning algorithms, such as decision trees, will generate a trivial model that always predicts the majority class and reports an accuracy rate of 99.5% [16]. However, data cases of the biased class often carries more significant meanings and are often the primary targets of mining.

Decision trees have been shown unsuitable for such tasks [10]. In Figure 1(c), we show the distribution of a synthetic dataset in a two-dimensional space, where the dark regions represent the data cases of the biased class. Data cases of the majority class are either clustered at different spots or simply distributed randomly and are not shown explicitly. A representative univariate decision tree learned from such a dataset without pruning is shown in Figure 1(d). The decision tree induction process keeps on partitioning the space either horizontally or vertically at each node, and the resulted decision tree often has a very large size. Furthermore,

Temp	Humid	Play?
cool	high	yes
mild	high	yes
mild	normal	yes
hot	dry	yes
hot	normal	yes
hot	normal	yes
hot	high	no
hot	high	no
hot	high	no
very hot	high	yes

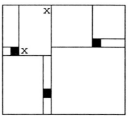

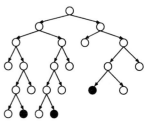

(a) Training Set   (b) C4.5 decision tree for (a)   (c) 2-dimensional biased dataset   (d) decision tree for (c)

Figure 1. Limitations of Decision Tree Classifiers

it is easy to see that the size of the tree will grow with the dimensionality of the data, as in a higher dimensional space more tests are required to locate the subspace region where the data cases cluster.

A decision tree that assigns an unknown instance a definite class label ('positive' or 'negative') or a probability based merely on the data distribution in the leaf nodes usually has a low predictive accuracy for instances of the biased target class. Furthermore, the model can hardly discriminate among data cases of the majority class on the basis of their closeness to the target class. For instance, the two 'X's in Figure 1(c) are in the same leaf node. Hence, they are assigned a same probability by the model, although one of them is much closer to the biased class. This causes problems in applications such as target marketing: the marketing department wants to send out promotions to 20% of the people in their database while only 1% of the people in the database are recorded buyers. The rest 19% has to be selected based on their closeness to the buyer class.

2 Our Approach: An Overview

It is clear from the examples in Figure 1 that univariate splitting conditions often results in undetected patterns or decision trees of formidable sizes. To build concise models, it is essential that more than one variables are taken into consideration in splitting the data. However, scalability requirements forbids us considering all possible combinations of these variables as OC1 [11] and LMDT [6] do.

We improve the decision tree induction process by providing an additional splitting criterion which results in more concise and more interpretable decision trees. The motivation is that, in datasets with biased class distribution, while the negative instances are distributed 'everywhere', instances of the target class tend to form clusters in some subspaces. These clusters are the foundation of accurate predictions of unknown instances. The proposed approach,

SSDT, uses an efficient multivariate search algorithm to locate subspace clusters so as to enable (multivariate) splitting based on weighted distances to the centroid of the clusters.

While it is computationally prohibitive to search for all the clusters, it is more feasible to search for clusters formed by points in the biased target class, since they only account for a small fraction of the data. Our algorithm detects candidate clusters from lower dimensions to higher dimensions, and prunes away all the candidates as soon as we find that partitions based on these clusters can not offer a better purity than the univariate splits.

Related Works Much work has focused on how to tackle the deficiencies of the decision tree discussed in the previous section. Among them, multivariate decision trees overcome a representational limitation of univariate decision trees [13, 4]. However, performing a multivariate partition often leads to a much larger consumption of computation time and memory, which may be prohibitive for large datasets.

The target selection problem also attracts lots of attention [9, 10]. Closeness estimations of an unknown instance to a certain class can be solved by clustering and nearest neighbor algorithms. A naive approach searches for clusters of the biased data and scores an unknown sample by its distance to the closest cluster. Association rule mining [3] is also used to solve the target selection problem. A potential problem with association rules is the combinatorial explosion of "frequent itemsets" [9, 10], which can be prohibitive for large datasets with biased data distribution even after sophisticated pruning.

Contributions of this Paper We use novel splitting criteria in building decision trees. We discover data clustering in correlated dimensions and partition the data by distance functions defined in the corresponding subspaces. With our multivariate splitting condition, decision trees can be built smaller, and more interpretable. However, unlike other multivariate decision tree algorithms that are usually prohibitive for large datasets or high dimensions, our approach is efficient and scalable.

3 Definitions

Let S denote the training set belonging to a node of a decision tree. Each point in S has n attributes in addition to the special attribute: class label. Let $C = \{x_1, ..., x_k\}$ be a cluster of points where each x_i has the same class label. The *centroid* of C is the algebraic mean of points in C.

To measure the closeness of a point to a cluster, we use weighted Euclidean distance function, $Dist(\vec{d}, \vec{p}, \vec{w}) = \sqrt{\sum_{i=1}^{n} \vec{w}_i(\vec{d}_i - \vec{p}_i)^2}$, where $\vec{d}$ is a point, $\vec{p}$ the centroid of a cluster, and $\vec{w}$ the weight vector. The Euclidean distance is indeed defined in a subspace that is specified by a set of dimensions whose weights are non-zero.

The Euclidean distance only works for numerical attributes. For ordinal attributes, we can map their values to the range of [0,1]. For categorical attributes, the heterogeneous Euclidean metric [15] defines the similarity of two values by their relative frequency of occurrences in the same class. However, for attributes with many values and a biased dataset, certain values may never occur in the training set. In our algorithm, we use a distance matrix M supplied by the user, such that the value $M(i, j) \in [0, 1]$ denotes the distance between categorical value i and j.

We use the *gini* index,

$$gini(S) = 1 - \sum_{j=1}^{c} p_j^2 \qquad (1)$$

where p_j is the relative frequency of class j in S, to measure the "goodness" of all the potential splits. If S is partitioned into two subsets S_1 and S_2, the index of the partitioned data $gini(S)$ can be obtained by:

$$gini(S) = \frac{n_1}{n_1 + n_2} gini(S_1) + \frac{n_2}{n_1 + n_2} gini(S_2) \qquad (2)$$

where n_1 and n_2 are the number of points of S_1 and S_2, respectively.

4 Scalable Decision Tree Classifiers

A decision tree classifier recursively partitions the training set until each partition consists entirely, or almost entirely, of records from one class.

The SPRINT algorithm has been proposed to build decision trees for large datasets [12]. The splitting criterion used by SPRINT is based on the value of a single attribute (univariate). For a continuous attribute, it has the form of $A \leq C$ where A is an attribute and C is a value in the domain of attribute A.

SPRINT avoids costly sorting at each node by presorting continuous attributes only once, at the beginning of the algorithm. Values of each continuous attribute are maintained by a sorted list. Each entry in the list contains i) a value of the attribute, ii) its record id (rid), and iii) the class label of the record. The node is split on the attribute which yields the least value of the $gini$ index (G_{best}). Based on the sorted list of the splitting attribute, a hash table is constructed to map each record (rid) to one of the subnodes which the record belongs to after the split. Entries in other attribute lists are moved to the attribute list of the subnodes after consulting the hash table as to which subnode this entry belongs to. The sorted order is maintained as the entries are moved in pre-sorted order.

5 The SSDT Algorithm

The core of SSDT lies in detecting subspace clusters of positive points. However, finding all such clusters is both time consuming and unnecessary. We are only interested in clusters that can offer a better split than univariate partitions. In Section 5.1, we prove an important property which enables us to narrow down our search to those clusters that have the potential. The actual clustering algorithm is introduced in Section 5.2, where we use an Apriori-like algorithm to find subspace clusters from lower dimensions spaces to higher dimensional spaces. In Section 5.3, we compute the exact $gini$ index for cluster-based partitioning by scanning a small proportion of the data, thus keeping the overhead of the multivariate partitioning to a minimum.

SSDT is based on the framework of SPRINT, where presorted attribute lists are maintained at each node. We consider only two class labels, `positive` and `negative`, and the target class (`positive`) is biased, usually accounting for only a small fraction of the data. We normalize the values on each dimension to the range of [0,1].

The SSDT approach is outlined in Algorithm 1. To partition a dataset, we first compute the $gini$ index on each of its attributes. While we scan through the pre-sorted attribute list, we also derive 1-dimensional clusters of the biased data for each dimension (described in detail later). Next, we locate subspace clusters of the positive data cases. The minimal $gini$ index produced by the univariate splits, G_{best}, is passed in as a parameter to $ClusterDetect()$ so that clusters can not possibly deliver a $gini$ index smaller than G_{best} are pruned as early as possible. We then compute the $gini$ index of splits based on the distance to each subspace cluster. The process, $DistanceEntropy()$, described in Algorithm 2, does not require globally reordering the data according to the distance. If the minimal $gini$ index is achieved by some subspace cluster, we partition

Algorithm 1 SSDT(Dataset: S)

1: $S_p \leftarrow$ points of the biased class in S;
2: **for each** attribute k **do**
3:     scan the sorted attribute list of k and compute:
4:     — I_k : the *gini* index on attribute k;
5:     — L_k : clusters of points in S_p on attribute k;
6: **end for**
7: $G_{best} \leftarrow \min_k I_k$;
8: $\mathcal{C} \leftarrow ClusterDetect(G_{best}, S_p, L)$;
9: **for each** cluster $c \in \mathcal{C}$ **do**
10:     $I_c' \leftarrow DistanceEntropy(c, S)$;
11: **end for**
12: **if** $\min_{c \in \mathcal{C}} I_c' < G_{best}$ **then**
13:     split S into two subsets S_1, S_2 based on the distance;
14: **else**
15:     split S into subsets on the attribute with G_{best};
16: **end if**
17: call SSDT(S_i) on each subset S_i if S_i does not satisfy the termination condition;

the dataset based on the distance to such a cluster. More specifically, given a point $\vec{d}$, instead of using a univariate test $\vec{d}_i \leq v$, we use a test in the form of $Dist(\vec{d}, \vec{p}, \vec{w}) \leq v$, where $\vec{p}$ is the centroid of the cluster and $\vec{w}$ is a weight vector of all the dimensions. As in the SPRINT algorithm, the partition process also keeps the sorted order of the attribute lists, so that no reordering is required. The partition stops when a node is composed entirely of negative points (100%) or almost entirely[1] of positive points.

5.1 Minimal Support of Subspace Clusters

To find subspace clusters of points (of the biased class), we need to find: i) the centroid $\vec{p}$ of the cluster, and ii) the weight $\vec{w}$ which defines the subspace ($\vec{w}_i = 0$ means dimension i is irrelevant) of the cluster. Several subspace clustering algorithms have been introduced in the literature. The CLIQUE algorithm [2] reports connected dense units in subspaces but the centroids of clusters are not detected. Another method, called PROCLUS [1], uses a hill climbing method to successively improve a set of centroids, and derives a set of dimensions for each cluster. This algorithm however, requires that the number of clusters k to be found is pre-known. Both methods are time consuming since they aim at discovering all the subspace clusters.

Given a found cluster, Algorithm 1 partitions a dataset S into 2 datasets, S_1 and S_2, such that S_1 contains points close to the centroid of the cluster. Instead of checking all

---

[1] We assign a higher weight to each positive point to balance the biased distribution. In our algorithm, we stop if more than 90% of the points in the node is positive.

the subspace clusters, we are only interested in those that can result in partitions with a *gini* index lower than G_{best}, the minimal gini index we get by partitioning the data on single attributes.

Proposition 1 tells us how to narrow our search on qualified clusters. We define the *support* of a cluster as P'/P, where P' is the number of (positive) points in the cluster, and P is the total number of positive points in S. We prove the following proposition:

Proposition 1. *If the gini index of a cluster-based partition of S is lower than G_{best}, then the cluster must have a support greater than $\frac{2q - 2q^2 - G_{best}}{2q - 2q^2 - qG_{best}}$, where q is the percentage of the positive points in S.*

Proof. Let N be the total number of points in S. Let P be the total number of positive points in S. Thus, $q = P/N$. Assume S is partitioned into S_1 and S_2, and S_1 contains the points in the cluster. According to Formula 2, we have:

$$gini(S) = \frac{P' + N'}{N} gini(S_1) + \frac{N - P' - N'}{N} gini(S_2)$$

where P' and N' are the number of positive points and negative points in S_1 respectively. Given $N \gg P'$, it can be shown that the lowest $gini(S)$ is achieved if S_1 contains only positive points, that is, $N' = 0$ and $gini(S_1) = 0$. That the partition produces a *gini* index lower than G_{best} means:

$$\frac{N - P'}{N} gini(S_2) < G_{best}$$

Expanding $gini(S_2)$ using Equation 1, we get:

$$\frac{-2NP' - 2P^2 + 2PP' + 2NP}{N(N - P')} < G_{best}$$

Substituting P/N with q, we get:

$$minsup = P'/P > \frac{2q - 2q^2 - G_{best}}{2q - 2q^2 - qG_{best}} \quad (3)$$

The *minsup* given by Formula 3 is a lower bound, because the cluster we find usually does not contain only positive points (i.e., $N' > 0$). □

5.2 Cluster Detection

To find subspace clusters of points in the biased class, we use an iterative approach that is very similar to the apriori algorithm [3] for finding frequent itemsets. A cluster whose support is lower than *minsup* in k-dimensional space can not have support larger than *minsup* in $(k + 1)$-dimensional space. We first find clusters in 1-dimensional spaces, then we combine them to form candidate clusters in 2-dimensional spaces. We count the number of points in each cluster and eliminate those candidate clusters whose support does not satisfy the constraint in Proposition 1. Then we combine clusters in the 2-dimensional spaces to form candidates in the 3-dimensional spaces, and so on, until no more qualified clusters can be found.

Figure 5.2(a) shows an example where points of the biased class form two clusters in a 3-dimensional space. We use a simple approach to detect 1-dimensional clusters. In Figure 3, the range of each attribute is divided into 10 bins and we keep the counts of points that fall in each bin. This is done when we scan through attribute lists to evaluate splits on single attributes, so there is minimal extra cost introduced. The horizontal line in Figure 3 indicates the average density and we regard each continuous region above the average density line as *one* cluster. Thus, we detect one cluster around .1 with radius .1 on attribute X, two clusters around .3 and .7 respectively both with radius .1 on attribute Y, and one cluster around .2 with radius .1 on attribute Z.

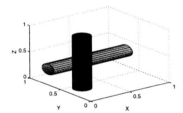

X	Y	Z
.1/.1	.3/.1	-
.1/.1	.7/.1	-
.1/.1	-	.2/.1
-	.3/.1	.2/.1
-	.7/.1	.2/.1

(a) Points of biased class form two clusters (b) Potential centroids of clusters

Figure 2. Cluster detection

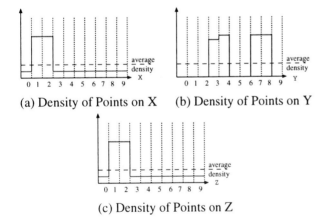

(a) Density of Points on X (b) Density of Points on Y

(c) Density of Points on Z

Figure 3. Histograms of positive points on each attribute

Assuming all the 1-dimensional clusters shown in Figure 3 has support larger than $minsup$, we then form a list of potential centroids in the 2-dimensional subspace as shown

in Figure 5.2(b). Each centroid is represented by values on two dimensions only, $(..., c_i/r_i, ..., c_j/r_j, ...)$, where c_i and c_j are centers of clusters on dimension i and j respectively, and r_i and r_j are their radius. Values on the other dimensions are unknown. Next, we make one scan through all the points in the biased class: for all points $\vec{d}$, $\vec{d} \in C = \{\vec{d}|r_i \geq |\vec{d_i} - c_i|, r_j \geq |\vec{d_j} - c_j|\}$, we compute the mean $c_k = \sum_{\vec{d} \in C} \vec{d_k}/|C|$, and the radius r_k on each of the dimension k.

Algorithm 2 ClusterDetect(GiniIndex: G_{best}, Biased Data: S_p, Center/Radius Lists: L)

1: $minsup \leftarrow$ derived by G_{best} (Formula 3);
2: $l \leftarrow 2; C_l \leftarrow \emptyset$;
    {*Step 1. find clusters in 2-dimensional space*}
3: **for each** center/radius c_i/r_i in L_i **do**
4:     **for each** center/radius c_j/r_j in $L_j, j > i$ **do**
5:         add $(..., c_i/r_i, ..., c_j/r_j, ...)$ to C_l;
6:     **end for**
7: **end for**
    {*Step 2. find clusters from lower to higher dimensions*}
8: **while** $C_l \neq \emptyset$ **do**
9:     scan the points in S_p and increase the count of cluster $c \in C_l$ for each point that belongs to c;
10:    eliminate cluster c from C_l if the number of points in c is less than $minsup$;
11:    $l \leftarrow l + 1$;
12:    $C_l \leftarrow$ combining clusters in dimension $l - 1$;
13: **end while**
    {*Step 3. return the clusters*}
14: **return** top-k leaf clusters;

After clusters whose support is less than the value given by Formula 3 are pruned, we explore clusters in higher dimensional spaces and repeat this process until no more clusters can be found. Finally, $ClusterDetect()$ returns the found clusters. We are only interested in *leaf* clusters, which are clusters that do not contain other clusters. Among all the leaf clusters, we return the top K clusters in the higher dimensions, where K is a user-specified parameter.

In order to compute the weighted Euclidean distance between a point and a cluster, we need to find out the weight on each dimension. For a non-clustered dimension i, we set $\vec{w_i} = 0$; otherwise, we set $\vec{w_i} = 1/r_i^2$, where r_i is the radius of the points' distribution on dimension i. Thus, the distance is normalized to reflect the span of the points on each dimension.

5.3 Split by Distance

For each cluster returned by $ClusterDetect()$, we derived a distance function $Dist(\vec{d}, \vec{p}, \vec{w})$. The next step is to find the value v so that the split by the test $Dist(\vec{d}, \vec{p}, \vec{w}) \leq v$ offers the minimum *gini* index.

A straight-forward approach is to reorder all the points by their distances to the center $\vec{p}$, and compute the *gini* index by scanning the ordered points. This is costly for large datasets. Another approach is to discretize the distance into intervals and for each interval we keep the counts of positive/negative cases whose distance to $\vec{p}$ are in that interval. One shortcoming of this approach is the loss of accuracy due to discretization.

Our approach, outlined in Algorithm 3, avoids reordering all the data and any loss of accuracy. This is achieved by making the following two observations: i) if point $\vec{d}$ is close to centroid $\vec{p}$, then $\vec{d_i}$, the coordinate on the i-th dimension, must also be close to $\vec{p_i}$; and ii) the best splitting position should be close to the boundary of the cluster.

Let N be the number of dimensions with non-zero weights (clustered dimensions). Let D be the set of points that are within an initial radius $r = \delta$ to $\vec{p}$. For any point $\vec{d} \in D$, the inequality $\vec{w_i}(\vec{d_i} - \vec{p_i})^2 \leq r^2$ must hold for each clustered dimension i. With the ordered attribute lists, it is easy to find D', points that satisfy the inequality on all the N clustered dimensions. Obviously $D' \supseteq D$, for D' can contain points whose distance to $\vec{p}$ is up to $r\sqrt{N}$. After sorting D' by distance, we compute the *gini* index up to radius r, and we keep the points in $D' - D$ and discard D.

We then increase the radius r by δ and repeat the process. However, we do not have to consider all the points. We are computing the *gini* index based on the distance to the cluster centroid we found. Thus, we expect a good *gini* index near the boundaries of the cluster. According to the weighting scheme discussed in the previous subsection, $\vec{w_i}$ is set to $1/r_i^2$ for each clustered dimension i, where r_i is the span of the points on that dimension. Thus, we have $\vec{w_i}(\vec{d_i} - \vec{p_i})^2 \leq 1$ for any point $\vec{p}$ that is inside the cluster. In addition to these points, we consider all points that satisfy $\vec{w_i}(\vec{d_i} - \vec{p_i})^2 \leq 2$ on each dimension i. Thus, the maximum radius of r is $\sqrt{\sum_i \vec{w_i}(\vec{d_i} - \vec{p_i})^2} \leq \sqrt{2N}$.

5.4 SSDT Examples

Let us review the two problems in Section 1. Unlike the C4.5 decision tree, which fails to detect pattern (hot,high) and builds a trivial decision tree in Figure 1(b), the SSDT algorithm accurately captures the pattern and constructs a compact decision tree in Figure 4(a). The second problem is introduced by datasets with biased class distribution. The decision tree model shown in Figure 1(d) used 11 tests to classify a 2-dimensional dataset shown in Figure 1(c). SSDT, shown in Figure 4(b), uses only 4 tests. Apparently, such differences tend to be more significant if the dataset has more than 2 dimensions.

Algorithm 3 distance_entropy(Dataset: S, Centroid: $\vec{p}$, Weight: $\vec{w}$)

1: $r \leftarrow \delta$;
2: $N \leftarrow$ # of dimensions with non-zero weights;
3: **repeat**
4:     **for each** relevant dimension i **do**
5:         find instances $\vec{d}$ that satisfies $(r - \delta)^2 \leq \vec{w_i}(\vec{d_i} - \vec{p_i})^2 < r^2$ using the ordered attribute lists;
6:         $\vec{d}$.count $\leftarrow \vec{d}$.count $+ 1$;
        {*check if $\vec{d}$ satisfies all the inequalities*}
7:         add $\vec{d}$ to the ordered set D' **if** $\vec{d}$.count $= N$;
8:     **end for**
9:     compute *gini*-index for splits by distance up to r;
10:    remove in tree D' the branch that represents data cases within distance r to $\vec{p}$;
11:    $r \leftarrow r + \delta$;
12: **until** $r > \sqrt{2N}$;
13: **return** I' and v;

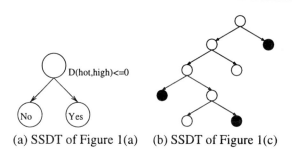

(a) SSDT of Figure 1(a)   (b) SSDT of Figure 1(c)

Figure 4. SSDT for datasets in Section 1

6 Evaluations

We evaluate the SSDT algorithm in various aspects. We study the size of the decision tree generated by the algorithm, the influence of the biased class distribution, the accuracy of predictions, as well as the efficiency and scalability issues. The tests were performed on a 700-MHz Pentium III machine with 256M of memory, running Linux.

Synthetic Data Generation We generate synthetic data in d-dimensional spaces with two class labels, positive and negative. Points have coordinates in the range of [0,1] and positive points account for $p = 1\% - 10\%$ of the total data.

To generate clustered points in subspaces, we use a method similar to [1]. The difference is that the number of positive points is controlled by the biased class ratio. Our method takes 4 parameters: n, the number of clusters; k, a Poisson parameter that determines the number of relevant dimensions in each cluster; p, the percentage (biased ratio) of positive points, and N, the total number of points.

First we determine the subspace for each cluster. For a given cluster i, the number of relevant dimensions, S_i, is picked from a Poisson distribution with mean k. However, an additional restriction, $2 \leq S_i \leq d$, must be observed.

We generate centroid $\vec{p}_i$ for each cluster i. We simply generate a uniformly distributed point in the d-dimensional space. We then decide the spread (radius) of the cluster on each dimension. We set $\vec{r}_{ij} = 0.5$ for irrelevant dimension j. For a clustered dimension, we fix a *spread parameter s* and choose the radius $\vec{r}_{ij} \in [0, s]$ uniformly at random. For our data generation, we use 3 values for $s = .1, .2, .5$.

We generate positive points in each cluster i in two different ways: i) points are distributed uniformly in the region; ii) for each dimension j, coordinates of points on the dimension follow a normal distribution with mean $\vec{c}_{ij}$ and variance $\vec{r}_{ij}^2$. We determine the size of each positive cluster by $N_i = pN \frac{v_i}{\sum_{i=1}^{n} v_i}$, where v_i is the volume of cluster i defined as $v_i = \prod_{j=1}^{d} (2 * r_{ij})$.

Finally, we generate $(1 - p)N$ negative points. The negative points either i) uniformly distribute at random in the entire space, or ii) form clusters in subspaces and are generated by the method described above with parameters $k = 0.8d$ and $s = 0.5$. If a negative point is generated inside one of the positive clusters, it is discarded with a probability δ. For our data generation, we choose $\delta = 0.5$.

Experiments: Tree Size and Scalability We generate 6 clusters (Table 1) of positive points out of a training set of total 100K records and 10 attributes. The total number of positive cases account for 2% of the training set. The average radius of the cluster on each clustered dimension is 0.05, and the negative points are uniformly distributed at random. The split at the root of the decision tree, for example, uses the distance function defined for Cluster 6. Total 5 clusters are used at different nodes for splitting, resulting in a tree of 37 leaf nodes before pruning, while the SPRINT algorithm uses 71 leaf nodes before pruning.

Cluster	Centroids	Points
1	(-, 0.35, -, -,-,0.62,-,0.77,-,0.26,0.27)	87
2	(-,0.74,-,0.11, -,0.85,-,-,-,-)	199
3	(0.92, 0.22, -, -, 0.81, -, -, -, -, -)	204
4	(-, -, 0.37, 0.12, -,-,0.63,-,-,-,-)	212
5	(-,-,-,-,-,0.32, 0.20,0.14,0.87,0.43)	83
6	(-,-,0.37,-,-,-,-,0.66,-,-)	1211

Cluster	Centroid Detected by SSDT	Points
6	(-,-,0.37,-,-,-,-,0.66,-,-)	1228
4	(-, -, 0.37, 0.11, -,-,0.62,-,-,-,-)	186
2	(-,0.74,-,0.13, -,0.85,-,-,-,-)	184
3	(0.92, 0.22, -, -, 0.81, -, -, -, -, -)	1124
1	(-, 0.34, -, -,-,0.62,-,0.74,-,0.26,0.27)	83

Table 1. 5 clusters are detected by SSDT. Un-clustered dimensions are denoted by '-'.

We compare the size of the decision tree (in terms of number of leaf nodes) generated by SPRINT and SSDT. The datasets we use have 10 attributes, and the 5 clusters of biased points account for 1%, 2% and 5% of the total data. Figure 6(a) indicates that trees built by SSDT are significantly smaller, and the sizes of the trees generally do not increase as the training sets become larger.

Next, we vary the number of clusters in the training sets and show the results in Figure 6(b). The datasets are generated with the same class ratio: 2%. The size of the tree increases significantly as there are more positive clusters in the dataset. The trees generated by SSDT are much smaller.

Figure 6(a) shows the scalability of SSDT as the size of the dataset increases from 0.1 to 2.5 million. The dataset has 10 attributes, 8 clusters with an average dimensionality of 4, and a biased class ration of 1%. The execution time increases linearly with the size of the dataset, since SSDT is able to detect the clusters and the resulted decision tree has similar heights, which means the number of passes through the database does not change. Figure 6(b) shows the scalability of SSDT when the average dimensionality of the positive clusters is increased from 2 to 12. The dataset used in the test has 1 million records, 8 clusters, 1% positive ratio, and a total of 20 attributes. It indicates that cluster dimensionality has little impact on the performance.

We study the impact of the number of positive clusters on the scalability. In Figure 6(c), we increase clusters from 4 to 20. The dataset has 1 million records, among which 1% are positive. There are 10 attributes and the clusters have an average of 5 dimensions. Since the number of positive data cases is kept unchanged during the test, each cluster contains fewer records as more clusters are used. The curve is steeper than in the previous cases because more scans of the dataset have to be performed. In Figure 6(d), using the dataset of the same size, dimensionality, and 8 positive clusters, we found the performance is stable.

We compare the performance of SSDT with SPRINT in Figure 6(c). The datasets have 10 attributes, 8 positive clusters, and a class ratio of 1%. In this case, SSDT has an advantage over SPRINT because SSDT trees are much smaller. As we increase the class ratio and the number of clusters, SPRINT becomes faster than SSDT. Indeed, SPRINT is 20% faster than SSDT when there are 20 clusters with a 15% class ratio, which means SSDT works best with biased class distributions. The association rule algorithm for mining datasets with biased class distribution does not scale well. Overall, SSDT is an efficient and scalable algorithm, despite the multivariate search it performs.

7 Conclusion

We presented a novel decision tree algorithm. The key idea is to take advantage of the subspace clusters formed by

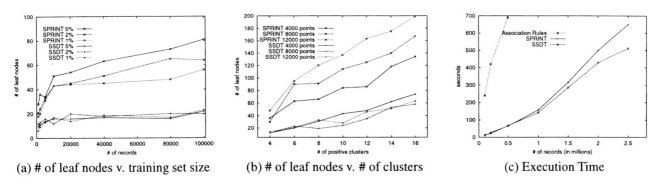

(a) # of leaf nodes v. training set size   (b) # of leaf nodes v. # of clusters   (c) Execution Time

Figure 5. Experiments and Comparisons

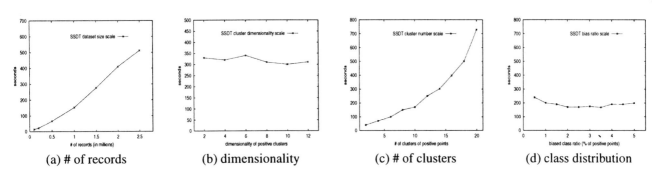

(a) # of records   (b) dimensionality   (c) # of clusters   (d) class distribution

Figure 6. Scalability

the data in the biased class. Once these subspace clusters are efficiently detected, a compact and accurate decision tree can be constructed by splitting a node based on the distance to such clusters. Our multivariate decision tree algorithm has proven to be scalable and efficient. Indeed, it has better performance over SPRINT for very skewed distributions.

References

[1] C. C. Aggarwal, C. Procopiuc, J. Wolf, P. S. Yu, and J. S. Park. Fast algorithms for projected clustering. In *SIGMOD*, 1999.

[2] R. Agrawal, J. Gehrke, D. Gunopulos, and P. Raghavan. Authomatic subspace clustering of high dimensional data for data mining applications. In *SIGMOD*, 1998.

[3] R. Agrawal and R. Srikant. Fast algorithms for mining association rules. In *VLDB*, 1994.

[4] J. Bioch, O. van der Meer, and R. Potharst. Bivariate decision trees. In *Principles of Data Mining and Knowledge Discovery*, 1997.

[5] L. Breiman, J. Friedman, R. Olshen, and C. Stone. *Classification and Regression Trees*. Wadsworth, 1984.

[6] C. E. Brodley and P. E. Utgoff. Multivariate versus univariate decision trees. In *Technical Report COINS-CR-92-8, Dept. of Computer Science, University of Massachusetts*, 1992.

[7] J. Gehrke, V. Ganti, R. Ramakrishnan, and W. Loh. Boat–optimistic decision tree construction. In *SIGMOD*, 1999.

[8] J. Gehrke, R. Ramakrishnan, and V. Ganti. Rainforest: A framework for fast decision tree constructionof large datasets. In *VLDB*, 1998.

[9] G. Guiffrida, W. W. Chu, and D. M. Hanssens. Mining classification rules from datasets with large number of many-valued attributes. In *EDBT*, pages 335–349, 2000.

[10] Y. Ma, B. Liu, C. K. Wong, P. S. Yu, and S. M. Lee. Targeting the right students using data mining. In *SIGKDD*, Zurich, Switzerland, August 2000.

[11] S. K. Murthy, S. Kasif, and S. Salzberg. A system for induction of oblique decision trees. In *Journal of Artificial Intelligence Research*, pages 1–32, 1994.

[12] C. Shafer, R. Agrawal, and M. Mehta. Sprint: A scalable parallel classifier for data mining. In *VLDB*, 1996.

[13] P. E. Utgoff and C. E. Brodley. An incremental method for finding multivariate splits for decision trees. In *ICML*, pages 58–65, 1990.

[14] H. Wang and C. Zaniolo. CMP: A fast decision tree classifier using multivariate predictions. In *ICDE*, pages 449–460, 2000.

[15] D. Wilson and T. Martinez. Improved heterogeneous distance functions. In *Journal of Artificial Intelligence Research*, pages 1–34, 1997.

[16] B. Zadrozny and C. Elkan. Learning and making decisions when costs and probabilities are both unknown. In *Technical Report CS2001-0664, Dept. of Computer Sci., UCSD*, 2001.

Meta-Patterns: Revealing Hidden Periodic Patterns

Wei Wang, Jiong Yang, and Philip S. Yu
IBM T. J. Watson Research Center
{ww1, jiyang, psyu}@us.ibm.com

Abstract

*Discovery of periodic patterns in time series data has become an active research area with many applications. These patterns can be hierarchical in nature, where a higher level pattern may consist of repetitions of lower level patterns. Unfortunately, the presence of noise may prevent these higher level patterns from being recognized in the sense that two portions (of a data sequence) that support the same (high level) pattern may have different layouts of occurrences of basic symbols. There may not exist any common representation in terms of raw symbol combinations; and hence such (high level) pattern may not be expressed by any previous model (defined on raw symbols or symbol combinations) and would not be properly recognized by any existing method. In this paper, we propose a novel model, namely meta-pattern, to capture these high level patterns. As a more flexible model, the number of potential meta-patterns could be very large. A substantial difficulty lies on how to identify the proper pattern candidates. However, the well-known Apriori property is not able to provide sufficient pruning power. A new property, namely component location property, is identified and used to conduct the candidate generation so that an efficient **computation-based** mining algorithm can be developed. Last but not least, we apply our algorithm to some real and synthetic sequences and some interesting patterns are discovered.*

1 Introduction

Periodicity detection on time series data is a challenging problem of great importance in many real applications. The periodicity is usually represented as repeated occurrences of a list of symbols in a certain order at some frequency [3, 6, 11, 12]. Due to the changes of system behavior, some pattern may be only notable within a portion of the entire data sequence and different patterns may present at different places and be of different durations. The evolution among patterns may also follow some regularity. Such regularity, if any, would be of great value in understanding the nature of the system and building prediction models. Consider the application of *inventory replenishment*. The history of inventory refill orders can be regarded as a symbol sequence. For brevity, let's only consider the replen-

ishment of the flu medicine. Figure 1(a) shows the history of refill orders of a pharmacy during 1999 and 2000 on a weekly basis. The symbol "r" stands for a refill order of flu medicine was placed in the corresponding week while "-" represents that no flu medicine replenishment was made in that week. It is easy to see that the replenishment follows a biweekly pattern during the first half of each year and falls into a triweekly cycle during the second half of each year. This seasonal fluctuation also forms a high level periodic pattern (The period length is one year). However, such high level patterns may not be expressible by any previous model (defined in terms of raw symbols) due to the presence of noise, even when the noise is very limited. In the above example, a major outbreak of flu caused a provisional replenishment at the 4th week of 1999 (Figure 1(a)). Afterwards, even though the replenishment frequency is back to once every other week, the occurrences of all subsequent replenishments become misaligned. Even though the biweekly replenishment cycle was notable in the first two quarters of both 1999 and 2000, the corresponding portions in the data sequence have different layout of replenishment occurrences. This characteristic determines that the representation of the above two-level periodicity is beyond the expressive power of any traditional model of periodic patterns that only takes raw symbols as components. In any traditional model, each symbol specified in a pattern uniquely matches its counterpart in the data sequence, and all occurrences of a pattern have to share a unique common layout. This inherent limitation would prevent many interesting high level patterns from being captured. Note that, even if the period length (i.e., 52 weeks) is given[1], the only annual pattern that is able to be generated under the traditional model via pairwise comparison of symbols corresponding to each week is shown in Figure 1(b). The symbol "*" denotes the don't care position[2] and can match any symbol on the corresponding position. Clearly, little information is conveyed in this pattern as the important two-level periodicity is completely concealed.

To tackle the problem, we propose a so-called **meta-pattern** model to capture high level periodicities. A meta-pattern may take occurrences of patterns/meta-patterns (of lower granularity) as components. In contrast, we refer to the patterns that contain

---

[1] Note that in many applications, e.g., seismic periodicity analysis, the period length is usually unknown in advance and is part of the mining objective.

[2] It is introduced to represent the position(s) in a pattern where no strong periodicity exhibits.

only raw symbol(s) as the **basic patterns**, which may be viewed as special cases of meta-patterns. In general, the noise could occur anywhere, be of various duration, and even occur multiple times within the portion where a pattern is notable as long as the noise is below some threshold. Even though the allowance of noise plays a positive role in characterizing system behavior in a noisy environment, it prevents such a meta-pattern from being represented in the form of an (equivalent) basic pattern. The model of meta-pattern provides a more powerful means to periodicity representation. The recursive nature of meta-pattern not only can tolerate a greater degree of noises/distortion, but also can capture the (hidden) hierarchies of pattern evolutions, which may not be expressible by previous models. In the previous example, the biweekly and the triweekly replenishment cycles can be easily represented by $P_1 = (r : [1,1], * : [2,2])$ and $P_2 = (r : [1,1], * : [2,3])$, respectively, where the numbers in the brackets indicate the offset of the component within the pattern. The two-level periodicity can be easily represented as $(P_1 : [1,24], * : [25,25], P_2 : [26,52])$ which can be interpreted as the pattern P_1 repeats at the first 24 weeks and the pattern P_2 repeats from week 26 to week 52. As shown in Figure 1 (c), each rectangle box denotes the portion where the corresponding low level pattern (i.e., either $(r : [1,1], * : [2,2])$ or $(r : [1,1], * : [2,3])$) is notable.

Unfortunately, the flexibility of meta-pattern poses serious challenges in the discovery process, which may not be encountered in mining basic patterns.

- While a basic pattern has two degrees of freedom: the period (i.e., the number of positions in the pattern) and the choice of symbol for each single position, a meta-pattern has an additional degree of freedom: the length of each component in the pattern. It is incurred by the fact that a component may occupy multiple positions. This extra degree of freedom would increase the number of potential meta-pattern candidates dramatically.

- Many patterns/meta-patterns may collocate or overlap for any given portion of a sequence. As a result, during the meta-pattern mining process, there could be a large number of candidates for each component of a (higher level) meta-pattern. This also aggravates the mining complexities.

Therefore, how to identify the "proper" candidate meta-patterns is very crucial to the overall efficiency of the mining process, and will be the focus of the algorithm part of the paper. To tackle this problem, we employ a so called *component location property*, in addition to the traditionally used Apriori property, to prune the search space. This is inspired by the observation that a pattern may participate in a meta-pattern only if its notable portions exhibit a certain cyclic behavior. A *computation-based* algorithm is devised to identify the potential period of a meta-pattern and for each candidate period, the potential components and their lengths within the meta-pattern. The set of all meta-patterns can be categorized according to their structures and are evaluated in a designed order so that the pruning power provided by both properties can be fully utilized.

In summary, we claim the following contributions in this paper.

- A model of meta-pattern is identified to capture the cyclic relationship among discovered periodic patterns and to enable a recursive construction of exhibited cyclic regularities.

- The *component location property* is proposed to provide further pruning power, in addition to the traditional Apriori property.

- A *computation-based* algorithm is designed to identify and to verify potential meta-pattern candidates.

The remainder of this paper is organized as follows. Section 2 gives a brief overview of recent related research. The general model is presented in Section 3. Section 4 outlines the major steps of our algorithm. Section 5 presents experimental results. The conclusion is drawn in Section 6.

2 Related Work

Most previous work on mining sequence data fell into two categories: discovering sequential patterns [1, 2, 4, 7, 8, 9, 10, 14] and mining periodic patterns[3, 6, 11, 12]. The primary difference between them is that the models of sequential pattern purely take into account the number of occurrences of the pattern while the frameworks for periodic patterns focus on characterizing cyclic behaviors. Due to space limitations, we will give a brief survey of the recent work on periodic patterns.

In [3], Han et. al. presented algorithms for efficiently mining partial periodic patterns. In practice, not every portion in the time series may contribute to the periodicity. For example, a company's stock may often gain a couple of points at the beginning of each trading session but it may not have much regularity at later time. This type of looser periodicity is often referred to as *partial periodicity*. We will see later that our model also allows partial periodicity.

To accommodate the phenomenon that the system behavior may change over time, a flexible model of asynchronous periodic pattern was proposed in [11]. In this model, a qualified pattern may be present only within a subsequence and whose occurrences may be shifted due to disturbance. Two parameters min_rep and max_dis are employed to specify the minimum number of repetitions that is required within each segment of non-disrupted pattern occurrences and the maximum allowed disturbance between any two successive valid segments. The intuition behind this is that a pattern needs to repeat itself at least a certain number of times to demonstrate its significance and periodicity. On the other hand, the disturbance between two valid segments has to be within some reasonable bound. Otherwise, it would be more appropriate to treat such disturbance as a signal of "change of system behavior" instead of random noise injected into some persistent behavior. The parameter

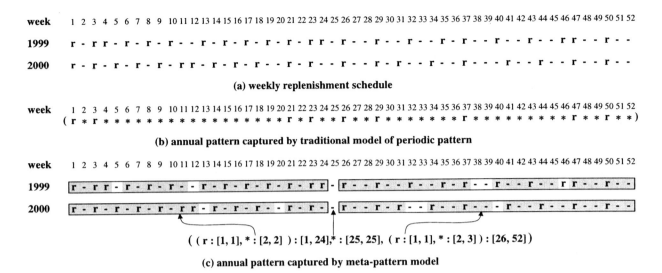

(a) weekly replenishment schedule

(b) annual pattern captured by traditional model of periodic pattern

(c) annual pattern captured by meta-pattern model

Figure 1. Meta Pattern

max_dis acts as the boundary to separate these two phenomena. For example, Figure 1(c) shows 6 valid segments of pattern $(r : [1, 1], * : [2, 2])$ (for both 1999 and 2000) if we set $min\_rep = 2$. (Each valid segment is indicated by a shaded region). Moreover, if we set $max\_dis = 3$, the three valid segments in 1999 (separated by a disturbance of 1 symbol) form a valid symbol subsequence of $(r : [1, 1], * : [2, 2])$ while the three valid segments 2000 form another valid symbol subsequence. Obviously, the appropriate values of these two parameters are application dependent and need to be specified by the user. Note that, due to the presence of disturbance, some subsequent valid segment may not be well synchronized with the previous ones. (Some position shifting occurs.) Upon satisfying these two requirements, the longest valid subsequence of a pattern is returned. A two phase algorithm is devised to first generate potential periods by distance-based pruning followed by an iterative procedure to derive and validate candidate patterns and locate the longest valid subsequence. Still, this paper only concerns patterns constructed from raw symbols and does not address the problem of meta-patterns. As we pointed out earlier, due to the extra degree of freedom possessed by meta-pattern and the massive amount of potential candidate components, no direct generalization of existing algorithm (designed for mining patterns consisting of only raw symbols) can be applied to mine meta-pattern efficiently. In fact, serious challenges exist in how to quickly identify the "proper" candidate meta-patterns so that unnecessary computation can be avoided. Thus, we will focus on candidate meta-pattern generation (rather than the candidate meta-pattern validation) in this paper.

Many patterns may occur frequently by nature and they are of no importance in many applications. In [12], instead of frequently occurred periodic patterns, the statistically significant patterns are mined. There is an occurrence probability associated with each pattern. If a pattern occurrence much more than the expectation, then this pattern is called statistically significant or surprising. An efficient algorithm is also proposed in [12] for

mining such patterns.

3 Model of Meta-Patterns

Let $\Im = \{a, b, c, \ldots\}$ be a set of literals. A traditional periodic pattern [3, 11] consists of a tuple of k components, each of which is either a literal or "*". k is usually referred to as the **period** of the pattern. "*" can be substituted for any literal and is used to enable the representation of partial periodicity. For example, $\ldots, a, b, c, a, b, d, a, b, b, \ldots$ is a sequence of literals and $(a, b, *)$ [3] represents that the incident "b following a" occurs for every 3 time instances in the data sequence. The period of this pattern is 3 by definition. Note that the third component in the pattern is filled by a "*" since there is no strong periodicity presents in the data sequence with respect to this component. Because a pattern may start anywhere in the data sequence, only patterns whose first component is a literal in $\Im$ need to be considered. In this paper, we refer to this type of patterns as **basic** patterns as each component in the pattern is restricted to be either a literal or a "*". In contrast, a **meta-pattern** may have pattern(s)/meta-pattern(s) as its component(s). This enables us to represent complicated basic patterns in a more concise way and to possibly reveal some hidden patterns among discovered ones. Formally, a **meta-pattern** is a tuple consisting of k components $(x_1, x_2, \ldots, x_k)$ where each x_i $(1 \leq i \leq k)$ can be one of the following choices augmented by the offsets of the starting and ending positions of the component with respect to the beginning of the meta-pattern: (1) a symbol in $\Im$; (2) "don't care" *; and (3) a pattern/meta-pattern. We also require that at least one position of a meta-pattern has to correspond to a non "*" component to ensure a non-trivial pattern. For example, $((r : [1, 1], * : [2, 2]) : [1, 24], * : [25, 25], (r : [1, 1], * : [2, 3]) : [26, 52])$ is

---

[3] Since each component corresponds to exactly one symbol, we do not have to explicitly record the offset of a component within the pattern as this information can be easily derived.

552

a meta-pattern with three components: $(r : [1,1], * : [2,2])$, $*$, and $(r : [1,1], * : [2,3])$. The **length** of a component is the number of positions that the component occupies in the meta-pattern. In the previous example, the component length of $(r : [1,1], * : [2,2])$ is 24. We also say that 52 is the **span** of this meta-pattern, which is equal to the sum of the length of all components in the meta-pattern. This pattern can be interpreted as "*the pattern $(r : [1,1], * : [2,2])$ is true for 24 positions (or weeks in previous example) followed by the pattern $(r : [1,1], * : [2,3])$ for 27 positions with a gap of one position in between, and such a behavior repeats for every 52 positions*". For brevity, we sometimes omit the augmenting offset of a component if the length of the component is only one position. For example, $(r, *)$ is the abbreviation of $(r : [1,1], * : [2,2])$ and $((r, *) : [1,24], *, (r, * : [2,3]) : [26,52])$ is equivalent to $((r : [1,1], * : [2,2]) : [1,24], * : [25,25], (r : [1,1], * : [2,3]) : [26,52])$. It is obvious that the meta-pattern is a more flexible model than the basic pattern and the basic pattern can be viewed as a special (and simpler) case of the meta-pattern. Because of the hierarchical nature of the meta-pattern, the concept of *level* is introduced to represent the "depth" of a meta-pattern. By setting the level of basic pattern to be 1, the **level** of a meta-pattern is defined as the maximum level of its components plus 1. According to this definition, the level of $(r, * : [2,3])$ is 1 and the level of $P_1 = ((r, *) : [1,24], *, (r, * : [2,3]) : [26,52])$ is 2. Note that the components of a meta-pattern do not have to be of the same level. For instance, $(P_1 : [1,260], * : [261,300])$ is a meta-pattern (of level 3) which has a level-2 component and a level-1 component.

All terminologies associated with the basic patterns [11] (i.e., level-1 patterns) can be generalized to the case of meta-patterns (i.e., higher level patterns). We now give a brief overview of terms defined in [11] for basic patterns. Given a symbol sequence $D' = d_1, d_2, \ldots, d_s$ and a basic pattern $P = (p_1, p_2, \ldots, p_s)$, we say D' **supports** P iff, for each $i (1 \leq i \leq s)$, either $p_i = *$ or $p_i = d_i$. D' is also called a **match** of P. Given a pattern P and a symbol sequence D, a list of j disjoint matches of P in D is called a **segment** with respect to P iff they form a contiguous portion of D. j is referred to as the **number of repetitions** of this segment. Such a segment is said to be a **valid segment** iff j is greater than or equal to the required minimum repetition threshold min_rep. A **valid subsequence** in D (with respect to P) is a set of disjoint valid segments where the distance between any two consecutive valid segments does not exceed the required maximum disturbance threshold max_dis. P is said to be a **valid pattern** in D if there exists a valid subsequence in D with respect to P. The parameters min_rep and max_dis, in essence, define the significance of the periodicity and the boundary to separate noise and change of system behavior. The appropriate values of min_rep and max_dis are application dependent and are specified by the user.

Similarly, given a symbol sequence $D' = d_1, d_2, \ldots, d_s$, for any meta-pattern $X = (x_1 : [1,t_1], x_2 : [t_1 + 1, t_2], \ldots, x_l : [t_{l-1} + 1, s])$, D' **supports** X iff, for each component x_i, either

(1) x_i is "$*$" or (2) x_i is a symbol and $d_{t_{i-1}+1} = \ldots = d_{t_i} = x_i$ or (3) x_i is a (mata-)pattern and $d_{t_{i-1}+1}, \ldots, d_{t_i}$ is a valid subsequence with respect to x_i. D' is in turn called a **match** of P. We can define *segment*, *subsequence*, and *validation* in a similar manner to that of a basic pattern. Given a meta-pattern X and a symbol sequence D, a list of j disjoint matches of X in D is called a **segment** with respect to X iff they form a contiguous portion of D. j is referred to as the **number of repetitions** of this segment. Such segment is said to be a **valid segment** iff j is greater than or equal to the required minimum repetitions min_rep. A **valid subsequence** in D (with respect to X) is a set of disjoint valid segments where the distance between any two consecutive valid segments does not exceed the required maximum disturbance max_dis. P is said to be a **valid pattern** in D if there exists a valid subsequence in D with respect to X.

In this paper, given a symbol sequence and two parameters min_rep and max_dis, we aim at mining valid meta-patterns together with their longest valid subsequences (i.e., the valid subsequence which has the most overall repetitions of the corresponding meta-pattern). Since a meta-pattern can start anywhere in a sequence, we only need to consider those starting with a non "$*$" component.

4 Algorithm Outline

The great flexibility of the model poses considerable difficulties to the generation of candidate meta-patterns. Therefore, we will focus on the efficient candidate generation of meta-patterns in the remainder of this paper. The well-known Apriori property holds on the set of meta-patterns of the same span, which can be stated as follows: *for any valid meta-pattern $P = (P_1 : [1, t_1], P_2 : [t_1 + 1, t_2], \ldots, P_s : [t_{s-1} + 1, t_s])$, the meta-pattern constructed by replacing any component P_i with "$*$" in P is also valid.* For example, let $X_1 = ((a, b, *) : [1, 19], * : [20, 21])$ and $X_2 = ((a, b, *) : [1, 19], * : [20, 21], (b, c) : [22, 27], * : [28, 30], X_1 : [31, 150])$. If X_2 is a valid meta-pattern, then the pattern $X_3 = ((a, b, *) : [1, 19], * : [20, 21], (b, c) : [22, 27], * : [28, 150])$ (generated by replacing X_1 with "$*$") must be valid as well. Note that X_2 is a level-3 meta-pattern which has three non "$*$" components: $(a, b, *)$, (b, c), and X_1; whereas X_3 is a level-2 meta-pattern that has two non "$*$" components: $(a, b, *)$ and (b, c). Intuitively, X_3 should be examined before X_2 so that the result can be used to prune the search space.

Nevertheless, because of the hierarchical characteristic of the meta-pattern, the Apriori property does not render sufficient pruning power as we proceed to high level patterns from discovered low level patterns. After identifying valid meta-patterns of level l, the brute force method (powered by the Apriori property) to mine patterns of level $l + 1$ is to first generate all possible candidates of level $l + 1$ by taking valid lower level patterns as component(s); and then, verify them against the symbol sequence. While the verification of a base pattern can be performed efficiently (e.g., in linear time with respect to the length of the symbol sequence [11]), the verification for a candidate meta-pattern may be a cumbersome process because of the typically complicated structure of the candidate meta-pattern. In fact, considerable difficulty lies on determining whether a certain portion of the raw symbol sequence corresponds to a valid subsequence of a component of the candidate pattern, especially when the component itself is also meta-pattern. One strategy to speed up the process is to store all valid subsequences of each valid low level pattern when the pattern is verified. Then the procedure of determining whether a portion of the sequence is a valid subsequence of a given component can be accomplished via table look-up operations. Even though this strategy requires additional storage space, it can usually lead to at least an order of magnitude of performance improvement. We will refer this method as the **match-based approach** in the remainder of this paper.

However, this match-based approach is still very cumbersome, and more specifically, suffers from two major drawbacks. (1) The number of candidate patterns of a certain level (say level l) is typically an exponential function of the number of discovered lower level meta-patterns. While a basic pattern has two degrees of freedom: the period and the choice of symbol at each position/component, a meta-pattern has an additional degree of freedom: the length of each component. This additional degree of freedom dramatically increases the number of candidate patterns generated. If there are v valid lower level patterns, the number of candidate patterns of span s and with exactly k components for level l is in the order of $\Theta(v^k \times (2k)^s)$. (2) There are typically a huge number of valid subsequences associated with each valid pattern even though only a few of them may eventually be relevant. Generating and storing all of them would consume a significant amount of computing resources and storage space, which in turn leads to unnecessary inefficiency. To overcome these drawbacks, we made the following observation.

Property 4.1 (Component Location Property) *A valid low level meta-pattern may serve as a component of a higher level meta-pattern only if its presence in the symbol sequence exhibits some cyclic behavior and such cyclic behavior has to follow the same periodicity as the higher level meta-pattern by sufficient number of times (i.e., at least min_rep times).*

In the above example, the meta-pattern X_1 can serve as a component of a higher level meta-pattern (e.g., X_2) only if the locations of valid subsequences of X_1 exhibits a cyclic behavior with a period equal to the span of X_2 (i.e., 150). Otherwise, X_1 could not serve as a component of X_2. This property suggests that we can avoid the generation of a huge number of unnecessary candidate meta-patterns by deriving candidates from qualified span-component combinations according to the component location property. To identify qualified span-component combinations, we need to detect the periodicities exhibited by the locations of valid subsequences of each low level meta-pattern. This can be achieved without generating all valid subsequences for a meta-pattern. In fact, only the set of **maximum valid segments** are sufficient. For a given pattern, a valid segment is a maximum valid segment if it is not a portion of another valid segment. For

example, if $min\_rep = 3$ and $max\_dis = 6$, $\{S_1, S_2, S_3, S_4, S_5 S_6\}$ is the set of maximum valid segments of basic pattern $(a, *)$ for the symbol sequence in Figure 2(a). Usually, the number of maximum valid segments is much smaller than the number of valid subsequences. The total number of distinct valid subsequences of $(a, *)$ in the symbol sequence given in Figure 2(a) would be in the order of hundreds. It is in essence an exponential function of the number of maximum valid segments. Furthermore, for each maximum valid segment, we only need to store a pair of location indexes indicating its starting and ending positions. In the above example, the segment S_1 occupies 8 positions (positions 1 to 8) in Figure 2(a) and its location indexes is the pair $(1, 8)$. The location indexes of maximum valid segments indeed provide a compact and ingenious representation of all necessary knowledge of a valid low level meta-pattern and is motivated by the following observations.

- Given the set of location indexes of maximum valid segments of a pattern, it is easy to compute all possible starting positions and ending positions of valid subsequences. Any starting position of a valid segment is also a starting position of a valid subsequence because a valid subsequence is essentially a list of valid segments. Given a maximum valid segment S containing r repetitions of the pattern, there are $r - min\_rep + 1$ distinct starting positions that can be derived from S. More specifically, they are the positions of the first $r - min\_rep + 1$ occurrences of the pattern in S, respectively. For instance, positions 1 and 3 are the two starting positions derived from S_1. Similarly, all possible ending positions can be computed as well.

- The starting positions of the valid subsequences that exhibit cyclic behavior also present the same periodicity and so do their ending positions. Figure 2(b) shows the set of possible starting positions and ending positions of valid subsequences of $(a, *)$. When $min\_rep = 3$, by careful examination, the potential periodicities of $(a, *)$ (i.e., the possible spans of meta-patterns that $(a, *)$ may participate in as a component) include 7, 9, 11, 18, and 20. The periodic behavior discovered on starting positions and ending positions for span $= 18$ is shown in Figure 2(c) and (d), respectively.

Thus, our strategy is to first compute the set of possible starting positions and identify, if any, the ones that exhibit some periodicity. The same procedure is also performed on the ending positions. If the same periodicity exists for both starting positions and ending positions, we then examine, for each pair of starting and ending positions, whether a valid subsequence exists and what is the possible format of the higher level meta-pattern (i.e., possible span of the meta-pattern and possible length of the component). Figure 2(e) shows some candidate components generated from $(a, *)$ and the valid subsequences that support them.

It is important to notice that the maintenance of the location indexes of maximum valid segments leads to a double-win situation. Besides its positive role in candidate generation, it also

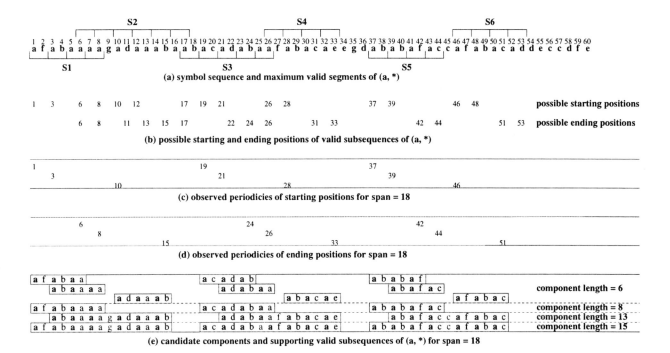

Figure 2. Computation Based Approach

enables the verification process to be accomplished efficiently without the expensive generation and maintenance of all valid subsequences nor the necessity of resort to the raw symbol sequence. As a result, we devise an efficient **computation-based** algorithm (as opposite to the traditional match-based approach) in the sense that the discovery of valid meta-patterns (other than base patterns) can be accomplished through pure computation (performed on the location indexes of maximum valid segments) without ever resort back to the raw symbol sequence. It has been demonstrated that this advantage offers at least two orders of magnitudes speed-up comparing to the match-based approach.

The component location property can provide substantial inter-level pruning effect during the generation of high level candidates from valid low level meta-patterns; whereas the traditional Apriori property can render some pruning power to conduct the mining process of meta-patterns of the same level. While all meta-patterns can be categorized according to their levels and the number of non "*" components in the pattern as shown in Figure 3, the pruning effects provided by the component location property and the Apriori property are indicated by dashed arrows and solid arrows, respectively. Consequently, the algorithm consists two level of iterations. The outer iteration exploits the component location property while the inner iteration utilizes the Apriori property. More specifically, each outer iteration discovers all meta-patterns of a certain level (say, level l) and consists of the following two phases.

1. *candidate component generation.* For each newly discovered valid pattern/meta-pattern of level l, generate candidate components for meta-patterns of level $l + 1$. The component location property is employed in this phase.

2. *candidate pattern generation and verification.* This phase generates candidate meta-patterns of level $l + 1$ based on the candidate components discovered in the previous step and validates them. This phase utilizes the Apriori property and contains an iteration loop. During each iteration, meta-patterns with a certain number (say k) of non "*" components are examined, which includes the following two steps.

   (a) If $k = 1$, the candidate singular meta-patterns[4] of level $l + 1$ are generated from candidate components derived in the previous phase. Otherwise, the candidate meta-patterns of level $l + 1$ with k non "*" components are generated based on the discovered level-$(l + 1)$ meta-patterns with $(k - 1)$ non "*" components.

   (b) The newly generated candidate patterns are validated.

   This inner iteration continues until no new candidate patterns of level $(l + 1)$ can be generated.

The entire procedure terminates when no new candidate components can be generated. Due to space limitations, we would not elaborate on the details of the algorithm. Interested readers please refer to [13].

5 Experimental Results

The meta-pattern discovery algorithm is implemented in C on an AIX workstation with 300 MHz CPU and 128 MB main

---

[4] A singular meta-pattern is a meta-pattern that has only one non "*" component. Otherwise, it is called a complex meta-pattern.

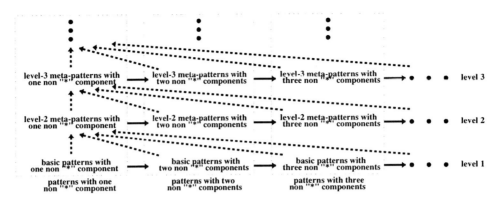

Figure 3. Pruning Directions

memory. A real trace log from the search engine *scour.net* is employed to evaluate the benefits of the meta-pattern model while four synthetically generated sequences are used to measure the performance of our algorithm.

5.1 Scour Traces

Scour is a web search engine specialized in multimedia content search whose URL is "http://www.scour.net". We apply the meta-pattern discovery algorithm to the traces of scour traces. Table 1 shows the number of patterns discovered from the Scour sequence with respective thresholds. There exist some interesting patterns. When min_rep and max_dis are set to 3 and 200, respectively, there is a level 3 meta-pattern. This level 3 pattern describes the following phenomenon. In a weekday between 4am and 12pm EST, there exists a pattern that the number of hits is between 10000 to 20000; and during 5pm to 1:30am EST, we found the pattern that the number of hits is between 40000 and 49999. Furthermore, this pattern repeated itself during each weekday within a week (i.e., level-2 pattern) and it also exhibits weekly trend (i.e., level-3 pattern). In addition, we also compute the meta-patterns that cannot be expressed in the form of basic patterns. We call these patterns *meta only* patterns and the number of these patterns is also shown in Table 1. From this table, we can see that most of the discovered level 2 and 3 patterns can not be expressed in the form of basic patterns, and thus can only be represented as meta-patterns.

To further understand the behavior of our proposed meta-pattern mining algorithm, we constructed four long synthetic sequences and the sensitive analysis of our algorithm on these sequences is presented in the following section.

5.2 Synthetic Sequences

The four synthetic sequences are generated as follows. Each sequence consists of 1024 distinct symbols and 20M occurrences of symbols. The synthetic sequence is generated as follows. First, at the beginning of the sequence, the level of pattern is determined randomly. There are four possible levels, i.e., 1, 2, and 3, 4. Next, the number of segments in this pattern is determined. The length l of each segment is selected based on a

geometric distribution with mean μ_l. The number of repetitions of a lower level pattern in a segment is randomly chosen between min_rep and $\lfloor \frac{l}{p} \rfloor$ where p is the span of the lower level pattern. The number of symbols involved in a pattern is randomly chosen between 1 and the span p. The number of valid segments is chosen according to a geometrical distribution with mean μ_s. After each valid segment, the length of the disturbance is determined based on a geometrical distribution with mean μ_d. This process repeats until the length of the sequence reaches 20M. Four sequences are generated based on values of μ_l, μ_s, μ_r, and μ_d in Table 2.

Data Set	μ_l	μ_s	μ_r	μ_d
$DS1$	5	5	50	50
$DS2$	5	5	1000	1000
$DS3$	100	1000	50	50
$DS4$	100	1000	1000	1000

Table 2. Parameters of Synthetic Data Sets

In our proposed algorithm, we use the component location property pruning to reduce the candidate patterns. Figure 4(a) shows the effects of the component location property pruning method. The pruning effect is represented as a ratio of the candidate patterns (after pruning) and the total number of potential patterns at each level. We compute the pruning effects of each data set individually and the average is shown in the figure. It is evident that the pruning effects increase with the min_rep threshold because more patterns would be disqualified. In addition, in the higher level, the pruning effects are more evident because more constraints are involved.

In our approach, we only store the maximum valid segments for each pattern. We compare the computation-based approach with the match-based approach. In the match-based approach, for each pattern, all valid subsequences are stored and used to mine higher level meta-patterns. For each level of pattern, we track the CPU time consumed by the computation-based approach and the match-based approach. (We assume that all information can be stored in main memory. Since the number of possible subsequences is much larger than that of maximum valid segments, the match-based approach has more ad-

556

min_rep	max_dis	Level-1 Patterns	Level-2 Patterns	Level-3 Patterns	Meta only Patterns
3	200	107	12	1	10
10	200	31	5	0	5
20	200	15	2	0	2

Table 1. Patterns Discovered in Scour Trace

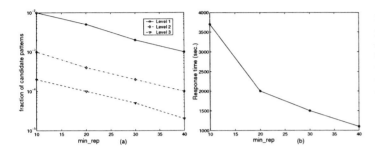

Figure 4. Performance of Meta-pattern Algorithm

vantages with this assumption.) The ratio of the CPU time of the computation-based approach over that of the match-based approach is calculated and presented in Table 3. It is obvious that the computation-based approach can save at least 95% of the CPU time comparing to the match-based approach. This is because the number of maximum valid segments is far less than that of valid subsequences as we explained in Section 5.

Level	$DS1$	$DS2$	$DS3$	$DS4$
2	0.02	0.02	0.04	0.01
3	0.05	0.03	0.01	0.02

Table 3. CPU Time Ratio

The overall response time is one of the most important criteria for evaluation of an algorithm. We mine the meta-patterns with different min_rep threshold. For a given min_rep, we mine the patterns on all four data sets and the average response time over the four data sets are taken and shown in Figure 4(b). The average response time decreases exponentially as min_rep increases. Although the average response time is a bit long when min_rep is small, but it is still tolerable (around 1 hour) due to the pruning effects of component location property and the computation-based candidate pattern generation. The meta-pattern mining algorithm is also applied to symbol sequences with different lengths. We found that the response time of our algorithm is linearly proportional to the length of the symbol sequence.

6   Conclusion

Meta-pattern is proposed to capture the hierarchical cyclic behavior exhibited in data sequence. A meta-pattern itself can serve as a component of some higher level meta-patterns. To accommodate noises in the data sequence, two parameters min_rep and max_dis are used to qualify a subsequence. The

number of candidates of meta-patterns could be very large. To minimize the response time of the pattern mining process, a pruning algorithm based on the component location property and Apriori property is proposed which can greatly to reduce the number of candidate patterns. In addition, a computation-based algorithm is designed to identify potential meta-pattern candidates. We use the meta-pattern mining algorithm on some real traces and some very interesting results are discovered.

References

[1] R. Agrawal and R. Srikant. Mining Sequential Patterns. *Proc. ICDE*, 3-14, 1995.

[2] M. Garofalakis, R. Rastogi, and K. Shim. SPIRIT: sequential pattern mining with regular expression constraints. *Proc. VLDB*, 223-234, 1999.

[3] J. Han, G. Dong, and Y. Yin. Efficient mining partial periodic patterns in time series database. *Proc. ICDE*, 106-115, 1999.

[4] J. Han, J. Pei, B. Mortazavi-Asl, Q. Chen, U. Dayal, and M. Hsu. FreeSpan: frequent pattern-projected sequential pattern mining. *Proc. SIGKDD*, 2000.

[5] L. Lin and T. Risch. Querying continuous time sequences. *Proc. VLDB*, 170-181, 1998.

[6] S. Ma and J. Hellerstein. Mining partially periodic event patterns with unknown periods. *Proc. ICDE*, 205-214, 2001.

[7] H. Mannila, H. Toivonen, and A. I. Verkamo. Discovery of frequent episodes in event sequences. *Data Mining and Knowledge Discovery*, vol. 1, no. 3, 259-289, 1997.

[8] B. Padmanabhan and A. Tuzhilin. Pattern discovery in temporal databases: a temporal logic approach. *Proc. SIGKDD*, 351-354, 1996.

[9] R. Srikant and R. Agrawal. Mining sequential patterns: generalizations and performance improvements. *Proc. EDBT*, 3-17, 1996.

[10] W. Wang, J. Yang, and R. Muntz. TAR: temporal association rules on evolving numerical attributes. *Proc. ICDE*, 283-292, 2001.

[11] J. Yang, W. Wang, and P. Yu. Mining asynchronous periodic patterns in time series data. *Proc. SIGKDD*, 275-279, 2000.

[12] J. Yang, W. Wang, and P. Yu. Mining surprising periodic patterns. To appear in *Proc. SIGKDD*, 2001.

[13] J. Yang, W. Wang, and P. Yu. Meta-Patterns: revealing hidden periodic patterns. *IBM Research Report*, 2001.

[14] M. Zaki. Sequence mining in categorical domains: incorporating constraints. *Proc. CIKM*, 422-429, 2000.

Using Boosting to Simplify Classification Models

Virginia Wheway
School of Mathematics and Applied Statistics,
School of Information Technology and Computer Science
University of Wollongong

NSW 2522 Australia
vlw04@uow.edu.au

Abstract

Ensemble classification techniques such as bagging, boosting and arcing algorithms have been shown to lead to reduced classification error on unseen cases and seem immune to the problem of overfitting. Several explanations for the reduction in generalisation error have been presented, with authors more recently defining and applying diagnostics such as edge and margin [4,9,10]. These measures provide insight into the behaviour of ensemble classifiers but can they be exploited further?

In this paper a four stage classification procedure in introduced, which is based on an extension of edge and margin analysis. This new procedure allows inverse sub-contexts and difficult border regions to be detected using properties of the edge distribution. It is widely known that ensemble classifiers 'balance' the margin as the number of iterations increases. However, by exploiting this balancing property and flagging observations whose edges (and margins) are not 'balanced', datasets can often be partitioned into subcontexts and classification made more robust as confounding within a dataset is removed. In the majority of cases, the subcontexts detected are inverse to each other, or quite possibly, the smaller subcontext contains mislabelled observations. The majority of classification techniques have not been adapted to detect contexts within a dataset and the generalisation error reported in studies to date is based on the entire dataset and can be improved by partitioning the dataset in question. The aim of this study is to move towards interpretability, and it is shown that by training on a subset of the original training data we gain simplicity of models and reduced generalisation error.

1 Introduction

The ability to classify unseen observations efficiently is a desirable property of many data mining algorithms. Numerous barriers may be present when an optimal classification model is being sought. In particular unavoidable dataset symptoms such as noisy data, outliers and 'fuzzy' boundaries inhibit a model's performance. Another such inhibitor is the presence of more than one context within a dataset. i.e. different sections of the dataset being classified according to significantly different models. If undetected, this results in increased generalisation error and a more complex model prone to overfitting. The undetected presence of such subcontexts has previously been attributed to noise and deterioration in generalisation error. If such situations can be detected and either removed or accounted for in the final modelling stage, significant gains may be made in both model simplification and generalisation ability.

This paper is concerned with the classification problem, whereby a learner is presented with a training set comprising of a series of n labelled training examples of the form $(\mathbf{x}_1, y_1), \ldots, (\mathbf{x}_n, y_n)$, with $y_i \in (1, \ldots, k)$. The learner's task is to use these training examples to produce an hypothesis, $h(\mathbf{x})$, which is an estimate of the unknown relationship $y = f(\mathbf{x})$. This 'hypothesis' then allows future prediction of y_i given new input values of $\mathbf{x}$. A classifier built by combining individual $h(\mathbf{x})$'s to form a single classifier is known as an ensemble. Whilst there are many ensemble building methods in existence, this discussion focusses on the method of boosting which is based on a weighted subsampling of the training examples.

Introduced by Freund and Schapire, boosting is recognised as being one of the most significant recent advances in classification [9]. Since its introduction, boosting has been the subject of many theoretical and empirical studies [3,8,10]. Empirical studies have shown that ensembles grown from repeatedly applying a learning algorithm over different subsamples of the data result in improved generalisation error.

This paper presents the results from an empirical study on boosting and edge analysis. Section 2 introduces the theory behind the study, which is tested in Section 3 on a selection of UCI [1] [1] datasets.

2 Boosting, Margin and Edge

Boosting is an iterative procedure which trains a learner over n weighted observations. Boosting begins with all with all training examples being given equal weight (i.e. $\frac{1}{n}$). At the $m + 1$-th iteration, examples which were classified incorrectly at the m-th iteration have their weight increased multiplicatively so that the total weight on incorrect observations is equal to 0.5. Hence, the learning algorithm will be given more opportunity to explore areas of the training set which are more difficult to classify. Hypotheses from these parts of the space make fewer mistakes on these areas and play an important role in prediction when all hypotheses are

---

1 URL = http://www.ics.uci.edu/~mlearn /MLRepository.html

Table 1. AdaBoost:M1 [9]

AdaBoost:M1

Input: n training instances x_i with labels y_i. Maximum trials, M. Base learner, H.
Initialization: All training instances begin with weight $w_i^0 = 1/n$.
Repeat for M trials:

- Induce classifier, h_m, using weighted training data and H.

- ϵ_m = weighted error for h_m on the training data. If $\epsilon_m > 1/2$, discard h_m and stop boosting. (If $\epsilon_m = 0$, then h_m gets infinite weight.)

- Classifier weight, $\beta_m = \log(\frac{1-\epsilon_m}{\epsilon_m})$

- Re-weight training instances:
  if $h_m(x_i) \neq y_i$ then,
  $w_i^{m+1} = w_i^m/(2\epsilon_m)$
  else, $w_i^{m+1} = w_i^m/2(1 - \epsilon_m)$

Unseen instances are classified by voting the ensemble of classifiers h_m with weights β_m.

---

combined via weighted voting. At each iteration, the weighted error is stored and used in the final voting weight when individual classifiers are combined to form the ensemble. Accuracy of the final hypothesis depends on the accuracy of *all* the hypotheses returned at each iteration and the method exploits hypotheses that predict well in more difficult parts of the instance space. An advantage of boosting is that it does not require any background knowledge of the performance of the underlying weak learning algorithm. Table 1 summarises the details of the boosting algorithm and its weight update methodology.

2.1 Margin and Edge

Recent explanations as to the success of boosting algorithms have their foundations in margin and edge analysis [4,10]. Schapire et al. [10] claim that boosting is successful because it creates a higher margin distribution and hence increases the confidence of correct classification.

Breiman, however, claims the high margin explanation is incomplete and introduces new ensemble techniques which actively improve margin distributions but do not result in improved generalisation error [4,5]. These two measures are defined for the ith training observation at trial m as follows:

> The edge is defined for each observation as the total weight assigned to the incorrect class, with the margin being defined as the total weight assigned to the correct class minus the maximal weight assigned to any incorrect class.

More formally, assume the ensemble comprises a combination of base learners, each of which produce $h_m(\mathbf{x})$ at the m-th iteration. From $h_m(\mathbf{x})$, an error indicator function $I(h_m(\mathbf{x})_i) \neq y_i)$ may be determined. Let c_m represent the vote for the m-th hypothesis with $\sum_m c_m = 1$. Then, for the i-th observation:

$$edge(m,i) = \sum_{j=1}^{m} c_j I(h_j(\mathbf{x}_i) \neq y_i) \quad (1)$$

Whilst the margin is a useful measure due to its interpretability, mathematically it is perhaps not as robust and tractable as the edge. In its pursuit of correctly classifying 'harder' sections of the data space, boosting tends to 'balance' the edge. In other words, the proportion of misclassifications for each observation becomes uniform as the number of iterations increases. This was demonstrated in [5,11]. By utilising this property, a method for detecting noise has been introduced in [11] whereby noisy of difficult observations could be detected via deviations in the overall edge distribution.

Instead of detecting single, unique outliers, the notion of deviation from the main edge distribution may be used to detect clusters of observations behaving differently to the rest of the data. By isolating these observations and attempting to determine their collective structure, we may gain insight into areas of the input space which should be segregated or at the least, treated with caution.

Section 3 extends this notion and describes a process for detecting clusters of noise within a dataset.

3 A Four Stage Classification Process

3.1 Stage 1: Detect Obvious Outliers

In the noise study discussed in [11], plots of $edge(10, i)$ versus observation number are drawn as the first step in detecting noise or anomolies in the data. Identified via a significant deviation from a 'balanced' edge distribution, such observations can be examined and if justified, removed. If observations are removed from the original dataset, boosting trials must be re-run as changes in the dataset results in adjustment of the edge values for all other observations.

3.2 Stage 2: Detect Clusters via Edge Diagnostic Plots

At the second stage of this process, obvious outliers have been removed and the edge values for each observation ($edge(m, i)$, $m = 1 \ldots 10$) stored at the completion of each iteration.

The best edge measure for the task of detecting clusters of observations with unique properties is unclear. Measures are sought which will capture and differentiate behaviour deviant from the main 'core' of the data.

Observations which are consistently classified correctly will have a low average edge and a low variance of the edge. Observations which are persistently misclassified will also have a low edge variance but high average edge. Groups of difficult observations which collectively behave in the same manner but differ in structure from the majority of observations will have a high edge variance as boosting will alternate between correct and incorrect classification. Such clusters of observations will fall in a common location when the mean edge is plotted against the variance of the edge.

It is therefore proposed to calculate the mean and variance of the sequence of edge values for each observation. Depending on the succession of correct or incorrect classifications for each observation, these edge statistics will vary greatly between observations. Observations which can be grouped together will have similar mean and variance of their edge values.

More formally, the edge measures for $m = 10$ boosting trials are calculated as:

- $\hat{E}[edge(10, i)] = \frac{1}{10} \sum_{m=1}^{10} edge(m, i)$

- $\hat{Var}[edge(10, i)]$
$= \frac{1}{10} \sum_{m=1}^{10} (edge(m, i) - \hat{E}[edge(m, i)])^2$

The next step in the classification process encompasses the plotting of $\hat{Var}[edge(10, i)]$ versus $\hat{E}[edge(10, i)]$. Any clusters or subcontexts within the dataset become apparent when this diagnostic plot is drawn. Signature behaviour is noted on all datasets tested but detail is restricted to the *colic* dataset only.

3.3 Stage 3 - Define a new Classification Problem to Differentiate Between Clusters

Analysis proceeds by separating the dataset into the clusters as appear on the variance versus mean edge plot. Cluster number is used as target class variable in a new classification problem. This may illuminate differences between the two clusters and improve classification accuracy as confounding on contexts (clusters) will be removed.

This process goes beyond simply selecting observations which were initially misclassified or by choosing observations with a high proportion of misclassifications. It is highlighting observations which have a certain variance and mean structure, symptomatic of flipping between correct and incorrect classification as boosting proceeds.

3.4 Stage 4 - Retrain the Classifier on a Subset of the Original Data

Once clusters have been identified, training new classifiers on each of the partitioned datasets will result in more generalisable models over these partitions. The difficulty arises for unseen observations

when the correct cluster is unknown. If the clusters identified in Stage 2 are able to be classified using only the predictor variables, it would be simple to use the resulting classifier to determine which cluster a new unseen observation would fall into. However, if the classification procedure fails to discriminate between clusters without using the original target variable, the optimal way to proceed is to assume all new observations are best modelled according to the classifier trained on the larger partition. This notion is shown to lead to reduced classification error as demonstrated in Section 5.

4 Demonstration on the UCI *colic* dataset

The 4-stage edge based procedure is now demonstrated on the *colic* dataset. (For more detail on this and other UCI datasets tested in this study, refer to Table 3.) The *colic* dataset requires binary classification pertaining to whether or not a horse had surgery (response = *yes/no*). A total of 23 input predictors are used in the classification process. Decreased generalisation performance has been observed on the *colic* dataset when boosting is applied. The four stage classification process suggested in this paper sheds some light on this phenomenon.

After detecting and removing an obvious outlier using the methodology from [11], a scatter plot of $\hat{Var}[edge(10, i)]$ versus $\hat{E}[edge(10, i)]$ is drawn and shown as Figure 1. Figure 1 shows 2 more possible outliers in observations *133* and *212*. After examining these observations there is no obvious reason as to why they should be considered outliers so they are retained in the *colic* dataset (in fact, it is seen in subsequent analysis that these observations are correctly classified by a model which is the inverse of the main model).

4.1 Stages 2 and 3 : Formulation of a new Classification Problem

The $\hat{Var}[edge(10, i)]$ versus $\hat{E}[edge(10, i)]$ plot is drawn for the *colic* data in Figure 1. Two clusters are ev-

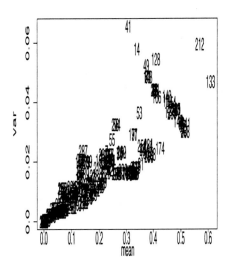

Figure 1. Plot of $\hat{Var}[edge(10,i)]$ **vs.** $\hat{E}[edge(10,i)]$ **:** *colic* **data.**

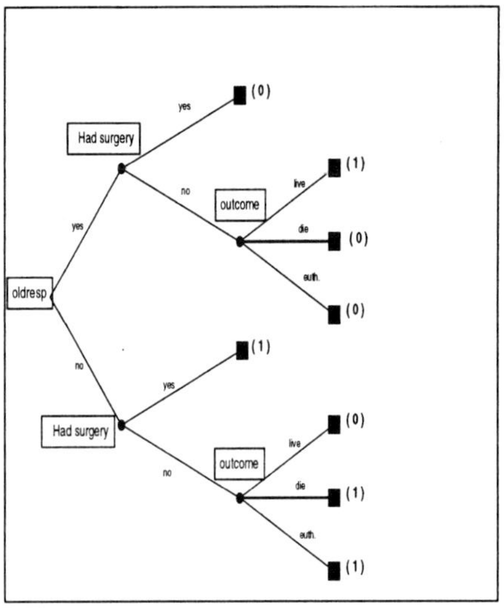

Figure 2. Decision tree for $edgeflag = 0/1$ **response :** *colic* **data.**

ident: one cluster being those observations exhibiting a positive relationship between $\hat{Var}[edge(10,i)]$ and $\hat{E}[edge(10,i)]$ and the others a negative one. Closer inspection reveals that all observations which were initially misclassified at iteration 1 fall into smaller 'negative' cluster, along with a small number of observations which were initally classified correctly.

A new dataset named *colicflag* is created for which a new response variable is appended to the *colic* dataset. This new response, *edgeflag* is assigned a value of 1 if an observation lies in the upper right hand cluster of Figure 1 and 0 otherwise. A total of 14.1% of the observations were flagged with $edgeflag = 1$. This creates a new classification problem with $edgeflag = 0/1$ as the new response variable. If *c4.5* or another classification algorithm can find repeatable structure in differentiating $edgeflag = 0$ from $edgeflag = 1$ using the available 23 predictor variables, then it may be concluded that such structure forms boundary regions of uncertainty, or differentiates between two contexts within the dataset. Because an aim of this study is interpretability, single trees are fitted as opposed to boosted ensembles, since boosted models become un-interpretable very quickly.

Several unsuccessful attempts to classify *edgeflag* using only the initial 23 predictor variables were made. Only when the original response is included in the predictors did a concise, highly accurate split result. The original *(yes/no)* response was returned as the initial split on the decision tree, indicating different mechanisms occurring for different values of the initial response, given identical input contributions.

This may seem intuitive as observations which are difficult to classify will naturally be predicted oppositely the main 'core' of data. However, in this and other UCI datasets tested we see that each cluster has equivalent input ($\mathbf{x}_i$) values but reversed y_i (class) values. Figure 2 shows the resulting decision tree for classification of the *edgeflag* variable. Note how the branches beyond the *Had Surgery* split are inverse to each other. Not only are the subtrees different on the initial split variable but are the exact inverse at greater depths in the decision tree.

Having a two stage model requiring prior knowledge of the original class variable will be futile in predicting unseen cases but leads us to hypothesise inverse models being present within a dataset.

4.2 Stage 4 - Retrain the Classifier on a Majority Subset of the *colic* Dataset

Using the *edgeflag* variable defined in Section 4.1, the *colic* dataset is split into two distinct datasets. Although we require the original target variable to do this, an important property is demonstrated. As will be shown, this results in a simple highly generalisable model fitting the majority of the data.

The partitioned datasets are labelled *horsec0* and *horsec1* respectively, with 0 and 1 representing the value of *edgeflag* determined in Section 4.1. The number of observations in each dataset is 262 and 37 respectively. The initial binary classification problem of *had surgery=yes/no* using 23 input predictors may then be re-estimated for each sub-dataset (*horsec0, horsec1*). For interpretability, a *c*4.5 decision tree using default values was used as the classification method. The results are encouraging with training error for the *horsec0* dataset being only 0.38% (as opposed to 14.99% on the entire *colic* dataset). Refer to Table 2 for detail of generalisation performance on the *colic* dataset. The figures presented in the final column refer to the average generalisation error estimated via 10-fold cross-validation , with bracketted figures giving the standard error of this estimate. The large standard errors evident for the *horsec1* dataset are based on test sets of 3-4 observations and may not be representative.

Table 2. Cross-validation results for *colic* dataset.

Dataset	Class	Method	Gen error
colic	(y/n)	*c*4.5 single	14.99(8.76)
colic	(y/n)	*c*4.5 10 boost	21.01(7.21)
colicflag	(0/1)	*c*4.5 single	0.34(1.08)
horsec0	(y/n)	*c*4.5 single	1.53(2.68)
horsec0	(y/n)	*c*4.5 10 boost	0.38(1.20)
horsec1	(y/n)	*c*4.5 single	3.33(10.25)
horsec1	(y/n)	*c*4.5 10 boost	3.33(10.25)

The decision tree is fitted on a reduced set of training data and the generalisation error on this partition will not be representative of the generalisation error for the entire dataset. Section 6 outlines logic for a new generalisation error estimate which encompasses error from both partitions of the dataset.

5 Generalisation Error Calculations

An empirical study is undertaken on a selection of UCI[2] [1] datasets to test the process outlined in Section 3. For all datasets, the term 'boosting' refers to the AdaBoost.M1 algorithm presented in Section 2. Unless otherwise described for a particular dataset, 10 boosting iterations were applied using *c*4.5 with default options as the base learner.

Table 3 gives a description of the UCI datasets used in this study.

Table 3. Summary of UCI datasets used in this study - as per [9])

Dataset	Cases	Num Classes	Cont. Attr.	Disc. Attr.
colic	368	2	10	12
credit	690	2	7	13
heart-h	294	2	8	5
heart-c	303	2	8	5
h'titis	155	2	6	13

Because it is proposed to use the simpler model trained on the majority partition for future prediction, generalisation error must be re-defined. Assume the proportion of observations falling into the main cluster is given as p. ($0 < p < 1$). Let e_1 represent the estimated generalisation error for the simple classifier trained on this cluster. 10 fold crossvalidation is used as the process for estimating e_1. 10 Now, since the remainder of the data is modelled in an inverse fashion to the main cluster, the generalisation errror for this section of the data will at worst be estimated at $1 - e_1$. Denoting the new overall generalisation error

---

[2]URL = http://www.ics.uci.edu/~mlearn/ MLRepository.html

Table 4. New estimates of generalisation error for a selection of UCI datasets.

dataset	% data with $edgeflag = 1$	e_{init}	$e_{cluster}$
colic	14.13	21.01	14.40
credit	9.3	18.24	12.17
heart-h	12.03	22.61	15.99
heart-c	9.9	18.41	16.64
hepatitis	7.1	16.00	14.98

estimate as $e_{cluster}$, we have:

$$e_{cluster} \approx (p*e_1) + (1-p)*(1-e_1) \quad (2)$$

Calculations of this generalisation error after applying the four stage classification process for a selection of UCI datasets are presented in Table 4. Note: e_{init} refers to the generalisation error as estimated on a 10 iteration boosted classifier trained on the entire dataset.

For the *colic, credit* and *hearth-h* datasets, this simplification of models results in an impressive reduction in generalisation error. For the *heart-c* and *hepatitis* datasets, reduction of error occurs but is less dramatic. In any case, this process certainly doesn't deteriorate generalisation error, and for all datasets we have gained model simplicity.

6 Discussion

In many cases, the $\hat{Var}[edge(10, i)]$ versus $\hat{E}[edge(10, i)]$ procedure identifies clusters no differently than simply selecting observations which were initially misclassified by a single decision tree on the entire dataset. Although discouraging, this phenomenon brings the following points to light:

- The usual practice of applying boosting to the entire dataset gives difficult observations an opportunity to be modelled correctly by the classifier. It was seen for the datasets tested, that even after 20 boosting iterations, the boosted ensemble was no closer to making consistent predictions on these groups of observations. The variance of the edge also

remains large as boosting flips between correct and incorrect classification on these observations.

- Closer inspection revealed these observations to occupy a similar region in predictor space to that of the 'core' data but the class labels are reversed. This could be attributed to mislabelling of the output or absence of a relevant predictor variable.

- In all datasets tested, the initial decision tree trained on the entire dataset was significantly more complex in its attempt to accommodate for the observations falling into the smaller cluster. A very simple robust tree with low generalisation error results when $c4.5$ is trained on the main cluster only. Using the tree trained on a subset of the data does not significantly deteriorate generalisation performance, as demonstrated in Table 4 for a selection of UCI datasets.

- Boosting is often successful within the 'core' data cluster, even when unsuccessful on the entire dataset.

7 Conclusion

This study has proposed a new multistage classification process which not only improves generalisation error but also results in easily interpretable classification models. In all datasets tested it was seen that a simple, highly accurate model built on the majority of the data was preferable to a more complex model trained on the entire dataset. The more complex model fitted to the entire dataset was a result of the need to accommodate noise and difficult observations. This additional detail was seen to cloud the underlying core classification model. It was also proposed that the UCI datasets tested contain sections of mislabelled data, or are lacking the measurement of a key predictor variable.

The clusters identified from the edge diagnostics are usually unable to be discriminated without the use of the initial class variable. However, if the simple tree trained on the majority cluster is applied to the entire dataset, the overall misclassification rate is reduced, sometimes substantially.

Further work will concentrate on automatic cluster detection and testing other possible edge measures across a varying number of boosting iterations and datasets.

References

[1] Blake, C.L. & Merz, C.J. (1988). UCI Repository of Machine Learning Databases. url=http://www.ics.uci.edu/~mlearn /MLRepository.html. University of California, Irvine, Dept. of Information and Computer Sciences.

[2] Breiman, L. (1996a). Bagging predictors. *Machine Learning, 26(2)*, 123–140.

[3] Breiman, L. (1996b). *Bias, Variance and Arcing Classifiers* (Technical Report 460). Statistics Department, University of California, Berkeley.

[4] Breiman, L. (1997). *Arcing the edge* (Technical Report 486). Statistics Department, University of California, Berkeley.

[5] Breiman, L. (1999). *Random Forests - Random Features* (Technical Report 567). Statistics Department, University of California, Berkeley.

[6] Freund, Y., & Schapire, R. E. (1996). Experiments with a new boosting algorithm. *Proceedings of the Thirteenth International Conference on Machine Learning* (pp. 148–156). Morgan Kaufmann.

[7] Freund, Y., & Schapire, R. E. (1997). A decision-theoretic generalisation to on-line learning and an application to boosting. *Journal of Computer and System Sciences , 55(1)*, 119–139.

[8] Quinlan, J. R. (1993). *C4.5: Programs for Machine Learning.* Morgan Kaufmann.

[9] Quinlan, J. R. (1996). Bagging, boosting and C4.5. *Proceedings of the Thirteenth National Conference on Artificial Intelligence.* (pp. 725–730). Menlo Park California, American Association for Artificial Intelligence.

[10] Schapire, R. E. , Freund, Y., Bartlett, P. & Lee, W. S. (1998). Boosting the margin:a new explanation for the effectiveness of voting methods. *Annals of Statistics, 26(5)*, 1651–1686.

[11] Wheway, V. L. (2000). Using Boosting to Detect Noisy Data *To appear in Lecture Notes in Computer Science 2112:AIApps 2000* Springer

Interestingness, Peculiarity, and Multi-Database Mining

Ning Zhong
Dept. of Information Engineering
Maebashi Institute of Technology
460-1, Kamisadori-Cho, Maebashi 371, Japan
E-mail: zhong@maebashi-it.ac.jp

Muneaki Ohshima
Graduate School
Maebashi Institute of Technology
460-1, Kamisadori-Cho, Maebashi 371, Japan

Y.Y. Yao
Dept. of Computer Science
University of Regina
Regina, Saskatchewan S4S 0A2, Canada
E-mail: yyao@cs.uregina.ca

Setsuo Ohsuga
Dept. of Infor. and Computer Science
Waseda University
3-4-1 Okubo Shinjuku-Ku, Tokyo 169, Japan

Abstract

In order to discover new, surprising, interesting *patterns hidden in data, peculiarity oriented mining and multi-database mining are required. In the paper, we introduce* peculiarity rules *as a new class of rules, which can be discovered from a relatively low number of peculiar data by searching the relevance among the peculiar data. We give a formal interpretation and comparison of three classes of rules:* association rules, exception rules, *and* peculiarity rules, *as well as describe how to mine more interesting peculiarity rules in multiple databases.*

1 Introduction

The goal of this work can be summarized in a phrase: *peculiarity oriented mining in multiple databases for discovering interesting patterns.* There are two keywords in this phrase:

The first keyword is *peculiarity*, which is a kind of interestingness, long identified as an important problem in data mining [10, 23, 24]. Peculiarity, unexpected relationships/rules (with common-sense) may be hidden in a relatively low number of data. Thus, we may focus on some interesting data (peculiar data), and then we find more novel and interesting rules (peculiarity rules) from the data. We argue that the *peculiarity rules* are a typical regularity hidden in a lot of scientific, statistical, and transaction databases. Sometimes, the ordinary association rules with common-sense cannot be found from numerous scientific, statistical or transaction data, or although they can be found, the user may be uninterested in the rules because data are

rarely specially collected/stored in a database for the purpose of mining knowledge in most organizations.

The second keyword is *multiple databases*, which are the objects of discovery and learning. So far the main stream in the KDD community is limited to rule discovery in a single universal relation (or an information table) [1, 11]. Multi-database mining is to mine knowledge in multiple related information sources. Generally speaking, the task of multi-database mining can be divided into three levels:

1. Mining from multiple relations in a database.

    Although theoretically, any relational database with multiple relations can be transformed into a single universal relation, practically this can lead to many issues such as universal relations of unmanageable sizes, infiltration of uninteresting attributes, loss of useful relation names, an unnecessary join operation, and inconveniences for distributed processing.

2. Mining from multiple relational databases.

    Some concepts, regularities, causal relationships, and rules cannot be discovered if we just search a single database because the knowledge hides in multiple databases basically [23].

3. Mining from multiple mixed-media databases.

    Many datasets in the real world contain more than just a single type of data [15, 23]. For example, medical datasets often contain numeric data (e.g. test results), images (e.g. X-rays), nominal data (e.g. person smokes/does not smoke), and acoustic data (e.g. the recording of a doctor's voice). How to handle such multiple data sources is a new, challenging research issue.

The rest of this paper is organized as follows: Section 2 discusses more detail on interestingness and peculiarity. Section 3 gives a formal interpretation and comparison of three classes of rules: association rules, exception rules, and peculiarity rules. Section 4 presents a method of peculiarity oriented mining. Section 5 extends the peculiarity oriented mining into multi-database mining. Finally, Section 6 gives concluding remarks.

2 Interestingness and Peculiarity

Generally speaking, hypotheses (knowledge) generated from databases can be divided into the following three types: incorrect hypotheses, useless hypotheses, and *new, surprising, interesting hypotheses*. The purpose of data mining is to discover new, surprising, interesting knowledge hidden in databases. Hence, the evaluation of interestingness (including peculiarity, surprisingness, unexpectedness, usefulness, novelty) should be done in pre-processing and/or post-processing of the knowledge discovery process [3, 5, 6, 9, 23]. Here, "evaluating in pre-processing" is to select interesting data before hypotheses generation; "evaluating in post-processing" is to select interesting rules after hypotheses generation. Furthermore, interestingness evaluation may be either *subjective* or *objective* [10]. Here, "subjective" means user-driven, that is, asking the user to explicitly specify what type of data (or rules) are interesting and uninteresting, and the system then generates or retrieves those matching rules; "objective" means data-driven, that is, analyzing structure of data (or rules), predictive performance, statistical significance, and so forth.

Zhong, Yao, and Ohsuga proposed *peculiarity rules* as a new class of rules [23]. A peculiarity rule is discovered from peculiar data by searching the relevance among the peculiar data. Roughly speaking, data are *peculiar* if they represent a peculiar case described by a relatively low number of objects and are very different from other objects in a dataset. Although it looks like the exception rule from the viewpoint of describing a relatively low number of objects, the semantic of the peculiarity rule is with common-sense, which is a feature of the ordinary association rule [1, 14].

Illustrative Example. The following rule is a peculiarity one that can be discovered from a relation called *Supermarket-Sales* (see Table 1) in a *Supermarket-Sales* database:

$rule_1$: *meat-sale(low)* $\wedge$ *vegetable-sale(low)* $\wedge$
fruits-sale(low) $\rightarrow$ *turnover(very-low)*.

We can see that this rule just covers data in one tuple on July-30 and its semantic is with common-sense. Hence, algorithms for mining association rules and exception rules may fail to find such useful rules. However, a manager of the supermarket may be interested in such rule because it

Table 1. Supermarket-Sales

Addr.	Date	meat-sale	vegetable-sale	fruits-sale	...	turnover
Ube	July-1	400	300	450	...	2000
...	July-2	420	290	460	...	2200
...	...	...	...	...	...	...
...	**July-30**	**12**	**10**	**15**	...	**100**
...	July-31	430	320	470	...	2500
...	...	...	...	...	...	...

shows that the turnover was a marked drop.

In order to discover such peculiarity rule, we first need to search peculiar data in the relation *Supermarket-Sales*. From Table 1, we can see that the values of the attributes *meat-sale*, *vegetable-sale*, and *fruits-sale* on July-30 are very different from other values in the attributes. Hence, the values are regarded as peculiar data. Furthermore, $rule_1$ is generated by searching the relevance among the peculiar data. Note that we use the qualitative representation for the quantitative values in the above rules. The transformation of quantitative to qualitative values can be done by using the following background knowledge on information granularity:

Basic granules:
$bg_1 = \{high, low, very\text{-}low\}$;
$bg_2 = \{large, small, very\text{-}small\}$;
$bg_3 = \{many, little, very\text{-}little\}$;
· · · · · · ··

Specific granules:
kanto-area = {*Tokyo, Tiba, Saitama, ...*};
chugoku-area = {*Yamaguchi, Hiroshima, Shimane, ...*};
yamaguchi-prefecture = {*Ube, Shimonoseki, ...*};
· · · · · · ··

That is, *meat-sale = 12, vegetable-sale = 10, fruits-sale = 15* and *turnover = 100* on July 30 are replaced by the granules, "low" and "very-low", respectively.

3 Interpretation of Rules

This section gives the formal interpretation and comparison of three classes of rules: *association rules, exception rules*, and *peculiarity rules*.

3.1 A Framework for the Interpretation of Rules

Typically, a rule can be expressed in the form, $\phi \Rightarrow \psi$, where ϕ and ψ are formulas of certain language used to describe objects (tuples) in the database. In order to have a precise interpretation of rules, we need a formal model in which various components of rules can be interpreted. We adopt the decision logic language (*DL*-language) studied by Pawlak [11], in Tarski's style through the notions of a model and satisfiability. The model is a database S consisting of a finite set of objects U. An object $x \in U$ either satisfies a formula ϕ, written $x \models_S \phi$ or in short $x \models \phi$, or does not satisfy the formula, written $\neg x \models \phi$. The satisfiability depends on the semantic interpretation of expressions and must be defined by a particular rule mining method. In general, it should satisfy the following conditions [11]:

(1) $x \models \neg\phi$ iff not $x \models \phi$,

(2) $x \models \phi \wedge \psi$ iff $x \models \phi$ and $x \models \psi$,

(3) $x \models \phi \vee \psi$ iff $x \models \phi$ or $x \models \psi$,

(4) $x \models \phi \rightarrow \psi$ iff $x \models \neg\phi \vee \psi$,

(5) $x \models \phi \equiv \psi$ iff $x \models \phi \rightarrow \psi$ and $x \models \psi \rightarrow \phi$,

where $\neg, \wedge, \vee, \rightarrow$ and $\equiv$ are standard logical connectives. If ϕ is a formula, the set $m_S(\phi)$ defined by

$$m_S(\phi) = \{x \in U \mid x \models \phi\} \qquad (1)$$

is called the meaning of the formula ϕ in S. If S is understood, we simply write $m(\phi)$. Obviously, the following properties hold [11]:

(a) $m(\neg\phi) = -m(\phi)$,

(b) $m(\phi \wedge \psi) = m(\phi) \cap m(\psi)$,

(c) $m(\phi \vee \psi) = m(\phi) \cup m(\psi)$;

(d) $m(\phi \rightarrow \psi) = -m(\phi) \cup m(\psi)$,

(e) $m(\phi \equiv \psi) = (m(\phi) \cap m(\psi)) \cup (-m(\phi) \cap -m(\psi))$.

The meaning of a formula ϕ is the set of all objects having the property expressed by the formula ϕ. Conversely, ϕ can be viewed as the description of the set of objects $m(\phi)$. Thus, a connection between formulas and subsets of U is established.

A formula ϕ is said to be true in a database S, written $\models_S \phi$, if and only if $m(\phi) = U$, namely, ϕ is satisfied by all objects in the universe. Two formulas ϕ and ψ are equivalent in S if and only if $m(\phi) = m(\psi)$. By definition, the following properties hold [11]:

(i) $\models_S \phi$ iff $m(\phi) = U$,

(ii) $\models_S \neg\phi$ iff $m(\phi) = \emptyset$,

(iii) $\models_S \phi \rightarrow \psi$ iff $m(\phi) \subseteq m(\psi)$,

(iv) $\models_S \phi \equiv \psi$ iff $m(\phi) = m(\psi)$.

Thus, we can study the relationships between concepts described by formulas based on the relationships between their corresponding sets of objects.

A rule, $\phi \Rightarrow \psi$, can be interpreted by logical implication, namely, the symbol $\Rightarrow$ is interpreted as the logical implication $\rightarrow$. In most cases, the expression $\phi \rightarrow \psi$ may not be true in a database. Only certain objects satisfy the expression, $\phi \rightarrow \psi$. The ratio of objects satisfying $\phi \rightarrow \psi$ can be used to define a quantitative measure of the strength of the rule:

$$T(\phi \Rightarrow \psi) = \frac{|m(\phi \rightarrow \psi)|}{|U|}, \qquad (2)$$

where $|\cdot|$ denotes the cardinality of a set. It measures the degree of truth of the expression $\phi \rightarrow \psi$ in a database. A problem with the logic implication interpretation can be seen as follows. For an object, if it does not satisfy ϕ, by definition, it satisfies $\phi \rightarrow \psi$. Thus, even if the degree of truth of $\phi \rightarrow \psi$ is very high, we may not conclude too much on the satisfiability of ψ given the object satisfies ϕ. In reality, we want to know the satisfiability of ψ under the condition that ϕ is satisfied. In other words, our main concern is the satisfiability of ψ in the subset $m(\phi)$. Obviously, logical implication is inappropriate in this case. For the same reason, the notion of conditional has been proposed and studied in the context of rule based expert systems [4].

3.2   Probabilistic Interpretations of Rules

In data mining, rules are typically interpreted in terms of probability. A detailed analysis of probability related measures associated with rules has been given by Yao and Zhong [19]. We review a few relevant measures. The characteristics of an rule, $\phi \Rightarrow \psi$, can be summarized by the following contingency table:

	ψ	$\neg\psi$	Totals
ϕ	a	b	$a+b$
$\neg\phi$	c	d	$c+d$
Totals	$a+c$	$b+d$	$a+b+c+d=n$

$$a = |m(\phi \wedge \psi)|, \qquad b = |m(\phi \wedge \neg\psi)|,$$
$$c = |m(\neg\phi \wedge \psi)|, \qquad d = |m(\neg\phi \wedge \neg\psi)|.$$

From the contingency table, different measures can be defined to reflect various aspects of rules.

The *generality* of ϕ is defined by

$$G(\phi) = \frac{|m(\phi)|}{|U|} = \frac{a+b}{n}, \qquad (3)$$

which indicates the relative size of the concept ϕ. A concept is more general if it covers more instances of the universe. If $G(\phi) = \alpha$, then $(100\alpha)\%$ of objects in U satisfy ϕ. The quantity may be viewed as the probability of a randomly selected element satisfying ϕ. Obviously, we have $0 \leq G(\phi) \leq 1$.

The *absolute support* of ψ provided by ϕ is the quantity:

$$\begin{aligned} AS(\phi \Rightarrow \psi) &= AS(\psi|\phi) \\ &= \frac{|m(\psi) \cap m(\phi)|}{|m(\phi)|} = \frac{a}{a+b}. \end{aligned} \qquad (4)$$

The quantity, $0 \leq AS(\psi|\phi) \leq 1$, shows the degree to which ϕ implies ψ. If $AS(\psi|\phi) = \alpha$, then $(100\alpha)\%$ of objects satisfying ϕ also satisfy ψ. It may be viewed as the conditional probability of a randomly selected element satisfying ψ given that the element satisfies ϕ. In set-theoretic terms, it is the degree to which $m(\phi)$ is included in $m(\psi)$. Clearly, $AS(\psi|\phi) = 1$, if and only if $m(\phi) \subseteq m(\psi)$.

The *change of support* of ψ provided by ϕ is defined by

$$
\begin{aligned}
CS(\phi \Rightarrow \psi) &= CS(\psi|\phi) = AS(\psi|\phi) - G(\psi) \\
&= \frac{an - (a+b)(a+c)}{(a+b)n}.
\end{aligned} \tag{5}
$$

Unlike the absolute support, the change of support varies from -1 to 1. One may consider $G(\psi)$ to be the prior probability of ψ and $AS(\psi|\phi)$ the posterior probability of ψ after knowing ϕ. The difference of posterior and prior probabilities represents the change of our confidence regarding whether ϕ actually relates to ψ. For a positive value, one may say that ϕ is positively related to ψ; for a negative value, one may say that ϕ is negatively related to ψ.

The generality $G(\psi)$ is related to the satisfiability of ψ by all objects in the database, and $AS(\phi \Rightarrow \psi)$ is related to the satisfiability of ψ in the subset $m(\phi)$. A high $AS(\phi \Rightarrow \psi)$ does not necessarily suggest a strong association between ϕ and ψ, as a concept ψ with a large $G(\psi)$ value tends to have a large $AS(\phi \Rightarrow \psi)$ value. The change of support $CS(\phi \Rightarrow \psi)$ may be more accurate.

3.3 Comparison of Association Rules, Exception Rules, and Peculiarity Rules

Within the proposed framework, we can easily analyze the ordinary association rules by a slightly different formulation. Let I denote a set of items and T denote a set of transactions. For each item $i \in I$, we define an atomic expression $F_{\{i\}} = (i = 1)$ with the satisfiability given by $t \in T$,

$$
t \models F_{\{i\}} \text{ iff } t \text{ contains } i, \tag{6}
$$

and

$$
m(F_{\{i\}}) = \{t \in T \mid t \text{ contains } i\}. \tag{7}
$$

For each subset $A \subseteq I$, we define a formula $F_A = \bigwedge_{i \in A} F_{\{i\}}$. A transaction satisfies the formula F_A if it contains *all* items in A. For two disjoint subsets of items A and B, an association rule can be expressed as $F_A \Rightarrow F_B$. The association rule, $F_A \Rightarrow F_B$, is interpreted as saying that a customer who purchases *all* items in A tends to purchase *all* items in B.

Two measures, called the support and the confidence, are used to mine association rules. They are indeed the generality and absolute support:

$$
\begin{aligned}
supp(F_A \Rightarrow F_B) &= G(F_A \wedge F_B) = G(F_{A \cup B}), \\
conf(F_A \Rightarrow F_B) &= AS(F_A \Rightarrow F_B).
\end{aligned} \tag{8}
$$

By specifying threshold values of support and confident, one can obtain all association rules whose support and confident are above the thresholds.

Association rules can be extended to non-transaction databases so that both the left hand and right hand sides are formulas expressing properties of objects in a database. With an association rule, it is very tempting to relate a large confidence with a strong association between two concepts. However, such a connection may not exist. Suppose we have $conf(\phi \Rightarrow \psi) = 0.90$. If we also have $G(\phi) = 0.95$, we can conclude that ϕ is in fact negatively associated with ψ. This suggests that an association rule may not reflect the true association. Conversely, an association rule with low confidence may have a large change of support. In mining association rules, concepts with low support are not considered in the search for association. On the other hand, two concepts with low supports may have either large confidence or a large change of support. In summary, algorithms for mining association rules may fail to find such useful rules. Other mining algorithms are needed.

Exception rules have been studied as extension of association rules to resolve some of the above problems [14]. For an association rule, $\phi \Rightarrow \psi$, with high confidence, one may associates an exception rule $\phi \wedge \phi' \Rightarrow \neg\psi$. Roughly speaking, ϕ' can be viewed as the condition for exception to rule $\phi \Rightarrow \psi$. To be consistent with the intended interpretation of exception rule, it is reasonable to assume that $\phi \wedge \phi' \Rightarrow \neg\psi$ have a high confidence and low support. More specifically, we would expect a low generality of $\phi \wedge \phi'$. Otherwise, the rule cannot be viewed as describing exceptional situations. Consequently, exception rules cannot be discovered by association rule mining algorithms.

Recently, Zhong, Yao, and Ohsuga [23, 24] identified and studied a new class of rules called *peculiarity rules*. In mining peculiarity rules, one considers the distribution of attribute values. More specifically, attention is paid to objects whose attribute values are quite different from that of other objects. This is referred to as peculiarity data identification. After the isolation of peculiarity data, peculiarity rules with low support and high confidence, and consequently high change of support, are searched. Although a peculiarity rule may share the same properties with an exception rule, as expressed in terms of support and confidence, it does not express exception to another rules. Semantically, they are very different. Furthermore, algorithms for ming peculiarity rules are different from mining association rules and exception rules. It should be realized that peculiarity rules only represent a subset of all rules with high change of support.

Based on the above discussion, we can qualitatively characterize association rules, exception rules, and peculiarity rules as shown in Table 2.

From the viewpoint of support, both exception rules and peculiarity rules attempt to find rules that are missed by association rule mining methods. While exception rules and peculiarity rules have a high change of support values, in-

Table 2. Qualitative characterization of association rules, exception rules, and peculiarity rules

Rule	G (supp)	AS (conf)	CS	semantic
Association rule: $\phi \Rightarrow \psi$	High	High	Unknown	common-sense
Exception rule: $\phi \Rightarrow \psi$ $\phi \wedge \phi' \Rightarrow \neg\psi$	High Low	High High	Unknown High	exception
Peculiarity rule: $\phi \Rightarrow \psi$	Low	High	High	common-sense

Table 3. A sample table (relation)

A_1	A_2	...	A_j	...	A_m
x_{11}	x_{12}	...	x_{1j}	...	x_{1m}
x_{21}	x_{22}	...	x_{2j}	...	x_{2m}
$\vdots$	$\vdots$		$\vdots$		$\vdots$
x_{i1}	x_{i2}	...	x_{ij}	...	x_{im}
$\vdots$	$\vdots$		$\vdots$		$\vdots$
x_{n1}	x_{n2}	...	x_{nj}	...	x_{nm}

Table 4. An example of peculiarity factors for a continuous attribute

Region	ArableLand		PF
Hokkaido	1209		134.1
Tokyo	12	$\Rightarrow$	60.9
Osaka	18		60.3
Yamaguchi	162		60.5
Okinawa	147		59.4

dicating a strong association between two concepts, association rules do not necessarily have this property. All three classes of rules are focused on rules with high level of absolute support. For exception rule, it is also expected that the generality of $\phi \wedge \phi'$ is low. For peculiarity, the generalities of both ϕ and ψ are expected to be low. In contrast, the generality of right hand of an exception rule does not have to be low.

From Table 2, one may say that rules with high absolute support and high change of support are of interest. The interesting on the generality of rules depends on the particularly application. The use of generality (support) in association rule mining is mainly for the sake of computational cost, rather than semantics consideration. Exception rules and peculiarity rules are two subsets of rules with high absolute support and high change of support. It may be interesting to design an algorithm to find *all* rules with high absolute support and high change of support.

4 Peculiarity Oriented Mining

The main task of mining peculiarity rules is the identification of peculiarity data. According to our previous papers [23, 24], peculiarity data are a subset of objects in the database and are characterized by two features: (1) very different from other objects in a dataset, and (2) consisting of a relatively low number of objects.

There are many ways of finding the peculiar data. In this section, we describe an attribute-oriented method.

4.1 Finding the Peculiar Data

Table 3 shows a relation with attributes $A_1, A_2, ..., A_m$. In Table 3, let x_{ij} be the ith value of A_j, and n the number of tuples. The peculiarity of x_{ij} can be evaluated by the *Peculiarity Factor*, $PF(x_{ij})$,

$$PF(x_{ij}) = \sum_{k=1}^{n} \sqrt{N(x_{ij}, x_{kj})}. \quad (9)$$

It evaluates whether x_{ij} occurs in relatively low number and is very different from other data x_{kj} by calculating the sum of the square root of the conceptual distance between x_{ij} and x_{kj}. The reason why the square root is used in Eq. (9) is that we prefer to evaluate closer distances for a relatively large number of data so that the peculiar data can be found from a relatively low number of data.

Major merits of the method are the following:

- It can handle both the continuous and symbolic attributes based on a unified semantic interpretation;

- Background knowledge represented by binary neighborhoods can be used to evaluate the peculiarity if such background knowledge is provided by a user.

If X is a continuous attribute and no background knowledge is available, in Eq. (9),

$$N(x_{ij}, x_{kj}) = |x_{ij} - x_{kj}|. \quad (10)$$

Table 4 shows the calculation of peculairity factor. If X is a symbolic attribute and/or the background knowledge for representing the conceptual distances between x_{ij} and x_{kj} is provided by a user, the peculiarity factor is calculated by the conceptual distances, $N(x_{ij}, x_{kj})$ [8, 18, 23, 24]. However, the conceptual distances are assigned to 1 if no background knowledge is available.

There are two major methods for testing if the peculiar data exist or not (it is called *selection of peculiar data*) after the evaluation for the peculiarity factors. The first is based on a threshold value as shown in Eq. (11),

$$threshold = mean\ of\ PF(x_{ij}) + \alpha \times$$
$$standard\ deviation\ of\ PF(x_{ij}), \quad (11)$$

where α can be adjusted by a user, and $\alpha = 1$ as default. The threshold indicates that a data is a peculiar one if its PF value is much larger than the mean of the PF set. In other words, if $PF(x_{ij})$ is over the threshold value, x_{ij} is a peculiar data.

One can observe that peculiar data can be selected objectively by means of the threshold we are proposing, and the subjective factor (preference) of a user can also be included in the threshold value by adjusting the α.

The other method for *selection of peculiar data* uses the chi-square test that is useful when the data size is sufficiently large [2].

4.2 Attribute Oriented Clustering

Searching the data for a structure of natural clusters is an important exploratory technique. Clusters can provide an informal means of assessing interesting and meaningful groups of peculiar data.

Attribute oriented clustering is used to quantize continuous values, and eventually perform conceptual abstraction [21]. In the real world, there are many real-valued attributes as well as symbolic-valued attributes. In order to discover the better knowledge, conceptual abstraction and generalization are also necessary. Therefore, *attribute oriented clustering* is a useful technique as a step of the peculiarity oriented mining process.

It is a key issue that how to do clustering in the environment in which background knowledge on information granularity can either be used or not according to whether such background knowledge exists. Our approach is to provide various methods in the mining process so that the different data can be handled effectively.

If background knowledge on information granularity as stated in Section 2 is available, it is used for conceptual abstraction (generalization) and/or clustering.

If no such background knowledge is available, the *nearest neighbor method* is used for clustering of continuous-values attributes [7].

4.3 An Algorithm

Based on the above-stated preparation, an algorithm of finding peculiar data can be outlined as follows:

Step 1. Execute attribute oriented clustering for each attribute, respectively.

Step 2. Calculate the peculiarity factor $PF(x_{ij})$ in Eq. (9) for all values in an attribute.

Step 3. Calculate the threshold value in Eq. (11) based on the peculiarity factor obtained in *Step 2*.

Step 4. Select the data that are over the threshold value as the peculiar data.

Step 5. If the current peculiarity level is enough, then goto *Step 7*.

Step 6. Remove the peculiar data from the attribute and thus, we get a new dataset. Then go back to *Step 2*.

Step 7. Change the granularity of the peculiar data by using background knowledge on information granularity if the background knowledge is available.

Furthermore, the algorithm can be done in a parallel-distributed mode for multiple attributes, relations and databases because this is an attribute-oriented finding method.

4.4 Relevance Among the Peculiar Data

A peculiarity rule is discovered from the peculiar data, which belong to a cluster, by searching the relevance among the peculiar data. Let $X(x)$ and $Y(y)$ be the peculiar data found in two attributes X and Y respectively. We deal with the following two cases:

- If both $X(x)$ and $Y(y)$ are symbolic data, the relevance between $X(x)$ and $Y(y)$ is evaluated by

$$R_1 = P_1(X(x)|Y(y))P_2(Y(y)|X(x)), \qquad (12)$$

  that is, the larger the product of the probabilities of P_1 and P_2 is, the stronger the relevance between $X(x)$ and $Y(y)$ is.

- If both $X(x)$ and $Y(y)$ are continuous attributes, the relevance between $X(x)$ and $Y(y)$ is evaluated by using the method developed in our KOSI system [22].

Furthermore, Eq. (12) is suitable for handling more than two peculiar data found in more than two attributes if $X(x)$ (or $Y(y)$) is a granule of the peculiar data.

5 Multi-Database Mining

Building on the preparatory in the previous sections, this section extends peculiarity oriented mining into multi-database mining.

5.1 Peculiarity Oriented Mining in Multiple Databases

Generally speaking, the tasks of multi-database mining for the first two levels stated in Section 1 can be described as follows:

First, the concept of a foreign key in the relational databases needs to be extended into a foreign link because we are also interested in getting to non-key attributes for data mining from multiple relations in a database [16]. A major work is to find peculiar data in multiple relations for a given discovery task while foreign link relationships exist. In other words, our task is to select n relations, which contain the peculiar data, among m relations ($m \geq n$) with foreign links.

The method for selecting n relations among m relations can be divided into the following steps:

Step 1. Focus on a relation as the *main table* and find the peculiar data from this table. Then elicit the peculiarity rules from the peculiar data by using the methods stated in Section 4.

Step 2. Find the value(s) of the focused key corresponding to the mined peculiarity rule (or peculiar data) in *Step* 1 and change its granularity of the value(s) of the focused key if the background knowledge on information granularity is available.

Step 3. Find the peculiar data in the other relations (or databases) corresponding to the value (or its granule) of the focused key.

Step 4. Select n relations that contain the peculiar data, among m relations ($m \geq n$). In other words, we just select the relations that contain peculiar data relevant to the peculiarity rule mined from the main table.

A peculiarity rule can be discovered from peculiar data hidden in multiple relations by searching the relevance among the peculiar data. If the peculiar data, $X(x)$ and $Y(y)$, are found in two different relations, we need to use a value (or its granule) in a key (or foreign key/link) as the relevance factor, $K(k)$, to find the relevance between $X(x)$ and $Y(y)$. Thus, the relevance between $X(x)$ and $Y(y)$ is evaluated by

$$R_2 = P_1(K(k)|X(x))P_2(K(k)|Y(y)). \quad (13)$$

Furthermore, the above-stated methodology can be extended for mining from multiple databases. A challenge in multi-database mining is a semantic heterogeneity among multiple databases because usually no explicit foreign key/link relationships exists among them. Hence, the key issue of the extension is how to find/create the relevance among different databases. In our methodology, we use *granular computing* techniques based on semantics, approximation, and abstraction for solving the issue [8, 20].

We again use the illustrative example mentioned at Section 2. If a manager of the supermarket found that the turnover was a marked drop in one day from a supermarket-sale database, he/she may not understand the deeper reason. Although $rule_1$ as a peculiarity rule (see Section 2) can be discovered from the supermarket-sales database, the deeper reason why the turnover was a marked drop is not explained well. However, if we search several related information sources such as a weather database as shown in

Table 5. Weather

Region	Date	...	Weather
Yamaguchi	July-1	...	sunny
...	July-2	...	cloud
...	...	...	...
...	**July-30**	...	**typhoon (no. 2)**
...	July-31	...	cloud
...	...	...	...

Table 5, we can find that there was a violent typhoon that day. Hence, we can understand the deeper reason why the turnover was a marked drop. For this case, the granule of *addr.* = *Ube* in Table 1 needs to be changed into *region* = *yamaguchi* for creating explicit foreign link between the supermarket-sales database and the weather database. This example will be further described in the next section.

5.2 Representation and Re-learning

We use the RVER (Reverse Variant Entity-Relationship) model to represent the peculiar data and the conceptual relationships among the peculiar data discovered from multiple relations (databases) [23]. Figure 1, as an example, shows the results mined from two databases on supermarket sales at Yamaguchi prefecture and the weather of Japan. The point of which the RVER model is different from an ordinary ER model is that we just represent the attributes that are relevant to the peculiar data and the related peculiar data (or their granules) in the RVER model. Thus, the RVER model provides all interesting information that is relevant to some focusing (e.g. *turnover* = *very-low*, *region* = *yamaguchi*, and *date* = *July-30* in the supermarket-sale database) for learning more interesting rules among multiple relations (databases).

Re-learning means learning more interesting rules from the RVER model. For example, the following rule can be learned from the RVER model shown in Figure 1:

$rule_2 : weather(typhoon) \rightarrow turnover(very\text{-}low).$

We can see that a manager of the supermarket may be more interested in $rule_2$ (rather than $rule_1$) because $rule_2$ shows a deeper reason why the turnover was a marked drop.

6 Concluding Remarks

We presented a method of mining peculiarity rules from multiple databases, and a formal interpretation and comparison of three classes of rules: *association rules, exception rules,* and *peculiarity rules.* We showed that such peculiarity rules represent a typically unexpected, interesting regularity hidden in databases.

Here we should mention that Liu's group systematically investigated how to analyze the subjective interesting-

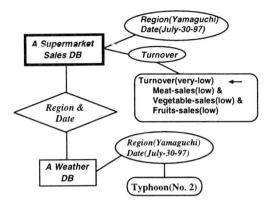

Figure 1. The RVER model mined from two databases

ness of association rules [9, 10]. The work of his group is about subjective evaluation of interestingness in post-processing (i.e. evaluating the mined rules). In contrast, our work is about objective evaluation of interestingness in pre-processing (i.e. selecting interesting data (peculiar data) before rule generation). In particular, our approach can mine a new class of rules: *peculiarity rules* in *multiple* databases.

So far, as examples with respect to the first two levels of the multi-database mining tasks mentioned in the Introduction, a number of databases such as Japan-survey, amino-acid data, weather, supermarket, web-log, have been tested for our approach. The results have been partly discussed in our papers [23, 24]. Currently, we are also working on the third level of the multi-database mining task, that is, mining from multiple mixed-media databases [17].

Our future work includes developing a systematic method to mine the rules from multiple databases where there are no explicitly foreign key (link) relationships, and to induce more interesting rules from the RVER model discovered from multiple databases by cooperatively using inductive and abductive reasoning.

References

[1] Agrawal R. et al. "Fast Discovery of Association Rules", *Advances in Knowledge Discovery and Data Mining*, (1996) 307-328.

[2] Bhattacharyya, G.K. and Johnson, R.A. *Statistical Concepts and Methods*, John Wiley & Sons (1977).

[3] Freitas, A.A. "On Objective Measures of Rule Surprisingness" J. Zytkow and M. Quafafou (eds.) *Principles of Data Mining and Knowledge Discovery*, LNAI 1510, Springer (1998) 1-9.

[4] Goodman, I.R., Nguyen, H.T. and Walker, E.A. *Conditional Inference and Logic for Intelligent Systems*, North-Holland (1991).

[5] Hilderman, R.J. *Mining Summaries from Databases using Domain Generalization Graphs and Objective Measures of Interestingness*, Ph.D. thesis, University of Regina (2000).

[6] Hilderman, R.J. and Hamilton, H.J. "Evaluation of Interestingness Measures for Ranking Discovered Knowledge", D. Cheung, G.J. Williams, Q. Li (Eds) *Advances in Knowledge Discovery and Data Mining*, LNAI 2035, Springer (2001) 247-259.

[7] Johnson, R.A. and Wichern, D.W. *Applied Multivariate Statistical Analysis*, Prentice Hall (1998).

[8] Lin, T.Y. "Granular Computing on Binary Relations 1: Data Mining and Neighborhood Systems", L. Polkowski and A. Skowron (eds.) *Rough Sets in Knowledge Discovery*, Vol. 1, Physica-Verlag (1998) 107-121.

[9] Liu, B., Hsu W., and Chen, S. "Using General Impressions to Analyze Discovered Classification Rules", *Proc. Third International Conference on Knowledge Discovery and Data Mining (KDD-97)*, AAAI Press (1997) 31-36.

[10] Liu, B., Hsu W., Chen, S., and Ma, Y. "Analyzing the Subjective Interestingness of Association Rules", *IEEE Intelligent Systems*, Vol.15, No.5 (2000) 47-55.

[11] Pawlak, Z. *Rough Sets, Theoretical Aspects of Reasoning about Data*, Kluwer Academic Publishers, Dordrecht, 1991.

[12] Ribeiro, J.S., Kaufman, K.A., and Kerschberg, L. "Knowledge Discovery from Multiple Databases", *Proc First Inter. Conf. on Knowledge Discovery and Data Mining (KDD-95)* (1995) 240-245.

[13] Silberschatz, A. and Tuzhilin, A. "What Makes Patterns Interesting in Knowledge Discovery Systems", *IEEE Trans. Knowl. Data Eng.*, 8(6) (1996) 970-974.

[14] Suzuki E.. "Autonomous Discovery of Reliable Exception Rules", *Proc Third Inter. Conf. on Knowledge Discovery and Data Mining (KDD-97)*, AAAI Press (1997) 259-262.

[15] Thrun, S. et al. "Automated Learning and Discovery", AI Magazine (Fall 1999) 78-82.

[16] Wrobel, S. "An Algorithm for Multi-relational Discovery of Subgroups", J. Komorowski et al. (eds.) *Principles of Data Mining and Knowledge Discovery*, LNAI 1263, Springer (1997) 367-375.

[17] Wu, J. and Zhong, N. "An Investigation on Human Multi-Perception Mechanism by Cooperatively Using Psychometrics and Data Mining Techniques", *Proc. 5th World Multi-Conference on Systemics, Cybernetics, and Informatics (SCI-01)*, in Invited Session on Multimedia Information: Managing and Processing, Vol. X (2001) 285-290.

[18] Yao, Y.Y. "Granular Computing using Neighborhood Systems", Roy, R., Furuhashi, T., Chawdhry, P.K. (eds.) *Advances in Soft Computing: Engineering Design and Manufacturing*, Springer (1999) 539-553.

[19] Yao, Y.Y. and Zhong, N. "An Analysis of Quantitative Measures Associated with Rules", N. Zhong and L. Zhou (eds.) *Methodologies for Knowledge Discovery and Data Mining*, LNAI 1574, Springer (1999) 479-488.

[20] Zadeh, L. A. "Toward a Theory of Fuzzy Information Granulation and Its Centrality in Human Reasoning and Fuzzy Logic", *Fuzzy Sets and Systems*, Elsevier Science Publishers, 90 (1997) 111-127.

[21] Zhong, N. and Ohsuga, S. "Discovering Concept Clusters by Decomposing Databases", *Data & Knowledge Engineering*, Vol.12, No.2, Elsevier (1994) 223-244.

[22] Zhong, N. and Ohsuga, S. "KOSI - An Integrated System for Discovering Functional Relations from Databases", *Journal of Intelligent Information Systems*, Vol.5, No.1, Kluwer (1995) 25-50.

[23] Zhong, N., Yao, Y.Y., and Ohsuga, S. "Peculiarity Oriented Multi-Database Mining", J. Zytkow and J. Rauch (eds.) *Principles of Data Mining and Knowledge Discovery*, LNAI 1704, Springer (1999) 136-146.

[24] Zhong, N., Ohshima, M., and Ohsuga, S. "Peculiarity Oriented Mining and Its Application for Knowledge Discovery in Amino-acid Data", D. Cheung, G.J. Williams, Q. Li (eds.) *Advances in Knowledge Discovery and Data Mining*, LNAI 2035, Springer (2001) 260-269.

POSTER

Discovering Similar Patterns for Characterising Time Series in a Medical Domain

Fernando Alonso, Juan P. Caraça-Valente, Loïc Martínez
Dept. Languages & Systems

Cesar Montes
Dept. Artificial Intelligence

Polytechnic University Madrid
{falonso, jpvalente,loic,cmontes }@fi.upm.es

Abstract

In this article, we describe the process of discovering similar patterns in time series and creating reference models for population groups in a medical domain, and particularly in the field of physiotherapy, using data mining techniques on a set of isokinetic data.

The discovered knowledge was evaluated against the expertise of a physician specialised in isokinetic techniques, and applied in the I4 (Intelligent Interpretation of Isokinetic Information) project developed in conjunction with the Spanish National Centre for Sports Research and Sciences and the School of Physiotherapy of the Spanish National Organisation for the Blind for muscular diagnosis and rehabilitation, injury prevention, training evaluation and planning, etc., of elite and blind athletes.

1. Introduction

An important domain for the application of data mining (DM) in the medical field is physiotherapy and, more specifically, muscle function assessment based on isokinetic data. Physicians collect these data using a mechanical instrument called an isokinetics machine. This machine can be described as a piece of apparatus on which patients perform strength exercises (in this case, knee extensions and flexions). This machine has the peculiarity of limiting the range of movement and the intensity of effort at a constant velocity (which explains the term isokinetic). Data concerning the strength exerted by the patient throughout the exercise are recorded and stored in the machine so that physicians can visually analyse the results using specialised computer software.

DM techniques on time series [1,2,3] were required to analyse isokinetic exercises in order to discover new and useful information for later use in a range of applications. Patterns discovered in isokinetic exercises performed by injured patients are very useful, in particular for monitoring injuries, detecting potential injuries early or discovering fraudulent sickness leaves. These patterns are also useful for creating reference models for population groups that share certain characteristics.

2. Discovering similar patterns in time series

One of the most important potential applications of DM algorithms for this sort of time series is to detect parts of the graph that are representative of an irregularity. As far as isokinetic exercises are concerned, the presence of this sort of deviations could be representative of some kind of injury, and the correct identification of the deviation could be an aid for detecting the injury in time. So, the identification of patterns (portions of data that are repeated in more than one graph) is of vital importance for being able to establish criteria by means of which to class the exercises and, therefore, patients.

Isokinetic exercises have a series of characteristics that cannot be overlooked when designing a pattern identification algorithm. Owing to the special characteristics of the individuals who complete isokinetic exercises, the graphs may have different amplitudes and be distant in time, even if the same pattern is observed. Therefore, some sort of distance has to be used to take into account not only the parts that are repeated exactly but also any that are more or less the same.

Another particular to be considered in pattern search is that there is no expert knowledge about the possible patterns and their length. Therefore, all the exercises have to be run through to get patterns of different lengths. The memory consumption and execution time of this process can be very high, and these are both factors that were considered in algorithm design.

The process of developing a DM method for identifying patterns that potentially characterise some sort of injury was divided into two phases:

1. Develop an algorithm that detects similar patterns in exercises.
2. Use the algorithm developed in point 1 to detect any patterns that appear in exercises done by patients with injuries and do not appear in exercises completed by healthy individuals.

The algorithm developed [4] is capable of detecting similar sequential patterns in a set of time series. It reuses some state-of-the-art ideas [1,5], like the A priori property to prune the search tree, but adds the Euclidean distance, used to level out insignificant differences between patterns possibly occurring in different series.

It is suitable for searching a large set of time series of non-homogeneous lengths, finding the patterns (time subsequences of undetermined length) that are repeated in any position of a significant number of series. Therefore, the algorithm will be useful for finding significant subsequences that are likely to characterise a set of non-uniform time series, even though important characteristics of these subsequences, like length or position within the time series, are unknown.

In order to test pattern discovery algorithm operation and effectiveness, a series of random curves were generated to simulate isokinetic strength curves. Figure 1 shows how long it takes the algorithm to execute depending on the number of values in the series used.

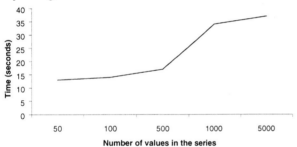

Figure 1. Execution time over number of values in the series

Algorithm execution time grows linearly as the number of elements in the time series increases. Thus, the number of values within the series would not appear to be too significant as regards algorithm execution time, as it takes the algorithm 15 seconds to execute with series that have 50 values and approximately 40 seconds with series containing 5000 elements.

Algorithm efficiency falls as the number of series increases (as shown in Figure 2). When the number of series is over 12, the time increases considerably. Thus, an increase in the number of series (as of 12) used to execute the algorithm raises algorithm execution time substantially. Therefore, it is the number of series used and not the number of elements in the series that has the biggest impact on algorithm execution time. However,

this is not a serious problem in our domain, as more than 10 series for the same injury and group of patients are seldom found.

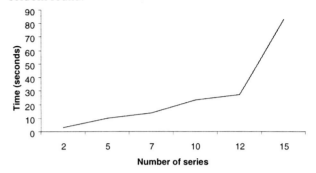

Figure 2. Execution time over number of series

It is clear that execution time also grows as the distance increases, because more patterns will be discovered when the distance is greater. If this distance is increased considerably, the tree cannot be retained in memory, and the time would rise to unsuspected levels. On the other hand, execution time is lower when the parameter ε increases. This is because the search space is smaller, as more branches are pruned.

The algorithm was applied to the data obtained from isokinetic exercises to detect injury patterns and create reference models.

3. Creating reference models for population groups

One of the most common tasks involved in the assessment of isokinetic exercises is to compare a patient's test against a reference model created beforehand. These models represent the average profile of a group of patients sharing common characteristics.

All the exercises done by individuals with the desired characteristics of weight, height, sport, sex, etc., must be selected to create a reference model for a particular population. However, there may be some heterogeneity even among patients of the same group. Some will have a series of particularities that make them significantly different from the others. Take a sport like American football, for instance, where players have very different physical characteristics. Here, it will make no sense to create a model for all the players, and individual models would have to be built for each subgroup of players with similar characteristics. Therefore, exercises have to be discriminated and the reference model has to be created using exercises among which there is some uniformity.

An expert in isokinetics used to be responsible for selecting the exercises that were to be part of the model. It is not easy to manually discard exercises that differ considerably from others. This meant that it was mostly not done. The idea we aim to implement is to automatically discard all the exercises that are different and create a model with the remainder.

The problem of comparing exercises can be simplified using the discrete Fourier transform to transfer the exercises from the time domain to the frequency domain. The fact that most of the information is concentrated in the first components of the discrete Fourier transform will be used to discard the remainder and simplify the problem. The advantage of the discrete Fourier transform is that there is an algorithm, known as the fast Fourier transform, that can calculate the required coefficients in a time of the order of $O(n \log n)$.

The number of comparisons to be made is drastically reduced using this technique, a very important factor in this case, since there are a lot of exercises for comparison in the database and comparison efficiency is vital.

Once the user has selected all the tests of the patient population to be modelled, the process for creating a new reference model is as follows:

1. Calculate the discrete Fourier transform of all the exercises.
2. Class these exercises, using some sort of indexing to rapidly discard all the exercises that are different from the one that we are searching for. R* trees [6], which divide the n-dimensional space geometrically into rectangles of n dimensions, are proposed as a very suitable indexing method for the problem. The system creates a search tree based on the R*-tree (this is an unbalanced tree) with the exercises of each class. Thus, the exercises are grouped into classes, and the groups of similar exercises are clearly identified.
3. Normally, users mostly intend to create a reference model for a particular group, and there is a clearly majority group of similar exercises, which represents the standard profile that the user is looking for, and a disperse set of groups of one or two exercises. The former are used to create a reference model, in which all the common characteristics of the exercises are unified.
4. An isokinetic exercise, or a set of isokinetic exercises, for a patient will later be able to be compared with the models stored in the database. Thus, we will be able to determine the group to which patients belong or should belong and identify what sport they should go in for, what their weaknesses are with a view to improvement or how they are likely to progress in the future.

The algorithm was implemented in the I4 project and is used in several kinds of isokinetic curve comparison. The project has produced two applications [7]: ES for Isokinetics Interpretation (*ISOCIN*), intended for any kind of patient and ES for Interpreting Isokinetics in Sport (*ISODEPOR*), which is being used at the National High Performance Centre to evaluate the muscle strength of Spanish top-competition athletes.

References

[1] R. Agrawal, C. Faloustsos and A. Swami, "Efficient similarity search in sequence databases", *Proc. of Foundations of Data Organisations and Algorithms FODO*, 1993.

[2] C. Faloutsos, M. Ranganathan and Y. Manolopoulos, "Fast subsequence matching in time series databases", *Proc. of SIGMOD 94*, Minneapolis, 1994, pp. 419-429.

[3] R. Povinelli, "Time series data mining: identifying temporal patterns for characterization and prediction of time series", Ph.D. Thesis, Milwaukee, 1999.

[4] J. P. Caraça-Valente and I. López-Chavarrías, "Discovering patterns in time series", *Proc of 6th Intl. Conf. on Knowledge Discovery and Data Mining KDD*, Boston, 2000, pp. 497-505.

[5] J. Han, G. Dong and Y. Yin, "Efficient mining of partial periodic patterns in time series database", *Proc. of Fourth International Conference on Knowledge Discovery and Data Mining*, AAAI Press, Menlo Park, 1998, pp. 214-218.

[6] N. Beckman, H.-P. Kriegel, R. Schneider and B. Seeger, "The R*-tree: an efficient and robust method for points and rectangles", *ACM SIGMOD*, 1990, pp. 322-331.

[7] F. Alonso, J. M. Barreiro, J. P. Valente and C. Montes, "Interpretation of Strength Data", *LNAI 1416*, vol. II (Proc. 11th IEA-AIE Conf. Benicassim, Spain), 1998, pp. 697-706.

Creating Ensembles of Classifiers

Nitesh Chawla, Steven Eschrich, and Lawrence O. Hall
Department of Computer Science and Engineering, ENB 118, University of South Florida
4202 E. Fowler Ave. Tampa, Fl 33620, USA
chawla, eschrich, hall@csee.usf.edu

Abstract

Ensembles of classifiers offer promise in increasing over-all classification accuracy. The availability of extremely large datasets has opened avenues for application of distributed and/or parallel learning to efficiently learn models of them. In this paper, distributed learning is done by training classifiers on disjoint subsets of the data. We examine a random partitioning method to create disjoint subsets and propose a more intelligent way of partitioning into disjoint subsets using clustering. It was observed that the intelligent method of partitioning generally performs better than random partitioning for our datasets. In both methods a significant gain in accuracy may be obtained by applying bagging to each of the disjoint subsets, creating multiple diverse classifiers. The significance of our finding is that a partition strategy for even small/moderate sized datasets when combined with bagging can yield better performance than applying a single learner using the entire dataset.

1. Introduction

Dataset sizes are continually increasing as more and more information is stored electronically. Machine learning techniques are being utilized to learn models over increasingly large feature and example spaces. Efficiently learning from these large datasets is difficult, as datasets can not always be completely loaded into a computer's memory. Reducing training set sizes to the size of available memory or less is a practical approach in machine learning. An attractive option for learning from large datasets is *distributed learning*: data and learning are distributed across different processors (and computers). Our expanded version of the paper [3] carries more detailed discussion on the related distributed learning work, and also more details on our work and experiments. The approach discussed here is to learn an ensemble of individual classifiers, with each learner creating it's own classifier from a subset of the total dataset. We examine both a random partitioning method

and a more intelligent partitioning method using clustering. With the addition of the bagging technique [2] applied to subsets contained in partitions, we show that disjoint dataset partitioning can actually yield better classifier performance than learning one model over the entire dataset.

2. Method

We describe below each of the methods used to partition a dataset into subsets from which an ensemble of classifiers can be built. In all instances, the ensemble of classifiers is composed of decision trees learned using C4.5 release 8 [4].

One of the simplest data partitioning approaches is to separate the dataset into n random disjoint subsets. The partitioning is done without respect to the class distribution within the dataset. Each disjoint subset is independently used in the generation of a decision tree classifier. This approach is well suited to distributed learning, since the entire dataset is never required to be loaded in memory at one time. Examples can be randomly chosen and distributed across a set of processors.

Fuzzy c-means (FCM) clustering [1] is used to examine the effects of intelligent partitioning of a dataset. A cluster-splitting FCM algorithm is applied to the dataset in order to create meaningful partitions of the data. The algorithm begins with two clusters ($c = 2$) and clusters until the fuzzy membership values are stable. The validity of the partition is evaluated and the "worst" cluster is split into two distinct clusters. This process is repeated until the stopping conditions are met. Since the number of clusters in the dataset is not known, values of c from 2 to 25 were used by the cluster splitting process. The splitting process is terminated early if the partition validity after clustering is worse than 5 times the best partition validity seen. This number was empirically observed to prune the search well, since a bad cluster split could almost never be improved by successive splits. Once the algorithm finishes clustering, the FCM step is repeated a final time with the best c found. A maximum membership function was used to harden the fuzzy clusters, creating a disjoint partition of the data.

3 Experiments

We evaluate the proposed approaches to learning by experiments on 7 well-known machine learning datasets. In all experiments, 10-fold cross validation is used. Results are reported as the mean classification performance over the 10 folds. The number of clusters found by FCM was taken as the number of random partitions to create. Comparisons between methods is done via a two-tailed paired two sample for means t-test among fold results, setting the confidence level, $\alpha = 0.025$.

In the random partition experiments, a simple majority vote is used to combine classification predictions. In the clustering experiments, an ask-expert combination method can be used. When FCM clustering of the training set is completed, the values of the cluster centroids are stored. When a test example is presented for classification, the closest centroid (using the Euclidean distance metric) is determined. This centroid corresponds to a cluster of training data, from which a decision tree was created. Only this decision tree (i.e. the expert) is consulted for a classification prediction.

The results of training and testing ensembles of classifiers according to the several partitioning methods described above can be seen in Table 1.

Dataset	Clusters	Full C4.5	Random	FCM
Page-block	2	96.90	96.82	96.95
Phoneme	5	86.50$^+$	83.44	85.99
Satimage	9	86.30	87.44$^+$	86.01
Pendigits	4	96.57$^+$	96.06	96.42
Mammography	2	98.50	98.51	98.40
Letter	2	88.10^{*+}	83.54	86.08
Shuttle	3	99.96$^+$	99.92	99.95

$^+$ C4.5/Random winner * C4.5/Cluster winner

Table 1. Partitioning Results vs. C4.5.

The next phase of experiments was to investigate the bagging phenomenon within our partitions. The resulting clusters and random partitions from Table 1 were bagged using 50 bags per partition (80% bag size). Most significantly, a random partition of a dataset, when combined with bagging performs better than a single decision tree learning the entire dataset.

4 Conclusion

In this paper, we present a novel approach to distributed learning using fuzzy clustering. This intelligent method of partitioning a dataset is compared to simpler, random methods of partitioning. In general, intelligent partitioning of a

Dataset	Full C4.5	Random Bag 50 bags	FCM Bag 50 bags
Page-block	96.90	97.11	97.26*
Phoneme	86.50	85.77	88.71*
Satimage	86.30	87.61$^+$	86.76
Pendigits	96.57	97.22$^+$	98.18*
Mammography	98.50	98.52	98.78*
Letter	88.10	90.82$^+$	93.01*
Shuttle	99.96^{*+}	99.89	99.93

$^+$ C4.5/Random winner * C4.5/Cluster winner

Table 2. Bagging Results.

dataset provides better performance than random partitioning, and generally performs as well as C4.5 over the entire dataset. The results presented in this paper suggest that for very large datasets, the creation of ensembles of classifiers can perform reasonably well.

Interestingly, our results indicate that bagging of individual partitions can yield better results than learning from the entire dataset. It is surprising as bagged classifiers created from subsets, in effect, see much less data. Even in the case of random partitioning, where any individual classifier created on a subset often performs significantly worse than a single classifier learned on the entire dataset, bagging on disjoint subsets can improve performance. We believe this is due to the same effects that cause bagging to improve performance in general - bagging produces diverse classifiers from the data partitions, despite the smaller number of examples within a partition. We have thus proposed a novel and effective three-stage learning technique - partition, bag each partitioned subset, and learn.

5 Acknowledgements

This research was partially supported by the United States Department of Energy through the Sandia National Laboratories ASCI VIEWS Data Discovery Program, contract number DE-AC04-76DO00789 and by Tripos, Inc.

References

[1] J. C. Bezdek and S. K. Pal, editors. *Fuzzy Models For Pattern Recognition*. IEEE Press, New Jersey, 1991.

[2] L. Breiman. Bagging predictors. *Machine Learning*, 24(2):123–140, 1996.

[3] N. Chawla, S. Eschrich, and L. O. Hall. Creating ensembles of classifiers. Technical Report ISL-01-01, University of South Florida, http://isl.csee.usf.edu/reports, 2001.

[4] J. Quinlan. *C4.5: Programs for Machine Learning*. Morgan Kaufmann, San Mateo, CA, 1992.

Association Rules Enhanced Classification of Underwater Acoustic Signal

Jie Chen[1], Haiying Li[2], Shiwei Tang[1]

[1] National Laboratory on Machine Perception, Peking University, P. R. China

[2] National Key Laboratory of Underwater Information Processing and Control, Northwestern Polytechnical University, P. R. China

chenjie@rdb01.pku.edu.cn, lizshun@nwpu.edu.cn, tsw@pku.edu.cn

Abstract

Classification of underwater acoustic signal is one of the important fields of pattern recognition. Inspired by the experience of training man experts in sonar, we propose a two-phase training algorithm to exploit the association rules to reveal the understandable intrinsic rules contributing to correct classification in the known misclassification datasets in this paper. Preliminary experimental results demonstrate the potential of classification association rules to enhance the accuracy of classification of underwater acoustic signals.

1. Introduction

Classification of underwater acoustic signal is one of the important fields of pattern recognition and has been extensively studied in the last ten years [1]. Researches on this topic fall into two categories: feature extraction and classification algorithm. Though many techniques of feature extraction have been developed, features from different classes are remarkably overlapped due to the complicated mechanism of vessel radiated noise [2]. Several kinds of neural networks have been used as classifiers of vessel radiated noises [3], yet the classification of underwater acoustic signal is still a tough problem owing to the complicated mechanism of subtle targets and their diverse environments. Bearing this problem in mind, we notice that some up to date research results on classification and association mining are beneficial to tackle the above problem.

Classification and association mining were studied in isolation for many years until recently. [4] discussed the use of association rule mining for the discovery of models of the data that may not cover all classes or all examples. [5] used association rules and prunes rules using both the minimum support and the pessimistic estimation to implement a classification algorithm called CBA (Classification Based on Associations). [6] proposed a method to build a decision tree from association rules.

However, the potential of these association rule based classification techniques has not been fully uncovered, and few papers using these techniques to the field of target recognition have been reported up to now. Learning from the experience of training man experts in sonar, we propose a two-phase training algorithm with association rules enhanced classifier for the classification of underwater acoustic signal. Usually training an expert need a long and laborious procedure. Sometimes they have to listen to and distinguish the records of some similar but often mistaken vessels. Inspired by this procedure, we aim to exploit the association rules to reveal the understandable intrinsic rules contributing to correct classification in the known misclassification datasets so as to build a classifier with high accuracy and robustness, which combines the advantages of both probabilistic neural networks (PNN) and association rules based classifiers.

2. CBA

The main idea of CBA algorithm is to build a classifier from the complete set of classification association rules that satisfy the user-specified minimum support and minimum confidence. Classification rules are a special subset of association rules whose right-hand-side are restricted to the classification class attribute. Compared with neural network classifiers, classification rule built classifiers are easy to understand and realize. Here we omit the detail of CBA algorithm that is composed of two parts, including a rule induction algorithm and a classifier-building algorithm.

3. Algorithm of association rules enhanced classification

Our objectives are (1) to separate the misclassification region of the feature space, and (2) to dig out the intrinsic rules that contribute to make correct classification in the misclassification region. Hence we propose a two-phase training algorithm to enhance the predicative accuracy of classifier.

For a given training set T, a portion of training cases is treated as an actual training set T' in the first phase. Because of ease of training and a sound statistical foundation in Bayesian estimation theory, we train a probabilistic neural network called PNN-1 to model the training set T'. Then input the whole set T into the trained network, thus T falls into two subsets noted by T_c and T_m respectively. The former is a set that has been correctly classified, and the latter is the rest that has been misclassified.

In the next phase, we suppose that there are effective low dimension patterns in the misclassification region though high dimension patterns in the misclassification region are overlapped. Intuitively, classification association rules can be exploited to discover these possible low dimension patterns. Thus the CBA algorithm is applied to mine the classification association rules in T_m and construct an association rules based classifier CBA-1, which is of the following format

$$< r_1, r_2, ..., r_n, default\_class >$$

where r_i is a classification association rule selected from all rules, which are both frequent and accurate. Obviously, CBA-1 is a local or partial classifier with respect to the whole feature space, therefore it is necessary to build a probabilistic neural network PNN-2 to perform a classification of two subsets T_c and T_m. For a new input case, the classifier PNN-2 is used to decide which sub classifier will be chosen as the final classifier. If the new case is classified as M, it will be classified by CBA-1, otherwise, it will be further classified by PNN-1.

Based on the partition of training set T and enhanced by classification association rules, it is reasonable that new cases within or near to the misclassification region T_m will be correctly classified by CBA-1. On the other hand, most other new cases classified into C class will tend to be correctly classified by PNN-1, or at least not to be more easily misclassified than using the PNN-1 to classify them directly.

4. Experimental results

A preliminary experiment applying the proposed algorithm to the classification of four classes of real vessel radiated noise data, which have 964 cases altogether, is carried out. Feature vectors extracted from these cases compose the whole dataset. We use a half of the set as training set T and a half of T as the actual training set T'. The left 482 cases are tested using the two-phase constructed classifies (PNN-2, PNN-1 and

CBA-1) compared with a straightforward probabilistic neural network classifier PNN-0 treating T as training set directly. Table 1 shows the results of 10-fold cross validation. All recognition rates of test set are the average of 10 folds, and we keep to use the same training and test sets for the PNN-0 and two-phase constructed classifiers during the cross validation. The class labels of four classes of vessel radiated noises are I, II, III, and IV respectively.

Table 1. Test results of two-phase constructed and PNN-0 classifiers.

Classifier	I	II	III	IV	Average
PNN-0	91.5%	82.2%	80.7%	86.9%	85.3%
Two-phase	92.1%	82.0%	84.3%	89.3%	86.9%

5. Conclusion

Inspired by the experience of training man experts in sonar, we propose a two-phase training algorithm to exploit the association rules to reveal the understandable intrinsic rules contributing to correct classification in the known misclassification datasets in this paper. Preliminary experimental results from real data demonstrate the potential of classification association rules to enhance the accuracy of classification of underwater acoustic signals. In our future work, we will focus on studying the impact of the partition of the feature space and discretization of continuous attributes. We suggest that using this algorithm as an incremental training algorithm and adding experts interfered selection of rules are beneficial to improve the performance of practical classification system for underwater acoustic signal.

References

[1] J. Huang, J. Zhao, and Y. Xie, "Source classification using pole method of AR model", IEEE ICASSP-97, 1997, Vol. 1, pp. 567 -570

[2] J. Chen, H. Li, J. Sun, and Z. Li, "Fractal feature of underwater acoustic signals in zero-crossing domain", WESTPRAC VII, Kumamoto, Japan, 2000, pp. 1129-132

[3] X. Li, F. Zhu, "Application of the zero-crossing rate, LOFAR spectrum and wavelet to the feature extraction of passive sonar signals", Proc. 3rd World Conf. Intell. Cont.& Auto., 2000, Vol. 4, pp. 2461-2463

[4] K. Ali, S. Manganaris, and R. Srikant, "Partial classification using association rules", KDD, 1997, pp. 115-118

[5] B. Liu, W. Hsu, and Y. Ma, "Integrating classification and association rule mining", KDD, 1998, pp. 80-86

[6] K. Wang, S. Zhou, and Y. He, "Growing decision tree on support-less association rules", KDD, 2000, pp. 265-269

Efficient Splitting Rules based on the Probabilities of Pre-Assigned Intervals

June-Suh Cho
IBM T.J. Watson Research Center
30 Saw Mill River Rd., Hawthorne, NY 10532
junesuh@us.ibm.com

Nabil R. Adam
CIMIC, Rutgers University
180 University Avenue, Newark, NJ 07102
adam@adam.rutgers.edu

Abstract

This paper describes new methods for classification in order to find an optimal tree. Unlike the current splitting rules that are provided by searching all threshold values, this paper proposes the splitting rules that are based on the probabilities of pre-assigned intervals.

1. Introduction

Most methods of classification repeatedly search for the best split of a subset by searching all possible threshold values for all variables [4, 1, 7, 5, 8, 6]. However, these methods do not efficiently find precise cutoff points when applied to continuous variables. In addition, they have computational complexity in split searching that requires long computation time.

We propose simple splitting rules based on minimizing the sum of variance and maximizing the difference of probabilities of intervals. Interval-based methods reduce the computational complexity of finding the optimal cutoff point since the number of intervals is less than the number of all possible threshold values.

In experiments, we demonstrate that our methods properly classify image objects based on new split rules. Our approach produces average recall and precision over 85% for experimental image data. We also describe the computational complexity of our split selection approach, which is better than exhaustive search methods. In continuous variables, $m-1$ is for our approach and $l-1$ is for the exhaustive search approach, where m is the number of intervals and l is the number of all possible threshold values. The number of possible splits is $l - 1 > m - 1$, where $l > m > 1$.

2 The Proposed Splitting Rules

In our approach, we assume that there are two classes, which are class 0 and class 1. We give definitions as follows:

$n = n_L + n_R$

n_L, n_R = the number of objects in the left and the right buckets
n^1, n^0 = the number objects of class 1 and 0 in the parent node
$n_L^1, n_R^1, n_L^0, n_R^0$ = the number of objects of class 1 and 0 in the left and right buckets

$p_L = \frac{n_L}{n}, p_R = \frac{n_R}{n}, p_L^1 = \frac{n_L^1}{n_L}, p_R^1 = \frac{n_R^1}{n_R}, p_L^0 = \frac{n_L^0}{n_L}, p_R^0 = \frac{n_R^0}{n_R}$

Given a split with left and right buckets, the probabilities of class 0 and class 1 on the left and the right satisfy $p_L^0 + p_L^1 = 1, p_R^0 + p_R^1 = 1$, respectively.

In this paper, we consider two kinds of splitting rule. One is to select an optimal cutoff point by minimizing the sum of variances of intervals. Minimizing the sum of variances is equivalent to maximizing the sum of weighted probabilities in the left and the right bucket as follows:

$$\min_c[1 - (q_L p_L^1 + q_R p_R^1)] \equiv \max_c[q_L p_L^1 + q_R p_R^1]$$

Another criterion for splitting maximizing the difference of probabilities between the left and the right bucket. This approach is based on the search for interesting regions of the data regardless of non-interesting regions. This criterion can be expressed as follows:

$$\max_c |p_L^1 - p_R^1|$$

In this section, the algorithm to select optimal cutoff point under each splitting rule and the method to combine these two rules are summarized. The hybrid splitting rule is to compromise the advantages and disadvantage in minimizing the variances and maximizing the difference of probabilities in the left and the right bucket.

- Splitting rule 1.

1. Split a predictor variable into I_i intervals, $1 \le i \le L$.

2. For each interval I_i, calculate $p_i^1 = P(\text{class } 1 \mid x \in I_i)$ and $q_i = P(\text{class } 1 \mid \text{class } 1 \text{ in parent node}, x \in I_i)$.

3. From the left, the right interval, or the interval which has the highest probability, add up the intervals to find a cutoff point c by maximizing the sum of weighted probabilities in each intervals as follows:

$$d_I = \max_c[q_L p_L^1 + q_R p_R^1]$$

- Splitting rule 2.

Classes	Plate	Cup	Pan	Pot
Minimum Error Rate	6.49%	5.32%	7.67%	10.88%

Table 1. Average Minimum Error Rate on Training Datasets.

Classes	Avg. Precision	Avg. Recall	F-score
Plate	95%	93%	93.9%
Cup	99%	94%	96.4%
Pan	94%	92%	92.9%
Pot	88%	89%	88.5%

Table 2. Performance evaluation with Precision, Recall, and F-score.

1. For each interval I_i, calculate $p_i^1 = P(\text{class } 1 \mid x \in I_i)$.

2. From the left, the right interval, or the interval which has the highest probability, add up the intervals to select a cutoff point c by maximizing as follows:

$$d_{II} = \max_c |p_L^1 - p_R^1|$$

- Hybrid splitting rule.

1. For each interval I_i, calculate $p_i^1 = P(\text{class } 1 \mid x \in I_i)$ and $q_i = P(\text{class } 1 \mid \text{class } 1 \text{ in parent node}, x \in I_i)$.

2. Calculate two statistics d_I, d_{II} and give a rank to them according to the grouping of the interval.

3. The average ranks for each group are given by two splitting rules. When the average ranks are the same, the priority is given to the first splitting rule because there is still a chance to split the other predictor variables later.

4. Take a cutoff point c with the highest rank.

We stop splitting the tree if the sample size in some bucket is less than a user-specified value or there is no significant different variables under the splitting rules.

3 Experimental Results

Experiment results are represented by 300 objects of images from image databases of electronic catalogs. The objects of images are categorized by semantics, such as pan, pot, cup, and plate. We have performed the feature extraction [2] for the electronic catalogs to extract the image parameters of the image objects.

We assigned the size of intervals as 20% of the total number of objects. We used 120 objects for the training data set, and 180 objects for the test data sets using Bootstrap [3] method because of the size of data. Table 1 shows the accuracy of classifier for plate and cup as well as pan and pot. This table shows average minimum error rate for plate/cup and pan/pot on the training set. Experiments have been implemented using Matlab for test the split rules.

We described recall and precision that are used to evaluate the effectiveness of classification as shown in Table 2.

Methods	Cup		Plate		Pan		Pot	
	train	test	train	test	train	test	train	test
Hybrid	94.6%	98.7%	93.5%	96.9%	92.3%	96.4%	89.1%	91.8%
CART	92.7%	96.2%	93.4%	97.2%	92.4%	96%	93.2%	94.5%
S-plus	90.3%	94.6%	89.8%	92.9%	91%	93.8%	88.7%	91.7%
C4.5	95.1%	99.1%	94.4%	96.4%	93.2%	96.2%	93.4%	94.2%

Table 3. The classification accuracy using our method and the existing methods.

Five test sets were run through the classifier, and the recall and precision scores averaged. We also evaluated performance using F-score to combine recall and precision with a single value metric. F-score is the method for calculating an appropriate value without being biased toward either recall or precision. If recall and precision score high at the same time, F-score becomes close to 1 in this case, the method has a good capability of classifying.

In Table 3, it shows simple comparison between our method and other existing methods such as CART, S-plus, and C4.5. It reports the classification accuracy using them for two cases, and classification accuracy is defined as follows: $accuracy = \frac{number\ of\ objects\ correctly\ classified}{total\ number\ of\ objects}$

4 Conclusion

In this paper, we have introduced the methods to perform classification that are new splitting rules based on the probabilities of pre-assigned intervals, and we used the binary tree splits to find cutoff points.

In this paper, new methods provided a means of finding the optimal cutoff points and a simple and fast classifier with reasonable accuracy to recognize the objects from a large image database.

References

[1] L. Breiman, J. Friedman, R. Olshen, and C. Stone. *Classification and Regression Trees*. Wadsworth, 1984.

[2] J.-S. Cho, A. Gangopadhyay, and N. Adam. Feature Extraction for Content-based Image search in Electronic Commerce. In *MIS/OA International Conference*, 2000.

[3] B. Efron. Estimating the error rate of a prediction rule: Improvement on cross-validation. *J. of the American Statistical Association*, 1983.

[4] D. M. Hawkins and G. V. Kass. *Automatic Interaction Detection*. Cambridge Univ Press, 1982.

[5] W.-Y. Loh and Y.-S. Shih. Split selection methods for classification trees. *Statistica Sinica*, 1997.

[6] S. K. Murty, S. Kasif, and S. Salzberg. A system for induction of oblique decision trees. *Journal of Artificial Intelligence Research*, 1994.

[7] J. R. Quinlan. *C4.5: Programs for Machine Learning*. Morgan Kaufmann, 1993.

[8] R. Rastogi and K. Shim. PUBLIC: A Decision Tree Classifier that Integrates Building and Pruning. In *Proceedings of the 24nd VLDB Conference*, 1998.

Inexact Field Learning:
An Approach to Induce High Quality Rules from Low Quality Data

Honghua Dai(*), **Xiaoshu Hang(**)** **Gang Li(*)**   HDAI@DEAKIN.EDU.AU

(*)School of Computing and Mathematics, Deakin University, 662 Blackburn Road, Clayton, VIC 3168, Australia
(**)Department of Automation, University of Science and Technology of China, Hefei, 230031, China

Abstract

To avoid low quality problem caused by low quality data, this paper introduces an inexact field learning approach which derives rules by working on the fields of attributes with respect to classes, rather than on individual point values of attributes. The experimental results show that field learning achieved a higher prediction accuracy rate on new unseen test cases which is particularly true when the learning is performed on large low quality data.

1. Introduction

Achieving higher prediction accuracy is the essential goal of almost all machine learning algorithms. Most traditional inductive algorithms perform learning by looking at each individual attribute (point) value of training instances (Shavlik, 1990) and trying to figure out a rule fitting the training data. Two major weaknesses of this approach are: (1) the learning could easily be misled by low quality data (LQD); and (2) the derived rules could overfit LQD. In addition, there is no way for these algorithms to provide a best estimation in the derived rules in the case of with many missing values in the training data. In opposite to deriving rules by looking at point values of training instances, one possible way is to induce rules by looking at the range of the possible values of each attribute in the instances.

2. Inexact Field Learning

Given set of training instances $D_{Training} = I = \{I_1, I_2, \ldots, I_m\}$, $b = (\gamma_i)^T$, $(1 \le i \le m)$ is called an *instance right hand vector*. We define

$$A = (a_1, a_2, \ldots, a_n) \qquad (1)$$

in which

$$a_j = \begin{pmatrix} a_{1j} \\ a_{2j} \\ \ldots \\ a_{mj} \end{pmatrix} \qquad (2)$$

$(1 \le j \le n)$.

Let $C = \{c_1, c_2\}$ be the set of two classes, let γ_i be the value of the output variable γ in the instance I_i, thus, $\gamma_i \in C (1 \le i \le m)$. A typical two class classification problem is that $c_1 = P$ and $c_2 = N$, where P refers to the positive class and N refers to the negative class. In formula (1), for each column in the instance matrix A, i.e, for each $a_j (1 \le j \le n)$, we classify all the elements in a_j into two subsets $a_j^{(1)}$ and $a_j^{(2)}$ according to the following rule: if $\gamma_i = c_1$ then put a_{ij} into $a_j^{(1)}$, otherwise, put $a_{ij} (i = 1, 2, \ldots, m)$ into $a_j^{(2)}$.

Let

$$h_{j_u}^{(1)} = \max_{a_{ij} \in a_j^{(1)}} \{a_{ij}|_{1 \le i \le m, 1 \le j \le n}\} \qquad (3)$$

$$h_{j_l}^{(1)} = \min_{a_{ij} \in a_j^{(1)}} \{a_{ij}|_{1 \le i \le m, 1 \le j \le n}\} \qquad (4)$$

Similarly we let

$$h_{j_u}^{(2)} = \max_{a_{ij} \in a_j^{(2)}} \{a_{ij}|_{1 \le i \le m, 1 \le j \le n}\} \qquad (5)$$

$$h_{j_l}^{(2)} = \min_{a_{ij} \in a_j^{(2)}} \{a_{ij}|_{1 \le i \le m, 1 \le j \le n}\} \qquad (6)$$

Thus, we have found the bounds (fields) $[h_{j_l}^{(k)}, h_{j_u}^{(k)}]$ $(k = 1, 2)$ for each attribute x_j corresponding to each class $c_k(k = 1, 2)$. Let $h_j^{(k)} = [h_{j_l}^{(k)}, h_{j_u}^{(k)}]$ That is, $h_j^{(k)}(k = 1, 2)$ is the field of attribute x_j which supports the class $c_k(k = 1, 2)$. By the above processing, we found the defining field $h_j^{(k)}(k = 1, 2)$ of each attribute $x_j(1 \le j \le n)$ with respect to each class $c_k(k = 1, 2)$. In general, for $k_1 \ne k_2$, $h_j^{(k_1)} \ne h_j^{(k_2)}$. That is for different classes c_{k_1}, c_{k_2}, the values of attribute x_j with respect to classes c_{k_1} and c_{k_2} would be different. This basic feature makes learning by working on fields possible. That is to say by using these fields we could construct rules to classify the classes. After all the fields have been found, we may apply a different learning methodology on them. Different learning methodologies may result in different field learning algorithms. The problem now is how do we apply these fields to induce a rule? The following formula (8) gives a way to derive inexact rules in field learning.

Let $h_j^{(P)} \cap h_j^{(N)} = [a, b]$, for any small number $\epsilon > 0$, if $b \pm \epsilon \in h_j^{(P)}$ and $a + \epsilon \notin h_j^{(N)}$ or $a - \epsilon \notin h_j^{(N)}$, then, a general formula can be applied for classification purposes,

$$\mu_{c_1}(x_j) = \begin{cases} 0 & x_j \in h_j^{(N)} - h_j^{(P)} \\ 1 & x_j \in h_j^{(P)} - h_j^{(N)} \\ \frac{x_j - a}{b - a} & x_j \in h_j^{(P)} \cap h_j^{(N)} \end{cases} \quad (7)$$

The formula (8) represents how strong the attribute x_j support the class c_k. It can be regarded as a general form of the six formulas described in (Dai, 1994; Dai & Ciesielski, 1995). It is obvious that the function $\mu_{c_1}(x_j)$ is a fuzzy membership function which describes how strong the attribute support the class c_1. Such a function is also known as a *contribution function* (Dai, 1994; Dai & Ciesielski, 1995). Therefore this learning approach is a fuzzy learning approach or an inexact learning approach. To avoid having a LPA problem, the rules can be formed in the way that when we apply the derived rule in solving a real world problem, the decision can be made not based on an individual attribute value nor on an individual field. It is made based on what the majority of the fields suggest. One way for achieving this purpose is instead of using a rule like

$$\mu_{c_1}(x_j) > \alpha_j$$

, We use

$$\bar{\alpha} = \frac{1}{\bar{n}} \sum_{j=1}^{\bar{n}} \mu_{c_1}(x_j) > \alpha \quad (8)$$

for all $\bar{n}$ attributes which contribute to class c_1.

In (Dai, 1994; Dai & Ciesielski, 1995) we introduced a specific field learning algorithm, the Fish_net learning algorithm(Dai, 1994). Suppose **I** is the instance space, **R** is the rules space, $I_n \subset \mathbf{I}$ is a set of n instances, then our Fish_net learning algorithm can be formally represented as:

FISH_NET LEARNING ALGORITHM (DAI & CIESIELSKI, 1995)

Input: I_n;
begin:
    Construct fish_net $\mathbf{F}_n$ from the given data set I_n;
    Contract the constructed fish_net $\mathbf{F}_n$;
    Pick a rule $r \in \mathbf{R}$ roughly consistent with I_n;
    Optimize the parameters and threshold to refine the discovered rule r;
    Output r;
end

In the Fish_net algorithm, the Fish_net is an extension of a field. The algorithm uses the formula (8) in the contraction of the constructed fish_net $\mathbf{F}_n$.

Theorem 2.1 *Let* $h_j^{(k)} = [h_{j_l}^{(k)}, h_{j_u}^{(k)}]$ $(k = 1, 2, \ldots, s)$ *be the field of the attribute* $x_j (1 \leq j \leq n)$ *with respect to the class* $c_k (1 \leq k \leq s)$. *If there is one and at least one attribute* x_{j_0} *whose value with respect to the class* c_{k_0} *makes* $c_{k_0} \neq c_k (k_0 \neq k, k = 1, 2, \ldots, s)$, *then it is possible to find a rule which can classify* c_{k_0} *within a limited time and using a limited number of instances.*

Proof:
According to the assumption, suppose that the values of attribute x_{j_0} with respect to the class c_{k_0} are within $[a, b]$, and $[a, b]$ makes $c_{k_0} \neq c_k$ for all k ($k_0 \neq k, k = 1, 2, \ldots, s$). In this case, at least one rule can be found:

$$(x_{j_0} \geq a) \wedge (x_{j_0} \leq b) \longrightarrow c_{k_0} \quad (9)$$

and the values within $[a, b]$ were derived from a limited number of instances, and of course, within a limited time.

$\square$

3. Complexity of Inexact Field Learning

We consider a basic field learning algorithm first. Let A_F be a field learning algorithm, $\|I\|$ be the number of instanc es provided to the learning algorithm A_F, $\|A\|$ be the number of attrib utes in each instance. For generating the field of each attribute, the instan ces are examined just once. Hence the total number of instances visited is $O(\|I\|)$. To generate the fields for all the attributes, in each instance $\|A\|$ attributes are examined. Therefore, the total number o f attributes examinations is $O(\|I\|.\|A\|)$. After the fields are generated, the rule will be derived by examining the generated fields. As each attribute has exactly one field with respect to each class, therefore altogether we have $\|A\|.\|C\|$ fields. In the expression $\|C\|$ is the total number of classes. The cost for this is almost equivalent to one instance examination which is a constant. So it can be ignored. This shows that a basic field learning is an order $\|I\|$ algorithm, i.e $O(\|I\|)$.

4. Field Learning Versus Point Learning

Field learning and point learning are different learning strategies. Under these learning strategies we may develop various learning algorithms. The main difference between these two learning strategies is that point learning induces rules through consistent generalization by looking at each individual point value a_{ij} $(i = 1, \ldots, m; j = 1, \ldots, n)$, whereas field learning induces rules through consistent generalization by looking at the fields $h_j^{(k)}(k = 1, 2, \ldots, s)$ of the attributes $x_j (1 \leq j \leq n)$.

Let r be a rule, I_i be an instance and $D_{Training}$ be the training instance set, field learning and point learning algorithms can be formally described as follows:

Algorithm 4.1 Point Learning
1. Let r be given the first positive instance;
2. If the next I_i is positive, do the consistent generalization on r and I_i, and form a new r (we need to look at each value of r and I_i, we assume that r is in some form or structure), otherwise, if the next I_i is negative, flush inconsistent elements from r (we also need to look at each value of r and I_i).
3. If $D_{Training}$ is not empty, go to 2.

Algorithm 4.2 Field Learning
1. Work out the fields $h_j^{(k)}(k = 1, 2, \ldots, s)$ of each attribute x_j from all instances $I_i(1 \leq i \leq m)$ in $D_{Training}$.
2. Induce rules by working on the derived fields $h_j^{(k)} = [h_{j_l}^{(k)}, h_{j_u}^{(k)}]$ $(k = 1, 2, \ldots, s; j = 1, 2, \ldots, n)$.

5. Experimental Results

We tested our inexact field learning algorithm on three very large real observational meteorological data bases, (1) Victorian rainfall data sets, (2) Latrobe valley rainfall data sets and (3) the Wuhan heavy rain data sets. Two of these data sets are LQD which contain noise, erroneous data, missing data and irrelevant features. Victorian Rainfall data set is a relatively good quality data set. It contains no missing data, and almost no noise and no erroneous data.

Accuracy. Table 1 shows that C4.5 achieved a better results on training data sets VD_{126}^{2000} and LD_{520}^{2000} which are 97% and 98.7% against 79% and 76.7% achieved by the inexact field learning algorithm, Fish-net. However Table 2 shows that on test data sets, the inexact field learning algorithm, Fish-net achieved better results on all three data sets which are 86.4%, 78% and 76.8% against 68%, 70% and 57% achieved by standard C4.5.

Time Cost. Experimental results also show that both FISH-NET and C4.5 are linear in number of instances. However as field learning visits instances once only, the time cost is significantly less than C4.5. The CPU time spent by C4.5 in constructing a decision tree from the

Data Sets	Ins #	Att #	FN	C4.5
VD_{126}^{2000}	2000	126	79%	97%
LD_{520}^{2000}	2000	520	76.7%	98.7%
WD_{8965}^{45}	45	8965	98.3%	98%

Table 1. General Accuracy Comparison Table on Training Data Sets

Data Sets	Ins #	Att #	FN	C4.5
VD_{126}^{1000}	1000	126	**78%**	**70%**
LD_{520}^{1000}	1000	520	**76.8%**	**57%**
WD_{8965}^{9}	9(*)	8965	**86.4%**	**68%**

(*) Using leave-9-out technique(Dai, 1994)

Table 2. General Accuracy Comparison Table on Test Data Sets

data set LD^{3000} is almost 9611 seconds, whereas it is only 335 seconds for the Fish_net algorithm. The CPU time used by C4.5 is more than 28 times that used by Fish_net.

6. Conclusions and Further Work

In conclusion, as a learning approach, field learning can derive rules from given data efficiently. Our experimental results show that the rules derived by the inexact field learning algorithm, Fish_net, achieved better prediction accuracy tested on new unseen LQD bases although C4.5 achieved a better accuracy rate on training data sets. The test results also show that field learning is a linear learning approach. The time cost of the inexact field learning algorithm Fish_net in finding rules is significantly less than that of C4.5.

Field learning could also be extensively implemented by introducing interval arithmetic and probability and statistics. We believe that this field learning approach would be more appropriate in the real application areas where high quality data are not available and all the condition variables are continuous.

References

Dai, H. (1994). *Learning of forecasting rules from large noisy meteorological data.* Doctoral dissertation, Department of Computer Science, RMIT University.

Dai, H., & Ciesielski, V. (1995). *Inexact field learning using the FISH-NET algorithm* (Technical Report 95/223). Department of Computer Science.

Shavlik, J. W. (1990). *Readings in machine learning.* San Mateo,California: Morgan Kaufmann Publishers,INC.

Incremental Support Vector Machine Construction

Carlotta Domeniconi   Dimitrios Gunopulos
Computer Science Department
University of California
Riverside, CA 92521
{carlotta,dg}@cs.ucr.edu

Abstract

SVMs suffer from the problem of large memory require-ment and CPU time when trained in batch mode on large data sets. We overcome these limitations, and at the same time make SVMs suitable for learning with data streams, by constructing incremental learning algorithms.

We first introduce and compare different incremental learning techniques, and show that they are capable of pro-ducing performance results similar to the batch algorithm, and in some cases superior condensation properties. We then consider the problem of training SVMs using stream data. Our objective is to maintain an updated represen-tation of recent batches of data. We apply incremental schemes to the problem and show that their accuracy is comparable to the batch algorithm.

1. Introduction

Many applications that involve massive data sets are emerging. Examples are: telephone records, sales logs, multimedia data. When developing classifiers using learn-ing methods, while a large number of training data can help reducing the generalization error, the learning process itself can get computationally intractable.

One would like to consider all training examples simulta-neously, in order to accurately estimate the underlying class distributions. Howerer, these data sets are far too large to fit in main memory, and are typically stored in secondary storage devices, making their access particularly expensive. The fact that not all examples can be loaded into memory at once has two important consequences: the learning algo-rithm won't be able to see all data in one single batch, and is not allowed to "remember" too much of the data scanned in the past. As a consequence, scaling up classical learning al-gorithms to handle extremely large data sets and meet these requirements is an important research issue [15], [4].

One approach to satisfy these constraints is to consider incremental learning techniques, in which only a subset of the data is to be considered at each step of the learning pro-cess.

Support Vector Machines (SVMs) [17] have been suc-cessfully used as a classification tool in a variety of areas [9, 2, 12]. The solid theoretical foundations that have in-spired SVMs convey desirable computational and learning theoretic properties to the SVM's learning algorithm. An-other appealing feature of SVMs is the sparseness repre-sentation of the decision boundary they provide. The loca-tion of the separating hyperplane is specified via real-valued weights on the training examples. Those training examples that lie far away from the hyperplane do not participate in its specification and therefore receive zero weight. Only training examples that lie close to the decision boundary between the two classes (support vectors) receive non-zero weights.

Therefore, SVMs seem well suited to be trained accord-ing to an incremental learning fashion [16, 11]. In fact, since their design allows the number of support vectors to be small compared to the total number of training examples, they provide a compact representation of the data, to which new examples can be added as they become available.

New optimization approaches that specifically exploit the structure of the SVM have also been developed for scal-ing up the learning process. See [1, 14, 3].

2. Incremental Learning with SVMs

In order to make the SVM learning algorithm incremen-tal, we can partition the data set in batches that fit into mem-ory. Then, at each incremental step, the representation of the data seen so far is given by the set of support vectors de-scribing the learned decision boundary (along with the cor-responding weights). Such support vectors are incorporated with the new incoming batch of data to provide the training data for the next step. Since the design of SVMs allows the number of support vectors to be small compared to the total number of training examples, this scheme should provide a compact representation of the data set.

It is reasonable to expect that the model incrementally built won't be too far from the model built with the complete data set at once (batch mode). This is because, at each incremental step, the SVM remembers the essential class boundary information regarding the seen data, and this information contributes properly to generate the classifier at the successive iteration.

Once a new batch of data is loaded into memory, there are different possibilities for the updating of the current model. Here we explore four different techniques. For all the techniques, at each step only the learned model from the previously seen data (preserved in form of support vectors) is kept in memory.

Error-driven technique (ED). This technique is a variation of the method introduced in [11], in which both a percentage of the misclassified and correctly classified data is retained for incremental training. The Error-driven technique, instead, keeps only the misclassified data. Given the model SVM_t at time t, new data are loaded into memory and classified using SVM_t. If the data is misclassified, it is kept, otherwise it is discarded. Once a given number n_e of misclassified data is collected, the update of SVM_t takes place: the support vectors of SVM_t, together with the n_e misclassified points, are used as training data to obtain the new model SVM_{t+1}.

Fixed-partition technique (FP). This technique has been previously introduced in [16]. The training data set is partitioned in batches of fixed size. When a new batch of data is loaded into memory, it is added to the current set of support vectors; the resulting set gives the training set used to train the new model. The support vectors obtained from this process are the new representation of the data seen so far, and they are kept in memory.

Exceeding-margin technique (EM). Given the model SVM_t at time t, new data $\{(\mathbf{x}_i, y_i)\}$ are loaded into memory. The algorithm checks if $(\mathbf{x}_i, y_i)$ exceeds the margin defined by SVM_t, i.e. if $y_i f_t((\mathbf{x}_i)) \leq 1$. If the condition is satisfied the point is kept, otherwise it is discarded. Once a given number n_e of data exceeding the margin is collected, the update of SVM_t takes place: the support vectors of SVM_t, together with the n_e points, are used as training data to obtain the new model SVM_{t+1}.

Exceeding-margin+errors technique (EM+E). Given the model SVM_t at time t, new data $\{(\mathbf{x}_i, y_i)\}$ are loaded into memory. The algorithm checks if $(\mathbf{x}_i, y_i)$ exceeds the margin defined by SVM_t, i.e. if $y_i f_t((\mathbf{x}_i)) \leq 1$. If the condition is satisfied the point is kept, otherwise it is classified using SVM_t: if misclassified it is kept, otherwise discarded. Once a given number n_e of data, either exceeding the margin or misclassified, is collected, the update of SVM_t takes place: the support vectors of SVM_t, together with the n_e

points, are used as training data to obtain the new model SVM_{t+1}.

3. Training SVMs using Data Streams

We consider here the scenario in which the example generation is time dependent, and follow the data stream model presented in [8], also used in [7], [6], [4]. A data stream is a sequence of items that can be seen only once, and in the same order it is generated.

We seek algorithms for classification that maintain an updated representation of recent batches of data. The algorithm therefore must maintain an accurate representation of a *window* of recent data [6]. This model is useful in practice because the characteristics of the data may change with time, and so old examples may not be a good predictor for future points. The algorithm must perform only one pass over the stream data, and use a workspace that is smaller than the size of the input.

The incremental learning techniques we discussed are capable of achieving these objectives. Our approach is similar to [5], and works as follows: We consider the incoming data in batches of a given size b, and maintain in memory w models representative of the last $1, 2, \ldots, w$ batches. Thus, the window size is $W = wb$ examples. The w models are trained incrementally as data becomes available. Let us call the models, at time t, SVM_1^t, SVM_2^t, $\ldots SVM_w^t$ respectively. When a new batch of data comes in, at step $t + 1$, SVM_w^t is discarded, the remaining SVM_1^t, $\ldots$, SVM_{w-1}^t are incrementally updated to take into account the new batch of data, producing SVM_2^{t+1}, $\ldots$, SVM_w^{t+1} respectively. SVM_1^{t+1} is generated using the new batch of data only. At each step t, SVM_w^t gives the in-memory representation of the current distribution of data, and it is used to predict the class label of new data. Any of the discussed techniques can be employed for the incremental updates.

Besides the w SVM models, only b data points need to reside in memory at once. Both b and w can be set according to domain knowledge regarding locality properties of data distributions over time.

4. Experimental Evaluation

We compare the four incremental techniques and the SVM learning algorithm in batch mode, to verify their performances and sizes of resulting classifiers, i.e. number of resulting support vectors. We have tested the techniques on both simulated and real data. The real dataset (Pima) is taken from UCI Machine Learning Repository at http://www.cs.uci.edu/ ~mlearn/MLRepository.html. We used, for both the incremental and batch algorithms, radial basis function kernels. We used SVM^{light} [10], and set the value of γ in $K(\mathbf{x}_i, \mathbf{x}) = e^{-\gamma \|\mathbf{x}_i - \mathbf{x}\|^2}$ equal to the optimal one determined via cross-validation. Also the value of C for the soft-margin classifier is optimized via cross-validation. For the incremental techniques we have tested different batch sizes and n_e values. In Tables 1- 2 we report the best performances obtained (B is for the batch algorithm). We also report, besides the average classification error rates and standard deviations, the number of support vectors of the resulting classifier, the corresponding size of the condensed set (%), and the number of training cycles the SVM underwent.

To test the incremental techniques with stream data, we have used the Noisy-crossed-norm dataset (generated as the Large-noisy-crossed-norm dataset described below), and generated streams in batches of size $b = 1000$, and set $w = 3$. We have employed the Fixed-partition technique for the incremental updates. At each incremental step, we have tested the performance of the current model using 10 independent test sets of size 1000. We report average classification error rates and classifier sizes over successive steps. For comparison, we have also trained a SVM in batch mode over $w = 3$ consecutive batches of data over time, and report average classification error rates obtained at each step.

The Problems: *Large-noisy-crossed-norm data*. This data set consists of $n = 20$ attributes and $J = 2$ classes. Each class is drawn from a multivariate normal distribution with unit covariance matrix. One class has mean $2/\sqrt{20}$ along each dimension, and the other has mean $-2/\sqrt{20}$ along each dimension. We have generated 200,000 data points, and performed 5-fold cross-validation with 100,000 training data and 100,000 testing data. Table 1 shows the results. The last column lists the running times (in hours). Experiments were conducted on a 1.3 GHz machine with 1GB of RAM. *Pima Indians Diabete data*. This data set consists of $n = 8$ attributes, $J = 2$ classes, and $l = 768$ instances. Results are shown in Table 2. We performed 10-fold cross-validation with 568 training data and 200 testing data.

Results: Tables 1-2 show that, for both the data sets we have tested, the performance obtained with the incremental techniques comes close to the performance given by the batch algorithm. Moreover, for each problem considered, more than one incremental scheme provides a much smaller condensed set. In particular, it is quite remarkable the condensation power (1.5%) that the Exceed-margin technique shows for the Large-noisy-crossed-norm, while still performing close to the batch algorithm. The fact that the classifier is kept smaller allows for a much faster computation (30 minutes). The results obtained with the Pima data are also of interest. All four incremental techniques perform better than the batch algorithm and, at the same time, compute a smaller condensed set.

In Figure 1, we plot the results obtained with the stream data for 12 time steps. The average estimator size for the

incremental and batch techniques, respectively, are 418 and 430. Since the data distribution is stationary, the performance and estimator size remain stable over time. We observe that the incremental technique employed (Fixed-partition) and the batch mode algorithm basically provide the same results, both in terms of performance and size of the model. These results provide clear evidence that, although the incremental techniques allow loss of information, they are capable of achieving accuracy results similar to the batch algorithm, while significantly improving training time.

Table 1. Results for Large-noisy-crossed-norm data.

	B	ED	FP	EM	EM+E
error (%)	3.2	9.1	3.2	4.5	6.7
std dev	0.18	0.05	0.001	0.02	0.02
#SVs	8321	4172	8452	1455	5308
Cond. set (%)	8.3	4.2	8.5	1.5	5.3
cycles	-	19	201	37	48
batch size	-	500	500	500	500
time	14	17	20	0.5	22

Table 2. Results for Pima data.

	B	ED	FP	EM	EM+E
error (%)	31.9	29.3	26.2	27.1	26.4
std dev	0.47	0.02	0.02	0.02	0.02
#SVs	547	291	405	394	399
Cond. set (%)	96	51.2	71.3	69.4	70.2
cycles	-	13	38	34	36
batch size	-	10	10	10	10

5. Related Work

The incremental techniques discussed here can be viewed as approximations of the *chunking* technique employed to train SVMs [13]. The chunking technique is an exact decomposition method that iterates through the training set to select the support vectors.

The incremental methods introduced here, instead, scan the training data only once, and, once discarded, data are not considered anymore. This property makes the methods suited to be employed within the data stream model also. Furthermore, the experiments we have performed show that,

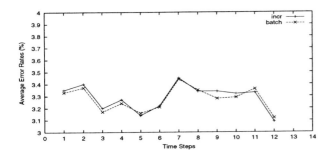

Figure 1. Noisy-crossed-norm data: Average Error Rates of Fixed-partition and batch algorithms for consecutive time steps.

although the incremental techniques allow loss of information, they are capable of achieving performance results similar to the batch algorithm.

6 Conclusions

We have introduced and compared new and existing incremental techniques for constructing SVMs. The experimental results presented show that incremental techniques are capable of achieving performance results similar to the batch algorithm, while improving the training time. We extended these approaches to work with stream data, and presented experimental results to show the efficiency and accuracy of the method.

Acknowledgments

This research has been supported by the National Science Foundation under grants NSF CAREER Award 9984729 and NSF IIS-9907477, by the US Department of Defense, and a research award from AT&T.

References

[1] J. C. Bennett, C. Campbel, "Support Vector Machines: Hype or Hallelujah?", *SIGKDD Explorations*, Vol. 2, No. 2, 1-13, 2000.

[2] M. Brown, W. Grundy, D. Lin, N. Cristianini, C. Sugnet, T. Furey, M. Ares, and D. Haussler, "Knowledge-based analysis of microarray gene expressions data using support vector machines," Tech. Report, University of California in Santa Cruz, 1999.

[3] G. Cauwenberghs and T. Poggio, "Incremental and Decremental Support Vector Machine Learning", *Advances in Neural Information Processing Systems*, 2000.

[4] Pedro Domingos, Geoff Hulten, "Mining high-speed data streams." *SIGKDD 2000*: 71-80, Boston, MA.

[5] Venkatesh Ganti, Johannes Gehrke, Raghu Ramakrishnan. "DEMON: Mining and Monitoring Evolving Data.", in *ICDE 2000*: 439-448, San Diego, CA.

[6] Sudipto Guha and Nick Koudas. "Data-Streams and Histograms.", In *Proc. STOC 2001*.

[7] S. Guha, N. Mishra, R. Motwani, L. O'Callaghan, "Clustering Data Stream", *IEEE Foundations of Computer Science*, 2000.

[8] M. R. Henzinger, P. Raghavan, and S. Rajagopalan, "Computing on data streams", *SRC Technical Note 1998-011*, Digital Research Center, May 26, 1998.

[9] T. Joachims, "Text categorization with support vector machines", *Proc. of European Conference on Machine Learning*, 1998.

[10] T. Joachims, "Making large-scale SVM learning practical" *Advances in Kernel Methods - Support Vector Learning*, B. Schölkopf and C. Burger and A. Smola (ed.), MIT-Press, 1999. http://www-ai.cs.uni-dortmund.de/thorsten/svm_light.html

[11] P. Mitra, C. A. Murthy, and S. K. Pal, "Data Condensation in Large Databases by Incremental Learning with Support Vector Machines", *International Conference on Pattern Recognition*, 2000.

[12] E. Osuna, R. Freund, and F. Girosi, "Training support vector machines: An application to face detection", *Proc. of Computer Vision and Pattern Recognition*, 1997.

[13] E. Osuna, R. Freund, and F. Girosi, "An improved training algorithm for support vector machines", *Proceedings of IEEE NNSP'97*, 1997.

[14] J. C. Platt, "Fast Training of Support Vector Machines using Sequential Minimal Optimization", Advances in Kernel Methods, B. Schölf, C. J. C. Burges, and A. J. Smola (eds.), MIT Press, 185-208, 1999.

[15] F. J. Provost and V. Kolluri, "A survey of methods for scaling up inductive learning algorithms", *Technical Report ISL-97-3*, Intelligent Systems Lab., Department of Computer Science, University of Pittsburgh, 1997.

[16] N. A. Syed, H. Liu, and K. K. Sung, "Incremental Learning with Support Vector Machines", *International Joint Conference on Artificial Intelligence (IJCAI)*, 1999.

[17] V. Vapnik, *Statistical Learning Theory*. Wiley, 1998.

Mining Generalized Association Rules for Sequential and Path Data

Wolfgang Gaul   Lars Schmidt-Thieme
Institut für Entscheidungstheorie und Unternehmensforschung,
University of Karlsruhe, D-76128 Karlsruhe, Germany
{Wolfgang.Gaul, Lars.Schmidt-Thieme}@wiwi.uni-karlsruhe.de

Abstract

While association rules for set data use and describe relations between parts of set valued objects completely, association rules for sequential data are restricted by specific interpretations of the subsequence relation: contiguous subsequences describe local features of a sequence valued object, noncontiguous subsequences its global features. We model both types of features with generalized subsequences that describe local deviations by wildcards, and present a new algorithm of Apriori type for mining all generalized subsequences with prescribed minimum support from a given database of sequences. Furthermore we show that the given algorithm automatically takes into account an eventually underlying graph structure, i.e., is applicable to path data also.

1. Introduction

Classical association rules describe dependencies between subsets of a large sample of set valued objects, e.g., market baskets. A typical association rule states that if a certain subset occurs in a set, then another subset is likely to occur in the same set (with estimated probabilities for the applicability and the strictness of the rule). For set valued objects subsets are natural substructures to consider.

To sequential data association rules can be applied in different ways. One can forget the sequence structure and map sequences on the sets of their elements, but looses ordering information. Or one looks for sequential association rules, i.e., pairs of subsequences that occur in order in a sequence. Here two different notions of substructures can be found in the literature: contiguous subsequences of elements, that occur one after the other in a sequence, and non-contiguous subsequences, where between two elements arbitrary noise may be interspersed. While the former describes local features of sequences, the latter describes global features of sequences. We combine both types of descriptions in generalized subsequences where possible noise is explicitly marked by a wildcard element.

The hard part of the computation of association rules is

the computation of frequent sets or subsequences. Frequent subsets of set valued objects can be mined by the standard Apriori algorithm (see Agrawal and Srikant (1994)). Frequent *contiguous or non-contiguous subsequences* can be mined by a well-known variant of the Apriori algorithm (see Agrawal and Srikant (1995) with modifications by Srikant and Agrawal (1996)). Borges and Levene (1999) have developed algorithms for sequence mining on aggregated data. Several algorithms exist to mine frequent *generalized subsequences of a specified type* (called templates, i.e., subsequences with prescribed positions of wildcards, see, e.g., Spiliopoulou (1999)). Other authors following a broader approach have constructed algorithms to find frequent subsequences of objects with attached attributes and relations (called generalized episodes, see Mannila and Toivonen (1996)). While those algorithms are perfectly suited for use in interactive analysis, a general algorithm mining *all* frequent generalized subsequences (of a given minimum support) as needed for association rule analysis is still missing. In this paper we describe a new algorithm that fills this gap.

If sequence data describes paths on a graph an algorithm mining frequent subpaths should take advantage of the underlying graph structure, i.e., only consider paths and no sequences of non-connected vertices. We show that our algorithm has this property automatically (by using a suitable join operator) and thus also solves the problem of mining frequent subpaths.

2. Formal background

Definition 1. Let R be an arbitrary finite set of (non-interpreted) items and $R^\star := \bigcup_{i \in \mathbb{N}} R^i$ the set of finite sequences of elements of R (with $\emptyset$ as the empty sequence). For a sequence $x \in R^\star$ the *length* $|x|$ is the number of symbols in the sequence ($|x| := n$ for $x \in R^n$, $|\emptyset| := 0$).

For $x, y \in R^\star$ we say that x *is a contiguous subsequence of* y ($x \leq_{ct} y$), if there is an index $i \in \{0, \ldots, |y| - |x|\}$ with $x_j = y_{i+j} \quad \forall j = 1, \ldots, |x|$.

We say that x *is a non-contiguous subsequence of* y ($x \leq_{nct} y$), if there is a strictly increasing map

$i : \{1, \ldots, |x|\} \to \{1, \ldots, |y|\}$ with $x_j = y_{i(j)}$ $\forall j = 1, \ldots, |x|$.

We use the neutral symbol $\leq$ to denote one of the two subsequence relations $\leq_{\mathrm{ct}}$ or $\leq_{\mathrm{nct}}$. x is called a *strict subsequence of y* ($x < y$), if it is a subsequence of y but not equal to y ($x \leq y \wedge x \neq y$).

Definition 2. A pair of sequences $x, y \in R^\star$ *overlaps on $k \in \mathbb{N}$ elements*, if the last k elements of x are equal to the first k elements of y ($x_{|x|-k+i} = y_i$ $\forall i = 1, \ldots k$). For such a pair of sequences $x, y \in R^\star$ overlapping on k elements we define the *k-telescoped concatenation of x and y* to be

$$
\begin{aligned}
x +_k y &:= (x_1, \ldots, x_{|x|-k}, y_1, \ldots, y_{|y|}) \\
&= (x_1, \ldots, x_{|x|}, y_{k+1}, \ldots, y_{|y|}).
\end{aligned}
$$

Note that any two sequences 0-overlap and the 0-telescoped concatenation of two sequences is just their arrangement one behind the other.

Definition 3. For a pair of sets of sequences $X, Y \subseteq R^\star$ we denominate the set of k-overlapping pairs $x \in X, y \in Y$ by $X \oplus_k Y$ and the set of k-telescoped sequences of all k-overlapping pairs as the *set of k-telescoped sequences of X and Y*:

$$
\begin{aligned}
X +_k Y &:= +_k(X \oplus_k Y) \\
&= \{ x +_k y \mid x \in X, y \in Y \text{ are overlapping on } k \text{ elements} \}.
\end{aligned}
$$

With this terminology an elegant formulation of the Apriori algorithm for sequences can be given that is omitted here for space restrictions (see Gaul/Schmidt-Thieme (2001)).

3. Mining frequent generalized subsequences

Definition 4. By a *generalized sequence in R* we mean a (finite ordinary) sequence in the symbols $R \cup \{\star\}$ with an additional symbol $\star \notin R$ called *wildcard*, so that no two wildcards are adjacent:

$$ R^{\mathrm{gen}} := \{ x \in (R \cup \{\star\})^\star \mid \nexists i \in \mathbb{N} : x_i = x_{i+1} = \star \} $$

The wildcard symbol $\star$ is used to model partially indeterminate sequences, matching arbitrary subsequences. For a generalized sequence $x \in R^{\mathrm{gen}}$ we define its *length* $|x|$ as the length of the sequence in the symbols $R \cup \{\star\}$, i.e., $|x| := n$, if $x \in (R \cup \{\star\})^n$.

Definition 5. Now let $x, y \in R^{\mathrm{gen}}$ be two generalized sequences. We say that *x matches y* or *y generalizes x* ($y \vdash x$), if there exists a mapping

$$ m : \{1, \ldots, |x|\} \to \{1, \ldots, |y|\} $$

(called *matching*) with the following properties:

1. m maps indices of elements of x to indices of elements of y that coincide or to a wildcard ($y_{m(i)} = x_i$ or $y_{m(i)} = \star$).

2. m covers all indices of y of non-wildcard elements ($y_i \in R \Rightarrow m^{-1}(i) \neq \emptyset$).

3. m is weakly increasing.

4. m is even strictly increasing at places where its image does not belong to a wildcard ($m(i) = m(i+1) \Rightarrow y_{m(i)} = \star$).

Note that as the set of ordinary sequences $R^\star$ is a subset of the set of generalized sequences R^{gen}, this also defines the notion of an ordinary sequence matching a generalized sequence. Obviously matchings are not uniquely determined by two generalized sequences x and y. A trivial example is $\star A\star \vdash AA$ with the two matchings $m_1 : 1 \mapsto 1, 2 \mapsto 2$ and $m_2 : 1 \mapsto 2, 2 \mapsto 3$. Finally we carry over the notions of subsequence and of k-telescoped concatenation from ordinary sequences to generalized sequences without any change. Note the difference between $A \star C$ not being a subsequence of ABCD but generalizing a subsequence of it (i.e. $A \star C \vdash ABC$ and $ABC \leq ABCD$). (For simplicity of notation we omit parentheses and commas in example sequences and just write ABC instead of (A,B,C).)

Definition 6. Let S be a finite (multi)set of ordinary sequences. For an arbitrary generalized sequence $x \in R^{\mathrm{gen}}$ we denominate the relative frequency of sequences containing a subsequence which matches x as *support of x with respect to S*:

$$ \sup_S(x) := \frac{|\{ s \in S \mid \exists y \leq s : x \vdash y \}|}{|S|} $$

Mining frequent generalized subsequences is the label for the task of finding all generalized sequences with at least a given minimum support. As subsequences actually are, what we are looking for, we can narrow our view to *closed generalized subsequences*, i.e. generalized subsequences without leading or trailing wildcard ($x \in R^{\mathrm{gen}}$ with $x_1, x_{|x|} \in R$).

At present no general algorithm for finding all frequent generalized subsequences in a (multi)set of sequences is known. We present a modification of the Apriori algorithm for sequences to generalized sequences. The idea is rather straightforward. As we restrict ourselves to closed generalized sequences, the support of any subsequence of such a closed generalized sequence again is greater than or equal to the support of the sequence itself. Adjacent wildcards are not allowed, therefore we obtain every closed generalized sequence of length $n + 1$ (for $n \geq 3$) as the junction of two overlapping closed generalized sequences of the kind described in table 1.

More formally we state:

	sequence	length		sequence	length
	ab...cd	n+1		a⋆b...cd	n+1
$=$	ab...c	n	$=$	a⋆b...c	n
$+_{n-1}$	b...cd	n	$+_{n-2}$	b...cd	n-1
	ab...c⋆d	n+1		a⋆b...c⋆d	n+1
$=$	ab...c	n-1	$=$	a⋆b...c	n-1
$+_{n-2}$	b...c⋆d	n	$+_{n-3}$	b...c⋆d	n-1

Table 1. Construction of closed generalized subsequences of length ≥ 4.

Lemma 1 (Generalized Sequence Construction). *For any closed generalized sequence $z \in R^{\mathrm{gen}}$ there are closed generalized sequences $x, y \in R^{\mathrm{gen}}$ with*

- *x and y are shorter than z ($|x|, |y| < |z|$) and*

- *z can be constructed from x and y (i.e., x and y are k-overlapping (for a suitable k) with $z = x +_k y$).*

Proof. Let $z = (z_1, \ldots, z_n)$. Depending on z_2 and z_{n-1} being in R or being a wildcard we distinguish four cases: (1) If $z_2, z_{n-1} \in R$ let $x = (z_1, \ldots, z_{n-1})$, $y = (z_2, \ldots, z_n)$, and $k = n - 1$. x and y are closed by assumption and obviously overlap on k elements and yield z. (2) If $z_2 \in R$, $z_{n-1} = \star$ let $x = (z_1, \ldots, z_{n-2})$, $y = (z_2, \ldots, z_n)$, and $k = n - 2$. As $z_{n-1} = \star$ and no adjacent wildcards are allowed, $z_{n-2} \neq \star$, i.e. x is closed. y is closed by assumption and again x and y obviously overlap on k elements and yield z. (3) If $z_2 = \star, z_{n-1} \in R$ let $x = (z_1, \ldots, z_{n-1})$, $y = (z_3, \ldots, z_n)$, and $k = n - 2$. As $z_2 = \star$ and no adjacent wildcards are allowed, $z_3 \neq \star$, i.e. y is closed. x is closed by assumption and again x and y obviously overlap on k elements and yield z. (4) Finally if $z_2, z_{n-1} = \star$ let $x = (z_1, \ldots, z_{n-2})$, $y = (z_3, \ldots, z_n)$, and $k = n - 3$. As $z_{n-1} = \star$ and no adjacent wildcards are allowed, $z_{n-2} \neq \star$, i.e. x is closed. As $z_2 = \star$ and no adjacent wildcards are allowed, $z_3 \neq \star$, i.e. y is closed. x and y obviously overlap on k elements and yield z. $\square$

We simply have to modify the join step of the Apriori algorithm for building new candidates of length $n + 1$ in such a way that we not only use the frequent (closed generalized) subsequences of length n but also those of length $n - 1$ from the previous step, and try all possible combinations. Closed generalized subsequences of length 3 containing a wildcard have the form $(x, \star, y)$ with $x, y \in R$, shorter closed generalized subsequences cannot contain wildcards.

The following algorithm gives the exact formulation of the necessary comparisons. Obviously, the computation of the support values of the candidate generalized sequences also has to be modified. The performance characteristics of the algorithm is the same as for the Apriori algorithm for

Apriori algorithm adapted for generalized sequences

Require: set of items R, (multi)set S of (finite) sequences of elements of R, minimum support value $\mathrm{minsup} \in \mathbb{R}^+$.

Ensure: set of frequent (closed) generalized subsequences $F := \bigcup_{n \in \mathbb{N}} F_n$ of the sequences of S with support of at least minsup.

$C := \{(r) \mid r \in R\}$ set of initial candidates,
$n := 1$, $F_0 := \emptyset$.
while $C \neq \emptyset$ or $F_{n-1} \neq \emptyset$ **do**
  compute $\sup_S(c) \quad \forall c \in C$ by counting the number of occurrences of each c in S (one loop through S).
  $F_n := \{c \in C \mid \sup_S(c) \geq \mathrm{minsup}\}$
  $C := F_n +_{n-1} F_n$ {compute new candidate sequences with length n+1}
  if $n = 2$ **then** {introduce wildcards}
    $C := C \cup \{(x, \star, y) \mid x, y \in F_{n-1}\}$
  else if $n > 2$ **then** {additional joins considering wildcards}
    $C := C$
    $\cup \{x +_{n-2} y \mid (x, y) \in F_n \oplus_{n-2} F_{n-1}, x_2 = \star\}$
    $\cup \{x +_{n-2} y \mid (x, y) \in F_{n-1} \oplus_{n-2} F_n, y_{|y|-1} = \star\}$
    $\cup \{x +_{n-3} y \mid (x, y) \in F_{n-1} \oplus_{n-3} F_{n-1},$
                      $x_2 = y_{|y|-1} = \star\}$
  end if
  $n := n + 1$
end while

ordinary sequences: to find sequences of length n, n loops through the database have to be accomplished.

We state some additional results for the special case of sequences describing paths on a graph. They apply to ordinary contiguous or noncontiguous sequences as well as to generalized sequences.

Definition 7. Let $G = (R, E)$ be a directed graph with vertices R and edges $E \subseteq R \times R$. A generalized sequence $x \in R^{\mathrm{gen}}$ of vertices is called a *path fragment*, if there are replacements for the wildcards that yield a path on G, i.e., for all $i = 1, \ldots, |x| - 1$ with $x_i \neq \star$:

- if $x_{i+1} \neq \star$ then $(x_i, x_{i+1}) \in E$.

- if $x_{i+1} = \star$ then there is a path $p^i \in R^\star$ connecting x_i and x_{i+2} (i.e., $p^i = (p_1^i, \ldots, p_n^i)$ with $p_1^i = x_i$, $p_n^i = x_{i+2}$ and $(p_j^i, p_{j+1}^i) \in E$ for all $j = 1, \ldots, n - 1$).

We denote as *set of path fragments of G* the set $R^{\mathrm{gen}}|_G := \{x \in R^{\mathrm{gen}} \mid x \text{ is a path fragment}\}$.

Lemma 2 (Path Fragment Construction). *If $x, y \in R^{\mathrm{gen}}|_G$ are path fragments on a graph G of length $|x|, |y| \geq 2$ that k-overlap with $k \geq 1$, then their k-telescoped concatenation $x +_k y$ again is a path fragment on G.*

The proof is omitted due to space restrictions (see Gaul/Schmidt-Thieme (2001)). The lemma guarantees that only path fragments are constructed during the candidate generation process.

4. Generalized association rules

As the retrieval of frequent (generalized) subsequences is the hard part of the generation of association rules, we can easily apply our algorithm to find association rules for generalized sequences with prescribed minimum support and confidence.

Definition 8. In analogy to ordinary association rules between sets a *contiguous generalized association rule* is (described by) a pair of 1-overlapping (generalized) sequences $x, y \in R^{\text{gen}}$ (written $x \to y$). One defines the *support of an association rule* $x \to y$ as the support of the concatenated sequence $x +_1 y := (x_1, \ldots, x_{|x|} = y_1, \ldots, y_{|y|})$ and its *confidence* as the fraction of the sequences containing $x +_1 y$ of the sequences containing x:

$$\begin{aligned} \sup_S(x \to y) &:= \sup_S(x +_1 y) \\ \mathrm{conf}_S(x \to y) &:= \frac{\sup_S(x \to y)}{\sup_S x} \end{aligned}$$

Speaking of association rules one has their interpretation as fuzzy rules in mind, i.e. that if the body x of the rule has occurred in a sequence, then the occurrence of x is continued by the head y of the rule, where occurrence is related to sequences from the underlying set S. The support gives a measure for the applicability of the rule, i.e. the overall percentage of sequences where it holds, while the confidence gives a measure for the strictness with which the rule holds, i.e., in what percentage of sequences that it is applicable to it holds.

Finding all association rules with a given minimum support and confidence means nothing else but finding all frequent sequences with at least the given minimum support and then trying the different splits of the found frequent sequences and checking the confidence of the resulting rules. — Please note that it is crucial for this application that the algorithm which finds the frequent subsequences also finds all subsequences of every subsequence returned and accordingly already has computed all support values needed.

The definition of an association rule can be extended to generalized sequences without any modification. But using generalized sequences opens an additional possibility:

Definition 9. A *non-contiguous generalized association rule* is (described by) a pair of generalized sequences x, y (written $x \rightsquigarrow y$). Its support and confidence are defined as follows:

$$\begin{aligned} \sup_S(x \rightsquigarrow y) &:= \sup_S(x_1, \ldots, x_n, \star, y_1, \ldots, y_m) \\ \mathrm{conf}_S(x \rightsquigarrow y) &:= \frac{\sup_S(x \rightsquigarrow y)}{\sup_S x} \end{aligned}$$

5. Outlook

Generalized sequences can be interpreted as non-contiguous subsequences of contiguous subsequences, i.e., as nested structures of second order. This interpretation opens the application of Apriori type algorithms to a huge range of new data and pattern structures. A unified framework for mining adequate substructures of such data will be presented in a forthcoming paper.

References

Agrawal, R. and Srikant, R. (1994): Fast Algorithms for Mining Association Rules. In: Bocca, J.B., Jarke, M., and Zaniolo, C. (eds.): *Proceedings of the 20th International Conference on Very Large Data Bases (VLDB'94)*, September 12-15, 1994, Santiago de Chile, 487–499.

Agrawal, R. and Srikant, R. (1995): Mining Sequential Patterns. In: Yu, P.S., and Chen, A.L.P. (eds.): *Proceedings of the Eleventh International Conference on Data Engineering*, March 6-10, 1995, Taipei, Taiwan, 3–14.

Borges, J. and Levene, M. (1999): Data Mining of User Navigation Patterns. In: *Proceedings of the Workshop on Web Usage Analysis and User Profiling (WEBKDD'99)*, August 15, 1999, San Diego, CA, 31–36.

Gaul, W., and Schmidt-Thieme, L. (2001): Mining Generalized Association Rules for Sequential and Path Data. Working paper, Unversity of Karlsruhe, 2001. http://www.webmining-research.com/working-paper/

Mannila, H., and Toivonen, H. (1996): Discovering generalized episodes using minimal occurrences. In: *The Second International Conference on Knowledge Discovery and Data Mining (KDD '96)*, Portland, Oregon, August 2-4 1996, 146–151.

Spiliopoulou, M. (1999): The Laborious Way from Data Mining to Web Mining. *Int. Journal of Comp. Sys., Sci. & Eng. 14 (1999)*, Special Issue on "Semantics of the Web", 113-126.

Srikant, R. and Agrawal, R. (1996): Mining Sequential Patterns: Generalizations and Performance Improvements. In: Apers, P.M.G., Bouzeghoub, M., and Gardarin, G. (eds.): *Advances in Database Technology - EDBT'96, 5th International Conference on Extending Database Technology*, Avignon, France, March 25-29, 1996, Proceedings. LNCS 1057.

Combining labeled and unlabeled data for text classification with a large number of categories

Rayid Ghani

Center for Automated Learning and Discovery
Carnegie Mellon University
Rayid.Ghani@cs.cmu.edu

Accenture Technology Labs
Northbrook, IL 60062
Rayid.Ghani@accenture.com

Abstract

We develop a framework to incorporate unlabeled data in the Error-Correcting Output Coding (ECOC) setup by decomposing multiclass problems into multiple binary problems and then use Co-Training to learn the individual binary classification problems. We show that our method is especially useful for classification tasks involving a large number of categories where Co-training doesn't perform very well by itself and when combined with ECOC, outperforms several other algorithms that combine labeled and unlabeled data for text classification in terms of accuracy, precision-recall tradeoff, and efficiency.

1 Introduction

A major difficulty with supervised learning techniques for text classification is that they often require a large number of labeled examples to learn accurately. One way to reduce the amount of labeled data required is to develop algorithms that can learn from a small number of labeled examples augmented with a large number of unlabeled examples.

There has been recent work in supervised learning algorithms using labeled and unlabeled data in problem domains where the features naturally divide into two disjoint sets, and algorithms that use this division, fall into the co-training setting (Blum & Mitchell, 1998).

Published studies on text classification with Co-training algorithms (Blum & Mitchell, 1998; Nigam & Ghani, 2000) have focused on small, often binary, problems and it is not clear whether their conclusions would generalize to real-world classification tasks with a large number of categories. On the other hand, Error-Correcting Output Codes (ECOC) are well suited for classification tasks with a large number of categories. However, most of the earlier work has focused neither on text classification problems (except our earlier work (Ghani, 2000) and (Berger, 1999)), nor on problems which deal with a large number of categories.

2 Combining ECOC and Co-Training

We propose a new algorithm aimed at combining the advantages that ECOC offers for supervised classification with a large number of categories and that of Co-Training for combining labeled and unlabeled data. Since ECOC decomposes a multiclass problem into multiple binary problems, we incorporate unlabeled data by learning each of these binary problems using Co-training.

The algorithm we propose is as follows:

- Training Phase
  1) Given a problem with m classes, create an m x n binary matrix M. 2) Each class is assigned one row of M. 3) Train n Co-trained classifiers to learn the n binary functions (one for each column since each column divides the dataset into two groups).
- Test Phase
  1) Apply each of the n single-bit Co-trained classifiers to the test example. 2) Combine the predictions to form a binary string of length n. 3) Classify to the class with the nearest codeword

Of course, an m-class problem can be decomposed naively into n binary problems and co-training can then learn each binary problem, but our approach is more efficient since by using ECOC we reduce the number of models that our classifier constructs and our approach scales up sublinearly with the number of classes (More details about using ECOC for efficient text classification using ECOC can be found in (Ghani, 2001). We also believe that our approach will perform better than the naive approach under the conditions that: 1) ECOC can outperform Naive Bayes on a multiclass problem (which actually learns one model for every class), 2)Co-Training can improve a single Naive Bayes classifier on a binary problem by using unlabeled data

The complication that arises in fulfilling condition 2 is that unlike normal binary classification problems where Co-Training has been shown to work well, the use of Co-Training in our case involves binary problems which themselves consist of multiple classes. Since the two classes in each bit are created artificially by ECOC and consist of many "Real" classes, there is no guarantee that Co-Training can learn these arbitrary binary functions.

If Co-training does not contain at least one labeled example from one of the original classes, it is likely that it will never be confident about labeling any unlabeled example from that class. Under the conditions that : 1) the initial

Table 1. Classification accuracies for the two datasets. Naive Bayes and ECOC do not use any unlabeled data whereas all the other algorithms have access to the same amount of labeled and unlabeled data.

Dataset	Naive Bayes		ECOC		EM	Co-Training	ECOC + Co-Training
	10% Labeled	100% Labeled	10% Labeled	100% Labeled	10% Labeled	10% Labeled	10% Labeled
Jobs-65	50.1	68.2	59.3	71.2	58.2	54.1	64.5
Hoovers-255	15.2	32.0	24.8	36.5	9.1	10.2	27.6

labeled examples cover every "original" class, 2) the target function for the binary partition is learnable by the underlying classifier, 3) the feature split is redundant and independent so that the co-training algorithm can utilize unlabeled data, theoretically, our combination of ECOC and Co-Training should result in improved performance by using unlabeled data.

3 Datasets

Hoovers dataset (used previously in (Ghani et al., 2001)) consists of web pages from 4285 corporate websites organized into 255 industry sectors (classes). Since there is no natural feature split, we randomly divide the vocabulary in two equal parts and apply Co-Training to the two feature sets. We have previously (Nigam & Ghani, 2000) shown that this random partitioning works reasonably well in the absence of a natural feature split.

We also use a dataset obtained from WhizBang! Labs consisting of Job titles and Descriptions organized in a two level hierarchy with 15 first level categories and 65 leaf categories. In all, there are 132000 examples and each example consists of a Job Title and a corresponding Job Description which we consider as two independent and redundant feature sets for Co-Training.

4 Experimental Results

All the codes used are BCH codes (31-bit codes for the Jobs dataset and 63-bit codes for the Hoovers Dataset) and are similar to those used in (Ghani, 2000).

Table 1 shows the results of the experiments comparing our proposed algorithm with EM and Co-Training. The baseline results with Naive Bayes and ECOC using no unlabeled data are also given, as well as those when all the labels are known which serve as an upper bound for the performance of our algorithm.

From results reported in recent papers (Blum & Mitchell, 1998; Nigam & Ghani, 2000), it is not clear whether co-training will perform well by itself and give us any leverage out of unlabeled data on a dataset consisting of a large number of classes. We can see that both Co-Training and EM did not improve the classification accuracy by using unlabeled data on the Hoovers-255 dataset; rather they had a negative effect and resulted in decreased accuracy. The accuracy reported for EM and Co-Training was decreasing at every iteration and since the experiments were stopped at different times, they are not comparable to each other. On

the other hand, our proposed combination of ECOC and Co-Training does indeed take advantage of the unlabeled data much better than EM and Co-Training and outperforms both of those algorithms on both datasets. It is also worth noting that ECOC outperforms Naive Bayes for both datasets and this is more pronounced when the number of labeled examples is small.

We also evaluate our results in terms of precision and recall but do not show the graphs because of space limitations. The figures can be found in (Ghani, 2001). We find that our method performs extremely well and can provide very high precision results unlike Naive Bayes and EM. This is a property of ECOC and is discussed further in (Ghani, 2001).

5 Conclusions

The results described in this paper lead us to believe that the combination of ECOC and Co-Training algorithms is indeed useful for learning with labeled and unlabeled data. We have shown that our approach outperforms both Co-Training and EM algorithms, which have previously been shown to work well on several text classification tasks. Our approach not only performs well in terms of accuracy but also provides a smooth precision-recall tradeoff which is useful in applications requiring high-precision results. Furthermore, we have shown that the framework presented in this paper results in text classification systems that are both computationally efficient (through the use of short error-correcting codes) and need very few labeled examples to learn accurately.

References

Berger, A. (1999). Error-correcting output coding for text classification. *IJCAI-99: Workshop on machine learning for information filtering.*

Blum, A., & Mitchell, T. (1998). Combining labeled and unlabeled data with co-training. *COLT 1998.*

Ghani, R. (2000). Using error-correcting codes for text classification. *ICML-00.*

Ghani, R. (2001). *Using error-correcting codes for efficient text classification with a large number of categories. masters thesis* (Technical Report). Center for Automated Learning and Discovery, Carnegie Mellon University.

Ghani, R., Slattery, S., & Yang, Y. (2001). Hypertext categorization using hyperlink patterns and meta data. *ICML-01.*

Nigam, K., & Ghani, R. (2000). Analyzing the applicability and effectiveness of co-training. *CIKM-00.*

Dependency Derivation in Industrial Process Data

Daniel Gillblad and Anders Holst
Swedish Institute of Computer Science
Box 1263, SE-164 29 Kista, Sweden
dgi@sics.se, aho@sics.se

Abstract

In many industrial processes, finding dependencies and the creation of dependency graphs can increase the understanding of the system significantly. This knowledge can then be used for further optimization and variable selection. Most of the measured attributes in these cases come in the form of time series. There are several ways of determining correlation between series, most of them suffering from specific problems when applied to real-world data. Here, a well performing measure based on the mutual information rate is derived and discussed with results from both synthetic and real data.

1 Introduction

Today, many companies keep close track of their systems by continuously recording the measurements of a large amount of sensors. The number of sensors used can range from just a few to tens of thousands depending on the type and technology level of the industry. Much of the recorded data is in the form of time series, with e.g. one measurement per minute and sensor. To gain thorough insight into the process, an understanding of how each measured sequence affects the others is necessary. Also important is to understand how long the delay is from a change in one sequence until there is any effect in another, dependent, sequence. More specific, the general task is to find how strongly the time series are correlated to each other, how long the time lag is between the correlations and, if possible, the causal direction [5]. Apart from the increased understanding of the process, this dependency derivation is important if for example a future value of some variable is to be predicted or if a virtual sensor is being constructed. Here, a measure based on the mutual information rate will be derived, which solves some of the problems encountered using other correlation measures.

2 Correlation measures

There is a number of applicable correlation measures, the perhaps most commonly used being Pearson's correlation coefficient and the covariance. These measure only the linear correlation, which means that they might not detect obvious dependencies simply because they do not point in the same direction for all values. Mutual information is a general correlation measure and can be generalized to all kinds of probability distributions [3]. It is also, given an appropriate model of the distributions, able to detect nonlinear dependencies between variables.

2.1 Mutual Information and Linear correlation

Before introducing the mutual information and the mutual information rate, we will give a brief review of some of the basic concepts of information theory. The *entropy* of a stochastic variable, which can be thought of as a measure of the amount of uncertainty or the mean information from the variable, is defined as

$$H(X) = -\sum_{k \in \chi} P(x_k) \log P(x_k) \qquad (1)$$

in the discrete case. The continuous case is analogue to the discrete definition, substituting the sum for an integral. If two variables X and Y are independent, $H(X,Y) = H(X) + H(Y)$. If the variables are not independent, $H(X) + H(Y)$ will be larger than $H(X,Y)$, that is some of the information in $H(X,Y)$ is included in both the marginal entropies. This common information is called the *mutual information*, $I(X;Y)$. It can also be thought of as the reduction in the uncertainty in one variable due to the knowledge of the other, or more formally

$$
\begin{aligned}
I(X;Y) &= H(Y) - H(Y|X) = H(X) - H(X|Y) \\
&= H(X) + H(Y) - H(X,Y) \qquad (2)
\end{aligned}
$$

The mutual information is symmetrical and is always larger than or equal to zero, with equality only if X and

Y are independent. The mutual information can also be written more briefly, here in the discrete case, as

$$I(X;Y) = -\sum_{x,y} p(x,y) \log \frac{p(x,y)}{p(x)p(y)} \qquad (3)$$

which follows directly from Eq. (2).

To be able to calculate the mutual information, we have to know both the variables marginal distributions and their joint distribution. First, we need a basic assumption of what the distributions will look like. If we assume a too complex model, where each data point essentially has to be considered on its own, we run the risk of over fitting the model so that all variables always look highly correlated. If we on the other hand assume a simple model such as that all data are normal distributed, we cannot detect anything but the linear part of the correlation. We have mainly tried two models of the distributions, normal distributions (Gaussians) and binning the data using a 2-dimensional grid.

If each measured variable is quantized into discrete values, or *bins*, it is very simple to calculate the mutual information between one variable and another using Eq. (3). Each marginal is discretized, and the joint distribution is modeled by the grid resulting from the two marginal distribution models. Then histograms are constructed from the data using this discretization and from these the probabilities are estimated.

Another simple assumption about the distributions is that they are Gaussian. This results in a measure where a linear correlation is assumed. To calculate the mutual information, we need to know the entropy of a Gaussian distribution. The entropy of an n-dimensional Gaussian distribution is

$$h(X_1, X_2, \ldots, X_n) = \frac{1}{2} \log(2\pi e)^n |C| \qquad (4)$$

where $|C|$ denotes the determinant of the covariance matrix. Using Eq. (2) and (4), it is easy to calculate the mutual information for Gaussian distributions. Naturally, there is a very close relation between the mutual information based on Gaussian distributions and the common linear correlation. The mutual information can be written as $I(X;Y) = -\log(1-\rho^2)/2$. Thus, the mutual information is in this case just a scaling of the correlation coefficient to a range between zero and infinity.

2.2 The Mutual Information Rate

Time series are sequential data; data that evolve in some random but prescribed manner. Simply from the statement that we are dealing with time series, we can make some very reasonable assumptions about the dependency structure of the data. This basic consideration can be used to construct a correlation measure specific for sequential data, unlike the general measures described in section 2.1. The result is a more sensitive and accurate measure of the dependencies in time series.

To construct this measure, we would like an expression for the uncertainty of a sequence, corresponding to the entropy of a single variable. Loosely speaking, if we have a sequence of n random variables, this uncertainty can be defined as how the entropy of the sequence grows with n. This is the entropy rate of the process and can be defined as

$$H_r(X) = \lim_{n \to \infty} \frac{1}{n} H(X_n | X_{n-1}, X_{n-2}, \ldots, X_1) \qquad (5)$$

which is the conditional entropy of the last variable given the past. Based on the entropy rate, we can also construct a measure of the *mutual information rate*. It can be defined as, for example,

$$I_r(X;Y) = \lim_{n \to \infty} I(X_n | X_{n-1}, \ldots, X_1; Y_n | Y_{n-1}, \ldots, Y_1) \qquad (6)$$

This can be seen as a measure of the total dependence, or the total amount of information in common, between sequence X and Y. To relate it to the entropy rate, we can also write the mutual information rate as

$$I_r(X;Y) = H_r(X) + H_r(Y) - H_r(X,Y) \qquad (7)$$

This can be derived directly from Eq. (6). Informally, it can be understood by considering the entropy rate of a sequence as analogous to the entropy of a stochastic variable and then applying Eq. (2).

Now we have the mutual information rate expressed in the entropy rates of the two sequences. This way, the mutual information rate measures the complete dependence between the sequences. In the limit, the shift between the sequences is irrelevant. Working with finite sequences though, the entropy rate of Eq. (5) is impossible to estimate perfectly, since the distributions used in the calculations contain infinitely many variables. When we restrict ourselves to the use a finite number of variables, the shift inevitably becomes important. Also, for some applications, we would actually like to have a localized measure that measures the direct dependence between one sequence and the other with a specific shift between them.

We can make a reasonable estimate using a Markov assumption, i.e. we assume that the process has a limited memory so that the value of a variable is dependent only on the closest earlier values. When we make the Markov assumption, we also have to take into account the shift of the sequences. If we denote this shift d, using a first order Markov assumption and assuming stationary sequences, the mutual information rate $I_r(X;Y;d)$, can be simplified to entropies of joint distributions as

$$
\begin{aligned}
I_r(X;Y;d) &= H(X_n|X_{n-1}) + H(Y_n|Y_{n-1}) - \\
&\quad H(X_n, Y_{n-d}|X_{n-1}, Y_{n-d-1}) \\
&= H(X_n, X_{n-1}) - H(X_n) + \\
&\quad H(Y_n, Y_{n-1}) - H(Y_n) - \\
&\quad H(X_n, Y_{n-d}, X_{n-1}, Y_{n-d-1}) + \\
&\quad H(X_n, Y_{n-d}) \qquad (8)
\end{aligned}
$$

using $H(X_{n-1}) = H(X_n)$ and $H(X|Y) = H(X,Y) - H(Y)$ [4]. The largest joint distribution that needs to be estimated contains four variables, which can be rather difficult depending on the model of the distribution used. A second order or higher Markov assumption can of course also be made, but the amount of data required to estimate the joint distributions will increase significantly.

Once again, like in section 2.1, the distributions can be modeled by discretizing the values using a multi-dimensional grid. First each marginal is discretized, and then two and four dimensional grids are constructed for the joint distributions based on these marginal grids. Instead of using bins, Gaussian distributions can be used, resulting in a linear measure tailored for time series. This is a much more robust measure; it requires much less data to estimate these gaussians reliably than to use a grid. The drawback is of course that still essentially only linear dependencies can be discovered.

The main drawback of the mutual information rate is that it needs more data to be estimated reliably. However, the Markov assumption also introduces another consideration. Dependencies that are visible at several shifts between the sequences will be handled correctly if this spread of the dependence is dependent on the Markov properties of the series. If the sequences on the other hand interact at two or more speeds this will not be considered and only the strongest correlation will show. In practice this is often sufficient.

3 Test results

The described correlation measures have been tested on both synthetic test data and real data from mainly two different process industries, a paper mill and a chemical industry. The experience from the tests on real data confirms those of testing on synthetic data, namely that the mutual information rate most of the time produces significantly better results than the ordinary mutual information.

3.1 Results on synthetic data

Synthetic data was generated for testing purposes and to illustrate the effects of the different models. The process generation model is depicted in Fig. 1, where $x(n)$

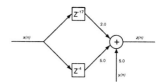

Figure 1. The model generating the synthetic data

and $y(n)$ are time series generated independently from each other using a model based on the movements of a particle in a potential well subjected to random forces. From $x(n)$, two new time series are generated, one that is delayed 17 time steps and multiplied by 2.0, and one that is delayed 4 time steps and multiplied with a factor of 5.0. The sum of these series as well as $y(n)$ multiplied by the factor 5.0 is the output of the model, called $z(n)$. The original series $x(n)$ can then be compared to the output series $z(n)$, trying to detect the correlations. $y(n)$ represents additive noise to the output signal.

Fig. 2 shows the correllograms generated from synthetic data. The diagrams show, from left to right, the linear Mutual Information, the linear Mutual Information rate, the binned Mutual Information and the binned Mutual Information rate. The x-axis represents the delay between the series and the y-axis the degree of correlation. A thin line in the center of each diagram shows delay 0. The linear mutual information diagram clearly shows a peak, although not very distinct, at delay 4. The other delay in the model of 17 does not show up as a peak in the diagram though. Using the linear version of the mutual information rate, the second peak is clearly detectable. The mutual information rate produces a much sharper and exact diagram than the mutual information, showing distinct peaks at both delay 4 and delay 17, the peak at seventeen being lower than the peak at 4. Looking at the process generation, this is what we would expect the correlation measure to produce.

The binned mutual information looks much the same as the linear mutual information, not detecting the second, weaker correlation at delay 17. The binned mutual information rate detects both peaks, although not very clearly. There is a large amount of noise and artifacts present, resulting from the binning of data. It is not very surprising, however, that the linear version of the measure performs better here since there are only linear dependencies present in the data.

3.2 Results on industrial process data

The measures presented here have all been used on several real data sets, mainly from a paper mill and a chemical plant. Here we will present a couple of examples, both

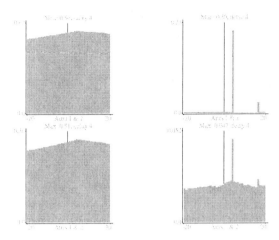

Figure 2. Results on synthetic data.

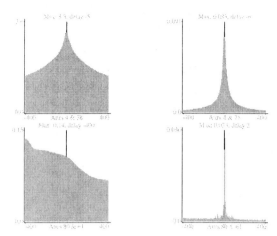

Figure 3. Results on chemical plant data.

taken from the chemical plant application. Only the linear versions of the measures are shown since they proved to be more useful than the binned versions. The names of the attributes were given as short abbreviations to not be directly recognizable. The delay is measured in minutes.

Fig. 3 shows correllograms generated for chemical plant data. The diagrams show, from left to right, the mutual information and mutual information rate between X3 and C63, and the mutual information and mutual information rate between X48 and Y. All measures are linear. The correlation between variable X3 and C63 is an example of a well behaved, linear correlation with a short and reasonable time delay. The mutual information correllogram shows just one clear peak at delay −5, and the mutual information rate correllogram for the same attributes shows the same behavior. It is a bit more peaky and shows much lower correlation, but the peak is at almost the same delay.

The correllogram for the linear mutual information between X48 and Y is very smooth, although somewhat low, but the measure is obviously fooled by some general trend in the data since it is constantly increasing with decreasing values of the delay. The mutual information rate on the other hand shows a clear peak at delay 2. That is a plausible value of the delay between the sequences, although the value of the correlation is rather low. The information rate diagram is not at all as smooth as the mutual information, showing several small spikes which are very likely effects of noise and oddities in the data.

4 Conclusions and practical considerations

Both the mutual information and the mutual information rate suffer from a tendency to be fooled by random effects in data, the information rate somewhat less so than the mutual information. Also, using mutual information or the normal correlation coefficient between time series tends to give a too high value of the correlation. This happens because that if the time series moves slowly enough, the relation between the series at one point in time is likely to be maintained for several time steps. This means that pure random coincidences between the series gets multiplied with a factor depending on how slow the series are, making that correlation seem more significant than it is. The mutual information rate on the other hand, which only considers the new information in every step, correctly compensates for that effect but instead requires a more complicated model to estimate, which makes it more sensitive to noise.

In practice it turns out that the diagrams using histograms have quite little interesting variation, whereas the linear diagrams show more features, some of which are clearly anomalous. As expected, the diagrams with information rates show much lower levels of correlations and more emphasized peaks, i.e. not so smeared out over several different delays, but also more noise in the form of random spikes in the correllogram. All in all it seems that the linear information rate is the one that gives the most reliable indications of correlations between the time series.

References

[1] Shannon C. E. (1948). The mathematical theory of communication. *Bell Syst. Tech. J.* **27**:379-423.

[2] Shannon C. E. (1951). Prediction and entropy of printed English. *Bell Syst. Tech. J.* **1951**:379-423.

[3] Li W. (1990). Mutual information functions versus correlation functions. *Journal of Statistical Physics.* **60**:823-837.

[4] Cover T. M., Thomas J. A. (1991). *Elements of Information Theory.* John Wiley and Sons, New York.

[5] Gershenfeld N. A., Weigend A. S. (Eds.). (1993). *Time Series Prediction: Forecasting the Future and Understanding the Past. SFI Studies in the Sciences of Complexity.* Proc. Vol. XV, Addison-Wesley.

Discovering Representative Episodal Association Rules from Event Sequences Using Frequent Closed Episode Sets and Event Constraints

Sherri K. Harms, Jitender Deogun
Department of CSCE
University of Nebraska
Lincoln, NE 68588-0115
sharms{deogun}@cse.unl.edu

Jamil Saquer
CS Department
SWMS University
Springfield, MO 65804
jms481f@smsu.edu

Tsegaye Tadesse
NDMC
University of Nebraska
Lincoln, NE 68588-0115
tadesse@unlserve.unl.edu

Abstract

Discovering association rules from time-series data is an important data mining problem. The number of potential rules grows quickly as the number of items in the antecedent grows. It is therefore difficult for an expert to analyze the rules and identify the useful. An approach for generating representative association rules for transactions that uses only a subset of the set of frequent itemsets called frequent closed itemsets was presented in [6]. We employ formal concept analysis to develop the notion of frequent closed episodes. The concept of representative association rules is formalized in the context of event sequences. Applying constraints to target highly significant rules further reduces the number of rules. Our approach results in a significant reduction of the number of rules generated, while maintaining the minimum set of relevant association rules and retaining the ability to generate the entire set of association rules with respect to the given constraints. We show how our method can be used to discover associations in a drought risk management decision support system and use multiple climatology datasets related to automated weather stations[1].

1. Introduction

Discovering association rules is an important data-mining problem. The problem was first defined in the context of the market basket data to identify customers' buying habits [1]. The problem of analyzing and identifying interesting rules becomes difficult as the number of rules increases. In most applications the number of rules discovered is usually large. Two different approaches to handle this problem have been reported: 1) identifying the association rules that are of special importance to the user, and 2)

minimizing the number of association rules discovered [2]. Most of these approaches introduce additional measures for interestingness of a rule and prune the rules that do not satisfy the additional measures, as a post-processing step. A set of representative association rules, on the other hand, is a minimal set of rules from which all association rules can be generated, during the actual processing step. Usually, the number of representative association rules is much smaller than the number of all association rules, and no additional measures are needed for determining the representative association rules [4].

Recently, Saquer and Deogun developed a different approach for generating representative association rules [6]. Similarly, Zaki [8] used frequent closed itemsets to generate non-redundant association rules in CHARM.

We use closure as the basis for generating frequent sets in the context of sequential data. We then generate sequential association rules based on representative association rule approaches while integrating constraints into our approach. By combining these techniques, our method is well suited for time series problems that have groupings of events that occur close together in time, but occur relatively infrequently over the entire dataset. We apply this technique to the drought risk management problem.

2. Frequent Closed Episodes

Our overall goal is to analyze event sequences, discover recurrent patterns of events, and generate sequential association rules. Our approach is based on the concept of representative association rules combined with event constraints.

A sequential dataset is normalized and then discretized by forming subsequences using a *sliding window* [5]. Using a sliding window of size δ, every normalized time stamp value x_t is used to compute each of the new sequence values $y_{t-\delta/2}$ to $y_{t+\delta/2}$. Thus, the dataset has been divided into segments, each of size δ. The discretized version of the

[1] This research was supported in part by NSF Digital Government Grant No. EIA-0091530 and NSF EPSCOR, Grant No. EPS-0091900.

time series is obtained by using some clustering algorithm and a suitable similarity measure. Each cluster identifier is an *event type*, and the set of cluster labels is the *class of events E*.

The newly formed version of the time series is referred to as an event sequence. An *event sequence* is a triple $(t_B, t_D, \mathcal{S})$ where t_B is the beginning time, t_D is the ending time, and $\mathcal{S}$ is a finite, time-ordered sequence of events [5]. That is, $\mathcal{S} = (e_{t_B}, e_{t_{B+1p}}, e_{t_{B+2p}}, \ldots e_{t_{B+dp}} = e_{t_D})$, where p is the step size between each event, d is the total number of steps in the time interval from time t_B to time t_D, and $D = B + dp$. Each e_{t_i} is a member of a class of events E, and $t_i \leq t_{i+1}$ for all $i = B, \ldots, D - 1p$. A sequence of events $\mathcal{S}$ includes events from a single class of events E.

A *window* on an event sequence $\mathcal{S}$ is an event subsequence $W = \{e_{t_j}, \ldots, e_{t_k}\}$, where $t_B \leq t_j$, and $t_k \leq t_D + 1$ [5]. The width of the window W is $width(W) = t_k - t_j$. The set of all windows W on $\mathcal{S}$, with $width(W) = win$ is denoted as $\mathcal{W}(\mathcal{S}, win)$. The width of the window is pre-specified.

An episode in an event sequence is a combination of events with a partially specified order. The type of an episode is *parallel* if no order is specified, and *serial* if the events of the episode have a fixed order. An episode is *injective* if no event type occurs more than once in the episode.

We extend the work of Mannila *et al.* [5] to consider closed sets of episodes. We use formal concept analysis as the basis for developing the notion of closed episode sets [6]. Informally, a concept is a pair of sets: set of objects (windows or episodes) and set of features (events) common to all objects in the set.

Definition 1 *An episodal data mining context is defined as a triple $(\mathcal{W}(\mathcal{S}, win), \mathcal{E}, R)$ where $\mathcal{W}(\mathcal{S}, win)$ is a set of all windows of width win defined on the event sequence $\mathcal{S}$, and $\mathcal{E}$ is a set of episodes in the event sequence $\mathcal{S}$, and $R \subseteq \mathcal{W} \times \mathcal{E}$.*

Definition 2 *Let $(\mathcal{W}, \mathcal{E}, R)$ be an episodal data mining context, $X \subseteq \mathcal{W}$, and $Y \subseteq \mathcal{E}$. Define the mappings α, β as follows:*
$$\beta : 2^{\mathcal{W}} \to 2^{\mathcal{E}}, \quad \beta(X) = \{e \in \mathcal{E} \mid (w, e) \in R \; \forall \; w \in X\},$$
$$\alpha : 2^{\mathcal{E}} \to 2^{\mathcal{W}}, \quad \alpha(Y) = \{w \in \mathcal{W} \mid (w, e) \in R \; \forall \; e \in Y\}.$$

The mapping $\beta(X)$ associates with X the set of episodes that are common to all the windows in X. Similarly, the mapping $\alpha(Y)$ associates with Y the set of all windows containing all the episodes in Y. Intuitively, $\beta(X)$ is the maximum set of episodes shared by all windows in X and $\alpha(Y)$ is the maximum set of windows possessing all the episodes in Y.

It is easy to see that in general, for any set Y of episodes, $\beta(\alpha(Y)) \neq Y$. A set of episodes Y that satisfies the condition $\beta(\alpha(Y)) = Y$ is called *a closed set of episodes* [6].

The *frequency* of an episode is defined as the fraction of windows in which the episode occurs. Given an event sequence $\mathcal{S}$, and a window width *win*, the frequency of an episode P of a given type in $\mathcal{S}$ is:

$$fr(P, \mathcal{S}, win) = \frac{\mid \boldsymbol{w} \in \mathcal{W}(\mathcal{S}, win) : P \text{ occurs in } \boldsymbol{w} \mid}{\mid \mathcal{W}(\mathcal{S}, win) \mid}$$

Given a frequency threshold *min_fr*, P is *frequent* if $fr(P, \mathcal{S}, win) \geq min\_fr$. A *frequent closed set of episodes (FCE)* is a closed set of episodes that satisfy the minimum frequency threshold. Closure of an episode set $X \subseteq \mathcal{E}$, denoted by $closure(X)$, is the smallest closed episode set containing X and is equal to the intersection of all frequent episode sets containing X.

To generate frequent closed target episodes, we develop an algorithm called *Gen-FCE*, shown in Figure 1. Gen-FCE is a combination of the *Close-FCI* algorithm [6], the *WINEPI* frequent episode algorithms [5], and the *Direct* algorithm [7]. *Gen-FCE* generates FCE with respect to a given set of Boolean target constraints B, an event sequence S, a window width *win*, an episode type, a minimum frequency *min_fr*, and a window step size p. The *Gen-FCE* algorithm requires one database pass during each iteration.

1) *Generate Candidate Frequent Closed Target Episodes of length 1 ($CFC_{1,\mathcal{B}}$);*
2) *$k = 1$;*
3) **while** *($CFC_{k,\mathcal{B}} \neq \emptyset$)* **do**
4) *Read the sequence S, one window at a time, let $FCE_{k,\mathcal{B}}$ be the elements in $CFC_{k,\mathcal{B}}$ with a new closure, and with a frequency $\geq min\_fr$*
5) *Generate Candidate Frequent Closed Target Episodes $CFC_{k+1,\mathcal{B}}$ from $FCE_{k,\mathcal{B}}$*
6) *k++;*
7) *return $\bigcup_{i=1}^{k-1} \{FCE_{i,\mathcal{B}}.closure$ and $FCE_{i,\mathcal{B}}.frequency\}$;*

Figure 1. Gen-FCE algorithm.

We incorporate constraints similar to the *Direct* algorithm [7]. This approach is known to work well at low minimum supports and in large datasets [7]. This approach requires an expensive cross-product operation, so for disjunctive singleton constraints, the candidate generation algorithm is used [5].

3 Representative Episodal Association Rules

We use the set of frequent closed episodes FCE produced from the *Gen-FCE* algorithm to generate the *representative episodal association rules* that cover the entire set of association rules [4].

The cover of a rule $r : X \Rightarrow Y$, denoted by $C(r)$, is the set of association rules that can be generated from r. That is, $C(r : X \Rightarrow Y) = \{X \cup U \Rightarrow V \mid U, V \subseteq Y, \quad U \cap V = \emptyset, \quad and \quad V \neq \emptyset\}$. An important property of the cover operator stated in [4] is that if an association rule r has support s and confidence c, then every rule $r' \in C(r)$ has support at least s and confidence at least c.

Using the cover operator, a set of representative association rules with minimum support s and minimum confidence c, $RAR(s, c)$, is defined as follows: $RAR(s, c) = \{r \in AR(s, c) \mid \not\exists r' \in AR(s, c), \quad r \neq r' \quad and \quad r \in C(r')\}$. That is, a set of representative association rules is a least set of association rules that cover all the association rules and from which all association rules can be generated. Clearly, $AR(s, c) = \bigcup \{C(r) \mid r \in RAR(s, c)\}$.

Gen-REAR shown in Figure 2, is a modification of the *Generate-RAR* [6] that generates $REAR$ for a given set of frequent closed episodes FCE with respect to a minimum confidence c.

1) k = the size of the longest frequent closed episode in FCE;
2) **while** *(k > 1)* **do**
3) *Generate $REAR_k$, by adding each rule $X \Rightarrow Z \setminus X$ such that $(Z.support/X.support \geq c$ and $X \Rightarrow Z \setminus X$ is not covered by a previously generated rule*
4) k + +;
5) return REAR;

Figure 2. Gen-REAR algorithm.

Using our technique on multiple time series while constraining the episodes to a user-specified target set, we can find relationships that occur across the sequences.

4 Empirical Results

We are developing an advanced Geospatial Decision Support System (GDSS) to improve the quality and accessibility of drought related data for drought risk management [3]. Our objective is to integrate spatio-temporal knowledge discovery techniques into the GDSS using a combination of data mining techniques applied to geospatial time-series data by: 1) finding relationships between user-specified target episodes and other climatic events and 2) predicting the target episodes. The REAR approach will be used to meet the first objective. In this paper we validate the effectiveness of the REAR approach to find relationships between drought episodes at the automated weather station in Mead, NE, and other climatic episodes, from 1989-1999. We compare it to the WINEPI algorithm [5]. We use data from nine sources, including satellite vegetation data and precipitation and soil moisture data.

We experimented with several different window widths, minimal frequency values, minimal confidence values, for both parallel and serial episodes. When using constraints, we specified droughts as our target episodes. The experiments were ran on a AMD Athlon 1.3GHz PC with 256 MB main memory, under the Windows 2000 operating system.

4.1 Gen-FCE vs. WINEPI

Tables 1 and 2 represent performance statistics for finding frequent closed episodes in the drought risk management dataset for Mead, NE with various frequency thresholds for injective serial drought episodes with a 2 month window using the *Gen-FCE* and WINEPI algorithms, respectively.

Table 1. Gen-FCE serial episode performance.

min-fr	Candidates	Freq. Closed Episodes	Iters	time (s)
0.05	525	77	3	2
0.10	335	24	2	1
0.15	153	10	2	1
0.20	93	6	2	0
0.25	83	5	2	0

Table 2. WINEPI serial episode performance.

min-fr	Candidates	Freq. Closed Episodes	Iters	time (s)
0.05	17284	3950	6	6932
0.10	4687	629	5	205
0.15	1704	229	4	10
0.20	807	102	4	1
0.25	567	58	3	1

Gen-FCE performs extremely well when finding the drought episodes. The number of frequent closed episodes decreases rapidly as the frequency threshold increases. For the sample dataset at a frequency threshold of 0.10 and a window width of 2 months, *Gen-FCE* produces 6 frequent drought serial episodes while WINEPI produces 1600% more (102) episodes.

Because we are working with a fraction of the possible number of episodes, our algorithms are extremely efficient. When finding all frequent drought episodes for the sample dataset using a window width of 5 months, the running time was 1 second for *Gen-FCE* and 6 hours for WINEPI. This illustrates the benefits of using closures and constraints when working with the infrequently occurring drought events.

As the window size increases, so does the frequent episode generation time and the number of frequent episodes. When using drought constraints, the increase is at a much slower pace than WINEPI. For the sample dataset and a window width of 3 months, *Gen-FCE* produces 53 frequent drought serial episodes while WINEPI produces 5779% more (3116) episodes.

4.2 Gen-REAR vs. WINEPI Association Rules

We next experimented with finding association rules in the drought risk management dataset for Mead, NE with various confidence thresholds and window widths using the *Gen-REAR* and WINEPI AR algorithms for injective parallel and serial episodes. The number of rules decreases rapidly as the confidence threshold increases and increases rapidly as the window width widens. In all cases, *Gen-REAR* produces fewer rules than the WINEPI AR algorithm. Using the *Gen-REAR* approach, all the rules can be generated if desired, even though the meaning of the additional AR's is captured by the smaller set of REAR's.

Gen-REAR performs extremely well when finding drought episodal rules as shown in Table 3. The number of REAR's decreases rapidly as the confidence interval increases. For the sample dataset at a confidence threshold of 0.20 and a window width of 2 months, *Gen-REAR* produces 24 drought parallel episodal rules while WINEPI AR produces 20892% more (5038) rules. With the same parameters, *Gen-REAR* produces 14 drought serial episodal rules while WINEPI AR produces 16257% more (2290) rules.

Table 3. Gen-REAR parallel and serial rules.

	Parallel	*Serial*
Confidence threshold	Distinct rules	Distinct rules
0.20	24	14
0.25	24	12
0.30	19	9
0.35	13	7
0.40	10	6
0.45	8	5

As the window width widens, *Gen-REAR* overwhelmingly produces fewer rules than the WINEPI algorithm. The number of REAR's increases as the window width. For the sample dataset at a window width of 3 months, *Gen-REAR* produces 30 parallel drought episodal rules while WINEPI AR produces 53763% more (16159) rules. With the same parameters, *Gen-REAR* produces 8 serial drought episodal rules while WINEPI AR produces 24825% more (1994). The savings are obvious. The *Gen-REAR* algorithm finds the drought REAR's for all reasonable window widths and confidence levels on the Mead, NE drought risk management dataset in less than 30 seconds. As the window

widens, the WINEPI AR algorithm quickly becomes computationally infeasible to use for the drought risk management problem.

5 Conclusion

This paper presents *Gen-REAR*, a new approach for generating representative episodal association rules. We also presented *Gen-FCE*, a new approach used to generate the frequent closed episode sets that conform to user-specified constraints. Our approach results in a large reduction in the input size for generating representative episodal association rules for targeted episodes, while retaining the ability to generate the entire set of association rules. We also studied the gain in efficiency of generating targeted representative episodal association rules as compared to the traditional WINEPI algorithm on a multiple time series drought risk management problem.

References

[1] R. Agrawal, T. Imielinski, and A. Swami. Mining association rules between sets of items in large databases. In *Proceedings of the ACM SIGMOD 1993 International Conference on Management of Data [SIGMOD 93]*, pages 207–216, Washington D.C., 1993.

[2] R. Bayardo, R. Agrawal, and D. Gunopupulos. Constraint-based rule mining in large, dense databases. In *Proceedings of ICDE-99*, 1999.

[3] S. K. Harms, S. Goddard, S. E. Reichenbach, W. J. Waltman, and T. Tadesse. Data mining in a geospatial decision support system for drought risk management. In *Proceedings of the 2001 National Conference on Digital Government Research*, pages 9–16, Los Angelos, California, USA, May 2001.

[4] M. Kryszkiewicz. Fast discovery of representative association rules. In *Lecture Notes in Artificial Intelligence*, volume 1424, pages 214–221. Proceedings of RSCTC 98, Springer-Verlag, 1998.

[5] H. Mannila, H. Toivonen, and A. I. Verkamo. Discovery of frequent episodes in event sequences. Technical report, Department of Computer Science, University of Helsinki, Finland, 1997. Report C-1997-15.

[6] J. Saquer and J. S. Deogun. Using closed itemsets for discovering representative association rules. In *Proceedings of the Twelfth International Symposium on Methodologies for Intelligent Systems [ISMIS 2000]*, Charlotte, NC, October 11-14 2000.

[7] R. Srikant, Q. Vu, and R. Agrawal. Mining association rules with item constraints. In *Proceedings of the Third International Conference on Knowledge Discovery and Data Mining [KDD97]*, pages 67–73, 1997.

[8] M. Zaki. Generating non-redundant association rules. In *Proceedings of the Sixth International Conference on Knowledge Discovery and Data Mining [KDD2000]*, pages 34–43, Boston, MA, USA, August 20-23 2000.

Text Clustering Based on Good Aggregations

Andreas Hotho
Institute AIFB
University of Karlsruhe
76128 Karlsruhe, Germany
hotho@aifb.uni-karlsruhe.de

Alexander Maedche
FZI Research Center at the
University of Karlsruhe
76131 Karlsruhe, Germany
maedche@fzi.de

Steffen Staab
Institute AIFB
University of Karlsruhe
76128 Karlsruhe, Germany
staab@aifb.uni-karlsruhe.de

1 Introduction

Text clustering typically involves clustering in a high dimensional space, which appears difficult with regard to virtually all practical settings. In addition, given a particular clustering result it is typically very hard to come up with a good explanation of why the text clusters have been constructed the way they are. In this paper, we propose a new approach for applying background knowledge (in terms of an ontology) during preprocessing in order to improve clustering results and allow for selection between results. The results may be distinguished and explained by the corresponding selection of concepts in the ontology. Our results compare favourably with a sophisticated baseline preprocessing strategy.

Thereby, the principal idea of our preprocessing approach, COSA (Concept Selection and Aggregation), is to use a simple, core ontology for restricting the set of relevant document features and for automatically proposing good aggregations. The aggregations are then exploited by the standard clustering algorithm K-Means. More precisely, we have compiled a heterarchy of concepts[1] that is used by a heuristic search algorithm to automatically construct a set of aggregations. The basic criteria of COSA include the computation of support for particular concepts and the top-down navigation of the heterarchy in a greedy manner. Based on COSA, a set of clustering results is produced without interaction by a human user of the system. The user may then decide to prefer the one over the other clustering result based on the actual concepts used for clustering as well as on standard quality measures (such as the silhouette measure).

2 Motivation example

Though standard mechanism for text clustering are well known, in typical applications (cf. [2]) they suffer from principal problems: First, background knowledge does not influence the interpretation of structures found by the clustering algorithms. Rather, irrelevant of the background knowledge existing clustering methods only compute one *"optimal"* result. Second, the term/concept vectors are too large. Therefore clustering takes place within a high-dimensional vector space leading to undesirable mathematical consequences, viz. all document pairs are similarly (dis-)similar. Thus, clustering becomes impossible and yields no recognizable results. Third, it is hard for the user to understand the differences between clusters.

Let us work through a detailed example to show you the problems and to give you an intuition for the proposed solution. In Table 1 you find a sample of (abbreviated) concept vectors representing web pages. In Figure 1 one may recognize the corresponding concepts highlighted in a small ontology. Our simplifying example shows the principal problem of vector representations of documents: The tendency that spurious appearance of concepts (or terms) rather strongly affects the clustering of documents. The reader may bear in mind that our simplification is so extensive that practically it does not appear in such tiny settings, but only when one works with large representations and large document sets. In our simplifying example the appearance of concepts PUBLICATION, KNOWLEDGE MANAGEMENT, and DISTRIBUTED ORGANIZATION is spread so evenly across the different documents that all document pairs exhibit (more or less) the same similarity. Corresponding squared Euclidian distances for the example document pairs (1,2), (2,3), (1,3) leads to values of 2, 2, and 2, respectively, and, hence, to no clustering structure at all.

When one reduces the size of the representation of our documents, e.g. by projecting into an subspace, one focuses on particular concepts and one may focus on the significant differences that documents exhibit with regard to these

---

[1] A heterarchy of concepts is a kind of "taxonomy" where each term may have multiple parents and — of course — multiple children.

Document #	("OTK")	("AIFB Publications")	("IICM Publications")
PUBLICATION	0	1	1
KNOWLEDGE MANAGEMENT	2	2	1
DISTRIBUTED ORGANIZATION	1	0	1

Table 1. Concept vector representations for 3 sample documents

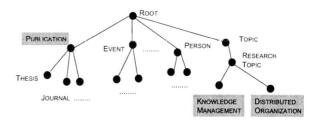

Figure 1. A sample ontology

concepts. For instance, when we project into a document vector representation that only considers the two dimensions PUBLICATIONS and KNOWLEDGE MANAGEMENT, we will find that document pairs (1,2), (2,3), (1,3) have squared Euclidean distances of 1, 1, and 2. Thus, axis-parallel projections like in this example may improve the clustering situation. In addition, we may exploit the ontology. For instance, we select features according to the taxonomy, choosing, e.g., RESEARCH TOPIC instead of its subconcepts KNOWLEDGE MANAGEMENT and DISTRIBUTED ORGANIZATION to built our aggregation. Then, the entries for KNOWLEDGE MANAGEMENT and DISTRIBUTED ORGANIZATION are added into one vector entry resulting in squared Euclidean distances between pairs (1,2), (2,3), (1,3) of 2, 0, and 2, respectively. Thus, documents 2 and 3 can be clustered together, while document 1 falls into a different cluster.

The algorithm GenerateConceptViews (described in [1]) acts as a preprocessing step for clustering. GenerateConceptViews chooses a set of interpretable and ontology-based aggregations leading to modified text representations. Conventional clustering algorithms like K-Means may work on these modified representations producing improved clustering results. Because the size of the vector representation is reduced, it becomes easier for the user to track the decisions made by the clustering algorithms. Because there are a variety of aggregations, the user may choose between alternative clustering results. For instance, there are aggregations such that publication pages are clustered together and the rest is set aside or aggregations such that web pages about KNOWLEDGE MANAGEMENT are clustered together and the rest is left in another cluster. The choice of concepts from the taxonomy thus determines the output of the clustering result and the user may use a view like Figure 1 in order to select and understand differences between clustering results.

Results

Our preprocessing approach COSA is a comprehensive approach using the background knowledge available in the ontology. In particular, we apply techniques from natural language processing to map terms to concepts. COSA selects aggregations by navigating top-down in the heterarchy. We use two other preprocessing strategies as baselines to evaluate the performance of COSA. To name but one, TES (Term selection) reduces terms considered "important" by information retrieval measures.

We have performed all evaluations on a set of 2234 HTML documents with a total sum of over 16 million words. For this purpose, we have manually modeled an ontology $\mathcal{O}$ consisting of a set of concepts $\mathcal{C}$ ($|\mathcal{C}| = 1030$).

The general result of our evaluation using the silhouette measure was that K-Means based on COSA preprocessing excelled the comparison baseline, viz. K-Means based on TES, to a large extent (more details in [1]).

3 Further Work

The preprocessing method, COSA, that we propose is a very general one. Our ontology-based text clustering approach has been implemented in a web-based knowledge management application supporting information brokering, viz. the FZI-Broker (cf. [2]). We have also applied our techniques on a high-dimensional data set that is not based on text documents, but on a real-world customer database with 24,156 customers in the telecommunications domain (cf. [3]). Preliminary results of applying our method on this complex transaction-oriented database show similar positive results.

References

[1] A. Hotho, A. Maedche, and S. Staab. Ontology-based text clustering. In *Proceedings of the IJCAI-2001 Workshop "Text Learning: Beyond Supervision"*, August, Seattle, USA, pages 30–37, 2001.

[2] A. Hotho, A. Maedche, S. Staab, and R. Studer. SEAL-II — the soft spot between richly structured and unstructured knowledge. *Journal of Universal Computer Science (J.UCS)*, 7(7):566–590, 2001.

[3] A. Maedche, A. Hotho, and M. Wiese. Enhancing preprocessing in data-intensive domains using online-analytical processing. In *DaWaK 2000*, LNCS 1874, pages 258–264. Springer, 2000.

Ad Hoc Association Rule Mining as SQL3 Queries

Hasan M. Jamil

Member, ACM and IEEE

jamil@acm.org

Abstract

Although there have been several encouraging attempts at developing methods for data mining using SQL, simplicity and efficiency still remain significant impediments for further development. In this paper, we propose a significantly new approach and show that any object relational database can be mined for association rules without any restructuring or preprocessing using only basic SQL3 constructs and functions, and hence no additional machineries are necessary. In particular, we show that the cost of computing association rules for a given database does not depend on support and confidence thresholds. More precisely, the set of large items can be computed using one simple join query and an aggregation once the set of all possible meets (least fixpoint) of item set patterns in the input table is known. The principal focus of this paper is to demonstrate that several SQL3 expressions exists for the mining of association rules.

1 Introduction

The motivation, importance, and the need for integrating data mining with relational databases has been addressed in several articles such as [3, 4]. They convincingly argue that without such integration, data mining technology may not find itself in a viable position in the years to come. To be a successful and feasible tool for the analysis of business data in relational databases, such technology must be made available as part of database engines and as part of its declarative query language. Some of the benefits of using existing relational machinery may include opportunity for query optimization, declarative language support, selective mining, mining from non-transactional databases, and so on. From these standpoints, it appears that research into data mining using SQL or SQL-like languages bear merit and warrant attention.

In this article, we demonstrate that there is a simpler SQL3 expression for association rule mining that does not require candidate generation such as in [6, 5] or any implementation of new specialized operators such as in [2]. We also show that we can simply add a mine by operator to SQL, with an optional having clause to facilitate filtering of unwanted derivations, in a fashion similar to the cube by operator proposed for data warehousing applications. The striking feature of our proposal is that we can exploit the vast array of optimization techniques that already exists and possibly develop newer ones for better performance. These are some of the advantages of our proposal over previous proposals in addition to its simplicity and intuitive appeal.

2 A Set Theoretic Perspective of Data Mining

In order to introduce a few ideas, let us consider a database, called the transaction table, **T** as shown in figure 1. Based on the traditional understanding of association rule mining we expect to obtain the "non-redundant" large item set table (l_table) and the rules table (r_table) shown in figure 1 below from the table **T** once we set the support threshold at 25%. The reasoning process of reaching to the large item set and rules tables can be explained as follows.

t_table

Tranid	Items
t_1	a
t_1	b
t_1	c
t_2	b
t_2	c
t_2	f
t_3	b
t_3	f
t_4	a
t_4	b
t_4	c
t_5	b
t_5	e
t_6	d
t_6	f
t_7	d

transaction table

l_table

Items	Support
{a, b, c}	.29
{b, f}	.29
{b, c}	.38
{f}	.43
{d}	.29
{b}	.71

large item set table

r_table

Ant	Cons	Support	Conf
{b}	{c}	0.38	0.60
{f}	{b}	0.29	0.66
{b}	{f}	0.29	0.40
{b,c}	{a}	0.29	0.66

association rules table

Figure 1: Source transaction database **T** is shown as t_table, large item set table as l_table, and finally the association rules as r_table.

We can think of **T** as the set of complex tuples shown in nested table (n_table) in figure 2 once we nest the items on transaction numbers. If we use a group by on the Items column and count the transactions, we will compute the frequency table (f_table) that will show how many times a single item set pattern appears in the transaction table (t_table) in figure 1. Then, let us assume that we took a cross product of the frequency table with itself, and selected the rows for which

- the Items column in the first table is a proper subset of the Items column in the second table, and finally projected out the Items column of the first table and Support column of the second table[1], or

---

[1] This will give us $< \{b, f\}, 1 >$ and $< \{d\}, 1 >$.

- the Items columns are not subset of one another, and we took the intersection of the Items of both the tables, created a new relation (int_table, called the intersection table) with distinct tuples of such Items with Support 0, and then finally computed the support counts as explained in step 1 now with the frequency table and intersection table[2].

This will give us the inheritance table (i_table) as shown in figure 2. Finally, if we took a union of the frequency table and the inheritance table, and then do a group by on the Items column and sum the Support column, we would obtain the count table (c_table) of figure 2.

n_table
nested table

Tranid	Items
t_1	{a,b,c}
t_2	{b,c,f}
t_3	{b,f}
t_4	{a,b,c}
t_5	{b,e}
t_6	{d,f}
t_7	{d}

i_table
inheritance table

Items	Support
{b,c}	3
{b,f}	1
{b}	5
{f}	3
{d}	1

f_table
frequency table

Items	Support
{a, b, c}	2
{b,c,f}	1
{b, e}	1
{b, f}	1
{d}	1
{d,f}	1

c_table
count table

Items	Support
{a, b, c}	2
{b,c,f}	1
{b,c}	3
{b, f}	2
{b, e}	1
{d, f}	1
{b}	5
{f}	3
{d}	2

Figure 2: n_table: t_table after nesting on Tranid, f_table: n_table after grouping on Items and counting, i_table: generated from f_table, and c_table: grouping on Items and sum on Support on the union of i_table and f_table.

The entire process of large item set and association rule generation can be conveniently explained using the so called item set lattice found in the literature once we enhance it with some additional information. Let us consider placing the transactions with item set I appearing in the frequency table with their support count t as a node in such a lattice as shown in figure 3. Notice that in the lattice, each node is represented as I_c^t, where it denotes the fact that I appears in exactly t transactions in the source table, and that I also appears as a subset of other transactions n number of times such that $c = n + t$. t is called the *transaction count*, or *frequency count*, and c is called the *total count* of item set I.

In the lattice of figure 3, the nodes marked with a solid rectangle are the nodes (or the item sets) in **T**, nodes identified with dotted rectangles are called the *intersection* nodes or the *virtual* nodes (as they do not appears in **T** explicitly), and the nodes marked with dotted ellipses are redundant. The solid ellipse nodes are redundant as well as

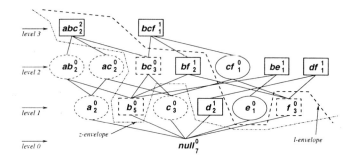

Figure 3: Lattice representation of item sets in the database **T**.

they are not large item sets. The nodes below the dotted line, called the large item set envelope, or *l-envelope*, are the large item sets. Notice that the node bc is a large item set but is not a member of **T**, while bcf, df and be are, yet they are not included in the set of large item sets of **T**. We are assuming here a support threshold of 25%. So, basically, we would like to compute only the nodes abc, bc, bf, b, d and f from **T**. This set is identified by the *sandwich* formed by the l-envelope and the zero-envelope, or the *z-envelope*, that marks the lowest level nodes in the lattice.

The concept of node redundancy, and consequently large item set and rule redundancy are formalized as follows.

Definition 2.1 Let $\mathcal{T}$ be a transaction table over item sets $\mathcal{I}$, $I \subseteq \mathcal{I}$ be an item set, and n be a positive integer. Also let n represent the frequency of the item set I with which it appears in $\mathcal{T}$. Then the pair $\langle I, n \rangle$ is called a *frequent* item set, and the pair is called a *large* item set if $n \geq \delta_m$, where δ_m is the minimum support threshold.

If for any large item set I, its frequency n can be determined from other large item sets, then I is redundant. Formally,

Definition 2.2 (Redundancy of Large Item Sets) Let L be a set of large item sets of tuples of the form $\langle I_u, n_u \rangle$ such that $\forall x, y (x = \langle I_x, n_x \rangle, y = \langle I_y, n_y \rangle \in L \wedge I_x = I_y \Rightarrow n_x = n_y)$, and let $u = \langle I_u, n_u \rangle$ be such a tuple. Then u is *redundant* in L if $\exists v (v \in L, v = \langle I_v, n_v \rangle, I_u \subseteq I_v \Rightarrow n_u = n_v)$.

The importance of the definition 2.2 may be highlighted as follows. For any given set of large item sets L, and an element $l = \langle I_l, n_l \rangle \in L$, I_l is unique in L. The implication of anti-monotonicity is that for any other $v = \langle I_v, n_v \rangle \in L$ such that $I_l \subset I_v$ holds, $n_v \leq n_l$ because an item set cannot appear in a transaction database less number of times than any of its supersets. But the important case is when $n_v = n_l$ yet $I_l \subset I_v$. This implies that I_l never appears in a transaction alone, i.e., it always appeared with other items. It also implies for all large item sets $s = \langle I_s, n_s \rangle \in L$ of I_v such that $I_s \supset I_v$, if it exists, $n_v = n_s$ too. As if not, n_l should be different than n_v, which it is not, according to our assumption. It also implies that I_l is not involved in any other sub-superset relationship chains other that I_v.

Because redundant large item sets exists, traditional mining algorithms such as apriori generates all possible rules, some of which are essentially redundant. For example, let $a \rightarrow b \langle \frac{s_{ab}}{m}, \frac{s_{ab}}{s_a} \rangle$ and $ab \rightarrow c \langle \frac{s_{abc}}{m}, \frac{s_{abc}}{s_{ab}} \rangle$ be two rules discovered from a any tracsaction table F_f, where s_X and m represent respectively the frequency of an item set X in

---

[2]The result of this will be tuple $< \{b, c\}, 3 >$, $< \{b\}, 5 >$, and $< \{f\}, 3 >$ in this example. Note that the intersection table will contain the tuples $< \{b, c\}, 0 >$, $< \{b\}, 0 >$, and $< \{f\}, 0 >$, and that these patterns are not part of the frequency table in figure 2. The union of step 1, and step 2 processed with the intersection table will now produce the inheritance table in figure 2.

the item set table and the number of transactions in the item set table $\mathcal{S}$. Then it is also the case that the set of discovered rules contains another rule (transitive implication) $a \to bc\langle\frac{s_{abc}}{m}, \frac{s_{abc}}{s_a}\rangle$. Notice that this last rule is a logical consequence of the first two rules that can be derived using the following inference rule, where $X, Y, Z \subset \mathcal{I}$ are item sets.

$$\frac{X \to Y\langle\frac{s_{X \cup Y}}{m}, \frac{s_{X \cup Y}}{s_X}\rangle \qquad X \cup Y \to Z\langle\frac{s_{X \cup Y \cup Z}}{m}, \frac{s_{X \cup Y \cup Z}}{s_{X \cup Y}}\rangle}{X \to Y \cup Z\langle\frac{s_{X \cup Y \cup Z}}{m}, \frac{s_{X \cup Y \cup Z}}{s_X}\rangle}$$

Written differently, using only symbols for support (δ) and confidence (η), the inference rule reads as follows.

$$\frac{X \to Y\langle\delta_1, \eta_1\rangle \qquad X \cup Y \to Z\langle\delta_2, \eta_2\rangle}{X \to Y \cup Z\langle\delta_2, \eta_1 * \eta_2\rangle}$$

Based on these observations, we take the position and claim that the table l_table shown in figure 1 is an information equivalent table of the large item set table produced by apriori on **T**, which essentially means that these tables faithfully imply one another (assuming identical support thresholds).

3 SQL3 Expressions for Computing Association Rules

Now that we have explained what non-redundant large item sets and association rules mean in our framework, we are ready to discuss computing them using SQL. The reader may recall from our discussion in the previous section that we have already given this problem a relational face by presenting them in terms of (nested) tables. We will now present a set of SQL3 sentences to compute the tables we have discussed earlier. We must mention here that it is possible to evaluate the final table in figure 1 by mimicking the process using a lesser number of expressions than what we present below. But we prefer to include them all separately for the sake of clarity.

For the purpose of this discussion, we will assume that several functions that we are going to use in our expressions are available in some SQL3 implementation, such as Oracle, DB2 or Informix. Recall that SQL3 standard requires or implies that, in some form or other, these functions are supported[3]. In particular, we have used a nest by clause that functions like a group by on the listed attributes, but returns a nested relation as opposed to a first normal form relation returned by group by. We have also assumed that SQL3 can perform group by on nested columns (columns with set values). Finally, we have also used set comparators in where clause, and set functions such as **intersect** and **setminus** in the select clause, which we think are natural additions to SQL3 once nested tuples are supported. As we have mentioned before, we have, for now, used user defined functions (UDFs) by treating set of items as a string of labels to implement these features in Oracle.

```
create view n_table as
(select Tranid, Items
from t_table
nest by Tranid)

create view f_table as
(select Items, count(*) as Support
from n_table
group by Items)
```

---

[3]Although some of these functions are not supported right now, once they are, we will be in a better shape. Until then, we can use PL/SQL codes to realize these functions.

The two view definitions above prepare any first normal form transaction table for the mining process. Note that these view definitions act as idempotent functions on their source. So, redoing them does not harm the process if the source table is already in one of these forms. These two views compute the n_table and the f_table of figure 2.

Before we can compute the i_table, we need to know what nodes in the imaginary lattice will inherit transaction counts from some of the transaction nodes in the lattice – Support value of Items in the f_table. Recall that nodes that are subset of another node in the lattice, inherit the transaction count of the superset node towards its total count. We also know that only those (non-redundant) nodes which appear in the f_table, or are in the least fixpoint of the nodes in f_table will inherit them. So, we compute first the set of intersection nodes implied by f_table using the newly proposed SQL3 create view recursive statement as follows.

```
create view recursive int_table as
((select distinct intersect(t.Items, p.Items), 0
from f_table as t, f_table as p
where t.Items ⊄ p.Items and p.Items ⊄ t.Items
    and not exists (select *
        from f_table as f
        where f.Items = intersect(t.Items, p.Items)))
union
(select distinct intersect(t.Items, p.Items), 0
from int_table as t, int_table as p
where t.Items ⊄ p.Items and p.Items ⊄ t.Items
    and not exists (select *
        from f_table as f
        where f.Items = intersect(t.Items, p.Items))))
```

We would like to mention here again that we have implemented this feature again using PL/SQL in Oracle. Notice that we did not list the int_table we create below in figure 1 or 2 because it is regarded as a transient table needed for the computation of i_table.

It is really important that we create only distinct set of intersection items and only those ones that do not appear in the f_table for the purpose of accuracy in support counting. Take for example three transactions in a new frequency table, f'_table, represented as $\{abc_0^1, bcd_0^1, bcf_0^1, bc_0^1\}$. Assume that we compute the set of intersections of the entries in this table. If we do not guard against the cautions we have mentioned, we will produce the set $\{bc_0^0, bc_0^0, bc_0^0\}$ using the view expression for int_table – which is not desirable. Because, these three will inherit Support from $\{abc_0^1, bcd_0^1, bcf_0^1\}$ giving a total count of 10, i.e., bc_{10}^1. The correct total count should have been bc_4^1. If we just ensure the uniqueness of a newly generated item set (but not its absence in the f_table) through meet computation, we still derive $\{bc_0^0\}$ instead of an empty set, which is incorrect. This means that not including the following condition (or its equivalent) in the above SQL expression will be a serious mistake.

```
not exists (select *
from f_table as f
where f.Items = intersect(t.Items, p.Items)
```

Once we have computed the int_table, the rest of the task is pretty simple. The i_table view is computed by copying the Support of a tuple in f_table for any tuple in the collection of f_table and int_table which is a subset of the tuple in the f_table. Intuitively, these are the nodes that need to inherit the transaction counts of their ancestors (in f_table).

```
create view i_table as
(select t.Items, p.Support
from f_table as p,
    ((select *
    from f_table)
    union
    (select *
    from int_table)) as t,
where t.Items ⊂ p.Items)
```

From the i_table, a simple grouping and sum operation as shown below will give us the count table, or the c_table, of figure 2.

```
create view c_table as
(select t.Items, sum(t.Support) as Support
from ((select *
    from f_table)
    union
    (select *
    from i_table)) as t
group by t.Items)
```

The large item sets of l_table in figure 1 can now be generated by just selecting on the c_table tuples as shown next. Notice that we could have combined this step with the c_table expression above with the help of a having clause.

```
create view l_table as
(select Items, Support
from c_table
where Support ≥ δ_m)
```

Finally, the (non-redundant) association rules of figure 1 are computed using the r_table view below. The functionality of this view can be explained as follows. Two item sets $u[Items]$ and $v[Items]$ in a pair of tuple u and v in the l_table implies an association rule of the form $u[Items] \rightarrow v[Items] \setminus u[Items]\langle v[Support], \frac{v[Support]}{u[Support]}\rangle$ only if $u[Items] \subset v[Items]$ and there does not exist any intervening item set x in the l_table such that x is a superset of $u[Items]$ and is a subset of $v[Items]$ as well. In other words, in the lattice, $v[Items]$ is one of the immediate ancestors of $u[Items]$. In addition, the ratio of the Supports, i.e., $\frac{v[Support]}{u[Support]}$ must be at least equal to the minimum confidence threshold η_m.

```
create view r_table as
(select a.Items, c.Items\a.Items, c.Support,
    c.Support/a.Support
from l_table as a, l_table as c
where a.Items ⊂ c.Items and c.Items/a.Items ≥ η_m
    and not exists
        (select Items
        from l_table as i
        where a.Items ⊂ i.Items and i.Items ⊂ c.Items))
```

The readers may verify that these are the only "generic" SQL3 expressions (or their equivalent) that are needed to mine any relational database (assuming proper name adaptations for tables and columns). The essence of this relational interpretation of the problem of mining, as demonstrated by the SQL3 expressions above, is that we do not necessarily need to think procedurally – in terms of number of iterations, candidate generation, space time overhead, and so on. Instead, we can now express our mining problems on any relational database in declarative ways, and leave the optimization issues with the system and let the system process the query using the best available method to it, recognizing the fact that depending on the instance of the database, the choice of best methods may now vary widely.

In another recent research [1] we have demonstrated that to implement apriori in SQL3, one need not be constrained by the complexity and availability of combination and GatherJoin [7, 6] operators. Without much discussion we present below the set of SQL3 queries (see [1] for details) that correctly implement apriori. Again, a comparison with the works in [6, 2] will expose the strength and simplicity of our proposal.

```
create view f_table as
(select Items, count(Items)/m as Support
from t_table
group by Items);

create sequence seq increment by 1 start with 1;

create view recursive l_table as
((select Items, sum(Support) as Support
from (flatten(select sub(Items, {}, 1) as Items,
        Support
    from f_table))
group by Items
having sum(Support) => δ_m)
union all
(select t.Items, sum(t.Support) as Support
from f_table as u, (flatten distinct(select
        sub(f.Items, l.Items, i.Degree) as Items
    from f_table as f, l_table as l,
        (select Seq.Nextval as Degree
        from iteration) as i,
    where sizeof(l.Items) = i.Degree − 1
        and l.Items ⊂ f.Items)) as t
where t.Items ⊆ u.Items
group by t.Items
having sum(t.Support) => δ_m));
```

References

[1] Hasan M. Jamil. On the equivalence of top-down and bottom-up data mining in relational databases. In *DaWaK*, Munich, Germany, 2001.

[2] Rosa Meo, Giuseppe Psaila, and Stefano Ceri. An extension to SQL for mining association rules. *DMKD*, 2(2):195–224, 1998.

[3] Amir Netz, Surajit Chaudhuri, Jeff Bernhardt, and Usama M. Fayyad. Integration of data mining with database technology. In *Proceedings of 26th VLDB*, pages 719–722, 2000.

[4] Amir Netz, Surajit Chaudhuri, Usama M. Fayyad, and Jeff Bernhardt. Integrating data mining with SQL databases. In *IEEE ICDE*, 2001.

[5] Karthick Rajamani, Alan Cox, Bala Iyer, and Atul Chadha. Efficient mining for association rules with relational database systems. In *IDEAS*, pages 148–155, 1999.

[6] Sunita Sarawagi, Shiby Thomas, and Rakesh Agrawal. Integrating mining with relational database systems: Alternatives and implications. In *Proc. ACM SIGMOD*, pages 343–354, 1998.

[7] Shiby Thomas and Sunita Sarawagi. Mining generalized association rules and sequential patterns using SQL queries. In *KDD*, pages 344–348, 1998.

Heuristic Optimization for Decentralized Frequent Itemset Counting

Viviane Crestana Jensen   Nandit Soparkar

Electrical Engineering and Computer Science

The University of Michigan, Ann Arbor, MI 48109-2122

{viviane,soparkar}@eecs.umich.edu

Abstract

The choices for mining of decentralized data are numerous, and we have developed techniques to enumerate and optimize decentralized frequent itemset counting. In this paper, we introduce our heuristic approach to improve the performance of such techniques developed in ways similar to query processing in database systems. We also describe empirical results that validate our heuristic techniques.

1. Introduction

The counting of frequent itemsets [1] is expensive, and research efforts concentrate on this step (*e.g.*, [2, 3, 5]). Available algorithms for partitioned databases (*e.g.*, see [4]) deal only with one single table partitioned horizontally. In contrast, decentralized schemas involve several tables that could be partitioned vertically as well. Our previous work [6] describes decentralized algorithms for finding frequent itemsets in a Star schema. Our algorithms run at individual tables separately, and the partial results are "merged" thereafter, thereby avoiding the expensive join of all tables required in typical centralized solutions.

2. Enumerating Alternatives

There are several alternatives to effecting the mining when dealing with decentralized tables (see [7]). Our "algebra" facilitates enumerating and choosing among alternatives – in a manner similar to an algebra for relational query processing. Our enumeration approach begins with an expression representing the join of all tables prior to finding the frequent itemsets. Thereafter, by using equivalence rules , we obtain alternative equivalent expressions that are often less expensive to compute (than using traditional techniques which first materialize the join). Each expression generated corresponds to different logical evaluation plans.

The basic notation for our "algebra"[1] has two terms: FI, frequent itemsets of a table (which could be a material-

---

[1]Due to space constraints, we use a simplified notation for FI and CI: we omit one parameter, the *weight table*, that carries the weight of the joined table when computing at separate tables. This weight table typically contains only foreign keys. For details, see [7].

ized join); and CI, frequent itemsets across tables (*i.e.*, the merging of results). Examples of equivalence rules are:

Eq1: $FI(X \bowtie Y) = FI(X) \cup FI(Y) \cup CI(\{X,Y\})$
Eq2: $CI(\{X,Y,Z\}) = CI(\{X, Y \bowtie Z\}) \cup CI(\{Y,Z\})$

To exemplify the use of our equivalences, consider a data schema composed of 4 tables: $Demographics$, $Product$, $Customer$ (which besides its attributes, has a foreign key to $Demographics$), and $ItemsBought$ (which contains only foreign keys to tables $Customer$ and $Product$). Since $ItemsBought$ does not contain any non-key attributes, it is only used as the *weight table*. Our goal is to find the frequent itemsets across all tables (from here on, referred to by the first letter in their names), *i.e.*, we want to compute

1. $FI(D \bowtie C \bowtie P)$

Using Eq1 and Eq2 subsequently we get various equivalent expressions:

2. $FI(D) \cup FI(C \bowtie P) \cup CI(\{D, C \bowtie P\})$
3. $FI(D) \cup FI(C) \cup FI(P) \cup CI(\{C,P\} \cup CI(\{D, C \bowtie P\})$
4. $FI(D) \cup FI(C) \cup FI(P) \cup CI(\{D,C,P\})$
5. $FI(D) \cup FI(C) \cup FI(P) \cup CI(\{D,C\}) \cup CI(\{D \bowtie C, P\})$
6. $FI(D \bowtie C) \cup FI(P) \cup CI(\{D \bowtie C, P\})$

3. Heuristic Optimization

When using cost models, database systems utilize heuristics to reduce the number of choices for which cost estimates are computed. Likewise, besides cost-based optimization (see [7]), we use heuristics to reduce the number of choices. Furthermore, in situations where cost estimates are not available, heuristics help decide which plans are more efficient. Here, we show a few heuristics.

Heu1: *When the table in an FI has joins between unrelated tables, use Eq1 to convert the expression.*
Heu2: *When tables have a direct relationship, merge them before merging with other tables.*

Applying our heuristics to the expressions listed in Section 2, we choose expression 5 over 1 and 2 (using Heu1), and over 3 and 4 (using Heu2). Our heuristics do not help in choosing between expressions 5 and 6.

A simple algorithm would be to enumerate all possible expressions, and then to use the heuristic rules to choose

---

among them. Given that the number of possible expressions is very large, this approach would be impractical (note that not all possible expressions for our example were listed). Instead, based on our heuristic rules, we developed an efficient algorithm (on the order of the number of tables, n) that develops a plan to merge efficiently the related tables only. The algorithm creates a decentralized logical plan with n FIs: one for each table. Since no tables are prejoined, Cartesian products (Heu1) are avoided, and only tables that are directly related by foreign keys get pre-merged (Heu2). The plan generated is then improved using other heuristic rules (see [7] for details). If cost estimates are available, they can be used where our heuristics do not help.

4. Empirical Validation

We base our dataset on the TPC-D benchmark [8], which reflects the decentralized schemas typical in a data warehouse, as shown in Figure 1. To incorporate customer buying patterns we replaced the $LineItem$ table with the transactions generated by the IBM Almaden synthetic data generator [2] with 1,500,000 transactions and 800,000 items, which we call $MyLineItem$. The table $MyLineItem$ had about 14 million records, and was approximately 120 Mbytes in size. The joined table was approximately 5.3 Gbytes in size.

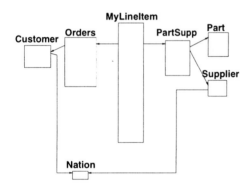

Figure 1. TPC-D benchmark schema.

We implemented the typical Apriori approach [2] for the centralized and the Memory saving [6] strategies. Our Memory saving strategy uses the same algorithm and data structure as used in any Apriori-like approach – with the added advantage accrued from decentralized counting. Therefore, any Apriori-like algorithm could be transformed, with expected savings comparable to the ones shown here. We also implemented our I/O saving strategy [6] for decentralized mining. The runtime for support 30% for each plan that we examined is shown in Figure 2, with Phase I corresponding to computing frequent itemsets locally, and Phase II to merging results across tables. Plans (a)-(f) are decentralized plans, whereas the Apriori is centralized. All 3-way and 2-way merges were performed by the Memory saving the I/O saving strategies, respectively. Our experiments were performed on a 200 MHz Pentium Pro with 256 Mbytes of RAM, running Linux.

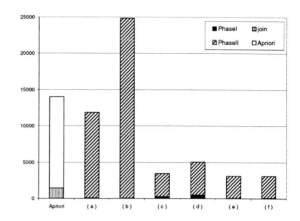

Figure 2. Runtime for 30% support.

Our heuristic algorithm would derive plan (e), where no joins were computed and tables were merged only when related directly. This plan was the second best plan (within 1%) for support 30%. The optimal plan (corresponding to plan (f)) differed from (e) in that it computed 2 prejoins. Again, cost estimates could be used here when deciding whether to prejoin any tables. It is important to notice that several plans with poor performance are usually precluded by our heuristics (*e.g.*, see [7]). For instance, plan (b), which was the worst performing (see Figure 2), would be discarded. We performed extensive experiments [7] and for all cases studied, our heuristic approach chose the best (or nearly best) strategy among those generated.

References

[1] R. Agrawal, T. Imielinski, and A. Swami. Mining association rules between sets of items in large databases. In *Proceedings of ACM SIGMOD Int'l Conference on Management of Data*, 1993.

[2] R. Agrawal and R. Srikant. Fast algorithms for mining association rules in large databases. In *Proceedings of the 20th Int'l Conference on Very Large Data Bases*, 1994.

[3] S. Brin, R. Motwani, J. Ullman, and S. Tsur. Dynamic itemset counting and implication rules for market basket data. In *Proceedings of ACM SIGMOD Int'l Conference on Management of Data*, 1997.

[4] D. Cheung, V. Ng, A. Fu, and Y. Fu. Efficient mining of association rules in distributed databases. *IEEE Transactions on Knowledge and Data Engineering*, 1996.

[5] J. Han, J. Pei, and Y. Yin. Mining frequent patterns without candidate generation. In *Proceedings of ACM SIGMOD Int'l Conference on Management of Data*, 2000.

[6] V. C. Jensen and N. Soparkar. Frequent itemset counting across multiple tables. In *Proceedings of the 4th Pacific-Asia Conference on Knowledge Discovery and Data Mining*, 2000.

[7] V. C. Jensen and N. Soparkar. Optimization and evaluation strategies for decentralized database mining. Technical Report. The University of Michigan, Ann Arbor, USA, June 2001. Consolidated version submitted for journal publication.

[8] Transaction Processing Performance Council. http://www.tpc.org., May 1995.

Evolutionary Structure Learning Algorithm for Bayesian Network and Penalized Mutual Information Metric

Gang LI   Fu TONG [*]   Honghua DAI

School of Computing and Mathematics, Deakin University, Victoria 3168, Australia

[*]School of Computer, Shanghai University, Shanghai 200072, China

gangli@deakin.edu.au   ftong@online.sh.cn   hdai@deakin.edu.au

Abstract

This paper formulates the problem of learning Bayesian network structures from data as determining the structure that best approximates the probability distribution indicated by the data. A new metric, Penalized Mutual Information metric, is proposed, and a evolutionary algorithm is designed to search for the best structure among alternatives. The experimental results show that this approach is reliable and promising.

1. Problem Definition and PMI Metric

Bayesian network is a powerful knowledge representation and reasoning tool under uncertainty [1]. However, the construction of a Bayesian network manually is usually time-consuming and subject to mistakes. Therefore, algorithms for automatic learning, that occasionally use the information provided by an expert, can be of great help [2]. Considering the fact that any Bayesian network for domain U uniquely determines a joint probability function over the domain U, the problem of structure learning of Bayesian network, can be viewed as finding the best approximate decomposition of the target distribution determined by the data. Let $\hat{p}$ be the probability distribution function represented by a Bayesian network, the KL difference [3] between $\hat{p}$ and the target probability distribution function p over the domain is

$$KL(p(v_1,\cdots,v_n),\hat{p}(v_1,\cdots,v_n))$$

$$= \sum_{v_1\cdots v_n} p(v_1,\cdots,v_n)\cdot\log p(v_1,\cdots,v_n) - \sum_{i=1}^{n} MI(v_i,Pa(v_i)) - \sum_{i=1}^{n}\sum_{v_i} p(v_i)\cdot\log p(v_i)$$

Where $MI(v_i,Pa(v_i))$ is the mutual information between node v_i and its parents $Pa(v_i)$. Since values of the other terms are independent of the Bayesian network structure, the KL difference between the Bayesian network structure and target distribution is minimized just when the total mutual information is maximized. However, it can be proved that this principle could lead to more complex structures. Our response to this problem is to incorporate some form of penalty for model complexity into the total mutual information like this:

$$\sum_{i=1}^{n} MI(v_i,Pa(v_i)) - f(N)\times\dim(S)$$

where $\dim(S)$ is the dimension, i.e. number of parameters needed to specify the Bayesian network with structure S, $f(N)$ is a non-negative penalization function. Based on the Bayesian Information Criterion [4], we set $f(N)=\dfrac{\log N}{2N}$, so we can get Penalized Mutual Information metric as follows:

$$\sum_{i=1}^{n} MI(v_i,Pa(v_i)) - \frac{\log N}{2N}\times\dim(S)$$

3. Structure Learning by Evolutionary Algorithm

In this section, we use evolutionary search methods to identify network structures with the highest score by selected metric. For a domain $U=\{v_1,v_2,\cdots,v_n\}$ with n variables, a Bayesian network structure can be represented by an connectivity matrix $M=[r_{ij}]_{n\times n}$, where r_{ij} equals 1 when v_j is a parent of v_i, or 0 if not.

Based on this representation, we defined two reproduction operators: *Intersection* results in a structure consists of the common of arcs in the parents; *Union* results in a structure consists of the union of the arcs in the parents.

In addition to these, five mutation operators are designed, they are : *Simple Mutation* randomly adds or removes an arc from the structure; *MI-Guided Mutation*, randomly selects arc to add or remove according its corresponding mutual information; *Arc Reversion* randomly selects an arc and reverses its direction; *Parent Shift* randomly selects an arc, and changes its starting point to another node; *Child Shift* randomly selects an arc, and changes its ending point to another node.

To assure the closeness of the reproduction and mutation operators, three repair operators, DAG Repair, Max-Parents Repair, and Partial Order Repair, are introduced to assure that each resulting structure during the evolution is a valid DAG, and do not violate the prior knowledge.

4. Experiment Results

In order to evaluate the performance of proposed algorithm, we present our experimental comparisons of structure learning by evolutionary algorithm and PMI metric (PMI-EA), with a genetic structure learning algorithm (MDL-GA) described in [5]. Both algorithms attempt to induce a Bayesian network structure from a database. Four databases are used in the experiment. Six values related to the behavior of algorithms are considered: Average PMI metric (APMI), Average MDL metric (AMDL), Average Total Mutual Information (ATMI), Average Number of Error Arcs (ANE), Average Number of Generations performed before the best structure is found (ANG), Times of Finding Original structure (TFO)

We give the result of ALARM databases in table 1. From the table we can see that the ANG for PMI-EA is significantly smaller than that of MDL-GA, and the ANE, AMDL for PMI-EA are smaller than those of the MDL-GA. This indicates that PMI-EA is capable of finding a better Bayesian network structure from the given data set. On the other hand, for the algorithm PMI-EA, we observe from the table that when use reproduction operators with a lower rate (0.1) the ANG is smaller than the ones that only use mutation operators. This indicates that the introduction of reproduction improves the convergence speed of the algorithm.

Table 5. Comparison result for ALARM database

	APMI	AMDL	AMI	ANE	ANG	TFO
MDL-GA	16.73291	1384269.41	17.01948	10.3	2102	1
PMI-EA (P_c=0.1 P_m=0.2)	17.23317	1357988.28	17.52483	2.6	3404	12
PMI-EA (P_c=0 P_m=0.2)	17.21954	1365633.73	17.48529	4.3	3260	7
PMI-EA (P_c=0.1 P_m=0.5)	17.23116	1362748.25	17.52091	3.1	2573	11
PMI-EA (P_c=0 P_m=0.5)	17.20188	1365975.11	17.46157	4.7	3081	9

The experimental results are very encouraging, which indicates that we are on the right way towards automated structure learning of Bayesian network. Clearly, what we have accomplished so far, is preliminary. In the future, we intend to incorporate other kinds of prior knowledge to increase the efficiency, as well as incorporate possibility theory to reduce the learning complexity especially when missing values exist.

Acknowledgements Related work is supported by Natural Sciences Foundation of China 69873031.

References

[1] Pearl, J. Probabilistic Reasoning in Intelligent Systems. Morgan Kaufmann Publishers, 1988

[2] Jordan, M.I. Learning in Graphical Models. MIT Press, 1999

[3] Kullback, S. and Leibler, R.A. *On Information and Sufficiency.* Annals of Mathematic Statistics. 22:79~86, 1951

[4] Schwarz, G. Estimating the Dimension of a Model. Annals of Statistics, 7(2):461~464, 1978

[5] Larranaga, P. et al. Searching for the best ordering n the structure learning of Bayesian networks. IEEE Transactions on Systems, Man and Cybernetics, 26c(4)487~493, 1996

[6] Wong, M.L. Lam, W. and Leung, K.S. Using Evolutionary Computation and Minimum Description Length Principle for Data mining of Probabilistic Knowledge. IEEE Pattern Analysis and Machine Intelligence, 21(2), 174~178, 1999.

[7] Wallace, C., Korb, K.B. and Dai, H. *Causal Discovery via MML.* Proceedings of the 13th International Conference on Machine learning (ICML'96), San Francisco: Morgan Kaufmann Publishers, 516~524, 1996

Applications of Data Mining in Hydrology

Xu Liang
Department of Civil and Environmental Engineering
University of California
Berkeley, CA 94720
Email: liang@ce.berkeley.edu

Yao Liang
Alexandria Research Institute
Department of Electrical and Computer Engineering
Virginia Polytechnic Institute and State University
Alexandria, VA 22314
Email: yaliang@vt.edu

Abstract

Long-term range streamflow forecast plays an invaluable role in water resources planning and management. In this study, the potential applicability and limitations of the time series forecasting approach using neural network with the multiresolution learning paradigm (NNMLP) are investigated. The predicted long-term range streamflows using the NNMLP are compared with the observations. The results show that the time series forecasting approach of NNMLP has good predicting skill. The NNMLP requires only historical streamflow information. The time series forecasting approach of NNMLP has great potential for being used alone in regions with limited available information, and for being combined with other approaches to improve long-term range streamflow forecasts.

1. Introduction

Long-term range (multi-season to one year or longer lead times) streamflow forecast, that is, the forecast of future available water, plays an invaluable role in water resources planning and management, and many environmental issues. It has been recognized that significant improvements have been achieved on short-term (a few hours to several days in advance) streamflow forecast due to advancements in short-term prediction of precipitation based on remote sensing measurements. Mid-term range (a few months to a season lead time) streamflow forecast is also improved, mainly for the cases where snowmelt plays a significant role in the composition of streamflow. However, the prediction of long-term range streamflow still suffers significant uncertainties. This is mainly due to the difficulty of the long-term prediction on precipitation and the increasingly sensitivity of streamflow to the accuracy of precipitation prediction during the forecast period with hydrological models.

In recent years, the long-term range streamflow forecast has received increasing attention. In principal, the predictions of streamflows can be classified into two general categories. One is to predict the future meteorological variables (such as precipitation) first and then to predict the streamflows; and the other is to predict the streamflows using a time series forecasting approach where future streamflows are predicted based on the past and current predicted streamflow time series. Most of streamflow forecast studies belong to the first category where the key for success is to obtain good prediction of future precipitation and/or other meteorological variables, a good hydrologic model, and a good estimation of model parameters. However, a large range of variation exists, with current state of art, for ensemble forecasts of streamflows using this approach.

This paper investigates the potential applicability of the time series forecasting approach on long-term range streamflow prediction by using neural network with multiresolution learning paradigm, and its limitations. Although there have been a number of studies of using neural networks to forecast streamflows, few of them employs the time series forecasting approach where past and current predicted streamflows are the only information that can be used as the input to the neural network. Instead, most of current streamflow forecast studies with neural networks belong to the first category, where their inputs to the neural network depend partially or entirely on the prediction knowledge or skills of other sources such as different climate modes, sea surface temperature, and precipitation.

617

In this paper, the approach of the neural network with multi-resolution learning paradigm (NNMLP) is briefly described in section 2. The results are described in section 3. Primary conclusions are presented in section 4.

2. Artificial Neural Network Approach
2.1. Neural networks and time series forecasting

Neural network models for time series forecasting have been developed rapidly. Research on approximation capabilities of multi-layer feed-forward neural networks has justified and motivated their use for non-linear time-series forecasting (e.g., [1]), since a feed-forward neural network with a single hidden layer is capable of approximating any continuous multivariate function uniformly to any desired degree of accuracy. The basic structure of a three-layer feed-forward neural network for time series forecasting, in general, is shown in Figure 1 where Δ denotes a time (unit) delay. The input layer employs $(x(t), x(t-1), ..., x(t-n+1))$ as inputs. The hidden-layer neurons employ the typical sigmoid activation

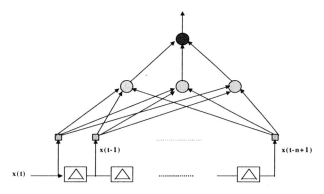

Figure 1. A feedforward neural network architecture for signal prediction

function, while the output neuron employs a linear activation function. A neural network trained for single-step forecasting can forecast multiple steps into the future through *iterated multi-step* prediction scheme, in which the current predicted output for a given step is used as an input for computing the time series at the next step, and all other network inputs are shifted back one time unit. With iterated multi-step prediction, the neural network can predict as many steps ahead as needed.

However, the current learning process in neural networks, referred to as conventional learning, limits the wide applications of neural networks to complex nonlinear systems. The main weakness of the conven-

tional learning is that a single representation of data is employed in the entire training, regardless of the individual learning algorithms used. Although some preprocessing techniques have been applied, a single representation of the training data is largely inadequate for difficult problems. In addition, the conventional learning process does not provide any mechanism for dividing and conquering the original difficult learning task. The conventional learning has two major limitations. First, with a single representation of training data during the entire training process, it is virtually impossible to represent every intrinsic facet of the information contained in the training data. For hydrological time series (e.g., streamflow) that shows different characteristics at different scales (e.g., [6], [2]), the weakness of conventional learning process of neural network would be particularly significant. Under such a condition, many important regularities existing in the training data might be hidden and not learned by the neural network. Secondly, the conventional training approach attacks the learning task as a whole. This lack of divide-and-conquer structure also results in poor learning quality and hence poor performance on the characteristics of generalization and robustness as the task becomes more complex. In other words, the conventional learning process does not offer good scalability to the complexity of a problem. In this paper, we will use the multiresolution learning paradigm (e.g., [3], [4], [5]), developed for and applied to signal prediction studies such as high-speed network traffic problems, to improve the applicability of the time series forecasting with neural network for long-term range streamflow forecast.

2.2. Multiresolution learning paradigm

Generalization is a key requirement and yet very difficult problem in neural network research and applications. Generalization refers to the ability of a network to yield appropriate responses for patterns that were not included in the concrete training set employed. Aimed at improving the generalization ability of neural networks for signal prediction, a new and effective learning paradigm, called *multiresolution learning*, has been presented [3]. Multiresolution learning is based on multiresolution analysis of wavelet theory. The multiresolution analysis framework is employed for decomposing the original signal and approximating it at different levels of detail. Unlike conventional neural network learning paradigm which employs a single signal representation for the entire training process, multiresolution learning paradigm exploits the approximation sequence representation-by-representation, from the coarsest resolution to finest resolution during the neural network training process. Consequently, the multiresolution learning paradigm can exploit the correlation structures in the training data at multiple resolutions, which otherwise could be obscured at the original resolution of the training data. It has been demonstrated that multiresolution learning can significantly improve neural network's generalization performance (e.g., [3], [5]) on difficult signal prediction tasks. The multiresolution learning paradigm has three important features: (a) a systematic way to hierarchically decompose the original learning task into subtasks so that each subtask can be learned more easily by the neural network; (b) a systematic and efficient way to make smooth transition among learning activities for subtasks and to integrate them together as an integral learning process; and (c) in each learning activity, a different representation is employed to exploit the different correlation structure of the problem to be learned.

3. Data and Results

The Clear Boggy watershed in Oklahoma is used in this study. The watershed has a drainage area of 1864 km^2. Forty years (1948-1988) of daily observed streamflow data is available at the site. However, the observed streamflow data has some problems (e.g., negative values) for the year of 1987-1988, thus, only thirty-eight years of data (1948-1986) is used in this analysis. The mean annual precipitation for the watershed is close to 1000 mm, and the runoff ratio is close to 0.20. Thirty-six years (1948-1984) of monthly streamflow data is used to train the neural network with multiresolution learning paradigm (NNMLP). Liang and Ming [2] showed that the streamflows at the studied watershed present characteristics over multiple scales. With the NNMLP method, monthly streamflow is the only information needed. The network is trained with 440 monthly data points and is then used to forecast monthly streamflows from June 1985 to October 1986. The predicted results are compared with the observed monthly streamflows. Figure 2a shows the monthly streamflow time series used to train the neural network for the Clear Boggy watershed. From the figure, it can be seen that the streamflow time series are complicated and irregular, suggesting that it presents a difficult time series prediction problem. Three common criteria are used to evaluate the prediction performance by the NNMLP. They are root-mean-square error (RMS), coefficient of determination (E_coeff), and the difference of annual total

volume between predicted streamflow and the observed one. The E_coeff is often used to measure the prediction skill of different methods, which is defined as,

$$E\_coeff = 1 - \frac{\sum\limits_{i=1}^{n}(Q_{i,f} - Q_{i,obs})^2}{\sum\limits_{i=1}^{n}(Q_{i,obs} - \overline{Q_{obs}})^2} \qquad (1)$$

where n is the number of monthly data points, $Q_{i,f}$ and $Q_{i,obs}$ are, respectively, the forecasted and observed streamflows for month i, and $\overline{Q_{obs}}$ is the monthly climatology streamflow which is obtained based on the monthly data from 1948-1984.

In our experiments with the NNMLP, the streamflow training data is decomposed into three sets of training data, with approximations at three coarser resolutions using Haar wavelet basis.

The 12-5-1 feed-forward neural network structure is used (notation 12-5-1 denotes a three-layered network having 12 input nodes, 5 neurons in the hidden layer, and a single output neuron), in which hidden neurons employ sigmoid activation functions, while the output neuron employs a linear activation function. Adjusting neural activation functions is adopted in the multiresolution learning paradigm. The training process was started with initial random connection weights. Back-propagation procedure was used in all learning activities. In each learning activity, 1000 training iterations were conducted. No momentum term was used.

Figure 2(b) shows the comparison between observed streamflows and the monthly predicted ones using the NNMLP approach at the Clear Boggy watershed. The method overpredicts the observations from June to November in 1985 and from July to October in 1986. The overprediction by the NNMLP during the period of July to October 1986 is mainly due to the long lead times. From December 1985 to June 1986, the NNMLP approach predicts quite well. The root-mean-square error is 19.9 mm/mo and the E_coeff is 0.84. The difference of annual total volume between predicted streamflows and the observed ones is 159.7 mm/yr. It should be mentioned that in the NNMLP, the historic monthly streamflows up to May 1985 are the only information used. No other information, either directly or indirectly related to the prediction period of June 1985 to October 1986, is used.

Based on the overall performance of the NNMLP at the test watershed, it can be seen clearly that the NNMLP has good potential for being used alone or combined with other approaches (e.g., the ones belong to the first category mentioned section 1) to improve long-term range monthly streamflow forecasts. The advantages of NNMLP are its generality, minimum data requirement, and simple and easy structure.

4. Conclusions

In this study the time series forecasting approach of neural network with multiresolution learning paradigm (NNMLP) is applied to forecast streamflows over a long-term range (over 12 months). The results show that the NNMLP has several good features. The NNMLP has good predicting skill as measured by the E_coeff, requires much less information than regular hydrological models, and is simple to use. The fact that the NNMLP requires only historical streamflow information makes it a good candidate to be applied to regions that are lack of other information and to the time periods during which the streamflows do not have strong dependence on large-scale climatic modes to make strong connections between the low-frequency climatic modes and meteorological variables. The NNMLP has a great potential for being used alone, and for being combined with other approaches to improve long-term range streamflow forecasts.

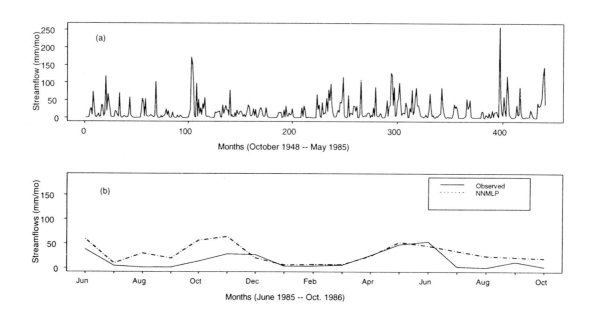

Figure 2. (a). Monthly observed streamflows used to train the neural network; and (b). Comparison of monthly predicted streamflows using NNMLP with the observations at Clear Boggy watershed.

5. References:

[1] Hornik, K., M. Stinchcombe and H. White, Multilayer feedforward networks are universal approximators, *Neural Networks*, Vol.2, pp. 359-366, 1989.

[2] Liang, X., and M. Chen, Application of multiresolution paradigm to automatic calibration of hydrologic models with multi-objective functions, *Water Resour. Res.*, submitted, 2001.

[3] Liang, Y., and E. W. Page, Multiresolution Learning Paradigm and Signal Prediction, *IEEE Trans. on Signal Processing*, Vol. 45, No. 11, 2858--2864, Nov. 1997.

[4] Liang, Y., Adaptive Neural Activation Functions in Multiresolution Learning, In *Proceedings of IEEE International Conference on Systems, Man, and Cybernetics*, Vol. 4, pp. 2601--2606, Nashville, Tennessee, USA, Oct. 2000.

[5] Liang, Y., and E. W. Page, VBR Video Traffic Prediction Using Neural Networks with Multiresolution Learning, In *Advances in Neural Networks and Applications*, pp. 98 – 103, WSES Press, 2001.

[6] Saco, P. and P. Kumar, 2000, Coherent modes in multiscale variability of streamflow over the United States, *Water Resour. Res.*, 36(4), 1049-1067.

RPCL-based Local PCA Algorithm

Zhiyong Liu and Lei Xu

Dept. of Computer Science and Engineering

The Chinese University of Hong Kong, Statin, N.T., Hong Kong, P.R. China

zyliu@cse.cuhk.edu.hk,lxu@cse.cuhk.edu.hk

Abstract

Mining local structure is important in data analysis. Gaussian mixture is able to describe local structure through the covariance matrices, but when used on high-dimensional data, fitly specifying such a large number of $d(d + 1)/2$ free elements in each covariance matrix is difficult. In this paper, by constraining the covariance matrix in decomposed orthonormal form, we propose a Local PCA algorithm to tackle this problem in help of RPCL competitive learning, which can automatically determine the number of local structures.

1. Introduction

Traditional clustering algorithms, e.g., k-mean algorithm, only divide data into several groups, but not consider the local structure of data during learning. The reason for considering local structure in clustering is at least justified from two points. The first is, of course, to get a better understand of data, and the second is that local structure information may play an important role during clustering, such as the covariance matrices in Gaussian mixture. So in this sense Gaussian mixture is a more powerful tool than traditional k-mean algorithm. However, as discussed in [1, 3, 6], fitly specifying such a large amount of $d(d + 1)/2$ (d refers to dimensionality of data) free elements in each covariance matrix is difficult when it is used on high-dimensional data. In this paper we constrain the covariance matrix in a decomposed orthonormal form to tackle this problem.

Another fundamental problem in clustering and also in Gaussian mixture is how to choose a proper number of clusters. Conventional approaches make it through a cost function, the main drawback of which is re-implementation of the whole algorithm is necessary for different k. Here we tackle this problem in help of the so-called RPCL competitive learning, which is able to automatically determine the number of clusters during learning [5].

2. RPCL Competitive Learning

Rival Penalized Competitive Learning (RPCL) was originally proposed in [5], the basic idea of which is that for each data sample, not only the winner component is pulled to be close to it, but also the rival one (the 2nd winner) is pushed to be slightly far away from this sample. The two-step algorithm is described as follows:

Step 1: $j_c = \arg \max_j d_j(x)$, $j_r = \arg \max_{j \neq j_c} d_j(x)$, $d_j(x)$ denotes distance between sample x and cluster j.

Step 2: $m_{j_c}^{new} = m_{j_c}^{old} + \eta_c(x - m_{j_c}^{old})$, $m_{j_r}^{new} = m_{j_r}^{old} - \eta_r(x - m_{j_r}^{old})$.

where the learning rate η_c is usually much greater than the de-learning rate η_r. The former part in step (2) is common in competitive learning, but the second part has the function of penalizing the rival. RPCL makes model selection in the sense of pushing the redundant components far away from the data.

Although the original RPCL was proposed for the MSE clustering, i.e., for the data with hyper-spheric shape, its elliptic extensions were also proposed [1, 2] to manage the data with hyper-elliptic shape. It should be pointed out that the original RPCL was proposed heuristically, but it has been shown that it is actually a special case of the general RPCL proposed in [6], which was obtained from harmony learning[6, 7] and with the ability of automatically determining the learning and de-learning rates.

3. RPCL-based Local PCA algorithm

We first consider Gaussian mixture model,

$$p(x|\theta) = \sum_{i=1}^{k} \alpha_i G(x|\mu_i, \Sigma_i) \quad (1)$$

where $\alpha_i > 0$ and $\sum_{i=1}^{k} \alpha_i = 1$. For the reasons discussed in section 1, we constrain each Σ_i as follows [1, 6]:

$$\Sigma = \sigma_0 I + W \Psi W^T \quad (2)$$

where $W = [\phi_1, \phi_2, ..., \phi_m], \Psi = \text{diag}(\sigma_1, \sigma_2, ..., \sigma_m)$, with the constraint: $W^T W = \text{I}, \sigma_0 > 0, \sigma_i > 0$. By setting so, the parameters needed to be specified are $\{\alpha_i, \mu_i, \sigma_{0,i}, W_i, \Psi_i\}_{i=1}^k$ and the number of free elements in each covariance matrix becomes $m(2d - m + 1)/2$. Usually, $m \ll d$ in high-dimensional case, so there are much less free elements need to be specified. It is easy to find that the m ϕ's are exactly the m PC's of the covariance matrix.

Conventionally, the parameters in Gaussian mixture are learned by *maximum likelihood learning* and EM algorithm, but this model has no model selection ability, so we adopt the RPCL competitive learning and at the same time, the updating rules for $\sigma_{0,i}, W_i, \Psi_i$ must be figured out.

By setting the "distance" $d(x) = -\ln[G(x|\mu, \Sigma)\alpha]$ as in [1], which is more general than the Mahalanobis distance, we can then use RPCL to update the parameters.

For the constraints of $\sigma_0 > 0$, $\sigma_i > 0$ and $\alpha > 0$. we introduce $\Theta = e^{\Xi}$ (including σ_0, σ_i, and α). So the gradient directions of σ_0 and Ψ become as

$$\triangle \sigma_{0,j} = 0.5 e^{\sigma_{0,j}} Tr(\Sigma_j^{-1} R_j)$$
$$\triangle \Psi_j = 0.5 \text{diag}(e^{\Psi_j}) \text{diag}(W_j^T \Sigma_j^{-1} R_j W_j)$$

where $R_j = (x_t - m_j)(x_t - m_j)^T \Sigma_j^{-1} - \text{I}$.

For $W^T W = \text{I}$, we adopted a method similar to the so-called Gradient Projection Method (see, for instance, [4]), where the first step is to project the gradient direction of each PC onto the subspace spanned by all of the other PC's, and the second step is to make the new W be orthonormal matrix. In practice, only the second step can almost always guarantee the convergency of the algorithm. The gradient direction of W is

$$\triangle W_j = \Psi_j \Sigma_j^{-1} R_j W_j \qquad (3)$$

Similar to the elliptic RPCL learning [1, 2], and based on the constraint analysis above, we get the EM-like iterations:

Step 1 Calculate distance $d_{tj} = -\ln[G(x_t|\mu_j, \Sigma_j)\alpha_j]$ based on the parameters $\{\mu_j, W_j, \sigma_{0,j}, \Psi_j, \alpha_j\}$, which are initialized at some proper values.

Step 2 $j_c = \arg\min_j d_{tj}, j_r = \arg\min_{j \neq j_c} d_{tj}$,
$$\sigma_{0_{j_c}}^{new} = \sigma_{0_{j_c}}^{old} + \eta_c \triangle \sigma_{0_{j_c}}, \sigma_{0_{j_r}}^{new} = \sigma_{0_{j_r}}^{old} - \eta_r \triangle \sigma_{0_{j_r}},$$
$$\Psi_{j_c}^{new} = \Psi_{j_c}^{old} + \eta_c \triangle \Psi_{j_c}, \Psi_{j_r}^{new} = \Psi_{j_r}^{old} - \eta_r \triangle \Psi_{j_r},$$
$$W_{j_c}^{new} = W_{j_c}^{old} + \eta_c \triangle W_{j_c}, W_{j_r}^{new} = W_{j_r}^{old} - \eta_r \triangle W_{j_r},$$
$$\mu_{j_c}^{new} = \mu_{j_c}^{old} + \eta_c (x_t - \mu_{j_c}^{old}),$$
$$\mu_{j_r}^{new} = \mu_{j_r}^{old} - \eta_r (x_t - \mu_{j_r}^{old}),$$
$$\alpha_{j_c}^{new} = \alpha_{j_c}^{old} + \eta_c, \alpha_{j_r}^{new} = \alpha_{j_r}^{old} - \eta_r,$$
$$\{\alpha_i = \frac{\alpha_i}{\sum_{y=1}^k \alpha_y}\}_{i=1}^k$$

The de-learning rate η_r are usually much smaller than learning rate η_c, and moreover, the learning and de-learning rates of different parameters can be different from each other.

4. Illustrations

We present two experiments to illustrate our algorithm. The first one is to demonstrate model selection for k. The second demonstrates model selection ability for m and makes a comparison with conventional Gaussian mixture.

Fig 1 (a) is the result obtained from *ML learning*-based local PCA algorithm and fig 1 (b) is from RPCL-based local PCA. From these two figures we can see that *ML learning* has no model selection ability whereas RPCL has by pushing the redundant one component far away.

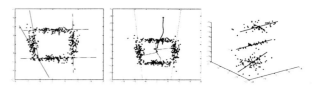

Figure 1. experiment results (a),(b),(c)

The second experiment is with 20-dimensional data and we compared the result obtained from Local PCA algorithm with that from conventional Gaussian mixture. The dimensionality of each local structure is determined by a cost function proposed in [7], from which we get a concise description as in fig 1 (c) with totally 6 PC's. We repeat the same experiment by using conventional Gaussian mixture but the eigen-decomposition of the obtained covariance matrices does not contain any local structure information shown in fig 1 (c). In fact, the most principal PC has almost the same property in all of the 20 dimensions.

References

[1] Lei Xu (2001), "An overview on Unsupervised Learning from Data Mining Perspective", *Advances in Self-Organising Maps: WSOM 2001 Proceedings*, 181-210.

[2] Lei Xu (1998), "Rival Penalized Competitive Learning, Finite Mixture, and Multisets Clustering", *Proc. of 1998 IJCNN 3*, 2525-2530.

[3] G.E. Hinton, P. Dayan, and M. Revow (1997), "Modeling the Manifolds of Images of Handwritten Digits," in *IEEE Trans. on Neural Networks*, Vol.8, No.1, 65-74.

[4] P. Y. Papalambros et al (2000), *Principles of Optimal Design*. Cambridge University Press, 190-194.

[5] Lei Xu, Krzyzak A, and Oja. E (1993), "Rival Penalized Competitive Learning for Clustering Analysis, RBF Net, and Curve Detection", in *IEEE Trans. on Neural Networks*, Vol.4, 636-649.

[6] Lei Xu (2001), "Best Harmony, Unified RPCL and Automated Model Selection for Unsupervised and Supervised Learning on Gaussian Mixture, Three-Layer Nets and ME-RBF-SVM Models", in *Int. Journal of Neural System* Vol. 11, No. 1, 43-70.

[7] Lei Xu (2001), "BYY Harmony Learning, Independent State Space and Generalized APT Financial Analyses," *IEEE Trans. on Neural Networks*, Vol. 12, No. 4, 822-849.

Learning Automatic Acquisition of Subcategorization Frames using Bayesian Inference and Support Vector Machines

M. Maragoudakis, K. Kermanidis, N. Fakotakis, G. Kokkinakis
Dept. of Electrical & Computer Engineering
University of Patras, 26500 Patras, Greece
Telephone: +30 61 991722
Fax: +30 61 991855
{mmarag,kerman,fakotaki,gkokkin}@wcl.ee.upatras.gr

Abstract

Learning Bayesian Belief Networks (BBN) from corpora and Support Vector Machines (SVM) have been applied to the automatic acquisition of verb subcategorization frames for Modern Greek. We are incorporating minimal linguistic resources, i.e. basic morphological tagging and phrase chunking, to demonstrate that verb subcategorization, which is of great significance for developing robust natural language human computer interaction systems, could be achieved using large corpora, without having any general-purpose syntactic parser at all. In addition, apart from BBN and SVM, which have not previously used for this task, we have experimented with three well-known machine learning methods (Feed-Forward Back-Propagation Neural Networks, Learning Vector Quantization and Decision Tables), which are also being applied to the task of verb subcategorization frame detection for the first time. We argue that both BBN and SVM are well suited for learning to identify verb subcategorization frames. Empirical results will support this claim. Performance has been methodically evaluated using two different corpora types, one balanced and one domain-specific in order to determine the unbiased behaviour of the trained models. Limited training data are proved to endow with satisfactory results. We have been able to achieve precision exceeding 80% on the identification of subcategorization frames which were not known beforehand.

1 Introduction

Verb subcategorization is an important issue especially for parsing and grammar development as it provides the parser with syntactic and/or semantic information on a verb's arguments, i.e. the set of restrictions the verb imposes on its arguments [1]. In many natural language interface applications, the syntactic-semantic information extracted from subcategorization frames (SF) could prove to be essential since it often clarifies the agent and the receiver of an action. Nowadays, with the impressive increase in the number of available text corpora and language resources in general, the need for fully annotated syntactic parsers could be alleviated by "mining" subcategorization frame information from large text corpora. Since building verb subcategorization classifiers is difficult and time-consuming, learning classifiers from examples is advantageous.

For the present work, we are incorporating two machine learning methods that have revealed great potential for learning classification functions and have not been previously used for the detection of verb SFs. We apply Bayesian Belief Networks (BBN) learning from corpora and use the extracting network as an inference tool that enables automatic acquisition of SF for Modern Greek. Furthermore, we experiment with Support Vector Machines (SVM), a recently well-founded technique in terms of computational learning theory that has been successfully applied in numerous classification problems including text categorization, pattern recognition, face detection, etc.

In order to obtain an inclusive view of the behaviour of the proposed methods, experiments with three additional machine learning techniques have been carried out. Namely Feed-Forward Back Propagation Neural Network, Learning Vector Quantization and Decision Tables. BBN outperforms all the other techniques and SVM follow with a variation of 1,5-3 % while by introducing supplementary parameters, precision increases considerably. 10-fold cross validation is used in order to retrieve results. The corpora used for our study are the balanced ILSP Greek Corpus, consisting of 1.6 million words and the DELOS corpus of economic news consisting of 1.7 million words. The complete set of frames for a particular verb was not known beforehand but it is learned automatically through the training process.

2 Corpus pre-processing.

Modern Greek is a 'free word-order' language. The arguments of a verb do not have fixed positions. They are basically determined by their morphology and especially by their case. Noun phrases (NP), prepositional phrases (PP), adverbs and secondary clauses may function as arguments to verbs. Weak personal pronouns may also function as arguments to verbs when occurring within the verb phrase either in the genitive or accusative case. As their arguments, verbs select specific prepositions (introducing a PP complement), specific types of secondary clauses, and/or specific cases (accusative or genitive) for their NP complements. Given that we want to avoid using a wide-coverage syntactic parser, limited linguistic resources have been utilized. Thus, pre-processing of the corpus consisted of the following tasks: basic morphological tagging, chunking, detecting the headword of the noun and prepositional phrases, and de-noise filtering. In our approach, a verb occurring in the corpus in both active and passive voice is treated as two distinct verbs. The same applies when the same verb appears with both a personal and an impersonal structure. We have carried out a number of experiments concerning the window size of the environment of a verb, i.e. the number of phrases preceding and following the verb. Windows of sizes (-2+3), i.e. two phrases preceding and three phrases following the verb, (-2+2) and (-1+2) were proved to provide better results. This phenomenon can be explained since it is rather unusual for an argument of a verb to be far away from it. This observation found to be true in both corpora used, since only in some literature texts we could found such verb-argument anomalies. For almost every environment, not the entire environment, but a subset of the environment is a correct frame of the verb. Therefore all possible subsets [2] of the above environments were produced and their frequency in the corpus was recorded.

3 Feature Selection

Features of our training data were categorized in grammatical and numerical ones. Grammatical Features consisted of the window size, varying from (-2+3) to (-1+2), along with seven more morphosyntactic categories, characterizing the type of phrase, the case, the preposition used, the presence or absence of an adverb, the type of verb, the tense, and category (personal or impersonal) of the structure.

As for the numerical features, our goal is to determine if a candidate SF is highly associated with a specific verb. In order to obtain our features, we proceed to the following postulation.

Making the hypothesis that the distribution of verb environment in the corpus is independent of the distribution of the verb, we compare the frequency of co-occurrence of a given environment with a certain verb (described by probability p1) to the frequency of its co-occurrence with the rest of the verbs (described by p2) and to its expected frequency in the input data (described by p). To this end the following counts are required:

- the count of a given environment of a given verb v, (k1).
- the count of a given verb v, (n1).
- the count of a given environment with every other verb except for v, (k2).
- the count of every other verb except for verb v, (n2).

Using the above values:

- $p1 = k1 / n1$
- $p2 = k2 / n2$
- $p = (k1+k2)/(n1+n2)$

We have also included one numerical feature, namely the Number of Distinct Elements (NDE) which are calculated as: NDE=number of distinct elements each environment has. e.g. NDE(N1 P5 N3)=3.

We should denote the initial features as "Standard Features" and as "Enhanced Features" the feature set added by NDE. As we should discuss in the results section NDE contribute to the improvement of the performance by a factor of about 3,1%.

4. Bayesian Networks-SVMs

A Bayesian Belief Network (BBN) is a significant knowledge representation and reasoning tool, under conditions of uncertainty [3]. We denote a network B as a pair B=<G,Θ>, where G is a DAG whose nodes symbolize the variables of D, and Θ refers to the set of parameters that quantifies the network.

Θ includes information about the probability distribution of a value x_i of a variable X_i, given the values of its immediate predecessors. In the process of efficiently detecting verb SF, prior knowledge about the impact each feature has on the classification of a candidate SF as valid or not, is not straightforward. Thus, a BBN should be learned from the training data provided. Learning a BBN unifies two processes: learning the graphical structure and learning the parameters Θ for that structure. In order to seek out the optimal parameters for a given corpus of complete data, we directly use the empirical conditional frequencies extracted from the data [4]. The probability a network B gives to the data can be extracted using the following formula [5]:

$$P(D \mid B) = \prod_{i=1}^{n} \prod_{j=1}^{q_i} \frac{\Gamma(\frac{\Xi}{q_i})}{\Gamma(\frac{\Xi}{q_i} + N_{ij})} \prod_{k=1}^{r_i} \frac{\Gamma(\frac{\Xi}{r_i q_i} + N_{ijk})}{\Gamma(\frac{\Xi}{r_i q_i})}$$

As a search algorithm, we follow greedy search with one modification: instead of comparing all candidate networks, we consider investigating the set that resembles the current best model most.

Support Vector Machines (SVMs) are learning models designed to automatically trade-off accuracy and complexity by trying to minimize an upper bound on the generalization error. The most important advantage of SVM is that contrary to other machine learning techniques, it behaves robustly even in high dimensional feature problems. SVMs are based on the *Structural Risk Minimization* principle [6]. The basic idea of this theory is to find a hypothesis h for which we could guarantee the lowest true error. By "true error" we denote the probability that a hypothesis will make an error when classifying a random unseen test vector. SVMs are a new machine learning technique that have been applied to numerous classification and pattern recognition problems such as text classification, shallow parsing and face recognition with noteworthy results. [7]. In our approach we investigate the use of polynomials and RBF networks as kernel functions.

5 Experimental Results

The primary training set used to learn a BBN was constructed by manually tagging the class for 4700 instances from the ILSP corpus and 3655 instances from DELOS corpus, with a window size of -2+3.

In each experiment two types of input data have been tested: a complete training corpus and a training corpus where all adverbs have been omitted. Table 1 tabulates precision from ILSP corpus, without adverbs. Performance is slightly reduced in DELOS corpus, due to the fact that is an economic corpus with a morphologically narrower set of elements surrounding a verb. BBN actually outperforms all other methods by a varying factor of 1,5-3% -compared to the performance of SVM- to almost 11-12% over the other three.

ILSP	METHOD				
	BBN	SVM	FFNN	LVQ	DT
W.S.	**Standard Feature Set**				
-1+1	81,8	78	62,6	63,4	70,9
-2+2	84,1	81,5	63	66,8	72,5
-2+3	82,4	80,2	63,2	66,6	71,9
	Enhanced Feature Set				
-1+1	84	81,4	64,7	65,3	73,4
-2+2	86,4	84,3	64,9	68,6	74,7
-2+3	84,6	83,1	65,2	68,6	74,1

Table1. Precision of the ILSP corpus

However, training time of BBN was much slower than that of SVM. Especially when using the enhanced feature set, the time for constructing the new Bayesian network was 4,3 times more than SVM's training time, a factor that is of insignificant impact since learning SFs is actually an off-line procedure.

6 Conclusion

In the present paper we introduced the idea of applying BBN and SVM, two machine learning techniques that have proven to perform well in various classification problems to text corpora in order to automatically identify SF. Our idea can be used for other languages as well with slight modifications. An obvious advantage of using BBN and SVM in corpora and not using a fully syntactic parsed tree bank is that the number of frames learned would grow as corpus size increases. Since more SF are learned, a dialogue system based on this information would be more robust.

Using minimal linguistic resources, i.e. basic morphological tagging and phrase chunking, verb environments were identified and every environment subset was formulated. Apart from BBN and SVM, Feed-Forward Neural Networks, optimized Learning Vector Quantization and Decision Tables were additionally applied to the task at hand, using balanced as well as domain-specific corpora and performance was evaluated. Experimental results supported the argument that BBN and SVM are well suited techniques for this task. Contrary to conventional verb subcategorization methods, BBN and SVM found to be very robust, thus eliminating the need for manual adjustment and expensive parameter tuning. Bayesian inference seemed to outperform all other approaches. The difference between SVM is estimated at about 1,5-3 % while it reaches almost 12% when compared to the other three. Various window sizes were experimented with and performance with a window size of -1+2 was slightly worse than with that of -2+2 and -2+3. It is also been demonstrated that adverbs appearing in verb environments are a significant cause of noise. New frames not known beforehand were learned throughout the training process.

References

[1] Basili R., Pazienza M.T. and Vindigni M. 1997. Corpus-driven Unsupervised Learning of Verb Subcategorization frames. *Proceedings of the Conference of the Italian Association for Artificial Intelligence*, AI*IA 97, Rome.

[2] Sarkar A. and D. Zeman, 2000. Automatic Extraction of Subcategorization Frames for Czech. *In Proceedings of the 18th Intl Conference on Computational Linguistics*, pp.691-697.

[3] Mitchell T. 1997. Machine Learning. Mc Graw-Hill

[4] Cooper J. and Herskovits E. 1992. A Bayesian method for the induction of probabilistic networks from data. *Machine Learning*, 9, pp.309-347.

[5] Glymour C. and Cooper G. (eds.). 1999. Computation, Causation & Discovery. AAAI Press/The MIT Press, Menlo.

[6] Vapnik V. 1995 The Nature of Statistical Learning Theory. *Springer, New York*

[7] Joachims T 1996. A probabilistic analysis of the Rocchio algorithm with TFIDF for text categorization. Carnegie Mellon University, Technical Report, pp 96-118

Bayesian Data Mining on the Web with B-Course

Petri Myllymäki, Tomi Silander, Henry Tirri, Pekka Uronen
Complex Systems Computation Group (CoSCo)
P.O.Box 26, Department of Computer Science, FIN-00014 University of Helsinki, Finland
URL: http://www.cs.Helsinki.FI/research/cosco/

Abstract

B-Course is a free[1] web-based Bayesian data mining service. This service allows the users to analyze their own data for multivariate probabilistic dependencies represented as Bayesian network models. In addition to this, B-Course also offers facilities for inferring certain type of causal dependencies from the data. The software is especially suitable for educational purposes as the tutorial style user-friendly interface intertwines the steps in the data analysis with support material that gives an informal introduction to the Bayesian approach adopted. Nevertheless, although the analysis methods, modeling assumptions and restrictions are totally transparent to the user, this transparency is not achieved at the expense of analysis power: with the restrictions stated in the support material, B-Course is a powerful analysis tool exploiting several theoretically elaborate results developed recently in the fields of Bayesian and causal modeling.

1. Introduction

In many domains, when practitioners in various fields apply data analysis tools, the underlying assumptions and restrictions are not clear to the user, and the complicated nature of the software encourages the users to a "black box" approach where default parameter values are used without any understanding of the actual modeling and analysis task. The B-Course tool (http://b-course.cs.helsinki.fi) is an attempt to offer a sophisticated multivariate modeling tool that can also be understood by applied practitioners. Although it is a first step in this direction, it makes a serious attempt to give an informal yet comprehensive introduction to the approach adopted.

One of the design choices for B-Course was to use the Bayesian framework as indicated by the fact that the dependency models constructed are represented by Bayesian

networks. B-Course supports inference on the constructed Bayesian network model as well as exporting the model for further use. We have chosen the Bayesian modeling framework, since we find it easier to understand than the classical statistical (frequentist) framework, and from our experience it seems that it is more understandable to the users also. We also feel that it has benefits over the classical framework, avoiding some of the anomalies caused by the hidden assumptions underlying the standard methods developed decades ago. This is not to say that Bayesian approaches do not have problems of their own — both theoretical and practical problems are lively discussed in the literature [1, 3, 5, 7, 11].

B-Course is implemented as an Application Service Provider (ASP), an architectural choice we feel is very natural in the context of data analysis: there is no downloading or installation of software, and the computational load for searching models is allocated to a server farm. B-Course can be used with most web-browsers (even Lynx), and only requires the user data to be a text file with data presented in a tabular format typical to statistical packages. In this paper we describe the main design principles of B-Course and present results of preliminary systematic empirical validation experiments performed with B-Course. For a more detailed discussion of the methodological aspects of the methods underlying the B-Course implementation can be found in [8]. We also strongly encourage the reader to experiment with B-Course by using the "ready-made trails" provided by the service, or with their own datasets if available.

2. Dependency modeling with Bayesian networks

In our context, dependence modeling means finding the model of the probabilistic dependences of the variables. In dependency modeling one tries to find dependencies between all the variables in the data. Since we are using probabilistic models, in more technical terms this means modeling the joint probability distribution. Dependencies can also be used to speculate about causalities that might cause them.

---

[1]B-Course can be freely used for educational and research purposes only.

Besides revealing the domain structure of the data, dependency models can be used to infer probabilities of any set of variables given any (other) set of variables. This will lead to a "game" where one can interactively study the model by probing it as implemented by the inference part in the B-Course software.

For the above purposes, in B-Course one will only need something that is called pairwise conditional dependencies, since that is the only type of dependency that appears in our models (it should be noted that this notion should not be confused with pairwise correlation). Saying that variables A and B are dependent on each other means that if one knows what the value of variable A is, it helps one to guess what the value of variable B is.

To illustrate the type of models B-Course searches for, let us look at a small example. For our present purposes it is not necessary to study the models in great detail , the example just tries to give an idea about the dependency models. So let us assume that our model has four variables A, B, C and D. Following list of statements is a dependency model:

- A and B are dependent on each other if we know something about C or D (or both).
- A and C are dependent on each other no matter what we know and what we don't know about B or D (or both).
- B and C are dependent on each other no matter what we know and what we don't know about A or D (or both).
- C and D are dependent on each other no matter what we know and what we don't know about A or B (or both).
- There are no other dependencies that do not follow from those listed above.

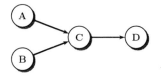

Figure 1. A Bayesian network representing the example list of dependencies.

This set of statements about dependencies is called a dependency model. Obviously, if the set of dependencies is large, such a descriptive list representation becomes impractical and hard to understand.

In its full generality the problem of finding the best dependency model in an arbitrary set of models is intractable (see the discussion in [11, 3]). In order to make the task of creating dependency models out of data computationally feasible, B-Course makes two important restrictions to the set of dependency models it considers. Firstly, B-Course

only considers models for discrete data and it discretizes automatically all the variables that appear to be continuous. Secondly, B-Course only considers dependency models where the list of dependencies can be represented in a graphical format using Bayesian network structures [9, 4]. For example, the list of dependencies in the example can be represented as a Bayesian network in Figure 1. An important property of Bayesian network models is that the joint probability distribution over the model variables factorizes to a product conditional probability distributions, one for each variable (see, e.g., the tutorial on Bayesian networks in data mining [6]).

This subset of models is interesting, but it has its limitations too. More specifically, if the variables of our model are in causal relationships with each other, and if in our domain there are no latent variables (i.e., variables that for some reason are not included in our data) that have causal influence on the variables of our model, then the dependencies caused by these causal relationships can be described by a Bayesian network. On the other hand, latent variables often induce dependencies, that cannot be described accurately by any Bayesian network structure. That can severely restrict our ability to automatically infer something about causalities just based on statistical dependencies.

Using the Bayesian approach provides for a way to recognize a good model when the software finds one: in the Bayesian framework a good dependence model is one with a high probability. Notice that it takes a Bayesian approach to speak about the probability of the dependencies. Further discussions on this topic can be found in [8].

3. Walking through B-Course

Using the B-Course data service follows a simple three step procedure (Data upload→Model search→Model analysis) for building a Bayesian Network dependency model. As B-Course is used via a Web-browser, user can freely use the browser features ("Back" and "Forward" buttons, resizing of the window etc.) during this procedure. In particular, a first time user is encouraged to follow the links leading to pages explaining many of the concepts discussed in the interface. These pages form the "B-Course library" that is maintained and updated every time a new feature is added to the analysis.

Of the three main steps, the last one is the most complex one as it allows the user to interactively use the inferred model, export both the graphical and textual representations of the model, check for strengths of the dependencies etc. It should be emphasized that there are no parameter settings involved except the fact that the user decides the length of the search phase by interactively inspecting the progress of search. Discretization, handling of missing data, setting non-informative priors and other technical details are handled automatically by the software. In the following we give a short description of each of these main steps.

Step 1: Data upload. B-Course attempts to give a simple, yet accurate description of the format of the data it accepts. In general it expects the data to be in tab-limited ASCII format with additional header line containing the names of the variables. This format is readily available in most of the database, spreadsheet and statistical software. B-Course also allows for missing data.

Uploading the data is implemented by standard HTML-form File input, that sends the data file to the server. As B-Course is currently implemented by using a server farm, the front end server directs the data to one of the servers in B-Course server pool in order to do load-balancing.

B-Course notifies user of the possible problems during the data upload. It also gives simple descriptive statistics of each variable so that the user can verify the upload was successful. At this point user can also exclude the variables he/she does not want to be part of the model, such as data ID etc.

Step 2: Model search phase. In the model search phase the user is first prompted to initiate the dedicated server to start searching for a good Bayesian network model for the data. Once the search is on, the user is lead to a page showing the current best model. User can now study the structure of this model, but she can also ask for an updated report on the search. B-Course then again shows the current best model together with a report how much better the current model is compared to the previous one (assuming some improvement has occurred). The search can be stopped any time — for example, if no progress in search has been gained for some time — or the user can wait until the system reaches the search time limit (currently 15 minutes). Searching for the dependency model is computationally very intensive (the problem is NP hard) and in any realistic case with many variables it is impossible to search exhaustively the whole search space.

Step 3: Analysis of the model found. Once the search has ended, B-Course gives the final report together with a list of ways to study the selected dependency model. The final report displays the constructed graph structure which the user can save if needed. The user is also given a report on strengths of the pairwise unconditional dependencies (i.e., arcs in the constructed Bayesian network) of the model. In addition to the standard Bayesian network representation, B-Course also offers two graphical representations describing the possible causal relationships that may have caused the dependencies of the model. These causal graphs are based on the calculus introduced by Pearl [10]. As far as we know this feature is unique to B-Course, we are not aware of any other software package supporting Pearl's causal analysis.

B-Course also provides interactive tools called "play-grounds" that allow user to perform inference on the constructed Bayesian network. Several playgrounds are offered in order to support browsers with various capabilities. The "Vanilla playground" is intended to be used with "low-end" browsers with restricted graphical capabilities and works even with text-only browsers such as Lynx. The "Java playground" requires a Java-enabled browser, but then offers a more flexible graphical user interface with zooming, pop-up displays of the distributions attached to variable nodes etc. In addition to using B-Course playgrounds online for model inspection, the model can also be exported in a format accepted by Hugin-software in order to allow off-line use of the model.

4. Empirical validation

When designing a learning algorithm to construct models from data sets with non-informative prior information (i.e., no preference for the structure in advance), a challenging and interesting task is to evaluate the "quality" of the learning algorithm. In addition to the theoretical justifications of the Bayesian model construction, with such an analysis tool as B-Course, empirical validation is a necessary step in the development process.

There are several possible ways to study the performance of a model construction algorithm, and many of the schemes are based on simulating the future prediction tasks by reusing the data available, e.g., with cross-validation methods. These approaches have problems of their own and they tend to be complex for cases where one is interested in probabilistic models for the joint distributions as opposed to for example classification. Therefore in many cases in the literature the so-called synthetic or "Golden Standard" approach is used to evaluate the learning algorithm. In this approach one first selects a "true model" (Golden standard) and then generates data stochastically from this model. The quality of the learning algorithm is then judged by its ability to reconstruct this model from the generated data.

In addition to the already quite extensive use with real data sets, B-Course was also tested using synthetic data sets generated from known Bayesian networks. In this case the particular interest in these experiments was to find out how well the B-Course learner can "recover" the Golden Standard network for Bayesian networks of varying complexity using data sets of different sizes. Following the dependency modeling aspects underlying B-Course, the main interest was in comparing the structural differences, not parameters. Several sets of tests were performed by varying the network size (5, 15, and 50 nodes) and the dependency structure complexity against the maximum of n^2 arcs (0%, i.e., all independent, 10%, and 40% of possible structural dependencies). In addition, the average node incoming/outgoing degree (i.e., the number of arcs pointing to or from a node) was varied (1, 3, and 5). Finally the construction rate (i.e., the "statistical power") was studied by varying the size of the generated data set from 100 to 10000 data vectors. The resulting Bayesian networks were compared to the generating network by comparing the skeletons, i.e., the underlying undirected structure, and the V-structures which together define an equivalence relation among the networks [9].

The results clearly validated that the model search in B-Course finds dependency structures present in the underlying data generating mechanism. For the small networks (5 nodes), regardless of the structure complexity in almost all the cases the correct network could be recovered with 100 to 1000 data vectors. Even if this was not the case, the differences in B-Course inferred network and the "true" dependency model were only 1-2 missing dependencies. Similarly the performance with 15 node random networks was comparable (typically 1-2 missing dependencies or 1 incorrect V-structure), albeit now the data set sizes needed to recover the network were typically 1000 as opposed to 100 sufficient for the smaller networks. As expected, when the network size was increased to 50 with a notable connection complexity (0.1 to 0.4), even the data set sizes of 10000 were sufficient to recover the generating structure only very approximatively. The typical amount of missing dependencies varied from 10% to 50%. However, one has to remember that the amount of data used for these cases is way too small for such complex models by any means (networks with more than 1000 arcs with 10000 to 15000 parameters!). The main purpose of the tests with larger networks was to find out, whether the model search produces "spurious dependencies", i.e., adds dependencies that only reflect the noise in the data. In this respect B-Course is extremely well-behaving — it almost never adds a dependency where there should not be one and prefers simpler models in the light of lesser amounts of evidence (i.e., smaller data sets).

5. Conclusions and future work

The two main design principles in building the current version of B-Course were transparency and ease of use. On one hand, we wanted to build a system where the modeling assumptions are explicitly visible so that applied practitioners can fully understand what the results of the analysis of their data mean. On the other hand, we wanted the data analysis to be fully automated so that the users would not have play with parameters the meaning of which would be clear only to modeling experts. These two requirements were met by adopting the Bayesian dependence modeling approach: the basic theoretical concepts in this probabilistic framework seem to be easier to understand than the concepts of classical frequentist statistics. By using a series of explicitly stated assumptions, we were also able to get rid of all the model parameters, leaving the user with a fully automated data analysis tool, as was the goal.

Nevertheless, although the initial goals of the B-Course development project have been met with the current version of the software, the current implementation leaves naturally room for many improvements. For example, the modeling assumptions allowing us to offer the users a "non-parametric" tool are not necessarily always very reasonable. Furthermore, the question of choosing an objective "non-informative" prior for the model parameters turned out to be a most complex issue, linking this superficially simple task directly to the most fundamental problems in statistics. On the other hand, as the chosen Bayesian approach offers an elegant framework for integrating subjective knowledge with empirical observations, it would be nice to be able to offer the more sophisticated users a possibility for expressing their expertise as a prior distribution on the dependency statements, or on the model parameters. Finally, it is evident that uncertainty on the result of the analysis should be expressed in a more elaborate manner than with the straightforward local analysis of the importance of the individual arcs. These issues will be addressed when developing future versions of the B-Course data analysis service.

Acknowledgments. This research has been financially supported by the National Technology Agency, and the Academy of Finland.

References

[1] J. Berger. *Statistical Decision Theory and Bayesian Analysis*. Springer-Verlag, New York, 1985.

[2] J. Bernardo, J. Berger, A. Dawid, and A. Smith, editors. *Bayesian Statistics 4*. Oxford University Press, 1992.

[3] J. Bernardo and A. Smith. *Bayesian theory*. John Wiley, 1994.

[4] R. Cowell, P. Dawid, S. Lauritzen, and D. Spiegelhalter. *Probabilistic Networks and Expert Systems*. Springer, New York, NY, 1999.

[5] A. Dawid. Prequential analysis, stochastic complexity and Bayesian inference. In Bernardo et al. [2], pages 109–125.

[6] D. Heckerman. Bayesian networks for data mining. *Data Mining and Knowledge Discovery*, 1(1):79–119, 1997.

[7] H. Jeffreys. *Theory of Probability*. Clarendon Press, Oxford, 1939.

[8] P. Myllymäki, T. Silander, H. Tirri, and P. Uronen. B-course: A web service for Bayesian data analysis. In *Proceedings of The Thirteenth IEEE International Conference on Tools with Artificial Intelligence*, Dallas, USA, November 2001. IEEE Computer Society Press.

[9] J. Pearl. *Probabilistic Reasoning in Intelligent Systems: Networks of Plausible Inference*. Morgan Kaufmann Publishers, San Mateo, CA, 1988.

[10] J. Pearl. *Causality: Models, Reasoning and Inference*. Cambridge University Press, 2000.

[11] J. Rissanen. *Stochastic Complexity in Statistical Inquiry*. World Scientific Publishing Company, New Jersey, 1989.

An Experimental Comparison of Supervised and Unsupervised Approaches to Text Summarization

Tadashi Nomoto
National Institute of Japanese Literature
1-16-10 Yutaka Shinagawa
Tokyo 142-8585 Japan
nomoto@nijl.ac.jp

Yuji Matsumoto
Nara Institute of Science and Technology
8916-5 Takayama Ikoma
Nara 630-0101 Japan
matsu@is.aist-nara.ac.jp

Abstract

The paper presents a direct comparison of supervised and unsupervised approaches to text summarization. As a representative supervised method, we use the C4.5 decision tree algorithm, extended with the Minimum Description Length Principle (MDL), and compare it against several unsupervised methods. It is found that a particular unsupervised method based on an extension of the K-means clustering algorithm, performs equal to and in some cases superior to the decision tree based method.

1 Introduction

The recent literature has witnessed a host of approaches, both supervised and unsupervised, to automatic text summarization [5, 12, 2, 7, 3, 1]. However to our knowledge, no prior work ever addressed the question of how supervised and unsupervised approaches compare in performance when they are set to the same task. A general perception seems to be that a learning based approach works better, since it is able to exploit information about the grand truth provided by humans, which is not available to an unsupervised approach. But it is well known that learning based approaches to summarization inherently suffer from the problem of "lack of uniqueness of a summary" [6] and the cost of creating a corpus large enough to train algorithms on.

Against this background, the present work sets out to investigate how the two varieties of approaches compare, by matching one against the other in the same summarization task. In the following, we will construct two summarizers, representing the two varieties; one based on decision tree and the other clustering. Although a precise component-by-component comparison between them would be infeasible, we will attempt to make a comparison as fair as possible by constructing them in such a way that they have best perfor-

mance within limits of a particular approach.

2 Summarization Methods

The decision tree based summarizer is based on C4.5. However we have made several modifications to it; one is a pruning optimization with the minimum description length principle (MDL).[1] Another has to do with the way the decision tree classifies data; in order to deal with a variable length summary, it was modified to output a class probability rather than a label, which allows a ranking of sentences according to the probabilistic strength. The use of MDL is motivated by our earlier study [9], which found that, in the natural language discourse domain, the extension of the decision tree with MDL produced performance comparable to AdaBoost [4].

Given a set of sentences (encoded in features) comprising a document, the decision tree outputs the probability that each sentence is included in a summary, which are used to generate a summary of a particular length. A feature description of a sentence contains information such as length, position, and linguistic cues; some of them are tailored to specifically deal with Japanese as we use a Japanese corpus for evaluation. Finally, one of two class labels, "Select" and "Don't Select", is assigned to a sentence, depending on whether it is to be included in a summary. The "Select" label is for a sentence which would be included in a summary, and the "Don't Select" label for other cases.

We consider an unsupervised approach along the lines of our earlier work [10]. There we developed what is called a diversity based method for summarization, which exploits the semantic diversity of contents in the document to generate a summary (hence the name *diversity*). We have found it effective with document retrieval tasks [10].

---

[1]The idea there is to regard a pruning operation as that of finding, among subtrees that comprise a decision tree, one with the shortest description length. See [9] for details.

The main part of the diversity based summarizer consists of two operations: **Find-Diversity** for building diverse topic clusters in text; and **Reduce-Redundancy** for finding a most representative sentence from each cluster. The summarizer takes sentences from Reduce-Redundancy to generate a summary.

Find-Diversity is a clustering algorithm based on an MDL-version of X-means [11] (we call it X^M-means). Given a set of data points, i.e. sentences in the text–which are represented as a vector of term weights–X^M-means begins by generating initial regions (clusters), which involves running K-means on the input data space, with $K = 2$.[2] For each region generated, X^M-means further splits the region into halves and examines whether the splitting is worthwhile in terms of MDL. The parent region is retained if it has a shorter description length than the sum of the description lengths of subregions given birth to. X^M-means searches the entire data space for a best region to split.

Reduce-Redundancy is a simple 'rank-and-select' algorithm, which ranks sentences according to some weighting scheme and selects those with top scores. We define the *weight* W of a sentence s as the sum of tfidf values of content words in the sentence, that is, $W(s) = \sum_{x \in s}(1 + log(tf(x))) \cdot idf(x)$, where x denotes a content word, $tf(x)$ is the frequency of term x in the document, $idf(x)$ is the inverse document frequency of x given as $\log \frac{N}{df(x)}$, where $df(x)$ is the number of documents with occurrences of x and N is the total number of documents.

3 Evaluation and Discussion

We asked 112 Japanese subjects (students at graduate and undergraduate level) to extract 10% sentences in a text which they consider most important in making a summary. The number of sentences to extract varied from two to four, depending on the length of a text. We used 75 texts from three different categories (25 for each category); column, editorial and news report. Texts were of about the same size in terms of character counts and the number of paragraphs, and were selected randomly from articles that appeared in a Japanese financial daily [8]. We had 19.98 sentences per text on the average. Since we were interested in how much subjects agree on their decisions, we assigned about 7 subjects to each article for annotation. We labeled with the "Select" class, every sentence marked as important by one or more subjects. Table 1 gives some statistical information on the test data; about a half of the data were labeled "Select."

---

[2]Each initial splitting of a region involved performing 200 runs of K-means with randomly generated initial points and selecting a clustering solution with the least distortion, which is the averaged sum of squares of Euclidean distances between objects in a cluster and its centroid.

Table 1. The Test Data. #SENT. **denotes the number of sentences in the test data.** #AGR. $\geq$ 1 **denotes the number of those marked as important by one or more subjects.**

#SENT.	#AGR. ≥ 1	NOT MARKED
1424	707	717

Table 2. 10-fold cross-validated error rates for C4.5. A figure in parentheses represents the size (the number of nodes) of a decision tree generated. The bottom row shows the baseline performance, also in error rate.

	NOT PRUNED	MDL-PRUNED
TRAIN	0.093 (527)	0.383 (4.6)
TEST	0.406 (527)	0.385 (4.6)
BASELINE	0.49	

In order to gain some insights into the classificatory accuracy of the decision tree trained on human coded data, we performed the 10-fold cross validation test; we split the test data into 10 blocks, reserve one for the test and use others for training. As Table 2 shows, the accuracy of classification for the test data is 59% without the pruning but increases to 61% with MDL. Though the figures are low, either is well above the baseline performance, which is 51%. The baseline performance is defined here as the chance probability that a given sentence is marked as "Select."

As for the diversity based summarizer with X^M-means (henceforth DBS/X^M), the only training involved was the estimation of the document frequency of a term used in sentence weighting, which was done using a collection of 14,391 articles selected from the same news paper corpus the test data came from. The summarizer was tested on the entire test data. Also for the purpose of comparison, we prepared other sorts of unsupervised methods. One is a diversity based summarizer (call it DBS/K) with X^M- means replaced with K-means; the number of K is given in proportion to a compression rate. For example, at compression rate of 0.2, K was set to 2 for a text of ten sentences.

Another method considered was Reduce-Redundancy itself, which can be turned into a summarizer by letting it applying to the entire text rather than some portion of it. We call Reduce-Redundancy as a summarizer Z-model or simply Z, since it closely resembles the idea in [12]. DBS/K, DBS/X^M and Z were all tested on the entire test set.

Table 3 shows performance in F-measure of summarizers at varying compression rates, where $F = \frac{2*P*R}{P+R}$ for precision P and recall R. It is interesting and even surprising to find that the decision tree based summarizer DT/MDL falls

Table 3. Performance at varying compression rates. Performance figures are in F-measure.

cmp.rate	DT/MDL	DBS/X(M)	DBS/K	Z
0.2	0.353	**0.394**	0.314	0.249
0.3	0.453	**0.477**	0.396	0.369
0.4	**0.535**	0.529	0.508	0.450
0.5	**0.585**	0.582	0.549	0.536

behind DBS/X^M at compression rates, 0.2 and 0.3, though they come closer at 0.4 and 0.5.[3] There could be a number of reasons for a relatively low performance of DT/MDL: the small corpus size, a choice of features to encode a sentence, etc.[4] But one could argue that in order for DT/MDL to get better of DBS/X^M, its performance in classification needs to be better than 61%, which is hard to beat, given that DT/MDL is among the best classifiers for a domain of the sort considered here and it is not clear whether there are features more effective in classification than those we have now.

A comparison of DBS/X^M, DBS/K and Z-model reveals significant effects of the diversity component on performance, particularly at lower compression rates. The former two methods outperforms Z-model at all points. DBS/X^M records twice as high performance as Z-model at 0.2. Moreover, the table shows that DBS/X^M outperforms DBS/K at every compression point, demonstrating the clear superiority of X^M-means over the simpler K-means.

To conclude, we have presented a comparison of several approaches, both supervised and unsupervised, to text summarization. We considered one supervised approach, C4.5 extended with MDL, and several unsupervised ones, including a simple tfidf based summarizer and diversity based summarizers based on K-means. We conducted experiments using test data collected from human subjects, and found an interesting result that a diversity based summarizer with X^M-means, which is unsupervised, was comparable to and even superior to the supervised approach at some compression rates. The results indicate that it is possible with an unsupervised approach to model subjective judgments by humans, at least as well as a learning (decision tree) based approach.

---

[3]Recall that DT/MDL generates a summary by way of selecting sentences whose probability of being "Select" category is among the highest.

[4]One may argue that DT/MDL and DBS/X^M are incomparable since they use different feature sets. However, it is not possible to restrict either to using the other's feature set without unreasonably hurting its performance. Our concern here is with comparing the two at their best.

References

[1] A. Berger and V. O. Mittal. Query-relevant summarization using FAQs. In *Proceedings of the 38th Annual Meeting of the Association for Computational Linguistics*, pages 294–301, Hong Kong, 2000.

[2] J. Carbonell and J. Goldstein. The use of MMR, diversity-based reranking for reordering documents and producing summaries. In *Proceedings of the 21th Annual International ACM/SIGIR Conference on Research and Development in IR*, Melbourne, Australia, 1998. 335-336.

[3] W. Chuang and J. Yang. Text summarization by sentence segment extraction using machine learning algorithms. In T. Terano, H. Liu, and A. L. P. Chen, editors, *Knowledge Discovery and Data Mining*, number 1805 in Lecture Notes in Artificial Intelligence, pages 454–457. Springer, 2000.

[4] Y. Freund and R. E. Schapire. Experiments with a new boosting algorithm. In *Proceedings of the Thirteenth International Conference on Machine Learning*, 1996.

[5] J. Kupiec, J. Pedersen, and F. Chen. A trainable document summarizer. In *Proceedings of the Fourteenth Annual International ACM/SIGIR Conference on Research and Development in Information Retrieval*, pages 68–73, 1995. Seattle, USA.

[6] I. Mani, D. House, G. Klein, L. Hirshman, L. Obust, T. Firmin, M. Chrzanowski, and B. Sundheim. The TIPSTER SUMMAC Text Summarization Evalutation Final Report. Technical report, MITRE, Virginia, USA, October 1998.

[7] D. Marcu. The automated construction of large-scale corpora for summarization research. In *Proceedings of the 22nd International ACM/SIGIR Conference on Research and Development in Informational Retrieval*, pages 137–144, Berkeley, CA, August 1999.

[8] Nihon-Keizai-Shimbun-Sha. Nihon keizai shimbun 95 nen cd-rom ban. CD-ROM, 1995. Tokyo, Nihon Keizai Shimbun, Inc.

[9] T. Nomoto and Y. Matsumoto. Comparing the minimum description length principle and boosting in the automatic analysis of discourse. In *Proceedings of the Seventeenth International Conference on Machine Learning*, pages 687–694, Stanford University, CA, June-July 2000. Morgan Kaufmann.

[10] T. Nomoto and Y. Matsumoto. A new approach to unsupervised text summarization. In *Proceedings of the 24th International ACM/SIGIR Conference on Research and Development in Informational Retrieval*, New Orleans, September 2001. ACM.

[11] D. Pelleg and A. Moore. X-means: Extending K-means with efficient estimation of the number of clusters. In *Proceedings of the Seventeenth International Conference on Machine Learning (ICML2000)*, pages 727–734, Stanford University, CA, June-July 2000. Morgan Kaufmann.

[12] K. Zechner. Fast generation of abstracts from general domain text corpora by extracting relevant sentences. In *Proceedings of the 16th International Conference on Computational Linguistics*, pages 986–989, 1996. Copenhagen, Denmark.

A Fast Algorithm to Cluster High Dimensional Basket Data *

Carlos Ordonez   Edward Omiecinski   Norberto Ezquerra
College of Computing
Georgia Institute of Technology

Abstract

Clustering is a data mining problem that has received significant attention by the database community. Data set size, dimensionality and sparsity have been identified as aspects that make clustering more difficult. This work introduces a fast algorithm to cluster large binary data sets where data points have high dimensionality and most of their coordinates are zero. This is the case with basket data transactions containing items, that can be represented as sparse binary vectors with very high dimensionality. An experimental section shows performance, advantages and limitations of the proposed approach.

1 Introduction

Clustering algorithms identify those regions that are more densely populated than others in multidimensional data [8, 13]. In general clustering algorithms partition the data set into several groups such that points in the same group are close to each other and points across groups are far from each other. It has been shown that high dimensionality [10], data sparsity [1] and noise [2] make clustering a harder problem.

In this work we focus on the problem of efficiently clustering binary data sets that are sparse and have very high dimensionality. This is precisely the case with basket data transactions, where transactions contain combinations of a few items out of thousands of items. Our approach can be used as an alternative data mining technique to association rule discovery [3].

1.1 Overview

We introduce a fast clustering algorithm for sparse high dimensional binary data (basket data) based on the well-known Expectation-Maximization (EM) clustering algorithm [7, 17, 6, 13]. The EM algorithm is a general statistical method of maximum likelihood estimation [7, 14, 17]. In particular it can be used to perform clustering. In our case we will use it to fit a mixture of Normal distributions to a sparse binary data set.

Our algorithm is designed to efficiently handle large problem sizes as typically encountered in modern database systems and it is guaranteed to produce high quality solutions as it will be shown by our experiments.

The proposed clustering algorithm builds a statistical model so that the user can understand transactions at a high level. Items are mapped to binary dimensions and transactions are thus mapped to binary data points. The basic idea is to group similar transactions. Clusters of transactions can have different interpretations. Each cluster can tell us what the typical transaction looks like; this is precisely the mean or average of transactions per cluster. Each cluster describes which items commonly appear together in each transaction. Since cluster centroids are averages of binary numbers the mean of a certain dimension can be interpreted as a probability or a percentage. If transactions are not well clustered in certain dimensions this can be explained by the deviation they have from the mean. The user will be able to compare several cluster models by looking at a quantity measuring their quality.

1.2 Contributions and paper outline

This is a summary of our contributions. We introduce a novel algorithm to cluster very high dimensional and sparse binary data sets. The proposed solution does not require complex data structures to store patterns or model parameters, but only matrices that in general can fit in memory. From a quality point of view the algorithm computes highly accurate clusters. From a performance point of view the algorithm is fast, having linear time complexity in data set size, in transaction size and in the desired number of clusters.

The rest of this paper is organized as follows. Section 2 provides definitions and statistical background. Section 3 contains the algorithm to cluster high dimensional and sparse binary data sets. Section 4 contains a brief experimental evaluation. Section 5 discusses related work. The paper concludes with section 6.

---

*This work was supported by grant LM 06726 from the National Library of Medicine

Matrix	size	contents
C	$d \times k$	means
R	$d \times k$	covariances
W	$k \times 1$	weights

Table 1. Output matrices

Matrix	size	contents
N	$k \times 1$	$|D_j|$
M	$d \times k$	$M_j = \sum_{i=1}^{N_j} t_i, \forall t_i \in D_j$

Table 2. Sufficient statistics

2 Definitions and statistical background

This section provides formal definitions that will be used throughout this work. First, basic statistical background on EM and the mixture problem are described. Second, additional definitions relating transactions and multidimensional binary vectors are introduced.

The multivariate normal density function for a d-dimensional vector $x = [x_1, x_2, \ldots, x_d]^t$ is:

$$p(x) = \frac{1}{(2\pi)^{d/2}|\Sigma|^{1/2}} \exp[-\frac{1}{2}(x - \mu)^t \Sigma^{-1}(x - \mu)],$$

where μ is called the mean vector and Σ is called the covariance matrix; μ is a d-dimensional vector and Σ is a $d \times d$ matrix. Our algorithm uses diagonal covariance matrices.

The input to EM are n d-dimensional points and k, the desired number of clusters. These n points are modeled as a mixture of normal distributions as defined above. This mixture has 3 parameters, namely, the means, the covariances and the weights. Data set size, i.e. number of points, is n. The desired number of clusters is k. Dimensionality is d. The parameters computed by the EM algorithm are stored in the matrices described in table 1. In the statistical literature all parameters are used as a single set called Θ, i.e. $\Theta = \{C, R, W\}$. To refer to one column of C or R we use the j subscript (i.e. C_j, R_j).

Since it is our intention to cluster basket data we will combine our previous definitions with additional definitions commonly used for association rules [3, 4]. Let $D = \{T_1, T_2, \ldots, T_n\}$ be a set of n transactions containing items, and let $\mathcal{I}$ be a set of d items, $\mathcal{I} = \{i_1, i_2 \ldots i_d\}$, where each item will be identified by its index, that is, an integer in $\{1, 2, \ldots, d\}$. Let $D_1, D_2, \ldots, D_k$ be k subsets of D (i.e. $D_j \subseteq D, j = 1 \ldots k$). s.t. $D_j \cap D_{j'} = \emptyset, j \neq j'$ (i.e. they are a partition of D induced by clusters). Each subset D_j represents one cluster. We use T_i to avoid confusion with t_i that will be used as a binary vector: T_i will be a set of integers and t_i will be a binary vector. Items will be mapped to binary dimensions. For each item $i_1, i_2, \ldots, i_d$ there will be a corresponding dimension b_l. Each transaction T_i will be given as a set of integers (items), $T_i = \{i_1, i_2, \ldots, i_K\}$, where $i_l \in \{1, \ldots, d\}$ and i (without subscript) denotes the number of transaction; $i \in \{1, 2, \ldots, n\}$. Then the notation t_i is used, meaning a binary vector, where each entry corresponds to one dimension (item). Then $(t_i)_l = 1$ for $l = i_1, i_2, \ldots, i_K$ and $(t_i)_l = 0$ otherwise. Each transaction becomes a sparse binary vector having d entries, but only K of them different from zero. So D in this case can be considered a huge and sparse $d \times n$ matrix. Each item i_l will be an integer, $i_l \in \{1, 2, \ldots, d\}$ to index matrices to refer to one dimension. Mathematically transactions will be points in $[0, 1]^d$ space, but for the algorithm they will be sets of integers.

3 A clustering algorithm for binary data sets with very high dimensionality

3.1 Improvements

We propose several improvements and changes on EM to deal with very high dimensionality, sparsity, null covariances, large data set size and slow convergence. Such improvements include suitable initialization for high dimensional data, sufficient statistics, covariance matrix regularization techniques, sparse distance computation and learning steps.

Initialization is based on the global statistics of the data set: the global mean and the global covariance. They are computed in a one-time pass over the data set and are available thereafter. Seed centroids are initialized based on the global mean and standard deviation of the data. Sufficient statistics [12, 11] (table 2) are used to summarize information about clusters; this reduces I/O time by avoiding repeated passes over the data and by allowing to make parameter estimation periodically as transactions are being read. The E step is executed for every transaction and the M step is executed a fixed number of times making convergence to the solution fast. The algorithm uses sparse distance computation and sparse matrix additions to make the E step faster. It uses regularization techniques [15] to deal with zero covariances, common with sparse data and specially with basket data. The algorithm requires two scans over the data per run. The main input parameter is only the desired number of clusters.

Input: $T_1, T_2, \ldots, T_n$ and k.
Output $\Theta = \{C, R, W\}$ and $L(\Theta)$
$\alpha \leftarrow (dk)^{-1}, L \leftarrow 50$
FOR $j = 1$ TO k DO   /* Initialize */
  $C_j \leftarrow \mu \pm \alpha r \, \mathrm{diag}[\sigma], \; R_j \leftarrow I, \; W_j \leftarrow 1/k$
  $\Delta_j = \delta(\bar{0}, C_j, R_j) = C_j^t R_j^{-1} C^j$
  $M_j \leftarrow C_j, \; N_j \leftarrow 1$
ENDFOR
FOR $scan = 1$ TO 2 DO
  $L(\Theta) = 0$
  FOR $i = 1$ TO n DO
    $t_i \leftarrow vect[T_i]$
    FOR $j = 1$ TO k DO   /* E step */
      $\delta_{ij} \leftarrow \delta(t_i, C_j, R_j)$,
      $p_{ij} \leftarrow ((2\pi)^d |R_j|)^{-1/2} exp(-\delta_{ij}/2)$
    ENDFOR
    Let m be s.t. $p_{im} \geq p_{ij} \forall j \in 1 \ldots k$
    $M_m \leftarrow M_m + t_i, \; N_m \leftarrow N_m + 1$
    $L(\Theta) \leftarrow L(\Theta) + ln(p_{ij})$
    IF($i \bmod (n/L) = 0$) THEN   /* M step */
      FOR $j = 1$ TO k DO
        $C_j \leftarrow M_j / N_j$
        $R_j \leftarrow M_j / N_j - M_j M_j^t / N_j^2 + I$
        $W_j \leftarrow N_j / \sum_{J=1}^{k} N_J$
        $\Delta_j \leftarrow C_j^t R_j^{-1} C_j$
      ENDFOR
    ENDIF
  ENDFOR /* Reset sufficient statistics */
  IF scan=1 THEN $M_j \leftarrow C_j, N_j \leftarrow 1$ ENDIF
ENDFOR

Figure 1. Clustering algorithm for sparse high dimensional binary data

3.2 Algorithm to cluster sparse binary data sets with very high dimensionality

The pseudo-code of our clustering algorithm is in figure 1. This is a high-level description. The input is a set of transactions $D = \{T_1, T_2, \ldots, T_n\}$ and k, the desired number of clusters. The output is $\Theta = \{C, R, W\}$, describing the mixture model, $L(\Theta)$ measuring model quality and a partitioning of D into k subsets. The constant α is used to seed C based on d and k. The global statistics μ and Σ are computed in a one-time scan and are available thereafter. Standard deviations are computed as $\sigma_{ll} = \sqrt{\Sigma_{ll}}$. The E step is executed for every transaction (n times). δ_{ij} is efficiently computed using Δ_j. The M step is periodically executed every n/L transactions (L times). L is typically a number between 10 and 100. The update formulas for C, R, W are based on sufficient statistics [12] M, N, shown in table 2, and regularization techniques [15]. M, N are the multidimensional version of the univariate sufficient statistics shown in [12] when points are binary; due to lack of space we do not explain how to derive their formulas. Sufficient statistics are reset at the end of the first scan. The goal of the first scan is to get accurate cluster centroids C_j and accurate

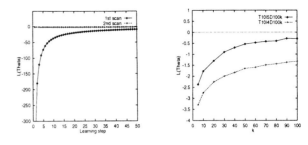

Figure 2. Quality of results

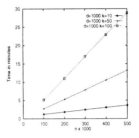 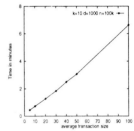

Figure 3. Performance

covariances R_j. The goal of the second scan is to tune Θ and recompute $L(\Theta)$. Dimensions (items) are ranked within each cluster by their value in C_j to make output easier to understand.

4 Experimental evaluation

This section includes experimental evaluation of our algorithm. All experiments were performed on a Sun Machine running at 600 MHz with 256 Mb of memory. This machine had several Gb of available disk space. Our algorithms were implemented in the C++ language and compiled with the GNU C++ compiler.

Our algorithm was evaluated with large transaction test files created by the well-known IBM synthetic data generator [4]. Test files are named after the parameters with which they were created. The standard way [4] is to use T (average transaction size), I (pattern length) and D (for us n) to label files since those are the most common parameters to change. The algorithm parameters were set as follows. $L = 50$ and $\alpha = 1/(dk)$.

In this paragraph we explain quality of results. The left graph in figure 2 shows how our algorithm converges on the 1st scan. The 2nd scan just tunes the solution without decreasing $L(\Theta)$. The right graph in figure 2 shows how model accuracy increases as k increases; the behavior is clearly asymptotic.

In this paragraph we describe performance with large data sets. Note that $d = 1000$ is a very high dimensionality. The left graph in figure 3 shows running as time as we vary n for several typical transaction files; the algorithm scales linearly. The right graph in figure 3 shows the impact of average transaction size (T) on performance; the algorithm is linear. Times varying k are also linear; this graph is not shown.

5 Related work

There has been so much work on both clustering and association rule mining that it is impossible to compare our approach with everybody else's. To the best of our knowledge there is no previous work on clustering *high dimensional and sparse large* binary data sets using EM. We do not know work where there are experiments with 1,000 or more dimensions [9, 10, 1, 2, 6]. Also, we believe that the idea of building a statistical model based on clustering for basket data has not been explored before. The only work that has analyzed how to cluster basket data transactions is [16]; their approach goes in the opposite direction since they mine associations and from them clusters are generated. We are not the first to propose a scalable and faster version of EM for data mining applications. One important work that also studied how to construct a faster and Scalable EM algorithm (SEM) is [6]. This work extended previous work on scaling K-means [5]. The authors present an algorithm, also based on sufficient statistics [12], that makes compression in two phases for dense and quasi-dense regions. The authors use it to build several models concurrently. SEM is significantly different from ours. It is designed for low dimensional continuous numerical data without zero covariance problems, and then it is not suitable for very high dimensional sparse binary data. It does not incorporate sparse distance computation, regularization techniques. Initialization is done by sampling and it keeps sufficient statistics on many subsets of the data, many more than k. Also, it uses an iterative K-means algorithm [14] to cluster data points in memory and then it does not make a fixed number of computations. One advantage over ours it that it only requires one scan over the data, but it makes heavier CPU use and it requires careful buffer size tuning.

6 Conclusions

This paper presented a new clustering algorithm. The proposed algorithm is designed to work with *large* binary data sets having *very high* dimensionality. The algorithm only requires two scans over the data to cluster transactions and construct a statistical model. Each cluster is a summary of a group of similar transactions and thus represents one significant pattern discovered in the data. Experimental evaluation showed transactions can be clustered with high accuracy. Model quality mainly depends on k, the desired number of clusters. The algorithm makes its best effort to get a high quality model given data characteristics. Performance

is linear and it is mainly affected by n, k and transaction size, and minimally by dimensionality since data sets are sparse. The algorithm is restricted to problem sizes whose model can fit in main memory.

A summary of future work follows. Evidently some of our results can be applied to cluster high dimensional numerical data, but data skew, noise and cluster overlap make the problem different and to some extent more difficult. We plan to adapt and modify our algorithm to cluster continuous numeric data and compare it with the simplification of Scalable K-means [5] discussed in [9]. We would like to analyze the possibility of mining association rules from the model without scanning transactions.

References

[1] Charu Aggarwal and Philip Yu. Finding generalized projected clusters in dimensional spaces. In *ACM SIGMOD Conference*, 2000.

[2] Rakesh Agrawal, Johannes Gehrke, Dimitrios Gunopolos, and Prabhakar Raghavan. Automatic subspace clustering of high dimensional data for data mining applications. In *ACM SIGMOD Conference*, 1998.

[3] Rakesh Agrawal, Tomasz Imielinski, and Arun Swami. Mining association rules between sets of items in large databases. In *ACM SIGMOD Conference*, pages 207–216, 1993.

[4] Rakesh Agrawal and Ramakrishnan Srikant. Fast algorithms for mining association rules in large databases. In *VLDB Conference*, 1994.

[5] Paul Bradley, Usama Fayyad, and Cory Reina. Scaling clustering algorithms to large databases. In *ACM KDD Conference*, 1998.

[6] Paul Bradley, Usama Fayyad, and Cory Reina. Scaling EM clustering to large databases. Technical report, Microsoft Research, 1999.

[7] Arthur P. Dempster, Nan M. Laird, and Donald B. Rubin. Maximum likelihood estimation from incomplete data via the EM algorithm. *Journal of The Royal Statistical Society*, 39(1):1–38, 1977.

[8] Richard Duda and Peter Hart. *Pattern Classification and Scene Analysis*, pages 10–45. John Wiley and Sons, 1973.

[9] Fredrik Fanstrom, James Lewis, and Charles Elkan. Scalability for clustering algorithms revisited. *SIGKDD Explorations*, 2(1):51–57, June 2000.

[10] Alexander Hinneburg and Daniel Keim. Optimal grid-clustering: Towards breaking the curse of dimensionality. In *VLDB Conference*, 1999.

[11] Alexander Mood, Franklin Graybill, and Duane Boes. *Introduction to the Theory of Statistics*, pages 299–320. McGraw Hill, NY, 1974.

[12] Radford Neal and Geoffrey Hinton. A view of the EM algorithm that justifies incremental, sparse and other variants. Technical report, Dept. of Statistics, University of Toronto, 1993.

[13] Carlos Ordonez and Paul Cereghini. SQLEM: Fast clustering in SQL using the EM algorithm. In *ACM SIGMOD Conference*, pages 559–570, 2000.

[14] Sam Roweis and Zoubin Ghahramani. A unifying review of Linear Gaussian Models. *Neural Computation*, 1999.

[15] Nononi Ueda, Ryoehi Nakano, Zoubin Ghahramani, and Geoffrey Hinton. SMEM algorithm for mixture models. In *Neural Information Processing Systems*, 1998.

[16] Ke Wang, Chu Xu, and Bing Liu. Clustering transactions using large items. In *ACM CIKM Conference*, 1999.

[17] Lei Xu and Michael Jordan. On convergence properties of the EM algorithm for Gaussian mixtures. *Neural Computation*, 7, 1995.

Metric Rule Generation with Septic Shock Patient Data

Jürgen Paetz

J.W. Goethe-Universität

FB Biologie und Informatik, Institut für Informatik

D-60054 Frankfurt am Main

paetz@cs.uni-frankfurt.de, www.informatik.uni-frankfurt.de/~paetz

Abstract

In this contribution we present an application of metric rule generation in the domain of medical research. We consider intensive care unit patients developing a septic shock during their stay at the hospital. To analyse the patient data, rule generation is embedded in a medical data mining cycle. For rule generation, we improve an architecture based on a growing trapezoidal basis function network.

1. Introduction

In abdominal intensive care medicine patients often develop a *septic shock*, a phenomenon that is related to mechanisms of the immune system and which is still an important research subject for medical experts and data analysts [1]. The septic shock is associated with a high lethality of about 50%. It is always related to measurements leaving the normal range and it is often related to multiorgan failure. Our data base D consists of 874 patients. 70 patients of the 874 patients developed a septic shock during their stay at the intensive care unit (ICU). 38.6% of the septic shock patients deceased.

We embedded our data analysis in a medical data mining cycle [2]: knowledge extraction, data collection, problem formulation, database operations, preprocessing, application of rule generation methods, interpretation.

One of the datasets we analysed after preprocessing is the subset F_{12} of the data base D, containing the measurements of the 12 most frequently measured variables. To limit the influence of missing values, we demanded the existence of a minimum of 10 out of 12 variables for each sample, so that 1698 samples remained out of 2068 (1177 survived, 521 deceased). We point out that we will classify the samples of the patients to generate warnings, we do not classify the outcome of the patients. We labeled all the samples of a deceased patient as "deceased".

2. Rule Generation

Initially, we chose the supervised algorithm [3] as a starting point for metric rule generation due to its easy adaptive geometrical rule generation process. The initial rule generation algorithm [3] is based on a 2-layer network that has neurons in the hidden layer with asymmetrical trapezoidal fuzzy activation functions. During the learning phase these neurons are adapted, i.e. the sides of the upper, smaller rectangles (= *core rules*) and the sides of the lower, larger rectangles (= *support rules*) of the trapezoids are adapted to the data. For every new training data point this happens in four phases: cover, commit, shrink committed neuron, shrink conflict neurons. Classification is done by a winner-takes-all mechanism. Details can be found in [3].

An *advantage* of the basic method is its simplicity that softens the combinatorical explosion in rule generation by its cover-commit-shrink-procedure. If a rule R has the format "... **and if** var$_j$ **in** $(-\infty, +\infty)$ **and** ... **then** class ...", the value of variable j is not relevant and so this variable could be omitted in the rule R. *Negative aspects* of the basic algorithm that weaken the quality of the rules are the dependency on presentation order of the training samples with an unfavourable expansion of core rules (P1), the immediate creation of new rules for outlier data (P2), the large overlapping of support rules (P3) and the extensive overlapping of core rules with different class labels (P4).

We approach the problems (P1), ..., (P4) before applying the algorithm to our data: (P1) by using a heuristic *nearby parameter*, (P2) by a counter (= weight) for every neuron *and every* class and an additional *insertion criteria*, (P3) by a *weak shrink*, (P4) by an additional subfunction that detects and avoids the *core conflict*, see our homepage for details.

To evaluate the performance of the rules generated by our improved algorithm we calculate the means of the well-known measures *frequency* and *confidence* for different fuzzy levels (= degrees of membership) on test data samples. A core rule has fuzzy level = 1 and a support rule has fuzzy level = 0. We also calculated all the rules for the

Table 1. Correct classifications on training and test data. In %.

	mean	std. dev.	min.	max.
train correct	74.62	3.82	68.85	78.66
test correct	69.00	4.37	61.20	72.66

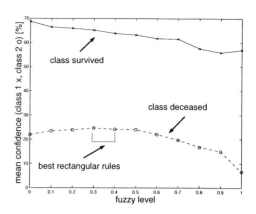

Figure 1. Dataset F_{12}: mean confidence of the rules per class in relation to the fuzzy level.

intermediate fuzzy levels 0.1, 0.2, ..., 0.8, 0.9. Every time a rule was not hit by any test data sample, its confidence was set conservatively to zero. Due to the fact that the core rules may be very small and so very inconfident because no test data hit the rules, it is interesting that the choice of *rectangular* rules of a fuzzy level < 1.0 could be a statistically better choice than rectangular rules of fuzzy level 1.0.

If you want to design fuzzy rules like "**if** heart frequency **is** high **and** systolic blood pressure **is** low **then** class deceased" the rectangular rules of different fuzzy levels are not interesting because the whole trapezoid is interpreted as one fuzzy rule in the defuzzification step. For us, fuzzy variables like "high", "middle" or "low" are not precise enough. Concerning the septic shock problem a physician could not draw a conclusion from these fuzzy variables without knowing the relevant values more exactly. The septic shock data is an excellent example where a "simple" fuzzy approach is not satisfying. This is the reason for analysing the underlying rectangular rules of the trapezoidal fuzzy activation functions with the frequency and confidence measures.

The classification results of 7 randomized repetitions of the entire training procedure is presented in Table 1. The testdata specifity is 92.26%, the sensitivity is 15.01%. Poor sensitivity performance could be interpreted in the way that deceased patients are not very critical all the time during their stay at the ICU, so that a warning should be generated only from the most confident rules.

The best rectangular rules we achieved at fuzzy level $\eta \in [0.3, 0.4]$ due to the class deceased, see Fig. 1.

There are many *local* rules covering areas of F_{12} with a good performance, many with a dimensionality < 12. These rules (for the class deceased) are good candidates for a warning to the physician. We give one example: "**if** heart frequency $\leq$ 110.00 [1/min] **and** systolic blood pressure $\leq$ 120.00 [mmHg] **and** CVP $\geq$ 11.00 [cmH$_2$O] **and** temperature $\geq$ 36.50 [°C] **and** leukocytes **in** (10.93, 37.00) [1000/μl] **and** sodium **in** (138.00, 146.00) [mmol/l] **then** class deceased **with** frequency 3.6% **and** confidence 64.7%". Interestingly, no better experience-based rules could be proposed by medical experts. So a rational data driven machine learning approach to metric rule generation is a benefit for physicians.

With our approach several interesting rules for human

interaction have been generated, although it was not possible to obtain an excellent *global* result covering the whole patient data. Further work will be the application of rule generation with additional categorical data, extending our previous results [4]. We also expect interesting results from analyses of more extensive data sets, currently collected in clinics all over Germany within the last three years, improving our early warning system prototype [5, 2].

Acknowledgement: The author like to thank all the participants of the MEDAN working group (www.medan.de), especially Dr. Brause and Prof. Hanisch for supporting my work.

References

[1] Wade, S., Büssow, M., Hanisch, E., Epidemiology of SIRS, Sepsis and Septic Shock in Surgical Intensive Care Patients, *Der Chirurg* **69**, 1998, pp. 648–655.

[2] Paetz, J., Hamker, F., Thöne, S., About the Analysis of Septic Shock Patient Data, *Proc. of the 1st Int. Symp. on Medical Data Analysis*, LNCS Vol. 1933, Springer-Verlag, 2000, pp. 130–137.

[3] Huber, K.-P., Berthold, M.R., Building Precise Classifiers with Automatic Rule Extraction, *Proc. IEEE Int. Conf. on Neural Networks* **3**, 1995, pp. 1263–1268.

[4] Paetz, J., Brause, R., A Frequent Patterns Tree Approach for Rule Generation with Categorical Septic Shock Patient Data. *Proc. of the 2nd Int. Symp. on Medical Data Analysis*, LNCS, Springer-Verlag, 2001.

[5] Hamker, F. et al., Erkennung kritischer Zustände von Patienten mit der Diagnose „Septischer Schock" mit einem RBF-Netz, Interner Bericht 04/00, FB Informatik, J.W. Goethe-Univ. Frankfurt am Main, 2000.

The Representative Basis for Association Rules

Viet Phan-Luong

L.I.M. CNRS FRE-2246, C.M.I. de l'Université de Provence

39, rue F. Joliot-Curie, 13453 Marseille Cedex 13, France

phan@gyptis.univ-mrs.fr

Abstract

We define the concept of the representative basis for interesting association rules, and an inference system which is purely qualitative. The representative basis is unique, and minimal with respect to (wrt) the inference system. On the representative basis, the inference system is correct and complete. Experimental results show that the number of rules in the representative basis is significantly reduced wrt the number of rules generated by other existing approaches.

1. Introduction

Faced with the exponential number of association rules extracted from a dataset, there is a trend searching for their concise representations, called generating sets or bases [1, 2, 4, 6]. A generating set is a small set of informative association rules from which all other interesting association rules can be derived. The concept of frequent closed itemsets [4, 6] is proposed as a theoretical basis for generating sets. These approaches have the main common points: (*i*) They distinguish the basis for exact rules from the basis for approximate rules. (*ii*) Rules that can be derived by transitivity or augmentation are discarded from the basis. As consequences, the inference on these bases has to use transitivity and augmentation. However, a rule derived by transitivity is not always interesting. Computing the confidence of the derived rule, basing on the confidences of the rules in the basis, is necessary to know if it is interesting. A rule derived by augmentation (on the left- or right-hand sides) is not always interesting. Only the augmentation using items obtained by Galois closure operators [3] can ensure the interestingness of the derived rule. We argue that these computations are not evident to the end users.

We present an approach to generating set, called the representative basis, which is different from the above approaches in these two points. In particular, we shall see the inference on the representative basis is very simple, and no computation of the confidences or closures is needed.

2. Preliminaries

Association rules are extracted from a dataset $\mathcal{D} = (\mathcal{O}, \mathcal{I}, \mathcal{R})$ where $\mathcal{O}$ is a finite set of objects, $\mathcal{I}$ is a finite set of items, and $\mathcal{R}$ is a binary relation on $\mathcal{O}$ and $\mathcal{I}$. A subset $I \subseteq \mathcal{I}$ is called an *itemset* of $\mathcal{D}$. For each $O \subseteq \mathcal{O}$ and each $I \subseteq \mathcal{I}$, let $g(I) = \{o \in \mathcal{O} \mid \forall i \in I, (o, i) \in \mathcal{R}\}$, and $f(O) = \{i \in \mathcal{I} \mid \forall o \in O, (o, i) \in \mathcal{R}\}$. The couple (f, g) is called a Galois connection [3] between $2^{\mathcal{O}}$ and $2^{\mathcal{I}}$. The Galois closure operators are the compositions: $h = f \circ g$ and $h' = g \circ f$. Let I be an itemset of $\mathcal{D}$, $h(I) = f(g(I))$ is called the *closure* of I. Indeed, $I \subseteq h(I) = h(h(I))$. An itemset I is *closed* if $h(I) = I$. The support of I is $sup(I) = card(g(I))/card(\mathcal{O})$, where $card(X)$ is the cardinality of X. Given a support threshold, denoted by $minsup$, $0 \leq minsup \leq 1$, an itemset I is frequent if $sup(I) \geq minsup$. I is *frequent closed* if it is frequent and closed [1, 6]. An itemset I is called a *frequent key* itemset [2] if there is no $I' \subset I$ with $sup(I') = sup(I)$.

An association rule r is an expression of the form $I_1 \rightarrow I_2$, where $I_1, I_2 \subseteq \mathcal{I}$. The support and confidence of r, denoted by $sup(r)$ and $conf(r)$, respectively, are $sup(r) = sup(I_1 \cup I_2)$, and $conf(r) = sup(I_1 \cup I_2)/sup(I_1)$. If $conf(r) = 1$, then r is called an *exact* rule. Otherwise, r is called an *approximate* rule. Let $minsup$ and $minconf$ be the thresholds for supports and confidences of associations rules, respectively. An association rule r is *interesting* if $sup(r) \geq minsup$ and $conf(r) \geq minconf$.

Example 1. The left part of Table 1 represents a dataset; in the right part are the itemsets with their supports.

Table 1.

Oid	Items		sup	Itemsets
1	A,C,D		1/5	D
2	B,C,E		2/5	AB,AE,ABC,ABE,ACE,ABCE
3	A,B,C,E		3/5	A,AC,BC,CE,BCE
4	B,E		4/5	B,C,E,BE
5	A,B,C,E		1	∅

We have $sup(AB \rightarrow CE) = sup(ABCE) = 2/5$,

$conf(AB \rightarrow CE) = 1$. And $sup(B \rightarrow CE) = 3/5$, $conf(B \rightarrow CE) = 3/4$. Wrt $minsup = 2/5$ and $minconf = 1/2$, $AB \rightarrow CE$ is exact and interesting, and $B \rightarrow CE$ is approximate and interesting. But wrt $minsup = 3/5$ and $minconf = 4/5$ these rules are not interesting.

3. Representative Basis

Definition 1 *The* representative basis *for interesting association rules extracted from a dataset $\mathcal{D}$ (called the representative basis of $\mathcal{D}$, in short), wrt the thresholds $minsup$ and $minconf$, is the set of interesting association rules $I \rightarrow J$ such that $I \subset J$ and there is no other interesting association rule $I' \rightarrow J'$ such that $I' \subseteq I$ and $J \subseteq J'$.*

The representative basis of the dataset in Table 1, wrt $minsup = 2/5$ and $minconf = 1/2$, consists of the following rules: $A \rightarrow ABCE, B \rightarrow ABCE, C \rightarrow ABCE, E \rightarrow ABCE, \emptyset \rightarrow BCE, \emptyset \rightarrow AC$.

Proposition 1 *The itemset on the right-hand side of every association rule in the representative basis is a frequent closed itemset.*

Proposition 2 *The itemset on the left-hand side of every association rule in the representative basis is a frequent key itemset.*

Proposition 3 Uniqueness. *The representative basis of $\mathcal{D}$ wrt $minsup$ and $minconf$ is unique.*

Definition 2 LD System. *Let I, J, K be itemsets. The* LD-System *consists of the inference rules:*

(1) Weak Left-Augmentation (wLa): If $I \rightarrow JK$ is interesting, then infer that $IJ \rightarrow JK$ is interesting.

(2) Decomposition: If $I \rightarrow I_1 I_2$ is interesting then infer that $I \rightarrow I_1$ and $I \rightarrow I_2$ are interesting.

Let $\vdash$ denotes the inference using the LD system. We have $\emptyset \rightarrow AC \vdash C \rightarrow AC, A \rightarrow AC$ (wLa). $C \rightarrow AC, A \rightarrow AC \vdash C \rightarrow A, A \rightarrow C$ (Decomposition). Similarly, we can infer all other interesting rules, approximate or exact, using the LD system on the representative basis.

Proposition 4 Soundness. *Given a set of interesting association rules $\mathcal{A}$, all association rules derived from $\mathcal{A}$ using the LD system are interesting.*

Proposition 5 Completeness. *All interesting association rules extracted from a dataset $\mathcal{D}$ wrt $minsup$ and $minconf$ can be derived from the representative basis of $\mathcal{D}$ wrt $minsup$ and $minconf$, using the LD system.*

Proposition 6 Minimality. *Let M be the representative basis of a dataset $\mathcal{D}$, wrt $minsup$ and $minconf$. Then for any association rule $r \in M$, r cannot be derived from $M \setminus \{r\}$ using the LD system.*

4. Experimental Results and Comparisons

An algorithm for computing the representative basis is implemented. In Table 2 are the numbers of rules in the representative basis, the structural basis [5], and the reduced basis [2] of the dataset Mushrooms (8124 objects coded on 128 items, http://kdd.ics.uci.edu), with $minsup = 30\%$.

Table 2.

$minconf$	Rep. Basis	Struct. Basis	Red. Basis
30%	63	424	1578
70%	440	384	1221

Notice that in order to represent all interesting association rules extracted from the dataset, the structural basis and the reduced basis need additionally the Duquenne-Guigues basis for exact rules [5], which consists of 69 rules.

Table 3 gives the numbers of rules in the representative basis and the generating set by [6] of the datasets Mushrooms, Chess (3196 objects coded on 76 items) and Connect-4 (67557 objects coded on 130 items, www.almaden.ibm.com/cs/quest/demos.html), with $minconf = minsup$.

Table 3.

Database	minsup	Rep. Basis	Generat. Set
Mushrooms	20%	158	5741
Chess	70%	891	152074
Connect-4	90%	222	18848

The representative basis is a very compact and faithful representation of the interesting association rules. each significant change on the support and confidence thresholds is reflected in the representative basis. It is not the case for other existing approaches.

References

[1] Y. Bastide, R. Taouil, N. Pasquier, G. Stumme and L. Lakhal, "Mining minimal non-redundant association rules using frequent closed itemsets", *the 6th Int'l Conf. on Ded. and Obj. Databases (DOOD'00), Stream of the 1st Int'l Conf. on Comput. Logics (CL'00)*, LNCS 1861:972-986, Springer Verlag, London, UK, 2000.

[2] Y. Bastide, R. Taouil, N. Pasquier, G. Stumme and L. Lakhal, "Pascal: un algorithme d'extraction des motifs fréquents", *Technique et Science Informatique - TSI*, 2001 (to appear).

[3] B. Ganter and R. Wille, *Formal Concept Analysis: Mathematiccal Foundations*, Springer, 1999.

[4] N. Pasquier, Y. Bastide, R. Taouil, and L. Lakhal, "Discovering frequent closed itemsets for association rules", *the 7th Int'l Conf. on Database Theory* (ICDT'99):398-416, 1999.

[5] N. Pasquier, Y. Bastide, R. Taouil, and L. Lakhal, "Closed Set Based Discovery of Small Covers for Association Rules", *15eme journées Bases de Données Avancées* (BDA'99):361-381, Bordeaux, France, 1999.

[6] M.J. Zaki, "Generating non-redundant association rules", *the 6th ACM SIGMOD Int'l Conf. on Knowledge Discovery and Data Mining* (KDD 2000):34-43, Boston, MA, August 2000.

Incremental Learning with Support Vector Machines

Stefan Rüping

Department of Computer Science, AI Unit
University of Dortmund, Germany
stefan.rueping@uni-dortmund.de

Abstract

Support Vector Machines (SVMs) have become a popular tool for machine learning with large amounts of high dimensional data. In this paper an approach for incremental learning with Support Vector Machines is presented, that improves the existing approach of [3]. Also, some insight into the interpretability of support vectors is given.

1 Incremental Learning with Support Vector Machines

Support Vector Machines (SVMs, [4]) have been successfully used for machine learning with large and high dimensional data sets. This is due to the fact that the generalization property of an SVM does not depend on the complete the training data but only a subset thereof, the so-called support vectors.

As the number of support vectors typically is very small compared to the number of training examples, SVMs promise to be an effective tool for incremental learning: When the data is presented to the learning algorithm sequentially in batches, one can compress the data of the previous batches to their support vectors. Then, for each new batch of data, a SVM is trained on the new data and the support vectors from the previous learning step.

This approach to incremental learning with SVMs has been investigated in [3], where it has been shown that incrementally trained SVMs compare very well to their non-incrementally trained equivalent. In the following this approach will be called the SV-incremental algorithm.

The principle behind this algorithm is this: The resulting decision function of an SVM depends only on its support vectors, i. e. training an SVM on the support vectors alone results in the same decision function as training on the whole data set. Because of this, one can expect to get an incremental result that is equal to the non-incremental result, if the last training set contains all examples that are support vectors in the non-incremental case. If a batch of data is a good sample, i. e. if the statistical properties of that batch and the whole data set do not differ very much, one can expect the resulting decision function to be similar to the final decision function. Therefore, a support vector in the final set is likely to be a support vector in previous iterations too.

The problem with this approach is the assumption that the batch of data will be an appropriate sample of the data. While this may be likely if the data is presented to the SVM in randomly drawn batches, there is no way to tell if this is the case if the examples are drawn in some other way. In real-world data, there may be artifacts of the way the data is presented to the learning algorithm, e.g. readings from a machine whose quality deteriorates, measurements from different kinds of patients or experiments following a certain test plan.

As an example, take examples distributed on $[-1, 1] \times [0, 1]$ and the decision function $f(x) = 1 \Leftrightarrow x_2 > |x_1|$ and assume training is done in two steps, first on the examples having $x_1 < 0$ and then on the rest. As the decision function in the first batch is very simple, only very few support vectors will be generated. When an SVM is trained on these support vectors together with the second batch of data, the old support vectors will have little influence in the result, because the empirical error on the second batch drastically outweighs the error on the old SVs (see Figure 1).

Usually, this is a desired property of the SVM algorithm, because it means that the SVM is robust against outliers in the data - only in this case the outliers are the old support vectors one would wish to take into account.

2 A New Incremental Learning Algorithm

To make up for the problem in the incremental learning algorithm stated in the last section, one needs to make an error on the old support vectors (which represent the old learning set) more costly than an error on a new example.

Fortunately, this can easily be accomplished in the support vector algorithm. Let $(x_i, y_i)_{i \in S}$ be the old support vectors and $(x_i, y_i)_{i \in I}$ be the new examples. Replace the

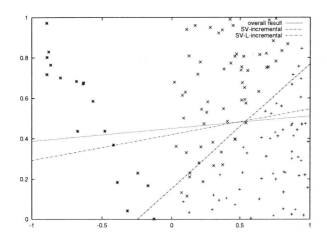

Figure 1. Results of both incremental learning algorithms on an example set

original defintion of the SVM target function by

$$\Psi(w, \xi, \xi^*) = \frac{1}{2}(w^T w) + C \left(\sum_{i \in I} \xi_i + L \sum_{i \in S} \xi_i \right).$$

This modification punishes the empirical error on the old support vectors by an extra factor L.

A natural choice for L is to let L be the number of examples in the previous batch divided by the number of support vectors. The idea is to approximate the average error of an arbitrary decision function over all examples by the average error over just the support vectors. This algorithm will be called the SV-L-incremental algorithm.

Figure 1 shows the result of the SV-L-incremental algorithm on the example problem of the last section. It is obvious that its result lies much closer to the overall result than the SV-incremental algorithm.

3 Interpretability of Support Vectors

The results so far give interesting insight into the question, how support vectors can be interpreted. It is often argued, that the support vectors provide a sufficient representation of the examples for the given classification task, because training an SVM on the support vectors gives the same decision function as training on the whole data set. But of course, this only means that the support vectors are a sufficient representation of the *decision function* on the examples, not the *examples* themselves.

Remeber that statistical learning theory formalizes the learning problem as finding a function f from a class of

functions $(f_\alpha)_{\alpha \in \Lambda}$, that minimizes the expected risk

$$R[f] = \int \int L(y, f(x)) dP(y|x) dP(x) \qquad (1)$$

with respect to a loss function L and unknown distributions of the examples $P(x)$ and their classifications $P(y|x)$.

The important difference here is, that in terms of the statistical learning principle, the support vectors provide an estimate of $P(y|x)$ (i. e. the decision function), but not of $P(x)$. If the support vectors are used to represent the entire data set this has to be taken into account.

4 Experiments

To compare the algorithms, some experiments on data sets from the UCI Repository of Machine Learning Databases [1] were made. A version of mySVM [2], modified to handle loss functions defined per example, was used.

The following table compares the 10-fold cross-validated accuracy of the classifier trained on all available data (non-inc.), the SV-incremental algorithm and the SV-L-incremental algorithm.

Dataset	non-inc.	SV-inc.	SV-L-inc.
australian	85.21	85.50	85.50
diabetes	70.94	70.80	70.42
german	74.90	75.80	76.70
heart	77.03	75.92	79.62
ionosphere	94.02	94.02	94.88
liver-disorders	69.61	69.92	71.05
monks2	85.03	85.03	85.03
monks3	96.38	96.38	96.38
promoter-genes	93.63	93.63	93.63
sonar	85.59	85.59	86.07

Acknowledgments

The financial support of the Deutsche Forschungsgemeinschaft (SFB 475, "Reduction of Complexity for Multivariate Data Structures") is gratefully acknowledged.

References

[1] P. M. Murphy and D. W. Aha. UCI repository of machine learning databases, 1994.

[2] S. Rüping. *mySVM-Manual*. Universität Dortmund, Lehrstuhl Informatik VIII, 2000. http://www-ai.cs.uni-dortmund.de/SOFTWARE/MYSVM/.

[3] N. Syed, H. Liu, and K. Sung. Incremental learning with support vector machines. In *Proceedings of the Workshop on Support Vector Machines at the International Joint Conference on Articial Intelligence (IJCAI-99)*, Stockholm, Sweden, 1999.

[4] V. Vapnik. *Statistical Learning Theory*. Wiley, Chichester, GB, 1998.

A Clustering Method for Very Large Mixed Data Sets

Guillermo Sánchez-Díaz[1] and José Ruiz-Shulcloper[2]
[1]Autonomous University of the Hidalgo State, Mexico
sanchezg@uaeh.reduaeh.mx
[2]Institute of Cybernetics, Mathematics and Physics, Havana, Cuba
recpat@cidet.icmf.inf.cu

Abstract

In the developed countries, especially over the last decade, there has been an explosive growth in the capability to generate, collect and use very large data sets. The objects of these data sets could be simultaneously described by quantitative and qualitative attributes. At present, algorithms able to process either very large data sets (in metric spaces) or mixed (qualitative and quantitative) incomplete data (missing value) sets have been developed, but not for very large mixed incomplete data sets. In this paper we introduce a new clustering method named GLC+ to process very large mixed incomplete data sets in order to obtain a partition in connected sets.

1 Introduction

In some areas such as finance, banking, marketing, healthcare, engineering and in diagnostic problems in several environments like geosciences, medicine among many others, the amount of stored data has had an explosive increase [1]. In these areas, there are many instances where the description of the objects is not numerical or exclusively categorical. Both kinds of values can appear simultaneously. It is well known that one of the most important tools to process data in order to extract knowledge from their is clustering algorithms, whose purpose is (in the KDD context) to solve the following problem. Given a similarity measure β (not necessarily a distance function) between pairs of object descriptions in the representation space and a collection of such descriptions in that space, find a structuralization of this collection. And, with the following additional constraints: i) the use of computing resources must be minimized and ii) the data set could be large or very large.

2 Related Works

Several techniques have been developed to cluster large and very large data sets. CLARANS [2], BIRCH [3]

and IncDBSCAN [4] have given solutions, with higher or lower efficiencies. One of the drawbacks of the mentioned algorithms is that they were not developed to cluster data sets defined in spaces in which the similarity relationships do not satisfy the triangle inequality and in some cases are not symmetric.

Also, Chameleon[5] and GLC [6] have been developed to cluster data sets and large data sets. These techniques handle objects defined in non-metric spaces, and use a similarity function S to compare two objects of the data sets. But these algorithms were not developed to cluster very large data sets.

In this paper, a new incremental clustering method for very large mixed incomplete data sets is presented. GLC+ handles data in any space and it is based on any similarity function β that compares two objects.

3 Connected Sets

Let $M=\{O_1,...,O_m\}$; $\beta(O_i,O_j)$ a similarity function between the objects O_i, O_j; and $\beta_0 \in V$ a similarity threshold, where V is a totally ordered set.

Definition 1. Let $G \subseteq M$, $G \neq \emptyset$, G is a β_0-*connected set* with respect to (wrt) β and β_0 if: $\forall O_i, O_j \in G$, $\exists\{O_{G1},O_{G2},...,O_{Gt}\}$ such that $O_i=O_{G1}$, $O_{Gt}=O_j$ and $\beta(O_{Gi-1},O_{Gi}) \geq \beta_0$, for all i=2,...,t.

Definition 2. Let $\beta_0 \in V$ and G be a β_0-connected set. We say that $S=\{O_1,...,O_t\}$, $S \subseteq G$, is a *skeleton* of G if $\forall O_i \in G$, $\exists O_j \in S$, $\beta(O_i,O_j) \geq \beta_0$.

Definition 3. Let G be a β_0-connected set and S_i be all possible skeletons of G. S_{min} is a *minimal skeleton* of G if $\forall S_i \subseteq G$, $card(S_{min}) \leq card(S_i)$, where card(A) is the number of elements in A.

4 The GLC+ Method

The GLC+ method has two phases. In the first phase, GLC+ clusters the objects in subclusters, which will be connected sets.

In the second phase, GLC+ gathers these generated sub clusters, giving the final clustering in connected sets.

The GLC+ method does not store all objects in the available memory. Instead, GLC+ only keeps the subset of these objects, which have a large number of similarity objects, named *skeleton objects*. Instead of comparing a new object with all of the objects in a cluster, this method only compares the new objects with the cluster's skeleton objects.

The GLC+ method uses the SCS algorithm (Skeleton of a Connected Set) in order to generate the skeletons of the connected sets. From each connected set generated, the SCS algorithm generates a minimal skeleton or approximates to it. The idea of the GLC+ method is to calculate a partition of the data set in connected sets, which approximates a partition in connected components (we can see a connected component as a maximal connected set). This approximation is due to the size of the available memory.

The GLC+ method works in the following way: in the first phase, all possible connected sets are calculated until the given percentage of objects is reached or the available memory is full. After that, the SCS algorithm processes these connected sets in order to find the skeleton of each one in its corresponding cluster, and all of the remaining objects not belonging to the skeletons are kept also in their clusters, but not in the available memory. These objects are marked, and will be used in the second phase of GLC+. The remaining objects are clustered, but they will be compared only with the objects stored in the available memory. This procedure is applied until all the objects have been gathered. In the second phase, GLC+ compares the border objects $O_b \in G_h$ and the skeleton objects $O_s \in G_l$, $h \neq l$. If O_b and O_s are similar, then the G_h and G_l clusters are merged.

Both phases of GLC+ are incremental.

5 GLC+ performances

We carried out a 2D projection of the Covtype data set (ftp://ftp.ics.uci.edu/pub/machine-learning-databases/covertype). This 2D data set is shown in Figure 1(a). The Figure 1(b) and 1(c) shows the clusters generated by a traditional hierarchical algorithm and CLARANS, respectively. Finally, the clusters discovered by GLC+ are shown in Figure 1 (d).

In this Figure, we can show that the 2D projection contains one cluster with high density and cardinality, formed by the majority of the objects in the data set. And the remainder clusters has low cardinality (i.e. there are formed by one, two, etc. objects). In this sense, the clusters discovered by GLC+ are genuine, because the method generate one cluster with high density and cardinality, and the remaining clusters obtained by GLC+, has low cardinality.

The traditional hierarchical algorithm and CLARANS, obtain four clusters, with high density and cardinality. These algorithms split (in four clusters) the cluster with high density and cardinality.

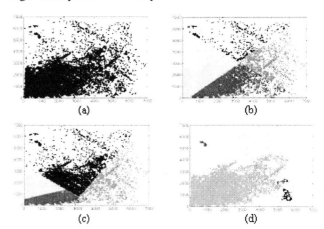

Figure 1. (a) Original data set; (b) clusters generated by a traditional hierarchical algorithm; (c) clustering obtained for CLARANS; and (d) clusters discovered by GLC+ method.

6 Conclusions

The GLC+ method allows the generation of β_0-connected sets from very large mixed incomplete data sets. The GLC+ method does not establish any assumptions about the form, the size or cluster density characteristics of the resultant clusters. This method could be used with any kind of distance, or symmetric similarity function. The objects in the data set to be clustered may be described by quantitative and qualitative (mixed) attributes and with the possible presence of missing data.

References

1. U. Fayyad, et al. Advances in knowledge Discovery in Databases. Cambridge, MIT Press, 1996.

2. R. Ng and J. Han. Efficient and Effective Clustering Methods for Spatial Data Mining. Proc. 20th Int. Conf. on VLDB, Santiago, Chile, pp. 144-155, 1994.

3. T. Zhang, R. Ramakrishnan and M. Livny. BIRCH: An Efficient Data Clustering Method for Very Large Databases. Proc. Int. Conf. on Management of Data, pp. 103-114, 1996.

4. M. Ester, et al. Incremental Clustering for Mining in a Data Warehousing Environment. Proc. of 24th VLDB, New York, pp. 323-333, 1998.

5. G. Karypis, E.H. (Sam) Han and V. Kumar. Chameleon: Hierarchical Cluster Using Dynamic Modeling. Computer, pp. 68-75, August, 1999.

6. G. Sánchez-Díaz, and J. Ruiz-Shulcloper. MID Mining: a Logical Combinatorial Pattern Recognition Approach to Clustering in Large Data Sets. Proc. of 5th SIARP, Lisbon, Portugal, September 2000, pp. 475-483.

Mining the Web With Active Hidden Markov Models

Tobias Scheffer[1,2], Christian Decomain[1,2], and Stefan Wrobel[1]
[1] University of Magdeburg, P.O. Box 4120, 39016 Magdeburg, Germany
[2] SemanticEdge, Kaiserin-Augusta-Allee 10-11, 10553 Berlin, Germany
{scheffer, decomain, wrobel}@iws.cs.uni-magdeburg.de

1 Introduction

Given the enormous amounts of information available only in unstructured or semi-structured textual documents, tools for *information extraction* (IE) have become enormously important. IE tools identify the relevant information in such documents and convert it into a structured format such as a database or an XML document. While first IE algorithms were hand-crafted sets of rules, researchers soon turned to learning extraction rules from hand-labeled documents. Unfortunately, rule-based approaches sometimes fail to provide the necessary robustness against the inherent variability of document structure, which has led to the recent interest in the use of hidden Markov models (HMMs) [1] for this purpose. Speech recognition and computational biochemistry are well-known applications of HMMs.

Markov model algorithms that are used for part-of-speech tagging, as well as known hidden Markov models for information extraction [1] require the training documents to be labeled *completely*, *i.e.*, each token is manually given an appropriate semantic label. Clearly, this is an expensive process. We therefore concentrate on the task of learning hidden Markov models, from *partially* (sparsely) labeled texts, and develop appropriate EM-style algorithms.

By using additional *unlabeled* documents as they are usually readily available in most applications, we can perform *active learning* of HMMs. The idea of *active learning* algorithms is to identify unlabeled observations that would be most useful when labeled by the user. Such algorithms are known for classification, clustering, and regression; we present the first algorithm for active learning of hidden Markov models.

2 Using HMMs for IE

The IE task is to attach a semantic *tag* X_i to some of the document tokens O_t. Observations can also be left untagged (special tag *none*). An extraction algorithm f maps an observation sequence $O_1, \ldots, O_T$ to a single sequence of tags (multi-valued assignments would have to be handled by using several IE models, one per label).

There are several natural ways to define the error criterion that an extraction algorithm has to minimize and that quantifies the algorithm's performance; which is appropriate depends on the application. For some applications, costs may arise for each false tag assigned to a token. The *per-token error* is the probability of an extraction algorithm assigning a false tag to a token in the document.

Precision and *recall* are other popular error criteria that can be defined for problems for which only tags $\{X, none\}$ are available. Precision refers to the amount of correct tags X assigned by f relative to the number of all (correct and incorrect) tags assigned. Recall reflects the amount of tags X correctly retrieved by f relative to the total amount of X tags that should have been assigned.

Hidden Markov models (see, [2] for an introduction) are a very robust statistical method for structural analysis of temporal data. An HMM $\lambda = (\pi, a, b)$ consists of finitely many states $\{S_1, \ldots, S_N\}$ with probabilities $\pi_i = P(q_1 = S_i)$, the probability of starting in state S_i, and $a_{ij} = P(q_{t+1} = S_j | q_t = S_i)$, the probability of a transition from state S_i to S_j. Each state is characterized by a probability distribution $b_i(O_t) = P(O_t | q_t = S_i)$ over observations. In the information extraction context, an observation is a token. The tags X_i correspond to the n target states $S_1, \ldots, S_n$ of the HMM. Background tokens without tag are emitted in all HMM states $S_{n+1}, \ldots, S_N$ which are not one of the target states. We might, for instance, want to convert an HTML phone directory into a database using an HMM with four nodes (labeled *name, firstname, phone, none*). The observation sequence "John Smith, extension 7343" would then correspond to the state sequence (*firstname, name, none, phone*).

How can the IE task be addressed with HMMs? Let us first consider what we would do if we already knew an HMM which can be assumed to have generated the observations. Given an observation sequence $O_1, \ldots, O_T$, which tag sequence should we return? If we want to minimize the per-token error, then we have to find, for each token, the state in which this token has most likely been emitted (index i with highest $\gamma_t(i)$). If this state is one of the target states, then the corresponding tag has to be assigned to the tokens; the token has to remain untagged otherwise.

When a desired balance between precision and recall is to be achieved, then a token has to be tagged if the probability of the single target state at time t given the observation sequence exceeds a given threshold θ. By adjusting θ, precision can be traded against recall.

Let us now briefly sketch how HMM parameters can be learned from data. In the standard model used in speech recognition, several HMMs are learned (*e.g.*, one for each word to be recognized) and each observation sequence is labeled only with the HMM that it is an example for. In our situation, it is important to achieve a correct assignment of the tokens to target states. We assume that a set of documents is available and the user then labels some of the *tokens* (not whole documents) with the appropriate tag. For each token O_t there is a set of candidate states σ_t; this set may contain one target state (the state corresponding to the label when the user has labeled the token), it can contain all background states (when the user has marked the token as not possessing one of the tags) or it may contain all states (token is unlabeled).

The algorithm which we use to adapt the HMM parameters to the partially labeled documents is an instantiation of the EM algorithm. The principle difficulty which this algorithm addresses is that, in order to determine the transition and emission probabilities, the states that correspond to the observations would have to be known. Unfortunately, the states of unlabeled tokens are hidden. In the E-step, the algorithm calculates, for each token, the probability distribution over the states based on the current estimate of the transition and emission probabilities, taking the labels into account. Based on these distributions over states, in the M-step we update the emission and transition probabilities.

In order to execute the E-step of the algorithm, we have to determine $P(q_t = S_i | O_1, \ldots, O_T, \sigma_1, \ldots, \sigma_T)$ – *i.e.*, the probability of being in state S_i at time t given the observation sequence $O_1, \ldots, O_T$ with labels that render states $\sigma_1, \ldots, \sigma_T$ possible. Note that labels can have non-local effects on this probability. Our principle result is a recursive algorithm which determines this probability exactly. The backward-forward-backward algorithm requires three passes over the observation sequence; in the first pass, the probability $\tau_t(i) = P(\sigma_{t+1}, \ldots, \sigma_T | q_t = S_i)$ is computed, in the second and third passes, α and β (which now depend on τ) are calculated. See [3] for details.

We have implemented this algorithm into a web mining tool. The system can be applied to a variety of tasks, such as extracting key information from emails, or spidering business information from the web.

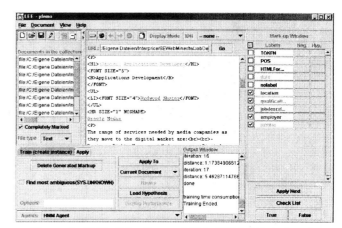

Figure 1. GUI of the SemanticEdge Web Mining tool.

3 Active Revision of Hidden Markov Models

Unlabeled documents can be obtained very easily for most information extraction problems; only labeling tokens in a document imposes effort. Our active learning algorithm selects the most "difficult" unlabeled tokens and asks the user to label them.

We can see the margin $M(q_t | O, \lambda) = \max_i \{ P(q_t = S_i | O, \lambda) \} - \max_{j \neq i} \{ P(q_t = S_j | O, \lambda) \}$ between the probability of the most likely and that of the second most likely state as the confidence of the state given O. Intuitively, the margin can be seen as quantifying how "difficult" (low margin) or "easy" (large margin) an example is. Our active HMM learning algorithm first learns an initial model λ_1 from a set of partially labeled documents. It then determines the margins of all tokens and starts asking the user to label difficult tokens which have a particularly low margin. The Baum-Welch algorithm is then restarted.

Our experiments [3] show that when the training is started by labeling randomly drawn tokens and the active HMM chooses difficult low-margin tokens after that initial phase, then a significant improvement is achieved over regular HMMs that can result in the sufficiency of many times fewer labeled examples.

References

[1] Andrew McCallum, Dayne Freitag, and Fernando Pereira. Maximum entropy Markov models for information extraction and segmentation. In *Proc. of the International Conference on Machine Learning*, 2000.

[2] L. Rabiner. A tutorial on hidden markov models and selected applications in speech recognition. *Proceedings of the IEEE*, 77(2):257–285, 1989.

[3] Tobias Scheffer and Stefan Wrobel. Active learning of partially hidden markov models. In *Proceedings of the ECML/PKDD Workshop on Instance Selection*, 2001.

A Simple KNN Algorithm for Text Categorization

Pascal Soucy   Guy W. Mineau
Department of Computer Science
Université Laval, Québec, Canada
{Pascal.Soucy, Guy.Mineau}@ift.ulaval.ca

Abstract

Text categorization (also called text classification) is the process of identifying the class to which a text document belongs. This paper proposes to use a simple non-weighted features KNN algorithm for text categorization. We propose to use a feature selection method that finds the relevant features for the learning task at hand using feature interaction (based on word interdependencies). This will allow us to reduce considerably the number of selected features from which to learn, making our KNN algorithm applicable in contexts where both the volume of documents and the size of the vocabulary are high, like with the World Wide Web. Therefore, the KNN algorithm that we propose becomes efficient for classifying text documents in that context (in terms of its predictability and interpretability), as will be demonstrated. Its simplicity (w.r.t. its implementation and fine-tuning) becomes its main assets for on-the-field applications.

1. Introduction

Text categorization (also called text classification) is the process of identifying the class to which a text document belongs. This generally involves learning, for each class, its representation from a set of documents that are known to be members of that class. This paper proposes to use a simple non-weighted features KNN algorithm to achieve this task. The simplicity of this algorithm makes it efficient w.r.t. its computation time, but also w.r.t. the ability for non expert users to use it efficiently, that is, in terms of its prediction rate and the interpretability of the results, as will be demonstrated below.

This paper presents a simple KNN algorithm adapted to text categorization that does aggressive feature selection. This feature selection method allows the removal of features that add no new information given that some other feature highly interacts with them, which would otherwise lead to redundancy, and features with weak prediction capability. Redundancy and irrelevancy could harm a KNN learning algorithm by giving it some unwanted bias, and by adding additional complexity. By taking into account both the redundancy and relevancy of features, we aim at providing solid ground for the use of KNN algorithms in text categorization where the document set is very large and the vocabulary diverse.

The KNN algorithm that we propose is presented in section 2. Our feature selection method is described in section 3. We tested the whole method on various corpora of text documents and we discuss the results of these experiments in section 4. In brief, it proved to be more accurate than Naive Bayes classifiers, and proved to be as accurate as other variants of the KNN approach but with a much smaller set of features, which helps the interpretability of the results and the speed of classifying new documents. Therefore we conclude that the KNN algorithm presented in this paper is highly relevant for the categorization of large corpora of text documents, and by its simplicity, could be easily implemented by non expert users.

2. Learning to categorize texts using KNN

Conceptually, each example document x, called an instance, is represented as a vector of length $|F|$, the size of the vocabulary:

$$<w_1(x), w_2(x), w_3(x), ..., w_F(x)>$$

where $w_j(x)$ is the weight of the jth term. That weight may be set according to different criteria, such as : frequency, *TFIDF* or a score assigned to the feature for its capability to divide the examples into some set of classes (e.g., the Information Gain). The simplest feature weighting function is to assign the same value to each term that occurs in the instance (let us say 1 for instance), and 0 to those that do not, which amounts to a non-weighted features approach. Our algorithm uses this latter simple weighting approach.

In our KNN algorithm, we used distance as a basis to weight the contribution of each k neighbor in the class assignment process. We define the confidence of having document d belonging to class c as:

$$\text{Confidence}(c,d) = \frac{\sum_{k_i' \in K \mid (Class(k_i')=c)} Sim(k_i',d)}{\sum_{k_i \in K} Sim(k_i,d)} \quad (1)$$

where *Sim* is the value returned by the similarity function used to compare the instance with its neighbors. That is, for each neighbor in the neighbor set K (of size k) belonging to a particular class c, we sum up their similarities to document d and divide by the summation of all similarities of the k neighbors with regard to d.

To compare document d with instance i, we choose the CosSim function which is particularly simple using our binary term weight approach :

$$\text{CosSim}(i,d) = \frac{C}{\sqrt{A*B}} \quad (2)$$

where C is the number of terms that i and d share, A is the number of terms in i and B the number of terms in d. The neighbor set K of d thus comprises the k instances that rank the highest according to that measure.

3. Feature Selection

Feature selection is the process of selecting a subset of all available features. With text documents, as mentioned before, text categorization may involve hundreds of thousands of features, most of them being irrelevant. Relevancy of a feature in text categorization is particularly hard to define since there may be much feature interaction that keeps irrelevant features from being identified as such.

Our findings are: 1) that the entropy-based Information Gain metric is good at finding relevant features in terms of its capability to discriminate between classes, and 2) that removing every feature occurring only once does not increase the error rate and should be used as a fast filter before computing the Information Gain. These results are consistent with similar findings in [1,2]. However, these latter methods do not allow feature removal based on the interaction between features. In our KNN experiments, we used *μ-Cooccurrence*, a recent feature selection method described in [3]. That feature selection method reduces aggressively the vocabulary size using feature interaction.

4. Results and conclusion

The data sets used in our experiments are summarized in Table 1. Tasks accompanied by * are data sets we have manually created, while the others have been studied in the literature. Each task involves two classes.

We conducted tests using a naïve bayesian classifier, and we ran comparisons with our KNN algorithm, as shown in Table 2. The best Bayes results are obtained using many features, but not all, a good value being the 2000 best features selected by the Information Gain.

Task name	Dataset	Train/Test Balance
WebKBCourse	WebKB	80/320
ReutersCornWheat	Reuters-21578	40/360
LingSpam	Ling-Spam	40/80
Prisoner*	WWW	40/20
Beethoven*	WWW	40/20
News1*	Usenet	40/27

Table 1 : Data sets used in our experiments.

However, despite the fact that Bayes performs quite well for these tasks, KNN does better (for any number of features). From these results, we claim that our very simple KNN algorithm can reach impressive results using very few features.

Task name	μCooc + KNN		μCooc + Bayes		Bayes 2000 Best	All Bayes	
	#f	%	#f	%	%	#f	%
Course	35	96.9	35	95	95,6	12150	94.2
Reuters1	8	98.3	8	97.4	89,2	3393	81.1
Spam	77	95	77	86.3	90	4484	86.3
Prisoner	9	90	9	70	80	5076	70
Beethoven	8	85	8	90	85	3327	90
News	130	85.2	130	92.7	96,3	8522	92.6
McrAvrg	95.5		92.7		93.1	90.3	
# feature	267		267		12000	36952	

Table 2 : Results summary. #f is the number of features, while % is the classification accuracy.

Future works include the use of meta-information such as the structure of the document, author name, presence of highlights, figure or image included, etc. KNN appears to be particularly fit to include meta-level information into its classification mechanism.

References

[1] I. Androutsopoulos, G. Paliouras, V. Karkaletsis, G. Sakkis, C. D. Spyropoulos & P. Stamatopoulos. Learning to Filter Spam E-Mail : A Comparison of a Naive Bayesian and a Memory-Based Approach. In *Proceedings of Machine Learning and Textual Information Access workshop*, 4th Eur. Conf. on Principles and Practice of KDD (PKDD-2000).

[2] T. Joachims. A Probabilistic Analysis of the Rocchio Algorithm with TFIDF for Text Categorization. *In Proceedings of the 14th International Conference on Machine Learning ICML97*. 1997.

[3] P. Soucy & G. Mineau. A Simple Feature Selection Method for Text Classification. In *Proceedings of the 17th International Joint Conference on Artificial Intelligence (IJCAI-01)*. 2001.

Measuring Real-Time Predictive Models

Samuel Steingold
Xchange Inc
Boston, Massachusetts, USA
sds@xchange.com

Richard Wherry
Xchange Inc
Boston, Massachusetts, USA
rwherry@xchange.com

Gregory Piatetsky-Shapiro
KDNuggets
Boston, Massachusetts, USA
gps@kdnuggets.com

Abstract

In this paper we examine the problem of comparing real-time predictive models and propose a number of measures for selecting the best model, based on a combination of accuracy, timeliness, and cost. We apply the measure to the real-time attrition problem.

1 Introduction

Comparing quality of different models is an important practical task. When the model deals with static data, this is a well-established area with many known model measures, like Lift, Response Ratio, L-quality etc (see [1], [2] and [3]).

Recently data miners have begun to deal with dynamic and real-time data. We can use the latest transactions to predict how likely the customer is to buy this product, click on that link, or disconnect the service. When using real-time data, in addition to traditional dimensions of accuracy and cost, we also have to compare models on the time dimension.

The difference from the usual setup is that it is important to identify the potential attritors as early as possible, so that some actions can be taken to retain the customer.

2 Desirable Properties of the Measure

A model $M(c, t)$ is a function of two arguments: the customer $c \in C$ and time $t \in [0; T]$, which means that the actual model scoring algorithm gets all the historical and demographical data for c as well as all transactions $x \in X$ up to time t. M returns (an estimate of) the probability $p \in [0; 1]$ of the predicted event ("attrition") by the end of the time period (say, a month, in which case $T = 30$). $M(t)$ is the model at time t. The boolean value $A(c)$ says whether the customer c will actually attrite by the end of the month.

As specified in the Introduction, the model which identifies the potential attritors early is better, thus, the model quality $Q(M)$ should satisfy the following property: if M_1 is *"better"* than M_2 in the following sense: for all t

$$\text{if } A(c) = 1 \text{ then } M_1(c, t) \geq M_2(c, t) \\ \text{if } A(c) = 0 \text{ then } M_1(c, t) \leq M_2(c, t) \qquad (1)$$

then $Q(M_1) \geq Q(M_2)$. In other words, if the model M_1 predicts *true* attritors *earlier* and *non-attritors later* than model M_2, then it is "better".

One of the simplest measures would be the L_q, as defined in [3]. If we define $L(M, t) := L_q(M(t))$ to be the L_q of the model M as run at time t, one can easily see that if the model M_1 is better than the model M_2 in the sense of 1, then for all t we have $L(M_1, t) \geq L(M_2, t)$, so a simple measure like $Q(M) := \sum_t L(M, t)$ would satisfy the requirement. Unfortunately, this measure does not capture the notion of *how much earlier* one model identifies the attritors than the other.

Thus, we need to generalize the current model quality measure to take the time aspect into account. While ultimately the cost/benefit matrix of the (in) correct prediction should be the deciding factor, in many cases it is not known, or subject to change. Thus we start with considering the value-free measures, based on time and accuracy, and will add the value consideration later.

3 Value-Free Measures

The full version [4] of this paper explains in details how we arrived at the non-normalized measure

$$Q_0(M) := \frac{1}{NT} \sum_{c \in C} \int_0^T M \left(3A - 1 - A \frac{2t}{T} \right) dt \quad (2)$$

where $N = \#C$ is the total number of customers and $M = M(c, t)$, $A = A(c)$.

Considering this formula separately for targets ($A(c) = 1$) and non-targets ($A(c) = 0$), one can see that 1 is satisfied.

The same consideration lets us interpret Q_0 as the mean "good time" (the advance warning the model gives us for the true attritors) minus mean "bad time" (the advance warning the model gives us for the non-attritors).

Let $N_a = \#\{c : A(c) = 1\}, b = \frac{N_a}{N}$ be the base rate, and compute Q_0 for four models: for "Always Negative" with $M(c,t) \equiv 0$, $Q_0 = 0$, for "Always Positive" with $M(c,t) \equiv 1$, $Q_0 = 2b - 1$, for "Perfect" with $M(c,t) \equiv A(c)$, $Q_0 = b$, and for "Random" with $M(c,t) = b$, $Q_0 = b(2b - 1)$.

It is better to normalize Q_0 so that the "Perfect" model always has $Q = 1$, while the "Random" model has $Q = 0$, i.e.,

$$Q(M) = Q_n(M) = \frac{Q(M) - b(2b - 1)}{b - b(2b - 1)} \quad (3)$$

Since the original measure 2 satisfies the requirement 1, this measure satisfies it too, and

Model	Q
Always Positive	$(2b - 1)/2b$
Always Negative	$(1 - 2b)/2(1 - b)$
Perfect	1
Random	0

4 Value-Based Measures

Business practice has shown that any data-mining effort should take the customer value into account, otherwise valuable resources would be wasted on retaining an unprofitable customer whose probably of attrition is high, while no effort would be made to retain a profitable customer with low attrition probability.

Thus we must ascribe a customer a value $V(c)$, take it into account during model training and evaluate the model using

$$Q(M) := \quad (4)$$
$$\frac{1}{2NTb(1 - b)} \sum_{c \in C} \int_0^T (M - b) V \left(3A - 1 - A\frac{2t}{T}\right) dt$$

Here $M = M(c,t), A = A(c)$, and $V = V(c)$ should be not the past value of the customer, but his projected total future value.

Again, this measure satisfies the requirement 1 when the value V is non-negative.

5 Real World Examples of Real-Time models

We use the measure 3 to compare two models. The data that we use is a combination of historical and transaction banking data. We compute the time integral in 2 using the Riemann sum with a step of 5 days (T is one month).

Both models were trained using the same dataset and are evaluated on the same held-out dataset.

Period	$Q_0(M)$	$Q_n(M)$ (Normalized)
Model 1	-0.0555	-0.8712
Model 2	-0.0013	0.0526
Random	-0.0282	0.0

Table 1. The quality measures for the experimental models

Table 1 summarizes the results.

With a base-rate of 0.03, both models perform poorly. Notice that for both Model 1 and Model 2, $Q_0(M) < 0$. This tells us that for both models, the mean "bad time" is greater than the mean "good time". Accordingly, both models are giving more weighted advanced warnings for non-attritors than for attritors. The fact that $Q_0(M) < 0$ is not necessarily bad. In fact, $Q_n(M_1) > 0$ indicates that Model 1 performs better than the random model.

5.1 Customer Value

It bears repeating the dictum of section 4 that the reason for data mining in the business setting is to increase the value of the customer to the company and vice versa. Therefore it is crucial to use the (reasonable estimate of the) customer value in the formula 4 if at all possible. Unfortunately, the data on which we performed our simulations did not have any value-related attributes.

References

[1] Foster Provost, Tom Fawcett "Analysis and Visualization of Classifier Performance: Comparison under Imprecise Class and Cost Distributions", *Proceedings of KDD-97*, pp. 43-48, AAAI Press, 1997.

[2] Gregory Piatetsky-Shapiro, Brij Masand "Estimating Campaign Benefits and Modeling Lift", *Proceedings of KDD-99*, pp. 185-193, ACM Press, 1999.

[3] Gregory Piatetsky-Shapiro, Sam Steingold, "Measuring Lift Quality in Database Marketing", *SIGKDD Explorations*, Vol. 2:2, (2000), 81-86

[4] http://www.podval.org/~sds/data/rt-modeling.pdf

Incremental Learning of Bayesian Networks with Hidden Variables

Fengzhan Tian   Hongwei Zhang   Yuchang Lu   Chunyi Shi

The State Key Laboratory of Intelligent Technology and System

The Department of Computer Science and Technology

Tsinghua University, 100084, Beijing, China

Abstract

In this paper, an incremental method for learning Bayesian networks based on evolutionary computing, IEMA, is put forward. IEMA introduces the evolutionary algorithm and EM algorithm into the process of incremental learning, can not only avoid getting into local maxima, but also incrementally learn Bayesian networks with high accuracy in presence of missing values and hidden variables. In addition, we improved the incremental learning process by Friedman et al. The experimental results verified the validity of IEMA. In terms of storage cost, IEMA is comparable with the incremental learning method of Friedman et al, while it is more accurate.

1. Introduction

In recent years there has been a growing interest in learning Bayesian networks from data[4][5]. Because of the disadvantages of the batch learning algorithm[3], it is of great importance and practical value to study incremental learning of Bayesian networks. Previous work on the incremental learning of Bayesian networks has been mostly restricted to updating the parameters assuming a fixed structure[7]. The approaches by Buntine[1] and by Lam and Bacchus[6] are two notable exceptions. While the most important contribution is the incremental learning algorithm by Friedman and Goldszmidt[3].

Nevertheless, there are some disadvantages in the incremental approach of Friedman et al. In this paper, a new method, called IEMA, is put forward. Compared with the work before, the following two improvements were made: (1) improve Friedman's incremental learning process. (2) introduce the evolutionary algorithm and EM algorithm into the process of incremental learning.

2. Incremental learning with Evolutionary Algorithm——IEMA

The incremental learning method by Friedman et al defines a *search frontier* at first. This frontier consists of all the networks it compares in the next iteration. We use F to denote this set of networks. We set S to contain all the sufficient statistics needed to evaluate the networks in F. After a new instance is received their procedure updates the values of the sufficient statistics in S and every receiving k instances, checks whether one of the networks in the frontier F is deemed more suitable than the current model. If this is the case, it adopts the new model as current model. And then it invokes the search procedure to determine the next frontier, and updates S accordingly[3].

However, when the initial network is far away from the generating network of the current dataset, the algorithm may stop before reaching the generating network and could not ensure to learn the golden network structure on the current dataset because it seeks only one step forward after reading k data.

Furthermore, through analyzing the algorithm above, we know that the newly added k cases dominate the evaluation results of the networks in the new search frontier and thereby lead the search direction. In this way, when k is larger, the efficiency of the algorithm is very low. When k is very small, the algorithm runs not very robust because its performance depends on the characteristic of these k cases. So, there is a contradiction in selecting the value of k. This accords with the experimental results by Friedman et al.

As for the problems mentioned above, we improved the incremental learning procedure as follows:

Set G to be initial network.

Let F initial search frontier for G.

While Not Empty (D)

  Read k cases

  Repeat

  Let $S = Suff(G) \cup \bigcup_{G' \in F} Suff(G')$

  Update each sufficient statistic record in S using the k cases.

  Let $G = \arg\max_{G' \in Nets(S)} \mathbf{S}(G' | S)$

Update the frontier *F*

Until a stop condition is reached.

Compute optimal parameters Θ for *G* from *S*.

Output $(G; \Theta)$.

In the above procedure, *Suff(G)* denotes the set of sufficient statistics for *G*. *Nets(S)* is the set of network structures that can be evaluated using the records in *S*.

From the above procedure, the value of k in the iteration should be as big as possible. In ideal situation, when the new dataset can be put into memory at one time, the *while* circulation in the above flow can be carried out only once and the time cost of the algorithm is only up to the *repeat* circulation. At this time, we can get the best incremental learning performance.

To avoid getting into a local maximum and learn Bayesian networks incrementally from incomplete data, we bring the evolutionary algorithm and EM algorithm into the process of incremental learning, transform the incomplete dataset to complete dataset by EM algorithm, and then learn Bayesian networks with evolutionary algorithms. In addition, for the purpose of learning the network structure with hidden variables, we introduce a new mutation operator and expand the function of the traditional crossover operator [2].

The whole process of the IEMA method is as follows:

Set the original evolutionary group *F*.

Select a good network *G* from *F* as the initial network.

While Not Empty (*D*)

Read k cases

Repeat

Evolve group *F* using crossover or mutation operations, and get the evolved group *F'*.

Let $S = \bigcup_{G' \in F'} Suff(G')$.

If there are missing values in the k cases, then compute the expected values of the sufficient statistics in *S* using these k cases by the current network *G* and EM algorithm. Otherwise, update the sufficient statistic records in *S* directly using these k cases.

Calculate the fitness $F_{G'}$ of each network *G'* in *F'*.

Choose λ individuals having the highest fitness from *F'* to form the next generation *F*.

Let $G = \arg\max_{G' \in F} F_{G'}$.

Until a terminative condition is reached.

Compute optimal parameters Θ for *G* from *S*.

Output $(G; \Theta)$.

3. Experimental Evaluation

We compared our method with the method by Friedman et al in terms of the normalized loss and the storage cost on condition of learning on the complete dataset. We use the same method as that by Friedman et al. to generate datasets.

The experimental results show that the normalized loss of IEMA is smaller than the method by Friedman et al. While in terms of storage cost, IEMA needs more storage than the method by Friedman et al, but there is not significant difference between these two procedures.

In addition, we also evaluated the increment learning ability of IEMA in presence of incomplete data and hidden variables. We took out respectively a certain percentage of values and several variables from the original datasets at random. The experiments illustrate that IEMA can learn networks with high accuracy in presence of incomplete data and hidden variables.

At last, in all the experiments, as expected, IEMA can learn more accurate networks and can be more robust by running with larger k.

4. Conclusions

The results of the experiments verified the validity of IEMA. In terms of storage cost, IEMA is comparable with the incremental learning method of Friedman et al, while it is more accurate.

It is expected that IEMA will cost more time than the method by Friedman et al. However, we believe that this time cost of IEMA can be decreased significantly by setting bigger value of k.

References

[1] Buntine, W.: Theory refinement on Bayesian networks. In UAI '91.

[2] Fengzhan Tian, Yuchang Lu, Chunyi Shi.: Learning Bayesian Networks With Hidden Variables Using the Combination of EM and Evolutionary Algorithm". In PAKDD 2001, Aril 2001, pp568-574

[3] Friedman, N., Goldszmidt, M.: Sequential update of Bayesian network structure. In Proc. 13th Conf. on Uncertainty in Artificial Intelligence, 1997

[4] Heckerman, D.: A tutorial on learning Bayesian network. Technical Report MSR-TR-95-06, Microsoft research (1995)

[5] Lam, W., Bacchus, F.: Learning Bayesian belief networks: An approach based on the MDL principle. Computational Intelligence 10 (1994) 269—293

[6] Lam, W., Bacchus, F.: Using new data to refine a Bayesian network. In UAI '94.

[7] Spiegelhalter, D. J., Lauritzen, S. L.: Sequential updating of conditional probabilities on directed graphical structures. Networks, 20, 1990.

Mining Frequent Closed Itemsets
with the Frequent Pattern List

Fan-Chen Tseng, Ching-Chi Hsu[*], and Henry Chen

Department of Computer Science and Information Engineering
National Taiwan University
Taipei, Taiwan, 106
cchsu@csie.ntu.edu.tw

Abstract

*The mining of the complete set of frequent itemsets will lead to a huge number of itemsets. Fortunately, this problem can be reduced to the mining of frequent closed itemsets (FCIs), which results in a much smaller number of itemsets. The approaches to mining frequent closed itemsets can be categorized into two groups: those with candidate generation and those without. In this paper, we propose an approach to mining frequent closed itemsets without candidate generation: with a data structure called the Frequent Pattern List (FPL). We designed the algorithm **FPLCI-Mining** to mine the frequent closed itemsets (FCIs). Experimental result shows that our method is faster than the previously existing ones.*

Keywords: *frequent closed itemset, frequent pattern list*

*Corresponding author: Fax: 886-2-23628167,
Tel: 886-2-2391-7406,
Email: cchsu@csie.ntu.edu.tw

1. Introduction and Problem Definitions

The mining of the complete set of frequent patterns often leads to a huge number of results, and the effectiveness of the association rules derived from them will be decreased. Fortunately, Pasquier et al. showed that this problem could be solved by mining only frequent closed itemsets (FCIs), which are a small portion of the complete set of solutions. They developed an *A-Close* algorithm [1], which took the generation-and-test approach, for mining FCIs. Recently, Pei, Han, and Mao designed an algorithm *CLOSET* [2] for mining FCIs without candidate generation by a combination of FP-tree and projected database. Here we use a simpler and more efficient data structure, the *frequent pattern list* (**FPL**) [3], for mining frequent closed itemsets without candidate generation. We redefine the **frequent closed itemset**, and then develop our approach, **FPLCI-Mining**, for mining the frequent closed itemsets.

Let I = {i1, i2, ...in} be a set of items. An itemset X is a non-empty subset of I. A transaction database DB is a set of transactions. Each transaction Tx is a pair <tid, X>, where tid is a unique transaction identifier, and X is an itemset. A transaction Tx = <tid, X> is said to contains an itemset Y, if Y $\subseteq$ X. Every item in Y is said to be contained in Tx if Y is contained in Tx. With these descriptions, we have the following definitions:

Definition 1. (Maximal frequent itemset).
A frequent itemset is called a **maximal frequent itemset** if there is no other frequent itemset to be its proper superset.

Definition 2. (Frequent closed itemset.)
A frequent closed itemset is either a maximal frequent itemset, or a frequent itemset whose support is higher than the supports of all its proper supersets.

2. Algorithm for mining frequent closed itemsets with FPL

Based on Definition 2, we take the following strategy for mining frequent closed itemsets (FCIs): finding frequent itemsets with items as many as possible, and with supports as high as possible. We formally define the algorithm FPLCI-Mining of mining frequent closed itemsets with FPL:

Algorithm FPLCI-Mining:

Input: FPL constructed using a transaction database DB and a support threshold *t*.
Output: The complete set of frequent **closed** itemsets.
Method: Call **FPLCI-Mining**(*FPL,n, t, ? , ?*)
FPLCI-Mining (*FPL, n, min_sup, parent_itemset, FCIS*)
{**For** *j = n* **to** *1*
{   // check the necessity to visit item node *j*
If (there is no existing FCI in *FCIS* that contains {*item j* }U *parent_itemset* and has a support equal to (*item node*

j).count) **Then** { // bit counting1. Examine the *bit-count array* of item node *j*, and ignore the LSB, which corresponds to item *j*, since it will always be included in the solution;2. Divide the surviving bits (whose counts are above *min_sup*) into two groups:

Group One: bit counts equal to (*item node j*).*count*.

Group Two: bit counts less than (*item node j*).*count*.;

   3. Generate a FCI, denoted as *fci_GroupOne*: *fci_GroupOne* = {*Group one* items}∪{*item j*}∪ *parent_itemset*, with count = (*item node j*).*count*;

   4. Use all the signatures in node item *j*, with the surviving bits in *Group Two* as filtering mask to keep their corresponding items, to form *fci_GroupOne*'s *conditional* database and construct a *conditional* FPL **FPL**$_{fci\_GroupOne}$ from this database; Let *FPL*$_{fci\_GroupOne}$ have *m* item nodes;

   5. Call **FPLCI-Mining** (*FPL*$_{fci\_GroupOne}$, *m*, *min_sup*, *fci_GroupOne*, *FCIS*);

} // end of bit counting

// conducting signature trimming and migration

For each transaction *Tx* in item node *j*, consider its full-length *j*–bit signature

   {1. Trim the LSB (corresponding to item *j*) and then trim all the trailing 0-bits;

   2. Find the least significant 1-bit and find *the item* corresponding to this bit;

   3. Migrate the trimmed signature to the item node containing *this item*;

   4. For the *bit-count array* of the target item node, increment the count values by one for the elements that correspond to the 1-bits in *Tx*.}

  Remove item node *j* from the FPL;

 // end of signature trimming and migration

 } // end of for loop of index *j*

} // end of procedure FPLCI-Mining

3. Experimental Results and Discussion

We test our algorithms on the synthetic data set T25.I20.D100K. There are 10K items. The number of transactions is set to 100K. The average transaction size and average maximal potentially frequent itemset size are set to 25 and 20, respectively. To compare our method with the existing ones: A-Close [1], CHARM [4], and CLOSET [2], we run our program on a Pentium 233-MHz PC with 128 megabytes main memory, running Microsoft Windows 98. The algorithms are implemented with Microsoft Visual C++ 6.0. The run time is the total execution time, including the time for disk I/O and the time for constructing the FPL from the original databases. The result is shown in Figure 1. From the result we see that FPLCI-Mining is much faster than A-Close and CHARM, and is also faster than CLOSET by 12 percent in average. The efficiency of our method is due to the following factors: no candidate generation and testing, simple data structures, and simple

operations. Besides, the optimization techniques of CLOSET can be implemented in our method. For optimization 1, we encode the database into the global FPL, and the conditional FPL can be derived directly in step 4 of FPLCI-Mining. Optimization 2 is implemented in step 2 and 3 of FPLCI-Mining to extract items appearing in every transaction of the item node; that is, the Group-One items. The single-path FP-tree of optimization 3 can also be detected in our FPL data structure, and the same technique can be used to speed up the mining process. Finally, for optimization 4, the checking before bit counting for the necessity to visit the item node prunes the search space.

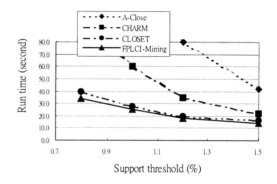

Figure 1. Experimental results

4 Conclusions

In this paper we proposed an efficient approach, FPLCI-Mining, to mining frequent closed itemsets with the simple structure FPL (frequent pattern list). There are several issues related to FPL-based mining. For example, the patterns in the transaction signatures should be studied to derive more efficient algorithms.

References

[1] Pasquier, N., Bastide, Y., Taouil, R., Lakhal, L., "Discovering frequent closed itemsets for association rules." Proc. 7th Int. Conf. Database Theory (ICDT'99), pp. 398-416, Jan. 1999

[2] Pei, J., Han, J., Mao, R., CLOSET, "An efficient algorithm for mining frequent closed itemsets." Proc. 2000 ACMSIGMOD Int. Workshop Data Mining and Knowledge Discovery (DMKD00), pp. 11-20, May 2000

[3] Tseng, Fan-Chen, Hsu, Ching-Chi, "Generating Frequent Patterns with the Frequent Pattern List." Proc. The Fifth Pacific-Asia Conference on Knowledge Discovery and Data Mining, pp. 376-386, April 16-18, 2001. Hong Kong.

[4] Zaki, M. et al, "An Efficient Algorithm for Closed Association Rule Mining." Technical Report 99-10, Computer Science, Rensselaer Polytechnic Institute, 1999

Classification through maximizing density

(Extended Abstract)

Hui Wang, Ivo Düntsch, David Bell

School of Information and Software Engineering

University of Ulster

Newtownabbey, BT 37 0QB, N.Ireland, UK

{H.Wang|I.Duentsch|DA.Bell}@ulst.ac.uk

Dayou Liu

Department of Computer Science

Jilin University

Changchun, 130023, P. R. China

dyliu@mail.jlu.edu.cn

Abstract

This paper presents a novel method for classification, which makes use of the models built by the lattice machine (LM) *[1, 3]. The LM approximates data resulting in, as a model of data, a set of hyper tuples that are equilabelled, supported and maximal. The method presented in this paper uses the LM model of data to classify new data with a view to maximising the density of the model. Experiments show that this method, when used with the LM, outperforms the C2 algorithm in [3] and it is comparable to the C5.0 classification algorithm.*

1 Introduction

The lattice machine is a general framework for supervised learning [1, 3]. It aims to find as a model of data a hyper relation, called the *LM-model*, such that each hyper tuple in the hyper relation is equilabelled, supported, and maximal. Being equilabelled means the model is consistent with data; being maximal means the model has generalisation capability; and being supported means the model does not generalise beyond the information given in the data. LM aims to approximate data while, in contrast, decision tree induction aims to partition data. Figure 1 illustrates LM and its difference to decision tree approach.

When such a model is obtained, classification can be done by the C2 algorithm [3]. This paper reports a different classification method, *LM/Dens*, based on LM-models.

LM/Dens starts with an LM-model (a hyper relation) of data, and classifies new data with a view to maximising the density of the hyper relation.

2 Density of hyper tuples

The main part of this work is a notion of density. Let $\mathbf{D}$ be a data table with a set of attributes $\Omega = \{x_1, \cdots, x_T\}$ and domains V_x of $x \in \Omega$. Let $\mathbf{M}$ be an LM-model, thus each $h \in \mathbf{M}$ is a hypertuple where $h(x) \subseteq V_x$. Note that $h(x)$ is the projection of h onto attribute x.

The *magnitude* of $h(x)$ is

$$\text{mag}'(h(x)) \stackrel{\text{def}}{=} \begin{cases} \max(h(x)) - \min(h(x)), \\ \qquad \text{if } x \text{ is numerical and } |h(x)| > 1 \\ |h(x)|, \qquad \text{otherwise} \end{cases}$$

Note that $\min(h(x))$ is the minimal value in $h(x)$ while $\max(h(x))$ is the maximal value.

We do not assume knowledge of significance of individual attributes, so we have to treat all attributes equally. Therefore we need normalisation: Let $\lambda \in \mathbb{R}^+$ be a number chosen by the user. For an attribute $x \in \Omega$, the *normalisation coefficient* is $s(x) \stackrel{\text{def}}{=} \lambda / \text{mag}'(V_x)$. The parameter λ relates to the granularity of attributes in the normalisation process so it is called the *granularity coefficient* of normalisation. The larger the λ the finer the granularity.

Given a granularity coefficient λ, the *measurement of a unit* of attribute $x \in \Omega$ is $u(x) \stackrel{\text{def}}{=} \text{mag}'(V_x)/\lambda = 1/s(x)$.

With a unit measurement for every attribute, a hyper tuple h can be *quantized* attribute by attribute as follows: if $\text{mag}'(h(x))$ is less than $u(x)$ the x-dimension of h should be treated as a unit; otherwise the x-dimension of t is treated as $\text{mag}'(h(x))/u(x)$ units. This gives us a *quantized magnitude* of $h(x)$, which is defined as

$$\text{mag}(h(x)) \stackrel{\text{def}}{=} \begin{cases} 1, \text{ if } \frac{\text{mag}'(h(x))}{u(x)} < 1 \\ \frac{\text{mag}'(h(x))}{u(x)}, \text{ otherwise.} \end{cases}$$

The *volume* of h is $\text{vol}(h) \stackrel{\text{def}}{=} \prod_{x \in \Omega} \text{mag}(h(x))$, and the *coverage* of h is $\text{cov}(h) \stackrel{\text{def}}{=} \{t \in \mathbf{D} : t \leq h\}$.

The *density* of h is

$$\text{den}(h) \stackrel{\text{def}}{=} \frac{|\text{cov}(h)|}{\text{vol}(h)}$$

The *density* of hyper relation H, $\text{den}(H)$, is then the average density of the hyper tuples in H.

Our definition of density applies to both numerical and categorical attributes and, since normalised and quantized, can be used to compare among hyper tuples and among hyper relations.

As for classification our philosophy is *classifying data into tuples to maximally increase the density of hyper tuples*. Based on this philosophy we have designed an algorithm, called *Dens*. Due to short of space we cannot include details of the algorithm.

3 Evaluation and conclusion

We implemented the *Dens* algorithm together with the LM algorithm [2, 3]. We refer to this implementation as *LM/Dens*. We experimented with *LM/Dens* using some public datasets and the results are shown in Table 1, along with C5.0 results on the same datasets. It is clear from this table that *LM/Dens* outperforms *LM/C2* and it is comparable to C5.0.

The *LM/Dens* classification method reported here was developed to improve the classification accuracy of the LM, and this objective has been achieved.

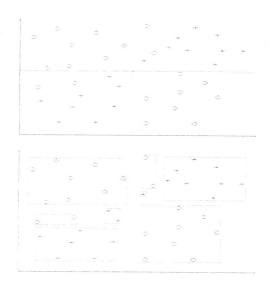

Figure 1. *(a) Partition of data – decision tree approach. (b) Approximation of data - LM approach. Each rectangle is a hyper tuple, which is equilabelled and supported.*

Dataset	Prediction success (%)		
	C5.0	LM/C2	LM/Dens
Annealing	96.6	93.6	96.1
Australian	90.6	83.5	92.7
Auto	70.7	76.1	73.2
Diabetes	72.7	71.7	69.9
German	71.7	72.5	69.3
Glass	80.4	82.7	83.6
Heart	77.0	77.0	78.1
Iris	94.7	92.7	95.3
Sonar	71.6	69.7	73.6
TTT	86.2	83.5	95.6
Vote	96.5	94.2	95.7
Wine	94.3	94.4	95.5
Average	83.6	82.6	84.9

Table 1. *Prediction success of C5.0, LM/C2 and LM/Dens. The validation method used is 5 fold cross validation in all cases.*

[1] H. Wang, W. Dubitzky, I. Düntsch, and D. Bell. A lattice machine approach to automated casebase design: Marrying lazy and eager learning. In *Proc. IJCAI99*, pages 254–259, Stockholm, Sweden, 1999.

[2] H. Wang, I. Düntsch, and D. Bell. Data reduction based on hyper relations. In *Proceedings of KDD98, New York*, pages 349–353, 1998.

[3] H. Wang, I. Düntsch, and G. Gediga. Classificatory filtering in decision systems. *International Journal of Approximate Reasoning*, 23:111–136, 2000.

An Immune Neural Network Used for Classification

Lei Wang, Licheng Jiao, *Senior Member, IEEE*
Key Lab for Radar Signal Processing, Xidian Univ., Xi'an, 710071, China

Abstract

Based on analyzing the immune phenomena in nature and utilizing performances of ANN, a novel network model, i.e., an immune neural network (INN), is proposed which integrates the immune mechanism and the function of neural information processing. The learning algorithm of INN is mainly about the selection of an excitation function and an adaptive algorithm of the network. This model makes it easy for an user to directly utilize the characteristic information of a pending problem and to simplify the original structure through adjusting the excitation function with the prior knowledge, and then the working efficiency and the searching accuracy are both improved. The analysis in theory and the simulating test for the twin-spiral problem show that, comparing with the artificial neural network, INN is not only effective but also feasible. INN can conducively simplify the structure of the existent model and show good working performances when dealing with a pending problem.

1. Introduction

It is well known that the artificial neural network (ANN) has been an important research field of people exploring and imitating the intelligent information processing mechanism of brain neural system. However, it is also necessary for us to note that these existing neural network models are all based on understanding of natural neural system, and established by highly simplifying and abstracting this system, which is propitious to its development and application in engineering practice, but losses some original functions of the natural system at the same time. With the development and wide spreading of ANN's applying, there continually appear some problems, such as the system is prone to plunging into locally extreme state when the learning algorithm is not selected suitably, there exists a conflict between the network complexity and its generalization and so on.

From the deep analysis of the existing network models and algorithms, we can learn about that their methods of setting parameters lack the capability of meeting an actual situation, so that some torpidity appears when solving problems, which is conducive to the universality of the structure or algorithm but neglects the assistant function of the characteristics or knowledge. The loss due to the negligence is sometimes considerable in dealing with some complex problems. Based on this consideration, this paper aims at introducing the concept of immunity into some existing artificial neural networks, so as to design a novel network model which can use the characteristic knowledge for solving problem. This model is presently called *immune neural network* (INN) and it is used for improving the capability of dealing with some difficult problems.

2. The Immune Neural Network Model

In the existing ANN models, an neuron is regarded as a unit which sums all the input signals at first, and then generates a output signal after comparing with a threshold. Distinctive features of this kind of models denote that they have simple structures and good versatility. However, these features simultaneously bring out a lack that they are not considered the active and assistant functions of characteristic information when dealing with a concrete problem. To be exact, there is no interface in these existing models. Based on this consideration, an *vaccinating unit* is designed in a novel model presented in this paper, which is used for utilizing characteristic information and prior knowledge to a pending problem, so as to improve the power of solving a concrete problem.

On designing this model, an neuron is firstly considered to take an important action during information processing, and secondly, all the neurons are similar in basic properties, but different in idiographic forms. Therefore, the excitation function of an neuron should be designed as an variable form. To be exact, basic properties of the function keep unchanged, but its concrete form can be changed through adjusting some of its parameters. To be more exact, the excitation function of any neuron i can designed as the following form, i.e.,

$$u_i = f_i(X, V) \qquad (1)$$

where, $f_i(\cdot)$ is a function family with a series of parameters V, and selections of a concrete function form and the concerned parameters have something to do with the pending problem, which is different from the fact that an excitation function of original models is usually selected as an universal threshold form or *S*-form. On the other hand, some features of the pending problem are contained in the information processing layer, therefore, the structure of this kind of network is usually more simple, and so as to make the time for network learning short and speed increased.

Taking an immune neural network with one hidden layer for example, suppose the weight matrixes of input layer to hidden layer and hidden layer to output layer are respectively $W^{(1)}$ and $W^{(2)}$, then the output vector *Y* is:

$$Y = W^{(2)} f(W^{(1)} X, V) . \qquad (2)$$

Suppose the real output of training samples is *Z*, then the error function can be defined as:

$$E = \frac{1}{2} \sum_{i=1}^{P} (z_i - y_i)^2 \qquad (3)$$

For the purpose of convenient operation, the gradient-descending method is used for network training. During the training process, for smoothing learning path and increasing learning speed, a synthetic approach of training group by group and the adding momentum items should better be used. In which, the training method group by group is proposed mainly for aiming to the method one by one, and used for increasing the training speed. It first adds all the modifying values produced by a group of samples, and then makes a modification for one time. The method of adding momentum items denotes using the modifying value produced by the former step to smooth the learning path, so as to avoid getting into local extremum. To be exact, the equation of modifying weight *W* and parameter *V* is shown as follows:

$$\left\{ \begin{array}{l} \Delta W^{(i)}(t+1) = \eta^{(i)} \sum \dfrac{\partial E}{\partial W^{(i)}}(t) + \alpha \left[W^{(i)}(t) - W^{(i)}(t-1) \right] \\[2ex] \Delta V^{(i)}(t+1) = \mu^{(i)} \sum \dfrac{\partial E}{\partial V^{(i)}}(t) + \beta \left[V^{(i)}(t) - V^{(i)}(t-1) \right] \end{array} \right.$$

where, α and β are all the momentum factors, and $\eta^{(i)}$ and $\mu^{(i)}$ are learning rates. It is necessary to point that effect of the learning rates $\eta^{(i)}$ and $\mu^{(i)}$ is relatively evident during the training process. If $\eta^{(i)}$ and $\mu^{(i)}$ are great, then the training process is more prone to convergence, but oscillation in the late process. Therefore, at the beginning of training, $\eta^{(i)}$ and $\mu^{(i)}$ are usually set great values, and then are decreasing with the training process.

3. Simulations

In actual test, we study the capability of INN with an example of the twin-spiral classification. At first, we generate 640 points with random noise which respectively belong to two spiral lines ρ_1 and ρ_2 (320 points per each). Where, the angular velocities of the two spiral lines are

same(both 4), and in addition, the starting distance are respectively 1 and 7. We select alternately half of the sample points for the training data, the rest are used for testing data. Finally, we use MatLab5.3 for programming and operate it on a Pentium-233 PC. When the trained network is used for classifying the testing data, there are 7 points in summon which are classified in error, and the correct distinguish ratio is 97.81%. If without noise, then the correct distinguish ratio is 100%, which is highly improved form what is reported in the references [3] and [4].

4. Conclusions

Based on analyzing the immune phenomena in nature and utilizing performances of the existent artificial neural network, a novel network model, i.e., an immune neural network, is proposed which integrates the immune mechanism and the function of neural information processing. This model makes it easy for an user to directly utilize the characteristic information of a pending problem and to simplify the original structure through adjusting the excitation function with the prior knowledge, and then the working efficiency and the searching accuracy are both improved. The analysis in theory and the simulating test for the twin-spiral problem show that, comparing with the artificial neural network, INN is not only effective but also feasible. INN can conducively simplify the structure of the existent model and show working performances when dealing with a pending problem. However, it is necessary to point out that there is also a lot of work to do on the theory of designing and optimizing this model, such as, the algorithm of optimizing excitation function of a neuron in hidden layer, the algorithm of adjusting parameters of the excitation function, the algorithm of network weight matrix training, etc.

References

[1] F. J. Varela and J. Stewart. *Dynamics of a class of immune networks. I) Global behavior.* J. Theo. Biol., Vol.144, 1990, pp.93-101.

[2] J. Stewart and F. J. Varela. *Dynamics of a class of immune networks. II) Oscillatory activity of cellular and humoral component.* J. Theo. Biol., Vol.144, 1990, pp.103-115.

[3] K. Takahashi and T. Yamada. *Self-tuning Immune Feedback Controller for Controlling Mechanical Systems.* Proceeding 1997 1st IEEE/ASME International Conference on Advanced Intelligent Mechatronics, Tokyo, Japan, 1997, pp.101-105.

[4] Y. Ishida and F. Mizessyn. *Learning Algorithms on an Immune Network Model: Application to Sensor Diagnosis.* Proceeding International Conference Neural Networks, China, 1992, pp.33-38.

α-Surface and Its Application to Mining Protein Data

Xiong Wang

Department of Computer Science
California State University, Fullerton
Fullerton, CA 92834-6870, USA
wang@ecs.fullerton.edu

Abstract

Given a finite set of points in three dimensional Euclidean space R^3, the subset that forms its surface could be different when observed in different levels of details. In this paper, we introduce a notion called α-surface. We present an algorithm that extracts the α-surface from a finite set of points in R^3. We apply the algorithm to extracting the α-surfaces of proteins and discover patterns from these surface structures, using the pattern discovery algorithm we developed earlier. We then use these patterns to classify the proteins. Experimental results show the good performance of the proposed approach.

1. Introduction

Protein classification is a very important research topic with deep implications [1, 2, 3]. Traditionally, proteins are classified according to their functions. However, recently, many approaches have been proposed to classify proteins according to their structures, e.g. sequences [3], secondary structures [3], and three dimensional structures [6]. In [5, 6], we developed an algorithm that discovers frequently occurring patterns in a set of 3D graphs. We applied the algorithm to protein classification. While we succeeded in classifying two families of proteins with high recall and precision, experimental results showed that it was difficult to extend the approach to classifying more than two families of proteins. One reason is that proteins are large molecules, typically with several hundreds or even thousands of atoms. Many of the substructures that occur frequently in multiple proteins are not specifically related to their functions.

Significant studies have shown that the structure of the surface of a protein relates more to the function of the protein. In this paper, we define α-surface of a finite set of points in R^3 and present an algorithm for extracting α-surfaces from finite point sets. We apply the algorithm to extracting α-surfaces of proteins. We then employ the

pattern discovery algorithm that we developed earlier to find frequently occurring patterns on the α-surfaces and use these patterns to classify the proteins. The rest of the paper is organized as follows: In Section 2, we define α-surface. In Section 3, we describe the surface extracting algorithm. Section 4 discusses how the surface extracting algorithm and the pattern discovery algorithm are applied to protein classification. Section 5 presents some experimental results. We conclude the paper in Section 6.

2. α-Surfaces

Definition 2.1 *Given a point O in R^3 and a real number α ($0 < \alpha < \infty$), an α-ball is the set of points $B(O, \alpha) = \{P | P \in R^3 \text{ and } ||P - O|| < \alpha\}$, where $||P - O||$ is the Euclidean distance between P and O. A closed α-ball $\overline{B}(O, \alpha)$ is the α-ball $B(O, \alpha)$ plus its bounding sphere, i.e. $\overline{B}(O, \alpha) = \{P | P \in R^3 \text{ and } ||P - O|| \leq \alpha\}$.*

Definition 2.2 *Given a finite set $\mathcal{D}$ of points in R^3 and a real number α ($0 < \alpha < \infty$), the α-surface $\mathcal{S}$ of $\mathcal{D}$ is defined as $\mathcal{S} = \{P | P \in \mathcal{D} \text{ and } (\exists O \in R^3 \text{ such that } B(O, \alpha) \cap \mathcal{D} = \emptyset \text{ and } P \in \overline{B}(O, \alpha))\}$. When $B(O, \alpha) \cap \mathcal{D} = \emptyset$ and $P \in \overline{B}(O, \alpha) \cap \mathcal{D}$, we say that α-ball $B(O, \alpha)$ touches P. $P \in \mathcal{S}$ is called a surface point with respect to α (simply a surface point when the context is clear).*

Fig. 1 illustrates the notion in R^2.

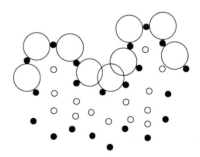

Figure 1. An α-surface in R^2.

The definition of α-surfaces is general. In the context of mining protein data, we need some adjustment. First of all, the surface of a protein is important to its function, because a protein reacts to its surrounding through its surface. Thus we are not concerned with those parts of α-surfaces that are not *visible*, namely those surface points that are enclosed inside the proteins. Secondly, when α is small, the α-surface of $\mathcal{D}$ could be split to two pieces. A protein is one molecule. Its surface should be in one piece. We specify the adjustment in the following definition.

Definition 2.3 *Let α $(0 < \alpha < \infty)$ be a real number and $\mathcal{S}$ be the α-surface of a finite set $\mathcal{D}$. $\mathcal{S}$ is connected, if for any two surface points $P_1, P_2 \in \mathcal{S}$ there are a finite number of α-balls: $B(O_1, \alpha)$, $B(O_2, \alpha)$, ..., $B(O_n, \alpha)$, such that:*

(i) $B(O_i, \alpha) \cap \mathcal{D} = \emptyset$ $(1 \le i \le n)$.

(ii) $\overline{B}(O_i, \alpha) \cap \overline{B}(O_{i+1}, \alpha) \cap \mathcal{S} \ne \emptyset$ $(1 \le i \le n - 1)$.

(iii) $P_1 \in \overline{B}(O_1, \alpha)$ and $P_2 \in \overline{B}(O_n, \alpha)$.

Notice that, (ii) requires two contiguous α-balls to touch at least one common surface point. Imagine that the α-ball is solid, so are the points in $\mathcal{D}$, and we roll the α-ball along the surface of $\mathcal{D}$. Intuitively, if an α-surface is connected, we can roll an α-ball from one surface point to another along the surface.

3. Extracting α-Surfaces

Starting from the point P_m with the maximum X-coordinate in $\mathcal{D}$, the surface extracting algorithm rolls the α-ball to any surface point that can be touched in a breadth first manner. Obviously, P_m is a surface point with respect to any α. Since the radius of the α-ball is fixed, the position of the α-ball is determined uniquely by the center. Thus rolling the α-ball means that given the current center of the α-ball O determine a new center O', such that the α-ball touches the next surface point. In R^2, this is an easy task, since there are only two directions to roll the α-ball. In R^3, however, determining the new center O' becomes a complicate problem. The difficulty comes from choosing the rolling direction. If we fixed the α-ball at one surface point, there are infinite directions in which we can roll the α-ball. We discuss three primitive ways of rolling the α-ball from the current position to the next surface point.

Case 1. Rolling from P_m: The first case occurs only once at the beginning, i.e. when the α-ball touches a single point P_m. Notice that the next surface point is within distance 2α of P_m (see Fig. 2). For each neighboring point P, we utilize the plane that is determined by O, P_m, and P to fix the rolling direction and pick up the next surface point to be the point that the α-ball can touch by rolling the smallest angle, e.g. P_1 in Fig. 2.

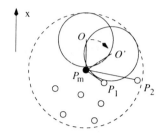

Figure 2. Rolling from P_m.

Case 2. Rolling side by side: In the second case, the α-ball touches at least two surface points. To determine the rolling direction, we pick up two of these points to be the current surface points. If we fixed the α-ball at both surface points, there are only two directions to roll the α-ball. In Fig. 3, suppose the α-ball currently touches P_0 and P_1, and P_c is the point in middle of P_0 and P_1. The next surface point is the point that the α-ball can touch by rolling the smallest angle from the plane determined by P_0, P_1, and O, namely $\angle OP_cO'$ is smallest.

Figure 3. Rolling side by side.

Case 3. Rolling away from one end: Rolling side by side does not guarantee to find all surface points that are within the neighbor of the current surface point, e.g. when the neighboring surface point is collinear with the two current surface points. In such cases we need to roll the α-ball away from one of the two current surface points. This is similar to the first case (Rolling from P_m).

The surface extracting algorithm maintains a queue $\mathcal{Q}$ which holds a subset of the α-surface $\mathcal{S}$ that are under expansion. The basic rolling procedure of the algorithm rolls the α-ball around one surface point in $\mathcal{Q}$, so that all its neighboring points in $\mathcal{S}$ will be touched at least once by the α-ball. These neighbors are added to $\mathcal{Q}$. Fig. 4 illustrates the procedure.

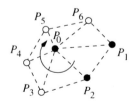

Figure 4. Rolling around one point.

Since the neighboring surface points are within distance 2α of the current surface point, to speed up the process, we partition $\mathcal{D}$ at the very beginning. Let x_{min} (x_{max}) be the minimum (maximum) X coordinate of all the points in $\mathcal{D}$, respectively. Let $x_0, x_1, ..., x_n$ be defined as the following:

(i) $x_0 = x_{min}$,

(ii) $x_{i+1} = x_i + 2\alpha$ $(0 \le i \le n-1)$, and

(iii) $x_{n-1} \le x_{max} < x_n$.

We cut the range $[x_{min}, x_{max}]$ to segments $[x_i, x_{i+1})$ $(0 \le i \le n-1)$ with length 2α. Similarly, let y_{min} (y_{max}) be the minimum (maximum) Y coordinate and z_{min} (z_{max}) be the minimum (maximum) Z coordinate, respectively. We cut the ranges $[y_{min}, y_{max}]$ and $[z_{min}, z_{max}]$ to segments with length 2α. Each partition $Pt_{i,j,k}$ is a cube $Pt_{i,j,k} = \{(x, y, z) | x_i \le x < x_{i+1}, \; y_j \le y < y_{j+1}, \; and \; z_k \le z < z_{k+1}\}$. For any given point $P = (x, y, z) \in \mathcal{D}$, let $i = \lfloor \frac{x - x_{min}}{2\alpha} \rfloor$, $j = \lfloor \frac{y - y_{min}}{2\alpha} \rfloor$, and $k = \lfloor \frac{z - z_{min}}{2\alpha} \rfloor$. P belongs to partition $Pt_{i,j,k}$ and the points that are within distance 2α of P are all located in the 27 partitions surrounding $Pt_{i,j,k}$.

Assuming that the points in $\mathcal{D}$ are evenly distributed, the complexity of the surface extracting algorithm is $O(\frac{|\mathcal{D}|^2}{N})$, where $|\mathcal{D}|$ is the size of $\mathcal{D}$ and $N = \lceil \frac{x_{max} - x_{min}}{2\alpha} \rceil \times \lceil \frac{y_{max} - y_{min}}{2\alpha} \rceil \times \lceil \frac{z_{max} - z_{min}}{2\alpha} \rceil$ is the total number of partitions.

4. Classifying Proteins

To evaluate the performance of the surface extracting algorithm, we applied it to classifying three families of proteins. We classified the proteins using the 10-way cross-validation scheme. That is, each family was divided into 10 groups of roughly equal size. Ten tests were conducted. In each test, a group was taken from a family and used as test data; the other nine groups were used as training data for that family. We first utilized the surface extracting algorithm to find the surfaces of the proteins in the training data. We then employed the pattern discovery algorithm we developed before to find frequently occurring patterns from these surfaces. Finally, we used these patterns to classify the proteins in the test data.

The pattern discovery algorithm proceeds in two phases to search for patterns on the surfaces. In the first phase, the algorithm decomposes the surfaces to substructures and hashes the substructures to a three dimensional hash table. Let $\mathcal{S}$ be a surface outputed by the surface extracting algorithm. For any point $P \in \mathcal{S}$, we consider P and its k-nearest neighbors in $\mathcal{S}$ as a substructure and attach a local coordinate system SF to P. We hash the node-triplets from the substructure to a three dimensional hash table. The hash bin address is determined by the lengths of the three edges

of the triangle formed by the triplet. The three edges are sorted ascendantly on their lengths. The basic idea is that if two triangles match each other the longest edge of a triangle must match the longest edge of the other triangle. Likewise, the shortest edge of a triangle must match the shortest edge of the other. Stored in the hash bin are a protein identification number, a substructure number, and the local coordinate system SF. By the end of the first phase, all surfaces are stored in the hash table. In the second phase, the algorithm considers each substructure as a candidate pattern and rehashes it to evaluate its number of occurrences in the training data. In this phase, we again take each node-triplet from the candidate pattern and utilize the lengths of the sorted three edges to access the hash table. All the triplets that were stored in the accessed hash bin are recognized as matches and their local coordinate systems SF are recovered based on the global coordinate system that defines the candidate pattern. The triplet matches are augmented to larger substructure matches if they come from the same substructure and their recovered local coordinate systems match each other. A candidate pattern M occurs on the surface of a protein if M matches any substructure from the surface within one mutation[1].

For each candidate pattern, let n_i ($i = 1, 2, 3$) be its occurrence numbers in the training data of family i. We exclude those candidate patterns such that $n_1 = n_2 = n_3$. All the other candidate patterns are collected as useful patterns. Each pattern is associated with a weight pro^i where

$$pro^i = \frac{n_i}{\min\{n_1, n_2, n_3\} + 1}$$

We add a denominator to the weight because we observed that some patterns are common to proteins from different families. Although they may still occur more frequently in some family, they really are not specific to any family.

When classifying a test protein Q, we first find its surface using the proposed surface extracting algorithm and construct substructures as described above. Let $M_1, M_2, \ldots, M_p$ be all the patterns found in the training data and $pro_1^i, pro_2^i, \ldots, pro_p^i$ be their corresponding weights for family i. Namely,

$$pro_j^i = \frac{n_{ji}}{\min\{n_{j1}, n_{j2}, n_{j3}\} + 1}$$

where n_{ji} is the occurrence number of pattern M_j ($j = 1, 2, \ldots, p$) in the training data of family i. Family i obtains a score

$$\mathcal{N}^i = \frac{\sum_{j=1}^p d_j \times pro_j^i}{\sum_{j=1}^p pro_j^i}$$

---

[1] A candidate pattern M matches a substructure S with n mutations if by applying an arbitrary number of rotations and translations as well as n node insert/delete operations to M, one can transform M to S (see [5, 6] for details).

where

$$d_j = \begin{cases} 1 & \text{if } M_j \text{ occurs in } Q \\ 0 & \text{otherwise} \end{cases}$$

The protein Q is classified to the family i with maximum $\mathcal{N}$. We add the denominator to make the score fair to all families. Notice that the maximum possible score for any family is 1. This is necessary because the three families do not have the same number of representatives in the training data. Furthermore, the sizes of the proteins are very different. If we can not decide a winner, then the "no-opinion" verdict is given.

5. Experimental Results

We have implemented the surface extracting algorithm using C++ on a Sun Ultra 10 workstation running Solaris 8 operating system. We selected three families of proteins from SCOP [2]. SCOP is accessible at `http://scop.mrc-lmb.cam.ac.uk/scop/`. The three families pertain to Transmembrane Helical Fragments, Matrix Metalloproteases – catalytic domain, and Immunoglobulin – I set domains. In determining the structure of a protein, we consider only the C_α, C_β and N atoms. These atoms form the polypeptide chain backbone of a protein where the polypeptide chain is made up of residues linked together by peptide bonds. We classified the proteins as discussed in Section 4. When adjusting α in the surface extracting algorithm, we found that $\alpha = 7.5$ yielded the best result. When constructing substructures (patterns), we found the substructures with 6 points yielded the best result. In each of these substructures, there was a surface point together with its 5 nearest neighbors on the α-surface. The algorithm produced a set of surface points that were on average 25% of the size of a protein.

We use recall ($\mathcal{R}$) and precision ($\mathcal{P}$) to evaluate the effectiveness of our classification algorithm. Recall is defined as

$$\mathcal{R} = \frac{\mathcal{T} - \sum_{i=1}^{3} \mathcal{M}^i}{\mathcal{T}} \times 100\%$$

where $\mathcal{T}$ is the total number of test proteins and $\mathcal{M}^i$ is the number of test proteins that belong to family i but are not assigned to family i by our algorithm (they are either assigned to family j, $j \neq i$, or they receive the "no-opinion" verdict). Precision is defined as

$$\mathcal{P} = \frac{\mathcal{T} - \sum_{i=1}^{3} \mathcal{M}^i}{\mathcal{T} - \mathcal{V}} \times 100\%$$

where $\mathcal{V}$ is the number of test proteins that receive the "no-opinion" verdict. With the 10-way cross validation scheme, the average $\mathcal{R}$ over the ten tests was 93.7% and the average $\mathcal{P}$ was 95.9%. It was found that 2.3% test proteins on average received the "no-opinion" verdict during the classification. In our previous work [6], we also tried to classify three families of proteins and the recall and precision dropped to 80%. The results reported here are much better.

6. Conclusions

We have given a formal definition of surface points of a finite point set in R^3 and presented an algorithm for extracting such surface points. We applied this algorithm, together with previously developed algorithms for 3D pattern discovery, to protein classification. In [4], we reported a preliminary result of this research without discussing the surface extracting algorithm. We also improve the classification approach in this paper, thanks to the comments from the reviewers. For our future work, we will conduct comprehensive experiments on more protein families to find interesting patterns on their surfaces. We will also extend our algorithm to applications in three dimensional visualization.

7. Acknowledgments

The author thanks Dr. Jason T. L. Wang for his comments and Dr. Jane Richardson for helpful discussion during the Atlantic Symposium on Computational Biology, Genome Information Systems & Technology. The author also appreciates the comments from the anonymous reviewers.

References

[1] R. King, A. Karwath, A. Clare, and L. Dephaspe. Genome scale prediction of protein functional class from sequence using data mining. In *Proceedings of the 6th ACM SIGKDD International Conference on Knowledge Discovery and Data Mining*, pages 384–389, Boston, MA, 2000.

[2] A. G. Murzin, S. E. Brenner, T. Hubbard, and C. Chothia. SCOP: a structural classification of proteins database for the investigation of sequences and structures. *Journal of Molecular Biology*, 247(4):536–540, 1995.

[3] J. T. L. Wang, B. A. Shapiro, and D. Shasha. *Pattern Discovery in Biomolecular Data: Tools, Techniques and Applications*. Oxford University Press, New York, NY, 1999.

[4] X. Wang. Mining protein surfaces. In *2001 ACM SIGMOD Workshop on Research Issues in Data Mining and Knowledge Discovery*, pages 20–24, Santa Barbara, CA, 2001.

[5] X. Wang, J. T. L. Wang, D. Shasha, B. A. Shapiro, S. Dikshitulu, I. Rigoutsos, and K. Zhang. Automated discovery of active motifs in three dimensional molecules. In *Proceedings of the 3rd International Conference on Knowledge Discovery and Data Mining*, pages 89–95, Newport Beach, CA, 1997.

[6] X. Wang, J. T. L. Wang, D. Shasha, B. A. Shapiro, I. Rigoutsos, and K. Zhang. Finding patterns in three dimensional graphs: Algorithms and applications to scientific data mining. *IEEE Transactions on Knowledge and Data Engineering*, To appear.

An Efficient Data Mining Technique for Discovering Interesting Sequential Patterns

Show-Jane Yen* and Yue-Shi Lee**

*Dept. of Computer Science and Information Engineering, Fu Jen Catholic University, Taipei, TAIWAN, R.O.C.
**Dept. of Information Management, Ming Chuan University, Taipei, TAIWAN, R.O.C.
Email: sjyen@csie.fju.edu.tw, leeys@mcu.edu.tw

Abstract

Mining sequential patterns is to discover sequential purchasing behaviors of most customers from a large amount of customer transactions. In this paper, a data mining language is presented. From the data mining language, users can specify the interested items and the criteria of the sequential patterns to be discovered. Also, an efficient data mining technique is proposed to extract the sequential patterns according to the users' requests.

1 Data mining language

The definitions about mining sequential patterns are presented in [1,2]. Our data mining language, which refers to [3], is defined as follows:

> **Mining** *<Sequential Patterns>*
> **From** *<TDB>*
> **With** *<{D₁},{D₂}, ...,{Dₘ}>*
> **Support** *<s%>*

1. In the **From** clause, *<TDB>* is used to specify the database name to which users query the sequential patterns.
2. In the **With** clause, $<\{D_1\},\{D_2\}, ...,\{D_m\}>$ are user-specified items which ordered by increasing purchasing time, Besides, the notation "*" can be in the itemsets D_i, which denotes any itemsets and $\{D_i\}$ can be the notation "*", which represents any sequence.
3. **Support** clause is followed by the user-specified minimum support $s\%$.

In order to find the interesting sequential patterns efficiently, we need to transform the original transaction data into another type. Each item in each customer sequence is transformed into a bit string. The length of a bit string is the number of the transactions in the customer sequence. If the ith transaction of the customer sequence contains an item, then the ith bit in the bit string for this item is set to 1. Otherwise, the ith bit is set to 0.

Suppose a customer sequence contains the two sequences S_1 and S_2. We present an operation called *sequential bit-string operation* to check if the sequence $S_1 S_2$ is also contained in this customer sequence. The process of this operation is described as follows: Let the bit strings for sequence S_1 and S_2 in customer sequence c is B_1 and B_2, respectively. Bit string B_1 is scanned from left to right until a bit value 1 is visited. We set this bit and all bits on the left hand side of this bit to 0 and set all bits on the right hand side of this bit to 1, and assign the resultant bit string to a template T_b. Then, the bit string for sequence $S_1 S_2$ in c can be obtained by performing logical AND operation on bit strings T_b and B_2. If the number of 1's in the bit string for sequence $S_1 S_2$ is not zero, then $S_1 S_2$ is contained in customer sequence c. Otherwise, the customer sequence c does not contain $S_1 S_2$.

2 Mining interesting sequential patterns

Suppose the user specifies a sequence which contains k itemsets D_1, D_2, ... and D_m in the **With** clause and $S = \{D_1\}\{D_2\}...\{D_m\}$. In the following, we describe the algorithm to find interesting sequential patterns:

Step 1. Find all the frequent (m+1)-sequences

Step 1.1. Scan the bit-string database, if all items in S are contained in a record, then output the items in this record and the bit string for each item into *1-itemset database*. If S is a frequent sequence, then find all frequent 1-itemsets. The frequent itemsets are found in each iteration. For the kth iteration ($k \geq 1$), the candidate $(k+1)$-itemsets are generated, and scan the $(k+1)$-itemset database to find $(k+1)$-frequent itemsets.

The method to generate the candidate $(k+1)$-itemsets is described as follows [1]. Suppose the two frequent k-itemsets X and Y in a record in the k-itemset database generate candidate $(k+1)$-itemset Z. We perform logical AND operation on the two bit strings for X and Y, and the resultant bit string is the bit string for Z. If this bit string is not zero, then output Z and its bit string into $(k+1)$-itemset database. Besides, we also output the frequent k-itemsets and its bit string in each record into the *frequent itemset database*.

Step 1.2. Each frequent itemset (i.e., frequent 1-sequence) is given a unique number, and replace the frequent itemsets in the frequent itemset database with their numbers to form a 1-sequence database.

Step 1.3. Generate candidate *k*-sequences (*k*=2,3), and scan (*k*-1)-sequence database to generate *k-sequence database* and find all the frequent *k*-sequences.

The candidate 2-itemsets are generated as follows: For each frequent 1-sequence *f* except D_l, if there is a notation "*" appears before the itemset D_l in the **With** clause, then the candidate 2-sequence *{f}{D_l}* is generated. If the notation "*" appears after the itemset D_l, then the candidate 2-sequence *{D_l}{f}* is generated. If the reverse order of a candidate 2-sequence is contained in the specified sequence S, then this candidate 2-sequence can be pruned. The method to generate candidate 3-sequences is described as follows: For every two frequent 2-sequences S_1=*{D_l}{r}* which is a sub-sequence of S and S_2=*{D_l}{t}* (or S_1=*{D_l}{r}* and S_2=*{t}{D_l}*), we can generate the candidate 3-sequences *{D_l}{r}{t}* and *{D_l}{t}{r}* (or *{t}{D_l}{r}*).

For each record in the (*k*-1)-sequence database, we use the frequent (*k*-1)-sequences in the record and apply the above method to generate the candidate *k*-sequences. Suppose that the two frequent (*k*-1)-sequences X and Y in a record generate the candidate *k*-sequence Z. We perform the sequential bit-string operation on the two bit strings for X and Y, and the resultant bit string is the bit string for Z. If this bit string is not zero, then output Z and its bit string into *k*-sequence database. After scanning (*k*-1)-sequence database, the *k*-sequence database can be generated and the candidate *k*-sequences can be counted.

Step 1.4. Frequent (*h*+1)-sequences (3≤*h*≤*m*) are generated in each iteration. For the (*h*-2)th iteration, we use frequent *h*-sequences to generate candidate (*h*+1)-sequence, and scan *h*-sequence database to generate (*h*+1)-sequence database, and find all the frequent (*h*+1)-sequences.

We use the following method to generate candidate (*h*+1)-sequences: For any two frequent *h*-sequence S_1={s_1}{s_2}...{s_{h-1}}{r} and S_2={s_1}{s_2}...{s_{h-1}}{t}, in which {s_1}{s_2}...{s_{h-1}} is a sub-sequence of S or {r} and {t} are contained in S, the candidate (*h*+1)-sequences {s_1}{s_2}...{s_{h-1}}{r}{t} and {s_1}{s_2}...{s_{h-1}}{t}{r} can be generated. If a generated candidate (*h*+1)-sequence contains more than one itemsets which are not contained in S, then the candidate (*h*+1)-sequence can be pruned. The methods to generate (*h*+1)-sequence database and the frequent (*h*+1)-sequences are the same as step 1.3.

Step 2. The frequent (*m*+*n*+1)-sequences (*n*≥1) which contain the specified sequence S are generated in each iteration. For the *n*th iteration, we use the frequent (*m*+*n*) -sequences to generate candidate (*m*+*n*+1)-sequences and scan the (*m*+*n*)-sequence database and 1-sequence database to generate (*m*+*n*+1)-sequence database in which the candidate (*m*+*n*+1)-sequences are contained in each

record but the bit string are not, and find the frequent (*m*+*n*+1)-sequences.

The method to generate candidate (*m*+*n*+1)-sequences is as follows: For every two frequent (*m*+*n*)-sequences S_1 = {s_1}{s_2}...{s_i}{r}{s_{i+1}}...{s_{m+n-1}} and S_2 = {s_1} {s_2}...{s_j}{t}{s_{j+1}}...{s_{m+n-1}} (i≤j), in which {r} is not contained in S_2 and {t} is not contained in S_1, a candidate (*m*+*n*+1)-sequence {s_1}{s_2}...{r}...{t}... {s_{m+n-1}} can be generated. For each record in (*m*+*n*)-sequence database, we also use every two frequent (*m*+*n*)-sequences in this record and apply the above method to generate a candidate (*m*+*n*+1)-sequence, and perform the sequential bit-string operations on the bit strings for the itemsets in the candidate (*m*+*n*+1)-sequence by scanning the 1-sequence database. If the resultant bit string is not zero, then output the candidate (*m*+*n*+1)-sequence into the (*m*+*n*+1)-sequence database, and count the support for the candidate (*m*+*n*+1)-sequence. After scanning (*m*+*n*)-sequence database, the (*m*+*n*+1)-sequence database can be generated and the frequent (*m*+*n*+1)-sequences can be found.

Step 3. For each frequent sequence, the code for each itemset in the frequent sequence is replaced with the itemset itself. If a frequent sequence is not contained in another frequent sequences, then this frequent sequence is a sequential pattern.

3 Conclusions

In this paper, we introduce a data mining language. From the data mining language, users can specify the items or the sequences and the minimum support threshold of the sequential patterns to be discovered, which they are interested in. We propose an efficient data mining technique to process the user requirement. Our algorithms can reduce the number of the combinations of itemsets or sequences in each customer sequence for counting the supports of the candidate sequences, and reduce the number of the candidate sequences according to the user's requests.

References

[1] Rakesh Agrawal, *et al*., "Mining Sequential Patterns," *Proc. of the Int'l Conference on Data Engineering*, pp. 3-14, 1995.
[2] Rakesh Agrawal, *et al*., "Mining Sequential Patterns: Generalizations and Performance Improvements," *Proc. of the 5th Int'l Conference on Extending Database Technology*, pp. 3-17, 1996.
[3] Show-Jane Yen and A.L.P. Chen, "An Efficient Data Mining Technique for Discovering Interesting Association Rules," *Proc. of the 8th Int'l Conference and Workshop on Database and Expert Systems Applications*, pp. 664-669, 1997.

Fast Parallel Association Rule Mining Without Candidacy Generation

Osmar R. Zaïane   Mohammad El-Hajj   Paul Lu
University of Alberta, Edmonton, Alberta, Canada
{zaiane, mohammad, paullu}@cs.ualberta.ca

Abstract

In this paper we introduce a new parallel algorithm MLFPT (Multiple Local Frequent Pattern Tree) [11] for parallel mining of frequent patterns, based on FP-growth mining, that uses only two full I/O scans of the database, eliminating the need for generating the candidate items, and distributing the work fairly among processors. We have devised partitioning strategies at different stages of the mining process to achieve near optimal balancing between processors. We have successfully tested our algorithm on datasets larger than 50 million transactions.

1. Introduction

Association rule mining algorithms currently proposed in the literature are not sufficient for extremely large datasets and new solutions still have to be found. In particular there is a need for algorithms that do not depend on high computation and repeated I/O scans. Parallelization is a viable solution. However, distributing and balancing the mining tasks between the processors without jeopardizing the global solution is not trivial. The problem of mining association rules over market basket analysis was introduced in [1]. Association rules are not limited to market basket analysis, but the analysis of sales, or what is known as basket data, is the typical application often used for illustration. The problem consists of finding associations between items or itemsets in transactional data. The data could be retail sales in the form of customer transactions or even medical images [12]. Association rules have been shown to be useful for other applications such as recommender systems, diagnosis, decision support, telecommunication, etc. This association-mining task can be broken into two steps: A step for finding all frequent k-itemsets known for its associated extreme I/O and a straightforward step for generating confident rules from the frequent itemsets.

1.1 Related Work

Several algorithms have been proposed in the literature to address the problem of mining association rules. One of the key algorithms, which seems to be the most pop-

ular in many applications for enumerating frequent itemsets, is the apriori algorithm [3] the foundation of most known algorithms whether sequential or parallel. Park et al. have proposed the Dynamic Hashing and Pruning algorithm (DHP) [9]. However, the trimming and the pruning properties caused some problems that made it impractical in many cases [13]. The partitioning algorithm proposed in [5] reduced the I/O cost dramatically . However, this method has problems in cases of high dimensional itemsets, and it also suffers from the high false positives of frequent items. FP-growth, was recently proposed by Han et al. [8]. This algorithm creates a relatively compact tree-structure that alleviates the multi-scan problem and improves the candidate itemset generation. The algorithm requires only two full I/O scans for the dataset. Our approach presented in this paper is based on this idea. In spite of the significance of the association rule mining and in particular the generation of frequent itemsets, few advances have been made on parallelizing association rule mining algorithms [6, 2]. Most of the work on parallelizing association rules mining on Shared-memory MultiProcessor (SMP) architecture was based on apriori-like algorithms.

Parthasarathy et al. [10] have written an excellent recent survey on parallel association rule mining with shared-memory architecture covering most trends, challenges and approaches adopted for parallel data mining. All approaches spelled out and compared in this extensive survey are apriori-based. These methods not only require repeated scans of the dataset, they also generate extremely large numbers of candidate sets easily approaching 10^{30} candidates in common cases [7].

1.2 Contribution

In this paper, we introduce a new parallel association rules mining algorithm MLFPT, which is based on the FP-growth algorithm [8]. We have implemented this algorithm on a 64 processor SGI 2400 Origin machine, where all experiments were tested using high dimensionality data that are of a factor of hundreds of thousands of items, and transactional sizes that range in tens of gigabytes. A special optimization step is added to achieve better load balancing with the goal of distributing the work fairly among processors for the mining process

2 Multiple Local Parallel Trees

The MLFPT approach we propose consists of two main stages. Stage one is the construction of the parallel frequent pattern trees (one for each processor) and stage two is the actual mining of these data structures, much like the FP-growth algorithm. However, in order to avoid false negatives, where locally infrequent itemsets are pruned inadvertently while they are frequent globally, we need global counters. Though global counters necessitate locking mechanisms for mutual exclusion, that would add significant overhead and waiting time. Our approach with interlinked local counters avoids the need for locking. Thus, we evade the famous ping-pong problem in parallel programs.

2.1 Construction of the Multiple Local Parallel Trees

The goal of this stage is to build the compact data structures called Multiple Local Parallel Trees (MLPT). This construction is done in two phases, where each phase requires a full I/O scan for the dataset.

A first initial scan of the database identifies the frequent 1-itemsets. In order to enumerate the frequent items efficiently, we divide the datasets among the available processors. Each processor is given an approximately equal number of transactions to read and analyze. As a result, the dataset is split in p equal sizes. Each processor locally enumerates the items appearing in the transactions at hand. After enumeration of local occurences , a global count is necessary to identify the frequent items. This count is done in parallel where each processor is allocated an equal number of items to sum their local supports into global count. Finally, in a sequential phase infrequent items with a support less than the support threshold are weeded out and the remaining frequent items are sorted by their frequency. This list is organized in a table, called header table, where the items and their respective global support are stored along with pointers to the first occurrence of the item in each frequent pattern tree. Phase 2 would construct a frequent pattern tree for each available processor.

Phase 2 of constructing the MLPT structures is the actual building of the individual local trees. This phase requires a second complete I/O scan from the dataset where each processor reads the same number of transactions as in the first phase. Using these transactions, each processor builds its own frequent pattern tree that starts with a null root. For each transaction read by a processor only the set of frequent items present in the header table is collected and sorted in descending order according to their frequency.

TID	Items Bought	Processor Number
1	A, B, C, D, E	
2	F, B, D, E, G	→ P_0
3	B, D, A, E, G	
4	A, B, F, G, D	
5	B, F, D, G, K	→ P_1
6	A, B, F, G, D	
7	A, R, M, K, O	
8	B, F, G, A, D	→ P_2
9	A, B, F, M, O	

Table 1. Transactional database example.

Figure 1. Steps of phase 1.

These sorted transaction items are used in constructing the local FP-Trees as follows: for the first item on the sorted transactional dataset, check if it exists as one of the children of the root. If it exists then increment the support for this node. Otherwise, add a new node for this item as a child for the root node with 1 as support. Then, consider the current item node as the newly temporary root and repeat the same procedure with the next item on the sorted transaction. During the process of adding any new item-node to a given local FP-Tree of a processor p, a link is maintained between this item-node in the tree and its entry in the global header table corresponding to processor p. The header table holds as many pointers per item as there are available processors.

For illustration, we use an example with the transactions shown in Table 1. Let the number of available processors be 3 and the minimum support threshold set to 4. The four steps in phase 1 are shown in Figure 1 and Figure 2 shows the result of the tree building process. For the sake of simplicity, only links from the items A and B are drawn from the header table.

2.2 Mining Parallel Frequent items using MLPT Trees

Building the trees in the first stage is not a final goal but a means with the purpose of uncovering all frequent patterns without resorting to additional scans of the data. The mining process starts with a bottom up traversal of the nodes on the MLPT structures, where each processor mines fairly equal amounts of nodes. The distribution of this traversal work is predefined by a relatively small sequential step that precedes the mining process. This step sums the global sup-

666

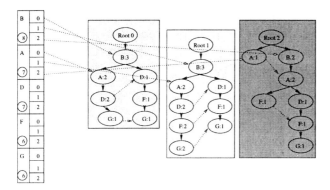

Figure 2. Phase 2 of the construction of the MLPT structure.

Items	Conditional Pattern Base	Conditional FP-Tree
G	(D:1, A:1, B:1) (F:1, D:1, B:1) (F:2, D:2, A:2, B:2) (F:1, D:1, B:1) (F:1, D:1, A:1, B:1)	(B:6, D:6, F:5, A:4)/G
F	(D:1, B:1) (D:2, A:2, B:2) (D:1, B:1) (D:1, A:1, B:1) (A:1, B:1)	(B:6, D:5)/F
D	(A:2, B:2) (B:1) (A:2, B:2) (B:1) (A:1, B:1)	(B:7, A:5)/D
A	(B2) (B:2) (B:2)	(B:6)/A
B	(∅)	

Table 2. Conditional Pattern Bases and the Conditional FPtrees (mining process).

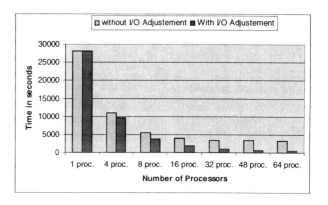

Figure 3. Comparison of execution time for 5 million transactions with and without I/O adjustement.

ports for all items and divides them by the number of processors to find the average number of occurrences that ought to be traversed by each processor. If A is this found average, this sequential step goes over the sorted list of items by their respective support and assigns items consecutively for each processors until the cumulated support is equal or greater than the average A. At this stage all frequent pattern trees are shared by all processors. The task of the processors, once assigned some items, is to generate what is called a conditional pattern base starting from their respective items in the header table. A conditional pattern base is a list of items that occur before a certain item in the frequent pattern tree up to the root of that tree in addition to the minimum support of all the item supports along the list. Since an item cannot only occur in many trees but also in many branches of the same tree, many conditional pattern bases could be generated for the same item. Merging all these conditional pattern bases of the same item yields the frequent string, a string also called conditional FP-Tree, that contains frequent itemsets and their support in the presence of a given item. The merge is based on the items in the patterns and all the supports of the same items are added up in the same manner as in [8]. If the support of an item is less than the minimum support threshold, it is not added in the frequent string.

Table 2 gives all conditional bases and conditional FP-Trees generated from the example in Table 1.

3 Experimental Results

A shared memory SGI Origin 2400 with 64 processors was used to conduct the experiments. We used synthetic transactional databases generated using the IBM Quest synthetic data generator [4]. The sizes of the input databases vary from 1 million transactions to 50 million using dimensions that are multiples of hundreds of thousands. Each

of these transactions has at least 12 items preceded by a unique transactional ID. The largest dataset is in the order 10 Gbytes.

In our experiments we studied the MLFPT algorithm with 4, 8, 16, 32, 48 and 64 processors and compared it to its sequential version. The sequential version was, of course, implemented without the summation phase and with only one tree. Speedup measures the performance of parallel execution compared to the sequential execution: $S_p = T_1/T_p$ where S_p is the speedup achieved with p processors, T_1 is the sequential execution time and T_p is the execution time using p processors.

I/O access is normally of an "embarrassingly parallel" nature. For instance, when data is stored on parallel disks with dedicated channels, twice as many processors should read twice as much data. In other words, with appropriate hardware, if it takes t time for one processor to read some data, it should take t/p for p processors to cover the same data.

Since our parallel machine had a sequential disk with one

shared head, to assess the real speedup of MLFPT, which does 2 I/O scans of the data regardless of the number of processors, we adjusted the I/O time assuming an "embarrassingly parallel" I/O access.

In our results we decided to adjust the I/O time of our algorithm as follows: The I/O time for parallel execution was estimated using the I/O time for sequential execution divided by the number of processors used. For instance, if using p processors the total execution time is T and the isolated I/O time is t, the execution time with I/O adjusted is calculated $TI = T - t + (S/p)$, where S is the isolated I/O time for a sequential execution. In other words, we replaced the 2 scans I/O time recorded with the expected real parallel I/O time.

Due to the space limitation we will only present figure 3 that depicts the significant time reduction with the increase of processors when mining 5 million transactions.

MLFPT operations are divided into two stages where most of the computation in the MLFPT algorithm is done during building the MLPT trees, and then mining them. Building the frequent pattern trees, which utilize most of the processing time, is shown to be of "embarrassingly parallel" nature and this indeed was the reason for the several-fold improvements achieved as we increased the number of processors in our experiments. This is due to the fact that the work is evenly partitioned among the processors and each unit of work is completely independent of each other where each processor builds a sub-tree representing its partition of transactions. There is no ping-pong effect where processors are waiting for each other.

Our experiments have shown that this creation and mining is almost linearly proportional to the number of processors and the size of the transactional datasets, where the speedup of the MLFPT algorithm increases as the problem size increases. These results suggest that the MLFPT algorithm would achieve speedups for extremely large datasets as well.

4 Conclusion and Future Work

In this paper, we have introduced an efficient parallel implementation of an FP-Tree-based association rule mining algorithm and have proposed a solution for load balancing among processors and resource sharing with minimum mutual-exclusion locking. We have discussed our experiments with this new parallel algorithm, MLFPT, for mining frequent patterns without candidate generation. The MLFPT algorithm overcomes the major drawbacks of parallel association rule mining algorithms derived from apriori, in particular the need for k I/O passes over the data.

Our experiments showed that with I/O adjusted, the MLFPT algorithm could achieve an encouraging many-fold speedup improvement.

The implementation of our algorithm and the experiments conducted were on a shared memory and shared hard drive architecture. We have recently acquired a cluster with 8 dual processor nodes and we plan to investigate the same approach with shared nothing architecture and devise a new protocol for sharing global resources while minimizing the message passing overhead. We are in the process of experimenting our algorithms with up to 1 billion transactions.

References

[1] R. Agrawal, T. Imielinski, and A. Swami. Mining association rules between sets of items in large databases. In *Proc. 1993 ACM-SIGMOD Int. Conf. Management of Data*, pages 207–216, Washington, D.C., May 1993.

[2] R. Agrawal and J. C. Shafer. Parallel mining of association rules: Design, implementation, and experience. *IEEE Trans. Knowledge and Data Engineering*, 8:962–969, 1996.

[3] R. Agrawal and R. Srikant. Fast algorithms for mining association rules. In *Proc. 1994 Int. Conf. Very Large Data Bases*, pages 487–499, Santiago, Chile, September 1994.

[4] I. Almaden. Quest synthetic data generation code. http://www.almaden.ibm.com/cs/quest/syndata.html.

[5] S. Brin, R. Motwani, J. D. Ullman, and S.Tsur. Dynamic itemset counting and implication rules for market basket data. In *Proc. 1997 ACM-SIGMOD Int. Conf. Management of Data*, pages 255–264, Tucson, Arizona, May 1997.

[6] D. Cheung, J. Han, V. Ng, A. Fu, and Y. Fu. A fast distributed algorithm for mining association rules. In *Proc. 1996 Int. Conf. Parallel and Distributed Information Systems*, pages 31–44, Miami Beach, Florida, Dec. 1996.

[7] J. Han and M. Kamber. *Data Mining, Concepts and Techniques*. Morgan Kaufmann, 2001.

[8] J. Han, J. Pei, and Y. Yin. Mining frequent patterns without candidate generation. In *ACM-SIGMOD*, Dallas, 2000.

[9] J. Park, M. Chen, and P. Yu. An effective hash-based algorithm for mining association rules. In *Proc. 1995 ACM-SIGMOD Int. Conf. Management of Data*, pages 175–186, San Jose, CA, May 1995.

[10] S. Parthasarathy, M. J. Zaki, and M. Ogihara. Parallel data mining for association rules on shared-memory systems. *Knowledge and Information Systems: An International Journal*, 3(1):1–29, February 2001.

[11] O. R. Zaïane, M. El-Hajj, and P. Lu. Fast parallel association rule mining without candidacy generation. Technical Report TR01-12, Department of Computing Science, University of Alberta, Canada, August 2001. ftp://ftp.cs.ualberta.ca/pub/TechReports/2001/TR01-12/TR01-12.pdf.

[12] O. R. Zaïane, J. Han, and H. Zhu. Mining recurrent items in multimedia with progressive resolution refinement. In *Int. Conf. on Data Engineering (ICDE'2000)*, pages 461–470, San Diego, CA, February 2000.

[13] M. J. Zaki. Parallel and distributed association mining: A survey. *IEEE Concurrency, Special Issue on Parallel Mechanisms for Data Mining*, 7(4):14–25, December 1999.

A comparison of stacking with meta decision trees to bagging, boosting, and stacking with other methods

Bernard Ženko, Ljupčo Todorovski, and Sašo Džeroski
Department of Intelligent Systems, Jožef Stefan Institute
Jamova 39, Ljubljana, Slovenia
{Bernard.Zenko, Ljupco.Todorovski, Saso Dzeroski}@ijs.si

Abstract. *Meta decision trees (MDTs) are a method for combining multiple classifiers. We present an integration of the algorithm MLC4.5 for learning MDTs into the Weka data mining suite. We compare classifier ensembles combined with MDTs to bagged and boosted decision trees, and to classifier ensembles combined with other methods: voting and stacking with three different meta-level classifiers (ordinary decision trees, naive Bayes, and multi-response linear regression - MLR).*

Meta decision trees. Techniques for combining predictions obtained from multiple base-level classifiers can be clustered in three combining frameworks: voting (used in bagging and boosting), stacked generalization or stacking [7] and cascading. Meta decision trees (MDTs) [5] adopt the stacking framework of combining base-level classifiers. The difference between meta and ordinary decision trees (ODTs) is that MDT leaves specify which base-level classifier should be used, instead of predicting the class value directly. The attributes used by MDTs are derived from the class probability distributions predicted by the base-level classifiers for a given example. An example MDT, induced in the image domain from the UCI Repository, is given below. The leaf denoted by an asterisk (*) specifies that the IBk classifier is to be used to classify an example, if the entropy of the class probability distribution predicted by IBk is smaller than or equal to 0.002369.

```
IBk:Entropy <= 0.002369:  IBk (*)
IBk:Entropy > 0.002369
|    J48:maxProbability <= 0.909091:  IBk
|    J48:maxProbability > 0.909091:   J48
```

The original algorithm MLC4.5 [5] for inducing MDTs was an extension of the C4.5 [3] algorithm for induction of ODTs. We have integrated the algorithm for inducing MDTs in the Weka data mining suite [6]. We have implemented MLJ4.8, a modification of J4.8 (the Weka re-implementation of C4.5): the differences between MLJ4.8 and J4.8 closely mirror the ones between MLC4.5

and C4.5. Integrating MDTs into Weka lets us perform a variety of experiments in combining different sets of base level classifiers, as well as comparisons to other methods for combining classifiers.

Experimental setup. In order to compare the performance of MDTs with that of other combining schemes, we perform experiments on a collection of twenty-one data sets from the UCI Repository of Machine Learning Databases and Domain Theories. Three learning algorithms are used in the base-level experiments: the tree learning algorithm J4.8, which is a re-implementation of C4.5 [3], the k-nearest neighbor (k-NN or IBk) algorithm and the naive Bayes (NB) algorithm. In all experiments, classification errors are estimated using 10-fold stratified cross validation. Cross validation is repeated ten times using different random generator seeds resulting in ten different sets of folds.

At the meta-level, the performances of seven algorithms for combining classifiers are compared. These are bagging and boosting of decision trees, voting, stacking with three different meta-level learning algorithms (J4.8, naive Bayes, and MLR), and stacking with MDTs. The performance of each of these algorithms is assessed in terms of its error rate. The performance of MDTs is compared to that of the other combining approaches. The relative accuracy improvement of classifier C_1 as compared to classifier C_2 is $1 - \texttt{error}(C_1)/\texttt{error}(C_2)$ (in our case $C_1 = $ MDTs). The average relative improvement is calculated using geometric mean: $1 - \texttt{geometric\_mean}(\texttt{error}(C_1)/\texttt{error}(C_2))$. The statistical significance of the difference in classification errors is tested using the paired t-test (exactly the same folds are used for C_1 and C_2) with significance level of 95%.

Results. Stacking with MDTs performs better than bagging and boosting of decision trees, which are the state of the art methods for learning ensembles of classifiers: In both cases MDTs are significantly better in 11 and worse in 3 domains, with a 20% and 15% relative accuracy improvement, respectively. A previous study of MDTs [5] shows that MDTs

Table 1. The performance of stacking with MDTs (error rate in %); the relative improvement in accuracy (in %) achieved by stacking with MDTs as compared to bagging, boosting, voting, stacking with J4.8, naive Bayes and MLR; and its significance (+/–: significantly better/worse, x: insignificant).

Data set	Sta. MDT abs. err.	Bag. J48 rel. im.	sig.	Boo. J48 rel. im.	sig.	Voting rel. im.	sig.	Sta. J48 rel. im.	sig.	Sta. NB rel. im.	sig.	Sta. MLR rel. im.	sig.
australian	13.77±0.38	-0.74	x	11.63	x	0.31	x	5.75	x	4.04	x	2.76	x
balance	8.51±0.19	50.83	+	60.39	+	4.49	+	-41.49	–	7.16	+	10.14	+
breast-w	2.69±0.07	45.98	+	27.41	+	22.31	+	3.09	+	6.93	+	1.57	+
bridges-td	16.08±0.84	-7.89	–	17.17	+	-1.86	–	4.09	+	7.34	+	-13.89	–
car	5.02±0.27	25.96	+	-20.75	–	22.73	+	-208.54	–	-89.30	–	10.62	+
chess	0.60±0.05	1.55	x	-56.55	x	59.10	x	20.42	x	20.42	x	0.00	x
diabetes	24.74±0.54	-0.48	x	13.28	x	-3.04	x	3.85	x	2.01	x	-4.05	x
echo	27.71±0.76	12.53	+	18.24	+	5.22	+	-4.31	–	1.09	+	3.20	+
german	25.60±0.30	2.92	+	12.42	+	-1.63	–	-0.51	–	5.50	+	-5.09	–
glass	31.78±1.19	-22.08	–	-37.10	–	-7.09	–	17.68	+	37.21	+	-2.72	–
heart	16.04±0.46	18.91	+	26.36	+	6.28	+	8.84	+	5.25	+	-4.84	–
hepatitis	15.87±0.84	10.22	x	13.07	x	8.89	x	16.04	x	8.55	x	-1.23	x
hypo	0.79±0.07	-1.62	x	24.62	x	40.09	x	4.56	x	32.34	x	-9.61	x
image	2.53±0.09	0.68	x	-37.65	x	13.72	x	22.92	x	61.16	x	10.82	x
ionosphere	8.83±0.62	-12.73	–	-37.78	–	-23.02	–	-44.86	–	-24.00	–	-20.16	–
iris	4.73±0.42	17.44	+	18.39	+	-12.70	–	22.83	+	5.33	+	-5.97	–
soya	7.06±0.14	2.43	x	0.21	x	-4.55	x	12.04	x	-7.59	x	2.23	x
tic-tac-toe	0.96±0.06	85.87	+	72.04	+	89.60	+	-130.00	–	20.69	+	-64.29	–
vote	3.54±0.17	9.94	+	21.03	+	50.16	+	12.99	+	30.00	+	0.00	x
waveform	14.40±0.11	20.00	+	22.50	+	9.44	+	-0.15	–	4.20	+	-0.53	–
wine	3.26±0.60	36.26	+	19.44	+	-87.10	–	14.71	+	6.45	+	-13.73	–
Average	11.17±0.39	19.89		14.78		18.34		-4.24		10.59		-4.07	
W/L			11+/3–		11+/3–		8+/6–		7+/7–		12+/2–		4+/9–

perform better than voting and stacking with ODTs. Our study confirms these findings and proves that they are independent of a specific implementation (we used their re-implementation in Java programming language) and the set of base-level classifiers (we used a different and smaller set). (Comparing MDTs to ODTs shows a 4% decrease in accuracy, but this is mostly due to the data sets car and tic-tac-toe, where all combining methods perform very well: if we exclude these two data sets a 7% increase is obtained; MDTs are also much smaller than ODTs).

Stacking with naive Bayes performs poorly. Stacking with MLR slightly outperforms stacking with MDTs (a 4% relative improvement in accuracy). Note that stacking with MDTs performs comparably while using less information (only aggregate data on the class probability distribution is used by MDTs, while the complete class probability distribution is used by MLR). The attributes used in MDTs are domain independent once we fix the set of base-level classifiers and the language of MDTs is the same for all domains. Another advantage of the MDTs is their understandability: they provide information about the relative areas of expertise of the base-level classifiers.

References

[1] Breiman, L. (1996) Bagging predictors. *Machine Learning*, 24(2): 123–140.

[2] Freund, Y. and Schapire, R. E. (1996) Experiments with a new boosting algorithm. In *Proceedings of the Thirteenth International Conference on Machine Learning*, pages 148-156. Morgan Kaufmann, San Francisco.

[3] Quinlan, J. R. (1993) *C4.5: Programs for Machine Learning*. Morgan Kaufmann, San Francisco.

[4] Ting, K. M. and Witten, I. H. (1999) Issues in stacked generalization. *Journal of Artificial Intelligence Research*, 10: 271–289.

[5] Todorovski, L. and Džeroski, S. (2000) Combining multiple models with meta decision trees. In *Proceedings of the Fourth European Conference on Principles of Data Mining and Knowledge Discovery*, pages 54–64. Springer, Berlin.

[6] Witten, I. H. and Frank, E. (1999) *Data Mining: Practical Machine Learning Tools and Techniques with Java Implementations*. Morgan Kaufmann, San Francisco.

[7] Wolpert, D. (1992) Stacked generalization. *Neural Networks* 5(2): 241–260.

Mining California Vital Statistics Data

Du Zhang, Quoc Luan Ha and Meiliu Lu

Department of Computer Science
California State University
Sacramento, CA 95819-6021
{zhangd, ha, mei}@ecs.csus.edu

Abstract

Vital statistics data offer a fertile ground for data mining. In this paper, we discuss the results of a data mining project on the causes of death aspect of the vital statistics data in the state of California. A data mining tool called Cubist is used to build predictive models out of two million cases over a nine-year period. The objective of our study is to discover knowledge that can be used to gain insight into various aspects of mortality in California, to predict health issues related to the causes of death, to offer an aid to decision- or policy-making process, and to provide useful information services to the customers. The results obtained in our study contain valuable new information.

Keywords: *vital statistics data, causes of death, data mining, predictive models, Cubist.*

1 Introduction

Several types of data constitute what are commonly known as vital statistics data. These include births, deaths, fetal deaths, marriages, and divorces. The most commonly used types of vital statistics data in public health are data on births and deaths. Birth and death data are derived from the information reported on birth and death certificates sent to the offices of local and state registrars.

One of the most important public health functions is the monitoring of a population's health status. Vital statistics data provide a valuable source of information regarding the health status of a population.

In this paper, we discuss the results of a data mining project on the causes of death aspect of the vital statistics data in the state of California. A data mining tool called Cubist [8] is used to build predictive models out of nearly two million cases over a nine-year period. The objective of our study is to discover knowledge that can be used to gain insight into various aspects of mortality in California, to predict health issues related to the causes of death, to offer an aid to decision- or policy-making process, and to provide useful information services to the customers. So far we have not found any published work in the literature on mining vital statistics data.

2. Data Preparation

Identifying Sources of Data. There are two main sources of data used in our study, namely, Death Statistical Master File (DSMF) and Estimated Population File (EPF). The DSMF data files contain data from the death certificates registered in California [4]. Each file contains a year worth of death data and includes detailed information concerning the decedent, the place of death, and the medical data related to the death. The total size of DSMF files used in the project is 1,995,398 records for the period of 1989-1997. The EPF is prepared by the Demographic Research Unit of the California Department of Finance [3], and is used for the purpose of calculating the death rates for the training and test sets in the project.

Data preprocessing. This step is the most time consuming one. After acquiring 1.99 millions of records from DSMF and 9090 records from EPF, data preprocessing in our study consists of *data consolidation and cleaning, data reduction*, and *data integration* and *transformation*.

Data cleaning is carried out by eliminating or handling noisy, missing or inconsistent data. Data reduction process results in six attributes being used in our study (out of 59 attributes in DSMF).

The causes of death (COD) in our study are coded according to the International Classification of Diseases, Ninth Revision, Clinical Modification (ICD-9-CM) [6].

To build predictive models from data, we need to have the death rate information in both the training and test data sets. Because the information is not explicitly contained in the original data files (DSMF, EPF), we derive the death rates from the data in DSMF and EPF through data integration and transformation.

Training/Test Data Sets Preparation. Before we can start the data mining process with Cubist, the *names, data* and *test* files must be in place.

3 Mining Process

The mining process is essentially COD-centric. It is geared toward generating models not only from the data of all-COD as a whole, but also from the data of each individual COD. There are several issues regarding how to carry out the mining process. How are training and test data sets selected and what are their respective sizes? What type of models is to be generated, rule-based or composite? Is a model generated just for a particular COD or for all-COD?

Data Selection Strategies. We adopt two strategies in selecting training and test data for the mining process. The first strategy (S1) uses the data collection from the period of 1989-1996 as the training set and the data from 1997 as the test set. The second strategy (S2), on the other hand, randomly selects both the training set data and the test set data from the entire period of 1989-1997.

Training and Test Data Partitions. In S2, we further define five different ways (T1, …, T5) of partitioning data into the training and test sets.

Model Generations. Of all the models generated in our study, 216 of them are defined according to the data selection strategies, training and test sets partitions, model types to be generated, and particular COD involved.

Committee Model. In addition to rule-based and composite models, Cubist can also generate what is referred to as the *committee* models out of several rule-based models. What a committee model does is that each member of the committee produces a target value for a case and the members' predictions are then averaged to yield a final prediction [8].

In our study, we select a best representative model (either rule-based or composite) for each COD based on considerations of prediction accuracy, average errors and relative errors. If a selected model is rule-based and its prediction accuracy is fairly high, we then turn on the committee model option to fine-tune the selected rule-based model for further performance improvements. Thus, 24 additional committee models were produced as a result of the fine-tuning process.

4 Result Analysis

Prediction Accuracy and Average Error. We compared the prediction accuracies and average errors under S1 and S2. There are some phenomena that depend on data selection strategies, and some that do not.

Impact of Training and Test Data Partitions. When data set sizes are small, the improvement of prediction accuracy is obvious as the training set size increases for some rule-based models.

Comparison of Rule and Composite Models. Composite models in general perform better than rule models (especially under S2). This is consistent with the observation that composite models are more effective when the number of attributes is small and all attributes are relevant to the prediction task.

Model Decomposition and Analysis. Once a model is generated, there are a number of issues pertaining to the rules in the model: their *objective* and *subjective*

interestingness [9], and reorganization for ease of analysis purpose [7]. In our study, we performed model decomposition and analysis on some obtained models to gain further insight.

Accuracy of Cubist Models. We compared the prediction results of Cubist models with those of the Vital Statistics of California Reports [1, 2]. Most of the Cubist results are consistent with the published reports.

Surprising Results. The models produced by Cubist also contain surprising results that are not found in the official published reports such as Vital Statistics of California [1, 2]. Most of those surprises represent valuable new information. Including marital status as an attribute during the mining process helped unearth valuable new information.

5 Conclusion

Our work pertains to a fertile ground for data mining. There is much to be done in the domain of vital statistics data. Future work can be pursued in several directions: generating and analyzing predictive models that include additional attributes such as individual underlying cause of death, place of occurrence, level of education, and place of residence, and that are from a subset of COD.

Acknowledgement. We would like to express our appreciation to Mike Quinn, Manager of VSS, Department of Health Services, State of California, for his help and comments

References

1   Center for Health Statistics, Department of Health Services, *Advance Report: Vital Statistics of California 1998*, February 2000.
2   Center for Health Statistics, Department of Health Services, *Vital Statistics of California 1997*, February 2000.
3   Department of Finance, State of California, http://www.dof.ca.gov.
4   Department of Health Services, Center for Health Statistics, State of California, http://www.dhs.ca.gov/hisp/chsindex.htm.
5   Q.L. Ha, *Knowledge Discovery on the State of California Health Statistical Data*, Master Degree thesis, Department of Computer Science, California State University, Sacramento, May 2001.
6   International Classification of Diseases 9th Revision, Clinical Modification (Volume One), http://www.mcis.duke.edu/standards/termcode/icd9/.
7   B. Liu, M. Hu and W. Hsu, Multi-Level Organization and Summarization of the Discovered Rules, Proceedings of *the Sixth ACM SIGKDD International Conference on Knowledge Discovery and Data Mining*, August 20-23, 2000, pp.208-217.
8   Rulequest web site, http://www.rulequest.com/cubist-win.html.
9   A. Silberschatz and A. Tuzhilin, What Makes Patterns Interesting in Knowledge Discovery Systems, *IEEE Transactions on Knowledge and Data Engineering*, Vol.8, No.6, December 1996, pp.970-974.

A Pattern Decomposition (PD) Algorithm for Finding All Frequent Patterns in Large Datasets

Qinghua Zou, Wesley Chu, David Johnson, Henry Chiu
Computer Science Department
University of California – Los Angele

Abstract

Efficient algorithms to mine frequent patterns are crucial to many tasks in data mining. Since the Apriori algorithm was proposed in 1994, there have been several methods proposed to improve its performance. However, most still adopt its candidate set generation-and-test approach. We propose a pattern decomposition (PD) algorithm that can significantly reduce the size of the dataset on each pass making it more efficient to mine frequent patterns in a large dataset. The proposed algorithm avoids the costly process of candidate set generation and saves time by reducing dataset. Our empirical evaluation shows that the algorithm outperforms Apriori by one order of magnitude and is faster than FP-tree. Further, PD is more scalable than both Apriori and FP-tree.

1. Introduction

A fundamental process in data mining is finding frequent patterns in a given dataset. Finding frequent patterns facilitates essential tasks such as discovering association relationships between items, correlation, and sequential patterns [7].

A significant problem with mining frequent larger patterns is that as the length of the pattern increases, the number of potential patterns grows at a combinatorial rate. Several different algorithms have been proposed to efficiently find all frequent patterns in a dataset [1,5,6,7]. Other algorithms output only maximal frequent sets, thus minimizing the number of potential patterns [2, 3, 4]. Max-Miner [2] uses a heuristic bottom-up search to identify frequent patterns as early as possible. Pincer-Search [4] uses a bottom-up search along with top-down pruning. Even though performance improvements may be substantial, maximal frequent sets have limited use in association rule mining. A complete set of rules cannot be extracted without support information of the subsets of those maximal frequent sets. FP-tree-based mining [9] is a different approach in that it first builds up an optimized data representation (FP-tree) from the dataset. All mining tasks are then performed on the FP-tree rather than on the dataset.

In this paper we propose an innovative algorithm called Pattern Decomposition (PD) that generates all frequent sets. The algorithm provides increased performance by reducing the dataset during each pass. The dataset is reduced by splitting transactions and combining similar transactions together, thus decreasing counting time and improving performance. In addition, the algorithm does not need to generate candidate sets; all subsets of any transaction in the reduced dataset are frequent thus should be counted. Intuitively, a transaction that contains infrequent itemsets can be decomposed to smaller itemsets if together they do not meet the minimum support threshold. Frequently, after splitting all the transactions in the dataset many itemsets are identical and can be combined, thus reducing the size of the dataset.

2. The Method

The PD algorithm shrinks dataset each time when infrequent itemsets are discovered. More specifically, it finds frequent sets by employing a bottom-up search. For a given transaction dataset D_1, the first pass has two phrases: 1) the algorithm counts for item occurrences to determine the frequent 1-itemsets L_1 and the infrequent 1-itemsets $\sim L_1$; 2) we decompose D_1 to D_2 such that D_2 contains no items in $\sim L_1$. Similarly, in a subsequent pass, say pass k, frequent itemsets L_k and $\sim L_k$ are generated by counting for all k-itemsets in D_k. Then, D_{k+1} is generated by decomposing D_k using $\sim L_k$ such that D_{k+1} contains no itemsets in $\sim L_k$.

Now let us illustrate the complete process for mining frequent patterns. In Figure 1, we show how PD is used to find all frequent patterns in a dataset. Suppose the original data set is D_1 and minimal support is 2. We first count the support of all items in D_1 to determine L_1 and $\sim L_1$. In this case, frequent 1-itemset $L_1=\{a,b,c,d,e\}$ and infrequent 1-itemset $\sim L_1=\{f,g,h,k\}$. Then we decompose each pattern in D_1 using $\sim L_1$ to get D_2. In the second pass, we generate and count all 2-item sets contained in D_2 to determine L_2 and $\sim L_2$, as shown in the figure. Then we decompose each pattern in D_2 to get D_3. This continues until we determine D_5 from D_4, which is the empty set and we terminate. The final result is the union of all frequent sets L_1 through L_4.

The example illustrates three ways to reduce the dataset as denoted by α, β, δ in Figure 1.

D_1
1: a b c d e f:
2: a b c g:
3: a b d h:
4: b c d e k:
5: a b c:

D_2
1: a b c d e: 1
2: a b c: 2
3: a b d: 1
4: b c d e: 1

L_1		$\sim L_1$				L_2		$\sim L_2$
IS	Occ	IS	Occ			IS	Occ	IS Occ
{a}	4	{f}	1			{ab}	4	{ae} 1
{b}	5	{g}	1			{ac}	3	
{c}	4	{h}	1			{ad}	2	
{d}	3	{k}	1			{bc}	4	
{e}	2					{bd}	3	
						{be}	2	
						{cd}	2	

D_3
1: abcd, bcde: 1
2: a b c: 2
3: a b d: 1
4: b c d e: 1

{ce} 2
{de} 2

D_4
1: b c d e: 2

L_3		$\sim L_3$		L_4		$\sim L_4$
IS	Occ	IS	Occ	IS	Occ	IS Occ
{abc}	3	{acd}	1	{bcde}	2	
{abd}	2					
{bcd}	2					
{bce}	2					
{bde}	2					
{cde}	2					

$D_5 = \Phi$

Figure 1. Pattern Decomposition Example

In α, when patterns after decomposition yield the same itemset, we combine them by summing their occurrence. Here, *abcg* and *abc* reduce to *abc*. Since both their occurrences are 1, the final pattern is *abc:2* in D_2.

In β, we remove patterns if their sizes are smaller than the required size of the next dataset. Here, patterns *abc* and *abd* with sizes of 3 cannot be in D_4 and are deleted.

In δ, when a part of a given pattern has the same itemset with another pattern after decomposition, we combine them by summing their occurrence. Here, *bcde* is the itemset of pattern 4 and part of pattern 1's itemset after decomposition, so the final pattern is *bcde:2* in D_4.

One simple way to decompose the itemset s by an infrequent k-item set t, as explained in [4], is to replace s by k itemsets, each obtained by removing a single item in t from s. For example, for $s = abcdefgh$ and $t = aef$, we decompose s by removing a, e, f respectively to obtain {*bcdefgh*, *abcdfgh*, *abcdegh*}. We call this method simple-split. When the infrequent sets are large, simple-split is not efficient. Thus PD needs Quick-split to decompose a pattern. [8]

3. Performance Study

We compare PD with Apriori and FP-tree since the former is widely cited and the latter claims the best performance in the literature. The test data sets were generated in the same fashion as the IBM Quest project [1]. We used two data sets T10.I4.D100K and T25.I10.D100K. For the comparison of PD with FP-tree, since PD was written in Java and FP-tree in C++ and we don't have time to implement PD in C++, their results are adjusted by a coefficient about 10.

Our study shows that PD is about 30 times faster than Apriori with minimal support at 2% and about 10 times faster than Apriori at 0.25%. The execution time for

Apriori linearly increases with the number of transactions from 50K to 250K. Better than that, the execution time for PD does not necessarily increase as the number of transactions increases.

Both FP-tree and PD have better performance than Apriori. FP-tree takes substantially more time than PD does when minimum support in the range from 0.5% to 2%. When minsup less than 0.5%, the number of frequent patterns increased quickly and thus the execution times are comparable. PD is about 9 times faster than FP-tree with minimal support at 2% and the gap reduces to 2 times faster at 0.25%. When the number of transactions ranged from 60k-80k, both methods took almost constant time (most likely due to overhead). When we scaled up to 200K, FP-tree required more than 1884M of virtual memory and could not run on our machine while PD finished the computation within 64M main memory. For more details, interested readers please refer to [8].

4. Conclusion

We propose a pattern decomposition (PD) algorithm to find frequent patterns. The algorithm significantly shrinks the dataset in each pass. It avoids the costly candidate set generation procedure and greatly saves counting time by using reduced datasets. Our experiments show that the PD algorithm has an order of magnitude improvement over the Apriori algorithm on standard test data and is faster than FP-tree.

References

[1] R. Agrawal and R. Srikant. Fast algorithms for mining association rules. In VLDB'94, pp. 487-499.

[2] R. J. Bayardo. Efficiently mining long patterns from databases. In SIGMOD'98, pp. 85-93.

[3] Zaki, M. J.; Parthasarathy, S.; Ogihara, M.; and Li, W. 1997. New Algorithms for Fast Discovery of Association Rules. In Proc. of the Third Int'l Conf. on Knowledge Discovery in Databases and Data Mining, pp. 283-286.

[4] Lin, D.-I and Kedem, Z. M. 1998. Pincer-Search: A New Algorithm for Discovering the Maximum Frequent Set. In Proc. of the Sixth European Conf. on Extending DatabaseTechnology.

[5] Park, J. S.; Chen, M.-S.; and Yu, P. S. 1996. An Effective Hash Based Algorithm for Mining Association Rules. In Proc. of the 1995 ACM-SIGMOD Conf. on Management of Data, pp. 175-186.

[6] Brin, S.; Motwani, R.; Ullman, J.; and Tsur, S. 1997. Dynamic Itemset Counting and Implication Rules for Market Basket Data. In Proc. of the 1997 ACM-SIGMOD Conf. On Management of Data, 255-264.

[7] J. Han, J. Pei, and Y. Yin. Mining Frequent Patterns without Candidate Generation. Proc. 2000 ACM-SIGMOD Int. Conf. on Management of Data, Dallas, TX, May 2000.

[8] Q. Zou, H. Chiu, W. W. Chu, D. Johnson. Pattern Decomposition Algorithm for Data Mining Frequent Patterns. Journal of Knowledge and Information Systems, 2002 (to appear).

Author Index